ENCYCLOPEDIA OF WORLD BIOGRAPHY

SUPPLEMENT

28

ENCYCLOPEDIA OF WORLD BIOGRAPHY

SUPPLEMENT

A
—————————— **28**
Z

GALE
CENGAGE Learning

Detroit • New York • San Francisco • New Haven, Conn • Waterville, Maine • London

GALE
CENGAGE Learning

REF
920
ENC

Encyclopedia of World Biography Supplement, Volume 28

Project Editor: Tracie Ratiner

Editorial: Jim Craddock, Jeffrey Muhr

Image Research and Acquisition: Leitha Etheridge-Sims

Rights Acquisition and Management: Mollika Basu, Jermaine Bobbitt, Jackie Jones

Imaging and Multimedia: Lezlie Light

Manufacturing: Drew Kalasky

For product information and technology assistance, contact us at
Gale Customer Support, 1-800-877-4253.
For permission to use material from this text or product,
submit all requests online at **www.cengage.com/permissions.**
Further permissions questions can be emailed to
permissionrequest@cengage.com

Gale
27500 Drake Rd.
Farmington Hills, MI, 48331-3535

ISBN-13: 978-1-4144-3366-0
ISBN-10: 1-4144-3366-2

ISSN 1099-7326

This title is also available as an e-book.
ISBN-13: 978-1-4144-3804-7
ISBN-10: 1-4144-3804-4
Contact your Gale sales representative for ordering information.

Printed in the United States of America
1 2 3 4 5 6 7 12 11 10 09 08

AUG   2008

CONTENTS

INTRODUCTION vii

ADVISORY BOARD. ix

ACKNOWLEDGMENTS xi

OBITUARIES. xiii

TEXT. 1

HOW TO USE THE INDEX 395

INDEX 397

INTRODUCTION

The study of biography has always held an important, if not explicitly stated, place in school curricula. The absence in schools of a class specifically devoted to studying the lives of the giants of human history belies the focus most courses have always had on people. From ancient times to the present, the world has been shaped by the decisions, philosophies, inventions, discoveries, artistic creations, medical breakthroughs, and written works of its myriad personalities. Librarians, teachers, and students alike recognize that our lives are immensely enriched when we learn about those individuals who have made their mark on the world we live in today.

Encyclopedia of World Biography Supplement, Volume 28, provides biographical information on 175 individuals not covered in the 17-volume second edition of *Encyclopedia of World Biography (EWB)* and its supplements, Volumes 18, 19, 20, 21, 22, 23, 24, 25, 26 and 27. Like other volumes in the *EWB* series, this supplement represents a unique, comprehensive source for biographical information on those people who, for their contributions to human culture and society, have reputations that stand the test of time. Each original article ends with a bibliographic section. There is also an index to names and subjects, which cumulates all persons appearing as main entries in the *EWB* second edition, the Volume 18, 19, 20, 21, 22, 23, 24, 25, 26, and 27 supplements, and this supplement—more than 8,000 people!

Articles. Arranged alphabetically following the letter-by-letter convention (spaces and hyphens have been ignored), articles begin with the full name of the person profiled in large, bold type. Next is a boldfaced, descriptive paragraph that includes birth and death years in parentheses. It provides a capsule identification and a statement of the person's significance. The essay that follows is approximately 2,000 words in length and

offers a substantial treatment of the person's life. Some of the essays proceed chronologically while others confine biographical data to a paragraph or two and move on to a consideration and evaluation of the subject's work. Where very few biographical facts are known, the article is necessarily devoted to an analysis of the subject's contribution.

Following the essay is a bibliographic section arranged by source type. Citations include books, periodicals, and online Internet addresses for World Wide Web pages, where current information can be found.

Portraits accompany many of the articles and provide either an authentic likeness, contemporaneous with the subject, or a later representation of artistic merit. For artists, occasionally self-portraits have been included. Of the ancient figures, there are depictions from coins, engravings, and sculptures; of the moderns, there are many portrait photographs.

Index. The *EWB Supplement* index is a useful key to the encyclopedia. Persons, places, battles, treaties, institutions, buildings, inventions, books, works of art, ideas, philosophies, styles, movements—all are indexed for quick reference just as in a general encyclopedia. The index entry for a person includes a brief identification with birth and death dates *and* is cumulative so that any person for whom an article was written who appears in the second edition of *EWB* (volumes 1–16) and its supplements (volumes 18–28) can be located. The subject terms within the index, however, apply only to volume 28. Every index reference includes the title of the article to which the reader is being directed as well as the volume and page numbers.

Because *EWB Supplement,* Volume 28, is an encyclopedia of biography, its index differs in important ways from the indexes to other encyclopedias. Basically, this is an index of people, and that fact has several interesting consequences. First, the information to which the index refers the reader on a particular topic is always about people associated with that topic. Thus the entry "Quantum theory (physics)" lists articles on people associated with quantum theory. Each article may discuss a person's contribution to quantum theory, but no single article or group of articles is intended to provide a comprehensive treatment of quantum theory as such. Second, the index is rich in classified entries. All persons who are subjects of articles in the encyclopedia, for example, are listed in one or more classifications in the index—abolitionists, astronomers, engineers, philosophers, zoologists, etc.

The index, together with the biographical articles, make *EWB Supplement* an enduring and valuable source for biographical information. As school course work changes to reflect advances in technology and further revelations about the universe, the life stories of the people who have risen above the ordinary and earned a place in the annals of human history will continue to fascinate students of all ages.

We Welcome Your Suggestions. Mail your comments and suggestions for enhancing and improving the *Encyclopedia of World Biography Supplement* to:

The Editors
Encyclopedia of World Biography Supplement
Gale, a Cengage Learning company
27500 Drake Road
Farmington Hills, MI 48331-3535
Phone: (800) 347-4253

ADVISORY BOARD

ACKNOWLEDGMENTS

Photographs and illustrations appearing in the *Encyclopedia of World Biography Supplement,* Volume 28, have been used with the permission of the following sources:

ALAMY: Shinzo Abe, Lou Andreas-Salome, Julius Axelrod, Hester Chapone, Ole Kirk Christiansen, Samuel Coleridge-Taylor, Alexandra David-Neel, Elizabeth of Bavaria, Joanna Baillie, Alphonse Laveran, Isabella Mary Mayson, Angela Merkel, Thomas Moore, Emma Magdalena Rosalia Maria Josefa Orczy, Eugene Ormandy, Jeanne-Antoinette Poisson Pompadour, Anita Roddick, Joshua Slocum, Marie Tussaud, Pauline Viardot, Elizabeth Woodville.

AP IMAGES: Kingsley Amis, Roberto Bolano, Lizzie Borden, Gordon Brown, Carlos E. Castaneda, Claude Chabrol, Frank Church, Martin Cooper, Herbert Dow, Drew Gilpin Faust, Stephen Frears, Klaus Fuchs, Deleuze Gilles, Merv Griffin, Alfred J Gross (Al Gross), Ernst Haefliger, Lucy Ware Webb Hayes, Robert Heinlein, Masaru Ibuka, Tove Marika Jansson, Garry Kasparov, Craig C. Mello, Helen Mirren, Hayao Miyazaki, Sven Nykvist, Orhan Pamuk, Les Paul, Arthur Rubinstein, Howard Stringer, Saint Therese of Lisieux, Granville T. Woods, Konrad Zuse.

CORBIS: Francois (Jean Pierre) Blanchard, Ole Bornemann Bull, Billy Collins, Manuel Maria Ponce.

GETTY: Mata Amritanandamayi, Ivie Anderson, Frederic-Auguste Bartholdi, Michael Bloomberg, William Seward Burroughs, Eddie Chapman, Nuruddin Farah, Ian Fleming, Pim Fortuyn, Kenneth Grahame, Florence Kling Harding, Rafiq Hariri, Benny Hill, Wenzel Hollar, Natalia Karp, Elizabeth Keckley, King Casimir III, Jacek Kuron, Bernard-Henri Levy, Wyndham (Percy) Lewis, Astrid Lindgren, Ian McKellan, Eddy Merckx, Bernard Moitessier, Olga Nikolaevna, Peyo (Pierre Culliford), Harriet Quimby, Hal Roach, Oral Roberts, Amalia Rodrigues, Adolphe Sax, Sidney Sheldon, Helen Herron Taft, Marie Taglioni, Danny Thomas, Rudy Vallee, Muhammad Yunus, Joe Zawinul.

JACK VARTOOGIAN: Max Roach.

LANDOV: Ellen Johnson-Sirleaf, Mikhail Kalashnikov, Sven Olof Joachim Palme, Wolfgang Sawallisch, Irena (Sendlerowa) Sendler, Bill Walsh.

PHOTO RESEARCHERS: Harold Eugene Edgerton.

OBITUARIES

The following people, appearing in volumes 1–27 of the *Encyclopedia of World Biography,* have died since the publication of the second edition and its supplements. Each entry lists the volume where the full biography can be found.

ANTONIONI, MICHELANGELO (born 1912), Italian filmmaker, died in Rome, Italy, on July 30, 2007 (Vol. 1).

BERGMAN, INGMAR (born 1918), Swedish filmmaker, died in Faro, Sweden, on July 30, 2007 (Vol. 2).

BHUTTO, BENAZIR (born 1953), Pakistani politician, died by suicide bombing in Rawalpindi, Pakistan, on December 27, 2007 (Vol. 2).

BUCKLEY, WILLIAM F., JR. (born 1925), American conservative pundit, writer, and editor, died in Stamford, Connecticut, on February 27, 2008 (Vol. 3).

CHANDLER, ALFRED D., Jr. (born 1918), American historian, died in Cambridge, Massachusetts, on May 9, 2007 (Vol. 3).

CLAIBORNE, LIZ (born 1929), American fashion designer, died of cancer in Manhattan, New York, on June 26, 2007 (Vol. 4).

CLARK, ARTHUR C. (born 1917), British science fiction writer, died in Colombo, Sri Lanka, on March 19, 2008 (Vol. 18).

CURIE, EVE (born 1904), French musician, author, and diplomat, died in New York, New York, on October 22, 2007 (Vol. 18).

DOUGLAS, MARY (born 1921), British anthropologist and social thinker, died on May 16, 2007 (Vol. 5).

EKWENSKI, CYPRIAN (born 1921), Nigerian writer, died on November 4, 2007 (Vol. 5).

FALWELL, JERRY (born 1933), American religious leader, died in Lynchburg, Virginia, on May 15, 2007 (Vol. 5).

FISCHER, ROBERT JAMES (BOBBY) (born 1943), American chess player, died in Reykjavik, Iceland, on January 17, 2008 (Vol. 5).

FOLKMAN, JUDAH M. (born 1933), American physician and medical researcher, died of a heart attack in Denver, Colorado on January 14, 2008 (Vol. 22).

HABASH, GEORGE (born 1926), founder of the Arab Nationalists Movement, died of a heart attack in Amman, Jordan, on January 26, 2008 (Vol. 7).

HALBERSTAM, DAVID (born 1934), American author, journalist, and social historian, died of injuries from a car crash in California on April 23, 2007 (Vol. 18).

HILLARY, EDMUND (born 1919), New Zealander explorer and mountaineer, died in Auckland, New Zealand, on January 11, 2008 (Vol. 7).

HUTT, WILLIAM (born 1920), Canadian actor, died of leukemia in Stratford, Ontario, on June 27, 2007 (Vol. 27).

KORNBERG, ARTHUR (born 1918), American biochemist, died of respiratory failure in Stanford, California, on October 26, 2007 (Vol. 9).

LEDERBERG, JOSHUA (born 1925), American geneticist, died of pneumonia in New York on February 2, 2008 (Vol. 9).

L'ENGLE, MADELEINE (born 1918), American author, died of natural causes in Litchfield, Connecticut, on September 6, 2007 (Vol. 18).

LEWITT, SOL (born 1928), American Minimalist and Conceptualist artist, died of cancer in New York on April 8, 2007 (Vol. 9).

MACCREADY, PAUL (born 1925), American aeronautical engineer, died in Pasadena, California, on August 28, 2007 (Vol. 20).

MACQUARRIE, JOHN (born 1919), Scottish Anglican theologian, died in Oxford, England, on May 28, 2007 (Vol. 10).

MAHARISHI MAHESH YOGI (born 1911), Indian guru and founder of the Transcendental Meditation movement, died of natural causes in Vlodrop, Netherlands, on February 5, 2008 (Vol. 10).

MAILER, NORMAN (born 1923), American author, producer, and director, died of acute renal failure in New York on November 10, 2007 (Vol. 10).

MARCEAU, MARCEL (born 1923), French practitioner of pantomime, died in Paris, France, on September 22, 2007 (Vol. 10).

OERTER, AL (born 1936), American discus thrower, died of heart failure in Ft. Myers, Florida, on October 1, 2007 (Vol. 21).

OUSMANE, SEMBENE (born 1923), Senegalese novelist and filmmaker, died in Dakar, Senegal, on June 9, 2007 (Vol. 12).

PALEY, GRACE (born 1922), American author and activist, died in Thetford Hill, Vermont, on August 22, 2007 (Vol. 22).

PAVAROTTI, LUCIANO (born 1935), Italian tenor, died of pancreatic cancer in Modena, Italy, on September 6, 2007 (Vol. 12).

PETERSON, OSCAR (born 1925), Canadian pianist, died of kidney failure in Mississauga, Ontario, Canada, on December 23, 2007 (Vol. 23).

PYM, FRANCIS (born 1922), British statesman, died in Bedfordshire, England, on March 7, 2008 (Vol. 12).

ROBBE-GRILLET, ALAIN (born 1922), French novelist and filmmaker, died in France on February 18, 2008 (Vol. 13).

ROBINSON, EDDIE GAY (born 1919), American college football coach, died of Alzheimer's disease in Ruston, Louisiana, on April 3, 2007 (Vol. 18).

RORTY, RICHARD M. (born 1931), American philosopher and man of letters, died of complications from pancreatic cancer in Palo Alto, California, on June 8, 2007 (Vol. 13).

ROSTROPOVICH, MSTISLAV (born 1927), Russian cellist and conductor, died in Moscow, Russia, on April 26, 2007 (Vol. 13).

SILLS, BEVERLY (born 1929), American soprano, died of lung cancer in New York on July 2, 2007 (Vol. 14).

SMITH, IAN (born 1919), African prime minister, died of a stroke in Cape Town, South Africa, on November 20, 2007 (Vol. 14).

SMUIN, MICHAEL (born 1938), American dancer, choreographer, and director, died of heart failure in San Francisco, California, on April 24, 2007 (Vol. 14).

STOCKHAUSEN, KARLHEINZ (born 1928), German composer, died on December 5, 2007 (Vol. 14).

SUHARTO (born 1921), second Indonesian president after independence, died of multiple organ failure in Jakarta, Indonesia, on January 27, 2008 (Vol. 15).

VALENTI, JACK (born 1921), American presidential advisor, copyright lobbyist, and longtime president of the Motion Picture Association of America, died of a stroke in Washington, D.C., on April 26, 2007 (Vol. 15).

VONNEGUT, KURT (born 1922), American author, died of brain injuries from a fall, in New York, on April 11, 2007 (Vol. 16).

WALDHEIM, KURT (born 1918), Austrian statesman and president, died of heart failure in Vienna, Austria, on June 14, 2007 (Vol. 16).

YELTSIN, BORIS (born 1931), Russian politician and former president, died of heart failure in Moscow, Russia, on April 23, 2007 (Vol. 16).

ZAHIR SHAH, MOHAMMAD (born 1931), Afghani king, died in Kabul, Afghanistan, on July 23, 2007 (Vol. 22).

Shinzo Abe

Shinzo Abe (born 1954) was Japan's prime minister for less than a year, from September 26, 2006, to September 12, 2007.

The first Japanese prime minister born after World War II, Abe faced problems that troubled Japanese society as a whole in the early 21st century. Like his predecessors, he tried to strike a balance between modern ideals of transparency and Japan's tradition of closed, clubby hierarchies in business and government. And he struggled with the issues of Japanese national pride and the country's still-conflicted attitudes toward its militaristic past and its World War II–era crimes. Those tensions, which bedeviled a succession of Japanese leaders, brought a quick end to Abe's reign as Prime Minister.

Born into Political Family

Shinzo Abe was born in Nagato Japan, in Yamaguchi Prefecture, on September 21, 1954. His family was immersed in Japanese politics on both its paternal and maternal sides. His maternal grandfather, Nobusuke Kishi, was a key military leader during World War II, serving as part of General Hideki Tojo's circle of advisers. Kishi was an American prisoner of war for three years but was released in 1948 and later favored a strongly pro-American foreign policy even as he attempted to rebuild the Japanese military. He was Japan's prime minister from 1957 to 1960. One observer, at least, detected traces of the grandfather's attitudes in the grandson. "Abe's beliefs and values are similar to Kishi's," Japanese Diet (legislature) member Katsuei

Hirasawa told Bryan Walsh of *Time*. "He's inherited his grandfather's political DNA."

On his father's side, too, Abe's family tree was filled with well-liked politicians. His father's father, Kan Abe, served in Japan's House of Representatives, and his father, Shintaro Abe, was the country's minister of foreign affairs from 1982 to 1986 and was often mentioned as a potential prime minister himself. Shinzo Abe was more distantly related to another Japanese prime minister, Eisuke Sato, who served from 1964 to 1972 and was later awarded the Nobel Peace Prize.

After studying political science at Seikei University in metropolitan Tokyo, Abe graduated in 1977. He headed for the United States in the late 1970s, taking English-language and political science classes at the University of Southern California. Abe returned to Japan in 1979 and worked for the Kobe Steel corporation for three years, but it was not long before he returned to the family vocation. In 1982 he entered the political world as an executive assistant in the foreign affairs ministry. After that he set his sights on ascending through the hierarchy of Japan's dominant Liberal Democratic Party, or LDP.

Abe was a part of the LDP's inner circle before he ever held formal political office. In the late 1980s he served as private secretary to the chair of the LDP's general council, and then as private secretary once again to the party's secretary-general—influential posts within the backroom environment of Japanese politics of the day. Abe's father died in 1991, and the son's political ambitions deepened. In 1993 he was elected by a landslide from a Yamaguchi Prefecture district to Japan's House of Representatives, the lower chamber of the Diet. At first he sometimes behaved like a pampered scion of a political dynasty. Hirasawa, one of his legislative mentors, once noticed him reading manga comic books during a Diet session—and was dismayed

when Abe refused to put the comic book down after his misstep was pointed out. Soon, however, Abe was angling for the party posts that were the well-trodden pathways to real power in Japan. One newspaper dubbed him the Prince of Politics.

Climbed Party Hierarchy

The LDP has been a "liberal" party in the classical sense of the word, favoring limited government intervention in free markets; it would be called conservative in Western terms, and Abe belonged to a powerful faction that was in the mainstream of the party's conservative beliefs. He rose quickly into the circle of party leaders from whom Japan's top government officials have traditionally been drawn. In 1999 he became director of the LDP's social affairs division, and the following year he was named deputy chief cabinet secretary. In 2003 he became secretary general of the LDP, and in 2005 he was appointed chief cabinet secretary under Prime Minister Junichiro Koizumi, a post regarded as a stepping-stone to that of prime minister.

A flamboyant figure who visited the Graceland mansion and sang karaoke versions of Elvis Presley songs during a trip to the U.S., Koizumi took Japan in new directions. He backed the U.S. invasion of Iraq and contributed several hundred members of the Japan Self-Defense Forces to the multinational forces serving in Iraq—the first foreign deployment of Japanese forces since World War II. He also stirred controversy with his visits to Tokyo's Yakusuni Shrine, a Shinto memorial to Japan's war dead; those visits

were seen as provocative by some in China, Taiwan, North and South Korea, and other countries that bore the brunt of Japanese expansionism during the war. On the home front, Koizumi tried to shake up some of the longtime government monopolies that he saw as impediments to Japanese productivity. In particular he attempted to privatize Japan Post, which in addition to delivery services also functioned as an insurance provider and as one of the world's largest savings banks. In 2006, after five years as prime minister, Koizumi stepped down, and Abe emerged as the consensus choice within the LDP to replace him. After being chosen in an election held among LDP members, he took office as Japan's 90th prime minister on September 26, 2007. He was the youngest prime minister in postwar Japanese history.

Abe had raised his public profile with strong criticisms of North Korea, a longtime nemesis of Japan. When the communist North Korean government confirmed in 2002 that agents of its secret services had kidnapped Japanese nationals and brought them to North Korea in the 1970s, Abe took a visible role in Japan's response, at one time urging a group of visiting abductees to defect to Japan. He took a hard line against North Korea's growing nuclear weapons program and its test-firing of missiles capable of reaching Japan. Abe frequently appeared on television in connection with these issues, creating the impression that he was a strong leader and helping to propel him to the prime ministership. At the same time, he carefully avoided tipping his hand on most key issues.

After becoming prime minister, however, Abe moved to quiet suspicions that he was a hard-line nationalist who might further worsen Japan's relationships with its neighbors. In October of 2006, shortly after taking office, he visited Beijing, China, and Seoul, South Korea, reassuring major Japanese trading partners of an atmosphere of stability. "Abe will stand up and make firm decisions for the Japanese people," LDP foreign-affairs specialist Ichita Yamamoto told Walsh. "But he's not a hard-liner against China or anyone. He's a strategist." Abe further calmed the waters by declining to announce any plans to visit the Yakusuni Shrine, and in fact he did not visit the shrine at all during his term in office. His approval percentage in public-opinion polls soared into the high 70s.

Readmitted LDP Renegades

Before long, however, Abe's popularity plunged. The heated debate over the privatization of Japan Post caused him problems: seeking to repair rifts within the LDP over the issue, he readmitted 11 Diet members who had left the party after Koizumi insisted on pushing privatization forward. But, noted the *Economist,* "[t]hat suggested Mr. Abe preferred back-room politics to pushing for change." (Japan Post finally dissolved into a group of private companies in October of 2007.) Behind the scenes, Abe worked to curb the system of *amakudari,* the revolving-door policy by which Japanese bureaucrats were often installed in high positions in the industries they had regulated while in government. However, much less colorful than the combative Koizumi, Abe was seen as a politician ready to revert to backroom dealings. Abe also suffered when his health minister, Hakuo Yanagisawa, said that Japanese women should function as "breeding machines" (in the *Economist*'s translation) in response to the country's low birthrate. Other scandals bedeviled the Abe administration in 2007: his agriculture minister committed suicide in May of that year (and his successor was later forced to resign), and the government was forced to admit that it had lost records pertaining to some 50 million pension accounts.

Although he had a successful summit meeting with Chinese leader Hu Jintao in 2007, Abe also had difficulties managing the more emotional aspects of Japan's relationships with neighboring countries. Japanese army records showed that Chinese and Korean women had been forced into sex slavery during World War II, but Abe at first denied that there was hard evidence that any coercion had occurred, and he refused to make official a 1993 apology for the episode by a lower-ranking government official. An international outcry ensued. The *New York Times* editorialized that "Mr. Abe seems less concerned with repairing Japan's sullied international reputation than with appealing to a large right-wing faction within his Liberal Democratic Party that insists that the whole shameful episode was a case of healthy private enterprise." Once again, less controversial Abe initiatives, such as the introduction of patriotic themes in Japanese primary education, were overshadowed, and he was forced to make an apology of his own before the Diet.

The cumulative result of these blows to Abe's popularity was a massive defeat for the LDP in parliamentary elections held on July 29, 2007. The party suffered through its worst showing since 1955 and lost not only its absolute majority, but also its traditional position of dominance within the Diet. Rural Japanese voters rejected Abe's party in favor of the opposition Democratic Party of Japan by especially large margins. The *Economist* opined that Abe "has shown himself to be diffident, patrician and out of touch with people's everyday concerns." On the other hand, some observers attributed the LDP's disastrous showing not to any failings on Abe's part but to the delayed impact of long-needed economic reforms initiated by the more persuasive Koizumi.

At first, with no clear mandate in place for any Japanese leader, Abe announced his intention to stay on as prime minister. Criticism of his leadership continued to mount, however, and Abe was also reported to be in poor health. On September 12, 2007, he abruptly announced that he would resign. The day after his announcement he was hospitalized, suffering from psychological stress and exhaustion. His resignation took effect on September 26, and he was replaced by Yasuo Fukuda. The victim of a period of general instability in Japan's political life, he was at least temporarily sidelined from the political sphere he had inhabited since he was a young man.

Periodicals

Economist (US), September 30, 2006; March 10, 2007; May 26, 2007; August 4, 2007.
Foreign Affairs, March-April 2007.
New York Times, March 6, 2007.
Time, September 11, 2006; September 24, 2007.

Online

"Abe in hospital after resignation," *Al Jazeera*, English edition, http://english.aljazeera.net/NR/exeres/EB74820F-3AC4-4455-B654-EE88C0DDE9B0.htm (October 11, 2007).
Biography Resource Center Online, Gale, 2006. http://galenet .galegroup.com/servlet/BioRC (October 11, 2007).
"Profile: Shinzo Abe," British Broadcasting Corporation, http://news.bbc.co.uk/2/hi/asia-pacific/4392480.stm (October 11, 2007).
Wiseman, Paul, and Naoko Nishiwaki, "Hard-liner looks set to lead Japan," *USA Today*, http://www.usatoday.com/news/world/2006-08-09-japan-prime-minister_x.htm (October 11, 2007). □

David Hayes Agnew

American physician David Hayes Agnew (1818-1892) trained a generation of surgeons through his involvement in several medical schools in the Philadelphia area.

One of the best-known surgeons of his era, he gained a national reputation after he treated the assassinated United States president James A. Garfield (1831-1881) in 1881. Agnew's career spanned an important era in the history of Western medicine, for he entered the profession when operating on live human beings had not yet shed some of its macabre reputation among the general public.

Agnew was born on November 24, 1818, in Nobleville, Pennsylvania, which later became the town of Christiana. His father, Robert, was a physician in private practice and came from a family that had been among the first settlers to the area. An only child, Agnew was raised in the Presbyterian faith and as a teenager he enrolled at Jefferson College in Canonsburg, Pennsylvania, in the western part of the state. Founded by a Presbyterian minister in the late eighteenth century, the school was the one of the first institutes of higher learning west of the Allegheny Mountains. It later combined with the another Presbyterian school, Washington College, to become Washington & Jefferson College.

Earned Medical Degree

Agnew left after just a year, transferring to Delaware College in Newark, Delaware, where a cousin was a professor. Again, he spent just a year before returning home to begin the study of medicine under his father's tutelage. Such professional apprenticeships were not uncommon in the 1830s, although the University of Pennsylvania had established the first formal medical school in the United States in 1765 and had become a renowned training ground for doctors. Agnew entered Penn's Medical School in the fall of 1836, just before he turned 18, and earned his M.D. degree two years later with a thesis titled *Medical Science and the Responsibility of Medical Character*.

Agnew returned to Nobleville and joined his father's practice, taking over in 1840 when his father retired. Yet Agnew dreamed of a more exciting career than that of a country doctor who treated fevers and delivered infants: he wanted to become a surgeon. This was an ambitious goal at the time, for formal surgery had become a legitimate and esteemed profession only during the previous century. His ambition would be thwarted by further delay when, in 1841, he married Margaret Creighton Irwin, the daughter of an iron foundry owner in Chester County. When Irwin's father died a year later, Agnew entered into a business partnership with her brothers to take over the foundry, which bore the name Irwin & Agnew Iron Foundry after 1843. A depressed world market for iron forced the firm into bankruptcy in 1846.

Thrown from Carriage

Reluctantly, Agnew returned to practicing medicine, first in Cochranville in Chester County, then in nearby Lancaster County, for the next two years. One day in the summer of 1848, while out driving with his wife, their horses were unnerved by a flock of sheep and reared up; Agnew was thrown from the carriage. His wife was also injured, but remained on board for nearly a mile before she managed to jump off and return to her husband. Agnew spent several weeks recuperating from a bad hip injury, which gave him a lifelong limp, but the event also served as a catalyst; he decided to move to Philadelphia to study anatomy, and his wife agreed to the plan, though they had suffered severe financial losses because of the foundry's failure. In Philadelphia he set up a small private practice while training in his spare hours to become a surgeon.

A proficient surgeon needed to have a detailed knowledge of human anatomy, and this was only possible by human dissection. An almost primordial human taboo against tampering with the dead, bolstered by centuries of Christian religious and burial practices, made this training requirement quite difficult for surgeons during this era. Agnew began studying anatomy on his own, utilizing the private dissecting rooms available to medical students, some of which also offered lecture courses in anatomy during the medical school breaks. One of these was the Philadelphia School of Anatomy, founded in 1820 as a separate training facility for University of Pennsylvania medical students. It was extremely difficult to obtain bodies for the purposes of dissection, however. Agnew's biographer, Jedidiah Howe Adams, in the 1892 volume *History of the Life of D. Hayes Agnew*, explained that among some working class, immigrant, and African-American quarters, prejudices against the medical profession at the time included "a common belief . . . that the authorities of certain hospitals murder their patients in order that they may be dissected by medical students."

Climbed into Mass Graves

Agnew began lecturing at the Philadelphia School of Anatomy, and would eventually take over the school outright in 1852. The availability of cadavers remained an issue, and as the school's director, "it was necessary for [Agnew] to be constantly on the outlook to obtain bodies for

his students' use," Adams wrote. He added, "he obtained them in a perfectly legitimate way; for example, during the terrible epidemic of Asiatic cholera in Philadelphia, in 1854, there were so many deaths daily, at the Philadelphia Hospital, that deep pits were dug in the neighboring fields, into which the bodies were rudely thrown. At that time, in order to render these bodies suitable for use, Dr. Agnew would descend into these pits, and, with the sun beating fiercely upon his head, he would inject a sufficient number of bodies for his purpose." The injection referred to was probably a syringe of glutaraldehyde, a preservative used to forestall decay before formaldehyde became the prevalent embalming fluid.

Agnew gained a reputation as an expert on human anatomy and as a teacher who delivered riveting lectures, and his school flourished, with medical students from both the University of Pennsylvania and from another top Philadelphia training ground for physicians, the Jefferson Medical College of Thomas Jefferson University. In 1854 Agnew founded the Philadelphia School of Operative Surgery at the same location on Chant Street, and continued to educate future surgeons—a subject on which he had some firm opinions, as evidenced by his *1857 Valedictory Address at the Philadelphia School of Anatomy*. In it, he provided the future doctors with several pieces of wisdom, including an injunction to have "a uniform, self-possessed, and cheerful manner." He also reminded the new graduates that "the sick read in the face of their medical attendant lessons of hope or despair, and he who understands the powerful influence which the mind exerts on the recuperative powers of the material organism, will appreciate the value of cultivating every agency calculated to secure its co-operation." Continuing on, he asserted that "a high moral tone should characterize professional intercourse. Such a deportment becomes the dignity of our calling, and secures a proper personal respect. Loose conversation and indelicate jests, aside from their being in themselves positively wrong, invite an unwarrantable degree of familiarity and freedom, and the assumption of eccentricities is altogether unbecoming an honorable practitioner, and, at best, only a charlatan trick to cover up the defects of education."

Aided Union Army Wounded

In 1854 Agnew attained his career ambition when he was appointed surgeon at Philadelphia Hospital, which was commonly referred to in its day as "Blockley," after the West Philadelphia neighborhood where it was located. It later became Philadelphia General Hospital, and when it closed in 1977 it had been the oldest continuously open medical care facility in the United States. There, he gained a reputation as a highly skilled surgeon who "was calm, never flurried in the face of emergencies," according to Walter Lincoln Burrage in the *Dictionary of American Biography*. "He could handle the knife with either hand, ambidextrousness having been acquired early in life."

Agnew found the Blockley hospital's pathological museum and served as its curator after 1860. During the American Civil War, Agnew was put in charge of the Hestonville Hospital, located on the outskirts of the city at the time, and also served as a consulting surgeon at the Mower Army Hospital in the Chestnut Hill section of Philadelphia. He gained a reputation as a specialist in gunshot wounds, one of the most pernicious causes of death and dismemberment during this particularly grisly military conflict.

In 1863 Agnew was elected surgeon at Wills Eye Hospital, was granted privileges at Pennsylvania Hospital two years later, and in 1867 became a surgeon at the Orthopaedic Hospital of Philadelphia as well. But it was with the prestigious University of Pennsylvania Medical School that he had the longest professional affiliation, serving on its faculty from 1863 to 1889. He became a professor of operative surgery in 1870, and a year later was named professor of the principles and practice of surgery. Within a decade his reputation had become a nationwide one, and when President James A. Garfield was assassinated on July 2, 1881, at the railway station in Washington, D.C., Agnew received a summons to Washington to serve as a medical consultant, along with prominent New York City physician Dr. Frank H. Hamilton (1813-1886). Like their predecessors on the case, Agnew and Hamilton were unable to pinpoint the exact location of the bullet, and agreed with their colleagues that the president was in no condition to undergo exploratory surgery. Over the next few weeks, Garfield's wound became infected, and the president died on September 19, after a period of great suffering. When government officials requested a bill from Agnew for his services, he refused to provide one.

Nevertheless, the intense newspaper coverage devoted to the president's wounds brought Agnew a degree of celebrity outside of Philadelphia and his professional circles, and those determined to obtain the best possible medical care—some from as far away as Europe—began flocking to his office, where he worked long hours to accommodate the increased demand for his expertise. In Philadelphia, Agnew and his wife spent the majority of their years in their home located at 1611 Chestnut Street; he also kept a country house in the Haverford area. He retired in 1889 as professor of surgery at the University of Pennsylvania, but continued to serve as an important influence on a generation of surgeons through his textbooks. These include *Anatomy in Its Relations to Medicine and Surgery*, published between 1859 and 1864, and *The Principles and Practice of Surgery* published in three volumes between 1878 and 1883.

Painted by Thomas Eakins

Agnew died on March 22, 1892, in Philadelphia. He was immortalized by the famous Philadelphia artist Thomas Eakins (1844-1916) in the 1889 painting *Agnew Clinic,* which hangs in the Medical School of the University of Pennsylvania. It was commissioned by the 1889 graduating class of the school and presented to him at that year's commencement ceremony. In art history scholarship, it is often compared to Eakins's earlier and better known painting, *The Gross Clinic* from 1875. Considered one of the most important paintings from this period of American art, *The Gross Clinic* depicts teacher-physician Dr. Samuel Gross (1805-1884) in the operating amphitheater at Jefferson Medical College in Philadelphia, with a surgery in progress. In comparing both paintings, the marked medical advances that occurred in the 1880s are apparent, with the operating attendants in Agnew's theater no longer wearing street clothes but more hygienic garments to guard against infection; a cone to administer anesthesia, rather than a rag soaked with ether, is another visible difference in the two tableaux. Eakins's earlier painting had provoked great controversy when it was exhibited back in 1875. "Well aware of the critical response to 'The Gross Clinic,' Dr. Agnew insisted that his hands and gown be free of blood," wrote Howard Markel in the *New York Times* more than a century later. "In the background, a constant of medical education over the millennia is on display: snoozing medical students."

Books

Adams, Jedidiah Howe, *History of the Life of D. Hayes Agnew,* The F.A. Davis Company, 1892.

Agnew, D. Hayes, *Valedictory Address to the Anatomical Class of the Philadelphia School of Anatomy, Delivered on Thursday Evening, February 19, 1857,* T. K. and P. G. Collins, 1857.

Burrage, Walter Lincoln, *Dictionary of American Biography Base Set,* American Council of Learned Societies, 1928-1936.

Simpson, Marc, "The 1880s," *Thomas Eakins,* Philadelphia Museum of Art, 2001.

Periodicals

New York Times, August 13, 2002.

Online

"Penn Biographies: D. Hayes Agnew," University Archives and Records Center (UARC), http://www.archives.upenn.edu/histy/people/1800s/agnew_d_hayes.html (January 3, 2008). ☐

Kingsley Amis

Kingsley Amis (1922-1995) became one of Britain's most daring and acclaimed new writers with the 1954 publication of his debut novel, *Lucky Jim*. Amis went on to write nearly two dozen more novels, as well as scores of other works, including discourses on science fiction, the detective novel, the English language, and even alcoholic beverages, for which he himself had a legendary and well-documented propensity. But it was his bitingly funny portrayal of a young but disillusioned college lecturer, Jim Dixon, that earned Amis enduring fame. *Lucky Jim*'s scathing critique of English culture and society would land the title on most surveys of the best English-language novels of the twentieth century. With that stellar debut, asserted Adam Gopnik in a 2007 article in the *New Yorker,* Amis "more or less invented the modern English comic novel—the small-scale satiric inspection, flavored with sexual malice, that dominates English fiction."

Kingsley William Amis was born on April 16, 1922, as the only child of William Amis, who worked in the London offices of Colman's, the mustard maker, and Rosa (Lucas) Amis. "It is a sad fate to be the child of the urban or suburban middle classes," Amis once wrote, according to Zachary's Leader's biography *The Life of Kingsley Amis.* Both parents were reportedly talented mimics of their friends, neighbors, and radio personalities, a trait that was passed on to their son, whose prose would feature an unusually nuanced degree of characterization through dialogue. While growing up in the southwest London area of Norbury, the young Amis also apparently inherited some nervous tendencies from his mother, who worried about his health, diet, and safety. "I used to tell myself stories all the time," he said in a 1988 London *Sunday Times* interview with John Mortimer, adding that he concocted the stories in part to quell his anxieties. "I was always nervous. Full of fear. I was afraid someone would come into my bedroom and murder me."

Served in British Army

Amis entered the City of London School at the age of 12, a boys' school that provided a university track education. In 1941, with Britain in the midst of World War II, he entered St. John's College of Oxford University and took part in a British Army officer training program over the next year while beginning his studies. In July of 1942 he entered the Royal Signal Corps, where he attained the rank of lieutenant and served at several different sites in the European field of combat. Returning to civilian life and Oxford, he

pursued an undergraduate degree in English, which he earned with first class honors in 1947, a year later receiving his master's degree. In between those two degrees, his first collection of poetry, *Bright November,* was published.

The years 1947 and 1948 were significant in Amis's life for another reason: he became romantically involved with a student from the Ruskin College of Art, Hilary "Hilly" Bardwell, whose middle class but eccentric family would become the model for the one so mercilessly skewered in *Lucky Jim.* In a letter he wrote to Philip Larkin (1922-1985)—a fellow Oxford student who became Amis's lifelong friend as well as an acclaimed writer in his own right—he described meeting Hilly's family, whose "dog smells of corpses. . . . And the father does folk dancing." Near the end of 1947 Hilly became pregnant, and the two wed in January of 1948. Their first child, whom they named Philip in honor of their friend Larkin, was born that August. At the end of 1948, Amis was hired by the University College of Swansea, Wales, as an assistant lecturer in English, and the family moved there in December. In August of 1949, a second son, Martin, was born.

Amis spent the next 12 years teaching at Swansea, and in the early 1950s began to work on his first novel, after working out some of *Lucky Jim*'s structure with Larkin. The novel was accepted for publication by the London publisher Gollancz in May of 1953, a prestigious house with whom he would remain for the first decade of his career. The novel's publication the following January prompted the *Times* of London to assert that "Mr. Amis could have afforded to give it a further polish, but he writes with such energy and enjoyment that it matters little."

Hailed as Voice of Generation

Lucky Jim recounts a few weeks in the life of Jim Dixon, a junior lecturer in history at a lesser university in northern England. He dislikes the job, finds his colleagues pretentious, and fears that he will be released from his contract at the end of the term when his probationary period ends. His success hinges upon Professor Welch, the department chair, though he secretly despises both his mentor and the man's family. "The novel's real comedy, and its originality, comes from its bracing contempt for culture and higher education—for madrigal singing, and lectures on 'organic' village life, and people who make a big deal of the difference between recorders and flutes," noted Gopnik. Dixon also finds himself romantically involved with two women, one pretty, the other plain, and is halfheartedly attempting to write his first serious treatise, an examination of medieval shipbuilding. In a February 12, 1954, review in the *Times Literary Supplement,* contributor Alan Ross compared the debut novel with the work of other up-and-coming writers who had come of age after the war. He commented that Amis's "dialogue and characterization are pointed and observant, and not the least of the genuinely funny things come from the imaginative gusto of Dixon's thoughts about what he would like to do with those around him."

Amis's debut novel was a tremendous success in Britain, and he was hailed as his generation's newest literary star. *Lucky Jim* seemed to touch a nerve in postwar Britain, with many of the once-mighty imperial nation's long-cherished notions giving way to a new, suddenly more mobile middle class. Amis was deemed one of Britain's new "Angry Young Men," a catchall phrase denoting a group of young novelists and playwrights who were unafraid to challenge and even mock long-held British traditions and beliefs. They included Larkin as well as playwrights Harold Pinter (born 1930) and John Osborne (1929-1994). Not surprisingly, Amis's novel and the whole movement also prompted some pointed backlash, including an essay by W. Somerset Maugham in December of 1955 in a yearly round-up of notable books in the *Sunday Times,* as quoted in *The Life of Kingsley Amis.* Maugham praised Amis and *Lucky Jim* but went on to discuss the larger issue of a new postwar Britain and its disappearing class boundaries. Noting that more than half of university graduates were by then earning their degrees thanks to new government grants, Maugham fumed that these youth "do not go to university to acquire culture, but to get a job." Maugham went on to remark that "they have no manners, and are woefully unable to deal with any social predicament. . . . Charity, kindness, generosity, are qualities which they hold in contempt."

Adultery and Alcohol

Lucky Jim was made into a film in 1957, as was Amis's second novel, *That Uncertain Feeling.* Published to great fanfare in 1955, the story centers on John Lewis, an adulterous librarian in a small town in Wales. It was made into a 1962 Peter Sellers film titled *Only Two Can Play.* In September of 1958, Amis took a year-long position as a lecturer and fellow in creative writing at Princeton University in New Jersey, where he also gave a series of lectures on science fiction. The entire family—which now included daughter Sally, born the same week *Lucky Jim* was published—went with him, and their rented house soon became the site of raucous, alcohol-fueled soirees. Amis had long dallied extramaritally, and years later his son Martin famously described his father as "a man who used to LIVE for adultery," according to *New York Times* writer A. O. Scott, in his review of Zachary Leader's book. During this reckless American period, Hilly reportedly conducted her own affairs as well.

Echoes of his affairs often found their way into Amis's fiction, such as descriptions of the vicious sexual games played by the male villain in his fourth novel, 1960's *Take a Girl Like You.* These affairs decimated Amis's marriage, which began a precipitous decline in early 1963 during his affair with novelist Elizabeth Jane Howard (born 1923), a former actress and model whose first marriage had been to the son of the noted Antarctic explorer Robert Falcon Scott (1868-1912). By the time they met, Howard was an acclaimed writer in her own right and, like Amis, rather unconventional and uncommitted in her romantic exploits. In somewhat uncharacteristic fashion, however, Amis seems to have fallen quite hard for her. The divorce from Hilly became final in June of 1965, and he wed Howard in London at the end of the month.

The union with Howard also served as a catalyst for severing ties with Gollancz, and he signed with his new wife's publisher, Jonathan Cape. His first title for them was written under the pseudonym Robert Markham, and was one of the James Bond adventure tales that continued on after the death of the original author, Ian Fleming (1908-1964). Amis's more serious literary efforts from this period include *I Want It Now,* published in 1968, followed by *The Green Man,* a tale of an alcohol-abusing, adulterous middle-aged proprietor of an English country inn who fears that the property is haunted. Subsequent titles published during the 1970s include *Girl, 20, Ending Up, The Alteration,* and *Jake's Thing.* These are the works "that most deeply divide Amis's admirers and his detractors," according to Gopnik. "To their fans, they are models of a disabused, cleanly written, and unsparingly Swiftian satire of mostly bad modern manners. To their non-fans, they seem like exhausting, increasingly alcoholic, right-wing rants."

Won Booker Prize

Amis had been a member of the Communist Party during his Oxford days, but his political ideals had traversed the full range from left to right by the 1980s, as he went from being a supporter of the Labour Party to admitting to a minor crush on prime minister Margaret Thatcher (born 1925), leader of Britain's Conservative (Tory) Party. He even wrote that Thatcher was "one of the best-looking women I have ever met," according to Scott, and he confessed that at times he seemed to find himself momentarily tricked "into thinking I am looking at a science-fiction illustration of some time ago showing the beautiful girl who has become President of the Solar Federation in the year 2220."

Amis's 1986 novel *The Old Devils,* about a novelist who returns to his Welsh hometown after many years and then dies in the middle of an evening of drinking with his longtime pals, won Britain's prestigious Booker Prize for Fiction. By then Amis's marriage to Howard had ended, and in his later years he lived in a rather unorthodox arrangement in the posh London neighborhood of Primrose Hill with Hilly and her third husband, Lord Kilmarnock. In 1991 Amis's autobiography, *Memoirs,* was published, followed by the novel *The Russian Girl* in 1994. In August of 1995 he fell and injured his back, which seemed to set off a rapid decline, and he died in London, England, on October 22, 1995. His twenty-third and final novel, *The Biographer's Moustache,* was published that year. "From young Turk to old Devil, he maintained an amazingly high standard, as well as that unerring ability to infuriate," noted Harry Ritchie, the writer of Amis's London *Guardian* obituary. Ritchie went on to quote Amis's own summation of his literary career: "I just enjoy annoying people."

Books

Leader, Zachary, *The Life of Kingsley Amis,* Pantheon, 2007.

Periodicals

Atlantic Monthly, May 2002.
Economist, March 9, 1991.
Guardian (London, England), October 24, 1995.
New Statesman, March 21, 1997.
New York Times, June 3, 2007.
New Yorker, April 23, 2007.

Sunday Times (London, England), September 18, 1988.
Times (London, England), January 27, 1954.
Times Literary Supplement, February 12, 1954. ☐

Amma

Mata Amritanandamayi (born 1953), known as Amma, is India's "Hugging Saint"—a spiritual leader who has given out hugs to some 30 million people in the course of her travels around the world.

When asked by Jesse Tarbert of the *Seattle Times* why she does it, Amma responded with a rhetorical question: "What is the motivation of a river? It just flows." India has produced a variety of spiritual leaders who have gained adherents in Western countries, but Amma has been unusual in several respects, both in the West and in India itself. She is female, for one thing; most Indian gurus, or religious teachers, are male. And it is uncommon for a single woman in India, much less one of a religious vocation, to touch a stranger, much less embrace one wholeheartedly. Amma's path extends beyond hugging to a variety of humanitarian undertakings that have earned her several major awards. Emerging from a background in the Hindu faith, she has also been honored as a figure who crosses religious lines.

Born in Fishing Village

Amma was born in a poor village called Parayakadavu, in south India's Kerala state, on September 27, 1953. Her father was a fish-seller. She was given the single name Sudhamani. The names by which she has been known as an adult were bestowed by her followers: Mata Amritanandamayi means "mother of immortal bliss," and Amma (or Ammachi) means "mother" in many south Indian languages. Amma's native tongue is Malayalam. She uses that language when traveling, relying on interpreters to communicate with attendees beyond her own retinue.

As is typical of writings about figures who are considered saintly, Web sites maintained by Amma's followers make various extraordinary claims about unusual spiritual powers and practices that manifested themselves during her childhood. When she was born, she smiled a beatific smile instead of crying. She is said to have been talking by the age of six months, singing by three years, and composing hymns and doing religious dances while still a young girl. Raised a Hindu, she heard a group of devotees discussing the god Krishna and went into a deep trance. Later, she carried a photographic image of Krishna in her pocket wherever she went. One account indicates that she spent hours in deep meditation as a child, another that her days were filled with hard physical labor to support her family after her mother fell ill.

Several facts emerge clearly from the tales of Amma's childhood. First, she was extraordinarily generous toward the frail elderly and other individuals suffering difficulties in the district where she lived. She cleaned their homes and helped them bathe, and she readily gave away food and clothing from her family's own meager stores. Her practice of giving hugs began during this period. Amma told Cathy Lee Grossman of *USA Today* that she decided to "make an offering of myself" to the poor and the sick. The second theme that recurs in discussions of Amma's early years is that her family was anything but supportive of her humanitarian endeavors. She was punished for giving the family's possessions away, and her spiritual intensity caused her father simply to conclude that she was insane.

Through her teens, Amma cultivated disciplines such as meditation, hymn singing, and yoga. When she was 21 she renounced the idea of marriage and dedicated herself to the spiritual life. At first, her deep trance states caused people to think of her as a medium, a channeler of souls from a world beyond. But before long a few began to regard her as a guru. Her father became convinced of her spiritual nature and bequeathed the family's small landholdings in Parayakadavu to her so that she could start an ashram, or spiritual community. By 1987, the ashram had more than 30 residents. Amma made her first foray abroad that year, stopping in France and Switzerland, and spending three months in the United States. Although the crowds that came to see her were small at the time, she succeeded in establishing the Mata Amritanandamayi Center (M.A. Center) in San Ramon, California, near San Francisco; it opened its doors in 1989.

Presided Over Interfaith Gathering

Amma slowly continued to gain followers beyond India, and in 1993 she served as president of the Centenary Parliament of the World's Religions, an interfaith gathering of 6,000 people in Chicago. In 1995 she addressed interfaith celebrations held in connection with the 50th anniversary of the United Nations in New York. While Amma continued to practice the Hindu faith, her message was a universal one. Her Web site (www.amma.org) proclaimed that "[m]y sole mission is to love and serve one and all. Amma's only wish is that her hands should always be on someone's shoulder, consoling and caressing them and wiping their tears." Amma's gatherings attracted devotees of various faiths, and attendees experienced no recruiting attempts on behalf of any religious denomination or organization. Amma's spokesman Rob Sidon told Erin Hallissy of the *San Francisco Chronicle* that Amma "firmly believes that all the religions are great and they all lead to the same path."

The growth of Amma's popularity to the level of worldwide phenomenon was due partly to her personal warmth and to the unique qualities of her encounters with her audience. Beginning around 1997, however, there was also an organized effort to "launch" Amma, as Amy Waldman put it in the *New York Times*. Sidon, a professional marketing specialist whose path to the position of spokesman began when he attended an Amma event (in Indian terms, a "darshan," or an audience with a saint), contacted media outlets to publicize Amma's appearances and later organized a billboard advertising campaign. The results were impressive. Amma attracted various high-profile devotees, including former *Dynasty* star Linda Evans and Yolanda King, a daughter of the Reverend Martin Luther King.

The backbone of Amma's popularity, however, was formed by the thousands of ordinary individuals who flocked to her events, seeking not only a hug but also a chance, if only for a few moments, to unburden themselves of their problems. Sidon told Hallissy that people might ask about anything from why their cows were not giving enough milk to "a priest wondering if he should remain a priest. Sometimes she'll whisper something"—translators were on hand at her appearances outside her home region—"or it could be as general as 'darling daughter, darling daughter.'" Simple as the encounters were, they had a powerful effect upon some devotees. Those receiving hugs from Amma were required to wipe their faces with tissue beforehand, for if they did not, Amma's sari would become streaked with makeup mixed with tears.

Amma's appearances began to fill large public spaces; on tour in the U.S. in 2004, she made a stop in one of the giant ballrooms at New York's Manhattan Center. Devotees might receive a small token that helped in keeping the lines flowing smoothly, but they would nevertheless have to wait for hours. Most were undisturbed by the long wait, and many returned year after year. "Every time I come I receive a blessing and a lesson, and I carry it with me for the year," suburban Seattle resident Gwendolyn Benedict told Tarbert. "Please do not hug Amma, let her hug you," a sign might read. After receiving their hugs, those leaving the stage where Amma sat might find themselves holding a flower petal or a candy kiss. Devotees reported a sense of calm and well-being after receiving their hugs.

Founded Hospital and Schools

Amma's mission, however, extended beyond her personal appearances. In her home state of Kerala, various charitable works owed their existence to her efforts. The most ambitious was the Amrita Institute of Medical Sciences, which opened in 1998 with more than 30 departments and ten specialty laboratories. The AIMS Hospital, with 1,300 beds, provided care for 751,098 patients between 1998 and 2006, and the Amrita Kripasagar hospice offered care for terminally ill patients—something usually out of reach of ordinary Indian families. Under the umbrella of the center in San Ramon, Amma operated soup kitchens in 30 American cities. She donated one billion rupees (about $23 million) to aid survivors of the 2004 Indian Ocean tsunami, and an additional $1 million for relief after Hurricane Katrina struck the U.S. Gulf Coast in 2005.

It was Amma's humanitarian activities that attracted Sidon and other devotees. "I was very impressed," he recalled to Eric Kurhi of the *Contra Costa Times* of his early meetings with Amma. "It wasn't so much just the hug, it was the whole philosophy, the humanitarian effort behind it. Amma is walking the talk." Many who came to Amma's appearances were drawn by sheer curiosity. And for others, she had an appeal on multiple levels. "You can take her as a sweet woman from India who gives you hugs up to the divine mother incarnate," Stella Petrakis of San Francisco told Hallissy. Her activities included the provision of social and medical services, spiritual teachings and secular education, and environmental protection under the auspices of her GreenFriends organization, which planted 100,000 trees annually in Kerala. As of 2005 the Amritanandamayi Charitable Trust operated centers in 15 countries, including Canada, France, Germany, Italy and Britain.

These activities earned Amma a variety of awards beginning in the early 2000s. She was given the Gandhi-King Award for Nonviolence in 2002 and the James Parks Morton Interfaith Award in 2006. In 2007 won a special humanitarian award at the Cinema Verité Film Festival in Paris, France, presented (by actress Sharon Stone) in connection with *Darshan,* a documentary that chronicled her life and activities. Several books of Amma's teachings, some of them in dialogue form, were translated from Malayalam and issued by the M.A. Center in San Ramon.

By 2007, not slowed by a 2005 attack by a man with a concealed knife, Amma had hugged an estimated 30 million people. She was noted for refusing to leave an event until all who had come for a hug had received one, even dispatching helpers into the crowd to tell visitors that she hoped they would not leave before she had a chance to meet them. In one 24-hour period in 2003, on her birthday, she reportedly hugged 75,000 people—three per minute with a few short breaks, but she showed few signs of tiring of her international schedule. "Just by feeling (someone's) pain you cannot resolve it," she told Grossman. "You have to do something. If you see a blind person who is crying, why suffer for him when you can hold his hand and help him across the street?"

Books

Amritanandamayi, Mata, *For My Children: Spiritual Teachings of Mata Amritanandamayi,* Mata Amritanandamayi Mission, 1986.
Religious Leaders of America, 2nd edition, Gale Group, 1999.
Swami Amritaswarupana, *Ammachi: A Biography of Mata Amritanandamayi,* M.A. Center, 1994.

Periodicals

Boston Herald, June 19, 2006.
Cincinnati Post, September 24, 2003; August 22, 2005.
Contra Costa Times (Walnut Creek, CA), June 7, 2007.
Daily News (Los Angeles, CA), June 22, 1996.
Daily Telegraph (London, England), July 22, 2004.
Grand Rapids Press (Grand Rapids, MI), January 9, 2005.
Independent (London, England), October 25, 2000.
New York Observer, July 25, 2005.
New York Times, September 29, 2003; July 18, 2004.
San Francisco Chronicle, June 11, 2003.
Seattle Times, June 6, 2003.
USA Today, July 19, 2006.

Online

"About Amma," Amma.org, http://ammachi.org/amma/index.html (October 21, 2007).
Contemporary Authors Online, Gale, 2007. http://galenet.gale group.com/servlet/BioRC (October 21, 2007).
"Devotees Flock to Hug Indian Guru," British Broadcasting Corporation, http://news.bbc.co.uk/1/hi/world/south_asia/3136524.stm (October 21, 2007).
"Film Award Honors 'Hug Guru,' " British Broadcasting Corporation, http://news.bbc.co.uk/2/hi/entertainment/7043185.stm (October 21, 2007).
"She was Sudhamani," The Homepage of Sri Mata Amritanandamayi Devi, http://www.amritapuri.org/amma/life/sud hamani.php (October 21, 2007). □

Ivie Marie Anderson

American singer Ivie Marie Anderson (1905-1949), one of the best vocalists of jazz's golden age, was the lead voice of jazz legend Duke Ellington's big band for 11 years. Her strong sense of timing, distinctive jazz phrasing, and genuine emotion made her performances of happy pop and sultry ballads equally affecting. Her most popular songs included "It Don't Mean A Thing (If It Ain't Got That Swing)," a defining song of the swing era, and the bluesy ballad "I Got It Bad and That Ain't Good."

A Trained Vocalist

I vie Marie Anderson (sometimes known as Ivy Anderson) was born in Gilroy, California, in 1905. Between the ages of nine and thirteen, she learned to sing at St. Mary's Convent in her hometown, and she sang in the choir and glee club at Gilroy elementary and high schools. She then spent two years receiving vocal training with Sara Ritt at the Nunnie H. Burroughs Institution in Washington, D.C.

Anderson returned to California around 1921, still a teenager, and began singing professionally, debuting at Tait's Club in Los Angeles and also performing at Mike Lyman's Tent Cafe. In 1922 she joined the Fanchon and Marco revue, a nationally touring vaudeville troupe led by Mamie Smith, performing as a singer and dancer. After singing in Cuba in 1924 and at the famed Cotton Club in New York City in 1925, Anderson joined the touring revue of *Shuffle Along,* a groundbreaking African-American musical. She returned to California and sang with several West Coast bandleaders, including Curtis Mosby, Paul Howard, and Sonny Clay. In the first five months of 1928, she toured Australia with Clay's band, then toured the West Coast of the United States for five months, headlining her own revue. She also sang with Anson Weeks at the Mark Hopkins Hotel in San Francisco in 1928, which may have made her the first black singer to perform with a white orchestra.

In mid-1930, Anderson joined jazz pianist Earl Hines's big band at the Grand Terrace in Chicago, Illinois. After five months performing there, she began performing with Duke Ellington, one of the country's most popular bandleaders. Ellington was booked to perform at the Oriental Theatre in Chicago, and the producer suggested that he add a female vocalist to his act. Before that, he had relied on clubs to provide singers or had his drummer, Sonny Greer, or trumpeter Cootie Williams sing. Ellington's producer suggested hiring a female singer. Ellington's autobiography revealed that Anderson was chosen over singer May Alix, who had recorded several successful records, including "Big Butter and Egg Man" with Louis Armstrong, because the producer felt the light-skinned Alix looked too white. Ellington, meanwhile, was impressed with Anderson's vocal sound and ability and, likely, her training and experience. Although he frequently hired self-taught musicians, he preferred trained vocalists. Anderson debuted with the band on February 13, 1931, performing live between showings of a film at the Oriental Theatre.

Her First Hits

Anderson quickly became a key part of the band's sound and appeal. Her first recording with the band, "It Don't Mean a Thing (If It Ain't Got That Swing)," became one of her best-known hits. Anderson's vocal included scatting, the jazz technique of playfully singing nonsense syllables to imitate musical instruments. "Anderson scats along with the band's introduction to the song like a jitterbug impatient to get the music moving," David Bradbury described in his book *Duke Ellington.* "She delivers the lyric as a passionate appeal, propaganda for a rhythmic revolution." Though the song had little melody and sparse lyrics, Anderson's catchy vocal proved a popular expression of the carefree, fun spirit of swing music.

At first the other band members found Anderson shy and awed by the fact that she was performing with Ellington. Soon, though, she and Greer, the drummer, started exchanging quick-witted banter onstage and developed a routine in which she would sing in response to his drumming. She stood out for "her showmanship, her fine understanding of song lyrics and her remarkable feeling for the way this band thought and felt and acted and played," wrote jazz critic Barry Ulanov, as quoted by Bradbury in *Duke Ellington.*

"Our Ivie wasn't a classic beauty, but how lovely she was as she sparkled through every scene, her small, shy smile unexpectedly quickening into an impish bump or dance step," trumpeter Rex Stewart later wrote, quoted by Bradbury. "When she sang a melancholy refrain such as 'Solitude' or 'Mood Indigo,' oft times the fellows in the band would get caught up in the tide of her emotional portrayal and look sheepishly at each other in wonder at her artistry." Anderson's winning onstage persona contrasted with her still charming but rougher personality out of the spotlight. On the band's train rides, Anderson proved herself a talented poker player, often winning a lot of money from the musicians in no-betting-limit games. "Off stage our Miss Anderson was another person entirely, bossing the poker game, cussing out Ellington, playing practical jokes or giving some girl-advice about love and life," Stewart recalled.

Veteran jazz critic Nat Hentoff once caught a glimpse of this side of Anderson, as he recounted in an article for *Jazz Times.* "I was talking with Duke Ellington in his dressing room when a slender, vivid, angry spirit swept in," Hentoff recalled. It was Anderson, "who had a grievance, which she expressed in remarkably inventive, salty language until she took note of me, stopped and vanished."

Anderson's second big hit for Ellington was the dark ballad "Stormy Weather." Her performance of the song at the London Palladium in June of 1933, during a two-month tour of England, the Netherlands, and France, was especially memorable. She sang the song without a microphone while dressed in a white gown and leaning against a marble pillar. "She stopped the show cold," Ellington recalled in his autobiography, *Music Is My Mistress.* "While she was singing 'Stormy Weather' the audience and all the management brass broke down crying and applauding." Anderson also sang the song in the film short *Bundle of Blues,* shot that year. Other early hits of hers included "Raisin' the Rent" and "I'm Satisfied," also released in 1933.

Anderson's Talent

Some critics felt Anderson had weaknesses as a singer, including poor intonation. But she sang with an authentic jazz feeling that made her very popular with Ellington's audiences. Ellington considered Anderson the singer "who best embodied the band's resilient spirit," according to Hentoff. She sang with a precise diction and was skilled with blues and scat phrasings, singing pop songs with a bright, piercing voice and ballads with a full, sultry tone.

"Ivie had an unerring sense of jazz time," wrote Hentoff. "Her phrasing was so musically that she fitted seamlessly into the band, and she had as strong a presence as the famed soloists in the orchestra." Hentoff judged her interpretations of the jazz standards "Solitude" and "Stormy Weather" the most affecting he ever heard.

In 1937 Anderson appeared in the Marx Brothers film *A Day at the Races,* singing "All God's Chillun Got Rhythm." Though she played a washerwoman, a stereotypical African-American job at the time, she still radiated dignity and joy. In the scene, she sings as a group of black children follow her, as well as Harpo Marx, who was playing a penny whistle.

Ellington, some feel, reached the peak of his creative powers around 1940 and 1941. Anderson recorded several significant songs with him during that period, including "Me and You," which Bradbury called one of her most joyful vocals. She also recorded vocal versions of "Solitude" and "Mood Indigo," which had long been theme songs for the band as instrumentals.

In 1941 Anderson and Ellington's band were featured in a groundbreaking revue in Los Angeles, *Jump For Joy,* which celebrated authentic African-American humor and culture and satirized sentimentality about the South and the theatrical stereotypes that white audiences expected black performers to re-enact. Anderson sang "I Got It Bad and That Ain't Good," which later became a hit, and two humorous social commentary songs, "Uncle Tom's Cabin is a Drive-In Now," which imagined the slave characters from the novel *Uncle Tom's Cabin* freed and running a Los Angeles restaurant, and "I've Got a Passport from Georgia," which celebrated the relative freedom of black Americans who left the South for New York City. The show played for three months in Los Angeles but did not tour elsewhere, likely because white audiences were not receptive to its positive message about blacks.

"I Got It Bad and That Ain't Good," a signature song for Anderson, told of an uncaring man who does not return the narrator's love: "Never treats me sweet and gentle, the way he should," Anderson sang. She, Ellington, and the band appeared in a film short featuring the song (now available on the DVD *Duke Ellington: The Big Band Feeling*). Anderson, clad in a plaid dress, sits forlornly on a windowsill, singing the title line directly to the camera. Another scene shows Anderson running her hands over Ellington's shoulders, then looking away, as he lies on a couch, drinking.

Retirement

By 1942 Anderson was suffering from chronic asthma, which made it difficult for her to sing. That summer, she and pianist and composer Billy Strayhorn scouted Chicago's nightclubs, looking for a new female singer to join Ellington's band. They recruited Betty Roche, a veteran vocalist who performed with the band for most of the 1940s. In August of 1942 Anderson retired from the band.

Returning to Los Angeles, Anderson opened Ivie's Chicken Shack with her husband, Marque Neal. She later divorced Neal, sold the restaurant, and married Walter Collins, an apartment building manager (the dates of the marriages and divorce are unknown). Anderson performed in nightclubs in California and recorded eight solo songs in 1946 with top jazz musicians, including Charles Mingus, Willie Smith, and Lucky Thompson. But her poor health kept her from recording or touring regularly.

Anderson died on December 28, 1949, in the Los Angeles apartment building her husband managed, after a three-week illness related to asthma. She was 45. Today her music is available on compilations from several record companies. The most comprehensive disc—Jasmine Records' 2000 release *I Got It Good and That Ain't Bad!*—includes some of her 1946 solo recordings as well as her work with Ellington. "She was really an extraordinary artist and an extraordinary person as well," Ellington recalled in *Music Is My Mistress*. "She had great dignity, and she was greatly admired by everybody everywhere we went, at home and abroad."

Books

Bradbury, David, *Duke Ellington,* Haus Publishing, 2005.
Collier, James Lincoln, *Duke Ellington,* Oxford University Press, 1987.
Ellington, Duke, *Music Is My Mistress,* Doubleday, 1973.
Notable Black American Women, Book 2, Gale Research, 1996.

Periodicals

Jazz Times, April 2001.
New York Times, December 30, 1949.

Online

"Ivie Anderson," Solid!, http://www.parabrisas.com/d_andersoni.php (December 16, 2007).
Kernfeld, Barry, "Anderson, Ivie," *American National Biography Online,* http://www.anb.org/articles/18/18-02718.html (December 16, 2007).

Wilson, Jeremy, "Ivie Anderson," *Jazz Standards History,* http://www.jazzstandards.com/biographies/ivie_Anderson.htm (December 16, 2007).
Yanow, Scott, "Ivie Anderson: Biography," *All Music Guide,* http://www.allmusic.com (December 16, 2007). □

Lou Andreas-Salomé

Russian-born German writer Lou Andreas-Salomé (1861-1937) has been known mostly as the lover of and inspiration to several of the most prominent male German authors of her time, including philosopher Friedrich Nietzsche, poet Rainer Maria Rilke, and psychoanalytic pioneer Sigmund Freud.

Andreas-Salomé was also a prolific writer on her own, however, and in matters of female independence and sexual liberation she was a trailblazer. Her novels, plays, stories, and essays, mostly forgotten today, are often thinly veiled treatments of her romantic and intellectual adventures with the men in her life. Yet as such, her writings are unique: she combined a strong female perspective, eroticism, and a spirit of independence, and in some ways she may be regarded as the forerunner of twentieth-century female intellectuals such as Simone de Beauvoir.

Doted On as Child

A native of St. Petersburg, Russia, Andreas-Salomé was born Louise Salomé on February 12, 1861. Her father, Gustav Ludwig von Salomé, was a distinguished Russian general who doted on his youngest child and only daughter, sometimes to an extent that disturbed Andreas-Salomé's mother, Louise Wilm von Salomé. Both French and German were widely spoken among the Russian aristocracy at the time, and Andreas-Salomé was raised speaking those languages. She spoke some Russian as well, but when she rebelled at the idea of studying that language in school, her father gave her the green light to study whatever she liked.

Fortunately, Andreas-Salomé proved to be a curious child who had little difficulty in educating herself. Lonely and given to fantasy, she finally found an effective teacher in a married Dutch-born minister named Hendrik Gillot. He instructed her in philosophy, languages, and religion, carried out her confirmation ceremony in the German Lutheran church, gave her the nickname of Lou (which would stick for the rest of her life), and inculcated in her a spirit of independence and self-regard. When the student-teacher relationship broke down, probably under the stress of Gillot's attraction to his young pupil (described as beautiful for most of her life), Andreas-Salomé fell ill. She and her mother headed for Zurich, Switzerland, where Lou would recuperate and continue her education at the University of Zurich.

In Zurich Andreas-Salomé immersed herself in studies of theology and art history. Professors at the university did not know quite what to make of the young Russian woman

fluenced the other as a writer, however; Andreas-Salomé is mentioned in Nietzsche's *Ecce homo* (Behold the Man), and *Also sprach Zarathustra* (Thus Spoke Zarathustra), written soon after the breakup, was directly credited to Andreas-Salomé's influence. ''My disciple became my teacher—the god of irony achieved a perfect triumph!'' Nietzsche wrote, according to the *Dictionary of Literary Biography*. ''She inspired me with the thought of Zarathustra: my greatest poem celebrates our union, and our tragic separation.''

As for Andreas-Salomé, her own writing career began to take off in the middle 1880s. While cohabiting with Rée in Berlin, she wrote the autobiographical novel *Im Kampf um Gott* (1885), using the male pseudonym Henri Lou (for later books she reverted to her own name). The novel features a character, clearly modeled on the blaspheming, life-affirming Nietzsche, who has destructive effects on three women, each of whom reflects an aspect of Andreas-Salomé's own personality. The novel won positive reviews and established Andreas-Salomé as a literary force independent of her famous boyfriends; her relationship with Rée ended in 1885.

In 1887 Andreas-Salomé married the linguistics scholar Friedrich Carl Andreas, after which she hyphenated her last name but put her own surname in the final position. Andreas was one of a number of men who took irrational steps—in his case stabbing himself in the chest with a penknife—during his courtship of Andreas-Salomé. According to many accounts, the marriage was never consummated, and by 1898 the two had separated, although they remained married until Andreas's death in 1930. Andreas-Salomé began to write about the growing Berlin theater scene, and in 1892 she wrote a book, *Henrik Ibsens Frauengetstalten* (Henrik Ibsen's Female Characters), about the pioneering feminist themes in the work of the Norwegian dramatist. Her 1894 study of Nietzsche, *Friedrich Nietzsche in seinen Werken* (Friedrich Nietzsche in His Works), was well received and consulted for many years. She also published a second novel, *Ruth,* in 1895.

That year, Andreas-Salomé embarked on an affair with a doctor from Vienna, Friedrich Pineles. Once again her love life provided material for her fiction, which took a decidedly erotic turn in such stories as ''Eine Nacht'' (One Night). A group of her stories appeared in book form in 1898 under the title *Fenitschka*. Another cycle, *Menschenkinder,* translated into English as *The Human Family,* appeared a year later. She had other sexual adventures and misadventures as well, including one with German playwright Frank Wedekind, in the wake of which the two engaged in mutual literary recriminations in the form of negative characters modeled on each other.

Became Muse to Rilke

The relationship with Pineles was interrupted (although it later resumed) when Andreas-Salomé met poet Rainer Maria Rilke in May of 1898. Although she was 36 and he was 22 years old at the time, the relationship soon turned serious. The two became lovers and traveled together twice to Andreas-Salomé's homeland of Russia, and Andreas-Salomé also exerted influence on Rilke's career just as his

but were unanimous in praising her brilliance. Andreas-Salomé, however, continued to suffer from the effects of a worsening lung disease that doctors had warned could cost her her life. She began coughing up blood. Her mother, alarmed, decided that a warmer climate might help, and the pair moved on to Rome, Italy, in 1882. The new location was helpful both physically and intellectually, for Rome was full of writers and thinkers from all over Europe.

Through a family friend, Andreas-Salomé met two young philosophers, Paul Rée and Friedrich Nietzsche. Rée was the first to fall under her spell, but both were soon in love with her. Andreas-Salomé, for her part, was pleased to be traveling Europe, healthy, and receiving romantic attention from some of the top thinkers of the day. Nietzsche set Andreas-Salomé's poem ''Hymnus an das Leben'' (Hymn to Life) to music in 1882. The love triangle evolved, and at one point the three planned to share a house, intended as a kind of intellectual commune they called the Trinity. The plan never bore fruit, but the tensions inherent in the situation were immortalized in a photograph by Jules Bonnet, of Andreas-Salomé atop a small cart, holding a whip that she wields over the ''horses,'' Nietzsche and Rée.

Rejected Marriage Proposal

Nietzsche saw Andreas-Salomé as something of an ideal woman whom he could mold into a disciple and partner. He proposed marriage but was rejected, and the relationship eventually deteriorated under the pressure of hostility from Nietzsche's sister Elisabeth. Each partner in-mature style was taking shape. She made suggestions that helped give his poetry its characteristic intensity, and she convinced him to take the German name of Rainer; formerly he had had been called René. In 1901 the relationship flamed out as quickly as it had begun, possibly because Andreas-Salomé felt uncomfortable with the degree of worship she was receiving from the younger man. She continued to be productive as a writer and published a novel, *Ma: Ein Portrait,* in 1901.

Andreas-Salomé wrote several other books in the first decade of the twentieth century, including *Im Zwischenland: Fünf Geschichten aus dem Seelenleben halbwüchsiger Mädchen* (In-Between Land: Five Stories from the Inner Life of a Half-Grown Girl, 1902) and the nonfiction *Die Erotik* (The Erotic, 1910), part of a major philosophy and sociology series edited by philosopher Martin Buber. Gradually, however, she began to feel the desire for a second career. The opportunity presented itself in 1911 when, at the Weimar (Germany) Congress of the International Psychoanalytic Association, she met psychoanalysis pioneer Sigmund Freud. At first he was amused by her desire to study psychoanalysis, but she quickly mastered Freud's ideas. According to the Books and Writers Web site, Freud observed that "all the tracks around her go into the Lion's den but none come out." Nevertheless, he remained the only one of Andreas-Salomé's three major intellectual mentors with whom she did not become romantically involved. The 50-year-old Andreas-Salomé began to attend the meetings of Freud's inner circle, to write essays on psychoanalytic theory and as of 1913, to practice psychoanalysis herself. Her friendship with Freud endured, and by the early 1920s she was widely recognized as an analyst, and, partly as a result of her continuing association with the depressive Rilke, she penned several forward-looking essays on the relationship between psychology and creativity.

Returning to writing in the 1920s, Andreas-Salomé penned a play, *Der Teufel und seine Großmutter* (The Devil and His Grandmother, 1922). Most of her later books, however, were nonfiction studies of the authors she had known well: *Rainer Maria Rilke* (translated as *You Alone Are Real to Me*) appeared in 1928, and *Mein Dank an Freud* (My Thanks to Freud) in 1931. In her last years, she wrote a *Grundriß einiger Lebenserinnerungen* (Outline of Some Life Reminscences, 1933) and a more extensive *Lebensrückblick* (Life Retrospective), not published until 1951. Andreas-Salomé underwent cancer surgery in 1935 but died of uremia on February 5, 1937, in Göttingen, Germany.

Andreas-Salomé's writings were well known during that time, but then were mostly forgotten. Even with the tremendous revival of interest in writings by women toward the end of the twentieth century, studies of Andreas-Salomé as a creative figure in her own right remain rare. As of the early 2000s, however, there were signs that scholars were beginning to reexamine Andreas-Salomés work. In 2005 University of Alberta professor Ralph G. Whitinger told the *Chronicle of Higher Education* that "the rediscovery of her fiction has given us an array of her documents that describe the nature of the 1890s second wave of the women's libera-

tion movement—some of the complexities of it, of course, but also the general thrust of it."

Books

Binion, Rudolph, *Frau Lou: Nietzsche's Wayward Disciple,* Princeton University Press, 1968.
Bloomsbury Guide to Women's Literature, Prentice Hall, 1992.
Dictionary of Literary Biography, Volume 66: German Fiction Writers, 1885-1913, Gale, 1988.
Peters, H. F., *My Sister, My Spouse: A Biography of Lou Andreas-Salome,* Norton, 1974.
Rilke, Rainer Maria, and Lou Andreas-Salomé, *The Correspondence,* tr. Edward Snow and Michael Winkler, Norton, 2006.

Periodicals

Chronicle of Higher Education, October 21, 2005.
Irish Times, September 7, 2002.
Library Journal, April 1, 2003.

Online

"Lou Andreas-Salomé (1861-1937)," Books and Writers, http://www.kirjasto.sci.fi/salome.htm (January 24, 2007). □

Agnes Arber

English botanist and plant morphologist Agnes Arber (1879-1960) was one of the eminent scientists of her time. She was the first female botanist (and only the third woman overall) to be elected to the Royal Society of London and the first woman to win the Gold Medal of the Linnean Society. The first of her seven books, *Herbals: Their Origin and Evolution: A Chapter in the History of Botany: 1470 to 1670* was published in 1912 and quickly became a classic. Arber's scientific work was further distinguished by its inclusion of her artistic, historical, and philosophical interests and sensibilities.

Early Life and Education

Arber was born in London, England, on February 23, 1879, the eldest of Henry Robert Robertson and Agnes Lucy Turner's eventual three children. Her father was an artist who began giving her drawing lessons when she was three years old, and her mother instilled in her an early interest in plants. Combined, those childhood influences would go on to play a crucial role in her education and professional life.

Arber's parents also had the intelligence and foresight to see that she was better educated than was the general fashion of the era for girls. Thus, she was sent to the North London Collegiate School for Girls, where education was taken seriously and the sciences were particularly emphasized. It was there that Arber met the botanist Ethel Sargant, who was to become a mentor and lifelong friend, and that she was exposed to the work of renowned German Johann Wolfgang von Goethe, who would also have a lasting impact on her.

In 1897, Arber began studying at University College in London. She received a bachelor of science degree, with First Class Honors, in 1899 before winning a scholarship to Cambridge University's Newnham College. She performed extremely well at Cambridge, again achieving First Class Honors, but the university did not grant degrees to women at the time, so the budding scientist was forced to obtain her doctorate elsewhere. First, beginning in 1902, she spent a year as Sargant's research assistant at the older botanist's private laboratory in her home. Arber then returned to University College as a Quain Student in biology. She was awarded a D.Sc. in 1905 and taught biology and botany at the university until 1909. In 1908, Arber had been made a fellow of the Linnean Society of London and in 1909, she married paleobotanist Edward Alexander Newell ("Newell") Arber. Her new husband was employed by Trinity College, Cambridge, so the young couple settled in a rented house there that Arber would inhabit for the next 51 years.

Beginnings and Endings

In Cambridge, Arber returned to Newnham College (one of only two women's colleges at the university then) to conduct her research at its Balfour Laboratory. Her primary specialty was the monocotyledon, or monocot, division of flowering plants. Monocots are the smaller of the two main flowering plant groups, the larger being dicotyledons (dicots), and are generally characterized as having a single seed leaf, narrow leaves with parallel veins, flower parts arranged in sets of threes, and hollow or soft stems. Their ranks include grasses, orchids, lilies, and palms.

As the newlyweds embarked upon their lives together, the world seemed to hold much promise. Arber's first book, *Herbals: Their Origin and Evolution: A Chapter in the History of Botany: 1470 to 1670,* was published in 1912 (a second edition appeared in 1938). Its attention to science and history, as well as the myriad beautifully detailed illustrations rendered by the author herself, quickly elevated the book to a classic of botanical literature. That success was followed by the unrelated, although surely just as welcome, happiness of the birth of the Arbers' only child, Muriel, on July 21, 1913. Sargant was named the godmother. But the joy was short-lived, as Arber's husband passed away on June 14, 1918, not yet nine years past their union as husband and wife.

The death of Arber's husband, unsurprisingly, left a great void and presented many challenges to the young widow. It is, perhaps, telling that she never remarried. Instead, she devoted her life to her work and her daughter, with whom Arber lived until her death in 1960. It may not have been an entirely blissful existence for the relatively nascent scientist, but it did prove to be a fruitful one.

Her Own Space

Arber continued her research at the Balfour Lab until the college closed the facility in 1927. During that time, she also wrote two more books, *Water Plants: A Study of Aquatic Angiosperms* (1920) and *Monocotyledons: A Mor-*

phological Study (1925). The former acknowledged her late husband as the instigator of the project in the preface and the latter was inherited from Sargant when the more senior botanist's health became too poor to write it. Both were rife with Arber's trademark illustrations and, although some of her ideas, such as the concept of parallel evolution, were controversial, the books were considered valuable contributions to the field of botany.

The closing of the Balfour Lab necessitated that Arber seek out new research facilities. She first asked permission to use the university's lab at its Botany School, but was refused, so cast about for another suitable location. Finally, as her mentor had done before her, Arber set up a laboratory in her home. And while the solution could hardly have been ideal, she rose to the challenge admirably. Indeed, Arber was well suited to the autonomy and solitude offered by such a working arrangement. Richard L. Hauke quoted her words from an address to Girton College students in 1926 in *Vignettes from the History of Plant Morphology* as, "The concentration of mind necessary for independent thought is far more easily achieved in a place where one can get a generous measure of solitude than in a populous laboratory where people are incessantly running in and out, and in Ethel Sargant's words 'Independence is the essence of research.' "

Head Full of Ideas

Whether Arber found her home laboratory facilities optimum or not, the situation did not affect her customary productivity. In 1934, her last major morphological (or that concerning the anatomy of plants) work, *The Gramineae: A Study of Cereal, Bamboo, and Grass,* was published. Later books included *The Natural Philosophy of Plant Form* (1950), *The Mind and the Eye: A Study of the Biologist's Standpoint* (1954), and *The Manifold and the One* (1957). Nor were her writing efforts limited to books. Arber also contributed historical pieces to such publications as *Isis* and *Chronica Botanica,* and wrote about such famous scientists as Nehemiah Grew, Marcello Malpighi, John Ray, and Sir Joseph Banks. In 1945, she drew upon her lifelong fascination with Goethe to publish a translation and commentary on his *Attempt to Interpret the Metamorphosis of Plants.* In all, Arber had written over 80 scientific articles, a great many historical and philosophical articles, plenty of book reviews, and, of course, her own seven books between 1903 and 1960. And that was in addition to conducting her scientific research and bringing up a child alone.

One of the most interesting things about Arber's writings was how they tracked her change of focus from strict morphology to the history and philosophy of scientific thought. In the *The Natural Philosophy of Plant Form,* for example, part of her preface reads, as quoted by Hauke, "I began by thinking of (the morphology of flowering plants) quite simply as a branch of natural science, but I have come finally to feel that it reaches its fullest reality in the region of natural philosophy, where it converges upon metaphysics." *The Mind and the Eye: A Study of the Biologist's Standpoint* explored the process of biological inquiry, with half the book dedicated to interpreting scientific research within the dual contexts of history and philosophy. *The Manifold and the One* went even further, as it delved into the paradox of the relationship of parts to a whole and brought mysticism into play. In fact, Arber's last book was such a departure from the mainstream literature of her field that it was not reviewed in the scientific press and was generally catalogued in libraries under "metaphysics," as opposed to the "botany" or "biology" classifications of her earlier work. Still, that later work retained relevance into the 21st century, as had much of her previous effort. Maura C. Flannery noted in a 2002 article for the *SHiPS Newsletter,* "As a new century and a new millennium get underway, it is easy to lose sight of the notable thinkers of the past . . . Agnes Arber is one such individual who deserves attention in the century ahead, particularly because she presented a view of biological inquiry that is still fresh and significant today."

A Woman of Firsts

Although Arber was considered one of the most important botanists of her time, she chose to live very simply. Her income was not large, and she never moved from the rented house she had come to as a young bride in 1909. Her preference for quiet and solitude, utter devotion to her work, and, undoubtedly, the demands on a single mother, did not lend themselves to a busy social schedule. But she found time to mentor various botany students, much as Sargant had helped her along so many years before, and she was known as a kind and gracious person. Arber's work, however, was what truly defined her, and the scientific community did not let it pass unremarked upon. In 1946, she became the first female botanist (and only the third woman overall) to be elected as a fellow of the Royal Society of London. Two years later, she became the first woman ever to be honored with the Gold Medal of the Linnean Society. In short, Arber's insight and contributions were recognized and rewarded by her peers.

Arber and her daughter, who grew up to be a noted geologist, lived together at 52 Huntingdon Road in Cambridge until Arber's death on March 22, 1960. She was buried with her late husband at St. Andrew's Parish in Girton. It is a testament to her impact and lasting legacy that her work and ideas were still being examined decades later. Kathryn Packer, for instance, wrote *A Laboratory of One's Own: The Life and Works of Agnes Arber, F.R.S. (1879–1960)* (1997), and the 1999 International Botanical Congress looked at her morphological work in relation to newer developments in vascular plant development. Simply put, Arber was gone, but her remarkable contributions lived on.

Books

Notable Scientists: From 1900 to the Present, Gale Group, 2001.

Online

"Agnes Arber: Morphology to Metaphysics and Mysticism," *Vignettes from the History of Plant Morphology,* 1996, http://members.aol.com/cefield/hauke/arber.html (November 29, 2007).

"Arber, Agnes Robertson (England 1879-1960)," Chrono-Biographical Sketch, http://www.wku.edu/~smithch/chronob/ARBE1879.htm (November 29, 2007).

"Monocotyledon," *Hutchinson Encyclopedia,* http://encyclopedia.farlex.com/Monocotyledons (January 2, 2008).

Packer, Kathryn, "A Laboratory of One's Own: The Life and Works of Agnes Arber, F.R.S. (1879-1960)," Royal Society Publishing, http://www.journals.royalsoc.ac.uk/content x8pfddhtv1t918wh/ (November 29, 2007).

"Plant Anatomy & Glossary," Texas A&M University, http://dallas.tamu.edu/weeds/anat.html (January 2, 2008).

"The Historical and Scientific Significance of Agnes Arber," http://socrates.berkeley.edu/~schmid/arber/ArberSummary.html (November 29, 2007).

"The Many Sides of Agnes Arber," *SHiPS Newsletter,* October 20, 2002, http://www1.umn.edu/ships/gender/arber.htm (November 29, 2007). □

Vera Atkins

British intelligence agent Vera Atkins (1908-2000), as principal assistant in Britain's Special Operations Executive (SOE) secret service, administered some of the most sensitive secret operations carried out by Allied forces during World War II.

Atkins's story is among the most striking illustrations of the collision between individual interpersonal ethics and the vast forces of worldwide conflict to be found in the annals of the entire World War II period. Atkins sent secret agents, drawn from all walks of life, into occupied France, to be dropped by parachute into an unknown fate. She knew, and they knew, that they faced a significant likelihood of being killed, yet that knowledge did not affect her precise implementation of a spy program that, at least until it was infiltrated, gave the Germans considerable trouble. After the war's end, Atkins embarked on a remarkable personal and professional odyssey, attempting to account for each and every one of the agents who had died in service to her mission, and she very nearly succeeded.

Concealed Jewish Background

Atkins was of Jewish descent, something she took pains to hide at various times in her life. She was born Vera-May Rosenberg on June 15, 1908, in Galatz, Romania. She later took her English mother's maiden name, which was Atkins, when she moved to England in the 1930s, and she replaced May with the more Christian-sounding Maria. (Obituaries reported her middle name as Maria but her biographer, Sarah Helm, unearthed and reproduced her original birth certificate, which reads as above.) Atkins's father, Maximilian Rosenberg, was a German-born Jew who moved from farming into the lucrative field of supplying lumber to industry, including South African diamond mines. Vera was born shortly after his return to Europe, by which time he had become a wealthy man. He purchased a substantial country estate.

The life of the young Vera Rosenberg gave few hints of the steel-willed spy runner to come. She was sent to Lausanne, Switzerland, and to Paris, to finishing schools, where she learned to speak faultless French, a skill that would later serve her well. These schools also required poetry and diction classes in English, and Rosenberg also learned to speak that language like a native, with an upper-class accent. Her life was a whirl of social events, aristocratic hunting parties, and numerous marital suitors. Some were highly placed landowners, sons of diplomats, and the like; her Jewish faith was sometimes an issue, sometimes not. Atkins took a job in London in the early 1930s, returned to Romania, perhaps because of a romance, and finally, as conditions deteriorated for Jews in central Europe, moved to London for good in 1937. As life for her family got worse, Atkins made a fateful compromise: in 1940, according to Helm, she paid a $150,000 bribe to a Nazi intelligence agent in Antwerp, Belgium, in order to help her cousin Fritz obtain a passport.

As with many other intelligence agents, Atkins had an ambiguous background. Other members of her family had trafficked in information across Europe during much of the period between the two world wars. That might have brought her to the attention of Britain's Secret Service as war loomed, and her linguistic competence—she spoke German well, in addition to English, French, and Romanian—would also have made her a candidate. She was recruited for the SOE, which she joined in the early stages of the war. She started as a secretary.

The SOE was a sabotage unit, set up at the direction of British prime minister Winston Churchill and told to set occupied Europe ablaze. The F section was the division assigned to France, which had been overrun by the Germans in 1940 and was under the control of a government at Vichy, administered by German military authorities and their French collaborators. Although she was an amateur in the business of intelligence operations, she first became an intelligence officer and then, in her early 30s, was made principal assistant to the SOE's director, Colonel Maurice Buckmaster, at the SOE offices at 62-64 Baker Street in London. Buckmaster was reputedly the model for "M" in novelist Ian Fleming's series of James Bond novels, while Miss Moneypenny, somewhat incongruously, was modeled on Atkins. A large portion of the operations planning for F section was left to Atkins herself, and, as subsequent events showed, the successes the unit accomplished were likely due to her own efforts rather than those of the chief to whom Adolf Hitler assigned an equal place with Churchill on his enemies list.

Staged Tea Party

Atkins's networks began with recruitment, during which candidates were interviewed in a hotel room with a single light bulb, quizzed to determine their fluency in French, and sent away to think, after being told that their chances of survival were 50-50. Since French general Charles de Gaulle refused to allow French citizens to participate, the new spies were mostly English citizens who had a French parent. Beyond their common ability to speak French, they represented a vast cross section of English society, from taxi drivers to a playwright. At their training camp, a sixteenth-century country house, they were trained in explosives and in the tradecraft of the spy. Atkins, who

reportedly worked 18-hour days, schooled them in the minutiae of French life and gave them realistic documents and other items such as ticket stubs, that could identify them as French.

Finally the candidate was summoned to have tea with a Miss Vivienne Thomas at 57 Wimpole Street. This was Atkins. She explained the agent's specific mission, handed over the appropriate identity papers, and sent him or her off with a shouted French expletive. She stood on the airfield runway to watch as each one departed. The agents she placed in the field became a remarkably cohesive and focused group. According to Julian Jackson, writing Atkins's London *Guardian* obituary, one agent who was distracted from his duties was chided by Atkins with the comment, "Oh the bloody English. . . . We never have this sort of bother with the French. . . . They copulate and that is that." Atkins was described by associates as businesslike, with never a hair out of place on her head.

Her inner experiences, however, were a different story. As she later admitted, according to Jackson, "The burden of stress was probably on the person who was seeing them off. The realisation that they were going out on a very dangerous mission . . . while you remained quite safely at the end. There was a considerable strain on one at this time. I think I must have been extraordinarily tough—I was extremely exhausted by it."

The exploits of some of Atkins's agents became part of Britain's World War II lore. Some were tortured and sent to German concentration camps. Accounts of those who survived told of extreme heroism under torture. Odette Sansom refused to tell Nazi interrogators her secrets even when her toenails were pulled out one by one. Most famous of all was the Indian-British Noor Inayat Khan, known as Nora, who was beaten to death by her captors and spoke only the single French word "liberté"—liberty. At the beginning of her training with Atkins she had been shy, childlike, and, according to her own testimony, incapable of lying.

Betrayed by French Pilot

The capture rate was as high as it was because a French pilot ferrying Atkins's agents into France had divulged the F section's secrets. The resulting problems were compounded when Buckmaster discounted mounting evidence that the operation had been compromised, at least until the Germans sent a thank-you note for the weapons and money they had seized. Of the 400 agents Atkins sent into the field, 118 were missing when France was liberated in the summer of 1944.

The next chapter in Atkins's story of secret service began after the war, when she applied for and, despite the misgivings of superiors who feared the malfeasance that might be exposed, was given the responsibility for interrogating defeated German soldiers and guards to find out what they might know about the disappearance of the 118 agents. She pointed out that she was the only person with the background knowledge to conduct the interviews most effectively. "I could not just abandon their memory," she said, according to Douglas Martin, in Atkins's obituary in the *New York Times*. "I decided we must find out what happened to each one, and where." In one of the most remarkable feats of investigation in military history, she discovered the fate of all 118 agents, 117 of whom had been killed. The last one had taken the Secret Service's money and fled to the casinos of Monaco. Captured Germans said that she was the most skilled interrogator they had ever faced, and she was also assigned to interrogate Auschwitz concentration camp commander Rudolf Höss. When Atkins asked him if it was true that he was responsible for the deaths of 1.5 million Jews, he corrected her with a figure of 2,345,000.

Atkins left the Secret Service in 1947 and, perhaps because of the Antwerp episode with her cousin, kept a low profile for many years, giving rise to rumors that she had spied for either Germany or the Soviet Union. She worked at the Special Forces Club. In 1987 she was named a commandant of the French Legion of Honor. Settling in a seacoast house in the town of Winchelsea in southeast England, she began to share her knowledge with historians late in her life, although even in 1998 the 90-year-old Atkins told her biographer Sarah Helm that "I have closed the book on many things in life." (Helm's biography supplements what she learned from Atkins with interviews of her relatives and associates, and with extensive investigation of source documents.) Atkins died in Hastings, East Sussex, England, on June 24, 2000.

Books

Helm, Sarah, *A Life in Secrets: Vera Atkins and the Missing Agents of WWII,* Nan A. Talese, 2006.
Millar, George, *Road to Resistance,* Little, Brown, 1980.
Stevenson, William, *Spymistress: The Life of Vera Atkins, the Greatest Female Secret Agent of World War II,* Arcade, 2006.

Periodicals

Guardian (London, England), July 6, 2000.
Independent (London, England), July 3, 2000.
New York Times, June 27, 2000.
U.S. News & World Report, July 10, 2000.

Online

"Her Life as a Spy," Salon.com, http://www.salon.com/books/review/2007/01/04/helm/index.html?source=search&aim=/books/review (February 3, 2008). □

Julius Axelrod

American scientist Julius Axelrod (1912-2004) shared the 1970 Nobel Prize in Physiology or Medicine (with Ulf von Euler and Sir Bernard Katz) for his research relating to the role that neurotransmitters play in the human body's sympathetic nervous system. Specifically, Axelrod and the co-recipients received the award for their discoveries concerning "the humoral transmitters in the nerve terminals and the mechanisms for their storage, release and inactivation."

Axelrod's research into the body's neurotransmitters has led to new discoveries in neurobiology and has enabled the development of chemical treatments for mental disease and nervous system disorders. For this reason, some people refer to him as "the father of Prozac Nation."

Axelrod was born on May 30, 1912, in New York City, New York, to Isadore and Molly Leichtling Axelrod. His parents were Polish immigrants who came to America in the early years of the twentieth century. They settled in the Jewish section of Manhattan's Lower East Side, where Isadore Axelrod supported his family by making flower baskets for local merchants.

Axelrod attended public elementary and high schools near his tenement home. Never one to let formal schooling interfere with his "real education," Axelrod spent many hours at the local public library. A voracious reader, he could finish several books in a single week. His literary interests were wide-ranging and included everything from contemporary pulp novels to important writers such as Upton Sinclair and Leo Tolstoy.

Obtained Master's After Medical School Rejections

After high school Axelrod spent a year at New York University, but he transferred to the tuition-free City College of New York (CCNY) when he ran out of money. He graduated from CCNY in 1933 with majors in biology and chemistry. Following college graduation, Axelrod applied to several medical schools, but was turned down. He claimed that the rejections stemmed from quotas for Jewish students. As quoted in the *Washington Post,* Axelrod said, "I wasn't that good a student, but if my name was Bigelow I probably would have gotten in."

Forced to seek work, Axelrod had difficulty finding employment in New York City, as the country was in the midst of the Great Depression. However, in 1933 he secured a position as a laboratory assistant at the New York University Medical School, where he received a meager $25-per-month salary. In 1935 he became a chemist at the Laboratory of Industrial Hygiene, a nonprofit organization established by the New York City Department of Public Health to test vitamin supplements added to foods.

On August 30, 1938, Axelrod married Sally Taub. The couple eventually had two sons, Paul Mark and Alfred Nathan. While supporting his family, Axelrod took courses at New York University toward his master's degree in chemistry, which he received in 1941. During this period, Axelrod lost the sight in one eye in a laboratory accident (a bottle of ammonia had exploded). For the rest of his life, he would wear a dark covering over the damaged eye. At first, he wore an eyepatch. Later he opted for a darkened eyeglass lens.

Research Assignment Led to Important Collaboration

Axelrod enjoyed working at the Laboratory of Industrial Hygiene, where he found the work interesting and the pay sufficient. But in 1946 his career received a boost when he was given the chance to do some substantial scientific research. The laboratory received a grant to determine why some people who took large quantities of acetanilide, a non-aspirin pain-relieving drug, developed methemoglobinemia, a blood disorder characterized by the body's inability to recycle hemoglobin (the oxygen-carrying molecule found in red blood cells) after it had been damaged. In severe cases of methemoglobinemia, the hemoglobin cannot carry oxygen to body tissues.

Inexperienced in such complex research, Axelrod consulted Dr. Bernard B. "Steve" Brodie of Goldwater Memorial Hospital of New York, who was a well known drug researcher. Brodie found the problem so fascinating that he decided to collaborate with Axelrod to determine a solution. In addition, through his relationship with Brodie, Axelrod became part of the New York University research staff.

Joined National Institutes of Health

Working together, Axelrod and Brodie made a significant contribution to the knowledge of the chemistry of analgesic medications. They learned that the human body either metabolizes acetanilide into a substance with an analgesic, or pain relieving, effect, or into another substance that causes methemoglobinemia. Therefore, they recommended that the analgesic substance be directly administered without acetanilde.

In 1949 Axelrod and Brodie, along with several other researchers from Goldwater Memorial Hospital, received an invitation to join the National Heart Institute of the

National Institutes of Health in Bethesda, Maryland. (The National Heart Institute later became the National Heart, Lung and Blood Institute.) At the institute, Axelrod conducted research on the physiology of caffeine absorption and drugs called sympathomimetic amines, which mimic actions of the sympathetic nervous system that prepare the body for strenuous activity. In addition, he studied several compounds including amphetamine, mescaline, and ephedrine. He then discovered a new enzyme group that enabled these compounds to metabolize in the body.

Obtained Doctoral Degree

Convinced that he needed to obtain a doctorate to advance in the National Institutes of Health, Axelrod sought an advanced degree in the mid-1950s. Taking a year's sabbatical from work, he prepared for comprehensive examinations at George Washington University in the District of Columbia. To meet his thesis requirements, he submitted the research from work he had already accomplished. In 1955 he received a Ph.D. in pharmacology. The degree did indeed provide new opportunities, and Axelrod did not return to the National Heart Institute. Rather, he joined the National Institute for Mental Health, which was another branch of the National Institutes of Health, where he was offered the chance to create a new pharmacology section within the Laboratory of Clinical Sciences. He became chief of the section, a position he held until he retired in 1984.

During this period, Axelrod's research included studies involving metabolism of lysergic acid diethylamide (commonly known as LSD) and the human body's pineal gland. In the course of his research, Axelrod determined that melatonin was the pineal gland's key hormone. In addition, working with collaborators, Axelrod determined the mechanism for glucocorticoid formation and demonstrated that congenital non-haemolytic jaundice is caused by a defect in glucocorticoid synthesis.

Focused on Neurotransmitters

In 1957 Axelrod began an area of research work that would culminate in a Nobel Prize. Working with colleagues and students, he focused on neurotransmitters, which are chemicals that transmit signals from one ending to another. Specifically, he studied how neurotransmitters worked inside the human body. During related research conducted the previous decade, Swedish scientist Ulf von Euler discovered that noradrenaline served as the neurostransmitter for the body's sympathetic nervous system. Now, in his own research, Axelrod looked at how the rapid deactivation of noradrenaline cleared the way for later nerve signal transmissions. This, he determined, happened in two ways: through the enzyme catechol-O-methyltransferase (which Axelrod discovered and named), which was essential to metabolism and, in turn, noradrenaline deactivation; and through the reabsorption and storage of noradrenaline by the nerves for later reuse. Axelrod's discoveries had significant impact. He was able to show that psychoactive drugs, such as antidepressants and amphetamines, achieved their effects by hindering the normal deactivation or reabsorption of noradrenaline and other neurotransmitters. This inhibition extended the impact the drugs had on the nervous system or the brain.

Axelrod's research would lead to numerous new discoveries in the emerging field of neurobiology and chemical treatment for mental disease and nervous system disorders. For instance, his work helped lead to selective serotonin reuptake inhibitors, which are antidepressant medications used to treat depression and anxiety. Perhaps the best-known selective serotonin reuptake inhibitor is Prozac.

Received Share of Nobel Prize

In 1970 Axelrod shared the Nobel Prize in Physiology or Medicine with Ulf von Euler and Sir Bernard Katz of the United Kingdom. Axelrod and the co-recipients were awarded specifically for their discoveries concerning ''the humoral transmitters in the nerve terminals and the mechanisms for their storage, release and inactivation.''

During his banquet speech, included on the Web site Nobelprize.org, Axelrod said, ''This award comes at a time when our young and many of our most influential people believe that basic research is irrelevant or is put to evil uses. The selection of chemical neurotransmission for a Nobel Prize this year, makes our work highly visible to the general public and gives us an opportunity to show how misinformed and mistaken they are. I think we can easily demonstrate that although our work is of a fundamental nature, it also gives us insight in explaining such illnesses as mental depression, Parkinson's disease, hypertension and drug abuse. It can also lead the way to the treatment of these terrible afflictions.''

After he was honored, Axelrod made a point of crediting von Euler for initiating the early work that eventually led to their recognition by the Nobel committee.

Axelrod has been described as a soft-spoken individual with a wry and often self-deprecating sense of humor. Also, with his highly visible darkened lens, he had a distinctive physical presence. ''I used to wear a black patch over my eye when I was young. It was very dashing, like Brenda Starr's husband,'' he quipped to the *Washington Post*, with characteristic wit.

Noted neuroscientist Solomon H. Snyder was quoted in *The Lancet* as saying, ''[Axelrod's] successes never went to his head. He still worked in the lab with his own two hands even when he'd won the Nobel Prize. He said he got his best ideas when he was washing glassware.''

Later Research

In his post-Nobel years, Axelrod continued with his biochemical and pharmacological research, in particular the study of hormones. Beyond his work on neurotransmitters, Axelrod also developed new experimental techniques that found wide application among his colleagues. In addition, he became well known and respected for the training and assistance he graciously provided to visiting researchers and postdoctoral students. It has been estimated that during his career he mentored about 70 younger scientists. Michael J. Brownstein, who did postdoctoral research in Axelrod's

laboratory in the 1970s, told *The Lancet*, ''He just loved to talk about science and think about science. . . . He had a special ability to see through biological phenomena when the rest of us couldn't.''

Even though Axelrod formally retired from the National Institute of Mental Health in 1984, he continued with his own research, despit failing health late in his life. Ironically, in 1993, when Axelrod was 80 years old, his life was saved through one of his own past scientific discoveries. He had suffered a massive heart attack and required immediate triple coronary-artery bypass surgery. But his blood pressure had fallen so low that the cardiologists at Georgetown University Medical Center, where he was being treated, feared that he could not survive such an operation. However, the physicians injected a synthetic form of noradrenaline to stimulate the contractions of his heart and raise his blood pressure to an acceptable level. Axelrod not only survived, but was able to go back to work in two months.

He continued to work regularly at his office at the National Institutes of Health until his death on December 29, 2004. Axelrod reportedly died in his sleep at his home in Rockville, Maryland. He was 92 years old. His wife of 53 years, Sally Taub Axelrod, had passed away 12 years earlier.

During his career he received numerous honors and awards. Along with his Nobel award, only a few of these included the National Science Foundation Travel Award (1958), The Gairdner Foundation Award (1967) and the Distinguished Achievement Award from George Washington University. He was a member of several distinguished scientific societies, and served on the editorial boards and committees of important scientific and medical journals, including *Journal of Pharmacology and Experimental Therapeutics, Journal of Medicinal Chemistry, Life Sciences, Circulation Research, Journal of Neurobiology, Pharmacological Research Communications, Journal of Neurochemistry,* and *International Journal of Psychobiology.*

Books

Notable Scientists: From 1900 to Present, Gale Group, 2001.

Periodicals

The Lancet, January 29, 2005.
Washington Post, December 30, 2004.

Online

''Julius Axelrod: The Nobel Prize in Physiology or Medicine,'' Nobelprize.org, http://www.nobelprize.org/cgi-bin/print ?from = %2Fnobel_prizes%2Fmedicine%2Flaureates %2F1970%2Faxelrod-bio.html (November 10, 2007).
''Julius Axelrod: The Nobel Prize in Physiology or Medicine - Banquet Speech,'' Nobelprize.org, http://www.nobelprize .org/nobel_prizes/medicine/laureates/1970/axelrod-speech .html (November 10, 2007).
''The Nobel Prize in Physiology or Medicine 1970,'' Nobelprize.org, http://nobelprize.org/nobel_prizes/medicine/ laureates/1970/press.html (November 10, 2007).
World of Health Online, http://www.galenet.galegroup.com/ servlet/BioRC (November 10, 2007). □

B

Bahá'u'lláh

Iranian prophet Bahá'u'lláh (1817-1892) founded the Baha'i faith in nineteenth-century Iran. Bahá'u'lláh, whose name in Arabic translates as "the Glory of God," claimed to have been anointed the "Promised One" for all the world's religions, the emissary who carried a message of world peace and unity for all of humankind.

Bahá'u'lláh was born Mírzá Husayn-'Ali' on November 12, 1817, in Tehran, Iran, into an aristocratic family. His father, Mírzá Buzurg, held an important post as vizier to Fath Ali Shah (1772–1834), the Persian emperor, and later served as governor of the Iranian provinces Burujird and Lorestan before being ousted when a new ruler, Muhammad Shah Qajar (1808–1848) came to power in Persia. After Mírzá Buzurg died in 1839, Bahá'u'lláh was offered a political appointment by a new vizier, but declined the post in order to tend to the sick and destitute.

Joined Bábist Sect

Around 1845, when Bahá'u'lláh was about 28 years old, he learned of a new sect known as Bábism. This had been founded a year or so earlier by Siyyid Mírzá 'Alí-Muhammad (1819–1850), a merchant from the Iranian city of Shiraz. Taking the name the Báb, (the Gate), 'Alí-Muhammad claimed to be the new *mahdi*, or "Guided One" that had been prophesied in Islam. Bábism, he asserted, would aid in the revival of Persia and its people, and from the Persians a new divine teacher would soon appear. Once that new prophet came, world peace would become possible.

Bahá'u'lláh joined the Bábi sect and began to preach its tenets in the province of Núr. Government officials, fearing the rise of this sect, began to target Bábi followers, and the Báb himself was executed in 1850. Two years later, Bahá'u'lláh learned of a plot to assassinate the Shah as vengeance for the death of the Báb, and advised against it. The plan went into motion anyway, was foiled by the Shah's agents, and brought a wave of reprisals against the sect. Bahá'u'lláh was jailed in the infamous Tehran dungeon jail known as *Síyáh-Chál*, or the Black Pit, where he experienced several religious visions. He was told, he claimed, that he was the Messenger of God of whom the Báb had spoken. Saying nothing of this revelation to anyone, Bahá'u'lláh was finally released thanks to an intercession from Russia's ambassador to Persia, and was sent into exile in Baghdad, Iraq.

Hid as a Dervish

In the ancient Iraqi city, Bahá'u'lláh joined other members of the now nearly defunct Bábi community. The Báb's appointed successor was Mírzá Yahya, but a power struggle erupted between the two, and not wishing to weaken the community any further, Bahá'u'lláh retreated to the mountains of Kurdistan in April of 1854. He spent the next two years living alone, dressed like a member of a Sufi Muslim sect called the dervishes, and began writing religious tracts. Soon, local leaders began to seek the advice of the wise man who called himself Darvish Muhammad, and word reached Baghdad of the visionary and his teachings. Both Bahá'u'lláh's family and the Bábi followers sent word to him requesting his return.

Bahá'u'lláh heeded the call to return to Baghdad, where the community was now bitterly divided because of Mírzá Yahya's marriage to the widow of the Báb. Still, Bahá'u'lláh was hesitant to reveal that he had been called

21

by God for another seven years, but nevertheless attracted unwelcome interest from Islamic clerics, who worried that he might lead his Bábi followers in an uprising. He was exiled once again, this time to Constantinople, in April of 1863. Before he departed, however, he went to nearby Garden of Ridván and spent twelve days there. Finally, he told his companions of his revelation, an act that ended the 11-year period in the Baha'i faith known as *ayyam-i butun* (days of concealment).

Once Bahá'u'lláh proclaimed himself the Messenger of God, the Bábis accepted him as their leader, an event that is considered the formal beginning of the Baha'i religion. His exile in Constantinople was a short-lived one, lasting just four months, and he was banished again to Adrianople (present-day Edirne, Turkey) in December of 1863. He remained there with his followers for more than four years. During this period, he and Mírzá Yahya continued their ideological battles, and the Bábis split into two branches: the Baha'i who followed Bahá'u'lláh, and the Azalís who remained loyal to Mírzá Yahya. At one point, Bahá'u'lláh suffered a near-fatal poisoning that was believed to have been an assassination plot ordered by his rival.

Sent Missives to World Leaders

In Adrianople, Bahá'u'lláh began codifying the tenets of the Baha'i faith. Its key beliefs were global unity and justice, and he wrote the *Súriy-i-Mulúk,* or Tablet to the Kings, which was sent out to various world leaders. In it, he urged them to recognize him as a guide for world peace and to work together to achieve that goal. The recipients of these missives included England's Queen Victoria (1819–1901); leader of the Roman Catholic Church Pope Pius IX (1792–1878); France's Napoleon III (1808–1873); Tsar Alexander II of Russia (1818–1881); and Kaiser Wilhelm I (1797–1888), the ruler of imperial Germany. In his *Súriy-i-Mulúk,* Bahá'u'lláh reminded the world leaders that "God hath committed into your hands the reins of the government of the people, that ye may rule with justice over them, safeguard the rights of the down-trodden and punish the wrong-doers. If ye neglect the duty prescribed unto you by God in His Book, your names shall be numbered with those of the unjust in His sight."

Bahá'u'lláh's activities resulted in his forcible deportation once more in August of 1868, this time to Akká, Palestine, which was a penal colony administered by British colonial authorities at the time. It later became the city of Acre, Israel. Here Bahá'u'lláh wrote the famous *Kitáb-i-Aqdas,* the book of laws of the Baha'i faith and its most important holy text. It was likely finished by 1873. "In the Aqdas, Bahá'u'lláh recognizes and honors the institution of human government, in the forms of monarchy, democracy, and republican government, and enjoins all people to obey 'those who wield authority,'" noted Sen McGlinn in the *Journal of Church and State.* The *Kitáb-i-Aqdas* also contained Bahá'u'lláh's reminder to world leaders that he had no ambitions to hold political power himself. "It is not Our wish to lay hands on your kingdoms. Our mission is to seize and possess the hearts of men. . . . To this testifieth the Kingdom of Names, could ye but comprehend it. . . . Forsake your pal-

aces and haste ye to gain admittance into His Kingdom. This, indeed, will profit you both in this world and in the next."

In another of the many religious texts Bahá'u'lláh authored, he cites Britain as a model of the ideal relationship between church and state. The *Lawh-I-Dunyá* (Tablet of the World) states that "the system of government which the British people have adopted in London peareth to be good, for it is adorned with the light of both kingship and of the consultation of the people." He also refers to his own persecution, asserting that "every man of insight will, in this day, readily admit that the counsels which the Pen of this Wronged One hath revealed constitute the supreme animating power for the advancement of the world and the exaltation of its peoples. Arise, O people, and, by the power of God's might, resolve to gain the victory over your own selves, that haply the whole earth may be freed and sanctified from its servitude to the gods of its idle fancies—gods that have inflicted such loss upon, and are responsible for the misery of their wretched worshippers."

Died in Akká

In the 1870s there was a lessening of restrictions on Bahá'u'lláh's movements, and after 1879 he resided in the Mansion of Bahjí in Akká, though he remained closely watched by authorities. In 1890, Bahá'u'lláh met with a respected British scholar of Middle Eastern religions, Edward Granville Browne, whose writings about the Baha'i faith roused interest in the religion elsewhere in the world. Bahá'u'lláh told Browne, according to the Web site Uplifting Words, "We desire but the good of the world and happiness of the nations; yet they deem us a stirrer up of strife . . . . [T]hese ruinous wars shall pass away, and the 'Most Great Peace' shall come. . . . Do not you in Europe need this also? Is not this that which Christ foretold? . . . Yet do we see your kings and rulers lavishing their treasures more freely on means for the destruction of the human race than on that which would conduce to the happiness of mankind. . . . These strifes . . . must cease, and all men be as one kindred and one family."

Bahá'u'lláh died in Akká on May 29, 1892. Survivors include the three wives he took, Navváb, Fatimih, and Gawhar, by whom he had fourteen children. The eldest of his ten sons was Abbas Effendi (1844–1921), known as Abdu'l-Baha, or "servant of the Glory." He had followed his father into exile and then assumed the leadership of the faith after Bahá'u'lláh's death. Abdu'l-Baha's missionary work served to spread the Baha'i faith in both Europe and North America. Adherents to the Baha'i faith recognize several significant principles set forth by Bahá'u'lláh. World unity is of paramount importance, and the creed also bans prejudice against others. Equality between the sexes is enshrined in its teachings, as are an eradication of the extremes of poverty and wealth. Universal compulsory education is another principle, as are good works in the forms of schools and clinics where the need is greatest.

More than a century after the death of Bahá'u'lláh, the Baha'i faith claims five million adherents in 235 nations. There are no clergy, and each community is a self-governing one that elects its own to members of a council. The administrative center of the faith is the Baha'i World

Centre in Acre, Israel, near the burial shrines of both the Báb and Bahá'u'lláh. There are Baha'i houses of worship on several continents, with a particularly splendid one in Evanston, Illinois, reflecting the blending of classical and Islamic elements that is a hallmark of Baha'i architecture. The religion uses its own calendar that begins with the date of March 19, 1844, a date set by the Báb in his original formulation of the Bábist faith. The main holy holiday of the Baha'i faith is the twelve-day Festival of Ridván, which begins on April 21 and commemorates the public declaration of Bahá'u'lláh as the Messenger of God. The Baha'i creed is notable for its recognition of other religions, believing that the founders of all the world's faiths that preceded it—Abraham, Moses, Jesus Christ, Muhammad, Zoroaster, Krishna, and Buddha—are the divine teachers in the pantheon that includes the Báb and Bahá'u'lláh.

Baha'i followers are still persecuted in Iran, a Muslim theocracy, where in the 1980s scores were arrested and 200 put to death. The recognition of Bahá'u'lláh as "a messenger of God," explained Laurie Goodstein of the *New York Times*, "violates the Islamic teaching that God sent many prophets before Muhammad, but none afterward."

Books

Palmer, Martin, "Baha'i," *World Religions*, Times Books, 2004.

Periodicals

Journal of Church and State, Autumn 1999.
New York Times, June 1, 2006.

Online

"Professor Brown's Visit to Bahá'u'lláh," upliftingwords.org, http://www.upliftingwords.org/browne.htm (December 30, 2007). □

Joanna Baillie

Scottish playwright and poet Joanna Baillie (1762-1851) was one of the most acclaimed literary figures of her day, despite the inescapable fact that she was female. Her work, which included over 25 plays and dozens of poems, was hailed by contemporaries in Great Britain and the United States, but fell largely into obscurity after her death on February 23, 1851. Happily, a resurgence of interest in the 20th century resulted in the artist finally receiving the long-term recognition she deserved.

Early Times

Joanna Baillie was born prematurely on September 11, 1762 in Bothwell, Scotland to the Reverend James Baillie and the former Dorothea Hunter. Her twin sister died shortly after birth, but she had two older siblings, Agnes and Matthew, with whom she would become very close.

Her father was a Church of Scotland minister who claimed descent from legendary Scottish patriot William Wallace (c. 1270–1305), whose story was told in the popular Hollywood movie *Braveheart* in 1995. Baillie's mother was a sister of the famous physicians and anatomists, William and John Hunter.

Fond of the outdoors, Baillie spent more of her early years horseback riding, swimming, and scaling roofs than immersed in schoolwork; there is speculation that she did not learn to read until she was 11 years old. This lack did not inhibit her active imagination however, as she reveled in listening to ghost stories and making up tales and playlets of her own. But it was not until she and her sister attended boarding school that she received the intellectual stimulation that allowed her inherent talents to blossom.

Baillie's family had moved to Hamilton in 1769 so that the reverend could take a position at the collegiate church. About three years later, the Baillie sisters were sent to Miss McDonald's Boarding School in Glasgow. There, Baillie finally developed an interest in books, as well as inclinations toward drawing, music, and, interestingly, mathematics. She also attended the theater for the first time giving rise to an overriding and lifelong passion for the stage. Although her natural high spirits remained intact, they were becoming tempered and enhanced by the benefits of a formal education.

Coped with Changes

In 1776, Baillie's father moved the entire family to Glasgow after he accepted a job as professor of divinity at

Glasgow University. Fate then took a sad turn when the reverend died just two years later, leaving three teenagers and a widow with very little inheritance. The family thus fell under the protection of Baillie's uncle, William Hunter, who took up his charge admirably. Brother Matthew was dispatched to Oxford to study medicine and engaged as an apprentice at his uncle's School of Anatomy, while Baillie's mother was provided with a lifetime allowance and a home (with her daughters) at her family's estate in Long Calderwood. The Baillie women were uprooted once again upon William Hunter's death in 1783. This time, they moved to London, England, to run the household on Windmill Street that Matthew had inherited from his uncle. After Matthew's marriage in 1791, his mother and sisters relocated to Hampstead, where they found domestic stability and lived out the remainder of their years.

Baillie thrived in London. Her aunt, Anne Hunter, wife of her mother's other brother, John, was a poet of some note. The niece was thus able to make the acquaintance of various members of the London literati, which surely gave her incentive to follow her dreams of writing. While still on Windmill Street, she read widely and began to write in earnest. Most of those maiden efforts never saw the light of day, but a volume of poetry with the improbable and unwieldy title *Poems: Wherein it is Attempted to Describe Certain Views of Nature and of Rustic Manners; and also, to Point Out, in Some Instances, the Different Influence Which the Same Circumstances Produce on Different Characters* was published in 1790. It appeared anonymously and received little notice at the time, but it did nonetheless mark the beginning of Baillie's career.

Anonymous to Famous

In 1798, a trio of plays was published under the once again unlikely title of *A Series of Plays: In Which it is Attempted to Delineate the Stronger Passions of the Mind, Each Passion Being the Subject of a Tragedy and a Comedy.* The lengthy introduction to the volume explained the author's intention to examine each of the major passions of humankind within a play, while dramatizing the often hidden psychological processes behind them. The author, however, remained anonymous, and London literary circles were instantly abuzz with speculation as to who could have come up with such a novel approach to the writing of plays. Naturally enough for the time, the initial consensus was that some erudite man of letters had penned the work. When that supposition failed to produce an author, lesser male lights were considered and then, finally, women. None though, considered the possibility that this new sensation might be the unassuming Scottish spinster of 36 who was often seen on the periphery of various literary gatherings around town. In fact, it was not until the work was rechristened with the shorter title of *Plays on the Passions* shortly after its original publication, was in its third printing in 1800 that Baillie revealed herself as the author. Astonished, the London literary in-crowd welcomed their newest genius with mostly open arms.

Volume 1 of *Plays on the Passions* consisted of *Basil,* a tragedy on love, *The Tryal,* a comedy on love, and *De Monfort,* a tragedy on hatred. *De Monfort* opened on April 29, 1800, at London's Drury Lane Theater with noted actor John Philip Kemble and his sister, Sarah Siddons, in the leading roles. Although the play became one of Baillie's most popular and most often staged, its run at the Drury Lane lasted only 11 nights and boded an ongoing problem the playwright would have with getting her work moved from the page to the boards. Still, the play and the volume in which it first appeared had secured Baillie's place as a preeminent author of her age.

Body of Work

A second volume of *Plays of the Passions* appeared under Baillie's name in 1802. It contained *The Election,* a comedy on hatred, *Ethwald,* a tragedy in two parts on ambition, and *The Second Marriage,* a comedy on ambition. That was followed up by *Miscellaneous Plays* in 1804 (reprinted in 1805) and the Scottish drama called *The Family Legend* in 1810. The latter included a prologue written by Baillie's friend Sir Walter Scott (1771-1832), the well known poet and novelist, and was staged in Edinburgh in 1810 and at the Drury Lane in 1815. In 1812, the third and final volume of *Plays on the Passions* was published. It was comprised of two tragedies, *Orra* and *The Siege,* and a comedy, *The Alienated Manor,* based on fear, and a musical drama on hope titled *The Beacon.*

After a hiatus of several years, Baillie began to expand her literary efforts beyond the theater. *Metrical Legends of Exalted Characters* (1821) was a work of narrative poetry that told the stories of such historical figures as her ancestor William Wallace and explorer Christopher Columbus. She then turned to editing, as she collected and prepared for publication an anthology of new poetry by leading writers of the day titled *A Collection of Poems, Chiefly Manuscript, and from Living Authors,* (1823). The collection was both philanthropic and therapeutic. It was produced for the financial benefit of a widowed friend and was compiled while Baillie was nursing her beloved brother through an illness from which he did not, sadly, recover. He died September 23, 1823.

Baillie's later work explored some new themes and styles, while revisiting themes found in her earlier works. *The Martyr* (1826), for instance was a tragedy about religion, while 1831's *A View of the General Tenour (sic) of the New Testament Regarding the Nature and Dignity of Jesus Christ* was a serious philosophical analysis of various religious doctrines. A second edition of 1823's collection of poems was published in 1832 and 1836 saw the release of *Dramas,* a three-volume set of plays. *Fugitive Verses,* which included writings from Scottish folk songs to hymns, elegies, and poetry (including some verses from her first publication in 1790), appeared in 1840. *Ahalya Baee: A Poem* (1849) was the last of the author's new material, but her collected works were compiled in what Baillie termed a "great monster book" entitled *The Dramatic and Poetical Works of Joanna Baillie, Complete in One Volume.* It was published in 1851, shortly before Baillie's death on February 23, and had two subsequent printings.

Life Well Lived

Although Baillie's long life was not without its disappointment and sorrow, it was also immensely productive and well-lived. Her writing had its detractors, of course, and she reportedly was always unhappy that her plays were so rarely staged. Nonetheless, her work was generally ranked among the very best of its time by her contemporaries, and its success provided the author with a comfortable income. That respect from the literati did not, however, extend as fully to the general public. Baillie's works were never as widely read as those of her friend Scott, for example, and that may be the reason she fell into relative obscurity after her death. She would thus undoubtedly be gratified by the resurgence of interest in her writing precipitated by Margaret S. Carhart's 1923 biography, *The Life and Work of Joanna Baillie,* and furthered by the republishing and publishing of her poetry, plays, and letters in the late twentieth and early twenty-first centuries. No author, but least of all one as diligent and prolific as Baillie, writes to become forgotten.

Baillie's personal life was also largely admired. After their mother died in 1806, Baillie and her sister were housemates and companions the remainder of their lives. Hospitable, intelligent, and modest, Baillie traveled throughout Europe, was an active correspondent, and maintained a busy social calendar. She was also a devoted daughter and sister, having cared for both her mother and brother during the illnesses that brought about their passing. Further, she had a lifelong commitment to philanthropy that was inspiring. Among her many laudable efforts in the last regard, Baillie customarily donated half of earnings to charity. And, as noted above, *A Collection of Poems, Chiefly Manuscript, and from Living Authors* was compiled to help out a friend. Yet another example of Baillie's good works was the Edinburgh staging of *The Family Legend,* the proceeds of which went to a different financially troubled family of her acquaintance. Clearly, the high regard that Baillie enjoyed was well deserved.

As interest in the professional and personal life of Baillie increases, her importance as a literary figure and female writer of the Romantic period is likely to continue to be reassessed and gain momentum. The long-term recognition she had worked for all her life appeared to, at long last, be close at hand.

Books

Dictionary of Literary Biography, Volume 93: British Romantic Poets, 1789-1832, First Series. A Bruccoli Clark Layman Book. Edited by John R. Greenfield, McKendree College. The Gale Group, 1990.

Periodicals

Sunday Times (London, England), May 26, 2002.
Times (London, England), February 23, 1990.

Online

"Baillie, Joanna," *Oxford Dictionary of National Biography,* http://www.oxforddnb.com/public/dnb/1062-print.html (November 30, 2007).

"First 100 Years," Juggernaut Theatre Company, http://www.juggernaut-theatre.org/first100years/bailliebio.html (November 30, 2007).
"Rounding the Circle: American Interest in Joanna Baillie (1762-1851)," *Scotland's Transatlantic Relations,* April 2004, www.star.ac.uk/Archive/Papers/Laidlaw_JoannaBaillie.pdf (November 30, 2007).
"Scott, Sir Walter," *Columbia Encyclopedia,* http://www.bartleby.com/65/sc/Scott-SirW.html (December 31, 2007).
"Sir William Wallace," *Britannica Online Encyclopedia,* http://www.britannica.com/eb/article-9075966/Sir-William-Wallace (December 31, 2007). □

Baroness Orczy

The Hungarian-British novelist known as the Baroness Orczy (1865-1947) wrote *The Scarlet Pimpernel,* a fast-paced and well-plotted tale of heroism during the French Revolution.

Orczy's story was originally a successful stage play in London, and went on to several feature film versions in the first half of the twentieth century. The title refers to a mysterious savior who rescues innocent French nobles from the guillotine, and who is eventually unmasked as Sir Percy Blakeney, an English fop and the unlikeliest of heroes. Orczy's first Pimpernel tale and its sequels, wrote *Times* of London journalist Will Gatti, "have an archetypal quality that becomes the base for other stories. Percy, with his dual identity, is the direct forerunner of heroes such as Superman, driven to save the world without letting the world see who they really are."

The Baroness Orczy was born Emma Magdalena Rosalia Maria Josefa Orczy on September 23, 1865, in Tarna-Ors, Hungary. Called "Emmuska" by her family and friends, she was born into the Hungarian aristocracy as the only child of Felix Orczy, Baron of Tarna-Ors, and Emma Wass, a countess. Felix was a gentleman farmer and music composer of minor renown who knew both Franz Liszt (1811-1886) and Richard Wagner (1813-1883). In 1868, in response to a new agricultural policy on the lands he owned, Felix was the target of a tenant uprising in Tarna-Ors, and the family had to flee to the safety of the capital, Budapest. The fear of the wrath of peasants would become a key element in his daughter's later Pimpernel tales, which centered upon the rescue of innocent nobles from mob justice.

Married a Fellow Artist

The Orczys lived in Brussels, Belgium, and Paris, France, before settling in London, England, by 1880. It was at this point that the Baroness, now 15, began learning English, the language in which she would make her career. Initially, however, she was drawn to music, and dreamed of following in her father's footsteps as a composer. After realizing she lacked musical aptitude, she switched to art, taking painting classes at the West London School of Art and at Heatherly's School of Art. It was at the latter that she met a

fellow student, Montagu Barstow, whom she wed in 1895. Their only son, John Montagu Orczy Barstow, was born four years later.

The Orczys were a titled family, but had little actual income, and Orczy and her husband were expected to support themselves financially. There were several lean years in which Barstow eked out a living as an illustrator and translator, and Orczy also ventured into publishing as the translator and illustrator for a volume of Hungarian fairy tales. For a time, the family lived as paying guests in a London home where the two daughters of the household earned a living by writing adventure tales for magazines. Orczy was fascinated that the young women churned out imaginative stories though they had barely ventured beyond the confines of their own home and native land, and decided that if they could pen such stories, then so could she. She completed a novel, *The Emperor's Candlesticks*, which centered around intrigue among Russian anarchists and aristocrats in Vienna, Austria, and St. Petersburg, Russia, but her 1899 literary debut attracted little notice and posted dismal sales figures.

A London Stage Hit

The story for *The Scarlet Pimpernel* came to Orczy while she was waiting at the London Underground subway station at Temple. When she finished the manuscript, she sent it to a dozen publishing houses, each of whom rejected it for publication. With help from her husband she rewrote it into a play, and *The Scarlet Pimpernel* made its theatrical

debut at the Theatre Royal in Nottingham in 1903. A well-known husband-and-wife acting team, Fred Terry and Julia Neilson, decided to stage it in London at the New Theater. Terry, known for his roles in swashbuckling dramas, rewrote the final act, and that alteration helped make *The Scarlet Pimpernel* a terrific success from its opening night in London in January of 1905. It would also mire the literary property in years of lawsuits between Terry and the Orczy/Barstows.

The Scarlet Pimpernel contained anti-French themes, which had always been popular with English audiences. The story is set during the French Revolution, specifically the ten-month period between 1793 and 1794 known as the Reign of Terror, when scores of French aristocrats were put to death by guillotine, a new invention that made death by beheading a dramatic public spectacle. The Pimpernel is a mysterious vigilante who saves blameless noble families from execution, and takes his moniker from a common English flowering plant that serves as his emblem. The Pimpernel's work is well-known on both sides of the English Channel, with much of London abuzz with speculation over his true identity. In Orczy's tale, the hero is actually Sir Percy Blakeney, an effete, rather shallow aristocrat whom no one would ever suspect of daring, altruistic deeds, The introduction to Orcyzy's book describes her hero: "Tall, above the average, even for an Englishman, broad-shouldered and massively built, he would have been called unusually good-looking, but for a certain lazy expression in his deep-set blue eyes, and that perpetual inane laugh which seemed to disfigure his strong, clearly-cut mouth".

As Orczy's tale relates, Percy has surprised many in his circle of friends—which included such prominent figures as the Prince of Wales—by marrying a lovely, spirited French actress, Marguerite St. Just, who has risen from a humble family to become the star of Paris's famed Comédie-Française. Lady Marguerite is unaware of her husband's secret identity and of the reasons behind his travels across the English Channel on his yacht, and the two have become estranged because Percy has learned that her humble family was responsible—although unintentionally—for the death of a family of nobles, the St. Cyr clan.

Wife Sets Off to Help

One of Percy's cohorts in the rescue missions is Marguerite's brother Armand, and when his role is discovered, his life is suddenly in grave danger. The French ambassador to England, Monsieur Chauvelin, blackmails Marguerite into providing information that leads to the discovery of the Pimpernel's real identity, though she still does not realize that she has just implicated her husband; like those who know Sir Percy, she believes he is too dim-witted to care about such matters. A series of events precipitating his departure for France finally leads Marguerite to realize that her husband is indeed the famous Pimpernel. According to the book, "She understood it all now—all at once . . . that part he played—the mask he wore . . . in order to throw dust in everybody's eyes. And all for the sheer sport and devilry of course!—saving men, women and children from death, as other men destroy and kill animals for the excitement, the love of the thing. The idle, rich man wanted some aim in life—he, and the few young bucks he enrolled under his banner, had amused themselves for months in risking their lives for the sake of an innocent few.''

To save her husband and her brother, Marguerite embarks upon her own secret mission to France. The couple, safely reunited on a ship bound for England, forgive one another. ''The rest is silence!—silence and joy for those who had endured so much suffering, yet found at last a great and lasting happiness,'' according to the final lines of Orczy's tale. The success of the stage version of *The Scarlet Pimpernel,* which broke London theater records in its four-year run, led to the publication of Orczy's written version later in 1905, and launched her career as an author. She wrote several sequels, including *The Elusive Pimpernel, The League of the Scarlet Pimpernel, The Scarlet Pimpernel Looks at the World,* and *Mam'zelle Guillotine: An Adventure of the Scarlet Pimpernel,* between 1908 and 1940.

Wrote Detective Fiction

Orczy also penned detective stories modeled after Sir Arthur Conan Doyle (1859–1930)'s fictional sleuth Sherlock Holmes. Hers was Bill Owen, the title figure in *The Old Man in the Corner,* the first volume of this series. In the 1908 collection and in subsequent stories, Owen solves notorious crimes with the help of budding journalist Polly Burton. Orczy's ill-tempered male protagonist, wrote Katherine Staples in the *Dictionary of Literary Biography,* ''compulsively knots and unravels a bit of string as he reveals the solutions to unsolved crimes publicized in newspaper accounts and spectacular trials. The Old Man's cases include the whole range of sensational and complex detective puzzles: grisly murder ('The Tremarn Case'), fiendish blackmail ('The Murder of Miss Pebmarsh'), perfect alibis ('The Case of Miss Elliott'), masked motive and identity ('The Regent's Park Murder'), and brilliantly planned thefts ('The Affair at the Novelty Theatre').''

Orczy penned seven collections of *Old Man in the Corner* tales, concluding with *The Old Man in the Corner Unravels the Mystery of the White Carnation and the Montmartre Hat* in 1925. The stories were not her only foray into crime fiction, however: Orczy also created one of the first woman sleuths in the genre, who appeared in a single 1910 volume, *Lady Molly of Scotland Yard.* ''The twelve tales narrated by Lady Molly's loyal maid praise her daring, intelligence, and savoir faire, but they do not develop a truly independent woman-detective character,'' wrote Staples in the *Dictionary of Literary Biography* essay. ''Lady Molly's cases all involve women and show her social insight into their sexually and socially motivated behavior. Lady Molly depends as much on her sensitivity and intuition as her brilliance and bravery. Her motivation as a crime solver lies in her wish to clear her falsely accused beloved.'' Orczy also created one final amateur detective, the Irish attorney Patrick Mulligan, who appeared in *Skin o' My Tooth* in 1928.

Term Fell into Common Usage

The success resulting from *The Scarlet Pimpernel* gave Orczy and her family permanent financial freedom. They

moved to a villa in Monte Carlo, in the Mediterranean principality of Monaco, following World War I, where she and Barstow defended their literary property in a series of lawsuits with the Terrys, primarily over film rights and compensation. There were actually several screen versions of the Pimpernel story, but the best known remains the 1934 production that starred British actor Leslie Howard (1893-1943) and Merle Oberon (1911-1979). The word ''pimpernel'' became synonymous with a person who is skilled in disguising his or her true identity. It was used in two famous instances during World War II, one involving an American man and the other a Scottish minister, each of whom saved civilians and military personnel from the threat posed by Nazi Germany and its anti-Semitic policies. Later, South African anti-apartheid activist Nelson Mandela (1918–) was dubbed the ''Black Pimpernel'' when he lived in hiding.

Orczy was widowed during the Second World War, and once its hostilities ended returned to England and a home in Henley-on-Thames. She died in London on November 12, 1947, at the age of 82.

Books

Orczy, Baroness, *The Scarlet Pimpernel,* [London], 1905.
Staples, Katherine, ''Emma Orczy,'' in *Dictionary of Literary Biography,* Volume 70: *British Mystery Writers, 1860-1919,* edited by Bernard Benstock, Gale, 1988.

Periodicals

Times (London, England), January 6, 1905; August 23, 1935; November 13, 1947; July 7, 2007. □

Agustín Pìo Barrios

Paraguayan musician and composer Agustín Barrios Mangoré (1885-1944) was one of the foremost classical guitarists of his day, and arguably the most important guitarist in South America. During his career, he toured incessantly, visiting practically every country in South and Central America as well as performing in Europe. His work blends traditional folk music with more sophisticated elements of classical music to create a unique sound. Long forgotten outside of Latin America, over the last few decades the music of Barrios has enjoyed an international revival.

Received Early Training in Paraguay

Born May 23, 1885, in the small town of San Juan Bautista de las Misiones in Paraguay, musician and composer Agustín Pìo Barrios (later called Barrios Mangoré) came from a humble background. His father, Doroteo, had come to Paraguay from Argentina and worked as Paraguay's commercial vice-consul; his mother, Martina Ferreira, was a native Paraguayan who worked as a schoolteacher. One of seven brothers, Barrios developed a love of guitar from his father and an interest in literature from his mother. Barrios first began playing guitar at the age of seven and quickly became known in his community as a child prodigy. Renowned guitarist Gustavo Sosa Escalada heard Barrios play during a trip to San Juan Batista and soon convinced Barrios' parents to send young Agustín to the Instituto Paraguayo in Asuncion, about 125 from San Juan Batista. There, the young Barrios developed his guitar talent under the tutelage of Escalada and learned music theory from Italian violinist Nicolino Pellegrini.

At the age of 18, Barrios played his first professional concert at the National Theater in Asuncion. His performance impressed both music fans and critics. Soon, Barrios began composing and performing his own pieces; Peter Sensier and Richard D. Stover noted in their *Grove Music Online* biography of Barrios that "although he lacked a formal musical education, Barrios . . . wrote guitar music of high quality that combined many of the characteristics of his predecessors, Sor and Tarrega." Barrios performed both with his instructor Sosa Escalada and with his brother, Francisco Martin, who had become a poet. Barrios and his brother toured Paraguay, writing and performing music.

Began Touring South America

In 1910, Barrios left Paraguay to give a week's worth of concerts in Argentina. He instead remained in Buenos Aires for the better part of two years, initially intending to save money so as to be able to marry a sweetheart in Asuncion who had bore him a son. However, Barrios was somewhat disorganized and carefree about business matters, and was unable to save money. Rather, he used the time to perfect his guitar technique and repertoire and studying the works of other guitarists, including Julio Sagreras, Domingo Pratt, and Miguel Llobet. Some time around late 1910 or 1911, Barrios seemed to have traveled to Chile and perhaps Peru. On this trip, he met Martín Gil, who was influential in Argentina's musical world and became an early supporter of Barrios's talent.

Barrios returned to Buenos Aires briefly, departing in 1912 to travel to Uruguay for a lengthy concert tour. There, he studied with Antonio Gimenez Manjon. Writing in "Minstrels of Magical Strings," Caleb Bach noted that "he also established an enduring friendship with a prosperous landowner, Martin Borda y Pagola, who . . . soon become something of an emotional anchor and confidant to the impulsive, passionate young man." Borda y Pagola also encouraged Barrios to write manuscripts of his compositions instead of carrying his music in his head, as he was inclined to do. Barrios remained in Uruguay for about three years; Richard D. Stover commented in *Six Silver Moonbeams: The Life and Times of Agustín Barrios Mangoré* that "these years . . . were no doubt a period of expansion and growth."

From 1916 to 1920, Barrios lived primarily in Sao Paolo, Brazil, performing there and in other cities in the area. Having left Paraguay, he was presumably surprised to learn that his own death was being reported in Paraguayan newspapers in September 1918. This strange event would recur later in Barrios's life; in 1934, he was reported to have

died first in a Mexican newspaper and then a few months later in the papers of Venezuela. This first false report seems to have stemmed from the death of an Argentine guitarist who happened to have the same name. The living Barrios, however, benefited from publicity generated by the many tributes made by those believing him to be deceased.

Enjoyed Successes and Faced Failures

Beginning in 1917 and lasting for about a decade, he experienced an outpouring of creative growth: aside from playing many concerts, he wrote 76 new compositions, transcribed 39 works, and added 20 pieces by other composers to his own repertoire. In 1919, he met renowned Italian conductor Gino Marinuzzi, who questioned his technical choice of using metal, rather than the usual gut, strings. Barrios—reputedly at Marinuzzi's suggestion—adopted the use of small rubber beads on some of his strings to eliminate the metallic twang. That same year, he performed a concert for the President of Brazil, an event which *Grove Music Online* claimed to be the beginning of "his first real successes."

After leaving Brazil in 1920, Barrios returned to Montevideo, Uruguay. He remained there for several weeks, performing concerts that combined classical European works with modern Latin American ones, including many of his own compositions. In 1921, Barrios traveled through parts of Uruguay and Argentina. During this tour, he became ill with what was probably typhus, a bacterial infection that plagued him for several months. Despite his illness, in 1921 Barrios composed the work that Stover claimed "is no doubt Barrios's most widely played composition, *La Catedral* . . . [which] figures among the concert guitar's greatest repertoire." In September 1921, Barrios—essentially recovered from his illness—voyaged to Buenos Aires to record music. While in Buenos Aires, Barrios became acquainted with famed Spanish classical guitarist Andrés Segovia. This year also marked Barrios's first published compositions.

The following year, Barrios toured parts of Chile and Brazil before at last returning to his native Paraguay. The first native Paraguayan to find success and fame outside of the country, he was a source of national pride for his fellow Paraguayans, who received him with much admiration. He spent the next few years primarily based there. During this era, he wrote two of his most important works, *Danza Paraguaya No. 1* and *Danza Paraguaya No. 2*. These pieces reflected traditional musical rhythms and sounds of his homeland. He also performed throughout the country, again accompanied by his brother Francisco Martin. In Paraguay he was also reunited with his former instructors Pellegrini and Escalada. However, the financial support Barrios had hoped to find in native country failed to materialize. Regretfully, he realized that could not remain permanently in Paraguay and left the country in 1925. He was accompanied by Tomás Salomini, who would serve as his patron for many years to come.

For the second half of the decade, Barrios split his time between Uruguay and Argentina. Despite his best efforts, Bach noted that "his reputation declined. Especially in Buenos Aires he was perceived as musician who clung to old-fashioned ways and as a provincial who could not compete with Segovia, who by then enjoyed an international reputation." Somewhat disheartened, Barrios moved to Brazil in 1929. He soon met a dancer named Gloria Seban; although the couple apparently never legally married, they presented themselves as man and wife for the remainder of Barrios's life.

Mangoré Caused Career Revival

From 1930, Barrios began performing under the pseudonym Chief Nitsuga Mangoré. Whether this persona stemmed from an attempt to garner a larger audience than he had as Agustín Barrios or simply from a whim, over the next few years it became that which Barrios publicly espoused. Basing this persona on a sixteenth-century chieftain from the indigenous Guarani culture, Barrios appeared in costume and employed poetry and props to enhance his guitar concerts. It seems likely that either Seban or Barrios's brother, who was traveling with Barrios at the time, made an influence on the creation and development of this character. Promoting himself as the greatest guitarist in the world, Barrios resumed touring. Over the next few years, Barrios took the Mangoré identity through much of South and Central America, parts of the Caribbean, and finally Mexico. There, Salomini convinced Barrios to give up the identity, believing it to be undignified. Barrios retired the character Mangoré in 1933, but retained the professional name of "Barrios Mangoré."

In 1934, Salomini arranged a performance for Barrios in Cuba. From there, Barrios, his wife, and the Salomini family traveled to Europe, fulfilling a dream of many years. Barrios spent several weeks in Brussels, Belgium, where he played at the Royal Conservatory of Music. On this trip, Barrios also met and befriended Igor Stravinsky. Leaving Brussels, the group traveled to Berlin, Germany, where they remained in an apartment rented for Salomini for about fifteen months. In Berlin, Barrios played no concerts, but did perform on Radio Deutschland. In late 1935, the Salominis returned to Paraguay while the Barrioses traveled to Spain. In Spain, Barrios performed a concert in Madrid and is reported to have played for Queen Victoria Eugenia. However, the encroaching Spanish Civil War forced Barrios and his wife to return to South America.

Barrios stayed briefly in Venezuela before embarking on a tour of the Caribbean. He visited Puerto Rico, the Dominican Republic, and Haiti before spending several months in Cuba. In financial difficulties, Barrios traveled to Costa Rica, but performed few concerts there.

Spent Final Years as Instructor

In July 1939, Barrios came to El Salvador to perform a concert series. That September he traveled to Guatemala, where he reportedly experienced a minor heart attack. Despite this, he soon ventured to Mexico City. There, he suffered a major heart attack; some claim that this happened while Barrios was performing and caused him to collapse onstage. After this heart attack, Barrios was advised to rest and never again regained complete strength. He returned to El Salvador and settled there, receiving a professorship at the National Conservancy from President Maximiliano Hernandez Martinez, an appreciator of guitar and a fan of Barrios.

Although Barrios continued to play occasional concerts, he dedicated the majority of his time to teaching. His pupils admired him, and he required them to play to the utmost of their abilities. Between 1940 and 1944, Barrios composed many guitar works, including some pieces for two and three guitars. His final work, *Una Limosna por el Amor de Dios* was composed in May 1944; Caleb Bach described this work as "a tremolo composition featuring a soprano line that rides above an ostinato motif said to represent a beggar's knocking at the door of heaven." That same year, RCA Victor asked Barrios to come to the United States to record. However, this long hoped for trip never occurred. On August 7, 1944, Barrios suffered heart failure and died. Stover reported that "the priest who attended him [at the time of his death] proclaimed, 'This is the first time I have witnessed the death of a Saint.'"

During Barrios's life, he composed something over 300 works for solo guitar. Primarily between 1912 and 1929, Barrios made over 30 recordings, including what may have been the first recording of a classical guitarist on vinyl record. These recordings are remarkably clear for the technology of their day. For many years after Barrios's death, however, his life and work were remembered only in his native Paraguay. However, beginning in the 1970s, his music again found a wider audience thanks to the performances of Australian guitar John Williams and American guitarist Richard Stover. Today, the music of Barrios is part of the classical guitar repertory and receives ever-increasing attention.

Books

Encyclopedia of Latin American History and Culture, 5 vols., Charles Scribner's Sons, 1996.
Stover, Richard P., *Six Silver Moonbeams: The Life and Times and Agustín Barrios Mangoré,* Querico Publications, 1992.

Online

"Barrios Mangoré, Agustín" *Grove Music Online,* http://www .grovemusic.com (November 26, 2007).
Student Resource Center—College Edition Expanded, http://find .galegroup.com/ips/start.do?prodId=IPS (November 26, 2007). □

Frédéric-Auguste Bartholdi

French sculptor Frédéric-Auguste Bartholdi (1834-1904) created the Statue of Liberty, the immense torch-wielding figure that rises out of New York Harbor as a welcoming beacon to the world.

The Statue of Liberty was designed as an expression of friendship and shared values between France and the United States, the work was planned as a gift from the French people to America on the one hundredth anniversary of the Declaration of Independence, but not erected

in the harbor until a dozen years later. "It is a consolation to know that this statue will exist thousands of years from now, long after our names shall have been forgotten," Bartholdi asserted on that day in 1886, according to Claudia Glenn Dowling in *Life.*

Bartholdi was born on August 2, 1834, in Colmar, Alsace, near France's southern border with Germany. His father, Jean-Charles Bartholdi, held a prominent position as counsellor to the prefecture of Colmar, but died when Bartholdi was two. A keen artist from an early age, Bartholdi began taking art classes during his teen years and moved from painting to sculpture. He went on to study under Eugene-Emmanuel Viollet-le-Duc (1814–1879), who had recently completed a restoration of Paris's landmark Notre Dame Cathedral, and also trained with Henri Labrouste (1801–1875), an architect who was trying out new methods of steel construction, which was a new and innovative building material at the time.

Visited the Pyramids

For the 1855 Universal Exposition in Paris, Bartholdi submitted a statue of Jean Rapp (1771–1821), a French general who served in the Napoleonic Wars. As the exhibition's opening date neared, however, Bartholdi's work proved too large to fit through the doors of the venue. Exposition officials gave him permission to leave it outside, and the enormous figure attracted a great deal of attention and favorable publicity for both the Universal Exposition and the young sculptor. It was later installed in

Bartholdi's hometown of Colmar to great civic fanfare. Later in 1855, Bartholdi traveled to Egypt to quench his curiosity about some of the largest structures ever created by humans—the ancient Sphinx and Pyramids.

Over the next decade Bartholdi's career continued its impressive upward trajectory. He won several notable commissions and was awarded France's Legion of Honor. Like many liberal-minded Europeans, he was unnerved by the assassination of U.S. president Abraham Lincoln (1809–1865) in 1865, viewing it as a blow to liberty in America. A friend of Bartholdi's, historian Edouard-Rene de Laboulaye (1811–1883), also expressed dismay over Lincoln's death, and over dinner one evening the two men discussed the possibility of some sort of gift that France might deliver to America on the upcoming centennial anniversary of her independence from Britain. The American Revolutionary War and its fight to end British tyranny had served as a source of tremendous inspiration for French revolutionaries who overthrew the monarchy in 1789 and installed a republican form of government.

Barred from Entering Colmar

Bartholdi and Laboulaye's plans were disrupted by the Franco-Prussian War of 1870–71, and the artist departed for National Guard service. His hometown of Colmar surrendered to German troops in the ten-month-long conflict, and much of the Alsace region was later absorbed into imperial Germany. New regulations made it impossible for him to return home—to either his studio or the home of his mother—for several more years, and so he settled in Paris. A month after the end of the hostilities, Bartholdi set sail for his first visit to the United States. The idea for a monumental statue to greet visitors came to him aboard his ship as it entered New York City's harbor, especially when he noticed a tiny, uninhabited island that seemed an ideal site for the base. Quickly, he sketched out a female figure with a crown of rays around her head, holding a torch aloft in one hand and clutching a tablet with the date of July 4, 1776, in the other. He called it *Liberty Enlightening the World.* It bore some resemblance to a figure he had already sketched for a proposed lighthouse for Egypt's Suez Canal back at its opening in 1867, which was an African-style female figure he titled *Progress Bringing Light to Asia.*

Bartholdi made a maquette, or small-scale sculptural model, of his proposed Statue of Liberty while in the United States, and introductions from Laboulaye paved the way for meetings with some influential Americans, among them the poet Henry Wadsworth Longfellow (1807–1882). Bartholdi traveled all the way to California and spoke to dozens of people about his and Laboulaye's proposal, and the end result was the establishment of a fundraising group, the Franco-American Union. It took several years, however, for the Union to raise the necessary funds.

Back in France in 1875, Bartholdi began working on what would be his largest statue in France, the *Lion of Belfort.* Perched near Belfort Castle atop a local hill, the work commemorated the town of Belfort's long standoff against a vastly superior number of German army forces during the Franco-Prussian War. Pierre Philippe Denfert-

Rochereau (1823–1878), the commander of the local French garrison, was hailed as the "Lion of Belfort" for his leadership, and Bartholdi's statue, made of pink sandstone, mythologized Denfert-Rochereau as a wounded but still fierce lion guarding the town.

Arm Caused Sensation in Philadelphia

While working to complete the *Lion of Belfort* in 1880, Bartholdi returned to his plans for the Statue of Liberty. Realizing that such a monumental figure would need a steel frame for its body of copper sheeting, he enlisted the help of Gustave Eiffel (1832–1923), a respected French bridge builder who later in the decade would create the Paris landmark tower that bears his name. Bartholdi and his team of assistants began the actual sculpting process in the Paris workshop of Gaget, Gauthier and Company. By 1876, her arm and the torch were finished, and were shipped to the United States in time for display at the Philadelphia Centennial Exhibition that summer. Visitors could climb inside and walk along the balcony surrounding the torch, and nearly ten million did so; the sheer size of the project and its novelty boosted the Franco-American Union's fundraising efforts immensely. Bartholdi accompanied the arm and torch to America, and the visit was also notable for his wedding to Jeanne-Emilie Baheux at the Newport, Rhode Island, home of John LaFarge. A highly regarded artist and writer, LaFarge had a New York City workshop in which Bartholdi's first Statue of Liberty maquette had been cast several years earlier.

In 1878 Lady Liberty's head was finished and exhibited at the Paris World's Fair. The seven points of its diadem, or crown, represent both the seven seas and the seven continents. The assembly process formally began in 1881, and was stalled for a few years because the fund-raising effort in America had not yet collected enough to erect the pedestal. "Ingrates grumbled about gift horses, pagan goddesses, revolutionaries and bad taste," wrote Dowling. "One suggested that the statue be immersed upside down in Central Park's reservoir. Everyone except New Yorkers felt that New Yorkers should bear the cost." The statue's strong classical inlfuence, which paid homage to the era of antiquity when Greek and Roman figures achieved their most impressive artistic perfection, was also somewhat controversial. Bartholdi seemed to have modeled his after a Roman goddess called Libertas. As Barry Moreno, author of *The Statue of Liberty Encyclopedia,* told *New York Times* journalist Glenn Collins, back then some "Roman Catholics objected to New Yorkers making obeisance to a 151-foot-high heathen goddess smack in the middle of New York Harbor."

Arrived to Major Fanfare

Bartholdi's statue was finished in January of 1884, and six months later a formal presentation of it was made to the American ambassador in Paris on July 4. It was then disassembled, packed into 214 cases, and loaded onto the frigate *Isere.* It arrived in New York on June 17, 1885, and was greeted by a crowd of 100,000. Journalists were allowed aboard the *Isere* to see the crates before they were unloaded. "The hold of the vessel was a curious sight," wrote a *New York Times* correspondent. "The diadem was in an arched frame large enough for a horse and wagon to drive under.... The eyes and nose filled one crate, the forehead another, an ear and part of the crown another, until every foot of space seemed to be utilized. A sheet iron curl looked large enough for the smokestack of a small steam launch. A sailor said that it was 8 feet long."

The pedestal had yet to be completed, however, and finally newspaper magnate Joseph Pulitzer (1847–1911) launched a campaign on the pages of his *New York World,* offering to print the names of anyone who sent in a donation. The dedication of the State of Liberty finally took place on October 28, 1886, presided over by President Grover Cleveland (1837–1908), all of his cabinet, and numerous French dignitaries. Bartholdi was present, too, and rejoiced to see the completion of his long-awaited project. It stood 151 feet in height from the foot to the top of the gold-plate torch, and weighed 225 tons. Years later, inside the visitors' center, a plaque was installed that was inscribed with the lines from *The New Colossus,* a poem by American writer Emma Lazarus (1849–1887), written back in 1883 during the fundraising campaign. It reads, in part, "Give me your tired, your poor, your huddled masses yearning to breathe free." By then, the Statue of Liberty was becoming a symbolic beacon for thousands of new immigrants who arrived weekly in New York City from all over Europe. Conversely, the statue also came to symbolize American imperialism abroad in political cartoons.

Bartholdi completed a few other impressive statues, none of them as grand as the Statue of Liberty, before he died of tuberculosis on October 4, 1904, in Paris. A century later, some historians disputed the story that Lady Liberty was meant as a purely noble gift from France to the United States to celebrate their shared respect for democratic values. Those familiar with the writings of Laboulaye—who played an important role in the planning and even the design of the statue—argued that it was more a statement against monarchy and slavery. Art historian Albert Boime told Collins that "as a gift, it was more accurately an instrument of statecraft on the French and American sides, intended to heighten interest in trade and to call attention to French technology." Nevertheless, Bartholdi's best-known work remains one of the most recognizable symbols on earth. "The Statue of Liberty may well be the single most seductive structure erected anywhere in the world during the past hundred years," declared John Russell in the *Smithsonian.* "It has a great location. It has stood up to everything that wind and weather can throw at it. It is part of a universal folklore. Yet when seen at firsthand, it never fails to astonish."

Periodicals

Life, July 1986.
New York Times, June 18, 1885; October 28, 2000.
Smithsonian, July 1984. □

André Bazin

The French film critic André Bazin (1918-1958) is considred by many to be the father of film criticism as it is practiced today.

Immensely influential in his native France and beyond, Bazin transformed film criticism from simple description and evaluation of the film under discussion into an evaluation of film as a serious art form, including detailed analysis of the techniques filmmakers used. Bazin had a strong perspective that was largely rejected by filmmakers and film critics who came of age in the decades after his death, but even that rejection testified to the depth of his influence. His writings on cinematic technique formed a basic vocabulary of film analysis that even his critics employed. Bazin showed, moreover, that criticism could change the course of cinematic history—at a time when American films were not taken seriously in France, his analyses of the realistic style of such directors as Orson Welles kindled a lasting French passion for American cinema, and he directly inspired François Truffaut and other directors who made French films a staple of almost every campus film society in the English-speaking world in the 1960s and beyond.

Collected Animals on Nature Walks

The son of a bank clerk, André Bazin was born on April 18, 1918, in Angers, France, but spent much of his childhood in the town of La Rochelle, near the Atlantic Ocean. He was a voracious reader as a youngster, and in school he was a top student. He displayed no special artistic enthusiasms as a child; his family, living in a small rustic home beside a stream, probably had only intermittent access to a movie theater. But Bazin had a childhood passion that would prove to be indirectly related to the thrust of his film criticism: both as a child wandering the surroundings of La Rochelle and as a mature writer, he was fascinated by nature and by the human power of observing it closely. He turned the balcony of his family home into a miniature jungle and filled it with lizards and other small animals he collected in the woods. When he was old enough to have a girlfriend, he once showed up for a date with her carrying a snake wrapped around his shoulders, and even as an adult he maintained a diverse menagerie of wild animals.

Bazin attended a school connected with a Catholic monastery and excelled in math and science. When he was 12 the family moved to Paris, where he received a strong public education at a high school in the suburb of Courbevoie and won several scholarships. His intention at this stage of his life was to become a teacher, and he moved back to La Rochelle to attend the Ecole Normale d'Institution, a teacher training school there. After graduating, he applied at the Ecole Normale Supérieure in St. Cloud, a top education school near Paris. On his second try he was admitted. Bazin seemed headed for a good teaching job or a post in France's government education bureaucracy.

At the school in St. Cloud, Bazin read widely in contemporary French thought. He favored philosophers of an idealistic Catholic tinge, especially Henri Bergson, whose writings often dealt with the topic of creativity and its place in the order of things, and the Catholic "personalist" or existentialist Emmanuel Mounier. Bazin often read the liberal Catholic journal L'esprit and admired the film writing of Roger Leenhardt, an early inspiration. Living near Paris on another scholarship, Bazin enjoyed the life of a top student immersed in the intellectual currents of the day.

Personal and geopolitical events combined to put that happy life to an end. First, the school at St. Cloud and every other aspect of life around Paris were disrupted by the outbreak of World War II and the invasion of France by Nazi Germany in May of 1940. Bazin reported for army duty but failed a physical exam that would have enabled him to pursue officer training. Before any other action could be taken, the French military collapsed after heavy losses, and fighting ceased as a pro-German regime was installed in the city of Vichy. Bazin returned to school in St. Cloud, but in 1941 he failed a key oral exam when he began stuttering during his response to one of the questions. He might have been able to retake the exam, but before he could do so the school mysteriously burned to the ground.

Formed Film Study Group

Despite the harsh life of occupied Paris and the beginnings of what would become a lifetime of poor health, Bazin flourished. He was chosen as one of the organizers of a student cultural group called the Maison des Lettres (House of Literature), offered by the Sorbonne university as a competitor to student groups set up by the pro-Nazi government. Bazin spent much of the war on the fringes of the resistance movement, writing articles that did not oppose fascism directly—that would have been impossible under the circumstances—but that avoided any hint of collaboration with Nazism. He immersed himself in theater, literary theory, and novels, particularly the American epics of Ernest Hemingway and John Dos Passos.

Most important for his future, he (along with a comrade who later joined the armed French resistance) started a cinema club. Although French directors such as Jean Renoir had made classic films during the 1930s, the world of film was disconnected from French intellectual life. "Once the sound film came into use," noted Bazin biographer Dudley Andrew, "most intellectuals placed the cinema beside the circus as a popular art not warranting reflection." The few newspapers and magazines still allowed to publish in Paris had no film columns, and Bazin faced an additional problem: getting films to show was difficult. German censors kept close control over the distribution of films, seeking to prevent the showing of American imports like Charlie Chaplin's The Great Dictator, which parodied dictator Adolf Hitler.

Due to all these factors, Bazin's cinema club tapped into a pent-up demand. Not only films but Bazin's lectures were well-attended. He began to write articles on film for newspapers and magazines, and one of them, quoted by Andrew, correctly prophesied that film studies would one day be ensconced in the university curriculum: "We will surely have someday a thesis of eight hundred pages on the function of comedy in American film between 1915 and 1917 or something approaching that. And who will dare maintain that this isn't serious?" After the liberation of Paris, Bazin was a logical choice to head a new Institute des Hautes Etudes Cinématographiques (Institute for Advanced Cinema Studies). He began writing regular columns for the newspaper *Le Parisien libéré* (Liberated Paris), and for the rest of his life he made a living mostly as an independent film critic.

Bazin wrote about two thousand short articles about film, using sources ranging from philosopher Jean-Paul Sartre's serious journal *Les Temps modernes* (Modern Times) to daily newspapers and magazines as outlets. A selection of these articles, titled *Qu'estce que c'est le cinema?* (What Is Cinema?), ran to four volumes in French (an English version containing a further-refined selection filled two volumes), and he wrote or co-wrote several books. Part of the reason for Bazin's feverish activity was that he had a family to support. He and his wife, Janine (who was partly responsible for the wide distribution of Bazin's ideas after his death), raised a son, Florent, who became a cinematographer working under such directors as François Truffaut and Roman Polanski.

Championed American Films

Part of what made Bazin's writing innovative was that he was interested in American films. Above all he admired *Citizen Kane* and the other ambitious creations of director Orson Welles, but also William Wyler's *The Little Foxes* (1941) and even Westerns—about which he co-wrote a book, *Le western; ou, Le cinéma americain par excellence* (The Western, or American Cinema at Its Best), which remains untranslated in English. He wrote a book-length study, *Orson Welles,* in 1950 and revised it in 1958. The book appeared in English as *Orson Welles: A Critical Study* in 1978.

Welles held particular appeal for Bazin because of the in-depth realism of his films. Bazin's criticism prized realism over experimental cinematic devices such as surreal imagery and montage (rapid editing, often enhanced by special effects). He admired Welles's use of depth of field to direct the viewer's attention to various parts of a scene at different perceived distances from the camera. "Let's take Susan Alexander Kane's suicide attempt," Bazin wrote in an analysis of *Citizen Kane* reproduced and translated in his book *Bazin at Work.* "We get it in a single shot on a level with the bed. In the left-hand corner, on the night table, are the enormous glass and the teaspoon. A little farther back, in shadow, we sense rather than see the woman's face. . . . Beyond the bed: the empty room, and completely in the background, even farther away because of the receding perspective created by the wide-angle lens: the locked door. Behind the door, we hear on the soundtrack Kane's calls and his shoulder bumping against the wood. This single shot, then, is built in depth around two dramatic centers of gravity, each consisting of sonorous and visual elements."

Few, if any, writers had analyzed film in this kind of detail before. Bazin applied similar analysis to the works of his favorite European directors, especially Renoir and the realist master of postwar French cinema, Robert Bresson. He also admired the Italian neorealist school, which focused an unsentimental lens on the poverty experienced by the lower classes in Italian cities after the war. Bazin was never particularly politically oriented, however; he believed that the camera should penetrate as deeply as possible into life as it is, leaving the viewer to form his or her own conclusions. The generation of so-called New Wave filmmakers that followed Bazin in the 1960s was both political and experimental, and many disagreed with Bazin on ideological grounds, but they could not escape his influence: he had virtually created a modern vocabulary for talking about film as a serious art form.

That influence was made manifest in several ways. Bazin served as a mentor to New Wave filmmaker François Truffaut, rescuing him twice from detention situations that resulted from acts of lawbreaking during Truffaut's teenage years. One of Truffaut's most famous films, *Les quatre cents coups* (1959), was dedicated posthumously to Bazin. Perhaps Bazin's most visible legacy was the magazine *Cahiers du Cinéma* (Cinema Notebook), which he co-founded in 1951 (it evolved from an earlier journal called *La revue du cinéma* or Cinema Review). The magazine remained central to the French film scene through the 1960s and beyond, and attacks on Bazin frequently used its pages as a medium, "an Oedipal rebellion if ever there was one," noted Bazin admirer John Lynch on his unofficial Bazin tribute Web site. *Cahiers du Cinéma* remains in existence today, now under the ownership of the newspaper *Le Monde.*

Bazin's health, never robust, steadily worsened during the 1950s, and finally he was diagnosed with leukemia. Working frenetically despite what was essentially a death sentence, he collapsed in August of 1958 and was admitted to a hospital. He recovered, and continued to work on what became his final book, *Jean Renoir.* The book was edited by Truffaut after Bazin's death and appeared in English under the same title in 1973. Bazin died of leukemia on November 11, 1958, in Nogent-sur-Marne, France,. He was widely mourned in the French film community, but his celebrity in the English-speaking world awaited the translation of his writings. *What Is Cinema?* (two volumes, 1967 and 1971) was followed by various other collections of Bazin's writings on specific topics.

Books

Andrew, Dudley, *André Bazin,* Oxford University Press, 1978.

Bazin, André, *Bazin at Work,* trans. by Alain Pierre and Bert Cardullo, Routledge, 1997.

Bazin, André, *What Is Cinema?,* 2 vols., University of California Press, 1967 and 1971.

Online

"André Bazin: A Brief Biography," André Bazin and François Truffaut," Unofficial André Bazin tribute site, http://www .unofficialbaziniantrib.com (November 20, 2007).

Contemporary Authors Online, Gale, 2007. http://galenet.gale group.com/servlet/BioRC (November 20, 2007).

"The Innovators 1950–1960: Defining the Real," British Film Institute, http://www.bfi.org.uk/sightandsound/feature/176 (November 20, 2007). □

Isabella Mary Beeton

The British author Mrs. Beeton (1836-1865), born Isabella Mary Mayson, was, in the words of Kathryn Hughes, author of *The Short Life and Long Times of Mrs. Beeton*, "the first domestic goddess." *Mrs. Beeton's Book of Household Management*, published in 1861, was a nearly universal fixture in British middle-class households for much of the next century.

In many ways, *Mrs. Beeton's Book of Household Management* was the predecessor to *Martha Stewart Living, The Joy of Cooking, Ladies' Home Journal* and other glossy magazines of its kind. Its chapters were originally published separately in issues of *The Englishwoman's Domestic Magazine,* largely the work of Mrs. Beeton and her husband, Samuel. Innovative in many ways, the book was also very much a product of its time, reflecting an England in which the women of a rising middle class lived independent of family ties and traditional domestic skills. Although not of substantial value to the modern homemaker ("First, catch your hare," begins one recipe), *Mrs. Beeton's Book of Household Management* has remained a treasure trove for historians and others curious about life in Britain's Victorian era.

Born into Racing Family

Isabella Mary Mayson was born on March 14, 1836, on Milk Street in London. She was the first of 17 siblings born to her mother, Elizabeth. Two husbands were involved; after the death of Isabella's father, Benjamin Mayson, Elizabeth's second husband, Henry Dorling, came to the marriage with four children of his own, and the couple had 13 more children. Isabella grew up as the eldest of a brood of 21 children, and was frequently responsible for cooking for, clothing, cleaning up after, and generally raising many of them. She had early training in domestic arts from another source, too; Henry Dorling was the clerk of the Epsom horse track 14 miles outside London, and she grew up watching the massive concession kitchens beneath the grandstands operating at full speed.

Isabella had a spotty education that was, on balance, a good one for a woman of her time and place. She was sent abroad in 1851 to a boarding school in Heidelberg, Germany, where she learned to speak fluent German and French. Back in Epsom she took piano lessons, which was expected of a marriageable young woman, but she also expressed a desire to study baking, which her family was less happy about, as a woman with social aspirations would be expected to leave that chore to servants. They relented—pastry cookery was on the border of acceptability—but her younger half-sisters recalled, according to Hughes, that her cooking lessons were regarded as "ultra modern and not quite nice."

Around 1855 Isabella met Samuel Beeton, a good-looking, cigar-smoking publisher with a slightly rakish past. All the cards were in place for her to fall in love. Beeton was the son of a family friend, and earlier in the decade he had made a bold and successful stroke: he traveled to the United States and persuaded author Harriet Beecher Stowe to sell his S.O. Beeton publishing firm the British rights to her novel *Uncle Tom's Cabin.* With the proceeds from that international success he had launched a pair of magazines that catered to the tastes of middle-class readers: *The Boy's Own Journal* and *The Englishwoman's Domestic Magazine.*

And fall in love Isabella did. The couple began a copious exchange of letters, escalating from Isabella's "I am so continually thinking of you that it seems to do me a vast amount of good even to do a little black and white business" to physical intimacies they described with code words such as "getting into a cab"—a horse-drawn hansom cab that allowed them privacy from Isabella's family. The reactions of her family were problematic, for the Dorlings disapproved of Beeton and his man-about-town image. The courtship was a long one by Victorian standards, but they were finally married on July 10, 1856. The couple moved into an apartment comprising half a spacious villa in the new London suburb of Pinner.

Suffered Miscarriages

The couple honeymooned in the south of France, and it soon became clear that Isabella had conceived a child. Samuel Orchart Beeton was born in the spring of 1857 but died on August 25, just three months old. Isabella became pregnant several times over the next few years, but each pregnancy ended in a miscarriage. A second son, also named Samuel, was born in 1859 but died at the age of three after a period of illness. This sequence of events, argued Hughes, "strongly suggests that [Isabella] was of the thousands of unfortunate young Victorian brides who were infected with syphilis on their honeymoon. . . . This is a classic pattern: syphilitic women have no trouble conceiving but . . . if a child *does* survive, it is only for a few sickly, miserable months." Samuel Beeton's known propensity toward frequenting prostitutes before his involvement with Isabella also supported Hughes's hypothesis.

Partly to deal with the emotional strain of these developments, Isabella threw herself into her work. That was an unusual solution for a woman of the Victorian age, but Isabella was an unusual woman, and she had found that her talents were in demand at her husband's busy publishing office. She began by translating German and French stories for *The Englishwoman's Domestic Magazine,* and soon appeared on the masthead as "editress." Around 1859 she began to write articles on cooking and other domestic skills. The assignment turned into a monthly column on those subjects, and Isabella found an enthusiastic audience among upwardly mobile women readers trying to manage busy households without the benefit of a traditional support structure. By 1860 Samuel Beeton had announced a circulation figure of 60,000 copies for the monthly magazine; a concrete indicator of its success was the appearance of a competitor, *Ladies' Treasury.*

Isabella became "Mrs. Beeton," and had already become a household name when Samuel Beeton issued her collected contributions to *The Englishwoman's Domestic Magazine* in book form in October of 1861. At first merely *The Book of Household Management,* its title soon acquired the more personal "Mrs. Beeton's" prefix. *Mrs. Beeton's Book of Household Management* had 2,751 entries, divided into sections covering "Information for the Mistress, Housekeeper, Cook, Kitchen-Maid, Butler, Footman, Coachman, Valet, Upper and Under House-Maids, Lady's-Maid, Maid-of-all-Work, Laundry-Maid, Nurse and Nurse-Maid, Monthly Wet and Sick Nurses, etc. etc.—also Sanitary, Medical, & Legal Memoranda: with a History of the Origin, Properties, and Uses of all Things Connected with Home Life and Comfort." An immediate bestseller, the book recorded sales in the millions of copies over the next several years.

Provided Historical Background

Mrs. Beeton's Book of Household Management included illustrations and a wealth of historical material. But the bulk of the book was given over to recipes. Noting correctly, for example, that asparagus was "light and easily digested, but is not very nutritious," Isabella then went on to offer a recipe for asparagus soup that ran as follows: "INGREDIENTS—1 1/2 pint of split peas, a teacupful of gravy, 4 young onions, 1 lettuce cut small, 1/2 a head of celery, 1/2 a pint of asparagus cut small, 1/2 a pint of cream, 3 quarts of water: colour the soup with spinach juice. Mode.—Boil the peas, and rub them through a sieve; add the gravy, and then stew by themselves the celery, onions, lettuce, and asparagus, with the water. After this, stew altogether, and add the colouring and cream, and serve."

Several aspects of this passage, which was typical of those in the book devoted to cookery, were novel at the time. Cookbooks of that period rarely listed ingredients at the beginning of a recipe (Mrs. Beeton, in fact, may have been the first to do so), even though such a configuration would be helpful indeed to a shopper in a hurry. Her notations on nutrition, while not uniformly accurate, played a role in promoting the deep modern linkage between dietetics and cuisine. Moreover, Mrs. Beeton's recipes were among the few available at the time that specified how long a dish should be cooked. Few things in Mrs. Beeton's book were original, for Isabella borrowed liberally from French cookbooks, other magazines, and classic writings on food and horticulture. Hughes noted that "there is scarcely a line in the book that can be said to belong to her." Yet, according to Hughes, "she did something unique with the material that she borrowed. She turned it into that thing most beloved by the mid-Victorians, a *system* which, if properly applied, would produce a guaranteed result—in this case domestic well-being."

By the mid-1860s, Isabella finally seemed on the way to domestic well-being herself. Her third child, Orchart Beeton, was born at the Beeton company offices on December 2, 1863, and grew into a healthy child. Again the pattern was typical of syphilis, a disease which would fall into dormant phases after several years of activity. In 1864 Isabella became pregnant with her fourth son, Mayson Moss Beeton. He was born healthy on January 29, 1865, but Isabella had fallen deathly ill by the next day. Her death on February 6, at age 28, was due not to syphilis but to another common scourge of Victorian women, puerperal fever, which, like syphilis, is easily treatable with modern antibiotics.

The Mrs. Beeton books did not die with their author. Samuel Beeton kept his wife's death quiet, issuing later editions of the *Book of Household Management* with new prefaces that suggested she was still alive. Over time, other Mrs. Beeton books appeared, and Mrs. Beeton became as much a brand name as an individual. Samuel Beeton himself was distressed by his wife's death, and his later years were unhappy ones. Editions of the once-wholesome *Englishwoman's Domestic Magazine* began to contain barely disguised episodes of sadomasochistic fantasy in the form of lengthy descriptions and discussions of whipping. Throughout much of the twentieth century, however, the name Mrs. Beeton served as shorthand for domestic quality in England and many other parts of the English-speaking world.

Books

Hughes, Kathryn, *The Short Life and Long Times of Mrs. Beeton,* Knopf, 2006.

Periodicals

Daily Mail (London, England), October 7, 2006.
Guardian (London, England), February 11, 2006; June 2, 2006; March 17, 2007.
Times (London, England), October 8, 2005.

Online

Mrs. Beeton's Book of Household Management, http://www.mrs beeton.com (January 19, 2008).

"Mrs. Beeton: The Stowmarket Connection," Stowmarket History, http://www.stowmarket-history.co.uk/Mrs_Beeton.htm (January 19, 2008). □

Jean-Pierre François Blanchard

French balloonist Jean-Pierre Blanchard (1753-1809), one of the first great hot-air balloon voyagers, or aeronauts, became famous in Europe and the United States for his high-altitude feats. He and American doctor John Jeffries crossed the English Channel by balloon, becoming the first international air travelers, and he was the first balloonist to fly over several European countries. His 1793 flight from Philadelphia to New Jersey, the first aerial voyage in the United States, captivated America's capital city and was witnessed by U.S. President George Washington.

Blanchard's ballooning career led him to occasional failures and great tragedy. He was not the first to create a hydrogen balloon, and his own aerial inventions, heavier-than-air vehicles and attempts to add wings and sails to balloons, were failures. He spent four years in the United States trying to interest Americans in ballooning, but struggled financially and only flew in his balloon once (or perhaps twice) in the United States. He, his son, and his wife all died of injuries related to their ballooning endeavors. But his showman's sense of drama, from his staging of events to his fancy dress and flair for ceremony, helped attract the public to share his fascination with journeying through the skies.

His First Ascension

Born in Les Andelys, France on July 4, 1753, the son of a skilled craftsman, Blanchard showed an early, if peculiar, interest in invention. At age 12 he built a rat trap around a firing pistol. As a teenager, he built an early velocipede—a predecessor to bicycles—and rode it to the city of Rouen. He designed a hydraulic system that pumped water into the Chateau Gaillard from the Seine River, 400 feet below.

Fascinated with the flight of birds, in 1781 Blanchard built an unsuccessful flying machine with four wings for the pilot to flap using levers and foot pedals. He attempted to demonstrate it in Paris, France, in 1782, but it did not work, and a member of the French Academy of Sciences publicly declared that Blanchard was foolish and that humans would never fly. When Jacques-Etienne and Joseph-Michel Montgolfier built a successful hot-air balloon and demonstrated it for King Louis XVI and Queen Marie Antoinette in 1783, however, Blanchard decided to turn to ballooning.

Blanchard built his own hydrogen balloon and flew it for the first time in Paris on March 2, 1784. He toured around Europe, staging balloon ascensions, and came to dominate the first decade of ballooning. He was the first balloonist, or aeronaut, to make ascensions in Germany, Belgium, Poland, Austria, and the Netherlands.

On January 7, 1785, Blanchard crossed the English Channel by balloon with American doctor John Jeffries, who financed the voyage. Traversing the 21-mile-wide channel made them the first international air travelers. They launched the balloon from the seaside cliffs of Dover, England. Attached were oars and a propeller, Blanchard's latest unsuccessful experiments meant to direct and propel his craft in the air. The two additions to the balloon did not work. In fact, about two-thirds of the way across the channel, the balloon began to leak. Blanchard and Jeffries threw the oars and propeller overboard, along with the bags of sand they had brought as ballast. As the balloon neared the French coast, it began to fall again, and the two men took off their coats and pants and threw them out, too, to lighten the load. They successfully touched down in Felmores Forest in France. Included in their cargo was a package of letters, the first international air mail, which they delivered successfully.

In August of 1785, Blanchard became the first aeronaut to travel more than 200 kilometers in the air with a flight from Lille to Servon. That same year, Blanchard also performed what is often credited as the first successful demonstration of a parachute. A basket attached to a parachute and containing a small animal, probably a dog, was dropped from a balloon and landed safely.

First In North America

After 44 flights in Europe, Blanchard took his balloon to the United States, intent on staging the first aerial voyage there. "The [Western] Hemisphere had as yet only heard of the brilliant triumph of aerostation [ballooning]; and the people who inhabit it appeared to me worthy of enjoying the sublime spectacle that it affords," he wrote later in his *Journal of My Forty-Fifth Ascension* (as quoted by C.V. Glines in *Aviation History*). Blanchard wrote that he wanted to "convince the New World that man's ingenuity is not confined to earth alone, but opens to him new and certain roads in the vast expanse of heaven." (Despite Blanchard's claim, a balloon ascension had already been staged in the United States. In 1784 in Baltimore, Maryland, 13-year-old Edward Warren had ascended in a small tethered balloon invented by lawyer and tavern-keeper Peter Carnes. But Blanchard's flight would be the first untethered balloon voyage in the country.)

Blanchard's American flight became his most celebrated and most thoroughly reported, surely because he staged it in Philadelphia, Pennsylvania, the capital of the United States at the time. For weeks, Blanchard ran an ad in *Dunlap's American Daily Advertiser,* announcing his intention to ascend over Philadelphia in his balloon on January 9, 1793. He set up his balloon and hydrogen generator inside the grounds of the Walnut Street Prison, near what is now the city's Independence Square, figuring the prison walls would protect his equipment from vandals and keep winds from damaging the silk balloon as it inflated. He also hoped to charge people $5 to watch his takeoff, but since the balloon would be visible outside the prison as soon as it ascended, only about 100 people bought tickets, even after Blanchard lowered the price to $2. Though several people asked to join him in the balloon, Blanchard insisted on ascending solo. In case the wind took him out of Philadelphia and across the nearby rivers and woods, Blanchard also discouraged anyone from trying to follow him on horseback.

Almost the entire population of Philadelphia came out to watch Blanchard's balloon ascend, as well as many people from the nearby countryside. Cannons fired every 15 minutes that day, starting at 6 a.m., to remind people of the launch. A brass band played military music inside the prison to heighten the drama. Blanchard, by now an experienced showman, dressed for the occasion in a blue waistcoat and knee breeches and a white-feathered hat. U.S. President George Washington arrived by carriage to witness the event and was greeted by a 15-cannon salute. The French ambassador to the United States attended as well. Washington presented Blanchard with a presidential letter that he could show to anyone he encountered after landing—practical help for the aeronaut, since he spoke no English. A visitor gave Blanchard a small black dog to take with him on the flight, which he accepted reluctantly.

Blanchard took off, rising straight above Philadelphia at first. "I could not help being surprised and astonished when, elevated at a certain height over the city, I turned my eyes towards the immense number of people who covered the open places, the roofs of the houses, the steeples, the streets and the roads," he wrote in *Journal of My Forty-Fifth Ascension* (as quoted by Glines in *Aviation History*). He waved a flag at the crowd.

The feat thrilled Philadelphians. "Seeing the man waving a flag at an immense height from the ground, was the most interesting sight that I ever beheld," General John Steele, comptroller of the U.S. Treasury, wrote in a letter (as quoted by Glines in *Aviation History*), "and tho I had no acquaintance with him, I could not help trembling for his safety." Dr. Benjamin Rush, a prominent Philadelphia citizen and friend of future U.S. President Thomas Jefferson, later wrote in a letter (as quoted by Glines): "The conversation in our city has turned wholly upon Mr. Blanchard's late Aerial Voyage. It was truly a sublime sight. Every faculty of the mind was seized, expanded and captivated by it, 40,000 people concentrating their eyes and thoughts at the same instant, upon the same object."

A slight breeze pushed Blanchard over the Delaware River, and he reached a height of about 5,800 feet. During the flight, he captured high-altitude air by pouring liquid out of six bottles and corking them. He also weighed a stone that had weighed 5 1/2 ounces on land and found it weighed 4 ounces. After traveling southeast, he released some hydrogen gas and some ballast and descended into a field near Woodbury, New Jersey, about 15 miles from Philadelphia. The voyage had lasted about 45 minutes. (The dog quickly ran away.) Some farmers, confused at first and unable to read the letter, but reassured by Blanchard's repetition of President Washington's name, transported him to a ferry that took him back to Philadelphia.

Financial Struggles

Blanchard remained in Philadelphia for some time after his flight, attempting to raise money to stage more ascensions, but bad fortune plagued his efforts. Ticket sales for his first flight and donations taken up outside the prison failed to raise the $1,500 in expenses he said the flight had cost. The governor of Pennsylvania allowed Blanchard to use an office in Philadelphia for free. There, Blanchard built a small museum, where he charged a small fee for visitors to see his balloon and basket, as well as a fanciful invention of his, a wheeled carriage that included an eagle with flapping wings, creating the illusion that the wings were powering the vehicle.

In June of 1793 Blanchard turned to another spectacle to attract customers: launching animals into the sky in tethered balloons. He sent a dog, cat and squirrel into the air attached to primitive parachutes, then propelled them out of the contraptions with small fuses and watched them float to earth. These ventures, too, raised little money. Blanchard finally left Philadelphia in 1795 during a yellow fever epidemic that made city residents afraid to go out in public.

That fall, Blanchard arrived in Charleston, South Carolina, where he attempted to raise money and interest in another balloon flight, with little success. He got a better reception in Boston, sparking serious interest in ballooning. But while he was there, Jeffries, his former co-voyager across the English Channel, sued him for $370 and won. In 1796, Blanchard moved to New York and took on showman

Gardiner Baker as his business partner, but financing was still scarce. Blanchard moved into a "balloon house" to construct a new balloon, but tragedy struck. A windstorm destroyed the house and killed Blanchard's 16-year-old son, Julien Joseph, who had been working on the roof. (Some sources suggest Blanchard flew in his balloon while in New York, but others disagree.)

Return to Europe

After staging a few more balloon flights with animal passengers, Blanchard returned to Europe in May of 1797. He returned to the sky, likely for the first time in four years, in Rouen, France, that August, one of 15 more balloon ascensions he staged in his life. He married his second wife, 18-year-old Marie-Madeleine-Sophie Armant, in 1798. She also became an aeronaut.

In 1808, Blanchard had a heart attack while on his 60th flight, over The Hague, in the Netherlands. He fell more than 50 feet from the balloon and never recovered from his injuries. He died in 1809. His wife, Marie, continued ballooning and became Europe's best-known female aeronaut. She died in Paris on July 16, 1819, falling out of her balloon to her death after fireworks set it on fire.

Books

Wallner, Alexandra, *The First Air Voyage in the United States: The Story of Jean-Pierre Blanchard,* Holiday House, 1996.

Periodicals

Aviation History, September 1996.
World & I, March 2006.

Online

"Blanchard, Jean-Pierre-François," *Encyclopedia Britannica,* http://library.eb.com/eb/article-9015591 (December 16, 2007).
"Celebrating a Century of Flight," NASA.gov, http://history.nasa.gov/SP-09-511.pdf (December 29, 2007).
"Jean Pierre Blanchard," *Microsoft Encarta Online Encyclopedia,* http://encarta.msn.com (December 29, 2007).
"Spring 2001 Newsletter," *FAI Ballooning Commission,* http://www.fai.org/ballooning/newsletter/2001-spr.htm (December 29, 2007). □

Harold Bloom

With the publication of his 1973 book *The Anxiety of Influence,* Harold Bloom (born 1930) became one of the most widely read literary critics in the English-speaking world.

His award-winning book dealt with poetry, and with the relationships of poets to their predecessors, but Bloom, whose erudition is legendary, has written on many other forms of literature. "I cannot think of a major work I have not ingested," he once told *Newsweek.* A longtime professor at Yale University, Bloom has written

densely theoretical texts in which he marshals terminology steeped in classic literature and philosophy in order to express his ideas. Almost alone among major scholars, however, Bloom has also sought to address a general readership. He has emerged as a defender of the canon (or generally accepted selection) of literary works as traditionally taught in Western countries, and he has been an indefatigable promoter of the idea that reading in general is a vital, creative, and even spiritual act. "His enthusiasm for literature is a joyous intoxicant. He scatters insight with manic profligacy," noted Adam Begley in the *New York Times.* A larger-than-life figure in many ways, Bloom has touched both students of literature and general readers with his enthusiasm.

Learned Three Languages as Child

Bloom was born in the New York City borough of the Bronx on July 11, 1930. His parents, William and Paula Bloom, were both working-class Eastern European immigrants who observed the Orthodox Jewish faith. They spoke Yiddish at home, and Harold, the youngest of five children, did not hear the English language regularly until he was six. By that time, however, his gift for absorbing language off the printed page had already begun to show itself. By age three he had taught himself to read Yiddish, and he added Hebrew at four. Starting in on English, he became fascinated with the mystical but rough poetry of English writer William Blake and with the difficult poems of the American author Hart Crane. "I remember my sister Esther at my request took me along to the Melrose branch of the New York Public Library—I couldn't have been more than seven or eight," Bloom recalled as quoted by Begley, "and I got her to take out the collected poems of Hart Crane, and I think a volume of T.S. Eliot's poetry, and Auden, and I went home and devoured them and fell even more violently in love with Hart Crane's poetry."

Bloom's prodigious powers of memory have spawned both true and apocryphal stories. He has said that when he was young he could read a thousand pages in an hour, and the encyclopedic nature of the literary references in his writing shows that he retained much of what he read. *The New Yorker* reported that as an undergraduate at Cornell University, he recited Crane's book-length poem "The Bridge" while drunk. Whatever his exact powers, it is clear that Bloom immersed himself in poetry and fiction as a young person, and that he committed many of the classics of English-language poetry to memory.

Attending the elite Bronx High School of Science, Bloom paid little attention to his classes and got generally poor grades. His academic career was rescued, however, when he turned in a strong performance on the New York State Regents examinations, a statewide standardized test. Admitted on a scholarship to Cornell University in Ithaca in rural upstate New York, he felt out of place at first—the first time he saw a cow in the flesh he was frightened, because he did not know what it was. But he soon began to soak up the university's offerings in the English department. "I came very much under the influence and the kind guidance of M. H. Abrams, Meyer Howard Abrams, who I'm delighted to say is still alive,"

Bloom recalled in an interview on the Web site of Barnes & Noble Books. "He's 88 years old now, one of the leading, perhaps the leading scholar of English Romantic poetry in the 20th century." When Bloom graduated with a B.A. in 1951, Cornell's faculty insisted they had no more to teach him and that he should go elsewhere for graduate study.

Accordingly, Bloom moved on to one of the citadels of East Coast literary studies, the English department at Yale University in New Haven, Connecticut. He would remain at Yale (and a New Haven resident) for the rest of his life, earning his Ph.D. in 1955 and joining the faculty as an instructor that same year. He did not completely fit in at Yale as a student among the university's tweedy professors. "And I," Bloom observed to Begley, "am very Jewish, and lower-class Jewish at that." Furthermore, Bloom was a specialist in Romantic poetry, while the intellectual fashion at Yale ran toward what was known as New Criticism—a school of analysis primarily oriented toward form and structure that favored the intellectual experimentation of modern poetry.

Published Books on Romantic Poets

Any disagreements Bloom might have had with his intellectual mentors at Yale, however (they included Frederick Pottle and William Clyde Devane), faded before his tremendous productivity. While many junior faculty members struggle to produce even one book, Bloom produced five between 1959 and 1971, beginning with *Shelley's Mythmaking* and proceeding through *The Visionary Company: A Reading of English Romantic Poetry* (1961), *Blake's Apocalypse* (1963), *Yeats* (1970), and *Ringers in the Tower: Studies in Romantic Tradition* (1971). Published by the major Doubleday house or by Oxford University Press, these works exerted a strong influence over literary studies, reawakening interest in Romantic poetry as a manifestation of visionary imagination. Bloom accomplished all this while starting a family; he married Jeanne Gould, a child psychologist, in 1958, and the couple had two children, Daniel and David.

Bloom advanced to the rank of assistant professor in 1960, was made associate professor in 1963 (after winning a prestigious Guggenheim fellowship the previous year), and became a full professor at Yale in 1965. Although his career seemed to be going brilliantly, Bloom was troubled by serious episodes of depression, beginning in 1965 and continuing intermittently after that. He sought various forms of intellectual refuge, reading the psychoanalytic works of Sigmund Freud voraciously, delving into philosophy, and exploring the Kabbalah tradition of Jewish mysticism and textual interpretation. Although he had always written very quickly, he labored for several years on a mysterious piece of writing that only piqued the curiosity of his associates—by the late 1960s, Bloom was viewed as an emerging intellectual star.

When the fruits of his labors were revealed, they changed the face of literary criticism. The title of Bloom's *The Anxiety of Influence* (1973) became part of the American intellectual vocabulary. The book was nothing less than a comprehensive theory of poetry, drawing on Freud's general ideas about the Oedipal competition between sons and fathers and amplifying them with a series of concepts drawn

from classical Greek rhetoric. A poem, Bloom argued, cannot be understood without referring to the poems that came before it. Furthermore, a poem represents a specific effort on the part of the poet—an effort to devalue a previous poem by making it seem a mere predecessor to the new poem. Poetry, in Bloom's view, was a constant struggle by poets to overthrow their forerunners. They accomplished this overthrow by what might be called creative misreading (Bloom's word was "misprision") of earlier poets, manipulating the ideas of the earlier in a variety of modes to which Bloom assigned Greek-derived names such as metalepsis.

Several of Bloom's books after *The Anxiety of Influence,* such as *A Map of Misreading* (1975), *Poetry and Repression: Revisionism from Blake to Stevens* (1976), and *Agon: Toward a Theory of Revisionism* (1982) further unpacked the ideas introduced in *The Anxiety of Influence.* Bloom also applied religious and philosophical ideas to literary studies in *Kabbalah and Criticism* (1975) and *Ruin the Sacred Truths: Poetry and Belief from the Bible to the Present* (1989). He himself became devoted to the philosophy of Gnosticism, an early offshoot of Christianity that held that the material world was an imperfect state created by a spirit known as a demiurge; the divine world could be glimpsed only through gnosis or spiritual knowledge.

Resisted New Trends in Criticism

The intensely theoretical nature of *The Anxiety of Influence* led readers to group Bloom with the hardcore literary theory known as deconstruction, but Bloom, who never lost his focus on the human content of poetry and fiction, rejected that association. Nor was he sympathetic to newer schools of criticism that viewed literature as a response to social conditions and often had strongly political content—he sometimes facetiously grouped Marxists, feminists, New Historicists, and other thinkers together as a "School of Resentment." A rebel in his earlier days, Bloom by the late 1980s was viewed as reactionary by some of his younger colleagues. He himself rejected any attempt to link his work to a particular political philosophy and had little use for overtly political literature of any kind. Disgusted by the increasing politicization of literary studies, he left Yale's English department in 1974 and took the designation of professor of humanities, becoming a department of one.

Bloom remained popular with students, giving lectures that were wide-ranging intellectual adventures in themselves. In his later years, his focus turned from literary theory (although he continued to expand on his earlier ideas) to writing books about literature for an audience beyond the academic community. He might have been motivated partly by financial considerations; Begley reported that one of Bloom's sons suffered from a disability that required ongoing medical care. (In 1988 Bloom began teaching at New York University on the side.) Bloom himself spoke, in his Barnes & Noble interview, of unease over the decline of reading. "I have reached the very sad conclusion that what most threatens the future of reading is the . . . real possibility of the disappearance of the book," he said.

Whatever his motivation, Bloom's second career as a public intellectual was remarkably successful. *The Book of*

J (1990), which suggested that parts of the Bible were written by a woman, as imaginative literature, was a bestseller. Bloom was paid an advance of $600,000 for his 1994 book *The Western Canon,* which surveyed the works of 26 writers from the anonymous author of the Sumerian *Epic of Gilgamesh* to contemporary playwright Tony Kushner. Among the most acclaimed of Bloom's later works was *Shakespeare: The Invention of the Human* (1998), in which he analyzed each of Shakespeare's 38 plays and argued that the modern understanding of personality has been crucially shaped by Shakespeare's plays. Bloom's *How to Read and Why* (2000) fell into a long tradition of books introducing American audiences to the art of reading classic literature.

In 1983 Bloom also set out on an ambitious editorial project: he collected essays on specific writers, publishing them in book form with a short introduction of his own. Issued by the small Philadelphia publisher Chelsea House, Bloom's series numbered some 600 volumes by the early 2000s. Although he admitted some contemporary works to the series, Bloom had little use for the major publishing phenomenon of the new millennium. In a widely noted *Wall Street Journal* article published in 2000, he attacked the Harry Potter series by British author J.K. Rowling. "The two Alice books by Lewis Carroll are the finest literary fantasies ever written," he told *Newsweek.* "They will last forever, and the Harry Potter books are going to wind up in the rubbish bin. The first six volumes have sold, I am told, 350 million copies. I know of no larger indictment of the world's descent into subliteracy." A rotund but charismatic figure who for some evoked the Shakespearean character Falstaff, Bloom was in demand as a speaker into old age and remained active in the mid-2000s, penning an introduction to an edition of Eugene O'Neill's play *The Iceman Cometh* in 2006. Literature had been his constant companion since early childhood, and he continued to expound its creative power to the wide public that, despite predictions of its demise, still cherished it.

Books

Allen, Graham, *Harold Bloom: Poetics of Conflict,* Harvester Wheatsheaf, 1994.
Dictionary of Literary Biography, Volume 67: Modern American Critics Since 1955, Gale, 1988.

Periodicals

New York Times Magazine, September 25, 1994.
New Yorker, September 30, 2002.
Newsweek, March 12, 2007.
Wall Street Journal, July 11, 2000.

Online

Contemporary Authors Online, Gale, 2007. http://galenet.galegroup.com/servlet/BioRC (November 1, 2007).
"Harold Bloom," Stanford University Presidential Lectures, http://prelectur.stanford.edu/lecturers/bloom/ (November 1, 2007).
"Meet the Writers: Harold Bloom," Barnes & Noble Books, http://www.barnesandnoble.com/writers/writerdetails.asp?cid=881671#interview (November 1, 2007). □

Michael Bloomberg

American politician Michael Bloomberg (born 1942) first gained renown as chief executive officer of Bloomberg L.P., the immensely successful financial data services and news media company.

Bloomberg was elected mayor of New York City in 2001, and during his second term rumors swirled that he would make a bid for the White House as an independent candidate in the 2008 presidential race. Buzz Bissinger, writing in *Vanity Fair,* called him "one of the most intriguing mayors the city of New York has ever had, in a boatload of bizarre and baffling and brilliant ones—not only because he's the first billionaire ever to hold the office, or the least popular, but also because, in his own idiosyncratic way, he's effective."

Born Michael Rubens Bloomberg on February 14, 1942, the future Wall Street media baron grew up in a lower middle class household in the Boston area. His father, Bill, was a bookkeeper, and his mother, Charlotte, was one of a minority of American women of the era who had earned a college degree. They were also a Jewish family in a city not known for its tolerance of ethnic groups outside of the white Anglo-Saxon Protestant model. In the late 1940s, Bloomberg's parents decided to move to a neighborhood closer to Bill's job in Somerville, just adjacent to Cambridge. They found a house in Medford, a city located on Somerville's other border, but the seller was reluctant to become the first person on the block to sell to a Jewish family. "And so he sold it to my father's Irish lawyer, who resold it to my father at the same table," Bloomberg recalled in an interview with *Newsweek*'s Jon Meacham.

Earned Harvard M.B.A.

At Medford High School, Bloomberg earned good grades, if the subject interested him, and he also attained the rank of Eagle Scout within the Boy Scouts organization after completing its demanding requirements. He went on to Johns Hopkins University, reportedly becoming the first openly Jewish member of the school's Phi Kappa Psi fraternity chapter, and earned his bachelor's degree in electrical engineering in 1964. He then went on to Harvard University for a graduate business degree. After completing his course of study there, he applied to the Officer Candidate School of the U.S. Armed Forces in 1966, at the height of the Vietnam War, but was rejected for having flat feet, or fallen arches.

Bloomberg went to work on Wall Street instead, joining the investment bank Salomon Brothers Inc., a major issuer and trader of bonds on the U.S. and international markets. At the time, Salomon was known for its meritocratic culture—meaning that the company hired and promoted based on talent and drive, not old-money or Ivy League connections, as was the case with many Wall Street investment banks. Bloomberg's first job was as a trading room clerk for a $9,000 annual salary. "It was a pretty lowly start for a Harvard MBA," he wrote in his 1997 autobiography, *Bloomberg on Bloomberg.* "We slaved in our underwear, in

a stand-alone computer terminal that let Merrill Lynch traders keep up-to-date on the Treasury bond market. The company expanded to develop a proprietary computer system that provided current bond and stock prices, and could also perform the notoriously complex government bond calculations.

In 1986 Innovative Market Systems became Bloomberg L.P., and its computer system was becoming a ubiquitous presence on Wall Street. The company contracted with investment banks and brokerage houses to supply them with the so-called Bloomberg Terminals, computers that provided access to current market prices and allowed users to execute on-the-spot trades. There was a hefty initial set-up charge, followed by a monthly fee per terminal. With more and more Wall Street firms using the terminals, and monthly user fees for each one that soared to $1,500 per month, Bloomberg became a millionaire several times over with his privately held company. He reinvested some of the profits in the early 1990s in media properties such as radio stations, creating the Bloomberg News Service. It, too, became a giant in the industry, and together the two properties became the world's largest financial news and data company.

By most accounts Bloomberg was a maverick boss, who ordered the chairs in the main conference room removed so that meetings did not drag on interminably. There were no doors to offices at the company's headquarters, nor official titles, and he expected the same long hours of work from his employees and managers that he himself put in. But by the late 1990s he had emerged as one of New York City's most generous new philanthropists, donating heavily to such institutions as the Metropolitan Museum of Art. Through the private foundation he set up, he also began giving millions to his alma mater, Johns Hopkins University; at the Harvard Business School, he endowed a professorship named in honor of his father, the William Henry Bloomberg Professorship, reserved for academics who specialized in philanthropic and nonprofit ventures management.

Long-Shot Mayoral Candidate

In late 2000 Bloomberg switched his longtime political affiliation from registered Democrat to registered Republican in order to give him a better chance in the following year's mayoral race in New York City. The Democratic field was historically a crowded one in the primary race, and Bloomberg won the public support of the city's outgoing mayor, Rudolph W. Giuliani (born 1944), a Republican. Despite that endorsement, few considered Bloomberg a serious contender. "His gifts on the stump were minimal: He was brusque, infelicitous, maladroit, utterly unvisionary," wrote John Heilemann in *New York* magazine.

New York City's Democratic and Republican mayoral primaries were scheduled for September 11, 2001, and were halted after just a few hours of polling when two airliners hit the towers of the World Trade Center and the city descended into chaos. As Heilemann noted, suddenly "the mood of the electorate darkened. What voters wanted now was an equable hand to keep the economy afloat and the city from unraveling." The primary was rescheduled, and Bloomberg bested his nearest Republican challenger,

an un-air-conditioned bank vault, with an occasional six-pack of beer to make it more bearable. Every afternoon, we counted out billions of dollars of actual bond and stock certificates to be messengered to banks as collateral for overnight loans. By the 1980s such practices would be as quaint as the horse-drawn carriage."

Bloomberg eventually became a bond trader, and was made a partner in 1972. By 1976, the year he married an English woman, Susan Brown, his title at Salomon was general partner in charge of equity trading and sales. A rising star known for coolly risking enormous sums in trades that nearly always proved profitable, Bloomberg was surprised in 1979 when he was given what appeared to be a demotion to director of the firm's computer operations division. Electronic trading was still in its infancy, and the job was not as prestigious as his previous title. However, Bloomberg determined that Salomon's in-house system had some flaws, and he went to work on designing a new one. In 1981, however, the privately held investment bank merged with the publicly traded Phibro Corporation, a commodity trading group. Bloomberg was let go with a $10 million severance package from Salomon, which he used to launch his own computer systems firm in October of 1981.

Launched Own Company

Bloomberg originally called his company Innovative Market Systems, and it landed its first major client in Merrill Lynch, another top Wall Street firm. Working with a team of just four employees, Bloomberg designed and programmed

former Bronx borough president Herman Badillo (born 1929). In the weeks leading up to the election, Bloomberg set a new record for New York City mayoral campaign spending at $74 million. He beat the Democratic challenger, the city's public advocate, Mark J. Green (born 1945), by a margin of two percentage points.

Bloomberg was inaugurated mayor in January of 2002, taking office at a time when New Yorkers were still traumatized by the events of 9/11 and the city was plunging into a steep economic decline that took the national economy along with it. Some of the new mayor's acts were popular, others were widely loathed: he found funding for thousands of new, affordable housing units, but also raised property taxes and wrested control of the city's ailing public school system from the Board of Education. He was commended for his handling of the East Coast blackout in August of 2003, and admired for accepting a mayoral salary of just $1 a year, but he was reviled for enacting a ban on smoking in the city's restaurants and bars. At many of Bloomberg's public appearances during his first term—especially in the more working-class boroughs of Queens, the Bronx, and Staten Island—he was jeered and booed. In his home territory of Manhattan, however, he was a popular leader, and could often be seen riding the subway to his City Hall office every morning.

"Mayor Gloomberg"

Early on, the city's tabloid newspapers dubbed Bloomberg "Mayor Gloomberg," and Bissinger theorized that the mayor might be a victim of what he termed "the Bloomberg Paradox, almost the inverse of" former U.S. president Bill Clinton (born 1946), a two-term Democrat. "While Clinton seemed to be all style and no substance, Bloomberg has substance but his style keeps getting in the way," Bissinger explained. "Much of the time he is unable to give the appearance of caring even when he presumably does, delivering bad news in such a bloodless hall-monitor buzz-saw drone that it often sounds worse than it already is."

Despite these failings, Bloomberg was reelected in 2005 and his approval ratings began to rebound. At times as low as 24 percent in his first term, the public opinion numbers rebounded and began to hit the 70 percent mark. Long rumored to have ambitions for a much higher office, Bloomberg seemed to give confirmation to the talk of a White House bid when on June 19, 2007, he formally resigned from the Republican Party. Declaring himself a political independent instead, Bloomberg refused to confirm or deny rumors as the year wound to a close, and with it his final year as New York City mayor (mayors are limited to two terms).

Remained Cagey about Plans

Some political pundits theorized that Bloomberg would not officially declare himself a candidate in the 2008 presidential race until March or April of 2008, explaining that unlike most candidates, Bloomberg could draw on his vast personal fortune—estimated by *Forbes* magazine at $11.5 billion in 2007—to finance a run that could cost up to $500 million; other presidential candidates must start their campaigns much earlier in order to raise that kind of money from supporters. As the uncertainty over a Bloomberg presidential run continued, Bloomberg reiterated that his focus remained on the stewardship of New York City, although he did tell Meacham that he believed the nation needed new leadership. "One of the sad things is that at the moment America is not liked around the world," Bloomberg reflected. "We have this view that we can do it alone, as we are getting more into a world where you can't."

Bloomberg and his wife, Susan, divorced in 1993, but remain on cordial terms and have two grown daughters, Emma (born 1979) and Georgina (born 1983). His mother, Charlotte, born in 1909, still lives in the same Medford house they bought in 1947, and the mayor reportedly phones her every morning before he leaves for work. Reflecting on his own background and achievements, he told Meacham, "I've been very lucky. . . . My academic record was never stellar, but it wasn't a disaster, either. I am a believer in what I learned in seventh-grade civics: I really down inside believe that everybody in this country has an opportunity—America is built around this premise that you can do it."

Books

(With Matthew Winkler) *Bloomberg on Bloomberg,* John Wiley & Sons, 1997.

Periodicals

Newsweek, November 12, 2007.
New York, December 11, 2006.
Vanity Fair, December 2003. □

Roberto Bolaño

The Chilean-born novelist Roberto Bolaño (1953-2003) earned international renown in the decade before his death with a series of colorful, sprawling, formally innovative novels steeped in the contemporary literary culture of Latin America.

Bolaño came of age among tumultuous political events—the student activism of Mexico in the late 1960s, and the overthrow of Chilean president Salvador Allende by forces loyal to military leader Augusto Pinochet in 1973. Although his writings addressed those episodes only tangentially, they breathed a spirit of freedom—from political restrictions, from stereotypes perpetuated by an entrenched literary establishment, from traditional social and sexual mores. Writing frantically before he was silenced by a progressive liver disease, Bolaño did not live to witness the expansion of his international reputation as his work was translated into English and other languages. Critic Susan Sontag, quoted by Larry Rohter of the *New York Times,* called Bolaño "the most influential and admired novelist of his generation in the Spanish-speaking world."

Moved Frequently as Child

In a Latin American literary world often characterized by intense national identification, Bolaño, who lived in Chile, Mexico, and Spain, often declined to claim a homeland other than Latin America in general. Born in the Chilean capital of Santiago on April 28, 1953, he moved often as a child among Chile's cities—his father was a truck driver and part-time boxer. His mother worked as a teacher. A voracious reader as a child, Bolaño was hampered by dyslexia and did poorly in school. The family moved to Mexico City in 1968, just as the city was becoming convulsed by huge student demonstrations.

That giant, chaotic metropolis awakened the creativity in the teenage Bolaño. He called the city, according to Daniel Zalewski of *The New Yorker,* "a vast, almost imaginary place where freedom and metamorphosis were a daily spectacle." The young Bolaño threw himself into the political and literary clamor of the Mexican capital, making friends with left-wing poets and embarking on a flirtation with a Communist political movement in nearby El Salvador. His political sympathies led him to return to Chile in 1973 to support the socialist Allende government, but he was arrested and jailed after the right-wing Pinochet coup. Through a sheer stroke of luck—a prison guard recognized him as a school friend—he was released, although thousands of Chilean leftists were killed. Bolaño returned to Mexico the following year.

Living in a low-rent but creatively oriented Mexico City neighborhood, Bolaño and some friends formed a literary group they called the Infrarealistas. Their activities were mostly subversive. For example, they attended readings by established authors such as Octavio Paz and interrupted them by reading their own poems loudly. In an interview quoted in *Contemporary Authors,* Bolaño called Infrarealism "a kind of Dada à la Mexicana." But the movement also stimulated him to begin writing poetry regularly and to publish it in small underground magazines. He issued two collections of poetry and also a sort of Infrarealist manifesto called *Déjenlo Todo, Nuevamente* (Leave Everything Behind Once More) before moving to Spain in 1977 to escape the despair brought on by a romantic breakup.

Bolaño traveled around western Europe and North Africa, styling himself a "poet and vagabond," and then settled in Barcelona. He edited an anthology of poetry by young Latin American writers and co-authored (with Antoni G. Porta) a short novel called *Consejos de un discípulo de Morrison a un fanático de Joyce* (A [Jim] Morrison Fan's Advice to a Joyce Fan). Dissatisfied with his own efforts and feeling that he was distracted by the sensuous, freewheeling atmosphere that flowered in Barcelona after the death of dictator Francisco Franco, Bolaño moved from place to place for several years and worked at low-wage jobs that included stints as a dishwasher, campground custodian, dockworker, grape picker, bellhop, and garbage collector. He began to abuse heroin during this period. Bolaño continued to write poetry that was set, as were most of his later fictional works, in Mexico.

Although many young Latin American writers emulated the so-called "magical realism" of writers who blended realistic and fantasy elements, Bolaño had little use for the style. According to Zalewski, Bolaño criticized the dean of Latin American literature, Colombia's Gabriel García Márquez, as "a man terribly pleased to have hobnobbed with so many Presidents and Archbishops" and called his countrywoman Isabel Allende a "scribbler" whose "attempts at literature range from kitsch to the pathetic." Allende returned the favor, describing Bolaño as an "extremely unpleasant" man and adding that "death does not make you a nicer person," as noted by Zalewski.

Entered Fiction Contests

Settling in a small town called Blanes on Spain's Mediterranean seacoast, Bolaño kicked his drug habit and married a local woman, Carolina López. The pair had a son, Lautaro (named for a Chilean resistance leader), and a daughter, Alexandra. Faced with the necessity of supporting his family, Bolaño decided that he might have more luck as a fiction writer than as a poet. He entered several short stories in Spanish regional literary contests and won cash prizes, sometimes recycling an earlier winner by retitling and lightly rewriting it. His 1993 novel *La Pista de Hielo* (The Ice Rink) brought in another prize.

The next major turning point in Bolaño's life came when he was 38, when he learned that he had an incurable liver disease. His response to this news was to begin to write furiously. Beginning in 1996 with *La Literatura Nazi en América* (Nazi Literature in the Americas), an "encyclopedia" of fascist writers Bolaño himself had invented, he wrote at least one book a year until his death in 2003. The theme of fascism recurred in *Estrella Distante* (Distant Star), Bolaño's next novel and one of his works set in his Chilean homeland; it dealt with a minor poet who attempts to ingratiate himself with the Pinochet regime by using a Nazi-era aircraft to compose poems in skywriting. Bolaño's 1997 short-story collection *Llamadas Telefónicas* (Telephone Calls) won the Premio Municipal (or Municipal Prize) of Santiago.

In Bolaño's next book the raw material of his unconventional earlier lifestyle, extremely imaginatively embroidered, began to permeate his writing. *Los Detectives Salvajes* (The Savage Detectives) appeared in 1998 and mixed elements of thriller, philosophical essay, and autobiography in a unique way. Its large cast of characters featured a pair of poets resembling those of Bolaño's Infrarealist group, here called the Visceral Realists. They go in search of a fictional female poet of the past who they think has been lost in the desert. They later experience outlandish adventures in Europe while a large group of observers (the "savage detectives" of the title) offer opinions on their activities and temporary disappearances. The book brought Bolaño fame across Latin America and won Venezuela's prestigious Rómulo Gallegos Prize. Paul Berman, writing in *Slate,* opined that *"The Savage Detectives* sings a love song to the grandeur of Latin American literature and to the passions it inspires. . . . "

In *Amuleto* (Amulet), published in 1999, Bolaño continued to draw on the Mexican literary scene of his youth, creating a Uruguayan female poet who immigrates illegally to Mexico, works as a housecleaner, and is swept up in the 1968 student riots. She hides out in a bathroom, where she writes poetry on toilet paper and narrates the events of the story. The poet first appeared as a minor character in *The Savage Detectives,* and Bolaño several times generated new novels from small pieces of earlier ones. The book's first line showed the indebtedness of Bolaño, an admirer of American genre fiction writers such as Philip K. Dick, to popular fiction forms: "This is going to be a horror story. A story of murder, detection and horror. . . . "

Novel Translated into English

Monsieur Pain, one of Bolaño's earlier novels, was reissued by his Spanish publisher, Anagrama, in 1999, and he published another short-story collection, *Putas Asesinas* (Murderous Whores), in 2001. That collection demonstrated an unusual feature of Bolaño's fiction: he sometimes created characters whose names were slightly altered versions of his own—although they are not necessarily those who actually resemble him most closely. Many of Bolaño's short stories remained untranslated into English by the mid-2000s (although a selection was published as *Last Nights on Earth* in 2007), but his next novel, 2002's *Nocturno de Chile,* appeared in the United States and Britain as *By Night in Chile* the following year and touched off a flood of Bolaño translations. That book, quite different in tone and structure from the expansive *The Savage Detectives,* offered a monologue by a dying Jesuit priest who had supported the Pinochet dictatorship.

Aware that his physical condition was deteriorating, Bolaño made plans to provide a consistent income for his family. He worked on a gigantic novel called *2666* (the date

had minor significance in some of his earlier writings that featured fanciful predictions), intending that it be published in five parts, one per year, after he died. The book was left finished but unedited as his condition worsened. "I'm not capable of doing the work that finishing *2666* requires. There are more than a thousand pages that I have to correct—it's a labor worthy of a nineteenth-century miner. For now, I'm going to do less taxing work. I will correct the novel after I have my liver operation . . . ," he said in an interview quoted by Berman. "I am third on the list to receive a transplant." By this time, he had lost most of his teeth.

The transplant did not come in time, and Bolaño died in a Barcelona hospital on April 28, 1953. After consulting with his widow, his publisher decided to issue *2666* as a single book rather than five of them. The book's 1,119 pages spanned eight decades narratively, centering on a factual story of serial murder: several hundred women, mostly factory workers, have been killed in city of Ciudad Juárez (renamed Santa Teresa by Bolaño). The book has hundreds of characters and like *The Savage Detectives* includes a search for an author thought to be missing in the northern Mexican desert. One section, written in the style of a police report, details some of the murders and examines the uncaring attitudes of local police (who have failed to solve most of the crimes). "More than three hundred pages long, it may be the grimmest sequence in contemporary fiction," Zalewski wrote of this part of the book.

Bolaño died just before his international reputation rose sharply. Translations of his books into French, German, and Italian appeared along with a host of English-language versions, and major profiles of his life and work began to appear in serious magazines such as *Harper's.* Deb Siddartha of that magazine pointed out that Bolaño's work grew from the same kinds of difficult conditions that had shaped great Latin American writing in the past: such conditions "include the idea that writing, and the life within which such writing is shaped, must often function without a safety net; that literature must engage with politics even when politics has foreclosed literature; and that a writer will often have to subvert established forms in order to capture the nature of contemporary reality." His unique blend of outrageous humor, lively political content, and sheer imaginative exuberance marked him as one of contemporary Latin America's most important writers.

Periodicals

Guardian (London, England), July 17, 2003.
Harper's, April 2007.
Library Journal, April 15, 2007.
New York Review of Books, July 19, 2007.
New York Times, November 9, 2005; April 12, 2007.
New Yorker, March 26, 2007.
World Literature Today, July-August 2007.

Online

Berman, Paul, "Mayhem in Mexico: Roberto Bolaño's Great Latin American Novel, *Slate,* http://www.slate.com/id/2173485 (November 1, 2007).

"Chilean Writer Bolano Dies," British Broadcasting Company, http://news.bbc.co.uk/2/hi/entertainment/3070879.stm (November 1, 2007).

Contemporary Authors Online, Gale, 2007. http://galenet.gale group.com/servlet/BioRC (November 1, 2007). □

Lizzie Borden

American alleged murderess Lizzie Borden (1860-1927) is claimed to have murdered her father and stepmother at the family's home in Fall River, Massachusetts, on August 4, 1892.

The crime, gruesome and undoubtedly sensational, spawned a trial that became a landmark in the annals of American crime and in the development of the American mass media. Borden's possible involvement in the murders was one of the first celebrated cases investigated with the help of modern forensic methods, and the trial brought the idea of the expert witness to the forefront in American jurisprudence. The murders remain one of history's great unsolved mysteries; Borden was acquitted of the crime, and debate over who killed Andrew J. Borden and Abby Durfee Gray Borden generated a vein of publishing activity that has proven enduringly profitable. That debate continues to this day, with modern writers attempting to explain the case by reference to child sexual abuse and other factors whose importance has only recently been clarified. "Lizzie Borden took an ax/ And gave her mother forty whacks," runs a nursery rhyme nearly universally known among Americans. "When she saw what she had done/ She gave her father forty-one." But the truth of the matter remains unknown.

Raised in Skinflint Household

Lizzie Andrew Borden (christened Lizzie, not Elizabeth), was born in Fall River, Massachusetts, on July 19, 1860, and lived in that city all her life. She was distantly related to the dairy-producing Borden family. Her mother, Sarah, died in 1862, whereupon her father, Andrew Borden, wed the never-married 38-year-old Abby Durfee Gray. Lizzie's older sister, Emma, did not accept her new stepmother, referring to her disrespectfully as Abby, and the tension soon transferred itself to Lizzie. There were other sources of tension in the household as well: though Andrew Borden was a wealthy man who had invested successfully in banks, cotton farms, and real estate, he was a miser who sold eggs from a basket to his business associates and refused to install running water in the family's Second Street home. Lizzie grew up with a slop pail and chamber pot in her bedroom—a fact that would prove significant in her eventual trial.

Neither Lizzie nor Emma Borden ever married. Lizzie graduated from a public high school in Fall River, and became involved with a variety of organizations consistent with the image expected of a young woman from a well-off family in a small New England city. She was a member in good standing of Central Congregational Church, where she taught Sunday school. Serving as secretary-treasurer of the Christian Endeavor Society, she was also active in the pro-Prohibition Women's Christian Temperance Union and in the antipoverty Fruit and Flower League. Both Lizzie and Emma lived at home, and in outward appearance Lizzie was an admirable and always composed young woman devoted to good works.

At home, though, the family dynamics steadily worsened. In 1887 Andrew Borden, who had wide real estate holdings, transferred ownership of a rental home he owned to Abby. The two daughters insisted that they should receive gifts of equal value. Andrew agreed, giving each daughter a $1,500 house, but the situation continued to fester. For Lizzie, everything given to Abby represented a diminution in her own inheritance, for the two sisters had never gotten along with their stepmother. Lizzie and Emma began to call Abby "Mrs. Borden" and to refuse to participate in family dinners—the household staff had to lay out two sets of place settings for each meal. In 1891 jewelry and cash disappeared from Andrew and Abby's master bedroom; the family went through the motions of a police investigation, although it was clear that Lizzie was the culprit.

After that, tensions began an increase toward the breaking point. " Everybody quietly bought lots of locks," noted Florence King in an article the *National Review.* "To supplement the key locks, there were bolts, hooks, chains, and padlocks." Abby locked and bolted the door that ran between her bedroom and Lizzie's (the labyrinthine house, today a bed-and-breakfast, had few hallways). Lizzie did the same, and escalated the conflict by pushing a writing desk up against the door. Andrew in turn bought a massive lock, but left the key on the living room mantelpiece, in effect daring Lizzie to steal it. Yet a facade of harmony was maintained at all times. Bridget Sullivan, the family's new Irish maid, later testified at Lizzie's trial that she never heard raised voices in the Borden household.

Tried to Purchase Poison

The summer of 1892 was a hot one (although the temperature during Lizzie Borden's fateful week has been a matter of dispute among researchers), and at the end of July both Borden sisters left Fall River: Emma went to Fairhaven, Massachusetts, while Lizzie went with some friends to a beach house on Buzzards Bay on the Massachusetts coast. While there, she tried to buy prussic acid (hydrogen cyanide) from a pharmacy, claiming that she wanted to use it to kill bugs that had infested a fur coat. Such behavior in midsummer attracted attention, and the druggist told her that the poison would be available only with a doctor's prescription.

Back in Fall River, Lizzie got wind of another major property transfer on Andrew's part: this time a farm was being put in his wife's name, and John Morse, the brother of Andrew's first wife, was to be installed as caretaker. Lizzie told a friend named Alice Russell that her father's ruthless business ways had left him with many enemies, and that she had a feeling something terrible was about to happen to him. Several members of the household, including Lizzie, became ill on the evening of August 3, and Andrew raised the possibility that they had been poisoned. On August 4, Andrew, Abby, and John Morse sat down to a breakfast of mutton soup, sliced mutton, pancakes, bananas, pears, cookies, and coffee, after which Morse and Andrew Borden departed. Abby sent Bridget outside to wash windows in the summer heat. Andrew returned home at about 10:40 a.m. for lunch.

Shortly after that, Bridget, whom Lizzie called Maggie, was resting after her exertions with the windows. "Maggie! Come down quick! Father's dead," she heard Lizzie cry out (according to her often-reproduced court testimony). "Somebody came in and killed him." Andrew had been hit, not 41 but 11 times with a heavy object, apparently an ax, and his head was mangled almost beyond recognition, with an eye and a tooth both split in two. Soon a neighbor made another gruesome discovery: the body of Abby was in an upstairs bedroom, in similar condition. Police summoned to the scene found no sign of forced entry. They concluded that Abby had been killed about an hour and a half before Andrew, a determination that has also been disputed. Questioned as to her whereabouts, Lizzie, who had no blood on her clothing or body, said that she had been in the barn behind the house, looking for lead weights to use as part of an upcoming fishing expedition.

The initial suspect was a Portuguese-born laborer who had wrangled with Andrew Borden over payment for a job and had visited the Borden home on the morning of the murders. Three days later, according to Russell's testimony before a grand jury in November, Lizzie burned a blue cotton dress in the kitchen stove, claiming she had ruined it by brushing up against some fresh paint. Police were skeptical of Lizzie's story, inasmuch as it would have required a killer other than Lizzie to remain inside the house or in the near vicinity for nearly two hours without being noticed, and a week later, after police remained unsatisfied with her answers to several questions at an inquest, she was arrested and charged with the double homicide. She awaited trial in jail for almost a year as police searched for a murder weapon and other evidence, and while prosecutors built a case against her.

Benefited from Well-Known Defender

The Borden murders were among America's first crimes to play out under the glare of the mass media. The case was covered extensively by New York's strenuously competing newspapers, and Lizzie Borden granted interviews in which she tried to influence public opinion. To forestall the impression that she seemed emotionless in the face of her parents' deaths, she told the *New York Recorder* (as quoted by King), "They say I don't show any grief. Certainly I don't in public. I never did reveal my feelings and I cannot change my nature now." When her trial finally began, on June 5, 1893, Borden had a celebrity attorney in her corner: former Massachusetts governor George Robinson. One of the prosecutors, Frank Moody, was a future U.S. attorney general.

The case against Borden seemed strong, but it was entirely circumstantial. No witness could testify to direct knowledge of her involvement, and no murder weapon was ever definitively located. An ax head, found without its handle in the Borden home's basement, was linked by an expert witness, a Harvard University professor, who testified that it matched the wounds inflicted on Andrew and Abby. No blood was found on the blade. It seemed possible that Borden, who was menstruating at the time of the murders, could have cleaned it off (and also cleaned her own hands and face) with one of the cloths that women of the time used as sanitary napkins; blood is much easier to remove from metal than from fabric. The cloth she used would then have blended in with those she had already accumulated over the course of her menstrual period when all were thrown in a bucket.

The all-male jury began its deliberations on June 20, and after an hour and a half it returned with a verdict of not guilty. Newspapers of the time generally praised the verdict and the painstaking cross-examinations that led to it, but a preponderance of later evaluations has concluded that Borden was the murderess. The view is far from unanimous, however, with other studies advancing Morse as the culprit; or other townspeople; or an illegitimate son of Andrew Borden; or that perhaps Bridget Sullivan, angered at having to wash windows on the hottest day of the year, did the deed. Lizzie's possible motive has also been dissected, with a group of modern commentators suggesting that the killing might not have been linked to money. Brown University psychiatry professor Eileen McNamara argued that incest could have played a role; it would explain both the family's fixation on locked doors and the extreme violence of the attacks—the first few ax blows were sufficient to kill each of the Bordens, but whoever killed them continued to swing the ax long past the point of death. "When an offspring kills a parent, there is usually a pattern of psychological, physical or sexual abuse," psychologist Steven Kane told Jo Ann Tooley of *U.S. News & World Report.*

Lizzie Borden, using the new name of Lizbeth, continued to live in Fall River after the trial's conclusion. She and Emma bought a substantial hilltop house they called Maplecroft; they were ostracized by many Fall River citizens, but opened their home to artists and traveling actors. Lizzie may have carried on a lesbian relationship with an actress named Nance O'Neill; a letter she wrote to O'Neill (quoted by King) read, "I dreamed of you the other night but I do not dare to put my dreams on paper." Author Evan Hunter has advanced the theory that the relationship between Lizzie and Bridget Sullivan was sexual, and that the murders resulted from Abby's discovery of the situation. Emma moved out of Maplecroft in 1905, and Lizzie lived there alone until her death from pneumonia on June 1, 1927. She left $30,000 in cash to the Animal Rescue League. An enormous variety of popular cultural treatments of Lizzie Borden remained unabated as of 2007, when New York actress Jill Dalton premiered her one-woman show, *Lizzie Borden Live.*

Books

Kent, David, ed., with Robert A. Flynn, *The Lizzie Borden Sourcebook,* Branden Publishing Co., 1992.
Masterton, William L., *Lizzie Didn't Do It!,* Branden Publishing Co., 2000.
Outlaws, Mobsters & Crooks: From the Old West to the Internet. Vol. 5. U*X*L, 2002.
Spiering, Frank, *Lizzie,* Random House, 1984.

Periodicals

Contemporary Review, December 1992.
National Review, August 17, 1992.
U.S. News & World Report, August 3, 1992.

Online

"The Trial of Lizzie Borden," Famous Trials, http://www.law .umkc.edu/faculty/projects/ftrials/LizzieBorden/bordenhome .html (January 29, 2008). □

Bertha Brainard

Bertha Brainard (died 1946) was a pioneering radio executive who became the first woman ever to hold an executive post at an American network.

Brainard's rapid rise occurred almost simultaneously with that of the fledgling medium itself during the 1920s, and in 1927 she became the first-ever head of programming for the newly created National Broadcasting Company (NBC). That same year, she wrote an article for the *New York Times* about the role of women in the new medium that was rapidly revolutionizing American life. "I have watched the increase of women's interest in broadcasting, realizing that it was one great factor which was working for the good of radio in general, demanding that the program managers arrange constantly better and more interesting programs," she asserted.

Brainard was born in New Jersey to Henry and Ada Brainard, and attended South Orange High School and Montclair Normal School. As a teen she was an avid moviegoer, fascinated by the new form of entertainment, and she hoped to become a screen star herself. During World War I she drove an ambulance for the American Red Cross. Back in New Jersey after the war, she was perplexed by the fascination her brother exhibited for his new hobby, the crystal set. These early radios were assembled by mail-order kits, and the quality of sound was often poor; Brainard, however, was more annoyed by the programming, which she thought was terrible.

Began at WJZ

Deciding to seek a career in radio, Brainard contacted a New York newspaper journalist, Heywood Broun (1888-1939). Broun spent most of the 1920s with the *New York World,* and had a nationally syndicated column called "It Seems to Me." Through his connections he set up an introduction for Brainard with a press agent for the Shubert Theater organization, a Broadway powerhouse. That person, in turn, knew someone at WJZ, one of the first commercial radio stations in the New York-New Jersey area. Located at 833 AM, WJZ was based in Newark, New Jersey, and took its call letters from the state's name. When it went on the air on October 1, 1921, its owner was the Westinghouse Electric Corporation. Four days later, it made radio history with its broadcast of baseball's World Series, the first ever to air.

Brainard finagled a meeting with WJZ executives and suggested to them that listeners might like to hear theater reviews. She offered to do the job herself, and by 1922 she was delivering a nightly program of theatre reviews and commentary called *Broadcasting Broadway* and had been made assistant manager at the station. A year later she became WJZ's program director, and in 1926 was made station manager. That same year, control of WJZ passed over to a newly formed parent company, the National Broadcasting Company (NBC), which was formed by a trio of companies with a common interest in creating a chain, or network, of radio stations. These were the Radio Corporation of America (RCA)—a manufacturer of radio sets—along with General Electric (GE) and Westinghouse.

Believed That Women Were Target Audience

From the start of her career, Brainard was firmly convinced that radio broadcasting needed to appeal to everyone in the household, not just the men. In the article she penned for the *New York Times* in 1927, she wrote of the medium's earliest era, when "women looked on the radio as something which occupied the entire attention of the men of the family while they were at home and kept them up until all hours of the night, making them cross and irritable the next day." Those first radio sets were unwieldy pieces of furniture whose inner workings were sensitive and thus easily rendered temporarily inoperable if jarred while dusting, for example; moreover, the batteries inside sometimes leaked acid and ruined furniture. Once loudspeakers on the units replaced headphones, more women began tuning in. "Women discovered that during the day, while the men were out of the house, they could gain a wealth of diversion from their radio sets," she wrote in the same 1927 article, adding, "I consider that [women's] opinions on broadcasting are very important . . . [and] I have found that most of them are constructive critics."

WJZ's first headquarters were a makeshift rooftop shack on a building at Orange and Plane streets in Newark, but with the NBC deal it moved to New York City and rented offices at the Aeolian Building, a concert hall on Times Square, later moving to a more elaborate setup at the newly completed Rockefeller Center in the early 1930s. NBC officially came into being on November 15, 1926, and on the first day of 1927 it began operating as two networks: NBC Red offered music and entertainment programming, while NBC Blue Network devoted its broadcasts to news and cultural programming. Brainard's talents as a radio executive impressed David Sarnoff (1891-1971), the head of NBC, who made her the commercial program director for the new Blue network, with WJZ as the flagship station. The Red and Blue divisions lasted until the 1940s, when the Federal Communications Commission ordered NBC to divest, and the Blue network eventually became the American Broadcasting Company (ABC).

Conceived Innovative Programming

Brainard championed several innovations at NBC that laid the groundwork for the future of American broadcasting, in both radio and television, especially after she became chair of NBC's programming board—a powerful position for a woman in that era. The forerunner of the television sitcom was one of her early successes, in the form of *The Goldbergs*, a 15-minute drama centered on a Jewish family in New York City that began in 1929 and later moved to television. That same year she put *The Fleischmann's Yeast Hour* on the air on NBC, which later became *The Rudy Vallée Show*. Hosted by popular singer-bandleader Rudy Vallée, the show had Brainard's backing and made it onto the air only when she managed to convince fellow NBC executives that Vallée's voice had a unique appeal to women that men could not grasp. The musical variety hour soon took the number two spot in the ratings for NBC, second only to the comedy *Amos 'n' Andy*. On being a woman in a male-dominated field, she said in a 1939 *New York Times* interview with Kathleen McLaughlin that "you can't beat men at their own game. You can bang your fist on the table and swear," she noted, but personally she found a softer approach worked best. Was it not wiser, she asked McLaughlin, to "be yourself and use feminine tactics? One of them I've always found effective in any impasse is to appeal for advice. What's more, I get it and like it."

The same article noted that Brainard regularly put in ten- to twelve-hour work days, and managed to go for a daily swim at a summer house she owned in the countryside. In the city, she lived in an "uptown penthouse apartment she shares with a sister who directs the household and relieves her of domestic responsibilities," according to McLaughlin. At the time, Brainard was one of the highest paid radio executives of either gender in American media. She retired in 1946 after 25 years in the business, and married advertising executive Curt Peterson. She died of a heart attack on June 11, 1946, at her home in Huntington, Long Island.

Brainard's influence on the medium stretched well into the next century in the form of weekly Saturday afternoon Metropolitan Opera broadcasts, which began in 1933. In the interview with McLaughlin, which mentioned that she earned a five-figure salary, she dismissed any notion that she had a gift for giving listeners what they wanted to hear. "The only smart thing I ever did in radio," she joked to McLaughin, "was to decide sixteen years ago that it was going to be as big as it is."

Periodicals

New York Times, January 1, 1922; September 18, 1927; January 22, 1939; June 12, 1946.

Online

"Bertha Brainard, Radio Executive," The Paley Center for Media, http://www.shemadeit.org/meet/biography.aspx?m=17 (December 17, 2007). □

Gordon Brown

Gordon Brown (born 1951) became British prime minister in the summer of 2007, after his longtime Labour Party colleague—and rival, some claim—Tony Blair (born 1953) relinquished power. Brown had served as Chancellor of the Exchequer, or finance and treasury minister, in Blair's government since 1997. Born in Scotland, the somewhat rakish, brooding politician had long been predicted to succeed Blair, and the perceived rivalry between the two men had even become the subject of a fictionalized television film in Britain in 2003, *The Deal.*

Brown was born on February 20, 1951, in Glasgow, Scotland, as one of three sons of the Reverend Dr. John Brown, a minister in the Church of Scotland. The family moved to the town of Kirkcaldy, in Fife, Scotland, when Brown was three years old, where his father became pastor of the local parish. Located on a narrow inlet called the Firth of Forth, Kirkcaldy experienced severe economic changes during Brown's youth, including the closing of one of its biggest employers, a linoleum factory. His charity-minded father was a beloved local pastor for his commitment to economic issues, and that sense of duty would be passed on to his son. Recalling the visitors who came to the St. Bryce rectory where the family lived, Brown later said that "as a minister's son you see every problem

that allowed surgeons to view the retina more clearly, and the sight in that eye was saved.

Brown's leftist political sensibilities were honed at the University of Edinburgh, where he became known as "Red Gordon." He earned his master's degree in history with top honors in 1972, and was elected rector of the school that same year. In this post, he chaired the school's governing body, although the rules were later changed to prevent students from holding the office. While working toward his doctorate in history, he challenged the school's administration on several fronts as rector, most notably over its investments in South Africa. At the time, South Africa's white government ruled by denying the black majority population their political rights, and the country was becoming an international pariah. The first mention of Brown's name in the venerable *Times* of London, Britain's newspaper of record, came on March 20, 1973, under the headline "University clash with student rector." Seeking support for his South African divestment campaign, Brown won an important ally in the form of the Duke of Edinburgh, also known as Prince Philip (born 1921), consort to Queen Elizabeth II (born 1926) and the University of Edinburgh's official patron. At the time, the rather dashing Brown, who remained a bachelor until age 49, was dating Princess Margarita, a member of the exiled Romanian royal family.

Elected to Parliament

Brown became a lecturer at the Glasgow College of Technology in 1976, a year after stepping down from his rector's post at the University of Edinburgh, where he continued to work toward his doctoral degree. He earned a Ph.D. in 1982 with a dissertation titled *The Labour Party and Political Change in Scotland, 1918-29*. He also became active in the Scottish Labour Party, which is part of the larger Labour Party of Britain, and stood for his first general election in May of 1979 as a candidate for the House of Commons from the Edinburgh South constituency. He lost to a Conservative (Tory) Party candidate in what was a major victory for the Tories that brought the first woman prime minister, Margaret Thatcher (born 1925), to power.

In 1980 Brown switched careers to journalism and became current affairs editor for Scottish TV, while also rising in the Scottish Labour Party to vice chair and then chair by 1983. In that year's 1983 general election, he again ran for a seat in the House of Commons, this time from Kirkcaldy's Dunfermline East riding, or district, and won, despite the fact that the final 1983 tally proved one of the worst ones for Labour in British electoral history. Also elected that year was an Oxford University graduate and left-wing lawyer named Tony Blair. The two shared an office in Westminster, where the Houses of Parliament meet. During the years that Labour remained in opposition, Brown held several successively higher posts as the "shadow" or opposition counterpart to various officials in the Tory government, including opposition trade and industry secretary and shadow Treasury chancellor.

Brown and Blair were part of a new generation of Labour Party politicians who sought to reform the organization from within by moving it away from its strongly

coming to your doorstep," as he told Paul Vallely in the London *Independent*. "You become aware of a whole range of distress and social problems."

"Red Gordon"

The Fife area where Brown grew up was a part of Scotland whose locals "pride themselves on being different from other Scots," Vallely described. "One cherished characteristic is, in Scots, that of being 'thrawn,' which translates as stubborn, cross-grained [contrarian] and defiant. Fifers have long memories, and brag of making good friends but bad enemies," with the journalist adding that among Brown's longtime colleagues in the center of government, "there are plenty in Westminster who will concur" with that assessment of Brown as a genuine Fifer.

Brown was a gifted student who was selected for a fast-track university entrance program, and he began his studies at the University of Edinburgh at age 16. His major was history, but he was also a talented rugby player for the school, as he had been back in Kirkcaldy. During his first year of college, however, he suffered a detached retina, which was likely a precondition exacerbated by the notoriously brutal sport. After three operations, he lost sight in his left eye. Following each of those surgeries, Brown later recalled in an interview with the London *Guardian*'s Suzie Mackenzie, "I'd have to lie, in darkness, for three maybe four weeks at a time." Later during his university period, he noticed the same symptoms in right eye, and this time underwent an operation with more advanced instruments

leftist, pro-union past. The party was led by Neil Kinnock until 1992, when a Scottish Labour Party veteran, John Smith (1938-1994) took over; Brown was said to have considered placing himself as a candidate for the leadership post that year, but decided against challenging the man who had been his mentor. Two years later, Smith died of a sudden heart attack, and two months later Blair stood for and won election to lead Labour at its 1994 party conference. Insiders venture that there had been a verbal agreement between Brown and Blair not to run against one another for the party leadership, and that if Labour did finally win a general election and Blair became prime minister, he would serve just one term before stepping down to let Brown take over.

Became Chancellor of the Exchequer

Blair and his coterie of Labour advisors did manage to retool the Labour platform enough to gain voters by the next general election, held in May of 1997. Under the banner "New Labour," Blair and Brown's party won a landslide victory for the party, giving it 418 out of 646 seats in the House of Commons. It marked a return of Labour to power for the first time since the Thatcher era had begun nearly 20 years earlier. Blair named Brown to be his Chancellor of the Exchequer, a post equivalent to that of minister of finance and the treasury department in other European countries, responsible for all economic and financial matters. As such, Brown was a key figure in helping Labour win a second victory in 2001 after having won effusive praise for his handling of the economy, which included reducing some taxes, granting the Bank of England more independence in setting interest rates, and settling the rancorous question over whether Britain would join the European Union's single-currency club. In this last matter, Brown decided that the Treasury Department would set five economic tests before Britain could adopt the Euro. Six years later, in 2003, the criteria set by Brown's ministry had yet to be met.

Brown's stint as Chancellor of the Exchequer set a new record in the history of the office. He remained on the job for ten years and 56 days, making him the longest Labour chancellor ever to hold the job and the longest consecutively serving chancellor in more than 200 years. There remained the question of the next step for him, however, and calls for Blair to step down increased considerably after Britain became the only major power to side with the United States in its 2003 invasion of Iraq, despite major public opposition.

Rumors of a deep rift between Brown and Blair resurfaced once again, as they had periodically since 1997, with the publication in 2005 of *Brown's Britain* by Robert Peston. The biography claimed that the two were not on speaking terms any longer, that Blair had not honored a promise to step down in 2004, and that Brown had told the prime minister, "There is nothing that you could ever say to me now that I could ever believe," according to Catherine Mayer in *Time International*. Blair's aides denied that Brown had uttered such words, but Brown's camp—some of whom are believed to have cooperated, at least off the record, with

Peston—refused to confirm or deny that the statement had been made. There were clamors from within the Labour Party for Brown and Blair to resolve their issues, lest the rift damage the party irrevocably, but the party did win its third consecutive victory in general elections in May of 2005. Sixteen months later, Blair announced that he would step down within the year. In May of 2007, he said in a speech that he would resign both as party leader and prime minister in June.

New Head of Labour Government

At a Labour Party conference on June 24, Blair handed over power to Brown, and the change in government was formally instigated when Brown accepted the Queen's invitation to form a government, as is the custom in Britain. He had already ascended to head of the Labour Party in May of 2007, after an uncontested bid. His first week in office was a challenging one, including the foiling of a terrorist plot with attacks planned in both London and at the Glasgow airport. Then came heavy rains that brought severe flooding to the north of England, and the new prime minister earned points for handling both "with unexpected deftness and assurance, radiating a newfound prime ministerial dignity," asserted *New York Times* writer Sarah Lyall.

On August 3, 2000, Brown married Sarah Jane Macauley, a former public relations executive. Their first child was a daughter, Jennifer Jane, born in December of 2001 two months prematurely; she died ten days later. The tragedy prompted an outpouring of sympathy for the family, and Brown spoke of the thousands of letters he and his wife received in support. In 2003 a son, John, was born, followed in 2006 by a second son, James. The younger boy was diagnosed four months later with cystic fibrosis.

Brown must call a general election by 2010. The man once dubbed the "Iron Chancellor" for his somewhat ruthless management style at the Treasury likely hopes to set another longevity record as prime minister, perhaps even surpassing Thatcher's modern-era record of eleven-and-a-half years. The college-era "Red Gordon" had not disappeared completely, despite his years in government and the requisite ideological compromises such careers often entail. Noting the achievements made since the early 1970s, when he and his peers were beginning their adult lives, he told Catherine Mayer in a *Time* article that Britain now might rise to a position of ethical leadership in the world. "We can be the first generation in history where every child has a chance of education. And we have the chance over the next few years to eradicate some of the most deadly diseases of the world: tuberculosis, polio, diphtheria, malaria. . . . That would be a great tribute to the concern and the moral sense of this generation."

Periodicals

Guardian (London, England), September 25, 2004.
Independent (London, England), June 28, 2007.
New York Times, May 10, 2007; December 5, 2007.
Time, May 21, 2007.
Time International, January 24, 2005.
Times (London, England), March 20, 1973. □

Sterling Brown

Though he has often been called a writer of the Harlem Renaissance—a period of cultural development among U.S. blacks, centered in New York City's Harlem in the 1920s—poet and literary critic Sterling Brown (1901-1989) rose to prominence during the early 1930s outside of New York's literary and intellectual circles. Other black writers and poets of the period sought inspiration from urban life and the exotic atmosphere of Harlem cabarets, whereas Brown embarked on a firsthand study of Southern blacks.

A graduate of the prestigious universities Williams and Harvard, Brown observed black dialect, music, and folktales with brilliant insight, attaining knowledge that emerged in a powerful poetic voice filled with rhythm and imagery cultivated from black oral and blues traditions. His critical works on black literature and drama published in the 1930s were the first in-depth studies of their kind, and they, like Brown's poetry of the same period, are among the most outstanding works by an African-American writer during the Depression era. His body of work remains a rich source for the study of African-American dialect and rural and folk culture.

Made Good Use of Elite Education

The youngest of six children, Sterling Allen Brown was born on May 1, 1901, on the campus of Howard University, in Washington, D.C. A Howard professor of religion and pastor of the Lincoln Temple Congregational Church, Brown's father, Reverend Sterling Nelson Brown, instilled in his son a sense of achievement and moral refinement. His stories of slavery in Tennessee and his subsequent struggle for a college education fueled his son's imagination. Brown's father was, as Arthur Fauset wrote in *Sterling Brown: A UMUM Tribute*, "characteristic of the race 'men' of his era. That indomitable drive to achieve, that quality of integrity and erudition possessed by him and his wife, were moulded into the character of their only son."

Raised on the Howard campus, near a section of the city known as "Foggy Bottom," Brown lived with his family on 11th Street, above the Lincoln Congregational Church. His contact with white youths was limited to a friendship with a boy whose father owned a nearby drugstore. In the rich intellectual environment of Howard, he met such noted black scholars as W.E.B. Du Bois and Howard professor of philosophy Alain Locke. At Dunbar High School, an institution noted for its prestigious instructors and graduates, Brown attended classes taught by abolitionist Frederick Douglass's grandson Haley Douglass and Jessie Redmon Fauset, the novelist and founding member of the National Association for the Advancement of Colored People (NAACP). At home, he received instruction in literature from his mother, Adelaide, a Fisk University graduate whose inspired reading of Henry Wadsworth Longfellow and Paul

Lawrence Dunbar had a profound impact on Brown's later career as a writer and literary scholar.

In 1918, at the age of 17, Brown received an academic scholarship and entered Williams College. Williams was segregated, so Brown spent most of his time with a small coterie of black students. He served on the debate team and played for the Common Club Tennis Team. Through the tutelage of instructor George Dutton, Brown discovered the works of Fyodor Dostoyevsky, Leo Tolstoy, Joseph Conrad, and Sinclair Lewis. He was impassioned by the words of these new literary figures and began to write poetry.

At the same time, Brown explored the rich world of African-American music. Unlike his father and most students at Williams, he did not view the blues and jazz as degenerate forms of artistic expression. In the dormitory at night, when everyone else was asleep, according to S. P. Fullinwinder in *The Mind and Mood of Black America*, Brown "found himself a secluded corner, before he dared to defy the current cannons of sensibility by listening to Mamie Smith sing the blues."

Unlike many other black thinkers and scholars, Brown did not experience an inner conflict between the influence of European culture and the artistic legitimacy of African-American music. As Fullinwinder explained, "His own success at breaking down the psychological barrier between himself and his people is probably due to the fact that, for him, the barrier never existed to begin with."

After graduating Phi Beta Kappa—as a member of the national honor society—from Williams, Brown entered Harvard University in 1922. Brown's instructors at Harvard included distinguished literary critic F. O. Matthiessen. There he was introduced to Louis Untermeyer's *Modern American Poetry*, which first exposed him to the work of the literary imagists, an Anglo-American poetic movement devoted to writing predicated on, as Henry May wrote in *The End of American Innocence*, "intensity, condensation, the use of images rather than abstractions, and the development of new cadences appropriate to the purpose of the particular poem." Poets Robert Frost and Edwin Arlington Robinson, however, had the most impact on Brown—their regional outlook and realistic view of the common man helped him to, as Sterling Stuckey wrote in his introduction to *Southern Road*, "take an uncondescending, that is to say a genuinely respectful, attitude toward the folk" he would later encounter in the South.

Shared Fascination with Folk Culture

After earning a master's degree from Harvard in 1923, Brown decided on a teaching career. He took a job teaching English at the Virginia Seminary and College in Lynchburg, Virginia, at the urging of his father and historian Carter G. Woodson. Exposed to the rural population of the South, he discovered the essence of what he described as a "people's poetry." At Virginia Seminary, Brown befriended Calvin "Big Boy" Davis, an itinerant musician and singer who would later serve as the catalyst for several of Brown's poetic works. "He was a treasure trove of stories, songs," wrote Brown, as quoted in *Sterling Brown: A UMUM Tribute*. "He was a wandering guitar player. . . . He knew blues, ballads, spirituals. He had a fine repertoire, and he'd sing, and although all of us were on starvation wages, we'd hand him a little money, buy him something to drink and that was the evening. . . . This wasn't my introduction, but this was my deepening awareness of the importance of music."

In 1926 Brown began a two-year teaching job at Lincoln University in Jefferson City, Missouri. Here, too, he spent time out of the classroom seeking out interesting individuals and local musicians. In an area bordering the campus known as the "Foot," he met "Preacher," a self-appointed prophet of doom. In Jefferson City he befriended a waiter called "Slim," a yarn-spinner who would become another important source for Brown's poetry. Affectionately known as "Prof" by his students, Brown emerged as a gifted educator, directing and often acting in plays by Eugene O'Neill.

After class, Brown would invite students to his home, where they listened to the blues and jazz and read poetry that was not part of the university's English curriculum. As one former student recalled in *Sterling Brown,* "In our in-home gatherings, some of us learned about poems of Robert Burns that don't appear in college textbooks. . . . And they were the sort that would have had Brown railroaded out of town if he had read them in class. In the early 1920s Brown was a rarity; professors were inclined to be stuffy rather than sparkling."

Brown next taught at Fisk University where, from 1928 to 1929, he further won the affection of students. Continuing his search for African-American culture, he would often make trips to Nashville, Tennessee, to watch blues singer Bessie Smith perform. He lived in an apartment on campus with his wife, Daisy Turnbull, whom he had married in 1927. One of Brown's Fisk colleagues recalled in *Sterling Brown*: "There was always a warmth in the greetings at the Brown's door. Daisy made us feel that we were expected. Sterling, with his pipe hanging loosely, had some quip to make. . . . His sardonic humor made the pomposity of some of his colleagues and the fancies and foibles of others tenderly amusing aspects of personality packages."

Emerged as Influential Poet and Writer

In 1925 Brown's poem "Roland Hayes," about the classical singer, became his first nationally published work, winning second prize in a contest sponsored by *Opportunity* magazine. Two years later, he won *Opportunity's* first prize for the poem "When de Saints Go Ma'ching Home," dedicated to Big Boy Davis. As the poem's narrator, Big Boy roams the landscape, his memory pouring forth images and characters from places where, as Brown concludes in the poem's last stanza, "we never could follow him."

Despite his growing profile as a poet and writer, Brown remained committed to his career as a teacher. He took a position at Howard University in 1929 and two years later, enrolled in the University's doctoral program. Brown's *Southern Road,* a collection of poems that had been published in various magazines between 1926 and 1929, including the prize-winning "When de Saints Go Ma'ching Home," was published in 1932. According to most critics, *Southern Road* ushered in a new era of black literary achievement.

Appearing during the wane of the Harlem Renaissance and the beginning of the Great Depression, Brown's volume featured symbolic folk heroes born during slavery and lone bluesmen, roustabouts, and convicts whose experiences transcended their race and region. In his assessment of the book's initial impact, Jean Wagner wrote in *Black Poets of the United States,* "If Sterling Brown succeeded in salvaging from despair what remained of man after the storm had subsided, it was essentially because he had drawn from past experience an unshakable faith in the eternal potentials of his race."

Brown's work in *Southern Road* represented a marked and conscious effort to break with an older African-American literary tradition. Brown and his younger contemporaries, like Richard Wright, did not, as James O. Young wrote in *Black Writers of the Thirties,* "see the need for proving the negro's humanity, they assumed it." In his few poems that address urban life, Brown avoids the celebration of Harlem nightlife and its vogue; instead, he reveals a more ominous side of city life.

An experimental poem, "Cabaret" revolves around the jazz musician and his exploitative white employers who, along with their jewel-studded friends, look on the entertainer solely as a means of amusement. But as Wagner observed in *Black Poets,* "the customers and performers . . . are only . . . elements in the counterpoint, for the poem, by opposing myth to reality and superiors to inferiors, also evokes the older polarity of masters and slaves. This is the historic dimension that endows the poem with its full depth of meaning."

Through well-crafted verse steeped in folkloric images, music, and authentic dialect, Brown shows the diversity of rural African Americans. Brown's characters live within a picturesque yet segregated and harsh land. The book's title poem portrays a convict laborer's travail, as told in the rhythm of the African-American worksong. Brown's repetitive use of the utterance "hunh"—the grunt of the worker's hammer as it falls—is used to punctuate certain lines, creating a haunting, chant-like rhythm. As Charles H. Rowell wrote in *The Harlem Renaissance Re-examined,* the poem "is a lyrical expression of powerlessness and despondency—one picture of 'the tragedy of the southern Negro.'" Together with the numerous other voices comprising the volume, the convict's lament, becomes, as Rowell explained, "a picture of the tragic condition of Southern black life."

Brown's poems in *Southern Road* also echo an ironic humor. His Slim Greer pieces, based on an acquaintance in Jefferson City, are modern "tall tales." When faced with racism and oppression, the character of Greer relies on cleverness and wit to disarm his white persecutors. Greer's ability to combat psychic pain with mirth reflects Brown's admiration for a people whose stubborn will to overcome and nobility of character emerged in powerful forms of creative expression.

Examined and Guarded Against Stereotypes

In 1937 Brown published the works *The Negro in American Fiction* and *Negro Poetry and Drama,* which were then the most extensive and in-depth studies of their kind. In *The Negro in American Fiction,* a survey of literature from the seventeenth century to the 1930s, Brown studied the image of blacks as presented by American authors. Examining various periods and locales, he identified stereotypes of what he called "The Contented Slave," "The Brute Negro," "The Wretched Freeman," "The Tragic Mulatto," "The Comic Negro," and "The Exotic Primitive." At the same time, he parallels the stereotypical portrayal of blacks in American fiction with caricatures created by writers of other cultures, the depiction by English writers of the "undesirable" Irish "Paddy," for example.

Brown served from 1936 to 1940 as Editor of Negro Affairs for the Work Projects Administration's (WPA) Federal Writer's Project—one of the few important positions bestowed on an African American as part of President Franklin D. Roosevelt's New Deal, which was designed to put the country back to work, among other goals, during the Depression. Overseeing a small staff of assistants, he supervised editorial operations concerning the contributions of black writers. As editor, he often protested the racist imagery of blacks found in WPA-sponsored state guidebooks. During his stay with the Federal Writers Project, he initiated the publication of the study *The Negro in Virginia* and the voluminous tour guidebook *Washington, City and Capital.*

In 1941 Brown, in collaboration with Arthur P. Davis and Ulysses Lee, compiled and edited *The Negro Caravan,* a comprehensive anthology of African-American essays, poetry, short stories, folklore, and drama. The editors amassed works from various eras and regions to demonstrate how the expression of black writers, despite their like-minded rejection of popular stereotypes and a common racial cause, represented no single literary form or "one unique cultural pattern." Their intent was to present a "truthful mosaic of negro characters" that would help represent the true black experience in America.

Among the work's many selections were Brown's poems "Long Gone," "Slim in Hell," "Ole Lem," "Break of Day," and "Strong Men." Brown also contributed to Swedish social economist Gunnar Myrdal's classic 1944 study of African Americans, *An American Dilemma.* Along with such scholars as Ralphe Bunche, Horace Cayton, Melville J. Herskovits, and Charles S. Johnson, Brown provided Myrdal with criticism and advice in the compilation of his more than one-thousand-page study of black American life.

Steadfast Dedication to Study of African-American Culture

While undertaking short-term teaching positions at the University of Minnesota in 1945, New York University from 1949 to 1950, and the University of Illinois from 1967 until 1968, Brown retained his position at Howard until his retirement in 1969. There he continued to expose students to African-American literature and music. Because Howard had forbidden the teaching of black American folk music, Brown held his own classes on blues and jazz music. Among his students at Howard were poet and writer Amiri Baraka, activist Stokely Carmicheal, and actor Ossie Davis. "His teaching had a very liberating effect on me," com-

mented Davis, as quoted in *Sterling Brown.* "He was a scholar, but Sterling was homey, Negro, grits and gravy."

In 1975 a small Detroit-based press, concerned that Brown's volume *Southern Road* had been out of print for several years, published *The Last Ride of Wild Bill,* which offered readers many of the poet's finest verse along with a new piece, "The Last Ride Of Wild Bill." A year later, a group of noted black writers and intellectuals from the Black History Museum Committee paid homage to Brown by publishing the compendium *Sterling Brown: A UMUM Tribute.* Among the book's contributors were several former students including Baraka and Leopold S. Senghor, president of the West African nation of Senegal. Brown greeted the republication of his work with glee, saying in 1979, according to the *Washington Post,* "I've been rediscovered, reinstituted, regenerated and recovered."

Brown's passion for the culture and music of his people is brilliantly captured in his writing. And it is through his poetry that he became most well known. His poetic subjects, like black folk heroes of the past, remain timeless symbols of a still universal struggle to preserve humanity. Describing the universality of Brown's poetry, James O. Young wrote in *Black Writers of the Thirties,* "Brown's genius is such that he sculpts simple, plain speech into poetry, as he unveils the value ensemble of a people. The reader will discover, almost in a flash, that he has entered a world as wonderously complex as life itself." In recognition of Brown's talent and influence as a poet, Washington, D.C., honored him as the city's poet laureate in 1984.

As poet, folklorist, and teacher, Brown's influence extended far and wide. His legacy lies in rebellion, the refusal to accept the stereotypical and romanticized image of blacks as put forth by both African-American and white writers. When black scholars and intellectuals dismissed blues and jazz as substandard folk art, Brown emerged as an outspoken champion of these unique forms. Reflecting on his experiences in the South, Brown explained in *The Harlem Renaissance,* "I learned the strength of my people. I learned the fortitude. I learned the humor. I learned the tragedy." After Brown's death of leukemia on January 13, 1989, his work remained as a champion of African-American culture.

Books

Dark Symphony: Negro Literature in America, edited by James A. Emanuel and Theodore L. Gross, Free Press, 1968.

Fullinwinder, S. P., *The Mind and Mood of Black America,* Dorsey Press, 1969.

The Harlem Renaissance: Revaluations, edited by William S. Shiver and Stanley Brodwin, with an introduction by Amritjit Singh, Garland, 1989.

Kramer, Victor A., *The Harlem Renaissance Re-examined,* AMS Press, 1987.

May, Henry, *The End of American Innocence: A Study of the First Years of Our Own Time,* Quadrangle Books, 1959.

Myrdal, Gunnar, with Richard Sterner and Arnold Rose, *An American Dilemma: The Negro Problem and Modern Democracy,* 1944.

Sterling Brown: A UMUM Tribute, edited by the Black History Museum Committee, 1976.

Wagner, Jean, *Black Poets of the United States: From Paul Lawrence Dunbar to Langston Hughes*, translated by Kenneth Douglas, University of Illinois Press, 1973.

Young, James O., *Black Writers of the Thirties*, Louisiana State University Press, 1973.

Periodicals

New York Times, January 17, 1989.
Washington Post, January 16, 1989. □

Ole Bull

Norwegian violinist and composer Ole Bull (1810-1880) was among the most celebrated musicians of the nineteenth century, a violin star who toured the world.

Bull was especially popular in the United States, which he visited multiple times. He lived for several long stretches in America, married an American woman, and attempted in the early 1850s to set up a Norwegian-American utopian community in the mountains of Pennsylvania. He was a larger-than-life figure of the kind American audiences have always admired. Yet Bull's fame was by no means limited to the United States. In Norway itself he was a key supporter of cultural and political nationalism, and he directly inspired two of Norway's greatest artists, playwright Henrik Ibsen and composer Edvard Grieg. Bull toured the rest of Europe as well. Opinions differed about his wild, unorthodox style of playing the violin, but in many countries he remained a household name for decades.

Tried to Use Yardstick as Bow

Ole Bornemann Bull was born in an apothecary shop, his family's business, on February 5, 1810, in Bergen, Norway. Several of his relatives were amateur musicians who came together to form a string quartet. When Bull's uncle Jens noticed that five-year-old Ole was imitating the violinists in the quartet by sawing on a small plank of wood with a yardstick, he gave his nephew his first violin. Bull's parents had hoped that he would learn Latin and go on to study Lutheran theology, but by the time he was eight he had filled in with the string quartet himself and had been made a student member of a local orchestra called the Harmonien.

Bull had no use for his Latin studies. One of his teachers, according to Bull biographer Einar Haugen, shouted in frustration: "Take hold of your fiddle, Ole. Don't waste your time here." A subsequent tutor fared even worse, as Bull and a group of classmates physically attacked him before being restrained by a maid wielding a set of fire tongs. Unsurprisingly, Bull failed the Latin exam that was given as part of his application to attend the University of Christiania (now the University of Oslo) in 1828. By that time, however, he was already a fearsomely talented violinist. When he was 14 he had persuaded a grandmother to buy him printed copies of the *Caprices of Niccolò Paganini*—works that the

great violinist had written for himself. Although despondent at the failure of his university application, Bull soon found work as a violinist with a local theater orchestra and was soon promoted to temporary conductor.

That was not the end of Bull's nonmusical education, however. He met and befriended the poet Henrik Wergeland, a writer and agitator for the cause of Norway as a distinct nation with its own literature and culture. After centuries of Danish control, Norway had been placed under the control of the Swedish crown as the map of Europe was redrawn in the wake of the Napoleonic Wars. Wergeland's ideas made a deep impact on Bull. After an initial foray to Copenhagen, Denmark, Bull headed for Paris in 1831 to launch his international career. With him he took a Hardanger fiddle, an unusual Norwegian folk instrument with features of both a violin and a hurdy-gurdy. Although never trained as a composer, he began to write music that evoked Norwegian folk airs. He filed down the bridge on his violin so that he could sound all four of its strings at the same time, producing an extremely unusual sound.

In 1832 Bull rented a room with a Madame Villeminot. Troubled with either poor health or hypochondria (or perhaps both) for much of his life, he took to his bed for a time and was nursed by his landlady's daughter, Félicie. In 1836 the two would marry and go on to raise five children. Bull heard his idol, Paganini, play a concert, and correctly concluded that an opening existed for a successor to the great Italian, but as of the early 1830s his talent was not yet equal to his ambitions. Bull gave his first concert in Paris in 1833.

Parisian critics treated the charismatic but undisciplined Bull as a kind of noble savage, but he began to gain admirers such as the critic Jules Janin and the great soprano Maria Malibran, whom he followed on tour in Italy in 1834. When she saw that one of her performances had moved him to tears, she stuck her tongue out at him. The violinist asked why, and Malibran replied, according an early Bull biography cited by Haugen, "It would have been fine if I too had burst into tears."

Toured Europe

By the end of 1835 Bull had become a major star in Paris, with the likes of painter Eugène Delacroix, author Eugène Scribe, and even king Louis-Philippe I attending his concerts. Positive reviews of his work flowed back to Norway and made him famous for the first time in his homeland. Bull extended his touring to England in 1836, impressing a recalcitrant orchestra with his rendition of a four-part arrangement of "God Save the King," in which he played all four parts simultaneously. In the year 1837 alone, Bull gave 274 concerts. He installed his family in Copenhagen and set off to conquer the rest of continental Europe. By 1838 he had reached Moscow, Russia, and the next several years saw successful Bull tours in Sweden and Eastern Europe. In 1840 he performed Beethoven's "Kreutzer" Sonata for violin and piano with Franz Liszt as his accompanist.

He also performed in the great German-speaking musical capitals of Berlin and Vienna (both in 1839), and only here was his success less than total. In those citadels of abstract music, where the symphonies of Beethoven and his successors were taken to be the pinnacle of musical art, Bull's showmanship was something of a liability, as showmanship had been a liability for Paganini a generation before. The opinions of critics mattered little to the general public, however, and Bull made several more tours of Germany and Austria during his lifetime.

In 1843, feted by a farewell poem from Wergeland, Bull set sail for the United States. He was not the first European artist to mount an American tour, but the scope of his activities in America (and also in Cuba and Quebec) exceeded anything that had been seen up to that point, and set the stage for the publicity extravaganza that later accompanied the arrival of Swedish opera star Jenny Lind. At the conclusion of one of his pieces, reported the New York *Herald* (according to Haugen), "the very musicians in the orchestra flung down their instruments and stamped and applauded like madmen." Bull's exploits as he traveled around the country gave rise to a variety of widely repeated stories, one of which held that he had been the victim of an attempted robbery on a Mississippi River paddleboat—but had thrown the robber overboard. He attracted the attention of writers such as Lydia Maria Child and Henry Wadsworth Longfellow, who based a character in one of his books (1863's *Tales of a Wayside Inn*) on Bull; Denmark's Hans Christian Andersen, France's George Sand, and other European writers would later do the same.

The requirements of touring had by this time caused Bull to try his hand at composition once again, and some of the pieces that became the most famous within his lifetime were written during his first stay in America. *Niagara* commemorated his visit to Niagara Falls, which he considered the most beautiful falls in the world, but *Solitude of the Prairies* was composed without benefit of an actual prairie visit. Later, while visiting a town in Minnesota, Bull decided that he should try to see a prairie and set out on horseback, but he quickly became lost and had to seek shelter in a nearby inn. Mostly his music was for violin and orchestra (including at least once full-scale violin concerto) or violin and piano, although he wrote several songs. Most of his compositions were forgotten (and many were destroyed) after his death, but there have been periodic attempts to revive them; violinist John Thomson told Chuck Haga of the Minneapolis *Star Tribune* that "his music deserves to be better known. It's beautiful—a combination of Norwegian folk style and the Italian style he learned from Paganini."

Fostered Norwegian Theater

At the end of 1845 Bull left New York and plunged into a fresh round of European touring that took him as far afield as Algiers in North Africa and the Balearic Islands of Spain. The revolutions of 1848 found him in Paris and inspired in him a fresh burst of Norwegian nationalism. He returned to Norway hoping to further the cause of Norwegian literature, and established a new Norwegian National Theater in Bergen, where he employed the young Henrik Ibsen as an administrator. Ibsen later modeled the title character in one of his greatest plays, *Peer Gynt,* on Bull, and Norway's greatest composer, Edvard Grieg, was also a Bull admirer and furnished Ibsen's play with a musical score. The poet Bjørnstjerne Bjørnson was also a Bull employee.

In 1852 Bull returned to New York to begin the second of an eventual five American tours. Soon, however, he was throwing his energy into a new project, a utopian community named New Norway. One of its four small communities was named Oleana. Bull purchased over 10,000 acres in a wooded area in northern Pennsylvania, inviting Norwegian immigrants to set up small farms as part of a larger cooperatively run organization. A few dozen Norwegian families took him up on his offer, but the venture was inadequately capitalized, and Bull was swindled by the original landowner—the only easily tillable farmland on the plot was excluded from the sale by an obscure provision in the deed. Within a few years the community had failed, and the Norwegians moved on to newer centers of settlement in the upper Midwest. A partially completed castle Bull had planned still stands today (although it suffered heavy fire damage in 1923) and is used as a forest ranger's residence at Pennsylvania's Ole Bull State Park.

For much of the rest of his life Bull divided his time between Norway and America, where, although newer virtuosi had come on the scene, he still commanded an enthusiastic following. Félicie died in 1862, and eight years later he married Sara Thorp of Madison, Wisconsin, whom he had met on an 1869 tour. The couple had one daughter. They separated for some time after a quarrel in the 1870s, and Bull purchased a Norwegian island, Lysøen, in 1872. He constructed an elaborate villa that displayed a hodgepodge of architectural features including an onion dome.

Bull and Sara reunited after she translated a Norwegian novel into English as a peace offering, and the couple lived in Boston for several years in the 1870s. Bull toured indefatigably, and he never lost his gift for public relations. In 1876 he climbed with his violin to the top of the Cheops Pyramid in Egypt and played a concert to the skies. Suffering from cancer, he played his one of his last concerts in Chicago in May of 1880. He died at his home on Lysøen on August 17, 1880, and was buried in Bergen.

Books

Baker's Biographical Dictionary of Music and Musicians, centennial ed., Nicolas Slonimsky, editor emeritus, Schirmer, 2001.

Haugen, Einar, and Camilla Cai, *Ole Bull: Norway's Romantic Musician and Cosmopolitan Patriot,* University of Wisconsin Press, 1993.

Periodicals

Star Tribune (Minneapolis, MN), October 16, 2000.

Online

"Ole Bull's New Norway," Pennsylvania Historical and Museum Commission, http://www.phmc.state.pa.us/ppet/olebull/page1.asp?secid=31 (January 14, 2008).

"Remembering Ole Bull's Dream," Norway: The Official Site in the United States, http://www.norway.org/News/archive/2002/200204bull.htm (January 14, 2008). □

William S. Burroughs

American inventor William Seward Burroughs (1855-1898) designed the world's first commercially viable adding machine, the Burroughs Registering Accountant, in 1892. Strong sales laid the foundation for the Burroughs Corporation, which was a Detroit manufacturing and computer powerhouse for much of the twentieth century.

Burroughs was born on January 28, 1855, in Auburn, New York, a town in Cayuga County. His parents were Edmund and Ellen Julia Burroughs, and he had an older brother and sister as well as a younger sibling. Edmund Burroughs was a model-maker for castings, which were used to create prototypes for new products. Burroughs left the Auburn public schools at the age of 15 to train as a bank clerk, and it was this professional beginning that inspired his later invention. Clerks had to spend long hours poring over ledger columns to find errors in addition or subtraction when the columns refused to balance, and finding these mistakes was a tedious chore which was done entirely by hand. Burroughs later went on to hold similar jobs in a retail establishment and later a lumber yard.

Moved to St. Louis

Around 1875, when he was about 20 years old, Burroughs moved to St. Louis, Missouri, and over the next decade he married, started a family, and worked for a manufacturer of woodworking tools and machinery. He began to think about his own ideas and how they might be realized, especially for an adding machine he called the arithmometer. In 1884 he found a financial backer in the form of Thomas B. Metcalf, whom he had met on visit to Metcalf's shop. By this point Burroughs's father had also relocated to the area, and the the younger Burroughs worked on the first prototypes for the adding machine in his father's model shop. By the end of 1885 he had had come up with a rudimentary device, and though it was not yet commercially ready, it did help him and Metcalf to find more backers, this time in the form of a pair of St. Louis merchants. Their new company, founded with start-up capital of $100,000, was called the American Arithmometer Company. It was incorporated in January of 1886 with Burroughs as vice president and Metcalf as president.

The funding helped Burroughs finish a new model, which he called the Burroughs Registering Accountant. It had a nine-key design, and to prevent human error the keys would lock up if two of them were pressed at once. Furthermore, the user could easily verify that the sum just entered was correct because each key would stay depressed until the user pulled the handle lever to record the transaction. It also had printing capabilities and glass panels that allowed the user to see the workings. Burroughs contracted with the Boyer Machine Company in St. Louis to serve as the manufacturer, and the initial order of 50 machines was finished late in 1887. The machines, however, proved problematic and consistently broke down, and at one point Burroughs threw several machines from the defective shipment out of his office window.

First Model Sold for $475

In 1892 Burroughs received patents for a machine that recorded each item in the tally and the final result. The first Burroughs Registering Accountant machines, in much-improved form, went on sale that same year for a price of $475 each. The exorbitant cost did not deter its sale to banks and other financial institutions, who were its first major customers once they saw that the device was both reliable and accurate. By 1895, 284 machines had been sold and the company opened a sales office in London. Unfortunately, Burroughs—whose health had been poor for much of his adult life—did not survive to see the impressive success his company would achieve. He died of tuberculosis on September 15, 1898, in Citronelle, Alabama, at the age of just 44. He and his wife, Ida Selover Burroughs, had four children: Jennie, Horace, Mortimer, and Helen. Mortimer's son was named in honor of his inventor grandfather, and went on to become a notable figure in American letters in the twentieth century as avant-garde novelist William S. Burroughs (1914-1997).

The company Burroughs founded would sell a stunning 1,500 adding machines in 1900. It soon moved its headquarters to Michigan, where it emerged as one of the mainstays of the local economy. The name was changed from the American Arithmometer Company to the Burroughs Adding Machine Company. Helmed by Joseph Boyer, who had owned the original company, it then contracted to manufacture the machines. The Burroughs Corporation, as it eventually became known, went on to develop impressive new technologies that paved the way for modern information science technology, including the first widely used mainframe computers. Its successes were often overshadowed by those of its nearest competitor, IBM, or International Business Machines, Inc. The company entered a new era in 1986 when it merged with the Sperry Corporation to become Unisys.

Online

"Introduction: William S. Burroughs," The Franklin Institute, http://www.fi.edu/learn/case-files/burroughs/ (April 15, 2008).

World of Computer Science, Online. Thomson Gale, 2006. http://galenet.galegroup.com/servlet/BioRC (April 15, 2008).
□

C

Minna Canth

Intrepid Finnish playwright and critic Minna Canth (1844-1897) is remembered as a forerunner of the Finnish realist writing movement as well as a symbol of Finland's modernist revolution.

Early Life

Minna Canth was born Ulrika Vilhelmina Johnson on March 19, 1844, in Tampere, Finland. Her working-class parents owned a shop in Kuopio, having moved there from Tampere when Canth was eight. Her father was Gustaf Wilhelm Johnson, and her mother was Ulrika Johnson. In an autobiographical sketch included in the book *Sanoi Minna Canth: Pioneer Reformer*, a 47-year-old Canth described her childhood relationship with her father: "From my infancy I was the apple of my father's eye; and I remember how he liked to brag a bit about my talents. . . . Though my father's circumstances at the time were humble, he nevertheless wanted to give me the best education a girl could hope for in our country."

Education

In keeping with her father's wishes, Canth first attended a Swedish language school for girls, and when the first Finnish teachers' college was established in 1863 at Jyväskylä, she enrolled in the same year but left before the completion of her studies, having met and married her natural science instructor, Johan Ferdinand Canth (nine years her senior), in 1865.

Life Learning

The Canths had seven children, and Canth recalled in *Sanoi Minna Canth*, "I now had to forget all my idealistic aspirations and instead do needlework, prepare meals and keep house and take care of my husband, all tasks that went against my grain. . . . For some time I denied myself all reading, except for newspapers, and I tried my best to dull my sense of loss." Canth had some opportunity to exercise her craft, writing the occasional article for a publication that was edited by her husband, but the majority of her time and energy went towards home and family. Canth's husband died unexpectedly of brain fever in 1877, while she was halfway through writing her first play and pregnant with their seventh child.

Writing for a Living

Undeterred by her misfortune, Canth struggled to support herself and her family. A shrewd businesswoman, she took over the Tampereen Lankakauppa, her father's draper's shop in Kuopio that sold Finlayson's fabrics. It had fallen on hard times since his passing a few years before, but she quickly revived the family business, all the while studying materials on the literature and social philosophies of the time. The business recovered so successfully that it allowed her the financial freedom to write more regularly. She published in minor journals and local newspapers like *Keski-Suomi* and *Päijänne*, addressing contentious issues like the temperance movement and women's rights. According to a biography of Canth on the Web site *Suomalaisen Kirjallisuuden Seura Biografiakeskus*, Canth "became the first Finnish-speaking female journalist to work independently as an editor. . . . [Her] journalistic writing [was] characterized by lively rhetoric: exclamations, questions, direct appeals to the reader; alert humour and sharp-witted irony, but also pathos and aggressiveness." The author might have continued her journalistic career, but was bitten severely by the drama bug after attending her first play.

From Businesswoman to Playwright

Canth began writing drama at the age of 40, after rigorous study that she conducted on her own. The folk play *Murtovarkens* (The Burglary, 1882) was her first foray into writing for the stage, and it was with this play that Canth began a decade of collaboration with Finnish Theatre founder Kaarlo Bergbom (1843-1906). She began to produce what *The Bloomsbury Guide to Women's Literature* described as "naturalist propaganda literature . . . [like] the drama *Työmiken vaimo* (The Workman's Wife, 1885)." Canth recalled the play in an autobiographical essay contained in *Sanoi Minna Canth,* saying that it "is filled with the sharpest satire from start to finish, but it has no deeper psychology or artistic ripeness either. Even so, it made a tremendous impact when, in 1885, it was performed for the first time at the Finnish Theater. . . . Criticism and abuse rained on me like hail. I was not spared. I was branded an atheist and a free-thinker; parents forbade their children to visit my house; I lost a large number of my friends, and it required a certain amount of moral courage from the rest who still dared to acknowledge me."

While Canth was critically and personally attacked on a regular basis for voicing her opinions, people were listening. As the book *Women in World History: A Biographical Encyclopedia* explained, Canth's "combination of powerfully depicted characters and a strong sense of social indignation appealed to a generation of Finns ready to change society and help create a new world based on justice and freedom." In 1872 a professional Finnish-language theater was established in Helsinki, deconstructing the nation's cultural stereotype as a society of "ignorant peasants and fishermen," and Canth stepped forward in the 1880s as a principal member of the Young Finns, an organization devoted to cultural awareness and social reform.

Success and Censure

Critics tended to condemn her work based on the external content, without acknowledging what the playwright was saying. The Web site *Suomalaisen Kirjallisuuden Seura Biografiakeskus* explained, "In the eyes of Finland's cultural elite, Canth was to be rejected and opposed not only because of the ideas that she championed . . . but perhaps even more so because of the ideas that she did *not* appear to champion. Nationality was the ideology of the era . . . and the further Canth went as a writer in the direction of psychological portrayal, the more clearly her art [showed] the ugly reality that [clipped] the wings of a national illusion."

A versatile writer, Canth also authored novellas, short stories and poetry. The 1888 play *Kovan onnen lapsia* (usually translated as Children of Misfortune or The Hard Luck Kids) was described in *Sanoi Minna Canth* as "a heart-rending description of the distress and misery of the proletariat, which ends up in desperation, crime and imprisonment." It was quickly banned by conservative and religious authorities. The play was staged only once, in the autumn of 1888, the year that it also appeared in print. Her 1889 short story

titled *Kauppa-Lopo* (Lopo the Peddler) was critically successful, but both productions were described in *Women in World History* as "shocking in their depiction of brutal exploitation and human degradation." However, both "were recognized as significant works of art . . . [that allowed] the Finnish stage [to] claim equality with that of Sweden."

Canth's early influences included Norwegian playwrights Henrik Ibsen (1828-1906) and Björnstjerne Björnson (1832-1910), as well as French naturalist Émile Zola (1840-1902), and in the 1890s she began to incorporate psychological and religious themes in her work after reading Russian author Leo Tolstoy (1828-1910). Canth's home became a haven for the young writers of her day. She even hired Heikki Kauppinen—later known as Kauppis-Heikki (1862-1920)—as an assistant in the shop and was able to guide his writing career.

Canth composed *Papin perhe* (The Vicar's Family) in 1891, *Sylvi* in 1893 and *Anna Liisa* (Anna-Liisa) in 1895. *Women in World History* stated that these plays mark the period where she became "the voice of the long-oppressed Finnish people, particularly its women, who had for centuries suffered not only from foreign oppression but also from the injustices at the hands of a patriarchal regime." Canth used her depictions and discussions of the family unit as a mirror held to bigger social issues. As Dennis and Elsa Carroll explained in an essay on Finnish Theatre in *The Drama Review,* the Finns as a people had a tendency to "nurture isolation and self-sufficiency" that leads to difficulty expressing feelings—a conflict that is well addressed through the rituals and ceremonies inherent in stage drama.

Canth's health started to spiral downwards in the 1890s, and she died on May 12, 1897, in Kuopio. Attempts to apply avant-garde translations to Canth's work have been met with interest as well as concern. According to *The Drama Review,* celebrated Finnish director Jouko Turkka's (born 1942) 1981 production of Canth's *Murtovarkaus* (The Burglary) "threw out all Canth's dialogue except seven sentences, and transformed the events, gestures and props of Finnish rural life into timeless and indelible icons."

Beloved

Canth was commemorated in 1944 on the centenary of her birth with a postage stamp bearing her portrait. There are statues of her in Kuopio, Tampere, and Jyväskylä, and productions of some of her more popular plays even appear in current internet movie databases. The Old Kuopio Museum has showcased historical interiors that include the room where Canth used to write, and tourist tours often begin in her room in the museum and end at a statue of her that stands in a nearby park, also named after her. Kuopio hosts a festival to celebrate Canth's "Name Day." In 2007 the festival included a morning picnic in the park, where trees were planted in her honor and the Kuopio University's Student Theater presented "What Would Minna Say Today?." The Kuopio Museum presented a drama titled "Mrs. C at the Old Kuopio Museum," after which the students of Minna Canth High School put on a play depicting local life at the end of the 1800s. Adult and child dance troupes performed folk dances included in Canth's stage works.

Despite her obvious and lingering popularity, Ritva Heikkil, editor of *Sanoi Minna Canth,* wrote, ''Incredibly, it is hard to find copies of her works anywhere. They have long been out of print. And published translations from the original Finnish into other languages are almost non-existent.'' According to *Sanoi Minna Canth,* Canth once acknowledged, ''To tell the truth, I am not satisfied with a single thing I have written so far, but I hope in the future to turn out better works, for I still have thirteen years left before I reach the age of sixty, the age, that is, at which every writer, I understand, ought to be clubbed.''

Canth's sharp, incisive and often fearlessly critical portraits of the lives and loves of her culture have become an integral part of Finnish and feminist literary history. According to *Sanoi Minna Canth,* the author had the last word, in a letter written to fellow Finnish writer Teuvo Pakkala in March of 1892, where she stated, ''That exactly is the important function of literature: to teach us to know and love one another.''

Books

Benét's Reader's Encyclopedia: Fourth Edition, edited by Bruce Murphy, Harper Collins Publishers, Inc., 1996.
Bloomsbury Guide to Women's Literature, edited by Claire Buck, Bloomsbury Publishing Ltd., 1992.
Cambridge Biographical Encyclopedia: Second Edition, edited by David Crystal, Cambridge University Press, 1998.
Cassell's Encyclopaedia of World Literature: Volume Two, edited by J. Buchanan, Brown, Cassell and Company Ltd., 1973.
Chambers Biographical Dictionary, edited by Melanie Parry, Chambers Harrap Publishers Ltd., 1997.
Penguin Companion to European Literature, edited by Anthony Thorlby, Penguin Books Ltd., 1969.
Sanoi Minna Canth: Pioneer Reformer, edited by Ritva Heikkilä, Werner Söderström Osakeyhtiö, 1987.
Women in World History: A Biographical Encyclopedia, edited by Anne Commire, Yorkin Publications, 1999.
Women's Firsts, edited by Caroline Zilboorg, Gale Research, 1997.

Periodicals

The Drama Review, Vol. 26, No. 3, Autumn 1982.
Educational Theatre Journal, Vol. 30, No. 3, October 1978.

Online

''Canth, Minna (1844–1897),'' *Suomalaisen Kirjallisuuden Seura Biografiakeskus,* http://www.kansallisbiografia.fi/english/?id = 2816 (December 8, 2007).
''Minna Canth,'' *Britannica Online Encyclopedia,* http://www.britannica.com/eb/article-9020060/Minna-Canth (November 27, 2007).
''Minna Canth (1844–1897),'' Famous Women on Stamps, http://home.online.no/~jdigrane/amd/finwomen/canth.htm (November 13, 2007).
''Minna Canth,'' Internet Movie Database, http://www.imdb.com/name/nm0134562/bio (December 8, 2007).
''Minna Canth,'' The Minna Project, http://www.minnaproject.net/java/Index?oid = 58 (December 13, 2007).
''Minna Canth (1844–1897),'' *Books and Writers,* http://www.kirjasto.sci.fi/mcanth.htm (November 27, 2007).
''Minna Canth Event,'' *Kuopion Setlementti Puijola ry,* http://www.puijola.net/monikulttuurikeskus_kompassi/multicultural_center_kompassi/minna_canth_event (November 13, 2007).

''Welcome to the Kuopio Region,'' Kuopio Info, http://www.kuopioinfo.fi/english/perussivut/vierailukohteet/museot.php?we_objectID = 1041 (December 8, 2007). □

Casimir III, King of Poland

King Casimir III of Poland (1310-1370) made major contributions to the growth of the Polish state as it is known today. Poland's growth under his peaceful reign was memorialized in a popular saying to the effect that he inherited a Poland built of wood, but left the world a Poland built of stone.

An oblong strip of land wedged among competing kingdoms when Casimir was crowned in 1333, Poland more than doubled in size during his reign. Casimir oversaw the founding and building of Poland's greatest university, and he put in place an administrative infrastructure that resulted in the growth of many Polish cities and towns. He brought about this era of growth not by the method of military conquest favored among medieval rulers but by skillful diplomatic maneuvers that transformed Poland from a small kingdom encroached upon by larger neighbors into a major European power in its own right. Casimir was also noted for his fair treatment of Poland's Jewish minority, and the preponderance of Polish ancestry among Jews with a European background today is attributable in part to his influence.

Early Years

Casimir (or Kazimierz) was born on April 30, 1310, in the town of Kowal, in Kujawy-Pomerania province in the central part of present-day Poland. He was the son of King Wladyslav I Lokietek, or Wladyslaw the Elbow-High. Despite his diminutive stature, Wladyslaw (or Ladislaus) had involved the Polish kingdom in a host of military adventures. One in particular, carried out around the time of Casimir's birth, ended disastrously. In order to repel an invasion by forces loyal to a pair of German noblemen, Wladyslaw called on aid promised by a group called the Teutonic Knights, a Roman Catholic order with a powerful army. After helping Wladyslaw to lift the German siege of the castle at Gdansk, the Knights proceeded to seize it for themselves. By the time of Casimir's coronation, although Wladyslaw embroiled them in a long war that seesawed for several years, they controlled a large portion of northern Poland.

What remained to Casimir was a narrow diagonal strip running southeastward along the Vistula River from the Poznan region in the northwest. Access to the Baltic Sea was controlled exclusively by the Teutonic Knights, and Poland was pressed by the Lithuanian kingdom and by Central Asian tribes on the east, by Hungarians and Bohemians to the south, and by German states on the west. The country, populated by about 800,000 people, included less than half of the area that was culturally Polish; what remained was unified but severely weakened, and military action as a way

of recovering lost territory seemed to be out of the question. And the new king was an unlikely candidate for leadership: he had been sent away to the court of Hungary's king Charles Robert, where he had a reputation as a playboy. In a battle against the Teutonic Knights at the northern Polish town of Plowce, Casimir fled the battlefield.

Nevertheless, Casimir confidently set out on a new course as he attempted to solve Poland's problems. In place of military campaigns he used statecraft. To quote the 1911 *Encyclopedia Britannica,* Casimir "belongs to that remarkable group of late medieval sovereigns who may be called the fathers of modern diplomacy, inasmuch as they relegated warfare to its proper place as the instrument of politics, and preferred the councilchamber to the battle-field." His first move was to placate the Teutonic Knights with a truce in 1333; the Treaty of Kalisz in 1343 restored some of Poland's northwestern territories, although not its Baltic seacoast. The Teutonic Knights remained entrenched in northern Poland until finally dislodged by a Polish-Lithuanian army in the early fifteenth century.

Charles Robert and his nephew Louis the Great were just two of the monarchs of surrounding states who harbored the ambition of taking over Poland themselves. Another was John of Bohemia. Casimir faced his first major diplomatic test in 1335 when all these rulers met at the Hungarian castle of Vyshegrad on the Danube River. Skillfully negotiating the murky intrigues inherent in the summit, Casimir bought off John, agreeing to pay him 400,000 groats (a groat was a silver coin) if he would relinquish his long-

standing claim on Poland. In turn, he conceded Bohemian sovereignty over Silesia, a region split mostly between present-day Poland and the Czech Republic. Resolution of Poland's tensions with Bohemia was formalized in the Treaty of Krakow in 1339, and Casimir was free to direct his own attention, and that of his uneasy ally Louis the Great, to the small principalities on Poland's eastern flank.

Launched War to Reclaim Eastern Region

In the late 1330s, Casimir declared war on the small states of Halych and Vladimir (now in western Ukraine), part of the Masovia (Polish: Mazowsze) region. The ruler of these states, Boleslaw-Iurii, who had no children, named Casimir as his heir, but he was then poisoned to death by a group of other noblemen from within his realm. The result was the single major military conflict of Casimir's long reign, undertaken in order to secure valuable trade routes and to provide a buffer against attacks from Tatars, Mongols, and the so-called Kievan Rus, the tribe that gave Russia its name.

Over a period of about two decades, Casimir made substantial progress, which he owed as much to diplomatic initiatives as to military command skills. To Poland's northeast he came into conflict with a group of Lithuanian kingdoms, wisely settling for vague acknowledgements of Polish suzerainty (overlordship) instead of attempting a full-scale conquest. With the tacit approval of Louis the Great, he conquered the Masovia region, including Halycz and the area around what is now Lviv, Ukraine, and Poland took on more of its characteristic square shape. Casimir constantly had to fend off a variety of other external pressures, including demands from the Pope that he renew the war against the Teutonic Knights, regarded by the Holy See as an unacceptable rival. He was aided by a stroke of luck in the late 1340s: the bubonic plague epidemic known as the Black Death, which according to some estimates killed more than half of Europe's population, left Poland mostly unaffected even as its neighbors suffered serious outbreaks.

Casimir's greatest accomplishments, perhaps, lay in the domestic sphere. "Almost every aspect of Polish life," wrote historian Norman Davies in *God's Playground: A History of Poland,* "was brought before the King's reforming and regulating gaze." Casimir put in place a modern government bureaucracy, replacing the administration by local fiefdom that had prevailed up to that time, and in 1347 he codified the laws of the kingdom, publishing them in two massive volumes. These so-called "Statutes" of Casimir the Great provided the basic framework of Polish law for centuries to come. Casimir embarked on a significant construction program that included 50 military fortresses and spun off into growth enjoyed by various Polish communities. The growth attracted immigration, most significantly from Jews who were suffering especially virulent persecution in German-speaking lands at the time.

That Jewish immigration was in many ways the beginning of a great center of European Jewish culture that lasted until its destruction by German Fascism during World War II. Casimir vowed to protect Jews as "people of the king," prohibited the common practice of kidnapping Jewish children in order to baptize them as Christians, and tried to mitigate the anti-Semitic thrust and frequent mob actions of the Catholic Inquisition in Poland. He put in place a measure limiting the interest rate charged by Jewish moneylenders to 8 1/3 percent, but even this had the effect of securing the place of the Jewish community within the country's legal framework. In the words of the online Jewish Encyclopedia, "This measure must not be ascribed to his animosity against the Jews, but should rather be considered as a wise act tending to the welfare of the country as well as of the Jews." The result of Casimir's protections was that, as of the early twenty-first century, about 70 percent of the world's Jews of European background, known as Ashkhenazi, could trace their ancestries to Poland.

Constructed University

Perhaps the most visible remnant of Casimir's realm today is the University of Krakow, for which the king issued a Charter of Royal Foundation on May 12, 1364. The charter specified the provision of 11 chairs or professorships: one in liberal arts, two in medicine, three in canon (church) law, and five in Roman law. Their income was guaranteed by an annual appropriation drawn from the profits realized by the royal salt monopoly. Although Casimir had had to petition the Pope for permission to establish the university, he placed the institution under secular administration, vesting control in the hands of a royal chancellor rather than that of the Bishop of Krakow. Several major Polish churches date from Casimir's reign, and the cathedral in Lviv was also begun at his direction.

Despite his successes, Casimir's domestic life was rarely a happy one. He failed to produce a legitimate male heir, effectively putting an end to the Piast dynasty of which he was a part. It was not for lack of trying: Casimir married three times, once bigamously, and embarked on several ill-concealed extramarital affairs. He had three sons, but all were illegitimate. All of Casimir's marriages were undertaken for political reasons, to cement alliances with friendly states, and the situations of the women involved were, as was typical at the time, not pleasant. After marrying his second wife, Adelheid of Hesse, Casimir essentially shut her away and began living with his mistress, Christina. When Casimir and Christina married, Adelheid charged him with bigamy, returned to Hesse, and pleaded her cause with Pope Innocent VI, all to no avail.

Casimir's reign was unusually long among those of monarchs in the violent medieval world. By the late 1360s he had lost none of his touch, concluding a new alliance with Louis of Hungary in the Hungarian capital of Buda (now half of the city of Budapest) in 1369. On November 5, 1370, however, he died from the aftereffects of a hunting accident. His funeral was a magnificent one, and as the monarchy passed into the hands of Louis (who had married Casimir's sister), Poles feared for the future. "And no wonder!" noted a Polish chronicler cited by Davies. "The death of the peace-loving king had caused them to fear that the peace to which they had all grown accustomed during his lifetime would now end." Casimir III remains the only Polish monarch known by the descriptor "the Great."

Books

Biskupski, M.B., *The History of Poland,* Greenwood, 2000.
Davies, Norman, *God's Playground: A History of Poland,* rev. ed., Columbia University Press, 2005.
Encyclopedia Britannica, 11th ed., Cambridge University Press, 1911.
Lukowski, Jerzy, and Hubert Zawadzki, *A Concise History of Poland,* Cambridge University Press, 2001.

Periodicals

New York Times, July 12, 2007.

Online

"Kazimierz III," Foundation for Medieval Genealogy: Poland, http://fmg.ac/Projects/MedLands/POLAND.htm#Kazimierz IIIdied1370 (February 3, 2008).
Rosenthal,Herman, "Casimir III: the Great," Jewish Encyclopedia .com, http://www.jewishencyclopedia.com/view.jsp?artid= 221&letter=C (February 3, 2008). □

Carlos Castaneda

The Latin American writer Carlos Castaneda (c. 1925-1998) gained international fame for a series of 11 books, beginning with 1968's *The Teachings of Don Juan: A Yaqui Way of Knowledge,* that recounted what he said were lessons in spirituality and perception imparted to him by a shaman of the Yaqui Native American tribe in the northern Mexican desert.

With the usage of peyote and other hallucinogenic drugs playing a major role in his teachings, Castaneda's writings arrived in tandem with the full flowering of the 1960s counterculture. His influence has proved more durable than that exerted by other writers of the 1960s, however. All his books have remained in print for decades and continue to sell well into the twenty-first century. Castaneda was an elusive figure who refused to be photographed, gave sparse accounts of his own life, and indeed argued that linear biographical details were unimportant to or even distorted his message. The veracity of the central accounts in his books has been widely challenged in recent years, but Castaneda's very elusiveness has made it difficult to fully discredit or confirm his writings.

Of Uncertain Nationality

The uncertainty over Castaneda's background begins with his place and date of birth. Among the few pieces of solid documentation of Castaneda's identity is a set of papers pertaining to his entry into the United States in 1951; they assign his birth to Cajamarca, Peru, on December 25, 1925. Castaneda himself, however, maintained that he was Brazilian, born in São Paulo on December 25, 1931, and other accounts date his birth as late as 1935. He said that he had been placed in a boarding school in Buenos Aires,

Argentina, where he would have learned to speak Spanish. Castaneda's defenders point to the publication of a 1975 interview in a Brazilian magazine in which he appeared to speak Portuguese fluently, among other details; his detractors cite records showing that he apparently attended several educational institutions in Peru, including the National School of Fine Arts in Lima. His father, a metalsmith of Basque descent, was (again according to immigration records) named César Arana Burungaray, but Carlos later began to use his mother's surname, Castaneda. The name, if indeed Spanish, would be spelled Castañeda, and it is sometimes given that way in Spanish books. In the United States, however, the author used only Castaneda.

Castaneda's decision to come to the United States may have been precipitated by the deterioration of a marriage or relationship in Peru, in the course of which he had fathered a daughter. He apparently lived in San Francisco for a time and then moved in with a family in Los Angeles. Beginning in 1955 he took courses at Los Angeles Community College, and he received an associate's degree from that institution in 1959, also studying creative writing. That year he married telephone company employee Margaret Runyon, a distant relative of the writer Damon Runyon, in a ceremony in Tijuana, Mexico; she recounted that he started working on a book called *Dial Operator* but did not finish it. The couple soon separated, but remained involved with one another and were divorced only in 1973.

In the fall of 1959, Castaneda enrolled at the University of California at Los Angeles (UCLA), studying anthropology.

He got an A for a paper he submitted in a California ethnography class, based on an interview he did with a local (but unnamed) Native American on the uses of the drug jimson weed (*datura stramonium*) in religious ceremonies. Castaneda was short on funds, and his education was interrupted several times by stints driving a taxi, working in a liquor store, and trips to the desert on both sides of the border to collect medicinal plants. However, he managed to graduate from UCLA in 1962 with a bachelor's degree in anthropology.

By that time, according to his own accounts in *The Teachings of Don Juan,* Castaneda had already encountered the figure who would change his life. His accounts place his first meeting with Don Juan Matus, an aging member of the Yaqui tribe, at a bus station in Nogales, Arizona, in the summer of 1960. Intrigued by the man's quizzical way of speaking, Castaneda visited him again, and after he had made several visits to Don Juan's home in the Mexican desert, the Native American, who spoke Spanish well, revealed that he was a *diablero,* or sorcerer. Castaneda dated the beginning of his apprenticeship to the year 1961. To Castaneda's teachers at UCLA, he seemed like solid gold—a student who had sought out a Native American informant with amazing forms of knowledge hitherto unknown outside his own community. Castaneda enrolled in the anthropology graduate program in 1962, receiving his master's degree two years later.

Described Drug Usage

Castaneda's first three books, *The Teachings of Don Juan, A Separate Reality: Further Conversations with Don Juan* (1971), and *Journey to Ixtlan: The Lessons of Don Juan* (1972), described the teachings he received from Don Juan and from another sorcerer (or *brujos*) to whom his teacher introduced him. *The Teachings of Don Juan* was initially published by the University of California Press; racking up superb sales for an academic title, it was acquired by the mainstream publisher Simon & Schuster, which issued the other two books, as well as almost all of Castaneda's later books. *Journey to Ixtlan* was accepted, with minor modifications, as Castaneda's Ph.D. thesis, and he was granted that degree in 1973.

Don Juan's sessions with Castaneda often began with drugs: peyote, jimson weed, and hallucinogenic mushrooms. With the help of those, the shaman led his student toward the apprehension of an alternate reality, only with difficulty described in words. Castaneda was, he said, identified by Don Juan as a nagual (pronounced na-WHAL), a spiritual leader; the word also meant a kind of spirit that existed in a realm beyond that of ordinary reality. Castaneda described how he communed and conversed with wild animals and entered into their existences, at one point being transformed by Don Juan into a crow and gaining the power of flight. Part of the appeal of Castaneda's books lay in the way he presented himself: he did not pretend to be a saint possessed of special enlightenment but rather depicted himself as something of a bumbler who had to be helped to enlightenment step by step. His descriptions of the Mexican desert environment were also natural and evocative, although some readers wondered how he could so consistently escape the risks of heat exposure and insect bites.

Castaneda said that his books were assembled from field notes, but he never actually produced the notes and later said that they had been lost. One big question mark that surrounded his books from the beginning was that no one else had seen Don Juan. Castaneda's admittedly detailed descriptions constituted the only evidence of his existence. Yaqui chieftains from the area were unable to remember any individual closely matching Don Juan's characteristics, and although other Mexican tribes, such as the Huichol ethnic group, used hallucinogenic drugs in some of the ways Castaneda described, the Yaquis themselves generally did not, and Yaqui individuals questioned by the *Arizona Daily Star* were unable to reconcile what they read in Castaneda's books with the traditional belief system they had learned. Another issue revolved around the fact that basic anthropological procedure would have involved learning the names of the plants Don Juan was giving to Castaneda, in Spanish or even in the Yaqui language, but Castaneda's books contained little such local detail.

Reviewers Reached Contrasting Conclusions

By the early 1970s Castaneda had received widespread praise from mainstream scholars, some of whom believed that he had expanded the frontiers of anthropology. According to *Contemporary Authors,* Paul Riesman, writing in the *New York Times Book Review,* asserted that "Castaneda makes it clear that the teachings of Don Juan do tell us something of how the world really is." Around that time, however, a contrary strain began to emerge in writing about Castaneda, with novelist Joyce Carol Oates leading the charge in a *New York Times* letter to the editor. She claimed that Castaneda's writings bore the mark of pure fiction. Among Castaneda's fiercest critics was Richard de Mille (the son of film director Cecil B. de Mille), who located passages in books by Mircea Eliade and other writers on the subject of transcendent experience that sounded similar to passages in Castaneda's writings. Castaneda's supporters rejoined that the language of mystical experience had shown similarities across the centuries as new writers rediscovered it. Many of de Mille's arguments were presented in his book *Castaneda's Journey: The Power and the Allegory.*

It was around the time that journalists began to look into his background that Castaneda withdrew from the public view. For about a decade after the Brazilian interview (published in a magazine called *Revista Veja*) he gave no interviews at all. He continued to write, however, extending the ideas of his previous books but focusing less on the figure of Don Juan. Instead, in books such as *Tales of Power* (1974), *The Second Ring of Power* (1977), and *The Fire from Within* (1984), Castaneda interwove personal observations with more general philosophical themes. Although he said in the 1970s that he was finished writing about Don Juan, he returned to the shaman for a another full-length book, *The Power of Silence: Further Lessons of Don Juan.*

In the early 1990s Castaneda resurfaced with a new book, *The Art of Dreaming* (1994), and a new system of body movements called Tensegrity that adapted elements of martial arts and tai chi to create what Castaneda promised would be the optimal conditions for the realizations of Don Juan's insights. The term "tensegrity" was borrowed from the writings of R. Buckminster Fuller, although as with "nagual" (and its companion, "tonal"), Castaneda attached his own meaning to the word. Charging fees ranging from $200 to $1,000, Castaneda often turned over Tensegrity seminars to his followers, who by the 1990s included a group of young women with whom he was alleged to have carried on sexual affairs. The Don Juan books were translated into 17 languages and amassed sales in excess of ten million copies, and Castaneda became a wealthy man with an estate valued at an estimated $20 million.

Suffering from liver cancer, Castaneda wrote a final book, *The Active Side of Infinity,* in which he seemed to foresee his own demise. His death was as mysterious as his life; he died on April 27, 1998, in the Westwood neighborhood of Los Angeles, but his passing was not announced until the following summer. His death certificate listed him as a teacher in the Beverly Hills, California, school district, which could produce no evidence that he had ever worked there. By the early 2000s, a preponderance of scholarly opinion held that the Don Juan books comprised an elaborate hoax. William W. Kelly, the chairman of the Yale University anthropology department, told the online magazine Salon that "I doubt you'll find an anthropologist of my generation who regards Castaneda as anything but a clever con man." His publishers and his many admirers, however, continued to assert the veracity of his remarkable experiences. Castaneda was, in the words of *Psychology Today,* "the 20th century's own sorcerer's apprentice. He is the invisible man, ephemeral, evanescent: now you see him, now you don't."

Books

De Mille, Richard, *Castaneda's Journey: The Power and the Allegory,* Capra, 1976.

De Mille, Richard, *The Don Juan Papers: Further Castaneda Controversies,* Wadsworth, 1990.

Sanchez, Victor, and Robert Nelson, The Teachings of Don Carlos: Practical Applications of the Works of Carlos Castaneda, Bear & Co., 1995.

Periodicals

Arizona Daily Star, June 20, 1998.

Guardian (London, England), June 23, 1998.

Independent (London, England), July 17, 1998.

International Herald Tribune, June 16, 2004.

Los Angeles Magazine, May 1996.

Psychology Today, March-April 1996.

San Francisco Chronicle, August 24, 2003.

Seattle Times, June 19, 1998.

Skeptical Inquirer, September-October 1999.

Online

"Carlos (Cesar Arana) Castaneda (1925-1998)," Books and Writers, http://www.kirjasto.sci.fi/castane.htm (January 19, 2008).

Contemporary Authors Online, Gale, 2008. http://galenet.gale group.com/servlet/BioRC (January 19, 2008).

"The Dark Legacy of Carlos Castaneda," *Salon,* http://www.salon.com/books/feature/2007/04/12/castaneda (January 19, 2008). □

Susanna Centlivre

Successful English playwright Susanna Centlivre (c. 1666-1723) crafted major comedies which became stock pieces of the British theater throughout the 18th century.

A Childhood Contested

Susanna Centlivre was born sometime between the years 1666 and 1680, of that sources seem sure. A review of biographical material for Centlivre produces no less than six possible years of birth and two likely countries—Ireland or England—so that her early life has settled firmly in the realm of legend rather than of record. Centlivre might have been born in Holbeach, Lincolnshire because she visited there frequently later in life. Then again, she might have been born in Whaplode, England . . . or perhaps in County Tyrone because her father owned a large parcel of land there. Centlivre's parentage is also a matter of mystery and myth. She may have been the daughter of commoners William (Edward) and Anne (Marham) Freeman, or her father may have been a Parliamentarian. Either both of Centlivre's parents died during her childhood, or her mother passed away early and her father remarried a woman who became a "wicked stepmother" of sorts and drove Centlivre to run away at age fourteen with a traveling acting troupe. Some claim Centlivre was a prodigy who wrote a song before she was seven and mastered French before she was twelve, while others marvel because she supposedly married at fourteen and was widowed at sixteen.

Many scholars believe that Centlivre ran away to Liverpool in 1682 at age fifteen, then attempted to travel to London by foot (with the assumption that she was born in England and not Ireland). The tale continues with Centlivre meeting Anthony Hammond (sometimes referred to by the name "Arthur"), who took her to Cambridge with him where Centlivre dressed as a young man and posed as Hammond's valet—known to his friends as "Cousin Jack." The young and adventurous Centlivre is believed to have had fun at Cambridge learning to fence as well as studying ethics, logic, rhetoric and grammar before choosing to continue on to London—or before being sent to London along with a sum of money provided by Hammond to help her get settled.

Accounts of Centlivre's later relationships are far from definitive. Most say Centlivre and a nephew of Sir Stephen Fox were married for all intents and purposes in 1683 or 1684 in London, with the ill-fated union being abruptly severed when the groom was killed in a duel mere months later. Centlivre is then said to have married an officer with the last name of Carroll in 1685 (rumored to go by the alias Rawkins), and he too fell in a duel within the year. Neither of these marriages are on record anywhere, but *Women in World History*'s Anita DuPratt suggested that while the "adventures associated with the young Susanna cannot be proved categorically; what can be assumed . . . is that she was self-educated, read at least one foreign language (French), and

that she developed a very independent spirit." Centlivre's professional future, although essentially well-documented, is also not without patches. Centlivre may have co-authored a publication called the *Female Tatler* from 1709–1710, and might have written anti-catholic essays in 1720—as well as penning a lost autobiography in 1761.

Centlivre Center-Stage

Early in her career, Centlivre took work as an amateur actress and often performed in roles that she had written herself. She commanded the heroine's role in her first play—published under the name Susanna Carroll—titled *The Perjur'd Husband; or The Adventures of Venice* (1700). The production premiered in Drury Lane's Theatre Royal that year, but quickly emerged as a failed tragicomedy. One problem was that many audience members were offended by the fact that some of the characters used coarse language, but Centlivre—as her entry in *Women in World History* recounts—maintained the integrity of her writing in a later preface to the play, "insisting that the characters were merely reflecting the manners and morals of London and that, until those were reformed, the stage would continue to follow suit. It is not 'reasonable,' she wrote, 'to expect a Person whose inclinations are always forming Projects to the Dishonour of her Husband, should deliver her Commands to her Confident in the Words of a Psalm.'" Centlivre also produced two volumes of fictional letters titled *Familiar and Courtly Letters of Monsieur Voiture* (1700) and *Volume II of Voiture's Letters* (1701)—both of which were critically, popularly and financially successful because epistolary novels were a popular and lucrative genre of the time.

Working Writer

Centlivre followed the disappointing reception of her first play by generating a solid body of new work. She wrote *The Beau's Duel: or, A Soldier for the Ladies* and *The Heiress: or, The Salamanca Doctor Out Plotted* in 1702 and *Love's Contrivance* a year later in 1703. Centlivre's ability to support herself financially with a writing career was genuinely remarkable. DuPratt explained, "there were three avenues for financial reward: theatrical benefits, the sale of copyright, and patronage," which meant that a successful playwright must manage to please a wide variety of people—from the average audience member to publishers of the day. Centlivre lived and worked in what was depicted by DuPratt as "a period of political and artistic transition . . . [from] the bawdy years of the Restoration, . . . [which] encouraged extravagant behavior and artistic license . . . [to] a greater sense of decorum. The new middle-class audience preferred farce, comedy of manners and intrigue. The 'celebrated Mrs. Centlivre' gained her reputation as a playwright of worth in this climate of change."

Necessary Anonymity

Centlivre wrote seventeen comedies and several tragedies in her lifetime, but published many works anonymously because she recognized a significant prejudice against women who tried to write for the stage. While her first play was published under the name Susanna Carroll, the two that followed were anonymous and by her fourth she was using the masculine initials *R.M.* as a pseudonym. Centlivre worked hard to refine her craft. She used English, French, and Spanish literature as inspiration and sources for her work and shrewdly analyzed all the responses to each of her plays—honing her writing and authorial judgment until she felt assured that she was succeeding in giving a broader audience what they wanted.

Centlivre released *Love's Contrivances* in 1703, but it was the 1705 *The Gamester* that made the playwright famous and fortified her credibility, as well as holding a place in London theater repertoires for close to half a century. DuPratt explained that *The Gamester* "was particularly popular with audiences because of its local color and Centlivre's command of the gambling lingo of the day." Gambling was a social and cultural obsession in the eighteenth–century, and Centlivre worked the theme into other plays, but never again as successfully. *The Basset–Table* (1705) featured a female protagonist in the grip of a gambling addiction, but did not come close to matching the success of *The Gamester*. Even after this success, which was authored "anonymously," her plays were recorded as being penned by "the Author of *The Gamester*."

Women's Works

Centlivre maintained a prolific output that included the 1706 *The Platonic Lady*, which was quoted from *Women in World History* and dedicated to " 'all the Generous Encouragers of Female Ingenuity.' " and further ranted that the "Vulgar World . . . think it a proof of their Sense, to dislike every thing that is writ by Women . . . And why this Wrath against the Womens Works? Perhaps you'll answer, because they meddle with things out of their Sphere: But I say, no; for since the Poet is born, why not a Woman as well as a Man?" In what must have become a last straw of sorts, Centlivre's colleague–actor and playwright Colley Cibber—has been accused of plagiarizing Centlivre's *Love at a Venture* (1706) in his successful production, *The Double Gallant*.

In 1706, Centlivre chose to travel with a troupe of players as an actress, and met Joseph Centlivre after a performance in Windsor. He had been a royal chef for the court of William and Mary, and was then a cook for Queen Anne (1665–1714), having received the title of "Yeoman of the Mouth." A widower with two children, he married Centlivre on April 23, in 1707 and she joined him in Buckingham Court—finally able to focus on perfecting her craft because she no longer had to support herself financially. Her next play—*The Busy Body* (1709)—was a popular and critical success. *Encyclopedia of British Women Writers'* Nancy Cotton described it as "a beautifully proportioned intrigue comedy in which two young couples outwit two comic old men." This production also marked the time when Centlivre once again began to sign her work, having effectively ascended above the prejudice of the day with multiple successes.

In 1714, Centlivre had her next big break with *The Wonder! A Woman Keeps a Secret*—a notable intrigue comedy that the *Biographical Dictionary of English Women Writers* noted "was translated into German and Polish, and

was chosen both by Kitty Clive and by [David] Garrick for their farewell performances." Cotton clarified that Centlivre's plays "focused on fast–paced, witty situations rather than witty dialogue. She was an adroit stage technician who wrote for actors rather than for readers." The successful author sold her plays and was given generous gifts from patrons that shared her political views. Centlivre was, DuPratt explained, "an ardent Whig, one whose loyalty to Parliamentary rule and a Protestant succession never wavered, [and] favor was bestowed upon her." Centlivre's next two plays—both written in 1715—were never staged in her lifetime. *A Gotham Election* was a politically inflammatory satirical farce about a corrupt election, and *A Wife Well Managed* (eventually staged in 1724) targeted Catholicism by mocking an impious priest.

The 1718 *A Bold Stroke for a Wife* was Centlivre's last comic triumph, but scholars agree that all of her stage successes featured animated dialogue, a broad variety of convincing characters from a range of backgrounds and skilled plotting—producing parts that actors relished and interpreted throughout the 18th and 19th centuries. Centlivre died on December 1, 1723 and was interred in St. Paul's Covent Garden in a simple grave without any monument.

Nameless No More

The *Dictionary of Literary Biography* remarked that "The successful revival of several of [Centlivre's] best comedies in this century is proof of their enduring appeal. *A Bold Stroke for a Wife*, for example, was successfully revived as recently as the summer of 1988 . . . Centlivre's comedies have long been recognized as . . . entertaining and lively, though earlier critics tended to deny them any solid literary merit. Later critics, however, have recognized much more fully the artistry of the plays." DuPratt pointed out that Centlivre "wrote during a time when few writers, either male or female, were able to earn a living in the theater . . . a highly acclaimed writer of the comedy of intrigue . . . [she] overcame the prejudice against women and succeeded where others had failed." Indeed a legacy that served as a foundation for scores of female playwrights given the opportunity to follow in Centlivre's footsteps.

Books

A Biographical Dictionary of English Women Writers: 1580–1720, edited by Maureen Bell, George Parfitt and Simon Shepherd, G.K. Hall and Company, 1990.

The Bloomsbury Guide to Women's Literature, edited by Claire Buck, Bloomsbury Publishing Ltd., 1992.

The Continuum Dictionary of Women's Biography: New Expanded Edition, edited by Jennifer S. Uglow, The Continuum Publishing Company, 1989.

Dictionary of Literary Biography, Volume 84: Restoration and Eighteenth–Century Dramatists, Second Series, edited by Paula R. Backscheider, The Gale Group, 1989.

An Encyclopedia of British Women Writers, edited by Paul Schlueter and June Schlueter, Rutgers University Press, 1998.

The Encyclopedia of World Theater, edited by Martin Esslin, Charles Scribner's Sons, 1977.

The Female Dramatist: Profiles of Women Playwrights from the Middle Ages to Contemporary Times, edited by Elaine T. Partnow and Lesley Anne Hyatt, Facts On File, Inc., 1998.

The Feminist Companion to Literature in English: Women Writers from the Middle Ages to the Present, edited by Virginia Blain, Patricia Clements and Isobel Grundy, Yale University Press, 1990.

International Dictionary of Theatre, Volume 2: Playwrights St. James Press, 1993.

The Lincoln Library of Language Arts: Volume 2, The Frontier Press Company, 1978.

Women in World History: A Biographical Encyclopedia, edited by Anne Commire, Yorkin Publications, 1999. ☐

Claude Chabrol

French filmmaker Claude Chabrol (born 1930) has long been regarded as a master of the suspense genre, and he was a founding father of the French nouvelle vague (French New Wave) film movement.

Few film directors have amassed such a large body of work as has Chabrol, who has averaged about a film a year over five decades beginning in the 1950s. Over his long career he has frequently focused on ordinary settings and favored emotionally detached characters, crafting classic French psychological thrillers with an underlying element of social critique.

Ran Wartime "Cinema"

Born on June 24, 1930, in Paris, Chabrol had his adolescence shaped by the German occupation of France during World War II. He and his family were forced to move from Paris to the village of Sardent in the Creuse département in central France. With an uncle who owned a chain of movie theaters, Chabrol was attracted to film from the start. He and some friends set up a homemade cinema in a barn, showing whatever movies they could get their hands on under Nazi restrictions.

Chabrol's parents expressed their disapproval toward his growing interest in film. Chabrol told Peter Lennon of the London *Guardian,* "My mother explained that the cinema was full of homosexuals. As far as I was concerned, either I was a homosexual or I wasn't, so making films would change nothing." His father, a pharmacist, convinced him to attend the Sorbonne university. Chabrol studied medicine and law, but eventually he left school altogether. He was offered a teaching job and turned it down—in favor, he told Lennon, of "an infernal life of drink and skirt-chasing."

At age 22, Chabrol developed a bad case of chicken pox and went to Switzerland to recover. While there, he ended up falling in love and marrying his first wife, Agnes Goute; the marriage produced two children but later ended in divorce. As his wife had a lot of money, Chabrol did not have to worry about finding work. Instead, he spent his days going to the burgeoning postwar cinema clubs, where he met filmmakers Franois Truffaut, Jean-Luc Godard, and Eric Rohmer. They invited him to write film criticism for *Cahiers du Cinéma,* the groundbreaking magazine of the French

New Wave. Chabrol later teamed with Rohmer to write a comprehensive book on Alfred Hitchcock, who became one of Chabrol's major cinematic influences, and to whom he has often been compared.

Chabrol also worked as an advisor on Godard's 1960 feature debut *A bout de souffle* (Breathless), one of the best-known films of the French New Wave. Chabrol's roles as a writer and advisor led him into work as a producer; after working with the public relations office of 20th Century Fox in France, Chabrol took charge of AJYM, the production company responsible for his first works as a director. When Chabrol heard that fellow *Cahiers* writer Roberto Rossellini wanted to help young filmmakers, Chabrol sent him a short script. Rossellini turned it down, but Chabrol made the film anyway. His 1958 directorial debut, *Le beau Serge* (Handsome Serge), was financed with money from his wife's recent inheritance.

Won Prize with Debut

Chabrol returned to his childhood village of Sardent to shoot the film, a simple story about a young man (Jean-Claude Brialy) who returns to his hometown to find that his old friend (Gérard Blain) has become an alcoholic. The film ended up winning the prestigious Prix Jean Vigo, providing enough prize money for Chabrol to begin work on his next film, *Les cousins* (1959). Teaming again with Brialy and Blain, Chabrol began using the character names of Charles and Paul, which he would continue to re-use over the next decade to describe a pair of contrasting characters. Often

Paul was the name for the troubled or isolated loner, while Charles was the conventional middle-class family man. *Les cousins* won an even more prestigious prize: the Golden Bear Award at the Berlin International Film Festival.

In his next project, 1960's *Les bonnes femmes* (The Good Girls), Chabrol set the tone of dry, emotional detachment that would become his trademark. In his first color film, *A double tour* (released in English as *Web of Passion*), he started to examine the psychological causes of violence and to relate them to the emptiness of bourgeois values. By 1962, when he released *L'oeil du malin* (Eye of the Devil), Chabrol had introduced a long-lasting formula: the love triangle story involving the recurrent female character Hélène, played by actress Stéphane Audran, whom Chabrol married in 1964. Chabrol's early films, often personal in nature, are considered central documents of the French New Wave.

To finance further films of a more personal stamp, Chabrol took on commercial assignments in the 1960s. Among theses were the spy films *Le tigre aime la chair fraiche* (released as *The Tiger Likes Fresh Meat*, 1964), *Marie-Chantal contre le docteur Kha* (Marie-Chantal vs. Dr. Kha, 1965), and *La route de Corinthe* (The Road to Corinth, 1967). He also did a Shakespearean parody called *Ophelia*. During the same period Chabrol collaborated with other major players in world cinema for several episodic films. In *Les plus belles escroqueries du monde* (The Most Beautiful Scams in the World) he teamed with Hiromichi Horikawa, Roman Polanski, and his old friend Godard to tell a story of four international con artists. He also collaborated with several of France's top directors for *Les sept péchés capitaux,* an investigation of the seven deadly sins. The Barbet Schroeder-produced *Paris vu par* (Paris as Seen By) featured six vignettes, each directed by a different filmmaker. Chabrol's segment "La Muette" starred himself and Audran as a husband and wife. Chabrol also tried his hand at war films with *La ligne de démarcation* (Line of Demarcation) starring Jean Seberg, the short-haired American beauty seen in *À bout de soufflé.*

In the late 1960s, Chabrol began what is generally regarded as a period of masterpieces, often employing variations of the love triangle story line featuring his stock characters Charles, Paul, and Hélène. With Audran as the calm, cool Hélène, actors Michel Bouquet and Jean Yanne often appeared as Charles or Paul. The rest of his crew also remained constant, with André Génovès generally serving as producer, Paul Gégauff as screenwriter, Jean Rabier as cinematographer, Pierre Jansen as composer, and Jacques Gaillard as editor. During this time he developed his own style of the psychological thriller that, as Terrence Rafferty discussed in the *New York Times,* "refuses to thrill," heavily influenced by directors Alfred Hitchcock and Fritz Lang. In Rafferty's words: "The icy, bemused manner he perfected in those years enabled him to generate tension in ways that didn't depend so heavily on satisfying the audience's desire for the resolution of a plot; the suspense was in the excruciating restraint of his direction, the scrupulous withholding of the artist's judgment on his often very, very naughty characters."

Launched Series of Triangle Tales

Chabrol's breakthrough film of this period was 1968's *Les biches* (The Does), the story of a lesbian couple in a love triangle with an outsider named Paul. Lennon wrote, "This could have been simply pandering to a classical male fantasy, and 1968 was not the best year to bring out a film with no political gloss, but it was given substantial depth by Chabrol's treatment. The critics liked it and it was a financial success." Stéphane Audran won the Best Actress Silver Bear at the Berlin International Film Festival for her performance. Chabrol's next film, *La femme infidèle* (The Unfaithful Woman), is considered a classic of love-triangle suspense; it was remade by director Adrian Lyne as *Unfaithful* in 2002.

Over the next several years, Chabrol continued to explore the ramifications of the basic scenario he had established. In *Que la bête meure* (The Beast Must Die, 1969), the Charles character finds out about Hélène and Paul as he investigates the death of his son. In *La rupture* (The Breakup, 1970), Charles and his wealthy parents hire the outsider Paul in a plot against Hélène. In 1970's *Le boucher* (The Butcher), among the most celebrated of all Chabrol films, Hélène is a schoolteacher and Paul is a butcher who returns from the war. They develop a friendship while a series of murders shake up the small town. In *Juste avant la nuit* (Just Before Nightfall, 1971), Charles is the one having the affair, while Hélène is the one compelled to turn to violence. In the last film of this period, *Les noces rouges* (Red Nights, 1973), the wife and her lover team up against Paul, the estranged husband.

Chabrol's films of the late 1970s and early 1980s were less consistent but more diverse, and he often worked in television and even commercials during this period. Written by and starring his longtime screenwriter Paul Gégauff, *Une partie de plaisir* (A Portion of Pleasure, 1975) was a dark psychological drama about the breakup of a family, co-starring Gégauff's own wife and daughter. Meanwhile, Chabrol's own marriage to Audran was breaking up, "because," Chabrol told Lennon, "I found myself becoming more interested in her as an actress than a wife."

He would soon find a new leading lady for his next era of films: Isabelle Huppert. In 1978's *Violette Nozière,* Chabrol investigated the true story of a young girl who killed her parents in the 1930s. A young Huppert played the title character, taking the Best Actress award at the Cannes Film Festival. Audran also had a role in the film. Chabrol also found a new production company in MK2, headed by Marin Karmitz. He also found a new composer, his son Matthieu Chabrol, and a new script supervisor, his third wife, Aurore.

Helmed World War II Abortion Film

While the careers of the other surviving members of the New Wave movement were finished or winding down, Chabrol returned to international distribution and critical recognition with 1988's *Une affaire des femmes* (An Affair of Women). Huppert portrayed a woman who was killed by the Vichy government for performing abortions during World War II. Despite a controversy at release time, it won international acclaim, including a Golden Globe nomination. In 1991 Chabrol took on the nineteenth-century literary subject Madame Bovary. He told Lennon, "I had wanted to do it for years, but was afraid. Then I said to myself, I am 60, if I don't do it now I never will—and I have the perfect actress: Isabelle."

In 1995's *La cérémonie* (The Ceremony), Huppert played a working class woman who befriends a shy maid, played by Sandrine Bonnaire. The film offers a strong example of a Chabrol story in which quiet desperation builds, here exploding in a violent attack against an upper-middle-class family. The film earned festival acclaim and several nominations for César awards, France's equivalent to the Oscars. Chabrol himself sat on the jury at the Venice Film Festival in 2000.

That year he teamed with Isabelle Huppert for *Merci pour le chocolat* (Thanks for the Chocolate, released in English as *Nightcap*), based on a crime novel by Charlotte Armstrong. In this slow thriller, Huppert took emotional detachment to an extreme level. According to Rafferty, "*Merci Pour le Chocolat* is as elegantly impersonal as a mathematical proof; a rigorous exercise in sang-froid. That description could, in fact, apply to a majority of [Chabrol's] 48 feature films, and to all the most celebrated ones." Featuring the director's son Thomas Chabrol in the supporting cast, *La fleur du mal* (The Flower of Evil, 2003) dealt with the criminal wrongdoing in three generations of a wealthy family. It was nominated for the Golden Bear Award at the Berlin International Film Festival, almost five decades after Chabrol was first honored there.

La demoiselle d'honneur (The Bridesmaid, 2004) was another typically slow-moving thriller involving a romance between Philippe, a middle-class man and Senta, a moody girl. Their relationship could be seen as a metaphor for Chabrol's films in general, argued Rafferty: "Philippe is attracted to Senta, then fascinated by her, then virtually obsessed with her, all without quite knowing why and without fully understanding who she is; she's ardent yet at times strangely affectless, opaque, and that opacity somehow both disturbs and excites him. That's what watching a Claude Chabrol movie is like."

In 2003 Chabrol was honored with a Lifetime Achievement Award from the European Film Awards, but he showed no signs of resting on his laurels. In 2006 Chabrol addressed current affairs with *L'ivresse du pouvoir* (The Comedy of Power), loosely based on the Elf affair, a real-life investigation of a corrupt oil company. Making a North American debut at New York's Tribeca Film Festival, the film showed Chabrol's continuing interest in exposing the corrupt values of the upper class. Chabrol returned in 2007 with the black comedy *La fille coupée en deux* (The Girl Cut in Two), winning the Bastone Bianco Award at the Venice Film Festival. Still at work in his eighth decade, Chabrol told Alison James of *Variety* that "when you get to my age, you have to accelerate, not slow down. I've still got a lot of films I want to make, and I don't want to tempt fate."

Books

International Dictionary of Films and Filmmakers, Volume 2: Directors, 4th ed., St. James, 2000.
Wood, Robin, and Michael Walker, *Claude Chabrol,* Praeger, 1970.

Periodicals

New Statesman, August 1, 2005.
New York Times, September 1, 2002; July 30, 2006.
Variety, August 22, 2005.

Online

"Claude Chabrol," Internet Movie Database, http://www.imdb.com (January 12, 2008).
"Claude Chabrol," Senses of Cinema, http://www.sensesofcinema.com/contents/directors/02/chabrol.html, (January 6, 2008).
"Surfer on the New Wave," *The Guardian,* http://film.guardian.co.uk/interview/interviewpages/0,6737,507603,00.html (January 6, 2008). □

Eddie Chapman

Eddie Chapman (1914-1997), a British criminal turned spy, was a double agent who so fooled the German government during World War II that it awarded him an Iron Cross for service. While not considered the most important double agent during the war, he "was probably the most colorful," Christopher Andrew wrote in London's *Times Online* of the safecracking womanizer. The false information Chapman—dubbed "Agent Zigzag"—provided the Nazis helped divert bombs from London and spare a vital aircraft factory.

Early Life

Chapman was born on November 16, 1914, in Burnopfield, a mining village near Newcastle, England. He worked in shipyards as an adolescent and briefly joined the Coldstream Guards, a regiment of the British Army, but was released in 1933; frequently he was in trouble. Chapman was part of a "jelly gang," a group that specialized in blowing up safes with gelignite and robbing them. He also engaged in extortion and blackmailed former paramours by showing them compromising photos. Once he even bragged about threatening to tell the parents of an 18–year–old, whom he had infected with venereal disease, that she had given it to him. "His skill as a thief made him a good deal of money and allowed him to live the life of a wealthy playboy in [London's] Soho, mixing with the likes of Noel Coward, Ivor Novello, and Marlene Dietrich," the British security service MI5 wrote on its Web site.

According to the *Times Online,* Chapman wrote years later: "I mixed with all types of tricky people, racehorse crooks, thieves, prostitutes, and the flotsam of the night–life of a great city." After he struck it rich as a safecracker, he drove a Bentley and wore Savile Row suits. "For Chapman, breaking the law was a vocation," Ben Macintyre wrote in his 2007 book, *Agent Zigzag,* as quoted in the *Times Online.*

Authorities arrested Chapman in Jersey early in 1939 and sentenced him to two years for breaking into a nightclub. They added an extra year for attempting to escape. While Chapman was imprisoned, the Germans occupied the Channel Islands, of which Jersey is a part, in July of 1940. Chapman was finally released about a year later.

Unhappy, Chapman yearned to return to Britain; he volunteered to help the Germans, who eventually accepted him into the Abwehr, their military intelligence organization. "The Abwehr was in a desperate position; it was getting only very low-quality intelligence out of Britain from its network of spies there," the British security service MI5 wrote on its Web site. MI5, in fact, had caught most of the German spies in the United Kingdom and were using some of them as double agents, though the Abwehr did not realize it at the time.

Chapman appealed to the Abwehr; he told the Germans he still harbored a grudge against the United Kingdom, where police still sought him for other crimes. The Abwehr felt he could recruit other agents through his underworld connections and commit sabotage, given his familiarity with explosives. The Abwehr trained him extensively in France and Norway, and called him "Fritzchen," or "little Fritz."

Parachuted Back into Britain

On December 16, 1942, Chapman, amid darkness of night, landed by parachute in Britain's Cambridgeshire countryside, near Ely. His assignment was to blow up the de

Havilland aircraft factory at Hatfield, where the British made the effective Mosquito bomber. Chapman carried fraudulent identity, €990 ($2,000) in used currency, a radio set, and a suicide pill. The Germans had also promised to commute the balance of his prison sentence.

Fritz Schlichting piloted Chapman to England for the flight. Years later, Schlichting, in an interview with Macintyre published in the *Times,* recalled the voyage. "Chapman seemed quite calm, although he asked lots of questions. On the way over the [English] Channel we sang songs," the former pilot said. There was one scary moment, when Chapman's parachute almost wouldn't open."

But Chapman, upon landing, instead called Scotland Yard from a farmhouse and offered to work as a double agent. "The British, having broken German codes, knew he was coming," Richard Goldstein wrote in the *New York Times.* Chapman wrote British officials a manifesto two days after his arrival. "I wish like hell there had been no war—I begin to wish I had never started this affair," Chapman wrote, according to documents MI5 released years later. "To spy and cheat on one's friends is not nice, it's dirty. However, I started this affair and I will finish it."

British military leaders interrogated him at Latchmere House, also called Camp 020, in west London. The skeptical camp commandant said Chapman considered himself "something of a prince of the underworld," as quoted on the British Broadcasting Company's BBC News Web site. The commandant added: "He has no scruples and will stop at nothing. He plays for high stakes and would have the world know it." In an internal memo, also posted on the MI5 site, a British captain urged Lieutenant Colonel Robin "Tin Eye" Stephens—named as such for his steel–rimmed monicle—to use Chapman immediately and "to the fullest extent."

Also drawing on Chapman's explosives background, the British devised a way to stage an explosion of the de Havilland factory that would convey the sight of "damage" from the air. "Rubble was strewn around the site and MI5 planted a story in the *Daily Express* about the "raid," BBC News reported. Chapman and others also used fake photographs. In another document that MI5 released (as chronicled by the MI5 site), British military official R.T. Reed wrote: "The camouflage was excellent and the impression gained was that aerial photography from any height above 2,000 feet would show considerable devastation without creating any suspicion. . . . The whole picture was very convincing, so much so that the operator in charge of the small boiler house near the swimming pool had arrived that morning in a state of great excitement; he thought that his machinery had been hit by a bomb during the night." MI5 wrote on its Web site: "Bomb–damaged transformers were created out of wood and paper–mache, and buildings were disguised with tarpaulins and corrugated iron sheets painted to appear from the air as if they were the half–demolished remains of walls and roofs."

The fooled Germans treated Chapman as a hero upon his return, giving him the Iron Cross for "outstanding zeal and success" at a secret ceremony in Oslo, Norway, in the spring of 1943. Chapman, the only Briton ever to receive this medal, also received 110,000 Reichmarks and a yacht.

"The Germans came to love Chapman," one MI5 officer said, as quoted in the British *Telegraph* newspaper. "But although he went cynically through all the forms, he did not reciprocate. Chapman loved himself, loved adventure, and loved his country, probably in that order."

MI5 Decided to Retire Him

After he returned to Germany, Chapman was dispatched to Norway to teach at a spy school in Oslo. After D–Day, the invasion of Normandy in June of 1944, the Abwehr sent him back to England to inspect damage from the V bombs. Chapman, who landed on concrete in his parachuting return and lost some teeth, continued to work as a double agent. His misinformation was said to help spare London, as German bombs fell on its periphery instead. Chapman also was credited with averting a German sabotage plot in Portugal; he had alerted a British captain about a bomb that resembled a lump of coal he had planted on a ship.

Chapman at one point admitted he had talked about his work to a Norwegian woman he was dating. "It was therefore thought too dangerous for him to continue," Michael Smith wrote in the *Telegraph*. Chapman, who had returned to Britain in 1944, was retired with a €6,000 payment from MI5, which let him retain €1,000 of the money the Nazis had given him. In addition, outstanding charges based on more than 40 safecracking jobs, which could have landed him another 20 years in prison, were stricken. According to MI5, he continued to date glamorous women and was seen in the company of a professional fighter of ill repute.

The British government attempted to keep Chapman's double–agent work under wraps, but when tried on a currency–related charge in 1948, a senior official from the War Office provided a character reference. The official, as quoted in the *New York Times,* called Chapman "one of the bravest men who served in the last war."

Books, Movies Followed

Chapman published three books about his work: *The Eddie Chapman Story* (1953), *Free Agent: The Further Adventures of Eddie Chapman* (1955) and *The Real Eddie Chapman Story* (1966). Also in 1966, the film "Triple Cross" was released, with Tony Award winner Christopher Plummer playing Chapman. Meanwhile, the Germans joined the British in forgiving Chapman. When Chapman's daughter was married, former German spy controller Baron Stefan von Grunen was a guest at the wedding. "The story of many a spy is commonplace and drab. The story of Chapman is different. In fiction it would be rejected as improbable," Smith wrote in the *Telegraph.*

Chapman died on December 11, 1997, at age 83 in a nursing home in Brickett Wood, near London. After his death, MI5 released its files on Chapman, and any person with a National Archives readers' ticket can view them. Macintyre added in *Agent Zigzag,* as quoted in a Carlo Wolff article in the *Chicago Sun–Times,* "He may have ascended heavenward or perhaps he headed in the opposition. He is probably zigzagging still."

In 2007, two more books about Chapman were published, though with different slants. While Macintyre's *Agent Zigzag* portrayed Chapman as a "rogue who so liked living on the edge that he threatened to fall over," Carlo Wolff wrote in the *Chicago Sun–Times,* Nicholas Booth, author of *Zigzag: The Incredible Wartime Exploits of Eddie Chapman,* pictured the double agent more heroically. "The life of a secret agent is dangerous enough, but the life of the double agent is infinitely more precarious. If anyone balances on a swinging tightrope it is her, and a single slip can send him crashing to destruction," Wolff said Macintyre wrote, quoting high–ranking MI5 official Major John Cecil Masterman. Wolff added: "Macintyre remains skeptical, while Booth winds up an apologist for Chapman despite his distaste for the man's philandering and tendency to embellish."

Macintyre, a writer–at–large for London's *Times,* was nominated for the 2007 Whitbread Book Awards, known more commonly as the Costa Book Awards. "Macintyre vividly brought Chapman to life after poring over hundreds of newly declassified MI5 papers-transcripts, wireless intercepts, reports, and letters," *Times* colleague Dalya Alberge wrote. "He painted a portrait of a man whose real–life story is the stuff of a screenwriter's imagination."

Chapman's Legacy

The release of the 2007 books revived interest in Chapman's work. After Macintyre published his book, old friends and enemies alike contacted the author. Journalist Peter Kinsley said, as quoted in the *Times:* "Eddie would have loved the publicity. His old friends said he should have worn a T–shirt emblazoned 'I am a Spy for MI5.' The last time I met him he described how he had missed a fortune in ermine [used in coronation robes] during a furs robbery, because he thought it was a rabbit."

Then, John Dixon contacted Macintyre. Dixon, an independent filmmaker, had six hours of interview footage with Chapman that he had begun shooting in 1996, intending to produce a documentary. Chapman, however, died one year later. Macintyre watched the footage from a screening room in Soho. "Meeting Chapman for the first time from beyond the grave was one of the strangest experiences of my life," Macintyre wrote in the *Times.*

Macintyre, though, caught Chapman in yet another lie, about how he was taken to meet British leader Winston Churchill in 1943. "Chapman could never have imagined that MI5 would release its records, and that the truth about his wartime service would be revealed," Macintyre wrote. "His own death is imminent, but here is Eddie Chapman still playing by his own rules: a grinning villain, spinning a yarn, looking you straight in the eye, and picking your pocket."

Online

"Ben McIntyre Shortlisted for Costa Book Awards 2007," *Times Online,* http://entertainment.timesonline.co.uk/tol/arts_and_entertainment/books/article2909485.ece (December 12, 2007).

"The Day Agent Zigzag Came Back from the Dead," *Times Online,* http://entertainment.timesonline.co.uk/tol/arts_and_entertainment/books/history/article1937243.ece (November 26, 2007).

"Eddie Chapman, 83, Safecracker and Spy," *New York Times,* http://query.nytimes.com/gst/fullpage.html?res = 980DE6D8 1F3FF933A15751C1A961958260 (November 26, 2007).

"A First–Class Double Cross," *Times Online,* http://entertainment .timesonline.co.uk/tol/arts_and_entertainment/books/ biography/article1272151.ece (November 26, 2007).

"History: Cases from the National Archives—Documents from the Chapman Case," MI5 Web site, http://www.mi5.gov.uk/ output/Page559.html (December 12, 2007).

"History: Cases from the National Archives—Eddie Chapman (Agent ZIGZAG)," MI5 Web site, http://www.mi5.gov.uk/ output/Page558.html (December 12, 2007).

"How Double Agents Duped the Nazis," BBC News, http://news .bbc.co.uk/2/hi/uk_news/1423826.stm (November 26, 2007).

"Meet Eddie Chapman: Double Agent," Bloomsbury, http://www .bloomsbury.com/ezine/Articles/Articles.asp?ezine_article_id = 1806&Quiz_id = 0 (November 26, 2007).

"The Spy with Two Faces," *Times Online,* http://entertainment .timesonline.co.uk/tol/arts_and_entertainment/books/article 1291912.ece (November 26, 2007).

"Welsh Spy Helped Defeat Hitler," BBC News, http://news.bbc .co.uk/2/hi/uk_news/1423605.stm (November 26, 2007).

"ZigZag, a Womanizer and Thief who Double–Crossed the Nazis," *Telegraph,* http://www.telegraph.co.uk/news/main .jhtml?xml = /news/2001/07/05/npro05.xml (November 26, 2007). □

Hester Chapone

18th century British writer Hester Chapone (1727-1801) defied the social standards of Georgian England by speaking up for a woman's right to a quality education.

Childhood, Interrupted

Hester Mulso was born October 27, 1727 in Twywell of Northamptonshire, England. She was the only surviving female child of country gentleman Thomas Mulso and his wife, Hester (Thomas) Mulso. She had three brothers, all of whom eventually lived out careers in the ministry. Carol Brennan's *Women in World History* biography reveals how as a girl, Chapone earned the nicknames "Hecky" and "linnet"—after the British songbird—for her beautiful voice. She displayed an early aptitude for writing, composing a romance at the age of nine that she called *The Loves of Amoret and Melissan.* Sources suggest that her mother disapproved of the accomplishment and speculate that the maternal reproach might have been borne of jealousy because the young girl was clearly gifted.

Jeannine Dobbs's 1976 *Frontiers* article titled *The Blue-Stockings: Getting It Together* explained that eighteenth-century English women from the working class "received little if any education . . . [while] Daughters of wealthy and/or aristocratic families were educated at the whims of their fathers." Indeed, Chapone's brothers enjoyed quality educations from an early age, and although

Chapone's mother discouraged her at first, when her mother passed away Chapone was free to pursue an edification of her own design. The young Chapone managed her father's estate and took on a curriculum for her own intellectual development with his blessing, during which she taught herself Latin, Italian, and French as well as music, drawing, and dancing.

In Sickness and in Health, Until Death . . .

In 1754, Hester Mulso and John Chapone—an attorney who was part of naturalist and epistolary novelist Samuel Richardson's (1689–1761) social set—began a long courtship. John Chapone was no stranger to smart, strong women. His mother, Sarah Chapone (1699–1764), was a celebrated feminist writer of her own time. Hester Mulso remained engaged to John Chapone for six years, during which time they struggled to obtain her father's approval. In 1760 they were married, and in a cruel stroke of fate nine or ten months later—in 1761—John Chapone died. Some sources claim their marriage was unhappy, while others argue that the affectionate content of their personal letters and the fact that the couple struggled so long and with such determination to gain approval for their union suggest a deep devotion, and Chapone keenly mourned its loss. Her husband's death left Chapone in dire economic circumstances. Unable to afford a home of her own, Chapone moved frequently, living in the homes of various friends as well as the estate of her uncle, the Bishop of Winchester.

Befit as a Bluestocking

Chapone never let her tenuous personal situation stand in the way of her evolution as a professional writer. She translated poetry as well as composed it, and chose to interpret verse on traditional subjects like the splendor of nature, the pleasures of solitude, and the perfection of friendship. Her own poetry also tended to celebrate the conventional, like her piece *To Stella*—written for British poet Susanna Highmore (1690–1750)—that champions the joys of female camaraderie over romantic relationships. Chapone's first poem was written in 1745—an ode to harmony titled *To Peace: Written During the Late Rebellion.* In her role as occasional literary critic, Chapone also extolled the novels *Evelina* (1778), *Cecilia* (1782) and *Camilla* (1796) written by Frances Burney d'Arblay, known as Fanny Burney (1752–1840)—praise that reportedly thrilled the celebrated author.

Chapone was quickly welcomed into the circle of female minds known as the "bluestockings" along with linguist Elizabeth Carter (1717–1806), feminist author Mary Wollstonecraft (1759–1797) and social reformer and critic Elizabeth Montagu (1718–1800), all of whom she admired and befriended. *Women in World History's* Carol Brennan described the Bluestocking Circle as "one of London's most celebrated societies for members of the leisured gentry . . . [that] began during the 1750s and 1760s as a conversation among friends, both women and men, who were interested in literature and other intellectual pursuits." The group earned their names when one of the initial gentry members began wearing the blue stockings normally seen only on the legs of peasants. Their discussions, which focused on literature instead of politics, became the seat for the most celebrated female society in London.

Chapone was first published in a 1750 issue of Samuel Johnson's *The Rambler*—a gentleman's magazine—to which she contributed an epistolary story in fictional letters. In 1753 she published *The Story of Fidelia*—the cautionary tale of a woman's descent into free-thinking and eventual salvation by religion—in Hawkesworth's *The Adventurer.* It was her *Letters on the Improvement of the Mind: Addressed to a Young Lady*, however—published anonymously in 1773—that secured her place in social and literary history.

Chapone's *Letters on the Improvement of the Mind* was one of the first of many such *conduct books* that followed in its wake. Linda Troost's biographical sketch in the *Encyclopedia of British Women Writers* describes the work as one that "presents a detailed plan for educating girls and includes a list of recommended books [in history, philosophy, poetry, geography and chronology as well as advice on] reading the Bible, controlling one's temper, managing finances, and acquiring accomplishments." The manuscript evolved over many editions in multiple countries before arriving in its final form in the 1851 edition, and was addressed to her niece, Elizabeth Montagu (named in honor of the elder bluestocking critic)—becoming a significantly influential handbook or primer on female comportment and education. Troost's biography told how "The queen revealed to [Chapone] in 1778 (both were visiting [Chapone's] uncle, the Bishop of Winchester) that even the

Princess Royal's education had been guided by the *Letters.*" The popular classic was still in print in 1840—reprinted often, with three editions released within just a year of publication. It even appeared in the fiction of the time when, in Irish playwright Richard Sheridan's (1751–1816) comedy of manners, *The Rivals* (1775), one character named Lydia Languish hides a stack of inappropriate novels she has been reading and pretends to be reading Chapone's *Letters.* While *Letters on the Improvement of the Mind* undoubtedly made Chapone famous, its release did not make her wealthy. She sold the copyright for a mere fifty pounds.

A Lifetime in Letters

In *Letters*—quoted extensively in the *Chambers's Cyclopaedia of English Literature*—Chapone stresses the importance of a young woman being "introduced into life on a respectable footing, and to converse with those whose manners and style of life may polish her behaviour, refine her sentiments, and give her consequence in the eye of the world." She advises intimacy between those equal in rank and suggests that one place oneself among one's "superiors" without becoming proud. She also warns against "intimacy with those of low birth and education," claiming that thinking of such connections as humble is, in fact, "the meanest kind of pride." Chapone suggests that the lower classes be treat[ed] "always with affability" and "an affectionate interest" but advises against allowing them to become "familiar."

In 1775 Chapone released *Miscellanies in Prose and Verse* and received two hundred and fifty pounds for the rights. It included her early poetry, some moral treatises and a reprint of *The Story of Fidelia.* Two years later, in 1777, she published what would be her final work, *A Letter to a New-Married Lady.* Chapone's combination of modesty and reason also inspired and motivated her contemporaries. In 1783, friends of the Earl of Carlisle asked for Chapone's help to influence Samuel Johnson to read and critique a tragedy the Earl had written, and Troost claimed that "Richardson used [Chapone] as a model for some of the 'genteel characters' in [his novel] *Sir Charles Grandison* (most likely Harriet Byron)."

Literary Legacy

Chapone died on December 25, 1801 in Hadley, Middlesex near London, England. Nothing beyond the date and place of death is recorded in most sources, suggesting how little was known about her personal life outside the details recorded by her correspondence. Chapone's relatives collected her work posthumously and put out a two-volume collection titled *Posthumous Works* and a four-volume collection simply titled, *Works and Life* in 1807. These collections showcased, among other things, the correspondence between Chapone and Samuel Richardson.

In the early 1750s, Chapone and Richardson used their correspondence to argue the merits of Richardson's 1748 novel *Clarissa.* Troost explained how Chapone felt that "a daughter should not marry without the consent of the parents but could refuse anyone the parents might propose" while Richardson claimed that "children must obey parents in all things and accept their choices of spouses." Scholar Julie Straight noted how Chapone used her writing to stand up for a woman's right to develop their rational minds by engaging in religious study and debate—a belief she supported in relation to all areas of study. Chapone's *Feminist Companion to Literature in English* biography noted that Richardson called her both "a spitfire and rebel," but admired the poise and modesty with which she maintained her own opinions. Johnson later shared that this friendship between Chapone and Richardson eventually faded because she let her poetry be read publicly and gained notariety—characteristics that Richardson supposedly found unbecoming.

Memoirs of Mrs. J. Chapone, from Various Authentic Sources—a biography written by descendants some time after her death—was published in 1839. Brennan explained how the term 'bluestocking' eventually developed into an insulting slight in the late 1790s, yet as recently as 1977 Harvard's Houghton Library underwent a renovation to establish an 18th-century enclave dedicated to England's Bluestockings. Chapone maintained that women were fully capable of rational thought, and did not have to relinquish morality or sentiment to achieve it. In her masterwork, *Letters on the Improvement of the Mind* Troost records how Chapone encouraged her niece and other young ladies to make choices by "listening to both heart and mind, but not to be 'afraid of a single life.' "—sound advice for anyone, regardless of their time or gender and the remarkable legacy of an extraordinary woman.

Books

The Blackwell Companion to the Enlightenment, edited by John W. Yolton, Blackwell Publishers, 1992.

The Bloomsbury Guide to Women's Literature, edited by Claire Buck, Bloomsbury Publishing Ltd., 1992.

The Cambridge Guide to Literature in English: Third Edition, edited by Dominic Head, Cambridge University Press, 2006.

Chambers Biographical Dictionary, edited by Melanie Parry, Chambers Harrap Publishers Ltd., 1997.

Chambers's Cyclopaedia of English Literature: New Edition, edited by David Patrick, W. & R. Chambers, Ltd., 1906.

The Continuum Dictionary of Women's Biography: New Expanded Edition, edited by Jennifer S. Uglow, Continuum Publishing Company, 1989.

The Dictionary of National Biography: The Concise Dictionary Part 1, Oxford University Press, 1953.

Eighteenth-Century Women Poets and Their Poetry: Inventing Agency, Inventing Genre, edited by Paula R. Backscheider, Johns Hopkins University Press, 2005.

An Encyclopedia of British Women Writers, edited by Paul Schlueter and June Schlueter, Rutgers University Press, 1998.

The Feminist Companion to Literature in English: Women Writers from the Middle Ages to the Present, edited by Virginia Blain, Patricia Clements and Isobel Grundy, Yale University Press, 1990.

The Oxford Companion to Children's Literature, edited by Humphrey Carpenter and Mari Prichard, Oxford University Press, 1984.

The Oxford Companion to English Literature: Sixth Edition, edited by Margaret Drabble, Oxford University Press, 2006.

Women in World History: A Biographical Encyclopedia, edited by Anne Commire, Yorkin Publications, 1999.

Periodicals

Frontiers: A Journal of Women Studies, Vol. 1, No. 3. Winter 1976.

The New York Times, November 27, 1977.

Nineteenth-Century Contexts, December 2005. □

George Cheyne

Scottish physician George Cheyne (1671-1743) is best known as a pioneering, eighteenth–century advocate for vegetarianism. He wrote several books that covered topics such as nutrition, exercise, and depression. His most famous work, "An Essay on Health and Long Life" was published in 1725.

Scottish physician George Cheyne can be considered the "diet and exercise guru" of his day. His popular publications about vegetarianism and nutrition were essentially the "self–help" lifestyle guides for his contemporaries. Despite his eccentricities and own health problems, Cheyne offered his readers some lifestyle advice that comes across as prudent and reasonable even today. This is remarkable, especially considering that he practiced medicine in the eighteenth century.

Not much is known about Cheyne's early life, but this much has been ascertained: He was born in Aberdeenshire in Scotland in 1671 into a good family. His parents envisioned for him a career in the church. However, Cheyne possessed a naturally curious and studious disposition, so he chose to enter the medical profession instead.

Earned Medical Degree

In his early years, Cheyne benefited from a formal and liberal education, and he eventually developed into a young man of considerable and wide–ranging knowledge.

He attended medical school in Edinburgh in Scotland, studying under Doctor Pitcairne, a well–known physician of the time. Cheyne was greatly influenced by Pitcairne. Later, when he wrote his most famous work, "Essay on Health and Long Life," he referred to Pitcairne in the preface as his "great master and generous friend."

After earning his medical degree, Cheyne moved to London, England, when he was about thirty years old. In 1702, he established his own medical practice. As it was a common method among contemporary physicians, Cheyne often called on his patients in the taverns that they frequented. During this period in his life, Cheyne himself engaged in an indulgent lifestyle. He reportedly possessed a cheerful disposition and was an entertaining conversationalist. As such, he became a popular figure in London's nightlife. In his own words, according to Paul Collins of the *New Scientist,* he associated with "Bottle companions, the younger Gentry, and Free–Livers . . . nothing being necessary for that Purpose, but to be able to Eat lustily, and swallow down much Liquor." Both of those Cheyne did quite well.

Indulgence Led to Poor Health

According to accounts, Cheyne consumed copious quantities of rich food and drink. But his lifestyle eventually took a physical toll, and his weight ballooned to more than four hundred pounds. Obese and unhealthy, he always felt short–winded and lethargic. In 1705, he nearly suffered an early death after a series of what Collins reported him naming "vertiginous Paroxysms." Translated into modern terms, he came close to suffering a heart attack or stroke. As such, he was forced to abandon his careless and extravagant habits. To revive his failing health, he attempted a regimen of vomiting purges. Unsurprisingly, this did little to improve his health or relieve the depression he frequently suffered.

He endured in this state until the winter of 1707, when, acting on the advice of a medical colleague, he traveled to Croydon in England to visit a Dr. Taylor, who became well known for advocating a unique diet. When Cheyne first met Taylor, the diet doctor was taking a meal that consisted of nothing more than a quart of milk. Taylor explained to the astonished Cheyne that after consulting with London physicians about his own poor health, he decided to abstain from alcohol and meat. Amazingly, for seventeen years, Dr. Taylor's only sustenance was milk. Cheyne was quite impressed and subsequently gave up everything but milk and vegetables. He had theorized that the two food items were essentially the same. "Milk being Vegetables immediately cook'd by Animal Heat and Organs," he explained and quoted by Collins.

In this way, Cheyne was able to start controlling his weight, and he began to feel better than he had for a long time. But when he tried to resume a more standard diet, he regained his weight and his health once again suffered. Thus, he went back to his vegetarian diet, which he adhered to for the rest of his life.

Reportedly, Cheyne's embracement of vegetarianism was also reinforced by the writings of Thomas Tryon, a self–taught philosopher and student of Protestant mysticism who died right around the time that Cheyne was first starting his medical practice. In 1691, Tryon had published a book, *The Way to Health,* that advocated a vegetarian diet. The work was very popular with educated people of the time. Benjamin Franklin had even been a "Tryonist" at one point in his life.

Revived Medical Practice

Reinvigorated, Cheyne re–established his medical practice in the famous spa town of Bath, England. He also began to put his health theories down on paper.

By the 1720s, Cheyne prospered as a physician in this fashionable setting. His clients were equally prosperous and included such well–known figures as poet Alexander Pope and the English novelist Samuel Richardson, who gained fame with early examples of the novel including *Pamela: Or Virtue Rewarded* and *Clarissa: Or the History of a Young Lady.* Another famous patient was John Wesley, the founder of the Methodist religion. Like Cheyne, Wesley had embraced vegetarianism. In part because of Cheyne's influence, and the powerful rapport Cheyne developed with his famous patients, vegetarianism became a trendy lifestyle option among the literary elite of England.

All the while, Cheyne still struggled with his own weight problem. Also, he suffered from excruciating headaches and severe gout blisters that made his skin appear, as the *New Scientist* article that quoted Cheyne once described it "burnt almost like the Skin of a roasted Pig." In addition, he was still plagued with bouts of depression.

Wrote Famous "Essay" on Health

Still, Cheyne was uplifted enough by his professional success that he felt compelled to write *Essay of Health and Long Life,* a 1724 publication that extolled the virtues of a vegetarian diet. It would become his most famous and influential work. The book went through six reprints in its first year, and it was translated into French, Dutch, Latin and Italian.

Cheyne based the book on his own professional and personal experiences, rather than existing medical literature. "I have consulted nothing but my own Experience and Observation in my own crazy Carcase and the Infirmities of others I have treated," he wrote in the preface of *Essay of Health and Long Life.* Departing from the contemporary conventional medical wisdom, Cheyne averred in the work that good health depended upon five critical components: diet, ample rest, exercise, plenty of fresh air and purgative vomiting. His recommendations included abstinence from red meat and alcohol (except for a moderate intake of wine); a diet consisting of milk, vegetables, poultry and mineral water; and an early–to–bed (10 p.m.), early–to–rise (6 a.m.) sleep schedule. As for dietary specifics, he suggested eating half a chicken a day and avoiding foods that were smoked, pickled or spicy. Recommended foods include plain portions of beans, oats, rice and potatoes. Further, Cheyne highly approved of green tea and disapproved of chocolate–flavored drinks, which he believed provoked "a false and hysterical appetite."

Exercise was an extremely important part of his health regimen. Cheyne felt that, with England's increasing urbanization, people were not getting enough physical activity, particularly academics and people who worked at sedentary desk jobs. "The Studious and the Contemplative . . . must make Exercise a Part of their Religion," he said, as quoted by Collins. As such, he recommended something called the "chamber horse," essentially an early example of indoor exercise equipment. Basically, it was a chair built with an elevated seat that moved by spring action. Users placed themselves on the seat, gripped the chair arms and vigorously bounced up and down. Surprisingly enough, this device became very popular, and physicians continued prescribing it for a century.

Ironically, as Cheyne's famous essay was being prepared for publication, he suffered a relapse into his old drinking and eating habits. The backsliding behavior almost caused his death.

Essay Created Controversy

Cheyne's work generated controversy among medical colleagues, particularly among his fellow members of the

Royal Society of London, where the *Essay of Health and Long Life* became a hot topic of debate. Medical professionals also were uneasy about Cheyne's popularity with his followers and its implications. They felt that health matters were too complex to be left in patients' own hands.

One Royal Society physician gave Cheyne the disparaging nickname of "Dr. Diet." Soon after Cheyne's book was published, a pamphlet appeared that accused Cheyne of offering bad medical device to promote his practice. However, not all physicians were critical: Dr. William Lambe concurred with Cheyne's ideas on vegetarianism and commented (as found in *Vibrant Life*) that "the use of the flesh of animals is a deviation from the laws of [mankind's] nature, and is universally a cause of disease and premature death."

Despite criticisms launched against it, Cheyne's book remained popular with the public, and it stayed in print for almost fifty years after its initial release.

Other Writings

In addition to that popular work, Cheyne had published previous papers on fevers, gout, hygiene and mathematics. At Dr. Pitcairne's request, he wrote "A new Theory of Acute and Slow continued Fevers; wherein, besides the appearances of such, and the manner of their cure, occasionally, the structure of the glands, and the Manner and Laws of Secretion, the operation of purgative, vomitive, and mercurial medicines, are mechanically explained." Pitcairne wanted to produce such a work himself, but he was far too busy with his own practice and teaching duties, so he encouraged Cheyne to write it. Though the work was well received, it was put together rather hurriedly, and Cheyne did not think the finished product was worthy of his name.

In 1715, Cheyne wrote "Philosophical Principles of Natural Religion," a work that combined spirituality with natural science. In it, Cheyne advanced the idea that life could not spring forth from inorganic matter; rather, it "must of necessity have existed from all eternity." The work was dedicated to the Earl of Roxburgh, and it is believed that Cheyne wrote it at his request. During this period, Cheyne also wrote "An Essay of the True Nature and Due Method of treating the Gout, together with an account of the Nature and Quality of the Bath Waters," which was reprinted in five editions.

In 1733, Cheyne wrote a book about depression, *The English Malady, or a Treatise on Nervous Diseases of all kinds, as Spleen, Vapours, Lowness of Spirits, Hypochondriacal and hysterical Distempers,* that described his own emotional bouts of melancholy and anxiety that troubled him for a large part of his life. In the work, Cheyne argued that such emotional turmoil only affected highly intelligent individuals, as "fools, weak or stupid Persons . . . are seldom troubled with Vapours or Lowness of Spirits." The work also described his own digestive troubles.

Cheyne published his last work, "The Natural Method of Curing the Diseases of the Body, and the Disorders of the Mind attending on the Body," in 1740. This very popular study of nutrition and natural living was dedicated to the Earl of Chesterfield, who was Cheyne's friend and correspondent. The book was so popular that it went into its third edition as early as 1742, the year before Cheyne died.

Died in England

Cheyne passed away on April 12 in 1743 in Bath. He was seventy–one years old. His advanced age was somewhat surprising, considering his weight problems. At the time of his death, however, he was completely sound of mind and in relatively reasonable sound physical health.

Cheyne's works on diet and health remained popular long after his death, and people continued reading his books for more than a century. Indeed, his "Essay of Health and Long Life" remained in print until 1834.

Cheyne became known as one of the founding fathers of modern vegetarianism. His work was often cited by vegetarians as well as animal–rights activists, who liked to quote one of Cheyne's passages in particular, which is found on the *all-creatures.org* Web site: "To see the convulsions, agonies and tortures of a poor fellow–creature, whom they cannot restore nor recompense, dying to gratify luxury and tickle callous and rank organs, must require a rocky heart, and a great degree of cruelty and ferocity. I cannot find any great difference between feeding on human flesh and feeding on animal flesh, except custom and practice."

During his life, not all of the ideas that Cheyne advanced or embraced survived beyond their time. For instance, Cheyne considered himself one of the "Iatro–mechanists," who developed the concept of "iatro–mathematics," a rather strange pseudo–science that blended the principles of Newtonian physics and astrology into medicine.

Through his health books, however, Cheyne did advance the notion of preventive medicine, a concept that is now accepted by virtually every modern healthcare professional. That appears to be Cheyne's greatest legacy.

Periodicals

New Scientist, October 7, 2006.
Vibrant Life, May–June, 1992.

Online

"Anxiety–panic History," AnxietyPanic.com, http://anxiety-panic.com/history/h-1600.htm (November 25, 2007).
"George Cheyne," Amazines.com, http://www.amazines.com/George_Cheyne_related.html. (November 25, 2007).
"George Cheyne (1671–1743)," Christian Vegetarian Association, http://www.all-creatures.org/cva/th-cheyne-george.htm (November 25, 2007).
"Significant Scots–George Cheyne," Electric Scotsman.com, http://www.electricscotland.com/history/other/cheyne_george.htm (November 25, 2007). □

Ole Kirk Christiansen

Danish toymaker Ole Kirk Christiansen (1891-1958) founded The LEGO Group, one of the world's largest toy manufacturers. A carpenter by training who be-

gan making wooden toys during the Great Depression, Christiansen devised the multicolored plastic blocks that could be fashioned into numerous combinations of colors and shapes and which went on to become one of the world's best-selling toys. Christiansen died in 1958, and his son inherited the company and turned it into a global powerhouse whose "brightly colored interlocking bricks have virtually revolutionized the worldwide toy market," wrote Robert D. Hershey in the *New York Times* in 1977.

Christiansen was born on April 7, 1891, in Vejle, a town in the Jutland peninsula of Denmark. He began tending his family's sheep in the fields at the age of six, and to pass the time during the long hours outside, he carved small wooden figures. Later, he trained under his older brother, Kristian Bonde Christiansen, to become a carpenter. Around 1916, he bought the Billund Woodworking and Carpentry Shop, and had several profitable years as a local home builder in the village of Billund, also in Jutland; during the slower winter months he made custom furniture. Along the way, he married and became the father to four sons.

Switched to Toymaking

The Great Depression did not impact Denmark's largely agricultural economy immediately when it began in 1929, but by 1931 a flattened market brought a subsequent slowdown in Christiansen's home-building and furniture-making business. He was also a widower by that point, and to make ends meet he began crafting more practical items in his woodshop. These included stepladders, stools for milking cows, and ironing boards, along with a few wooden toys that were made primarily from wood scraps. The yo-yos, cars, and animals he carved out of wood proved such a hit that he came up with a brand name around 1934 for them. Taking the Danish phrase *leg godt,* or "play well" he called the line LEGO.

After World War II, Christiansen became intrigued by the possibilities offered by a relatively new material, plastic. In 1947, he acquired one of the first plastic injection-molding machines in Denmark to make a new series of toys, such as a rattle shaped like a fish. His sons, now grown and working with him, cautioned that the new space-age material was too expensive and the possibilities too limited, but they were proven wrong over the next few years. In 1949, Christiansen introduced the first LEGO Automatic Binding Bricks, which in 1953 was shortened to just LEGO Bricks. When he visited a toy fair in England in 1954, one toy buyer for a retail chain told him there was no "system" in the world of toys, and this gave Christiansen the idea to create a series of LEGO items that could be purchased separately, but used with one another.

Won Patent for Brick Design

In 1955, the LEGO System of Play was introduced, which featured little cars and miniature people that children could use to create a town. The first "Town Plan No. 1" package also came with a large plastic sheet that provided a basic urban layout with roads and sidewalks. Altogether, the line grew to include 28 separate sets, which were a hit with children in Denmark and neighboring Scandinavian countries. The company still produced the LEGO bricks, but there were complaints that the bricks did not stay together. In 1958, Christiansen's son Godtred Kirk Christiansen devised a radical innovation in the design for each brick: there were already eight studs on the top, to which three tubes were added to the bottom. This made them click together neatly, and the company even applied for and was granted a patent for this, which was called a stud-and-tube coupling.

Unfortunately, Christiansen did not survive to witness the phenomenal growth of his company. He died on March 11, 1958, in Ribe, Denmark's oldest town. A year later, the company ended production of all wooden toys, and began moving into the larger European toy market over the next few years. In 1967, it introduced a Duplo line of plastic building blocks which were easier for younger children to put together. An agreement with Samsonite, the U.S. luggage manufacturer, to sell LEGO products in the United States proved to be an unwise strategy for conquering the vast American toy market, but Christiansen's sons had exited it by 1974 and moved to set up their own subsidiary in Enfield, Connecticut. This site began producing its own LEGO bricks in the early 1980s.

LEGO's World Domination

Adding a vast array of other LEGO products to the company's wares, Christiansen's heirs witnessed the cult-like status that their mainstay achieved among youngsters around the world, who avidly collected each of the sets of any new line. As Hershey wrote in the *New York Times* article, "Lego's bricks . . . are said by the company's psychologists to meet many of children's needs. One of their needs is to learn hand-eye coordination. Another is to make something of their own. (Lego says that, although the results may seem awkward to an adult, they satisfy a child, whose critical sense is not as well developed as his imagination.) And the bricks are designed to provide a harmless outlet for the basic urge to destroy as well as to create."

LEGO bricks are manufactured on several continents, including South America and Asia, and the bricks themselves are built from specially made injection-molding machines, which are engineered "to achieve tolerances within two-thousandths of a millimeter, so precise that the bricks are said to lock a bit stiffly the first nine times but thereafter to grip perfectly for years," wrote Hershey in the 1977 *New York Times* article. The LEGO Group headquarters are still located in Billund, Denmark, and Christiansen's grandson Kjeld Kirk Kristiansen (the spelling differs because of an error in the Danish vital records office), served as chief executive officer until 2004.

LEGO also opened fantastical theme parks, first in Billund in 1968 followed by sites in Windsor, England, Carlsbad, California, and Günzburg, Germany, where international landmarks are created entirely from LEGO bricks, among other attractions. The statistical record for the company is equally impressive: the Billund factory alone produces some 19 billion bricks per year, or 36,000 per minute. The core set of six LEGO bricks can be combined into 915,103,765 possible configurations. Since they first went into production in 1949, some 400 billion LEGO bricks have been manufactured and sold since 1949, which in 2006 meant that there was an average of 62 LEGO bricks for each person on earth. Only years later did the name that Ole Kirk Christiansen gave to his line of toys prove eerily prophetic in a universal language: in Latin, *lego* means "I put together" or "I assemble."

Books

Company Profiles for Students, edited by Donna Craft and Amanda Quick, Volume 1, Gale, 1999.

Periodicals

Investor's Business Daily, April 24, 2000.
New York Times, December 25, 1977.
Saturday Evening Post, October 1984.
Times (London, England), November 13, 1981; May 14, 1985. □

Frank Forrester Church, III

Elected to the U.S. Senate in 1956, Frank Church (1924-1984) spent 24 years in Congress as an advocate for progressive causes, including civil rights,

equal rights for women, wilderness preservation, and opposition to the Vietnam War. In the mid-1970s he gained notoriety for overseeing a Senate investigation that exposed some of the CIA and FBI's more controversial activities. Church's inquiry paved the way for passage of the Intelligence Oversight Act of 1980, which requires the agencies to report covert activities to an oversight committee in an effort to curb abuses of power.

Born to Middle-Class, Catholic Family

Frank Forrester Church, III, was born on July 25, 1924, in Boise, Idaho. His pioneering grandfather, raised on the East Coast, had relocated to Idaho at the height of the gold rush that followed the Civil War. Church was the second of two boys born to Frank and Laura Bilderback Church. His parents ran a modest but profitable sporting goods store in Boise. As a child, Church developed an affection for the outdoors, which was later reflected in the environmental legislation he supported. Church's father took him and his brother, Richard, on fishing expeditions and duck hunting trips. The wilderness around them also provided for plenty of swimming and hiking excursions.

As a student, Church impressed teachers with his interest in politics—he read the paper daily and was always eager to discuss current events. In the Frank Church biography *Fighting the Odds,* classmates described Church as a witty and confident, yet humble peer. "You always felt better being around him," one classmate recalled. As such, the Church home was the place neighborhood kids came to study, chat and play ping pong.

As an eighth grader, Church wrote an editorial letter to the *Boise Capital News,* laying out reasons the United States should stay out of the impending war in Europe. He touted the benefits of isolationism and noted that since U.S. territories were not at stake, the United States need not intervene. Church warned that winning the war would cost countless American lives and would not necessarily pave the way for democracy abroad. Skeptical that a 14-year-old could write such an articulate letter, the editor contacted Church's teachers to verify authorship, then printed the letter on the front page.

Intrigued by Politics

With a love for words, an interest in politics, and superb speaking abilities, Church joined the Boise High School debate team, then led it to a state championship. As a junior he won the 1941 American Legion National High School Oratorical Contest with a speech titled "The American Way of Life," in which he warned against the dangers of economic monopolies and recommended that American freedoms be preserved for future generations. The $4,000 scholarship prize allowed him to attend Stanford University.

During his senior year of high school, Church befriended Bethine Clark, the Democratic governor's daughter, and began hanging out at the governor's mansion. Church's interest in politics—and in the Democratic Party in particular—were born out of a desire to debate his father, a staunch Republican. As noted in *Fighting the Odds,* Church once said, "I learned all about the Democrats so I could argue with Dad. I ended up by converting myself."

Church's idealistic views on democracy and reason got him into trouble during his senior year. One evening a fight broke out after a basketball game and a classmate was arrested. Church rushed down to the jail to admonish authorities for violating the boy's civil liberties. Buoyed by his success on the debate team, Church believed he could win any argument. When Church arrived, the police chief grabbed him by the collar and threw him in jail. From behind bars, Church continued his tirade, quoting the Constitution and Declaration of Independence and insisting that his civil rights were being violated. He was freed, along with the other boy, a few hours later.

Battled Cancer

After graduating from high school in 1942, Church attended Stanford University. By then, Japan had attacked Pearl Harbor and the United States had joined World War II. Church enlisted in the Army and encouraged his friends to do the same. In early 1943 he completed basic training and was eventually commissioned as a second lieutenant. He was deployed to Asia, where he served as a military intelligence officer.

After returning from the war in 1946, Church finished his political science degree at Stanford and married Bethine Clark on June 21, 1947. The newlyweds road-tripped to Mexico, then headed to Boston so Church could start classes at Harvard Law School. That first semester, Church suffered severe back pains, which doctors attributed to long hours spent hunched over books. Church's health continued to deteriorate and he decided to transfer to the Stanford Law School, figuring California's warmer weather might make him feel better. In February of 1949, Church's groin swelled and a surgeon recommended a hernia operation. During the operation, the doctor discovered a cancerous testicular tumor, which he removed along with several lymph nodes.

Doctors told Church the cancer was incurable and gave him six months to live. He and Bethine Church fell into a deep depression—they had just become parents to a baby boy. They contemplated leaving the baby with grandparents in Boise and embarking on one last hurrah to Italy. There, they would drive off a cliff to end it all. A week after the initial diagnosis, another doctor was more optimistic and suggested the cancer might respond to new experimental radiation therapy. For several weeks doctors doused Church's torso daily with radium that burned his flesh and left him so nauseous he dry-heaved relentlessly. At one point, the 6-foot-tall Church was hospitalized and put on a feeding tube because he had dropped to 90 pounds.

Bethine Church read to her husband and helped nurse him back to health. According to *Fighting the Odds,* Church said that after surviving cancer, he felt compelled to take more chances in life. "I'd had a sentence of death passed upon me—a sentence that had been lifted. I was determined to make my life the better for it—personally, with my wife and children, and professionally in my career."

Won U.S. Senate Seat

Church finished law school in 1950 and returned to Boise to practice law and teach public speaking at the junior college. Two years later, he ran for a seat in the state legislature, but lost. Undaunted—and eager to take chances—Church set his sights higher and launched a campaign for the U.S. Senate in 1956.

As a virtual unknown who had never held public office, Church faced an uphill battle. He hit the road, shaking some 75,000 hands over the course of the campaign. During one campaign stop, Church spoke to a group of high schoolers and one of the teachers suggested he dust a little grey into his hair to set himself apart from the students. He went on to beat the state's incumbent Republican and become the fifth youngest member in the Senate's history.

Once in Washington, Church befriended Senate Majority Leader and future president Lyndon B. Johnson, helping push through the 1957 Civil Rights Act. Though the legislation dealt primarily with voting rights, it was the first civil rights legislation passed since the Reconstruction legislation that followed the Civil War. A noted voice in the Senate, Church became a national figure at 36 when he delivered the keynote address at the 1960 Democratic National Convention.

Opposed U.S. Involvement in Vietnam

By the early 1960s, U.S. troops were being sent into Vietnam to shore up the anti-Communist South Vietnamese army, which was locked in battle with North Vietnam. Church was one of the first politicians to protest U.S. involvement in the conflict. In 1965 he gave a speech on the Senate floor titled "Going from Bad to Worse in Vietnam." As deployment continued, Church began to publicly denounce the administration's insistence on sending U.S. troops to the area.

In November of 1965 the *New York Times* published a commentary by Church titled "How Many Dominican Republics And Vietnams Can We Take On?." In the article, Church suggested that the United States should not try to impose a solution to every insurgency abroad. "No nation—not even our own—possesses an arsenal so large, or a treasury so rich, as to damp down the fires of smoldering revolution throughout the whole of the awakening world," he wrote.

In 1969 Church joined forces with Republican Sen. John Sherman Cooper of Kentucky to co-sponsor the Cooper-Church Amendment. This measure prohibited U.S. troop deployment to Cambodia, touching off an extensive filibuster and a six-month debate. Though it eventually passed the Senate, the measure died in the House of Representatives. A watered-down version eventually passed—monumental because it was the first bill to curb presidential powers during a war situation. Church continued to call for the withdrawal of U.S. troops, and in April of 1975 the last U.S. soldiers left Saigon. South Vietnam fell within hours.

During the mid-1970s, Church gained national attention for his involvement in the so-called "Church Committees," which investigated U.S. intelligence agencies and multinational corporations for abuses of power. In 1975 Church headed the Senate's Select Committee to Study Governmental Operations With Respect to Intelligence Activities. The committee uncovered assassination plots by the CIA and found that the FBI had harassed dissident groups, conducted break-ins and illegally spied on U.S. citizens. The committee also found evidence of illegal wiretapping. The committee's findings led to the formation of a permanent oversight committee.

In 1976 Church entered the presidential primary, seeking the Democratic Party's nomination. He won primaries in Idaho, Nebraska, Oregon, and Montana before dropping out and endorsing former Georgia Governor Jimmy Carter, who went on to win the presidency. Realizing Church was an able diplomat, Carter leaned on him to negotiate relations with Cuban leader Fidel Castro in the late 1970s. In 1979 Church was named chairman of the Senate Foreign Relations Committee, a position he had aspired to for years.

Lost Senate Seat after 24 Years

As the 1980 elections neared and a wave of conservatism swept the country, Church found his Senate seat in jeopardy. He was placed on the short list of Democratic senators chosen for defeat by the Virginia-based National Conservative Political Action Committee. As a Democrat in a traditionally Republican state, Church was an ideal target. Months before the election, the committee launched an

"Anybody But Church" ad campaign across Idaho. Some of the accusations leveled against the Senator were erroneous, including one ad that said he voted to increase his pay by $13,000 in 1977. Church actually voted against the increase.

Antiabortion groups also jumped on the bandwagon. Church had a record of opposing abortions and had denied federal funding for the procedure. He did, however, approve of abortion in cases of incest or rape, or when a mother's health was at risk. One antiabortion group, Americans for Life, launched a mail campaign titled "Stop the Baby Killers," which targeted Church.

Church had a long record of opposing gun control and supporting agricultural interests in Idaho, which pleased constituents. He had also played a pivotal role in ensuring that Idaho's water was not diverted to surrounding states. In the end, these actions were not enough to carry him through, and he lost to GOP candidate Steve Symms by less than one percent of the vote. Analysts at the time said that Church was a capable politician whose only downfall was being too liberal for the conservative state he represented. After his defeat, Church practiced international law in Washington, D.C.

Died of Cancer

Four years after his election defeat, Church became ill with a pancreatic tumor and died at his home in Bethesda, Maryland, on April 7, 1984. He was 59. Survivors included his wife and two sons, F. Forrest Church and Chase Clark Church. In an effort to commemorate Church's years of service in the U.S. Senate, Congress in 1984 designated a 2.2-million-acre area of land the Frank Church River of No Return Wilderness area in his home state of Idaho.

Books

Ashby, LeRoy, and Rod Gramer, *Fighting the Odds: The Life of Senator Frank Church,* Washington State University Press, 1994.
Boise State University Library Special Collections Department, *The Frank Church Papers,* Boise State University, 1988.
Hall, Bill, *Frank Church, D.C., & Me,* Washington State University Press, 1995.

Periodicals

New York Times, November 7, 1956; May 25, 1960; November 28, 1965; December 27, 1979; April 8, 1984.
Wall Street Journal, August 28, 1979.
Washington Post, April 8, 1984. □

Samuel Coleridge-Taylor

The British composer Samuel Coleridge-Taylor (1875-1912) was the first major classical composer of African descent.

C oleridge-Taylor's 1898 choral work *Hiawatha's Wedding Feast* was extraordinarily widely known among British classical listeners in the early years of the twentieth century. Although it was later eclipsed in

popularity, it was performed all over the English-speaking world for several generations. Coleridge-Taylor was equally important as an early example of a composer who investigated the idea of an art rooted in the experience of the African diaspora, and his influence on African-American culture in the early decades of the twentieth century is just now beginning to gain its proper appreciation. Largely forgotten in the years after his untimely death, Coleridge-Taylor's works have been performed and recorded more and more often in recent times.

Early Years

The circumstances of Coleridge-Taylor's early life are tangled. Named for the British poet Samuel Taylor Coleridge, he was born on August 15, 1875, in London. His father, D.P.H. (Daniel Peter Hughes) Taylor, was African. Originally from Freetown, Sierra Leone, he was part of a Krio (or Creole) family that had been rescued from transport into American slavery by the British navy after the abolition of slavery in Britain. The elder Taylor came to London to study medicine, but his background apparently discouraged potential patients. He returned to Africa, apparently before his son was born, and he may not even have known of his existence. He later became a physician in Banjul, Gambia, and died there in 1904.

Coleridge-Taylor was raised in the London suburb of Croydon by his mother, whose name was Alice. She used various surnames, including Taylor's, even though they were probably never married. (He might have been a renter

in the boarding house her family operated.) She was also known as Alice Hare Martin, and she was later taken in by a family named Holmans. The patriarch of this family, Benjamin Holmans, was referred to by Coleridge-Taylor as his grandfather, and he may in fact have been Alice's father. It was Holmans who gave the young Coleridge-Taylor his first violin.

Suffering racial insults at school, including one incident in which his curly hair was set on fire, Coleridge-Taylor devoted himself to the violin with extra intensity. It was unusual for an English working class family to let a potential money-earning offspring take music lessons, but some of the Holmans family were musicians, and Coleridge-Taylor apparently showed enough talent to justify the outlay. He was given lessons with a local violinist named Joseph Beckwith, and in 1890 he entered the Royal College of Music in London.

By that time, Coleridge-Taylor had become interested in composition as well as violin performance. He had heard a number of classical concerts, probably at the Crystal Palace in south London not far from his home. In 1892 Coleridge-Taylor was accepted as a student by Royal College of Music professor Charles Villiers Stanford, one of the top composers in England at the time. In teaching Coleridge-Taylor about the music of German composer Johannes Brahms, Stanford made the assertion that it would be impossible to write a quintet for clarinet and strings without being influenced by Brahms's own sterling composition for that combination of instruments. Coleridge-Taylor took that as a dare and produced his own clarinet quintet, which has received several recordings in recent years. Stanford was forced to concede the originality of the young man's work, and Coleridge-Taylor became one of the school's star students. He received the Royal College of Music's sole composition fellowship in 1893. By the time he finished his studies in 1897, several of his student works, mostly chamber pieces (pieces for small groups of instruments), had been performed there.

Help From Hiawatha

Coleridge-Taylor also impressed Edward Elgar, the dean of British composers at the time, and Elgar recommended Coleridge-Taylor's Ballade in A minor for orchestra for presentation on the program at the 1898 Three Choirs Festival, one of Britain's most prestigious venues. Coleridge-Taylor followed that up with what was to be his greatest success: the giant cantata *Hiawatha's Wedding Feast,* set to a section of the "Song of Hiawatha" by American poet Henry Wadsworth Longfellow. A cantata is a work for chorus, soloists, and orchestra in which the singers often embody specific characters and make dramatic statements without the work being staged in the manner of an opera.

Hiawatha's Wedding Feast won rave notices in London newspapers and was an immediate smash hit; musical organizations all over England placed it on their schedules without having heard it. It became a staple of the choral-orchestral repertoire all over the English-speaking world, was performed as far afield as South Africa and New Zealand, and also became well known in the United States. In addition to its purely melodic qualities, Norman Lebrecht pointed out in the London *Evening Standard* that ideological factors that could have contributed to its success: "To its composer, *Hiawatha's Wedding Feast* paid tribute to native North Americans, dignified in defeat. To his audiences, it celebrated the white man's triumph, the superiority of his culture." During Coleridge-Taylor's lifetime the work remained a frequent presence on English concert programs; several sources state that it was equaled in popularity only by two similarly ambitious religious works, Handel's *Messiah* and Mendelssohn's *Elijah.*

Coleridge-Taylor set poetry by Shakespeare, Christina Rossetti, and other English writers to music, and many of his works stylistically resembled those of white English composers. However, even in his student days, he also showed an interest in creating an idiom that more closely reflected his African background, and in this enterprise he turned to African-American models. He heard the touring Fisk Jubilee Singers chorus from Nashville, Tennessee, and in 1896 he met the African-American poet Paul Lawrence Dunbar in London. He went on to set some of Dunbar's poems to music, and the two even collaborated in 1898 on a stage work, *Dream Lovers,* subtitled "An Operatic Romance." Coleridge-Taylor also wrote several orchestral works oriented toward Africa, including an *African Suite* and a set of *Symphonic Variations on an African Air.* Even the overture to *Hiawatha's Wedding Feast* incorporates the African-American spiritual "Nobody Knows the Trouble I've Seen."

In this tendency Coleridge-Taylor also took after another major white musician of the time: the Czech composer Antonin Dvorak, who on his visits to the United States had urged American composers to seek out African-American musical materials as inspiration for their own music. Coleridge-Taylor made three tours of the United States, in 1904, 1906, and 1910. A similar duality between English and African appeared in his experiences and music-making on those voyages. He often conducted the *Song of Hiawatha* so energetically that American observers dubbed him the Black Mahler after the famous Austrian composer and conductor. In 1904 he conducted the combined forces of the United States Marine Band and an African-American choir, which was called the Coleridge-Taylor Society in his honor. Subjected to racial epithets on a train, he answered angrily that he was an Englishman. He was invited to visit President Theodore Roosevelt in the White House, a rare honor indeed for a black person at the time. Coleridge-Taylor's 1906 tour took him through the Midwest to St. Louis, Detroit, and Milwaukee, and also to Toronto, Canada.

Coleridge-Taylor also furthered his activities in support of an emerging black classical music and of what was known as Pan-Africanism: the view that the works of African-descended creative artists were tied together by common qualities derived from their creators' African backgrounds. In the words of Stuart Jeffries of the London *Guardian,* Coleridge-Taylor "was regarded as an icon by pan-Africanists, the early 20th-century movement that contended that black people share an origin and that their cultural products should express particularly fundamental beliefs."

Coleridge-Taylor admired W.E.B. DuBois's 1903 book *The Souls of Black Folk,* calling it one of the best books he had read by any author, white or black. He was honored in turn by black American creative figures, and when he visited Washington, D.C., students at the M Street School for Girls presented him with a baton made from a cedar tree on the estate of abolitionist leader Frederick Douglass. Even today, many American communities have schools named for Coleridge-Taylor, and according to an essay by Blydon Jackson quoted on the Web site of the Cambridge Community Chorus, "American Negroes who were born in the earlier years of this century grew up in black communities where the name of Samuel Coleridge-Taylor was as well known then as now are such names as Martin Luther King Jr. and Malcolm X." Coleridge-Taylor's set of *Twenty-Four Negro Melodies, Op 59* were based on melodies such as "Deep River," many of which he had heard in performances by the Fisk Jubilee Singers. His program notes for those piano pieces, quoted on the AfriClassical Web site, stated that "what Brahms has done for the Hungarian folk music, Dvorak for the Bohemian, and Grieg for the Norwegian, I have tried to do for these Negro Melodies."

Despite these successes in America, Coleridge-Taylor's career in England was somewhat hampered by the lack of a fund of inherited wealth on which he could draw. In 1899 he married fellow Royal College of Music student Jessie Walmisley, and the pair had two children: a son, Hiawatha, born in 1900, and a daughter, Gwendolyn, known as Avril, born in 1903. Coleridge-Taylor took on a variety of high-profile but time-consuming posts in order to support his family. From 1904 until his death he was principal conductor at the Handel Society of London, and he held professorships at Trinity College of Music, the Crystal Palace School of Art and Music, and the Guildhall School of Music. He could never turn down a commission, and he continued to compose voluminously, providing incidental music for a London production of Shakespeare's *Othello* and writing an orchestral *Petite Suite* among other works. He never equaled the success of *Hiawatha's Wedding Feast.* Critics disagree about the musical value of his later works, with some venturing the opinion that they might have lacked inspiration because of the financial and time pressures that affected the composer.

On August 28, 1912, while waiting for a train at the West Croydon railway station, Coleridge-Taylor collapsed. He died on September 1 from pneumonia, the effects of which were likely compounded by exhaustion. He was just 37 years old. Coleridge-Taylor remained popular after his death, and several biographies of the composer appeared, including one by his wife. As the grandiloquent choral style represented by *Hiawatha's Wedding Feast* fell out of fashion, Coleridge-Taylor was largely forgotten, but the end of the twentieth century saw a tremendous revival of interest in his work. But *Dream Lovers,* which would potentially seem to be an important document in the evolution of the African-American musical, had not yet been recorded as of 2008, and the significance of Coleridge-Taylor's example in the evolution of urban African-American culture remained a fertile field of investigation.

Books

Baker's Biographical Dictionary of Music and Musicians, centennial ed., Nicolas Slonimsky, ed. emeritus, Schirmer, 2001.

Sayers, W. C. Berwick, *Samuel Coleridge-Taylor, Musician: His Life and Letters,* Cassell, 1915.

Self, Geoffrey, *The Hiawatha Man,* Scolar, 1915.

Tortolano, William, *Samuel Coleridge-Taylor: Anglo-black composer, 1875–1912,* Scarecrow, 1977.

Periodicals

American Record Guide, March-April 1996; July-August 1999.

Black Music Research Journal, Fall 2001.

Evening Standard (London, England), April 7, 2004.

Guardian (London, England), January 3, 2003.

News & Record (Piedmont Triad, NC), February 2, 2001.

Online

"Samuel Coleridge-Taylor," AfriClassical.com, http://www.africlassical.com (February 4, 2008).

"Samuel Coleridge-Taylor," Cambridge Chorus, http://www.cambridgechorus.org/docs/comps/SC-Taylor.html (February 4, 2008).

"Samuel Coleridge-Taylor," 100 Great Black Britons, http://www.100greatblackbritons.com/bios/samuel_coleridge-taylor.html (February 4, 2008). □

Billy Collins

American poet Billy Collins (born 1941) has worked to craft a poetic art that is accessible without being sentimental or crass.

Named poet laureate of the United States in the early 2000s, Collins became the public face of American poetry and embarked on an ambitious effort to insert poetry—not the teaching of poetry so much as the raw material of poems themselves—into American secondary schools. His own books have enjoyed a rare combination of popular and critical success, selling tens of thousands of copies and earning Collins large advance payments unheard-of for practitioners of poetic art. A distinctive feature of Collins's career is that his serious activity as a poet began only when he was well into middle age; he published his first substantial collection when he was 47. Collins blamed the prevalence of the idea that poetry should be difficult to understand for the weakness of his earlier efforts. "I wrote poems I hoped no one could understand," he told Bob Keefer of the Eugene, Oregon, *Register-Guard.* "If they did there would be no point in writing poetry. We still have to get over our mild hangover from that kind of modernism."

Nurtured Writing Ambitions

Billy Collins was born on March 22, 1941, in New York, to William S. Collins, an electrician, and Katherine S. Collins, a nurse. His parents were both over 40 when he was born, and he was an only child. The family's financial situation improved after his father landed a job with a Wall Street insurance brokerage, and they were able to move to subur-

ban Westchester County. From the start, Collins was enamored of the idea of becoming a writer. He wrote his first poem at age 12, and later joined the staff of his high school literary magazine.

English classes at school did not stimulate Collins's imagination, however. He recalled to *Teachers & Writers* magazine that the curriculum focused on "these rather antique poetry voices, mostly dead men with three names—William Cullen Bryant, Henry Wadsworth Longfellow, etc." Instead, it was Collins's father who steered him in the right direction—he noticed that copies of *Poetry* magazine were being discarded from the collection of publications at his Wall Street office, and he began bringing the magazine home. Collins enjoyed the contemporary poetic voices he found inside. "I remember reading a poem by Thom Gunn about Elvis Presley," he told *Teachers & Writers,* "and that was a real mindblower because I didn't know you could write poems about Elvis Presley. I thought there was poetry—what you read in class, you read 'Hiawatha' in class—and then when you left class there was Elvis. I didn't see them together until I read that poem."

Collins attended the College of the Holy Cross in Massachusetts, graduating in 1963. He moved west to the University of California at Riverside and worked toward a Ph.D. in English, studying nineteenth-century poetry of the Romantic era. He was still nurturing the idea of becoming a poet, and began emulating various contemporary poets in his own writing. One was the durable San Francisco poet Lawrence Ferlinghetti, whose free-verse style was rooted in the era of the Beat Generation. Another was the counterculture fiction writer and poet Richard Brautigan. "He was a real influence on me," Collins told Keefer. "I wrote bad imitative Richard Brautigan poems for a couple years in the 1970s. . . . He took the lessons of the French surrealists like [Guillaume] Apollinaire and gave them this Western American spin."

Nothing in those experiences, however, steered Collins toward a style of his own, and he remained unsatisfied with his work. "My bad poems were bad in the beginning because they were emotionally heavy, brooding, then profound and ponderous," he told *Newsweek*. Part of the problem was that he was gifted with an innate sense of humor, which his training in the works of the brooding Romantics had taught him to avoid—and humor was not a quality prized in the world of modern poetry, either. Collins sold some poems to *Rolling Stone* magazine for $35 each in the 1970s, and he published two small collections, *Pokerface* (1977) and *Video Poems* (1980). Newly married to his wife, Diane, an architect, he settled into a teaching job at Lehman College, part of the City University of New York.

Work Appeared with Major Publisher

Through the 1980s Collins's output was sparse. He reemerged with *The Apple That Astonished Paris,* published by the University of Arkansas Press in 1988, the title itself indicating a new attitude in his poetry. Collins's breakthrough to national prominence came with his next book, *Questions About Angels,* which won the 1990 National Poetry Series competition. As a result, the book was issued by the major Morrow publishing house in 1991, giving Collins access to an audience beyond academic readers and poetry specialists. As Collins's fame grew, the university presses that issued his first books jockeyed with commercial publishers for control of his poems; the University of Pittsburgh Press, one of his early supporters, was unwilling to give up the rights to what had become some of the most profitable items in its catalog.

Questions About Angels (1991) attracted mixed reviews, but it accomplished what most of his contemporaries had failed to do—it attracted a wide readership. *The Art of Drowning* (1995) and *Picnic, Lightning* (1998), along with *Questions About Angels,* sold tens of thousands of copies, almost unheard-of totals in a world where a volume of poetry selling 5,000 copies is considered a strong success. For three books beginning with 2001's *Sailing Around the Room: New and Selected Poems,* Collins received payment in six figures from the publisher Random House, which found its investment repaid when *Sailing Around the Room* passed the 100,000 sales mark.

The secret to Collins's success did not lie in any special simplicity or in any overt attempt to popularize his poetry. He used plain language and wrote about details of everyday surroundings, but some of his poems referred obliquely to poetic classics (opening *Poetry* magazine, he told *Teachers & Writers,* was "like looking into Chapman's Homer," echoing a famous work by British poet John Keats), and he relied in general on drawing readers into his works rather than making his writing transparent. One aspect of Collins's

appeal hinged on his ability to mix humor and seriousness in the same work. The title poem of *The Art of Drowning* imagines a drowning person who sees life flashing before his eyes, and suggests that a full-scale slide presentation would be more desirable, but later turns serious, describing the moment of death, the water's "surface now covered with the high/travel of clouds."

Collins's poetry flourished in live performance, and he gained added exposure when he appeared on the radio program *A Prairie Home Companion,* hosted by his friend Garrison Keillor. He seemed able to ennoble everyday scenes with poetry—as in "Snow Day," which described "the government buildings smothered/schools and libraries buried, the post office lost/under the noiseless drift. . . . In a while I will put on some boots/and step out like someone walking in water/and the dog will porpoise through the drifts. . . . But for now I am a willing prisoner in this house/a sympathizer with the anarchic cause of snow."

Named Poet Laureate

In 2001 Collins was named United States Poet Laureate (officially Poet Laureate Consultant to the Library of Congress), succeeding Stanley Kunitz. The position of poet laureate has been treated differently by its recipients, with some opting to use it as an opportunity to write. Collins, however, followed Robert Pinsky and many of his other predecessors in using the position as a platform from which to try and increase awareness of poetry in America, specifically in American schools. Collins's efforts were chronicled in a DVD, *On the Road with the Poet Laureate,* that chronicled his travels and readings. In 2002 Collins was reappointed as Poet Laureate for a second one-year term.

One of Collins's most visible initiatives as Poet Laureate was the creation of Poetry 180, a selection of 180 poems by various authors (the name and number were derived from the fact that an American school year consists of roughly 180 days), designed to be read aloud to students via public address system, one per day. Collins asked school personnel not to analyze the poems or give students assignments based on them, but merely to read them aloud—"no discussion, no explication, no quiz, no midterm, no seven-page paper—just listen to a poem every morning and off you go to your first class." The poems were posted on the Library of Congress Web site and also issued as a book, *Poetry 180: A Turning Back to Poetry.* They were so successful in that form that it was followed by a sequel, *180 More: Extraordinary Poems for Every Day.* Collins was partly motivated by his own almost accidental discovery of poetry as a young man—he believed that putting students in direct contact with accessible poems was the best way to interest some of them in the art.

Meanwhile, Collins continued to publish new poetry of his own and to find an enthusiastic audience for his work. *Sailing Alone Around the Room* was followed by *Nine Horses* in 2003, after which the poet took a detour into the world of children's literature with *Daddy's Little Boy* (2004). In 2006 he issued *The Trouble with Poetry,* which began with the wry lines, "The trouble with poetry/is that it encourages the writing of more poetry." In 2004 he served as

New York State Poet. He continues to live with his wife in Somers, New York.

Books

Authors and Artists for Young Adults. Vol. 64, Thomson Gale, 2005.

Periodicals

Buffalo News, December 1, 2003; November 17, 2006.
Commonweal, January 11, 2002.
Independent (London, England), May 31, 2003.
News & Record (Piedmont Triad, NC), March 28, 2004.
Newsweek, July 9, 2001.
Register-Guard (Eugene, OR), September 21, 2006.
Teachers & Writers, March-April 2002.
Writer, April 2006. □

Martin Cooper

American engineer Martin Cooper (born 1928) is often dubbed the father of the mobile phone. In November of 1972, he and a team of associates at the Motorola Company began working on a proto-type of the Dyna-Tac phone, and five months later Cooper stood on a Manhattan street and placed the world's first call from a mobile phone. "There were a lot of naysayers over the years," Cooper admitted in an interview with *Investor's Business Daily* writer Patrick Seitz. "People would say, 'Why are we spending all of this money? Are you sure this cellular thing will turn out to be something?' "

Cooper was born on December 26, 1928, in Chicago, Illinois, the son of Arthur and Mary Cooper. He was a tinkerer from an early age, recalling in an interview with *Seattle Times* journalist Yukari Iwatani, "I'd been taking things apart and inventing things since I was a little kid. . . . I still have memories as a child trying to really understand how things work." He graduated from the Illinois Institute of Technology in 1950, and from there enlisted in the U.S. Naval Reserves, serving on destroyers and a submarine. His first job was with the Teletype Corporation of Chicago, which made the units that provided remote communications services to media outlets.

Worked on New Police Radios

Cooper joined Motorola, Inc., of Schaumburg, Illinois, in 1954, and earned his master's degree in electrical engineering from the Illinois Institute of Technology three years later in 1957. At Motorola, he was assigned to the division that was working on the first portable handheld police radios, which were introduced in Chicago in 1967. By then he had advanced to the position of operations director, and over the next nine years he made his most significant contri-

bution to the future of mobile communications while serving the company.

Car-based mobile phones had been in limited use in large U.S. cities since the 1930s. By the early 1970s, they were used with a communications system called the Mobile Telephone Service, which carried signals over the same VHF (very high frequency) that FM radio stations used. Calls were placed not by dialing telephone numbers, but by locking onto specific channels. The system was unreliable and prone to congestion in urban areas, where it was impossible for more than 24 channels to operate on a given network. Moreover, the phones cost between $2,000 and $4,000 and had to be installed in an automobile because of the power source and antenna that were both required for use; waiting lists for an available account—which usually only came up when a subscriber chose to disconnect the service—could be as long as three years. Cooper believed that car phones were impractical from a deeper standpoint, however. "Our basic dream was that people didn't want to talk to cars," he told Iwatani, the *Seattle Times* writer. "They didn't want to talk to a desk or a wall (where phones were generally placed). They want to talk to other people."

Motorola's main competitor was Bell Laboratories, the research division of American Telephone & Telegraph Company (later known as AT&T). At the time, AT&T had a monopoly on traditional (so-called "landline") telephone service in the United States, and was working on a new form of mobile communication that it could offer its subscribers. An important technological breakthrough came with the idea that the phone's signal would be carried over a geographical area, passing from transmitter to transmitter in individual "cells" of territory. "AT&T announced they had a solution called a cellular phone for personal communications," Cooper explained about the battle between the two in an *Electronic Design* interview in 2003. "It had two attributes that were totally abhorrent to us: One that AT&T would operate a new cellular service as a monopoly; the other that the solution was car telephones. We had to prove to the world that both of these attributes were not in the public interest."

The Dyna-Tac

Motorola's legal team began working on a proposal to the Federal Communications Commission to win approval for private companies like itself to operate communications networks over radio frequencies, which would be a necessary step in entering the mobile-phone service market and prevent AT&T's continued monopoly. Motorola also needed to show the government agency that a working mobile phone was indeed feasible from a practical standpoint, despite AT&T's claims that car-based units were the future of communications. In November of 1972, Cooper and his team began working on a portable phone, and ran their first tests in Washington. The result was the Dyna-Tac, which the Motorola staffers dubbed "the shoe phone" for its design profile. It weighed 30 ounces, or nearly two pounds, and measured ten inches long, three inches deep, and one-and-a-half inches wide.

The public demonstration for the world's first mobile phone came on April 3, 1973, in New York City. Cooper and engineers at Motorola installed the first cellular transmitter atop the Burlington Consolidated Tower (later renamed the Alliance Capital Building) on Sixth Avenue. Prior to walking into a scheduled press conference at the New York Hilton, Cooper took out the Dyna-Tac prototype and pressed the off-hook button, which connected him to a base station. From there, he dialed into the landline system and, ignoring curious looks of passers-by, called his rival at Bell Labs, Joel Engel, and "told him: 'Joel, I'm calling you from a "real" cellular telephone. A portable handheld telephone,' " Cooper recalled in an interview with BBC correspondent Maggie Shiels. Asked what Engel's response was years later, Cooper could not remember the exact words, but admitted to *New York Times* writer Ted Oehmke that Bell Labs was "a little bit annoyed. They thought it was impertinent for a company like Motorola to go after them."

The *New York Times* duly ran an article the next day, on April 4, with the headline "Motorola Introduces Wire-Less Telephone." The reporter assigned to cover the Motorola press conference, Gene Smith, related that journalists were allowed to make calls from the phone, and predicted that the network would probably be ready for subscribers by 1976. Monthly costs would be $60 to $100 a month, but could drop to $10 a month by the early 1990s, Smith reported. Of Cooper's device itself, the newspaper quoted him as saying that it "eliminates the phone cord. All information today goes on the wire, including dialing and hanging up the phone. Through the use of a few integrated

circuits, chips, and devices, we are performing the functions of tens of thousands of parts in the normal phone system."

Became Vice President

Cooper's Dyna-Tac appeared on the July 1973 cover of *Popular Science* magazine, and the technological breakthrough helped Motorola achieve its goal of winning FCC permission for private companies to operate a wireless communications network over radio frequencies. The achievement also boosted his profile within the company, and he was made a division manager at Motorola in 1977 and then vice president and corporate director for research and development a year later. In 1983, the same year that the first commercial cellular phone service began operation in the United States, Cooper left Motorola to found his own company, Cellular Business Systems, Inc. This Chicago-area software company handled billing for cellular phone service providers, and was sold to Cincinnati Bell in 1986.

In the earliest years of wireless communication phone service, Cooper and Motorola appeared to have lost their ideological battle with AT&T, as car phones dominated the market. Smaller, lightweight portable mobile phones did not make significant inroads with consumers until the early 1990s. He remained convinced of the practicality of his original concept, however. "A telephone number shouldn't represent a home or a car or a restaurant, but instead a person," he explained to Peter Meade in *America's Network* in 1997. "That vision is not complete. That is why I'm still working." He noted that avid users of mobile phones in Japan, for example, were canceling their residential landline phone service. "Why would anyone want any other phone but one with their own personal phone number? It's the dream of AT&T realized: When you're born, you are assigned a phone number—and if you don't answer, you're dead," he told Meade.

Envisioned Wireless Internet

By then Cooper had served as chair and chief executive officer of another company, Cellular Pay Phone Inc., and in 1992 signed on with Arraycomm Inc., in Del Mar, California, as chair and chief executive officer. The firm was founded by two other inventors and was working on wireless Internet applications, which Cooper saw as the next breakthrough in mobile communications services. "Cellular was the forerunner to true wireless communications," he told Oehmke in the *New York Times* in 2000. "And just as people got used to taking phones with them everywhere, the way people use the Internet is ultimately going to be wireless. With our technology, you will be able to open your notebook anywhere and log on to the Internet at a very high speed with relatively low cost . . . when people get used to logging on anywhere, well, that's going to be a revolution."

Cooper is not a household name, but is well-known inside wireless technology circles. For years, he was often photographed with that Dyna-Tac prototype he had used to make the world's first mobile phone call back in 1973. Often asked if he was surprised at the ubiquity of the device for which he was granted U.S. Patent No. US3906166 for a "Radio telephone system" on October 17, 1973, he conceded that seeing scores of mobile-phone callers on that same Manhattan sidewalk 30 years later might have indeed seemed a bit far-fetched at the time, noting that even "in 1983 those first phones cost $3,500, which is the equivalent of $7,000 today," he told Shiels, the BBC correspondent. "But we did envision that some day the phone would be so small that you could hang it on your ear or even have it embedded under your skin." He also admitted to a certain satisfaction that his original idea for a wireless telephone had caught on with the rest of the world. "Freedom is what cellular is all about," he said in the same interview. "It pleases me no end to have had some small impact on people's lives because these phones do make people's lives better. They promote productivity, they make people more comfortable, they make them feel safe and all of those things."

Cooper went on to win several more patents, and was still active in the wireless technology business in 2007. He had two children from his first marriage, and in 1991 he married Arlene Harris, a co-founder of Cellular Business Systems. An avid skier and fitness enthusiast, he claims to keep his mind active by completing *New York Times* crossword puzzles. He still gave press interviews—over a standard phone line, ironically—and admitted to Todd Wallack of the *Houston Chronicle* that "I am talking now on a land line. I get as frustrated as you do with wireless service. I get infuriated because I know what the technology is capable of."

Periodicals

America's Network, March 1, 1997.
Business Week, June 19, 2000.
Electronic Design, October 20, 2003.
Electronic News, August 22, 1983.
Houston Chronicle, April 13, 2003.
Investor's Business Daily, September 27, 2005.
New York Times, April 4, 1973; June 23, 1985; January 6, 2000.
Seattle Times, April 7, 2003.
Telecommunications, August 1998.

Online

Shiels, Maggie, "A Chat with the Man Behind Mobiles," BBC News, http://news.bbc.co.uk/2/hi/uk_news/2963619.stm (December 28, 2007). □

Nancy Cunard

Poet, publisher, and professional radical Nancy Cunard (1896-1965) used both craft and cunning to fight for the equality of races, of sexes, and of classes.

The Reluctant Heiress

Nancy Clara Cunard was born at the 13,000–acre estate of Nevill Holt on March 10, 1896 in Leicestershire, England—the only child of third baronet Sir Bache Edward Cunard and Lady Maude Alice (Burke)

Cunard. Sir Bache had inherited the wealth of the Cunard family shipping line, while Lady Cunard—an American–born socialite from San Francisco living in England—stirred passionate opinions in everyone she met, both celebrated later in her daughter's obituary from *The Times* as a "brilliant hostess, conversationalist and patron of the arts" and maligned in the *Encyclopedia of Women Social Reformers* as an "outrageous snob, and wit, famous for her put–downs." She included her daughter Nancy in the parties and gatherings of prominent aesthetes of the time—writers, artists, politicians and musicians.

In 1910, Cunard's mother left Sir Bache and took her daughter to London where she became involved with conductor Sir Thomas Beecham and changed her name to Lady "Emerald" Cunard. While in Europe, Cunard attended schools in London, Paris and Germany. It was in London, in 1914 however, that Cunard began to assert herself and gather the circle of friends that would later be known as the "Corrupt Coterie"—Iris Tree, Dianna Manners, Osbert Sitwell, Augustus John and Ezra Pound. In 1916, Edith Sitwell printed Cunard's poetry in the publication *Wheels,* and on November 15 of that same year she married Sidney George Fairbairn—a wounded Grenadier Guard soldier. The openly rebellious heiress's conventional marriage shocked and puzzled everyone, but the relationship evaporated twenty months later and was legally annulled in 1925, at which point she took back her maiden name.

Cultural Awakening

In 1919, Cunard suffered through a bout of the Spanish flu epidemic that left her permanently weakened, but her fragile health failed to dampen what would prove to be an adventurous interest in gifted men. Cunard was reported to have had affairs with a wealth of talented male colleagues, including authors Michael Arlen and Aldous Huxley and surrealist intellectual Louis Aragon. In 1920 Cunard moved to Paris and met the Dadaists, Surrealists, and other expatriate American artists and authors living there at that time. She lived with Arlen, during which time she had a mysteriously unexplained hysterectomy and appendectomy that almost killed her. It was rumored that she was affiliated with the Communist party, and some sources confirm that it was at this time that Cunard developed what would become a life–long addiction to drugs and alcohol.

Cunard also attended Virginia Woolf's private London school, where she excelled as a student and eventually became friends with the famous author and her husband, Leonard. She published two poetry collections, *Outlaws* (1921) and *Sublunary* (1923). In 1925 the Woolfs' Hogarth Press published Cunard's third and final poetry collection titled *Parallax*—a single poem about estrangement and belonging that ran for more than 500 lines. It was approved by some, but largely dismissed by critics as being too imitative of T.S. Eliot's *The Waste Land* (1922).

Cunard was a faithful member of avant–garde literary and artistic circles in both France and England in the 1920s. She was living with Aragon, who had attempted suicide when Cunard left him in 1926, when she saw African–American jazz musician Henry Crowder perform in a night club and they began a public and controversial relationship that quickly tuned her in to the problems of racism in the United States.

From Poet to Publisher

In 1927, Cunard bought a farmhouse in Reanville, just outside of Paris, and set up a press that would give her the opportunity to publish inventive and contentious works of her choosing. In 1928 she established The Hours Press and published, among others, Richard Aldington, Ezra Pound, Samuel Beckett, Louis Aragon, George Moore, Robert Graves, and Laura Riding. The Hours Press was active for only four years because Cunard quickly became an aggressive and outspoken advocate for the rights of African Americans, which prompted her to devote all her time and efforts to a new project that would address issues of prejudice and race.

Cunard and Crowder suffered significant and sometimes violent discrimination when they moved to New York and lived in Harlem briefly, where she spoke to blacks about their rights and experiences. Cunard was impressed with the Harlem renaissance, but openly critical of blacks for what she saw as a disinterest in their African heritage. She also became deeply involved in the Scottsboro Boys trial, organizing public protests in an effort to support nine young black boys—aged thirteen to nineteen—who had been falsely accused but convicted and sentenced to death in Montgomery, Alabama for reportedly assaulting a pair of young white girls on a train.

Some sources claim that Cunard successfully transformed or evolved from mere aesthete to political activist, calling other writers and artists of the time to stand up and take a side on controversial issues. In 1931 Cunard wrote and published an opposition piece titled *Black Man and White Ladyship*, described in *The Feminist Companion to Literature in English* as a "bridge–burning attack" in response to her mother's negative reaction to Cunard's relationship with Crowder. But it was in 1934 that Cunard edited and published *Negro*—described by *The Bloomsbury Guide to Women's Literature* as a "civil liberties plea," whereas Caroline Weber of the *New York Times* called it "an anthology of black history and culture," and "a call to 'condemn racial discrimination and appreciate the . . . accomplishments of a long–suffering people.'"

Negro tipped the scales at close to 900 pages written by over 150 benefactors—including "Harlem Renaissance man" Langston Hughes, activist and scholar W.E.B. Du Bois, authors Theodore Dreiser and Claude McKay and folklorist Zora Neale Hurston. It contained poetry, history, photographs, manifestos, rants, ethnographies, hate mail, confidential military material, ads, comics, folk songs and scores, maps and reproductions of artworks. Cunard wrote the preface and published the broad volume at her own expense, but it was met with critical disdain and included material that pleased some but also managed to offend most people in one way or another. As Laura Winkiel explains in *Nancy Cunard's NEGRO and the Transnational Politics of Race*, the anthology was essentially a collection that attempted to "reconstruct a past that is lost . . . that, if recontextualized and recirculated, might compose an alternative future." She noted how "Cunard herself commented very little on the . . . [scandals]" she was personally involved in, believing that the " 'sex–scandal' [was] merely an effort to detract from antiracist work."

From Publisher to Activist

Cunard, who had lived through World War I, followed her passion for fighting fascist regimes to Spain where she served as a relief worker during that country's civil war, organizing the transfer of food parcels from Britain to Spain. Cunard also acted as a journalist for the *Manchester Guardian* and the *Associated Negro Press* while in Spain. In a *Columbia University Press* interview about her 2007 biography, *Nancy Cunard: Heiress, Muse, Political Idealist* (hailed by the *International Herald Tribune* as the "first substantial study to be published in almost 30 years"), Lois Gordon—English professor at Fairleigh Dickinson Unversity—described how Cunard served in the Spanish Civil War by "carry[ing] the wounded to safety. . . feed[ing] the hungry . . . walk[ing] with refugees . . . brib[ing] guards to give food to starving . . . soldiers . . . [seeking] homes for the refugees in Central America . . . work[ing] with underground organizations . . . [and engaging] in guerilla activities."

In 1937 she and Chilean poet Pablo Neruda invited British writers to take a stand on the Spanish conflict and published the results in the booklet *Authors Take Sides*. In 1937 Cunard joined the British Delegation to the Second Congress of the International Association of Writers for the Defense of Culture in Madrid, Spain—campaigning for the rights of Republican prisoners and Spanish refugees in France following Franco's conquest. She also traveled as far as South America, the Caribbean and Tunisia to better understand the imprint left by colonialism, always returning to raise the issues of race and class in Britain.

In 1944 Cunard put out an anthology of poems honoring France and its people that got her included in Adolf Hitler's list of enemies. Following its release, her home in Reanville was vandalized by locals and occupying German soldiers, and as a result, she took to traveling.

Debutante in Decline

Cunard wrote two memoirs, the 1954 *Grand Man* about Norman Douglas, and *G.M.*, about George Moore two years later, but her physical and mental health declined rapidly and she suffered from episodes of drunken paranoia that drove away friends and antagonized police. She was arrested, among other things, for throwing her shoes at police officers and eating a train ticket rather than giving it to the conductor of a train traveling across France. She was ordered to check into the Holloway Sanatorium for four months, after which she lived a grim life until, broken both in body and mind, she cut herself off from even her closest friends. Cunard died alone in the Hopital Côchin—a charity hospital in Paris—on March 17, 1965. She was 69 years old. The official cause of death was natural causes and severe emphysema from years of heavy smoking. She was cremated and her remains were buried in the Père Lachaise Cemetary in Paris.

Those who knew Cunard assert that she was never comfortable with the fact that she became a symbol of the "roaring twenties" rather than being taken seriously. In *Contemporary Authors*, Critic Chris Hopkins pointed out that Cunard's personal life tends to be discussed more widely than her prose and her poetry, but despite any judgments about the merit of her writing, Cunard's works are important because they offer "insights . . . into the aesthetic and political possibilities of poetry in the period 1916 to 1940" and provide "a unique perspective on some of the most important issues of her time." The posthumously released *These Were the Hours* (1969) added to Cunard's substantial legacy.

While Cunard was an infamous figure in her lifetime, her work remains little known to modern readers. Labeled in *The Bloomsbury Guide to Women's Literature* as an "indomitable rebel" and portrayed in the *International Herald Tribune* as an "unconventional child of privilege," many sources are surprisingly disparaging. Cunard's biographical entry in *The Feminist Companion to English Literature* states that she "left her mother's fashionable, establishment circle to conduct a sexually and socially unorthodox life." and her *Women in World History* biographical sketch describes Cunard as "the archetypal spoiled English upper–class rich girl . . . [who] often suffered from lack of direction and purpose in life . . . [and] engaged in shocking behavior, alienated friends and family, and treated her many lovers as sexual objects to be used and discarded." The author also describes Cunard as "beautiful, tall, slender, aggressive, reckless, sexually promiscuous, unconventional to an extreme, and an immutable hater."

Advocate and Muse

One fact remains irrefutable, however: Nancy Cunard inspired. Dadaist playwright Tristan Tzara dedicated a play to her. Sculptor M. Constantin Brancusi crafted a wooden image of her, and photographer Man Ray chose her as a subject repeatedly—producing, among others, the iconic portrait of Cunard wearing stacks of African ivory bracelets and looking away from the camera. Samuel Beckett infused a long, notable speech with her name in his famous play *Waiting for Godot*, and male authors of the day—from T.S. Eliot and Michael Arlen to Ezra Pound, Aldous Huxley and Ernest Hemingway—created fictional characters based on her, many of which have since been given the weight of personal accounts. As quoted from the Spartacus Schoolnet Web site, Langston Hughes wrote in 1965 that Cunard was "kind and good and catholic and cosmopolitan and sophisticated and simple all at the same time and a poet of no mean abilities and an appreciator of the rare and the off–beat . . . she had an infinite capacity to love peasants and children and great but simple causes across the board and a grace in giving that was itself gratitude."

Whether marginalized or completely ignored, scorned or celebrated, Nancy Cunard fought conventions in ways that many felt made her dangerous. George Seldes wrote—as recorded by the Spartacus Schoolnet Web site—that "We who talk and write about nonconformity rarely have the courage to live the lives of nonconformists, but Nancy Cunard had the courage and paid the price society still demands." One might argue that Cunard's character and historical status is still paying the price.

Books

Beckett in Black and Red: The Translations for Nancy Cunard's NEGRO (1934), edited by Alan Warren Friedman, University Press of Kentucky, 2000.

The Bloomsbury Guide to Women's Literature, edited by Claire Buck, Bloomsbury Publishing Ltd., 1992.

Contemporary Authors: Volume 219, The Gale Group, Inc., 2004.

Dictionary of Literary Biography, Volume 240: Late Nineteenth– and Early Twentieth–Century British Women Poets, edited by William B. Thesing, The Gale Group, 2001.

An Encyclopedia of British Women Writers, edited by Paul Schlueter and June Schlueter, Rutgers University Press, 1998.

Encyclopedia of Women Social Reformers, edited by Helen Rappaport, ABC–CLIO, Inc., 2001.

The Feminist Companion to Literature in English: Women Writers from the Middle Ages to the Present, edited by Virginia Blain, Patricia Clements and Isobel Grundy, Yale University Press, 1990.

The New York Times: Sunday Book Review, April 1, 2007.

Obituaries from the Times 1961–1970, compiled by Frank C. Roberts, Newspaper Archive Developments Limited, 1975.

Women in World History: A Biographical Encyclopedia, edited by Anne Commire, Yorkin Publications, 1999.

Periodicals

Biography, Summer 2007.

Cineaste, v25 no4, 2000.

The Globe and Mail (Canada), June 16, 1979.

Modernism/modernity, vol 13 no 3, 2006.

Online

"Interview with Lois Gordon," Columbia University Press, http://www.columbia.edu/cu/cup/publicity/gordoninterview.html (November 13, 2007).

"Nancy Cunard," Spartacus Schoolnet, http://www.spartacus.schoolnet.co.uk/Wcunard.html (November 13, 2007).

"Nancy Cunard, 1896–1965 Biographical Sketch," Harry Ransom Humanities Research Center, http://www.hrc.utexas.edu/research/fa/cunard.n.bio.html (November 13, 2007).

"Nancy Cunard: A troubled heiress with an ideological mission," *International Herald Tribune,* http://www.iht.com/articles/2007/03/29/arts/IDSIDE31.php (November 13, 2007).

"Nancy Cunard: Heiress, Muse, Political Idealist," Columbia University Press, http://www.columbia.edu/cu/cup/publicity/cunardexcerpt1.html (November 13, 2007).

"Poster-Man Ray: Nancy Cunard," Image Exchange, http://www.imageexchange.com/featured/manray/6900.shtml (November 13, 2007). □

D

Alexandra David-Néel

French explorer and author Alexandra David-Néel (1868-1969) led a remarkable life. A scholar of Buddhism and Eastern religions, David-Néel traveled into the hidden kingdom of Tibet in 1924 and is believed to be the first Western woman ever to visit the holy city of Lhasa, the center of Tibetan Buddhism. It was one of several impressive journeys she made during her lifetime, some of which she chronicled in the more than two dozen books she authored in her later years.

David-Néel claimed to have been plagued by wanderlust from her earliest memories. She was born Louise Eugénie Alexandrine Marie David in Saint-Mandé, a suburb of Paris, France, on October 24, 1868. Her father was a French journalist and teacher, and her mother was a native of Belgium, to which the family moved when David-Néel was six years old. Even back in Saint-Mandé, David-Néel said she was eager to explore further than the confines of her yard, and recalled years later that she made her first break for the street when she was just two years old. Later in her youth, she was distressed by the long, idle vacations her family took, which were common among the European middle classes of the era. "I cried bitter tears more than once, having the profound feeling that life was going by, that the days of my youth were going by, empty, without interest, without joy," David-Néel wrote, according to a Web site devoted to her works, Alexandra-David-Neel.org. "I understood that I was wasting time that would never return, that I was losing hours that could have been beautiful."

Bicycled Across Europe

At the age of 17, David-Néel boarded a Switzerland-bound train at the Brussels station, and managed to venture across the Saint Gotthard Pass in the Swiss Alps and made her way to Lake Maggiore in Italy, where her mother came to collect her. A year later, at the age of 18, she tied her possessions onto the handlebars of a bicycle and set off for Spain. On that trip she also made her way to London, where she became involved in a study group associated with the Theosophical Society of Madame Blavatsky (1831–1891). Blavatsky was a well-traveled Russian émigré interested in Eastern religions and the occult and whose Society and celebrity status served to arouse curiosity among Britons and other Europeans in non-Western belief systems.

When David-Néel turned 21 in 1889, she was considered an adult and able to live as she pleased. She moved to Paris, where she audited courses in Eastern religions at the Sorbonne University—women were not permitted as degree-earning students at the time—and spent hours devoted to the same subject at the reading room of the Guimet Museum of Asian art. Her desire to visit exotic lands was finally quenched in 1890, when she went to India after receiving an inheritance from her grandmother. She stayed until her funds ran out, and for the next few years earned a living by singing in a traveling opera company under the stage name Mademoiselle Myrial. The company visited many of France's far-flung colonies—likely the appeal of the job for David-Néel—including North Africa, where in Tunis, Algeria, she met Philippe Néel, a railroad engineer. They wed in 1904, but spent many years apart due to David-Néel's extended journeys. She also kept her maiden name but added her husband's and created a hyphenated name, a relatively rare practice at the time.

David-Néel began to gain some renown in France as an authority on Eastern religions, and earned money by giving lectures. In 1911, she returned to India, this time with the help of a grant from the French Ministry of Education, and studied Sanskrit in Benares, the Hindu holy city. On this trip she was introduced to the thirteenth Dalai Lama (1876–1933), born Thubten Gyatso, who had recently fled Tibet when Chinese troops invaded the neighboring mountain kingdom. For centuries the Dalai Lamas had been the heads of government in Tibet, and were considered to be the incarnation of the Buddhist god of compassion, Avalokiteśvara. Rarely constrained by the deference expected of her gender in either Western or Asian cultures, David-Néel was able to ask and receive answers to several questions on spiritual enlightenment from the Dalai Lama, which is believed to have made her the first white woman ever to address the leader of Tibetan Buddhism on such topics.

Lived in a Cave

David-Néel went on to the royal monastery in the nearby kingdom of Sikkim, where she met the crown prince, Sidkeong Tulku Namghyal, who would ascend to the throne of the tiny land that was wedged between Nepal and Tibet, in 1914. There were rumors the two were romantically involved. From 1914 to 1916, hoping to journey further on her quest for Buddhist enlightenment, David-Néel spent more than a year in a cave in Sikkim, though assigned helpers camped nearby and brought her one meal a day. One of them was a Sikkimese monk named Aphur Yongden,

who would spend the remainder of his life at David-Néel's side as her traveling companion and later her adopted son.

In 1916, David-Néel and Yongden became trespassers when they crossed the border into Tibet. The country had been closed to foreigners for several decades by then, because its leaders feared the encroaching Russian and British empires and were wary of permitting the country to become part of the trade route to India, which would have destroyed its unique character. British colonial authorities, who had jurisdiction over Sikkim, learned of the transgression and deported her and Yongden. They were unable to return to Europe, however, because World War I had disrupted passenger-ship travel, and so they traveled to Japan instead. There they met Ekai Kawaguchi (1866–1945), a Buddhist monk of Japanese birth and some renown. He had visited Tibet's holy city of Lhasa back in 1901 after having disguised himself as a Chinese physician.

David-Néel decided they, too, would disguise themselves and venture into the forbidden city of Lhasa, which was populated largely by monks. She and Yongden began to make their way across China, a trip of some two thousand miles that was conducted partially on foot. For a time in the early 1920s they stayed at a famed monastery called Kum-Bum, considered the birthplace of Tibetan Buddhism, where she translated Tibetan sacred texts into French. During the winter of 1922–23, David-Néel and Yongden were discovered traveling in the Gobi Desert region near Tibet, and were expelled by authorities. They did, however, manage to arrive in Lhasa in 1924, this time via the southeast route along with a group of other Buddhist pilgrims. David-Néel had disguised herself as a Tibetan woman, with Yongden claiming to be her son, and she darkened her face each morning by rubbing her hand on the bottom on the only pot they had brought with them.

Book Captivated French Readers

David-Néel spent two months in Lhasa, and returned to France in the spring of 1925. The magazine articles she wrote about her journey became the book *Voyage d'une Parisienne a Lhassa à Pied et en Mendiant de la Chine à l'Inde à Travers le Thibet,* which caused a sensation when it was published in France in 1927 along with its English version, *My Journey to Lhasa: The Personal Story of the Only White Woman Who Succeeded in Entering the Forbidden City.* Reviewing it in the *New York Times* on June 12, 1927, Alma Luise Olson found it a fascinating, if a bit vague read, wishing that David-Néel might have provided more details on how Buddhist monks endured freezing cold conditions by raising their internal body temperature, for example, which the explorer claimed to have mastered. Despite these lack of details, Olson wrote that David-Néel's "journey reveals amazing and almost incredible powers of physical endurance. . . . In peasant homes she slept on the floors on greasy sackcloth and drank nauseating, evil-smelling broths from her bowl that she must later cleanse, native fashion, by licking with her tongue." Though David-Néel claims to have visited the royal palace of Potala, she did not remove her disguise and renew her acquaintance with the Dalai Lama.

David-Néel was awarded the Gold Medal of the Geographical Society of France, and named a chevalier of the French Legion of Honor. With the proceeds from her book's sales she bought a house in Digne-les-Bains, in the south of France, where Yongden lived with her. She was still married to Philippe Néel, and though they lived apart for some time he remained supportive, both financially and emotionally, until his death in 1941. Though she was nearing her seventieth birthday, David-Néel was far from retired, and spent several years writing more books on Tibet and Buddhism. In 1937, at the age of 69, she decided to return to the part of western China where the Kum-Bum monastery was located, in the remote Qinghai area, and she and Yongden journeyed across the Soviet Union to China. They were forced to remain in the country several years longer than planned, however, when World War II erupted.

Inspired Beat Poets

The titles of works written by David-Néel include *Buddhism: Its Doctrines and Its Methods,* published in the United States in 1939, and *The Secret Oral Tradition in Tibetan Buddhist Sects,* published by San Francisco's famed City Lights bookstore in 1964. City Lights played a vital role in the rise of the Beat poets like Allen Ginsberg (1926–1997). Ginsberg asserted that it was David-Néel's writings that deepened his interest in Buddhism and led him to formally convert to the religion, and the influential poet and counterculture figure in turn influenced a generation of young adults who, like David-Néel had been so many years before, deeply skeptical of the middle-class values and tenets of her parents' world.

David-Néel's long-time traveling partner Yongden was said to have drank heavily for many years, and died in 1955. David-Néel lived to a remarkable age of 100, dying in Digne-les-Bains just six weeks before her next birthday. In 1973, her ashes—along with Yongden's—were scattered on the waters of the Ganges River near Benares. Her house is now the Alexandra David-Néel Museum, open year round to visitors.

Periodicals

Geographical, July 2005.
New York Times, June 12, 1927.
World and I, September 2004.

Online

"Biography," Alexandra-David-Neel.org, http://www.alexandra-david-neel.org/anglais/biog2.htm (December 1, 2007). □

Shah Waliullah Dehlavi

Indian religious leader Shah Waliullah Dehlavi (1703-1762) was an influential Islamic reformer who sought to regenerate Muslim society in Asia. A prolific writer, he produced 51 important Islamic texts.

Through his writings and his teachings, as well as the life he led, Shah Waliullah Dehlavi inspired subsequent generations of Islamic followers who carried on his reformation mission after his death. Today people consider his writings to represent his most important achievement, especially his translation of the Holy Quran into a popular language, which made that religious text more accessible to a greater number of people.

Shah Waliullah Dehlavi was born on February 21, 1703, in the town of Phulat in Muzaffarnagar, Uttar Pradesh, India, as the reign of Aurangzeb, the Mughal emperor of India, was nearing its end. (Four years later, Aurangzeb died.) He was born as Qutb-ud-Din, but he would come to be better known as Shah Waliullah, an appellation that indicated his inherent goodness and spirituality.

His grandfather, Sheikh Wajihuddin, was a high-ranking military officer in the army of Shah Jahan, who sided with Prince Aurangzeb in the war of succession. His father, Shah Abdur Rahim, was a Sufi and an illustrious scholar who helped compile the *Fataawa-i-Alamgiri,* the huge written work of Islamic law. He taught at the Madrassa-i-Rahimiya, a theological college, or seminary, that he helped establish. The institution would become an important part of the religious emancipation of Muslim India, as it provided a starting point for later religious reformers.

Precocious Scholar

Shah Waliullah received his basic education from his grandfather, but his father later provided him with his academic and spiritual education. When he was only five years old, Shah Waliullah was introduced to Islamic education. Two years later he could recite the Holy Quran. Obviously, he was a precocious scholar. He was only ten years old when he was able to read from the *Interpretation by Ja'mi,* an acclaimed grammar book. Around this time he also gained knowledge of Tafseer, Hadith, spiritualism, mysticism, metaphysics, logic, and Ilm-ul-Kalam. Once introduced to Persian and Arabic languages, he was able to complete his lessons in one year. After that he concentrated on grammar and syntax. On top of all that, he studied medicine.

After his father died, Shah Waliullah, who was then 17 years old, became an educator at the Madrassa-i-Rahimiya. He taught there for 12 years, providing guidance to fellow Muslims on their spirituality and reformation. A deeply devout person, Shah Waliullah adhered to the Islamic custom of offering prayer five times a day. The Madrassa-i-Rahimiya would become the center of the Islamic Renaissance in the Indian subcontinent, as it attracted scholars from all parts of the country. After their training, they carried the seminary's teaching throughout the region.

Experienced Vision in Arabia

In 1730 Shah Waliullah went on to pursue higher studies in Arabia. He studied at Makkah and Madina, two renowned educational institutions, where he developed a reputation as a brilliant scholar. In all, he studied for 14 years in Madina, where he received his Sanad in Hadith (the oral traditions related to the teachings and the life of the Holy Prophet Muhammad). At the time, he also became aware that the Marathas (invading warriors from the Maratha Empire) staged continuous attacks within India, where they looted the wealth of the Muslims.

According to accounts, while he was in Arabia, Shah Waliullah received a vision of the Holy Prophet Muhammad, who commanded that he work to organize and then emancipate the Muslim community in India. Apparently in response to this vision, Shah Waliullah returned to Delhi on July 9, 1732, where he began what he considered to be his life's mission.

Became a Muslim Leader

In pursuing this mission, Shah Waliullah faced a formidable task. At the time, Muslim India was in chaos socially, politically, economically and spiritually. But Shah Waliullah identified the causes of the problems and indicated appropriate remedies. He was critical of the non-Islamic customs that had become integrated into Muslim society, mostly as a result of the Muslim society's exposure to Hinduism. Specifically, he denounced extravagant marriage ceremonies and festivals. Also, he determined the causes of the economic erosion in the Muslim society and proposed appropriate changes, including greater distribution of wealth, a concept that predated the economic theories of Karl Marx, the nineteenth-century philosopher and economist who denigrated capitalism and became known as the father of communism.

But the larger, underlying problem, Shah Waliullah believed, was a lack of knowledge on the part of Muslims about Islam and the Holy Quran. This ignorance, he felt, was the source for all of the troubles that the Muslims endured.

Once settled in Delhi, Shah Waliullah began teaching students in the many varied branches of Islamic learning, as well as preparing them to be missionaries who would go out and reveal to the masses the true nature of Islam. Further, to help promote Islamic teachings and make the Holy Quran more comprehensible to laypeople, he translated the Quran into Persian, which was the common language at the time. He also tried to help settle the differences that separated Muslims into various sectarian groups. In this way, he rose to become a great leader as well as a scholar, and his followers recognized in him certain saintly qualities. His ambitions were great yet selfless, and he saw his own mission as engineering the revival of Islam in India. A humble man, Shah Waliullah sought no personal reward but only greater glory for his fellow Muslims.

Besides being a deeply spiritual and noted academic, Shah Waliullah was also politically astute. He helped create a united Muslim front to oppose the rising Marhatta power, which threatened the already deteriorating Muslim influence in the northern part of India. To forestall the eradication of Muslim power, he prevailed upon the national leaders of the time, including Ahmad Shah Abdali, Nizam ul Mulk, and Najibuddaula. In particular, he wrote to Ahmad Shah Abdali, asking him to help the Muslims of India defeat the Marhattas, as well as their constant threat to the declining Mughal Empire. As a result of the plea, Ahmad Shah Abdali appeared on the battlefield of Panipat in 1761 and, with his army, halted the Marhatta ambitions to control the Indian subcontinent. Shah Waliullah's letter to Ahmad Shah

Abdali is now regarded as one of the most important historical documents related to the eighteenth century, as Shah Waliullah perceptively described the grave political circumstances in India as well as the numerous dangers the Muslim society faced from all sides.

Shah Waliullah not only had a keen grasp of regional and national politics; he also clearly understood the profound impact of economics. Based on what he saw, he promoted the concept of socio-economic equilibrium, and he deplored the accumulation of wealth, viewing it essentially as the proverbial root of all evil in the world. Further, he advocated a social order that embraced Islamic principles of equality, fraternity, and brotherhood.

Prolific Writer

As his letter to Ahmad Shah Abdali suggests, Shah Waliullah exerted a great deal of influence through his use of the written word. A prolific writer, he assumed a lifetime task of producing standard works on Islamic learning. Within a period of 30 years, he wrote 51 books (23 in Arabic and 28 in Persian). Today, some of his works are still regarded as being unmatched in the entire sphere of Islamic literature.

Scholars tend to classify Shah Waliullah's written works into six categories: those works that deal with the Holy Quran (which includes his Persian translations), those that deal with Hadith, works related to "Fiqh" (or Islamic jurisprudence), works based on mysticism, works dealing with Muslim philosophy and Ilm-i-Kalam, and, finally, the writings that focused on the Shia-Sunni division that had become quite acute during his time.

His most famous works include *Fath ur Rahmaan Fee Tarjumatul Qura'an,* a translation of the Holy Quran in Persian, and *Al Fauzul Kabeer Fee Usool at Tafseer,* a booklet written in the Persian language that communicates the core of the Holy Quran and its rules for interpretation. It also reviewed interpretations of the Holy Quran made by other scholars.

Many regard his most renowned work to be the *Hujjat-ullah-il-Balighah,* a two-volume manuscript penned in Arabic that detailed jurisprudence for the Hadith, as well as aspects of Islam shared in all Muslim countries. It is still taught in seminaries. The Studying Islam Web site quoted Shah Waliullah in his introduction to this work: "Some people think that there is no usefulness involved in the injunctions of Islamic law and that in actions and rewards as prescribed by God there is no beneficial purpose. They think that the commandments of Islamic law are similar to a master ordering his servant to lift a stone or touch a tree in order to test his obedience and that in this there is no purpose except to impose a test so that if the servant obeys, he is rewarded, and if he disobeys, he is punished. This view is completely incorrect. The traditions of the Holy Prophet (sws) and consensus of opinion of those ages, contradict this view."

One chapter in the work described the evils of capitalism, which Shah Waliullah believed led to the fall of the Roman and Sassanid empires. Many of his theories relating to economics and socialism are now deemed revolutionary, and he is considered to be a forerunner to Marx. Shah Waliullah criticized the exploitation of the poor and saw it as a fomenter of bloody revolution, which he deplored. Revolution, he felt, should be of a peaceful and intellectual nature, and he believed that an intellectual revolution needed to precede any lasting form of political change. In *Izaalat-ul-Khifaa,* another of his best-known works, Shah Waliullah fully described the idea of the political revolution that he envisioned.

Shah Waliullah's ideas and values no doubt came in response to the time in which he was born, which has been described as an era of decadence. His ideal vision for the Muslim society was one where all individuals enjoyed complete freedom and rulers based their decisions on the Holy Quran. He was critical of the idle rich, such as the Mughal rulers and India's nobility. The Studying Islam Web site further quoted him writing about this element of society: ''Oh Amirs! Do you not fear God? (How is it that) you have so completely thrown yourself into the pursuit of momentary pleasures and have neglected those people who have been committed to your care! The result is that the strong are devouring the (weak) people.''

Influence Lasted Beyond Death

After a lifetime devoted to teaching and writing about Islam, Shah Waliullah died on August 20, 1762. The Muslim leader and reformer was 59 years old. He was buried in ''Munhadiyan,'' a famous graveyard in India, next to his father. After his death, his son, Shah Abdul Aziz, along with his followers and generations of successors, continued his mission to regenerate the Muslim faith.

Today, he is still highly respected by Muslims throughout Asia. His teachings and tradition live on with the Deoband and Barelvi movements. Later, Shah Abdul Aziz, following in his father's footsteps, translated the Holy Quran into Urdu, the language of the Muslim masses in India. Meanwhile, Shah Waliullah's influence continues to be felt in many religious, social, and political matters.

Online

''Famous Personalities of the Global Islamic Movement Throughout History,'' The Khilafah Movement, http://www.khilafah movement.org/shahwaliullah.htm (November 1, 2007).

''Shah Wali Ullah,'' Story of Pakistan, http://www.storyof pakistan.com, (November 1, 2007).

''Shah Wali Ullah,'' Studying Islam, http://www.studying-islam .org/articletext.aspx?id=642 (November 1, 2007).

''Shah Wali Ullah's Reform Movement [1707-1762],'' Story of Pakistan, http://www.storyofpakistan.com/articletext.asp ?artid=A021 (November 1, 2007).

''Shah Waliullah,'' AllExperts, http://en.allexperts.com/e/s/sh/ shah_waliullah.htm (November 1, 2007).

''Shah Waliullah,'' CSSForum, http://www.cssforum.com.pk/css-compulsory-subjects/islamiat/7388-shah-waliullah.html (November 1, 2007). □

Gilles Deleuze

French philosopher Gilles Deleuze (1925-1995) has come to be regarded as one of the most important figures in European contemporary thought.

Many of Deleuze's ideas ran counter to the strain of so-called postmodern philosophy in vogue during the last decades of the twentieth century, and there was a positive, life-affirming strain in his writings that stood in sharp contrast to the pessimism of postmodernists who held, to borrow a formulation from the film *Pump Up the Volume,* that all the great themes have been used up and turned into theme parks. Deleuze believed that philosophy should be a positive act, not a neutral and detached observation of the world and the mind. One of the key concepts in his work was that of immanence, which he borrowed from the realm of theology to denote the unity of thought, mind, and the world, as opposed to the rising-above-the-world indicated by the idea of transcendence. Deleuze's writings were notable among those of modern philosophers for their wide range. He wrote about the history of philosophy, politics, literature, and visual arts (including cinema) with equal enthusiasm. Deleuze was also an unusual example of a truly collaborative writer, co-authoring several books with psychoanalyst Felix Guattari.

Rooted in Specific Neighborhood

Gilles Deleuze was born on January 18, 1925, in the 17th arrondissement, in the northwestern part of Paris, France. He lived in that same neighborhood for much of his life, but he spent much of World War II in Normandy after his family was stranded there when German forces overran France in the summer of 1940. Deleuze's father, an engineer, was a conservative with anti-Semitic leanings, but his older brother joined the French Resistance and was captured by the

Germans and sent to the Auschwitz concentration camp, dying or being killed en route. The 15-year-old Deleuze, who to that point had showed no special academic talent, took classes with a tutor in Normandy who challenged him to read the classics of modern French literature, and Deleuze later cited that teacher as his first major influence.

Back in German-controlled but pacified Paris, Deleuze attended two specialized high schools, the Lycée Carnot and the Henri IV School. By the time he enrolled at the latter, he had been identified as a talented student and was put through a yearlong top-notch college preparatory curriculum known as the kâgne. He enrolled at the Sorbonne university in 1944. There he encountered a second major set of intellectual influences: the university's philosophy faculty included Descartes specialist Ferdinand Aliquié, Jean Hippolyte (an adherent of the ideas of German philosopher G.W.F. Hegel), and Georges Canguilhem, who also served as an adviser to the famed French thinker Michel Foucault. Deleuze finished a philosophy degree called an agrégation (which qualified him as a secondary school teacher) at the Sorbonne in 1948 and went on to teach philosophy at top high schools in Amiens, Orléans, and Paris in the late 1940s and early 1950s.

Deleuze married Fanny Grandjouan, who had translated the works of British author D.H. Lawrence into French, in 1956, and the pair raised a son, Julien, and a daughter, Emilie. By that time he had already embarked on his writing career with a study of the works of Scottish philosopher David Hume, published in 1953. That book, *Empirisme et subjectivité* (Empiricism and Subjectivity), was typical in one way and unusual in another. Like Hegel, and like many of his peers, Deleuze started out believing that philosophy advanced in an orderly way, and that by writing about the history of philosophy one might pave the way to new breakthroughs—an attitude he was later to decisively reject. His choice of Hume as a subject, however, was less common for a French writer, and it pointed to an unusual aspect of his thought: unlike most of his compatriots, Deleuze over his entire career evinced a preference for English, German, and American philosophy and literature over the productions of French writers.

In 1957 Deleuze began teaching courses in the history of philosophy at the Sorbonne, and from 1960 to 1964 he held a position at the National Center of Scientific Research. In the 1960s he taught at the University of Lyon. He was a young scholar, not yet well established, and in each of these positions he held the post of assistant professor or another similar position. He followed up his Hume book with studies of other philosophers: Friedrich Nietzsche (in 1962), Emmanuel Kant (in 1963), and Henri Bergson (in 1966), and his reputation grew.

Gained Attention with Nietzsche Book

The most important of these works was *Nietzsche et la philosophie,* which appeared in English as *Nietzsche and Philosophy* in 1983. With that book Deleuze almost single-handedly elevated Nietzsche's reputation in France from that of an aphoristic essayist to that of a thinker who had subtly and concisely derived a multifaceted (although

nonsystematic) philosophy of life from the idea of a life force, and had influenced many aspects of modern thought. Deleuze caught the attention of other French thinkers who were looking for ideas that were progressive, even radical, but who were uncomfortable with the orthodoxy of the still-powerful French Communist party. Among his new admirers was Foucault, and the two developed a close friendship that, although interrupted by political disagreements, lasted until Foucault's death from AIDS-related complications in 1984.

Nietzsche became one of the two major influences on Deleuze's mature writing. The other was the Portuguese-Dutch-Jewish seventeenth-century philosopher Baruch Spinoza, who became the subject of half of Deleuze's 1968 doctoral dissertation. The other half, *Difference et Répétition,* is regarded as Deleuze's most significant work of pure academic philosophy. By the late 1960s Deleuze was a full-fledged member of the French academic elite. But his life took a sharp turn in 1968, as a result of two unrelated events. One was the onset of a chronic lung disease from which he would suffer for the rest of his life. The other was the eruption of left-wing student protests in France in May of that year, which rapidly grew more intense and culminated in a national general strike. Deleuze emerged as the philosopher of the 1968 generation, not in its Marxist guises but as a result of his status as an experimental but rigorous thinker who could provide an intellectual underpinning to the project of overturning the established order.

Deleuze took a job teaching at the new and experimental University of Paris VII (now Denis Diderot University) in 1969, remaining there until his retirement in 1987. Around that time he met Guattari, a radical psychoanalyst who believed in putting his ideas into practice in actual therapy situations. The two collaborated on several books that became among Deleuze's best known, including *Anti-Oedipus* (1972), *Kafka: Pour une litterature mineure* (1975, translated as *Kafka: Toward a Minor Literature*), and *Mille plateaux* (1980, translated as *A Thousand Plateaus*). These books were not co-authored in the usual sense; rather, they represented a true meeting of the minds in which it is often impossible to tell where one author's voice leaves off and the other's begins. "So close was the association between the philosopher and the psychiatrist," noted David Macey of the London *Guardian,* "that they were sometimes described as a 'bicephalous scientist.' "

The most celebrated of these books was *Anti-Oedipus,* in which Deleuze and Guattari, writing in a dense but freeform prose, gleefully attacked several of the theorists and thinkers who had been central to much of twentieth-century French thought, including Sigmund Freud and his French intellectual descendant Jacques Lacan, and Karl Marx. The two writers were hostile especially to the systematizing tendencies of these thinkers, and they affirmed the unquantifiable aspects of the human mind in their analysis of Freudian ideas. To quote Macey in relation to the book's analysis of the Freudian idea of the unconscious: "The unconscious is no longer seen as a theatre, as in Freud, or as a text, as in Lacan, but as a psychic factory in which desiring machines pulsate and throb. It does not produce stable structures, but operates like a rhizome, constantly bifurcating and putting out shoots at unpredictable intervals.'' Despite the fact that it was extremely difficult to read, the book became a bestseller in 1970s France.

Was Active in Gay Rights Movement

Part of the new trend in Deleuze's thinking was that philosophy was, and ought to be, a form of direct action. Accordingly, despite the disapproval of his wife, he often took part in street demonstrations. In the 1970s, although he himself is thought to have been heterosexual, he was active in the early French gay rights movement. He was a member of the group FHAR (Front Homosexuel d'action Révolutionnaire, or Revolutionary Front for Homosexual Action), which was short-lived but exerted heavy influence on later gay activists in France. In 1972 he worked with Guattari and Foucault on a special issue of the influential philosophical journal *Récherhces*, titled ''Trois milliards de pervers'' (Three Billion Perverts). The publication of the journal resulted in Guattari's arrest (and subsequent conviction) by French police on obscenity charges, but the quieter and more prestigious Deleuze escaped sanction.

The freewheeling style of Deleuze's writing has sometimes led to his being grouped among the thinkers of the French postmodernist movement, who included Jean Baudrillard and Jean Lyotard. Major postmodernist thinkers themselves rejected that categorization, however, and Deleuze's essentially activist stance entailed an intrinsic rejection of the postmodernist ideas of blank pastiche and the death of ideology. Toward the end of the twentieth century Deleuze emerged as an alternative to postmodernism, just as he had become an alternative to Marxism and Freudianism in his younger years. His recurring philosophical ideas had a revolutionary but not dogmatic ring: he created the concept of deterritorialization to describe an individual's attempt to free himself or herself from social categories, and he used the term nomadism to describe the act of resistance to repressive state structures. He was also active on behalf of prisoners' rights, and he became a staunch supporter of the Palestine Liberation Movement.

In the 1980s Deleuze wrote several books on the arts, including *Francis Bacon* (1981), *Cinéma 1: Mouvement-Image* (Cinema 1: The Movement-Image, 1983), and *Cinéma 2: L'image-temps* (Cinema 2: The Time-Image, 1985). He argued, however, that these books should not be understood as film or art criticism. In Deleuze's own words, quoted in the Internet Encyclopedia of Philosophy, ''Let's suppose that there's a third period when I worked on painting and cinema: images on the face of it. But I was writing philosophy.'' Deleuze retired from teaching in 1987 after his already fragile health began to deteriorate.

In the last decade of his life Deleuze worked with Guattari on a book that followed from many of his ideas, even though it did not exactly summarize them: *Qu'est-ce que c'est la philosophie?* (What Is Philosophy?), published in 1991, ironically questioned the historical primacy accorded to pure thought, generally regarded as a key basis of philosophy itself. Hospitalized repeatedly and suffering badly after undergoing a tracheotomy, Deleuze committed

suicide by jumping out the window of his Paris apartment on November 4, 1995. He was the sole author of 25 books, plus several more written as part of his unique collaboration with Guattari. Numerous explications of his work by other scholars have appeared in the years since. In the United States his writing has been particularly influential among theorists of contemporary art.

Books

Badiou, Alain, *Deleuze: The Clamour of Being,* trans. Louise Burchill, University of Minnesota Press, 2000.
Hardt, Michael, *Gilles Deleuze: An Apprenticeship in Philosophy,* University of Minnesota Press, 1993.
Patton, Paul, *Deleuze and the Political,* Routledge, 2000.

Periodicals

Artforum International, March 1996; April 2003.
Guardian (London, England), November 7, 1995.
New York Times, November 7, 1995.

Online

''Biography: Gilles Deleuze,'' European Graduate School, http://www.egs.edu/resources/deleuze.html (February 2, 2008).
''Gilles Deleuze,'' The Internet Encyclopedia of Philosophy, http://www.iep.utm.edu/d/deleuze.htm (February 2, 2008). □

Philip K. Dick

American science fiction writer Philip K. Dick (1928-1982) gained acclaim across genres with novels and short stories that anticipated major aspects of life in the late 20th century and beyond.

Prolific in the extreme, Dick wrote about the nature of consciousness and reality in a world in which each could be altered through the use of drugs or by the machinations of hidden powers in society. His heroes were ordinary men (and they were always men) trying to act humanely in a world in which they experienced constant destabilization. The experience of reading Dick's fiction has been described as similar to the feeling of falling through a series of trap doors, as new realities beneath the apparent surface reverse everything that his characters, and his readers, believe to be true. Dick used science fiction less as a medium for adventure stories than as a way of addressing philosophical questions. In his last years he created a series of novels in which he explored a set of bizarre hallucinations he had experienced. Critics disagree over the merits of those books, and indeed of much of Dick's fiction—''While most critics agree that Philip K. Dick has written some of the best SF [science fiction] novels and some of the worst, few agree on which is which,'' quipped the *St. James Guide to Science Fiction Writers.* But Dick's literary reputation has been rising steadily since his untimely death at age 53, and his works, rich in ideas, have served regularly as sources for cinematic adaptations.

Suffered Loss of Twin

Philip Kindred Dick was born in Chicago on December 16, 1928. His father, Edgar Dick, was a federal employee; his middle name, Kindred, was his mother Dorothy's maiden name. The new parents were inept at caring for their twin babies, and Dick suffered a serious trauma when he was just five weeks old: his twin sister, Jane, died of malnutrition. Much of Dick's childhood, spent largely in the San Francisco Bay Area, was unhappy; his parents divorced when he was five, and his relationship with his mother was poor. She did, however, encourage his first attempts at writing.

Dick first encountered the still–young science fiction genre in 1940, when he was 12; looking for a copy of the magazine *Popular Science* at a newsstand, he picked up *Stirring Science Stories* instead. "I was most amazed," he was quoted as saying on his official Web site. "Stories about science? At once I recognized the magic which I had found, in earlier times, in the Oz books—this magic now coupled not with magic wands but with science. . . . In any case my view became magic equals science . . . and science (of the future) equals magic."

The creative atmosphere of Berkeley, California, was another major shaping force in Dick's work. He attended Berkeley High School, graduating in 1947; science fiction writer Ursula LeGuin was a member of his graduating class, but the two did not know each other personally. Dick moved on to the University of California at Berkeley, beginning a major in German, but he soon dropped out in favor of a job in a Berkeley record store called Art Music and a brief gig as a classical radio DJ on station KSMO. As a young man he showed enthusiasm for the surreal novels of Czech writer Franz Kafka and their frightening yet darkly comic depictions of individuals who find themselves powerless in the face of unseen forces, and his own writings have been seen as responses to the dehumanizing qualities of life in suburban postwar California. In 1948 Dick married Jeanette Marlin; the marriage, the first of Dick's five, lasted only six months.

Writing almost constantly, as he would do throughout his life, Dick worked at Art Music until 1952. He began submitting short stories to science fiction magazines and got nowhere at first, once receiving 17 rejection slips in a single day. But in 1951 a Dick story called "Roog" was accepted for publication in the *Magazine of Fantasy and Science Fiction,* and it seemed to open the floodgates. By the time it appeared in print, seven more of Dick's stories had already been published. Sometimes he wrote under the name of Richard Phillips. In 1954 he met the established science fiction writer A.E. Van Vogt at a convention and was advised that novels, even given the notoriously low pay rates of science fiction publishers, were more lucrative than short stories. Dick's first novel, *Solar Lottery,* appeared in 1955; it concerned a corrupt lottery that determined the life courses of the participants.

Breakthrough Novel Turned Heads

Married to his second wife, Kleo Apostolides, and so broke, he admitted, that he could not even afford library fines, Dick wrote rapidly. Between 1959 and 1964 he published 16 science fiction novels, plus several non–science fiction works that Dick, although he defended the validity of science fiction as an art form, hoped would be his path to literary respectability. His agent returned those to him as unpublishable (although *Confessions of a Crap Artist* was eventually published, and several others appeared after his death), and Dick applied himself with new energy to science fiction. He was married for a third time in 1959, to Anne Williams Rubinstein, and he had a young daughter, Laura.

As of the early 1960s, Dick was best known among hardcore science fiction fans. His breakthrough came in 1962 with the novel *The Man in the High Castle,* which presented his characteristic theme of alternate realities in a relatively conventional setting: the novel imagined a United States that had lost World War II to the Axis powers. Unlike most of Dick's novels, which take place on a fantastic plane, the book relied on several years' worth of historical research and won praise from mainstream as well as science fiction critics. The Chinese *I Ching* book of fortune telling was used by Dick in formulating the plot and also appeared as an element in the story. Dick's 1964 novel *Martian Time–Slip,* one of four Dick novels published that year, was also especially successful; it featured a character whom Dick described as an ex–schizophrenic, and it was one of a number of Dick novels in which mental illness played a significant role.

Perhaps Dick's first fully characteristic novel was *The Three Stigmata of Palmer Eldritch* (1965), the story of colonists on Mars who have had to leave Earth due to deteriorating environmental conditions. They amuse themselves with a drug called Can–D that allows them to experience an idyllic Earthlike setting temporarily. They come under the control of the title character, who purveys a more powerful drug called Chew–Z. The novel was identified with the rise in the use of LSD in the mid–1960s; although Dick rarely used LSD he consistently abused methamphetamines. Dick's *Do Androids Dream of Electric Sheep?* (1968) was adapted into the film *Blade Runner* in 1982 and was later republished under that title. Dick at first refused to cooperate with filmmaker Ridley Scott. The book tells the story of a bounty hunter among androids, introducing the favorite Dick theme of what is definitively human—the book's androids closely resemble humans but can be distinguished from them through their inability to show empathy toward others. The book offered a nightmare vision of the near future in which most real animals have gone extinct and have been replaced by mechanical replicas.

Ubik (1969) took the idea of alternate realities to an extreme, imagining a world in which the dead seem to come back to life and a warring group of psychics move among a group of parallel realities. The following year *A Philip K. Dick Omnibus* was published in London, signaling a new level of popularity for Dick outside the United States. His works have been translated into a wide variety of European and Asian languages, and he has had an especially strong following in France. Dick married twice more; his marriages to Nancy

Hackett (1966) and Tessa Busby (1973) each produced a child (Isolde and Christopher, respectively).

Anticipated Governmental Security Apparatus

Dick's novel *Flow My Tears, the Policeman Said,* published in 1974, mixed themes of drug use, alternate realities, and malevolent government control in a story widely considered one of the author's best. The title comes from that of a song ("Flow My Tears") by English Renaissance composer John Dowland, a name that appears in several other Dick works; his novels contain various obscure references that his increasingly devoted fan base ferreted out. *Flow My Tears, the Policeman Said* tells the story of a television talk show host, Jason Taverner (Taverner is the name of another English Renaissance composer), who finds that his identity has disappeared from California state records—a serious problem in the near–future police state depicted in the book. Later it becomes clear that his lack of an identity is due to the fact that he is actually a drug–induced hallucination in the mind of one of the other characters. The novel earned Dick science–fiction's John W. Campbell Memorial Award.

The year 1974 marked a turning point in Dick's life and writing. In February of that month, recovering from dental surgery that had involved the administration of sodium pentathol, he opened the door to a young woman who was delivering him a prescription. She was wearing a medallion with the Christian fish symbol, which Dick asked about. At that point he experienced one of a series of visions that he believed added up to a major revelation about himself and the nature of the world he was living in. These visions continued through February and March of 1974; he referred to them as the two–three–seventy–four or 2–3–74 experiences. Briefly, Dick came to believe that the world around him was an illusion, and that time had stopped in the year 70 C.E. He and the prescription deliverer were actually early Christians being persecuted by the Roman government; his first–century name was Thomas. His visions sometimes came in the form of laser beams or geometric patterns, and he believed that not only he but also God had a dual existence, with one half of the divine duality being a female who had created the illusory world. Some of his ideas had affinities with the group of early Christian philosophies collectively known as Gnosticism.

In a series of often bizarre novels written over the rest of his life, most notably *Valis* (1981), Dick tried to flesh out the implications of his visions. "Valis" was an acronym for Vast Active Living Intelligence System, the entity Dick believed was sending his visions and was responsible for the nature of the reality he was experiencing. "Without Dick's name," noted Adam Gopnik in the *New Yorker,* the book "almost certainly wouldn't have been published—it's just too static and strange. Yet, once you force yourself to read it, and read past the really nutty bits, it emerges as perhaps the most emotional and in an odd way the most artistically achieved of all his books." The book's narrator is once again divided into a duality, alternating between Horselover Fat and the more dispassionate Philip Dick, who questions the accuracy and occasionally the sanity of Horselover Fat and by

extension Philip K. Dick himself—the name Horselover Fat is a translation of his own name (he derives Philip from a pun on the Latin roots "phil hippo," or horse lover, and Dick is German for fat or thick).

Dick continued to write at a rapid pace; *Valis* was the first part of a vast trilogy that continued with *The Divine Invasion* (1981) and *The Transmigration of Timothy Archer* (1982), the last work to appear during Dick's life. In all, he wrote 36 novels and more than 100 short stories. A chronic sufferer from high blood pressure, Dick died from a stroke on March 2, 1982, in Santa Ana, California. Sadly, he missed by just a few months the enormous success of the film *Blade Runner,* which marked the beginning of a consistent rise in his posthumous reputation. Collections of Dick short stories and republications of his earlier novels proceeded at a steady clip.

Perhaps the surest indicator of Dick's continuing influence was the frequency with which his writings were adapted as movies. After *Blade Runner* came *Total Recall* (1990, based on Dick's short story "We Can Remember It for You Wholesale"), *Screamers* (1995, based on the story "Second Variety"), *Minority Report* (2002, based on the story "The Minority Report"), *Paycheck* (2003, based on a story of the same name), *A Scanner Darkly* (2006, based on a novel of the same name), and a 1992 French film *Confessions d'un Barjo* (based on Dick's mainstream novel *Confessions of a Crap Artist*). Various television programs and stage plays also took Dick's work as a point of departure. By the mid–2000s Dick had become the subject of several biographies (including a partly fictionalized one in French) and numerous literary studies, and in 2007 he became the first science fiction writer included in the popular Library of America series of classic literature.

Books

Rickman, Gregg, *To the High Castle: A Life of Philip K. Dick, 1928–1962,* Fragments West–Valentine Press, 1989.

St. James Guide to Science Fiction Writers, 4th ed., St. James Press, 1996.

Sutin, Lawrence, *Divine Invasions: A Life of Philip K. Dick,* Harmony, 1989.

Periodicals

Book, July–August 2002.

Economist (U.S.), April 17, 2004.

New Yorker, August 20, 2007.

Publishers Weekly, February 27, 1995.

Time, June 24, 2002.

Online

Contemporary Authors Online, Gale, 2007. http://galenet.gale group.com/servlet/BioRC (December 21, 2007).

"Philip K. Dick—Author—Official Biography," Philip K. Dick official Web site, http://www.philipkdick.com/aa_biography .html (December 21, 2007).

"Philip K(indred) Dick (1928–1982)," Books and Writers, http://www.kirjasto.sci.fi/pkdick.htm (December 21, 2007).

☐

Dionysius Exiguus

Roman scholar and theologian Dionysius Exiguus (c. 465 A.D.-c. 530 A.D.) is best known for his creation of a calendar that led to the modern Gregorian calendar. From his calendar stem the designations "B.C." and "A.D." Dionysius championed the system that is still used to determine the date of Easter, and his many translations and writings have influenced canon law and helped preserve early Church texts for study.

A Life Shrouded By History

Dionysius Exiguus, the man, is something of a mystery to modern scholars; Writing in *Anno Domini: The Origins of the Christian Era,* Georges Declercq argued that "the epithet 'exiguus' was adopted by Dionysius himself as a sign of intellectual humility, not because he was small of stature ('the Short')." Beyond this issue of nomenclature, the details of the early life and career of Dionysius have been lost over the centuries. Modern scholars do know that Dionysius originally came from Scythia—an area that in antiquity covered parts of present-day Russia, Ukraine, and Kazakhstan—where he was reputedly raised by a sect of Gothic monks before becoming a monk himself. A preface to one of his translations seems to indicate that Dionysius came from Scythia Minor, which today encompasses a portion of Romania that borders the Black Sea.

Regardless of his place of origin, sometime around 496 Dionysius came to Rome; he was by that time already a well-known scholar who had been summoned by Pope Gelasius I to the city to organize the internal archives of the church, and, according to the *New Catholic Encyclopedia,* "to compile a collection of texts of incontestable worth and authenticity." However, Dionysius did not arrive until after the Pope's death in November of 496. Because he was a respected scholar by then, it seems likely that Dionysius was born sometime around the 460s. The *Catholic Encyclopedia* noted that despite his origins, Dionysius was considered by contemporary Cassiodorus to be "a true Roman and thorough Catholic." Dionysius seems to have remained in Rome for the remainder of his life. There, he lived as a monk; one sixth-century source claimed that Dionysius had been the abbot of a Roman monastery, but no evidence exists to support this assertion. Because modern scholars know that Dionysius constructed a set of Easter tables in the year 525, his death must fall at some time after that year; however, no evidence points to a date more specific than that.

Translated Important Church Documents

During his career, Dionysius worked in several fields of study. He translated many of the decrees issued by the Council of Nicaea, which created the first standard Christian doctrine; decrees by the Council of Constantinople, which created the first major revision of that doctrine; decrees by the First Council of Ephesus, which declared Mary to be the mother of God; and finally, decrees by the Council of Chalcedon, which established the difference between Jesus Christ the human and Jesus Christ the divine. These translations were published as three separate editions, including one dual Greek-Latin collection created at the behest of Hormisdas, who served as Pope from 514-523. The *New Catholic Encyclopedia* called this collection, the *Dionysiana,* "the first canonical collection worthy of the name." Dionysius also collected letters written by fourth-century Popes. These letters, together with his collections of council decrees, later served as important resources for the creators of canon, or church, law.

Dionysius also translated a number of texts describing the lives of saints, as well as theological works that recount early doctrinal debates among different groups within the Church. The *New Catholic Encyclopedia* claimed that "Dionysius's perfect knowledge of Greek and Latin is proved by his translations."

In addition to translating important Church texts, Dionysius himself was a theologian who wrote on the early history of the Catholic Church. His biography in *Science and Its Times* stated that "he is credited with writing a collection of 401 ecclesiastical canons . . . that would become important historical documents about the early years of Christianity."

Calculated Dates of Easter

According to the *New Catholic Encyclopedia,* "the entire work of Dionysius had but one purpose: the reconciliation of the Churches of the Orient and the West." At the time of Dionysius, Christian doctrine was not yet standardized; the Christian world had divided into eastern and western branches due to disagreements on doctrinal matters.

One of Dionysius's efforts to reunite the divided Church related to the calculation of the dates of Easter, the most important Christian feast day, on which believers celebrate the resurrection of Jesus Christ from the dead. This date was one of much contention in the early Church, and was one cause of the split between the eastern and western branches of the Church. At the time, two methods competed for supremacy. One, the Alexandrine rule, had been created by the Council of Nicaea in 325. The other, used by the Church authorities in Rome at the time of Dionysius, declared that Easter must fall between March 25 and April 21 and relied on an 84-year cycle.

Dionysius was trained as a mathematician and an astronomer, and these skills surely helped him as he conducted studies into the calculation of dates. His work with the calendar stemmed from a request from Pope John I in 525 to extend the existing Easter tables for an additional 95 years. To do this, Dionysius chose to employ the Alexandrian method and to base his calculation on the Easter tables of St. Cyril, who had used the Alexandrian method, rather than those of Victorious of Aquitaine, which employed the cycle then endorsed by the Roman Church.

A number of bishops asked Dionysius to explain this decision, and Dionysius responded to this request in the preface to his *Book on Easter Reckoning,* as quoted by Declercq. Declercq noted that Dionysius believed firmly that the Council of Nicaea endorsed the Alexandrian method, and summarized Dionysius's explanation of the criteria of that method thus: "The beginning of the first lunar month, Nisan, from 8 March to 5 April inclusive; the lunar limits 15-21 for Easter Sunday; the theory of the spring equinox on 21 March as the earliest possible date for the Paschal [spring] or 14th moon; the calendar limits for the Paschal full moon (21 March to 18 April) and those for the festival of Easter itself (22 March to 25 April)."

These criteria dictated that Easter would occur on the first Sunday following the 14th day of the lunar cycle—the full moon—that falls on or after the spring equinox. Despite the controversy caused by Dionysius's use of this method, his tables noting the dates of Easter for the years 532-626 stood. Western Christianity still calculates the date of Easter using this method, showing the lasting impact of Dionysius's work.

Created the Christian Era

In the course of determining the date of Easter, Dionysius also created the Christian Era calendar, commonly used today and recognizable by its B.C./A.D. ("Before Christ"/"*Anno Domini*") designations. The calendar in the era of Dionysius differed from the modern calendar. Instead of relying on the modern Gregorian calendar, people of Dionysius's time determined the year using the Julian calendar. This calendar was created by famed Roman statesman Julius Caesar in an attempt to correct the highly inaccurate Roman calendar of his day. (The Gregorian calendar, introduced in 1582, would later perfect the Julian system's minor errors, primarily regarding the placement of leap days.) This calendar numbered years commencing from either the foundation of the city in Rome, or from the first year of the reign of the Roman Emperor Diocletian; using the former system, the year in which Dionysius's Easter tables would take effect would be called 1285, and by the later, 248.

The Diocletian dating system was at the fore in the era of Dionysius. Preferring not to memorialize Diocletian, who had been a somewhat tyrannical emperor and had persecuted Christians, by basing the calendar upon his reign, Dionysius decided to renumber the years. In *The Oxford Companion to the Year: An Exploration of Calendar Customs and Time Reckoning,* Bonnie Blackburn and Leofranc Holford-Strevens quoted Dionysius as stating that he wished to date the year "from the Incarnation of our Lord Jesus Christ, in order that the beginning of our hope should be better known to us and the cause of our recovery, that is the Passion of our Redeemer, should shine forth more clearly." Dionysius thus renumbered the years beginning with the incarnation of Jesus Christ, beginning with the year 1 as the Roman numbering system had no way to indicate a zero. This meant that his Easter tables began with the year 532, instituting the Christian Era (also called the Incarnation Era) still used for reckoning the number of the year.

However, Dionysius incorrectly calculated the year of Christ's birth. Both ancient and modern scholars placed this event some time between 6 and 2 B.C. The reason for Dionysius's error is unclear. Some scholars have speculated that the inaccuracy may have stemmed from Dionysius placing the first day of the year in September rather than January; basing the indicator of the year on the number of elapsed years, rather than noting the date of the current year; and considering the incarnation to be the moment of birth, rather than the moment of conception. Alternatively, Dionysius may have simply misinterpreted a document listing the names of consuls, for whom the Romans named the year at the time of Christ, and made some minor miscalculation that resulted in the date shift.

Legacy

The legacy of Dionysius Exiguus is evident throughout the world. His dating system, incorporated into the standard Gregorian calendar, is the most common reckoning of the year around the globe. The Alexandrian rule of calculating the date of Easter, introduced by Dionysius, remains the method used by Western Christianity to set this feast day. Although the details of his life are unknown, the effects of that life affect human society at all levels.

Books

Blackburn, Bonnie, and Leofranc Holford-Strevens, *The Oxford Companion to the Year: An Exploration of Calendar Customs and Time-reckoning,* Oxford University Press, 1999.

Declercq, Georges, *Anno Domini: The Origins of the Christian Era,* Brepols, 2000.

New Catholic Encyclopedia, Gale, 2002.

Science and Its Times, Vol. 1: 2000 B.C. - 700 A.D., Gale Group, 2001.

Online

"Dionysius Exiguus," *Catholic Encyclopedia,* http://www.new advent.org/cathen/05010b.htm (November 26, 2007). □

Herbert H. Dow

American chemist Herbert H. Dow (1866-1930) founded the chemical company that bears his name, in 1897 in Midland, Michigan. He was both a gifted chemist and a savvy entrepreneur, and held more than 90 patents for his research, achievements that represented both significant scientific advances and the beginning of American dominance in the field of modern industrial chemistry. Harrison E. Howe, who profiled the company founder in the *Dictionary of American Biography,* noted that "Dow was an early exponent of the philosophy that a company should make more cheaply and better than anyone else the product in which it is interested, then pass the benefits of that advantage to the consumer."

Born on February 26, 1866, in Belleville, Ontario, Canada, Herbert Henry Dow was the son of an inventor and mechanical engineer, Joseph Henry Dow. The family's roots in America stretched back to 1637 and an ancestor who was listed as a resident of Watertown, Massachusetts. When Dow was still an infant, the family—which would expand to include his three younger sisters—moved back to their original hometown of Derby, Connecticut. Joseph Dow went on to work for the Derby Shovel Manufacturing Company, and in 1878 the family moved once again, this time to Cleveland, Ohio, where the senior Dow was hired by the Chisholm Shovel-Works.

Fascinated by Brines

Dow inherited his father's knack for mechanics and invention, and devised an early prototype of a chicken egg incubator when the family was still living in Connecticut. After graduating from high school in 1884, Dow remained close to home for college, enrolling at Cleveland's Case School of Applied Science, which later became Case Institute of Technology and finally Case Western Reserve University. His major was chemistry, and during his time at Case he became intrigued by brine, or water with a high salt content. Brines can be made by adding salt to water, and from ancient times it was used by humans as a food preservative. Ocean saltwater is also considered a brine, and eons earlier, the shifting of land masses resulted in large underground deposits of sea water from the time when there were immense inland oceans in North America. The area that stretched from Ontario south and west to Kentucky was known to contain large underground deposits of this type of brine.

Brines contained bromine, the chemical element on the periodic table with the symbol "Br." In Dow's childhood, bromines were used to make sedative medications, and later new applications were discovered for its use in the nascent photographic film-developing industry. As a college student, he was interested in even more future possibilities, and began to conduct his dissertation research on the Ohio-area underground brines. His professors suggested that Dow write a paper on his brine analysis and present it at a coming meeting of the American Association for the Advancement of Science in Cleveland. He found that both Canton, Ohio, and Midland, Michigan, were brine-rich sites. Michigan had become a major salt producer at the time, with brine pools left to evaporate in the mid-state Saginaw Valley area and the resulting salt packaged and sold on the consumer market.

Dow earned his bachelor of science degree from Case in 1888 and was hired by the Huron Street Hospital College in Cleveland as a chemistry professor. In 1889 he applied for and received his first patent, which involved a more efficient way to extract bromine from brine. He founded a company to exploit this process, but it soon failed. Despite the setback, the young chemist still had some financial supporters, and in 1890 they funded a second venture, this time in Midland, Michigan. Dow moved there in August of 1890 to establish a plant and offices for this venture, which was called the Midland Chemical Company.

Fired from Company

In 1891, after more experimentation, Dow had a new breakthrough in bromine extraction, and earned another patent. This one came to be called the "Dow process," and was the first to use electrolysis, or the application of electrical current. This eliminated several steps in bromine manufacturing and represented a significant breakthrough in industrial chemistry. "A direct current generator was required for this Dow process," noted Howe, "and although it was a most difficult piece of equipment to obtain at that time, one was installed in 1892 and may be regarded as the first commercially successful installation of an electrochemical plant in America." Dow thought that electrolysis could be used in other chemical manufacturing applications, but his financial backers disagreed, and they fired him.

Returning to Cleveland, Dow continued his experiments on his own, this time in extracting chloride and caustic soda from salt in its pure form, the element sodium chloride, or NaCl on the periodic table. Caustic soda, otherwise known as lye or sodium hydroxide, had also been used by humans for centuries, particularly in the making of soap, but it was also coming into use as a bleaching agent in paper production, which had begun to soar in the nineteenth century. Chloride was also used to make chlorine, another potentially lucrative product for the industrial and consumer markets. Dow asked several friends and alumni from Case for financial help in backing a new company. In 1896 he moved back to Midland, this time with his wife and children, and in May of 1897 formally established the Dow

Chemical Company. Its manufacture of both bleaching powder and bromine using the Dow process proved such a success that by 1900 the company bought Midland Chemical, the firm that had fired him just five years before.

Broke the German Cartel

Dow's company sold bromine in the United States for 36 cents per pound. In its first years in business, looking to expand internationally, Dow was warned not to challenge a major European supplier, a German government-subsidized group of several industrial-chemical manufacturers known as Die Deutsche Bromkonvention, or the German Bromine Cartel. The Bromkonvention had fixed the price of bromine at 49 cents per pound on the world market, and threatened to flood the United States market with bromine at an even cheaper price than Dow's 36 cents, should Dow Chemical try to move beyond the U.S. borders with the product. In 1904 Dow decided to ignore the threat, and started to export his company's bromine to England and then Japan. The European cartel was so irate that it sent an executive, by ship and then railway, all the way to Midland, a trip of several weeks at the time. The company president, however, told the Bromkonvention ambassador, Hermann Jacobsohn, that he was unaware of any formal agreements that fixed the price of bromine on the world market, or a list of who could and could not sell it.

In response, the Bromkonvention followed through and reduced the price of their bromine in the United States to just 15 cents per pound. In a masterful stroke of business acumen, Dow had agents of his in New York City secretly buy it as it came off the cargo ships. Dow Chemical then repackaged it, marked it up to 27 cents per pound, and exported it overseas. At the same time, the company's U.S. bromine sales were put on hold. Dow began to reap enormous profits from the ruse, which went undiscovered by the Bromkonvention for some time. They kept reducing their price per pound, and were finally selling bromine below cost. Finally, the two sides entered into an agreement that the Bromkonvention would be allowed to retain its lucrative German market rights, while Dow Chemical would keep its American clients—but all other markets were open to competition.

Profited from Modern Warfare Needs

As he had predicted, Dow found many other uses for brine, and developed methods of extracting caustic soda, calcium, magnesium, and other minerals from it. During World War I his company enjoyed an extraordinary stroke of luck when the British Royal Navy set up a formidable naval blockade of all German ports, which prevented Dow's biggest competitors—Bromkonvention members such as BASF, Hoechst, and Bayer—from accessing markets outside Europe. Dow Chemical further benefited from wartime production needs, such as tear gas, which used bromine in its manufacturing process. Magnesium was used in making incendiary flares, and phenol, also known as carbolic acid, was used in explosives manufacturing. This later became one of the building blocks for Bakelite, the first synthetic resin and the predecessor of plastic.

After World War I, Dow guided his company into an ever-expanding array of processes and products. One division discovered that magnesium was ideal when combined with other metals in making automotive engine pistons, and DowMetal was established to capitalize on this growing market. Dow's earliest experiments in the chicken coop progressed later in his life to gardening, and he experimented with a number of chemicals on his home garden and orchard dating all the way back to the 1890s. In 1907 Dow Chemical introduced lime sulfur, a fruit tree fungicide, and by 1910 had established an agricultural chemicals division that went on to develop some of the world's first synthetic pesticides.

Dow died on October 15, 1930, of cirrhosis of the liver, in Rochester, Minnesota. He had traveled there for treatment at the Mayo Clinic, but fell into a coma after surgery, from which he never recovered. He was survived by his wife, the former Grace Ball, with whom he had seven children. By this point he had established such a strong leadership model that the scores of researchers and executives who succeeded him at Dow Chemical Company continued to press forward and make it the world's second largest chemical manufacturer a century after its founding. In the post-World War II years, the company ventured into consumer products, and held the first U.S. patents for such ubiquitous items as Saran Wrap, Ziploc bags, and Styrofoam.

Books

Doyle, Jack, *Trespass Against Us: Dow Chemical & the Toxic Century*, Common Courage Press, 2004.
Dictionary of American Biography, Supplements 1-2: to 1940, American Council of Learned Societies, 1944-1958.

Periodicals

Chemical Week, December 22, 1999; November 21, 2007.
New York Times, October 16, 1930.

Online

"Herbert Dow, the Monopoly Breaker," Mackinac Center for Public Policy, http://www.mackinac.org/article.aspx?ID = 31 (January 3, 2008).
"Herbert H. Dow," Ohio History Central, http://www.ohiohistorycentral.org/entry.php?rec = 109 (January 3, 2008). □

Cornelius Drebbel

Dutch inventor Cornelius Drebbel (1572-1633) earned a place in nautical history as the builder of the world's first navigable submarine. A self-taught engineer, Drebbel spent much of his career in the service of two of Europe's most powerful monarchies early in the seventeenth century, and it was for England's King James I that he built and tested several leather-clad, submersible rowboats between 1621 and 1624.

Was Apprentice to an Engraver

Drebbel was born in 1572 in Alkmaar, a town in West Friesland, Netherlands. His father was believed to have been one of the town's burghers, or group of merchants and leading citizens who held political authority in the city. He had little formal education, learning to read and write in English and Latin—the latter the universal language of science, religion, and scholarship at the time—only later in life. In his teens he entered the engraving workshop of Hendrick Goltzius in Haarlem as an apprentice. Goltzius was also an alchemist, an amateur chemist of medieval and Renaissance Europe in the era before the field was fully established as a science. Alchemists were primarily engaged in attempting to transform base metals such as iron, nickel, and zinc into gold. In 1595, Drebbel married Goltzius's younger sister, Sophia Jansdochter, with whom he would have four daughters.

The newlyweds soon returned to Drebbel's hometown of Alkmaar, where he opened an engraving business that made maps and pictures using early printing technology. A tinkerer by nature, he also began working on his own inventions, and in 1598 applied for and received an official patent for a perpetual-motion clock. His device needed no winding, for it was driven by gears that moved on their own via naturally occurring changes in atmospheric pressure. He also devised a way to supply Alkmaar's water needs, and a fountain of his design was constructed in Middelburg, a town in Zeeland, in 1601. In 1602, he received another patent, this one for a new type of chimney.

Word of Drebbel's inventions, especially that of the perpetual-motion clock, began to spread through Europe, and in 1604 he published a book, *Een cort Tractat van de Naturae de Elementen* ("On the Nature of the Elements"), which outlined his theories about the four elements of life— earth, fire, water, and air. He dedicated the English-language edition to King James I of England and Scotland (1566–1625), who was known for his devotion to alchemy and the occult. James invited Drebbel and his family to move to England, and gave them living quarters in Eltham Palace in London, where there were also rooms specifically given over to displays of Drebbel's inventions. Drebbel received an annual stipend and was technically a member of the royal court, but had been given responsibility for fireworks displays, which relegated him to the entertainers' section of official pageants, along with musicians and court jesters. One of his novelties was a magic lantern, the demonstration of which he described in a 1608 letter: "I am clad first in black velvet, and in a second, as fast as a man can think, I am clad in green velvet, in red velvet, changing myself into all the colors of the world . . . and I present myself as a king, adorned in diamonds, and all sorts of precious stones, and then in a moment become a beggar, all my clothes in rags," he claimed, according to Tom Shachtman's *Absolute Zero and the Conquest of Cold*.

Boasted of Secret Powers

Drebbel had confided to James that he was working on a perpetual-motion machine, a mythical device that had intrigued Europe's thinkers for several centuries by then. Scientists and engineers attempted to create a device featuring parts that moved entirely on their own, with no human interaction or source of external energy. Drebbel did manage to produce a timekeeping device, described in a book by his contemporary Thomas Tymme as an enormous globe, mounted atop pillars and ringed by a water chute made of crystal; it provided the time, day, month, year, season, astrological period, phases of the moon, and tide patterns. Like his earlier clock, it was probably powered by atmospheric pressure, but Drebbel apparently claimed that he had uncloaked the mysteries of the universe, and reportedly told only King James the secret of its motion.

Around 1610, Drebbel and his family departed for Prague after receiving an invitation from Emperor Rudolf II (1552–1612), the Holy Roman Emperor. Like James, Rudolf was intrigued by alchemy, and had become the patron of several of Europe's most notable seekers of the so-called Philosopher's Stone, the mythical substance that was believed to have the power to transform base metals into gold and perhaps even reverse the aging process in human beings. Drebbel became the chief alchemist at Rudolf's court, with quarters at the magnificent Prague Castle that Rudolf enlarged to hold the extensive royal collections of exotic animals and mechanical inventions. During his time in Prague, Drebbel probably worked on a pump device for Rudolf, whose Bohemian kingdom held extensive Central European mountain ranges whose mineral wealth was just being discovered at the time. Devising a method of removing water from mine shafts also occupied several engineers of the era.

In 1611, Rudolf was ousted and Drebbel was taken prisoner by Frederick V's army at the start of the Thirty Years' War. Rudolf died a year later, and Drebbel appealed to James in England for help, who agreed to intercede as well as provide funds for the journey back to England for the inventor and his family. Drebbel seemed to have built an impressive automated fountain for the king, which played music and featured animated statues of sea deities from classical mythology. He also worked on a microscope which had two convex lenses, the first ever to feature a pair of optical lenses.

World's First Air Conditioner

In the summer of 1620, Drebbel demonstrated what he called a cooling machine—the prototype for the world's first air conditioner—to a royal audience in the Great Hall of Westminster Abbey. The site of the presentation is notable, for it was literally the largest room in all of the British Isles at the time, with a massive vaulted ceiling and a length of 332 feet. Inside the sacrarium, a smaller chamber, Drebbel chilled the air by unknown artificial means so well that the king began shivering and quickly exited back into the July heat.

Drebbel was already working on his next impressive feat of entertainment magic, the world's first navigable submarine, which he demonstrated on the Thames River in 1621. The design for a submersible vessel dated back to a proposal by English mathematician William Bourne in his 1578 work *Inventions and Devises,* but the problem of maintaining enough of an air supply to keep the crew alive proved the most daunting obstacle. But Drebbel's craft made a round trip from Westminster to Greenwich and back, which took three hours, as James and a crowd estimated in the thousands watched. He had modified a rowboat into upper and lower chambers, with its wooden exterior clad in greased leather to promote buoyancy.

Intensely secretive and always cautious to protect his position at court from usurpers, Drebbel kept no scientific notebooks, and left no drawings behind of any of his devices, so there are only educated guesses—some made hundreds of years later—on how his marvels actually functioned. There are two theories of how Drebbel solved the oxygen question on the submarine. One is that his submarine had pigskin bladders stashed underneath the seats where the crew of twelve rowers were stationed, and these bags were attached by pipe to the exterior. "Rope was used to tie off the empty bladders," a BBC report explained, and "in order to dive, the rope was untied and the bladders filled. To surface the crew squashed the bladders flat, squeezing out the water." But this seems an inadequate explanation for how the 13 humans had enough air to last three hours, and it is thought that Drebbel's more impressive feat was the isolation of the element of oxygen. His writings hint that he devised a way to produce it by heating saltpeter, a nitrate, and he probably worked on this during his time in Prague with another alchemist at Rudolf's court, Michael Sendivogius (1566–1636). His isolation and manufacture of oxygen—the element necessary to sustain human life—took place 150 years before a British scientist, Joseph Priestley (1733–1804), officially discovered it.

Worked for Royal Navy

Drebbel built three craft, each one larger than the previous, between 1621 and 1624, and was given a position with the British Royal Navy to develop his ideas further. But the court magician lost his most important patron when King James died in 1625. James's successor, Charles I (1600–1649) gave Drebbel a post with the Office of Ordnance, where he worked on developing a floating bomb. In 1627 he was put in charge of the British Navy's fireships. This was a most spectacular form of floating bomb, and was loaded up with even more combustible materials then the average warship of the era, which contained sails, grease, tar, and gunpowder. The fireships were then set aflame by a skeleton crew near the enemy's ships, an act that could destroy an entire flotilla in a harbor. There was an attempt to use this tactic to help the Huguenots (French Protestants) at their enclave of La Rochelle, a port in the Bay of Biscay. But the English effort to aid La Rochelle in its defiance of the French king and Roman Catholic Church ended disastrously. The mission had been led by George Villiers (1592–1628), the first Duke of Buckingham, who was also a patron of Drebbel's. Villiers was assassinated by a disgruntled wounded army officer while attempting to organize a sec-

ond campaign, and with the death Drebbel lost another influential patron.

Some accounts note that Drebbel may have been involved in one of the first serious schemes to drain the fenlands, or wetlands, of East Anglia, a project headed by a noted Dutch engineer Cornelius Vermuyden (1590–1677). Drebbel had earned significant amounts of money in his lifetime, but both he and his wife were said to have squandered their income, she on a series of adulterous affairs. In 1629, he took over the management of an ale house, and died four years later on November 7, 1633. Two of his daughters married Abraham and Johannes Kuffler, a pair of German brothers who founded a dye house in the Dutch city of Leiden. The manufacture of their popular bright red dye known as "color Kufflerianus" was a closely guarded trade secret discovered accidentally by Drebbel years before. In crafting one of his thermometer devices, he realized that tin chloride made from naturally occurring carmine (at the time, ground-up insects known as cochineal) made the color much brighter and more durable.

Books

Science and Its Times, Volume 3: *1450–1699,* Gale, 2001.
Shachtman, Tom, *Absolute Zero and the Conquest of Cold,* Houghton Mifflin, 2000.

Online

"Cornelius Drebbel," BBC Historic Figures, http://www.bbc.co .uk/history/historic_figures/drebbel_cornelis.shtml (December 1, 2007).
"Who Was Cornelius J. Drebbel?" (Based on a text of Brett McLaughlin), University of Twente, http://www.drebbel .utwente.nl/main_en/Information/History/History.htm (December 1, 2007). □

Jean Baptiste Pointe du Sable

The African-American explorer Jean Baptiste Pointe du Sable (c. 1745-1818), despite a long period during which his contributions were minimized, is now recognized as the founder of the city of Chicago.

I n the 1770s, du Sable and his wife established a farm and trading operation on the north shore of the Chicago River, near Lake Michigan. The swampy site was previously uninhabited; it was known to local Native Americans as Eschecagou, or the land of wild onions. An 1856 account of Chicago's pioneer days (quoted in *The Devil May Care: Fifty Intrepid Americans and Their Quest for the Unknown*) noted that "the first white man who settled here [in present-day Chicago] was a Negro," for du Sable was partly of African descent; his mother was probably a Congolese-born slave. His life, though not well documented, offers insights into the world of the North American interior in the eighteenthth century, a land where interracial cooperation had existed for many decades before the culture du Sable represented was displaced by the advance of the new American nation.

Benefited from Biracial Background

The early facts of du Sable's biography are not completely clear, and even a correct spelling of his name is uncertain and may well be impossible to establish definitively, inasmuch as he lived much of his life in places where full literacy was rare. He was probably born in the port town of St. Marc in western Haiti, which was then the French colony of St.-Domingue, in the year 1745, although one account gives his birthplace as Montreal, Canada, and the determination of his birth year seems to rest on testimony that he was 73 years old when he died in 1818. His father was apparently a French seaman (or pirate) named du Sable, and his mother was of West African descent, probably a Haitian slave whose freedom had been purchased by her husband. She appears nowhere in accounts of du Sable's early life and may have been killed during his early childhood. Du Sable enjoyed privileges beyond those accorded the majority of blacks in Haiti, and he may have been sent to France for a formal education.

It was said that du Sable could speak French, Spanish, English, and several Native American languages. Such skill in learning languages suggests that he acquired some education in grammar, but this too is unsubstantiated, and one study has argued that he never learned to read and write. Du Sable arrived in North America around 1765, perhaps planning to settle in the French colony of Louisiana. During the sea passage he lost his identification documents and was worried that he would be enslaved upon landing. Du Sable hid out at a Catholic mission run by the Jesuit order, offering to work as a groundskeeper.

This stratagem enabled du Sable to establish himself in New Orleans, and he also benefited from his connection with a white French-Haitian friend, Jacques Clemorgan, whom he had known since childhood. However, having experienced the long military conflict between France and Spain over the island of Hispaniola, he would have been dismayed to find that the city of New Orleans had just been ceded by treaty to the Spanish, whom he considered his enemies. Du Sable, probably accompanied by Clemorgan and by a member of the Choctaw Native American tribe, decided to make their way north on the Mississippi River.

They stopped for a time in what is now Missouri, where du Sable established some enduring contacts. Clemorgan may have stayed on or later returned to Missouri, becoming an important figure in the early judicial history of St. Louis. But du Sable continued northward, perhaps traveling as far as Canada but then returning southward and living as a hunter and fur trapper in the lands of the Potawatomi tribe. He owned a barge that he used to transport furs down the river to New Orleans, and for a time he contributed a portion of his profits to the Jesuit mission that had sheltered him there.

Accepted by Potawatomis

Over time, like some of the other French hunters who lived among Native Americans, du Sable became more and more involved in Indian life. He learned to speak the Potawatomi language and those of several neighboring tribes. Du Sable is said to have met the great Ottawa chief, Pontiac, and to have served as his emissary to the Midwestern tribes Pontiac was trying unsuccessfully to unite against British expansionism. The unusual degree to which du Sable was accepted as a member of Potawatomi society was demonstrated when he was permitted to marry a Potawatomi woman named Kittihawa. Potawatomi women were generally forbidden to marry outside the tribe, to say nothing of marrying non-Indians. The two married in a traditional ceremony, much later (in 1788) undertaking a second ceremony officiated by a Catholic priest. Kittihawa acquired the new name of Catherine, and they raised a daughter, Suzanne (or Susanne), and a son, Jean.

Du Sable farmed land in the Peoria area for a time and probably arrived in the area now called Chicago near the beginning of the Revolutionary War; dates through the 1770s are given in various sources. What is certain is that he was quickly able to establish a prosperous farm and trading post. He constructed a solid frame house (measuring 40 by 22 feet) and was soon able to send for his wife and children. Later accounts enumerated 44 large hens, baking and smokehouses, 30 head of cattle, and other outbuildings among his possessions, and he raised and was apparently able to export wheat, hay, and other agricultural commodities. His trading post on the riverbank, located on the site of the present-day *Chicago Tribune* newspaper offices (and commemorated by a nearby plaque), served explorers, trappers, Native Americans, and military troops of several nationalities.

Visitors to du Sable's home, impressed by furnishings that included several paintings and an imported French coffee grinder, believed that he was a government official of some sort. Undoubtedly du Sable owed the success of his endeavors partly to the help of his adopted Potawatomi tribe, and the cultural coexistence he practiced stood in sharp contrast to what was to come in northern Illinois. In the words of historian Christopher Robert Reed in his book *Black Chicago's First Century*, du Sable "represented a model for all times in that his life embodied a humanistic concern for intergroup coexistence balanced against the eighteenth century's avaricious commercial spirit." Some Potawatomi started hundred-acre farms near du Sable's trading post, contributing to his prosperity.

Du Sable, who spoke English well by the late 1770s, visited Detroit and the British garrison at Fort Michilimackinac in northern Michigan, meeting the British commander, Colonel Arent Schuyler de Peyster. But that was not enough to keep him out of trouble when the tide turned against the British during the Revolutionary War— Americans of French background were presumed, correctly in most cases, to be anti-British. After du Sable refused to allow de Peyster to construct a fort in Chicago (he had likewise refused an American colonel), du Sable was arrested in August of 1779 and taken to a British prison in Port

Huron (or, according to one source, to Fort Michilimack-inac). Some sources also implicate the Wisconsin-based French nobleman Charles-Michel Mouet de Langlade, who resented du Sable's success, in the mulatto's downfall; du Sable may have fled to Michigan City, Indiana, and been arrested there after fighting flared between American and British troops.

Managed Trading Post

Du Sable remained technically a British prisoner until the end of the war, but he impressed Michigan's British governor, Patrick Sinclair, and he was apparently held under a kind of house arrest. He was even given a commission to manage a British trading post, the Pinery, and he may have served as an unofficial monitor of the military activities of Native American tribes in the region. After the British were expelled from America, du Sable returned to Chicago. Fresh sources attested to the vigor of his trading post in 1790, when a Detroit-based agent reported that he was doing a brisk business in pork, bread, and flour. His daughter married that year, and he became a grandfather in 1796. Du Sable maintained his connections with Native American culture, and around 1796 he apparently tried to obtain a minor chieftancy among some Michigan clans but was unsuccessful.

In 1800, du Sable decided to leave Chicago. Among the items the family put up for sale in the growing town were two mirrors, two paintings, 20 large wooden plates, and the coffee grinder; they were reported to have had as many as 23 paintings at one time, and they no doubt kept many possessions for themselves. The reason du Sable left Chicago has not been definitively established, but Reed has argued that it would have been connected with increasing American influence, bringing a deterioration in the region's racial attitudes. It is significant that du Sable moved southward, into regions where the French, more tolerant in racial matters, retained greater influence. The family settled once again in Peoria. After the death of Kittihawa in the early years of the nineteenth century, du Sable moved south once again, to St. Charles, Missouri.

In the last decade of his life, du Sable turned over most of his possessions to his offspring. He transferred ownership of his home in St. Charles to his granddaughter, Eulalie, in exchange for her commitment to care for him in his old age and arrange a Catholic burial after his death. Whether Eulalie fulfilled those duties is unclear. Du Sable was briefly arrested and imprisoned on charges of nonpayment of debts in 1814, and he lived out the rest of his life in poverty. He died in St. Charles on August 28 or 29, 1818.

Du Sable's contributions to Chicago's growth were expunged throughout much of the nineteenth century, but black Chicagoans, especially, worked to recover his memory in the twentieth. Du Sable High School opened in the Bronzeville neighborhood on the city's South Side in the 1930s, and a downtown harbor was later given his name. The Du Sable Museum of African American History opened in 1961, and in 1968 he was finally recognized officially as Chicago's founder. Du Sable was honored with a stamp in the U.S. Postal Service's Black Heritage series in 1987.

Books

Cortesi, Laurence, *Jean du Sable: Father of Chicago,* Chilton, 1972.
The Devil May Care: Fifty Intrepid Americans and Their Quest for the Unknown, edited by Tony Horwitz, Oxford, 2003.
Notable Black American Men, Gale, 1998.
Reed, Christopher Robert, *Black Chicago's First Century,* University of Missouri Press, 2005.

Periodicals

Jet, February 23, 1987.
St. Louis Post-Dispatch, March 7, 2000.

Online

"1779: Jean Baptiste Point DuSable," Chicago Public Library, http://www.chipublib.org/004chicago/timeline/dusable.html (February 1, 2008). □

Eugène Dubois

Dutch anatomist and paleoanthropologist Eugène Dubois (1858-1940) was the first scientist to actively search for human ancestral fossils. His efforts led to the discovery of the so-called "Java man," which was the first fossil discovery of *Homo erectus*, a direct descendent of modern humans.

Eugène Dubois gained international fame through his discovery of the *Pithecanthropus erectus*, which is now called *Homo erectus*. This discovery, as well as Dubois's related scientific claims, generated a great deal of controversy. Dubois's value to the field of anthropology, however, is inarguable.

Dubois was born on January 28, 1858 as Marie Eugène Francoise Thomas Dubois at Eijsden, in the province of Limburg, Netherlands. His parents were Jean Joseph Balthasar Dubois and Maria Catharina Floriberta Agnes Roebroeck.

Dubois was born within a period of important scientific discovery and research related to natural history and human origins. In particular, in 1856, two years before Dubois was born, primitive human fossils were uncovered in the Neander Valley in Germany. Then, in 1859, naturalist Charles Darwin published his controversial work *On the Origins of Species.* The new scientific knowledge would greatly influence Dubois's interests, education and career.

As a boy, Dubois demonstrated a great fascination for the natural world, especially the flora that flourished in the area where he grew up. He was encouraged in this direction by his father, who was a pharmacist. Later, as a high school student, he developed an interest in human origins.

Became a Teacher

In 1877, Dubois enrolled at the University of Amsterdam and studied medicine. An excellent student, Dubois

tion efforts near the Neolithic flint mines in his own country, but he found nothing of substantial scientific value.

Now, Dubois chose the Dutch East Indies because of its plentiful caves. Up to this point, all human fossils had been found in caves. Moreover, the Dutch East Indies attracted Dubois because, like Darwin and other scientists, he believed that humans could only evolve in a warm climate, such as that afforded by the tropics. In addition, he believed that humans were closely related to gibbons, which live in Indonesia.

To gain passage to his destination, Dubois enlisted in the Royal Dutch East Indies army as a surgeon. He arrived, with his wife and very young son, on October 29, 1887, and was assigned to a post on Sumatra. The area was rampant with disease, and Dubois could only search for fossils during spare time from his medical responsibilities. Still, his early efforts revealed promise, and the government provided him with the services of two engineers and 50 enforced laborers. Despite these assets, Dubois's subsequent efforts were disappointing. In addition, uncovering fossils proved difficult, as Dubois was stationed in a harsh, dangerous environment, where foliage was dense and water was in limited supply. Also, illness beset his crew. One of his engineers became sick and the other died. Some of his laborers died, too, and many abandoned the fossil-finding enterprise.

In May of 1888, Dubois transferred to the Sumatran village of Pajakombo, which led to his discovery of animal fossils in the Lida Adjer Cave. In turn, the government subsidized further research on Java, where a human skull fossil had recently been unearthed in Wadjak Cave. Dubois was excited by the prospect of digging up more fossils.

Uncovered Important Artifacts on Java

Dubois began searching the same area on Java and, in 1890 at Koedoeng Broeboes, his workers found a second but less complete skull. Their find included the right side of the chin and three attached teeth. This discovery compelled Dubois to move beyond caves and into more open areas. A year later, he and his workers focused their efforts near Trinil, located along the Solo River. The site had yielded many mammal fossils. In August of 1881, they found a fossilized molar of a primate. In October of that year, they made a most interesting discovery: a skullcap that appeared not quite human but not quite ape. Dubois believed the molar and the skullcap came from a chimpanzee that possessed obvious human attributes.

Later that year, Dubois's crew found a whole skullcap, a discovery that would come to be known as "Java Man." In August 1892, they made another significant discovery in the same area: a nearly complete left thighbone. Dubois proposed that all of the finds came from the same human-like chimpanzee. Further, as the thighbone's structure resembled a human femur, Dubois believed its owner had walked erect. This discovery, along with a later recalculation of the skull capacity, led Dubois to believe that he indeed had found the "missing link." He named the specimen *Pithecanthropus erectus*, which means the "ape-man who walked upright."

Dubois also felt his discoveries confirmed two popular, contemporary theories: that upright posture was the first

became an assistant to Dutch morphologist Max Furbinger in 1881, an arrangement that further directed his education and career into anatomy. In college, he wrote a paper about the human larynx. The work discussed the organ's structure and suggested that the mammalian larynx evolved from the gill cartilage of fish. Dubois graduated from Amsterdam as a doctor in 1884. In 1886, he was appointed a lecturer in anatomy at the university. That same year, he married Anna Geertruida Lojenga.

Dubois's early post-graduate years were marked by resentments and frustrations. He was not a particularly enthusiastic educator (he entered his lecture appointment with some reluctance) and his relationship with Furbinger eventually became contentious. Meanwhile, he became even more interested in human origins, due to his discussions with Dutch botanist Hugo De Vries, who had studied Darwin and Charles Lyell, as well as Ernst Haeckel, who had come up with the name *Pithecanthropus alalus* for Darwin's proposed "missing link" between man and ape. As a result, Dubois wanted to prove Darwin's theories by finding the so-called missing link. The best way to do this, he reasoned, was through evidence of evolution afforded by human fossils.

Sought Fossils In the East Indies

To pursue his scientific passions, Dubois gave up his position at the University of Amsterdam in 1887 to travel to the Dutch East Indies (now Indonesia), where he believed he had the best chance to find transitional human fossils. Earlier in 1876 and 1877, Dubois conducted fossil excava-

stage in the evolution that gave rise to humans, and that the East Indies (and not Africa, as scientists including Darwin had proposed) was the birthplace of the human race.

In addition, more precise examination of the fossils, which had been estimated to be about a half-million years old, led Dubois to develop a saltationist theory about human evolution. The theory advanced the idea of a more rapid and punctuated rate of evolution than presumed in Darwin's gradualist theory.

While Dubois's discoveries in the East Indies and Java had helped advance the understanding of human evolution, his search proved to be an adventure fraught with peril. He had almost met with death due to malaria, tigers and collapsing caves. Most tragically, he lost a son to tropical fever. Later, a return trip from Java to Europe proved nearly as perilous. The ship that carried Dubois, his wife and his three children got caught up in a storm so violent that the captain ordered all passengers into the lifeboats. Reportedly, Dubois told his wife that if anything happened to their lifeboat, she would have to assume the responsibility of the children. He explained to her that he would have to concentrate on saving the important fossils that he had found.

Encountered Criticism in Europe

In August 1894, after he returned to Europe, Dubois published his findings and theories in a thirty-nine page paper titled *Pithecanthropus erectus, eine menschenaehnliche Uebergangsform*. In it, he described the *Pithecanthropus erectus* as neither ape nor human, but something in between (a "missing link"). As with most new ideas that broke from conventional thought, Dubois's work generated strong criticism. The main point of controversy involved Dubois's contention that the molar, skull cap and thighbone belonged to the same individual. However, while his ape-to-man theory was ridiculed, Dubois was praised for discovering a new species of gibbon as well as for placing human existence in the Pliocene epoch, some five million years earlier than had been believed.

Dubois strongly defended his interpretation, backing up his assertions with more information about his fossils. Also, he pointed out that some scientific experts felt the skull was ape-like while others thought it to be more human-like. This, he believed, only underscored his theory that the skull presented a mix of both ape and human characteristics.

In 1895, Dubois traveled throughout Europe to lecture about and present the fossils. On September 21, 1895, the fossils were displayed at the Third International Congress of Zoology held in Leiden.

Settled in Amsterdam

In 1897, Dubois and his wife made their home in Haarlem, located west of Amsterdam, where he took the position as curator of the Teylers Museum. He would retain the position until he died. That same year, Dubois received an honorary doctorate in botany and zoology from the University of Amsterdam. In 1899, he became a professor of crystallography, mineralogy, geology and paleontology at the University. Despite the recognition, Dubois's appointments didn't carry much prestige, especially considering the import of his work and discoveries.

As the nineteenth-century drew to a close, scientific consensus started to shift in Dubois's favor. Some previously dissenting critics had begun to concur with his interpretations. In particular, they agreed with Dubois's age determination and genealogical positioning for the ape-man. Still, Dubois harbored bitterness about the overall experience that he would hold throughout his later years. By 1900, he refused to discuss the *Pithecanthropus erectus* any longer. According to accounts, he stored the fossils in his home and focused on other research.

After 1900, Dubois conducted research into the evolution of the mammalian brain size as it corresponded to body size. Earlier, he came up with calculations that he felt revealed that brain size doubled with each evolutionary stage. However, these calculations did not fit into his theory that the *Pithecanthropus erectus* provided the missing link between man and ape. Thus, he was now compelled to modify his methodology. But his revised method has been deemed as an expedient way to support his saltationist theory of evolution. Specifically, critics pointed out that Dubois enhanced the body weight of the *Pithecanthropus erectus* to fit the theory.

In 1923, responding to strong entreaties from scientists, Dubois brought the Java Man fossils out of storage. By this time, the discoveries of similar fossils had made Dubois's fossils a popular topic of discussion once again. In 1929, the partial skull of Peking (or Beijing) man was found in China. Three more were found in 1936. Also, due to the increased acceptance of Dubois's Java Man interpretations, a Dutch anatomist, Ralph von Koenigswald, traveled to Java on his own fossil expedition. He eventually dug up fossil remains for almost forty individuals that strongly resembled the *Pithecanthropus erectus*. As it turned out, the new evidence unearthed demonstrated that Dubois's Java Man was not an intermediate species (or a missing link) but a direct ancestor to the modern human. As a result, these newer fossils, along with Dubois's fossils, were eventually reclassified as *Homo erectus*.

Died in the Netherlands

In the meantime, Dubois had officially retired in 1928, but he continued conducting scientific research. He died in his Haarlem home in the Netherlands on December 16, 1940. He was eighty-three years old. Dubois's discovery, the *Pithecanthropus erectus* eventually reclassified as *Homo erectus*, is regarded as one of the most important finds in history.

Online

"Biographies: Eugène Dubois," *Talkorigins.org*, http://www.talk origins.org/faqs/homs/edubois.html (October 31, 2007).

"Fossil Hominids, Human Evolution: Thomas Huxley & Eugène Dubois," Understanding Evolution, http://evolution.berkeley .edu/evolibrary/article/_0/history_17 (October 31, 2007).

"Rocky Road: Eugène Dubois," Strangescience.net, http://www .strangescience.net/dubois.htm (October 31, 2007).

World of Biology Online, Thomson Gale, 2006, http://galenet .galegroup.com/servlet/BioRC (October 31, 2007).

World of Scientific Discovery Online, Thomson Gale, 2006, http://galenet.galegroup.com/servlet/BioRC (October 31, 2007). □

E

Harold Eugene Edgerton

Harold Edgerton (1903-1990) the inventor of the Stroboscopic flashbulb, created a revolutionary way of looking at the world. He was responsible for inventing a bulb that could flash rapidly in conjunction with a high-speed camera. Edgerton captured motion on high-speed film, producing some of the most expressive photographs that the artistic community had ever seen.

Early Life

Harold Eugene Edgerton was born on April 6, 1903, in Fremont, Nebraska. From a young age, Edgerton showed an interest in all things mechanical. As a young boy he got his first taste of electricity when he bought some old Ham Radio equipment from a friend. Using some items found around the house, he crafted his own antenna for the Ham equipment, and then wanted to take a picture of what he had done. The art of photography was a young science at the time, not to mention expensive. The first few photos Edgerton managed to take were rather devoid of life because he could not get enough light onto the scene. His interest in photography would stay with him throughout his life, and soon he would invent a device that would effectively banish the problems of photographic lighting.

Invented the Stroboscopic Bulb

Edgerton attended the University of Nebraska for his undergraduate studies, earning a degree in electrical engineering. He went on to work for General Electric in New York, and soon entered the Massachusetts Institute of Technology (MIT) for graduate studies. Edgerton received both his master's and doctoral degrees in electrical engineering from MIT, and remained there to become a tenured professor.

While working with power generators, Edgerton noticed that when light would flash onto the spinning rotors, they appeared to stand still for a split second. The flash would illuminate one small moment in time, making everything seem to be at rest. This happy accident is what gave Edgerton the inspiration to create the first reusable flash bulb.

Edgerton created his first electric flash bulb in 1928. At the time, the technology was not available to create fluorescent lighting. The stroboscopic bulb that Edgerton invented contained mercury gas that emitted light when a pulse of high voltage electricity was passed through the tube itself. However, Edgerton switched from Mercury gas to Argon and Xenon, because these other gases provided just as much light as Mercury, and were easier to control while lasting for longer periods of time.

On January 14, 1932, during the height of the Great Depression, Edgerton approached a patent attorney and offered up his invention, called the Stroboscope, for a patent. Edgerton had no money, and told the attorney that he could not afford to pay for a patent. This man was so impressed by Edgerton's invention that he decided to put the patent forward for review immediately. Edgerton would go on to create a multitude of different devices, from the sonar that is used in deep sea diving to a bulb bright enough to illuminate the ground from 1500 feet in the air. However, the Stroboscope was the invention that would lead to Edgerton's continued success in the areas of both science and the arts.

Art Met Science

The Stroboscope bulb was soon being used in factories and plants all around the United States to gauge the revolution rates of fans and turbines that could only be seen if captured on film with this high frequency flash bulb. Edgerton set up a photo laboratory and experimented by taking high frequency pictures of his assistants and others doing things like swinging a golf club, throwing a baton high in the air, and jumping rope. He was able to capture every movement of the human being as well as the object on one piece of film, and thus created mosaics that captured not only the beginning and end of the action, but also the actions in the middle that moved too fast for slower light sources to capture. The stroboscopic bulb could be set to different intervals of flashing, and was sensitive enough to capture a millisecond of history. The bulb could make faster objects seem much slower, or could make them appear to be going in reverse. The bulb was a powerful invention, not only for artistic pursuits but also in the realm of scientific discovery.

Edgerton was asked to use his stroboscopic light to capture athletes in action at the Boston Garden indoor sports arena. This would be the first time that anyone outside of Edgerton or his assistants had seen the device work. Even the patent lawyer had not seen it. Edgerton and his assistants moved the Stroboscope into the arena and set it up to take pictures of the athletes while they performed.

This was a momentous occasion, not only for Edgerton and his new invention, but also for the art of photography. Before Edgerton had invented his bulb, the only way to get sufficient light to take a good photograph indoors was to use flash powder, a mixture of magnesium and other chemical substances. The powder was activated as soon as the camera shutter opened to expose the film. The resulting flash was bright, but dangerous to be near. The powder was actually set on fire, and burned out in the instant that the picture was taken. These flashes were powerful, but because of the chemicals used, there were worries about its danger to humans, specifically to the nervous system. The flash powder had to be held close to the photographic subject, so there was no escaping the burst of powder as the picture was taken.

The stroboscopic bulb changed all of this. It was safe to use at close range, did not interfere with the activities of the photographic subjects, and was bright enough for illumination both indoors and out. After Edgerton was finished capturing the athletes at the Boston arena, the newspapers raved about this new technology, proclaiming that Edgerton's "high speed graphic camera" was creating the photography of the future.

Edgerton himself believed that his pictures were records of events, and not just a picture in time. Edgerton wanted to reveal the hidden activities of nature, and through his Stroboscope was able to produce pictures that captured these actions very clearly. One of his most famous images is that of a milk droplet that splashes into a puddle of milk and creates a corona, or crown, above the puddle. He programmed his camera to flash in the milliseconds of this event. Edgerton also captured the images of a bullet penetrating an apple, a balloon, a light bulb and other objects. He was able to capture the very instant when the bullet entered and left the object. The resulting image showed just how the laws of nature worked during these kinds of events. Just like the milk splash, the pictures of the bullet piercing an apple showed that there was just as much of an impact at the entry point of the bullet as there was when the bullet exited the apple. Before this kind of photography, these images could not have been captured. Edgerton supplied scientists and artists with a way to explore the hidden world of "in-between," where events could be seen from all points of view, and not just from before and after.

Wider Uses of the Stroboscopic Bulb

Edgerton's high-powered lights not only helped to illuminate the movements of athletes and bullets, but also served to light the territories of Germany and France during World War II. Edgerton was approached by the U.S. government and asked if his new invention would be powerful enough to illuminate the ground from above. Edgerton ran a test to verify the technology. The test involved flying a plane above Stonehenge in Britain, and flashing a light down on the ancient structure from 1500 feet above. A camera was situated at ground level, and was programmed to take a picture at the same time that the overhead bulb flashed. The resulting picture showed Stonehenge illuminated from above, just as if a beam of light from above was shining down on it. This proved that the flash bulbs could be used to illuminate enemy territory at ground level, and it provided helpful reconnaissance during night spy flights.

Edgerton received a U.S. Medal of Freedom for his work with the war effort. After the war ended, Edgerton used his knowledge of engineering to create a sonar version of his Stroboscope. He was able to use sound in the same way he used light, and gave deep water explorers the first tools that could be used to measure the depth of a body of water. The device itself was called the pinger, and is still used today to measure water depth. The pinger sonar was also used to locate shipwrecks on the bottom of the oceans, by sending down pulses of sound to identify differences of depth in the waters. Edgerton also invented the camera that took some of the first pictures of the Titanic when it was discovered on the ocean floor. The bulbs used in underwater sea diving were also Edgerton's creation.

Edgerton formed a friendship with the famous undersea explorer Jacques Yves Cousteau (1910-1997), and he would accompany Cousteau on many of his voyages beneath the waters, taking pictures of discoveries along the way. Edgerton had a passion for underwater photography, and developed tools to aid him in the taking of underwater pictures. Edgerton's moniker was "Papa Flash," and it was an accurate one, because in many ways he was was the father of the modern flashbulb technology that is used today.

Legacy

Edgerton was one of the most prolific inventors in history. His inventions greatly advanced the science of high-speed imagery, as well as the artistic world of photography, and earned him much fame and reputation in the artistic and scientific worlds. Through his discovery of the strobo-scopic bulb, as well as its many uses and adaptations, Edgerton showed that the milliseconds of every activity could be captured clearly, and this opened up a realm of discovery that had to that point been unseen by the human eye.

Books

Contemporary Photographers, 3rd ed. St. James Press, 1996.
Edgerton, Harold, *Stopping Time: The Photographs of Harold Edgerton.* New York: Harry N. Abrams, 1987
Notable Scientists: From 1900 to the Present. Gale Group. 2001.

Online

Contemporary Authors Online, Gale, 2007, http://galenet.gale group.com/servlet/BioRC (February 27, 2008).
World of Invention. Online. Thomson Gale, 2006. http://galenet .galegroup.com/servlet/BioRC (April 14, 2008). □

Elisabeth, Empress of Austria

The German-born Elisabeth, Empress of Austria (1837-1898), was the beloved "Sisi," one of the most famous royal celebrities of her day. As the consort of the emperor of Austria—a land that dominated the map of Europe at the time—Elisabeth was a well-known figure whose exploits were avidly chronicled

in the nineteenth-century press much in the same way that Britain's Diana (1961-1997), Princess of Wales, would be a hundred years later.

The future empress was born Elisabeth Amalie Eugenie von Wittelsbach on December 24, 1837, in Munich, Bavaria. Her father was Maximilian Joseph, a duke from one of Germany's oldest aristocratic families, the House of Wittelsbach. In possession of vast estates throughout southern Germany, the von Wittelsbachs had been the ruling dynasty in the area since 1180, and played a key role in shaping the region's political destinies. During Elisabeth's lifetime, Bavaria was a kingdom ruled by perhaps the most famous Wittelsbach, her cousin King Ludwig II (1845–1886), often referred to as "Mad Ludwig." Eight years her junior, he ascended to the throne in 1864 and built the fairy-tale castle of Neuschwanstein, later used as the model for the castle of Sleeping Beauty in the Disney theme parks. As cousins, Elisabeth and Ludwig were close, and though she later defended him when he was declared mentally ill, she reportedly feared that she had inherited the same strain of mental illness that ran through their side of the family.

Whirlwind Courtship

There is some speculation that such genetic conditions may have been exacerbated by a tradition of intermarriage in the royal dynasty. Elisabeth's father, for example, married his cousin, Ludovika, Royal Princess of Bavaria and daughter of King Maximilian I. The pair raised their family at Possenhofen Castle on Lake Starnberg outside Munich, and would have ten children in all. Elisabeth was close to her older sister, Helene, who married into an equally powerful old German family, the Thurn und Taxis. Helene was dubbed "Nene" as a child, while Elisabeth bore the nickname "Sisi."

In the summer of 1853, when Elisabeth was 15, she and her sister, accompanied by their mother Ludovika, traveled to Bad Ischl, the Austrian resort. Ludovika made notable matches for nearly all of her children, and was eager to introduce 18-year-old Helene to the new Emperor of Austria, Franz Josef (1830–1916). The handsome young emperor, who had ascended to the throne in 1848, was the son of Ludovika's sister, Princess Sophia and was a popular young ruler also considered to be Europe's most eligible bachelor at the time. He was instantly smitten with Elisabeth, not her sister, and their engagement was announced just a week later. The wedding took place in Vienna on April 24, 1854, and Elisabeth would later say that she deeply regretted accepting the marriage proposal after such a whirlwind romance. Franz Josef's mother, Princess Sophia, was also reportedly uneasy with the plan to marry the younger Wittelsbach niece, but gave her permission anyway.

After a honeymoon that included a tour of Austria and Hungary, Elisabeth—now the Empress of Austria—settled into life at the Habsburg court. The Habsburg dynasty had the richest, most opulent royal court in Europe at the time, in an era when nationalism and the ideas of the Enlightenment were giving way to liberal reforms elsewhere on the continent, and clung dearly to its long-cherished protocols and rigid etiquette. Still a teenager, Elisabeth disliked the stiff formality that regulated her public appearances, and her unease was compounded by the disdain that many Austrian nobles at court held for Bavarians, whom they considered inferior. One such custom that she found tiresome concerned her boots: the empress was expected to wear a pair just once, and then give them to one of her ladies in waiting. Instead, Elisabeth wore hers for a month. On one occasion, she shocked an aristocrat seated near her at a formal dinner by removing her gloves. When the older woman asked why she did so, Elisabeth replied, "Why not?" to which the woman answered, "Because it is a deviation from the rules." At that, cognizant of her power as empress, Elisabeth retorted, "Then let the deviation henceforth be the rule," according to A. De Burgh's biography, *Elizabeth, Empress of Austria: A Memoir.*

Devastated by Daughter's Death

Elisabeth produced three children in the first four years of her marriage: Archduchess Sophie, born in March of 1855; Archduchess Gisela, born in July of 1856, and Crown Prince Rudolf, born in August of 1858. Sophie died while the family was on an official visit to Hungary, which was part of Franz Josef's empire. It was in May of 1857 when both royal infant daughters fell ill with diarrhea. Gisela recovered, but Sophie died in Budapest. The empress was reportedly grief-stricken over the loss of her first child, and sunk into a deep depression that was only alleviated by the birth of Rudolf, the long-awaited male heir, in the summer of 1858.

It was uncommon for parents among Europe's royalty to actively participate in the rearing of their children, and Elisabeth's family was no exception. The care and supervision of Gisela and Rudolf were largely given over to a team of staffers supervised by her mother-in-law, Princess Sophia. Elisabeth was thus free to travel, and she eagerly seized any opportunity to be away from the stifling protocol of the Habsburg court. She spent time in England, and on the Mediterranean isle of Corfu, and also on Madeira, an island in the Atlantic Ocean midway off the coasts of Portugal and West Africa. Hungary was also a rather unexpected favorite destination, for there was strong nationalist sentiment against the ruling Habsburgs in the country and a concerted independence movement. Elisabeth's husband had even been the target of a political assassination by a Hungarian activist just months before they met, but the stiff, high collar of his uniform apparently saved him from bleeding to death from the stab wound.

Elisabeth's exploits were avidly chronicled in the burgeoning new journalism aimed at a newly literate, mass-market readership. Her fashion sense, exuberant lifestyle, and rumors of romantic liaisons were all reported on in great detail, and the time she and Franz Josef spent apart spurred rumors that their union was over in all but name. In this respect, Elisabeth shared many similarities to Princess Diana of England, whose marriage similarly imploded after a spectacular 1981 royal wedding to the most eligible bachelor in Europe. Like Diana, Elisabeth was also plagued by rumors that she suffered from an eating disorder. The empress was indeed conscious about maintaining her figure and reported 20-inch waist, and did daily gymnastic exercises, including stunts on flying rings. She also studied Greek and wrote verse, giving herself the literary pen name of Titania, from Shakespeare's *Fairy Queen,* and some of her poems featured sly rebukes to the Habsburgs. In her later years she became one of the most widely traveled European royals of her day, venturing into the Middle East and North Africa.

Mysterious Death of Son

Elisabeth and Franz Josef had a brief reconciliation, occasioned by his decision to establish a double monarchy, which created the Austro-Hungarian Empire in 1867. She was given a new title, Queen of Hungary, in addition to that of Empress of Austria. A coronation was held for both in Budapest, and their fourth child, Archduchess Marie Valerie, was born in April of 1868. Elisabeth took a much more involved parenting role this time, and she and her youngest child became quite close. There were rumors that Marie Valerie was perhaps the result of an extramarital affair, but she strongly resembled Franz Josef. The gossip likely stemmed from the fact that both the parties conducted extramarital affairs during the course of their marriage. The emperor was linked for many years to Austria's best-known actress, while Elisabeth carried on with a dashing British noble, George Middleton, who was an attendant to an ancestor of Princess Diana's. He and Elisabeth—an accomplished equestrienne—met while riding at the Spencer estate, Althorp. He visited her at her Hungarian summer estate, Gödöllö, on at least two occasions between their first meeting in 1876 and his 1882 marriage.

The spectacular Gödöllö, an immense Baroque palace, was located outside Budapest. Elisabeth also began building a castle, called Achilleion, on Corfu, which was completed in 1890. This was the year that Marie Valerie married the man of her choice, the Archduke of Austria-Tuscany, rather than one of the more powerful dynastic scions of Europe which might have cemented a new diplomatic alliance for the Austro-Hungarian throne. Elisabeth backed Marie Valerie's choice of spouse, and their intransigence was said to have angered Crown Prince Rudolf, who had several years earlier complied with pressure to marry the daughter of the King of Belgium. On January 30, 1889, the 31-year-old Rudolf and his 17-year-old mistress, Baroness Mary Vetsera, were found dead at his Mayerling hunting lodge in Lower Austria in what was claimed to have been a double suicide. Revelations in the 1990s, however, suggest that a third party may have been involved, which is tied to speculation that the more liberal-minded Rudolf was planning to seize the throne from his father with the help of foreign conspirators.

Rudolf's death plunged the Empress into a period of deep mourning. She spent the remaining eight years of her life clad in a long black gown, with a white leather parasol and a fan to hide her face from the public. Her final years were spent at Gödöllö or aboard her steamer, the *Miramar*. She died at age 60 on September 10, 1898, in front of the Beau Rivage Hotel in Geneva, Switzerland, in one of the more bizarre incidents of nineteenth-century European history: a 25-year-old anarchist named Luigi Lucheni rushed at her with a needle file in hand, and delivered a fatal stab wound to her heart. In an eerie similarity with the assassination attempt on her husband years before, Elisabeth's corset stanched the bleeding, but once physicians removed the tightly laced undergarment, the bleeding intensified and she died. Lucheni claimed to have not known who she was, only that she was royal and he intended to kill a member of that class.

The "Sisi" Cult

Elisabeth's assassination is viewed by many historians as the foreshadowing of a more famous one 16 years later, the 1914 shooting of her nephew, Archduke Franz Ferdinand, who was heir to the Austro-Hungarian throne. The archduke's death unleashed World War I (1914–18), which finally brought down the Habsburgs. News of Elisabeth's death prompted an outpouring of public mourning in Hungary, for many Hungarians considered her the only member of the royal family worthy of their respect. In the decades to follow, the Empress Elisabeth has become a sentimental icon in both Austria and Germany. A 1955 film which starred a young Romy Schneider enshrined her in the public imagination as *Sissi* and became an instant classic, along with its two equally successful sequels, "Sissi: The Young Empress" and "Sissi: Fateful Years of an Empress." In a less kitschy 1968 movie, Elisabeth was portrayed by Ava Gardner in the tale of Rudolf's doomed romance, *Mayerling*, which also starred Omar Sharif and Catherine Deneuve. Even in the twenty-first century Elisabeth's iconic status seemed to endure, with her life becoming the subject of a 2003 stage musical in Vienna.

Books

De Burgh, A., *Elizabeth, Empress of Austria: A Memoir*, Lippincott, 1899. □

F

Nuruddin Farah

Somali writer Nuruddin Farah (born 1945) is one of Africa's most acclaimed contemporary writers, as well as the sole Somali author whose works have achieved international renown. Farah has lived in exile from his homeland since 1976, when the content of his second novel was deemed treasonous by Somalia's ruling dictatorship. After learning that he was persona non grata that day in Rome in 1976, he vowed that "if I couldn't go back home then I would systematically make the rest of Africa my country," he explained in a *Publishers Weekly* interview with Stephen Gray.

Farah was born on November 24, 1945, in the south-central Somali city of Baidoa. At the time of his birth, the area was under British jurisdiction in the months just following World War II; prior to this, Somalia had been a colonial possession of Italy, along with neighboring Ethiopia and, beyond that, the nation of Eritrea. The alliances and animosities in this region, known as the Horn of Africa, along with decisions made by foreign powers in this postwar era, would play a large role in shaping the long and deadly descent into chaos that marked Somalia's late twentieth-century history.

Studied in India

In addition to his first language, Somali, Farah became fluent in English, Italian, Arabic, and Amharic—the predominant tongue of Ethiopia—reflecting the cosmopolitan, multicultural nature of the region. Somalia's capital was Mogadishu, which had been a trading port connected to the Indian subcontinent since the first century C.E. Farah's father, Hassan, was a merchant, and his mother, Aleeli, was a poet whose work was presented orally, according to the literary tradition of Somalia at the time. The Somali tongue, part of the Cushitic family of languages spoken in the Horn of Africa, was not codified into a written language until the early 1970s, just when Farah was beginning his career as a writer.

Farah attended school in Kallafo, a city located in Ogaden, which was a largely Somali-populated region that bordered Ethiopia and figured prominently in a long-running dispute between the two nations. His family had settled there when he was a toddler, but when the border war flared up once again, they were forced to flee to Mogadishu. As a young man, he took a job as a clerk-typist with Somalia's Ministry of Education in 1964, but two years later went to Punjab University in Chandigarh, India, to spend the next three years studying philosophy, literature, and sociology.

Farah returned to Somalia in 1969, the same year that a military coup led by a Somali army officer, General Siad Barre (1919-1995), ousted the regime which had administered the country since the World War II era, installed when the area achieved independence from Britain. Initially Marxist in fervor and progressive in outlook, the new Barre regime was greeted with enthusiasm by many young Somalis, Farah among them, for its revolutionary goals. One of Barre's first official acts, for example, was to end the reliance on colonial languages in Somalia's educational system, and he ordered linguists to rush a written form of the Somali language into development.

Published First Novel

Though Farah initially took a job as a secondary school teacher when he returned from India, he was also aiming for a literary career, and in 1970 his first novel, *From a Crooked*

Rib, was published in English by the Heinemann publishing house in London as part of its influential African Writers Series. Farah's story centers on Ebla, a young Somali woman who struggles to break free of the constraints that keep her from an independent life and will force her into an arranged marriage. He took the title of the novel from a well-known Somali proverb, "God created woman from a crooked rib; and any one who trieth to straighten it, breaketh it," according to an article that appeared in London's *Independent* in 2005."

In the early 1970s, Farah taught comparative literature at the university level in Mogadishu while working on his second novel, which for a time was serialized in a new Somali-language newspaper but then halted. This would be the sole work that he wrote in the Somali language. The Barre regime, now firmly allied with the Soviet Union, was becoming an increasingly repressive one, and Farah decided to leave for a time in order to study playwriting in England. He spent time at the University of London and the University of Essex, and in 1976 served a stint at London's acclaimed Royal Court Theatre. His next book, *A Naked Needle,* appeared that same year under the Heinemann imprint. Its plot centers around a marriage discussed between a teacher in Mogadishu and an English girl he meets while studying abroad. When she arrives in Somalia, the young, idealistic Somali has second thoughts about the interracial match.

Forced into Exile

A Naked Needle contained descriptions of life in contemporary Somalia that the Barre regime deemed unaccept-

able, and this precipitated the events that would change Farah's life in a major way. In 1976 he was at the Fiumicino airport in Rome awaiting a flight home to Somalia, and he phoned his brother in Mogadishu to arrange an airport pickup. His brother warned him not to board the plane, telling him that the authorities were so incensed about his novel that it was advisable to instead "forget Somalia," and to "think of it as if it no longer exists for you," Farah recalled during an interview with Maya Jaggi in the London *Guardian.* From that point forward, Farah lived in several African nations, including Uganda, the Gambia, and Nigeria. Freed from the fear of political reprisals, he began writing a trilogy called "Variations on the Theme of an African Dictatorship." The first novel was *Sweet and Sour Milk,* published in Britain in 1979. The story centers on Loyaan, a dentist who learns that the recent death of his twin brother was tied to the latter's underground political activities in opposition to an authoritarian regime of a ruler known only as "the General."

Maps Lauded by Academia

Farah's next novel in the trilogy was *Sardines,* published in 1981. Its protagonist is Medina, a former journalist who finds herself in trouble with the General's regime. In the third and final work, *Close Sesame,* a man is released from prison after decades of political dissent under various regimes. When he learns that his son is now involved in a coup plot, he attempts to halt the ill-conceived plan. *Close Sesame* appeared in 1982, the same year that all three works in the first trilogy first appeared in print in the United States. By this point Farah had become well-known in European literary circles, and he emerged as an important new discovery among American academics in 1986 with *Maps,* the first in his "Blood in the Sun" trilogy. The work attracted major attention in academia, and immediately became part of the standard reading list for courses on postcolonial literature.

Maps focuses on the coming of age of Askar, who is a boy in Ogaden before moving to Mogadishu during his teens. "At the same time as he discovers the 'territory of pain' connected with the necessary separations that lead to manhood, he becomes aware of the border conflict between Somalia and Ethiopia," explained Jacqueline Bardolph in an essay on Farah that appeared in *Research in African Literatures.* "The two themes, the personal and the political, are woven in a complex manner, all the more striking as the narrative sequences follow one another in the first-, second-, and third-person pronouns, 'I,' 'you,' 'he.' "

Won Neustadt Prize

In 1996 Farah was finally able to return to Somalia for the first time in 22 years, when he made a brief visit to family members who had remained there. Barre had finally been ousted in January of 1991, but the country had erupted into civil war in the interim. In 1998 Farah won the Neustadt International Prize for Literature, a highly prestigious literary award given by the University of Oklahoma and its journal, *World Literature Today.* With its $40,000 prize purse, the Neustadt is considered the literary world's second most coveted honor after the Nobel Prize. Farah joined an impressive list of past Neustadt recipients, including Colombian novelist Gabriel García Márquez (born 1927) and Poland's Czesław Miłosz (1911-2004).

Later in 1998 Farah moved to Capetown, South Africa, with his wife, Nigerian academic Amina Mama, with whom he has a son. *Secrets,* the second work in his "Blood in the Sun" trilogy, also appeared that year. Again, the story features a powerful female protagonist, in this case Sholoongo, who is abandoned by her mother and raised by lions, later moves to New York City, and returns to Somalia in the early 1990s, just as Barre's dictatorship is winding down. The third work in Farah's trilogy was *Gifts,* which appeared in 1999. Its protagonist is Duniya, a nurse who worries about her family as Somalia's civil war looms. She also recalls her own struggle for independence as a young woman, when a marriage to an elderly blind man was arranged by her family.

Farah began a new trilogy in 2004 with *Links,* the story of Jeebleh, a Somali immigrant to the United States who returns to his homeland after two decades' absence. He becomes enmeshed in the terror experienced by the family of his long-time friend, whose young daughter appears to have been kidnapped by the local warlord. The next work in the trilogy was 2007's *Knots.* Its heroine is Cambara, a Somali immigrant to Canada whose young son has drowned in a swimming pool because of the negligence of her adulterous husband. Grief-stricken, she returns to Mogadishu determined to retake possession of her family's former home, now the lair of one of the notorious warlords who dominated Somali politics until just before the novel's actual publication.

Briefly Ventured into Diplomacy

The author himself reluctantly returned once again to Somalia when he was asked to serve as go-between to settle a conflict between the transitional government and an Islamic fundamentalist group. His mission was unsuccessful, but he wrote of it in a 2007 *New York Times* article titled "My Life as a Diplomat," in which he concluded that "the only way out of the current impasse is to resume dialogue between the two principal parties to the conflict. I now know from personal experience how difficult this is."

Farah also spoke about the experience in an interview with Jeffrey Brown of *News Hour,* a Public Broadcasting Service (PBS) news program. Brown asked Farah about an oft-repeated quote the author had made many years before, when he asserted that his mission was "to keep my country alive by writing about it." Farah replied, "When I said that, I was a young man. You could say that, being young, I was also ambitious. I dreamt that this is what I was going to do. And now that I am older, the only thing I can say is that I have tried my best to keep my country alive by writing about it, and the reason is because nothing good comes out of a country until the artists of that country turn to writing about it in a truthful way."

Periodicals

Guardian (London, England), April 3, 1993; May 3, 1996.
Independent (London, England), March 11, 2005.
New York Times, July 19, 1998; May 19, 2004; April 8, 2007; May 26, 2007.

Publishers Weekly, August 23, 1999.
Research in African Literatures, Spring 1998.

Online

"Somali Author Reflects on Conflict in Native Country," PBS, http://www.pbs.org/newshour/bb/africa/jan-june07/farah_02-27.html (January 10, 2008). ☐

Drew Gilpin Faust

In 2007 American scholar Drew Gilpin Faust (born 1947) became Harvard University's first woman president. A longtime scholar of American history and a specialist in feminist and American Civil War studies, Faust had spent her entire career in the academic world, and her appointment to the Harvard presidency became a benchmark moment in U.S. higher education. Among the eight schools of the Ivy League—the oldest, most prestigious colleges and universities in the United States—fully half were now led by women presidents. Just 50 years earlier, many of those same schools barred women from enrollment.

Born Catharine Drew Gilpin on September 18, 1947, in New York City, Faust was raised in the wealthy Shenandoah Valley area of northern Virginia. Her father, McGhee Tyson Gilpin (died 2000), was a thoroughbred horse breeder whose grandfather, Lawrence Tyson (1861-1929), had been a prominent senator from Tennessee. Her mother's family were denizens of Far Hills, New Jersey, a similarly elite enclave. Faust and her three brothers grew up in a part of Clarke County that had been home to several generations of Gilpins known for their prize-winning racehorses. Like most affluent families of the area, they had African-American employees in their household, and Faust recalled that at around the age of nine she became aware of the school segregation issue. The matter had been decided three years earlier, in the landmark 1954 *Brown v. Board of Education* case, but the state and local authorities in Virginia were still resisting the federal order. She recalled asking the family handyman whether if she painted her face black—as his was—was it true that she would not be allowed to enter her elementary school?.

Civil Rights Activist

The nine-year-old Faust wrote a letter to President Dwight D. Eisenhower (1890-1969) to voice her concern on the matter. Years later, as a scholar she wondered about her plea, and contacted the Eisenhower Library in Abilene, Kansas. She was astonished when her letter was found and a copy returned to her in the mail. "Dear Mr. Eisenhower," it began, according to an article Faust wrote on it for *Harvard Magazine,* "I am nine years old and I am white, but I have many feelings about segregation." She urged the president to bring

school segregation to an end, asserting that "colored people aren't given a chance. . . . So what if their skin is black? They still have feelings but most of all are God's people!"

The letter to the White House marked Faust out as a rebel at an unexpectedly early age. As she noted in the same *Harvard Magazine* essay, in Virginia in the 1950s, discussions about race in households like hers were tantamount to talking about sex—both were taboo topics. Her parents found out about the letter "only when a formulaic acknowledgement arrived from the White House," she wrote. "They were stunned—both that I should have written to the president and that I should have expressed the thoughts that I did."

Faust's independent streak continued in her adolescent and teen years, when she fought bitterly with her mother over the freedoms her brothers were permitted while she was expected to conform to an idealized notion of young Southern womanhood. The rules for her included wearing dresses, not jeans, adopting a demure manner, and being "presented" to society at a debutante ball. Her mother frequently reminded her that her protests were futile ones. "It's a man's world, sweetie, and the sooner you learn that the better off you'll be," her mother often told her, as Faust recalled in an interview with *New York Times* reporter Sara Rimer.

Earned History Degree

Faust began to break free of some of the conventions of her upbringing when she entered the Concord Academy, a private boarding school in Concord, Massachusetts, at the time an all-girls school. She excelled academically, and had

she been born a boy, she might have entered Princeton University, from which her father, two of her brothers, two uncles, and a great-uncle had earned degrees. But the Ivy League school did not admit women as undergraduate students at the time. Instead, Faust's options were limited to either state schools or one of the so-called "Seven Sisters" schools formed in response to that long history of discrimination. These were the septet of elite women's colleges in the Northeast, and Faust chose Bryn Mawr in Pennsylvania, which she entered in 1964. She was a rule-challenger there, too, and was active in the student campaign to repeal the campus's "parietal rules." These rules governed the hours at which young women were expected to be inside their dormitories every evening, and they also restricted visits by men to the women's dormitories.

Faust went on to earn a master's degree from the University of Pennsylvania in Philadelphia in 1971, and a doctorate in American civilization in 1975. She joined that school's faculty a year later as an assistant professor, and progressed to a full professorship there eight years later. Penn, as it was known, was one of the Ivy League schools, but had a much longer history of admitting women and of hiring them as faculty members. In 1996 she was named director of the school's women's studies program, which was the same year that her seventh work of scholarship, *Mothers of Invention: Women of the Slaveholding South in the American Civil War,* was published. She was also active in numerous faculty committees at Penn, as well as within the larger community of academic professionals. In 2001 she was hired by Harvard University in Cambridge, Massachusetts, as a professor of history.

Faust's new job came with a second title in addition to her duties as a researcher and teacher: that of dean of the Radcliffe Institute for Advanced Study. Harvard had once been a single-sex institution, but its adjacent Radcliffe College—one of the Seven Sisters—had educated several generations of women before Harvard became a coeducational school. The remaining Radcliffe address on campus was the Radcliffe Institute for Advanced Study, and its focus was on postgraduate research on women in society and on gender issues. As director, Faust helped revive the fortunes of the Institute, raising funds and recruiting new names to its fellows program.

Harvard President Scorned

Faust advanced to the Lincoln Professor of History chair at Harvard in 2003. In early 2005 a serious controversy erupted involving remarks made by Harvard's president, Lawrence H. Summers (born 1954). In a speech before a conference of the National Bureau of Economics Research, Summers addressed the issue of why there were so few women who served as chairs of science, math, and engineering departments at U.S. colleges and universities. Summers discussed several theories, one of which mentioned research into "intrinsic aptitude"—or the idea that women simply did not possess the same intellectual abilities as men. His remarks spread first throughout academia and then made national headlines, most of them centering around the inflammatory idea that the president of the most prestigious college in the United States did not believe that women were as smart as men. Women in academic positions across the country voiced vehement protests in the media, recounting the challenges and biases they had faced in their professional careers.

Harvard students and professors of both genders voiced criticism of the school's president for his remarks, and Summers subsequently chose Faust to head two newly established committees charged with the task of attracting more women to the sciences and to academia's top ranks. The rancor on campus continued, however, and Summers—who had been an unpopular leader even before the controversy—announced his resignation in 2006. A nationwide search for his replacement was launched, and Faust became the surprise frontrunner among several well-qualified candidates. In February of 2007, Harvard made the announcement that Faust was to become its next president, effective the following October. "Faculty members and officials familiar with the search said Dr. Faust's leadership style—her collaborative approach and considerable people skills—would be vital for soothing a campus ripped apart by the battles over Dr. Summers, whom many accused of having an abrasive, confrontational style," noted Rimer.

"Education Is the Engine"

Faust's promotion once again thrust Harvard into the headlines, this time favorably. The appointment of a woman to lead the first institution of higher learning in the United States, founded in 1636, was deemed a historic turning point for American higher education. She was also the first Harvard president without a degree from the school in 335 years. Faust was sworn into office on October 12, 2007, and just weeks later she issued a new policy that again made positive headlines for the school: Harvard announced a new financial aid package that would provide tuition help to a much greater number of students, not just academically gifted ones from the lowest income households. "We've all been aware of increasing pressures on the middle class," the *New York Times* quoted her as saying. "We hear about this in a number of ways—housing costs, both parents working, the difficulty of amassing any kinds of savings, just the increasing pressures as middle class lives have become more stressed. . . . Education is the engine that makes American democracy work. And it has to work, and that means people have to have access." Harvard was able to take such steps in part because of its massive endowment of nearly $35 billion. (Endowments are donations made by alumni, and Harvard's had been wisely invested over the years).

Faust took office at Harvard just as her latest book was going to press. *This Republic of Suffering: Death and the American Civil War,* was published by Knopf in January of 2008, and received more media coverage than had her previous titles. Its focus was on the 600,000-plus casualties of the U.S. Civil War, and how such an enormous death toll impacted American society. *Newsweek* writer Malcolm Jones explained, "The Victorian idea of the 'good death,' in which the dying faced their demise with a peaceful frame of mind and in the company of loved ones, was intrinsic to beliefs about the primacy of home. Then, suddenly, the

unthinkable—the notion that a son or husband could die hundreds of miles distant—became the reality." During the Civil War, neither the Union nor the Confederate side had any identification system for its soldiers, nor were there any rules or guidelines in place about burying the war dead. In many cases, fleeing armies had to leave fallen comrades behind on the battlefield.

Years later a federal effort was made to establish national cemeteries in several states near famous battle sites, such as Gettysburg, Pennsylvania; the government also began to provide pensions for veterans and war widows. At the time, these actions reflected a major step in the responsibilities that the federal government assumed with regard to its citizens. During interviews about her book, Faust related that reading the letters of soldiers who had managed to write a letter back home as they lay dying was one of the most heartbreaking aspects of her research, but that "in some ways I don't find this book a depressing book," she told Jones. "I find it an inspiring book, as I watch people struggle to deal with extraordinarily difficult circumstances and retain their humanity and affirm that humanity in the face of suffering and loss."

Faust is married to Charles Ernest Rosenberg, an authority on the history of American medicine who teaches at Harvard. Their daughter, Jessica, is a Harvard graduate. Faust has often thought about her mother's words to her as a young woman, that the world was not a fair place, and considers herself fortunate to have been witness to such immense changes. As she told Rimer, "I think in many ways that comment—'It's a man's world, sweetie'—was a bitter comment from a woman of a generation who didn't have the kind of choices my generation of women had."

Periodicals

Christian Science Monitor, February 12, 2007.
Harvard Magazine, May-June 2003.
Newsweek, January 21, 2008.
New York Times, February 10, 2007; February 12, 2007; December 11, 2007. □

Celia Fiennes

Celia Fiennes (1662-1741) made her mark as the foremost female travel writer of her day, providing one of the most inclusive personal accounts of England since the Elizabethan era.

Rebellious Roots

Celia Fiennes (pronounced *fines*) was born June 7, 1662 at the manor of Newton Toney in Wiltshire, England—not far from Salisbury. Her father was Colonel Nathaniel F. Fiennes, a member of the Council of State and Keeper of the Great Seal under Cromwell. Her mother—Nathaniel's second wife—was Frances (Whitehead) who came from a family of parliamentarians and dissenters. Both of Fiennes's parents were anti–monarchical activists descended from regicidal families and they brought their political views to bear in the raising of their children. Fiennes's grandfather was the 1st Lord Saye and Sele, a nobleman who led the House of Lords in what *Who Was Who in World Exploration's* Waldman and Wexler define as "the Puritan cause against the monarchy from 1628 to 1642."

From Noblewoman to Journeyman

Fiennes—identified later in life by various sources as both a Presbyterian and a Protestant—grew up in a prestigious puritan family with daunting Parliamentary ties and contacts. Her siblings included two half–brothers from her father's first marriage and a younger sister, Mary, who eventually married and settled in London. It was the travels that Fiennes undertook, however—remarkable for her time, and even more so for her gender—and their eventual recounting that sealed her name in the annals of British history.

Sources vary on what year Fiennes began her treks into greater England. The first noted date of departure ranges from 1685 to 1690—making her age at the onset of her travels anywhere between twenty–three and twenty–eight. This discrepancy is attributed to a disconnect between her largely undated notes and posthumous attempts by scholars to establish a timeline. All agree that she ended her roving in 1702, having at that time traversed every county in England as well as having engaged in additional short explorations of portions of Scotland and Wales.

Fresh Air Bred Refreshing Perspectives

Fiennes initially claimed that her decision to travel was prompted by ill health—explaining in the preface to her original manuscript that she began her trips for the "change of aire and exercise," according to the *Vision of Britain* Web site, as well as a desire to broaden her mind, since she felt that a person's body and brain should be equally occupied whenever possible, especially in reference to the fact that, at the time, women were discouraged from occupying either with vigor.

Her early trips—made in the company of her mother and various servants—took her to the southern English counties like Oxford, Bath and London. Fiennes's 1697 tour of the north of England and her 'Great Journey'—undertaken in 1698 and covering over a thousand miles through Newcastle and Cornwall—were achieved on horseback and by coach, accompanied only by a few servants. Fiennes rode side–saddle, keeping detailed notes of her experiences and later compiled the material in a manuscript around 1702. In Margaret Willy's 1964 publication *Three Women Diarists*, the author explained how dates and times for Fiennes's recollections must be "deduced from internal evidence" because only one actual date is mentioned in the original manuscript.

Giantess Among Men

While travel writing was decidedly in fashion during Fiennes's day and she shared the spotlight with more famous counterparts like Charles Dickens and Daniel Dafoe,

the intrepid diarist was the only female in this genre claiming mainstream attention. She usually stayed at inns or lodged with relatives and friends of friends, and despite its rough nature, her manuscript rewarded readers with accurate illustrations of the towns she visited—everything from the domestic, including prices and the virtues and inadequacies of the inns she stayed in, to detailed commentary on the political and religious climate of local life.

Fiennes's biographical entry in *The Dictionary of National Biography Missing Persons* described her unique attributes as a travel writer in a genre and country that normally defers to the culturally entrenched, "She was interested in the modern rather than the ancient, preferring Nottingham to York . . . formal gardens and waterworks to ancient houses. The sharpness of her observations on numerous aspects of contemporary life has made her journal a prime source for social and economic historians."

The attention that Fiennes paid to industry and progress made her accounts unusual and valuable in their own right, and whether she was taking her readers into a cave or a cathedral, her writing garnered praise for its readability and natural style—in *The Cambridge Guide to Literature in English,* her style is described as "quirky", "opinionated", and "enthusiastic." Willy admitted that Fiennes "tends to prattle on about all she sees and does with a fine disregard for spelling and punctuation and a tumbling breathlessness," yet pointed out that "this in itself is part of her appeal, communicating far better than any more polished narrative the eagerness of her exploration."

As reviewer James Munson noted, history and travel writing in particular have a tendency to overlap. Fiennes was traveling during a time of expansion for England's middle classes in the midst of a movement bent on discovering the treasures of one's native land rather than the previous age's focus on and curiosity in more exotic destinations. Fiennes's accounts proved valuable because she immersed herself in that changing social environment, including descriptions of the dangers and discomforts she endured on her travels—from riding accidents that unsaddled her to inns so crowded that people slept three to a bed amid "froggs and slow–worms and snailes." She became an expert judge of products and services like spa waters, beer and local architecture and prefaced her manuscript by saying that while she hoped to correct and improve the writing, she hoped it is helpful despite the fact that her female status may have resulted in access to fewer sources than that which a gentleman might have enjoyed. As the *Cambridge Guide to Literature in English* explained, however, the accounts penned by Fiennes "constituted the most comprehensive impression of the [English] countryside since the work of [William] Camden."

Rough Road to Publication

Fiennes's finished manuscript was first excerpted in a Southey miscellany, then eventually transcribed and published under the title *Through England on a Side Saddle in the Time of William and Mary* in 1888 by a relative who had acquired it. This first official edition is described by scholars as both coarse and incomplete, and it wasn't until

1947 that Christopher Morris edited and released a scholarly edition titled, *The Journeys of Celia Fiennes* that separated her travel into four geographical components (considered by academics to be the "definitive" edition). Another edition titled *The Illustrated Journeys of Celia Fiennes* was published in 1982 and described in a December, 1982 *Choice* review as a "a well–produced edition that makes the energetic and enlightening travels of Celia Fiennes more accessible." The reviewer, however, also criticized the fact that *The Illustrated Journeys* was an abridged edition (trimmed to make room for color plates)—maintaining that the 1947 and 1949 Morris editions are still the best choice for true scholars.

Private Life

Fiennes never married and had no children, and in fact, very little is known about her personal experiences between the close of her travels and her death. It is known that Fiennes's mother died in 1691, and the author moved to London to be near her sister Mary's family. Fiennes died in 1741 on the 10th of April in Hackney, London and was interred in Newton Toney. She is believed to have died in the home of one of her nieces.

Willy found it ironic that so little can be established about Fiennes's later years, despite the fact that she found fame as a diarist. She theorized that Fiennes's original claims of fragile health as the impetus to travel were "the excuse of an unconventional spirit, in an age when the English gentlewoman was still so restricted in mobility, to satisfy a restless itch for action and her lively impulses of curiosity in everything going on around her."

Departed, but Not Forgotten

Fiennes's lively travel accounts went on to inspire Nicholas Crane to host an edition of the television program *Great British Journeys* for the BBC that aired on August 28, 2007 in which he rode and pushed his bicycle along Fiennes's 1698 tour, "puffing away as he regales [the audience] with anecdotes and Fiennes's no–nonsense prose" according to the London *Times* television viewing guide. In addition, the March 2, 2007 edition of the *Liverpool Echo* invited would-be authors to write contributions for a new publication that would emulate the style of Fiennes in describing Liverpool as part of a celebration of the city's 800th birthday. The winning authors would have their writing published in the same work along with some of Fiennes'.

Rings on her Fingers and Bells on her Toes?

On a more whimsical note, sources continue to bicker when faced with the disputed suggestion that the "Fine lady upon a white horse" of the children's rhyme *Ride a Cock Horse to Banbury Cross* was, in fact, referring to or inspired by Celia Fiennes. On June 1st, 1988 travel writer Alison Payne—astride a white horse—followed a police escort out of Hyde Park to re–enact Fiennes's 'Great Journey' as part of that year's tercentenary celebrations of William and Mary's reign. Payne participated in the event to raise money for a skin treatment and research charity, and in reports Fiennes

is identified as "linked" to the nursery rhyme. Others argue that it is a possibility because she had relatives who owned Broughton Castle near Banbury—and contend that the term *fine* in the rhyme is a distortion of *Fiennes*.

A reader of the London *Times*, however, (in response to a later claim published by that paper) stated that the roots of the nursery rhyme lie in pagan fertility rites, and because "the 'High Cross' at Banbury was destroyed in 1602"—sixty years before Fiennes' birth—the connection between the diarist and the fine lady of rhyme was nothing more than so much "cock and bull."

Free Spirit

Described by Waldman and Wexler as "one of the first women known to have traveled for the express purpose of seeing and experiencing new places at a time when most overland journeys were difficult," Fiennes will be remembered not only for having the courage and determination to satisfy her curiosity and wanderlust, but for expending the time and energy to record her experiences for posterity. While the work of her colleagues might always move to the front of the line, most seem to agree with Willy, who closes her book's section on Fiennes with the suggestion that her manuscript "forms a social picture quite as absorbing as any drawn by her more famous contemporaries." After all, historians must capture the attention of the reader before they can pass on their knowledge, so the engaging nature of Fiennes's accounts assure them pride of place among the achievements of her generation.

Books

A Biographical Dictionary of English Women Writers 1580-1720, edited by Maureen Bell, George Parfitt and Simon Shepherd, G.K. Hall & Co., 1990.

The Bloomsbury Guide to Women's Literature, edited by Claire Buck, Prentice Hall General Reference, 1992.

The Cambridge Guide to Literature in English, Third Edition edited by Dominic Head, Cambridge University Press, 2006.

Cambridge Guide to Women's Writings in English, edited by Lorna Sage, Germaine Greer and Elaine Showalter, 1999.

Chambers Biographical Dictionary, edited by Melanie Parry, Chambers Harrap Publishers Ltd., 1997.

The Continuum Dictionary of Women's Biography, edited by Jennifer S. Uglow, Continuum Publishing Company, 1982.

The Dictionary of National Biography Missing Persons, edited by C.S. Nicholls, Oxford University Press, 1993.

The Feminist Companion to Literature in English Women Writers from the Middle Ages to the Present, edited by Virginia Blain, Patricia Clements and Isobel Grundy, Yale University Press, 1990.

Merriam-Webster's Biographical Dictionary, Merriam-Webster, Inc., 1995.

Merriam-Webster's Encyclopedia of Literature, Merriam-Webster, Inc., 2002.

The Oxford Companion to English Literature: Sixth Edition, edited by Margaret Drabble, Oxford University Press, Inc., 2000.

Who Was Who in World Exploration, edited by Carl Waldman and Alan Wexler, Facts on File, Inc., 1992.

Willy, Margaret, *Three Women Diarists: Celia Fiennes, Dorothy Wordsworth and Katherine Mansfield*, edited by Geoffrey Bullough, Longmans, Green and Co., 1964.

Women in World History: Volume Five, edited by Anne Commire, Yorkin Publications, 2000.

Periodicals

Choice, December 1982.
Contemporary Review, January 1996.
Liverpool Echo: Liverpool, England, March 2, 2007.
The Times: London, England, June 1, 1988; August 6, 1999; August 28, 2007.

Online

"Celia Fiennes," *London Borough of Hackney,* http://www .hackney.gov.uk/ep-celia-fiennes.htm (October 14, 2007).
"Celia Fiennes, Through England on a Side Saddle in the Time of William and Mary," *A Vision of Britain Through Time,* http://www.visionofbritain.org.uk/text/contents_page.jsp?t_id=Fiennes (October 14, 2007).
"Did Celia's 17th C Rides Inspire a Nursery Rhyme?" *Travellers Tales,* http://www.port.ac.uk/research/gbhgis/media resources/freearticles/filetodownload,23047,en.pdf (October 14, 2007). □

Rudolph Fisher

American writer Rudolph Fisher (1897-1934) gained widespread notice during the Harlem Renaissance era for his realistic depictions of urban African-American life.

Although he had a few champions among African-American critics, Fisher's works were largely forgotten after his untimely death. His eclipse came partly because his tone and outlook were primarily satirical—a generation raised on the epic struggles of the civil rights movement looked to writers who tackled big themes. As the twentieth century neared its end, however, Fisher's works were rediscovered by a new generation of readers. Among the first African Americans to write a mystery novel, Fisher was seen as a precursor to such contemporary masters of African-American genre fiction as Walter Mosley. His writing in general was praised for its sharp observations on the social dynamics of New York City's predominantly African-American Harlem neighborhood and its relationship to the still largely white city that surrounded it. In addition to writing fiction, Fisher was also a physician. His works, noted the *New York Post,* have "a special intelligence and humor and knowledge of life—qualities familiar from such other physician-writers as Anton Chekhov and William Carlos Williams."

Excelled in School

Fisher did not grow up amid the colorful street life he depicted in his Harlem stories. He was born Rudolph John Chauncey Fisher on May 9, 1897, in Washington, D.C., and raised in Providence, Rhode Island. His father, John Wesley Fisher, was a minister. A top student at Providence's Classical High School, Fisher was one of the few African Americans allowed to follow a rigorous college preparatory curriculum. He graduated with honors in 1915 and was admitted to prestigious Brown University on a scholarship, majoring in English at first but later switching to biology. College friends nicknamed him "Bud" after *Mutt and Jeff* cartoonist Bud Fisher.

At Brown, Fisher continued to excel academically. He won several oratory (public speaking) prizes, including one, the Caesar Misch Premium, given for a speech in the German language during his freshman year. He also won an intercollegiate oratory contest held at Harvard University. Fisher graduated from Brown in 1919 with a host of honors. He was the commencement speaker and was inducted into three honor societies, including Phi Beta Kappa. Also on stage was Paul Robeson, who went on to a distinguished career as a singer of spirituals and opera; the two exchanged congratulations and promised to keep in touch. Fisher earned a master's degree at Brown in 1920, and then enrolled at Howard University Medical School in Washington, D.C.

At that institution, the flagship of the American network of historically black colleges and universities, he worked his way through the program by serving as an instructor in embryology for four years. Despite his busy schedule, Fisher's creative side began to flower during this period; he arranged music for Robeson and accompanied him on the piano in concert. Fisher finished the program at Howard in 1924, graduating summa cum laude after an internship at Washington's Freedmen's Hospital during his senior year. He married schoolteacher Jane Ryder that year.

In the fall of 1924 Fisher moved to New York, settling in Harlem and winning a research fellowship at the nearby Columbia University College of Physicians and Surgeons. He remained there for two years, doing work in the fields of bacteriology, pathology, and what was then called roentgenology—the study of the technology and uses of X-rays. But he was also furiously at work on a series of short stories that reflected his new milieu. Fisher wrote to Carl Van Vechten, a prominent white patron of African-American literature, about the conflicting demands of his dual careers. The 1925 publication in the *Atlantic Monthly* of Fisher's first story, "The City of Refuge," did nothing to resolve his dilemma, for it was critically acclaimed and was included in the influential annual anthology *Best Short Stories of 1925.*

Explored Harlem Setting

"The City of Refuge," like many of Fisher's other early stories, explored the migration of Southern blacks to New York City in the 1920s, casting a jaundiced eye on the dreams of the newcomers but never succumbing to bitterness. Its central character is King Solomon Gillis, an African American who has fled to New York to escape a murder charge in North Carolina. Instead of the "city of refuge" of the title, he finds in Harlem a nest of corruption where he is ensnared in a drug dealing operation by con men. Fisher followed up that success with a group of linked stories, *The South Lingers On,* in which he furthered his observations of the tensions between country and city in African-American society. One story within the set introduced a Southern character, Grammie, who sees Harlem as a place of sin and vice; she was one of a several similar characters to appear in Fisher's fiction.

The South Lingers On was included in the influential 1925 anthology *The New Negro* (under the new title *Vestiges: Harlem Sketches*), and Fisher reaped still more honors that year with *High Yaller,* a story that addressed discrimination based on skin tone within the African-American community. It won the Amy Spingarn fiction contest sponsored by the W.E.B DuBois-edited magazine *The Crisis.* Fisher's story *Ringtail,* also published in the *Atlantic Monthly,* dealt with a different kind of conflict: that between Southern-born blacks and those of Caribbean descent. The story framed blacks' differing reactions to the black nationalist leader Marcus Garvey within the perspective of a love triangle. Other Fisher stories over the next several years were published in mainstream periodicals of the day such as *McClure's* and *Redbook,* as well as black-owned newspapers and other publications oriented toward African-American audiences.

In 1926 Fisher's son, Hugh, was born; Fisher dubbed him "the New Negro." In between his medical studies and responsibilities at home, he found time to critique Van Vechten's novel *Nigger Heaven* (whose title referred to the segregated balcony seating in movie theaters of the day) before its publication that year. Fisher opened his own medical practice in 1927 and published an article on the response of bacteria to ultraviolet light in the *Journal of Infectious Diseases.* He also returned to fiction writing with a vengeance, publishing four stories, "The Promised Land," "Blades of Steel," "The Backslider," and "Fire by Night."

Those stories, loaded with detail about life in Harlem ("The Promised Land," for instance, depicted a rent party, a paid-admission party with musical entertainment staged in order to help a family pay the monthly rent on its dwelling), attracted white as well as black readers with the windows on black life they offered. Fisher responded to white attention, as well as the more general white fascination with African-American entertainment, in a 1927 nonfiction essay titled "The Caucasian Storms Harlem," published in the *American Mercury* magazine edited by humorist and social critic H.L. Mencken. Fisher continued to feel and express tension between his writing and medical careers, but neither seemed to suffer; in 1928 he took a job as a roentgenologist (or radiologist) with the New York City Department of Health.

Wrote Novel

Fisher's corpus of short stories up to that point had encompassed a wide variety of Harlem characters, from doctors and lawyers to those operating criminal enterprises on the fringes of society. With the literary and cultural movement known as the Harlem Renaissance at its height, Fisher was challenged by a friend to write a novel that would weave the disparate elements of Harlem society together into a book-length story. The result was *The Walls of Jericho* (1928), which, in the words of Clifford Thompson of the *Black Issues Book Review,* "comically but convincingly evokes the worlds of three Harlem strata: educated elite, small-business owners, and rank-and-file workers." The book was published, at Van Vechten's urging, by the major

Knopf publishing house. Its central character is a prosperous black lawyer who suffers ostracism from both whites and blacks when he attempts to move into an all-white neighborhood and enter the upper echelons of white society. Despite its serious theme, the novel is filled with sharp satirical observations of both the black and white characters.

The *New York Times* reviewed *The Walls of Jericho* positively, noting that Fisher "writes from the inside. Consequently his piano movers, poolroom hangers-on, gamblers, bootleggers, 'kitchen mechanics,' and other colored persons who are still permitted to talk their native dialect—however mixed with the special lingo of Harlem—have authentic quality and carry conviction."

In 1929 Fisher became superintendent of Manhattan's International Hospital. The following year he joined the U.S. Army and was commissioned as a first lieutenant in the legendary all-black 369th Infantry Regiment, otherwise known as the Harlem Hellfighters. A well-known figure in the black literary scene by that time, he served on the literature committee of the Harlem YMCA and frequently gave lectures at the New York Public Library's 135th Street branch. During this time he was at work on his second novel, *The Conjure-Man Dies: A Mystery Tale of Dark Harlem.* The book was published in 1932, and was one of the first mysteries by an African-American author, and probably the first with an all-black cast of characters. The book tells the story of a police detective and a physician who investigate the possible death of an African king who is moonlighting in Harlem as a fortune-teller and psychiatrist.

After the publication of *The Conjure-Man Dies,* Fisher wrote several more short stories; two of them, *Ezekiel* and *Ezekiel Learns* (both 1933), were for children and featured a 12-year-old boy from Georgia as a central character. In addition, two of his best realizations of the figure of the Southern grandmother coming to terms with the careers of her descendants in the city, "Miss Cynthie" and "Guardian of the Law," appeared in 1933. Fisher worked on a stage version of *The Conjure-Man Dies* but began to suffer the symptoms of stomach or intestinal cancer in 1934; the disease was possibly the result of his frequent use of radioactive materials in his X-ray work, undertaken without safeguards in the days before the dangers of radioactivity were fully understood. The stage version of *The Conjure-Man Dies* was completed by Harlem Renaissance writers Countee Cullen and Arna Bontemps. Fisher died on December 26, 1934, in New York.

Books

Afro-American Writers From the Harlem Renaissance to 1940, Ed. Trudier Harris-Lopez and Thadious M. Davis, *Dictionary of Literary Biography Vol. 51,* Detroit: Gale Research, 1987.

American Short-Story Writers, 1910-1945: Second Series, Ed. Bobby Ellen Kimbel, *Dictionary of Literary Biography Vol. 102,* Detroit: Gale Research, 1991.

Bontemps, Arna, *The Harlem Renaissance Remembered,* Dodd, Mead, 1972.

Brown, Sterling, *The Negro in American Fiction,* Arno, 1969.

Lewis, David Levering, *When Harlem Was in Vogue,* Penguin, 1997.

Notable Black American Men, Gale, 1998.
The Short Fiction of Rudolph Fisher, edited by Margaret Perry, Greenwood, 1987.

Periodicals

Black Issues Book Review, May-June 2003.
New York Post, February 8, 2001.
New York Times, August 5, 1928.

Online

Contemporary Authors Online, Gale, 2007, http://galenet.gale group.com/servlet/BioRC (December 10, 2007).
"Rudolph Fisher (1897-1934): A Brief Literary Biography," Per-spectives in American Literature (California State University at Stanislaus), http://web.csustan.edu/english/reuben/pal/chap9/fisher.html (December 10, 2007). □

Ian Fleming

British writer Ian Fleming (1908-1964) was the cre-ator of James Bond, the fictional British spy in a series of novels that became one of the most profitable film franchises in cinema history. Fleming shared a few similarities with his rakish hero, Agent 007, and some of Bond's daring exploits were based on actual stories of British spies that Fleming had gleaned firsthand during World War II as a high-ranking officer with the British naval intelligence service. The first Bond novel was published in 1953, and until his death 11 years later, Fleming wrote 11 more books plus two short-story collections. "I wanted to show a hero without any characteristics," Fleming once explained about his creation, according to his *Times* of London obitu-ary, "who was simply the blunt instrument in the hands of the government."

Fleming was born on May 28, 1908, in London, En-gland. He came from prominent, wealthy families on both sides. His father's family, the Flemings, were respected bankers whose deals included the Anglo-Saudi venture that became BP (British Petroleum). Among his mother's ancestors were members of the House of Lancaster, the royal dynasty that lost power during the War of the Roses in the 1470s to the rival House of York. Fleming's father, Valentine, was a Member of Parliament and friend of future British prime minister Winston Churchill (1874-1965), but died in combat during World War I while serving with a regiment called the Queen's Own Oxfordshire Hussars.

Failed Foreign-Office Exam

Fleming was one of four sons, and it was his older brother Peter of whom great achievements were expected. Peter was a gifted student, and would go on to enjoy a career as a espionage agent, explorer, and travel writer. Fleming, by contrast, disliked school and earned dismal grades. He followed Peter into elite Eton College, but was

allegedly forced to leave after his dalliance with a maid was discovered. After a stint at the notoriously tough Sandhurst military academy, Fleming eschewed the "Oxbridge" route—taking a degree at either of England's top schools, Oxford or Cambridge universities—and instead spent sev-eral semesters studying languages in Austria, Germany, and Switzerland. He achieved fluency in German, French, and Russian, all of which would later serve him well during his career as a journalist.

Fleming was aiming for a job with the Foreign Office, the British Empire's diplomatic corps and policy-setters, but he failed its notoriously rigorous exam. In 1929 he took a job with Reuters, the British news agency, and was posted to its Moscow bureau for a time. In 1933 he moved on to a new career in merchant banking, working first for Cull & Company before spending the final four years of the decade with Lon-don stockbrokers Rowe & Pitman. Fleming's contacts with members of the Foreign Office did lead to his first actual quasi-espionage assignment in early 1939, when he was asked to file some reports on the potential military and indus-trial capabilities of Russia and Poland while on a trade mis-sion to those countries. Europe was on the verge of world war once again, and the conflict began in earnest in the late summer of 1939 when Nazi Germany invaded Poland.

Fleming spent most of the war years as a personal assis-tant to the director of Britain's naval intelligence division. The post was a highly placed one that required an immense amount of trust, but did not involve the feats of derring-do apparently carried out by his brother Peter in Asia. Fleming did conceive of a rather fantastical plot to break the German encryption codes used for radio communication, however: his idea was to install a British crew aboard an already-captured German plane, send it out over the English Channel and then crash it, where a German ship would rescue it, believing it to be one of their own. The British crew would then attack their rescuers and hijack the ship, obtaining access to the encryption machine and its codes. Devising such schemes for the Royal Navy would later serve as excellent training ground for Agent 007's exploits.

Wrote Novel in Jamaica

After the war's end, Fleming returned to civilian life and took a job as the foreign news service manager for the Kemsley newspapers chain (later Thomson-Reuters). At the time, the Kemsley holdings included the *Daily Telegraph* and several other properties. Fleming spent the next 14 years on the job, although it did come with a generous two months' vacation each winter that he successfully negotiated into his contract. He had acquired property in Jamaica and built a home there he called Goldeneye; this was also the name of a contingency plan he wrote during his wartime service for maintaining contact with the British enclave of Gibraltar on the coast of Spain, in the event that the Germans invaded the Iberian peninsula.

Fleming had been a committed bachelor for much of his adult life, avoiding marital or other long-term entanglements. For many years he carried on with Ann, Lady Rothermere, who had been born into an old Scottish titled family and then married into an Irish one; that husband died during the war. When she became a widow, Ann reportedly hoped to marry Fleming, but he refused. Instead she wed the Viscount Rothermere, a friend of Fleming's and, coincidentally, owner of the *Daily Mail,* rival paper to Fleming's employer the *Daily Telegraph.* She allegedly became pregnant with Fleming's child, but the child died shortly after its birth. When she became pregnant a second time—again, purportedly by Fleming—a divorce was arranged and she joined him in Jamaica in January of 1952. They were married that March. In the interim, Fleming wrote his first spy story, which he later said was done to calm his nerves. The impending nuptials, he claimed, seemed to be "a very painful thing to do at the age of 44; so to take my mind off the whole business, I sat down and wrote a novel," according to his *Times* of London obituary.

Casino Royale was the first James Bond novel, and was based on an actual incident that took place at a casino in Estoril, Portugal, in 1941. It is not known if Fleming was actually in Portugal at the time, but his job with naval intelligence certainly gave him classified details of the legendary roulette win made by a British double agent named Dusko Popov against a passel of German spies. Popov was a notorious rake whose code name "Tricycle" referred to his penchant for *ménage à trois* encounters with the opposite sex. He would become one of a long list of little-known but legendary espionage figures who reportedly provided inspiration for Fleming's Bond.

The plot of *Casino Royale* follows Bond, who has recently received "007," or license to kill, designation from

his British spymasters. Agent 007 becomes enmeshed in a high-stakes baccarat game with Le Chiffre, the first of several vicious foes determined to either outwit or kill the clever Bond. Fleming's debut sold nearly 5,000 copies in its first month after it was published in April of 1953. He went on to churn out at least one more in the series every year until 1959, when he quit his newspaper job in order to devote himself to screenplay adaptations. The James Bond tales include *Live and Let Die, Diamonds Are Forever, From Russia, with Love,* and *Goldfinger.*

Became British Icon

Fleming's fictional creation had no predecessor in spy fiction. He was a drinker, a brawler, and a rake, but his cleverness kept him one step ahead of his enemies. In the novels the emphasis on luxury goods gave Bond discerning upper-crust tastes at a time when many consumer goods were still under wartime rationing in England, including butter and coal. In a review of the sixth Agent 007 tale, *Dr. No,* the *New Statesman*'s Paul Johnson coined the famous descriptive phrase about Fleming's novels, derisively enshrining them as paeans to "sex, sadism, and snobbery." Johnson's review described "three basic ingredients in Dr. No, all unhealthy, all thoroughly English: the sadism of a schoolboy bully, the mechanical, two-dimensional sex-longings of a frustrated adolescent, and the crude, snob-cravings of a suburban adult. Mr. Fleming has no literary skill ... but the three ingredients are manufactured and blended with deliberate, professional precision."

Fleming's Bond books were also published in the United States, sometimes under different titles, such as *You Asked For It* for the book *Casino Royale.* Sales remained somewhat moribund until American president John F. Kennedy (1917-1963) cited them as among his favorite reads, and the titles suddenly began rocketing up the bestseller lists. The transatlantic appeal was a somewhat ironic note for Bond fans who recognized one of Fleming's most obvious themes throughout the tales: with the end of World War II, Britain lost much of its mighty empire and world power, while the United States, bolstered by the use of the world's first atomic weapon, suddenly moved to a leadership position on the world stage. As William Cook explained years later in the *New Statesman,* Fleming's hero "pandered to Britain's inflated and increasingly insecure self-image, flattering us with the fantasy that Britannia could still punch above her weight." Cook added that Bond "epitomised the cosy fiction of the lopsided Anglo-American alliance. The Yanks might have become the masters, but only the Brits really knew how to behave."

The Bond Girls

In addition to the reliance on luxury items in the Bond stories, Fleming also created a bevy of vixens on the page who occupied varying roles in the plots. Sometimes Bond rescued them from danger, while at other times they were enemy agents who battled wits with him before ultimately submitting to his powers of seduction. These "Bond girls" were later immortalized in the film adaptations by such actresses as Honor Blackman, Ursula Andress, Jane Seymour, Diana Rigg, Michelle Yeoh, and Eva Green. Fleming himself played little role in the film versions, save for developing the story for the first true Bond film, *Dr. No,* which introduced Scottish actor Sean Connery (born 1930) as Agent 007. The actual film rights became a complicated legal morass that took more than three decades to untangle, finally ending in 1999 when one Hollywood movie studio exchanged revenues from the upcoming *Spider-Man* franchise for the rights to *Casino Royale,* which had originally been filmed in 1967 as a spoof starring David Niven (1910-1983). The outcome of that studio deal was the 2006 version of *Casino Royale,* featuring the newest in a long list of screen Bonds, British actor Daniel Craig (born 1968), whom critics considered ruthless and icy enough to become perhaps the closest match with Fleming's original villain ever to appear on screen.

Fleming had apparently never planned to devote the remainder of his life to writing the Agent 007 takes, and "soon tired of his hero, whom he described as 'a cardboard booby,' " noted the *Guardian*'s Adrian Turner. "He wanted to kill him off, but the books were selling too well. Instead, Bond became as jaded, as introspective, and as disillusioned as his creator." Fleming did write a children's book, *Chitty-Chitty-Bang-Bang: The Magical Car,* based on a story he had invented to entertain his son, Caspar. It was published in 1964, the same year that Fleming died of a heart attack on August 12 at Kent and Canterbury Hospital in Canterbury, England. Tragically, Caspar died in an apparent suicide in 1975, and Ann died in 1981.

That the rakish and ruthless agent that Fleming created would prove such an enduring success would have no doubt perturbed him had he lived to see the success that came later in the 1960s and beyond, thanks to the movie versions. "Apart from the fact that he wears the same clothes that I wear, he and I really have very little in common," Fleming once said, according to his *Times* of London obituary. "I do rather envy him his blondes and his efficiency, but I can't say I much like the chap."

Books

Winder, Simon, *The Man Who Saved Britain: A Personal Journey into the Disturbing World of James Bond,* Farrar, Straus and Giroux, 2006.

Periodicals

Guardian (London, England), August 15, 1992.
Independent on Sunday (London, England), September 5, 2004.
New Statesman, April 5, 1958; June 28, 2004.
Sunday Times (London, England), November 5, 2006.
Times (London, England), August 13, 1964. □

Pim Fortuyn

The Dutch politician Pim Fortuyn (1948-2002) altered the terms of political debate in his country during his short career in the electoral arena, which ended with his assassination in May of 2002. His murder was, in

the words of London's *Daily Telegraph,* "the most prominent political assassination in the Netherlands since that of William the Silent in 1584."

Fortuyn defied traditional political classifications, and his maverick ways were part of his appeal. His strong stance against immigration to the Netherlands by foreigners, which historically has come mostly from predominantly Islamic countries, caused political observers to group him with other European politicians who had spearheaded far-right political movements based on strongly nationalist sentiments and mistrust of foreigners. But Fortuyn, who rejected such comparisons, did not fit the far-right mold. He was openly gay, and many of the values he championed in Dutch culture, including full rights for homosexuals, were contrary to those of many anti-immigration parties in other countries. Fortuyn aroused strong opinions among the Dutch populace, with some calling him a neo-fascist while others hailed him for overturning a stagnant political system and stirring up useful debate about the country's future.

Born into Religious Family

Wilhelmus Simon Petrus Fortuyn, nicknamed Pim, was born on February 19, 1948, in the small city of Velsen in northwestern Holland. His father was a salesman, his mother a housewife, and the family, adherents of the Roman Catholic faith, attended mass regularly. Even though he led a flamboyant lifestyle later in his life, stating that he preferred gay bars to the inside of a church, Fortuyn never rejected his identification with Catholicism. According to an article by Roger Boyes in the London *Times* following the assassination, Catholic priest Father Louis Berger, to whom Fortuyn went for confession, characterized him as "a religious man with a warm heart who cared about vulnerable people." Fortuyn was a talented student who was quickly marked for university studies. Another major aspect of his life, the realization of his homosexuality, was also set in place early, after he had a relationship with another altar boy at the church his family attended.

Fortuyn enrolled at the Universiteit Nyenrode (the Netherlands Business School) in Breukelen, graduating in 1970 after studying history, sociology, law, and economics. He moved on to the University of Amsterdam for graduate study, and when he entered into the liberated life of the Dutch capital of Amsterdam, he soon felt freer to express his sexuality. According to Boyes, Fortuyn described himself as a "self-proclaimed homosexual, more feminine than every woman in the Cabinet, an aesthete and grass roots democrat, a desperado, a Dadaist with a skull of a gladiator." He became involved near the end of a period of left-wing student activism in Amsterdam, and rejected the conservative beliefs of his parents in favor of the writings of Communist philosopher Karl Marx, Russian revolutionary Vladimir Lenin, and Chinese leader Mao Tse-tung.

Embarking on a series of advanced degrees that seemed designed to lead toward an academic position in the Dutch university system, Fortuyn received a doctorate (comparable to a master's degree in the United States) in sociology from the University of Amsterdam in 1971. He then enrolled at the University of Groningen, working as a lecturer in Marxist theory and writing a Ph.D. thesis on economic development in the Netherlands after World War II. He received a degree at Groningen in 1980. Joining the Dutch Labor Party, a center-left party that had enjoyed a long dominant role in the nation's affairs, Fortuyn spent the 1980s in research posts with the Dutch government, working on education and railway policy issues.

In 1990 he landed a job as a professor at Erasmus Universiteit (Erasmus University) in Rotterdam. As a teacher, Fortuyn was a skillful showman who was popular with students. But his off-the-cuff style did not always sit well with his colleagues, and all through his life he had a tendency to antagonize his employers to a point where his position was in jeopardy—a tendency his friends referred to as Fortuyn's Law. He left Erasmus University in 1995, having already put in place the next stage of his career. In 1992 he formed a political consulting firm called Fortuyn BV and began a successful stint as a lecturer, commanding fees of some $500 for a single appearance. He also began writing a column for the magazine *Elsevier*. These occupations proved lucrative, and Fortuyn began to adopt a swank personal style.

Swung Strongly in Conservative Direction

By this time, Fortuyn had abandoned his Marxist beliefs and turned strongly in the direction of free-market conservatism. He had also begun to identify immigration as a key issue in Dutch politics, although criticism of immigrants and their values was mostly considered taboo in Dutch society. In Rotterdam Fortuyn found himself at the epicenter of a brewing controversy: in the Netherlands as a whole (as of 2002), Turks and Moroccans, the largest immigrant groups, made up only 6 percent of the population, but in the industrial city of Rotterdam the figure was 30 percent. Social services were strained by the large number of newcomers, who did not always learn the Dutch language, and the crime rate rose. In 1997 Fortuyn published a book, *Against the Islamicization of Our Culture.*

In the summer of 2001 Fortuyn joined the small Leefbar Nederland (Livable Netherlands) party, which had its greatest strength in Rotterdam. His initial intention was to stir up the political world by provoking debate. From the start he showed an ability to galvanize a crowd, and he was quickly named the party's leader. Just as quickly, controversy broke out over Fortuyn's often incendiary statements. He called for a temporary shutdown in immigration to the Netherlands, saying (all quotations appeared in London's *Independent*), "Full is full, and you can't mop the floor while the tap is running." He commented that "in Holland, homosexuality is treated the same way as heterosexuality. In what Islamic country does that happen?" (The Netherlands legalized gay marriage in 2001.) Fortuyn cast himself as a defender of free speech. After a fundamentalist Islamic imam condemned homosexuals as a life form lower than pigs, Fortuyn said, "An imam should be able to say about me that homosexuals are worse than pigs. My only demand is that you mustn't incite violence."

Fortuyn did not fit the traditional image of a Dutch politician. The Netherlands had long been governed by a group of centrist parties known as the purple coalition, with officeholders generally being career politicians who had painstakingly worked their way up through the various party hierarchies. Fortuyn, by contrast, thrived on making headlines. He was a flamboyant figure who was chauffeured in a luxury German limousine adorned with an elaborate but imaginary Fortuyn family coat of arms, usually accompanied by a pair of King Charles spaniels named Kenneth and Carla. To the charge that he was a racist, Fortuyn rejoined that young Arab men were among his numerous lovers.

All this was anathema, even to the right-wing leadership of Livable Netherlands, and by the end of 2001 Fortuyn had been asked to leave the party. By that time, however, he was at a stage where publicity only magnified his success. "He was a genius performer, a pop-star kind of populist," Dutch journalist Hans Wansink told Elizabeth Kolbert of *The New Yorker*. Fortuyn quickly announced that he was forming a party of his own, the immodestly named Lijst (List) Pim Fortuyn. Moderating some of his stands when challenged, but sticking to others, such as requiring immigrants to learn Dutch, Fortuyn became internationally known in the first months of 2002. Supportive of Jews in general and the state of Israel in particular, he denied any connection with other European right-wing leaders, such as France's Jean-Marie Le Pen and Austria's Jörg Haider, whose rhetoric sometimes had anti-Semitic overtones. Second in command in the Lijst Pim Fortuyn was a Dutch citizen of African descent, Cape Verde native João Varela. Other List candidates included a chauffeur, several students, a former beauty queen, and an Internet pornography entrepreneur.

Party Notched Startling Results

Fortuyn confidently predicted that the Dutch parliamentary elections of 2002 would culminate in his selection as prime minister, but few observers took the boast seriously. That changed in March of 2002, when the Lijst Pim Fortuyn, emphasizing anti-crime and anti-immigration rhetoric, won municipal elections in Rotterdam, ending the 80-year rule of the Dutch Labor Party. Suddenly polls suggested that Fortuyn's party was running neck and neck with more established parties, and that Fortuyn could hold the balance of power in determining the next prime minister—or might even become prime minister himself.

Protests against Fortuyn turned ugly. The politician needed a police escort to make it to the polls in Rotterdam, and he was hit by urine-soaked cream pies while making a speech. After receiving death threats, he told friends about an upsetting visit he had made to a fortune teller two years before. "Now I think I will tell you what the fortune-teller said. She told me that I would end up in an ugly way," Fortuyn was quoted as saying in *Newsweek International.*

The prophecy proved accurate. On May 6, 2002, as he was leaving a radio interview in the Amsterdam suburb of Hilversum, Fortuyn was shot five times in the head and chest. Police arrested animal-rights activist Volkert van der Graaf, who later confessed to the crime and was convicted of Fortuyn's murder, but given only an 18-year prison sentence. Immigrant Netherlanders were initially relieved that Fortuyn's killer had not emerged from among their ranks, and police were confused as to the assassin's motives: Fortuyn, although he had made general statements opposing Holland's environmental movement, had not specifically addressed the issue of animal rights. Van de Graaf's 2003 trial reopened tensions when he asserted that he had killed Fortuyn in an attempt to protect Dutch Muslims. "I could see no other option than to do what I did," he was quoted as saying in the *Independent.* Muslims in the Netherlands were being used as "scapegoats," and he "saw it as a danger, but what should you do about it? I hoped that I could solve it myself."

Fortuyn's influence in the Netherlands manifested itself in forms beyond the statue that was erected in Rotterdam in his honor. The Lijst Pim Fortuyn won 28 seats in the Dutch parliament and became part of the Dutch government in a coalition with the Christian Democratic Party in the elections of May 15, 2002, despite the death of its founder. Without the charismatic Fortuyn at the helm, the party was soon weakened by internal disagreements. More important was that several of Fortuyn's positions, once considered extreme, had become part of the political mainstream by the next cycle of national elections in 2006. A ban on the Islamic head covering for women called the burqa was in the works. Enrollment in Dutch language classes was made compulsory for new immigrants, and restrictions were placed on family reunification as a justification for entry into the country. In late 2006, David Charter of the London *Times* wrote that "an uncompromising approach towards immigration has become the new orthodoxy in a country known for its tolerant social attitudes." That change was largely Fortuyn's handiwork.

Periodicals

Daily Telegraph (London, England), May 7, 2002; May 8, 2002; May 24, 2003.
Economist, November 30, 2002.
Europe, May 2002.
Global Agenda, May 16, 2002.
Guardian (London, England), May 8, 2002; April 16, 2003.
Herald (Glasgow, Scotland), May 11, 2002.
Independent (London, England), May 7, 2002; March 28, 2003.
Irish Times, May 19, 2003.
New York Times, May 14, 2002.
New Yorker, September 9, 2002.
Newsweek International, May 20, 2002.
Times (London, England), May 8, 2002; November 21, 2006.

Online

Biography Resource Center Online, Gale Group, 2002, http://galenet.galegroup.com/servlet/BioRC (November 12, 2007). □

Stephen Arthur Frears

British filmmaker Stephen Frears (born 1941) has directed critically acclaimed films in both the United Kingdom and the United States, showing an eagerness to explore new themes in a wide range of film genres.

Training Combined Film, Theater, and Television

Frears was born on June 20, 1941, in Leicester, England. As a child he attended Gresham's School, a prestigious boarding school in Norfolk. After studying law at Trinity College, he decided to enter the film industry instead. He had some theatrical training at London's Royal Court Theatre, and in the 1960s he worked as an assistant under top British directors Lindsay Anderson and Karel Reisz, both known for their ambitious films covering a wide swath of English society.

In the late 1960s Frears, like several of his British cinematic contemporaries, worked in television as a director and producer. At the time, the British Broadcasting Corporation (BBC) often espoused a progressive agenda that encouraged content pertaining to ordinary British citizens. Out of this era came filmmakers Ken Loach and Mike Leigh, who built their careers making socially conscious slice-of-life films. Although he has not kept strictly to social-realist styles in his own films, Frears has approached his films with class consciouness in mind. As he reflected to Cynthia Lucia of *Cineaste,* "I come from the privileged middle classes. I can

see that working-class people who have to struggle more in their lives are better equipped to deal with life.''

In 1971 Frears made his feature film debut with the mystery comedy *Gumshoe,* starring Albert Finney. A satire of detective films of the 1940s, the film features a score by the legendary songwriting team of Andrew Lloyd Webber and Tim Rice. Returning to British television, Frears worked on a series of films with writer Alan Bennett. Frears would continue to work closely with writers, making his own contribution as a director almost invisible in order to showcase the screenplay. ''I do come second,'' Frears told Lucia, of his relationships with writers. ''I don't invent the films. I have a clear sense of that. What the writer has done, I admire. Maybe it has become less like that in recent years. Maybe it's a completely dishonest position. For all I know, it may just be entirely an act of self-concealment on my part.''

Frears frequently switched between television and feature films, a practice he would continue throughout his career. ''All directors should be made to shoot pilots or B movies,'' he told Tobias Grey of *Variety.* ''It keeps you on your toes, and it's an antidote to self-importance.'' In the late 1970s, Frears learned that his mother was Jewish, a fact that had been hidden from him during his childhood. He was brought up Christian and his mother died before he could talk to her about the subject. The moment was a creative turning point for Frears: he stopped making films about the England he grew up in and moved away from personal projects. Frears told Lucia that ''I'd . . . grown up to

be a rather secretive person. If I think about it, since secrets were being kept from me, I'm not surprised.''

Depicted Immigrant Family

In his next few movies, Frears explored issues of race, class, and sexuality. In 1985 he received international attention for *My Beautiful Laundrette.* Written by first-time screenwriter Hanif Kureishi, the film was made with a modest budget and intended for BBC television. Set in a crumbling London during the prime ministership of Margaret Thatcher, the film follows a young man caught between his Pakistani immigrant family and his lover, a homeless thug played by a then-unknown Daniel Day-Lewis. *My Beautiful Laundrette* was later released theatrically and earned Kureishi an Academy Award nomination for Original Screenplay.

Kureishi and Frears joined forces again in 1987 for the comedy *Sammy and Rosie Get Laid,* which likewise explored the sexual underground in lower-class London. In the same year, Frears directed *Prick Up Your Ears,* a biography of playwright Joe Orton, played by Gary Oldman. Based on a book by theater critic John Lahr, the film follows the short, troubled life of Orton, who is killed by his abusive lover, played in the film by Alfred Molina.

Frears made his Hollywood debut in 1988 with the costume drama *Dangerous Liaisons,* starring Glenn Close, John Malkovich, and Michelle Pfeiffer. This frequently adapted story involves a cruel game of sexual deception played between beautiful and vicious aristocrats. The film won three Academy Awards and earned several nominations. An international success, *Dangerous Liaisons* was also recognized by the British and French film academies. In 1990 Frears stayed in Hollywood to make the post-noir film *The Grifters.* Based on a novel by Jim Thompson, the film follows the exploits of three con artists, played by John Cusack, Anjelica Huston, and Annette Bening. *The Grifters* received attention at the Independent Spirit Awards and the Academy Awards, including a Best Director nomination for Frears.

Just as Frears seemed to be on the brink of establishing himself solidly in Hollywood, however, he suffered setbacks. The media satire *Hero* and the costume drama *Mary Reilly* both failed at the box office. Frears continued to experience success with the British made-for-television features *The Snapper* (1993) and *The Van* (1996). Based on books by Roddy Doyle, the two comedies concluded the so-called Barrytown trilogy that had begun with *The Commitments,* directed by Alan Parker. The stories are set in the tightly knit community of working-class Dublin. With its bittersweet tale of a scandalous pregnancy and a stellar ensemble cast including Colm Meaney, *The Snapper* earned a theatrical release and several awards in both Britain and the United States.

Adapted Hit Novel of Music Shop

Back in Hollywood, Frears tried his hand at Westerns with *The Hi-Lo Country,* featuring actors Woody Harrelson and Billy Crudup as cowboys in love with the same woman. Some critics thought Frears was out of his element in this typically American genre, but with *High Fidelity* (2000), based on the popular novel by Nick Hornby, Frears was back on familiar territory. With his old colleague John

Cusack as producer, co-screenwriter, and leading man, Frears seamlessly adapted the novel's original North London setting to Chicago, Illinois. Cusack appeared as a melancholy but charming record store owner trying to keep up with adult relationships. With excellent musical references and a supporting cast that included Jack Black, *High Fidelity* was a commercial success.

For his next challenge, Frears revived the long-dormant practice of live television drama with *Fail Safe,* starring George Clooney. Hosted by Walter Cronkite, the dramatic thriller was aired live in black-and-white on CBS, on April 9, 2000, and received several nods at the Emmy Awards. In the same year, Frears was honored with a tribute at the Toronto Film Festival. He remained modest about his success. He told Grey, "Personally, I make films for people who go to the pictures, ordinary people, the kind of people who don't often get to go to festivals."

Over time, Frears established a balance between his British and American activities. Several of his British films of the early 2000s explored racism and class divisions. Made for the BBC, *Liam* (2000) looked at the anti-Semitism brewing among the working class in 1930s Liverpool. "It's absolutely inappropriate for the commercial cinema, but it's the kind of film I grew up making for the BBC," Frears told Matt Wolf of *Variety*. For the first time in years, Frears was making a movie about life in the England he grew up in. *Liam* was also his first film to take on a Jewish subject since the point when he learned his mother was Jewish. In response to critics who charged that the film was anti-Semitic, Frears told Lucia, "I was insistent on casting Jewish actors. I wouldn't cast non-Jews to play Jews. Maybe that is a sort of anti-Semitism, I don't know; but I got into trouble." Like *My Beautiful Laundrette* and *The Snapper* before it, the made-for-television *Liam* received a theatrical release.

In 2002 Frears explored the theme of illegal immigration in the thriller *Dirty Pretty Things,* starring Audrey Tautou and Nigerian-British actor Chiwetel Ejiofor. Returning to the social-realist themes of his earlier films, Frears worked with a multicultural cast to create a tense thriller rooted in unusual raw material: the brutal exploitation of immigrant service workers in London. Steven Knight, creator of the original *Who Wants to Be a Millionaire,* wrote the Oscar-nominated screenplay, and *Dirty Pretty Things* won a British Independent Film Award for Best Independent Film.

Frears's *The Deal* (2003), originally aired on Britain's Channel 4, was a docudrama—a film that recounted actual events but lightly fictionalized them and used professional actors to portray the individuals involved. Based on the book *The Rivals* by James Naughtie, the film follows the politicians Gordon Brown (played by David Morrissey) and Tony Blair (played by Michael Sheen). Next, Frears teamed with British superstars Judi Dench and Bob Hoskins for the comedy *Mrs. Henderson Presents* (2005), based on a true story about nude shows at the historic Windmill Theater in London. Frears then reunited with screenwriter Peter Morgan for *The Queen,* a follow-up to *The Deal.* Starring Helen Mirren as Her Majesty Queen Elizabeth II, the film traces the political aftermath of the death of Princess Diana. Originally made for television, *The Queen* received a theatrical release

in 2006. It was showered with awards, including five Academy Award nominations and an Oscar for Helen Mirren.

After *The Queen* rose to international success, Frears found himself receiving honors and film festival retrospectives. However, he continued to work on small personal projects for British television. Few directors have been associated with as many high-profile, ambitious international successes as has Frears, yet general evaluations of his art are rare. As John Woodward told Maev Kennedy of the London *Guardian,* "Stephen Frears has been so modest about his success over the years, and about the range of genres that he has completely mastered, from *Gumshoe* to *The Queen* by way of *The Grifters* and *Dangerous Liaisons,* that sometimes he seems to have made himself almost invisible."

Frears has been married twice, to Mary-Kay Wilmers and then to painter Anne Rothenstein. Each marriage produced two children; his son Will Frears, born to Frears and Wilmers in 1973, is a theatrical director. In addition to filmmaking, Frears has taught at the National Film & Television School in Beaconsfield, England, where he holds the David Lean Chair in Fiction Direction. He also taught a master class at the Zurich Film Festival in 2006, where he was presented with a Lifetime Achievement Award. Explaining the attraction of teaching, Frears told Grey that "If I was doing nothing I'd make another film, and I don't always want to make a film. So it provides work for idle hands." In May of 2007, he became the first British director to serve as jury president of the Cannes Film Festival. Despite his high-ranking status in the world of cinema, Stephen Frears went on that year to direct the television series pilot *Skip Tracer* for CBS.

Books

International Dictionary of Films and Filmmakers, Volume 2: Directors, 4th ed., St. James, 2000.

Periodicals

Cineaste, Fall 2003.
Guardian (London, England), May 18, 2007.
Variety, September 4, 2000; April 26, 2004; September 25, 2006; May 14, 2007.

Online

"Like Pulling Teeth (Or Stealing Kidneys): Stephen Frears On Dirty Pretty Things." Indiewire, http://www.indiewire.com/people/people_030718frears.html (January 3, 2008). □

Klaus Fuchs

The German-born physicist Klaus Fuchs (1911-1988) was one of the Soviet Union's most effective spies operating in Britain and the United States in the critical period during and after World War II.

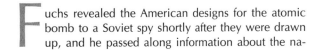

Fuchs revealed the American designs for the atomic bomb to a Soviet spy shortly after they were drawn up, and he passed along information about the na-

scent hydrogen bomb as well. He is thought to have speeded construction of a Soviet nuclear device by perhaps three years. Fuchs's eventual exposure was the first in a long line of incidents that revealed grave flaws in Britain's national security apparatus, and his story, which reads in places like a spy thriller, bears on the difficulty of combating the nuclear proliferation in the world today.

Of Quaker Background

Klaus Emil Julius Fuchs was born on December 29, 1911, in Rüsselsheim, Germany, near Darmstadt in the German state of Hesse. He was influenced heavily by his father, Emil, a Quaker minister with a strong socialist and idealist orientation that he impressed upon all his children. When the family later moved to the city of Kiel they became known as the Red Foxes of Kiel, both for their red hair and their left-wing philosophies (the name Fuchs means "Fox" in German). Fuchs became interested in politics as a student at the University of Leipzig in 1930. He joined the socialist Social Democratic Party but was disillusioned after that party made accommodations with conservatives in the maneuvering that accompanied Adolf Hitler's rise, and his politics moved leftward. At the University of Kiel he joined the Communist Party of Germany, which he and many other leftist Germans felt represented the last bastion of resistance to Hitler.

Conditions for Fuchs and his family deteriorated rapidly as the Nazis' grip on Germany tightened, and harassment caused Fuchs's mother to commit suicide. Fuchs and his siblings scattered, and Fuchs decided to leave Germany.

In September of 1933 he arrived in England. By that time he was a committed Communist who took orders from the Communist Party in Moscow, and he left Germany only to escape persecution. "I was sent out by the Party," he was quoted as saying by biographer Robert Chadwell Williams in *Klaus Fuchs: Atom Spy*. "They said that I must finish my studies because after the revolution in Germany people would be required with technical knowledge to take part in the building up of the Communist Germany."

Fuchs took his instructions seriously. He enrolled in a Ph.D. program at the University of Bristol, receiving his degree in 1936 after writing a thesis titled "The Cohesive Forces of Copper and the Elastic Constants of Monovalent Metals." His Communist leanings were noted by British officials, but in 1930s Britain, with many Britons viewing the Soviet Union as a bulwark against German fascism, his political positions were not thought to represent a significant threat. Fuchs moved on to the University of Edinburgh and continued to do physics research. Supporting himself on a fellowship stipend, he published a series of articles in 1939 and 1940 dealing with electromagnetic radiation and wave functions.

After war broke out, Fuchs fell under more suspicion because he was German than because he was a Communist. In 1940 he was questioned in Edinburgh, arrested, and sent to an internment camp run by the Canadian army near Quebec City, Quebec. Later he was transferred to another Quebec camp near Sherbrooke. Conditions were difficult in these camps; in the Sherbrooke facility, only five faucets and six latrines were provided for the 720 prisoners. However, Fuchs and other prisoners organized a camp university at which he gave physics lectures. Fuchs was released from the internment camp and taken back to Britain at the behest of two British scientists: Max Born, his former advisor in Edinburgh, and Rudolf Peierls, a scientist working on Britain's atomic research program centered at Birmingham University. Their intercession was successful because Fuchs was on a list of scientists wanted for work on Britain's atomic bomb enterprise, which was code-named the Tube Alloys project.

Contacted Soviet Embassy

According to John Crossland of the *Times* of London, an MI5 security service agent named Griffiths wrote to his superiors: "If anything very serious against Fuchs should come to light we could consider the cancellation of his permit. In the meantime perhaps it would be as well to warn the Ministry of Atomic Production of this man's communist connexions." Although disregarded owing to the growing alliance between Britain and the Soviet Union, the warning was a pertinent one. Fuchs quickly made contact with the Soviet Embassy in London and informed personnel there that he had been assigned to sensitive atomic work. They placed him in contact with a female Soviet military intelligence agent, Ruth Beurton, code-named Sonia.

Fuchs became a naturalized British citizen in 1942, enhancing his security credentials despite continuing misgivings from British intelligence agencies. His value as a Soviet resource increased dramatically in 1943 when he became one of a group of British scientists chosen to join the U.S. atomic bomb project in Los Alamos, New Mexico, known as the Manhattan Project. Soviet intelligence had its own code name for the project, "Enormoz," and Fuchs was referred to as agent Charles. Fuchs made important contributions to the atomic bomb as it developed, focusing on detonation devices, and he was present at the Trinity test, the world's first test of a nuclear weapon, on July 16, 1945. He had close working relationships with Edward Teller and other designers of American nuclear weaponry.

Fuchs's contact in America was a Soviet spy named Harry Gold, whom he knew as Raymond. Their initial meeting took place in New York City, where Fuchs arrived before traveling to New Mexico. They agreed to meet on a Saturday afternoon, identifying each other as follows: Gold carried a pair of gloves and a green-covered book, and Fuchs carried a handball. Subsequent meetings after Fuchs went to Los Alamos were often accomplished during Fuchs's vacation time, with his sister Kristel, who lived in Cambridge, Massachusetts, sometimes serving as intermediary. Fuchs passed along detailed drawings of American nuclear weapon designs, enabling the Soviet Union to build its own atomic bomb well in advance of the timeline its own capabilities would have permitted.

In 1946 Fuchs returned to Britain and was assigned to the Harwell Atomic Research Establishment as senior principal scientific officer. He continued to meet with Sonia and other Soviet handlers, using as rendezvous points a country road and a south London pub called the Spotted Horse. Fuchs was instructed to leave chalk marks on a sidewalk near a railway station to confirm a meeting, and for emergency meetings he was supposed to throw a copy of the magazine *Men Only* into the garden of a specific house. During this period he transmitted to Soviet intelligence what he knew of the incipient hydrogen bomb, which he had heard Teller discuss. Fuchs's hydrogen bomb information is thought to have been less useful than the materials he passed along about the atomic bomb, as the eventual hydrogen bomb tested by the Americans was based on a design that was different from the ones developed while Fuchs was in Los Alamos. He did help the Soviets keep abreast of developments in the American hydrogen bomb program.

Experienced "Controlled Schizophrenia"

Fuchs did all this because he was devoted to the Soviet Union and its aims. The stress of leading a double life began to take its toll on him, however, and he was troubled by the increasing brutality of Soviet dictator Joseph Stalin's reign in the late 1940s. "I used my Marxist philosophy to establish in my mind two separate compartments," he said in his eventual confession, as quoted by Williams. One compartment was the sphere of his British identity "in which I allowed myself to make friendships, to have personal relations, to help people and to be in all personal ways the kind of man I wanted to be." The other compartment contained his status as a loyal Communist. "It appeared to me at the time that I had become a 'free man' because I had succeeded in the other compartment to establish myself completely independent of the surrounding forces of society. Looking back at it now the best way of expressing it seems to be to call it a controlled schizophrenia."

In 1949, in poor health and with these questions weighing on his mind, Fuchs made a fatal mistake. He was already under close surveillance as a possible source of unexplained leaks of information on Britain's nuclear program. His father, Emil, had moved to Communist East Germany, and Fuchs reported this fact to Harwell security officers, warning that the Soviets might use that information to try to blackmail him. He was subsequently questioned by MI5 investigator Jim Skardon. Fuchs initially denied knowledge of the leaks, but on January 24, 1950, he asked Skardon to meet for lunch at a pub near the Harwell establishment. Skardon noted that Fuchs seemed to be under a good deal of stress, and Fuchs began to lay out his story. Curiously, Fuchs believed that he would still be able to maintain his position at Harwell.

Fuchs was put on trial and convicted of espionage. On March 1, 1950, he was sentenced to 14 years at the Old Bailey prison, a sentence lightened by the fact that Britain and the Soviet Union had been allies during the time most of the crimes had been committed. Fuchs was a model prisoner who taught classes and wrote articles for the Old Bailey prison magazine. He was released after nine years, in 1959, for good behavior and was deported to East Germany. A few days after his arrival there he married Greta Keilson, whom he had met in France in the 1930s. Fuchs became a member of the Central Committee of the East German Communist Party and served until 1979 as deputy director of the country's nuclear research institute. He died in East Berlin on January 28, 1988.

Books

The Cold War, 1945-1991, 3 vols., edited by Benjamin Frankel, Gale Research, 1992.

Moss, Norman, *Klaus Fuchs: The Man Who Stole the Atom Bomb,* Grafton, 1987.

Williams, Robert Chadwell, *Klaus Fuchs: Atom Spy,* Harvard University Press, 1987.

Periodicals

Daily Mail (London, England), May 22, 2003.

Daily Telegraph (London, England), May 22, 2003.

Mirror (London, England), September 13, 1999.

Science, November 6, 1987.

Time, January 15, 1990.

Times (London, England), January 29, 1988; May 22, 2003.

Online

"Klaus Fuchs (1911-1988)," Atomic Archive, http://www.atomic archive.com/Bios/Fuchs.shtml (February 4, 2008).

"Klaus Fuchs (1911-1988)," Public Broadcasting Service: *The American Experience,* http://www.pbs.org/wgbh/amex/ bomb/peopleevents/pandeAMEX54.html (February 4, 2008).

"1 March 1950: Communist spy jailed for 14 years," British Broadcasting Corporation, http://www.news.bbc.co.uk/onthisday/ hi/dates/stories/march/1/newsid_4222000/4222261.stm (February 4, 2008). □

G

Galerius, Emperor of Rome

The emperor Galerius (c. 250-311 A.D.) ruled over a disintegrating Roman Empire in the years just prior to its conversion to Christianity. The six-year period of his reign, from 305 to 311, marked the last official persecution of Christians in the Roman world. In the work *De Mortibus Persecutorum* (Of the Manner in Which the Persecutors Died), the historian Lactantius, a contemporary of the emperor, described Galerius as "worse than all the bad princes of former days. In this wild beast there dwelt a native barbarity and a savageness foreign to Roman blood."

Galerius's full Latin name is Gaius Galerius Valerius Maximianus, but he was not born a citizen of Rome proper, nor was he of noble status. Historians place the date of his birth around the year 250, in Serdica, which is near Sofia, the present-day capital of Bulgaria. At the time, Serdica was the capital of Dacia Aureliana, a Roman province comprising the area south of the Danube River. The region was populated by Thracians, an Indo-European people who were influenced by contact with ancient Greece. Galerius's father was Thracian and a herdsman by profession, a job that Galerius apparently took up in his younger years. It is known that Galerius's mother was called Romula, and was of Dacian birth, meaning that she had originally come from what is now Romania after the region was subject to raids by Carpians, a Dacian tribe that often attacked Roman settlements.

Proclaimed Caesar

Joining the Roman legion was almost the sole avenue for professional advancement during Galerius's time, and historical records hint that he served in the army under the emperors Lucius Domitius Aurelianus (214–275) and Marcus Aurelius Probus (c. 232–282). He apparently advanced rapidly through the ranks, for on March 1, 293, a new Tetrarchy, with four joint rulers, was set up by Diocletian (c. 236–316). In this scheme, Diocletian ruled as Augustus with the general Marcus Aurelius Valerius Maximianus Herculius, known as Maximian (c. 250–310), over respective Eastern and Western regions of the empire, with two junior emperors, known as Caesars. Galerius was designated one of these Caesars, that of the East, with Constantius Chlorus (c. 250–306) named to be Caesar of the West. With the honor came Galerius's betrothal to Diocletian's daughter, Valeria.

Galerius was responsible for overseeing Illyricum, the Roman provinces comprising lands that include present-day Albania, Croatia, Slovenia, and Bosnia. When the Romans went to war with their Sassanid neighbors in the east at the renewal of the Persian Wars in 296, Galerius commanded a legion that took to the field near the Euphrates River region. The first major battle of the war was here at Callinicum (also called Carrhae), near Turkey's border with Syria, but Galerius's troops lost heavily, and with that loss the Roman Empire was divested of its holdings in Mesopotamia. A year later, however, came a significant reversal of fortunes, as Galerius led troops into Armenia and won a decisive victory against the Persian shah. He seized the ancient city of Ctesiphon near Baghdad as well as a large cache of goods plundered from the enemy, including the shah's extensive harem. The victory returned Roman rule to Mesopotamia for the time being, and the lands taken east of the Tigris River marked the furthest eastern boundary ever touched by Roman rule.

Urged Persecution of Christians

Galerius was a pagan, and his mother Romula's intense devotion to certain pagan cults and distrust of the new religion of Christianity was said to have greatly influenced him. For much of Diocletian's rule, Christians had been allowed to practice their religion, but Galerius urged the aging emperor to launch a renewal of persecutions. In an edict dated February 24, 303, Christian scriptures were ordered to be destroyed, as were Christian houses of assembly. Later that year, Diocletian's palace in Nicomedia—at that time the eastern capital of the empire and now the city of İzmit, Turkey—was engulfed by flames, and harassment of the minority sect intensified as a result. All Christians in the city were ordered to be put to death as punishment, but some scholars posit that Galerius himself was behind the arson attack as a way to incite further attacks on Christians.

As Diocletian's health declined, Galerius likely persuaded him to resign jointly with Maximian. They abdicated on May 1, 305, and with that, Galerius received the title of Augustus along with Constantius Chlorus. Below them were two newly appointed Caesars, Flavius Valerius Severus and Galerius's nephew, Maximinus Daia. Constantius died the following year in York, England, during a campaign against the Picts in Britain, and Galerius reportedly planned to become sole emperor. But Constantius had appointed his son Constantine to serve as his successor, which the Roman troops with him immediately recognized. Galerius's ambitions were further thwarted by Maximian Herculius and his son Marcus Aurelius Valerius Maxentius (c. 278–312), who also supported the rise of Constantine as Emperor of the West.

In direct conflict with Constantine's claim to the throne, Galerius made Severus the new Augustus in the West, and ordered him to Rome to suppress a rebellion led by Maxentius. Severus's forces invaded Italy in 307, but failed to take the imperial city, and Severus was put to death on orders of Maxentius. In the midst of the disarray, Galerius ordered a reorganization of the empire in 308 at a conference in Carnuntum, a Roman army camp in what is present-day Austria. There he named his friend Licinius as the new Augustus in the East, and retired to a city he was in the process of building in honor of his mother, which he called Felix Romuliana (Gamzigrada, Serbia).

Died Gruesome Death

The Roman historian Lactantius wrote about Galerius and his turbulent reign in *De Mortibus Persecutorum,* noting that the emperor considered himself a Dacian, not a Roman—an important distinction in an empire when Roman ideals were the strongest common bond for denizens of the far-flung empire and its long line of rulers. Lactantius wrote that Galerius called himself the enemy of the Roman name, and wanted the empire to be renamed the Dacian empire. In the work, Galerius was described as "tall, full of flesh, and swollen to a horrible bulk of corpulency; by his speech, gestures, and looks, he made himself a terror to all

that came near him," and the historian also noted that Diocletian "dreaded him excessively."

The persecutions of Christians begun under Diocletian continued under Galerius. They continued for eight years until a general edict of tolerance was proclaimed by Galerius at Nicomedia in April 311, just a month before his death. By this point he had been ill for some time in what appears to have been bowel cancer. Lactantius wrote that "a malignant ulcer formed itself low down in his secret parts, and spread by degrees." Galerius underwent operations, but his condition worsened. Lactantius claimed that this illness was so dire that it compelled Galerius to revise his beliefs about Christianity and issue the new edict of tolerance.

The Last Pagan Emperor

Galerius died on May 5, 311. He was succeeded by Constantine I, his longtime rival. Constantine's rule marked a significant turning point for the Roman Empire, for he was the first emperor to convert to Christianity, but even prior to that had strengthened the original 311 edict of tolerance with his own Edict of Milan in 313, which banned all forms of religious persecution in the empire. Galerius was buried in Felix Romuliana, where the ruins of his palace were designated a World Heritage site in 2007. In Thessaloniki, Greece, the Arch of Galerius that commemorates his victory over Persia still stands. That Greek city is also home to the Church of St. Dimitrios, named for an early Christian martyr. Dimitrios was a Greek-born officer in the Roman army who was a secret convert to Christianity. When this was discovered, he was arrested and jailed, and while incarcerated came to know another Christian and urged him to battle a well-known gladiator. The gladiator died, and when Galerius learned of Dimitrios's role in it, he ordered the prisoner to be executed by spear. Legend holds that Dimitrios's body was then thrown into a well, which then began to emit holy oil, and miracles were attributed to site, which became the crypt of St. Dimitrios, the patron saint of Thessaloniki.

Another tale of Christian persecution related to Galerius supposedly concerns two of his bodyguards, Sergius and Bacchus. They, too, were accused of secretly practicing Christianity. They confessed when confronted by the emperor, and were paraded through the streets while dressed in women's clothing. In prison, Bacchus was beaten to death over several hours, and when Sergius refused to recant his faith, nails were driven into his boots and he was ordered to run. Some historians believe the pair of martyrs were actually lovers, and a group of gay Roman Catholic activists now uses their image as a symbol during their community events.

Books

Costelloe, M. J., "Galerius, Roman Emperor," *New Catholic Encyclopedia,* Volume 6, second edition, Gale, 2003.

Periodicals

New York Times, July 2, 1982; September 17, 1995.
Star Tribune (Minneapolis, MN), February 26, 2005.

Online

Lactantius, *Of the Manner in Which the Persecutors Died,* http://www.ucalgary.ca/~vandersp/Courses/texts/lactant/lactpers.html (December 27, 2007). □

Rasul Gamzatov

Dagestan's "most famous son," poet Rasul Gamzatov (1923-2003) composed a flood of poetry, prose and analytical work that has been passed on to future generations in many of the world's languages.

Welcomed by Bullets

Rasul Gamzatovich Gamzatov was born September 8, 1923 in the village of Tsada in the Hunzahskogo district of Dagestan. Practically a poet at birth, Gamzatov's father—Tsadasa Hamzat (1877–1951)—had also held the title of People's Poet of Dagestan and had been awarded the USSR State Prize for poetry in his lifetime as well.

Gamzatov recalled his naming in his lyric novel, *Moi Dagestan* (My Dagestan, 1967–1971). He was the third son, and according to Dagestani tradition, because he was a boy, pistols were pointed at the ceiling inside the house and bullets were shot in his honor. The family's male names had been given to his two older brothers, and there had been no deaths of revered men in the community to provide a namesake, so his mother handed the infant Gamzatov to an elder, who chose the name "Rasul"—which means messenger or representative—then whispered the name in one of the babe's ears and shouted it in the other.

Early Learning

Gamzatov's father served as his first tutor in the literary arts and remained a mentor throughout the poet's life. He listened eagerly when his father recited memorized stories—from folk legends and fairy tales to epic songs—and read everything he could get his hands on. While many sources say Gamzatov was composing poetry at the age of nine, some claim it was not until the ripe old age of eleven that the Dagestani boy began working on his craft. His poems began to appear in local newspapers and other cultural publications and in 1940 he graduated from a pedagogical college in Buynaksk and taught in the school in his village for a short period before taking work assisting the director of the Avarskogo State Theatre. He followed this work with a position as department head and correspondent for the newspaper *Bolshevik Mountains,* while also acting as editor for the radio program Avar Transmission in Dagestan.

Love and Hate: The Poet's Muses

Gamzatov's first collection of poetry was written in the Avar language, which is spoken by only approximately 500,000 people. The book was released in 1943 and its title,

Plamennaia liubov' i zhguchaia nenavist, proved to be an interpretational challenge with translations ranging from "Flaming Burning Love and Hatred" to "Love Inspired and Fiery Wrath." In the biography on Gamzatov's official Web site, the poet remembers when this first collection was released, and recalled that "He was overjoyed when girls in the mountains who read it wrote to him—and to this day he cannot forget his pain on seeing a shepherd in winter pastures using a page to roll a cigarette."

Gamzatov was 20 when he joined the Union of Writers of the USSR. Sometime in 1945 Gamzatov's poem "Children Krasnodona" was translated into Russian by Ilya Selvinskim and its influence earned him an invitation to attend the Gorky Literary Institute located in Moscow. The institute's director at the time noted Gamzatov's poor Russian, but also recognized the young poet's nimble yet powerful style. While Gamzatov read a variety of poets as a student, he remained partial to Russian Romantic author Alexander Pushkin (1799–1837), Caucasus poet Mikhail Lermontov (1814–1841) and Russian poet, critic and publisher Nikolay Nekrasov (1821–1878). Gamzatov graduated from the Gorky Literary Institute in 1950, publicly grateful for the immersion in Russian literature that he received while there. *Love Inspired and Fiery Wrath* was translated into Russian in 1947, and the prolific poet followed his primary work with more than twenty books of poetry and prose—a versatile wealth of epigrams, long narrative poems, philosophical octaves, ballads, and short love lyrics.

The Road to Celebrity

Gamzatov's fame as a poet was well–earned and well–known, but he was also a gifted translator and is credited with introducing the work of Pushkin to a Dagestani readership with such enthusiasm that said author's work became a national phenomenon that enriched the culture of the Avar people. In fact, every year on June 6—Pushkin's birthday—all of Dagestan celebrates Pushkin Poetry Day. Gamzatov translated a wealth of works from their native languages into Avar, including the creations of Mikhail Lermontov (1814–1841), Nikolay Nekrasov (1821–1878), Taras Shevchenko (1814–1861), Alexander Blok (1880–1921), Vladimir Mayakovski (1893–1930) and Sergei Yesenin (1895–1925). Much of Gamzatov's poetry and prose gained additional momentum when it was turned into popular songs or adapted for the stage and the opera.

Cranes

Gamzatov's poetry often showcased and praised the heroism of soldiers because he lost his two older brothers in the Great Patriotic War, the term that was used almost exclusively in the Soviet Union for World War II. The most famous of Gamzatov's poems, "Cranes," was composed after a visit to Japan where he saw the monument to Sadako—a Japanese girl who survived Hiroshima only to die of cancer at the age of twelve. Gamzatov was profoundly moved by the monument and the tale, and further shaken by news in a telegram of his own mother's death. He composed the piece while in flight to Moscow—

recalling his father and brothers, then deceased, and thinking about the casualties of war. The poem was crafted into a stirring song which appeared in the 1957 award–winning film *Flying Cranes* and continues to serve as a requiem for the dead in all wars. The reach of Gamzatov's imagery remains vast. "The Moscow Circus's celebrated aerialists The Flying Cranes are considered exceptional the world over, and their [performance] enacts the words of a Russian song, 'Cranes.' " Glenn Collins wrote in his 1990 *New York Times* piece about the troupe. "The Cranes use their safety net as both a trampoline and, in the context of their narrative performance, a symbol of the earth. Their text, derived from a poem by Rasul Gamzatov, celebrates the souls of soldiers who have perished and who are transformed into white cranes that ascend to the sky. It is a powerful, traditional Russian image." Indeed, the symbol is so strong that many of Gamzatov's contemporaries, when interviewed at the time of the poet's death, shared that they pictured Gamzatov's spirit as a white crane circling those he left behind on earth and a memorial—aptly titled, "White Cranes"—was erected next to the poet's grave.

Beyond Fame

Rasul Gamzatov married Patimat Saidovna (1931–2000) and they had three daughters—Zarema, Patimat and Salihat. After becoming a widower, Gamzatov lived in Makhachkala—the capital of Dagestan, located on the shores of the Caspian sea—with his daughters and grand-daughters Shahrizat, Madina, Tawus, and Aminat. Gamzatov's literary and eventually political popularity rose into the cultural stratosphere, and "poetical" events honoring the modern bard were always well attended. An avenue bears his name in Makhachkala, and his obituary in the *Caucasus Reporting Service* pointed out that to the younger generation, Gamzatov was "a more remote figure, a poet laureate constantly caught up in one celebration or commemoration [or] another." He was showered with awards, honors, titles and medals—serving as chairman of the Union of Writers of Dagestan from 1950 until his death in 2003. His 80th birthday celebrations were extravagant to the extreme, with more than a million dollars spent by the government and a hectic schedule of proceedings and appearances that led mourners to suspect that the event might have inadvertently killed the people's poet. In fact, 2003 was declared the Year of Rasul Gamzatov in Dagestan even before his death.

A simple mountain bard at heart, Gamzatov never got used to his celebrity. Janice Turner quoted the poet in her 1989 *South Magazine* interview, "If writers and speakers were previously prone to boasting and being surrounded by the pomposity and privileges accompanying the position of a writer, they are now surrounded by wicked bureaucracy and admiration and never have time to write, look at the stars and cry on the graves of those who died." Further into Turner's interview, Gamzatov went on to say, "I like individuality in literature and don't mind what nationality it comes from. Poetry is the passport of the country one belongs to. I come to the world as Rasul Gamzatov, who tells of . . . his village and his people. That is what I represent. And when I return to my village, I speak the language of the world."

Despite Gamzatov's humility, his influence was profound. Russian poet Robert Rozhdestvensky (1932–1994) recalled the way Gamzatov's compassionate perceptions seemed truly ownerless, so that millions of readers in a multitude of languages felt like "citizens" of his unique poetic world. He never cultivated fluency in Russian, a fact that allowed him to maintain his simple image and meant he could travel in times when Russians were often discouraged from going abroad. Thousands wrote of their sorrow at his passing, some marveling at how the mention of Gamzatov or the recitation of his poetry had acted as an identifier for those who found it hard to explain where they came from—unity in just a handful of words. Dagestani President Mukhu Aliyev (1940–) also used Gamzatov's words to address a security conference, and, according to the *BBC World Monitoring Trans Caucasus Unit,* reminded the crowd, "As you remember, Rasul Gamzatov used to say that a small nation needs either a big knife or a big neighbour. The people of Dagestan have a big neighbor. We are part of the Russian state." It is clear that Gamzatov's words were for everyone, however. An opposition leader also used a quotation from *My Dagestan* to express his hope that the authorities would not use excessive force during a planned opposition rally in April of 2007. As recorded in *BBC Monitoring Central Asia Unit* That same leader went on to say, "I am confident that they will not resort to force. To rephrase the words of the famous poet, Rasul Gamzatov, by shooting with a gun, they will get a blow from a cannon. Because shooting people means that you have given yourself the death sentence." The lyricism and wisdom of Gamzatov's words seemed to charm everyone who read them.

Private Passing

Gamzatov was discharged from the Central Clinical Hospital on November 3, 2003 with no explanation of what he had been treated for, or how his health was at the time of release. He died at home on November 3, 2003 at the age of 80, and the cause of death was never released. The Dagestani culture is famous for its hospitality, but devoted about maintaining the privacy of its people—heros included. Little has been written about Gamzatov's personal life beyond what he offered in his own autobiographical work, out of respect to his family. He was buried on November 4, 2003 in the Tarky–Tau Mount Cemetery in Makhachkala, Dagestan and is remembered, above all, as an international man. In the obituary released by the *Caucasus Reporting Service*, the journalist explained that Gamzatov "represented a certain kind of Dagestani who was loyal to the communist system, but was also modern and internationally–minded." His jovial verses, weighted with a dark undercurrent, are likely to be read and recited for lifetimes to come. Even the inscription Gamzatov composed for a tombstone embodies his frank simplicity (as quoted from his official Web site), "A thousand roads you build, but one thing's clear: Whichever road you take, you end up here!"

Books

The International Authors and Writers Who's Who: 11th Edition, edited by Ernest Kay, Melrose Press Limited, 1989.

The International Who's Who: 67th Edition, Europa Publications Ltd., 2003.

Who's Who in the Socialist Countries, edited by Borys Lewytzkyj and Juliusz Stroynowski, K.G. Saur Publishing Inc., 1978.

Who's Who in the World: 7th Edition 1984–1985, Marquis Who's Who, Inc., 1984.

Periodicals

BBC Monitoring Central Asia Unit, April 2, 2007.

BBC Monitoring Former Soviet Union–Political, June 14, 2007.

BBC Monitoring Trans Caucasus Unit, June 8, 2007.

The Globe and Mail (Canada), November 5, 2003.

The New York Times, December 30, 1990.

South Magazine, December 1989.

Online

"Biography," People's Poet of Daghestan Rasul Gamzatov, http://www.gamzatov.ru/bioeng.html (November 20, 2007).

"Dagestan Mourns National Poet," Caucasus Reporting Service, http://iwpr.net/?p = crs&s = f&o = 159035&apc_state = henicrs2003 (December 15, 2007).

"Gamzatov, Rasul Gamzatovich," *Encyclopedia of Soviet Authors,* http://www.sovlit.com/bios/gamzatov.html (November 27, 2007).

"My Dagestan," People's Poet of Daghestan Rasul Gamzatov, http://www.gamzatov.ru/nadpiseng.html (November 20, 2007).

"Rasul Gamzatov," Blog of Death, http://www.blogofdeath.com/archives/000527.html (November 27, 2007).

"Rasul Gamzatov," Find A Grave Memorial, http://www.findagrave.com/cgi-bin/fg.cgi?page = gr&GRid = 8081660 (December 15, 2007).

"Rasul Gamzatov," Peoples.ru, http://translate.google.com/translate?hl = en&sl = ru&u = http://www.peoples.ru/&sa = X &oi = translate&resnum = 1&ct = result&prev = /search%3Fq %3Dpeoples.ru%26hl%3Den (December 15, 2007).

"Rasul Gamzatov," Pipl: People Search, http://pipl.com/directory/people/Rasul/Gamzatov (December 15, 2007).

"Rasul Gamzatov," Rusnet, http://www.rusnet.nl/encyclo/g/gamzatov.shtml (November 27, 2007).

"Rasul Gamzatov," Thinkers Network: Modern Indian Writings, http://thinkers.net/forum/showthread.php?t = 1145 (December 15, 2007).

"Well–known poet Rasul Gamzatov passed away," *Pravda: News From Russia,* http://newsfromrussia.com/accidents/2003/11/03/50990.html (November 27, 2007). □

Bashir Gemayel

Lebanese political and military leader Bashir Gemayel (1947-1982) served as the commander for the Lebanese Forces and, in 1982, was elected president of Lebanon. However, the charismatic yet ruthless Gemayel was assassinated only days before he was scheduled to assume office. During his rise to power, he established a covert relationship with Israel that led to that country's invasion of Lebanon in 1982. He also served as an informant for the United State's Central Intelligence Agency.

ashir Gemayel was born into political power. His father was Sheikh Pierre Gemayel, a founder and main leader of the Lebanese Phalange (al-Kataeb al-Lubnaniah), the paramilitary organization that became a potent political force in Lebanon's national affairs. But because he was his family's youngest child among six children, Bashir Gemayel was not expected to rise to a position of prominence and power. Rather, it was anticipated that his brother, Amin, would precede him. However, by the time he was thirty-four years old, the charismatic Gemayel had defied expectations to become one of the most important leaders in Lebanon's history. In 1982, he became president of the country. Despite realizing an ambition that, at that point, had eluded both his father and his brother, he never served in that role as he was assassinated before he had a chance to assume office.

Early Life

Bashir Gemayel was born on November 10, 1947 in Bikfaya, Lebanon, a mountain village near Beirut. He had four sisters and an older brother, Amin. The organization that their father founded, the Lebanese Phalange, was a right–wing organization that was primarily supported by Maronite Christians, even though it was officially considered secular. Its vision included the establishment of a strong Lebanese state.

While growing up, Bashir Gemayel benefited from an excellent education. He completed his primary and intermediate studies at Notre–Dame de Jamhour, a leading educational institution in Lebanon, and his secondary studies at the Lebanese Modern Institute. In 1962, he joined the Kataeb party and became a member in the Kataeb Student Section. He later attended Saint Joseph University in Beirut and received degrees in law and political science. While attending the university, he taught intermediate– and secondary–level civil education at the Lebanese Modern Institute for three years (1968–1971).

Rise to Power

Gemayel's rise to power began in the early 1970s. Relatively young but politically shrewd, he engineered a swift ascent through the ranks of the right–wing Phalange organization. He had a strong base within his country's Maronite Christian community, and he was able to use this to his advantage. Lebanon was an unevenly divided country, and its Muslim population outnumbered the Christian segment. Even so, the country's political system tended to favor the Christians, a situation established as far back as 1943, when Lebanon's National Pact established the modern state as a sectarian democracy with a Christian president and a parliament comprised of more Christians that Muslims.

The decade started off in grim fashion for Gemayel when, in 1970, Palestinian militants kidnapped him from Dekwaneh to the Tal el–Zaater camp. He was released, however, after eight hours. On a better note, that same year, he was invited to Egypt to meet Khaled Abdul–Nasser, the son of President Jamal Abdul–Nasser.

In 1971, he was appointed inspector in the Kataeb Regular Forces, the para–military branch of the Kataeb party. That same year, he traveled to the United States to take a law course. In 1972, he received a degree from the American and International Law Academy in Plano, Texas. During the early 1970s, when he worked in a Washington, D.C. law firm, he was recruited by the U.S. Central Intelligence Agency (CIA) to be an informant. At first, Gemayel served the CIA on a straight exchange basis, providing information for money. However, when Gemayel later took charge of the Maronite militia in 1976, his importance to the CIA substantially grew and his payments increased. (Later, during the administration of Ronald Reagan, Israeli defense minister Ariel Sharon urged President Reagan to authorize $10 million in covert aid to Gemayel's militia).

During this period, Gemayel, who become a member of the bar association, opened a law office in West Beirut, which operated from 1972 to 1975. In 1973, Gemayel was appointed to be political director of the Phalange office in Ashrafieh. In 1974, he established the "B.G." squad, which became a core faction of the Lebanese Forces. Comprised of university students, the squad sought to address the dangers posed by the Palestinian Liberation Organization (PLO), which had been setting up armed barricades and kidnapping and attacking civilians.

In 1976, the Maronite forces staged a siege at Tel al–Zaater, a Palestine refugee camp set up in East Beirut. The battle and aftermath would propel Gemayel to national prominence. During the siege, Gemayel became deputy commander of the Phalange militia. Then, on July 13 of that year, he was promoted to the position of chief of the militia's military council after previous leader William Hawi was killed in the Tal el–Zaater battle. The refugee camp eventually fell. The Christian militias recognized the need for a unified front. Gemayel met with Druze leader Kamal Jumblatt to unify the Lebanese ranks to forestall an increased presence of the Syrian army in Lebanon. Afterward, Gemayel became head of the joint command council of the newly united Lebanese Forces, which had combined the Maronite militias.

As events continued unfolding, renowned *Washington Post* journalist Bob Woodward (who gained fame when he teamed with fellow reporter Carl Bernstein to break the story of the Watergate break–in in Washington, D.C.) described Gemayel as "a baby–faced ruthless warlord," as recorded in *The Cold War, 1945–1991*. The colorful description indicated the harsh tactics Gemayel deployed in his rise to power: he sometimes dispatched opposition by having his rivals killed. In this way, he became the top Maronite figure. Attacks on his enemies could be particularly vicious. In June of 1978, when Gemayel attacked the home of Tony Frangieh, a Christian leader and son of former Lebanese president Suleiman Frangieh, he reportedly slaughtered the rival along with his family and servants.

During the period, Gemayel also worked on strengthening his relationships with the United States and Israel. Both countries considered him an "asset" in the Middle East, as he was a Christian leader in a Muslim part of the world. Further, they supported his aim to modernize Lebanon, no matter the cost. "We have not spilled the blood of thousands of young men in order to move backward,"

Gemayel told Israeli and U.S. leaders, from *The Cold War, 1945–1991*.

In 1978, the Syrian army arrested Gemayel in Sassine Square, but only held him for a short period. That same year, he launched the "100 days war" against Syrian forces that had attacked Ashrafieh and Ain el–Remaneh. Also in 1978, Gemayel's first daughter, Maya, was born (he had married Solange Toutoungi the previous year).

At the time, Gemayel continued strengthening his relationship with Israel. This relationship was a covert one, and Gemayel's primary objective was to use it to rid his country of Syrian militia and PLO guerillas. In turn, Israel supported Gemayel in his efforts to reorganize and build up the Phalange militia. The militia was Gemayel's power base, and it bolstered his political position within Lebanon.

Daughter Killed in Assassination Attempt

In 1980, Gemayel's daughter Maya was killed by a car bomb that had been intended for him (he and his wife later had another daughter, Youmna, and a son, Nadim).

In July of that year, Gemayel struck against another rival. His militia initiated a surprise attack on the Tigers of Dany Chamoun, an oppositional Christian militia faction. Chamoun was the son of a former Lebanese president Camille Chamoun. During the attack, eighty soldiers were killed, along with Chamoun. Gemayel then offered Camille Chamoun $1 million in reparations, a move critics described as a buy–off.

Also in 1980, Gemayel unified military forces in his country's Eastern sector, which put a stop to the military strife in that region. He also became a member of the Lebanese Front, an organization that enjoyed the greatest political power in the sector.

Communicated the Lebanese Cause

Gemayel returned to the United States in 1981, to visit with President Reagan and to define the Lebanese cause, which Gemayel had already been advancing through Radio Free Lebanon, a media outlet he established in 1978. He later established another radio station, Radio 102, a commercial enterprise designed to help ease the financial burdens of war.

The following year, he organized the first international conference of solidarity with Lebanon. Also, he joined the National Salvation Front, an organization that included both Lebanese Christian and Muslim leaders. He also visited Saudi Arabia to meet with foreign ministers of the Arab countries.

Assassinated after Presidential Election

In an interview with ABC television on July 9, 1982, Gemayel explained his vision and purpose as leader. "We are looking for the liberation of our country. We are looking that all the foreigners get out—Syrians, Palestinians and Israelis and even UNIFIL—we don't need any foreign, armed presence in this country. As Lebanese, as a strong central government, as a strong central army, as once again the nation reunited, we will take care of the security of our own country. We don't need anybody in this country, and [PLO leader Yassir] Arafat should understand that.''

His statement was in part contradictory, as it essentially denied the covert relationship he had established with Israel. A month earlier, on June 6, 1982, Israel had finally responded to Gemayel's previously expressed wish: It invaded Lebanon to wage war against the PLO within his country. The invasion virtually secured Gemayel's chances of becoming president of the Lebanese Republic. Indeed, on August 23, 1982, the Lebanese parliament elected him president.

However, only eight days before he would assume office, Gemayel was assassinated in a bomb blast on September 14, 1982. The explosion occurred as he was making a speech at the Phalange party headquarters in Ashrafieh. Now the president–elect of his country, Gemayel would have to resign his party post, and he wanted to express his thanks to the organization as well as offer an official farewell.

The bomb, an electronic device, was detonated from outside the building, in an East Beirut neighborhood called Nasrah, located almost a mile from Ashrafieh. It was later determined that the assassination was accomplished by Syrian agents who objected to Gemayel's aim to force Syrian troops out of Lebanon.

The bomb, which was comprised of 450 pounds of dynamite, was planted and detonated by Habib Tanous Chartouni, a twenty–six–year–old Lebanese who was a member of the National Syrian Socialist party and an operative for Syrian intelligence. He had planted the bomb the night before Gemayel's speech, in a room on the building's second floor, right above the central meeting hall.

Chartouni had little problem planting the bomb, as he used to live in an apartment in the building. Further, his family, who still resided there, had close ties with the Gemayel family. Chartouni's uncle served as a bodyguard for Gemayel's father. As such, Chartouni was a familiar figure in the area. Reportedly, the blast, which could be heard for miles, destroyed the three–story building. Twenty–six people were killed and more than a hundred were wounded. Gemayel's body was so badly disfigured that it took hours before his death could be officially announced.

Following Gemayel's assassination, his brother Amin Gemayel became president of Lebanon. He was elected the same month that his brother was killed and served until September 1988. During his tenure, Amin Gemayel downgraded the relationships his brother had established with Israel and the United States. For the most part, his administration was an ineffective one and, when his tenure as president ended, he left the government with a significant internal division.

While Bashir Gemayel was a ruthless leader and ambitious politician, his presidency did achieve certain advances for his nation, particularly in the area of civil infrastructure. He employed the Lebanese Forces to establish and maintain public services in the areas of water, electricity, highways, garbage collection and social relief.

Along with establishing two radio stations, Bashir Gemayel set up a non–commercial television station in 1980 (LBC) that served as a national, educational and cultural media outlet. He also created Help Lebanon, a group focused on helping children and alleviating the consequences of war, and the Gamma Group, designed to help build a modern state in all national sectors. In 1982, he helped create the Lebanese Cultural Association, which focused on intellectual and artistic matters; the Ashrafieh Merchants Committee, to help revive economy and trade; and the Ashrafieh Festival Committee, which organized fairs and exhibitions and encouraged artistic activities.

Bashir Gemayel was survived by his wife and two children.

Books

The Cold War, 1945–1991, Gale Research, 1992.

Online

"Bachir Gemayel," Experiencefestival.com, www.experience festival.com/a/Bachir_Gemayel/id/1925041 (December 8, 2007).

"Bachir Gemayel Biography: The Timeline," Lebaneseforces .com, http://www.lebaneseforces.com/bachirbiography.asp (December 8, 2007).

"Bashir Gemayel," LexicOrient.com, http://i-cias.com/e.o/ gemayel_b.htm (December 8, 2007).

"Historical Fact: The Assassination of Bashir Gemayel," Lebanese forces.com, http://www.lebaneseforces.com/blastfromthepast 013.asp (December 8, 2007).

"Interview with Bashir Gemayel on ABC television- 9 July 1982," Israel Ministry of Affairs, http://www.israel-mfa.gov.il/MFA/ Foreign%20Relations/Israels%20Foreign%20Relations %20since%201947/1982-1984/42%20Interview%20with %20Bashir%20Gemayel%20on%20ABC%20television (December 8, 2007). □

Kenneth Grahame

Scotland-born British writer Kenneth Grahame (1859-1932) remains known above all for a single work for children, *The Wind in the Willows,* with its perennially popular Toad, Ratty, Mole, Badger, and a host of subsidiary characters.

*T*he Wind in the Willows originated in a set of stories Grahame told aloud to his son, Alastair, and part of its appeal lies in the way it brings the surprise of oral storytelling to the printed page. But there is more to the popularity of *The Wind in the Willows* than that. In many ways the book, published in 1908, inaugurated the modern era of literature for children. In contrast to earlier children's books, it was not particularly moralistic; one of its central plot developments, a car theft carried out by the irrepressible Mr. Toad, is presented in a spirit of adventure. And it seemed to define a realm akin to that of a child's imagination, one in which the real world of adults was kept at bay.

Contracted Scarlet Fever

Kenneth Grahame was born on March 8, 1859, in Edinburgh, Scotland. His father, James Cunningham Grahame, moved the family to Inverary in the western Scottish Highlands so that he could take up a judicial post as sheriff-substitute. Grahame's early years were happy ones, but the life of his family was completely disrupted in 1864 when both Grahame and his mother contracted scarlet fever. His mother, Bessie, died after giving birth to her fourth child. Grahame himself took months to recover from the disease, and his respiratory health remained fragile for the rest of his life. The episode sent Grahame's father into a tailspin; he began to drink heavily, and Grahame and his three siblings were sent to live with their maternal grandmother in England's Berkshire region, in a town called Cookham Dene.

Grahame's existence over the next few years set the pattern for many of his attitudes in later life. His grandmother was not an especially devoted foster parent; she discharged her duties but did little more. But Grahame loved her impressive old house and, even more, the gardens and woodlands along the nearby Thames River. The house burned down at the end of 1865, and Grahame was moved to a nearby town, Cranbourne, then briefly back to Inverary. However, by that time his father's alcoholism had progressed to a point where he was unable to care for the children. Grahame was sent back to Cranbourne, and when he was nine he entered St. Edward's preparatory school in Oxford, England.

In school, Grahame became more outgoing socially while maintaining an active inner life that he mostly kept hidden. He won several student prizes and became captain of the rugby team. Continuing on to Oxford University would have been the expected course for Grahame, but his uncle, who controlled the family purse strings, refused to finance his education any further. Grahame was forced to apply for a job with the Bank of England. His application involved an essay section on which he received a top score, an unprecedented accomplishment in the bank's history. In 1879 Grahame was offered and accepted the position of clerk at the bank's headquarters on London's Threadneedle Street.

The move to London was beneficial, for it put Grahame at the center of England's literary culture. He was steadily promoted (by 1898 he had reached the top executive rank of Secretary), giving him increasing amounts of free time in which to cultivate acquaintances with London writers and editors. He traveled to Italy, and he was the only one of the Grahame children to put in even a perfunctory appearance at their father's funeral in France in 1887. After a time, he began to write down poems, short stories, and especially essays, one of which appeared in the *St. James's Gazette* in 1888. The writings also became a frequent feature of the *National Observer* in the early 1890s. In 1894 Grahame collected some of his essays and stories into a book titled *Pagan Papers.*

Extolled Value of Nature

The *Pagan Papers,* written in a florid nineteenth-century style, are rarely read today, but they pointed toward Grahame's future accomplishments in interesting ways. The title referred not to the pagan religion, but more generally to an appreciation of nature and natural forces, the themes of many of the essays. The book also included some fictional pieces in which a group of orphaned children operate under the radar of their guardians, whom Grahame called the "Olympians," a scenario that both pointed backward to the circumstances of Grahame's own childhood and looked forward to his coming fictional efforts.

Grahame must have realized that he was moving in a new direction, because he removed the Olympians stories from subsequent editions of *Pagan Papers* and began accumulating a separate collection of stories about the children, some of which appeared in an innovative literary magazine called the *Yellow Book.* In 1895 Grahame published 18 short stories about these children in a book titled *The Golden Age.* The collection met with acclaim from Britain's literary establishment. It also found a wide readership in the United States, where future president Theodore Roosevelt was one of its many admirers.

The Golden Age was popular for several reasons. First, Grahame's youthful characters struck a sharp contrast with the obedient lesson-learners of Victorian children's literature of the day—literature which set out "patterns of conduct to which the young reader is invited to conform," according to R.J. Dingley, writing in the *Dictionary of Literary Biography.* "Grahame's children, conversely, inhabit a world with largely autonomous values and regard the precepts of their elders (the 'Olympians') with puzzled disdain,'' Dingley added. He noted that the children in the stories learn, not through "adult instruction," but from "experience and observation." Grahame's second innovation also foreshadowed modern works (*The Simpsons* would be one of many examples) with children as central characters, that could be enjoyed equally by children and adults, reading them in different ways. "The Argonauts," for example, worked equally well as a story about a group of children who embark on a river trip and meet a strange woman when they debark, and as a retelling of the ancient Greek story of Medea.

Grahame's sole work unconnected with children, a satire called *The Headswoman,* was published in the *Yellow Book* in 1894 and issued in book form in 1898. It was not a success with audiences, and Grahame decided to focus again on his trademark children. He wrote eight more long stories in the same vein as those in *The Golden Age,* and they were published in 1898 as *Dream Days.* That book included one of Grahame's most acclaimed short stories, "The Reluctant Dragon," a reworking of the St. George and the Dragon tale in which dragon and saint agree to stage a battle in order to fulfill the expectations of villagers. In 1899 Grahame married Elspeth Thompson. The marriage was never a happy one, but it produced a child, Alastair, who was born prematurely in 1900.

Raised Child with Disabilities

Alastair was born blind in one eye and with impaired vision in the other, but his late-marrying parents doted on him and predicted a great future for him. Grahame began telling him stories about animals that posssessed human qualities, and these gradually evolved into the stories featured in *The Wind in the Willows.* This novel took another step toward completion when Alastair was sent on vacation with relatives, and Graham continued the stories in written form, as letters to his son. Grahame polished the book as he cut back his activities at the bank (he retired completely in 1908), but it still retained the qualities of a loose, episodic collection of stories in its finished form—which was perhaps one of its strengths.

Despite Grahame's previous success, he had difficulty finding a publisher for *The Wind and the Willows.* Several publishers turned it down before it was accepted by Methuen Publishing, partly as the result of a campaign by U.S. president Theodore Roosevelt, who asked to meet Grahame when he came to Oxford University to deliver a lecture. The book was published in 1907 and was immediately recognized as a classic. A.A. Milne, the author of *Winnie-the-Pooh,* later wrote that he loved to read the book aloud to guests (presumably of all ages), and he adapted it into a play called *Toad of Toad Hall.* The book received a fresh lease on life when it was republished with illustrations, the most famous of which are by E.H. Shepard, in an edition that appeared in 1931, although there have been many editions illustrated by different artists.

The story of *The Wind in the Willows,* although it holds no great complexities, is action-packed. The opening chapters introduce some principal members of a settled community of animals, such as Ratty (actually a vole), Mole, and

Badger; they are friends and join together to try to reform the more reckless Mr. Toad, who likes cars but has a tendency to both crash them and steal them. One of Mr. Toad's misadventures lands him in prison, and to make things worse, his mansion, Toad Hall, is taken over by weasels and stoats. But he escapes from prison and begins to change his ways. As with *The Wizard of Oz,* various interpretations, each adding to the fun of the tale for adult readers, have been proposed: the animals' mini-society has been said to resemble the rural England of the nineteenth century in its outlines, or to allegorically represent class conflict, among other analyses.

Grahame edited *The Cambridge Book of Poetry for Children* in 1916 and furnished introductions for other books, but in general he wrote very little after the publication of *The Wind in the Willows.* His inactivity was partly the result of domestic problems. Alastair Grahame struggled in school despite several moves from one institution to another, and he was increasingly plagued by what would now be called depression. In 1920 he walked in front of a train in Oxford and was killed. The death was ruled accidental, but many of Grahame's biographers have suggested that he committed suicide.

Grahame died on July 6, 1932, after suffering a cerebral hemorrhage at his home in Pangbourne, England. He was free of financial worries in his later life, for *The Wind in the Willows* had become one of the best-loved children's books in the world. Its fame only increased in the years after his death. It was made, among many other adaptations, into a film (*The Adventures of Mr. Toad,* 1949); a television musical (1985); a series of comic books published in France as well as England; the animated *The Adventures of Toad* (Disney Channel, 2000); and a live-action (non-animated) version broadcast on both British Broadcasting Corporation (BBC) television and the U.S. Public Broadcasting System (PBS) in 2007.

Books

British Fantasy and Science-Fiction Writers Before World War I, Darren Harris-Fain, ed. *Dictionary of Literary Biography Vol. 178,* Detroit: Gale Research, 1997.

British Novelists, 1890-1929: Traditionalists, Ed. Thomas F. Staley. *Dictionary of Literary Biography Vol. 34,* Detroit: Gale Research, 1984.

Green, Peter, *Beyond the Wild Wood: The World of Kenneth Grahame,* Webb & Bower, 1982.

Major Authors and Illustrators for Children and Young Adults, 2nd ed., 8 vols., Gale Group, 2002.

Milne, A.A., *Not That It Matters,* Methuen, 1927.

Prince, Alison, *Kenneth Grahame: An Innocent in the Wild Wood,* Allison & Busby, 1994.

Online

"Biography," Kenneth Grahame Society, http://www.kenneth grahamesociety.net/ (January 4, 2008).

Contemporary Authors Online, Gale, 2008. http://galenet.gale group.com/servlet/BioRC (January 4, 2008).

"Kenneth Grahame (1859–1932)," Books and Writers, http://www.kirjasto.sci.fi/grahame.htm (January 4, 2008). □

Grand Duchess Olga Nikolaevna

Grand Duchess Olga Nikolaevna (1895-1918) of Russia was the eldest daughter of the last tsar of Imperial Russia, Nicholas II (1868–1918). She died at age 22, along with her three sisters, younger brother, and parents, on a night in July of 1918, when the royal family—then under house arrest after Nicholas's abdication in the midst of a Communist revolution—was taken into a basement room and shot on orders of the local Bolshevik regional government.

Olga was born on November 15, 1895, at Tsarskoye Selo ("Tsar's Village"), the imperial family's estate outside of St. Petersburg. On her father's side she was a Romanov, the dynasty that had ruled Imperial Russia since 1613, and this first child of the tsar's marriage was named in honor of Grand Duchess Olga Alexandrovna (1882-1960), the tsar's sister, who spent a great deal of time with her nieces and nephew during their youth and young adulthood. On her mother's side, Olga descended from the venerable German dynasty that produced England's Queen Victoria, who was Olga's great-grandmother. Olga's mother was Alix of Hesse, who wed Nicholas in April of 1894 and became Empress Alexandra of Russia. As a ten-month-old, Olga visited Queen Victoria when her parents took her to Balmoral, the royal castle in Scotland.

"The Big Pair"

Olga was an only child for 19 months, until the birth of her sister Tatiana in June of 1897. Two years later came Maria, followed by Anastasia in June of 1901. The Romanovs ruled by the right of male primogeniture, which meant only a male heir could become tsar; there was immense relief, therefore, in August of 1904 when a son was born to Nicholas and Alexandra, whom they named Alexei. The little Tsarevich, as he was known, soon showed signs of hemophilia, an incurable genetic disorder that had already afflicted several in his mother's family. Hemophilia is characterized by a lack of clotting agents in the blood, which meant that a simple injury could lead to fatal internal bleeding. In this era, there were no remedies for hemophiliacs, and few lived past the age of 20.

Olga and her sisters doted on the Tsarevich, and with few friends outside of their royal circles all five siblings were a close-knit family. Olga shared a bedroom with Tatiana, and the two were referred to as "the big pair." Maria and Anastasia were also dressed in matching outfits and dubbed "the little pair." Like their father before them, the girls lived in austere conditions despite the opulence of the imperial household. When they were little, they slept on camp beds and were required to take a cold-water bath each morning. As they grew into their teens, however, the quartet of daughters successfully petitioned for a few more luxuries, and later took baths in a solid silver tub with water both heated and perfumed. Olga's signature scent was reportedly Rose Thé from the French perfumer Coty. They spoke Russian amongst themselves, with their father, and to members of the household staff, and English with their mother. Like her sisters, Olga was educated at home by a governess and tutors. She was known as high-spirited and somewhat willful, though not as mischievous as the youngest sister, Anastasia.

Mother Influenced by Odd Monk

Empress Alexandra spent much of her children's lives in poor health. She suffered from both migraines and sciatica, and was confined to a dark room for the former and a wheelchair at times because of the latter. She had renounced her Lutheran faith as required for her marriage, and became a devout convert to the Russian Orthodox faith. Her weakened state, exacerbated by worry over Alexei's always-precarious health, led her to fall prey to an unusual spiritual advisor. Grigori Rasputin (1869-1916) was a bearded, unkempt Russian peasant known as a wandering monk, who had impressive powers as a faith healer. The Empress requested his help for her son, and the improvement in Alexei's condition secured Rasputin's link to the royal family for several years. The household staff, however, was resentful of the uncouth, disheveled peasant's access to the Romanovs, and those close to the family were also wary. For years gossip circulated that Rasputin was conducting an affair with Alexandra, and had even seduced all four daughters. He was finally murdered by a posse of aristocrats in December of 1916.

Olga had been briefly engaged to one of the men who killed the monk, Grand Duke Dmitri Pavlovich, back in 1912, but they drifted apart and Russian history scholars posit that the influence of Rasputin likely caused Dmitri to distance himself from the family. Another marital prospect was Prince Edward of England (1894-1972), eldest son of Britain's George V (1865-1936), who remained a bachelor when he assumed the throne as Edward VIII in 1936, then famously abdicated eleven months later to marry a twice-divorced American woman. There was also a halfhearted attempt to unite Olga with a member of the Romanian royal family; she and her sisters visited Romania in the summer of 1914, but Olga was reportedly unimpressed with Crown Prince Carol. She revealed to intimates that her parents had promised to allow her some input into her future spouse and would not compel her to marry someone she did not love.

Became War Nurse

In November of 1915, Olga celebrated her twentieth birthday, was given access to her personal fortune at the milestone year, and began making charitable bequests. By this point Russia was fully engaged in a large-scale war with her mother's homeland of imperial Germany in the conflict that became known as World War I. Olga trained as a Red Cross nurse and tended the wounded in a St. Petersburg military hospital for several months. Her mother and Tatiana also joined in the war effort, while their father—against all advice, and with no combat experience—insisted upon commanding Russian troops in the field. Russia was losing badly, and the number of horrific injuries began to weigh on Olga. She became alternately depressed and prone to angry outbursts, was given arsenic injections as treatment, and finally moved to an administrative job at the hospital.

As nurses at the hospital, the "big pair" were able to meet regular young women their own age for the first time in their lives, and exhibited a keen curiosity about what life was like outside the royal enclave. The duchesses usually traveled back and forth to their duties with a lady-in-waiting, but on one occasion the carriage came with just the driver, whom Olga and her sister Tatiana ordered to stop in St. Petersburg's retail district. They ventured into a store, thrilled that they were not recognized in their nurse uniforms, and tried to buy something but had no money. The next day, they asked one of their fellow nurses exactly how such store transactions were conducted.

Millions of Russians, meanwhile, lived in the most abject poverty. The Romanovs had freed the entirety of the peasants just 50 years earlier; for several generations the poorest farmers had essentially lived as sharecroppers, bound to the estate of the local landowning noble and prohibited from moving elsewhere. During his reign, Olga's father was famously resistant to calls for further democratic reforms, yielding only when absolutely cornered while ordering a growing state-security apparatus to deal harshly with political opponents of the monarchy. The war only worsened anti-Romanov sentiment, with the Tsar blamed for the mounting casualties and resentment focused on his already-disliked wife, unpopular because of her German heritage, haughty airs, and devotion to Rasputin. Revolu-

tionary groups used the growing unrest in both the armed forces and in the civilian populace as an opportunity to seize power in March of 1917. Nicholas finally agreed to abdicate in order to prevent outright civil war.

Sixteen-Month House Arrest

When Olga and her sisters lost their royal status, they were at Tsarskoye Selo and were guarded by royal troops in an uneasy truce for several days before their father was able to join them there. They were suddenly at the mercy of a revolutionary village council, who now made all decisions about their daily routine, diet, access to books, and other details. They were held there for five months as the country descended into civil war, with the Red Army fighting on the side of the new Communist Soviet state. On the other side was the White Army, made up of troops loyal to the Romanovs and the monarchy. In August the family was moved to a governor's mansion in the Siberian city of Tobolsk. In the spring of 1918, after more than a year of house arrest, the family was moved once more, this time to Ekaterinburg, a city in central Russia. Before the trip, Olga and her sisters sewed their jewels into the lining of their clothes.

In Ekaterinburg the family was placed under guard in Ipatiev House, a once-grand residence commissioned by the Ural Soviet, the regional governing council. With them there were a retinue of close servants, including the maid Anna Demidova; Alexei's physician, Dr. Eugene Botkin; Trupp, Nicholas's valet, and two cooks. Olga walked twice a day in the yard with her father, a brief respite from being shut up in the house, whose windows were locked and painted white except for one; this was done to prevent the family from signaling to the outside for rescue.

There was indeed a concerted effort to make contact with the Romanovs and rescue them. When the White Army advanced toward Ekaterinburg, the Ural Soviet decided to put to rest fears that the family would be freed (and restored to the throne, which would likely result in mass executions of Communists) by eliminating them altogether. On the night of July 16-17, 1918, Botkin was told to wake the family just after midnight and assemble them. The order was given by Yakov Yurovsky, the newly installed commander of the Cheka, the Bolshevik government's secret police. He told the family that there was unrest in the town and that they needed to be taken to the basement for their protection. They walked through a courtyard—with their retinue and Jemmy, Anastasia's King Charles spaniel—and entered a room with no furnishings. Yurovsky arranged them in two rows, informing them that a photograph needed to be made to quell rumors circulating that they had escaped from custody. Then he gave an order, and eleven soldiers brandishing revolvers entered the room. Yurovsky took out a piece of paper and read aloud from it: "In view of the fact that your relatives are continuing their attack on Soviet Russia, the Ural Executive Committee has decided to execute you," according to Robert K. Massie's *The Romanovs: The Final Chapter.*

At that, Nicholas turned to look at his family as he said, "What? What?" and was shot first by Yurovsky. The other weapons were fired immediately. Olga was shot in the head and died quickly, having attempted to make the sign of the cross before she fell. Her sisters, however, seemed impervious to the bullets. The executioners had been told to fire at the hearts, but after the first bullets did not pierce their dresses, the soldiers panicked and fired a volley of shots. Only when the bodies were buried were the jewels they had sewn into their corsets discovered, which had appeared to make them bulletproof; a stunning 18 pounds of diamonds alone were found. The bodies were dismembered, then burned, a process which reportedly took three days. Five days after that, the Ekaterinburg fell to the Whites. Their graves were not discovered until 1991, and subsequent DNA tests confirmed the identities of Olga, her parents, and two of her sisters. In 1998 their remains were interred at Sts. Peter and Paul Cathedral in St. Petersburg.

Books

Martin, Russell E., "Romanov Dynasty," *Encyclopedia of Russian History,* edited by James R. Millar, volume 3, Macmillan Reference USA, 2004.

Massie, Robert K., *Nicholas and Alexandra,* Atheneum, 1967.

Massie, Robert K., *The Romanovs: The Final Chapter,* Random House, 1995. □

Chabuca Granda

The Peruvian singer and songwriter Isabel Granda Larco (1920-1983), known as Chabuca Granda, was an icon of popular music in her country although, unlike other South American vocal stars, she never sought stardom in the United States and has remained little known among English-speaking music listeners.

Chabuca Granda's voice, a powerful low contralto combining nostalgia with a hint of a weary groan, was inimitable. She began her career singing in the traditional Peruvian folk style known as Creole music, but she had a command of rhythm that would have been at home in American jazz, and later in life she served as a primary inspiration for Susana Baca and the other singers who brought Afro-Peruvian music to international prominence. She sometimes said she had the voice of a dog, but with swing. Granda was also unusual among Latin American female performers in that she wrote much of her own material. Several of Granda's songs, such as "Fina Estampa," are regarded as classics of Peruvian music.

Born in Andes

Though identified with the Peruvian capital of Lima, Isabel Granda Larco was born on September 3, 1920, in the Andes mountains, in the small town of Cotabambamba in the Apurimac region. She called herself a proud sister of the condor who could wash her face with the stars. Her father, Eduardo Granda y Esquivel, was an engineer who supervised a copper mine in the area; her mother, Teresa Larco

Ferrari, came from the city of Trujillo. Granda's family was shaken by the sudden death of her brother, and they decided to move back to Lima. They settled in the Barranco neighborhood where Granda grew up, and where a statue of her stands today. In Lima Granda she encountered the music of black Peru, very different from the mountain sounds of her early childhood.

Granda attended the Colegio Sophianum, a private girls' high school in Lima, where she sang in the choir. At that point she had a fine soprano voice, but a throat operation lowered it by an octave and left her with the smoky alto heard on her recordings. She took a few guitar lessons, but as a teenager she was more interested in sports, especially tennis. In 1942 Granda married Demetrio (or Henry) Füler da Costa, an aviator. The marriage produced two sons, Gustavo and Eduardo, and a daughter, Teresa, before it dissolved in 1952. In Catholic and conservative Peru, divorce was almost unheard of, and Granda's caused a scandal in Lima social circles.

Granda's performing career began during the final stages of her marriage when she started singing at clubs and parties (although she had written her first song, "Callecita Escondida" (Hidden Little Street), at 18). She was part of a duo called Luz y Sombra (Light and Shade) as well as other groups, working days at a Helena Rubinstein cosmetics counter in Lima. In contrast to nearly every other Latin American female vocalist as well as many from other countries, she was a singer-songwriter almost from the start of her career. She wrote her first hit song, "Lima de Veras" (Truly Lima), in 1950, when she was 30. A friend, Maria Isabel Sanchez Concha, initiated her into a small group of leading entertainers in Lima, and her popularity began to grow. The music from the first part of Granda's career was in the Creole genre, sometimes described as folk music in English-language obituaries of Granda, but more accurately called old-style pop, with a vocalist accompanied by a small, quiet instrumental ensemble.

Penned Song as Tribute

The Estacion tierra world music Web site described her early compositions as "evocative and painterly," suggesting the vanished world of Lima's nineteenth-century high society. Her lyrics rarely had the conventional romantic themes of popular song; instead, she had literary ambitions. A good example of Granda's style, and one of the songs for which she remains best known, is "La Flor de la Canela" (Cinnamon Flower). The song was inspired by an Afro-Peruvian woman named Victoria Angulo, the sister of two of Peru's leading singers of the day; Granda wrote it as a kind of homage, or thank-you, for her growing acceptance in Peru's creative circles.

"La Flor de la Canela" was a song about a city and about a woman. "Déjame que te cuente, limeño," it opens, over a rhythmically free guitar accompaniment: "Let me tell you a story, resident of Lima, about the dream that evokes memories of the old bridge over the river, and of the poplar grove." Angulo is described this way: "Jasmine in her hair and roses in her face / The cinnamon flower walked gracefully / Exuding charm as she passed, leaving / The mixed aromas that she carried in her breast." "La Flor de la Canela" remains perhaps Granda's most popular song; it has been translated into many languages and recorded by major contemporary artists, including opera star Plácido Domingo. Today it serves as Lima's—or even Peru's—unofficial anthem.

Granda had other major hits in Peru in the 1950s and 1960s, including "José Antonio," "Zeño Manué," and "Estampa Fina" (Good Looks). The last of these was written on the occasion of Granda's father's death in 1963. Granda occasionally recorded in French ("La Vals Créole") and English ("Tickertape"), but she remained less well known outside of South America than more politically-oriented roots singers such as Chile's Violeta Parra and Victor Jara. Other major Granda recordings included "Mi Canción de Ausencia" (My Song of Absence), "Mi Ofrenda" (My Offering), "El Fusil del Poeta Es una Rosa" (A Poet's Rifle Is a Rose), "Amor Viajero" (Traveling Lover), and "Bello Durmiente" (Beautiful Sleeper, also referring to Peru). Various reissue compilations of Granda's work have appeared on compact disc and Internet download sites.

Mentored Younger Artists

Granda's home in Lima was a sort of artistic meeting place, attracting creative writers, visual artists, journalists, historians, and musicians on a regular basis. As she herself had been helped along, she nurtured the careers of younger musicians such as vocalist Rubén Flórez, father of the tenor Juan Diego Flórez. Often these included black Peruvians such as percussionists Carlos "Caitro" Soto and Rodolfo Arteaga, and guitarists Felix Casaverde and Alvaro Lakes. The rhythmic and melodic freedom of Granda's songs had always seemed to push the boundaries of older song forms, and later in her career her music took a turn toward Afro-Peruvian rhythms. Susana Baca and other Afro-Peruvian singers from the late twentieth century invariably cited her as an influence.

Granda's music also took a more political turn later in her career. She dedicated a set of songs to Violeta Parra, and another to the poet Javier Heraud, who was killed in 1963 after joining a leftist guerrilla faction. She deplored the extremes of wealth and poverty in her country, saying in an interview quoted by United Press International that "I tried to contribute to the making of Peru, and I deplore the fact we are facing the birth of a generation of minds limited by hunger."

Suffering from ill health due to a series of heart attacks beginning in 1974, Granda nevertheless continued to perform. She was hospitalized in Lima in February of 1983 and transferred to a hospital in Fort Lauderdale, Florida, for further treatment. Five days after undergoing open heart surgery, she died on March 8, 1993, with her three children at her side. Her body was flown back to Lima, where performances in the city's clubs were called off in mourning. In a review of a Granda reissue disc, Spain's El País noted that "her compositions, with their refined poetry, incorporated Afro-Peruvian percussion and raised the Creole waltz to a level where it transcended national boundaries. One can speak of a before and after when regarding her appearance

in the musical panorama of her country, where many people consider her the greatest popular composer of the century." Her Order of Merit award from the Peruvian government, given in 1994, was posthumous.

Periodicals

Associated Press, March 8, 1983.
Miami Herald, March 9, 1983.
El Nuevo Herald (Miami, Florida), March 9, 1983; March 26, 1983.
El País (Madrid, Spain), December 23, 1999.
United Press International, March 8, 1983.

Online

"Chabuca Granda," Estacion tierra, http://www.estaciontierra .com/artistas/artista.php?id=184 (February 17, 2008).
"Homenaje a Chabuca Granda," http://www.trazegnies.arrakis .es/chabucagranda.html (February 17, 2008).
"Maria Isabel Granda Larco—Chabuca Granda," Criollismo, http://criollismo.perublogs.com/2006/10/MARIA-ISABEL-GRANDA-LARCO-----CHABU.html (February 17, 2008). □

J.J. Grandville

French artist J.J. Grandville (1803-1847) was an influential and prolific illustrator. Today remembered primarily for his political cartoons in pioneering publications such as *La Caricature* and for his somewhat fantastical illustrations of people and animals, Grandville created a body of work that served as inspiration for later Surrealist artists. In recent years, renewed interest in Grandville's art has led to the publication of many of his original drawings as well as public exhibitions of his work.

Developed Early Interest in Art

Jean-Ignace-Isidore Gérard was born on September 15, 1803 in Nancy, France into an artistic family. His paternal grandparents had been actors at the court of Lorraine; from their stage name of "Gérard de Grandville," Gérard would later take his own professional name, J.J. Grandville. His father, Jean-Baptiste Gérard, painted miniatures and passed this skill on to his son. Stanley Appelbaum noted in his introduction to *Fantastic Illustrations of Grandville* that "several critics have traced the mature Grandville's finicky draftsmanship and crowded compositions to this early training." Grandville began drawing at a young age and published his first lithograph, *The Cherry Seller* in 1824 or 1825 in Nancy. (Lithography was a printing technique that transferred text or pictures from a printing plate to paper that had been invented shortly before the time of Grandville's birth.) From this early age, Grandville's style was heavily influenced by the satirical drawings that appeared in popular English and French publications.

Léon-André Larue, a relative and lithographer who worked under the name of Mansion, liked the young Grandville's work and encouraged him to travel to Paris to pursue a career. Grandville took this advice and went to Paris in about 1825. In Paris, Grandville worked with costume designer Hippolyte Lecomte to produce a series of lithographs, *Costumes*, in 1826. Grandville's family maintained connections to the theatrical world—a cousin was stage manager of the Opéra-Comique—and there, Grandville found both early work and inspiration. Grandville continued to publish series of lithographs through the remainder of the decade. Some notable works were the 1826 series *Sundays of a Paris Bourgeois* and the 1827 series *Every Age Has its Pleasures,* which he produced for the printer Langlumé.

In 1829, Grandville published a successful series of 70 lithographs entitled *The Metamorphoses of the Day*. These works depicted animals in human attire and participating in human activities. Michel Melot commented in Grandville's *Grove Art Online* biography that in this series, "[Grandville's] penchant for fantasy was already obvious," while Appelbaum stated that the series "instantly established his fame and determined much of his future activity."

Considerably less successful was Grandville's next series, the 1830 *Voyage pour l'éternité* (A Trip to Eternity). This series shows a skeleton appearing before a variety of people as a harbinger of their deaths. Writing in *The Charged Image*, Beatrice Farwell described one on the pieces of the series thusly: "A quaking who just admitted Death says, 'Monsieur le Baron . . . on vous demande?' (Monsieur le Baron . . . someone asking for you?) The fat and gouty baron replies, 'Dites que je n'y suis pas' (Say I'm not in)." The somewhat macabre series, probably inspired by a similar, earlier series by the artist Thomas Rowlandson, stopped publication after only nine were printed. Despite the lack of popular support for the series, it drew the admiration of contemporary notables such as writer Honoré de Balzac and art critic Champfleury.

Became "King of Caricature"

Around 1830, Grandville's career took a new direction. The previous year, he had begun working for the satirical publication *La Silhouette*. At *La Silhouette*, Grandville met publisher Charles Philipon and draw caricatures of the increasingly unpopular French king, Charles X. A staunch Republican, Grandville may have actively participated in the Revolution of 1830, in which Charles X was removed from power and replaced with his more populist cousin, Louis-Philippe. Grandville continued producing caricatures for *La Silhouette* until the journal ceased publication in January 1831. He then joined the staff of Philipon's new publication, *La Caricature*. In 1832, the journal declared Grandville to be the "king of caricature."

Soon, the government sought to close *La Caricature* down. In order to raise money to support the paper, its publisher began a series of politically-charged lithographs called the *Monthly Association*. Grandville contributed 17 of the 24 prints published under this title. Philipon brought a new publication, *Le Charivari*, in 1832. This journal was less politically strident than was *La Caricature,* but still provided opportunity for politically-charged material. At *La Caricature* and *Le Charivari*, Grandville—joined by such notables as Honoré Daumier—expressed his displeasure with Louis-Philippe's government through his cartoons, singling out the King's support for causes that Grandville believed were anathema to the Republican movement. Melot noted that these cartoons were "among the most powerful published at that time, especially in defence of the freedom of the press." During the early 1830s, Grandville created about 100 cartoons, but this number dropped sharply with the reintroduction of government censorship on the press in 1835.

Success in Book Illustration

From 1827 on, Grandville produced works for book illustration; after 1835, due to the new laws that essentially barred Grandville from making his living creating political caricatures, he turned away from the creation of contemporary cartoons to focus more closely on illustration. His first significant illustrated work of this era was a volume of song lyrics by popular French songwriter Pierre-Jean de Béranger. In 1838, Grandville produced illustrations for two major works, an edition of Jonathan Swift's *Gulliver's Travels* and an edition of the fables of Jean de La Fontaine. The former showcased Grandville's ability to mix the fantastic with the commonplace, one of his great contributions to the field of book illustration. The latter led to further work illustrating the texts of two more French fable writers, Lavalette and Florian, in 1841 and 1842, respectively. Grandville also illustrated an edition of Daniel Defoe's *Robinson Crusoe* in 1840.

Around 1840, Grandville received a major commission from publisher Pierre-Jules Hetzel. Impressed by Grandville's previous drawings of animals, Hetzel created a project that would showcase this style; Appelbaum called this commission "the first book specifically conceived as a vehicle for Grandville's genius." *Scènes de la vie privée et publique des animaux* (Scenes of the Private and Public Life of the Animals) used story frameworks to highlight Grandville's drawings depicting animals in situations relevant to the lives of contemporary people, as announced by the subtitle *Etudes de moeurs contemporaines* (Studies of Contemporary Manners). For example, one story tells of a drawn-out court case concerning the killing of a sheep by a wolf; another describes the dog of a drama critic who himself becomes a critic, only to die of boredom. Four of the stories were written by Balzac, and the majority of the rest by Hetzel under the pseudonym P.J. Stahl. Published first in 100 installments between November 1840 and December 1842, the book was later collected into two volumes and published in full; in 1866, the book reappeared in a somewhat altered form under the alternate title *Les Animaux peints par eux-mêmes et dessinés par un autre* (The Animals Painted by Themselves and Drawn by Another). The satire was such a popular success that small statues depicting characters from the stories were being sold without the consent of the publisher.

Following the completion of this work, Grandville illustrated a book entitled *Les petites misères de la vie humaine* (The Petty Sorrows of Human Life). Close on the heels of this project, he received a commission from publisher Henri Fournier, who had previously published Grandville's illustrations in the 1838 La Fontaine collection. Beginning in 1844, Fournier published the thirty-six installments of *Un Autre Monde* (Another World), which many consider to be Grandville's masterpiece and which Peter A. Wick, writing in his introduction to Grandville's collection *The Court of Flora,* called "almost a forerunner of *Star Wars*." This collection featured the stylized, exaggerated images of people, plants, and animals that characterized much of Grandville's work. Linked loosely by a text by Taxile Delord, a writer and editor for *Le Charivari,* Grandville's illustrations are here at their most fantastic, whimsical, and imaginative. Melot commented that "Grandville abandoned the logic of the conscious mind to depict the world of dreams, in which perspective, viewpoint, shape and size undergo peculiar metamorphosis and distortion." Although this piece was greeted with both confusion and respect in its time, it is today considered Grandville's most significant work; Appelbaum called it "a summation of all that had gone before, Grandville's artistic testament."

Personal Difficulties and Legacy

Despite professional achievements, Grandville suffered from personal difficulties that aged him before his time; he reportedly became hunched and gray-haired before his fortieth birthday. In 1833, Grandville had married a relation from Nancy, Marguerite Fischer, who had a strong and somewhat overbearing personality. However, the couple had three children. Two of these children died young, and Fischer followed in July 1842. He remarried a Miss Lhuillier in 1843, apparently at the behest of his wife, who had requested that he marry again while on her deathbed and selected Lhuillier as a suitable choice for Grandville.

Grandville's final months were marked by personal tragedy. Sometime around late 1846 or early 1847, his surviving child by Fischer passed away suddenly, and Grandville was affected by a severe bout of melancholy. Shortly after this, Granville seems to have contracted a throat infection of some sort that ultimately resulted in his admittance to a private medical clinic near Paris; some stories suggest that this clinic was a mental institution, although this seems unlikely. Soon after entering the clinic, Grandville died as a result of his illness on March 17, 1847. Appelbaum noted that Grandville had composed his own epitaph: "Here lies Grandville; he loved everything, made everything live, speak, and walk, but could not make a way for himself."

In some ways artistically ahead of his time, Grandville had what Melot called "the boldness of a visual imagination that anticipated the Surrealists." Because of the extreme topicality and intellectual sharpness of his political cartoons and their accompanying descriptive captions, the modern reader may face challenges in determining their meaning or relevance; however, Grandville's work is for the most part accessible to the modern viewer. His works somewhat superficially resemble the illustrations that depict the nonsense fantasies of his approximate contemporary Lewis Carroll, whose *Alice's Adventures in Wonderland* was published nearly 20 years after Grandville's death, but his themes reflect the psychological and social explorations of artists working in the 20th century. From the time of Grandville through today, opinions on the quality of his work have often been mixed; however, recent revivals in interest have led to some exhibitions as well as publications showing the unique style of this innovator.

Books

Farwell, Beatrice, *The Charged Image: French Lithographic Caricature 1816–1848,* Santa Barbara Museum of Art, 1989.
Grandville, J.J., *The Court of Flora* George Braziller, 1981.
———, *Fantastic Illustrations of Grandville* Dover, 1974.

Online

Melot, Michel, "Grandville, J.J.," Grove Art Online, http://www.groveart.com (December 8, 2007). □

Merv Griffin

Once called by CNN's Larry King a "Merv of all trades," former big band singer Merv Griffin (1925-2007) achieved his greatest fame hosting his self-titled talk show from 1962 to 1986. The bulk of his wealth, however, came via packaging such long-running game shows as *Jeopardy* and *Wheel of Fortune* and several high profile real estate deals.

Born Mervyn Edward Griffin Jr. on July 6, 1925 in San Mateo, California, he was the son of Mervyn and Rita Griffin, who nicknamed him "Buddy." Surrounded by members of his mother's family who exhibited strong interest in music, young Griffin first showed interest in playing piano at age four. Soon after, his aunt Claudia Robinson began giving him lessons, which was kept secret from his father, a tennis pro, who believed that the life of a musician was not a manly one. Indeed, the elder Griffin did not know that his son could actually play piano until the youngster was quite accomplished on the instrument. At a family gathering, when he was commanded by his father to play the piano, the teenager charmed him with a rendition of "Tea for Two," that he was asked to play repeatedly.

In his 1980 autobiography, Griffin recalls always being show-biz bound, putting on pretend shows with neighborhood kids, and orchestrating the choir at his local Catholic church. During the Depression, the industrious youngster also exhibited a knack for earning extra cash when his family lost their home and moved in with Aunt Claudia. At age seven, he collected neighborhood gossip and sold it in a hectograph printed sheet called *The Whispering Winds.* He also mowed lawns, sold Christmas wreaths, and worked as an organist for hire at local weddings and funerals.

Morgan, Gene Vaughn, and Helen Ward. At the time Martin hired Griffin, the singer was earning more in a day than the bandleader paid in a week, but the opportunity to expand into a national market proved irresistible.

Griffin quickly became a popular addition to Martin's show where the singer's most popular romantic songs were "Wihelmina," "Never Been Kissed," "My Truly, Truly Fair," "Music, Music, Music" and "Am I Love." However, Griffin's main claim to fame as a recording artist rests with his RCA-Victor release "I've Got a Lovely Bunch of Coconuts." Sung with an unconvincing cockney accent, the bouncy novelty peaked at number 8 on the national charts in 1949. Although Griffin never liked the number, it made him a star, leading to well-attended bookings for Martin at the Cocoanut Grove in Los Angeles. In late 1951, Griffin hit the Top 40 under his own name with "The Morning Side of the Mountain" and "Twenty-Three Starlets (and Me)," the latter recorded with Hugo Winterhalter's Orchestra. In retrospect, Griffin proved a less distinctive vocalist than fellow Irish crooners Dennis Day or Mike Douglas. However, the upside of his short string of hits was a legitimate shot at a mainstream movie career.

According to Griffin in his autobiography, none other than Doris Day arranged his screen test with Warner Bros. in late 1952. As a result, the singer appeared in a handful of feature films during the early 1950's, most notably *So This is Love* with Katheryn Grayson and *The Boy from Oklahoma* starring Will Rogers Jr. Sick of studio politics and inactivity between pictures, Griffin opted out of his contract with Warner Bros. in 1955. There was something better on the horizon for Griffin: television.

Legendary Talk Show Host

While touring with Martin's band and with the big band days rapidly coming to a close, Griffin worked on network television whenever possible. Starting in 1951, he appeared on the summer replacement series *The Freddy Martin Show* which led to regular appearances on *Arthur Murray's Dance Party, The Robert Q. Lewis Show,* and the Sunday morning religious program *Look Up and Live.* Griffin also co-hosted a summer replacement series with Jane Froman called *Snapshots on a Summer Day* and was one of the regular vocalists on the Dick Van Dyke CBS series *The Morning Show.* "Well, I served my time as an apprentice in television," Griffin told Larry King in a 2006 interview. "I did a lot of shows in New York. I was kind of a utility singer. If a show like Ken Murray or some of them had a waterfall in their vault and they'd say, 'Let's put the waterfall on this week, who knows waterfall? Get Merv Griffin. He knows all the waterfall songs.' So, I'd come and do the waterfall songs."

Griffin hosted his first televised talk show in 1956, the Miami-based *Going Places.* His big break, however, came when he filled in for Bill Cullen as the host of *The Price is Right* for CBS in 1959. His quick mastery of game show rules and ease in front of the microphone wore well with daytime audiences. He was subsequently hired as the second of three hosts of a *To Tell the Truth* knock-off called *Play Your Hunch.* During the interview portions of the

By his own admission, Griffin was overweight as a teen, and tried to deflect the taunts of his classmates with humor and song. Later, his abilities as a pianist and a singer made him a favorite at local talent shows and U.S.O. events, but his career didn't really get rolling until 1944 when he was hired by radio station KFRC in San Francisco. Hoping to latch on strictly as a pianist, the 19-year-old was asked to sing at his audition. Imitating popular crooner Dick Haymes singing "Sleigh Ride in July," he impressed station management, who gave him his own 15-minute, three-times a week radio show. Billed as "America's New Romantic Singing Star" and publicized as "the romantic mystery voice," Griffin became a local sensation, although his 240-pound frame was seldom seen by the public. Finally, after Joan Edwards, one of the singing stars from *Your Hit Parade,* sang on his show, she told the budding star (as Griffin recalled in his autobiography *Merv—an Autobiography*), "Merv, honey, you sing great, but the blubber has to go." Griffin dieted strenuously until he was a svelte 160 pounds, but he would struggle with weight fluctuations the rest of his life.

Sang with Freddy Martin's Orchestra

When KHJ, the Mutual Broadcasting outlet in Los Angeles, picked up Griffin's show, his star rose higher, and attracted the attention of bandleader Freddy Martin. Best remembered for his transformation of Tchaikovsky's B-Flat Piano Concerto and Grieg's Piano Concerto into the lush pop hits "Tonight We Love" and "I Look at Heaven," respectively, Martin had a good ear for vocalists and at one time or another employed the likes of Buddy Clark, Russ

show, Griffin impressed NBC's late-night talk show king Jack Paar, who eventually offered the former singer a semi-regular substitute host slot on The *Tonight Show.* These stints, including a two week run after Paar left the show, drew surprisingly strong ratings. As a result, before they chose Johnny Carson for the permanent job, NBC seriously considered hiring Griffin as Paar's replacement. Instead, the network gave him his first daytime talk show, which they subsequently canceled after 26 weeks.

Rebounding quickly, Griffin signed on with Westinghouse, who syndicated his talk show nationwide. This version became a ratings hit. Part of the show's charm came via the host's interplay with sidekick/announcer Arthur Treacher. A former Hollywood feature player renowned for playing butlers, Treacher introduced Griffin with great affection, saying, "Now here's the dear boy himself, Mervyn." When a guest dropped out, Treacher could regale Griffin's audience with stories of old Hollywood, offer a withering comedic insult, or charmingly express an opinion about his adventures in modern society. During the show's early run, Treacher became so popular, that he eventually lent his name to a fast food franchise—Arthur Treacher's Fish & Chips. When Treacher died of heart failure in 1975, the show began changing formats and locations on a regular basis in an attempt to make up for the loss of interpersonal chemistry.

Although Griffin had his own low-key style, he often followed Paar's lead by scooping up some of his retired mentor's favorite guests, such as Dody Goodman, Jack Douglas and Reiko, Genevieve, and sprinkling famous authors and newsmakers throughout programs laden with movie stars and comedians. Indeed, Griffin made television history hosting the likes of Dr. Martin Luther King, Henry Kissinger, Robert Kennedy, Richard Nixon, Spiro Agnew, etc. Even counter-culture icon Abbie Hoffman appeared on the show, but his appearance was broadcast audio-only because the hippie provocateur was wearing a shirt made from an American flag. Griffin courted controversy more actively than his late-night rival Johnny Carson, but it should be noted that for every famous newsmaker on his program, Griffin featured dozens of appearances by the likes of Totie Fields, Monte Rock III, Charro, Rip Taylor, and dozens of other c-list celebrities that only he could showcase amusingly. Further, Griffin provided the first serious, continuing exposure for such up and coming comics as Richard Pryor, George Carlin, and Jerry Seinfeld.

In late 1969, Griffin was enticed to move his show to CBS and take on ratings king Johnny Carson. The program, basically a glitzier version of the Westinghouse show, easily beat out Joey Bishop and Dick Cavett's late-night chat-fests on ABC, but with far less CBS affiliates signed up for the show than NBC boasted, Griffin's show lagged far behind Carson's. Ironically, one of Griffin's chief strengths during this period was his director Dick Carson—Johnny Carson's brother—the former director of the *Tonight Show.* In February of 1972, Griffin left CBS and went back to doing a daytime talk-show, this time for Metromedia, where he did episodes that were much more theme-oriented, until he retired the program in 1986.

Game Show and Real Estate Tycoon

Although Griffin stayed active making cameo appearances in movies, taping occasional television specials, and recording for Pat Boone's Gold label, he had no pressing need to work. A lover of puzzles, he began packaging game shows during the early 60's, including *Wordplay* and *Jeopardy.* For the latter—one of the most enduring game show hits in television history—Griffin's wife Julann came up with the idea to answer every statement of fact with the appropriate question. Griffin himself wrote the "thinking music" played while contestants wrote their answers, and the composition is said to have earned him over seventy million dollars in royalties.

Griffin's company also produced *Wheel of Fortune,* another long-running smash that appeared in network and syndicated versions. Originally hosted by Chuck Woolery from 1975 to 1982, the program really took off when Pat Sajak took over hosting chores and was aided by letter-turning Vanna White, whom Griffin personally championed. Another syndicated hit was a *Dancing with the Stars* forerunner called *Dance Fever.* In 1986, Griffin sold his production company to Columbia Pictures television for $250 million dollars and a continuing share of his shows' profits.

During the late 80's, Griffin grew bored with being idle and began a third career as a real estate mogul. In 1989 he made a decision which was recounted in his MSNBC.com obituary years later. "I said 'I'm not going to sit around and clip coupons for the rest of my life.' That's when Barron Hilton said 'Merv, do you want to buy the Beverly Hilton?' I couldn't believe it." In the years to come, he would make headlines when he wrested control of the Resort International hotels and Casinos in Atlantic City away from mogul Donald Trump. Even Griffin's interest in horse racing proved profitable. In 2005, his colt Stevie Wonderboy won a $1.5 million dollar purse at the Breeder's Cup Juvenile Stakes. By 2003, his net worth was estimated at over $1 billion dollars.

Generous and cordial, the retired talk show host also worked hard for various charities, most notably serving as Chairman of the Board of the Young Musicians Foundation and deeding a $10 million dollar property to Childhelp USA. In 2007, just as his company completed the first week of production on a new game show, *Merv Griffin's Crosswords,* Griffin was diagnosed with a recurrence of the prostate cancer he had successfully beaten ten years earlier. The disease rapidly spread to other organs and the singer/actor/composer/business tycoon and last of the great 1960's talk show hosts died on August 12, 2007. Divorced from wife Julann in 1973 after twenty years of marriage, he was survived by his son and business partner Anthony Patrick Griffin, who currently runs his estate.

Books

Griffin, Merv with Barsocchini, *Merv—An Autobiography,* Simon & Schuster, 1980.

———, *Merv Griffin's Book of People,* Arbor House, 1982.

Griffin, Merv with Bender, David, *Merv—Making the Good Life Last,* Simon & Schuster, 2003.

Knopper, Steve, editor, *MusicHound Lounge—The Essential Album Guide to Martini Music and Easy Listening* Visible Ink, 1998.

Whitburn, Joel, editor, *Pop Memories 1890 - 1954: The History of American Popular Music* Record Research, 1991.

Online

''About Merv,'' The Griffin Group, http://www.merv.com, (October 11, 2007).

''Hollywood Legend Merv Griffin dies,'' *Variety,* http://www.variety.com, (August 12, 2007).

''Interview with Merv Griffin,'' CNN.com, http://www.transcripts.cnn.com/TRANSCRIPTS/0605/11/1kl.01.html, (May 11, 2006).

''Merv Griffin,'' *All Movie Guide,* http://www.allmovie.com (October 11, 2007).

''Merv Griffin,'' *All Music Guide,* http://www.allmusic.com, (October 7, 2007).

''Merv Griffin,'' Internet Movie Database, http://www.imdb.com (October 11, 2007).

''Merv Griffin dies at 82,'' MSNBC.com, http://www.msnbc.com/id/20236685/from/ET/print/1/displaymode/1098/, (August 12, 2007). □

Al Gross

Al Gross (1918-2000) was way ahead of his time. Gross introduced the wireless telephone, pager, and similar gadgets in the 1940s and 1950s, long before wireless became a worldwide buzzword. "I was born too soon," Gross once told a reporter, according to an article by David Hawley in the *Pioneer Press* in St. Paul, Minnesota. "If I still had the patents on my inventions, Bill Gates would have to stand aside for me."

Early Years

Gross was born Alfred J. Gross on February 22, 1918, in Toronto, Ontario, Canada. His father was a Russian immigrant tailor. The family moved to Cleveland, Ohio, when Gross was an infant.

When Gross was nine and his family was on a cruise along Lake Erie, he wandered into the steamship's radio room. "I heard the noise of the spark transmitter, and I saw the radio operator and all his radio gear," he said, as quoted in London's *Daily Telegraph.* Boy, did that impress me." The operator invited Gross into the room and briefly let him don the headphones. From then on, Gross was hooked.

At age 12, Gross assembled a ham radio with parts he took from a junkyard and assembled in his basement. He earned his amateur operator's license four years later. His next progression would be a so-called walkie-talkie, when he found his basement equipment clunky. "I wanted to walk around and talk to other hams," he said, according to the *New York Times.*

After some experimenting, in 1938 he completed what was essentially the prelude to the citizens band radio. He used Phineas Thaddeus Veeblefetzer as his handle, based on offbeat inventor Phineas Fogg from the book *Around the World in 80 Days* by Jules Verne. His ham radio signature was W8PAL.

Gross graduated in 1939 with a degree in electrical engineering from the Case School of Applied Sciences in Cleveland, Ohio, the predecessor to Case Western Reserve University. Meanwhile, he kept working to improve his portable receivers, with an eye toward a breakthrough—using frequencies above 100 megahertz (MHz). By 1938 he had invented and patented the walkie-talkie, making miniature vacuum tubes that operated between 200 and 300 MHz. "Convinced that trial and error worked, Gross spent hours in his workshop, fiddling with radio parts to improve performance. To get the clearest signal, he created small transceivers using circuit boards he etched himself, something unheard of," Reinhardt Krause wrote in *Investor's Business Daily.*

"He was a tinkerer, a true experimenter. He just fiddled with things. He was a freethinking person. He just played with things. He thought anything was possible. It just hadn't been done yet," Fred Maia told *Investor's Business Daily.* Maia for 25 years was editor of the *W5YI Report,* a ham radio newsletter.

Military Took Interest During War

Word of Gross's achievements filtered to the U.S. military by the onset of World War II. The communications unit of the U.S. Office of Strategic Services (OSS), the forerunner of the Central Intelligence Agency (CIA), was eager to develop a ground-to-air system and recruited Gross. The inventor won over General William J. Donovan, who converted him from a civilian to a captain. "Donovan liked the idea," Gross said in the *New York Times.* By 1941 Gross had designed military ground and air units, which he called "Joan" and "Eleanor," respectively. They communicated with each other through Hertzian radio waves, working at 260 MHz, which enemies could not penetrate.

The units had a roughly 30-mile range. The ground unit had a transceiver weighing just three-and-a-half pounds, a collapsible antenna, and two B and two D batteries for power. "It could easily be carried and hidden by a soldier on hostile ground," the Massachusetts Institute of Technology's MIT School of Engineering wrote on its Web site. "The airborne unit, carried most often in British 'Mosquito' bombers, was more complicated, heavier, and fitted with an adjustable, external antenna to transmit and receive at pre-arranged polarization."

The U.S. Joint Chiefs of Staff called it among the best intelligence-gathering methods ever. In 1944 and 1945, the last two years of World War II, intelligence teams in the Netherlands and Germany were able to signal Mosquito planes six miles above them. "The device later formed the basis for all kinds of wireless communications," the Institute of Electrical and Electronics Engineers (IEEE) Communications Society wrote on its Web site.

Ran Successful Businesses after War

When World War II ended, Gross launched Gross Electronics, which designed and constructed communications products, including those under government contract. Gross also founded Citizens Radio Corporation, which made personal wireless receivers, after the Federal Communications Commission (FCC) allocated him frequencies for personal radio service. In 1948 his company received FCC approval to use its "Citizens Band" equipment. Gross himself sold roughly 100,000 units, mostly to farm owners and to the U.S. Coast Guard. In addition, he licensed the technology to electronics companies. He also gave cartoonist Chester Gould permission to use Gross's concoctions in his detective comic strip *Dick Tracy,* paving the way for the Dick Tracy two-way radio.

Gross surfaced with yet another innovation in 1949. He adapted the two-way radios for cordless remotes. "That is, he invented and patented the telephone pager, by building discriminating circuitry into a pocket-sized wireless receiver that responded selectively to specific signals," according to the MIT Web site. Doctors were initially the inventor's target group, but he faced initial resistance while marketing it at a medical convention in Philadelphia, Pennsylvania. "The doctors hated it. They complained that it would interrupt their golf games," he said in an award acceptance speech at MIT, as quoted in the *New York Times.* The pagers caught on, however; an estimated 300 million were sold worldwide in 2007.

Throughout the 1950s, Gross vainly attempted to sell U.S. telephone companies on his contraptions but struck out, largely due to opposition from Bell Telephone. The FCC, though, did approve his pager transceivers in 1958. In the 1960s, such companies as Sperry and General Electric hired Gross as a consultant for microwave and other communications systems after Gross gave up as an entrepreneur. "Gross excelled as an inventor. But he knew his shortcomings—one of which was his lack of salesmanship," Krause wrote. In addition, he provided technology for digital timing devices for Titan, Atlas, and Minuteman missiles while the aerospace industry was in massive growth mode. Gross, who enjoyed teaching, frequently discussed technology and invention with elementary and high school students. He said on MIT's Web site that he enjoyed working with adolescents, "to make them realize that math and science can be great fun, and help them to make a difference through applying their ideas."

Won Many Awards and Accolades

The patents on Gross's technologies expired in 1971. "I guess I was born 35 years too soon to be a millionaire today, but the thrill of inventing is not just about the money, it's about having fun and making a difference for your fellow humans," he said, as quoted on MIT's Web site. Accolades poured in over the years, including a commendation from President Ronald Reagan in 1981.

Gross also received the Fred B. Link Award from the Radio Club of America in 1992, the Marconi Memorial Gold Medal of Achievement from the Veteran Wireless Operators Association in 1996, and the Edwin Howard Armstrong Achievement Award from the IEEE in 1999. In 2000 he won the Lemelson-MIT Lifetime Achievement Award for invention and innovation.

Gross worked during the 1990s as an electrical engineer at Orbital Sciences Corporation in Chandler, Arizona. There he worked on space exploration programs, overseeing the analysis of electromagnetic elements of satellite, military, and aerospace systems. "Al was our radio frequency guru. He knew everyone, everywhere, in the radio world, and was a real joy to work with," Gross's manager at Orbital Sciences, Chuck Smith, said on the IEEE Communications Society Web site.

Workaholic Disdained Small Talk

Gross kept himself busy and had little spare time. His hobbies included visiting Civil War battlegrounds and searching for relics. Not surprisingly, he designed his own metal detector. He stumped three of four panelists when he appeared on the television game show "To Tell the Truth" in 1977. That year he also met Ethel Stanka in Cleveland while arranging for his tax preparation. He eventually moved to Sun City, Arizona, to join her and they married in 1982. He toured Europe extensively while receiving many awards, and met privately with Pope John Paul II.

While congenial, Gross would often go wordless at a party unless someone asked him about his work. Gross and his wife vacationed every May on the west coast of Florida, where he collected shells and observed sunsets while strolling along the beach. In his later years, he also took an interest in ancient Egyptian history and the history of religion. Though generally serious, Gross would laugh extensively at Three Stooges episodes.

Felt Satisfied as an Innovator

Gross died at age 82 on December 21, 2000, at a hospice in Sun City after a brief illness. He was still on the Orbital Sciences payroll at the time of his death. "His fascination for communication thrilled Gross to the very end," Krause wrote. The *New York Times* called Gross the "granddaddy of citizens' band radio, who tinkered with all manner of electronic gear before people just had to have them." The London *Economist* added, "Of all the ingenious people who have had a hand in developing the pager, the cordless phone, and other urgent instruments of modern life, Al Gross could take much of the credit, or, if you like, the blame."

"Al Gross was reluctant to call himself an inventor," the *Economist* added. "He doubted whether there was any such being who could devise something on his own from scratch. But if you had thought up something that looked different from anything else, you might be justified in calling it an innovation." Citing the technological discoveries by Germans in cars and by Britons in computers, the *Economist* pointed out that the likes of Henry Ford and Bill Gates enriched themselves from marketing them. "It is the entrepreneurs . . . who tend to profit from discoveries," the newspaper added.

Hawley added to the plaudits for Gross. "Depending on how they look at it, [working people's] lives are either a little easier or a little more hectic because of an electronics genius named Al Gross." Noting the death of Gross in almost the same year of Cliff's Notes' academic preparation creator Cliff Hillegass, Hawley added: "Hillegass and Gross died. . . . You've probably never heard of them, and it's unlikely that their names will show up on the typical year-end obituary lists of notable people. But they have made it to this list of lesser-knowns who touched many lives."

David Coursey of the Web site Zdnet.news recalled getting an e-mail about Gross shortly after the inventor died. "The story is so interesting and the accomplishment so great that I'd like to share it with you," Coursey wrote. "First, though, I'll need to shut off the cordless phone, put the pager in silent mode, and turn down the volume on the walkie-talkie I use in my volunteer work. It is startling to realize how much I owe to the inventions of a guy I didn't even know about."

Periodicals

Daily Telegraph (London, England), January 16, 2001.
Economist (London, England), January 6, 2001.
Investor's Business Daily, June 8, 2006.
Pioneer Press (St. Paul, MN), December 31, 2001.

Online

"Al Gross, Inventor of the Gizmos with Potential, Dies at 82," *New York Times,* http://www.query.nytimes.com/gst/full page.html?res = 9A00E4DA123BF931A35752C0A96 79C8B63 (December 13, 2007).

"Al Gross: 2000 Lemelson-MIT Lifetime Achievement Award Winner," Lemelson-MIT Program, http://www.web.mit.edu/ invent/a-winners/a-gross.html (December 13, 2007).

"Al Gross, The Walkie-Talkie," Lemelson-MIT Program, http://www.web.mit.edu/invent/iow/gross.html (December 17, 2007).

"In Memory of Al Gross," IEEE Communications Society, http://www.comsoc.org/socsTR/org/operation/awards/algross mem.html (December 17, 2007).

"Passing of a Wireless Pioneer," Zdnet News, http://www .retrocom.com/Al%20Gross.htm (December 6, 2007). □

Ernst Haefliger

The Swiss tenor Ernst Haefliger (1919-2007) was termed "one of the finest of all lyric tenors" by London's *Daily Telegraph*.

Haefliger never achieved the superstar status of tenors like Luciano Pavarotti or Plácido Domingo. Yet among connoisseurs of classical vocal art his reputation remained at the highest level over a career that lasted more than 60 years. Haefliger's strength was his versatility. While most singers in the field of classical music specialize in a single area, such as opera, classical songs, or oratorios like Handel's *Messiah*, Haefliger performed music from all of these areas with equal confidence and with a characteristic grace and sensitivity to text. He sang music from the classical tradition's eighteenth- and nineteenth-century mainstream, newly composed works, and, often, the music of Johann Sebastian Bach. According to the *Daily Telegraph*, words, Haefliger "brought to his elegant performances an intellectual Teutonic Romanticism, following in the great tradition from Schumann, Schubert and Goethe."

Studied in Switzerland, Austria, Czechoslovakia

Haefliger (pronounced HEFF-ligger) was born on July 6, 1919, in the small Swiss city of Davos. His father, Jakob, was a salesman. Attending Switzerland's Wettinger Seminary he began to show vocal talent and moved on to the Zurich Conservatory. His first teacher there was Leni Haefely, and he rounded out his vocal education with top-flight instruction in various European cities: in Vienna, Austria, he studied with tenor Julius Patzak, a connoisseurs'

favorite of the era of 78 rpm records whose style Haefliger's somewhat resembled. He also studied in Prague, Czechoslovakia, and in the Swiss city of Geneva with veteran vocal instructor Fernando Carpi. His first small concert appearances came in 1940.

Although the careers of most European singers were disrupted by World War II, Haefliger was fortunate to be living in neutral Switzerland and thus had the chance to develop his vocal talents fully. His official debut came in 1942 in Zurich in the part of the Evangelist, or narrator, in a performance of Bach's St. John Passion. The music, consisting of recitation of biblical texts was not technically difficult, but it demanded a singer who could enter with a high level of conviction into the words being sung. Haefliger toured Switzerland during the war, often appearing in the St. John Passion and Bach's related St. Matthew Passion, and he remained closely identified with those two works.

In 1943, at the urging of Hungarian conductor Ferenc Fricsay, Haefliger joined the cast of the Zurich Opera and he appeared with the company in a wide variety of subsidiary roles before departing in 1952. Fricsay became another key mentor, and Haefliger's recording career began with appearances on Fricsay's recordings of Wolfgang Amadeus Mozart's operas. After the war, Haefliger's reputation spread and he was engaged to sing the role of the blind seer Tiresias in German composer Carl Orff's *Antigonae* at Austria's prestigious Salzburg Festival in 1949. The work, in a neo-primitive style that had what today would be called minimalist elements, was a complete change of pace from Bach and from Haefliger's earlier operatic experience.

Haefliger joined the cast of the Berlin Städtische Opera (Berlin City Opera), later renamed the Deutsche Oper or German Opera, in 1952. He was named the company's principal lyric tenor, a lighter variety of tenor voice than the

a music administration career and became executive director of Switzerland's Lucerne Festival. The couple also had a daughter, Christine. Haefliger's career in North America began in 1959 with an appearance at Canada's Vancouver Festival in Mahler's symphony-with-vocals *Das Lied von der Erde* (The Song of the Earth), and included two sojourns in the United States. In 1966 he appeared at Chicago's Lyric Opera as Tamino in *The Magic Flute,* and a tour involving performances of the two Bach Passion settings included stops in Boston, Hartford, Princeton, New York City, and Washington, D.C.

Although well established by the 1960s, Haefliger took notice of new trends in Bach performances. He returned to his trademark Evangelist roles in Bach performances led by German conductor Karl Richter with his Munich Bach Orchestra, one of the first performing organizations to use a small ensemble appropriate to Bach's music instead of a full-sized symphony orchestra. Haefliger traveled to the Soviet Union with Richter's group in 1968, and enlarged his discography with numerous recordings of Bach's music under Richter's baton.

Haefliger was also much more active than most of his vocal peers in championing contemporary music. He sang, in several world premieres, works by his countryman Frank Martin and by German composer Boris Blacher. The Russian-French-American composer Igor Stravinsky praised Haefliger's interpretation of one of his works. Haefliger continued to experience success with mainstream operatic repertory as well. He made a series of critically praised recordings, under Fricsay and others, of operas by Mozart and Ludwig van Beethoven in the 1960s. One of his most famous performances of that decade came in the vocal finale of Beethoven's Symphony No. 9 with England's New Philharmonic Orchestra, on the occasion of the group's founding.

Began Teaching Career

Haefliger retired from the operatic stage in 1974 after beginning a new career as a professor at the Hochschule für Musik in Munich, a university-level music school, three years earlier. Another beneficiary of Haefliger's musical example was his son Andreas, whose career as a piano soloist featured appearances in Europe, the United States, and East Asia. Haefliger taught at the Hochschule für Musik until 1981 and in 1983 he authored a textbook, *Die Singstimme* (The Singing Voice).

Leaving the world of opera did not signal the end of Haefliger's singing career, however. His recitals in England in the 1980s drew enthusiastic crowds, and a 1981 performance at London's Wigmore Hall in 1981 broke new ground with the use of a fortepiano, a piano from the time of Mozart and Beethoven, as the accompanying instrument. In 1995 Haefliger, with his son Andreas as accompanist, returned to Wigmore Hall for a performance of *Die Winterreise.* He was 76 years old, a nearly unthinkable age for a classical singer (most classical vocal careers end by the performer's 50s). Tom Sutcliffe, writing in London's *Guardian,* described Haefliger, "standing with rheumatic stance and marble face, quite frank about the fragility of his vocal resources—occasionally quavering, often almost toneless. Yet the in-

so-called Heldentenor or heroic tenor. In Berlin, Haefliger undertook a variety of roles that required him to sing in languages other than his native German: French in Claude Debussy's Pélléas and Melisande, Italian (in several Mozart operas and in Ferruccio Busoni's *Turandot*), and Czech (in Bedrich Smetana's *The Bartered Bride*). He took guest roles at opera houses around Europe, including the lead role of Tamino in Mozart's *Die Zauberflöte* (The Magic Flute) at England's Glyndebourne Opera House in 1956.

Specialized in Schubert Song Cycles

As his name became better known in Europe through these performances, Haefliger also began to receive invitations to give song recitals—concerts of songs (known in German as lieder) for voice and piano (or voice and orchestra) from the classical tradition. He became particularly identified with two song cycles—groups of related songs that collectively tell a story—of nineteenth-century Austrian composer Franz Schubert. Both cycles, *Die schöne Mülerin* (The Beautiful Miller's Daughter) and *Die Winterreise* (The Winter Journey), depicted the flowering and subsequent breakup of love affairs, using unusual harmonies to depict the psychological states of the male protagonists. Haefliger was particularly enamored of the bleak *Die Winterreise,* continuing to sing it for much of his long career.

At times during the later part of his career he was accompanied on the piano by his son, Andreas Haefliger, the product of his marriage to architect and interior designer Anna Hadorn in 1954. Another son, Michael, embarked on

tensity with which he pursued both the meaning of the text, and the beauty and inspiration of the musical line was distilled and sweet."

Haefliger recorded *Die Winterreise* that year, once again using a fortepiano. But even that did not mark the end of his career. In 2001 he appeared across the United States in Arnold Schoenberg's *Gurrelieder,* a large piece for chorus and orchestra that features a spoken part at its climatic movement. Haefliger was the speaker. He performed in the same work in 2002 at Britain's Royal Albert Hall and in London's annual Proms concerts. Haefliger also remained active as an educator, giving master classes in Switzerland, Japan, and the Marlboro Music Festival in Vermont.

A singing competition named for Haefliger was established in Switzerland in 2006. The singer died in his birthplace of Davos, of acute heart failure, on March 17, 2007. "Whether it was an opera by Mozart, a Passion by Bach or a song-cycle by Schubert, he always found the appropriate style for the music and treated the words with wonderful expressiveness," noted the London *Independent* in his obituary. His work remained well represented on recordings that dated back as far as the 1950s but continued to sound fresh in reissues, and that seemed to point back to an era in which celebrity was less important in classical music that craft.

Books

Baker's Biographical Dictionary of Musicians, Centennial ed., Nicolas Slonimsky, ed. emeritus, Schirmer, 2001.

Periodicals

American Record Guide, July-August 1993.
Daily Telegraph (London, England), March 23, 2007.
Guardian (London, England), June 5, 1995; March 20, 2007.
Independent (London, England), June 6, 2007.
New York Times, March 21, 2007.
Times (London, England), March 31, 2007.

Online

"Ernst Haefliger," Bach Cantatas Web site, http://www.bach-cantatas.com/Bio/Haefliger-Ernst.htm (November 5, 2007).
"Swiss Tenor Ernst Haefliger Dies," Canadian Broadcasting Corporation, http://www.cbc.ca/arts/music/story/2007/03/18/haefliger-tenor-obit.html?ref=rss (November 5, 2007). □

Lloyd Augustus Hall

American chemist and inventor Lloyd Hall (1894-1971) created an innovative method of preserving meat known as "flash-drying." He also worked to find methods to combat spoilage and rancidity in various food products such as spices and oils; in all, he published more than 50 scientific papers and received about 105 patents. An active supporter of scientific and civic causes, in 1955 Hall became the first African American to sit on the board of directors of the American Institute of Chemists.

Discovered Interest in Chemistry

Lloyd Augustus Hall was born on June 20, 1894, to Augustus and Isabel Hall in Elgin, Illinois, about 40 miles northwest of Chicago. Augustus Hall was a high school graduate and a Baptist minister; his own father had come to Chicago in the 1830s and had become the first pastor of the Quinn Chapel African Methodist Episcopal Church, the city's first African-American congregation, in the 1840s. Isabel Hall was also a high school graduate—uncommon for women, especially African-American women, in the late 1800s. Her mother had escaped slavery on the Underground Railroad as a teenager and settled in Illinois.

The Hall family moved to nearby Aurora, Illinois, when Lloyd Hall was a child. He attended East Side High School in Aurora, and there became interested in chemistry. He was also active in activities such as debate, track, football, and baseball. During his high school years, Hall was one of only five African-American students at the school. In 1912 he graduated as one of the top ten students in his class and received scholarship offers from four Illinois universities. Hall entered Northwestern University in nearby Chicago. There he studied chemistry while working his way through school. He graduated with a bachelor of science degree in 1916 and began pursuing graduate studies at the University of Chicago.

Early Career

Despite Hall's academic qualifications, racism affected his employment prospects; for example, he was hired for a job sight unseen with the Western Electric Company, but turned away when he arrived for work in person. Many other companies unwilling to employ an African-American chemist also rejected Hall, before he found a job with the Chicago Department of Health Laboratories in 1916. There, Hall quickly was promoted to senior chemist. During World War I, Hall served as assistant chief inspector of powder and high explosives in the Ordnance Department of the U.S. Army, primarily inspecting the output of a Wisconsin explosives plant. After the war ended in 1919, Hall was offered a position as chief chemist with the Ottumwa, Iowa-based meatpacking firm John Morrell & Company. On September 23 of that same year, Hall married Myrrhene E. Newsome, a schoolteacher from Macomb, Illinois. The couple later had two children, Kenneth and Dorothy.

Hall worked at John Morrell & Company until 1921, when he returned to Chicago to take the position of chief chemist with the Boyer Chemical Laboratory. He worked there only briefly before becoming president and chemical director of a consulting laboratory, Chemical Products Corporation.

During these early years of his career, Hall developed an interest in food-related chemistry, and this area of expertise would ultimately make his name as a chemist. In the early 1920s, many companies sought ways to cheaply and safely preserve food. One of Hall's clients was Griffith Laboratories, run by a former Northwestern classmate and lab partner of Hall's, Carroll L. Griffith. In 1924 Griffith Laboratories offered Hall laboratory space where he could conduct research while maintaining his consulting business. The following year, Hall became Griffith Laboratories' chief chemist, director of research, and, according to his biography on the Griffith Laboratories Web site, its "first technical mastermind." In 1929 Hall gave up his consulting business. He remained with Griffith until his retirement in 1959.

Created Flash-Drying Technique

At Griffith Laboratories, Hall turned his interest in food chemistry specifically to the science of meat curing. Curing techniques intended to preserve and enhance the flavor and appearance of meat had been used for some time; table salt mixed with chemicals such as sodium or potassium nitrate was a well-known curing compound. Hall sought to improve upon this method by combining sodium nitrite, sodium nitrate (saltpeter), and sodium chloride (table salt). However, a significant problem arose: because the sodium nitrite and sodium nitrate affected the meat considerably more quickly than did the sodium chloride, the meat fell apart before it was preserved. Hall considered possible methods to delay the effects of the sodium nitrite and sodium nitrate, so that the sodium chloride would have sufficient time to fully preserve the meat.

Hall's solution to this challenge revolutionized the meat-curing industry. He determined that by including small amounts of sodium nitrite and sodium nitrate within crystals of sodium chloride, the quicker-acting chemicals would not reach the meat until after the slower-acting sodium chlorite had dissolved. This meant that the meat was fully preserved before it was exposed to the curative properties of the sodium nitrite and sodium nitrate. In order to encapsulate the chemicals within the sodium chloride crystals, Hall developed a "flash-drying" technique. First, he made a strong mixture of sodium chloride containing small amounts of sodium nitrite and sodium nitrate. He then quickly evaporated the mixture over heated metal rollers, leaving only the flash-dried crystals. These crystals looked like salt, but had the capability to quickly and safely preserve meat, locking in its freshness.

Despite this great success, Hall's work was not complete. He discovered that the flash-dried crystals tended to absorb moisture from the air when stored, rendering them less effective. To solve this problem, Hall sought a way to deter the absorption of moisture by the crystals. He struck upon the idea of adding a combination of glycerin and alkali metal tartrate to the prepared flash-dried crystals. This changed their consistency from a salt-like one to a powdery one, and increased their ability to effectively preserve the meat. Finally, Hall determined that using chemically softened water in the flash-drying process improved its efficacy.

Experimented in Food Chemistry

After finalizing the flash-drying process, Hall turned his attention to other areas of food chemistry. At the time, food packers pre-seasoned their meats with such various spices as garlic powder and paprika before shipment, thinking that this pre-seasoning would improve the preservation of the

meat during transport. However, this seasoned meat usually deteriorated more, rather than less, quickly. Hall found that the spices used in the seasoning process contained bacteria that hastened the spoilage of the meat, and began seeking a way to, as Louis Haber wrote in *Black Pioneers and Science and Invention,* "effectively sterilize these foodstuffs and at the same time preserve their appearance, quality, and flavor with no noticeable change."

Hall researched this problem for some time. Finally, he discovered that by using the gas ethylene oxide, he could kill germs in food. Because naturally-occurring moisture and gases in the meat prevented the ethylene oxide from fully reaching every surface, Hall first introduced the meat into a vacuum. This removed all barriers to the ethylene oxide, which he then used to sterilize the various foodstuffs. This discovery led to the invention of food products that contained not only spices, but also proteins, baking ingredients, and others. James Michael Brodie observed in *Created Equal: The Lives and Ideas of Black American Innovators* that this method "still is utilized throughout the world by hospitals for such items as bandages, dressing, drugs, sutures, and cosmetics," showing its lasting effects on chemical products.

Hall soon returned to the question of food preservation by working with fats and oils. These spoiled quickly, often due to contact with oxygen. Hall began experimenting with different antioxidants to prevent this contact. Eventually, he isolated some chemicals that were effective as antioxidants, but was faced with a new challenge: these often did not dissolve in fats such as those Hall hoped they would preserve. To solve this problem, Hall contained the antioxidants in chemicals that did dissolve in fats. This process greatly increased the amount of time refined fats and oils could be safely stored without turning rancid. Eventually, he replaced some of the original materials used, creating an antioxidant salt mixture.

Hall made other important chemical discoveries during his years at Griffith Laboratories. He worked with proteins, finding a way to break them down to extract their flavoring materials. An entry on Hall in *Contemporary Black Biography* commented that this was "among Hall's most successful and most widely used products.... [It] convinced Griffith Laboratories to open a large manufacturing facility devoted to protein hydrolysates." During World War II, Hall again worked the U.S military, this time serving on a food research committee for the scientific advisory board of the Quartermaster Corps of the Army. Haber maintained that Hall was "invaluable in solving problems of maintaining military food supplies in pure and palatable form."

One of Hall's last great food discoveries occurred in 1951. He improved the process for curing bacon from one that took up to two weeks to one that took only hours. Like Hall's other food discoveries, this process also enhanced the appearance and safety of the cured meat.

Retirement and Legacy

In 1959 Hall retired from Griffith Laboratories. That same year he received an honorary membership award from the American Institute of Chemists, honoring his leadership in food chemistry. After retirement, Hall and his wife relocated to Pasadena, California, where he resided for the rest of his life.

Haber noted that "Hall does not separate the chemist from the citizen." Hall's dedication to civic affairs lasted throughout his life. In the 1930s, as a supporter of civil rights, Hall first served on the Chicago Executive Committee of the National Association for the Advancement of Colored People (NAACP) and later on the Board of Directors of the Chicago Urban League. He served on the Illinois State Food Commission and consulted with the George Washington Carver Foundation in the 1940s, and worked with the Institute of Food Technologists, serving on the organization's board in the early 1950s. During the late 1950s, Hall was active in the Hyde Park-Kenwood Conservation Community Council, an organization that worked for urban renewal in Chicago. From 1959 to 1960, Hall served as a member of the Board of Trustees of the Chicago Planetarium Society, acting as a science and education adviser to the Adler Planetarium.

After his official retirement in 1960, Hall continued his scientific and educational pursuits. Shortly after his retirement he traveled to Indonesia to serve as a consultant to the United Nations' Food and Agricultural Organization. In 1962 President John F. Kennedy appointed Hall to the American Food for Peace Council, which oversaw the donation of food to developing nations. Hall remained in this position until 1964. He was also active in organizations such as the American Red Cross, and worked on the SEED project, which aimed to educate underprivileged youth who were interested in chemistry careers.

Hall died on January 2, 1971, in Altadena, California. By the time of his death he had received 105 patents, covering areas such as solid seasonings, flavoring compounds, and protective food coatings. He had also received honorary doctorates from Virginia State University, Howard University, and the Tuskegee Institute. In 2004 Hall was posthumously inducted into the Inventors' Hall of Fame in honor of his pioneering contributions to the field of food preservation and science.

Books

Brodie, James Michael, *Created Equal: The Lives and Ideas of Black American Innovators,* William Morrow and Co., 1993.

Haber, Louis, *Black Pioneers of Science & Invention,* Harcourt, Brace & World, 1970.

Contemporary Black Biography, Volume 8. Gale Research, 1994.

Notable Black American Scientists, Gale Research, 1998.

Online

"Dr. Lloyd Augustus Hall," Griffith Laboratories, http://www.griffithlaboratories.com/United_States/en-US/people/Profiles + In + Excellence/Dr + Lloyd + A + Hall.htm (November 29, 2007).

"Lloyd Hall," The Black Inventor Online Museum, http://www.blackinventor.com/pages/lloydhall.html (November 29, 2007).

Scientists: Their Lives and Works, Vols. 1-7. Online Edition. U*X*L, 2006. http://galenet.galegroup.com/servlet.BioRc (November 26, 2007).

World of Chemistry, Online, Thomson Gale, 2006, http://galenet.galegroup.com/servlet.BioRc (November 26, 2007).

World of Invention, Online, Thomson Gale, 2006, http://galenet.galegroup.com/servlet.BioRc (November 26, 2007). ☐

Hanna and Barbera

William Hanna (1910-2001) and Joseph Barbera (1911-2006) are the single most successful producing/directing team in animation history. For nearly two decades, their work on MGM's Tom & Jerry cartoons rocked movie houses with laughter. However, when the duo brought their knack for sight gags and sure sense of parody to television, they became giants in the field of limited animation.

Met at MGM

Hanna and Barbera started out at opposite ends of the country before they met at MGM in 1937. The son of William John and Avice Joyce Hanna, William Denby Hanna was born on July 14, 1910, in Melrose, New Mexico. The dictates of his job as a construction superintendent for the Santa Fe Railroad caused the elder Hanna to move his family to Logan, Utah, in 1915, and then to California in 1917. One of seven children, young Hanna was the only boy and an enthusiastic member of the Boy Scouts of America. While growing up, he was encouraged to express himself both musically and artistically by his mother, who wrote poems for the family, and by his sister Lucille, who passed her piano lessons on to her only brother.

Initially, Hanna studied journalism and engineering at Compton Junior College, and hoped to become an engineer. He worked briefly as a surveying assistant before the financial hardships of the Great Depression compelled him to take any paying work he could find. Fortunately for Hanna, his sister Marian was dating Jack Stevens, who worked for Warner Bros. animation producer Leon Schelesinger. Stevens advised the youngster to seek employment with the animation/production team of Hugh Harman and Rudolph Ising.

Starting out at the bottom, Hanna earned $18 a week as a janitor at Harman and Ising's studio. Besides sweeping up and emptying the trash, he also washed the ink off the acetate sheets or production cels, so they could be reused. Hard working and a quick study, Hanna enjoyed the sociable animation shop and was quickly put in charge of the ink and paint department. Harman and Ising, who got their start with Walt Disney, proved valuable mentors. While working on the *Merrie Melodies* and *Looney Tunes* series, Hanna learned every aspect of the business. By 1933 he was skilled

enough to begin working as a story editor, lyricist, and occasional director. When Harman and Ising's company broke up in 1937, Hanna joined MGM as a cartoon writer and director. It was there he met Joseph Barbera.

The son of an Italian immigrant, Joseph Roland Barbera was born on March 24, 1911, in New York City. Growing up in the Flatbush area of Brooklyn, the youngster discovered his love of theater and writing while attending Erasmus Hall High School. A high school graduate at the age of 16, Barbera studied accountancy at the American Institute of Banking, which resulted in a position filing income tax forms at the Irving Trust Bank on Wall Street. Later, Barbera jokingly told Ted Sennett, author of *The Art of Hanna-Barbera,* "To this day, they must be still looking for my mistakes."

When not working at the bank, Barbera secretly longed to become a cartoonist and magazine illustrator. Drawing all night and refining his skills through instruction at the Pratt Institute, he eventually sold a few cartoons to *Collier's* for $25 apiece. Although not enough money to quit his job over, the sales encouraged the young artist, and he sought full-time employment in his chosen field. In 1934 he briefly worked as a cel painter and inker at the Fleischer Brothers's New York studios, where he was occasionally paid $1 per gag idea for *Popeye* cartoons. A far better opportunity came at the Van Buren Studios, best remembered for their animated version of the *Toonerville Trolley* comic strip, where animator Tom Goodson showed him the fine points of the craft before the studio abruptly closed its doors in 1936.

Subsequently, Barbera applied for a job at the Disney studios in California, but Paul Terry, of *Terrytoons* fame, promptly hired Barbera as an animator and storyboard editor. A year later, Barbera and most of Terry's staff were asked to join MGM's new cartoon unit. Hanna and Barbera began to share story conferences. Few animators understood comedic timing as well as Hanna, who had refined his skills alongside such giants as Friz Freleng and Tex Avery. For his part, Barbera was clearly the superior artist. "He was the best cartoonist I'd ever seen," Hanna told Ted Sennett. "I had a lot of respect for his artistic abilities and I knew how much he contributed to the stories." By the end of 1938, they were officially a creative team.

Made Hit With Tom & Jerry

Most of Hanna and Barbera's early work at MGM was done under the aegis of producer Fred Quimby. After backing an unsuccessful series of cartoons based on the *Captain and the Kids* newspaper strip, Quimby was reluctant to allow Hanna and Barbera to produce a cartoon about a squabbling domestic cat and mouse they privately named Jasper and Jinx. However, when the 1940 release *Puss Gets the Boot* proved a rollicking laugh-getter, exhibitors clambered for more.

Hanna and Barbera refined their characters, making the cat sleeker and less sinister and the mouse cuter and chubbier. Finally they changed the name of the cartoon duo to Tom and Jerry. Consistently funny and action packed, the Tom and Jerry cartoons remain among the very few movie-based series that still hold up as entertainment. Hanna and Barbera adhered to a simple formula: The cat and mouse were "the best of enemies." Jerry never provoked a fight, but always got the last laugh. When a common enemy menaced both cat and mouse, they displayed fierce loyalty and teamwork. Both characters were devoid of human speach, but all of Tom's screeches and yowls and purrs were provided by co-creator Hanna.

Working closely with animators Irven Spence, Eddie Barge, Ken Muse, Ray Patterson, and Bick Bickenbach, Hanna and Barbera created well over a hundred Tom and Jerry cartoons. Further, they added animated sequences to several live action feature films, most notably *Anchors Aweigh* (1945), in which actor Gene Kelly appeared to be masterfully dancing with Jerry the mouse. Both Tom and Jerry swam with Esther Williams in *Dangerous When Wet* (1956). However, the cartoon shorts were Hanna and Barbera's bread and butter, and their popularity with audiences and critics resulted in seven Academy Awards and eight other nominations. Producer Fred Quimby took home the Oscars, but it was Hanna and Barbera's work and vision that made the seven-minute cartoons so enduringly entertaining.

Both men would have happily spent the rest of their days making Tom and Jerry cartoons for MGM, and the studio rewarded them by making them head of the studios cartoon unit in 1955. However, facing stiff competition from television, MGM closed the theatrical cartoon unit in late 1957. With other studios also cutting back or closing their cartoon units outright, it seemed that the outlet for their creative talents was television.

Created Early Television Cartoons

Early cartoons made for television faced significant budgetary hurdles that demanded cut-backs in the number of drawings used per frame in each film. The result was a technique called limited animation, which showed characters talking more than moving, and a lot of herky-jerky movement accompanied by sound effects and music to provide an illusion of action. Such kiddie fare as *Crusader Rabbit, Clutch Cargo,* and Captain Kangaroo's regular feature *Tom Terrific* had their respective charms, but were often poorly drafted and pitifully animated. Hanna and Barbera, with their superior sense of draftsmanship and storytelling, brought most of their MGM staff with them when they set a new, high standard for limited animation.

In late 1957, Hanna and Barbera debuted their new Saturday morning series, *The Ruff and Reddy Show,* on NBC. Made under the auspices of H-B Productions, a freelance animation company, the black-and-white show remained a staple of the network's programming for several years. Far more iconic was the floodgate of characters that came under the Hanna-Barbera Productions imprint, each with his own catch-phrase and high concept storyline. The good-natured fool, Huckleberry Hound, introduced Yogi Bear, who was "smarter than the average bear" and lusted after forbidden picnic baskets. Quick Draw McGraw, a dim-witted palomino who stood upright, parodied TV's abundance of westerns with the aid of long-suffering burro Baba Looey. One-upping their own Tom and Jerry movie cartoons, the duo also introduced Pixie & Dixie, cute cartoon mice who constantly outsmarted the Brooklyn-esque cat Mr. Jinx. Each creation became a major hit with kids and parents alike.

The Hanna-Barbera TV cartoons followed a certain formula. Voiced predominantly by Daws Butler and Dale Messick, each storyline had to play out in six minutes or less. In 1963 they altered the format to suit their 30-minute rendition of Phil Silvers and his *You'll Never Get Rich* sitcom for their cat cartoon *Top Cat.* However, the team's greatest success came with the creation of the perfect stone-age suburban family, *The Flintstones.*

Loosely based on Jackie Gleason's *The Honeymooners,* and starring the voice of Alan Reed, previously of radio's *Duffy's Tavern* and *The Fred Allen Show,* the show became the first successful animated prime-time sitcom. After its six-year run on ABC (1960-66), the show eventually spawned several televised spin-offs, two live action films, and a plethora of licensed merchandise.

The late 1950s through the mid-1960s were Hanna and Barbera's most creative era, and the merchandise licensing, advertising tie-ins and theme parks made them wealthy overnight. Even relative failures like *The Jetsons,* which lasted only one full season on CBS, proved popular enough in reruns to warrant a revival 17 years later. In his book *A Cast of Friends,* Hanna attributed his successful relationship with Barbera to the fact that the duo seldom socialized and intuitively worked out the allocation of their duties. Hanna concentrated on the logistics of production while Barbera developed the writing staff. Even a move into

action-adventure with *The Adventures of Jonny Quest* paid off, but their creative hot streak would not last forever.

Returned to Full Animation

At the peak of their success in 1967, Hanna and Barbera sold their production company to Taft Broadcasting, who promptly installed the former owners as co-presidents and co-directors of operations. The move allowed them to expand and place Saturday morning shows on all three networks. Consequently, the look and quality of the product suffered, and only a few of their shows—most notably the many incarnations of *Scooby Doo, Where Are You?*—had the staying power of old. Yet some of their lesser efforts, such as *Space Ghost, Birdman and the Galaxy Trio,* and *Sealab 2020* were repurposed and freshly voiced for the ironic satire of the Cartoon Network's late night *Adult Swim* programming during the early 2000s.

Always active, Hanna and Barbera had been dabbling in feature-length cartoons since 1964, but their most enduring—and least typical—work in the field was their adaptation of E. B. White's *Charlotte's Web* in 1973. At the insistence of Barbera, the duo also began producing and directing live action films for television and theatrical release, the best of which was *The Gathering,* an Emmy-winning drama.

The fortunes of Hanna and Barbera took another leap forward during the home video boom of the late 1980s, as they re-released old favorites and created new animated series, including *Greatest Adventure Stories from the Bible.* Hanna and Barbera worked together as animators for the last time on the 1990 feature-length cartoon *Jetsons: The Movie.* After creating 138 series in 30 years, their final major credit as a team came when they co-produced the live action *Flintstones* movies in 1994 and 2000, respectively. Suffering from heart problems, Hanna died on March 22, 2001, leaving behind his wife, Violet, and children Bonnie and David.

Barbera was credited as executive producer on the live action *Scooby Doo* movies of the early 2000s, but he enjoyed one final spurt of brilliance in 2005 when he created the first new Tom & Jerry cartoon short in 45 years. It proved to be his swan song. Joseph Barbera died on December 18, 2006. He was survived by second wife Sheila, and by his three children from his first marriage to Dorothy; Earl—Jayne, Neal, and Lynn. "Animation is relief from what's going on in the world," Barbera was quoted as saying on IMDB.com. "You get up in the morning and turn on the radio and you hear a bridge goes out in Albany, a bomb has exploded here and there's a flood on the East Coast. Then, you turn on the TV and see it all visualized. In living color, no less. Where's the relief? That's what we do: Provide relief in a fantasy product. It's important to make people forget what's really happening."

Books

Fischer, Stuart, *Kids' TV: The First 25 Years,* Facts On File Publications, 1983.

Hanna, Bill, with Tom Ito, *A Cast of Friends,* De Capo, 1996.

Sennett, Ted, *The Art of Hanna-Barbera—Fifty Years of Creativity,* Viking Studio Books, 1989.

Online

"Hanna, William, and Joseph Barbera," The Museum of Broadcast Communications, http://www.museum.tv/archives/etv/H/htmlH/hannawillia.htm (December 20, 2007).

"Joseph Barbera," *All Movie Guide,* http://www.allmovie.com (December 19, 2007).

"Joseph Barbera," *Internet Movie Database,* http://www.imdb.com (December 20, 2007).

"The Lives They Lived: William Hanna, B. 1910; Stone-Age Visionary," *New York Times Magazine,* http://www.query.nytimes.com/gst/fullpage.html?, (December 30, 2006).

"William Hanna," *All Movie Guide,* http://www.allmovie.com (December 19, 2007).

"William Hanna and Joseph Barbera," Film Reference.com, http://www.filmreference.com (December 20, 2007).

"William Hanna and Joseph Barbera," Hollywood.com, http://www.hollywood.com (December 21, 2007).

"William Hanna," Internet Movie Database, http://www.imdb.com (December 21, 2007). ☐

Florence Kling Harding

American First Lady Florence Kling Harding (1860-1924) used her determined, strong personality to support the political aspirations of her second husband, President Warren G. Harding. Harding survived early setbacks, including a teenage pregnancy and estrangement from her family, to become one of the best-known women of her time as First Lady. After her husband's much-criticized Presidency was cut short by his death, Harding burned many of his papers, causing a controversy that followed her into history.

Showed Youthful Determination

Neither of Florence Kling Harding's parents were native Ohioans. Her father, Amos Kling, originally came from a farming family in Lancaster, Pennsylvania. In his youth he settled in Ohio, and at the age of 24 purchased his first business in Marion, Ohio. He later became a banker and real estate owner. Both his business acumen and his difficult, somewhat tyrannical nature were widely acknowledged. Harding's mother, Louisa Bouton Kling, came from a colonial family that had helped found the city of New Canaan, Connecticut. She left her family's home in 1859 to marry Amos Kling. The couple had met earlier that year during a visit Kling made to a friend in New Canaan. The couple's first child, Florence Mabel Kling, was born on August 15, 1860, in Marion.

Amos Kling had hoped his first child would be a boy, and was determined to raise his daughter as though she were a son. Indeed, Florence—soon nicknamed "Flossie"—became a tomboy with an assertive, willful temperament to match her father's. Even after the births of her brothers, Clifford Bouton and Vetallis Hanford, in 1861 and 1866, respectively, the young girl remained her father's favorite. Louisa

Kling had become something of an invalid as a result of illness or perhaps depression, and Amos became the primary presence in his daughter's life. From the local schools, young Florence learned math, science, English, history, philosophy, and other academic subjects; from her father, she learned banking and business practices. Her mother's only apparent contribution to her psyche was a talent for music. Following her education in Marion, Harding spent a year studying at the Cincinnati Conservatory of Music.

Survived Difficult Years

After returning to Marion, Harding became involved with a young local man named Henry "Pete" DeWolfe. This involvement led to a pregnancy in 1880, and the couple left Marion together for the state capital with the intent of marrying. Contrary to popular legend, no records exist to confirm that Harding and Pete DeWolfe ever legally married. However, the couple did live together as husband and wife in the town of Galion, Ohio. Their son, Eugene, was born in September of that same year. However, the DeWolfes' marriage was a difficult one; Pete DeWolfe drank heavily, and after only two years deserted his wife and child. Left alone and impoverished, Harding returned to Marion.

There, she lived apart from her family, teaching piano in order to support herself and her son. Amos Kling was enraged at his daughter's behavior and refused to support her, although Louisa Kling and the DeWolfe family did provide some financial support. In 1884 Amos Kling offered to take Harding's son—called Marshall rather than Eugene by his family—and raise him as his own. Harding accepted the offer. As Carl Sferazza Anthony noted in *Florence Harding: The First Lady, the Jazz Age, and the Death of America's Most Scandalous President,* "although there would be holidays, vacation trips, and overnight visits with her in a new life, when she let go of Marshall in 1884, she essentially ended her obligations of motherhood." In June of 1886, Harding filed for divorce from DeWolfe.

Married a Budding Politician

In 1890 Florence met Warren G. Harding, the new owner of a local newspaper, the *Marion Star,* and became romantically interested in him. Five years younger than Florence, Harding was an easygoing, attractive womanizer who seemed an odd match for the driven, plain divorcee. Neither the Kling nor the Harding family approved of the couple's relationship; when the pair married on July 8, 1891, Amos Kling did not attend the wedding.

Their marriage was one based more on business than on romance. Florence Harding became head of the circulation department of the *Marion Star,* and according to her biography in *Biography Resource Center Online,* "She was a penny-pincher and a domineering force who reportedly spanked a newsboy on at least one occasion." She managed the business side of the newspaper effectively, building circulation and allowing her husband the freedom to focus on his editorial duties. Florence Harding brought the same fierce persona to her marriage, and Warren Harding often complained that his wife nagged him incessantly; he called her "The Duchess" and she referred to him as "Wurr'n." However, her determination buoyed Harding as he embarked on his political career.

In 1899 Warren Harding was elected to the Ohio state senate, bolstered by the success of the *Marion Star.* Five years later he became Ohio's lieutenant governor. Florence Harding was well aware of her husband's failings: laziness, indecisiveness, and an inclination to drink and womanize. Warren Harding also suffered from heart problems and nerves, while Florence Harding had significant kidney problems-she may have had a kidney removed in the early 1900s-as well as a weak heart. Despite any misgivings she may have had about her husband's abilities, Florence Harding helped manage Warren Harding's election campaigns and gave him political advice while he was in office. As Robert P. Watson commented in *First Ladies of the United States: A Biographical Dictionary,* after Warren Harding lost the 1910 election for governor of Ohio, Florence Harding "pushed him back into the political scene, and even courted important contacts for him." The loss caused Warren Harding to consider leaving politics; without Florence Harding's efforts of his behalf, it seems unlikely that he would have successfully run for a seat in the United States Senate in 1914.

Moved to the Capital

In 1915 Florence Harding moved to Washington, D.C., with her husband. At first she felt isolated from the social and political life of the capital. However, she became a close friend of Evalyn Walsh McLean, a prominent hostess and socialite who was married to the owner of the

Washington Post and the *Cincinnati Enquirer.* McLean helped Florence Harding become acquainted with other important Washingtonians and build her personal network.

As a political wife, Harding supported the war effort after the United States' entry into World War I in 1917. She helped women from her native Ohio locate housing in the capital, and passed out coffee and sandwiches to men preparing to depart for the front in Europe. However, Florence Harding found her calling when accompanying McLean on visits to Walter Reed Naval Hospital in Washington. There, veterans wounded in European combat recuperated; for the rest of her life, Harding maintained an interest in veterans' affairs, hoping to help her "boys" as much as possible. Anthony commented that "the 'boys' became her work and purpose. . . . She found a sense of personal satisfaction that had long been sorely lacking in her life."

After the close of World War I, Warren Harding decided to run for President, encouraged by leading Ohio Republican politician Harry Daugherty. At first, Florence Harding was against her husband's candidacy, perhaps believing him incapable of winning or even effectively serving should he attain the office. Watson noted Warren Harding's "lackluster Senate career marked more by missing votes than by legislative leadership." In early 1920, however, she visited an astrologer, Madame Marcia Champrey, who told her that Warren Harding would one day become President but not live to complete his term. After this visit—although perhaps not necessarily due to it—Florence Harding began working with Daugherty on her husband's campaign.

Florence Harding was instrumental in creating her husband's public persona as a regular American during his "Front Porch" campaign; whether she knew that the campaign paid out a large sum of money to Carrie Phillips, Warren Harding's longtime mistress, in order to ensure her silence, seems debatable. In November of 1920, Florence Harding joined the wide majority of voters who selected Warren G. Harding over fellow Ohioan and newspaper publisher James M. Cox as the twenty-ninth president of the United States. Because the Nineteenth Amendment, which granted women the right to vote, had become law only months before the election, Florence Harding was the first woman to vote for her husband in a presidential election.

As First Lady, Florence Harding was both publicly prominent and privately influential. She helped her husband select Cabinet members prior to his inauguration in March of 1921. Throughout Harding's presidency, his wife advised him on policy matters and wrote his speeches. As an advocate of gender equality, she helped bring continued public attention to women's issues. Florence Harding's support for her "boys" surely helped bring about the creation of the Veterans' Bureau (the precursor of the United States Department of Veterans Affairs) during the Harding administration. She became greatly popular with the general public, reopening the White House to tours (it had been closed during World War I) and often appearing in newsreels with her dog, Laddie.

However, Florence Harding—called "Ma" or "the boss" by those close to the President—also served as bartender for her husband and his friends during their frequent poker games. She disliked Vice President Calvin Coolidge and his wife, and treated them poorly; many of the president's staff disliked the First Lady intensely. Warren Harding's affairs continued during his presidency, and his wife often helped silence the women involved. Neither of the Hardings could halt the growing corruption within the administration. Although Harding himself apparently did not profit from any of the scandalous deals that occurred during his administration, he could not control the members of his Cabinet. During the summer of 1923, as Warren Harding became concerned about the increasing possibility that the corruption within his White House would become public knowledge, the Hardings traveled to the western part of the United States. Years of poor health, exacerbated by food poisoning and stress, finally caught up with the president, who died from heart failure and a cerebral hemorrhage on August 2, 1923.

Death and Scandal

After Warren Harding's death, speculation that he had been poisoned by one of many people—including his wife—became common. Some suspected that Florence Harding had poisoned her husband, either to protect him from potential impeachment proceedings or to punish him for his continued marital infidelities. However, no evidence exists that his death was not a natural one.

Florence Harding returned to Marion, Ohio, to arrange for her husband's funeral. After his funeral, however, she immediately returned to Washington, D.C., where she stayed with McLean. While in Washington, she destroyed many of the president's papers, presumably hoping to salvage some of the remaining shreds of his dignity. In Anthony's biography Harding is quoted as saying, "We must be loyal to Warren and preserve his memory."

Soon after burning her husband's papers, Florence Harding returned to Ohio. Her health had been poor for years and continued to deteriorate. On November 21, 1924, Harding died as a result of her failing heart and kidneys. Watson noted that Harding "is remembered as an active, assertive, nontraditional woman but also as a failed first lady." Florence Harding's unusual life, from single mother to controversial First Lady, often seems overshadowed by the somewhat dramatic circumstances of her husband's presidency and death. However, Florence Harding's influence on history and on the office of the First Lady cannot be ignored.

Books

American First Ladies, edited by Robert P. Watson, Salem, 2002.

Anthony, Carl Sferrazza, *Florence Harding: The First Lady, the Jazz Age, and the Death of America's Most Scandalous President,* William Morrow and Company, 1998.

Watson, Robert P., *First Ladies of the United States: A Biographical Dictionary,* Lynne Rienner Publishers, 2001.

Online

Biography Resource Center Online, Gale Group, 2002, http://galenet.galegroup.com/servlet.BioRc (November 19, 2007).

"Florence Kling Harding," *The White House: Biography of Florence Kling Harding,* http://www.whitehouse.gov/history/first ladies/fh29.html (November 19, 2007). □

Rafic Hariri

Lebanese politician Rafic Hariri (1944-2005) helped rebuild his country after its long civil war, both as a billionaire businessman and as its prime minister from 1992-1998 and 2000-2004. Hariri amassed his fortune in Saudi Arabia in the 1970s and 1980s, then returned to Lebanon and became its dominant political leader of the 1990s and 2000s. After emerging as an opponent of neighboring Syria's occupation of Lebanon, Hariri was assassinated by a massive car bomb, causing an international dispute that led to the occupation's end.

Hariri relished his public role as "Mr. Lebanon," the international leader of his nation's recovery. "He was as extravagant in his charitable works as he was in his big-game hunting, yachts, private jets and multimillion-dollar real estate projects," wrote Susan Sachs of the *New York Times.* "Always impeccably dressed, he was stout with bushy eyebrows and a commanding manner."

A Self-Made Billionaire

Hariri was born on November 1, 1944, in Sidon, a town on the Mediterranean coast in southern Lebanon. He was the third child of a Sunni Muslim grocer and farmer. Hariri studied in Egypt as a teen and then attended the Arab University in Lebanon, studying accounting. He left without graduating, probably unable to afford the tuition. In 1965 he moved to Saudi Arabia, like many ambitious Lebanese of his generation. He became a math teacher in Jeddah and worked part-time as an accountant for a contracting company. While living in Saudi Arabia, he married Nazik Audeh Hariri.

In 1969 or 1970, Hariri founded a construction company, Cisconest, intent on getting involved in the oil-financed Saudi building boom of the time. He quickly amassed a fortune by building palaces, hotels, and convention centers for wealthy Saudis. He became the owner of Saudi Arabia's largest construction company in the late 1970s by taking over the French firm Oger. He became close to Saudi Crown Prince Fahd and to Jacques Chirac, the once and future French prime minister and future French president. Saudi Arabia granted Hariri citizenship in 1978.

Hariri's business interests expanded into telecommunications, insurance, and real estate. He bought mansions around the world. In the 1990s *Forbes* magazine named him one of the world's richest men. His wealth was conservatively estimated at $4 billion.

A dedicated philanthropist, Hariri founded the Hariri Foundation for Culture and Higher Education, based in Beirut, in 1979. The foundation has given scholarships to 30,000 Lebanese students for education at home and abroad, and provides social services to the needy in Lebanon. Hariri's wife, Nazek, oversaw many of his charitible projects. She has served as head of the Children's Cancer Center of Lebanon.

From the mid-1970s through the 1980s, a brutal civil war among several political and religious factions in Lebanon killed 150,000 people. Hariri became directly involved in trying to end the war in 1983, when he returned to his home country as a mediator representing Saudi Arabia's King Fahd. He played a major role in convening conferences of various Lebanese groups in Switzerland in 1983 and 1984. Meanwhile, his company, Oger, helped tear down buildings destroyed during Israel's 1982 invasion of Lebanon.

Since Syria exerted strong control over Lebanon, Hariri attempted to win over its president, Hafez Assad, by building a palace for him in the Syrian capital, Damascus, as a gift. In 1985 and 1987, Hariri tried to convince Lebanese Christians to accept Syria's influence over Lebanon, but failed. In 1989 Hariri paid for dozens of Lebanese leaders to attend a peace conference in Taif, Saudi Arabia, that brought an end to the civil war, but with a price: The agreement allowed Syria's army to remain in Lebanon and occupy its capital, Beirut, and essentially gave Syria substantial control over Lebanon's government.

Leading His Nation

In 1992 Hariri was elected to Lebanon's parliament and became prime minister. Hariri named a cabinet equally balanced between Muslims and Christians, an attempt to bring Lebanon's various religions and factions together. In the delicate balance of Lebanese politics during the Syrian occupation, Hariri had complete freedom over the coun-

try's economy, but Syria's army and intelligence services were responsible for Lebanon's security, and Hariri had to run major appointments past them. He did not have much control over the country's foreign policy. Also, the militant group Hezbollah, supported by Syria and Iran, controlled much of southern Lebanon.

"I want to go down in the history books as the man who resurrected Beirut," Hariri declared upon taking office, according to Sachs. Using his many business ties to benefit his country, Hariri convinced financial partners of his to invest in Lebanon. He regularly visited Washington, D.C., and European capitals to lobby for aid for his country, and was usually successful. In December of 1996, for instance, he co-chaired an international "Friends of Lebanon" conference to attract foreign aid and private investment.

Thanks to the new investment, Lebanon's currency gained value and the country became more prosperous. Hariri also implemented a $10 billion program to rebuild Lebanon's infrastructure. He helped set up a company, Solidere, to rebuild Beirut's downtown, especially along the ravaged Green Line, which had been the border between fighting factions during the civil war. He set up a new government department, the Ministry for the Displaced, in 1993 to help refugees from the civil war resettle in their former towns.

Hariri's rebuilding plan was controversial. His business allies and many Syrians profited greatly from government contracts. Lebanon accrued a massive foreign debt, about $35 billion, and a large budget deficit. Critics argued that his focus on reconstructing Beirut and regaining Lebanon's former status as a financial and trading center neglected poor and rural areas. Several government officials were investigated for possible corruption. His administration had mixed success managing the economy, since the government's deficit drove up interest rates and slowed growth. However, the rebuilding effort created tens of thousands of jobs, and Beirut, once a center of Middle Eastern culture, regained some of its former health.

Mindful of Syria's power over his country, Hariri carefully avoided direct criticism of its president, Hafez Assad, and his son, Bashar Assad, who succeeded him. Occasionally, though, Hariri's frustration with Lebanon's occupier showed. In 1993, for instance, a *Boston Globe* reporter asked Hariri if he minded the fact that many copies of the elder Assad's portrait hung in Beirut's airport. "It's not a problem to put it up," Hariri said, according to Sachs. "It's a problem to take it down."

Hariri resigned as prime minister in 1998 after a dispute with Lebanon's pro-Syrian president, Emile Lahoud. He returned to the post in October of 2000 and continued working to improve Lebanon's economy. He also had to rebuild a part of southern Lebanon that Israel had occupied for two decades. While he was prime minister in the 2000s, tourism increased greatly, especially due to visitors from Persian Gulf states. He represented Lebanon at the second "Friends of Lebanon" conference to attract international aid and investment in 2001.

Confrontation With Syria

Hariri, ever mindful of Syria's power, never openly called for Syria to withdraw from Lebanon, but he allied himself with factions in parliament that did. In 2004 he defied Syria's will during a political crisis, a stance that may have led to his death. The presidential term of Lahoud, Hariri's longtime rival, was scheduled to expire, but Syria pressed the Lebanese parliament to pass a constitutional amendment that would allow Lahoud to stay in the office. Hariri commanded enough support in parliament that he could have resisted, but after visits to Damascus and the office of Syrian intelligence in Lebanon, Hariri agreed not to block the change.

Later, a United Nations investigation reconstructed Hariri's meeting with Syrian President Bashar Assad in Damascus in August of 2004. Assad told Hariri he wanted to extend Lahoud's term by three years, and when Hariri refused, Assad threatened him, according to recollections of Hariri's aides and family in the UN report. Though Hariri allowed the constitutional amendment to pass, he resigned as prime minister in October of 2004, a move widely interpreted as a protest of Syrian influence and a final break with Syria. Meanwhile, the United Nations Security Council passed a resolution calling on Syria to respect Lebanon's sovereignty.

As 2005 began, Hariri was organizing a new political movement called Al Mustaqbal (The Future). Observers believed he would be elected prime minister again in May. However, Hariri felt that he had endangered his life by crossing Assad and the many Syrian business associations that benefited from the occupation of Lebanon. On February 1, according to the UN report, Hariri told a Syrian deputy foreign minister, Walid Mouallem, that Lebanon would no longer be ruled by Syria. Mouallem replied that Syrian security forces had cornered Hariri and that he should not take the situation lightly, the UN report said. On February 13, Hariri told an ally, Walid Jumblat, leader of Lebanon's Druze party, that he believed his days were numbered.

Hariri's Assassination

On February 14, Hariri was assassinated by a massive car bomb explosion next to his motorcade in Beirut. He was 60 years old. He is survived by his wife, Nazek, and six children. More than a dozen other people were also killed in the bombing.

Hundreds of thousands of people, including members of normally feuding political parties, attended Hariri's burial in Beirut's Martyr's Square. During the funeral ceremony in the Sunni Muslim al-Amine Mosque, the neighboring St. George Cathedral, a Maronite Christian church, rang its bells in an unprecedented display of solidarity across Lebanon's religions. The funeral procession became a massive rally against Syria.

Though Syria denied any involvement in Hariri's death, many Lebanese blamed Syria and the Lebanese security forces allied with it for the assassination. The United States recalled its ambassador to Syria, and French President Jacques Chirac demanded an international investigation into the murder when he arrived in Beirut for the funeral.

The following month, a preliminary United Nations report by Patrick Fitzgerald, an Irish police official, charged that Assad had personally threatened Hariri. It called for a thorough international investigation.

Syria withdrew its troops from Lebanon in April of 2005, in response to the massive protests and pressure from the United Nations. It was the end of a 29-year occupation. In October of 2005, a second United Nations report, from German prosecutor Detlev Mehlis, provided detailed accounts of Hariri's conversations with Assad and Mouallem. The report declared that high-ranking Syrian and Lebanese intelligence officers were responsible for Hariri's assassination.

Periodicals

New York Times, February 15, 2005; March 25, 2005.
Times (London, England), February 16, 2005.
Washington Post, February 17, 2005; October 21, 2005.

Online

"Biography: Mr. Rafic Hariri," Rafic Hariri, The Official Web site, http://www.rhariri.com/general.aspx?pagecontent =biography (December 16, 2007).
"Hariri, Rafiq Bahaa Edine al-Hariri," *Encyclopedia Britannica Online Library Edition,* http://www.library.eb.com/eb/article-9438460 (December 16, 2007).
"Obituary: Rafik Hariri," BBC.com, http://www.news.bbc.co .uk/go/pr/fr/-/1/hi/world/middle_east/4264359.stm (December 16, 2007). ☐

Lucy Webb Hayes

American First Lady Lucy Ware Webb Hayes (1831-1889) was considered by many of her era to be the most successful First Lady to date. Remembered equally for her strict adherence to the temperance movement and for her dedication to her husband and family, Hayes was also remarkably well-educated and progressive for her time. At a young age, Hayes became an adherent of abolitionist beliefs; from the Civil War on, she was especially interested in the welfare of soldiers and their families. Her influence on her husband, Rutherford B. Hayes, was evident throughout his life and career.

Early Life and Education

Lucy Ware Webb was born into a politically progressive family. Her father, James Webb, was a medical doctor originally from Lexington, Kentucky. James Webb was a supporter of the abolitionist movement who freed the slaves he inherited from his Kentucky family. After completing his medical training in Lexington, he moved to Chillicothe, Ohio—then the state capital—where he met Maria Cook, the daughter of politician and Ohio pioneer

she would become the first college-educated woman to serve as First Lady of the United States.

Married a Cincinnati Lawyer

A native of Delaware, Rutherford B. Hayes reportedly first noticed Lucy Webb in the summer of 1847, when she was only 15 years old. In *First Lady: The Life of Lucy Webb Hayes,* Emily Apt Geer wrote that Hayes considered Lucy "a bright sunny hearted little girl not quite old enough to fall in love with—and so I didn't." However, both Sophia Hayes, Rutherford's mother, and Maria Webb thought that the match would be a good one and encouraged contact between the two families. Hayes practiced law in Cincinnati, and seems to have met Lucy socially at least once before her graduation from college. Lucy and her mother left Cincinnati for several months following her graduation, but after their return to the city during the winter of 1851, Hayes began courting Lucy. In June of that year the couple became engaged; on December 30, 1852, they married at the Webb home in Cincinnati.

The couple remained in Cincinnati, first at the Webb home and then in their own residence nearby. During the early months of their marriage, Lucy Hayes convinced her husband to support abolitionist ideas; Geer noted that "by 1854, Rutherford, bolstered by the convictions of his wife and aware of the inhuman plight of slaves trying to escape through the gateway city of Cincinnati, was available at all hours to give legal aid to trapped or fugitive slaves." That same year, Lucy Hayes became interested in politics due to the emergence of the new anti-slavery Republican political party. Her husband, already inclined towards politics and encouraged by his wife's interest, let it be known that he was interested in public office. The Cincinnati city council appointed him to an unexpired term as head of the city's law department in 1858, and soon thereafter he won election to the post for a two-year term. From her college years onward, Lucy Hayes was also interested in the growing women's rights movement; she attended speeches on the matter with her sister-in-law, Fanny Platt, until Platt's death in 1856.

As the Hayes family grew in importance, it also grew in size. Hayes gave birth to their first son, Birchaud Austin, in November of 1853. In March of 1856, the couple had a second son, James Webb Cook. He was followed by Rutherford Platt in June of 1858. Shortly following childbirth, Hayes contracted a severe case of rheumatism, which occasionally recurred throughout the rest of her life. The strain of motherhood sometimes caused Hayes to suffer from migraine headaches, which also plagued her through the years to come.

Civil War Years

By early 1861, the first stirrings of the conflict that would become the grueling American Civil War had begun. Shortly after the first shots of the war were fired at Fort Sumter, Rutherford Hayes decided to enlist in the Union army. He was made major of the 23rd Ohio Volunteer Infantry, and was soon committed to lengthy service. Lucy Hayes, then pregnant with the couple's fourth child, remained in Cincinnati; she gave birth to Joseph Thompson in late December. Despite her husband's frequent letters, Lucy Hayes worried

settler Isaac Cook. The couple married on April 18, 1826, at the Cook family farm. The following year Maria gave birth to their first son, Joseph Thompson; another son, James Dewees, was born in 1928. Lucy Ware, named for her paternal grandmother, became the youngest member of the Webb family on August 28, 1831.

During the summer of 1833, James Webb traveled to Kentucky to conduct business and visit his father. There he contracted cholera and died; his father, mother, and brother also died during this cholera outbreak. Left fatherless at the age of two, young Lucy turned to her maternal grandfather, Isaac Cook. From him, she came to value the importance of temperance and signed a pledge to avoid drinking alcohol. The Webb family was financially secure, and all three Webb children attended school in Chillicothe.

In 1844 the Webbs moved to Delaware, Ohio, so that Joseph and James could attend the recently-founded Ohio Wesleyan University. Hayes attended college preparatory classes at the school and even some university courses; writing in *First Ladies of the United States: A Biographical Dictionary,* Robert P. Watson noted that Hayes "was something of an educational pioneer, as very few women of the time enrolled in universities alongside men." Soon, however, Maria Webb transferred her daughter to the Wesleyan Female College in Cincinnati, where Hayes did well academically and enjoyed her college years. In 1850 she was admitted to a college society, the Young Ladies Lyceum, before taking her degree. In an era when women rarely received a college education, Hayes was an anomaly; later,

about him and about the other soldiers fighting and dying in the conflict. In 1862 Rutherford Hayes was wounded during battle, and his wife set out for the capital to visit him in the hospital. Unable to find him at first, she traveled to many hospitals in the area before locating her husband. The following year she and her children relocated to Camp White to be with Rutherford Hayes. Shortly after their arrival, the youngest Hayes child died. While living at the camp, Lucy Hayes helped tend to wounded soldiers; she earned their respect for her compassion, becoming known as "Mother Lucy." In 1864 the fifth Hayes son, George, was born.

The Civil War drew to a close in 1865 and Rutherford Hayes returned home as a hero. His war record helped lead to his election to the United States Congress in 1865. Lucy Hayes was an active and supportive partner throughout her husband's political career; she regularly accompanied him to Washington, D.C., during sessions of Congress and became interested in Reconstruction. The following year three deaths struck the Hayes's immediate family: first toddler George, then Lucy Hayes's mother, Maria Webb, and soon after that, Rutherford Hayes's mother Sophia. However, Hayes was not reelected to Congress that year. In 1867 he resigned his seat to successfully run for Governor of Ohio as a supporter of the Congressional Radical Republicans, who stridently called for legal racial equality and hard-line reform in the South. That same year, Lucy Hayes gave birth to the Hayes's sixth child and only daughter, Fanny. Geer wrote that serving as governor's wife prepared Hayes for her years as First Lady, commenting that "she learned to identify herself completely with her husband's career and to balance her activities as a hostess with the demands of a young family."

Became Wife of a Governor

Because Rutherford Hayes was a Republican governor and both houses of the Ohio Congress had a Democratic majority, he had little hope of accomplishing significant legislative action. Instead, he worked to reform prisons, hospitals, and other public institutions in the state. Lucy Hayes visited many public institutions to raise public awareness of and support for her husband's programs, and on her own helped a group of volunteers establish a home for soldiers' orphans near Xenia, Ohio. Rutherford Hayes won reelection as governor in 1869, but did not run for a third term in 1871. The Hayes family—recently expanded by the addition of one final child, Scott—returned to private life for only a short time before Rutherford Hayes's interest in politics led him to campaign for office. He narrowly won election to a third gubernatorial term in 1875. This election practically guaranteed that Hayes would be a strong contender for the Republican presidential nomination the following year.

Rutherford Hayes was nominated for and won the Presidency in 1876, carrying the electoral—although not the popular—vote. His win was contested for months, and until the time of his inauguration, Hayes questioned whether he would take office. Despite this, Hayes and his wife enjoyed popular support upon entering the White House. With the Hayes administration came the end of Reconstruction, as the nation—and Congress—lost its drive for reform more

than a decade after the close of the Civil War. Few other notable events marked Hayes's years in office.

Presided Over a Happy White House

Lucy Hayes's official White House biography commented that "she entered the White House with confidence gained from her long and happy married life, her knowledge of political circles, her intelligence and culture, and her cheerful spirit." She quickly became recognized as a successful First Lady, admirably performing her duties as hostess and offering private and public support to her husband. The Hayes' often entertained friends, creating what Watson called "a fun and active White House" that was home to three children, two dogs, a Siamese cat, a bird, and a goat. In 1877 the Hayes celebrated their silver wedding anniversary at the White House.

Because of Lucy Hayes's dedication to the temperance movement, she and her husband barred all alcohol from the White House. This act earned Hayes the nickname of "Lemonade Lucy" as well as some public derision, and remains one of her most-remembered acts. Evidence suggests that the rule of temperance may have been suspended for visiting dignitaries on a handful of occasions. Lucy Hayes also initiated the annual White House Easter Egg Roll, a popular activity for children to this day.

Later Years and Legacy

Hayes, along with her husband, returned to Ohio at the end of Rutherford Hayes's term in 1881, Hayes not wishing to run for a second term. They settled at Spiegel Grove, a family property in Fremont. Although Lucy Hayes was invited to take an active role in the Women's Christian Temperance Union, she declined participation, aside from leading a few prayers at local meetings, most likely because the organization was somewhat controversial. She served as president of the national Woman's Home Missionary Society of the Methodist Episcopal Church from 1880 until her death. In this role she continued her lifelong work to improve the lives of other members of society.

Hayes died on June 25, 1889, at Spiegel Grove, as the result of a stroke. She was buried at Spiegel Grove State Park in Fremont. Today, scholars and historians primarily remember her for her abilities as hostess and supportive partner during her husband's political career, particularly his time in the White House. Geer also noted that Lucy Hayes's educational background, concern for social welfare, and active interest in politics "enhanced the role of women in the American social and political structure." Although Hayes never assumed the mantle of "new woman" that some of her day tried to assign to her, she was nonetheless in some ways a pioneer and an example for later generations of women to follow.

Books

American First Ladies, edited by Robert P. Watson, Salem, 2002.

Davis, Mrs. John, *Lucy Webb Hayes: A Memorial Sketch,* Cranston & Curts, 1892.

Geer, Emily Apt, *First Lady: The Life of Lucy Webb Hayes,* Kent State University Press, 1984.

Watson, Robert P., *First Ladies of the United States: A Biographical Dictionary,* Lynne Rienner Publishers, 2001.

Online

Biography Resource Center Online, Gale Group, 2002, http://galenet.galegroup.com/servlet.BioRc (November 26, 2007).
"Lucy Ware Webb Hayes," The White House, http://www.white house.gov/history/firstladies/fh29.html (December 13, 2007).
☐

Robert A. Heinlein

American science fiction writer Robert A. Heinlein (1907-1988) was among the critical figures of the science fiction genre, advancing it beyond adventure stories in extraterrestrial settings. In Heinlein's hands, science fiction became a vehicle for exploring serious philosophical and social themes.

Heinlein had a strongly libertarian streak that led him into seemingly contradictory outlooks in his fiction. The militaristic themes of one of his most popular novels, 1959's *Starship Troopers,* led some critics to classify him as an adherent of extreme right-wing views. Yet in the 1960s Heinlein, thanks to the exploration of unconventional sexuality in his *Stranger in a Strange Land* (1961) and other books, was lionized by members of the leftist student counterculture in the United States. Heinlein himself, however, saw no contradiction. In a letter to writer Alfred Bester, quoted by Brian Doherty in *Reason,* he wrote that both *Starship Troopers* and *Stranger in a Strange Land* dealt with the idea that "a man, to be truly human, must be unhesitatingly willing at all times to lay down his life for his fellow man. Both [novels] are based on the twin concepts of love and duty—and how they are related to the survival of our race."

Drawn to Astronomy

Robert Anson Heinlein was born in Butler, Missouri, on July 7, 1907, while his family was living in the home of his mother's father, Alva Lyle, a physician whose strong moral example influenced Heinlein greatly as a young man. The family soon moved to Kansas City, Missouri. The spectacular appearance of Halley's Comet in 1910 had a major impact on Heinlein, stimulating an interest in astronomy that lasted all through his childhood and youth. He hoped for a time to become an astronomer, and he was a voracious consumer of astronomy books at the Kansas City Public Library.

Although Heinlein did not turn to writing himself until he was in his early 30s, he had already become interested in science fiction as a student at Kansas City's Central High School. He read both new works and classics of the genre such as those by Jules Verne and H.G. Wells, "whose influence on his work," noted the *Times* of London, "is clear."

After briefly attending the University of Missouri, Heinlein entered the U.S. Naval Academy in 1925. After graduating four years later he was commissioned as an ensign and shipped out on the U.S.S. Lexington battleship. In 1933, however, while serving on the U.S.S. Roper, he contracted tuberculosis and was discharged as medically unfit for service, having reached the rank of lieutenant.

Heinlein cast about for a new career in the 1930s, trying out several different ventures in an effort to support himself and his wife Leslyn, whom he had married in 1932. He attended the University of California at Los Angeles briefly; owned and operated the Shively & Sophie Lodes silver mine in Silver Plume, Colorado, in 1934 and 1935; sold real estate; and, in 1938, ran for the California State Assembly from the district that included his home in Southern California's Laurel Canyon. Heinlein's venture into politics went nowhere, and his financial situation worsened.

In late 1938 Heinlein spotted a notice in the magazine *Thrilling Wonder Stories,* urging unknown authors to submit stories and offering a $50 prize (which was actually just the publication's normal pay rate). Within four days he had written "Life-Line," a story about a machine that can predict when a person will die. Pleased with the story, Heinlein sent it not to *Thrilling Wonder Stories* but to the more prestigious *Astounding Science Fiction.* The story was accepted, and Heinlein, earning $70 on its publication, applied himself industriously to his writing. He published so many stories over the next three years that he had to use pseudonyms— editors tended to avoid publishing two stories by the same author in the same issue of a magazine, but by using names such as Anson McDonald, Lyle Monroe, Caleb Saunders, John Riverside and Simon York, Heinlein was able to increase his income. From the beginning, Heinlein's stories were more than adventures of dueling spaceships; many of them imagined aspects of a potential future human society. In fact, as a biography of Heinlein in the *St. James Guide to Science Fiction Writers* contended, "One could argue that all of Heinlein, all of his themes and obsessions, are fully developed in these early stories and novella. The magic years, in fact, are 1939–42."

Served as Engineer in Wartime

Heinlein took time off from writing during World War II, attempting to enlist in the military after the Japanese attack on Pearl Harbor. He was rejected due to lung scarring, so he signed on as a civilian engineer at the Mustin Field Naval Experimental Air Station near Philadelphia. Heinlein convinced fellow science fiction writers Isaac Asimov and L. Sprague de Camp to join him at the station, and the three worked on projects that turned out to have applicability to their fiction; Heinlein worked on high-altitude pilot suits (one of his most successful postwar novels was *Have Space Suit— Will Travel*), and near the war's end he wrote two letters unsuccessfully urging the U.S. Navy to become involved with space travel. The space program eventually fell under the administrative umbrella of the Air Force.

After the war Heinlein returned to writing full-time, quickly building on his former successes. In the heady atmosphere of the late 1940s, when the future seemed full of limitless possibilities but also dangers (Americans first began to come to grips with the threat of nuclear annihilation), his audience grew, and he succeeded in placing stories not only in science fiction periodicals but also in the *Saturday Evening Post* and other general-interest magazines. His marriage to his wife Leslyn dissolved, and he married biochemist and Navy officer Virginia "Ginny" Gerstenfeld. She became an important collaborator in Heinlein's career, often discussing potential story ideas with him.

Beginning with *Rocket Ship Galileo* in 1947, Heinlein also wrote stories for young readers. For the most part these differed from his books for adults only in their omission of sexual material, and several of them were later reissued in editions aimed at adult audiences. Heinlein helped foster the modern science fiction film industry, co-writing a screenplay for *Rocket Ship Galileo;* the film was released as *Destination Moon* in 1950. Heinlein's second young adult novel, *Space Cadet*, served as the basis for the television series *Tom Corbett: Space Cadet*, which ran from 1951 to 1956. Many of Heinlein's young adult novels, which included *Farmer in the Sky* (1950), *The Rolling Stone* (1952), and *Starman Jones* (1953), helped to stoke American excitement about the coming era of space exploration, which began with the launch of the Soviet Union's Sputnik orbiter in 1957.

The last of these young adult novels was *Starship Troopers* (1959), which told the story of an infantryman of the future who goes into battle against a race of giant alien bugs. The novel frankly expressed Heinlein's admiration for

the armed forces as an institution; responding to charges that he had glorified the military, Heinlein (as quoted in the *National Review*) retorted, "I hope I accomplished [just] that. . . . The infantryman . . . needs some glorifying. That's the least I can do." *Starship Troopers* embodied Heinlein's strong opposition to Communism—the alien insects, a regimented force lacking in individuality, symbolized the forces of the totalitarian Communist state—but perhaps its most controversial feature was Heinlein's depiction and seeming endorsement of a society in which only members of the armed forces and those involved in other forms of public service are allowed to vote. In 1997 *Starship Troopers* was made into a hit film by Dutch-American director Paul Verhoeven.

Wrote Novel of Free Love

Heinlein's next book, however, was anything but militaristic, and it was unlike anything that had been published in the science fiction field thus far. *Stranger in a Strange Land* (1961) told the story of a Martian named Valentine Michael Smith who comes to Earth and establishes a religious movement called the Church of All Worlds, whose members live in communes and engage in a variety of non-monogamous sexual practices, including group sex. Heinlein was writing well in advance of the full flowering of the 1960s student counterculture, but sales of the book shot upward in the mid-1960s as students began to question established lifestyles. The 1967 Crosby, Stills & Nash song "Triad" was a Heinlein tribute. To get *Stranger in a Strange Land* published Heinlein had to excise some of the sexual material and shorten the book considerably, but an unexpurgated version was issued in 1990. Both *Starship Troopers* and *Stranger in a Strange Land* won science fiction's Hugo awards; Heinlein had already won for *Double Star* in 1956 and would win again with *The Moon Is a Harsh Mistress* in 1967.

Heinlein and his wife moved back to California in 1967, settling in the Santa Cruz area, and, as they had in Colorado, designing a unique new house of their own. Later they moved to Carmel. In 1969 Heinlein and his contemporary Arthur C. Clarke appeared as guests on CBS television news coverage of the Apollo spacecraft moon landing that year. By that time he was regarded, along with Clarke and Isaac Asimov, as one of the three greatest living science fiction writers, but he did not rest on his laurels; despite mounting health problems, he published several major novels in the 1970s and 1980s. Most of them, like mainstream fiction releases but unlike most science fiction, initially appeared in hardback editions.

I Will Fear No Evil (1970), another book in which Heinlein speculated on the possibilities opened up by unconventional social arrangements, dealt with a young woman who has received a brain transplant from a dying businessman and is then impregnated with his frozen sperm. He nearly died from a peritonitis infection just as the book was being published but recovered to write *Time Enough for Love* (1973) and *The Number of the Beast* (1980), both massive in scope. Heinlein's novel *Friday* (1982) was one of several Heinlein books with female protagonists, or important female characters, who went beyond the sidekick roles to which they were frequently assigned in early science fiction. Heinlein published three more novels in the 1980s: *Job: A Comedy of Justice* (1984), *The Cat Who Walks Through Walls: A Comedy of Manners* (1985), and his swan song, *To Sail beyond the Sunset: The Life and Loves of Maureen Johnson, Being the Memoirs of a Somewhat Irregular Lady* (1987). The recipient of numerous awards in his final years, including the first-ever Grand Master Nebula Award from the Science Fiction Writers of America in 1975, Heinlein died in his sleep on May 8, 1988. He was cremated, and his ashes were scattered at sea with military honors. In 2003 a trust established in Heinlein's name inaugurated the Heinlein Prize, gives a periodic award of $500,000 for advances in the commercial uses of space flight. The Heinlein Archives, housed at the University of California at Santa Cruz, were posted online beginning in 2007 with an installment of 106,000 pages. As of that year, a two-volume biography of Heinlein by William H. Patterson Jr. was in preparation.

Books

Franklin, H. Bruce, *Robert A. Heinlein: America as Science Fiction,* Oxford, 1980.
St. James Guide to Science Fiction Writers, 4th ed., St. James Press, 1996.

Periodicals

Guardian (London, England), December 19, 1997.
National Review, June 10, 1988.
New York Times, March 10, 2004; October 2, 2005.
Reason, August-September 2007.
San Jose Mercury News, September 20, 2007.
Times (London, England), May 11, 1988.

Online

Contemporary Authors Online, Gale, 2007, http://galenet.gale group.com/servlet/BioRC (December 23, 2007).
''Heinlein,'' http://www.wegrokit.com/bio.htm (December 23, 2007).
''Robert A. Heinlein: A Biography by William H. Patterson Jr.,'' Robert A. Heinlein Society, http://www.heinleinsociety.org/ CentennialReader/robert.html (December 23, 2007). □

Frank Herbert, Jr.

The novels of American author Frank Herbert (1920-1986), particularly the series that began with *Dune* (1965), set new standards of complexity in the field of science fiction, imagining entire worlds and drawing on diverse fields of human knowledge in an attempt to depict large interconnected systems.

*D*une itself is widely regarded as a masterpiece. ''Described as 'science fiction for people who do not read science fiction,' '' noted the *Times* of London, England, the novel ''ranged widely over biology, astronomy, philosophy, politics, physiology, religion, psychology and ecology, and was rated by devotees as one of science fiction's most comprehensively realized achievements.'' *Dune* was one of several Herbert books that explored linkages among ecological structures, and social and political conflicts, including religion. He foresaw in his writings many aspects of ecology as a general idea, and his works in general are marked by a seriousness and ambition that were new to the science fiction genre.

Planned Writing Career Early

Frank Herbert Jr. was born in Tacoma, Washington, on October 8, 1920. His father moved from job to job in the southern Puget Sound area in the 1920s, working as a salesman, motorcycle patrol officer, and bus line operator. In 1928 the family moved to a farm near Burley, Washington. The younger Frank Herbert grew up tending to chickens and cows but was intellectually curious. He carried books with him wherever he went, and his classmates thought of him as a genius type who knew everything. Herbert liked adventure stories and read science fiction classics by Edgar Rice Burroughs and H.G. Wells when he was very young. When Herbert was eight, he announced to his family that he wanted to be a writer.

At first that ambition took the form of preparing for a journalism career. World War II interrupted his plans, and he served as a photographer in the United States Naval Reserve until his discharge in 1943. Herbert then landed a job as a copyeditor with the *Oregon Journal* newspaper in Portland. From then on, until the runaway success of *Dune* made him self-sufficient, Herbert worked in the journalism field even though his energies were focused elsewhere; new jobs were easy to find in the burgeoning cities of the West. He moved from job to job, going as far afield as Glendale in southern California and working for a time for the *San Francisco Examiner.* Herbert's journalism career was interrupted by stints as an oyster diver and as a jungle survival instructor. His restlessness also showed up in his attitude toward classes at the University of Washington, where he took classes in 1946 and 1947 but failed to graduate, believing that he should study only subjects in which he was interested.

Herbert's first publications were adventure stories he sold to *Esquire* and *Doc Savage* magazines in the 1940s. Those had already been published by the time he took creative writing classes at Washington, and in his class he met another published author, Beverly Ann Stuart, who had landed a slot in *Modern Romance.* The two were married in 1947; Herbert had been married once before, to teenager Flora Parkinson in 1941, but that marriage had ended in divorce after producing a daughter, Penny. Beverly Herbert served as her husband's editor, sounding board, and confidante, and her work as an advertising copywriter often paid the family's bills during slow periods during Herbert's career—of which there were many during the early years. They had two sons, Brian and Bruce.

Working as a feature writer for the *Tacoma Times* in the late 1940s, Herbert wrote science fiction short stories and sent them to magazines. *Startling Stories* published Herbert's ''Looking for Something'' in 1952, but for the most part he accumulated rejection slips. He continued to write short stories through much of the 1950s, but only about 20 of them were published over his entire career—a small number in comparison with most of his successful contemporaries in the science fiction field. He had more luck, however, when he turned to the longer form of the novel, where he could let his imagination run wild. His very first science fiction novel, *The Dragon in the Sea,* won the International Fantasy Award in 1956.

Explored Undersea Setting

The Dragon in the Sea had an adventure setting that was typical of science fiction of the period: a small submarine or "subtug" is assigned to intercept fuel shipments in a future world war between the U.S. and a group of fictitious Eastern Powers with affinities to the Communist East Bloc. But the focus of Herbert's novel was not really on adventure, nor on international politics. Instead Herbert examined the behavior of a totally closed society—his undersea subtug crew, which is threatened by tensions and divisions. The book foreshadowed Herbert's later work in several respects, including his attention to detail: his description of submarine controls was so thorough that parts of it were later incorporated into designs used by Britain's Naval Intelligence Service.

"Despite his skillful handling of technical description," noted the *St. James Guide to Science Fiction,* "Herbert, in the tradition of American romanticism, opposes the mechanistic with the natural and organic to show the superiority of the intuitive biological organism." The limits of human technical intelligence interested him throughout his career, and the theme of the understanding of biological systems, at a time when the idea of ecology was still quite new, played a major role in his next novel, *Dune.* For this sprawling work, Herbert spent six years writing and doing research, expanding on an idea he had while observing a sand dune preservation project being carried out on Oregon's coastline. His research encompassed the 12-volume *The Golden Bough,* a classic anthropological study of mythology and religion, and the *Lotus Sutras* of Mahayana Buddhism.

Dune, like most of Herbert's fiction, was not particularly easy to read; its virtues lie in its complexity, detail, and originality rather than in tale-spinning skills. The book accumulated 23 rejections before it was serialized in *Analog Science Fiction* in 1963 and published by Chilton two years later, with Herbert earning an advance of $7,500. Eventually the novel would be translated into 14 languages, with sales of approximately 12 million copies worldwide. Herbert rewrote much of the text between the periodical and book publications. *Dune* was made into a film in 1984 by acclaimed director David Lynch, but many admirers of the original novel criticized the film adaptation.

The vast plot of *Dune* cannot be successfully summarized in a few words. The novel spans several worlds, describing the evolution of an intergalactic empire and its ruling House of Atreides; it tells the story of a new leader, Paul Atreides, who visits a desert planet called Arrakis that is the source of a spice called Melange. Melange is a fuel necessary for galactic travel and can confer special talents,

such as psychic powers, on those who use it. "Metaphorically," noted the Minneapolis *Star Tribune,* "it is everything that the human race has ever valued and fought over, from salt to diamonds, from precious metals to atomic secrets." The core of the novel is formed by Herbert's elaborate descriptions of Arrakis and its inhabitants, the Fremen, whose society was modeled by Herbert partly on Arab societies and their adaptations to desert life. Melange, Paul Atreides learns, is closely connected with a species of giant sandworms he found on Arrakis—and he comes to understand the Web site of life on the planet in intricate detail. No similar description of an intricate biological system had ever been attempted before in science fiction, and Herbert's originality was recognized with a Nebula award in 1965. The following year he shared the Hugo award with author Roger Zelazny.

Expanded Themes in Series

Herbert remains known for *Dune* above any of his other novels, of which there are about 30 in all. He never again took the time to conceptualize the plot and background of a novel in such detail, and most of his other books received mixed critical receptions. Some critics, however, believe that an understanding of the other five books that constitute the so-called Dune Chronicles is necessary for a full appreciation of Herbert's intentions; the later books continue the story of *Dune* and expand upon themes of the original book. The five *Dune* sequels completed by Herbert were *Dune Messiah* (1970), *Children of Dune* (1976), *God Emperor of Dune* (1981), *Heretics of Dune* (1984), and *Chapterhouse: Dune* (1985). At his death Herbert was at work on a seventh *Dune* novel in collaboration with his son Brian, who completed it in 1999 as *Dune: House Atreides.* Brian Herbert and Kevin J. Anderson issued an eighth *Dune* novel, *Sandworms of Dune,* in 2007.

In between the volumes of this mammoth series, Herbert wrote numerous other books between the appearance of *Dune* and the end of his life. This collection included other books linked into series; *Whipping Star* (1970) and *The Dosadi Experiment* (1977) featured a secret agent named Jorj X. McKie who has been married 55 times. McKie must contend with the phenomenon of adaptation in alien cultures; *The Dosadi Experiment* deals, like *Dune,* with a race of beings that has evolved superior powers in response to the harsh environment in which they live. Herbert's Pandora series began with *Destination: Void* (1966) and continued with *The Jesus Incident* (1979) and *The Lazarus Effect* (1983; the latter two books were co-written with Bill Ransom). *Destination: Void,* among Herbert's most popular novels, tells of a spaceship crew that can survive only if it can raise the ship's computer to the level of human intelligence.

Herbert's *The White Plague* (1982), unlike most of his books, was set on a recognizable Earth in the near future. It is narrated from the point of a view of a scientist who, deranged by the deaths of his wife and children at the hands of terrorists, becomes a terrorist himself: through genetic manipulation he develops a new bubonic plague virus that affects only women. After he unleashes the virus, nations and their scientists must put aside their usual ways of interacting in order to contain it. Of all of Herbert's novels, only one, 1972's *Soul Catcher,* was not science fiction; it was set among Native Americans.

Herbert died in Madison, Wisconsin, on February 11, 1986, after a long struggle with cancer. But the influence of his writings, *Dune* above all, only increased after his death. *Dune* itself was made into a five-hour television miniseries in the year 2000, eliciting more positive reviews than the 1984 film had received; one reason for its success was that the novel's complex three-part structure was much better suited to a five-hour miniseries format than to the two and a half hours to which a big-screen adaptation was restricted. By that time, *Dune* had become one of the most successful science fiction novels of all time, and top science fiction writers who had once lived hand-to-mouth in the 1950s could command six-figure advances for major projects. Herbert was seen as one of the thinkers whose ideas had spawned the environmental movement, and the *Dune* novels had become the center of a small subculture with its own reference text, *The Dune Encyclopedia* (1984). Brian Herbert issued a biography of his father, *Dreamer of Dune,* in 2003.

Books

Concise Dictionary of American Literary Biography Supplement: Modern Writers, 1900-1998, Gale Research, 1998.

Herbert, Brian, *Dreamer of Dune: The Biography of Frank Herbert,* Tor Books, 2004.

McNelly, Willis E., *The Dune Encyclopedia,* Putnam, 1984.

St. James Guide to Science Fiction Writers, 4th ed., St. James Press, 1996.

Touponce, William F., *Frank Herbert,* Twayne, 1988.

Periodicals

Detroit Free Press, June 10, 2002.

Seattle Post-Intelligencer, August 3, 2007.

Star-Tribune (Minneapolis, MN), December 1, 2000.

Times (London, England), February 13, 1986.

Online

"Biography: Frank Herbert," The Dune Novels official Web site, http://www.dunenovels.com/bios/frank.html (December 24, 2007).

Contemporary Authors Online, Gale, 2007, http://galenet.gale group.com/servlet/BioRC (December 24, 2007).

"Frank (Patrick) Herbert (1920-1986)," Books and Writers, http://www.kirjasto.sci.fi/fherbert.htm (December 24, 2007).

□

Benny Hill

The cherub-faced master of slapstick and double-entendre, Benny Hill (1924-1992) revived the nearly forgotten art of burlesque comedy for British audiences during his forty-year run on British television. When his works were re-edited and syndicated during the late 1970s and early 1980s, he became an international comedy star. As his worldwide fame

peaked, Hill's occasionally bawdy humor was deemed politically incorrect in certain quarters, and his comedic career ended in controversy.

Began As a Music Hall Performer

Born Alfred Hawthorn Hill on January 21, 1924, he was the son of Alfred Hill Sr., a manager of a surgical goods store in Canal Walk, Southampton, and the former Helen Cave, a clerk at Toogoods Rolling Mills. The senior Hill had previously harbored show-business ambitions, running away from home to join the circus when he was 16 years old. Although he mainly cleaned animal cages and put up tents, Hill's father was allowed a few treasured turns as a clown before his World War I army enlistment cut his brief career short. Later, the elder Hill would dress up his young namesake as a clown and the boy would entertain his mother, father, and older brother Leonard with his antics.

A self-professed show-off, young Alfie Hill first began performing in school, teaming up with friends to do impersonations of the Mills Brothers or in solo turns, Louis Armstrong and Jack Buchanan. Besides being an excellent mimic, Hill was a fairly accomplished musician who—at his father's urging—sang and played guitar and drums. The Hill family often took the youngster to nearby Music Halls to see variety shows laden with pretty girls and top-flight comedians. In later years, Hill would claim that he was not a music hall performer in the classic tradition, but he listed among his early influences an obscure British comic named Peter Waring and "cheeky chappie" Max Miller, as well as American movie comic Danny Kaye. These variety performers quickly moved from sketch to song to monologue with the same sort of ease that Hill himself later exhibited. Under the approving eye of his family, the youngster donned a red-checkered suit and began performing jokes and routines that he heard at the music halls. This led to several semi-pro appearances at local working men's clubs where he impressed onlookers with his confident delivery and timing.

Despite occasional bookings, Hill—who finished school at age 14—found it necessary to take employment as a coal company clerk, stockroom clerk, and milkman, where he was subjected to the ire of housewives fed up with war-time rationing. These short-lived jobs only added to his ardor to be in show-business full-time. At the age of 16, he hired on as a guitarist, drummer, and occasional singer for an aggregation called Ivy Lilywhite and Her Boys. Never a great vocalist, Hill could croon hits of the day passably enough, but his mind continually wandered back to comedy. Before Hill arrived, the comedy had been handled by the group's trumpeter, but always looking for an opening, the youngster began working more bits of business into the show. Playing Boy Scout huts and working men's clubs, he developed enough confidence to strike out on his own in war-torn London.

Hill was turned down by every working show in London, but eventually he found regular employment as a property man and assistant stage-manager at the East Ham Palace. When many of the town's actors left the stage to fight in World War II, the 17-year-old performer got the chance to take on bit parts and even play straight man to comedian Hal Bryan during the runs of Follow That Fun and Send Him Victorious. Constant moving about to various cheap rooming houses resulted in the youngster missing his draft notice until he was 19 years old. Once conscripted, he served in Royal Electrical Mechanical Engineers as a driver. Hill proved an unremarkable and undecorated soldier, but he was able to forge a connection with the post-war touring company of Stars in Battledress where he garnered valuable experience doing his stand-up routines and emceeing the show. It was during this era that the young comic began to bill himself as Benny Hill, after one of his American comedy favorites, Jack Benny.

The late 1940s was a tough time for Hill. He worked for small pay when he worked at all, but he dreamt big. Occasionally he would latch on to a small part in a traveling variety show, but he made his biggest early splash as a straight man for comic Reg Varney. "As a 'feed,' Benny was brilliant," Varney told John Smith, author of The Benny Hill Story. "We became very close, and in fact we became so good that he had only to look at me and he knew just what was required when we were on the stage together." Working for three seasons in a show called Gay Times, Hill and Varney proved a successful team. Afterwards, they were hired for a 1950 show called Sky High. As a bonus, Hill was given a solo spot during the show's first half, but he bombed horribly. "I know it's awful to say," Varney told Smith, "but Benny's act was always the weak link in that show." When the spot was canceled, Hill decided that he did not want a career as a straight man, and after finding a replacement, he and Varney parted ways.

Made His Name on Radio and Television

Hill made his first television appearance in 1949 on a show hosted by Alfred Marks and Vera Lynn called Music-Hall, but his still undeveloped monology style fell flat. Although television was fast making in-roads in London, radio was still the mass media powerhouse and Hill secured guest appearances on such programs as Henry Hall's Guest Night, Listen My Children, The Third Division, Variety Bandbox, Beginners Please, and Midday Music Hall. These low-paying spots did little for his languishing career as a solo performer and he was desperately in need of a showcase. Despite the disparaging attitude of his peers concerning the new medium, Hill began to write comedy sketches with television in mind. Finding a sympathetic ear at the British Broadcasting Corporation's (BBC) television division, he filmed several sketches, gags, and black outs based on his observation of everyday people for the 1951 program Hi There! Compared to his stage act, the show—which featured an early version of his Fred Scuttle character—was well received. Subsequently, the BBC offered the 26-year-old comic a regular spot on their radio show Anything Goes.

Although Hill understood that television was his future, he continued to take roles on radio sitcoms such as Educating Archie and its follow up Archie's the Boy. His popularity on the rise, he emceed such televised programs as The Centre Show (1953) and Showcase (1954), live variety shows that smartly showcased his ability to jump in and out of quick sketches and underplay jokes. By 1955, Hill was given a series of variety specials dubbed The Benny Hill Show. Working double-entendre and non-sequitors into his monologues and wacky mime into his sketches, his work earned him the London Daily Mail's TV Personality of the Year Award. Steady television work ensured his rise in popularity as stage performer and he proved quite a success starring with Shani Wallis in the live production of Fine Fettle. However, disquieted by audiences who favored the routines he performed on television over new material, the comic eventually eschewed live performance altogether.

Like his contemporary Peter Sellers, Hill hoped to parlay his popularity on radio and television into success on the big screen. The seldom seen 1956 mystery spoof Who Done It? proved to be his only starring cinematic appearance, however. In later years, he was smartly used as a character actor in such films as Those Magnificent Men in Their Flying Machines, (1965) Chitty Chitty Bang Bang, (1968) and The Italian Job (1969). Showing a good business head, Hill also re-used the better audio comedy moments from his television work as part of a series of BBC radio Light Programme's titled Star Parade, Benny Hill Time, and Benny's Bandbox.

Apart from a long series of filmed commercials for various products, Hill's most successful spin-off came as a recording artist. Starting in 1961, he began recording a series of novelty songs for the Pye l that routinely earned him airplay and included such hits as "Gather in the Mush-rooms" (#24 UK, 1961), "Transistor Radio" (#12 UK, 1961), and "The Harvest of Love" (#20 UK, 1963). Later recording for EMI, Hill's song about one of his own characters, "Ernie (Fastest Milkman in the West)," became a number one hit in the UK in 1971 and was successfully revived after his death (#29 UK, 1992).

Dubbed King Leer

Television comedy exploded in Britain during the 1960s the same way it had previously in American during the 1950s. Hill was mindful, however, of how quickly television ate up material and he limited his output to several specials each year. Initially hosting standard variety format episodes, the BBC persuaded the comic to appear in his own sitcom for three seasons. The show was successful, but Hill preferred to work in sketch comedy and negotiated his way back to a BBC variety show by 1967. The deal allowed him complete creative control over the entire product he delivered for air.

From that point onward, Hill wrote everything for his televised specials without filtering or interference from the BBC. The comic's creative method was deceptively simple. He traveled widely, obsessively writing gags and visual sequences as they occurred to him. When he compiled enough material, he began filming and editing shows. The resultant product mixed filmed segments, quick sketches, monologues and silly songs in a zingy, speedy format that predated the American smash *Rowan and Martin's Laugh-In.* Indeed, the cheeky comic hoped he could parlay his UK success into an American series, but his two summer replacement specials for CBS's enormously popular *Red Skelton Show* proved to be ratings failures.

Hill stunned the British entertainment world in 1969 when he allowed his contract with the BBC to lapse and then signed with newly licensed Thames Television channel. Now filming in color and working with his dependable stock company of second bananas which included Henry McGee, Bob Todd, and the little bald-headed man Jackie Wright, Hill fashioned the work that would eventually introduce him to comedy fans worldwide. In 1979, Thames re-edited many of Hill's specials into half-hour programs and began to syndicate them around the globe. This, along with the emerging home video trend of the of the 80s, made Hill an international star.

The comedian's act, based in burlesque and music hall double-entendre, had always featured scantily clad females as props. During a silent movie type chase scene with Boots Randolph's hit "Yakety Sax" blaring in the background, some fetching female was inevitably featured in various stages of undress for a quick moment or two. When standards for family entertainment changed during the late 70s, however, Hill amped up his use of women as props. In 1979, he hired four beautiful show girls and dubbed them Hill's Angels—actress Jane Leeves from *Frasier* was briefly a member—and began building his more suggestive brand of comedy wound them. His longtime fans, who had seen no worse on Dean Martin's old variety show, loved it. Younger viewers either dismissed him as out-dated or complained of his crude insensitivity. For their part, the press began to refer to Hill as King Leer. Although Hill did cut back on the raunchier material, the damage to his reputation had been done. By 1989, despite strong ratings, Thames Television terminated the comic's contract. His last batch of specials were independently produced and distributed.

Heart problems hospitalized the 67-year-old comedian on at least two occasions, but he rejected the idea of surgery. On April 20, 1992, he was found dead in his home by his friend/director Dennis Kirkland. Next to him was an unsigned contract to create a new series for ITV. At the time of his death, Hill was reportedly worth ten million pounds, yet he lived like a member of the suburban working class. He did not own a car and—always a loner—he never married or spawned any children. The comedian's will left everything to his parents, brother and sister, all of whom had passed away before he did.

Death has neither curtailed Hill's popularity nor controversy. The DVD age brought all of his works into the marketplace again, but in late 2007, BBC America announced that it would no longer air Hill's shows because they were seeking a different image. The prior year Jemima Lewis, writing for *The Independent,* questioned the politically correct forces that brought the twinkly-eyed comic down before concluding, "Hill wanted us to laugh at lechery, not condone it. Men who lusted after women usually came to a sticky end: Ernie the Milkman was slain with a rock bun hurled by his love rival, Two-Ton Ted from Teddington. It's old-fashioned and nostalgic, surprisingly clean fun[.]"

Books

Brown, Tony, Kutner, Jon & Warwick, Neil, *The Complete Book of the British Charts* Omnibus Press, 2000.
Smith, John, *The Benny Hill Story,* St. Martin's Press, 1989.
Smith, Ronald L., *Comedy on Record - The Complete Critical Discography,* Garland Publishing, 1988.

Online

"Benny Hill," *All Movie Guide,* http://www.allmovie.com (October 11, 2007).
"Benny Hill," *All Music Guide,* http://www.allmusic.com, (December 27, 2007).
"Benny Hill," Internet Movie Database, http://www.imdb.com (December 27, 2007).
"Benny Hill," Laughterlog.com, http://www.laughterlog.com, (December 27, 2007).
"Benny Hill," The Museum of Broadcast Communications, http://www.musuem.tv/archives/etv/H/htmlH/hillbenny/hillbenny.htm (December 27, 2007).
"Jemima Lewis: Why did the British disown Benny Hill?," *The Independent,* http://www.comment.independent.co.uk/commentators/article620206.ece, (May 26, 2006). □

Lewis Wickes Hine

During a career that spanned nearly four decades, photographer Lewis Wickes Hine (1874-1940) created some of the most unforgettable images of twentieth-century America.

Hine considered himself less an artist than a documentarian of both the social ills and industrial achievements in the United States. His photographs of children laboring in factories at the turn of the century helped sway public opinion in favor of new federal laws restricting the employment of minors. But Hine's best-known work may be the series of photographs he took each day during the construction of New York City's majestic Empire State Building. "Hine's photographs sealed its status as a stunning human endeavor," noted *New York Times* contributor Jim Rasenberger, "animating its steel and brick with something like soul."

Hine was born on September 26, 1874, in Oshkosh, Wisconsin, as the last of three children of Douglas Hill Hine and Sarah Hayes Hine. His father ran a restaurant in Oshkosh, but earlier had been a sign painter and Union Army soldier. Hine quit school at age 15, though he later completed his education with night school classes while holding down various jobs. He found a mentor in the form of an Oshkosh educator named Frank A. Manny, who encouraged him to pursue teaching as a career. In 1900, the year he turned 26, Hine entered the University of Chicago.

Immortalized Ellis Island Immigrants

Hine moved to New York City when Manny was named head of the Ethical Culture School, a progressive school that prided itself on serving as an academy for children from the working classes, as well as those from wealthy families whose parents were keen on the ideals of social justice. Manny hired Hine to teach nature studies and geography, while Hine continued his education at both Columbia University and New York University. In 1905 he earned the equivalent of a master's degree in education from New York University, which was called a master in pedagogy (Pd.M.). By this point he had also married a woman from Oshkosh, Sara Ann Rich, with whom he would have a son, Corydon Lewis Hine.

Hine took his first photographs around 1903, when Manny gave him a camera to document classes and events at the Ethical Culture School. Hine was so intrigued by the medium that he began devoting much of his spare time to mastering it. From 1904 to 1909 he regularly visited Ellis Island, the debarkation point for the thousands of new immigrants to America who had often spent their life savings on the journey. Hine's images would later serve as a crucial witness to this period of U.S. history, with *Antiques* writer Barbara Head Millstein calling his work here "perhaps the most complete pictorial examination of the great tide of humanity that entered this country at the turn of the century."

Hine quit his teaching job at the Ethical Culture School in 1908 in order to become a full-time photographer. Another of his most important photo essays was completed that year when he visited Pittsburgh, Pennsylvania, and photographed its impressive industrial architecture, particularly that of its steel plants. Back in New York City, he photographed the tenements where new immigrants lived, often in the most abject, squalid conditions. Many of these appeared in the magazine *Charities and the Commons,* which later changed its name to *Survey* but retained its focus as a journal of the settlement movement. This was a well-organized mission to improve the lives of the poor by establishing neighborhood centers that offered such services as child care and English language lessons.

Depicted Children in Factories

Hine's work came to the attention of the National Child Labor Committee (NCLC), a nonprofit organization set up in 1904 to end the practice of using children in factories and other workplaces. The use of children as menial laborers was an entirely legal practice at the time and would remain so well into the 1930s in many U.S. states. Like other progressive Americans, Hine was appalled at the conditions under which these youngsters toiled, often for a fraction of the wages paid to adults doing the same job. Not long after the NCLC received official government sanction to investigate and report on abuses, Hine was hired as its art director and began sneaking his camera into factories to document conditions. Taken on the sly in more than 20 different states, the photographs accompanied official reports submitted by the NCLC to bolster support for new labor laws—bitterly opposed by corporate America at the time—that would restrict what employers considered their right: to hire cheap child labor.

What made Hine's images all the more remarkable was that he never had permission from the employers to take the photographs, and instead talked his way into these workplaces by pretending to be a Bible salesperson or insurance agent. Once he made sure a manager was enough of a distance away, he quickly set up his camera on a tripod and snapped the shutter. At the time, this kind of indoor photography required the use of noxious flashlight powder, which left a cloud of telltale smoke. Hine would usually take some notes on the child's age, name, and job, often writing the details inside his pocket. Hine's images of boys working in the deadly coal mines in Pennsylvania and of little girls working the massive textile looms at cotton mills in the South were some of the first widely disseminated images of children at work in America. They were used for NCLC posters that featured slogans such as "Everybody Pays But Few Profit by Child Labor."

The American public was fully aware that many children never went to school, instead being forced to enter the working world because of their family's dire poverty. In large cities, it was a common sight to see young children selling newspapers or other goods on street corners, but few newspaper readers had ever been inside a genuine industrial workplace, with its massive machinery, where children as young as six were employed in the filthy and often dangerous conditions, nor were they privy to the many home-based sewing businesses which were common in New York City at the time. "Because of Hine, comfortable middle-class Americans were forced to look at children embroidering lace in airless tenements on New York's Lower East Side [or] cutting sardines in Eastport, Maine," wrote Elizabeth Winthrop in the *Smithsonian.*

Documented New Skyscraper

In 1918 Hine accepted a job offer from the American Red Cross to visually document the flood of refugees displaced in Europe in the aftermath of World War I. He spent several months between 1918 and 1919 shooting some 600 images, some of which were shown at exhibits he later organized for the American Red Cross Museum in Washington, D.C. Most of them, however, were lost for decades in the Red Cross archives until they were unearthed in the 1980s. They appeared in the 1988 volume *Lewis Hine In Europe: The Lost Photographs* by Daile Kaplan.

Hine preferred to call himself an interpretive photographer, a tag he seemed to have adopted not long after a 1920 show at the National Arts Club of New York City titled *Interpretation of Social and Industrial Conditions Here and Abroad.* But as the reform movement of the early decades of the twentieth century gave way to the postwar prosperity of the 1920s, Hine found himself out of step with the times. His only income came from freelance work over the next decade. In 1930 he was offered a job by an old friend named Belle Moskowitz (1877-1933), who had once been a New York City social worker and active in the settlement house movement. Moskowitz went on to a job as campaign manager for liberal New York State governor Al Smith (1873-1944) when he ran for the White House in 1928, but by 1930 she was serving as the publicist for New York City's most highly anticipated construction project, the Empire State Building.

At 102 stories, the Empire State Building was planned as the world's tallest building, and it kept that title for the first 40 years of its existence. Moskowitz offered Hine a job as the official photographer for the project, and he accepted. As the building's stories went up between May and November of 1930, he made a daily visual record of the construction. He was particularly fascinated by the ironworkers, who walked the beams without any fear of heights, and dubbed them the "sky boys." Many were Irish immigrants, but some came from Mohawk Indian communities in upstate New York and Canada, and were known for what seemed to be a genetic predisposition for fearlessness in the air. Hine's own task was challenging: he took his heavy camera and tripod up with him as the stories climbed higher, and finally resorted to locking himself in a makeshift steel box suspended from a crane. One of his images near the end of the project showed a final rivet being driven in a girder. Among the images was the now-famous *Icarus atop Empire State Building,* which shows a worker suspended from a giant loop of cable so far up that the Hudson River and part of New Jersey are visible in the background.

Hine's Empire State photographs were published in book form in 1932 as *Men at Work.* He wrote in the book's introduction, "Cities do not build themselves, machines cannot make machines, unless back of them all are the brains and toil of men. We call this the Machine Age. But the more machines we use the more do we need real men to make and direct them. . . . The more you see of modern machines, the more may you, too, respect the men who make them and manipulate them." As Rasenberger wrote, "Hine gave the men a degree of honor and immortality that is rarely bestowed on blue-collar workers. They, in turn, lent his photographs their exhilarating pride and grace, and inspired some of the greatest work of his life."

Worked for WPA

The rest of the 1930s were a moribund period for Hine and his camera. In 1933 he photographed Alabama dam-building projects in Wilson and Muscle Shoals on behalf of the Tennessee Valley Authority, but failed to receive credit when they were published. Between 1936 and 1937 he worked for the National Research Project of the Works Progress Administration (WPA), a federal agency created to alleviate massive unemployment during the Great Depression via large-scale public-works projects. For the WPA he photographed Rural Electrification Administration sites in Pennsylvania, Ohio, and New York State. Later in the decade he revisited the textile mills in North Carolina, New Hampshire, and other states he had photographed years before on behalf of the National Child Labor Committee. By contrast to his earlier images, "these later photographs are a poignant reminder that the worker was no longer simply a slave to the machine but had become subsumed by it," wrote Millstein. "The assembly line had triumphed."

One of Hine's last assignments, to depict life on America's railroads, came from *Fortune* magazine, and appeared in its June 1939 issue. In his last years, friends paid the rent on his house in Hastings-on-Hudson, New York, where he died after abdominal surgery on November 3, 1940. Decades later, as his work was rediscovered, his works began to rise significantly in value, some prints commanding as much as $50,000 at auction. In the late 1990s, an art world scandal over some of his prints erupted after rumors arose that Hine photographs purportedly sold as "vintage" prints had actually been printed from negatives long after Hine's death, by Walter Rosenblum, a young photographer he had once mentored.

Periodicals

Antiques, November 1998.
Atlantic Monthly, June 2003.
New York Times, April 23, 2006.
People, July 4, 1988.
Smithsonian, January 2002; September 2006. □

Xuan Huong Ho

Late eighteenth-century Vietnamese poet Ho Xuan Huong (fl. late 18th century-early 19th century) used her poetry to speak her mind against polygamy and the constraints on women in a male-dominated world.

Life or Legend?

While there is no record of Ho Xuan Huong's birth or death, scholars agree that she lived in a historically tumultuous time. In *Spring Essence:*

The Poetry of Ho Xuan Huong, translator John Balaban wrote that Ho was "born at the end of the second Lê Dynasty (1592-1788), a period of calamity and social disintegration," but that "warfare, starvation and corruption did not vanquish ... [her], but deepened [her] work." He added that "whatever the facts of her life, a legend of rich cultural significance and consistency has emerged."

Ho is believed to have been born in the Nghe An province and raised in Thang Long (now Hanoi). Most assume she received a classical literary education at the hands of her mother (whose given name may have been Ha), and that her father was Ho Phi Dien (1703-1786), or Ho Si Danh (1706-1783). Both were noted and respected scholars. According to Balaban, Ho's name, *Xuan Huong,* "may derive from the village in which she was raised, [and] means 'spring essence,' as in 'perfume' or 'scent of spring.'" The majority of details accepted as fact regarding Ho's life are pulled from the lines of her poetry or gleaned from verse written by her contemporaries. There are poems that mention her death, and various pieces of correspondence that link her with certain people at particular times. Some scholars have stated that she was not particularly attractive, that she was embarrassed by her relative poverty, and that she teased and taunted her husbands, but none of these assertions are proven.

Her father is thought to have died early, prompting the end of her attempts to educate herself and restricting her marriage choices. Most agree that she oversaw a popular tea shop, and was renowned for her wit and skill with words. Ho is said to have challenged a young man—identified as the Prefect of Vinh-Tuong—by giving him an intricate verse to finish. He completed it to her satisfaction, and she supposedly married him, taking the position of concubine or second wife. Upon her first husband's death, her second marriage was also as a second wife or concubine to an official whom she openly ridiculed in her poetry. Some scholars have produced chronological evidence that she could not have been married to the Prefect, while others, according to Balaban, have argued that "she never existed but was the fictional creation of some literary man-of-letters, sort of an Earl of Oxford argument." But Balaban asserted that "too much dense biographical evidence emerges from the poems for this to be true, along with her habitual way of looking at things and a unique range of diction."

A "Momentous Invention"

To understand the unique place Ho inhabits within the history of Vietnamese literature, one must look first at the script she wrote in, known as *Nom,* and described in *Poetry for Students* as a "nearly extinct ideographic Vietnamese script" that, today, can only be deciphered by a handful of people. In the *Anthology of Vietnamese Poems From the Eleventh through the Twentieth Centuries,* translator Huỳnh Sanh Thông explained that "Vietnamese scholars selected Chinese graphs for either their semantic equivalence or their phonetic similarity to Vietnamese words and, through various combinations, devised a writing system that they named the southern script.... As an instrument for representing the sounds of Vietnamese, [*Nom*] suffered from many limitations

and defects.... It presupposed a considerable knowledge of Chinese graphs on the part of both writers and readers. Then, too, it was never rigorously standardized but remained dependent on the skill and whim of anyone who chose to write in it; its inconsistencies and obscurities bedeviled anyone who tried to decipher it. [But] for all its shortcomings, it was a momentous invention. It freed Vietnamese poets from complete reliance on an alien medium [Chinese] and allowed them to speak in their own voice at last."

Poems as Riddles Wrapped in Enigmas

Ho's decision to compose and record her poetry in *Nom* was both spirited and unusual, considering that the majority of literature at the time was written in the dominant Chinese script, but it was perhaps not entirely unexpected, considering the pride Vietnamese culture places on its poetic heritage. As scholar Michael Wiegers suggested in *American Poetry Review,* "Centuries of war and invasion have seen physical art objects taken out of [Vietnam], and a harsh climate has made it difficult to preserve what remains. But poetry, portable and passed along by individual voices, has remained the most lasting of Vietnam's arts." In the *Journal of Asian Studies,* scholar John Spragens Jr. explained, "Vietnam is a country where poems still appear regularly in the pages of daily newspapers and popular magazines. Poetry is not incidental to the literary tradition of the country but its very heart and soul. It is impossible to study either the literature or the intellectual history of Vietnam without delving into Vietnamese poetry."

Vietnamese poetry, technically speaking, is a delicate and exacting practice and a demanding lyrical form. Balaban wrote that "with a music of pitches inherent in every poem, an entire dynamic of sound—inoperable in English—comes into play. And since like-sounding words can mean vastly different things, a whole world of double meanings also is possible in any poem." This was particularly true in the case of Ho's work, which was infamous for its erotic duality. Ho even hid additional messages and allusions that could only be revealed by reading parts of the poem vertically as well as horizontally.

Thông described how Ho was believed to have composed her poem "Scolding Some Dunces" on the spot and "hurled" it "at some naughty students or young men to put them in their places." He also noted, in Ho's poem "An Unwed Mother," the interplay between the physical characters and each line's content, as well as the nuances between the Chinese and Vietnamese pronunciations.

Meant What She Said and Said What She Meant

Thông described how, historically, while "the Chinese regulated poem maintained its outward structure virtually unscathed ... in the hands of Vietnamese poets, the very nature of the poem underwent changes so profound that they altered it beyond recognition. In its original habitat it remained an aristocratic medium, the embodiment of Confucian decorum and restraint.... In Vietnam, by contrast, the regulated poem shed its haughty reserve ... and went native.... It lifted all taboos and welcomed any word, however vulgar, that circumstance might justify.'' Ho seemed to possess a poetic skill that was unmatched by her male contemporaries. In *An Introduction to Vietnamese Literature,* authors Maurice M. Durand and Nguyen Tran Huan noted that Ho preached ''free love, equality of the sexes and the cause of unmarried mothers; [and derided] social conventions, ignorant scholars and high officials, and impious monks. Her poems contain virtually no Chinese literary allusions, being essentially Vietnamese in inspiration and form.''

Ho's poems were often controversial for their sensual content. Balaban noted that ''Traditionally, Vietnamese women wielded considerable economic and political power, but by 1800 the condition of women had deteriorated.... Many women could choose only between struggling alone and becoming concubines.... Men, meanwhile, could have many wives.'' Confucian culture was rigidly patriarchal and morally conservative. Balaban posed the question, ''So, in a time when death and destruction lay about, when the powerful held sway and disrespect was punished by the sword, how did [Ho] get away with the irreverence, the scorn, and the habitual indecency of her poetry? The answer lies in her excellence as a poet and in the paramount cultural esteem that Vietnamese have always placed on poetry. &hellip: Quite simply, she survived because of her exquisite cleverness at poetry.'' While the quantity of Ho's poetry may not have matched that of her contemporaries, the quality of writing was so exceptional that she is always given a lofty position in the Vietnamese literary cannon.

Bawdy, Brilliant, or Both?

Ho seems to have defied a multitude of conventions. It was unusual that, as a woman in a man's world, she wrote at all, and it seems astonishing that her poetry spoke in such a bold voice. The general popularity of her poems has kept the contentious spirit of her work very much alive. Ho's poems are often found in high school texts, used as lessons in context and close reading. They are considered by most to be a vital part of the Vietnamese cultural and aesthetic tradition, although her work has also been prohibited and treated as pornographic.

Eternal Voices Do Not Fade

Opinions and discussions on the merit of different translations of Ho's poetry have strongly suggested that the challenge her work poses is as tantalizing today as it must have been in her time, perhaps more so. In *The Heritage of Vietnamese Poetry* she is called the ''most remarkable woman poet in Vietnamese literature,'' and her fame has enjoyed a broad reach, with a man-made lake in Dalat and a Hanoi street named after her. In 2004 a traditional operetta about Ho's life and legend was staged in Hanoi and broadcast on live television. The piece, which bears Ho's name as a title, was first staged in 1988 and has been a controversial production ever since. Balaban dedicated ten years of his life to the faithful representation of Ho's poetry, but as a reviewer in *Booklist* remarked, such achievements ''pale in the presence of [her] saucy voice, vital imagery,

and nimble, teasing, sexy, and wise protestations and philosophical observations.'' Balaban himself praised Ho's ''lonely, intelligent life, ... her exquisite poetry, her stubbornness, her sarcasm, her bravery, her irreverent humor, and her bodhisattva's compassion. She is a world-class poet who can move us today as she has moved Vietnamese for two hundred years.'' Celebrated or scorned, Ho can rest confident that her poems have truly left their mark on the world of words.

Books

An Anthology of Vietnamese Poems from the Eleventh through the Twentieth Centuries, edited and translated by Huỳnh Sanh Thông, Yale University Press, 1996.
Chambers Biographical Dictionary, edited by Melanie Parry, Chambers Harrap Publishers Ltd., 1997.
Dictionary of Oriental Literatures: Volume II: South and South-East Asia, edited by Jaroslav Prusek, Basic Books Inc., 1974.
Durand, Maurice M., and Nguyen Tran Huan, An Introduction to Vietnamese Literature, Columbia University Press, 1985.
The Heritage of Vietnamese Poetry, edited and translated by Huỳnh Sanh Thông, Yale University Press, 1979.
Historical Dictionary of Vietnam, 2nd Edition, edited by William Duiker, Scarecrow Press, Inc., 1998.
The Penguin Book of Women Poets, edited by Carol Cosman et al, Penguin Books, Ltd., 1978.
Poetry for Students, Thomson Gale, 2003.
Spring Essence: The Poetry of Hô Xuân Huong, edited and translated by John Balaban, Copper Canyon Press, 2000.

Periodicals

The Advertiser, (Australia), January 13, 2007.
American Poetry Review, September 2000.
Booklist, October 1, 2000.
The Hudson Review, Autumn 1984.
International Herald Tribune, June 16, 2006.
Journal of Asian Studies, November 1980.
Journal of Southeast Asian Studies, October 2002.
New York Times, June 15, 2006.

Online

''The Cake That Drifts in Water,'' Rice University, http://www.cs.rice.edu/~ssiyer/minstrels/poems/617.html (December 8, 2007).
''Ho Xuan Huong,'' Dang Anh Tuan, http://perso.limsi.fr/dang/webvn/ehoxuan.htm (November 27, 2007).
''Ho Xuan Huong Biography,'' Famous Poets and Poems, http://famouspoetsandpoems.com/poets/ho_xuan_huong/biography (November 27, 2007).
''Live broadcast: Legendary poet takes screen,'' Vietnam Net Bridge, http://english.vietnamnet.vn/features/2004/05/155464/(December 8, 2007). □

Ted Hoff

American engineer Ted Hoff (born 1937) is credited with changing the face of the world as one of the key people behind the creation of the first microprocessor. While working for Intel in 1969, he developed the architecture that made a single-chip Central Pro-

cessing Unit (CPU) possible. That product came on the market as the Intel 4004 in 1971 and the microprocessor industry was born. Exaggerating the impact of Hoff's invention is nearly impossible, as it became integral to a staggering array of modern conveniences and necessities that included CD players, personal computers, and medical devices.

Science Was His Game

Hoff was born Marcian Edward Hoff, Jr. on October 28, 1937, in Rochester, New York. His father, who worked in railway signaling and his uncle, a chemical engineer, were big influences on him as a boy, and encouraged his early interest in science. Chemistry was his first love, but that affection waned after Hoff was told there was no practical career to be had in research. His uncle's gift of a subscription to *Popular Mechanics,* however, soon filled the void with electronics. By the time Hoff was 12 years old, he was ordering books on electronics from the magazine, and a Christmas present of a radio-building kit from his parents soon sealed the deal. Electronics would be Hoff's future.

The aspiring young scientist tasted his initial success at only 15, when he was awarded a $400 scholarship and a trip to Washington, D.C., from the Westinghouse Science Talent Search. He continued that winning streak after graduating from high school in 1954 and starting to work as a laboratory technician for his father's company, the General Railway Signal Company, during summer breaks from college. While still a sophomore at Rensselaer Polytechnic Institute in Troy, New York, he designed two circuits, one that detected trains via audio frequencies and one that absorbed energy to protect against lightning, for General Railway. Those innovations led to an inaugural pair of patents for the nascent inventor (a group that would eventually number 17).

Hoff received a bachelor's degree in electrical engineering from Rensselaer in 1958 and then headed to the West Coast to complete his graduate work. As a National Science Foundation Fellow at Stanford University, he earned an MS (1959) and Ph.D. (1962) in electrical engineering. Hoff stayed on at Stanford for six years as a research associate in adaptive systems, until a start-up company named Intel began pursuing him, and soon after, the world would change forever.

Hired at Intel

In 1968, Robert Noyce, Gordon Moore, and Andrew Grove founded the Intel Development Corporation (Intel was shorthand for integrated electronics). Noyce, who served as the start-up's president, had helped invent the integrated circuit. The new company had been established with the idea of developing semiconductor memory, but Hoff was not aware of that as he was sitting in Noyce's living room being interviewed for his first real job. "When I inter-

viewed with Bob Noyce(,) he asked me what I thought would be the next big thing for semiconductors," Hoff recalled for a 2006 Stanford School of Engineering Alumni Profile. "I said memory—a lucky guess because that was before I knew why Intel was being founded." His good instincts paid off by landing him the position of manager of applications research in September of 1968. He was Intel's 12th employee.

Although Intel's early mandate was memory, it was decided that it would be a sensible idea to take on some custom work to make money while the memory business was being built up. An opportunity presented itself when a Japanese calculator company contacted Intel about developing chips for a line of calculators. A deal was struck in April of 1969, and Hoff was assigned to act as liaison for the Japanese engineering team. He had no design responsibilities on the project. Instead, his role was to facilitate and streamline interactions between the Japanese engineers and the applicable Intel counterparts. His natural curiosity and fiscal consciousness, however, prompted Hoff to become more deeply involved. In this, history was soon in the making.

Birth of the Microprocessor

It is important to note that the computers of the 1960s were quite different animals from those of later years. They were huge, for instance, often requiring acre-sized rooms. Circuit chips were needed for each application a computer performed, as opposed to a single chip, or "brain," that could run programs. Personal computers did not exist, and few imagined that consumers would ever have a desire for one. The London *Sunday Times'* Simon Sebag Montefiore cited Hoff's quoting the chairman of Digital, Ken Olson's, decidedly less than prescient remarks on the subject as, "There is no reason anyone would want a computer in their home." Even scientists were often suspicious or intimidated by the machines. Thus, given such an atmosphere, it is hardly surprising that Hoff's proposal to give Intel's Japanese customers what was, in essence, a computer chip rather than a calculator chip was initially not met with delight.

Hoff's inspiration mainly stemmed from simple economic considerations. The Japanese design required about a dozen different chips to get the calculators up and running. Hoff became concerned about Intel's ability to meet its cost targets while implementing such a complicated project. As he contemplated the problem and sought a way to simplify matters, his inventor's intuition and years of technical training took over. Surely it would be better to combine functions, thereby reducing the necessary number of chips. The clients were not impressed with Hoff's idea, but Noyce encouraged him to proceed anyway, believing that having a back-up design would be prudent.

So, Hoff continued his efforts over the summer of 1969. Simply put, he was designing a chip that would act as a CPU, which could run programs on its own. It would be, in effect, a computer on a sliver of silicon. Chip designer Stan Mazor joined Intel in September, and the two began to move beyond overall architecture into specific chip design. And this time, when the skeptical clients reviewed the proposal in October, they gave the single-chip concept the green light. The chip was dubbed the 4004 in honor of the approximate number of transistors it would replace.

A design, however groundbreaking, did not equal an end-product though. Thus, another talented chip designer, Federico Faggin, was brought in to oversee implementation. He arrived at Intel in April of 1970 and brought his own expertise to bear on the project. In February of the following year, working kits were delivered to the clients and in November of that year, the Intel 4004 made its debut on the market. The era of the microprocessor had begun.

The ramifications of the microprocessor were immense and far-reaching. Many, including the advent of the personal computer, could not have been foreseen by Hoff and his colleagues back in 1971. Jerry Sanders, Chief Executive Officer of Advanced Micro Devices, succinctly characterized the chip's impact when he presented Hoff, Faggin, and Mazor with the Semiconductor Industry Association's highest honor for leadership, the Robert N. Noyce Award, in 2000. *Business Wire* quoted his words as, ''One of the most important developments of the last half of the 20th century has been the microprocessor. Semiconductors are found in virtually every automobile, medical device, and computer in the modern world. Who knows where we would be today without the vision, passion(,) and unyielding tenacity of these three men?'' Indeed, overestimating the Hoff team's effect on the world is nearly impossible to do.

Accolades and Later Career

Following up his opening career act could hardly have been an easy matter, but Hoff was not one to rest on his laurels. He was, for example, involved with the second and third generations of the 4004, the 8008 and 8080, respectively, as were Mazor and Faggin. In 1975, he turned his considerable abilities toward the telephone industry, at the behest of Noyce. He led a team that explored possible applications of semiconductor technology on telephones. The result, according to Hoff's biographical sketch found on the Computer History Museum Web site, was the production of ''the first commercially available monolithic telephone CODEC (for coder/decoder), a device which converts voice signals between analog and digital representations, and the first commercially available switched-capacitor filter for use with the CODEC.''

In 1980, Hoff was named the first Intel Fellow, the highest technical position within the company. But his tenure with the one-time start-up was nearing an end. After he declined to move to Arizona with Intel's telephone group, he was contacted by a recruiter for Atari. Intrigued by what he perceived as that company's advanced ideas, Hoff signed on as vice president of corporate technology early in 1983. It was not a long-lived association however, as financial troubles forced Atari's sale in 1984. Hoff then became a private consultant. In 1986, a former colleague of Hoff's from Atari founded a company called Teklicon to engage in intellectual property litigation consulting. Hoff began using the outfit as an agent for his own consulting business until joining Teklicon's ranks as chief technologist in 1990. There may have appeared to be a large disparity between engineering and consulting, but Hoff had come to recognize the merits of having a business, as well as a creative, sense. The Stanford School of Engineering's Alumni Profile quoted some of his thoughts on the subject. ''So(,) now I look back and wish I had appreciated business more than I did . . . Even though science and technology are wonderful, what really gets them out there for people to use is to have businesses built around them. It takes savvy businessmen as well as savvy technologists to make that work.''

Whatever success Hoff enjoyed as a businessperson and consultant later in his career, it was his technological achievements for which he will be best remembered. In addition to being listed as inventor or co-inventor on 17 U.S. patents, he received myriad honors for his pioneering work. Those included the 1979 Stuart Ballantine Medal of the Franklin Institute, the 1980 Cledo Brunetti Award and the 1984 Centennial Medal (both from the Institute of Electrical and Electronics Engineers), induction into the National Inventors Hall of Fame in 1996, and, as previously noted, the Robert N. Noyce Award of Semiconductor Industry Association in 2000. His contributions were delineated in Paul Freiberger and Michael Swaine's book *Fire in the Valley: The Making of the Personal Computer,* published in 1984 and revised in 2000, and in a DVD called the *Microprocessor Chronicles* in 2006. Justly so, there was no shortage of praise for or interest in the man who had been integral in altering the face of the modern world. The promise of Hoff's youth had been fulfilled in a manner that few could equal, but to which many could aspire.

Periodicals

Business Wire, November 2, 2000.
Investor's Business Daily, November 5, 2001.
San Francisco Chronicle, June 29, 1996.
Sunday Times (London, England), November 3, 1996.

Online

''Fascinating Facts About Ted Hoff Inventor of the Microprocessor in 1968,'' Idea Finder, http://www.ideafinder.com/history/inventors/hoff.htm (November 29, 2007).

Freiberger, Paul and Swaine, Michael, ''Development of the Microprocessor,'' *Fire in the Valley,* http://www.fireinthevalley.com/fitv_book1.html (November 29, 2007).

Freiberger, Paul and Swaine, Michael, ''The Making of the Personal Computer,'' *Fire in the Valley,* http://www.fireinthevalley.com/fitv_press.html (November 29, 2007).

''Marcian E. (Ted) Hoff,'' Inventor of the Week, http://Web site.mit.edu/invent/iow/hoff.html (November 29, 2007).

''Marcian E. (Ted) Hoff,'' National Inventors Hall of Fame, http://www.invent.org/hall_of_fame/79.html (November 29, 2007).

''Marcian (Ted) Hoff: Teenage Prodigy, Still Going Strong,'' Electronic Design, http://electronicdesign.com/Articles/Index.cfm?AD=1&ArticleID=2854 (November 29, 2007).

''Ted Hoff,'' Computer History Museum, http://www.computerhistory.org/events/index.php?spkid=1&ssid=1162597290 (November 29, 2007).

''Ted Hoff: The Birth of the Microprocessor and Beyond,'' Stanford School of Engineering Alumni Profile, http://soe.stanford.edu/alumni/profile_hoff.html (November 29, 2007).]

World of Invention. Online. Thomson Gale, 2006, http://galenet.galegroup.com/servlet/BioRC (April 15, 2008). □

Felix Hoffmann

German scientist Felix Hoffmann (1868-1946) is credited as the inventor of aspirin, the first mass-produced and mass-marketed consumer drug product. Hoffmann was a young chemist working for Bayer, the German chemical company, when he came up with a synthesized form of the chemical found in extract of willow-tree bark, which had been known for centuries as a pain reliever. Aspirin is notable as "the world's first truly synthetic drug," according to an article in the *Economist* commemorating the centenary of Hoffmann's discovery, which was a product that "paved the way for the modern pharmaceuticals industry."

Hoffmann was born on January 21, 1868, in Ludwigsburg, Germany, a city near Stuttgart. He was the son of Jakob, an industrialist, and went on to earn a science degree—magna cum laude—from the University of Munich in 1891. In 1893 he completed work on his doctorate, also awarded with magna cum laude honors, after writing a dissertation on the properties of dihydroanthracene, a source of hydrogen that could be used in industrial chemical applications such as hydrogenation. A year later Hoffmann joined the staff of Bayer, a manufacturer of dyes that had been founded in the northern city of Wuppertal, Germany, in 1863.

Began Researching Pain Relievers

Bayer was named after one of its two founders, Friedrich Bayer (1825-1880), a dye salesperson. Its first products were synthetic forms of chemical dyes whose mass-scale industrial production methods had only recently been discovered, and which proved much cheaper than the production of dyes made from natural sources. By the time Hoffmann began working for Bayer, it had expanded into other areas, and he was assigned to the company's state-of-the-art research facility in Elberfeld, a city near Wuppertal, to work in its pharmaceutical research division.

Hoffmann's father was plagued by severe arthritis, and there were few pain relievers on the market that did not also have unpleasant or even adverse effects. Like many arthritis sufferers, Jakob Hoffmann disliked the taste of artificial salicylic acid, the most reliable remedy at the time and known as sodium salicylate. A chemical whose discovery had been made at Germany's University of Marburg in 1859, sodium salicylate was by the 1870s being mass-produced in the city of Dresden by the Heyden Company, but it had a terrible taste and could irritate the stomach lining to the point of causing ulcers. Scientists at Bayer and elsewhere were searching for a way to replicate the original salicylic acid in a more stable chemical form that would reduce its irritant properties.

Salicylic acid is derived from the bark and leaves of the willow tree, and this plant had been known for centuries as having analgesic, or pain-relieving, properties. It was depicted in clay tablets made by the ancient Sumerians, whose Mesopotamian settlements in the years between 5000 B.C.E. and 4000 B.C.E. are the first evidence of human civilization. Centuries later, the Greek physician Hippocrates (c. 460 B.C.E.-c. 370 B.C.E.) recommended chewing the bark or leaves of the white willow tree for pain relief.

Formulated Heroin in Bayer Lab

Hoffmann's breakthrough came on August 10, 1897, in the Elberfeld laboratory after he investigated the records and notes that had been written by a French chemist, Charles Frédéric Gerhardt (1816-1856). In 1853 Gerhardt mixed acetyl chloride—a corrosive liquid used by chemists as a reagent which gave off a white smoke—with sodium salicylate, but it was an unstable compound that to him did not seem to have much practical use. Hoffmann studied scientific notes on these experiments, and managed to come up with a variant by using two slightly different ingredients: he mixed a different form of salicylic acid derived from *spirea alba*—the Latin name for meadowsweet, a perennial herb—with acetic anhydride instead of acetyl chloride. This resulted in a far more stable form that could be used for medicine, and Hoffmann named it acetylsalicylic acid (ASA).

Bayer reportedly tested the compound on animals, then conducted a study on patients—said to be one of the first pharmaceutical trials involving human subjects—at Deaconess Hospital in Halle an der Saale, a town in the German state of Saxony-Anhalt. Executives at Bayer came up with the trade name Aspirin, with "a" referring to acetyl, plus "spir" for the spirea plant, and began distributing it in powder form to doctors as a pain reliever and fever reducer in 1899. The first water-soluble tablets were introduced a year later, and became the first medicine ever sold in tablet form. For the first several years of its existence, aspirin was available only through doctors, but it became an over-the-counter drug in 1915.

Oddly, the second major breakthrough of Hoffmann's career came just 11 days after the discovery that led to aspirin: heroin. This was the brand name that Bayer marketing executives gave the drug, and it was sold as a cough suppressant and even as a cure for morphine addicts from 1898 to 1910. Again, he was replicating the work of an earlier chemist, in this case C.S. Alder Wright at St. Mary's Hospital in London, England, in 1874. Heroin's addictive properties and harmful nature soon became apparent, and in contrast to the success of aspirin, this proved to be a major public relations embarrassment for the Bayer company.

Found to Prevent Blood Clots

For reasons still unclear, Hoffmann left his research position at Bayer and moved to an executive post in the company's marketing division not long after these breakthroughs. He remained there until he retired in 1928, and spent his final years in Switzerland. Never married, he died on February 8, 1946. Bayer went on to become a major international pharmaceutical corporation thanks to the success of aspirin, though its American aspirin franchise was seized by the U.S. government during World War I and deemed "enemy property." The franchise was later sold at auction, and in 1920 Sterling Drug paid $5.3 million for the franchise to sell Bayer aspirin in the United States.

For the first several decades of the twentieth century, Bayer aspirin dominated the analgesic market. Its main competitors were sold under the brand names Excedrin, Anacin, and Bufferin, all of which used aspirin as the main ingredient, but Excedrin and Anacin also contained caffeine. Paracetamol, also known as acetaminophen, became part of a new class of pain relievers in the 1950s that were first sold in the United States under the brand name Tylenol. Ibuprofen, marketed as Advil, followed in the 1980s, along with naproxyn, which was introduced as the over-the-counter (non-prescription) remedy Aleve in 1994. The companies that introduced these pain relievers were Bayer's biggest competitors in the consumer drug market, and included Johnson & Johnson and Procter & Gamble.

With the newly crowded field of pain relievers, aspirin's share of the over-the-counter market declined precipitously until the late 1980s, when medical studies began to appear that showed its remarkable effectiveness in preventing the risk of heart attacks. Further research proved it could serve as a blood-thinning agent that could reduce the risk of a deadly blood clot immediately following a heart attack or stroke. At the turn of the twenty-first century, aspirin was the most widely studied drug in the history of medicine, with scientists investigating its other uses, including its possibilities as a cancer preventative, in more than 3,000 research studies that appeared annually.

Scientific Dispute over Credit

Bayer, which eventually regained the rights to its U.S. aspirin franchise, celebrated aspirin's hundredth anniversary in 1997. Two years later, a scientist at Strathclyde University in Scotland, Walter Sneader, presented a paper at the Royal Society of Chemistry's annual conference, in which he claimed that Bayer had been falsely attributing the discovery of aspirin to Hoffmann, when it was actually Hoffmann's lab colleague, Arthur Eichengrün (1867-1949), who deserved the credit. In the paper, which was published in the *British Medical Journal* in December of 2000, Sneader asserted that there were no company documents or records prior to 1934 that linked Hoffmann to aspirin's discovery, and instead the earliest records seemed to hint that Heinrich Dreser, head of the pharmaceutical research division at Elberfeld, had made some initial tests. "In a paper published in *Pharmazie* in 1949, Eichengrün claimed that he had instructed Hoffmann to synthesise acetylsalicylic acid and that the latter had done so without knowing the purpose of the work," Sneader wrote. Another supervisor of Hoffmann and Eichengrün's disagreed over its potential, and so "Eichengrün tested it on himself, experiencing no ill effects. He stated that he then surreptitiously gave a supply of it to his colleague Dr. Felix Goldmann, who then recruited physicians to evaluate the drug in strict secrecy. Their reports were most encouraging."

Sneader pointed out that Eichengrün had left Bayer in 1908 and founded his own successful chemical company which made flame-retardant materials. He was also Jewish, which put both him and his thriving Berlin factory in danger once Adolf Hitler (1889-1945) and the Nazi Party came to power in Germany in 1933 and began enacting anti-Semitic laws. Sneader asserted that the first mention of Hoffmann as aspirin's discoverer did not appear until a year after this, in 1934. "I believe the whole story was concocted so the Germans did not learn the most successful drug in history was discovered by a Jew," Sneader told Rosemary Free, a journalist with the *Herald* of Glasgow, Scotland.

At the age of 76, Eichengrün had been deported to the Theresienstadt concentration camp in the present-day Czech Republic, but survived his 14-month internment. He died in December of 1949, the same month his article in the journal *Pharmazie* appeared. Both Bayer and other scientists disputed Sneader's claims, including Axel Helmstädter, the general secretary of the International Society for the History of Pharmacy, who sent a letter to the *British Medical Journal* stating, "There is no actual need for a reappraisal of Aspirin history. There are at least two sources earlier than Sneader's article reporting the development precisely," one that discusses Eichengrün's claims, and one that "relies on a laboratory journal written and signed by Hoffmann in 1897," according to Helmstädter.

Periodicals

American Medical News, October 20, 1997.
British Medical Journal, December 23, 2000.
Economist, February 21, 1998; August 9, 1997.
Herald (Glasgow, Scotland), September 2, 1999.
New York Times, August 9, 1997.
People, September 15, 1997.

Online

"Felix Hoffmann," Bayer, http://www.bayer.com/en/Felix-Hoffmann.aspx (January 11, 2008).
"Felix Hoffmann," The Great Idea Finder, http://www.ideafinder.com/history/inventors/hoffmann.htm (January 11, 2008).
"Rapid Responses to History: Walter Sneader, The Discovery of Aspirin: A Reappraisal," *British Medical Journal,* http://www.bmj.com/cgi/eletters/321/7276/1591#12342 (January 10, 2008). □

Wenceslaus Hollar

Bohemian etcher Wenceslaus Hollar (1607-1677) was one of the principal topographical engravers of the seventeenth century. His plates depicting views of London before and after the Great Fire (1666) are some of the most valuable printmaking accomplishments in the world.

Early Years

Wenceslaus Hollar was born on July 13, 1607, in Prague, Czechia (also referred to as Bohemia), as the eldest of three sons. His mother, Marketa (died c. 1613), was identified by the *Oxford Dictionary of National Biography* as being "of Löwengrün and Bareyt in

the upper Palatinate." His father, Jan Hollar (died 1630), was an upper middle-class public official, and although not much is known about Hollar's youth, most agree that he was expected to follow his father into the legal field. However, despite any demands his father may have made, Hollar chose to pursue the printmaking trade as an amateur. Richard Godfrey's *Wenceslaus Hollar: A Bohemian Artist in England* (1994) explained, "Our knowledge of Hollar's beginnings as an etcher—probably as an interested young amateur rather than a fledgling professional—has been enlarged by . . . [the] discovery of a cache of juvenile prints . . . nervously scratched on little scraps of leftover copper . . . hesitantly executed, snatched too quickly from the acid, but their subjects are revealing."

Exodus or Exile?

Hollar's colleague and friend John Aubrey (1626-1697) wrote a biography of the etcher that identified Hollar's father as a protestant Knight of the Empire who "forfeited his estate, and was ruined by the Roman Catholiques" when Prague was captured in the Thirty Years' War, according to the Web site *She Philosopher*. While Hollar did leave Prague in 1627 at the age of 20, sources disagree as to whether it was to seek opportunities as an artist against his father's wishes, or as a self-imposed exile prompted by the governmental changes happening at the time. Emperor Ferdinand II (1578-1637) issued an edict on July 31, 1627, that obligated Bohemian nobility, like Hollar's family, to convert and become Catholics or go into exile, but most scholars agree that Hollar left Prague of his own volition.

Where Hollar Went

Almost every biography of Hollar favors a timeline that claims he went straight from Prague in 1627 to Frankfurt, Germany, and entered training with renowned Swiss engraver Matthäus Merian the Elder (1593-1650). In an article written for *The Art Bulletin,* however, John Pav made a strong argument that "in the latter part of 1627, during 1628, and perhaps even in the early part of 1629, Hollar's presence can be positively documented only in Stuttgart and its immediate vicinity. . . . In 1629 and 1630, the artist was active mainly in Strasbourg. From 1633 until 1636, Hollar's center of activity was Cologne . . . [and] for over a year (during 1631 and probably also the major part of 1632) Hollar's whereabouts cannot be traced at all. . . . The most plausible explanation of this temporary 'disappearance' . . . is that he entered a studio, probably Merian's workshop in Frankfurt, where he became an anonymous member of a team of engravers."

This timeline appears to be well supported and has been adopted by many scholars. Rather than go straight to Frankfurt, it is believed that Hollar spent 1627-1628 in Stuttgart, but found the township to be too small to support his growing career and skills. In Strasbourg from 1629-1630, according to Godfrey, Hollar "seriously commenced his profession, and . . . undertook his first commissions for print publishers." Godfrey further described Hollar's technical prowess at that time, explaining how the etcher "rapidly evolved a delicate technique that employed careful modulations of acid bites." Not until 1631-1632 did Hollar travel to Frankfurt to work with Merian, whose workshop was the heart of German print publishing, and where Hollar mastered the bird's eye view. From Frankfurt he stopped in Holland briefly in 1634, and then spent the next two years in Cologne, where he focused on landscape and costume, publishing his first collection of etchings there in 1635 at the age of 28.

A Rewarding Collaboration

In 1636 Hollar met the Earl of Arundel—Thomas Howard, 21st Earl of Arundel, 4th Earl of Surrey and 1st Earl of Norfolk (1585-1646), a renowned English courtier who is remembered as an art collector rather than as a politician. Godfrey explained, "Whether Hollar had offered his services to Arundel or whether Arundel had sought him out is not known, but the meeting was felicitous for both." Hollar accompanied Arundel on a tour of Europe that allowed him to return briefly to his native Prague, and he then continued to Vienna, eventually returning to England. The tour was a diplomatic mission, technically speaking, but most who were involved knew it would not be successful as anything more than an opportunity to expand the Earl's already vast collection. According to the *Folger Exhibitions* Web site, Arundel wanted to "create a visual inventory of his collection, a 'paper museum' of etchings that would be an enduring record." This was never achieved, although Hollar's plates and watercolors are all that remain of some famous works of architecture and pieces of art.

Hollar was not required to work exclusively for Arundel, and he accepted work from print sellers and other patrons while part of Arundel's retinue. In 1637 the tour ended and Hollar settled in London, England, as a member of Arundel's household, and Aubrey described the artist's time there as idyllic. In 1640 Hollar served as a drawing instructor to the Prince of Wales—the future Charles II. Godfrey summarized Hollar's professional position at that time, saying that "he was a skilled but conservative etcher and a first-class topographer . . . a fine draftsman of costume . . . [and] a master on a small scale, a talent highly amenable to English taste." While Hollar may not have been the first landscape engraver to be active in England, he was definitely a primary source of introduction for etching methods and techniques.

No Head For Business

Hollar was not a businessman by nature, and was frequently taken advantage of. According to Hollar's *NNDB* biography, buyers would pretend "to decline his work that he might still further reduce the wretched price he charged." Eventually Hollar began to charge by the hour and kept meticulous track of his time with a sand glass. Aubrey remembered seeing him set it on its side whenever his work was interrupted for any reason.

An Artist At War

Some confusion clouds Hollar's activities and whereabouts between 1642 and 1645. The Arundel household left England for Antwerp, Belgium, without Hollar in tow, and he is believed to have served in a Royalist regiment during the English Civil War period. According to the *NNDB* Web site, the engraver "passed into the service of the Duke of York, taking with him [his] wife and two children" in 1642 and "stood the long and eventful siege of Basing House" with "other royalist artists." Hollar was either released or he escaped, and made his way to Antwerp. Other sources have claimed that he could not have been part of the siege at Basing because all who were involved were executed.

Wherever he was, Hollar's work suggests that he used this period away from Arundel to focus on the depiction of women's costumes. From 1643 to 1644 Hollar fashioned full-length studies of female figures dressed to represent the seasons, and they became some of his most famous plates. He arrived in Antwerp in 1645, where he once again worked with the Earl of Arundel, who had begun selling off his collection. Hollar's bank of drawings and watercolors provided ample material for him to make etchings of some of the Earl's fleeting treasures.

It was during his eight years in Antwerp that Hollar had the opportunity to address a broad array of personal artistic interests, and his original etchings of fur muffs, insects and sea shells set him apart from other artists of that time. Godfrey believed that Hollar "transcends plain prose and draws and etches with poetic spirit." His plates from this period still amaze with their attentive and refined ability to reproduce the lacy pattern of veins in a butterfly wing or the intricate spirals and glossy efficiency of a rare shell.

Return to England

In 1652 the restoration of Charles II allowed for Hollar to return to England, where he began what would become a life's labor for various print sellers and publishers, mainly publisher John Ogilby and antiquarian Sir William Dugdale. While there seem to be no accounts to clarify the fate of Hollar's first wife and children, records do show that on July 3, 1656, Hollar married Honora Roberts and is believed to have had more several children. But Hollar soon discovered that the shine had worn from his adopted home. Aubrey stated, "I remember [Hollar] told me that when he first came into England, (which was a serene time of peace) that the people, both poore and rich, did looke cheerfully, but at his returne, he found the countenances of the people all changed, melancholy, spightfull, as if bewitched." The *Oxford Dictionary of National Biography* noted that "in 1660 Hollar issued a prospectus for a large-scale map of London which he hoped would be his financial salvation." Godfrey further described the project as "a map that would transcend all others in scale and detail, a task of vaulting ambition for which [Hollar] alone was qualified." In 1665 Hollar's son James died of the plague, and in 1666 Hollar was appointed with the title of "His Majesty's Designer."

The Great Fire: Blessing or Curse?

Hollar was most likely in London during the Great Fire of 1666, and the topographical scenes of the city that he recorded from Southwark before and after the fire made him famous. The plates became very valuable as one of the few direct sources of information from that time. Some claimed that Hollar sketched the fire while it burned, but scholars have maintained that this is unlikely because Hollar, as a foreigner, would have been in hiding rather than out in public where roving bands of vigilantes swarmed the streets looking for foreigners who were rumored to have started the fire. While it did make Hollar's London plates legendary, the fire also rendered his work for a large map of London obsolete.

In 1669 Hollar petitioned to be assigned as the official artist on Lord Henry Howard's trip to Tangier, Africa. He traveled with Howard's retinue and returned a year later. Wenceslaus Hollar died on March 28, 1677, at his home on Gradner's Lane in Westminster, and was interred at St. Margaret's Church. Considered one of the most skilled etchers of any time, Hollar did not let the fact that he had lost most of the sight in one eye deter him from cultivating an attention to texture and displaying his gift for translating it into the etched medium.

Carving History into Copper

Hollar produced well over 2,000 pieces in his lifetime, ranging from classical, historical, and religious subjects to portraits, costumes, still-lifes, and topography. His seemingly inexhaustible work ethic assured a prolific turnout in a time before photography when painting and engraving were vital methods of preserving history. The Folger Library hosted an exhibition of Hollar's work from October of 1996 through February of 1997, and the *Folger Exhibitons* Web site noted in the introductory material that "If Hollar were alive today, he might well be a freelance photographer" because "his eye was his camera lens, [and] his copper-plates the film. . . . His etchings permit us to witness the spectacle of coronations and executions, to pour over the detail of costume and buildings, and to view a terrain that was shifting even as Hollar rendered it and that has since been irrevocably altered." Godfrey suggested that "it is the gentle modesty of [Hollar's] work, the affectionate curvature of his delicate etched lines, that has assured him a lasting place in our affections."

Books

Cambridge Biographical Encyclopedia: Second Edition, edited by David Crystal, Cambridge University Press, 1998.

Chambers Biographical Dictionary, edited by Melanie Parry, Chambers Harrap Publishers Ltd., 1997.

Dictionary of the Arts, Helicon Publishing Ltd., 1994.

Godfrey, Richard T., *Wenceslaus Hollar: A Bohemian Artist in England,* Yale University Press, 1994.

McGraw-Hill Dictionary of Art, edited by Bernard S. Myers, McGraw-Hill Publishing Co. Ltd., 1969.

Oxford Companion To Art, edited by Harold Osborne, Oxford University Press, 1970.

Oxford Companion To Western Art, edited by Hugh Brigstocke, Oxford University Press, 2001.

Oxford Dictionary of Art: Third Edition, edited by Ian Chilvers, Oxford University Press, 2004.

Oxford Dictionary of National Biography, edited by H.C.G. Matthew and Brian Harrison, Oxford University Press, 2004.

Van Eerde, Katherine S., *Wenceslaus Hollar: Delineator of His Time,* University Press of Virginia, 1970.

Yale Dictionary of Art and Artists, edited by Erika Langmuir and Norbert Lynton, Yale University Press, 2000.

Periodicals

The Art Bulletin, Vol. 55, No. 1, March 1973.

Online

"Impressions of Wenceslaus Hollar," Folger Exhibitions, http://www.folger.edu/html/exhibitions/wenceslaus_hollar/ (December 8, 2007).

"Wenceslas Hollar," Storm Fine Arts, http://www.stormfinearts.com/framesindex.htm (December 8, 2007).

"Wenceslaus Hollar: A Bohemian Artist in England," Yale University Press, http://yalepress.yale.edu/yupbooks/book.asp?isbn=9780300061666 (December 8, 2007).

"The Wenceslaus Hollar Digital Collection," University of Toronto Libraries, http://link.library.utoronto.ca/hollar/ (November 27, 2007).

"Wenceslaus Hollar (1607–1677)," She Philosopher, http://www.she-philosopher.com/ib/bios/hollar.html (December 8, 2007).

"Wenceslaus Hollar (1607–1677)," World Wide Arts Resources, http://wwar.com/masters/h/hollar-wenceslaus.html (December 8, 2007).

"Wenzel Hollar," *Encyclopaedia Britannica,* http://www.britannica.com/eb/article-9040801/Wenzel-Hollar (November 27, 2007).

"Wenzel Hollar," NNDB, http://www.nndb.com/people/741/000103432/ (November 27, 2007).

"Wenzel Hollar," University of Liege (Belgium), http://translate.google.com/translate?langpair=fr en&u=http://www.wittert.ulg.ac.be/fr/flori/opera/hollar/hollar_notice.html (November 27, 2007). □

I

Masaru Ibuka

As co-founder and longtime president of the Sony Corporation, Japanese executive Masaru Ibuka (1908-1997) conceived of and brought to fruition several of the most popular and fundamentally influential consumer electronics innovations of the twentieth century.

The public face of Sony for decades was its chairman and marketing wizard, Akio Morita, but Ibuka was the company's leader on the technical side. The two men worked closely together. Ibuka's son Makoto was quoted as saying in the London *Daily Mail* that the pair "were bound together by a tie so tight it was more like love than friendship." The miniaturization of the tape recorder, the transistor radio, the Trinitron color television, the Betamax videotape system, and the video projector were among the Ibuka projects that reshaped consumer culture globally.

Dubbed "Student Inventor of Genius"

Born on April 11, 1908, in Nikko, Japan, in Tochigi Prefecture, Ibuka was interested in radio from the time he was young, and was an avid "ham" or amateur radio operator. His father was a beer brewer, and it was expected that young Ibuka would take over the family business. Ibuka attended Waseda High School and Waseda University, where he studied chemical engineering. He stayed on at the university as a researcher, and in 1933 one of his discoveries, a form of the element neon with applications in the transmission of light, won a prize at the Paris Exhibition, an international science fair. According to James Kirkup of the London *Independent*, Ibuka was described at the time as a "student inventor of

genius." He moved on to become manager of the radio telegraphy department of the Japan Audio Optical Industrial Corporation from 1937 to 1940, and was then managing director and chief engineer of the Japan Measuring Apparatus Company from 1940 to 1945. But his early orientation toward pure research had left its mark.

In 1936 Ibuka had married Sekiko Maeda, the daughter of a man with close connections to the Japanese monarchy. The marriage produced two daughters and a son. It ended in divorce, but helped propel Ibuka into Japan's military-industrial complex; during World War II he did research on heat-seeking missiles and created an amplifier designed to help aircraft pilots detect submarines. In the course of his company's involvement in military research, he met Morita, then a representative of the Japanese navy, and the two stayed in touch.

Ibuka and his fellow engineers did not fall into that portion of the Japanese population willing to sacrifice everything for victory in the war. Ibuka and Morita, who listened to shortwave radio broadcasts from the United States, became convinced that Japan's loss was certain, and when the Emperor Hirohito announced the country's surrender on the radio, many members of Ibuka's team were happy at the chance to get away from developing military technology. Amid the ruins of postwar Tokyo, Ibuka formed a new company called Tokyo Tsushin Kogyo, or Totsuko for short. The name meant Tokyo Telecommunications Engineering, and the company, with headquarters in a bombed-out department store, was incorporated on May 7, 1946. Morita, who was teaching engineering at the time, soon signed on as general manager, and Morita's father invested the then-enormous sum of $60,000 in the new firm. As of the late 1990s, the family's return on that investment was about $5 billion.

Things got off to a slow start. Disposable income was almost nonexistent in postwar Japan. And the company's

first product, an electric rice cooker, was a flop. But Ibuka and his staff of 20 engineers continued to develop ideas, experimenting with a ferric oxide compound that they heated in a frying pan at first. That produced a magnetic paste that they brushed by hand onto strips of paper. The end result, by 1950, was Japan's first tape recorder, which weighed in at 100 pounds. Within a year, however, the weight had been reduced by 80 percent.

Bought Rights to Transistor

Ibuka visited the United States in 1952, hoping to explore new recording technologies. While there, he encountered a then-obscure device called a transistor, a miniature semiconductor that could be used to amplify electronic signals. The transistor's U.S. manufacturer, Western Electric, marketed it primarily for use in military applications and hearing aids, but Ibuka had other ideas, and he paid $25,000 for the rights to manufacture them in Japan. "American companies were using transistors to make hearing aids, but even today Japanese don't like to wear hearing aids," Ibuka told Brent Schlender of *Fortune.* By 1955 his staff had perfected the world's first transistor radio, and two years later they released a shirt-pocket model—actually slightly too big for most shirt pockets, but Morita dispatched a sales staff outfitted with specially tailored shirts that would hold the radios.

This development catapulted Ibuka to the top of the worldwide consumer electronics industry. Radios, which had been at least of tabletop size and were often major

pieces of furniture, could now be carried anywhere. Transistor radios were a runaway success and became an icon of worldwide youth culture in the 1960s. In 1958, with the company's Western markets rapidly expanding, Tokyo Tsushin Kogyo changed its name to Sony, a meaningless but easy-to-remember hybrid of the Latin root *sonus* (sound) and the "Sonny" moniker often used for young Japanese by occupying American troops.

A series of other innovative Sony products followed, lasting for much of the rest of the twentieth century. The company introduced the world's first transistor television in 1959, spelling the end of the use of cumbersome vacuum tubes, and another invention equally important for television, the videotape recorder, appeared in 1961. In many cases the ideas for these products were Ibuka's own, and the engineers who perfected them worked under his direct supervision. The invention of which he was proudest was the Trinitron color television, which appeared in 1967 and transformed the fuzzy outlines of earlier color TV systems into sharply focused images. Sony invested heavily enough in the technology that failure could have meant its demise, but the Trinitron emerged as a market leader. In the fast-moving world of video electronics, the basic Trinitron technology remained in use for many years.

In 1971 Ibuka became president of Sony. The pace at which forward-looking new products appeared was undiminished over the next decade, as Sony pioneered two more key technologies. The company's Betamax home video system was released in 1975. Although it was eventually eclipsed by the competing VHS format, it was a key development in the introduction of video devices into homes all over the world. In 1976 Ibuka retired, taking the title of honorary chairman (and eventually supreme founder and consultant). But there were more devices in the pipeline, developed by the engineering staff he had put in place, that reshaped the electronics marketplace: the portability of music, a trend with enormous implications for the future, took a significant step forward with the introduction of the Sony Walkman in 1979, and it was Sony, in collaboration with the Dutch company Philips, that pioneered the compact disc. Ibuka was also responsible for numerous electronics-manufacturing devices with lower profiles. Toward the end of his career he approved the development of a Sony lab that would investigate the possibility of extrasensory perception.

Attributed Success to U.S. Military Orientation

Ibuka's consistent record of innovation flew in the face of conventional wisdom, which held that while Japanese manufacturers were efficient at developing existing ideas to perfection, they generally lacked creativity. Ibuka pointed to Sony's consumer orientation as an explanation. "The American electronics industry is spoiled by the emphasis on military and space applications," he told Schlender. "In the U.S. you put your energy into fundamental research to develop technologies that you apply first to military uses. Only later does it make its way into business and consumer products. " He recalled visiting a U.S. professor who had developed a big-screen television. "I told him it was a natural consumer product, and he became upset with me. He didn't want his superb technology used in a lowly consumer product."

In Japan itself Ibuka became a widely revered figure, a sort of national folk hero roughly comparable in stature to Alexander Graham Bell or Thomas Edison in the United States. He made headlines for a non-electronic accomplishment in 1966 when he married his childhood sweetheart, Yoshiko Kurosawa. Ibuka maintained a variety of interests outside work; he was an avid golfer, and from 1985 to 1994 he served as chairman of the Boy Scouts of Nippon. In later years he also served as president of the Japan Institute for Invention and Innovation, and of the Japan Audio Society. He visited his old office at Sony at least weekly, and received audio summaries of company reports.

The major project of Ibuka's later life resulted from his vision of creating a new corps of creative Japanese engineers through an emphasis on early childhood education. Even before becoming Sony president he had written two books, *The Zero-Year Child* (1970) and *Kindergarten Is Too Late!* (1971). After his retirement, the pace of his writing accelerated as he penned ten more books. Most were on educational and child-rearing topics, but he also wrote the biography *Good Mileage: The High-Performance Business Philosophy of Soichiro Honda,* about the founder of the Honda automobile company, a personal friend. *Kindergarten Is Too Late!* and *Good Mileage* were translated into English.

In 1992 Ibuka received one of Japan's highest awards, the Order of Culture, bestowed by the emperor himself.

That year he was hospitalized with a serious heart arrhythmia; Morita, who suffered a stroke at nearly the same time, was put in an adjoining room, and the two were seen sitting together, holding hands and weeping silently. Ibuka died in Tokyo on December 19, 1997. "Mr. Ibuka has been at the heart of Sony's philosophy," Sony president Nobuyuki Idea was quoted as saying in the *New York Times.* "He has sowed the seeds of the deep conviction that our products must bring joy and fun to users. Mr. Ibuka always asked himself what was at the core of 'making things,' and thought in broad terms of how these products could enhance people's lives and cultures."

Books

Business Leader Profiles for Students. Vol. 1, Gale Research, 1999.

Periodicals

Daily Mail (London, England), October 4, 1999.
Fortune, February 24, 1992.
Fresno Bee, December 20, 1997.
Guardian (London, England), December 20, 1997.
Independent (London, England), December 22, 1997.
New York Times, December 20, 1997.
Times (London, England), December 29, 1997.

Online

Contemporary Authors Online, Gale, 2007, http://galenet.gale group.com/servlet/BioRC (December 6, 2007). □

J

Tove Marika Jansson

Finnish artist and author Tove Jansson (1914-2001), whose widely translated work spoke to children and adults alike, is often compared to such timeless authors as J.R.R. Tolkein and A.A. Milne.

Creative Beginnings

Tove Marika Jansson (pronounced *TOH-vay YAN-son*) was born on August 9, 1914, in Helsinki, Finland. The eldest of three, Jansson shared her childhood with two younger brothers, Per and Lars. Their father was sculptor Viktor Jansson, and their mother was Signe Hammarten-Jansson, a successful Swedish graphic artist. All three children were raised to speak and write in Swedish, making the family a part of the country's Swedish-speaking Finnish minority.

According to *Major Authors and Illustrators for Children and Young Adults,* Jansson recalled in her 1968 autobiographical novel *Bildhuggarens dotter* (The Sculptor's Daughter), "We lived in a large, dilapidated studio in Helsinki, and I pitied other children who had to live in ordinary flats . . . nothing like the mysterious jumble of turn-tables, sacks with plaster and cases with clay, pieces of wood and iron constructions where one could hide and build in peace. A home without sculptures seemed as naked to me as one without books." Jansson spent her youth immersed in the imaginings of other authors. Her mother brought home samples of books she had been hired to design covers for, and Jansson read them avidly. Even when forced to play

outside or told to go to bed, Jansson remembered hiding "behind a trash container in the yard" to read, or reading "by flashlight under the covers."

Early Accomplishments

Jansson began sharing her unique talents at a young age. Her first official publication, a cartoon titled *Prickinas och Fabians äventyr* (Prickina and Fabian's Adventure), told the story of a pair of caterpillars falling in love and appeared in the children's magazine *Lunkentus* in 1929 when Jansson was just 15 years old. Four years later, in 1933, Jansson used the pseudonym Vera Haij to publish a picture book she wrote and illustrated, titled *Sara och Pelle och Neckens bläckfiskar* (Sara and Pelle and the Water-Sprite's Octopuses). While her mother undoubtedly had a strong hand in her early success—Signe Hammarten-Jansson was a standout in her field with strong literary contacts and the ability to financially support the family with her design work—Jansson had the skill and drive required to fruitfully publish on her own.

An Education in Invention

Jansson later applied herself at multiple art schools. From 1930 to 1933 she studied lettering, heraldry, ceramics, drawing, painting, and book design among other subjects at Konstfack in Stockholm, Sweden. In 1933 she continued to study multiple mediums at the Finnish Art Society in Helsinki, Finland, and in 1938 Jansson took advantage of an opportunity to attend the Ecole d'Adrien Holy and the Ecole des Beaux Arts in Paris, France. She even supplemented this European exposure with a short period of study in Florence, Italy. In 1943 Jansson had her first private exhibition in Helsinki, a popular and critical success that quickly identified her as a young artist to watch.

The Moomins Are Born

Despite a varied authorial career, Jansson is best remembered as the creator of the Moomintrolls, a gentle family of hippo-esque creatures who lived in an idyllic valley and survived both natural and emotional disasters, from raging floods to the more subtle echoes of personal loss. She began writing the first Moomin book, *Smatrollen och den stora översvämningen* (The Small Troll and the Large Flood), in 1939, claiming in a later interview that she consciously chose to avoid the typical protagonists of children's literature in favor of the strange but engaging troll figures.

There are eight novels and four picture books in the Moomin anthology, all written and published in Swedish between 1945 and 1970 and later translated into a wealth of languages. Described in terms like "simple," "spritely," and "mythical," Jansson's Moomin images became the foundation for a surprisingly vast international fan base.

The Moomins evolved into a lucrative comic strip that ran in the London *Evening News* from 1953 to 1960. Eager to prove herself capable of conceptualizing beyond Moominvalley, Jansson also contributed political cartoon work for nearly 20 years to *GARM,* described by Boel Westin in the *Dictionary of Literary Biography* as a satirical, political mouthpiece with a Finno-Swedish audience. Westin remarked that Jansson's "drawings and her sharp satirical portraits of Adolf Hitler (as well as of Joseph Stalin) contributed to the tough profile of the magazine and were on some occasions censored by the authorities."

In 1958 Jansson's father died, and a year later her brother, Lars, took over the Moomin comic strip. Years later, Jansson's London *Times* obituary described how the Moomintrolls "developed a life of their own which outlasted their creator's interest in them. . . . As [Jansson] found, the marketing of a successful idea brought its own form of slavery, and she was heartily glad when . . . her brother Lars stepped in, releasing her to pursue other interests." While she never truly shed what some scholars see as the "Moomin Shroud," Jansson's later work took readers far from the halcyon days of Moominvalley and introduced her remaining audience to the thought-provoking and sometimes trying existence of an aging life. Acknowledged as a gifted artist in her day, Jansson's position meant she also enjoyed more than one opportunity to illustrate the work of classic children's authors she admired, and she provided art to accompany the words of both Lewis Carroll and J.R.R. Tolkien.

Jansson's Sapphic Reputation

Jansson is lauded by many sources as a prominent lesbian figure. Johanna Pakkanen commented in *Who's Who in Contemporary Gay and Lesbian History* that "homosexual characters, both female and male, appeared first in [Jansson's] short stories." Tuulikki Pietilä, a graphic artist and Jansson's life partner, was the inspiration for the Moomin character Too-Ticky, described as "much addicted to bathing-houses, the sea-side in every particular in fact, and quite a philosopher in a way." Jansson and Pietilä met when they were both art students in the 1930s, and their relationship developed quickly when they met again some 20 years later in 1954. The women eventually settled on Klovharu island in the Finnish archipelago, an environment that provided the setting for the Moomin stories because it was rich with Jansson's memories of childhood summers spent on one of the Porvoo islands with her grandparents.

Moominvalley had been brought to life at a time when the Second World War loomed large on the historical horizon. The *Dictionary of Literary Biography* recorded a diary entry written by Jansson that revealed how she "longed to get away so much that she [felt] she could go to pieces," and it was then that she began to create a "happy society and a peaceful, if fictional, world," as a way of struggling against her anguish. No stranger to the soothing effects of storytelling, Jansson's mother had been a gifted storyteller who spun tales in a way that made Jansson and her siblings feel safe. In an article on the Web site Sybertooth, Literary scholar K.V. Johansen explained, "In many fantasies of the fifties the fantastic is used to create a world that is more comforting, more contained, than the author's own times, or ours. Many children's writers of the . . . fifties used fantasy as a way of looking back to another time when the world did not seem so threatening, or of creating another world, as Jansson did, in which the dangers were of a scale to be grappled with and overcome."

More Than the Moomins

Scholars and reviewers alike agree that Jansson's classification as a writer of children's literature is narrow at best. She revealed her authorial intentions in a 1971 interview cited in the *Reference Guide to Short Fiction*, explaining that she wrote for "the people who find it hard to fit in anywhere, those who are outside and on the margin, rather as when one says 'small and dirty and frightened of the train.' The fish out of water. The inferior person one has oneself succeeded in shaking off or concealing."

Apart from the wildly popular Moomin material, Jansson was also a gifted writer of short fiction. A collection of her novellas titled *Meddelande* (Messages) was released in 1997 to considerable critical acclaim. The *Reference Guide to Short Fiction* described the Moomin books as works that developed a "blend of an adult consciousness of evil and inadequacy with the child's experience of fear and joy," also noting that the final Moomin book, *Sent i november* (Moominvalley in November), is "intended almost exclusively for adults, and focuses on the problems of old age, loneliness, obsession, and change."

National Treasure

Jansson died on June 27, 2001, at the age of 87. That same year, Sort Of Books hired poet Sophie Hannah to re-translate Jansson's *Hur gick det sen? Boken om Mymlan, Mumintrollet och Lilla My* (The Book about Moomin, Mymble and Little My) and released a full-color version of the children's classic as the first in a series of forgotten favorites. Jansson's niece, Sophia Jansson, was present to promote the new book celebrating her aunt's talents. The same publisher has continued purchasing the rights to Jansson's works and plans to release English translations until 2014, when they intend to publish something special to celebrate the author's centenary.

Jansson's legacy includes a Finnish museum in Tampere dedicated to her art and books that span numerous countries, translated into more than 35 languages, from Persian to Korean. The popularity of Jansson's troll world posthumously developed into a full-blown cultural craze in Japan, thanks to an animated television series starring the Moomins that became popular in 1980. This "Moomin-mania" produced everything from dolls and ceramics to towels, pens and postcards. The "Scandinavian beasties" have also been featured in opera, theater and radio, and fans can travel to a small Baltic island near Turku to visit "Moomin World," where they will meet characters from Jansson's stories and immerse themselves in the details of Jansson's fantasy. Jansson was commissioned to paint frescoes on the basement walls of Helsinki's City Hall, and she donated many paintings to the Aurora Children's Hospital in the capital. Her Moomin illustrations have graced everything from Finnish postage to wallpaper, jewelry, and chocolates, and scholars remain fascinated and inspired by Jansson's work, which still appears regularly in doctoral-level dissertations.

According to the *Dictionary of Literary Biography*, Jansson loved "borders because they imply expectations to be on one's way, representing the important movement forward." The entry praised the author's skill at both crossing and erasing a multitude of borders in her writing and art. Whether it be the meeting of water and land epitomized by island life, or the moments when an artist steps from drawing to writing and back again, Tove Jansson proved a nimble negotiator of many borders. Jansson's London *Daily Telegraph* obituary quoted her as saying, "I've had an exciting, varied life that I am glad of, though it has been trying as well. If I could live it all over again, I'd do it completely differently. But I won't say how."

Books

The Cambridge Biographical Encyclopedia: Second Edition, edited by David Crystal, Cambridge University Press, 1999.
Children's Literature Review: Volume 125, Gale Research, 1976.
Dictionary of Literary Biography, Volume 257: Twentieth-Century Swedish Writers After World War II, edited by Ann-Charlotte Gavel Adams, The Gale Group, 2002.
Jansson, Tove, *Finn Family Moomintroll*, Farrar, Straus and Giroux, 1952.
Jansson, Tove, *Moominsummer Madness*, Penguin Books, 1955.
Major Authors and Illustrators for Children and Young Adults: Second Edition, Gale Group, 2002.
Reference Guide to Short Fiction, edited by Noelle Watson, St. James Press, 1994.
Short Story Criticism: Volume 96, Gale Research, 1988.
Who's Who in Contemporary Gay and Lesbian History: From World War II to the Present Day, edited by Robert Aldrich and Garry Wotherspoon, Routledge, 2001.

Periodicals

The Bookseller, September 21, 2001; February 2, 2007.
Daily Telegraph (London, England), June 28, 2001.
Independent (London, England), June 28, 2001.
New York Times, July 9, 2001.
Sunday Herald, December 2, 2001.
Times (London, England), June 28, 2001.
World Literature Today, Spring 1999.

Online

"Famous Finnish Women on Stamps," Famous Women on Stamps, http://home.online.no/~jdigrane/amd/finwomen/jansson1.htm (October 25, 2007).
Johansen, K.V., "The Fifties: Mary Norton, Edward Eager, Lucy Boston, and Tove Jansson," http://www.sybertooth.com/kvj/rl7.htm#tove (October 25, 2007).
"The Rhythm of Texts: Translating for Children," *The Lion and the Unicorn*, http://muse.jhu.edu/journals/lion_and_the_unicorn/v019/19.2br_oittinen.htm (October 25, 2007).
"Tove Jansson," Fantastic Fiction, http://www.fantasticfiction.co.uk/j/tove-jansson/ (October 25, 2007).
"Tove Jansson Biography," Essortment, http://www.mimi.essortment.com/tovejanssonbio_rwpd.htm (October 25, 2007).
"Tove (Marika) Jansson," Books and Writers, http://www.kirjasto.sci.fi/tjansson.htm (October 25, 2007). □

K

Mikhail Kalashnikov

Russian inventor Mikhail Kalashnikov (born 1919) designed the most ubiquitous gun in the history of modern armaments, the AK-47. Known more fully as the *Avtomat Kalashnikova* Model 1947, the infamous Kalashnikov rifle was developed for Soviet army soldiers by one of their own, and went on to become the most manufactured gun in the history of weaponry, with an estimated 100 million produced by the start of the twenty-first century. Interviewed in 2003 by British journalist Nick Paton Walsh for the *Guardian* newspaper, Kalashnikov expressed no regret about the ultimate human cost his invention unleashed on the world. "I sleep soundly," he told Walsh. "The fact that people die because of an AK-47 is not because of the designer, but because of politics."

Kalashnikov was born in 1919 in the town of Kuriya in the Altai Republic in Siberia. He came from a poor peasant family in this steppe region, and was one of 17 children born to his mother, but one of just eight who survived to adulthood. The Soviet Union's forced collectivization of agriculture a few years after his birth brought severe hardships for the family, as their meager land and livestock holdings were seized by the state and they were ordered to work on large collective farms instead. His father was one of the many who resisted, and died in a labor camp in the more frigid part of central Siberia.

Fled into Kazakhstan

Kalashnikov was a tinkerer from an early age, and claimed to have made his first gun at the age of ten, which fired matchsticks. He quit school after word spread in his village that he was fixing an old Browning pistol that he had found—possessing a firearm in the Stalinist-era Soviet Union was tantamount to a death sentence—and fled to neighboring Kazakhstan, though he did not possess the necessary international travel documents and residency papers. He lived underground, but managed to obtain work as a clerk for the Turkistan-Siberian railroad.

At the onset of World War II in 1939, Kalashnikov was drafted into the Soviet Army, and by the time the Germans invaded the Soviet Union in the summer of 1941, he had reached the rank of tank sergeant. In his spare moments, he worked on improvements for the T-34 tank vehicles of his division, such as a device that counted the number of rounds fired from the machine gun mounted on the tank that let the personnel know when ammunition was running low. The German-Soviet encounters in the western regions of the Soviet Union were some of the most pitched and long-lasting battles in the entire war, with heavy civilian casualties and vicious reprisals carried out by both sides. Thanks to Germany's long history of industrial development, the Nazis went to war with excellent rifles that were known as *Sturmgewehr 44,* abbreviated as the StG44, with *Sturmgewehr* translating as "assault rifle." The Soviet Red Army, by contrast, still used an archaic single-shot rifle.

Kalashnikov was wounded in the Battle of Bryansk in October of 1941, a 19-day fight that took place about 200 miles from Moscow. The Germans annihilated Bryansk, and Kalashnikov suffered a shrapnel hit to left shoulder, but it took another week for him to reach medical facilities because of the fighting. Given a six-month leave by the Army

to recuperate, he went to Almaty, the main city in Kazakhstan, and visited his former colleagues at the rail yard. He had already been thinking of a new kind of assault rifle, and manufactured a prototype with the help of the metal workers at the yard. When he showed it to a Red Army officer, Kalashnikov was recommended for a new assignment, this one with the firearms lab of the Aviation Institute in Kazakhstan.

Won National Competition

In 1943, Soviet arms engineers created a new gun cartridge—the cylindrical case that holds an explosive charge along with ammunition and is inserted into a gun—and asked him to develop a prototype for a gun that it would fit. He worked on that project until the war's end, when the Red Army announced a contest to create a new automatic weapon, and Kalashnikov beat out several other professionals with the winning design. He called it the "Mikhtim" after his first and middle names, Mikhail Timofeyevich, though the second name is known as a patronym in Slavic nomenclature and is the name of one's father. The rifle went into production in 1947 as the AK-47. Two years later, it became the standard-issue weapon for the entire Soviet Army.

Kalashnikov's rifle was easy to manufacture, requiring few advanced technical skills, and had just eight moving parts, which made it easy to take apart, clean, and put back together. Even if not maintained properly, however, it still fired accurately. The Soviets put it into production at several sites, and also licensed its manufacture in countries that were

its Cold War allies, including Poland, Bulgaria, China, Iraq, and North Korea. Kalashnikov, meanwhile, spent much of his career with the Red Army as a designer of small arms working out of Izhevsk, a city in the southern Ural Mountains that was the Soviet Union's center of weapons manufacturing and closed to visitors. He was known to have supervised two famous German weapons experts, Hugo Schmeisser and Werner Grüner, who were forcibly relocated there in the years following World War II but released in the early 1950s. He also developed the PK *Pulemyot Kalashnikova* or Kalashnikov machine gun, as well as the RPK, the *Ruchnoi pulemyot Kalashnikova* or Kalashnikov light machine gun.

Meanwhile, Kalashnikov's AK-47 began to achieve a certain level of notoriety. In 1964, rebels in the African nation of Congo were using them in a struggle that pitted them against U.S.-backed forces, and in the late 1960s they became a status symbol for Arab commandoes across the Middle East. A factory in Egypt manufactured them for Syrians, who in turn provided aid to Al Fatah and other guerrilla organizations that were fighting Israel. *Esquire*'s Guy Martin explained their impact on the developing world, asserting that "Kalashnikovs have decided the fates of nations by enabling people who could not afford to determine the shape of a battlefield to decide where war was possible."

Beloved by Soldiers

Kalashnikov's rifle was used by the North Vietnamese Communist forces during the Vietnam War, and their superiority was well-known to U.S. soldiers, some of whom preferred to trade their inferior, problem-plagued assault-rifle counterpart, the M16, for the Soviet-made gun when AK-47s were captured along with enemy troops. Writing in *Field & Stream* C.J. Chivers noted that the name Kalashnikov had become synonymous with "functionality. Kalashnikov's series of rifles, now ubiquitous, achieved global circulation in part because of two reasons central to their design. They are simple to use. And they almost never fail."

At the 1972 Summer Olympics in Munich, Germany, an Arab group took several Israeli athletes hostage with the help of the barrels of their AK-47s, which they used to break into the Israeli team members' rooms in the Olympic Village dormitory compound. Later that decade, when the Soviet Union invaded neighboring Afghanistan, the resistance movement of mujahadeen fighters were backed by the United States, which sent Kalashnikov rifles into Afghanistan via Pakistan. Those weapons were later used by the Taliban fighters in their attempt to establish an Islamic theocracy in Afghanistan in the 1990s. By that point, the Kalashnikov had even made its way to the United States, and was the weapon of choice in urban gang warfare. In cities like Los Angeles or New York City, they fetched prices as high as $600 each. Fifty years after they first went into production, the official count for the number of Kalashnikovs produced was 70 million, but unofficial totals added at least another 30 million to that number.

Kalashnikov never benefited financially from his invention, since it took place in the Soviet era of collective labor. He was lauded, however, as "Hero of Socialist Labor" and was given a seat on the Supreme Soviet, and remained a celebrated figure. His milestone birthdays became occasions for civic celebrations in Izhevsk, and in 1994, when he turned 75, Russian President Boris Yeltsin (1931–2007) said that a patent might be in the works. That never happened, but the cash-strapped former Soviet state found other ways to capitalize on the world-famous Kalashnikov name, including a vodka brand and a line of hunting knives. The city also opened two museums dedicated to his invention, and honoring his lifetime of service.

Regretted Mass Production Numbers

In the interview with Walsh for the *Guardian* years later, Kalashnikov—having risen to the rank of general—was able to speak freely about his thoughts on the matter. "I made it to protect the motherland. And then they spread the weapon [around the world]—not because I wanted them to. Not at my choice. Then it was like a genie out of the bottle and it began to walk all on its own and in directions I did not want." He repeated the same sentiments when Chivers, writing for the *New York Times,* visited Izhevsk for the general's 80th birthday celebrations in 2004. Noting that the AK-47 was designed to save the Soviet Union from the Nazi threat, he reflected that "it is a pity it was used in other inadmissible conflicts." Chivers found Izhevsk an aging city, no longer closed to outsiders but struggling with the loss of manufacturing jobs. "Like the city he helped put on the map, General Kalashnikov still flashes fondness for much of the socialist ideal," Chivers wrote. "As he worked the crowd this week, he used the word *tovarishch,* or 'comrade,' not with the bitter irony of some post-Soviet Russians but with casual sincerity. He wore a medal bearing Lenin's intense, jaw-forward gaze. He spoke of the value of labor, not just to state but to self. 'Work—and only work—can bring you to a high position,' " he was quoted as saying.

Periodicals

Esquire, June 1997.
Field & Stream, March 1, 2006.
Guardian (London, England), October 10, 2003.
New York Times, November 11, 2004. □

Natalia Karp

In 1943 Jewish concert pianist Natalia Karp (1911-2007) arrived at Poland's Plaszow concentration camp expecting to be executed by the German soldiers in command. Instead, her musical talents saved her life. The camp's commandant summoned Karp to play for him and was so impressed with her piano playing that he halted her execution. Karp survived the war, then resumed her musical career. By the 1950s, Karp was playing with the London Philharmonic and touring Europe, where she earned recognition for her mastery of Chopin. She continued public performances into her 90s.

Earned Reputation as Child Prodigy

The gifted pianist was born Natalia Weissman on February 27, 1911, in Krakow, Poland. She was the second of four children born to the Weissmans, an upstanding Polish-Jewish family. Her father, Isidor, was a successful businessman. He owned a knitwear factory and several properties scattered throughout Berlin. With plenty of wealth, the family enjoyed vacations at some of Europe's leading spa resorts. Karp developed her interest in music from her mother, who sang opera arias to her children at home. Karp taught herself to play the piano by ear, and by the time she was four, the child's musical abilities were known throughout her neighborhood. When Karp was a youngster, a woman came to the door, saying she had heard rumors there was a musical prodigy living at the address. She offered to give Karp lessons. Later, Karp studied with the brother-in-law of famed Polish pianist Arthur Rubenstein.

Karp attended Hebrew school and at 13 decided that she wanted to make a career out of the piano. Her musical grandfather helped persuade her parents to let her go to Berlin to take lessons with Austrian classic pianist Artur Schnabel. Karp had to audition for Schnabel before he would take her on as a student. After hearing Karp play, Schnabel agreed to tutor her and at 16, she relocated to Berlin. Schnabel's son taught Karp about harmony and musical theory. What she yearned to study, however, was technique, which Schnabel did not cover, so she switched teachers and began studying under Georg Bertram.

In 1929 the teenage virtuoso, playing alongside the Berlin Philharmonic, wowed Germans with a performance of Chopin's E minor concerto. Karp's career was just taking off when her mother became ill and died of kidney failure, forcing Karp to return to Poland to care for her younger siblings. In 1933 Karp married a lawyer and fellow pianist named Julius Hubler. He recognized her talents but discouraged her public performances, preferring that his wife stay at home.

The War Began

By 1939, World War II was heating up as German forces invaded Poland. Hubler left at the start of the war, answering a call to join the Polish Army. He died when his train was bombed, though Karp did not know she was a widow until after the war ended six years later. As German soldiers moved into Poland, the Jewish population faced increasing persecution. Karp's father and brother fled Krakow.

In time, Karp and her sister, Helena, relocated to Tarnow, a predominantly Jewish city 45 miles east of Krakow. Karp thought it might be safer there, out of the big city and in the company of fellow Jews. At the time, thousands of Jewish refugees were fleeing to Tarnow. Tarnow, however, was eventually turned into a ghetto surrounded by a high fence and patrolled by German troops. There was scarcely enough food. Routinely, German troops came in to round up Jews for deportation to labor camps—or death camps. During the "selection" process, soldiers randomly gunned down Jewish people. Karp witnessed the massacre of thousands of Jews. Over the course of one single day, she watched as German soldiers shot 5,000 people in the square.

If they were to survive, Karp and her sister knew they had to leave. Accompanied by two friends, the sisters fled Tarnow in 1943, after dying their hair blonde, hoping to hide their darker Jewish features. Once outside the ghetto walls, they headed for Warsaw and obtained false papers, which they thought would get them out of Poland and into Slovakia. Polish police captured them, however, and turned the sisters over to the German Gestapo. They were sent to the Plaszow concentration camp outside Krakow, knowing full well that they would likely be shot upon arrival. Plaszow had a reputation for mass shootings. The Plaszow concentration camp was built on a Jewish cemetery and the Germans had removed the gravestones, using them to pave the roads.

After Karp's arrival, the callous commandant, Amon Goeth, got wind that a talented pianist was among the prisoners. He summoned Karp. It was December 9, 1943, the commandant's birthday, and he needed entertainment for his party. "A hairdresser did my hair, and they took me past screaming inmates to the villa," Karp recalled in a 1994 article in the London *Guardian*. "There was a party, uniformed German officers, women in evening dresses, Goeth in a white dinner-jacket, drinking and food. I was so frightened, and I hadn't played for so many years because of the war that my fingers were almost stiff."

Karp chose to play Chopin's Nocturne in C sharp minor. She was frightened during the entire performance, knowing that at any moment Goeth might pull a gun and kill her. She made it through the piece, and afterward Goeth declared,

"Sie soll leben"—she shall live. Karp asked that her sister be spared, too, and Goeth agreed. Over the course of the war, Goeth was responsible for some 10,000 Jewish deaths. Steven Spielberg's 1993 haunting epic *Schindler's List* featured the Plaszow camp, with Ralph Fiennes portraying Goeth.

Survived the Holocaust

While at Plaszow, the sisters were forced to labor in a factory that made goods to support the German war effort. Other times, they spent entire days doing meaningless manual labor, like moving rocks in the nearby quarry. After about ten months, the sisters were stuffed into a crowded train and shipped to Auschwitz, a concentration camp where 75 percent of the prisoners were executed. Auschwitz was the largest World War II death camp, a place where Hitler carried out mass murders as part of his forced annihilation of the Jewish population. When she arrived at Auschwitz, Karp was branded with the number A27407 seared into her arm. After being branded, she knew she was not immediately going to the gas chamber. Her clothes were taken and she was issued a short, black dress and wooden clogs.

At the camp, Karp and her sister were given one meal a day, consisting of bread and potato-peel soup. They worked all day long, beginning at 5 a.m. It was cold and miserable and Karp knew that any day she might be selected for death. In a 2005 interview with David Cohen of the London *Evening Standard,* Karp described the experience this way: "My sister and I clung to each other. We scavenged for any food we could find. We hardly interacted with the other prisoners. It was the bleakest place on earth—everyone weak and starving, with empty, staring eyes—and you did what you could to survive." Karp spent each day listening to the constant screams of children and their parents being separated. Upon arriving at the camps, young children, unable to do labor like adults, were usually executed. During this time, Karp prayed that the Allied Forces would bomb the camp to end their suffering.

Toward the end of the war, the sisters were transferred to another camp, in Sudetenland, an area of western Czechoslovakia that was occupied by the Germans. She was set free in May of 1945. Weighing 35 pounds less than she did before the war, Karp returned to Poland with her sister, but things were not the same in Krakow. Karp never found her brother or father or learned what had happened to them. Speaking to the London *Times*, Karp described the surreal experience this way: "One was walking in the streets like in a strange place because before the war Cracow had had 65,000 Jews . . . so when you went out to town you met people you knew all the time. But now you didn't meet anybody."

Revived Music Career

After the war, Karp assisted orphans in Krakow and experienced a renewed interest in music. She scrounged a piano from a bombed-out house and began practicing. Her first post-war performance, in 1946, was broadcast on Polish radio, with Karp playing alongside the Krakow Philharmonic Orchestra. For this event, she performed the Tchaikovsky Piano Concerto No. 1. "I chose it because it is one of the hardest and needs the strength of a man, and I wanted to show the Poles and Germans that they didn't destroy me,'' she told the London *Evening Standard.* She married Josef Karpf in 1946 and the couple moved to London, where he worked in the Polish embassy. They had two daughters, Eve and Anne. Anne Karpf grew up to be a journalist and wrote a 1996 book, *The War After,* which included firsthand accounts from Holocaust survivors, including passages from her parents. Eve Karpf took an interest in music, becoming a voice actress.

After settling in Britain, Karpf Anglicized her name, dropping the ''f'' and using Karp as her stage name. By the 1950s she was playing extensively, giving recitals at London's famed Wigmore Hall. Over the next 20 years, she gave hundreds of concerts for the BBC and played alongside the London Philharmonic Orchestra and the London Symphony. Karp toured Europe and earned a reputation for her mastery of Chopin's music, although she also played Beethoven and Schubert. While performing, Karp played in an impersonal, direct manner, believing the music should speak for itself and come through the performer. She thought the performer's personality should be secondary to the music. When performing, Karp was known to place a pink handkerchief on her piano. This plain piece of fabric, purchased for a nominal fee after the war, served as a reminder of the luxury and femininity that was lost during her years in the concentration camps. Besides performing with orchestras, Karp played with a small ensemble that included Regina Schein on cello and Henriette Canter on violin. The musicians, who performed under the name the Alpha Trio, recorded a disc of the Tchaikovsky Piano Trio for German-based Vox Records.

As Karp grew older, she was dismayed that genocide and war continued around the globe. According to the London *Independent,* Karp lamented, ''When we came out of the camps, we thought, 'Now we'll never need any passports, there will never be any more wars,' we were sure of it. What a disappointment that so many Holocausts happen again in the world, like Rwanda and Yugoslavia. . . . When I see the ethnic cleansing and how the refugees cry and leave and go with the bundles—exactly the same as the Jews during the war. I see the same pictures again, and I can't believe it repeats itself.''

Karp continued performing into her 90s. She died July 9, 2007, in London. Her husband preceded her in death in 1993. She was survived by her two daughters.

Periodicals

Daily Telegraph (London), July 11, 2007.
Evening Standard (London), January 19, 2005.
Guardian (London), February 17, 1994; July 11, 2007.
Independent (London), July 17, 2007.
Times (London), July 14, 2007. □

Garry Kasparov

Russian chess master Garry Kasparov (born 1963) dominated the game of chess as few others had be-

fore him, reigning as world champion from 1985 to 2000. His struggles against chess-playing computers gained international publicity.

After a career marked by clashes with chess authorities, Kasparov embarked on what was perhaps an even greater challenge upon his retirement from professional chess in 2005: he entered the troubled world of Russian politics. Within two years he had emerged as leader of the opposition Other Russia coalition, posing direct challenges to the continued influence of the powerful Russian president Vladimir Putin. Even during his years as an international representative of the Communist-ruled Soviet Union, Kasparov's chess feats had become imbued with political significance: in his world championship matches against Anatoly Karpov, the first of which ranks among the most bizarre chess matches ever played, he was seen as a freewheeling challenger to an orthodox player backed by the Communist establishment. However, despite his tremendous celebrity—in Russia, chess players are national celebrities—Kasparov faced enormous difficulties in his quest to alter Russia's political course.

Turned to Chess After Father's Death

Kasparov was born Garry Weinstein (both his birth name and the name Garry Kasparov have been transliterated from Russian Cyrillic characters in many ways) on April 12, 1963, in Baku, now in Azerbaijan but then part of the

Soviet Union. He was of mixed ethnic background; his father, Kim Weinstein, was Jewish, and his mother, Clara Kasparova, was Armenian. In Baku, dominated by ethnic Azerbaijanis and Russians, he was therefore a double minority. Kasparov's parents, both engineers and chess enthusiasts, noticed their son's skills when, at the age of six, he solved a newspaper chess puzzle even though he hardly understood the rules of the game. Shortly after that, Kim Weinstein died of cancer, and his young son began to immerse himself in chess.

Clara Kasparova channeled her energies into her son's promising chess career, taking out loans so that the pair could travel to important tournaments. Kasparov was enrolled in a government-sponsored chess academy run by former world champion Mikhail Botvinnik, who, like Kasparov, had Jewish ancestry. Botvinnik suggested to Kasparov that in order to further his career in a country plagued by anti-Semitism, he should take the masculine form of his mother's surname, which did not sound Jewish. Weinstein did. Kasparov was winning tournaments even as a preteen, and in 1980 he became the junior chess champion of the world. Chess watchers had already identified him as a future star; Leonard Barden, chess columnist for London's *Guardian,* wrote that "there is a clear favorite for the world championship in 1990. He is 11-year-old Garry Weinstein from Baku."

The pressure of competitive chess permanently shaped Kasparov's personality. "The loss of my childhood was the price for becoming the youngest world champion in history," he told David Remnick in *The New Yorker.* "When you have to fight every day from a young age, your soul can be contaminated. I lost my childhood. I never really had it. Today I have to be careful not to become cruel, because I became a soldier too early." Kasparov became Soviet champion in 1981, and he qualified for the arduous series of elimination matches that would select a challenger for world champion Anatoly Karpov in 1984.

After the epic clash between American Bobby Fischer and the Soviet Union's Boris Spassky in 1972, top-flight international chess became freighted with political significance. The two players could not have been more different in their styles on the chessboard and in their general attitudes. "Kasparov represented a new generation," noted Remnick. "At twenty-one, he was ironic, full of barely disguised disdain for the regime. He was a member of the Communist Party until 1990—his chess ambitions required it—but no one saw him as subservient. Rather, he was cast, in his challenge to Karpov, as a champion of the young and of the outsiders. His chess style was swift, imaginative, daring—sometimes to the point of recklessness. Karpov painted academic still-lifes; Kasparov was an Abstract Expressionist. He prepared thoroughly, but at some point, he once said, he played by instinct, "by smell, by feel."

Came Back from 5–0 Deficit

When Kasparov and Karpov met in Moscow to play for the championship in September of 1984, the match followed a course unlike almost any other that had ever been played. A player needed six victories to win the match;

draws (tied games) did not count. Kasparov lost five games without a single win and appeared headed for a crushing defeat. He nearly lost the fifteenth game, but held on for a draw after 93 moves. Kasparov, wrote Remnick, "was figuring out Karpov the way an astute hitter, after repeated, chastening strikeouts, figures out a pitcher." He began to wear his opponent down, forcing draws in 20 consecutive games at one point. Karpov lost weight as the match dragged on through the long Russian winter. Finally Kasparov notched two quick victories in a row, in games 47 and 48. Karpov seemed to be crumbling.

At that point, under Soviet pressure, international chess authorities cancelled the match, claiming that Karpov was exhausted. (Karpov, for his own part, insisted that he wanted the match to continue.) Kasparov was angered, believing that Soviet chess authorities had conspired to circle the wagons against him. In the end, the decision did not matter. He defeated Karpov unambiguously in a return match, winning the world championship with a slashing attack on November 9, even though he was playing the black pieces—a slight disadvantage. Kasparov and Karpov fought several more closely contested matches over the rest of the 1980s, with Kasparov retaining his title each time. The new champion saw his victories in political terms, telling Remnick, "The 80s were purely dominated by two players. Karpov and myself. But our fight was also about ideological differences. We represented different values. It was communism versus democracy." Kasparov's successes came in spite of petty interferences from Soviet chess authorities; he sometimes found, for example, that his seconds, or helpers, had been drafted into the Soviet army and had to report for duty days before an important match.

Indeed, Kasparov was a proto-capitalist thinker off the chessboard as well. In 1987 he filmed an advertisement for Schweppes soft drinks in Switzerland. He insisted on keeping all of his chess prize money, becoming the first Soviet competitor in any sport to do so. Using Western contacts, he was instrumental in beginning what became a steady stream of Russian hockey players who signed lucrative contracts in North America's National Hockey League; he introduced Soviet hockey team captain Slava (Vyacheslav) Fetisov to the general manager of the New Jersey Devils team. After Communism fell, Kasparov started trading and consulting firms, and he became wealthy. By 1993 his annual income was estimated at $3 million. Something of a playboy (although he neither smoked nor drank), Kasparov married three times, enjoyed a two-year affair with the well-known Moscow stage actress Martina Neyelova, and had two children. Another key female presence in his life was his mother, Clara, who served as his manager all through his years as a chess champion and continued to advise him as he entered politics.

The chaos that accompanied the last years of the Soviet Union brought Kasparov upheaval as well as profit, however. Kasparov was preparing for a match in January of 1990 near his hometown of Baku when fighting intensified between Armenians and Azerbaijanis over the disputed Nagorno-Karabakh region. Ethnic Armenians were attacked by roving gangs in Baku, and Kasparov found himself trapped when transport out of the city was shut down. Finally Kasparov, amid rumors that he had been targeted by the gangs, managed to charter a plane to Moscow. Rushing to his childhood home, he collected some family pictures and chess notebooks he had used as a child. He filled his charter airliner with 68 Armenian friends and fled. As of 2007 he had never returned to Baku.

Kept World Championship

Kasparov continued to roll over his human chess opponents in the 1990s, defeating Nigel Short in 1993 and Viswanathan Anand in 1995 to keep his world championship. The latter match took place on the 107th floor of the World Trade Center. Increasingly, however, Kasparov was also interested in facing a new kind of opponent: a chess computer. In the mid-1980s he had become involved with early attempts to develop a computer capable of competing with top-flight human grandmasters, and he defeated a state-of-the-art machine, Deep Thought, in 1989. Even while humans were clearly superior to computers, though, he seemed to have problems in a situation where his mastery of chess's psychological aspect did him no good—a machine was unfazed by his intimidating attacking style. In 1994 Kasparov lost a game to a computer called ChessGenius 2, and was reportedly devastated by the loss. Other players in the exhibition defeated the computer without trouble.

In 1996 Kasparov lost another game to the Deep Blue machine constructed by computer maker IBM, a computer that could analyze 200 million chess positions per second. His 1997 rematch against Deep Blue was a milestone in the relationship between human and machine. With international attention focused on the contest, the computer won by a score of 3 1/2 to 2 1/2; the computer won two games, Kasparov won one, and the rest were draws. While Steve Forbes editorialized in *Forbes* magazine that Kasparov's loss was "about as significant as an Olympic gold medalist's losing a weight-lifting contest to a crane or a forklift," Kasparov, whose play was uncharacteristically poor, was depressed by his loss. Computers and top grandmasters remained closely matched into the mid-2000s, and chess master Boris Gulko, writing in *Commentary,* suggested that once again psychological factors were responsible for Kasparov's loss: "There is some evidence to suggest that the same champion who shows no mercy whatsoever when dispatching ordinary mortals does have special psychological difficulties meting out similar punishment to machines."

Kasparov finally lost the world championship in 2000 when he was defeated by one of his own chess students, Vladimir Kramnik. That year he launched a new online chess site, KasparovChess.com (now defunct, but the chess lectures are still in circulation), and he continued to play competitively. In 2003 he played a short match against another computer, X3D Fritz, also known as Deep Junior. This time Kasparov emerged in a tie with the computer, winning one game, losing one, and drawing one. In 2005, after winning a chess tournament in Linares, Spain, he retired.

By that time, Kasparov had become deeply committed to his new career as a political leader—or resistance figure,

for he was one of the few voices in Russia opposing the monopolistic power of President Vladimir Putin and his colleagues in politics and industry. Although his own politics tended toward the conservative side, Kasparov joined Drugaya Rossiya, or the Other Russia, an umbrella group of liberal groups opposed to the Putin regime; he felt it was necessary for Russians opposed to Putin to make common cause with each other. Kasparov did not plan to run for the Russian presidency himself, but he emerged as leader of The Other Russia after winning several internal elections.

Kasparov's chances of displacing Putin or one of his handpicked successors in the 2008 presidential elections were slim. Mostly denied access to television time, he was forced to take his message on the road across the sprawling nation of Russia. He was harassed by Russian intelligence services, arrested once, and roughed up by right-wing youth gangs. But Kasparov felt he was speaking for Russians left behind by the new prosperity of Russian capitalism. He pointed to poverty outside Russia's large cities, human rights violations, and the gap between rich and poor as "the key reasons this regime will inevitably collapse" (as he told Remnick). He had no plans to return to chess. "I don't want to look back," he told *Time.* "I have a new life now."

Books

Kasparov, Garry, *Child of Change: The Autobiography of the World Chess Champion,* HarperCollins, 1990.
Newsmakers, Issue 4, Gale, 1997.

Periodicals

Atlantic Monthly, December 2005.
Commentary, July 1997.
Forbes, June 2, 1997.
Guardian (London, England), February 20, 1993.
Independent (London, England), October 2, 2007.
Insight on the News, August 19, 1996.
New Scientist, July 12, 2003.
New Yorker, October 1, 2007.
Observer (London, England), August 21, 2005; September 30, 2007.
Sports Illustrated, December 20, 2004.
Time, February 26, 1996; April 9, 2007.
Times (London, England), September 1, 1990; March 24, 2007.
□

Elizabeth Hobbs Keckley

American slave, seamstress, and author Elizabeth Keckley (c.1818-1907) had a close friendship with First Lady Mary Todd Lincoln during her time in the White House. Keckley's autobiography *Behind the Scenes; or, Thirty Years a Slave and Four Years in the White House* caused considerable controversy at the time of its publication, with some accusing Keckley of betraying the confidence of Mrs. Lincoln. However, this book and its unique perspective remain valuable for researchers and historians today.

Born Into Slavery

Elizabeth Keckley was born into slavery as Elizabeth Hobbs on the estate of Colonel Armistead Burwell in Dinwiddie County, Virginia. The exact date of her birth is unknown. Sources place it as early as 1818 and as late as 1840; based on records from the Burwell household, February 1818 seems the most likely date, although other evidence from Keckley's lifetime suggests that 1824 or 1825 may be the correct year.

Details of her family are better known. Agnes Hobbs was the Burwells' house slave, caring for the Burwell children and acting as the family's seamstress. Unlike most slaves—and in violation of laws forbidding slaves to be educated—Agnes Hobbs had been taught to read and write. George Pleasant Hobbs, Agnes's "abroad" husband, was a slave who lived on his owner's property in the area. For all that Agnes Hobbs gave her first child the family name of her husband, it seems unlikely that George Hobbs was actually Elizabeth's father. Like many children born into slavery, Elizabeth Keckley was probably the child of Agnes Hobbs's owner, Colonel Burwell. George Hobbs remained devoted to his wife and her daughter, despite being permitted to see them only occasionally. When Keckley was about seven or eight years old, George Hobbs's owner's family moved away, taking Hobbs with them. Keckley never saw the man she believed to be her father again.

Keckley's childhood was difficult. When about four years old, Keckley began looking after the youngest Burwell daughter, Elizabeth. She also performed household chores and began learning to sew from her mother. As a child, she received her first severe beating, and the memory of it never left her. Writing in her memoirs, *Behind the Scenes; or Thirty Years a Slave and Four Years in the White House,* Keckley remembered, "The blows were not administered with a light hand . . . doubtless the severity of the lashing has made me remember the incident so well. This was the first time I was punished in this cruel way, but not the last."

As a teenager, Keckley went to live with the Burwells' oldest son, Robert, and his new wife. The family moved to North Carolina, where Keckley suffered beatings by a local schoolmaster and learned to handle her temperamental mistress. She was also sexually abused by a man named Alexander Kirkland, who fathered her only child, George. In the early 1840s, Keckley and her baby son returned to Virginia to live with the Burwell family, now a resident at a farm belonging to Hugh A. Garland, who had married Anne Burwell. She remained with the Garland family for over twenty years, becoming close to the Garland children. Jennifer Fleischner noted in *Mrs. Lincoln and Mrs. Keckley: The Remarkable Story of the Friendship Between a First Lady and a Former Slave* that "if Lizzy ever experienced something like happiness as a slave, it was with the Garlands."

Gained Freedom

In 1847, the Garlands moved their household to St. Louis. Here, Keckley saw a number of free African Americans and began to long for freedom, believing it now to be a possibility. She began working independently as a seamstress to help support the Garland family's often inadequate income. In 1850, she became reacquainted with James Keckley, whom she previously met in Virginia. He told her he was a free man and proposed marriage, but she refused, not wanting to bring any children into the world as slaves, as any of her children would have automatically been. However, this proposal made her determined to acquire her own freedom. Deciding against escaping, she instead began badgering Garland with questions about, as she said in her memoirs, "whether he would permit me to purchase myself, and what price I must pay." On one occasion, Garland offered her a small amount of amount so she could cross the river with her son and thereby gain her freedom, but she refused, preferring to legally purchase her freedom. Garland finally set the price for the freedom of Keckley and her son at $1200. Keckley then agreed to marry James Keckley, but soon discovered that he was a slave like herself as well as an alcoholic.

Keckley continued to work as a seamstress, hoping to earn enough money to buy her freedom. By the time Garland died, Keckley had not raised the sum; however, the women for whom she sewed banded together to lend her the money and Keckley and her son became free in August 1855. She soon saved enough money from her earnings to repay the loan. In 1860, Keckley left St. Louis for Baltimore, Maryland. She stayed there only briefly before continuing to Washington, D.C. There, she began her own sewing business, working for a time with Varina Howell Davis, wife of the future President of the Confederacy Jefferson Davis. (Keckley recounted in her memoirs that after the Civil War, she observed a wax figure depicting Davis in the dress he was reported to have been wearing when captured and recognized it as one she had made for his wife.) Keckley hired other young women to work for her, building her sewing business and expanding her clientele. Keckley's biography in *Notable Black American Women* commented that her "business success was derived not only from her sewing and teaching skills, but also from her bearing and personality."

Developed Friendship with Mrs. Lincoln

Upon her arrival in Washington, D.C., Keckley dreamed of working for the women of the White House. This hope was realized shortly after the arrival of Mary Todd Lincoln, wife of newly-elected President Abraham Lincoln, in the capital in 1862. One of Keckley's clients knew Mrs. Lincoln and recommended Keckley's services to her. Over the next several months, Keckley made several dresses for the new First Lady. Soon, Keckley became a confidante of Mrs. Lincoln, acting not only as dressmaker but as personal maid, nurse, traveling companion, and general sounding board. When the Lincolns' son Willie became ill, Keckley sat with him and later helped dress him after his death. Keckley had lost her own son George, who had enlisted in the Union army and died in a battle in August 1861. Mrs. Lincoln had written Keckley when she heard of the death; Keckley said in her memoirs that "the kind womanly letter that Mrs. Lincoln wrote to me . . . was full of golden words of comfort." The two women supported each other through their losses, building a basis for their friendship. Fleischner noted that "after Willie died, Lizzy was one of the few people Mary admitted to her presence."

Keckley soon became an integral part of Mary Todd Lincoln's retinue. Mrs. Lincoln, somewhat like Keckley's former North Carolina mistress Mrs. Burwell, was a temperamental woman given to outbursts of emotion and fits of depression, and Keckley was someone on whom she could rely. In turn, Mrs. Lincoln supported Keckley in her endeavors; when Keckley helped a relief organization for recently-freed slaves in Washington, D.C., Mrs. Lincoln provided both moral and financial support for the venture. When Abraham Lincoln was assassinated in April 1865, Keckley came to the assistance of his bereaved wife. During Mary Lincoln's period of mourning, Keckley was again one of the few people whom she wished to see. Keckley later helped Lincoln gather her belongings and return to Illinois; Lincoln wanted to employ Keckley, but could not afford to, so Keckley returned to her business in Washington, D.C. However, the two women corresponded and met again in 1867 when Lincoln tried to sell some of her personal effects in the hopes of raising money to cover debts. However, this action brought considerable criticism upon both women.

Published Controversial Memoirs

In 1868, Keckley's memoirs, *Behind the Scenes,* were published by G.W. Carlton and Company. Keckley wrote the book hoping to defend both herself and Mary Lincoln from the recent criticism. She also hoped to raise money to support Lincoln. The book contained Keckley's account of the personal lives of the Lincolns, and displayed both Mary Lincoln's strengths and failings. Keckley provided much private detail about private events and opinions; in doing so, she revealed many things that the Lincolns would have preferred to keep out of the public eye. In *Disarming the Nation: Women's Writing and the American Civil War,* Elizabeth Young argued that the book was an effort to "[leave] Mary Todd Lincoln symbolically naked and the seamstress herself holding needle." Whatever the intent, the effect of the book was to end all future contact between Keckley and the Lincoln family. Robert Lincoln publicly condemned the work and may have even tried to stop its publication; Mary Lincoln, feeling betrayed by her friend, no longer even corresponded with Keckley.

Keckley's life continued to be quiet for the next several years. She remained in Washington, D.C., and continued with her sewing business, training many young seamstresses. Despite being in her 70s, Keckley moved to Wilberforce, Ohio, in 1892 to teach sewing and head the domestic arts program at the historically African-American Wilberforce University. The following year, she represented the university at the 1893 Columbian Exposition in Chicago.

In 1898, Keckley returned to Washington, D.C., where she lived in the Home for Destitute Women and Children. During her years at the shelter, she spent much of her time in her room, apparently mourning the circumstances that had estranged her from Mary Todd Lincoln. Her only income during this time was the $8 (later $12) a month she received as a pension from her deceased son, George. She remained at the home until her death from a stroke on May 26, 1907, following a brief illness. Keckley was buried in Harmony Cemetery in Washington, D.C. On her tombstone, the words "For so he giveth his beloved sleep" from Psalm 127 were engraved. This tombstone marked Keckley's grave until 1959, when Harmony Cemetery was relocated from Washington, D.C. to Landover, Maryland; because Keckley had no relatives to claim her remains, she was reburied in an unmarked grave.

After her death, Keckley's very existence was called into question. In 1935, journalist David Rankin Barbee argued that not only was Keckley not the author of *Behind the Scenes,* but that no such person as Elizabeth Keckley had ever lived; he claimed that the true author of the autobiography was a woman named Jane Swisshelm. However, people who had known Keckley personally came forward to dispute his claims, and Barbee was ultimately forced to recast his accusations to say, according to Fleischner, that "no such person Elizabeth Keckley wrote the celebrated Lincoln book."

Despite the controversy regarding *Behind the Scenes,* this account of White House life remains valuable to scholars today. Although many have challenged Keckley and her account over the years, her place in history seems assured.

Books

Fleischner, Jennifer, *Mastering Slavery: Memory, Family, and Identity in Women's Slave Narratives,* New York University Press, 1996.

Fleischner, Jennifer, *Mrs. Lincoln and Mrs. Keckly: The Remarkable Story of the Friendship Between a First Lady and a Former Slave,* Broadway Books, 2003.

Keckley, Elizabeth, *Behind the Scenes; or, Thirty Years a Slave, and Four Years in the White House* Cartleton & Co., 1868.

Notable Black American Women, Book 1. Gale Research, 1992.

Young, Elizabeth, *Disarming the Nation: Women's Writing and the American Civil War,* University of Chicago Press, 1999.

Online

Contemporary Authors Online, Gale, 2008, http://galenet.galegroup.com/servlet/BioRc, (November 26, 2007). □

W. K. Kellogg

American food industrialist Will Keith (W. K.) Kellogg (1860-1951) founded the company that bears his name after creating the world's first flaked cereal. His "Toasted Corn Flakes" laid the foundation for the later success of The Kellogg Company, which dominated the packaged breakfast food market in America for much of the twentieth century. Kellogg bested his competitors in a crowded field by relying heavily on advertising and promotional gimmicks, but he was an early pioneer in brand management, and more than a century after his company came into being in 1906, Kellogg cereal boxes still bear his distinctive signature as a logo.

Kellogg was born on April 7, 1860, in Battle Creek, Michigan, a city located about 110 miles west of Detroit. He was the seventh of sixteen children born to John Preston Kellogg and Ann Janette Kellogg, both of whom joined a burgeoning new religious group in the city known as the Seventh Day Adventists. This Protestant Christian denomination was known for observing its Sabbath, or holy day, on Saturday instead of Sunday, and members were urged to follow the church's recommended diet, which forbade meat, alcohol, and caffeine.

Dropped Out of School

Kellogg's father owned a broom manufacturing company in Battle Creek, and young Will went to work there at the age of 14, after leaving school. In marked contrast to his sixth grade education was Kellogg's older brother, John Harvey Kellogg (1852-1943), who graduated from New York University's Medical School in 1875, the year Will Kellogg turned 15 and was working as a broom salesperson. John Kellogg then returned to Battle Creek and took over what was known as the Adventist Health Reform Institute in 1876; he renamed the Battle Creek Sanitarium and it emerged as an internationally renowned center of holistic health. Taking the Adventist principles to a new level, John Kellogg advocated a lifestyle that relied on a vegetarian diet, fresh air, and plenty of exercise.

Kellogg went to work at the Sanitarium not long after completing a three-month program at Parson's Business College in nearly Kalamazoo in the early 1880s. With the fame of the Sanitarium spreading, John Kellogg had less time for its day-to-day operations, and he hired his younger brother to serve as business manager. "While Dr. Kellogg basked in celebrity and adulation, Will essentially ran the operation, working 15 hours a day, seven days a week," wrote *FSB* journalist Paul Lukas. "He kept the books, bought supplies, answered correspondence, served as handyman and janitor, and filled mail orders for the sanitarium's many products. For his trouble, W.K. earned $6 a week (the most he would ever earn in 25 years of toiling for his brother was $87 a month)." Other accounts noted that when they were younger, John sometimes caned Will, and when they were older, the doctor also added "personal valet" to the list of his brother's duties, requiring him to give him his daily shave and shoeshine.

Accidentally Invented Flaked Cereal

Dr. Kellogg had some radical ideas about food and diet at the time, including a reliance on colonic irrigation for optimum health, and the belief that a diet rich in nut proteins was the key to longevity. In 1877 John devised a type of dry cereal he called Granula, to distinguish it from Granola, a name already trademarked by a New York State physician, and he and Will experimented with other grains. By 1894 the two were working with a boiled wheat paste that the doctor hoped would be more easily digestible for some sanitarium patients. One of the batches was accidentally left out for several hours, and dried out. They put it through the cereal-making rollers anyway and "were surprised to discover that instead of coming out in long sheets as it always had in the past, every wheat berry came out flattened into its own thin flake," explained Rod Taylor, a writer for *Promo* magazine "After baking the flakes, the two realized—much to their delight—that they had stumbled on a whole new type of food." This became the first world's first "flaked" cereal.

The Kellogg brothers sold the new cereal under the brand name Granose as part of the doctor's side venture, the Sanitas Nut Food Company. Patients at the sanitarium liked it so much they bought it by mailorder, too. Soon Will Kellogg became convinced that the factory, a barn located on the sanitarium grounds, needed to be moved to a separate location in order to safeguard their trade secret. The doctor, always conscious of a promotional opportunity, exhorted the sanitarium clients to visit the facility and watch how the beloved cereal was made. This led to a notorious incident in the history of American industrial espionage, when a man named C. W. Post (1854-1914) visited the sanitarium for health reasons, saw how the flaking process worked, and was inspired to start his own cereal company. Post Cereals, which later became General Foods, emerged as a major competitor to the Kelloggs, with its Grape Nuts cereal.

The long-simmering tensions between the two brothers began to reach a crisis point: Kellogg was so irate at his brother that he decided to establish a company separate from the sanitarium, but his doctor brother refused to finance it. They did, however, agree to try a new grain, and using corn instead of wheat to make the cereal proved a wise decision. They launched Sanitas Toasted Corn Flakes in 1898, which featured a picture of the Battle Creek Sanitarium on the box. In 1900, when John was out of the country for several weeks, Kellogg had a new factory built. When the doctor returned, he was reportedly so angry that he demanded Kellogg repay the amount immediately. But as Lukas explained, the cereal business was becoming immensely profitable. "A ten-ounce box sold for 15 cents, which meant the Kelloggs were turning a 12-cent bushel of grain into $6 worth of cereal."

Founded Kellogg Company

As the company neared its ten-year anniversary, Battle Creek had become the cereal manufacturing capital of America, with scores of competitors, and the Sanitas brand lagged behind Post's products. Finally, John agreed to finance an entirely new company in return for a two-thirds share of its stock, and the Battle Creek Toasted Corn Flake Company was incorporated in February of 1906. Kellogg was now able to put into practice some ideas he had about advertising and promotion, and one of the first moves he made was to add his autograph to the box, with the tagline, "Beware of Imitations. None Genuine Without This Signature, W.K. Kellogg." Corn Flakes were touted as a healthy breakfast food at a time when well-to-do Americans ate eggs and meat at that meal; the majority ate toast or various hot cereals such as porridge, farina, and gruel. To promote Corn Flakes in cities where it was about to set up a distribution channel, Kellogg took out newspaper ads in advance, which created demand for a product not yet on grocers' shelves. He even advertised nationally in women's magazines such as *Ladies' Home Journal,* which was extremely expensive, but the strategy worked and sales soared.

The first promotional giveaways in the cereal industry began with Kellogg, as a way to distinguish himself in a crowded field. It started with *The Funny Jungleland Moving Pictures Book,* an interactive picture book of animals for children. The books were delivered along with Kellogg cereal shipments to grocers, who gave one to every customer who bought two boxes of Corn Flakes. Later the boxes themselves had coupons that could be clipped and sent in for the book, which went through various editions and remained in print until the late 1930s. By 1912 the Kellogg Company had an advertising budget of $1 million, and it pioneered another strategy that year when it hired teams of marketers to give out samples of its newest cereal, Krumbles.

Kellogg continued to have serious conflicts with his brother over strategy and even corporate mission—John was strongly opposed to adding sugar to any of the products, for example. Finally, on another occasion when John was out of the country, Kellogg began buying up shares of the company stock that the doctor—still a notoriously frugal boss—had been using to pay some of his sanitarium em-

ployees. This gave him an ownership share of the company, but precipitated a falling-out between the brothers that worsened over time. Before John died in 1943, he wrote Will a conciliatory letter apologizing for some of his behavior, but the younger brother refused to open or read it until shortly before his own death in 1951.

Established Philanthropic Foundation

Sadly, the family problems continued through the next generation. Kellogg, who married in the early 1880s, had a son named John L. who joined the company as a young man. Like his father, he had an innovative mind and invented the wax-paper lining now common to all cereal boxes. However, he incurred his father's wrath when he divorced his wife to marry a Kellogg secretary. Kellogg forced John L. out of the company and groomed grandson John Jr. to take over, but the boy also proved a disappointment. John Jr.'s resignation precipitated the young man's mental breakdown, and he died by his own hand in 1938.

Kellogg believed that inherited wealth corrupts, and he used his private fortune to lavishly endow a private philanthropic foundation, which began attracting notice for funding various cancer studies. In 1932 he funded a school in Battle Creek for elementary students whose concept was so radical it earned this *New York Times* headline in 1932: "Normal and Handicapped Pupils Put Side by Side in New School." Kellogg's one indulgence was a large ranch in Pomona, California, where he bred prized Arabian thoroughbred horses. Kellogg later donated this property as well, and the parcel of land eventually became California State Polytechnic University at Pomona.

Died at Age 91

In his later years, Kellogg experienced severe vision loss, and was completely blind by 1937. Two years later he retired as president of the Kellogg Company, as it was formally known by then, but remained on its board of directors. At his W.K. Kellogg Foundation, he kept an office and was still going there on a daily basis at the time of his ninety-first birthday, April 7, 1951. He died almost six months later, on October 6, 1951.

The W.K. Kellogg Foundation, including its original endowment of $60 million, became one of the top ten richest philanthropic organizations in the United States, and has been especially generous to its hometown of Battle Creek. Its assets were estimated at more than $7 billion in 2005, but a large part of that was in Kellogg Company stock, which had suffered financial hits in the late 1990s as consumers seemed to tire of the higher prices for Corn Flakes, Rice Krispies, and Frosted Flakes, especially when private-label competitor brands were much cheaper. The company, wrote Dana Canedy and Reed Abelson in the *New York Times* in 1999, "has been unable to get a grip on just how much people are willing pay for its cereals, especially when other boxes of corn flakes seem more like its brand than ever before. A few years ago, the company set off a price war, hoping to make up the lost profits through volume, but then struggled to raise prices again. In the end, the approach gave consumers sticker shock at grocery checkout lanes and benefited competitors like General Mills, whose strategy depended less on its pricing." The same article noted that the management team in Battle Creek seemed paralyzed on how to move forward. "Kellogg is a funny company," said a former executive who spoke with Canedy and Abelson only on the condition of anonymity. "As recently as the mid-90's, we were still asking what Mr. Kellogg would have done."

Books

Business Leader Profiles for Students, volume 1, Gale, 1999.

Periodicals

FSB, April 1, 2003.
New York Times, January 3, 1932; October 7, 1951; January 24, 1999.
Promo, September 1, 2003. □

U. G. Krishnamurti

Indian philosopher and writer Uppaluri Gopala (U.G.) Krishnamurti (1918-2007) has been described as the "anti–guru." Throughout his life, this unique spiritual figure repeatedly and vehemently insisted that he could not help anyone seeking enlightenment. Ironically, he attracted a large following through his lectures and books.

Krishnamurti's main message to those who looked to him for illumination was that he had no message at all to offer. Appropriately, he has been described as the anti–guru, a spiritual nihilist and a philosopher without a philosophy. During his long, personal spiritual quest, Krishnamurti, widely known as U.G. Krishnamurti, rejected the paths presented by well–known spiritual leaders throughout history. Though he inspired others, he did not want fellow seekers to forge a template that matched his own experiences. "I have no particular message for mankind, except to say that all holy systems for obtaining enlightenment are nonsense and that all talk of arriving at a psychological mutation through awareness is rubbish," he once stated, as quoted on the *Mystic Missal* Web site. "Psychological mutation is impossible. The natural state can happen only through biological mutation."

Interestingly enough, his rebellious stance resonated with a great many people who drew upon his wisdom as they proceeded on their individual paths toward this desired "natural state."

Early Life

Krishnamurti was born on July 9, 1918, in South India, into a Brahmin family that lived in Masulipatam, a coastal town in the state of Andhra Pradesh. His mother died only seven days after she gave birth to the future spiritual sage, but before she passed away, she predicted a remarkable destiny for her son.

Krishnamurti was raised by his maternal grandparents, and he never really knew his father, who remarried soon after his wife's death and left his son in the care of the grandparents. Krishnamurti's maternal grandfather, Tummalapalli Gopala Krishnamurti (T.G. Krishnamurti), was a wealthy Brahmin lawyer and prominent member of the Theosophical Society. He believed in his daughter's prediction about her son, and he gave up his thriving law practice to devote himself to U.G. Krishnamurti's upbringing and education. Grandparents and family friends believed that Krishnamurti was a *yogabhrashta,* someone who had come close to enlightenment in a past life. As such, Krishnamurti received a thorough education in classical Hindu literature and was raised to become a great spiritual leader, a role that he would eventually renounce.

Awakening of a Spiritual Rebel

As T.G. Krishnamurti was both a Theosophist and an orthodox Brahmin, U.G. Krishnamurti's early education included a diverse, incongruous mixture of the orthodox and unorthodox, including both Hindu religious beliefs and Theosophical spiritual beliefs. U.G. Krishnamurti later said that his grandfather was a "mixed up" man. The educational dichotomy, coupled with his grandfather's apparent spiritual confusion, would affect Krishnamurti's own belief system in later years.

To help with his grandson's spiritual upbringing, T.G. Krishnamurti invited many so–called holy men into his home. When U.G. Krishnamurti was only three years old, he forsook typical childhood pastimes to spend his time in meditative postures, imitating the celebrated visitors. Further, during the entire course of each day, he was taught from the major holy books, including the *Upanishads, Panchadasi,* and *Naishkarmya Siddhi,* as well as the commentaries on these works (and even the commentaries on the commentaries). By the time he was seven, he could recite important passages from these complex books.

With his early indoctrination into both the Hindu scriptures and spiritualism, Krishnamurti came to a realization: By embracing their respective beliefs, both Hindus and Theosophists were kept from comprehending the real truth. Further, truth is something they had to discover for themselves. This realization formed the basis of the message he would later deliver to the world, and it underscored the nature of his character. From childhood to adulthood, he was rebellious and could even be brutally honest.

In 1925, when he was seven years old, U.G. Krishnamurti lost his faith in the power of prayer and found the concept of God irrelevant when he perceived a contradiction in a personal prayer request. Essentially, he came to believe that prayer fulfillment resulted from sheer strength of his own desire rather than the power of prayer itself.

His disillusionment also resulted from the hypocrisies he perceived in his teachers. For instance, he once witnessed T.G. Krishnamurti administer a harsh beating to a crying great–grandchild who had disturbed his concentration during meditation. About this incident, as recorded on the ugkrishnamurti.net Web site dedicated to him, U.G. Krishnamurti later commented: "There must be something funny about the whole business of meditation. [The practitioners'] lives are shallow and empty. They talk marvelously. But there is a neurotic fear in their lives. Whatever they preach does not seem to operate in their lives. Why?'' Such questions formed the basis of his own spiritual search, which lasted a good part of his life.

Further Youthful Disillusionment

After his home schooling, U.G. Krishnamurti received his formal education in the town of Gudivada. Between the ages of fourteen and twenty–one, he practiced a wide assortment of spiritual exercises to determine if *moksha*, a state of total liberation, truly existed. As many great spiritual leaders preached extensively about this particular concept, Krishnamurti wanted to experience it for himself. He later recalled: ''I was so young, but I was determined to find out if there was any such thing as *moksha*, and I wanted that *moksha* for myself,'' as quoted in the *Mystic Missal* Web site. ''Everybody is talking about *moksha*, liberation, freedom. What is that? I want to know for myself. These are all useless fellows, yet there must be some person in this world who is an embodiment and apostle of all those things. If there is one, I want to find out for myself.''

As far as his efforts toward achieving *moksha*, the *Mystic Missal* Web site recorded his observation that ''[n]obody can give that state; I am on my own. I have to go on this uncharted sea without a compass, without a boat, with not even a raft to take me. I am going to find out for myself what the state is in which that man is. I wanted that very much, otherwise I wouldn't have given my life.''

At various times throughout this early period of his life, he studied classical Yoga with Hindu evangelist Swami Sivananda Saraswati in Rishikesh: practicing yoga and meditation, led to several spiritual visions and experiences. These were the kinds of experiences described in the sacred texts and were called ''samadhi,'' ''super samadhi,'' and ''nirvikalpa samadhi.'' However, Krishnamurti questioned the validity of his own experiences, as he felt these were not entirely revelatory but based on prior knowledge. The Web site dedicated to him documented his beliefs that ''[t]hought can create any experience you want—bliss, beatitude, ecstasy, melting away into nothingness—all those experiences. But this can't be the thing, because I have remained the same person, mechanically doing these things.''

After all his searching up to this point, he concluded that he had not found what he had been looking for. Appropriately, he looked to other directions.

Graduated from College and Joined Theosophical Society

In 1939, Krishnamurti enrolled in the University of Madras. By this time, he was leaning toward atheism. At the university, he studied psychology, philosophy (both Eastern and Western), mysticism and modern sciences. Eventually, he received bachelor's degrees in philosophy and psychology. Still, formal studies of various philosophical and psychological systems left him unimpressed.

As he continued maturing, he evolved into a spiritual cynic. He questioned all accepted dogmas and philosophies, denounced the ''hypocrisy of the holy business,'' according to his Web site, and continued challenging accepted spiritual authorities. Furthermore, he came to believe that all of mankind's greatest spiritual teachers (e.g., Buddha, Jesus, Sri Ramakrishna) were self–delusional and, as such, only deluded their followers.

In 1941, after he left the university, he joined the Theosophical Society, which was co–founded in 1873 by Helena Petrova Blavatsky, a Russian immigrant to the United States. The Society was formed on a basis of Buddhism, Hinduism and various occult teachings, and it attracted freethinkers, agnostics and atheists, providing believers and non–believers with spiritual order and support. Krishnamurti became a public speaker and lectured extensively on Theosophy, helping the Society introduce the Western world to Eastern spiritual thought.

Moved to the United States Following Marriage

In 1943, when he was twenty–five years old, Krishnamurti married Kusuma Kumari. They eventually had four children, but he continued to work with the Theosophical Society, giving lectures throughout Europe.

In 1955, he moved his family to the United States so that his son could receive medical treatment for his polio condition. By this time in his life, Krishnamurti never really had to seek work, as he benefited from his grandfather's inheritance. However, by the mid–1950s, his funds began to dwindle, so he began lecturing for a fee in the United States, giving talks for the Theosophical Society about the world's major religions and philosophers. During this period, he met some of the greatest living spiritual teachers, including Ramana Maharshi and Judda Krishnamurti (who was not related to U.G.). Even so, he still felt that no one had anything to offer him in regards to answers to his questions. His spiritual dissatisfaction intensified, which led to personal, professional, financial, and marital turmoil. After about two years of lecturing, he lost interest in public speaking. It was also at this time that his marriage came to an end. After his wife and children returned to India, Krishnamurti entered a period in his life when he drifted from one place to another. His inheritance had run out, and he was virtually penniless. His wife eventually died in a mental institution, and he would not establish contact with his family again until much later in his life.

A Homeless Wanderer in Europe

In his destitute and rambling state, he eventually ended up in Paris, France and London, England in 1961. ''I was a bum practically, living on the charity of some people and not knowing anything,'' he later described, quoted on the *Sentient Publications* Web site. ''There was no will. I didn't know what I was doing. I was practically insane.''

He lived like this for six more years. All the while, he continued concerning himself with *moksha* and asking himself ''What is the state.'' Ultimately, he came to believe he was living that state, due to his property–less and ego–less existence. The experience informed his later radical philosophy.

During his wanderings, he eventually found his way to the Indian embassy in Geneva, Switzerland, and asked for transportation back to India. At the embassy, he met Valentine DeKervan, who took him into her home. She would become his lifelong friend, benefactor and traveling companion.

In this period, Krishnamurti had a mystical experience that changed his life and became part of his legend. It took place in 1967, on his 49th birthday. As he related, for seven days his body underwent confounding physical changes that led him into what he called the "Natural State." He referred to the experience as the "calamity," and described it as a "sudden explosion inside, blasting, as it were, every cell, every nerve and every gland in my body," as the *Mystic Missal* Web site recounts. Characteristically, he downgraded the importance of the event. "I call it the 'calamity' because from the point of view of one who thinks this is something fantastic, blissful, full of beatitude, love, ecstasy and all that kind of a thing, this is physical torture," he said, from the same Web site. "This is a calamity from that point of view. Not a calamity to me, but a calamity to those who have an image that something marvelous is going to happen. It's not the thing that you had sought after and wanted so much, but totally different. What is there, you really don't know—you have no way of knowing anything about that—there is no image here."

Post–"Calamity" fame

During the 1970s, he began to become more of a public figure, even though his lecturing came to an end. In 1972, he gave his first and last talk at the Indian Institute of World Culture. The event would prove to be the last time he gave a public talk. But, by this time, people had begun to seek him out for answers to their own personal questions. He willingly received their questions and accommodated them with answers based on his own viewpoint. People from all over the world felt drawn to him, even though he repeatedly said that he had no message for the masses. He gave no lectures, had no organization, was headquartered in no offices and, of course, never had a fixed address. Rather, he got his message out through books and television.

He published his first book, *The Mystique of Enlightenment,* in 1982. In 1986, he gave his first television interview, which led to many other television and radio interviews across the world. Despite his increasing fame, he still lived an austere lifestyle. As far as living arrangements, he stayed either with friends or in small, rented apartments. He never stayed in one place longer than six months.

As far as his published works, he made the unusual move of not allowing any of his books to be copyrighted. "My teaching, if that is the word you want to use, has no copyright," he explained, as reprinted in the Web site dedicated to him. "You are free to reproduce, distribute, interpret, misinterpret, distort, garble, do what you like, even claim authorship, without my consent or the permission of anybody." This arrangement exposed his ideas to even more people.

Some of his other published works include *The Mind is a Myth* (1988), *The Sage and the Housewife* (1990), *Thought is Your Enemy* (1991), and *Courage to Stand Alone* (1997). Because these books are not copyrighted, they are readily available via download at various Web site sites on the Internet.

Died in Italy

In early 2007, Krishnamurti injured himself in a fall. It was the second such occurrence for the aging anti–guru in two years, only this time he refused any medical treatment. Experiencing failing health and believing that his end was coming soon, he did not want to burden his friends with his physical problems. Rather, he decided to let nature run its course. He remained in his bed, which was situated in an apartment that had been built for him by friends in Vallecrosia, Italy. As he awaited death, he consumed very little food and water.

He died on March 22, 2007. Reportedly, in his final days, he demonstrated no fear about death. Nor did he request any special funeral rites or ceremonies. Furthermore, he did not care about how his body would be disposed, even going so far as to tell his friends that they could throw it away, nihilistic right to the very end. Friends had his body cremated the day after he died.

Described as someone who could be both cruel and loving, U.G. Krishnamurti remained an enigma. He rejected the role of spiritual leader in life, and he wanted no one to worship his memory after he died. "After I am dead and gone," he said to his friend and biographer, filmmaker Mahesh Bhatt, from his Web site, "nothing of me must remain inside of you or outside of you. I can certainly do a lot to see that no establishment or institution of any kind mushrooms around me whilst I am alive. But how do I stop all you guys from enshrining me in your brains?"

Books

Bhatt, Mahesh, *U.G. Krishnamurti: A Life*, Viking, 1992.

Online

"Remembering U.G. Krishnamurti," U.G. Krishnamurti, http://ugkrishnamurti.net/ (December 15, 2007).

"U.G. Krishnamurti," Actualfreedom.com, http://www.actualfreedom.com.au/library/topics/ug.htm (December 15, 2007).

"U.G. Krishnamurti," Mysticmissal.org, http://www.mysticmissal.org/u_g__krishnamurti.htm (December 15, 2007).

"U.G. Krishnamurti," Sentientpublications.com, http://www.sentientpublications.com/authors/ug.php (December 15, 2007). □

Jacek Kuroń

Polish political dissident Jacek Kuroń (1934-2004) spent nearly a decade imprisoned for his actions and speeches during his country's long, often bleak experiment with one-party state socialism.

He was a key figure in Poland's Solidarity trade union movement in the late 1970s and early 1980s, then rose to the post of labor minister in his country's first non-Communist, freely elected government in 1989. A noted historian and onetime ardent Communist Party member who grew disillusioned with the regime's increasingly totalitarian aspects, "Kuroń was instrumental in bringing together the two previously separate strands of industrial unrest and intellectual opposition to the Communist regime" in the mid-1970s that gave rise to the Solidarity trade union, noted Gabriel Partos, the writer of his obituary in London's *Independent* newspaper.

Kuroń was born on March 3, 1934, in Lviv, Poland, a city that would later became part of the Soviet Union as the Ukraine republic at the end of World War II. He came from a middle-class family with leftist leanings who relocated westward to Poland after the war when the borders of the region shifted, and in 1949 the 15-year-old Kuroń joined the Polish Youth Union (ZMP). The ZMP was the youth branch of the Polish United Workers Party (PZPR), known less formally as Poland's Communist Party, and the PZPR was emerging as the dominant political force in a war-ravaged country still under occupation by Soviet troops. Kuroń was a committed Marxist during these young-adult years, for many Poles of his generation believed allegiance to the Soviets—and to the socialist state model—was the appropriate response to preventing the rise of fascist alternatives like Nazi Germany and its genocidal policies, which had included a plan for turning Poland into a nation of slave-laborers.

Active in Scouting

As the Soviet apparatchiks tightened their control of the PZPR in an effort to firmly establish Poland as a Communist ally, debate and dissent within the Polish party's ranks became impermissible. Once Kuroń began to question the party's draconian control, he was quickly cast out of its ranks. In the early 1950s, for example, he was serving as president of the ZMP affiliate at the Warsaw University of Technology, and in an official report he submitted as required, he was critical of the parent party's direction. Called to answer for his defiance, he stood by his claims and refused his superiors' orders to submit a boilerplate "self-criticism" report in order to atone for his transgression. As a result, he was dismissed from his posts in both the ZMP and the PZPR.

Kuroń was allowed to rejoin the PZPR in 1956 after a thaw that year, and earned his degree in history from Warsaw University a year later. He went on to become a professor at the school, and was also active in the *Związek Harcerstwa Polskiego* (ZHP, or Polish Scouting Association). His attempts to establish political debating societies in such workplaces like the Warsaw Steel Factory in the early 1960s were rebuffed by the party, and that prompted him and another professor to pen their "Open Letter to the Party." In it, he and Karol Modzelewski "argued that control of the economy gave communist planners powers of exploitation over society which surpassed those held by capitalists," Kuroń's *Times* of London obituary noted. The pair were both arrested on sedition charges for the document in 1965, and Kuroń spent two years in prison.

In 1968, during a period of unrest in March, Kuroń helped organize a student strike during demonstrations that had started at the university level. The student revolt had no support among ordinary workers in Poland, though both groups were equally dissatisfied with the Communist regime. Two years later, workers in Poland's Baltic sea ports staged a series of demonstrations to protest price hikes of consumer goods, and this time the students and intellectuals failed to join in. Kuroń was actually in jail again at the time, having been arrested on charges related to the 1968 disturbances, but began to realize that Poland's leadership seemed to be playing these two groups against one another. This manipulation actually kept dissent to a manageable, nonthreatening level in the country.

Argued for New Approach

Kuroń was jailed again in 1975 after signing a manifesto in protest of proposed constitutional changes that contained controversial wording noting Poland's "special relationship" with the Soviet Union. A year later, workplace labor unrest erupted when the government was forced again to raise the price of basic food staples, and major strikes took place at industrial centers in Warsaw and in nearby Radom. Government troops responded with force, and scores were arrested and jailed. Kuroń became the co-founder of the *Komitet Obrony Robotników*, or Worker's Defense Committee (KOR), which was set up to aid those arrested and their families. The KOR offered legal help, medical treatment, and even financial help for detainees and their families, and served as an inventive new merger of the intelligentsia and the workers and their common cause.

Kuroń's other significant contribution to shaping Poland's postwar history was his belief that new organizations could be formed that would supplant the tightly controlled, state-sanctioned ones. "During the protests in Radom, angry workers had set fire to the building of the local Communist Party committee," noted Partos in London's *Independent*. "Kuroń later told them: 'Don't burn committees: found your own.'" In 1979, KOR evolved into a new body, called the Committee for Social Self-Defense (KSS-KOR). Its focus was to establish just these types of independent groups. One of the ones it encouraged to form was a workers' self-defense committee at the massive Lenin Shipyard in the Baltic port city of Gdansk, where several workers had died during the 1970 protests and anti-government resentment lingered. As part of this activity, Kuroń came to know one of the workers who had agreed to risk their jobs and lives to distribute an illegal newsletter called "The Coastal Worker." That man was an electrician named Lech Wałęsa, who soon rose to lead the illegal strikes that erupted at the Lenin Shipyard in the summer of 1980.

The Gdansk workers' actions were quickly copied by workers at other shipyards and factories throughout Poland, and captured worldwide attention. In September of 1980 the trade union called *Solidarność*, or Solidarity, was formed. This was the first-ever independent organization in the Soviet bloc. Kuroń was recruited to serve as an advisor to the top leadership as part of its national coordinating commission. "As one of Walesa's chief advisers, Kuron was keen to steer Solidarity along a moderate course," explained Partos in the *Independent*. "It involved negotiating—and striking—for better pay, working conditions and social benefits, as well as for a freer society. In the process Solidarity gained a key role it what became a de facto power-sharing arrangement—without ever explicitly challenging the Communist Party's notional monopoly to rule which would have held out the danger of Soviet military intervention."

Jailed Once Again

Solidarity quickly turned into a social movement over the next year, but Polish authorities declared martial law in December of 1981, and dozens of ringleaders, Kuroń and Wałęsa included, were arrested. In September of 1982, Kuroń was given a four-year prison term on charges of conspiring to overthrow the regime. When authorities finally relented and granted a general amnesty in 1984, he was one of the last to be released. Solidarity and other unofficial organizations had been outlawed under martial law, but its membership remained active despite government surveillance and harassment. When strikes erupted again in the spring and summer of 1988, Wałęsa formed the Solidarity Citizens Committee, and Kuroń was given a seat. With a new Soviet leader, Mikhail Gorbachev (born 1931) in power and signs that the formerly tightly controlled Soviet bloc alliance was crumbling, Polish authorities agreed to hold the famous Round Table talks between Solidarity lead-

ers, the PZPR, and military officials. Kuroń took part in these historic negotiations on Poland's future, which were held in February of 1989.

In June of 1989, Kuroń was elected to the Sejm, the lower house of Poland's parliament, in the country's first free, multiparty elections in decades. He and other Solidarity-backed candidates won several seats, and were able to form a government in August of 1989 headed by new prime minister Tadeusz Mazowiecki (born 1927). Mazowiecki, a longtime Solidarity activist, named Kuroń to serve as the country's minister for labor and social policy. On his first day of work, wrote *Times* of London correspondent Roger Boyes, "an official and vaguely sinister looking car drew up outside" Kuroń's Warsaw apartment building. It was a familiar sight, Boyes noted, for by then Kuroń had been arrested between 50 and 60 times, and was "accustomed to the early morning arrival of the secret police. Usually, the car stays parked for a while and a neighbour rings Mr. Kuron to warn him to pack his prison gear." But on this day, the car was an official vehicle from the Ministry, and in place of a police officer it was helmed by a chauffeur.

The ride to and from the office may have been the only tranquil part of Kuroń's job as government minister. Poland's looming economic crisis had been the catalyst for the Round Table talks, and the situation had only worsened. The country's transition from a planned, heavily subsidized system to a new, free-market economy brought massive unemployment and terrible hardships for the majority of Poles. Kuroń appeared regularly on television to discuss the changes and offer reassurances that the difficulties were temporary, while working behind the scenes to bring actual relief in the form of soup kitchens and hardship stipends. He even staffed the lines at the soup kitchens on occasion, and the unemployment benefit instituted during his term became known informally as the *kuroniówka,* or "Kuroń's soup."

Made Failed Presidential Bid

Mazowiecki's government lasted just over a year, but in 1992 Kuroń returned to his minister's post under a new prime minister after three more governments failed. That cabinet lasted a year and three months before dissolving in October of 1993. In 1995, Kuroń became a candidate in presidential elections, but took third place in the contest in which a former Communist, Aleksandr Kwasniewski (born 1954) bested Wałęsa. A year later, Kuroń reunited with Karol Modzelewski to publish another open letter, this time claiming that the Polish intelligence services—rife with holdovers from the Communist era, it was said—was still actively working to quash dissent in the country, only this time in the form of undermining legitimate political opposition.

Kuroń was known for his informal, iconoclastic demeanor. He wore jeans, even as a government minister and even when accepting France's prestigious Legion of Honor medal. His apartment door in Warsaw was famously left unlocked for years as an open invitation to anyone who needed to speak with him or sought a place of refuge. He died on June 17, 2004, in Warsaw, at the age of 70. Survivors included his second wife, Danuta, and a son, Maciej, from his first marriage. His first wife, Grazyna, died during the period of martial law, when Kuroń was jailed. Upon news of Kuroń's death, Wałęsa reflected, "without him, the events of August 1980 would have been impossible," Michael T. Kaufman in the *New York Times* quoted him as saying.

Books

The Cold War, 1945-1991, 3 volumes. Edited by Benjamin Frankel, Gale, 1992.

Periodicals

Independent (London, England), June 21, 2004.
National Review, October 18, 1985.
New York Times, January 23, 1996; June 18, 2004.
Times (London, England), September 22, 1989; June 18, 2004. □

L

Alphonse Laveran

French medical researcher and physician Alphonse Laveran (1845-1922) discovered the parasite that causes the endemic tropical disease of malaria. He also guessed correctly that the disease was transmitted by mosquitoes.

The story of Laveran's discoveries was a remarkable one in several respects. They took shape not in the pure realm of laboratory research but in the field: Laveran was a military physician and surgeon posted to Algeria, where he observed the ravages of malaria firsthand. Laveran's hypotheses about malaria flew in the face of established scientific theories of his time, when the recently discovered role of bacteria in many other diseases was assumed to apply to malaria as well. Most remarkable of all was his ability to interpret what he saw under his primitive microscope: it was not a bacterium but a single-celled animal, trailing long filaments, that, in the early years of microscopy, appeared to be an entirely mysterious entity. Laveran's discovery of the malaria parasite was a scientific triumph combining patient observation, strong intuition, and the ability to synthesize diverse preexisting insights and ideas.

Spent Part of Childhood in Algeria

Charles Louis Alphonse Laveran was born on June 18, 1845, in Paris. His eventual choice of career followed that of his father, Louis-Théodore Laveran, who was a French military physician. His mother, the former Marie-Louise Anselme Guénard de la Tour, was herself descended from high-ranking army officers. When Laveran was five, the

family was sent to Algeria, then a French colony where resistance to European rule was simmering. His first lessons in medicine came from his father, augmented by impressions gathered from the eyes of a child living in a tropical war zone. In 1856 the family returned to Paris, and the elder Laveran became a professor at the Ecole de Val-de-Grâce, a Paris military medical school.

Laveran attended two private schools in Paris, the Collège Saint Baube and the Lycée Louis-le-Grand, planning on following his father into the medical profession. To that end he enrolled in a military medical college in Strasbourg, France, in 1863, graduating in 1867 with a thesis on the repair of nerve damage. After that he joined the French military as a physician, and by the time the Franco-Prussian War broke out in 1870 he had reached the rank of medical assistant-major. He saw action as an ambulance officer during several major battles, including the disastrous siege of Metz, when he was briefly imprisoned by the Germans. After the French surrendered that city, he was moved to hospitals in Lille and then Paris. In 1874 he bested several other physicians in competitive exams and was appointed to a term as chair of Department of Military Diseases and Epidemics at the Ecole de Val-de-Grâce.

After completing his term as chair, Laveran was sent to the city of Bône in Algeria (now Annaba). Soon after that he moved to the city of Constantine (Qusantînah). Working in military hospitals in these two cities, Laveran was confronted by wards full of patients suffering from malaria, a common and serious tropical disease that was (and remains) potentially fatal and is invariably accompanied by extreme discomfort such as joint pain, intense flashes of fever and cold, and nausea. The disease took its toll on French military recruits, who sometimes dropped dead before they could be assembled into platoons. Laveran began making cultures of soil

samples, doing autopsies, and drawing patients' blood with pinpricks in order to learn what he could about the disease.

At the time, malaria was poorly understood, and techniques for examining blood under a microscope were poorly developed. Laveran could see in the blood of his patients some small black granules or pigments that were already known to result from infection with malaria, but he had no idea what produced these pigments or caused the disease. By the third quarter of the nineteenth century, the germ theory of disease, and specifically the role of bacteria—single-celled organisms called prokaryotes, or organisms without a nucleus—in causing infectious diseases, had become generally accepted after experiments conducted by France's Louis Pasteur and Germany's Robert Koch had shown their widespread applicability. Malaria was thought by most scientists to be the result of an as-yet-undiscovered bacterium, and they were busily combing the air, water, and earth in malaria-infested regions in search of it.

Spotted Motile Bodies

Laveran patiently continued his observations, and finally, early in the morning of November 6, 1880, he struck pay dirt: he spotted a moving organism on a slide he was examining under a high-powered microscope. It had long filaments that propelled it through the patient's blood like the legs of a swimmer, something no bacterium would do. According to an article published on the Malaria Site Web site, Laveran wrote, "In 1880, at the military hospital in Constantine, I discovered on the edges of the pigmented

spheric bodies, in the blood of a patient suffering from malarial fever, thread-like elements resembling whips which were scurrying about with great vivacity, displacing neighboring erythrocytes [red blood cells]; from then on, I had no further doubts as to the parasitic nature of the elements I had found."

The organism Laveran had seen was a protozoan, a single-celled microbe that contains a nucleus and shares certain characteristics with higher orders of animals—it can move, and it consumes other organic matter. Laveran found these protozoa in the blood of 148 of 192 malaria patients he examined, and he correctly concluded that they were the primary cause of malarial infection. Furthermore, he identified other small spherical organisms he had also found in patients' blood as stages in the development of the full-fledged motile protozoan that, he thought, lived on the surface of red blood cells and disrupted them (another researcher soon showed that the parasite actually grew inside cells). He named the new organism *Oscillaria malariae* and published his findings in an article titled "A new parasite found in the blood of malarial patients. Parasitic origin of malarial attacks."

Laveran's ideas were not immediately accepted. Several other scientists claimed to have observed a *Bacillus malariae* or malaria bacterium, and Laveran's protozoan was an enigma with an appearance unlike any other microscopic organism that had yet been discovered. Many scientists looked to the familiar idea of bacteria as the most likely explanation, but experiments over several years in the early 1880s began to confirm Laveran's findings. An American military physician, George Sternberg, made an exhaustive search of air and mud from marshes in clearly malarial areas and found no trace of anything resembling *Bacillus malariae*. Other scientists observed parasites related to Laveran's protozoan in animals. In 1884 two Italian researchers named Ettore Marchiafava and Augusto Celli spotted blood organisms in malaria patients that were actually among the earlier stages of the malarial parasite Laveran had discovered, but they did not realize they were looking at the same organism. They named their new discovery *Plasmodium,* and that name, although technically inaccurate, continued to be used.

New techniques of microscopy yielded findings that expanded Laveran's own, and he continued to defend his ideas. He replicated his own results during a trip to Rome, Italy, in 1882, where he collected large numbers of blood samples from Italian soldiers who had served in the Roman Campagna, a swampy area south of Rome that was a notorious reservoir of the disease, and he then returned to Paris and the Ecole de Val-de-Grâce in 1884. That year Pasteur became the first big-name researcher to sign on to Laveran's theory, and by the end of the decade it had gained general acceptance. In 1889 Laveran was given the prestigious Brént Prize by the French Academy of Sciences.

Suggested Mosquitoes as Host

"After having discovered the parasite of malaria in patients' blood," Laveran wrote, as quoted on Malaria Site, "there remained an important question to be solved: in what form did the hemacytozoon [the protozoan] exist in the exterior environment and how did the infection come about? The solution to this problem required long and laborious research." He made extensive studies of air, water, and earth at sites known to be infested with malaria, but failed to find his parasite. "I was convinced that the microbe existed outside the human body, in a parasitic state, and most probably in the shape of a parasite of mosquitoes."

Laveran presented this hypothesis in a new *Treatise on Malarial Fevers* and delivered it in report form to the International Congress on Hygiene at Budapest, Hungary. Once again, his ideas were generally rejected, but experiments by British researcher Ronald Ross, working in India, showed that the Plasmodium parasite did indeed develop inside mosquitoes. Soon malaria was understood to be a disease transmitted by mosquito bites, and was therefore almost impossible to eradicate.

The French military did not substantially reward Laveran for his accomplishments. In 1894 he was moved from the Ecole de Val-de-Grâce to the position of chief medical officer at the military hospital in Lille, and then to that of director of health services of the 11th Army Corps at Nantes. These were administrative posts where Laveran neither interacted with patients nor had access to a laboratory to do his beloved research. Offended, Laveran took a position as chief of the honorary service at the Pasteur Institute in 1896, heading a research lab of his own. For the next ten years he did research on trypanosomes—parasitic protozoa with a single flagellum (or whiplash tail) that live inside insects. He explored their role in several major diseases, including African Sleeping Sickness. In 1908 he founded a new Society for Exotic Pathology, remaining its president until 1920. He was inducted into major scientific societies in France, England, the United States and many other countries. In 1907 he was awarded the Nobel Prize in Physiology or Medicine. He donated half his prize money to the Pasteur Institute. In 1912 Laveran was made a Commander of the Legion of Honor, a French honor roughly comparable to a knighthood in England.

Laveran was a man entirely devoted to science. In 1885 he married Sophie Marie Pidançet, but the pair had no children. He spent most of each day doing research, but during World War I he served on committees devoted to protecting and improving the health of French soldiers. He continued to work until a few weeks before his death, sending assistants to inform him of the day's happenings at the Pasteur Institute's labs even after he lost the strength to visit the labs himself. Laveran died on May 18, 1922, after a long illness.

Periodicals

Journal of Medical Biography, May 2002.

Online

"Alphonse Laveran," Nobelprize.org, http://nobelprize.org/ nobel_prizes/medicine/laureates/1907/laveran-bio.html (December 14, 2007).

"Charles Louis Alphonse Laveran (1845-1922)," Malaria Site, http://www.malariasite.com/malaria/laveran.htm (December 14, 2007).

"Laveran and the Discovery of the Malaria Parasite," U.S. Centers for Disease Control, http://www.cdc.gov/Malaria/history/ laveran.htm (December 14, 2007).

World of Anatomy and Physiology. Online. Thomson Gale, 2006, http://galenet.galegroup.com/servlet/BioRC (April 16, 2008). □

Florence Lawrence

Canadian-born American actress Florence Lawrence (1886-1938) was a familiar face in the early years of motion pictures, even though most viewers had no way of putting a name to the face because few of her several hundred films credited her or any of the other actors involved.

Sometimes Lawrence was known simply as the "Biograph Girl," after the company for which she did much of her onscreen work. Audiences were sure to recognize her, for her face was everywhere motion pictures were shown. At the peak of her career around 1910, she was featured in several dozen films each year. Lawrence was the subject of perhaps the first major publicity stunt associated with an onscreen personality, and she was the first to be courted with a bidding war between rival studios. In other ways, too, Lawrence anticipated the lives of numerous future stars: her later life was unhappy, her marriages were unsuccessful, she burned through a large fortune she had accumulated, and she came to a terrible end.

Perfected Whistling Act at Four

Lawrence was born Florence Annie Bridgwood on January 2, 1886. She was one of a group of early Canadian-born movie stars, including Mary Pickford and Marie Dressler. She was part of a family that made a living in traveling vaudeville; her mother, Charlotte, used the name Lotta Lawrence (and billed the troupe as the Lawrence Dramatic Company). Florence took that surname as well. Her performing career began at age four, when she took the stage as Baby Flo, the Child Wonder Whistler. While she was still a child, the family emigrated from Hamilton to nearby Buffalo, New York. Lawrence attended school there and perfected a variety of other skills that might help her in the theatrical business, such as ice skating and, with Wild West shows on the rise, horseback riding.

Continuing to appear in stage productions throughout her teens, Lawrence found herself in New York City in 1906 after the Lawrence Dramatic Company disbanded. She had no luck finding work on Broadway, but her timing was fortunate. Film production was expanding in New York as the art of cinema advanced beyond the status of novelty and began to tell stories aimed at creating an ongoing audience. Thanks to her horseback riding skills, Lawrence won a part in *Daniel Boone,* one of cinema's early adventure landmarks. The single-reel film, which simply depicted Boone's capture by Indians after an ill-fated attempt to rescue his daughter (played by Lawrence), was released by Thomas Edison's

Edison Manufacturing Company. She soon found additional work with Vitagraph, a rival New York studio that was attempting to capitalize on Edison's improvements to the movie camera. She had to do costume-sewing work in addition to appearing on screen, but she preferred that to the grind of touring in an unheated carriage with a theatrical troupe.

One Reelers

In 1908 Lawrence made 38 films for Vitagraph. Most of these were so-called "one-reelers," about ten minutes in length, and were melodramas featuring a single dramatic plot twist. Some had Western or other exotic settings (location filming was out of the question, but Lawrence sometimes had to work outdoors), and her skill on horseback again set her apart from the crowd. That same year Lawrence married fellow Vitagraph actor Harry Solter, who also directed some of her films. The pair set out to give Lawrence a higher profile than the other young actresses who labored anonymously in the growing industry.

They got a major break when the pioneering director D.W. Griffith spotted Lawrence in one of her Vitagraph films and decided to cast her in *The Girl and the Outlaw*, filmed in Fort Lee, New Jersey, from August 2 through August 4, 1908. This time Lawrence portrayed a Native American princess who is beaten and left for dead but is rescued by a white rancher and his daughter. The entire group is attacked by Indians, and Lawrence's character is killed as she tries to help her rescuers escape. Griffith signed Lawrence to a $25-a-week contract with his Biograph studio, and she appeared in his increasingly ambitious productions such as *Outpost in Malaya* and the tearjerker *Romance of a Jewess*.

In terms of the sheer number of her performances shown on screen, the year 1909 marked the high point of Lawrence's career. She starred in 65 films, including such pathbreaking Griffith releases as *Resurrection*, a 12-minute adaptation of an entire novel by Leo Tolstoy in which she plays a girl on trial in court who inspires a jury member, who had seduced and abandoned her years earlier, to reform his ways. She was also the cinema's first Juliet, appearing in the female lead role in the first of many films of Shakespeare's *Romeo and Juliet*. It was in 1909 that Mary Pickford, following Lawrence's example, decided to emigrate to the United States. Lawrence was still an unknown name to moviegoers, but it was around this time that they dubbed her the "Biograph Girl" or "The Girl of a Thousand Faces."

In 1910 Lawrence was lured to yet another new studio, the IMP Company of executive Carl Laemmle, who later founded Universal Studios. Laemmle not only offered Lawrence a raise but also raised her profile with a publicity stunt of nationwide scope: he planted rumors that she had been killed in a St. Louis trolley accident but then ran full-page newspaper advertisements, headed "We Nail a Lie," debunking his own rumors and announcing her signing to IMP. Lawrence was unveiled in a St. Louis ceremony that outdrew an appearance by U.S. President William Howard Taft. The moviegoing public continued to refer to Lawrence with the anonymous "Imp Girl" title, but she was also known by her actual name. She is often regarded as the first true movie star.

In her first IMP film, 1910's *The Broken Oath*, Lawrence's name was featured in the credits and publicity. Executives who had previously resisted this practice now embraced it, realizing that a star's name on a marquee could build business. Lawrence continued to try to convert her fame into a better financial deal, moving to the Lubin studio and then, with support from Laemmle, establishing her own studio, Victor, in Fort Lee, New Jersey. Solter, still her husband and director, was her partner in the enterprise as well. Between 1910 and 1914 Lawrence made about 140 films. All were one- or two-reelers, and many of them, capitalizing on her new fame, featured a character named Florence or Flo.

Lawrence bought a New Jersey home with a formal garden, and she had disposable income left over to buy the new rich person's toys of the moment: automobiles. "A car to me is something that is almost human," she said in an interview quoted in *Technology Review*, "something that responds to kindness and understanding and care, just as people do." She even invented an early turn signal—an arm and flag, attached to the back bumper, that could be raised by pressing a button inside the passenger compartment. A similar brake warning button raised an arm with a stop sign. Unfortunately Lawrence failed to patent these inventions and received no credit for them when similar devices became standard equipment. Lawrence's mother, however, received a patent for a primitive type of electric windshield wiper.

Work Related Injury

Lawrence's period of stardom came to an end with a horrific accident in 1914: during the filming of a stunt scene in *Pawns of Destiny*, a fire broke out on the set. Lawrence's hair ignited and she fell, injuring her back and going into shock. Lawrence's recovery was slow, and the implosion of her career coincided with the dissolution of her marriage to Solter. She tried to make a comeback with the feature-length *Elusive Isabel* in 1916, in which she played a secret agent from an unnamed Latin American country who is sent to destabilize the U.S. government. The film, competing with Griffith's mammoth three-hour epic *Intolerance*, was unsuccessful, and Lawrence continued to battle poor health.

Nor was her marital life happy. She married car salesman Charles Woodring, but that married ended with her husband's death. A third marriage, to Henry Bolton, lasted for only a few months in 1932. Lawrence moved to Hollywood and tried out several new enterprises, including a line of cosmetics and a second abortive comeback, but she had little success; the public had forgotten her. Financial losses during the stock market crash of 1929 wiped out much of her fortune.

Through the 1920s and 1930s, screen personalities from the early days of film were often given bit parts in new films as a form of tribute and that often providing financial support in the pre-Social Security days. She appeared in the 1936 screwball comedy *One Rainy Afternoon* but, as in the beginning of her career, was not credited. Suffering chronic pain, she committed suicide on December 28, 1938, by eating ant poison. The total number of films in which she appeared is difficult to estimate, for some have been lost, but estimates range between 250 and 300. Lawrence was buried at Hollywood Cemetery, in a grave that remained unmarked until 1991. That year, actor and film preservation activist Roddy McDowall funded the placement of a gravestone that, although it mistakenly listed her birth year as 1890, correctly identified her as ''The Biograph Girl'' and ''The First Movie Star.''

Books

Brown, Kelly R., *Florence Lawrence, the Biograph Girl: America's First Movie Star,* McFarland, 1999.

Periodicals

Technology Review, July-August 2002.

Online

''Florence Lawrence,'' *All Movie Guide,* http://www.allmovie .com (January 28, 2008).
''Florence Lawrence: The Biograph Girl,'' Biograph Company, http://www.biographcompany.com/celebrity/lawrence.html (January 28, 2008).
''Florence Lawrence,'' Internet Movie Database, http://www .imdb.com (January 28, 2008).
''Florence Lawrence,'' Northern Stars, http://www.northernstars .ca/actorsjkl/lawrencebio.html (January 28, 2008). □

Aldo Leopold

American forester, conservationist, and author, Aldo Leopold (1887-1948), a father of wildlife management, deeply influenced the modern environmental movement a generation after his death. His collection of essays, *A Sand County Almanac,* published posthumously in 1949, expressed the need for people to develop an ethic around preserving the natural balance of wild land.

L eopold was born on January 11, 1887, in Burlington, Iowa. His father was a desk manufacturer and his grandfather was a landscape architect who had designed several of Burlington's buildings. He grew up in a mansion overlooking the Mississippi River, learning about nature. The trees and flowers on his family's land needed constant attention because of the thin and stony soil. Meanwhile, the Mississippi provided a migration route for vast numbers of North America's ducks and geese, and Leopold and his brothers and father often went down to the river valley to hunt them. Young Leopold became a curious observer of birds and natural history and began recording his experiences with nature every day in a journal, a habit he kept up all his life.

Leopold the Forester

After attending Lawrenceville Prep in New Jersey, Leopold enrolled in Yale University in 1905, graduated from the Sheffield Scientific School at Yale in 1908, then earned a master's degree from the Yale Forest School in 1909. The Forest School was the first in the country, and the profession of forestry was growing thanks to the 1905 creation of the U.S. Forest Service. Leopold joined the service after graduation, and he was put in charge of a crew sent into the Apache National Forest in Arizona Territory to map the forest and look for timber.

In 1912, Leopold was promoted to supervisor of New Mexico's million-acre Carson National Forest. That same year, he married Estella Bergere, whose prominent Santa Fe family had been active in settling the Southwest. Leopold spent 18 months in 1913 and 1914 recovering from a severe case of nephritis, a sometimes fatal inflammatory kidney disease, and afterwards he accepted a less physically strenuous position as acting head of grazing at the Forest Service's district headquarters in Albuquerque.

In 1915, Leopold began pressing Forest Service employees to enforce fish and game laws—limitations on hunting—in New Mexico. Americans had hunted the country's native wildlife so aggressively in the late 1800s that many species were in danger of extinction, and hunters were advocating strict hunting laws to preserve deer, turkeys, and other commonly hunted wildlife. New Mexico and Arizona had agreed to let Forest Service rangers enforce their game laws when they became states in 1912, but rangers had not arrested a single person for violating them. Leopold created a handbook defining forest rangers' powers to limit hunting. He also traveled across New Mexico and Arizona to talk with citizens and local forest officers about forming local game protection associations, establishing wildlife refuges, and restocking lakes with trout. In addition, he founded a newspaper, *The Pine Cone,* the official bulletin of the New Mexico Game Protective Association.

To protect deer and other game, as well as cattle ranches, Leopold argued forcefully during the 1920s for completely eradicating populations of predatory animals: wolves, coyotes, bobcats, and mountain lions. ''It is going to take patience and money to catch the last wolf or [mountain] lion in New Mexico,'' he said in a 1920 speech to the National Game Conference (as quoted in Susan Flader's book *Thinking Like A Mountain*). ''But the last one must be caught before the job can be called fully successful.'' Leopold's efforts gained the admiration of former U.S. President and avid hunter Theodore Roosevelt, who sent him a supportive letter.

Between 1915 and 1924, Leopold worked in various administrative jobs with the forest service in the Southwest. In 1916 and 1917, he helped implement a new policy that added summer homes, campgrounds, and other recreational areas to the forests. From 1919 to 1924, he was placed in charge of operations for the Arizona and New Mexico forests, including personnel, finances, roads, trails, and fire control. Reluctant to see all forests opened to roads, he worked on a successful 1924 proposal to set aside a halfmillion acres in the Gila National Forest as a roadless wilderness preserve, an approach that eventually evolved into the National Wilderness Preservation Act of 1964. Meanwhile, Leopold wrote many newspaper and journal articles about game preservation and the health of wild land.

Moving to Wisconsin

In 1924, Leopold accepted a position as associate director of the U.S. Forest Products Laboratory in Madison, Wisconsin. The job did not fit his interests in game management and wilderness protection, however, so he dedicated his spare time to those pursuits. He worked on a book-length manuscript, *Southwestern Game Fields,* which included life histories of wildlife in the Southwest, but changes in the region, including an explosion in the deer population, made the work outdated, and he abandoned the project. He joined a local conservation group and helped push for the passage of Wisconsin's Conservation Act of 1927, which created a department that oversaw the state's hunting laws and forests.

Leopold left the Forest Service in 1928 for a new project: compiling game surveys of the Midwest. He secured funding from hunting-gun manufacturers and traveled through nine states, consulting with hunters and local officials and scientists. He published his findings in his 1931 *Report on a Game Survey of the North Central States,* making him one of the country's top experts in hunted wildlife.

Leopold's second published book, *Game Management,* finished in 1933, became a classic wildlife management textbook. It promoted a new approach to dealing with game animals, instead of relying only on wildlife refuges and hunting limits or on breeding efforts. Leopold argued that wildlife managers had to understand animals' biology and their relationship to their habitats, and preserve, manage and restore those habitats. "The central thesis of game management," he wrote in the book (as quoted by Flader in *Thinking Like A Mountain*), "is this: game can be restored by the *creative use* of the same tools which have heretofore destroyed it—axe, plow, cow, fire, and gun."

In August of 1933, Leopold joined the faculty of the University of Wisconsin. He and his students performed field research on wildlife and worked on wildlife-preservation programs that encouraged cooperation between farmers and hunters. In 1935, Leopold bought an old farm on the Wisconsin River in central Wisconsin's "sand country" that would become his retreat and muse for the rest of his life. He and his family planted thousands of trees there in an effort to restore its natural state.

Changing Philosophies

Later in 1935, Leopold traveled to Germany to observe forest and wildlife management there. He found the highly managed German forests too artificial. They had no predators or independent wildlife. Rangers fed deer on straw bales. Brick walls surrounded rivers. Fences protected recently planted trees. Leopold also saw that clear-cutting forests and letting them re-grow, as he had in the Southwest, produced inferior trees compared to forests with small, selective annual harvests. "We, Americans, have not yet experienced a bearless, wolfless, eagleless, catless woods," Leopold wrote after his trip to Germany (as quoted in Marybeth Lorbiecki's biography, *Aldo Leopold: A Fierce Green Fire*). "We yearn for more deer and more pines, and we shall probably get them. But do we realize that to get them, as the Germans have, at the expense of their wild environment and their wild enemies, is to get very little indeed?"

The trip to Germany convinced Leopold that forests could not be controlled, but that foresters should preserve wild lands' natural balance. In 1939, Leopold presented a paper, "A Biotic View of Land," arguing against old methods of wildlife management, which saw species as competing with each other and intervened to favor species people found useful (deer for hunting, corn for harvesting). Instead, he argued, conservationists needed to encourage diversity of species and stable, healthy land—wilderness that could always renew itself.

In 1943, Leopold was named a conservation commissioner in Wisconsin. He campaigned in favor of reducing deer herds and against eradicating wolves. It was a complete reversal from his public position of two decades earlier, but Leopold was putting his new views into action to address a concrete problem. With their natural enemies exterminated, deer were dying of starvation, their populations grown too large. Yet Leopold faced strong public opposition in Wisconsin, as the public was not ready to change its mind and allow predators to live freely.

The Classic Essays

World War II drew most of Leopold's graduate students out of school, so he spent more of his time writing literary and philosophical essays about wildlife and the land. In early 1944, Leopold began writing his landmark essay "Thinking Like A Mountain," in which he vividly admitted that his years of wanting to eradicate predators were a mistake with terrible consequences for nature. In poetic language, he recalled shooting a wolf in the southwest decades earlier.

"We reached the old wolf in time to watch a fierce green fire dying in her eyes," he wrote (as quoted in Flader's book *Thinking Like A Mountain*). "I was young then, and full of trigger-itch; I thought that because fewer wolves meant more deer, that no wolves would mean hunters' paradise. But after seeing the green fire die, I sensed that neither the wolf nor the mountain agreed with such a view." Between then and the 1940s, he went on, "I have lived to see state after state extirpate its wolves." As a result, he had seen mountains with "every edible brush and seedling" eaten to death by deer, followed by "the starved bones of the hoped-for deer herd." Nature replaces deer killed by wolves within a few years, he said, but a mountain range's overeaten vegetation still might not be replaced decades later.

By the 1940s, Leopold was famous in conservation circles, consulted on nearly every conservation issue of his time by more than a hundred government agencies, activist groups, professional societies, and journals. In 1947, he was elected president of the Ecological Society of America. In late 1947 or early 1948, he wrote his most important essay, "The Land Ethic," which argued that people needed to develop a new ethic around preserving the health and integrity of natural areas. The essay would later become an important statement of the goals of the environmental movement. "A thing is right with it tends to preserve the integrity, stability and beauty of the biotic community," he wrote (as quoted in Flader's *Thinking Like A Mountain*). "It is wrong when it tends otherwise."

In January of 1948, the federal government invited Leopold to help represent the United States at a 1949 United Nations conference on conservation. That April, he learned that Oxford University Press had accepted a collection of his essays, including "Thinking Like A Mountain" and "The Land Ethic," for publication as a book. A week later, on April 21, 1948, Leopold died of a heart attack while helping to fight a grass fire on his neighbors' farm. He was 61.

Leopold's book of essays, titled *A Sand County Almanac* in tribute to the land where he wrote and set his writing, was published in 1949. His blending of natural history, scientific knowledge, and narrative and literary skill eventually made the work a classic. Though it fell out of print in the 1950s, it was republished as a mass-market paperback in the 1960s, and a new generation of people concerned about the environment discovered it. It has sold more than a million copies. "We abuse land because we regard it as a commodity belonging to us," Leopold wrote in the book's foreword (as quoted by Curt Meine in an *American National Biography* article on him). "When we see land as a community to which we belong, we may begin to use it with love and respect."

Books

Brown, David E., and Neil B. Carmony, editors, *Aldo Leopold's Wilderness*, Stackpole Books, 1990.
Flader, Susan L., *Thinking Like A Mountain*, The University of Wisconsin Press, 1994.
Loribiecki, Marybeth, *Aldo Leopold: A Fierce Green Fire*, Falcon Press, 1996.

Online

Meine, Curt, "Leopold, Aldo," *American National Biography Online*, http://www.anb.org/articles/13/13-00983.html (December 16, 2007). ☐

Bernard-Henri Lévy

French philosopher Bernard-Henri Lévy (born 1948) is one of the best known writers in contemporary France, notable for his sheer celebrity as well as for the range and depth of his writings.

Lévy has a level of public visibility perhaps unmatched by any philosopher outside of France; he is popularly known simply by his initials, BHL. Deeply concerned with political and cultural issues in most of his writings, he has rejected and challenged the extremes of both left- and right-wing philosophies, in France and around the world. Unusual for French thinkers, Lévy has been generally supportive of the United States, and several of his books, including *Who Killed Daniel Pearl?* and *American Vertigo*, have brought him a wide readership in the English-speaking world.

Born in Algeria

Bernard-Henri Lévy was born on November 5, 1948, in Beni-Saf, in what was then French-controlled Algeria. His father, André, was a member of Algeria's small French-Jewish population who saw military action both with republican forces during the Spanish Civil War and in the underground anti-Nazi resistance in Italy during World War II. After the war's end he returned to Algeria and started a lumber wholesale business called Becob, which proved spectacularly successful; the father grew up poor, but the son and his two siblings grew up wealthy. The family moved to Morocco and then, in 1954, to the Paris suburb of Neuilly, where Bernard-Henri attended the Lycée Pasteur. Quickly identified as a top student, he was placed in the special yearlong *kâgne* classes that identify top French students and groom them for elite university studies. As a young man he obtained a black belt in judo.

Lévy attended the Ecole Normale Supérieure, a French university known for the large number of intellectuals it has graduated. Among his teachers were Jacques Derrida and Louis Althusser, two of the most important French philosophers of the twentieth century. Althusser especially was of a Marxist orientation, and Lévy was pushed in that direction as well by the eruption of left-wing French student activism in the spring of 1968. From the start, however, he was uncomfortable with the positions of the far left. He traveled extensively during and just after his student years, visiting Mexico, the Middle East, and the Indian subcontinent. He received his philosophy degree from the Ecole Normal

Supérieure in 1971 and was selected as part of a French government "Groupe des Experts" by Socialist party leader and future French president François Mitterand.

In the 1970s Lévy taught at a high school near Paris and then joined the philosophy faculty at the University of Strasbourg. He tried his hand at fiction and wrote a book about Bangladeshi nationalism. The book that put Lévy on the intellectual map was 1977's *La barbarie à visage humain* (Barbarism with a Human Face), in which he broke decisively with Marxist thought. Entertainingly written in a polemical style that attracted readers despite the philosophical density of the subject matter, the book sold well in the United States as well as in France, and even landed Lévy on the cover of *Time* magazine. In France, he became identified with a group of young thinkers, known as the New Philosophers, who rejected leftist thought.

Leftist writers attacked Lévy furiously, accusing him of being a media creation, of lacking originality, and even of being an agent of the American Central Intelligence Agency. But Communism was on the decline in France, and Lévy was ahead of the trend. His writings were treated with equal hostility by the French right wing, which Lévy placed under scrutiny in his 1981 book *L'idéology française.* Lévy argued that France's rightist politics had roots in French collaboration with Nazi rule during World War II. "I put my finger into the wound, and it provoked such convulsions—it was like the Devil convulsing when faced with the truth," he recalled to Joan Juliet Buck of *Vanity Fair.* Once again, Lévy proved prescient; his warnings of a resurgent extreme right in France were borne out by the electoral success of the National Front party in the 1980s and 1990s.

Supported Solidarity Labor Union

These twin controversies made Lévy irresistible to the French media, and he was a frequent guest on television talk shows. In 1981 he became a columnist for the left-leaning daily newspaper *Le Matin,* where he wrote essays supportive of the Solidarity labor union in Poland. Lévy married his first wife, Isabelle Doutreligne, in 1973; that marriage produced a daughter, Justine (named after the central figure in a novel by the Marquis de Sade). Lévy married Sylvie Bouscasse in 1980, and the two had a son, Antonin-Balthazar. Both children have pursued literary careers, Justine as a novelist and Antonin-Balthazar as an editor and columnist.

In the late 1980s Lévy began to express concern at the rise of militant Islam. He was one of the first supporters of Indian-born British writer Salman Rushdie, whose death had been ordered by Iran's Ayatollah Ruhollah Khomeini. In 1989, acting under the auspices of the French Secretary of State for International Cultural Relations, Lévy began visiting the countries of Eastern Europe as they emerged from decades of Communist rule.

In 1992 Lévy became one of the first writers to raise the alarm over the outbreak of genocidal violence that followed the formation of the new nation of Bosnia and Herzegovina, part of the former Yugoslavia. He made two documentaries, *Bosna!,* about the general chaos in Bosnia, and *A Day in the Death of Sarajevo,* about the siege of Sarajevo by Yugoslav and Bosnian Serb forces between 1992 and 1996. His per-

sistence in highlighting the breakdown of order in the former Yugoslavia contributed to the European and American military intervention that ended the regional conflict in the Balkans. Divorced from Bouscasse, Lévy married actress Arielle Dombasle in June of 1993.

Lévy and Bouscasse were a glamour couple, dividing their time between France and Morocco, where they lived in an elaborate villa they acquired from French actor Alain Delon. Lévy, with his usually partially unbuttoned white silk shirt, did not fit the public image of an intellectual. He had never learned to drive, and traveled in chauffeured limousines, staying in luxury hotels. Once, in Afghanistan, he was forced to choose between a secure hotel room that had no hot water or a more dangerous building where the water heater was operating. He chose the hot water.

Lévy's 1997 film *Le jour et la nuit* (Day and Night) was both critically and commercially unsuccessful, and he returned to writing. He took up the cause of his Algerian homeland, now beset by Islamic fundamentalist attacks, and in 2000 his book *The Century of Sartre,* a biography and evaluation of philosopher Jean-Paul Sartre, was critically acclaimed. Among Lévy's most controversial books was *Who Killed Daniel Pearl?* (2003), which used a mixture of fiction and reportage to explore the world of the Al Qaeda-affiliated terrorists who beheaded *Wall Street Journal* reporter Daniel Pearl in 2002.

Visited United States

Through this entire period, Lévy clashed with thinkers on both sides of the political spectrum in his staunch support for the United States. Dombasle had been born in the United States, and Lévy admired the country's strong traditions of democracy and pluralism. Furthermore, he mistrusted the roots of anti-Americanism in France. "I'm not pro-American as much as anti-anti-American," he told Buck. "When the French begin to feel a mad visceral hatred toward an imagined America, I know the cauldron is boiling and the filthy genie is about to jump out again." In 2004, at the request of *Atlantic Monthly* magazine in Boston, Lévy made a tour of the United States, loosely retracing the route of another famous French political philosopher and observer of America, Alexis de Tocqueville.

Lévy's observations were serialized in *Atlantic* and then appeared in book form as *American Vertigo* in 2006. Mixing anecdote (he is cited by a state highway patrolman for public urination but then discovers that the officer is well acquainted with Tocqueville's writings) with deeper reflections on such matters as sport as an American religion, the book won wide attention in both the United States and France. I have strong links with the U.S.," Lévy observed to Donald Morrison of *Time International.* "Yet I discovered on this trip that I did not know anything. Every single step was a surprise, every moment a paradox, every meeting an education. Europeans have a poor understanding of the U.S., not because they don't spend time here, but because of a smog of cliché and prejudice."

By that time Lévy had published more than 30 books and, despite ups and downs in his career, had demonstrated a knack for identifying hot topics and making contributions, buttressed by his background as a philosopher, that advanced the debate regarding those topics. Several of Lévy's other books were translated into English in the early 2000s: *Sartre: The Philosopher of the Twentieth Century* appeared in 2003, and the set of essays *War, Evil and End of History* followed in 2004. In 2006 and 2007 Lévy was at work on the hottest of all hot topics, the conflict between Israel and its Arab neighbors.

Books

Lévy, Bernard-Henri, *American Vertigo,* Random House, 2006.

Periodicals

Chronicle of Higher Education, October 24, 2003.
Europe, April 1995.
Publishers Weekly, December 12, 2005.
Time International, May 12, 2003; February 7, 2005; March 6, 2006.
Vanity Fair, January 2003.

Online

Bernard-Henri Lévy Official Web site, http://www.bernard-henri-levy.com (February 22, 2008). □

Edmonia Lewis

American sculptor Edmonia Lewis (c. 1840-c. 1909), of African-American and Native American background, overcame tremendous odds and the effects of a terrorist attack she survived as a young woman to become a successful artist working in Rome, Italy.

Long forgotten, Lewis's sculptures have found their way back into museum collections through remarkable routes of rediscovery. Even though the contributions of minority artists have long been undervalued, art historians were quick to realize what had been lost: Lewis, although she worked in the highly conventionalized style known as neoclassicism, injected elements of her own background into her works. Triply disadvantaged as an African American, a Native American, and a woman, she drew on history and classical mythology to create sculptures that expressed her feelings and her perception of her own position.

Raised in Native American Tribe

Both the earliest and final years of Lewis's life are shrouded in mystery, deepened by questionable statements she gave to interviewers as she attempted to expand the foothold she had gained in the art market after moving to Italy. Birth years from 1840 to 1845 appear in various accounts of her life, with the earlier part of that range seeming the most likely: she is known to have entered Oberlin College in 1859, and while she could certainly have matriculated at the age of 14 or 15, she also attended another secondary or post-secondary institution, New York Central College, for several years before that, and it is unlikely that

she did so as a preteen. Lewis's father was African American, probably an immigrant from Haiti who worked as a servant; her mother was Native American, a member of the Chippewa tribe. Lewis's birthplace is also unknown. Contemporary accounts have stated that she was from Albany, New York, or the nearby town of Greenbush (now East Greenbush), but she told an English interviewer that she was from Greenhigh, Ohio. She also apparently spent time in Newark, New Jersey, and may have been born there.

Lewis went by several different names during her life. Born Mary Edmonia Lewis, she dropped her first name later in life. She also said she had a Native American name, Wildfire, and that after her parents died she had been brought up among the Chippewa—leading a "wandering life, fishing, swimming and making moccasins," she told the London art critic Henry Wreford in 1866, as quoted in *History Today.* Some corroboration for Lewis's account surfaced in the form of records showing that a Chippewa woman named Catherine had married an African American named John Mike on a reservation in what is now Mississauga, Ontario.

Lewis also had a brother, 12 years older than she, who was called Samuel Lewis or Sunrise. He headed west during the Gold Rush years of the late 1840s and apparently struck it rich, for he sent money back east to provide for his sister's education. When Edmonia was 12, she enrolled at the New York Central College in McGrawville, a Baptist-affiliated school known for its sympathy to abolitionist ideas. After about three years of study there, she was, she told Wreford, "declared to be too wild." She moved on to Oberlin College in Oberlin, Ohio, which in 1835 had become the first college in the United States to admit women and African Americans.

Despite Oberlin's progressive ideals there was still plenty of racial tension at the school, and especially in the surrounding community. Edmonia did well at Oberlin for several years, finishing the college preparatory part of the curriculum and beginning to take liberal arts courses. She lived with two white girls, Christine Ennes and Maria Miles, in a boarding house owned by an abolitionist minister. But her environment began to unravel on January 27, 1862, when her two roommates went out for a sleigh ride with male friends after all three girls had drunk some spiced wine—Edmonia apparently barely touched hers. During the ride, both Christine and Maria complained of abdominal pains and then collapsed. Doctors concluded that they had been poisoned, and both blamed Lewis. The poison was cantharides, popularly known as Spanish Fly; it was used in small doses for its supposed effect as a sexual stimulant.

Left for Dead

Put on trial, Lewis was defended by lawyer and Oberlin graduate John Mercer Langston, who was himself shot at by the father of one of the poisoned girls (both survived) while preparing to try the case. In his autobiography, quoted in *History Today,* he recalled that Lewis "was seized by unknown persons, carried out into the field lying at the rear, and after being severely beaten with her clothes and jewellery [sic] torn from her person and scattered here and there, she was left in a dark obscure place to die." Searchers found her, but it took almost two weeks before she was well enough for the trial to begin. When it did, Langston moved successfully for dismissal without calling any witnesses, arguing that the contents of the girls' stomachs had never been analyzed, and thus the charges against Lewis could not be proved. It was never established whether she had poisoned the two girls, given them the stimulant as a prank, or been entirely unjustly accused. Neither Lewis's nor Langston's attackers were ever charged.

Troubles continued to plague Lewis at Oberlin. She was accused, and again exonerated, in two petty theft cases, and other students taunted her with whispers of "Watch out for Spanish Flies!" She thought of returning to her mother's tribe. Finally, aided by a letter of introduction to abolitionist leader William Lloyd Garrison, she headed for Boston without finishing her degree. After arriving there in January of 1866, she saw a bust of Benjamin Franklin in a shop window and decided she wanted to become a sculptor. Garrison arranged an apprenticeship in the studio of sculptor Edward Brackett, and Lewis made rapid progress. By 1865 she had created a sculpture of Colonel Robert Gould Shaw, the slain commander of the otherwise all-black 54th Massachusetts Infantry and a local hero of the Civil War. Lewis sold some one hundred copies of the Shaw bust to prominent Boston abolitionist families, and she decided to use the proceeds to finance further art studies in Rome.

Lewis was not alone in her decision to go to Rome. Many young artists, male and female, traveled to the city seen as the seat of the European artistic tradition, a city whose streets were a living museum of sculpture. But Lewis stated that she had another motivation as well: in Italy she was less likely to be judged solely on the basis of her skin color. She was quickly befriended by another female sculptor, Harriet Hosmer, and became part of an inseparable all-female circle of artists who dressed in shirts and caps. That association, together with the lack of any hint of romance with a man in surviving records of Lewis's life, has led some historians of gay life to conclude that she was a lesbian. Lewis was also supported by the Abolitionist Lydia Marie Child, who was living in Rome at the time.

Setting to work in Rome, Lewis sculpted *Freedwoman and Her Child,* the first sculpture on the theme of emancipation by an African-American artist. Shortly after that, she was profiled in the *Atheneum* and another London publication, the *Art-Journal.* While she frequently addressed African-American themes in her art, she also stressed her Native American ancestry. The poems of Henry Wadsworth Longfellow, notably "The Song of Hiawatha," were reaching a peak of popularity in both the United States and Europe, and art involving Native American imagery was marketable. Lewis's major work based on Native American themes was *The Old Arrow-Maker and His Daughter (The Wooing of Hiawatha)* (1867), which was purchased by a wealthy patron, donated to the Boston YMCA, and finally acquired by the Smithsonian Museum of American Art in Washington, D.C.

Opened Roman Showrooms

With commissions for copies of busts coming in from American patrons, Lewis prospered. She opened a show-room on the Via della Frezza in Rome and attended the Paris Exposition, a major arts exhibition. Books and travel guides about Rome, such as John Murray's *Handbook of Rome and Its Environs,* began to mention her studio as an important stop for visitors to the city, and one of the visitors who came to see her was Longfellow himself, in 1868. The poet's family thought highly of the bust that resulted. In 1870 Lewis made a small medallion bearing the likeness of the composer Franz Liszt. Lewis also revealed that she had joined the Roman Catholic church in 1868.

Some of Lewis's sculptures, such as *Poor Cupid* and a bust of the Roman emperor Diocletian, took up themes typical of neoclassical art, but remarkably often she took up subjects that reflected her own background. The Egyptian woman Hagar from the biblical Book of Genesis, who would have been considered black from a nineteenth-century perspective, became the subject of Lewis's *Hagar in the Wilderness* (1868). She created that work, as well as some others, without a commission from a rich buyer and with no prospect of immediate financial gain, and was rebuked for doing so by Child. Lewis began to travel to the United States to meet with buyers and promote her works; *Hagar in the Wilderness* was set up in Chicago's Farwell Hall. She billed herself as the Young and Gifted Colored Sculptress from Rome, and charged visitors 25 cents to see the sculpture. In America, Lewis found a ready market for busts of abolitionist heroes like John Brown and Senator Charles Sumner. Although most sculptors hired teams of assistants to help with the heavy work of moving hundreds of pounds of marble, Lewis did all the work on her sculptures herself, partly to forestall expected suggestions that a black woman could not possibly have created works of such skill and accomplishment.

Lewis's most ambitious work, and by most accounts her masterpiece, was the two-ton *The Death of Cleopatra,* finished in time for the Centennial Exposition in Philadelphia in 1876. While many sculptures of the Egyptian queen showed her as a power-hungry seductress, Lewis showed the moment of her death, a tragic and vulnerable figure slumped in a chair after being bitten by the poisonous snake she is said to have used to cause her own death. The statue had a powerful emotional quality that both attracted and repelled viewers in Philadelphia and then at the Chicago Interstate Exposition, where it was moved in 1878 after it failed to sell in Philadelphia. One Philadelphia journalist, quoted in *History Today,* noted that the work "excites more admiration and gathers larger crowds around it than any other work of art in the vast collection of Memorial Hall." But in Chicago, as well, it went unsold and Lewis finally placed the sculpture in storage and returned to Europe.

Much of Lewis's work was neglected for decades before its ultimate rediscovery, but the odyssey of *The Death of Cleopatra* was especially unusual. It resurfaced in a saloon on Chicago's Clark Street and was later acquired by gambler "Blind John" Condon, who placed it atop the grave of a favorite racehorse named Cleopatra. There the sculpture remained (in accordance with a legal writ executed by the dying Condon in 1915) until a U.S. postal service building was constructed on the site in the 1970s. At that point it was moved to the grounds of a construction company in Cicero, Illinois, where a fire inspector became intrigued by it and instructed his son's Boy Scout troop to paint it. Local newspaper accounts of this episode brought the sculpture to the attention of the Forest Hills (Illinois) Historical Society, which moved it to a storeroom at a shopping mall. The Forest Hills group made inquiries to try and determine what it was they owned, and through a chain of museum curators who heard about it, the sculpture found its way to the National Museum of American Art in Washington, where it resides today.

Lewis made several more important sculptures; she traveled to Syracuse, New York, and Cincinnati, Ohio, in 1879 to exhibit *The Veiled Bride of Spring* (it, too, had been relegated to a scrap yard but was rescued by people who knew nothing more about it than that they liked it), and in 1883 she executed a remarkable altarpiece featuring a multiracial set of cherubs for a Baltimore church. Neoclassical sculpture was falling out of fashion, however, and her career slowed. Lewis continued to live in Rome, where Frederick Douglass visited her in 1887. In 1893 a pair of Lewis sculptures, *Hiawatha* and *Phillis Wheatley* (an eighteenth-century African-American poet who was little known in Lewis's day), were exhibited at the Columbian Exposition world's fair in 1893 in Chicago. Records of Lewis's later life are sparse; she visited New York in 1898 and apparently lived in London and Paris for a time. A Catholic magazine reported in 1909 that she was still alive, but the date and place of her death are unknown. In the early 2000s, Lewis's life became the subject of a play, *Wildfire: Black Hands, White Marble,* by Linda Beatrice Brown.

Books

Gay & Lesbian Biography, St. James, 1997.
Notable Black American Women, Book 1, Gale, 1992.

Periodicals

History Today, October 2007.
Lexington Herald-Leader (Lexington, KY), June 30, 2007.
News & Record (Piedmont Triad, NC), April 12, 2002.
Smithsonian, September 1996.

Online

"Edmonia Lewis," http://www.edmonialewis.com (November 23, 2007).
"Edmonia Lewis," Lakewood (OH) Public Library: Women in History, http://www.lkwdpl.org/wihohio/lewi-edm.htm (November 23, 2007).
"The fascinating journey of a 19th-century sculpture . . .," PBS Newshour, http://www.pbs.org/newshour/bb/entertainment/edmonia_8-5.html (November 23, 2007).
"Lewis, Mary Edmonia (1844-1907)," An Encyclopedia of Gay, Lesbian, Bisexual, Transgender, and Queer Culture, http://www.glbtq.com/arts/lewis_me.html (November 23, 2007). □

Wyndham Lewis

Infuriating and erratic, but brilliantly creative, the Canadian-born British artist and writer Wyndham Lewis (1882-1957) was an always controversial pres-

ence in the British cultural scene for much of the first half of the twentieth century.

Lewis's talent ranged across painting, fiction, criticism, and social thought. He had a knack for finding sheer celebrity, as a troublemaker who consistently made himself into a topic of informed conversation. His output as a whole is difficult to summarize, for he developed, espoused, and then rejected quite a number of ideas over his long career, both in his visual and his verbal productions. "Contradict yourself," he wrote, according to the Flux Europa Web site. "In order to live, you must remain broken up." As an artist, Lewis introduced abstract styles to Britain with his so-called Vorticist style, and he is considered one of Britain's most important visual artists of the Modernist period. He was a brilliant satirist who attacked what he saw as negative trends in modern society, and he had an obsession with greatness that, perhaps, prevented him from really achieving it. In the decade preceding World War II, Lewis made a crucial political misjudgment in praising Adolf Hitler, and his reputation suffered as a result. He soon renounced his pro-Fascist ideas, however, and in the late twentieth century his fragmented but aggressive personality began to assert its attraction over readers and visual artists once again, and his popularity grew.

Off to London

Percy Wyndham Lewis was born November 18, 1882, on a ship anchored off Amherst, Nova Scotia, Canada. Although he retained a Canadian passport, his upbringing had little to do with that country. His father, Charles Lewis, was an American military officer, while his mother, Ann, came from south London, England. An only child, Lewis was sent to England for the best private school education available at the time.

The plan did not work out as intended. Enrolled at the posh Rugby School in Britain's Warwickshire region, Lewis caused trouble from the start. According to William Scammell of the London *Independent on Sunday* newspaper, he later bragged to Canadian media theorist Marshall McLuhan that he was "the only Rugby man until his time who had ever been given the 'sixth licking'—six full-scale lashings by a prefect in one day." Lewis moved on to the Slade School of Art, University College, in London, attending classes from 1898 to 1901 and receiving strong basic training, but he was eventually asked to leave that institution as well.

Most of the period between Lewis's late teens and his mid-twenties was spent in Paris, where he lived the stereotypical life of a young bohemian artist. He wrote sonnets about lust and pursued it in real life as well, becoming involved with a long series of mistresses. Lewis would marry Gladys Anne Hoskyns in 1930. That marriage produced no children, but Lewis had at least five illegitimate children by other women. In 1909 he returned to England, where he created paintings that began to spread his name around the art world. At first he was associated with the Bloomsbury Group of artists that followed French Post-Impressionist developments, but soon he went his own way. Among his first distinctive works was a set of drawings intended for a production of Shakespeare's play *Timon of Athens*. In place of the realistic quality of most theatrical drawings, Lewis provided figures that had a mechanical look and the two-dimensional quality of African masks.

Around 1914 Lewis became associated with the artistic movement known as Vorticism. Later in life he sarcastically defined Vorticism as whatever it was he had been doing around that time, but the term "Vorticism" was actually coined by Lewis's poet friend Ezra Pound, and it involved other artists as well. Allied in its harsh look with the Italian Futurist movement but lacking the focus on machinery of that school, Vorticism was a semi-abstract style that used bright colors and angular geometric forms. The "Vortex" was an abstractly conceived focus of primal energy. In 1914 Lewis and Pound founded a Vorticist journal called *The Blast*. It lasted for only two issues, but the influence of its aggressively irregular block typography and daring use of color has continued to resonate for nearly a century. *The Blast* published a Vorticist manifesto, quoted by Tom Lubbock in the *Independent on Sunday*, that contained, among others, these proto-punk broadsides: "Our Vortex is fed-up with your dispersals, reasonable chickenmen. . . . Our Vortex rushes like an angry dog at your Impressionistic fuss. . . . Our Vortex is white and abstract with its red-hot swiftness."

Took Artillery Fire

Lewis enlisted in the British army during World War I, and in 1917 he was sent to the front in France and joined an artillery unit. He saw fierce fighting in action around Ypres, but unlike other artists he did not seem overly dismayed by it. "I am here (in the firing line) since yesterday," he wrote to Pound, as quoted on the Spartacus Web site. "Battery split up, and I have come as reinforcements. Whizzing, banging and swishing and thudding completely surround me, and I almost jog up and down on my camp bed as though I were riding in a country wagon or a dilapidated taxi. I am in short, my dear colleague, in the midst of an unusually noisy battle." Lewis was made an official War Artist by the Canadian army and produced one of his most renowned paintings, *A Battery Shelled*. Lewis's war paintings anticipated the theme of dehumanization that ran through much of his later work. He later wrote extensively about his war experiences in his autobiography, *Blasting and Bombardiering*.

In 1918, Lewis's first novel, *Tarr*, was published. It looked back to his youthful experiences in Paris's hip Montparnasse neighborhood, but it also looked forward to one of the themes of his writings in the 1920s: the position of the artist in a contemporary society ruled by mass culture. Lewis found after the war that his Vorticist style had run its course. He withdrew from the cultural scene for several years, although he continued to associate closely with Pound, James Joyce, and other writers, and he read extensively in the fields of philosophy and literature. He emerged around 1925 with a series of fiction and nonfiction works that expressed criticisms of modern society. His first broadside was the 1926 nonfiction book *The Art of Being Ruled*, which imagined an authoritarian society that gave artists special status. The book touched on other strikingly modern topics: homosexuality, the cult of youth, and racial conflict. Although Lewis's views were generally retrogressive, he displayed a keen grasp of emerging social trends.

One of Lewis's most extensive books of the 1920s was *Time and Western Man*, published in 1927. The book was an attack on various targets, including many of Lewis's fellow writers, as well as on advertising, cinema, and other manifestations of modern mass culture. Many of Lewis's writings could be classified as right wing but had an iconoclastic flavor that set him apart from other conservative thinkers. Lewis further explored some of the ideas from *Time and Western Man* in his 1928 novel *Childermass*, intended as part of an allegorical fantasy trilogy to be titled *The Human Age*.

In 1927 Lewis founded another new periodical; this one was called *The Enemy*, and indeed he made enemies galore with his vituperative attacks on fellow writers, many of whom had been supportive of him in the past. Likewise irritating to the British cultural establishment was his 1930 novel *The Apes of God*, a 625-page book for which he furnished his own illustrations. The central figure was a young man on the point of entering modern literary society, but its real focus was a set of thinly disguised and savagely satirical portraits of other writers of the day, this time including T.S. Eliot, ironically one of his biggest admirers, and Gertrude Stein. Whatever hopes Lewis had for the rehabilitation of his reputation were dashed with the publication of *Hitler* in 1931; the book unwisely suggested that Hitler's National Socialist party represented the best hope for future peace in Europe.

Renounced Fascist Ideas

It should be noted that Lewis was not alone among British writers in his flirtation with fascism; Pound expressed longer-lasting fascist sympathies, and such views were by no means uncommon in Britain in the early 1930s. By the end of the decade, Lewis realized the error of his ways and published two anti-Hitler tracts, *The Hitler Cult* and *The Jews: Are They Human?* a tract critical of Nazi Germany whose title satirized that of an earlier book, *The English: Are They Human?* Lewis returned to painting in the 1930s and 1940s, creating several well-known works including *The Surrender of Barcelona,* a Spanish Civil War counterpart to Picasso's *Guernica,* and also sympathetic portraits of many of the literary figures he had treated so roughly in prose. His portraits were slated for a major retrospective at the National Portrait Gallery in London in 2008.

Low on funds, in 1939 Lewis was stranded in the United States, where he had gone to paint a commissioned portrait. He spent most of World War II in Canada, living in Toronto, a city he detested and later satirized mercilessly in his novel *Self-Condemned* (1954). He also taught at Assumption University in Windsor, Ontario, where he enjoyed debating the school's priest administrators and flirted with Catholicism, although he never converted. At Assumption Lewis met the young Marshall McLuhan; the future author of *Understanding Media* was heavily influenced by Lewis's views on the nature of mass culture.

Lewis and his wife (whom he married in 1930) took the first boat back to London from New York after the war ended in 1945. Suffering vision problems as the result of a slow-growing brain tumor, he was forced to give up his new career as an art critic for *The Listener.* He continued to write fiction, sometimes using a dictation device in later years. Lewis died in London on March 7, 1957. His reputation was temporarily eclipsed, but British museums mounted several major retrospectives of his artworks in the late 1990s and early 2000s, and even his fiction found new readers. According to Flux Europa, "He is now quite widely acknowledged as England's greatest and most original artist of the first half of the twentieth century." Lewis also wrote nine novels, three books of short stories, a play, two collections of poetry, and some 30 nonfiction books on topics ranging from America to architecture.

Books

Dictionary of Literary Biography, Volume 15: British Novelists, 1930-1959, Gale, 1983.

Edwards, Paul, *Wyndham Lewis: Painter and Writer,* Yale, 2000.

Kenner, Hugh, *Wyndham Lewis,* New Directions, 1954.

O'Keeffe, Paul, *Some Sort of Genius: A Life of Wyndham Lewis,* Cape, 2000.

Pritchard, William, *Wyndham Lewis,* Twayne, 1968.

Wyndham Lewis: A Revaluation, edited by Jeffrey Meyers, Athlone, 1980.

Periodicals

Design Week, February 24, 2005.

Evening Standard (London, England), March 1, 2005.

Guardian (London, England), July 23, 1992; November 18, 2000; February 26, 2005.

Independent (London, England), December 4, 2001; October 26, 2004.

Independent on Sunday (London, England), October 15, 2000; February 13, 2005.

Online

"The Art and Ideas of Wyndham Lewis," Flux Europa, http://www.fluxeuropa.com/wyndhamlewis-art_and_ideas .htm (February 5, 2008).

Contemporary Authors Online, Gale, 2008. http://galenet.gale group.com/servlet/BioRC (February 5, 2008).

"Percy Wyndham Lewis," Spartacus, http://www.spartacus .schoolnet.co.uk/ARTlewis.htm (February 5, 2008).

Wyndham Lewis Society, http://www.time-space.net/wyndham lewis (February 5, 2008). ☐

Astrid Lindgren

Swedish author Astrid Lindgren (1907-2002) is one of the most widely translated authors of all time. She was catapulted to fame in the 1940s after creating the famed storybook character Pippi Longstocking. Over the course of her lifetime, Lindgren wrote more than 40 children's books, selling some 145 million copies worldwide.

Enjoyed Carefree Upbringing

Lindgren was born Astrid Anna Emilia Ericsson on November 14, 1907, in a red wooden house located in small-town Vimmerby, Småland, Sweden. She was the second of four children born to Hanna Jonsson and Samuel August Ericsson. The farm where the Ericssons lived, called Nas, had been around for 500 years, and the Ericsson family had been renting the land for three generations. When Lindgren finished her farm chores, she was allowed to run free in the fields and surrounding woods. Along with her siblings, she enjoyed tree-climbing, swimming in the river, and frolicking in the barns. The joy of childhood freedom Lindgren experienced is replicated in her fiction, particularly with the carefree Pippi Longstocking.

Lindgren discovered the magic of words at the age of five, when one of the farmhand's daughters read her a story. She received her first book, *Snow White,* from a teacher and was delighted whenever she was able to get a new one. In *Astrid Lindgren,* author Eva-Maria Metcalf included a quote from Lindgren concerning her love of books: "I can still remember how these books smelled when they arrived fresh from the printer. Yes, I started by smelling them, and there was no lovelier scent in all the world. It was full of foretaste and anticipation."

Growing up, Lindgren read everything she could find, from English castaway *Robinson Crusoe* to the precocious adolescent *Anne of Green Gables.* She also wrote a number of creative essays that caught the attention of her teacher. One of them was published in the local paper, causing

Lindgren's classmates to tease her. Afterward she vowed never to write again.

In 1924 Lindgren began working for the local paper, the *Wimmerby Tidningen*. She caused an uproar in town when she cut her hair in a bob to match the "flappers" of her day. A flapper was a term used to describe liberated women of the 1920s who cut their hair short and bucked the societal norms of the day. Pregnant at 19, Lindgren moved to Stockholm to avoid the scorn of the Vimmerby villagers. Her son, Lars, was born in 1926 and Lindgren was forced to place him in foster care because she could not support him.

In Stockholm, Lindgren studied stenography, then found work as a secretary. The money, however, was barely enough for food, rent, and train tickets to Copenhagen, Denmark, to visit Lars. For a while Lindgren worked for the Royal Swedish Automobile Club writing tour guides for car owners. There she met Sture Lindgren, whom she married on April 4, 1931. Afterward, Lindgren was able to gain custody of Lars. A daughter, Karin, followed in 1934.

Developed Pippi to Entertain Daughter

Despite her natural ability, Lindgren never pursued writing seriously until the 1940s. Pippi Longstocking came into being in 1941 when Lindgren's seven-year-old daughter—bored and bedridden with pneumonia—asked Lindgren to tell her a story about "Pippi Långstrump" (Longstocking). Karin made the name up but it was so inviting that Lindgren instantly pictured the character and began formulating tales about the wiry, spirited, freckle-faced Pippi, whose braids stuck out in either direction. Pippi became an instant hit with Karin and her friends.

The Pippi tales remained an oral tradition until 1944, when Lindgren fell on the ice and sprained her ankle. Laid up during recovery, Lindgren decided to put Pippi's adventures on paper, figuring they would make a nice birthday gift for her daughter. After completing the manuscript, Lindgren sent it to a publisher, who rejected it. Undaunted, Lindgren continued writing because she found she enjoyed it. Later that year she entered a manuscript titled *Britt Mari lättar sitt hjärta* (Confidences of Britt-Mari) in a writing contest sponsored by Stockholm publishing house Rabén and Sjögren. Britt-Mari won second place and was published in 1944. The book, written in diary form, delves into the life of a proper, well-behaved girl.

Lindgren revamped Pippi, and in 1945 her revised manuscript won first prize in Rabén and Sjögren's children's book competition. *Pippi Longstocking* hit the shelves in 1945 and over the next several decades went on to capture the attention of multitudes of children around the globe. More volumes followed, including *Pippi Goes on Board,* 1946, *Pippi in the South Seas,* 1948, and *Pippi on the Run,* 1971.

Pippi, short for Pippilotta Delicatessa Windowshade Mackrelmint Efraim's Daughter Longstocking, represented a new kind of heroine for the children's book world. Pippi was loud, boisterous, and brave and did not care what others thought of her. She wore mismatched stockings and oversized shoes. Her mother was dead and her father was a sea captain who had never returned from his last voyage. Thus, Pippi lived alone with no adults telling her what to do. With a supply of never-ending gold, she lived a grand life. Pippi threw parties, downed entire chocolate cakes and lived in a ramshackle cottage with a monkey named Mr. Nilsson and a horse, Alfonso. She was so strong she could even lift the horse. Pippi had terrible manners, too. She slept upside-down in her bed with her feet on the pillow, and rolled out biscuits on the kitchen floor. Pippi took on bullies, refused to go to school, and mocked adults, especially those who were condescending toward children.

Children loved and admired Pippi because she was able to do many things they wished they could do themselves. Many parents, however, criticized Pippi's manners and general lack of respect for adults. Deemed an unsuitable role model, Pippi even sparked letters to the editor in the newspaper, where letter writers chastised the publishing company for honoring the book. Pippi sold well, however, and was soon translated into other languages. Pippi appeared in the United States in 1950 and in England in 1954. Eventually the book was translated into more than 70 languages, including Arabic, Hindi and Spanish. Pippi is known as Pippi Toong-Taw Yao in Thailand, Nagakutsushita-No-Pippi in Japan and Pippi Langkous in Holland.

Showed Versatility in Writing

By 1946 Lindgren was writing full-time. For Lindgren, writing became a vehicle for reclaiming her happy childhood. For the next 30 years, she averaged about one book per year for Rabén and Sjögren. The company also made her an editor and head of the children's book department. As such,

Lindgren's job was to track down popular American books for translation. She helped with some translations, using the pseudonym Anna Ericsson or Emilia Ericsson. Throughout the bulk of her career, Lindgren spent mornings writing her own books, film manuscripts, radio plays, and theater adaptations. The afternoons were devoted to editorial jobs for Rabén and Sjögren, and evenings were spent with her family. During the summer, the family stayed at their vacation home on a small island outside Stockholm, where Lindgren woke at dawn to write on her balcony overlooking the Baltic.

Lindgren developed many popular children's book protagonists, including *Bill Bergson, Master Detective,* who appeared in 1946; *Mischievous Meg* in 1960; and the boy hero Emil, who came into being in 1963. Her second most popular character after Pippi was *Karlsson-on-the-Roof.* This series of fairy tales hit bookshelves in 1955. Short and tubby, Karlsson has a propeller on his back that allows him to fly from his rooftop apartment. Much of the storyline revolves around the friendship between Karlsson and Lillebror—which translates literally to Little Boy—who lives with his family in the same house as Karlsson. Karlsson, playful and slightly naughty, often gets Lillebror in trouble. In the 1960s Lindgren created the *Noisy Village* books, which covered the lives of several Swedish children living on countryside farms. Another hit, *Ronja Rövardotter* (Ronia, the Robber's Daughter), came out in the 1980s.

Over the course of her writing career, Lindgren pushed the bounds of what was considered acceptable literature for children. *Mio, My Son,* published in 1954, dealt with fatherlessness. This fantasy tale follows an orphan who, with the help of a genie trapped in a bottle, is reunited with his father in a magic place called Farawayland.

In 1973 Lindgren published *The Brothers Lionheart,* a book that dealt with death. The story centers around two brothers, Karl and Jonatan. Nine-year-old Karl is ill and facing death. Jonatan comforts Karl by telling him that when he dies, he will go to a magnificent place called Nangijala. The brothers face a terrible fire in which Jonatan dies while saving Karl. In time, they are reunited in Nangijala, but the place is not as wonderful as Jonatan had described. The book delves into evil and fear, as the brothers battle dark forces. Under the guise of a fantasy tale, the book also explored the emotional growth of the brothers. Critics said the book was not suitable for children because death was too heavy of a topic for them to digest. Lindgren, however, maintained that death was a real part of life with which children had to deal. Many of her fans credited the book with helping them resolve issues surrounding death. *The Brothers Lionheart* became a movie in 1977.

In the early 1970s Lindgren retired from the publishing company, but continued writing. In 1976, facing a huge tax burden as a self-employed writer, Lindgren published a satirical fairy tale titled *Pomperipossa in the World of Money.* The piece struck a chord with fellow Swedes and helped lead to the demise of the ruling Social Democrats, who lost the next election. Tax laws were amended, with Lindgren credited for the change. In the 1980s Lindgren turned her attention to the plight of farm animals, publishing a series of newspaper articles that depicted God coming to earth to assess living conditions and becoming appalled at the way animals were forced to live. In turn, the government introduced legislation to protect livestock animals.

Revered by Fellow Swedes

In Sweden, Lindgren is a household name. She was voted "Swede of the Century" in 1999. Generations of Swedish children have grown up reading her books and hearing her tell her stories in recordings and on the radio. Several of her characters sparked Swedish movies and television series, some earning worldwide syndication. Pippi herself was featured in three Swedish feature films. In 1989 a theme park, called Astrid Lindgren's Varld, opened in her hometown and draws about 300,000 tourists annually. The theme park depicts many of the settings of her books. There is a model of Pippi's house, in which children are allowed to play.

Despite her monetary success, Lindgren never moved from the modest Stockholm apartment she had settled into during the 1940s. Toward the end of her life, Lindgren's eyesight began to fail and she wrote sparingly. She died on January 28, 2002, at the age of 94. Her husband preceded her in death in 1952 and Lars in 1986.

In 2007, to commemorate the centennial anniversary of Lindgren's birth, Britain's Oxford University Press issued a fresh edition of Pippi Longstocking with a new translation by Tiina Nunnally and illustrations by Lauren Child, creator of the popular Charlie and Lola series. When approached to do the artwork, Child jumped at the chance. Speaking to the London *Daily Telegraph,* Child discussed the character's universal appeal: "Pippi is all-powerful. She's completely independent and doesn't have to answer to anybody. She has a chest of gold so she can buy whatever she wants. She's a comic-book superhero with super-human strength, so nobody can frighten her. She just doesn't care what anybody thinks about her." Pippi translations have continued into the twenty-first century. In 2007 Pippi was tapped for translation into Arabic by the groundbreaking Kalima project, which seeks to translate leading books from across the world for Middle East readers. Pippi reached the list, along with classics by other authors, including John Milton, William Faulkner and George Eliot.

Books

Hurwitz, Johanna, *Astrid Lindgren: Storyteller to the World,* Viking Kestrel, 1989.
Metcalf, Eva-Maria, *Astrid Lindgren,* Twayne Publishers, 1995.

Periodicals

Daily Telegraph (London), September 29, 2007.
Guardian (London), June 18, 1994.
Horn Book Magazine, November 2007.
Irish Times, February 2, 2002.
New York Times, January 29, 2002.
Times (London), January 29, 2002.

Online

"How Pippi Longstocking and John Milton Went Arabic," *TimesOnline,* http://www.entertainment.timesonline.co.uk/tol/arts_and_entertainment/books/article2917627.ece (December 8, 2007). □

Dinu Lipatti

Romanian pianist and composer Dinu Lipatti (1917-1950) had a brief but exceptional career. Remembered mostly for his technical and interpretative skills, Lipatti was considered an exceptional performer of the works of Chopin, Mozart, and Bach among others. An inveterate perfectionist, Lipatti gave numerous well-received performances and, on a smaller scale, recorded music from his adolescent years up to a short time before his early death from cancer.

Showed Early Musical Talent

Constantin Lipatti, called "Dinu" from a diminutive of his baptismal name, was born on March 19, 1917, in Bucharest, Romania. His family was a musical one. His grandfather—for whom he was named—played the guitar and the flute; his father, Theodor, studied the violin in Bucharest and Paris before becoming a diplomat in Romania. Throughout his life, he collected rare violins. Lipatti's mother, Anna Racoviceanu, was a talented pianist. Throughout his childhood, Lipatti was surrounded by music and perhaps unsurprisingly showed a particular talent for it. In their book *Lipatti*, Dragos Tanasescu and Grigore Bargauanu claimed that "at six months [Lipatti] was clapping time to the melodies and Czardes dances. . .he became highly excited by the sound of a hurdy-gurdy being played by an old man passing in the street. By the age of two he could imitate any sound from the clinking of glass to the horn of an automobile."

Because Theodor Lipatti was concerned that his young son might damage one of his old and valuable violins, the family instead encouraged Dinu Lipatti to take up playing the piano. By the time of Lipatti's christening at the age of four, he was able to play one of Mozart's *Minuets* and Bach's *Prelude in C*. Georges Enusco, perhaps Romania's foremost musician of the twentieth century, was Lipatti's godfather. As a child, Lipatti studied first with Mikhail Jora; in 1928, he entered the Royal Academy of Music and Drama in Bucharest to study under Floria Musicescu. These two teachers were greatly influential in Lipatti's development, both as a musician and as a young man.

Continued Studies in Paris

Lipatti was a dedicated, self-disciplined student. While still in school, he made his solo debut at Bucharest's Opera House, and graduated in 1932 having received the prestigious Paul Ciuntu Prize. In 1933, he won second prize in the Georges Enusco Composition contest for his "Sonatina for Violin and Piano" and second prize at the Vienna International Piano Competition. Alfred Cortot, a renowned Swiss pianist, quit the jury in Vienna because he believed Lipatti was unfairly denied the First Prize. Cortot soon invited Lipatti to study with him in Paris, where he arrived in August 1934. There, Lipatti studied piano under Cortot as well as pianist

Yvonne Lefebure and composition under famed instructor Paul Dukas. After the death of Dukas in 1935, he went on to study with Nadia Boulanger, whom, according to Lipatti's *Grove Music Online* biography, he called his "musical guide and spiritual mother." During this time, Lipatti also developed friendships with several rising French composers and musicians, such as Pierre-Octave Ferroud.

Although Lipatti's instructors and peers considered him a fine musician and composer, Lipatti himself suffered from self-doubt. Tanasescu and Bargauanu wrote that "the search for perfection continued to dominate Dinu's life, and his torments while finding himself as a composer became a leit-motif in every letter." Even after highly successful performances such as his 1934 recital of Liszt's *First Concerto in E flat* with the orchestra of the Ecole Normale de Musique, conducted by Cortot, Lipatti focused only on Cortot's suggestions for improvement, rather than his strong praise for the overall performance. The following year, Lipatti played the Paris debut of Enesco's *Piano Sonata in F sharp minor* to much acclaim. Also in 1935, Lipatti gave his first Paris recital, playing works by Bach-Busoni and Johannes Brahms. The skill he displayed in this debut was such that the Director of the Ecole Normale invited him to sit with faculty members of the school to judge candidates for its Diploma of Virtuosity. In October of that year, Lipatti performed two concerts in Switzerland, one for radio broadcast and the other at Montreuz with the well-respected Manhattan Quartet.

The year 1936 marked other notable accomplishments for Lipatti. In January, his symphonic suite *Satrarii* (The Gypsies) was performed for the first time at a concert of Romanian music in Bucharest. Lipatti's *Sonatina in E minor for Violin and Piano* made its debut in March as part of another concert dedicated to Romanian music, this time in Paris. Lipatti remained in Paris, continuing his studies and composing and performing music, until summer 1936 when he returned to his native Romania. There, he first gave a recital with Enesco; in November, he performed as a soloist with the Bucharest Philharmonic in one of Mozart's *Concertos*.

In 1937, Lipatti returned to Paris to continue his studies with Cortot and Boulanger. He often played with Boulanger and began receiving offers to record music. At first, he refused these offers, but then changed his mind, turning his self-discipline and driving need for perfection to his recording sessions. According to *Grove Music Online*, Lipatti's "recorded legacy is small but beyond price." During the summer of 1937, Lipatti participated in the festival of Romanian classical that was organized as part of the *Exposition Internationale de Paris*. He returned to Romania in the fall for a series of concerts, then returned briefly to Paris to complete a recording of Brahms with Boulanger before traveling to Italy in early 1938 for a series of concerts. Back in Paris, he gave a recital featuring the debuts of many works by Romanian composers, including Enesco and his former teacher Jora, in February. At about this time, Lipatti began studying conducting at the Ecole Normale under Diran Alexanian and Charles Munch. However, he soon determined that he could not effectively focus on the three fields of piano, composition, and conducting, and so gave up the latter.

Returned to Romania

In March 1939, Lipatti gave a significant recital at the Salle Chopin-Pleyal in Paris. This performance marked the first time critics evaluated Lipatti's work as that of an adult master, and not that of a talented youth. However, the rising tensions that would lead to World War II drove Lipatti to return to Romania, which remained his home for the duration of the conflict. He quickly became active in the Romanian musical scene, performing concerts and, in April 1940, acting as conductor for the only time in his career during a radio concert. In 1941, Lipatti toured with the Bucharest Philharmonic as a soloist, visiting major eastern European cities including Prague, Berlin, and Munich. After his return, he spent much of his time composing, giving occasional performances for special events. Around the close of the year, he again traveled with the Bucharest Philharmonic, visiting Austria, Bulgaria, and Slovakia. In early 1942, he gave several recitals with George Enesco; that March, a concert was given featuring his and fellow Romanian composer Silvestri's compositions. Later that year, he returned to Berlin, Vienna, and Rome to perform.

In 1943, Lipatti recorded one of his compositions, *Concertino in Classical Style,* in Berlin. Shortly afterwards, he began making plans to tour Scandinavia. Despite the difficulties of war, he gave a series of performances primarily in Sweden in the fall of 1943. He then traveled to Geneva, Switzerland, for a recital and wound up settling in the city with the intention of working with Swiss pianist, Edwin Fischer. Toward the end of the year, he fell so ill that he could not get out of bed. Angered and concerned by the mysterious sickness, Lipatti was forced to cancel performances and found himself seeking a way to remain in Geneva. He was soon made a professor at the Geneva Conservatory. About a year later, Lipatti found himself continuing to battle his mysterious illness; he believed that a cure was in sight when X-ray therapy briefly lessened his symptoms. Despite his poor health, Lipatti continued to perform not only in Switzerland, but also in France, Belgium, and Italy.

Diagnosed with Cancer

Around the beginning of 1946, Lipatti experienced a brief period of good health. However, this soon deteriorated and Lipatti embarked on a course of biopsies and x-rays and altered his playing style to put less stress on his painfully swollen arms. Tanasesco and Bargauanu noted that "when playing the piano his movements became more deliberate and economical ... no one imagined that the beautiful tones, precision and subtleties of his interpretations were the result of such great effort." Increasingly, Lipatti found some works too exhausting to perform and was forced to cancel a planned tour of the United States. Despite his illness, he was able to travel to Belgium to give some performances. Also in 1946, he signed a contract with Columbia Records to make a series of recordings; he recorded some pieces at his home in Geneva.

Against the advice of his doctors, Lipatti continued touring throughout Europe in 1947. These activities were halted somewhat due a new diagnosis of malignant lym-

phogranulomatosis, a generic description of the cancer of the lymph nodes now referred to as Hodgkin's disease. After a brief period of rest, Lipatti gave concerts in Italy and Switzerland in the spring; that fall, he performed in England, Switzerland, and the Netherlands. Around the end of 1947, Lipatti underwent radiation treatment for his cancer and suspended musical work. By spring, he was again touring around Europe but was unable to accept offers to perform in such far-flung destinations as Egypt and South America.

During the summer of 1948, Lipatti's condition worsened and he began treatments in a hospital in Geneva. The following year, Lipatti married his longtime companion, pianist and teacher Madeleine Cantacuzene. His health continued to worsen, and in 1949, he suffered from complications arising from the aggressive treatments.

Death and Legacy

A brief improvement of his condition, in 1950, permitted Lipatti to play some concerts in Switzerland and to make recordings for Columbia; ultimately, more than half the planned recordings were completed. On September 19 of that year, Lipatti gave his final concert at Besançon in France; *Grove Music Online* stated that "he gave incomparable performances" at this concert while Dragos Tanasesco, writing in *Dinu Lipatti Remembered,* said that it "might be compared to a sacrifice offered by the performer on the altar of art." Lipatti died from cancer at his home on December 2, 1950, at the age of 33. He was buried at Chêne-Bourg, Switzerland.

Lipatti's career could be characterized as short but brilliant. His technical and interpretative skills, particularly while playing the works of composers such as Frédéric Chopin and Johan Sebastian Bach, were considered top-notch by his contemporaries. His composition abilities were also strong, although a relatively small portion of his 41 works are readily available today. Music lovers still admire Lipatti and this is evident in the 2004 creation of the Lipatti-Haskil Foundation, dedicated to the preservation of the works of Lipatti and fellow Romanian pianist Clara Haskil. It seems unquestionable that Lipatti's great talent would have continued to flourish if not for his unfortunate early death.

Books

Almanac of Famous People, 9th ed., Thomson Gale, 2007.

Baker's Biographical Dictionary of Musicians, Centennial Edition. Nicolas Slonimsky, Editor Emeritus, Schirmer, 2001.

Tanasescu, Dragos, *Dinu Lipatti Remembered,* Musical Score Publishers, 1971.

Tanasescu, Dragos, and Grigore Bargauanu, *Lipatti,* Kahn & Averill, 1996.

Online

"About the Foundation," Lipatti-Haskil Foundation, http://www.lipatti-haskil-foundation.com/02/foundation.php (December 16, 2007).

"Lipatti," Bloomingdale School of Music, http://www.bsmny.org/features/lipatti/index.php (December 16, 2007).

"Lipatti, Dinu" *Grove Music Online,* http://www.grovemusic.com (December 5, 2007). □

John Avery Lomax

American song collector John Lomax (1867-1948) helped set in motion the tradition of studying and performing folk music in the United States.

Songs that seem to be timeless elements of the fabric of American music—"Home on the Range" and "Git Along Little Dogies," to name two—actually owe their preservation and popularization to Lomax's efforts. Beginning in the area of cowboy music, which he knew as a boy and continued to study for his entire life, Lomax also studied African-American music extensively, and his books are standards used alike by academic researchers and groups of singers who enjoy gathering around a guitarist or piano player. The archive of some 10,000 recordings he deposited at the Library of Congress remains a definitive core sample of the music of ordinary Americans.

Moved to Texas in Covered Wagon

John Avery Lomax was born into a farm family on September 23, 1867, in Goodman, Mississippi. Although he was born in Mississippi and died there, he was identified strongly with the state of Texas for almost his entire life; his family moved to a farm near Meridian, Texas, in the central part of the state, when he was a baby. From the *Old Time Herald* Web site, in his book review of Nolan Peterfield's work, Robert Cantwell noted that the Lomaxes were, he sometimes said, "the upper crust of the poor white trash"— he grew up driving a mule team, but his hardworking family mostly avoided the trials of poverty. Lomax's childhood was shaped by a variety of musical influences. He heard the stirring hymns of rural Methodism at camp meeting. And, most important, the family farm was located near a branch of the Chisholm Trail on which cattle were driven from range to rail yard, and he often heard folk ballads and cowboy songs as they were sung by actual cowboys. When he was in his teens, he began to write some of them down.

Lomax's schooling was sporadic, but he took to education enthusiastically when he had the chance, and his schooling was marked by a variety of influences—religious, financial, and cultural. He attended Granbury College (a Methodist school that would be called a high school today) for a year in 1887 and 1888. That was enough to qualify him, in Texas frontier days, to teach at Weatherford College, a new school that evolved from Granbury, and at Clifton Lutheran College. But Lomax was intent on finding upward mobility. In the summers he headed north for further education, attending Poughkeepsie Business College and spending three summer term at the Chautauqua Institution, an adult education resort in western New York State whose lecture series brought in speakers in the mainstream of progressive thought in the late nineteenth century.

In 1895 Lomax enrolled at the University of Texas. His literature professors there frowned on his habit of collecting cowboy songs, believing that he should direct his attention toward the classics. But Lomax's enthusiasm for learning was undiminished, and he finished the coursework for a B.A. in two years and received his degree in 1897. He stayed on at the university as secretary to the president, registrar, and steward of the men's dormitory, with other job duties as needed, for a total salary of $75 a month, and then began teaching at Texas Agricultural and Mechanical College (now Texas A&M University) in 1903, remaining there until 1910. Married to Bess R. Brown since 1904, and in the early stages of raising four children, he hardly had time for graduate studies but carved it out nonetheless, receiving a master's degree in literature in 1906, at age 38.

After he received that degree, Texas A&M granted Lomax a one-year sabbatical to study at Harvard University, where he received a second master's degree. The year at Harvard proved to be a crucial intellectual turning point for Lomax, who found faculty members there, principally Barrett Wendell and George Lyman Kittredge, fascinated rather than contemptuous of his song-collecting efforts. Between 1907 and 1910 they steered him toward fellowships that allowed him to spend summers traveling through Texas with a notebook and a primitive wax-cylinder recording rig. Lomax placed ads in cattle-industry newspapers soliciting reminiscences, and he haunted nightspots that seemed likely places to find singers. At the White Elephant Saloon he heard "The Old Chisholm Trail" from a group of cowhands. An African-American bar owner and former trail cook sang him "Home on the Range," and from a Gypsy woman who lived in a car he learned "Git Along, Little Dogies."

Published Groundbreaking Song Collection

These songs and the others Lomax collected were not well known at the time, but thanks to his efforts they became part of the musical folklore of a country absorbed by the image of the cowboy. They came from a variety of sources, some unknown; "Home on the Range" had appeared in print in 1873. But all had entered oral tradition—and all, with the gradual disappearance of the way of life of the free-roaming cowboy, might have been forgotten if it had not been for the publication of Lomax's *Cowboy Songs and Other Frontier Ballads* in 1910. A pioneer publication in a country where the study of folklore was in its infancy, the book was dedicated to President Theodore Roosevelt.

After the book's publication Lomax gradually became recognized as America's foremost authority on the cowboy song. He often gave lectures at colleges and universities, illustrating them with a ringing yodel that, as one friend (quoted by Cantwell in his book review) noted, made the listener "feel the dust, the great grass ocean, the harrowed bellowing steers" of the plains. He landed a post as alumni association secretary at the University of Texas in 1911, but he was fired in 1917 after becoming caught in a political tug-of-war between Texas governor James "Farmer Jim" Ferguson and the university administration. With four young children to support, Lomax worked for two years selling bonds in Chicago, but friends helped him continue his research. A second Lomax volume of cowboy songs, *Songs of the Cattle Trail and Cow Camp* was published in 1919.

In the 1920s Lomax worked mostly in banking, becoming an executive in the bond department at Dallas's Republic Bank in 1925. The go-go financial world of the 1920s circumscribed his collecting activities as academics never had, but he did keep in close touch with the members of the Texas Folklore Society, which he had co-founded in 1910. Lomax also made friends with the poet Carl Sandburg and began to correspond with other folklore collectors, some of whom he had directly inspired.

Lomax's first wife died in 1931, and the collapse of the bond market during the Great Depression put an end to his financial career. He turned 65 in 1932, but, at an age when most people would have considered retirement, he instead embarked on yet another new phase of his career, one that was perhaps the most influential of all. Urged on initially by his sons John Jr. and Alan, who wanted to help revive his spirits after his wife's death, he began touring once again as a lecturer. Lomax's two daughters Bess and Shirley also later became involved with his musical efforts, as did Ruby Terrill Lomax, whom he married in 1934. In New York, Lomax pitched the idea for a comprehensive anthology of American folk songs to the Macmillan publishing firm. He then headed for the Library of Congress in Washington D.C., to do research at its Archive of American Folk Song. He offered to travel the country collecting songs for the archive in exchange for the loan of recording equipment. His proposal was accepted, and he was named honorary curator of the archive.

Embarked on Mammoth Collecting Expedition

Several factors came together to produce the remarkable accomplishments Lomax notched over the next several years. One was financial: Lomax was awarded a fellowship by the prestigious American Council of Learned Societies to support his work. Another was technological: sound recording equipment, though still bulky and inconvenient, had advanced dramatically in terms of portability since Lomax's previous collecting trips. In July of 1933 he acquired a 315-pound recording machine that made acetate discs—78 rpm records—and mounted it in the trunk of his Ford sedan, giving him what was in effect a portable recording studio. A third was ideological: Lomax, along with other folklorists, had come to believe that traditional folk arts were under attack from modern recorded music. He saw it as his mission to preserve as much music as he could, and he was especially interested in seeking out locations where he thought there would be music mostly untouched by the outside world. Chief among such locations were prisons and prison camps; others included work camps of various kinds and isolated rural communities.

Although he recorded music of various genres, Lomax brought a new focus on African-American music to his 1930s research. He recorded work songs, spirituals, ballads, and early blues, capturing the heavily African-influenced music that black fieldworkers had carried through the generations since the end of slavery. Again Lomax added songs that became standards to the repertory of American music: "John Henry" and "Rock Island Line" were among the pieces he recorded. He was also responsible for the emergence of a figure who became a major star in his own right: Huddie Ledbetter, known as Leadbelly (also spelled Lead

Belly), was first recorded by John and Alan Lomax at the Louisiana State Penitentiary. They later arranged tours for him in the northern states after his release from prison, and he became a key figure in the folk music revival of the 1950s and 1960s.

In all, Lomax logged about 200,000 miles on the road in the 1930s, visiting all but one of the 48 states. He was often accompanied by his son Alan, who continued his research independently, becoming one of the world's foremost authorities on African-American music and expanding his research into such issues as the relationship between social structure and voice production on a global scale. The sum total of his fieldwork efforts was impressive: he single-handedly added more than 10,000 recordings to the Archive of American Folksong, documenting aspects of the African-American musical tradition that have continued to occupy scholars ever since.

Much of the last decade of Lomax's life was spent assembling the fruits of his research into new publications, all of which sold well and remain fixtures of home and library music collections to this day. With Alan Lomax he edited *American Ballads and Folk Songs* (1934), *Negro Songs as Sung by Lead Belly* (1936), *Our Singing County* (1941), and *Folk Song U.S.A.* (1947). The Leadbelly volume was the source of enduring controversy, much of which occurred after Lomax's death. Lomax had copyrighted (or part-copyrighted) many of the bluesman's songs, including "Goodnight Irene," which later became a major hit for the Weavers—and Leadbelly in turn commented in his lyrics on the profits Lomax reaped from his work. After writing an autobiography, *Adventures of a Ballad Hunter* (1947), Lomax died in Greenville, Mississippi, on January 26, 1948, just after singing a dirty song called "Big Leg Rose."

Books

Lomax, John A., *Adventures of a Ballad Hunter,* Macmillan, 1947.

Porterfield, Nolan, *The Last Cavalier: The Life and Times of John A. Lomax,* University of Illinois Press, 1996.

Online

Cantwell, Robert, (review of Nolan Porterfield) *Last Cavalier: The Life and Times of John A. Lomax, Old Time Herald,* http://www.oldtimeherald.org/archive/back_issues/volume-6/6-4/reviews.html#lomax (December 17, 2007).

"John Avery Lomax," Library of Congress, http://memory.loc.gov/ammem/lohtml/lojohnbio.html (December 17, 2007).

"Lomax, John Avery," Handbook of Texas Online, http://www.tsha.utexas.edu/handbook/online/articles/LL/flo7.html (December 17, 2007). □

Ignacy Lukasiewicz

The Polish inventor and pharmacist Ignacy Lukasiewicz (1822-1882) was the inventor of the kerosene lamp and an important figure in the early European oil industry.

Lukasiewicz belonged to the tail end of the age of the amateur inventor. He was fascinated by petroleum and its possibilities, but not because he had any education in the fields of geology or mining. He operated simply on an accurate instinct that petroleum would prove immensely important to industrial development, and although he died young, he lived long enough to see his intuitions validated and to profit from them. His breakthroughs on the design of the kerosene lamp were accomplished while he was working days behind the counter of a pharmacy.

Life and Learning

Ignacy Lukasiewicz was born on March 8, 1822, in the small town of Zaduszniki, Poland. He was the youngest of seven children. His parents, Josef and Apolonia Lukasiewicz, were landowners whose fortunes had declined; his father belonged to a noble family and had taken part in a rebellion against Russian rule led by Thaddeus Kosciusko in 1794. After that he moved to the Galicia region in southern Poland and leased a large farm where Ignacy spent the first part of his childhood. In 1830 the family moved to Rzeszow, where they purchased an apartment building and rented out rooms. Despite their aristocratic background, they never had money to spare.

Lack of money hampered Lukasiewicz's education, but he nevertheless had a zest for learning and pursued it as rigorously as he could whenever he had the chance. He was enrolled in a Catholic grammar school in 1832, gaining a good grounding in Latin and German, but after his father's death he had to drop out of school. Interested in chemistry, he chose the profession that seemed nearest to that field and still allowed him to make a living: he apprenticed himself to a pharmacist, Antoni Svoboda, in the town of Lancut.

As a young man Lukasiewicz was involved in political activities in Galicia, at that time under the control of the Austro-Hungarian Empire. Lukasiewicz joined a group called the Polish Democrats' Conspiracy that aimed to educate the Polish people about the goal of independence; one of Lukasiewicz's compatriots was arrested and imprisoned, and Lukasiewicz himself narrowly escaped a prison sentence. After passing an exam that qualified him to work as a pharmacist, he was hired at a pharmacy in Rzeszow. There again he was involved with independence organizations; he became an agent of the Polish Democratic Society, which hoped to foment regional uprisings. He used the pharmacy where he worked as an after-hours meeting place for himself and his co-conspirators. This conspiracy was also a failure, and this time Lukasiewicz was arrested by Austrian authorities and imprisoned for much of 1846 and 1847. He was released on condition that he not leave the city of Lvov (now Lviv, Ukraine, where he had been arrested) and that he check in regularly with police.

Lukasiewicz found work at the Under the Golden Star pharmacy of Piotr Mikokaj in Lvov. There he compiled an almanac titled *Manuscript* that summarized the pharmaceutical knowledge of the day. Hungry for more education, he moved to Krakow and enrolled in pharmacy courses at the Jagiellonian University. He then moved to Vienna, Austria, and completed a doctoral degree in pharmacy in the summer of 1852, after which he returned to the Under the Golden Star pharmacy. Around that time Lukasiewicz became fascinated by petroleum, which at the time had been the subject of just a few experiments trying to determine how it might be exploited as an energy source. Obtaining small amounts of petroleum was not a problem, for it came to the surface of the earth in "seeps" all over the Carpathian mountain region of southern Poland.

Refined Seep Oil

In 1852 Lukasiewicz and Jan Zeh, a lab assistant in Mikolaj's pharmacy, joined forces to work on the problem of converting petroleum into a form in which it would burn slowly and steadily. Zeh remembered a local peasant who had experimented on his own with petroleum distillates that would remove volatile compounds, essential for the creation of a lamp that would not explode when lit. They tried various ways of removing other impurities in order to create a constant-burning flame, working through the night on experiments that more than once ended in small explosions. Lukasiewicz is widely credited with this research, but the relative contributions of Lukasiewicz and Zeh are a matter of historical dispute.

At the time, the only lamp illumination available came from whale oil, a substance that was difficult to transport and that was in increasingly short supply as whale stocks were depleted. Lukasiewicz and Zeh also had help from a local tinsmith. After a year's worth of work, they were ready to present the first prototype of a kerosene lamp. It was first exhibited in Mikolaj's window, where it became the focus of intense public attention. The new lamp was cylindrical, with transparent mica windows running around its top. Openings in the tube above and below the flame provided air sources for a burning wick. Lukasiewicz's creation essentially resembled the kerosene lamps of today. Lukasiewicz also sent a shipment of the new lamps to the Lvov hospital, which used them to illuminate its operating room and make nighttime surgery possible. The lamps were installed on July 31, 1853, a date that has been used as a symbolic marker of the beginning of the Polish petroleum industry.

Lukasiewicz and Zeh patented their invention, and by the winter of 1858-59, when the Emperor Ferdinand Northern Railway began to replace candles with Lukasiewicz's kerosene lamps in its railway stations, Lukasiewicz was on his way to a new level of financial success. Lukasiewicz continued to work as a pharmacist for a few more years, but now he had the opportunity to indulge his interest in oil exploration on a bigger scale. Beginning in the mid-1850s he worked with Titus Trzecieski, a philosopher, farmer, miner, and estate owner to develop an oil field near the village of Bobrka, where a Polish oil industry museum stands today.

The wells Lukasiewicz constructed were among the world's first. The earliest wells at Bobrka, 1.2 by 1.2 meters square, were dug with picks and shovels and reinforced with wood beams. At first the wells were only 15 meters deep, but Lukasiewicz soon succeeded in increasing the depth to 60 meters, and then, in the case of a well named

Izydor, to 150 meters. Each well had its own name; two of them, Franek and Janina, are still in existence.

Petroleum Estate

Lukasiewicz moved with his wife to the town of Jaslo in the late 1850s (he suffered through the birth and death of an infant daughter that year), continuing to work in a pharmacy (this time one that he leased) and manage the Bobrka field. He also opened several new oil fields and refineries. Purchasing a large estate in Chorkowka, he constructed a state-of-the-art refinery there. His estate became an informal headquarters for petroleum specialists from across eastern Europe, and his wells and refineries were considered the best in the Carpathian-Galician region, the center of the early eastern European oil industry. He finally gave up the practice of pharmacy in the early 1860s.

Even in addition to these varied activities, Lukasiewicz once again became involved in Polish independence causes, generously funding the unsuccessful January Uprising against Russian rule in 1863. He provided housing and jobs for defeated soldiers and their families, and opened several schools around Bobrka, including an oil industry trade institute and a lace-making school for girls. He founded churches and community organizations, built roads, donated money to charity, and offered free kerosene lamps to Orthodox and Catholic churches and monasteries near his home. In 1876 he became a deputy in Poland's parliament. Awarded the papal Order of St. Gregory in 1873, he became a figure of national renown in Poland.

In 1880 he was named head of Poland's National Petroleum Society, a lobbying group. Lukasiewicz's frenetic pace, maintained over much of his adult lifetime, may have weakened his health. He died of pneumonia on January 7, 1882, and was buried in Chorkowka, near a church he and one of his business partners had founded. He is considered the father of Poland's oil industry. Lukasiewicz's memory survives today in the names of various schools and monuments, and the petroleum industry museum in Bobrka also bears his name. In 2003 the Polish government issued coins in 2-zloty and 10-zloty denominations, bearing Lukasiewicz's portrait and commemorating the lighting of his kerosene lamps in the Lvov hospital. They bore the Polish inscription "150 Years of the Oil and Gas Industry."

Online

"The First Kerosene Lamp in the World," Government of Poland, http://www.poland.gov.pl/Ignacy,Lukasiewicz:,the,first ,kerosene,lamp,in,the,world,1985.html (February 10, 2008).

"Ignacy Lukasiewicz (1822–1882)," http://www.gim2jaslo.edu .pl/patron/english.html (February 10, 2008).

"The Ignacy Lukasiewicz Memorial Museum of the Oil Industry," Bobrka, http://www.geo.uw.edu.pl/BOBRKA/ LUKASIEWICZ/lukasiewicz.htm (February 10, 2008).

"The Oil Field at Bobrka," Bobrka, http://www.geo.uw.edu.pl/ BOBRKA/MINE/mine.htm (Feburary 10, 2008).

"Polish Coins Commemorating 150 Years of the Oil Industry," http://www.geo.uw.edu.pl/HOBBY/MONEY/poland4.htm (February 10, 2008). □

Madame de Pompadour

French mistress Madame de Pompadour (1721-1764) came to fame as the paramour of King Louis XV (1710-1774). She was a woman of great beauty, tremendous talent, and enormous influence, despite her humble origins. Often reviled by the court for her bourgeois background, the public for her profligate spending, and sometimes by both for each reason, Pompadour nonetheless remained in the king's favor throughout most of her life and wielded enormous power in eighteenth-century France. From politics to the arts, her stamp was indelible and lasted far beyond her comparatively short time on the earth.

Groomed for a King

Pompadour was born Jeanne-Antoinette Poisson on December 29, 1721, in Paris, France. Her mother was Louise-Madeleine de La Motte, a lovely dark-haired woman with a certain *"joi de vivre."* Her legal father was Francois Poisson, who had made a fortune as a steward for powerful financiers the Paris brothers (Paris de Montmartel and Paris-Duvereny). Poisson traveled a great deal in his work, and even lived abroad for nearly ten years in order to avoid a prison sentence for speculating in wheat during a famine. Those frequent and sometimes prolonged absences, coupled with his young wife's comeliness and alleged taste for the company of the opposite sex, rendered the identity of Pompadour's biological father less than certain. Biographers, historians, and Pompadour's contempo-

raries have put forth several candidates, including Paris de Montmartel and tax collector Charles-Francois Lenormand (also known as le Normant) de Tournehem. Nor, of course, could Poisson himself have been ruled out completely. But the true paternity of the pretty little girl remained a topic of debate and conjecture into the twenty-first century.

No matter who Pompadour's sire really was, it was certain that she was born to please. From the Ursuline nuns with whom she spent the first few years of her life to her maybe, or maybe not, papa, Tournehem, she apparently captivated all who came across her path. When Pompadour was nine years old, the famous fortune teller Madame Lebon predicted that she would become the mistress of Louis XV, then a dashing young man of 20. Such a prophecy might have been dismissed by another family, but Pompadour's mother took it at face value and set about grooming her daughter accordingly. Tournehem saw to it that she was properly and thoroughly educated, not a difficult task with such an apt student. He then arranged her marriage to his nephew Charles-Guillaume Lenormand (le Normant) in March of 1741, and sponsored the new bride's entrance into society. (Tournehem had given the newlyweds the estate Etoiles as a wedding gift, and they were known thereafter as "Monsieur and Madame d'Etioles.)

The fetching young matron bewitched Parisian society much as she had the companions of her childhood. Pompadour became a welcome fixture at fashionable salons, hobnobbing with the aristocracy and intellectuals alike. It was during this period that she embarked upon a lifelong friendship with famed author and philosopher Voltaire (1694-1778), who, naturally, found her charming and amiable. But Pompadour had higher aspirations than merely conquering polite society. Indeed, she had been bred to strive for the most royal of prizes. And that is precisely what she did.

Mission Fulfilled

Even royal blood had not protected Louis XV from having a particularly difficult childhood. He had lost his entire immediate family to disease when he was just two, in 1712. At the age of five, he had inherited the French throne from his redoubtable great-grandfather Louis XIV (1638-1715). He had been married to the Polish Princess Marie Leczinska when he was but 15 years old, and although she had borne him seven children, the union was nobody's idea of a love match. Thus, the king had grown to become a moody, pessimistic soul, easily given to flights of boredom and melancholy. This was not to imply that he did not have his strong points or the love of his people (at least at one time), but rather suggests possibilities as to why he might have been especially susceptible to a woman of Pompadour's energies and talents. Or perhaps it was simply love.

Whatever Louis XV's psychological makeup, the keeping of an official mistress was, in itself, nothing more than a long tradition of the monarchy. In 1745 the king was in the market for a new favorite after the untimely death of his previous one. Pompadour, given her social circles, could hardly have been unaware of that fact, and perhaps believed that her moment had come at last. Her chance came in February at a masked ball at Versailles in honor of the nuptials of the Dauphin. The king did not fail to notice the enchanting Madame d'Etioles, and before very long, all the careful planning and fondest hopes of the Poisson family were fulfilled as Pompadour was installed as the mistress of Louis XV.

Before Pompadour's actual elevation to the coveted role, however, at least one obstacle had to be overcome, and further training was in order. The first was the circumstance of her birth. Custom dictated that the king's mistress must be high-born, certainly not a commoner who had risen to the disdained ranks of the bourgeoisie through money alone. This problem was dispatched by making the new favorite the marquisate of Pompadour, thus a commoner no more. The second was the polishing of the fresh mistress's already considerable gifts to be appropriate to her rise in station. So, with Voltaire in attendance as one of her tutors, Pompadour set about mastering court etiquette and the manners of a noble lady. This, too, was accomplished, after which Pompadour was presented at court and settled into quarters at Versailles. Her unhappy husband, understandably, reportedly never spoke to her again.

The First Five Years

At court, Pompadour quickly demonstrated a shrewd grasp of the king's needs. Interestingly, one of the most prominent of these appeared to be simple entertainment or distraction. And Pompadour was admirably suited to providing such things. She rode, played cards, toured palaces, and gave intimate dinner parties for the king. The pair shared interests in architecture, the decorative arts, botany, ornithology, and animals as well. Pompadour was also a gifted singer and actress. She organized over 120 court theatricals of exceptional quality, including operas, plays, and ballets, that she both starred in and directed. In short, Pompadour brought liveliness and fun to a court that had once tended toward the dour.

Pompadour also displayed a flair for domestic politics, establishing a polite relationship with the queen that Louis XV's former mistresses had never bothered with. Early in her relationship with the king, for instance, she convinced him to pay off Her Majesty's gambling debts and redecorate her apartments. Perhaps more important, she displayed a deference to the queen that must have been soothing, if not gratifying, to the older woman's sensibilities. The royal children, however, proved invulnerable to Pompadour's charms. They called her "Mommy Whore."

Finally, one cannot disregard the nature of Pompadour's position at Versailles—that of the king's mistress. Although she fulfilled the duties inherent to that role, suffering several miscarriages in the process, she was reportedly quite indifferent to sex. This may have been because of an ongoing gynecological illness from which she suffered, or even the miscarriages themselves, but it was certainly an odd situation for a woman who was depicted as one of great seductresses of all time.

Stranger still, it became apparent after a while that Pompadour's hold over her master had little to do with her beauty or sexual wiles. This was demonstrated when it became clear that Pompadour and Louis XV had rendered their relationship platonic around 1750. Colin Jones of *History Today* may have offered the best (and certainly most understated) comment on this surprising development when he said, "It was unusual for a royal mistress to be distinguished by chastity, sexual abstention being the shortest chapter in the annals of French royal mistresshood.'' Yet, much to the disappointment of various courtiers and much of the public, not only was the king's mistress not dismissed, she actually gained in power and prestige in palace business.

Increased Influence

The demands of the royal bed behind her (although she did make certain that the king's new dalliances remained just that and were not the sort who could be presented at court), Pompadour became increasingly valuable to her sovereign in other ways. As Judith Thurman put it in the *New Yorker,* ''There was virtually no high commission, ministerial portfolio, alliance, diplomatic post, important public-works project, royal favor, invitation, or marriage contract authorized against the will of the Marquise.'' She even interfered in military tactics, although that was hardly her strong point, as she was widely seen as having orchestrated the changes in alliances that led to France's involvement in the Seven Years' War.

Pompadour also continued her patronage of the arts, surrounding the king with portraits (many of her) and objects of beauty. Two of her pet projects championed local craftsmanship and valor, the porcelain factory in Sevres and the Ecole Militaire. Her collection of books was vast, as were the decorative treasures in her various homes. She favored the French rococo style, especially encouraging its premier painter, Francois Boucher (1703-1770). Writers, sculptors, scientists, painters, and philosophers—all came under Pompadour's patronage and efforts to promote French culture at one time or another.

And despite frequent hopes and predictions that she would fall, Pompadour never lost the king's esteem. She had successfully evolved from an infatuation to an indispensable part of the king's world and, as Jones said, ''bucked her sexual and social handicaps to become a major political player.'' For a woman, a commoner no less, of her time, Pompadour's influence and accomplishments were unprecedented.

A Hummingbird's End

By the late 1750s, Pompadour's famous looks were fading. And by the early 1760s, her health was failing as well. She had always been rather frail. Appearances notwithstanding, she had long suffered from chronic migraines and lung ailments, not to mention the gynecological troubles mentioned earlier. Pompadour died on Palm Sunday, April 15, 1764, at Versailles. The cause was either tuberculosis or congestive heart failure. She was just 41 years old.

Louis XV made no public expression of regret at Pompadour's passing. Nor was there any outpouring of grief from a public that had seen her as a spendthrift who dabbled in disastrous foreign policy. The latter would hardly have surprised her, as her energies had always been geared towards the king, not his people. Jones wrote, ''Her assiduous cultivation of her own image had muddied her appreciation of the wider public just as much as it muddied the public's view of her.'' But perhaps Thurman characterized the remarkable mistress's legacy best as a mystery. ''Did Pompadour fulfill a great destiny or betray one?''

Periodicals

History Today, November 2002.

Online

''A Brief Biography by the Late Lamented Mario Frejaville Taken from His Book: *Madame de Pompadour Mi Ha Detto* (Mme. de Pompadour Told Me),'' Madame de Pompadour, http://www.madamedepompadour.com/_eng_pomp/home .htm (December 3, 2007).
''Eminence Rose,'' *New Yorker,* October 7, 2002, http://www .newyorker.com/archive/2002/10/07/021007crbo_books (December 3, 2007).
''Madame de Pompadour,'' Visit Voltaire, http://www.visit voltaire.com/v_pompadour.htm (December 3, 2007).
''Madame de Pompadour, Francois Boucher (1759),'' *Guardian,* September 8, 2001, http://www.arts.guardian.co.uk/portrait/ story/0,,740343,00.html (December 3, 2007).
''Madame Pompadour,'' Everything2, http://www.everything2 .com/index.pl?node_id=1169401 (December 3, 2007).
''Voltaire: Author and Philosopher'' Lucid Cafe, http://www .lucidcafe.com/library/95nov/voltaire.html (January 4, 2008). □

Nazik al-Mala'ika

Innovative Iraqi poet and literary critic Nazik al-Mala'ika (1923-2007) was instrumental in the evolution of free Arabic verse and in her vigorous cultivation of Arabic women's rights.

Child Poet

Nazik al-Mala'ika was born on August 23, 1923, in Bagdad, Iraq, as the eldest of seven siblings. In an autobiographical essay contained on the Kool Pages Web site, al-Mala'ika admitted that she wrote ''some poems, in Iraqi slang, when I was seven years old,'' and confirmed that she wrote her first classical poem ''in the Arabic language when I was ten years old.'' The gifted youth's mother was the confrontational poet Um Nizar al-Mala'ika—who was, in turn, the daughter of a famous male Iraqi poet. Al-Mala'ika's father taught Arabic language and grammar in secondary schools, and was the editor of a 20-volume encyclopedia on the Arabic language. Some sources also identified him as a poet. Sources also mention an uncle as well as one of al-Mala'ika's brothers as being poetically talented.

A Comprehensive Education

Al-Mala'ika graduated high school in 1939, and then studied Arabic literature and music, learning to master the Arabic lute, called an *oud.* She earned a degree from Bagdad's Higher Teachers' Training College in 1944. While attending college al-Mala'ika contributed poems to local publications, taught herself French, and studied Latin, reading literature in all of these languages and in English. She investigated philosophy and classical Greek works that she committed to memory. Al-Mala'ika also translated the work of other poets, sculpting the likes of Byron into Arabic rhyming quatrains. In 1952 she won a scholarship to study for a year at Princeton University in New Jersey, and she was the first female student to attend that institution. In 1954 al-Mala'ika entered the University of Wisconsin at Madison, where she earned a master's degree in comparative literature.

Woman and Wordsmith

A biography of al-Mala'ika on the Jehat.com Web site classified her poetry as "characterized by its terseness of language, eloquence, original use of imagery, and delicate ear for the music of verse." While a variety of specific poems are mentioned, the majority of attention goes to her 1947 poem "Cholera," which describes the epidemic that spread across Egypt and into Iraq. It was her first poem in free verse. Al-Mala'ika's family did not share her excitement over the poem's style. Kool Pages quoted her description of her mother's reaction as "What is this strange rhythm, the lines are not of equal length, and the music is weak." Al-Mala'ika recalled, "My brothers and sisters were laughing as I retorted, 'Say what you will. I am sure that this poem will change the map of Arabic poetry.'"

Al-Mala'ika was on the Map

The young poet was right. Since her first collection of poems, *Ashiqat al-ayl* (Night's Lover or Lover of the Night), was published in 1947, she has been credited by many with creating the first successful free verse Arabic poetry. Arguments have circulated regarding which Arabic poet was the "first" to use free verse, with recognition being given to both al-Mala'ika and the poet Badr Shakir al-Sayyab. The *Encyclopedia of the Modern Middle East* explained, "This issue was complicated because both poets published their first collections of poems in the new form . . . in December 1947"—a mere two weeks apart.

In an article in the *International Journal of Middle East Studies*, Issa J. Boullata told readers that "it has already been shown that the first poet in Iraq to write in such free verse was Badr Shakir al-Sayyab and that the first to publish a poem in it was Nazik al-Mala'ika." Both poets are usually given equal acclaim by scholars for their contributions to the popularization of the free verse movement. Al-Mala'ika was said to have practiced a more logical approach to free verse than other founders, and all agree that she was uniquely qualified to defend her theoretical opinions, thanks to her educational roots in theory, grammar, and music, and a consummate understanding of the Arabic language.

Al-Mala'ika's second poetry collection, *Shadaya wa-ramad* (Sparks and Ashes, Splinters and Ashes or Ashes and Shrapnel, 1949), included a skillfully argued preface that fortified her theory on the technical aspects and poetic merits of free verse. Al-Mala'ika, despite her gender and her boldness, was highly respected for her work. In an article in *Die Welt des Islams*, Wiebke Walther suggested that poetry "utters social criticism in a way differing from that of stories or novels . . . playing with words, with rhythms and rhymes, appealing with aesthetic, with lingual means to the emotions of their readers or hearers." Perhaps it was her gift for

lyrical analysis that helped al-Mala'ika earn such a prominent place in the hearts and the minds of her people.

Feminist Foot Forward

According to *Cultures of the World: Iraq,* "Iraqi literature experienced a rebirth in the 1950s. . . . Epic stories were replaced by short stories that were filled with the everyday struggles and experiences of people in Iraq." In a culture that had traditionally believed that educating women would surely have dire moral and social consequences, al-Mala'ika became a feminist voice to be reckoned with. In 1954 she published an essay, *Al-mar'a baina 'l-tarafain, al-salbiyya wa'l-akh-laq* (Women Between the Extremes of Passivity and Ethical Choice), now considered a feminist classic. In its obituary on al-Mala'ika, ALARAB Online recalled the well-known essay's thesis that Arabic women should not be allowed to take an ethical stance, "since [that] presupposes a certain amount of intellectual and material freedom, the ability to make decisions for one self, make money, have an education, and choose one's husband and lifestyle." Her short stories, too, depicted "a rich world of feminine experience and relationships seldom noticed by other Arabic authors," according to the Web site.

Al-Mala'ika's third collection of poems, *Qararat al-mawjah* (Bottom of the Wave) was released in 1957. In 1961 she married Abdel-Hadi Mahbouba, an academic colleague who eventually helped her found the University of Basra. Her next publication was an essay titled *Qadaya al-Shi'r al-Mu'asir* (Issues of Contemporary Poetry, 1962), and in 1968 her fourth poetry collection, *Shajarat al-qamar* (Tree of the Moon), was released.

After Saddam Hussein's Baathist regime took power in 1968, "Literature and films [became] equally censored under the Baathists," according to *Cultures of the World: Iraq.* The book went on to state that "artists were careful to avoid any negative reflections on the government. . . . some authors . . . preferred to sacrifice artistic integrity rather than risk punishment by the Iraqi government." Al-Mala'ika therefore left Iraq in 1970 and moved to Kuwait City, where she published *Ma'sa al-Haya wa-Ughniya li al-Insan* (The Tragedy of Life and a Song for Man, 1970).

She continued to publish poetry, and in 1974 she published *Al-tajzi'iyya fi'l-mujtama al-Arabi* (Fragmentation in Arab Society), which, according to the *Bloomsbury Guide to Women's Literature,* "[dissects] the inherent contradiction of men calling for freedom while wishing to keep women in chains." Al-Mala'ika stayed in Kuwait until 1990, returned briefly to Iraq after the Gulf War, but fled again in 1991 to Cairo, Egypt. She chose to move to Cairo during what a biography on the One Fine Art Web site described as a "period of convalescence," when al-Mala'ika, "for reasons best known to herself, put up a barrier against the press, which few journalists were able to penetrate." As the years passed, she began to put some distance between herself and poetic experimentation. Her later poetry often used the old form and espoused more morally conservative views. The *Encyclopedia of the Modern Middle East* commented that "al-Mala'ika came to feel that the new generation of Arab poets interpreted the form of free verse with too much license, and she advocated a more careful approach to what seemed to her a chaotic use of the form.''

The Poet Who Died Twice

A number of biographical sources list the year of al-Mala'ika's death as 1992—an oddity described in an article in the *British Journal of Middle Eastern Studies* by Ronak Hussein and Yasir Suleiman, who noted that ''early in 1993 the Arab press carried the news that Nazik al-Mala'ika was dead. Letters of condolence started to pour in at her home address in Baghdad, and it is even reported that obituaries appeared in some Arabic newspapers. . . . A few days later friends and admirers . . . heaved a sigh of great relief when it transpired that the news of her death was false and that she was still alive and well.'' Another collection of poems, *The Sea Changes Its Colors*, was completed in 1974, but it wasn't published until 1999, when it brought her renewed notoriety while she was living in seclusion in Cairo. Al-Mala'ika suffered from a number of physical maladies, the most debilitating of which was Parkinson's disease, and she died on June 20, 2007, at age 84, of natural causes in a Cairo hospital. She was buried in Cairo next to her husband, who died in 2005. They were survived by a son.

The Woman Who Faced the Fear of Words

While the *Dictionary of Oriental Literatures* claimed that ''although [al-Mala'ika's] poetry is popular . . . she is not the poet of the wide public,'' an entry in the *Encyclopedia of World Literature in the 20th Century* praised al-Mala'ika's technical prowess as a poet, describing her as ''versatile, inventive and unique, producing poems of high quality that lay bare the general dilemma of life in the Arab world.'' The entry called her vocabulary ''sensuous, fresh, and unadulterated by use.'' A *festschrift*—a German term meaning ''celebration publication,'' or a book presented to a respected academic during his or her lifetime as a token of honor—was prepared in 1985 to celebrate her work, and included 20 pieces about her theory and poetry. Her death and burial in Egypt raised an outcry from Iraqi intellectuals, who accused the government of neglecting ''Iraq's greatest surviving symbol of literature,'' according to ALARAB Online.

According to Jehat.com, al-Mala'ika once asked in a poem, ''Why do we fear words?/ Some words are secret bells, the echoes of their tone announce the start of a magic/ And abundant time steeped in feeling and life,/ So why should we fear words?'' Books that provide a cultural overviews of Iraqi history and culture uniformly mention al-Mala'ika by name in their literary overviews, a memorial of sorts for a poet who wrote without fear, challenging and changing the very words that made her voice so influential.

Books

The Bloomsbury Guide to Women's Literature, edited by Claire Buck, Bloomsbury Publishing Ltd., 1992.
The Continuum Dictionary of Women's Biography: New Expanded Edition, edited by Jennifer S. Uglow, Continuum Publishing Company, 1989.
Dictionary of Oriental Literatures, edited by Jaroslav Prusek and Jiri Becka, Basic Books, Inc., 1974.
Encyclopedia of the Modern Middle East, 4 vols., Macmillan Reference USA, 1996.
Encyclopedia of the Modern Middle East & North Africa, edited by Philip Mattar, Thomson Gale, 2004.
Encyclopedia of World Literature in the 20th Century, edited by Steven R. Serafin, St. James Press, 1999.
Foster, Leila Merrell, *Enchantment of the World: Iraq,* Children's Press, 1992.
Hassig, Susan M., and Laith Muhmood Al Adely, *Cultures of the World: Iraq,* Benchmark Books, 2004.
Marquis Who's Who, Marquis Who's Who, 2007.
Who's Who in Contemporary Women's Writing, edited by Jane Eldridge Miller, Routledge, 2001.
Women in World History: A Biographical Encyclopedia, edited by Anne Commire, Yorkin Publications, 1999.

Periodicals

Arab Studies Quarterly, Fall 1997.
BBC Monitoring Europe, September 25, 2007.
British Journal of Middle Eastern Studies, 1993.
Die Welt des Islams, July 1996.
International Herald Tribune, June 28, 2007.
International Journal of Middle East Studies, July 1970.
Los Angeles Times, June 22, 2007.
New York Times, June 27, 2007.
Research in African Literatures, Summer 1982.
Washington Report on Middle East Affairs, September/October 2007.

Online

''Iraqi Poet Nazik al-Malaika Passes Away,'' ALARAB Online, http://english.alarabonline.org/display.asp?fname=2007%5C06%5C06-21%5Czculturez%5C971.htm&dismode=x&ts=21/06/2007%2002:13:24%20%C3%A3 (November 27, 2007).
''Nazik al Malaika,'' One Fine Art, http://www.onefineart.com/en/artists/nazik_al_malaika/index.shtml (November 27, 2007).
''Nazik al-Mala'ika (1922-2007),'' Books and Writers, http://www.kirjasto.sci.fi/malaika.htm (November 20, 2007).
''Nazik al-Malaika: A Tribute Page,'' Kool Pages, http://www.koolpages.com/almalaika/images/nazikpage.html (November 27, 2007).
''Not an Obituary for Nazik al-Malaika,'' *Guernica,* http://www.guernicamag.com/blog/354/not_an_obituary_for_nazik_alma/ (November 27, 2007).
''Obituary: Nazik al-Malaika,'' Al-Ahram Weekly Online, http://weekly.ahram.org.eg/print/2007/851/cu5.htm (November 27, 2007).
''Renowned Iraqi Poetess Nazik al-Malaika,'' Jehat.com, http://www.jehat.com/Jehaat/en/Poets/Nazek-al-Malaika.htm (November 27, 2007). □

J. Willard Marriott

American executive J. Willard Marriott (1900-1985) founded the internationally successful Marriott hotel chain. He exerted strong influence on the development of both the food service and lodging industries in the United States.

The Marriott empire began in 1927 with a single A&W root beer stand, located in Washington, D.C. From there, Marriott's empire grew, gradually but consistenty, until by the end of the twentieth century the Marriott Corporation had become the thirteenth-largest employer in the United States. The secrets of the company's growth were simple: Marriott worked hard, he had a gift for developing clear and fair company procedures, and, from the beginning, he had a keen instinct for new business opportunities. President Ronald Reagan, quoted by Richard Papiernik in *Nation's Restaurant News,* called Marriott "a living example of the American dream."

Worked on Sheep Ranch

The second of eight children, John Willard (Bill) Marriott was born on September 17, 1900, in Marriott, Utah, a town established by his great-grandfather. Marriott's father, Hyrum, was a farmer who raised sheep and sugar beets, and Marriott grew up as a real-life cowboy, riding a horse from age five, carrying a gun, and herding sheep. The family, adherents of the Mormon faith, stressed hard work but also independent thinking, and young Marriott was always encouraged to work out problems for himself. When he was 13, he planted lettuce on some unused land and turned a $2,000 profit, which he presented to his father. At 15, he handled the sale and transport to San Francisco of 3,000 Marriott sheep.

Marriott was, in short, ready to take over the family ranch. But he wanted to see more of the world, and the Mormon emphasis on missionary work gave him the opportunity. He spent two years as a missionary in New England before returning to Utah and enrolling at the University of Utah. He graduated in 1926, having met his future wife, Alice (Allie) Sheets, during his senior year. The two frequented a local A&W root beer stand. The following year, Marriott went to visit a friend, Hugh Colton, who was studying law at Georgetown University in Washington, D.C. He observed that the national capital's humid summer heat might make it an ideal location for an A&W stand. Back in Utah, he convinced A&W founder Roy Allen to open up a new Washington-area territory, to which he and Colton, who put up $3,000, would have franchise rights. Marriott's own $3,000 share consisted of $1,500 in savings and a $1,500 loan.

Marriott and Sheets married in 1927 and, for their honeymoon, drove from Salt Lake City to Washington in a Model T Ford. On May 20 they opened the doors to their nine-seat A&W shop at 3128 14th St. NW in Washington, treating their first customer to a mug of root beer on the house. The first day's business was strong, thanks to street celebrations marking the successful transatlantic flight of aviator Charles Lindbergh, and the pair earned $16,000 in gross receipts in their first year. Alice Marriott, then and for many years afterward, served as bookkeeper in addition to being chief cook. "We joked around that Mom had the sticky-nickel job," J.W. Marriott, Jr. (born in 1932) told Papiernik. "That syrup would somehow always wind up on the coins. And there she would be, with $50 in nickels sticking together, trying to clean them up to get to the bank."

Soon, in order to attract business year-round, Marriott, who waited tables, added hot foods like beef barbecue to the menu. He changed the name of the restaurant to Hot Shoppe. From the start, Marriott included Mexican standards like tacos and tamales among his offerings, using recipes obtained at the nearby Mexican embassy. He had become familiar with Mexican food in Utah, but he was among the first restaurateurs—the very first, according to Charles Bernstein of *Nation's Restaurant News*—to offer it in the northeastern United States. Another East Coast first was a drive-in Hot Shoppe, among Marriott's first operations. The unique operation presented logistical challenges. "There were no cuts in the curbs to allow cars to pull up for drive-in service," Marriott Jr. told Papiernik, "and Dad had to go to the district council to get special approval. He got the first permits for off-street parking in Washington." The Marriotts decided on new locations by personally staking out intersections and counting cars.

Opened Airline Catering Operation

The Hot Shoppes were successful from the start, thanks to such novel marketing techniques as hiring people to pass out coupons on street corners. They were air-conditioned, and in the sweltering Washington summer they drew customers in droves. By 1929 there were three restaurants, and Marriott had incorporated the business under the name Hot Shoppes Inc. Colton sold his original stake back to Marriott that year for the original amount he had paid. By 1932 the chain had grown to seven locations in Washington, plus one in Baltimore, Maryland. One location was near Hoover Field, an airport at the site of the present-day Pentagon.

The manager of that shop passed on word to Marriott that air passengers were buying takeout meals for their flights, and Marriott once again saw an opportunity. After negotiations with Eddie Rickenbacker, head of the Eastern Transport Co. (later Eastern Airlines), he signed a contract to cater in-flight meal service, and in 1937 the In-Flite Catering division of Hot Shoppes opened for business with Eastern, American, and Capital airlines as customers. In-Flite grew into the largest airline catering business in the world, and in 1945 it branched out into airline terminal food service with an operation at Miami International Airport.

New Hot Shoppes opened steadily through the 1930s, and the company scored another coup in 1939 with a contract to provide catering services to the U.S. Treasury building. The frenetic pace Marriott insisted on for himself—he reportedly worked 15-hour days—took its toll on his health, however. In 1931 he suffered from a bout with Hodgkins' disease, and in 1933 he was sidelined for six months with a lymph disease and had to rely on family members to keep operations going. In later years he suffered multiple heart attacks, a ruptured brain blood vessel, and a hepatitis infection, but he always refused to delegate anything more than he had to. Business slowed at the Hot Shoppes themselves during World War II, but the company was positioned well to prosper from its growing government catering operations, and after the war's end, growth began anew.

In 1948 Marriott became president of the National Restaurant Association, and by the early 1950s Hot Shoppes had reached annual sales of $20 million. Among Marriott's few non-business activities were spiritual ones: he became second counselor in the Mormon church's Washington Stake (a divisional entity broadly comparable to a diocese in the Catholic church), and he later became president of that body. Although he had always resisted turning over any aspect of the company to outsiders, Marriott realized that a stock sale was necessary if expansion was to continue. In January of 1953, Hot Shoppes Inc. publicly offered 229,880 shares of common stock at $10.25 a share, plus 18,000 more shares to company employees at $7.54 a share. The Marriott family still owned two-thirds of all the Hot Shoppes shares, and Marriott held the titles of chairman and president.

Persuaded to Open Hotel

The Hot Shoppes scored one more major coup: in 1957 they broke the dominance of archrival Howard Johnson over the lucrative food service operations on the New York State Thruway toll highway. Hot Shoppes remained a visible presence in the northeastern dining scene for several decades; the last one did not close until 1999, although by then both the Hot Shoppes and the original airline catering operation had been sold. The year 1957 also marked a major turn in the company's operations: the 365-room Twin Bridges Motor Hotel opened in Arlington, Virginia, near Washington National Airport. Marriott had originally purchased the land for a new corporate office. Ironically, he was skeptical about the plunge into the hotel business that would bear his name. Two decades earlier he had been vividly impressed by the mass failures of hotels during the Great Depression. He was persuaded to change his mind by his son Bill Jr., who spearheaded the development of the Marriott hotel chain as it is known today.

The first hotel specifically designated a Marriott was the Key Bridge Marriott, also in Arlington, which opened in 1959. The Marriott hotels offered a new kind of space for lodging and conferences that competed successfully with older downtown hotels; they catered to business travelers and tended to be located near airports and other transportation hubs. Marriott specifically preferred locations near bridges, reasoning that while highways and intersections might undergo extensive redesign, bridges generally stayed put. The company's emphasis on thorough training was especially visible in its hotel operations; housekeeping staff had a prescribed set of 66 operations that they had to complete before they could consider a room cleaned.

Marriott relinquished the role of president to Bill Jr. in 1964, remaining as chief executive officer. At that point the company was still known as Hot Shoppes Inc., but a name change to Marriott Corporation in 1967 confirmed the company's new direction. Bill Marriott, Jr. assumed the role of CEO as well in 1972, but the senior Marriott continued to keep close tabs on the company's day-to-day operations. He witnessed the company he had begun with a single root beer stand expand internationally with the opening of a Marriott hotel in Amsterdam, the Netherlands, and extend its reach domestically with the creation or acquisition of several new restaurant chains, including Roy Rogers and one Big Boy entity.

In his later years, Marriott continued to be active in the Mormon church, with his annual tithe (or contribution of 10 percent of his income) establishing him as one of the church's major donors. A staunch Republican, he grew close to President Richard Nixon, serving as chairman of his inaugural committees after both the 1968 and 1972 elections. At Nixon's behest, he tried to counter the influence of the student counterculture by sponsoring an "Honor America Day" on July 4, 1970. Marriott died on August 13, 1985, in Wolfeboro, New Hampshire, after suffering a heart attack at the family vacation home. Shortly before his death, he admitted to *Dun's Business Month* that he did have one regret. "My dad always told me to take time to smell the flowers," he said, "but these days I just don't have the time."

Books

Business Leader Profiles for Students, Vol. 1, Gale Research, 1999.

Periodicals

Caterer & Hotelkeeper, May 23, 2002.
Dun's Business Month, December 1984.
Investor's Business Daily, February 15, 2000.
Nation's Restaurant News, August 26, 1985; September 16, 1985; October 7, 1985; February 1996.
Travel Weekly, August 22, 1985.

Online

"The Marriott Timeline," Marriott Corp, www.marriott.com (January 30, 2008). □

Ian Murray McKellen

English actor Ian McKellen (born 1939) has delighted audiences and critics from his first professional appearance in 1961 to stage and film performances in the twenty-first century. One of the premier Shakespearean performers of his time, he attained widespread fame in the role of Gandalf in the *Lord of the Rings* movie trilogy that opened in 2001. He was also noted for his public avowal of his homosexuality in 1988, and his activism for gay rights thereafter. Knighted in 1991, his sexual revelation did nothing to hamper his career or, certainly, his legendary talents. It instead became another thing for which he was greatly admired.

Early Years

McKellen was born on May 25, 1939, in the Northern English town of Burnley. His father, Denis Murray, was a civil engineer who also played the piano and his mother, Margery Lois (Sutcliffe), a housewife who dabbled in amateur theater. An older sister, Jean, com-

Shakespeare was deepened by summer camps at Stratford-upon-Avon, where he watched performances by such luminaries as Edith Evans, Paul Robeson, and John Gielgud. He was also successful in other areas, becoming Bolton's Head Boy in 1957 and winning a scholarship to study English at Cambridge University upon graduation. So, at 18, McKellen set out for new adventures.

Became An Actor

At Cambridge, McKellen soon felt at home among an undergraduate body of would-be show business aspirants that included Corin Redgrave, Derek Jacobi, Trevor Nunn, and David Frost. Even such talented fellows did not, however, prevent McKellen's stage work being singled out for praise by the student and national press while he was still in his first year. His studies suffered as he completely immersed himself in theatrical pursuits (21 productions during his undergraduate tenure). He did manage to squeak by enough academically to receive an English degree in 1961, but his heart was clearly not in it. He had decided to act professionally. Thus, without the benefit of any drama school training, McKellen pursued a career on the stage.

McKellen first landed at London's storied Old Vic Theater, then under the leadership of the eminent actor Laurence Olivier. On the plus side, the company was comprised of some of the most wonderful young performers of the day, including Maggie Smith, Joan Plowright, Lynn Redgrave, Michael York, Anthony Hopkins, and Michael Gambon. Invigorating as having such colleagues undoubtedly was though, the extent of their gifts also presented a problem. That is, of course, as there was only a finite number of leading roles to be had and there was a tremendous amount of potential star power vying for each one. McKellen was too young and impatient to wait his turn, so he left for slightly less august circles in which he had better hopes of actually plying his craft.

McKellen made his professional debut in 1961 as Roper in *A Man for All Seasons* at the Belgrade Theater Company in Coventry. After a year with that company, he moved on to the Arts Theater Company in Ipswich and the Nottingham Playhouse before winding up in London again in late 1964. The smaller companies had given him many opportunities to perform, but he felt it was time to seek a bigger spotlight. His professional debut in London was in 1964, as Godfrey in the Duke of York's production of *A Scent of Flowers*. The role won McKellen the Clarence Derwent Award for best supporting actor. In 1965, he returned to the Old Vic as Claudio in *Much Ado About Nothing*. 1967 saw his Broadway debut in *The Promise*, which led to a small part in the 1969 movie version. In short, and with very little downtime, McKellen had forged the very career he had vowed to pursue when he had been fresh out of college.

Gay Pride

For the next twenty years, McKellen built a repertoire and reputation on the stage. Shakespeare was a specialty, and he played almost every one of the Bard's great roles at one time or another, from Hamlet to Iago to Richard III to

pleted the family unit. Shortly before the onset of World War II, the McKellens relocated to a coal mining town called Wigan, where their son slept under the makeshift bomb shelter of the dining room table.

McKellen's parents were fans of the theater and encouraged his early interest in it. They took him to see his first play, *Peter Pan*, at the Manchester Opera House when he was three years old. At nine, he received a toy theater for Christmas. His sister was theatrically inclined as well, and exposed McKellen to Shakespeare at a Wigan's Little Theater performance of *Twelfth Night*. With all that familial influence, it is hardly surprising that McKellen took to the boards himself, starting in grammar school.

When he was 12, McKellen began attending the Bolton School (Boys' Division) in the town of the same name. Unhappily, it was also in that year that his world was shaken by the premature death of his mother. Over 50 years later, when most memories of her had faded, he still felt the loss keenly, telling Emma Brockes of the London *Guardian*, "If I could rewrite my life(,) it would be that, a) my mother didn't die when I was 12, because if so she might even be alive now . . .'' His father remarried quickly, and McKellen did have the good fortune to enjoy a long and warm relationship with his stepmother, Gladys.

Back at Bolton, McKellen did well despite the recent upheaval in his domestic life. The senior English master, who directed the annual spring play, supported his theatrical aspirations and McKellen made his Shakespearean debut at 13 as Malvolio in *Twelfth Night*. His appreciation for

Macbeth to Romeo to, most recently, King Lear. In 1980, he took Broadway by storm with his portrayal of Antonio Salieri in *Amadeus*. The part earned him a Tony Award for best actor, as well as other accolades. In England, his efforts had already been recognized with myriad honors by that time, including being named a Commander of the British Empire in 1979. But all his success did not soothe the internal battle he was fighting over his sexuality.

McKellen had been openly gay among his colleagues and friends since the middle 1960s, but he had hidden that reality from his family and the public, and the secret became increasingly wearing on him. That all changed in 1988 however, when, at age 49, he publicly came out as a gay man during a BBC Radio discussion about a law to prevent the "promotion of homosexuality." McKellen's world changed almost immediately and, quite surprisingly to him, mainly for the better. As he told Brockes, "Once you come out, all the problems go away, because the problem becomes somebody else's. It's not yours anymore. I was emotionally freed up, not only in life(,) but in work. Acting became easier because I was unedited." The newfound sense of freedom also prompted him to become an activist and vocal proponent of gay rights. He was, for instance, a co-founder of "Stonewall," a group that promotes social and legal equality for gays and lesbians. But perhaps even more unexpected than his newfound sense of liberation and purpose was the reaction of the public and impact on his career, both of which were quite positive. Rather than being reviled or mocked by his fans, he was hailed for his bravery. And far from putting a damper on the kinds of roles he was offered, 1989 found him starring as notorious womanizer John Profumo in the feature film *Scandal*. To top it all off, McKellen was knighted in 1991, making him one of the country's very few openly-gay knights.

As McKellen's father had died just 12 years after his mother, coming out to his family mainly entailed telling his Quaker stepmother, Gladys. Gratifyingly to the actor, she was accepting. "Not only was she not fazed," McKellen told Bruce C. Steele of the *Advocate*, "but as a member of a society which declared its indifference to people's sexuality years back, I think she was just glad for my sake that I wasn't lying anymore." Thus having rid himself of his albatross of deception and secrecy, McKellen carried on with his distinguished career.

Stage and Screen

McKellen began to get more widespread attention from American television audiences in the 1990s with such projects as Armistead Maupin's *Tales of the City* (1993) and *And the Band Played On* (1993). He then picked up a Golden Globe Award for the 1996 TV production of *Rasputin*. Feature film notice started to increase with 1993's *Six Degrees of Separation*, 1995's *Richard III*, and 1997's *Bent*, in which he had starred in the London production of the original play in 1989. But his portrayal of James Whale in 1998's *Gods and Monsters* kicked that newfound visibility up to another level, as critical acclaim, including an Academy Award nomination for best actor, poured in. More popularized appeal was the result of 2000's *X-Men*, but

McKellen unquestionably hit international celebrity paydirt with his unforgettable (and also Oscar-nominated) portrayal of Gandalf in the *Lord of the Rings* trilogy that began in 2001. Once a hero primarily to his countrymen, McKellen had risen to worldwide fame.

Although his success on the big screen could not have been unwelcome, McKellen still considered himself a stage actor. He returned to Broadway in 2001, for example, to appear with Helen Mirren in a revival of *Dance of Death*. Even more notably was his 2007 star turn in one of Shakespeare's most challenging roles, King Lear, which opened in London and went on tour in conjunction with Anton Chekhov's *The Seagull*. Asked by the *Economist* why he chose such an ambitious project rather than bask away in Hollywood, McKellen answered, "This is what I do. This is what I've been doing a long time . . . I'm not living full(–)time in Hollywood and I don't think of myself as a film actor. Why would I not want to do what I have spent 40 or more odd years discovering how to do, which is to act in these extremely difficult plays by William Shakespeare, which are more rewarding in personal achievement." Movies were still in the mix as well though, including 2007's *The Golden Compass* and *The Colossus*, which was expected to be released in 2008. It was just such a mixture of projects that McKellen found appealing, but the stage remained his first home.

McKellen turned 69 in 2008, and had the impressive resume and myriad awards that came with such a long and stellar career. (The latest accolade was having been made a Companion of Honor in December of 2007.) But he remained spry and showed no signs of slowing down. His world tour of *King Lear* ended in January, but he had other undertakings in the works, including a recording of some of William Wordsworth's poetry and the aforementioned film, *The Colossus*. His attitude was well reflected in his remarks to Catherine Shoard of the *Sunday Telegraph* in 2004, when queried on how old he felt. "I feel like everything's to come, like I'm just over halfway," McKellen said. "I'm aware of the end, but it's not in sight. Maybe I just need my glasses."

Periodicals

Entertainment Weekly, November 13, 1998.
Sunday Telegraph (London, England), May 16, 2004.

Online

"An Interview with Sir Ian McKellen," *Economist*, June 14, 2007, http://www.economist.com/books/PrinterFriendly.cfm?story_id=9332808 (January 6, 2008).
"Every Inch a King," *Guardian*, November 24, 2007, http://arts.guardian.co.uk/print/0,,331328697-123425,00.html (November 30, 2007).
"Ian McKellen: Biography," MSN Movies, http://movies.msn.com/celebs/celeb.aspx?c=118500&mp=b (January 6, 2008).
Ian McKellen.com, http://www.mckellen.com (November 30, 2007, January 6, 2008).
"Ian McKellen," IBDB, http://www.ibdb.com/person.asp?id=6425 (November 30, 2007).
"Ian McKellen," IMDb, http://www.imdb.com/name/nm0005212/ (November 30, 2007).

"The Knight's Crusade: Playing the Wizard Gandalf in *The Lord of the Rings* May Make Sir Ian McKellen the World's Best-Known Gay Man," *Advocate,* December 25, 2001, http://findarticles.com/p/articles/mi_m1589/is_2001_Dec_25/ai_83451265 (January 6, 2008). □

Ladislas J. Meduna

Hungarian neurologist Ladislas J. Meduna (1896-1964) was a pioneer in the treatment of schizophrenia and other psychosis-type disorders with what is known as convulsive therapy. Meduna used drugs to induce convulsions in his first trials in the 1930s, but the practice was soon replaced by a more reliable way to induce seizures via the application of electric current to the patient, which became known as electroshock therapy. Meduna later emigrated to the United States and taught at Loyola University in Chicago, Illinois.

Meduna was born in Budapest, Hungary, on March 27, 1896, to Francis and Gisela (Eissler) Meduna, and grew up in relative middle-class comfort during the waning years of the Austro-Hungarian Empire. In 1914 he began studies at the Royal University of Science in Budapest, but left a year later to serve in the army of the Austro-Hungarian Empire as World War I erupted in Europe. He served on the Italian front, and resumed his studies at the war's end in 1918. Three years later he earned his medical degree, and began specialty training in neurology. In 1924 he accepted a teaching position at the Budapest Interacademic Institute for Brain Research.

Became Intrigued by Mental Disorders

Meduna's initial research investigated disorders of the pineal gland, the endocrine gland that plays a role in human sexual development at puberty and later produces melatonin, a chemical that regulates sleep patterns. But in 1927 he began a new position as associate professor at the University of Budapest's Clinic for Mental and Nervous Diseases, and became intrigued by the emerging field of clinical psychology and its ties to neurological disorders. He began sitting in on autopsies conducted on recently deceased clinic patients. There was talk at the time that the mentally ill had marked differences in their brain structures, though there were few diagnostic tools available to prove this theory.

Schizophrenia was a disorder that mental health professionals believed to be incurable. It was characterized by delusions, hallucinations, disordered speech patterns, and distorted perceptions of reality, and patients often sank into a catatonic state. Among medical professionals, rumors arose in the late 1920s that some schizophrenics who suffered epileptic seizures—an entirely separate and unrelated neurological disorder—seemed to have been cured of their mental disorder by the violent convulsions. Meduna began to research the matter further, and discovered that there were very few patients with epilepsy who also exhibited signs of psy-

chosis. He also tracked 6,000 known schizophrenics, and found that just 20 of them also had epilepsy. Postmortem investigations seemed to show that those who suffered from epilepsy had more neuroglia—the network of supporting tissue and fibers found in the brain and spinal cord—than the average person. In autopsies on schizophrenics, by contrast, Meduna believed he saw far fewer neuroglia cells. He theorized that convulsive seizures caused formation of the neuroglia, and that inducing the production of more of these cells might prove to be the cure for schizophrenia.

A Remarkable Outcome

Meduna conducted his first experiments in inducing seizures on animals using camphor dissolved in oil. He injected it in his first human patient on January 23, 1934, at the Budapest State Hospital. The 33-year-old male patient, named L.Z., had been at the institution since 1930 after he began to hear voices that he claimed came from his ears as well as his stomach; the man also believed that when he was out in public people were waving at him. He spent all of 1933 in his bed under the covers, the hallmark of a genuinely catatonic patient. Meduna injected him with camphor six times over the next 18 days, and L.Z.'s symptoms began to abate. "On the morning of February 10, the patient spontaneously arises from bed, is lively, speaks, and asks for something to eat," Meduna's notes reported, according to Edward Shorter's book *A History of Psychiatry: From the Era of the Asylum to the Age of Prozac.* "He is interested in everything going on about him, asks about his illness and realizes that he has been sick. He asks how long he has been in the hospital, and as we tell him that he has already been there four years he cannot believe it."

In an autobiographical piece that was not published until the 1980s in the journal *Convulsive Therapy,* Meduna provided an interesting sidenote to L.Z.'s seemingly miraculous recovery. Following the treatment with camphor, the man actually escaped from the Budapest State Hospital and returned home to find "that the cousin living with his wife was not a relation at all but his wife's lover. He beat up the cousin and kicked him out of the house; proceeded to beat up his wife and told her that he . . . preferred to live in the state mental hospital where there is peace and honesty," according to Shorter's book. To Meduna and other professionals, however, the exit from a catatonic state was indeed nothing short of remarkable, and had only occurred through two other forms of treatment for schizophrenia: one was insulin coma therapy, in which schizophrenics were given high doses of insulin, which produced convulsions then coma. This was pioneered in Vienna, Austria, by Dr. Manfred Sakel (1900-1957) just a few years before Meduna's camphor trials. Insulin coma therapy replaced sleep therapy, which had come into use in the first years of the twentieth century. In this treatment, patients were given heavy doses of barbiturates for up to nine days, but there was a risk of death from circulatory collapse.

Treatment Had Serious Drawbacks

Meduna continued his Budapest trials with 26 more patients, and reported signs of remission in half of them. He submitted his first published report on the trials in January of 1935, but soon switched to using another convulsion-inducing chemical compound known by its trademarked name, Metrazol, and sold under the brand name Cardiazol in Europe at the time as a circulatory and respiratory stimulant. It had some benefits over camphor, whose intramuscular injections were painful. Vomiting also sometimes accompanied the usual state of great anxiety that camphor induced in patients before the seizures began, which could take up to 45 minutes. Metrazol had similar disadvantages, because it, too, caused extreme distress for patients before they lost consciousness, and the treatments were described as stressful for even the medical professionals involved; aversion to second dosages was so strong that patients had to be restrained by force. Another drawback to Metrazol was that the convulsions could not be halted once they were underway—unlike insulin coma therapy, where a saline solution could be given that began to reverse the shock almost immediately—and spinal fractures occurred in some patients.

Meduna treated 110 patients with Metrazol, and presented his study results in 1937 at a meeting of psychiatry professionals in Münsingen, Switzerland. Within a year, however, a team of researchers led by Dr. Ugo Cerletti (1877-1963), chief of the University of Rome's Clinic for Nervous and Mental Diseases, had devised a new method of inducing convulsions that was much less barbaric. It was called electroconvulsive therapy, and became the standard treatment for schizophrenia and other psychosis-type disorders for the next several decades. It fell out of favor in the 1970s, but is still sometimes used to treat depression.

Settled in the Chicago Area

Meduna fled the encroaching threat of Nazi Germany in the late 1930s, emigrating to the United States and becoming associate professor of psychiatry and neurology at Loyola University in Chicago in 1939. Four years later he joined the faculty at the University of Illinois's Neuropsychiatric Institute in Chicago as an associate professor of psychiatry, and remained there until his death in 1964. Later in his career he devised carbon dioxide therapy as a course of therapy for schizophrenics. His formula of 30 percent carbon dioxide and 70 percent oxygen was known as the "Meduna mix," and caused unconsciousness and in some cases near-death experiences reported later by patients, who reported feeling a sensation of moving through a tunnel toward a light source while under the influence.

Even Metrazol was banned by the U.S. Food and Drug Administration in 1982 because of the danger of convulsions, but a quarter-century later there were new theories that it could reverse the effect of mental retardation for those afflicted with Down syndrome. Meduna's ideas about neuroglia were later proven to have been in error, though scientists were still unsure about the root causes of schizophrenia. He was a respected colleague in his day, however, serving as editor-in-chief of the *Journal of Neuropsychiatry* and as president of both the American Society of Medical Psychiatry and the Society of Biological Psychiatry. The latter group was founded after World War II, partly in response to the then-fashionable theories of Austrian psycho-

analysis pioneer Sigmund Freud (1856-1939), which focussed on the unconscious mind and its fixation on inanimate objects that Freud argued were representative of repressed sexual desires. When the Society was founded, Meduna said, according to a *New York Times Magazine* article by Mike Gorman, "Our flag is a flag of revolution upon which I should like to write the rebellious, the defiant motto: 'A telegraph pole is a telegraph pole.'"

Books

Science and Its Times, edited by Neil Schlager and Josh Lauer, Volume 6: *1900 to 1949,* Thomson Gale, 2000.

Shorter, Edward, *A History of Psychiatry: From the Era of the Asylum to the Age of Prozac,* John Wiley & Sons, 1997.

Periodicals

American Journal of Psychiatry, November 1999.

New York Times Magazine, January 13, 1957. □

Craig Cameron Mello

American molecular biologist Craig C. Mello (born 1961) shared the 2006 Nobel Prize in Medicine with Andrew Fire for their discovery of RNAi. As a result of their co-research, the two men shared numerous other awards that underscored the impact, both immediate and potential, of their discovery.

In 2006 Craig Cameron Mello and Andrew Fire opened up new doors for gene technology and treatment of human diseases at the cellular level with their discovery of RNAi, also known as RNA interference or gene silencing. Mello was born on October 19, 1961, in New Haven, Connecticut. He is the son of James and Sally Mello and was the third child in a family of four children. His father was a paleontologist and his mother was a homemaker and artist.

Mello became interested in science through his father, who completed his doctorate in paleontology at Yale University in 1962. Upon receiving his doctorate, James Mello moved his family to Falls Church, Virginia, to take a position with the U.S. Geological Survey in Washington, D.C. A short time later the family moved to Fairfax, Virginia, when James Mello accepted the position of assistant director at the Smithsonian Museum of Natural History, also located in the nation's capital. Craig Mello would later recall that his fondest childhood memories involved family camping trips to the Blue Ridge Mountains in Virginia and to Colorado and Wyoming. During these vacations, he hiked and searched for fossils. He also fondly remembered family discussions around the campfire. Mello recalled that his family had a strong tradition of discussions, especially around the dinner table. The experience was extremely important to him, both emotionally and intellectually. The Nobelprize.org Web site quoted from Mello's autobiography: "I learned to argue, to listen, and to admit (sometimes grudgingly) when I was wrong about something," he remembered. "These were often lively

discussions, and my parents did a great job of allowing each of us to be heard. At a time when I was not performing so well in school, these daily discussions helped to build my confidence and self esteem."

A Late Bloomer

Despite his obvious inquisitiveness and evident intelligence, Mello struggled through grade school. By his own account, he did not start to blossom as a student until he reached his middle school years. However, during his early education he possessed a certainty that he would grow up to become a scientist. That idea began to take firm root when he entered the seventh grade and was first exposed to a formal science education. For the first time in his life, he began to truly apply himself to his studies. In his spare time he enjoyed reading science fiction and he became an amateur astronomer.

A precocious adolescent, he already possessed an intuitive grasp of humanity's position within the earth's natural history, and he was mystified—even disappointed—by his elders' short-sighted views on science and the human condition. "I was amazed that so few adults (including my teachers) understood basic concepts such as deep (geologic) time, the vastness of the universe, and the common evolutionary origins of life," he recounted, according to Nobelprize.org.

Further, while he was raised as a Roman Catholic, Mello rejected ideological elements of religion. Even at an early age, he found it hard to accept concepts such as the

inerrancy of the Bible and of intelligent design (especially as it was presented to him as a counterargument to evolution). Because he had been exposed to the world's rich pageant of natural history through his father's workplace (the Smithsonian Institution), he found it impossible to unconditionally embrace religious dogma. "The 'absolute knowledge' offered was, in my view, inadequate to explain the world around me," he recalled in the autobiography he penned when he received the Nobel Prize, on Nobelprize.org.

At the same time, he had no problem reconciling science with spirituality. "I believe that there is no more spiritual and worthwhile undertaking than that of trying to understand the world around us, and our place in it," he stated in his Nobel autobiography.

When he entered Fairfax High School, he took all of the science courses the school offered, except for advanced physics. In 1978, when he was 18 years old, he became particularly interested in molecular biology after reading an article in the *Washington Post* that described the cloning of the human insulin gene in bacteria. The article explained how the bacterial cells read the human genetic code and produced functional human insulin. Mello was intrigued that bacterial cells could speak the same genetic language as human cells to produce a human protein useful for diabetic patients. Mello began to grasp the potential for treating disease at the genetic level and for molecular treatments such as gene therapy. After Mello earned a bachelor of science degree in biochemistry at Brown University in 1982, he did post-graduate work at the University of Colorado from 1982 to 1984, studying molecular, cellular, and developmental biology.

Earned Doctorate at Harvard

While in Colorado, he worked in the laboratory of Dr. David Hirsh, where he was introduced to C. elegans. As Mello recalled, at that time no one had yet succeeded in introducing DNA (deoxyribonucleic acid), into C. elegans, a method called DNA transformation. Also, researchers working with yeast had identified functional DNA elements that direct the replication and partitioning of chromosomes. Collaborating with Dan Stinchcomb, Mello took on a project to identify such elements from the worm. Project goals included understanding these essential functional chromosomal elements and then using them to produce stable artificial chromosomes for worm molecular genetics.

When Hirsh later accepted a position in industry, Mello transferred to Harvard University, where he continued his work with Stinchcomb, who was establishing an independent laboratory. Mello earned his Ph.D. in cellular and developmental biology from Harvard University in 1990.

After earning his doctorate, Mello became a postdoctoral fellow at the Fred Hutchinson Cancer Research Center in Seattle, Washington. He joined the laboratory of Jim Priess, a scientist. Mello learned about genetics, which would later help advance his work on RNAi. While working with Priess, Mello identified genes that act as regulators of the early development of C. elegans.

In 1992 Mello married Margaret Hunter. The couple had one child, Melissa. The couple separated and divorced, amicably, in 1994. When he remarried in August of 1998, to Edit Kiss, he became the stepfather of David and Sarah Apotheker. In 2000 the couple's daughter, Victoria, was born.

Began Research with Andrew Fire

In 1995 Mello joined the University of Massachusetts Medical School as a professor of molecular medicine and as a researcher. Throughout the late 1990s he worked on a project, through e-mail and the Internet, with Andrew Fire, who was employed at the Carnegie Institution of Technology in Baltimore, Maryland. In his autobiography, found on Nobelprize.org, he wrote, "We were both working on developing techniques for DNA transformation in worms," recalled Mello. "Andy had some early success and developed a number of clever methods. I followed up with some improvements. And together we made DNA transformation a routine procedure for the worm. We developed the mutual trust and respect that ultimately led to our collaboration on RNAi."

Working together, they discovered that RNA (ribonucleic acid) could do a great deal more than realized. Up until then, it had been thought that RNA only carried out the genetic instructions given by DNA. Working with small worms (nematodes), Mello and Fire discovered that double-stranded RNA (dsRNA) could be directed to turn off specific genes. This action was called RNA interference or RNAi. More specifically, in the technique, dsRNA triggers sequence-specific silencing of (or interfering with) gene expression, essentially tricking the cell into killing messenger RNA before it can produce a protein. In this way, the RNAi mechanism can destroy gene products that a virus needs in order to replicate itself. Essentially, it can stop the progression of invading viral infection.

Within a few years, it had been demonstrated that the RNAi process could work in mammalian cells and that the process could be reversible. Soon, scientists began deploying the process in laboratories throughout the world, trying to develop ways that it could be used in humans to combat genetic disease.

Shared Nobel Prize

Mello and Fire published a paper about their work with RNAi on February 19, 1998, in the scientific journal *Nature*. In 2006 they shared the Nobel Prize for Medicine for their discovery. Mello was only 47 years old when he received the prestigious international award.

The publication in *Nature* was followed by accolades. In 2002 Mello and Fire's work had been named the "Breakthrough of the Year" by *Science* magazine. In 2003 Mello and Fire won the Wiley Foundation Prize in the Biomedical Sciences from Rockefeller University, the National Academy of Sciences Award in Molecular Biology, and the fourth Annual Aventis Innovative Investigator Award at the Drug Discovery Technology World Conference. In 2004 the pair received the Warren Triennial Prize, the highest research honor bestowed by Massachusetts General Hospital. At the time, it was commented that the collaborators had opened up an entirely new area of biology. RNAi is now widely and routinely used in research

and is expected to lead to medical breakthroughs in the fight against cancer and other diseases.

In awarding the Nobel Prize to the two men, the Nobel committee pointed out, according to Nobelprize.org, that RNAi had opened up exciting possibilities for use in gene technology, stating that the method "has already become an important research tool in biology and biomedicine. In the future, it is hoped that it will be used in many disciplines including clinical medicine and agriculture.... Plans are underway to develop silencing RNA as a treatment for virus infections, cardiovascular diseases, cancer, endocrine disorders and several other conditions."

The year before the two men received the Nobel Prize, Mello and Fire were named to the National Academy of Sciences. In addition, they received several additional honors, including Brandeis University's Lewis S. Rosenstiel Award for Distinguished Work in Medical Research, the Canadian government's Gairdner International Award, and the Massry Prize.

In 2006 Mello and Fire traveled to Germany to accept the Paul Ehrlich and Ludwig Darmstaedter Prize, which is one of the highest and most internationally renowned awards conferred by the Federal Republic of Germany in the field of medicine. That same year, Mello became the first-ever recipient of the Dr. Paul Janssen Award for Biomedical Research, which was established by Johnson & Johnson in 2004.

Eventually, the University of Massachusetts Medical School and the Carnegie Institution of Technology were issued a patent, "Genetic Inhibition by Double-Stranded RNA," (US Patent 6,506,559 B1). It is anticipated that the patent will have tremendous licensing potential both in the laboratory and for drug development. To their credit, both institutions were enthusiastic about making RNAi as widely available as possible, to help accelerate genetic research. As such, they developed a licensing policy that enables companies to easily obtain, for a basic fee, a broad and non-exclusive license for research scientists to use the technology. As a result, many companies have licensed the invention and many others continue to express interest.

In assessing recent research as well as his own accomplishments, Mello, who became the Blais University Chair in Molecular Medicine at the University of Massachusetts Medical School and was designated an Investigator of the Howard Hughes Medical Institute in 2000, said that with RNAi and the completion of the genome sequences for humans and numerous other organisms, "we now have unprecedented opportunities to develop new, life saving therapies and to advance the basic understanding of our biology," according to Nobelprize.org.

He added that he feels mankind has a potentially bright future, but also faces significant challenges that need to be addressed and overcome. "The biological mechanisms at work inside our cells are truly ancient and remarkably stable, more stable even than the positions of continents and oceans on the face of the Earth. However, in my view, our thriving global economy has engendered serious problems. Climate change and other forces beyond our control could easily disrupt our economies causing widespread human suffering at unprecedented levels," he said.

Books

"Craig C. Mello," *Marquis Who's Who,* Marquis Who's Who, 2007.

Online

Biography Resource Center Online. Gale, 2007. http://galenet .galegroup.com/servlet/BioRC (October 15, 2007).

"Craig C. Mello—The Nobel Prize in Physiology or Medicine 2006: Autobiography," Nobelprize.org, http://www.nobel prize.org/nobel_prizes/medicine/laureates/2006/mello-autobio.html (October 15, 2007).

"Craig C. Mello, Ph.D," Bio International Convention, http://www .bio2007.org/Attendees/educational_sessions/CraigMello.htm (October 15, 2007).

"The Nobel Prize in Physiology or Medicine 2006," Nobel prize.org, http://www.nobelprize.org/nobel_prizes/ medicine/laureates/2006/mello-autobio.html (October 15, 2007). ☐

Eddy Merckx

Belgian cyclist Eddy Merckx (born 1945) dominated the sport of professional cycling during a 13-year career that ended with his retirement in 1978. Many observers of the sport consider him the greatest cyclist who ever lived.

Merckx has had a competitor for that title: American cyclist Lance Armstrong, who won cycling's premier race seven times to Merckx's five. But the two athletes are difficult to compare. Armstrong, especially after his bout with cancer, restricted his racing mostly to the Tour de France. Merckx, by contrast, competed in hundreds of races, entering a full season of competitions during the European cycling season of February 1 through October 1 every year. Merckx won a staggering total of 476 races over his professional career, 54 of them in 1971 alone. He once raced for 54 days in a row and sometimes entered two races in a single day. He entered multi-day endurance tests, single-day races, mountain bike races, and short track races with equal enthusiasm. Never considered the strongest or most technically gifted cyclist on the European circuit, Merckx amassed his impressive record partly through a sheer competitive drive that led his opponents to bestow upon him the nickname "the Cannibal."

Began Riding at Four

Edouard Louis Joseph Merckx was born on June 17, 1945, in the small town of Meenzel-Kiezegem, Belgium, to Jules and Jenny (Pittomvils) Merckx. The following year, the family moved to Sint-Pieters-Woluwe, a suburb of the Belgian capital of Brussels, where they lived above a small grocery store they operated. Merckx's father served as an example when it came to the virtues of a competitive spirit.

"His life consisted of work, work and more work," Merckx was quoted as saying by Amy Reynolds Alexander in *Investor's Business Daily.* "The shop was open every day, even all day Saturday and Sunday morning." Merckx got his first bicycle at age four, and was soon a familiar sight riding around the neighborhood. To the questions of passers-by as to whether he intended to ride in the Tour de France someday, he confidently answered that he did.

As a child, Merckx became more or less obsessed with cycling. He hated school, and he was determined to pursue the sport at a competitive level despite an unpromising pudgy build. When he was about ten a friend ridiculed him aims, predicting that in five years he would be too fat to fit through the door of the family shop, but Merckx continued to respond to the questions of worried teachers about his career plans by saying that he wanted to be a cyclist. In 1962 he asked and received his parents' permission to drop out of school to pursue competitive cycling full-time.

It did not take Merckx long to justify his choice of career. As an amateur in 1962 he entered 55 races and won 23 of them, including Belgium's national championship. Curiously, that was his only career victory in that race, but he soon began to dominate cyclists in other European countries besides Belgium. In 1964 he won the Amateur World Championship Road Race, and the following year he turned professional. His first major victory came in 1966 at the Milan-San Remo cycle race in Italy, at which time he had not yet reached his twenty-first birthday.

From then until his retirement in 1978, Merckx dominated the sport of cycling "like no one else has before or since," in the words of his entry on the Cycling Hall of Fame Web site. Between 1969 and 1975 he won about 35 percent of the races he entered&mdash, a staggering percentage in a sport where athletes push their bodies to the limit and generally need plenty of recovery time. Merckx's tolerance for pain was legendary, and experiments conducted at the Sports Academy of Cologne, Germany, showed that he had an unusual ability to maintain his pace even when his blood contained high levels of lactic acid, a normally painful byproduct of intense physical activity.

Accomplished Unique Feat at Tour de France

One joke reported in a BBC biography of Merckx illustrated the general attitude toward Merckx as an athlete: "Today," it ran, "Eddy Merckx, Fausto Coppi and Gino Bartali [the strongest competitors in the Tour] were all fined by the cycling authorities. Coppi and Bartali were caught hanging onto the back of a truck and allowing it to pull them up a mountain. Merckx was pulling the truck." Merckx's period of greatest dominance began around 1968, when he won the Paris-Roubaix Race. The following year he notched his first Tour de France victory, and in the process he accomplished an unprecedented and still-unmatched feat: in a grueling race marked by strategies of conceding in one area in order to gain strength in another, Merckx won the Yellow Jersey (for the overall victory in the race), the Green Jersey (for the winner on points), and the Polka-Dot Jersey (for fastest mountain climb).

The year 1969, however, also marked a low point in Merckx's career. Toward the end of the season, he agreed to participate in an exhibition race paced by a motorbike known as a derny. A crash involving the bicycle and derny in front of Merckx involved him in a chain reaction accident that killed Merckx's pacer and left Merckx himself unconscious and bleeding heavily from the head. He suffered a concussion, a cracked vertebra, and a twisted pelvis that for the remainder of his career made climbing hills even more painful than usual. Merckx recovered, however, and the majority of his triumphs were still ahead of him.

Those triumphs included wins that made Merckx a superstar all over Europe, where competitive cycling enjoys a larger audience than in the United States. His wins included the Giro d'Italia in 1970, 1972, and 1974, and the Vuelta d'España in 1973—races that, together with the Tour de France, make up a so-called Grand Tour. Merckx remains one of just a few cyclists who has won all three races over the course of his career, and his 1974 triple victory in the Giro d'Italia, Tour de France, and World Championship Road Race is even rarer; the only other cyclist to accomplish it was Stephen Roche in 1987. One of Merckx's greatest accomplishments came in the difficult high-altitude environment of Mexico City in 1972, where he set a new record for the greatest distance traveled by a cyclist in one hour: 49.431 kilometers, or about 30.715 miles. That record stood for several years before finally being broken by cyclists riding bikes technically superior to the one Merckx had used; his record

was restored when such bikes were banned, and no one using similar equipment exceeded Merckx's distance until Britain's Chris Boardman did it in 2000.

Part of Merckx's mastery could be credited to his inexhaustible attention to the small details of cycling. He was said to have a basement full of bicycle tires, and he would sometimes get up in the middle of the night to adjust his bicycle seat. Although he was "never afraid to have a beer or a cigarette," as quoted by the London *Guardian,* Merckx was in every way a fierce competitor who hated to lose in any contest, even after he retired from professional cycling. He amassed his unprecedented win total mostly by entering every race he could and going all out for victory, while most of his competitors were making trade-offs among themselves and cutting deals to help each other. "He was called 'The Cannibal' by frustrated opponents because he would try to win every race, whatever the time and place," noted the BBC. "This is not the way to win friends in cycling, where the handing out of a few favors to call back in later is an essential part of the competitors' armory."

Punched by Spectator

Merckx's 1974 victories in the Tour de France and Giro d'Italia were to be his last Grand Tour wins. In 1975, during one of the legendary climbing stages of the Tour de France, he was punched in the stomach by a spectator, and later in the race he fractured a cheekbone in a crash. In neither situation did he consider giving up, but he did lose the race to Bernard Thevenet by three minutes. Merckx turned 30 in 1976, and his victories became rarer and more restricted to smaller events. In 1978, plagued by back problems, he retired.

Merckx was an example of a single-minded athlete who found himself at loose ends after his competitive career came to and end. Used to eating 3,500-calorie breakfasts as a competitor on his way to annual training distances variously estimated at 30,000 kilometers and 30,000 miles, he was often described as rotund or even corpulent by the 1990s. Merckx snapped out of his malaise by throwing himself into bicycle manufacturing with the same energy that had consumed him as a racer. At first he concentrated on custom made bicycles for other racers, but by the early 1990s he had branched out into general sales of high-end bicycles, and Eddy Merckx bicycles were produced at a factory in Meise, Belgium, that Merckx himself oversaw.

Merckx was quick to befriend Lance Armstrong, the brilliant American cyclist who invaded the traditionally European sport of cycling. The two met after Armstrong chose a Merckx bicycle for competition at the 1992 Summer Olympics in Barcelona, Spain. Merckx encouraged Armstrong, telling him that he would be able to win the Tour de France if he lost weight, and when Armstrong was stricken with testicular cancer Merckx visited him in the hospital. Armstrong's dogged determination to fight his way back to the top after beating the cancer into remission appealed to Merckx, who said in an interview, as quoted by William Fotheringham in the London *Observer,* "[Armstrong] was determined to come back to what he had been and I was impressed. No one believed in him at the time. Even I would never have thought he was capable of coming back and winning the Tour de France." Merckx's friendship with Armstrong was tested only when Armstrong competed against one specific cyclist—Merckx's son Axel, who began racing in the 1990s and won a stage of the Giro d'Italia in May of 2000.

Merckx, who continued to ride a bicycle a few days a week, remained a superstar in Belgium and much of the rest of Europe, widely recognized when he walked down the street as a result of television cycling commentary and the fame he had accumulated. Two decades after his retirement, he could still turn out a line of fans two hours long for an autograph session in Boulder, Colorado. "I have no regrets at all," he explained to *Bicycling* magazine on that occasion. "With all the races I won, what regrets could I possibly have?" The year 2006 saw the release of a DVD biography, *Eddy Merckx: Hunger for Glory.*

Books

Vanwallaghem, Rik, *Eddy Merckx: The Greatest Cyclist of the 20th Century,* translated by Steve Hawkins, Inside Communications, 2000.

Periodicals

Bicycling, May 26, 1997.
Guardian (London, England), January 3, 1997.
Independent on Sunday (London, England), July 24, 2005.
Investor's Business Daily, March 27, 2000.
New York Times, August 2, 1998; July 12, 2000.
Observer (London, England), July 7, 2002.

Online

"Cannibal's Recipe for Success," British Broadcasting Corporation, http://news.bbc.co.uk/sport2/hi/other_sports/992257 .stm (December 27, 2007).
"Eddy Merckx," Cycling Hall of Fame, http://www.cyclinghalloffame.com/riders/rider_bio.asp?rider_id=1 (December 27, 2007).
"Eddy Merckx," Milan–San Remo Title, http://www.milansanremo.co.uk/merckxpalmares.htm (December 27, 2007).
"Eddy Merckx—The Cyclist," British Broadcasting Corporation, http://www.bbc.co.uk/dna/h2g2/A1006525 (December 27, 2007). □

Angela Merkel

Angela Merkel (born 1954) became the first woman ever to lead Germany as chancellor. Merkel and the party she chairs, the Christian Democratic Union (CDU), formed a coalition with two other parties in 2005, and the agreement installed the former physicist as head of government. Perhaps more notable than her gender is Merkel's background: she is the first person to lead a reunified Germany who comes from the formerly Communist eastern states, a division that endured for more than four decades following the end of Germany's defeat in World War II. "My life changed completely in 1989," Merkel said

once at a rally, according to Judy Dempsey in the *International Herald Tribune.* "I have had many opportunities in the last 15 years. I would like to give my country back what I myself have gained in terms of the opportunities from reunification."

Merkel was born Angela Dorothea Kasner on July 17, 1954, in Hamburg, Germany. This was one of the largest cities of West Germany, but her parents moved east just a few months later to the German Democratic Republic, or GDR, as Communist East Germany was called. The decision was made by Merkel's father, Horst, a Lutheran pastor, who was offered a job at a seminary in the state of Brandenburg, about an hour north of Berlin. Berlin was surrounded by the GDR, but had a Western sector that remained technically part of West Germany. Soviet and U.S. troops monitored the different Berlin zones, but in 1961 the East Germans, with Soviet aid, began constructing a massive wall that divided the city into East and West, like Germany itself. East German border guards patrolled the no-man's land adjacent to the Wall, with orders to shoot on sight any trespassers. Nearly all of those who died were East Germans seeking freedom in the West instead of the strictly regulated state socialism of the East.

A Prize-Winning Student

Merkel was raised as the eldest of three children in the Brandenburg city of Templin. After she became chancellor, a biography was published in Germany which revealed that her father had been instrumental in the creation of a separate Protestant church in the GDR—allowing GDR officials to keep a closer watch on its members—and his tacit support of the German Communist Party likely gave the family the few perks they were able to enjoy. These included two cars—when one automobile was an almost unheard-of luxury in much of Communist Eastern Europe—and travel visas that permitted them to visit relatives back in West Germany and even vacation in Italy.

As a youth, Merkel was nicknamed "Kasi" from her surname, Kasner, and was a studious high schooler who excelled in languages, as had her mother, who had been a teacher of English back in Hamburg. Merkel became so fluent in Russian that she even won a prize trip to Moscow. Like nearly all other college-bound East German teens, she was a member of the *Freie Deutsche Jugend* (Free German Youth, or FDJ), the official socialist youth organization in the GDR, but most reports of her young adult years portray her as a dutiful East German who avoided political rhetoric of any stripe. "I would have loved to have become a teacher," she once reflected, according to a profile written by Ruth Elkins in London's *Independent*. "But not under that political system." Instead she chose to study the sciences, remarking that "physics was harmless and uncontroversial," according to Elkins.

Merkel entered the University of Leipzig in 1973. According to a German-language biography by Gerd Langguth published in Germany as *Angela Merkel: Aufstieg zur Macht* (Angela Merkel: Rise to Power), her father's "pro-regime attitude helped Angela's career," noted Luke Harding, correspondent for London's *Observer*. Horst's status with GDR authorities permitted his daughter "to study at an elite comprehensive school and go on to university, at a time when the children of clergy were routinely refused places." During her student years, Merkel worked as a barmaid in a discotheque, and a year before earning her degree married a fellow student, Ulrich Merkel. They moved to an apartment with neither toilet nor hot water in the Prenzlauer Berg district of East Berlin, and began renovating it while Merkel also went to work on her doctorate in quantum chemistry at the Central Institute for Physical Chemistry of the Berlin Academy of Sciences. The marriage ended in 1982.

Joined Nascent Democracy Movement

Merkel earned her doctorate in 1986 and remained affiliated with the Central Institute for Physical Chemistry as a researcher. In 1989 she became involved in pro-democracy groups that were suddenly being allowed to operate in East Berlin and other GDR cities. One of them was Demokratischer Aufbruch (Democratic Awakening), which had its roots in several pacifist Protestant church groups in the GDR. The pro-democracy movement escalated, leading to the opening of the Berlin Wall in November of 1989, when the wall was demolished and thousands of East Berliners jubilantly streamed through, signalling the beginning of the end for the GDR. Merkel's first mentor in politics was Lothar de Maizière (born 1940), who headed

the East German branch of the Christian Democratic Union (CDU). The East Germany Communist Party allowed the CDU to operate as a token nod to a multiparty electoral system, but parties like the CDU had little power until the fall of the Berlin Wall. Soon de Maizière was named head of a caretaker government in the lead-up to reunification, and in March of 1990 Merkel became the deputy spokesperson for his government.

The former East German *Länder*, or states, were reunified with the rest of Germany in October of 1990. Two months later the first post-reunification parliamentary elections were held, and Merkel won a seat in the Bundestag (Germany's lower house) from the state of Mecklenburg-Vorpommern. The East German branch of the CDU merged with its West German counterpart that same year, and Merkel became a rising star in the party when its powerful leader, German chancellor Helmut Kohl (born 1930), made her his protégé. Kohl had served as chancellor of West Germany since 1982, and was heralded as the architect of reunification, which just three years earlier had been considered an entirely unfeasible hope by most Germans. Kohl famously dubbed Merkel *das Mädchen,,* or "the Girl," and made her a member of his cabinet in 1991 as minister for women and young people. In December of 1991, thanks to Kohl's support, she was elected deputy party leader.

Elected Head of CDU

Merkel became the first politician from the former East to become a government minister in a newly reunited Germany. In 1994 Kohl gave her a more significant cabinet assignment, this time as minister for the environment and reactor safety, but Kohl was ousted in 1998 elections and stepped down accordingly. Weeks later, she was elected a secretary-general of the CDU, the first woman to attain that post in party history, and over the next two years she distanced herself from Kohl and older members of the CDU when a series of financial misdeeds came to light. In 2000 she bested the latest CDU chair, Wolfgang Schäuble (born 1942), in a leadership contest, and became the first woman ever to lead the party.

At the time, the CDU was relegated to one of its rare periods out of power. Its main rival, the center-left Social Democratic Party of Germany (SPD), had won in 1998 and Gerhard Schröder (born 1944) succeeded Kohl as chancellor. Schröder and the SPD held onto power in the 2002 elections, but by 2005 the German public appeared ready to shift their political allegiances once again. In parliamentary elections that year, voters gave the CDU a small margin of victory. Schröder refused to concede power, however, and finally a so-called "Grand Coalition" was negotiated, with Merkel becoming chancellor on November 22, 2005. She agreed to form a government comprised of cabinet members from her own party as well as its counterpart in the southern German state of Bavaria, the Christian Socialist Union (CSU), and members of Schröder's SPD.

Political pundits often compare Merkel to Margaret Thatcher (born 1925), who served as British prime minister from 1979 to 1990. Like Merkel, Thatcher had enjoyed an impressive career in the sciences before becoming the first woman to head her country's leading center-right party, the Conservative (Tory) Party. The reforms enacted during Merkel's years in office also had echoes of the Thatcher era: Merkel instituted some sweeping tax cuts for German businesses and began to move Germany to a more active role as a leader in foreign policy. Her accomplishments in this realm included a reworking of the compact between France and Germany that gave both powers a shared leadership role in the powerful European Union (EU), but for the first time since the end of World War II the new arrangement meant that more decisions were made in Berlin, not Paris.

Friendly with Texan President

In other foreign-policy initiatives, Merkel has established more cordial relations than her predecessor with the United States, meeting several times with U.S. president George W. Bush (born 1946). Unlike her predecessor Schröder, she has been a vocal critic of Russian president Vladimir Putin (born 1952), despite the fact that she is modern Europe's first leader to speak fluent Russian. Political analysts have wryly noted that while Merkel was busy with the pro-democracy movement in East Germany in 1989, Putin was serving as a station agent for the KGB, the Soviet state-security apparatus, in Dresden East Germany.

In 2007 Merkel took over two temporary posts in addition to her duties as chancellor of Germany: the rotating presidencies of both the EU and the G8 (Group of Eight, an international forum comprised of the world's most powerful nations). As chair of the latter, she proposed a transatlantic free trade zone that might become known by the acronym TAFTA. "I consider it my job to express to America what's in the interest of Europe," *New York Times* correspondent Mark Landler quoted her as saying about TAFTA. "And for me, the trans-Atlantic partnership, in general, is in the European interest. Europeans know that we cannot accomplish things without America," but she added, "America must also know that Europe is needed in many areas."

Merkel earns consistently high marks in public opinion polls, receiving the highest approval ratings among all post-World War II German chancellors. In 2007 *Forbes* magazine ranked her at the top of its list of the world's most powerful women for the second year in a row. In 1993 she married her former doctoral advisor, Joachim Sauer, a chemistry professor. Like many German women of her generation, she is childless; the country has regularly posted some of the world's lowest birth rates since the 1980s. On the domestic front, this demographic shortfall may keep her in power—as the median voter age in Germany remains close to her own actual age—but may also portend disaster for the country's future. "If birthrates continue to decline, the country will one day have a workforce too small to support the social and medical programs that its elderly will need," explained Andrew Purvis in *Time International.* "Previous governments have sounded the alarm about this scenario—and then done little or nothing about it. . . . If Merkel uses her leadership to find ways in which women can be better integrated into the economy, she will go down in history for a lot more than her gender."

Periodicals

Economist, November 18, 2006; June 30, 2007.
Independent (London, England), June 19, 2005.
International Herald Tribune, October 8, 2005.
Maclean's, December 3, 2007.
New Statesman, July 25, 2005.
Newsweek International, May 1, 2006; May 14, 2007.
New York Times, October 11, 2005; January 12, 2007.
Observer (London, England), June 26, 2005.
Time International, January 30, 2006.

Online

"Angela Merkel," *Forbes,* http://www.forbes.com/lists/2007/11/biz-07women_Angela-Merkel_34AH.html (January 4, 2008). □

John Milne

Although little known today in his native Britain, scientist and inventor John Milne (1850-1913) arguably contributed more than any other single individual to the understanding and remote detection of earthquakes.

"Earthquake Milne," as he was sometimes known, invented one of the first modern seismographs and put in place the beginnings of the worldwide network of earthquake measuring stations that exists today. It is noteworthy that many of his pioneering discoveries were accomplished while he was living and working in Japan, a country where awareness of earthquakes was and remains more immediate and urgent than in Milne's homeland. Milne also made important contributions to Western scholarship on Japan during his nearly two decades of residence in that country. He had a colorful life, wrote several books (including two textbooks on seismology that were used for decades), and generally deserves more attention than he has been accorded in the English-speaking world.

Financed Trip with Pub Appearances

John Milne was born on December 30, 1850, in Liverpool, England, but grew up in Rochdale, near Manchester. He was the only child of John Milne Sr. and Emma Twycross. A talented student from the start, he enrolled at Liverpool Collegiate Institute when he was 13 and won a series of academic prizes there. One of them carried a cash award that Milne used to take a trip around northwest England's Lake District. He extended the journey all the way to Ireland essentially on foot, living on apples that he filched from orchards along the way and making extra money by entertaining patrons at roadside pubs by playing the piano.

When Milne was 17 he moved to London and resumed his education, entering King's College and taking a diverse curriculum that included mathematics, mechanics, theology, geology, chemistry, geometrical drawing and, most important, surveying and mineralogy. Interested in a career as a mining engineer, he enrolled at the Royal School of Mines in London and also studied mining further in Freiburg, Germany. In his early twenties Milne participated as a field geologist in mining expeditions in Europe, Iceland, the Canadian province of Newfoundland, and the Sinai region in the Middle East. With this wide experience under his belt by 1875, Milne was offered a job still farther away: the Japanese government in Tokyo had just formed a new public works department and offered Milne the position of consulting engineer, which he accepted. Later he became professor of geology and mining at the Imperial College of Engineering in Tokyo.

Rather than sailing for Japan, Milne traveled overland through Scandinavia, Russia, Central Asia (where part of the journey involved travel on camelback), and China, a grueling journey he summarized in his 1879 book *Across Europe and Asia*. Reportedly Milne insisted on the land journey because he suffered from seasickness. On Milne's first night in Japan he experienced the first of the many earthquakes that would menace the island nation, which is located in the active earthquake zone that surrounds the Pacific Ocean.

The scientific understanding of earthquakes was still in its infancy in the 1870s. Supernatural explanations had given way to the hypothesis that earthquakes were somehow connected to volcanic eruptions. The interest of European scientists in earthquakes had been heightened by a group of major quakes that struck England and Portugal in the 1750s, and measurements of earthquake intensity had been made for more than a century. But few researchers had analyzed the collected data systematically. Early in his career in Japan, Milne made close observations of Japanese volcanoes and correctly concluded, according to the Web site of the Department of Earth & Atmospheric Sciences at Saint Louis University that "the majority of earthquakes which we experience do not come from volcanoes nor do they seem to have any direct connection with them."

Investigated Aboriginal Japanese

Beyond his purely scientific pursuits, Milne took a keen interest in his new home and made several important contributions to the study of Japanese prehistory and to the description of Japan's aboriginal inhabitants, the Ainu. He traveled to Japan's northernmost island, Hokkaido, to make his ethnological observations, and many of his guesses about the movements of peoples in early Japan were proven correct by artifacts recovered later during anthropological expeditions.

A major earthquake that struck the Yokohama area in 1880 focused Milne's energies on seismology. That year he and two other British scientists in Japan, James Alfred Ewing and Thomas Gray, devoted their efforts to seismology research. They founded the Seismological Society of Japan, which was the first scientific seismology organization anywhere in the world; Milne was asked to be the group's leader but chose to edit and to contribute articles to its journal instead. The society also funded Milne's research. Working again with Ewing and Gray, Milne quickly perfected the horizontal pendulum seismograph, one of the first modern precision instruments for the measurement of the duration and intensity of earthquakes. It was not the first

seismograph—earthquake-measuring instruments were known in ancient China—but modern seismographs trace their ancestries ultimately to Milne's instrument. The horizontal pendulum seismograph enabled Milne to distinguish primary and secondary waves ("P" and "S" waves) in the vibrations resulting from motion along a fault line; the two waves produced different patterns on Milne's seismograph, and interpretations of those patterns allowed scientists to determine exactly where a quake's epicenter was located.

Living through and observing another major Japanese quake, the Mino-Owari earthquake of 1891, Milne offered the correct hypothesis that earthquakes were caused by the release of energy along fault lines in the Earth's crust. He published several major books about earthquakes in the 1890s, including one that documented the effects of the 1891 quake in photographs. His summaries of his Japanese earthquake observations were published in the books *Earthquakes and Other Earth Movements* (1898) and *Seismology*; these remained standard texts in the field of seismology for many years. For his efforts in search of an understanding of earthquakes in Japan, Milne was given the Order of the Rising Sun award by the Japanese emperor; he was one of very few foreigners ever to receive that honor. Milne married Toné Horikawa, a Japanese geologist. They solemnized their marriage in two separate ceremonies, one Japanese and one recognized under British law.

After Milne's home, laboratory, and books were destroyed in an 1895 fire, he decided to return to Britain. His wife and an assistant, Shinobu Hirota (known as Snowy), accompanied him to the Isle of Wight off England's southern coast, where they moved into an old estate called Shide Hill House and renovated its barn into a seismological laboratory. Milne oversaw the pouring of a precision-specified concrete floor before installing his array of instrumentation. Shide Hill House attracted scientists and researchers from around the world for the rest of Milne's life. The location had an additional attraction for Milne: the nearby Carisbrooke Castle owned another seismograph, and by 1900 Milne had added several more of his own, creating in effect the world's first major seismographic research center. Milne formed a new British Seismological Investigation Committee, which communicated with other seismographic stations around the world to form a global network that in vastly refined and expanded form still exists today. Milne's network included observation stations in Russian, the United States, Canada, and later Antarctica.

Burned Gap in Mustache

Milne's earthquake observatory occasioned wonderment among residents of the still rural Isle of Wight. Milne, with a distinctive mustache featuring a gap burned by decades of chain-smoked cigarettes, could be a startling figure, and the strange illumination caused by his various nighttime experiments led to the local belief that his observatory was haunted. Milne's household consisted of Milne, his wife, Hirota, an astronomer named Herbert Turner, a cook, and a housemaid. He had no children.

Prior to his death, Milne collaborated with John Johnson Shaw on another important advance in seismograph technology known as the Milne-Shaw Seismograph. Advances in electronic technology eventually superseded the designs of Milne's instruments, but the basic look of Milne's seismograph, with its weighted base and recording needles sweeping across paper and inscribing wave forms, persisted for decades. Milne served as secretary of the seismological committee of the British Association for the Advancement of Science (BAAS) in the 1910s. He died from kidney disease on July 31, 1913. After his death, what remained of his laboratory became the property of Oxford University. Surprisingly little known in Britain today, he is venerated in Japan as a scientific pioneer.

Books

Herbert-Gustar, Leslie, and Patrick A. Nott, *Earthquake Milne and the Isle of Wight*, Vectis, 1974.

Herbert-Gustar, Leslie, and Patrick A. Nott, *John Milne: Father of Modern Seismology*, 1980.

Kabrna, Paul, *John Milne: The Man Who Mapped the Shaking Earth*, Craven & Pendle Geological Society, 2007.

Online

"Earthquake Milne: 1850-1913," Isle of Wight Rock Archives, http://www.iowrock.demon.co.uk/profiles/iow_profile_milne.html (February 9, 2008).

"Inventor of the Week: John Milne," Massachusetts Institute of Technology, http://www.web.mit.edu/invent/iow/milne.html (February 9, 2008).

"John Milne (1850-1913)," Department of Earth & Atmospheric Sciences, Saint Louis University, http://www.eas.slu.edu/People/BJMitchell/TextPages/milne.html (February 9, 2008).

□

Helen Mirren

British actor Helen Mirren (born 1945) has starred in roles ranging from racy to regal over her career of more than 40 years. Mirren is best known for earning Emmy and Academy awards as Queen Elizabeth I and II, respectively. "Indeed, there's something quite haughty about her that suits such parts," Ryan Gilbey wrote in the British *Guardian* newspaper.

Early Life

Mirren was born Ilyena Lydian Mironoff on July 26, 1945, in London's Chiswick section. Neither Mirren nor her older sister, Katherine, knew about their Russian blood until after the Soviet Union dissolved in 1991. Mirren is a descendant of field marshal Mikhail Kamensky, a hero of the Russo–Turkish war of the late 1700s.

Mirren was the middle child among three. Her father, Basil Mironoff, was a musician and former Russian nobleman who drove a cab in London. Her mother, Kitty Rogers, was a woman from a blue–collar family who claimed gypsy

heritage, and whose grandfather was the butcher to Queen Victoria. Mirren's grandfather was Russian aristocrat Pyotr Vasielvich Mironov, who was stranded in London while negotiating a World War I arms deal in 1917, at the start of the Bolshevik revolution. Basil Mironoff strove to integrate the family into English society, anglicizing the surname to Mirren and refusing to teach any of his children Russian.

The young Mirren was educated in Westcliff–on–Sea, at St. Barnard's High School for Girls. Even early on, Shakespearean drama captivated her. At age 13, she played Caliban in a school production of *The Tempest.* When she left school, she worked briefly as a carnival barker of sorts at a local amusement park called The Kursaal, coaxing people onto rides.

When Mirren told her parents she wanted to pursue acting as a career they frowned on it, encouraging a more secure living. At age 18, she enrolled in a teacher's college in Hampstead, but soon left for the stage. The National Youth Theatre accepted her after an audition, and she made her acting debut in *Antony and Cleopatra* in 1965. "She was a sensation as Cleopatra and was deemed a revelation due to her sexual presence onstage," the British Broadcasting Corporation wrote on its Web site.

Within two years, she joined the Royal Shakespeare Company (RSC), its personnel having noticed her in a Youth Theatre play. She first appeared for RSC in *Coriolanus.* Later in her early acting years, she made connections with the likes of Patrick Stewart and Ben Kingsley. While in her 20s, Mirren left London in the early 1970s to perform worldwide with stage director Peter Brook's experimental troupe, the

International Centre of Theatre Research, and performed in Africa and the United States. It was during this rather wild phase of her life when she got a tattoo. "I was visiting this native American reservation in Minnesota. I got very drunk on brandy and woke up with it the next day," she told Gilbey. "I haven't had it removed because it's a reminder that I was sometimes a bad girl in the past."

"Mirren's sexual presence, her passion for her roles and her willingness to show how an intelligent woman had the strength to use her sexuality all became her trademark in the business," BBC wrote on its Web site. "However, Helen still had to run the gauntlet and ignore the smutty remarks and seedy attitudes of those she was trying to alter."

Broke into Film

Mirren made her film debut in 1969 as Hermia in *A Midsummer Night's Dream,* and appeared in the satirical *O Lucky Man!* in 1973. During the 1970s, Mirren worked in both film and television, in several made–for–TV dramas. In 1979, she played a female lead in a borderline porno-graphic film *Caligula,* produced by *Penthouse* magazine publisher Bob Guccione, Sr. The *Guardian's* Gilbey called the film "a blight on the [resumes] of all who appeared in it, including Peter O'Toole and John Gielgud." Andrew Walker wrote for BBC News: "There have been turkeys . . . most notably the shambolic sub–pornography of *Caligula,* but Helen Mirren has always redeemed herself with spell-binding performances at just the right time." In her early years, Gilbey added: "She seemed to be playing up to her off–screen image as a free spirit happy to hang out with the hippies, while her more serious work . . . was restricted to the stage."

Mirren took on more serious roles in the 1980s. She co–starred with Bob Hoskins, playing the tough–as–nails moll to a gangland leader in *The Long Good Friday* and made a name for herself in Hollywood with her appearance beside Harrison Ford and River Phoenix in *The Mosquito Coast.* She was also a moll, working with Michael Gambon, in *The Thief, His Wife & Her Lover.* In addition, Mirren played Morgana opposite Nicol Williamson's Merlin in *Excalibur.* There, director John Boorman effectively drew on the dislike Mirren and Williamson developed a few years back while working together on *Macbeth.*

While filming *Excalibur,* Mirren met another rising ac-tor, Liam Neeson, and they had a brief relationship. In 1984, she met Taylor Hackford, who directed *An Officer and a Gentleman.* She moved in with him in 1986 and they mar-ried on New Year's Eve, 1999, at Ardesier Parish Church in Scotland. Hackford first met her when she appeared in his 1985 movie, *White Knights;* at the time, he said she ema-nated "cold disdain," as reported in the *Guardian.*

From 1990 to 2006, she played detective inspector Jane Tennison in the *Prime Suspect* series. Tennison alter-nated between confused and ruthless, and frequently made waves with male police officers. The ratings success of *Prime Suspect* in the 1990s was an effective transition for a Mirren approaching her 50s. It ran from 1990 to 2006— ending with her retirement from the force—and earned her Emmy, Golden Globe, and British Academy of Film and Television Arts (BAFTA) nominations. "It allowed me finally to step forward to the next generation, to catch up with who I really was," she told Gilbey. "It was a huge relief not to have to play even one year younger."

Juggled On–Screen Personas

Though Mirren has best shone in her more sophisti-cated roles, she downplays that with a down–to–earth per-sona. "Sometimes, she will accomplish this by making very un–Hollywood, off–the–cuff statements such as: 'I've al-ways been a bit of a wild thing and have the scars to prove it," Gilbey wrote. She has freely discussed her relationships with Neeson and Williamson, both stormy at times.

She is also active politically, battling the sex–slave trade in Asia, working for Oxfam International against the buildup of arms, and pleading to the British government on behalf of Ugandan children ensnared in civil war. About aging, she told the *Guardian:* "There's a difficult period between 44 and 58 when you're no longer a mature, good–looking woman and not yet an old bird, but after that it's fine."

Mirren continued to star in productions in the new millennium. She appeared on Broadway in *Dance of Death* in 2001 and played the title role in a remake of the Tennes-see Williams classic, *The Roman Spring of Mrs. Stone,* in 2003. She also starred in *Pride* (2004), a BBC One produc-tion, which featured computer animation.

Won Acclaim as Queen

Mirren's roles have also included Lady Macbeth, and as a contrast, a cruel teacher in *Teaching Mrs. Tingle* (1999). She also played the mother of a hunger–striking Irish Re-publican Army (IRA) prisoner *Some Mother's Son* (1996). She "can switch with aplomb between classical drama, hard–boiled thrillers and breezy comedy," Gilbey wrote. In the television miniseries *Elizabeth I,* produced by Tom Hooper and released in 2005, she played Britain's aging queen juggling her public and private personas. Mirren, who had turned 60 around the time, won three Golden Globe awards and an Emmy, among her many accolades. Pauline Kael, as quoted by Gilbey, wrote in the *New Yorker:* "Probably no other actress can let you know that she's playing a distinguished and important woman."

She finally won an Academy Award in 2007, for best leading actress in *The Queen.* In that film, she portrayed Queen Elizabeth II as the royal family coped with aftermath of the death of Princess Diana in an automobile accident in Paris, France. Mirren had already won BAFTA, Golden Globe, and Screen Actors Guild awards for her perform-ance. Her Oscar win surprised no one. Bookmaking com-pany William Hill began paying out bets one week before the ceremony, and Oscar host Ellen DeGeneres quipped during the event, according to BBC News: "It's exciting because you don't know who's going to win—unless you're British, and then you know you've a pretty good shot."

Mirren, who was named a Dame of the British Empire in 2003, said on BBC News: "I had to recognize the person that I was playing and everything that she means to us and to me and to the history of our country and all the rest of it." She received a congratulatory phone call from the queen herself and an invitation for her, director Stephen Frears, and screenwriter Peter Morgan to join her for lunch at Buckingham Palace. "I think it's wonderful that I live in a country that allows us to make a film like this," she said, also on BBC News.

Former British Prime Minister Tony Blair only added to the praise. "It takes a very special kind of actress to take on a role of this kind and to do so to universal acclaim. Helen Mirren is a very special kind of actress and her Oscar is well deserved," Blair said in a statement published on BBC News. Michael Sheen played Blair's character in the movie.

Mirren also went on to give struggling British television network Independent Television, commonly known as ITV, an inadvertent shot in the arm. ITV partially underwrote *Elizabeth II.* The network also carried a two–part, four–hour sequel to *Prime Suspect,* with Mirren in her old role as Jane Tennison. ITV carried *Elizabeth II* in the fall of 2007. *Prime Suspect: The Final Act* also won an Emmy.

Breath of Fresh Air in Hollywood

Cashing in on her fame, later in 2007 Mirren published her autobiography, *In the Frame,* published by Orion/McArthur. "It just flew off the page and it's not been changed," she told the Web site of Canadian cable television network CTV. She was so prolific she threw her publishers into a tizzy. "They wanted 20,000 words but before I knew it I'd written 56,000 and they were screaming stop. We've got too many words. It'll be too big a book. Stop writing," she told the CTV.ca Web site. Constance Droganes of CTV.ca praised the down–to–earth tone in Mirren's book, which includes Russian family roots, personal anecdotes, dumpy apartments, and life–learning experiences. "Mirren's story is rich, entertaining, and one that makes 'life apprenticeship,' not 15 minutes of fame, the real prize at the end of this page–turner," Droganes wrote.

Mirren will not slow down. In *National Treasure, Book of Secrets,* released in 2007, she starred with Nicholas Cage in a film about missing information related to the 1865 assassination of President Abraham Lincoln. She also appears in *Inkheart,* scheduled for release in March of 2008 and set in medieval times. Future movie projects include *State of Play,* an adaptation of the British miniseries, and *Love Ranch,* directed by her husband, and involving Nevada's first legalized brothel.

Mirren and Hackford live in Los Angeles; she is the stepmother of Hackford's two sons, Rio and Alex. Being fluent in French, Mirren also owns houses in London and southern France. In recent years the couple sold their estate in New Orleans, Louisiana. "In a scandal–happy showbiz fueled by botox–junkie actresses, rehab–hotties, and jail–bound badsters, Mirren, 62, has done the impossible by today's Hollywood standards: not just last, but blast her career into a level of super stardom that's rarely ever seen," Droganes wrote.

Online

"Dame Helen Crowned Best Actress," BBC News, February 26, 2007, http://news.bbc.co.uk/2/hi/entertainment/6396179 .stm (December 23, 2007).

"Dame Helen Mirren—Actress," BBC, May 1, 2007, http://www .bbc.co.uk/dna/h2g2/A21388494 (December 6, 2007).
"Helen Mirren," Internet Movie Database, http://www.imdb .com/name/nm0000545/ (December 6, 2007).
"Helen Mirren Dishes about Life 'In the Frame,' " CTV, December 3, 2007, http://www.ctv.ca/servlet/ArticleNews/story/ CTVNews/20071130/ENT_Mirren_071130/20071202?hub =Entertainment (December 6, 2007).
"Helen Mirren: In Her Prime," BBC News, June 13, 2003, http://news.bbc.co.uk/2/hi/entertainment/2988112.stm (December 6, 2007).
"Helen Mirren: The Queen of All She Portrays," *Guardian,* August 13, 2006, http://film.guardian.co.uk/features/feature pages/0,,1844293,00.html (December 6, 2007). □

Hayao Miyazaki

Japanese filmmaker Hayao Miyazaki (born 1941) is considered to be one of the world's greatest animators. His naturalistic style has shaped the genre of animation both in Japan and around the world.

Art Had Wartime Origins

Born in Tokyo on January 5, 1941, Miyazaki spent his early childhood amid the chaotic political climate of World War II. His father manufactured fighter airplane parts, which led the young Miyazaki to start drawing airplanes and to develop a lifelong passion for aviation. His mother was ill with tuberculosis and confined to her bed for most of his childhood, yet she remained a positive presence in his life.

During the occupation of the postwar years, Japanese comic books, or manga, started to emerge as a new medium. Miyazaki began drawing his own manga by studying the work of Osamu Tezuka, the creator of *Astro Boy.* Animation, or anime, was also growing in popularity in Japan in the years following World War II. Miyazaki first became interested in becoming an animator after seeing the feature-length color anime film *The Tale of the White Serpent* while he was still in high school.

He furthered his interest in animation by joining a children's literature club at his college, Gakushuin University. After earning degrees in political science and economics in 1963, Miyazaki joined Toei Animation, where he received basic animation training and met his future collaborators. There he would also meet his wife, fellow animator Akemi Ota, alongside whom he worked on the early animated films *Gulliver's Travels Beyond the Moon, Flying Phantom Ship,* and *Animal Treasure Island.* The pair raised two sons, Goro (now a filmmaker) and Keisuke.

Miyazaki started as an in-between artist, drawing the pictures in between the key frames (the most important frames) to make the images flow smoothly. He soon moved up to the key animation department as well as the writing department, and became heavily involved with the animator's union. As a member of a new team of progressive

animators, Miyazaki was able to work on *Hols: Prince of the Sun,* the directorial debut of Isao Takahata. Containing socialist themes and innovative animation techniques, the film caused a stir when it was released in 1968 and remains a landmark in anime history.

Directed Animated Television Series

Miyazaki and Takahata left Toei Animation in 1971, starting what would become a lifelong collaborative relationship. During the 1970s, Takahata and Miyazaki worked together at several production studios for both film and television. At A Pro, the team co-directed several episodes of the animated television series *Lupin III,* based on the popular manga by Kazuihiko Kato (also known as *Monkey Punch*).

The team also worked together on the short films *Panda! Go, Panda!* and *Panda! Go, Panda!: Rainy Day Circus* for Tokyo Movies Shinsha. In 1978 Miyazaki directed his first television series, *Future Boy Conan,* for Nippon Animation. *Future Boy Conan* was an adaptation of Alexander Key's novel *The Incredible Tide,* and the series followed the adventures of two children looking for hope amid world destruction. Miyazaki would return to the themes of ecological disaster in his later films.

During this time, Miyazaki was also practicing his craft as a scenic design artist. He traveled around Europe to observe landscapes and backgrounds for projects based on Western literature. In 1979 Miyazaki made his directorial feature film debut with *Lupin III: The Castle of Cagliostro.* Lupin III, the fictional grandson of the master thief Arsène

Lupin, was originally a character created by French novelist Maurice Le Blanc. Miyazaki was able to use his experiences traveling in Europe to inform the detailed settings and background scenery. Although commercially successful, the film was still mostly a genre exercise, and Miyazaki was left with a desire to expand the horizons of the art of animation.

In the early 1980s Miyazaki began writing an epic manga series about Nausicaä, a fearless princess who defends her peaceful valley from a toxic jungle and inevitable war. A fusion of figures from Japanese folklore with a character in the *Odyssey* of ancient Greece, Nausicaä struggles to defend her people's way of life as well as respect the dangerous environment she has come to understand. The feature film *Nausicaä of the Valley of the Wind* was released in 1984 (the manga series continued into the late 1990s). Miyazaki did the writing, directing, and storyboarding, with Takahata as the producer.

Emerged as Anime Auteur

The first major work done in the classic Miyazaki style, *Nausicaä,* marked Miyazaki as a filmmaking auteur. With its strong female protagonist, realistic depictions of nature, and ecological themes, the film set a standard for his career and for animation in general. Miyazaki did away with the common association between anime and a metalllic, high-tech look, offering fungus-covered forest trees instead. In the 1980s, a heavily cut version of *Nausicaä* was released in dubbed English on video under the name *Warriors of the Wind.* The Disney studio later re-released a more thorough English-language version with a new voice cast, including Patrick Stewart and Uma Thurman.

After nearly two decades of working together, Miyazaki and Takahata decided to start their own production company within the parent company of Tokuma Shoten. They named it Studio Ghibli, after the nickname for a kind of Italian airplane. Studio Ghibli was founded in 1985 as a completely in-house animation studio, just when other companies began to outsource work to cheaper animators overseas. Miyazaki was thus able to maintain his dedication to high-quality work. As Melanie Goodfellow wrote in *Variety,* ''Miyazaki is an old-fashioned craftsman who insists that all his characters and backgrounds are drawn by hand.''

Studio Ghibli's first feature, *Castle in the Sky,* followed a boy who fights a destructive power active on a beautiful ancient floating city. Miyazaki based this film on events he observed during a trip to Wales in Great Britain, where he witnessed a miners' strike. Miyazaki told Xan Brooks of the London *Guardian,* ''I admired the way they battled to save their way of life, just as the coal miners in Japan did. Many people of my generation see the miners as a symbol, a dying breed of fighting men.'' In this film, Miyazaki was able to showcase his love of aircraft by creating meticulously detailed flying machines. The film also expanded on the ecological themes of nature in relation to technology, made poignant in a particular scene featuring a giant robot soldier (later reproduced in a statue placed in the rooftop garden of Studio Ghibli's museum) gently caring for his garden.

In 1988 Studio Ghibli released a double bill of two starkly different films: the joyously amusing *My Neighbor*

Totoro (directed by Miyazaki) and the downbeat *Grave of the Fireflies* (directed by Takahata). Neither did well at the box office, so the studio decided to release stuffed Totoro toys as a marketing strategy. The cute creatures became Studio Ghibli trademark icons, and remain popular toys. *My Neighbor Totoro* was a gentle story of two sisters who move to the country with their father while their mother is in the hospital. They discover Totoro, a giant magical creature who rules the forest.

My Neighbor Totoro again embodied the spirit of environmentalism, but this time with an innocent sense of wonder and amazement. While remaining a beloved family film, Totoro resists the sugary sweetness of typical American animation aimed at kids. An essay in *Authors and Artists for Young Adults* commented that "Miyazaki does not simply replicate the cutesy cartoon antics of critters as in the golden age of cartooning. Instead, he ponders timeless themes from Asian folklore and mythology, [and] delves into the psyche of his characters." An English-language version was released in the United States on home video. Disney's 2005 English re-release featured the voices of Dakota and Elle Fanning as the sisters.

Directed Features with European Settings

In 1989 Miyazaki directed *Kiki's Delivery Service*, based on a fiction series by Eiko Kadono. The lighthearted story follows a young witch seeking independence and self-reliance: Kiki leaves home and settles in a seaside town where she starts a delivery service by flying around on her broomstick with her black cat, Jiji. With a warm-hearted storyline and a European-style setting, the film was a commercial success in Japan and marked a new stage in the growth of Miyazaki's popularity with international audiences. Disney's 1998 English version featured the voices of Kirsten Dunst, Phil Hartman, and Janeane Garofalo.

Miyazaki also employed a European setting for his next feature, *Porco Rosso* (1992), which he based on a manga of his own, titled *The Age of the Flying Boat*. Set in Italy between the two world wars, the story follows an anti-Fascist fighter pilot who happens to be a pig. The English-language Disney release featured the voices of Michael Keaton and Cary Elwes. Craig Butler wrote in the *All Movie Guide* that "*Porco* is nothing short of splendid, featuring a vibrant palette that never turns garish, beautiful backgrounds and settings, delicate but forceful line work, and forceful character design." Taking a break from writing and directing, Miyazaki took on producer duties for the ecological adventure *Pom Poko* and wrote the screenplay and storyboard for the romantic drama *Whisper of the Heart* (1995).

Although he had achieved mainstream success in Japan, Miyazaki was relatively unknown in the United States outside of anime fan circles. That changed with the release of *Princess Mononoke* (1997), an epic adventure set in feudal Japan at the beginning of the Industrial Revolution. The story concerns a traveler who finds himself interposed between two powerful women: Lady Eboshi, the ruler of Iron Town, who is determined to kill the forest spirit, and the wild wolf-girl San, a proud member of the wolf tribe and protector of the forest. *Princess Mononoke* broke Japanese box-office records and received a North American theatrical release by Disney's Miramax division. It was also the first Miyazaki film to contain computer animation, although Miyazaki personally hand-drew many of the animation cells. When asked about the fate of hand-drawn animation, Miyazaki told Brooks, "If it is a dying craft we can't do anything about it. Civilization moves on."

Nearly 60 years old and losing his eyesight, Miyazaki was considering retiring after the wide international success of *Princess Mononoke.* But he re-emerged in 2001 with *Spirited Away*, a story inspired by a a friend's ten-year-old daughter, on whom he based the main character, Chihiro. The story follows Chihiro as she learns self-reliance in a magical world by working in a bathhouse for the spirits. Highly anticipated, *Spirited Away* became Japan's largest-grossing film up to that time. The film received a wide international release, festival acclaim, and a 2003 Academy Award for Best Animated Feature. Miyazaki was not entirely ready to receive the Oscar. As he told Devin Gordon of *Newsweek*, "Actually, your country had just started the war against Iraq, and I had a great deal of rage about that. So I felt some hesitation about the award."

Miyazaki continued making animated shorts exclusively for the visitors of the Studio Ghibli Museum, such as *Koro's Big Day Out* and *Mei and the Kitten Bus*. He also served as producer for *The Cat Returns,* a sequel to *Whisper of the Heart.* In 2004 he issued a new film, *Howl's Moving Castle,* adapted from a science fiction adventure by Welsh author Diana Wynne Jones. The story follows Sophie, a young girl who is put under a spell by the Witch of the Waste. She then joins the young wizard Howl on a strange journey in order to break the spell. Disney released an English version featuring the voice talents of Christian Bale, Billy Crystal, and Lauren Bacall.

Though it received a wide international release, the film had a complicated storyline that was misunderstood by many audiences. Miyazaki told Steve Daly of *Entertainment Weekly*, "I don't provide unnecessary explanations. If you want that, you're not going to like my movie. That's just the way it is." Indeed many of Miyazaki's films, although made for and enjoyed by children, have matched narrative complexity with intricate visual detail. *Howl's Moving Castle* was nominated for the 2006 Academy Award for Best Animated Feature, but lost the Oscar to *Wallace & Gromit in The Curse of the Were-Rabbit.*

Somewhat inappropriately nicknamed the Walt Disney of Japan, Miyazaki has proven himself to be more of an animation virtuoso than a business entrepreneur. As Tim Morrison wrote in *Time,* "Miyazaki is Walt Disney, Steven Spielberg, and Orson Welles combined, with a dash of Claude Monet in his sumptuous landscapes and more than a smidgen of Roald Dahl in his sly, sophisticated understanding of children." In 2005 Miyazaki was honored with a Golden Lion for Lifetime Achievement from the Venice Film Festival. Miyazaki's son Goro has released his first animated feature, *Tales From Earthsea,* based on the works of author Ursula K. LeGuin. With no plans for retirement as of 2007, Hayao Miyazaki continued to work as CEO of Studio Ghibli and was at work a new feature, *Ponyo on a Cliff.*

Books

Authors and Artists for Young Adults, Volume 37, Gale Group, 2000.
Cavallaro, Dani, *The Animé Art of Hayao Miyazaki,* McFarland, 2006.
International Directory of Business Biographies, 4 vols., St. James Press, 2005.
Newsmakers, Issue 2, Thomson Gale, 2006.

Periodicals

Chicago Sun-Times, December 23, 2001.
Entertainment Weekly, June 24, 2005.
Guardian (London, England), September 14, 2005.
Newsweek, June 20, 2005.
Variety, August 29, 2005.

Online

''Hayao Miyazaki,'' *All Movie Guide,* http://www.allmovie.com (November 25, 2007).
''Hayao Miyazaki,'' *Time,* http://www.time.com/time/magazine/article/0,9171,1554962,00.html (November 25, 2007). □

Bernard Moitessier

One of the greatest seafaring adventurers of all time, French sailor and author Bernard Moitessier (1925-1994) gained notoriety in 1969 after completing a solo, 10-month, nonstop trip in which he circled the globe one and a half times, logging 37,455 miles without setting foot on land. An avid skipper and gifted writer, Moitessier wrote about his journeys at sea, and his books remain favorites among maritime enthusiasts.

Raised in French Indochina

Moitessier was born on April 10, 1925, in what is now Vietnam, but at the time was known as French Indochina. His parents hailed from France but had relocated to Southeast Asia a few weeks before his birth. Back then, Vietnam was a French colony filled with plantations that exported cash crops like tobacco, indigo, tea and coffee. Moitessier's mother had studied art at the École des Beaux Arts in Paris. His father, Robert, had a business degree from the Paris-based Hautes Études Commerciales. Once in Vietnam, Moitessier's father ran a small importing business in Saigon.

The oldest of five children, Moitessier grew up in a privileged household that included a nanny and cook, and rides to elementary school in a rickshaw. Their home was enormous, complete with offices and storerooms for Robert Moitessier's business. The place overflowed with Ovaltine and barrels of wine. In the courtyards, workers washed and refilled bottles with wine, then crated them for delivery to shopkeepers. Despite their father's success, the children

grew up in a Spartan household without amenities like mattresses. They slept like the Vietnamese, on little mats atop wooden pallets. A strict disciplinarian, Robert Moitessier admonished his children for poor posture and whipped them for misbehavior and especially for poor grades.

One of Moitessier's favorite childhood activities was shooting his slingshot. In Saigon the streets were lined with fruit trees bursting with mangoes and tamarinds. Moitessier and his friends knocked down the fruits with their slingshots, making sure to hit the stem so as not to bruise the fruit. He also enjoyed visiting the market, where the streets were clogged with peddlers and artisans, bicycles and horse-drawn carts. He rarely saw a motorized vehicle in Saigon.

Drawn to the Sea

Moitessier sometimes skipped school to stroll the riverbanks and watch the Chinese sailing vessels known as junks. He was particularly intrigued by the boats from the Annam coast, which resembled the fish baskets he saw at the market. The bow—or front part—was made of wood, but the majority of the hull was constructed from woven bamboo sealed with a mixture of cow manure, a tar-like resin known as pitch, and wood oil. One day, Moitessier befriended a sailor from one of the vessels and was invited on board. The man demonstrated how the rudder worked and told Moitessier the vessel could carry 50 tons of rice. Moitessier told the man he would give anything to sail away with him. When they finally said goodbye, the man gave Moitessier a replica of his boat, carved from a coconut.

The Moitessier family spent summer vacations in a village close to the Cambodian border on the Gulf of Siam, where Robert Moitessier had received a land grant to plant rice. The village where they stayed consisted of a mile-long stretch of about 20 mud huts with thatched roofs. For the villagers, fishing was a way of life. The community owned about five junks, which everyone shared. Fascinated with all things nautical, Moitessier helped the village men repair and caulk the boats at the start of each fishing season. His favorite part was going out on the open sea with them.

For Moitessier, trips to the remote village became the most vibrant part of his childhood. ''There, my brothers and I lived in almost limitless freedom, a freedom of the senses and the body so intense we practically turned into little jungle animals,'' he recalled in his memoir, *Tamata and the Alliance.* Returning to Saigon each fall for school was rough on Moitessier. During class, he gazed out the windows and daydreamed about life beyond the school walls, covering his notebooks with sketches of boats. In his memoir, Moitessier wrote that a teacher once remarked: ''You are not only a lazy dunce, but a cretin and an incorrigible. Boys like you never amount to anything in life. Given to anarchy.'' By age 15, Moitessier had been kicked out of all the local schools and ended up at a newly opened agriculture school that sat 30 miles from Saigon on the edge of the jungle.

Fought in the Indochina War

After finishing school, Moitessier, just 18, landed a job at the Indochinese Rubber Plantation Company, where he supervised some 300 workers. Each day he covered more than 20 miles on his bicycle, overseeing every aspect of the operation, from the planting to the harvesting of the latex. One day, as Moitessier was studying a stately tree, he had a vision that prompted him to leave the job. Writing in his memoir, Moitessier recalled the experience of telling his boss he was leaving. ''I told him that my father needed me in his business in Saigon and also for his rice paddies, which was true. But I didn't tell him about the tree I had found in the forest while hunting. . . . The tree that climbed to the sky as I looked at it . . . and which became planks . . . which became a junk . . . and which was telling me that the world is limitless.''

Moitessier returned to Saigon and settled into life running the family business, though the job felt suffocating to him. World War II was in full swing, and tensions in Southeast Asia mounted as Japanese and French forces jockeyed for control of the area. The war ended in 1945, but the fighting was far from over in Vietnam, as the pro-Communist Viet Minh continued their war for independence, seeking unification of the area. Anti-French demonstrations became common and the Viet Minh killed off Frenchmen and pro-French Vietnamese. Moitessier and his brothers joined the Volunteer Liberation Group, which was composed of French and Eurasian soldiers who sought to overthrow the Viet Minh. Eventually, Moitessier landed aboard the *Gazelle,* a 600-ton gunboat operated by the French military. He was taken on board as an interpreter because he spoke Vietnamese fluently, and spent the next several months patrolling the waters of Southeast Asia. After being discharged from the military, he rejoined his father's business.

Took to the Winds

In 1952 Moitessier's dream came true—he finally procured his own boat, the *Marie-Thérèse,* and set sail from Kampot, Cambodia, in search of life on the open sea; he was 27. Less than a year later, he encountered a monsoon and wrecked his boat on the Chagos atoll in the Indian Ocean. A British naval ship rescued Moitessier and delivered him to the island of Mauritius, where he worked odd jobs and built a new ship from scratch. Around 1955 he set sail in his new ship, the *Marie-Thérèse II.* He sailed to South Africa, Brazil, and the West Indies before wrecking near Trinidad in 1958. At 34, Moitessier found himself a penniless, shipwrecked castaway. He returned to France and took a job as a drug salesman. At around this time he began writing, and published *Vagabond des Mers du Sud* (Sailing to the Reefs) in 1960, which described his early sea misadventures.

While in France, Moitessier met and married a woman named Françoise. He also procured another ship—the twin-masted, steel-built, 39-foot-long, red-bottomed *Joshua.* Ready for another adventure, Moitessier and his wife set sail in 1963. During one leg of their ''honeymoon'' trip, they sailed 14,216 miles from the French Polynesian Island of Moorea to Alicante, Spain, in 126 days without stopping at any ports. Their journey ended in Europe in 1966 and Moitessier settled down to write a book about the trip, *Cap Horn à la Voile* (Cape Horn: The Logical Route). In this book, Moitessier gives a firsthand account of the delights and dangers that come with sailing around Cape Horn, the southernmost tip of South America, in some of the ocean's most treacherous waters. In nautical circles the book became a must-read, not only for its practical advice, but also for its eloquent passages.

Raced Around the World

In 1968 Moitessier entered the Golden Globe competition—a solo, around-the-world, nonstop yacht race sponsored by Britain's *Sunday Times.* The course included sailing around Africa's Cape of Good Hope, Australia's Cape Leeuwin and South America's Cape Horn. There were nine contestants. Moitessier set sail from Plymouth, England, on August 21, 1968, aboard the *Joshua.* In 200 days he covered 33,000 miles. By this time, many of the other sailors had dropped out of the race. Many struggled to weather the storms, gear failures and loneliness of the voyage, all while Moitessier enjoyed the sail immensely. He entertained himself by doing yoga poses naked on the deck, listening to the waves, and communing with nature. Moitessier had a substantial lead as he passed around Cape Horn and had only to sail north, back to England, to win the race and claim the cash prize and celebrity that awaited his arrival. Instead he turned around, deciding he wanted to circle the globe twice.

Moitessier's decision surprised the sailing world, as well as his wife, who suggested seven months of solitude might have driven him mad. Another competitor had committed suicide during the race. Only one man finished.

Moitessier finally ran out of supplies and docked at Papeete, Tahiti, on June 21, 1969, having completed a journey of 37,455 miles in 303 days. This is believed to be the world's longest recorded nonstop solo sailing voyage. According to the London *Times,* Moitessier explained his actions to reporters this way: "You have to understand that when one is months and months alone, one evolves; some say people go nuts. I went crazy in my own fashion. For four months all I saw were the stars. I didn't hear an unnatural sound. A purity grows out of that kind of solitude." For Moitessier, the purity was so perfect he did not want the feeling to end, so he sailed on.

After the voyage, Moitessier settled in Ahe, Tahiti, and lived in a bamboo beach cottage. He spent the next few years writing *La Longue Route* (The Long Way), a memoir of the race. It was published in 1974 and Moitessier donated all royalties to the Pope. While in Tahiti, he met Iléana, a French-Romanian woman in search of adventure who was traveling the world with a suitcase full of poetry books. Their son, Stephan, was born in 1971. Moitessier continued sailing, visiting New Zealand in 1973 and Israel in 1974. In 1975 he settled down in Ahe to spend more time with his son. He spent the next few years sailing between the nearby islands and promoting ecological issues. In 1982 he lost the *Joshua* in a shipwreck near Cabo San Lucas, Mexico, and within a year had acquired the *Tamata,* which he sailed until the end of his life.

During the 1980s Moitessier was a vocal opponent of France's underground nuclear test program, which was detonating devices in French Polynesia. He also wrote hundreds of letters to U.S. publications urging nuclear disarmament. During the last years of his life, Moitessier was busy writing his memoir, *Tamata et l'Alliance* (Tamata and the Alliance), which he finished in 1993. Moitessier died on June 16, 1994, in Paris, France, and was buried in Brittany, France, in a cemetery filled with sailors and fishermen.

Books

Moitessier, Bernard, *Tamata and the Alliance,* Sheridan House, 1995.

Periodicals

Globe and Mail (Canada), February 15, 2003.
New York Times, June 22, 1969; June 3, 2001.
Times (London), June 23, 1994. □

Thomas Moore

The Irish poet Thomas Moore (1779-1852) gave popular music a strong flavor of his native country with his *Irish Melodies,* lyric poems of love and nostalgia that he set to traditional Irish tunes or new music he had composed himself.

I n his own time, Moore was considered a major figure in the literature of the British Isles, comparable in stature to such poets as Lord Byron and Percy Bysshe Shelley, both of whom he numbered among his friends. His output ranged from epic poetry to satire, and he was an energetic writer of prose who authored the first major biographies of several important figures of nineteenth-century literature and politics. But it is the *Irish Melodies,* which appeared between 1807 and 1835, for which Moore remains best known today. They include such evergreen melodies as "The Last Rose of Summer," "Believe Me, If All Those Endearing Young Charms," and "The Minstrel Boy."

Published Poems at 14

Thomas Moore was born on May 28, 1779, in Dublin. His background might be called lower middle class today; his father, John Moore, was a shoemaker and grocer and later the manager of an army barracks. His mother, Anastasia Codd Moore, had a strong interest in the arts, and young Thomas was placed in Dublin's top private schools, including (from 1786) the English Grammar School, considered the best in the city, and later Dr. Carr's Latin School, which prepared him for a university education. He was a top-notch student who had his first poems published in the Dublin magazine *Anthologia Hibernica* in 1793 when he as just 14. He also appeared in stage plays; he was always an enthusiastic performer and would later help popularize many of the *Irish Melodies* himself by singing them in concert.

Despite his academic accomplishments, Moore faced discrimination as a Catholic in a British and Protestant-controlled Ireland. His application at Trinity College ranked high among those of incoming students, but he was ineligible to receive a scholarship for which he otherwise would have qualified, and his father had to pay his tuition. At Trinity, Moore became friends with two other Irish students, Robert Emmett and Edward Hudson, who became leaders in a 1798 rebellion against English rule. Moore, who had written an anonymous pamphlet in support of the rebel cause, was questioned by British officers and described his own activities but did not name those of his friends. He was allowed to remain at Trinity.

Moore's collegiate career was nevertheless successful in spite of these upheavals. He received a bachelor's degree in 1799, by which time he had already begun his translation of the Odes of the ancient Greek poet Anacreon. His translation was published in 1800 and sold well. Moore worked on a law degree in London, but abandoned it and never practiced law. He settled on a career as a writer but rejected the title of Irish Poet Laureate, arranged for him by an influential friend, because he felt it would cramp his ability to express controversial political ideas. Instead, in 1803, Moore took a British government post as Registrar of the Admiralty Prize-Court for the colony of Bermuda. He sailed for the New World in the fall of 1803, arriving in 1804 via Norfolk, Virginia. On this trip Moore toured the United States and Canada, leaving a deputy in charge in Bermuda. He was impressed by Niagara Falls but disliked the New World and its egalitarian atmosphere; the young United States would be a prime target of his satirical writings in years to come.

In 1801 Moore published some of his youthful poems in a volume called *The Poetical Works of Thomas Little Jr.,* the pseudonym probably referring to his short stature—he stood only slightly over five feet tall. In 1806 Moore published a second book, *Epistles, Odes, and Other Poems.* Both books contained romantic passages that by the standards of the time were considered risqué. They succeeded in spreading his name in the literary world but attracted some negative reviews. The worst came from Francis Jeffrey, the editor of the *Edinburgh Review.* Moore challenged Jeffrey to a duel that became famous for its incomplete status; police were called to break it up before it could begin, and when it was revealed that Jeffrey's gun had been unloaded the whole time, Moore became the subject of ridicule.

Published *Irish Melodies*

Moore bounced back in 1807 with the first volume of the *Irish Melodies,* originally written at the suggestion of the publishers James and William Power. Folk song collections like Moore's were not uncommon at the time; even the German composer Ludwig van Beethoven published several collections of folk songs from the British Isles. Moore's *Irish Melodies* were also prefigured by the folk song collecting activities of Sir Walter Scott in Scotland, but Moore, who was assisted in the musical arrangements of the songs by his friend Sir John Stevenson, outstripped his predecessors commercially. The songs were immediately successful in Ireland, and then in England; over the first half of the nineteenth century

they spread across Europe and were translated into many languages. In the United States, Moore's *Irish Melodies* inspired a whole tradition of Irish-flavored melodies running through the works of Stephen Foster (whose "I Dream of Jeannie with the Light Brown Hair" strongly resembles Moore's compositions) and beyond.

Moore's 124 melodies contained 40 about love, 30 about Ireland, 15 about wine and friendship, 20 on miscellaneous life topics, 10 on people and events of the times, 6 about nature, and 6 on autobiographical topics (some of which overlapped with other categories). In years to come they would give Moore the general distinction of being the "Poet of the People of Ireland," with such lyrics as " 'Tis the last rose of summer / Left blooming alone / All her lovely companions / Are faded and gone." Unlike the works of Scottish poet Robert Burns, Moore's Irish music was adapted for English and assimilated Irish consumption; he did not use the Gaelic language or heavy Irish dialect in his texts. With his financial status assured, Moore married actress Elizabeth (Bessy) Dyke in 1811. For the rest of his life he lived in England, not Ireland. The pair had five children whom they raised Protestant, and in later years Moore would be criticized by hardcore Irish nationalists as insufficiently devoted to the cause.

However, Moore worked to embed messages supportive of the Irish cause in some of his writings. Chief among these was the long poem *Lalla Rookh,* published in 1817 and acquired from Moore by the publisher Longmans for $15,000, the highest price ever paid for a poem up to that time. The poem consists of four shorter tales set in the Middle East and centering on a military struggle between Persians and their Arab rulers. The poem was hailed by British travelers for its realistic depictions of life in the Middle East, but for Irish readers it carried overtones of Ireland's long struggle against Great Britain. Despite the profits from *Lalla Rookh,* Moore suffered a financial setback when it came to light that his deputy in Bermuda had embezzled and absconded with $30,000, for which Moore was held responsible. Rather than allow friends to help, Moore fled England and spent three years in Paris.

In 1813 Moore published the first in a series of satirical books, *Intercepted Letters, or, The Twopenny Post Bag.* He followed that up with tales of the perambulations of a fictitious Fudge Family that allowed him to focus on whatever targets he chose at a given time. An example was 1818's *The Fudge Family in Paris.* Moore used the pseudonym Thomas Brown the Younger for these books, but the real identity of the author was no secret. The Fudge Family books presume a body of topical knowledge that few readers have today, but they were quite successful in their own time and enabled Moore and his family to move to an old country house called Sloperton Cottage in the Wiltshire region. He continued to issue satirical works such as *Odes upon Cash, Corn, Catholics, and Other Matters* (1828).

Moore took up the cause of Irish peasants directly in 1824 with a prose story called *Memoirs of Captain Rock,* a satirical work in which he created a Robin Hood-like Irish folk hero who takes the side of peasants against their landlord. Another Moore work identified with his Irish sympathies was *The Life and Death of Lord Edward Fitzgerald,* a biography of one of the leaders of the 1798 revolt of the United Irishmen. Moore continued to write new *Irish Melodies* and also began new musical collections of *National Airs* and *Sacred Songs.* In 1827 he produced a novel, *The Epicurean,* which was set in third-century Egypt and in which he attempted to justify his own unorthodox approach to Christianity. He reflected on his own Catholic faith in his 1833 book *Travels of an Irish Gentlemen in Search of a Religion.*

Penned Biography of Byron

In addition to the Fitzgerald work he wrote a biography of the 18th-century comic playwright Richard Brinsley Sheridan (*Life of Sheridan,* 1825), and, in 1830, *Life of Byron,* about the British poet George Gordon, Lord Byron. Moore was uniquely situated to write a biography of Byron because he had been in possession of the poet's letters, but he is thought to have burned those letters because of their controversial content. Moore is considered one of England's greatest literary biographers.

In later life, Moore worked on a giant *History of Ireland* that remained unfinished at his death. In 1841 he issued a collection of his own works in ten volumes, writing an autobiographical preface to each volume. He outlived all five of his children, several of whom died young; his son Thomas lived a dissolute life and died in Africa in 1845. Moore himself did not see Ireland after 1838. In 1846

Moore's health began to decline, and he suffered from senile dementia, which began very suddenly, during the last three years of his life. He died at Sloperton Cottage on February 25, 1852. New editions of the *Irish Melodies* continued to appear throughout the nineteenth century, and they were translated into languages as distant as Hungarian, Polish, and Russian. In the words of The Contemplator Web site, "Thomas Moore's work popularized Irish music throughout the world."

Books

Baker's Biographical Dictionary of Music and Musicians, centennial ed., edited by Nicolas Slonimsky, Schirmer, 2001.
Dictionary of Literary Biography, volume 144, Gale, 1994.
Jones, Howard Mumford, *The Harp That Once—A Chronicle of the Life of Thomas Moore,* Holt, 1937.
Strong, L.A.G., *The Minstrel Boy: A Portrait of Tom Moore,* Knopf, 1937.
White, Terence de Vere, *Tom Moore The Irish Poet,* Hamilton, 1977.

Online

"The Contemplator's Short History of Thomas Moore," The Contemplator, http://www.contemplator.com/history/tmoore.html (February 8. 2008).
"Thomas Moore (1779-1852)," Books and Writers, http://www.kirjasto.sci.fi/tmoore.htm (February 8, 2008).
"Thomas Moore: 1779-1852," http://www.lang.nagoya-u.ac.jp/~matsuoka/Moore.html (February 8, 2008). □

N

Andre Norton

American author Andre Norton (1912-2005) was among the most prolific and successful writers of the twentieth century in the science fiction and fantasy genres, with some 150 novels and 100 short stories to her credit.

Norton was one of just a few female science fiction writers to reach the top echelon in the genre and, unlike most of her male counterparts, she had little interest in the technologies of space propulsion and weaponry that were central to so many science fiction tales. Instead, Norton tended to use the exotic settings of science fiction and fantasy as vehicles for coming-of-age stories and explorations of personal growth and psychology. Over a writing career spanning more than 75 years, Norton created a stunning variety of imaginary worlds, often, especially in her later years, working with collaborators in order to provide a constant flow of new literary products.

Edited School Newspaper Section

A native of Cleveland, Ohio, Alice Mary Norton was born on February 17, 1912. Her father, Adalbert Freely Norton, was a carpet salesman. Norton's mother, Bertha, began to read her stories and poetry when she was two. Norton attended Collinwood High School on Cleveland's east side, where she was editor of the fiction section of the school's newspaper, the *Collinwood Spotlight.* During her senior year she wrote her first novel; it was revised and later published in 1938 as *Ralestone Luck.* Like her other early books it was not science fiction but a historical romance.

After graduating from high school in 1930, Norton enrolled at Western Reserve University (now Case Western Reserve University), hoping to become a history teacher. The Great Depression hit her family hard, however, and Norton was forced to drop out after her freshman year. She got a job at the Cleveland Public Library, continuing to study creative writing in night classes. In 1932 Norton was promoted to the post of children's librarian and gained a broad familiarity with the field of literature for young people. With only a brief interlude during World War II, when she moved to Washington, D.C., to work for the Library of Congress (and to briefly operate a bookstore of her own in Maryland), Norton worked for the Cleveland Public Library for the next 18 years. At one point or another she put in work time at 38 of the library's 40 branches.

In the early 1930s Norton continued to write historical fiction. Her first published novel, *The Prince Commands,* was published by Appleton Century in New York in 1934, when she was 22. It was at that time, at a publisher's suggestion, that she took the name Andre; it was thought that the audience for her stories would be primarily male, and that she should have a name to match. Norton actually thought of the name as something of a compromise. "As to Andre," she said in an interview quoted on the Web site of the Science Fiction and Fantasy Writers of America, it was "just a properly ambiguous either-sex name to be worn by a female who makes a living writing male adventure stories." Radio interviewers were sometimes quite surprised when Norton showed up wearing a skirt. After the publication of *Ralestone Luck,* Norton wrote several spy novels during World War II, including *Follow the Drum* (1942) and *The Sword Is Drawn* (1944). The latter book marked a new level of success for Norton; it was published in the United States by the major Houghton Mifflin house, and in England by the even more prestigious Oxford University

Press. She remained equally popular in England and the United States. Later, in the early 1960s, she wrote a few Western novels.

Began Writing Science Fiction

As the science fiction genre expanded in the 1930s and 1940s, Norton became an avid reader, and she began writing science fiction herself. Once again using a new name, Andrew North, she published her first science fiction story, "People of the Crater," in 1947. She continued to use the name Andrew North for her science fiction writings until the mid-1950s. In 1950 Norton finally left the Cleveland Public Library to take a job as an editor at Gnome Press, a science fiction publisher in New York City. She remained there until 1958, when her growing success allowed her to become a full-time writer.

Norton's turn to science fiction was well timed, for the market for science fiction novels, often appearing in paperback editions, exploded in the 1950s. Her first science fiction novel was *Starman's Son: 2250*, published by Harcourt in 1952; by the time Norton left Gnome in 1958 she had written 23 novels. *Starman's Son* contained traits characteristic of Norton's fiction as a whole: it told of a being named Fors who has been turned into a mutant on a strange planet and is in search of a city free of the radiation that has damaged him and ruined his life. Through success in a series of tests he learns to believe in himself. For a companion, Fors has a cat, with whom he can communicate through telepathy, a feature that appeared in several of Norton's later books.

Like many of the early novels of science fiction giant Robert A. Heinlein, Norton's books of the early 1950s were at first published as novels for young adults. There was nothing about them thematically, however, that precluded their having an appeal to adult readers, and Ace Books editor Donald A. Wollheim acquired the rights to *Starman's Son* and retitled it *Daybreak 2250*. The book sold well among adults, and many of Norton's subsequent novels appeared in Ace's adult line.

The only downside to this arrangement was that Norton stayed largely under the critical radar, even among science fiction critics, because she was regarded as a young adult author. In general, the deeper themes of her books, often concerned with the inner lives of their characters rather than with high tech razzle-dazzle, remained unappreciated by critics and readers simply because she had such an effective talent for pure storytelling. Often the only technological element in a Norton novel was the spaceship that had transported the characters to the field of action. She was not only indifferent to technology as a writer but actively disliked it. "I think the human race made a bad mistake at the beginning of the Industrial Revolution," she said in an interview quoted by Christopher Lehmann-Haupt of the *New York Times*. "We leaped for the mechanical things. . . . People need the use of their hands to feel creative." Her work generally balanced on the fuzzy dividing line between science fiction and fantasy, and some of it fell firmly into the fantasy category.

Succession of Hits

Norton hit her stride commercially in the late 1950s with a succession of hit novels, including *The Beast Master* (1959, adapted into a film in 1982), *Catseye* (1961, which again explored telepathy between humans and animals), and *Lord of Thunder* (1962). Norton became most famous, however, not for any of these individual books but for a series, *Witch World,* which began in 1963 with a single novel simply entitled *Witch World.* The series eventually grew to encompass more than 30 novels, depicting in detail many aspects of a fantasy world called Estcarp, entered by the English protagonist Simon Tregarth through a metaphysical gate he has found in a large old stone in England's Cornwall region. Estcarp is a vaguely medieval world, ruled by witches with special powers gained from jewels. The stories tell of the exploits of Tregarth, his wife, Jaelithe, and their three children, often moving into sword-and-sorcery action but still keeping Norton's focus on young people and their psychological growth. Norton began several other series during her best-selling years from the 1960s through the 1980s; these included *Halfblood Chronicles, Time Traders, Solar Queen,* and *Magic.*

As these series developed, Norton often began to work in collaboration with younger writers, beginning around the late 1970s. Her collaborators included Phyllis Miller, Susan Shwartz, Marion Zimmer Bradley, and Mercedes Lackey. Norton did more than just provide her collaborator with an outline and then exit the scene; she was closely involved in every stage of the collaboration. In the words of John Clute of London's *Independent,* "It seems clear that she maintained a strict overview, and often a hands-on control of detail; but it does also seem that most of these co-signed works were not in fact substantially written by her." In Clute's opinion, "no one can pretend that the flood of titles in the last few decades enhanced her reputation. They are respectable hack work; but they do not have the Norton glow."

Norton, who apparently never married or had children, was always reticent about her personal life. Living alone, she moved to Winter Park, Florida, in 1966, and to Murfreesboro, Tennessee, in 1997, where she was cared for by a friend, Sue Stewart. For companionship she lived with large numbers of cats, and she edited a group of anthologies of science fiction and fantasy cat stories under the series title *Catfantastic.* In 1999 Norton founded a writers' retreat and library called High Hallack; the center was closed in 2003 or 2004, but many younger science fiction writers, including Ursula K. LeGuin, testified after Norton's death to the inspiration they had received from Norton early in their careers.

Norton kept writing into her early 90s. At her death in Murfreesboro (from congestive heart failure) on March 17, 2005, she had completed a novel she had written entirely herself, *Three Hands for Scorpio*; its publisher, Tor Books, printed one copy of the book before her death so that she could see it. The story told of a group of sisters who are kidnapped and escape an underground world by their own wits and through the help of a young man and his powerful catlike sidekick. Several Norton collaborations were also underway at the time of her death and were completed and published posthumously. Norton asked to be cremated with copies of her first and last books. In her later years she had amassed a large collection of science fiction and fantasy awards, including the Grand Master Nebula award in 1983, and before her death she approved the creation of an Andre Norton Award for young adult novels, to be presented by the Science Fiction and Fantasy Writers of America.

Books

Dictionary of Literary Biography, volume 8, Gale, 1981.
Schlobin, Roger C., *Andre Norton,* Gregg Press, 1979.
St. James Guide to Fantasy Writers, St. James Press, 1996.
Stephensen-Payne, Phil, *Andre Norton: Grand Master of the Witch World—A Working Bibliography,* Galactic Central, 1991.

Periodicals

Daily Telegraph (London, England), March 19, 2005.
Guardian (London, England), March 29, 2005.
Independent (London, England), March 21, 2005.
New York Times, March 18, 2005.

Online

"Andre Norton (1912–2005)," Science Fiction and Fantasy Writers of America, http://www.sfwa.org/news/anorton.htm (February 10, 2008).
"Andre Norton dies at age 93," Andre Norton Official Web site, http://www.andre-norton.org (February 10, 2008).
Contemporary Authors Online. Gale, 2008, http://galenet.gale group.com/servlet/BioRC (February 10, 2008). □

Said Nursî

Turkish religious leader Said Nursî (1876-1960) was an Islamic philosopher who authored the Risale–i Nur Collection, a huge Quranic commentary of more than five thousand pages. A man of enormous influence in Middle Eastern politics and religion, he is credited with helping to inspire resurgence in the Islam faith through his writings and teachings.

In his rich, full life, Said Nursî witnessed and experienced much. As both an observer and participant during his eighty–four years, he lived through the decline of the Ottoman Empire, World War I and the emergence of the modern Turkish Republic. An influential Islamic teacher and philosopher, he also endured religious oppression and suffered through prolonged periods of exile and imprisonment. He was resilient, however, and emerged as an important teacher and philosopher who inspired generations of students who embraced his writings.

Early Life

Said Nursî, later known as Bediüzzaman Said Nursî, was born in 1876 in Nurs, a small village in the province of Bitlis in eastern Turkey. The middle child in a family of seven children, he was raised in a sun–dried brick

house. His parents were Kurdish farmers who were devout and humble.

In the agricultural setting, Nursî lived in close harmony with nature, aware and curious about his natural surroundings. Considered an exceptionally child bright, he memorized the manuals of the classical Islamic fields of knowledge in a short time. His remarkable academic accomplishments earned him the title "Bediüzzaman," which means "the wonder of the time."

Nursî received his basic, formal education from the best–known scholars in his region. He became a popular student with his teachers, due to his high intelligence and large capacity for learning. When he reached adolescence, he remained an enthusiastic student and continued exhibiting his characteristic sharp memory. By the time he was fourteen, he completed the traditional Turkish madrasah education. At sixteen, he could hold his own in debates with distinguished scholars.

Following his madrasah education, Nursî studied the physical sciences, mathematics and philosophy. As his learning progressed, he came to the conclusion that the traditional Turkish madrasah education was inadequate. Essentially, he believed that the world was entering a new age that would place high value on science and logic, and he felt that the classical theological curriculum was ill–equipped to remove the doubts an individual might experience regarding the Quran and Islam. Possessing extensive scientific knowledge, Nursî would always strive to integrate science with theology throughout his life, via his writings and teachings. According to his worldview, modern physical sciences and the Quran were not irreconcilable. Indeed, he felt that science made it easier for people to better understand the truths revealed in the Quran.

Based upon his own copious learning, Nursî developed an Islamic educational curriculum that combined both theological teachings and modern sciences, both of which he felt should be provided at religious and modern schools alike, as this would simultaneously eliminate disbelief on one hand, and fanaticism on the other. He even developed a plan to establish a university, called Medrestu'z Zehra (the Resplendent Madrasah), where both of these disciplines would be taught. In 1917, he went to Istanbul to promote the plan to Sultan Abdul Hamid. Subsequently, he received funding for the construction of the university. However, it only got as far as the building's foundation. Further construction was halted with the outbreak of World War I.

Commanded a Volunteer Regiment

During the war, Nursî served as the commander of a volunteer regiment assigned to the Caucasian front in eastern Anatolia, where he demonstrated heroism in battle. To maintain his regiment's morale, he entered the trenches that were besieged by constant shelling. Later, he received a medal.

While serving in the military, Nursî began composing what would become a celebrated commentary on the Quran. Written in the Arabic language, the work combined religious and natural sciences. Reportedly, Nursî wrote it while traveling on horseback and in the trenches on the front line. These efforts proved to be the beginnings of his major work, the *Risale–i Nur* (Epistle of Light), which eventually was endorsed by eminent scholars.

Work was interrupted, however, when Nursî became a prisoner of war. While fighting in a battle against invading Russian forces, he was captured along with ninety other officers and sent to a camp in Kostroma, in the northwestern region of Russia. At one point during his two–year internment, he was sentenced to death by firing squad after insulting a Russian General, Nicola Nicolaevich, the commander of the Caucasian front who was Czar Nicholas II's uncle. But the death sentence was rescinded at the very last moment, just as Nursî was reciting his prayers before the firing squad.

In early 1918, when Russia succumbed to chaos during the communist revolution, Nursî escaped from the prison camp and, after a long and arduous journey, made his way back to Istanbul. Upon his return to his homeland, he received a war medallion and was offered a government position, which he turned down. Instead, he accepted an appointment at Dar al–Hikmat al–Islamiya, a religious academy.

After World War I, British forces swept into Turkey, and Nursî again faced threats on his life, this time for denouncing the invaders in daily newspapers. His invectives were bitter and vehement, and, as quoted by the Islamic Information Service Web site, included, ''You dogs, who are more basely and utterly dog–like than any dog!!'' and ''Spit at the shameless face of the damned British!'' and made him a target of the occupiers.

But he survived and entered into what he considered the second phase of his life. In his mind, the historic period that included the end of the World War, the defeat of the Ottoman Empire and the occupation of Turkey marked his existence with a deep demarcation. He referred to the period leading up to and including these turbulent times as the ''Old Said,'' as he experienced a profound personal change and became deeply dissatisfied with the world. The next phase of his life would include isolation and spiritual solitude, not entirely self imposed.

Arrested and Exiled

During the Turkish War of Independence, which took place between 1919 and 1922 and displaced British rule, Nursî supported Turkish General Mustafa Kemal. In 1922, General Kemal, who now was part of the new Turkish military elite that came to power following the British occupation, invited Nursî to Ankara, so that he could take part in the reconstruction of the so–called New Turkey. But Nursî, realizing that the military sought to establish a secular republic that shunned Islam, declined the offer. Instead, to find peace through prayerful solitude, he relocated to Van.

His peace was shattered in 1925 when he was accused of participating in a rebellion in eastern Turkey. He was arrested and sent to Barla, a remote village located in the mountains of the Isparta province. Actually, Nursî played no part in the rebellion. The rebels had sought his help because of the strong influence he had over people, but he turned down their requests. ''The Sword is to be used against the outside enemy; it is not to be used inside,'' he told them, as reported on the Islamic Information Service Web site. ''Give

up your attempt, for it is doomed to failure and may end up in the annihilation of thousands of innocent men and women because of a few criminals.''

Despite his innocence, Nursî, along with hundreds of fellow Turkish citizens, was sent into exile. This would begin a twenty–five year period in his life in which he endured oppression and imprisonment.

Resumed work on *Risale–i Nur*

During his exile, Nursî resumed work on the *Risale–i Nur,* which would eventually form the basis for a religious–intellectual movement called Nurculuk. In his monumental work, Nursî attempted to establish links between Quranic verses and the natural world as well as to demonstrate that no contradictions existed between religion and science. Also, Nursî advanced the radical idea of God as the divine artisan of a mechanistic universe.

Risale–i Nur was actually a collection of dictated thoughts and sermons. In the eight and a half years that he spent in Barla, Nursî wrote approximately three–quarters of the *Risale–i Nur* collection. His followers made handwritten copies that they secretly circulated, as Turkey's new secular regime banned all religious writings. The collection was distributed in this fashion until 1946, when Nursî's students gained access to duplicating machines. It is estimated that previous to the automation, 600,000 handwritten copies were created and disseminated.

In this way, Nursî became the founder of the Nurcu movement. Even though he was exiled in a remote region and without money or property, Nursî still managed to have substantial impact on millions of Turkish men and women, due to the powerful effect of his writings. The movement quietly grew until 1950, and efforts to crush it proved fruitless. Afterward, it spread more openly. Nursî's influence would later extend beyond Turkey.

During his exile, which Nursî referred to as the second part of his life (the ''New Said''), he also wrote an essay about God and resurrection as well as thirty–three other pieces that were eventually collected as *Sozler* (The Words). He also compiled letters written to students in a collection called *Maktubat* (Letters). In addition, he wrote two more works: *Lem'alar* (The Flashes) and *Sualar* (The Rays).

In 1943, his essay on God got him into political trouble. He was arrested again and sent to prison. While awaiting his trial, he continued his work from prison, writing new essays and helping criminals to reform. Eventually, he was acquitted, but he was not granted his freedom. Instead, he was sent to Emirdag, another remote village, where he was arrested yet again. This time, he was sent to Afyon prison, a brutal place where Nursî endured great suffering. By this time, he was in his seventies and afflicted with several illnesses. He was placed in an isolation cell with broken windows, where he spent two harsh winters. Reportedly, he was also poisoned, but he survived this attempt on his life and his conviction was eventually overturned.

He received a reprieve of sorts in the new Turkish era that ensued. In 1950, the first free elections were held in Turkey, and a multi–party political system was established.

The newly formed Democratic Party, which Nursî supported, deposed the secular Republican People's Party and its hostile attitudes toward religion. In this new era of religious freedom, the first session of the new parliament revoked the ban over Adhan (the call to prayer). This new period in the Turkish Republic marked the beginning of a new, personal period in Nursî's life, which he called the "Third Said." During this period, his major works were published in Latin script, and the number of Nursî's students increased both within and outside of Turkey.

Died in Turkey

After a brief illness, Nursî died on March 23, 1960 in Urfa, in southeastern Turkey. Later that year his grave was moved to an unknown location in Isparta, where he had been exiled for so long during his life. Following his death, he continued to be an honored figure in Turkey and other Muslim nations. It has been commented that his *Risale–i Nur* helped keep the Muslim faith alive in Turkey during the period of religious oppression, and it played a part in the subsequent resurgence of Islam in that region of the world. Once a forbidden text, the *Risale–i Nur* is now available in many languages.

Online

"The Author of the Risale–i Nur: Bediuzzaman Said Nursî," risale-inur.com, http://www.risale-inur.com.tr/rnk/eng/tarihce/bsn.htm (November 10, 2007).

"Badiuzzaman Said Nursî (1877–1960)," Center for Islam and Science, http://www.cis-ca.org/voices/n/Nursî.htm (November 10, 2007).

"A Brief Biography of Said Nursî," Islamic Information Service, http://www.islamicinformationservice.com/Biography%20text.htm (November 10, 2007).

"A Brief Look at the Life of Bediuzzaman Said Nursî," Ummah.com, http://www.ummah.net/Al_adaab/biography/Nursî.html (November 10, 2007). □

Sven Nykvist

Swedish cinematographer Sven Nykvist (1922-2006) was among the most widely recognized and influential practitioners of his art in film history, with a distinctive style that added impact to Swedish art house classics and American movie hits alike.

Nykvist's camera work was particularly identified with the films of Ingmar Bergman (1919-2007), and he developed his style largely in the films he made with that legendary Swedish director. His style depended heavily on natural light, avoiding the use of complicated studio lighting effects, and he was a master at using ambient surroundings to deepen the psychological content of a scene. Often Nykvist's brilliance lay merely in his ability to find simple solutions. "The gaffers we work with can't believe how few lights Sven uses," American television commercial director Cal Bernstein, for whom Nykvist

often worked, told Robert Goldrich of *Back Stage*. "Sven looks at the trucks, asks 'What do you need all these lights for?' . . . He puts one light here, one there and he's ready to go." Bernstein also recalled a cinematographer friend who became obsessed with figuring out how Nykvist had set up the lighting in a particular scene in the film *Sacrifice*. Finally Bernstein agreed to ask Nykvist how he had done it, and Nykvist replied that he had lit the scene entirely with natural light, using no electric lights at all.

Saw Parents at Four-Year Intervals

Sven Vilhem Nykvist was born in Moheda, in Sweden's Smaland province, on December 3, 1922. His parents, Natanael and Gerda Nykvist, were Lutheran missionaries working in the Belgian Congo (now the Republic of Congo). They feared that their son would contract malaria in Africa, so they boarded him with relatives or in a home he shared with the children of other missionaries. As a child he lived with them for only one year of every five. Nykvist's parents sent word to his guardians that he was forbidden to go to the movies, which they considered sinful. The ban may have intensified the young Nykvist's interest in the burgeoning art form, and Nykvist's father also influenced his son in another way, as he was an avid photographer of African wildlife. Nykvist acquired a box camera and then a small movie camera, which he used to have himself filmed by a friend while practicing the high jump with his school track team.

There was no film school in Sweden in the late 1930s, so Nykvist enrolled at the Municipal School for Photographers in Stockholm. He landed his first film job at age 19, in 1941, as an assistant cameraman with Sandrews, the large Swedish studio that later issued many of Ingmar Bergman's films, working on a film called *The Poor Millionaire.* Unsure of his career choice, he went to visit his parents in Africa. While he was there, he shot footage for a documentary called *In the Footsteps of the Witch Doctor.* Back in Sweden, studio owner Anders Sandrew offered to acquire the documentary and distribute it. Nykvist then became an apprentice with Julius Jaenzon, the top Swedish cinematographer of the time, and he worked through the 1940s on a series of films that are now mostly forgotten. He never had any formal education in film, but he broadened his cinematic experience by working for a year as a cameraman at the Cinecittà studio in Rome, Italy.

Serious Swedish filmmakers of the time were often influenced by the Expressionist style, which featured heavy shadows, dramatic lighting and makeup, and sometimes surreal effects. As Nykvist gained greater experience, he began to win assignments with prominent directors such as Alf Sjöstrom. His path crossed that of Ingmar Bergman when he worked as a cinematographer filming the interior quarters of a circus troupe for Bergman's expressionist 1953 film *Sawdust and Tinsel.* At the time, Bergman was still working primarily with cinematographer Gunnar Fischer, but according to London's *Daily Telegraph* he remarked to Nykvist, "I think we should work a whole life together."

Nykvist continued to find his skills in demand in Sweden, working on seven films during the year 1956 alone. His breakthrough came in 1960 when Bergman became dissatisfied with Fischer's harsh style, on display in such stark classics as *The Seventh Seal,* and turned to Nykvist as he prepared to film the naturalistic revenge fable *The Virgin Spring.* From then on, Nykvist would work as director of photography on all of Bergman's films and television productions, except for his final film, *Saraband* (2003). The two men, who shared the experience of growing up in families headed by remote religious figures, worked so closely together that in many films it is difficult to tell where Bergman's inspiration ends and Nykvist's begins.

Observed Light Conditions Closely

Among the first films on which Nykvist worked with Bergman were a bleak trilogy dealing with the theme of loss of religious faith. One of the films, *Winter Light* (1963), dealt with a minister in a northern Swedish town, where there might be only three hours of daylight in winter. Nykvist remarked to Bergman that there would not be a great variety of lighting conditions on location, but Bergman replied, as Nykvist recalled in an American Film Institute seminar quoted on the Fathom Web site, "That's what you think. Let's go to the churches in northern Sweden." The pair spent weeks in the frozen Swedish north, "looking at the light during the three hours between eleven and two o'clock. We saw that it changed a lot, and it helped him in writing the script because he always writes the moods."

Thus Bergman helped Nykvist develop his famed sensitivity to natural light. Likewise, Nykvist helped devise several of Bergman's most famous cinematic images. One

came in *Persona* (1966), a study of schizophrenia in which the personalities of two women seem to merge at one point in the film. "Nykvist," noted the *Daily Telegraph,* "illustrated this in a single shot that can haunt the viewer for days afterwards. He took the left half of one girl's face and the right half of the other's and spliced them together to form a composite image that was spookily non-human." Nykvist worked with other Swedish filmmakers during the 1960s, such as Mai Zetterling on *Loving Couples* in 1964, but it was his work with Bergman that began to bring his name before international audiences.

All these films were in black and white, and Nykvist and Bergman approached the use of color gingerly after the failure of their comedy *Now About These Women,* shot "according to the Kodak rule book," as Nykvist said, according to the *Daily Telegraph.* When Nykvist did begin to work in color, however, he achieved some of his most brilliant successes. Bergman's *Cries and Whispers* (1972), a grim drama about a woman dying of cancer, featured powerful scenes bathed in the color red. Again Nykvist and Bergman spent several weeks observing the lighting in the house where the film was made. The amount of planning might seem excessive, but as Nykvist observed to Goldrich, "Everything [in production] goes much quicker. We finished 'Cries And Whispers' in 42 days." The film brought Nykvist his first Academy Award for Best Cinematography. Other Bergman films of the 1970s, including *Autumn Sonata* and the made-for-television *Scenes from a Marriage* also brought Nykvist critical acclaim.

When he began to work in the United States, Nykvist had to make several adjustments to his methods. Leisurely preproduction of the kind he enjoyed with Bergman was impossible. And, although it was a relaxation in union regulations that allowed U.S. directors to hire Nykvist as director of photography in the first place, he was still not allowed to actually operate the camera himself, as that still had to be done by a union employee. Nykvist's first American film was *Pretty Baby,* made in New Orleans by French director Louis Malle; despite the new restrictions under which he worked, the firm was critically acclaimed.

Talents Stimulated Demand

Nykvist found his services in great demand in the 1980s. Bergman's output was slowing, but Nykvist worked on two of the great films of the director's later years, *Fanny and Alexander* (which earned Nykvist his second Oscar in 1982) and *After the Rehearsal* (1984). In the United States, Nykvist served as cinematographer for various high profile films, including a 1981 remake of the film noir thriller *The Postman Always Rings Twice,* a 1988 film adaptation of Milan Kundera's Czech novel *The Unbearable Lightness of Being,* and several films by director Woody Allen, including *Crimes and Misdemeanors.*) Nykvist's marriage to his wife, Ulla, which began in 1952, dissolved in 1968; it produced two sons, one of whom committed suicide. His surviving son, Carl-Gustav Nykvist, became a film director and in 2000 made a documentary, *Light Keeps Me Company,* about his father's work.

Even after he became widely recognized as one of the greatest cinematographers alive, Nykvist continued to work on television commercials periodically. "When you make too long a stop in between features, you can lose touch," he explained to Goldrich. "A cinematographer is like a pianist, he has to train always. Otherwise you get like a boxer who hasn't been able to box for a long time. Commercials can help keep you sharp." He also set down his ideas on cinematography in a series of articles for *American Cinematographer,* France's *Positif,* and other magazines in the late 1980s.

Nykvist remained active almost until the end of his long life, and he was associated with several major hits in the 1990s, among them the 1993 comedy *Sleepless in Seattle.* He worked closely with Swedish directors after Bergman, making *What's Eating Gilbert Grape?* and other films with Lasse Hallström and *Kristin Lavransdotter* with actress-turned-director Liv Ullmann. Cinematography, like other aspects of filmmaking, was increasingly impacted by computer technology in the 1990s, but Nykvist had little interest in reinventing his art in old age. "Computers are now creating new traditions of cinematography, but I'm frankly happy I was born at the time I was and was able to experiment as I have done," he told Marlene Edmunds of *Variety.* In 1996 he was honored with a Lifetime Achievement Award by the American Society of Cinematographers. Returning to work with Woody Allen on *Celebrity* in 1998, he began to show signs of aphasia, a form of dementia, while working on the film. The last of his approximately 120 films was *Curtain Call* (1999). Nykvist died in Stockholm on September 20, 2006.

Books

International Dictionary of Films and Filmmakers, Volume 4: Writers and Production Artists, 4th ed., St. James Press, 2000.

Periodicals

Back Stage, February 5, 1988.
Daily Telegraph (London, England), September 21, 2006.
Guardian (London, England), September 22, 2006.
Independent (London, England), September 22, 2006.
New York Times, September 21, 2006.
Quadrant, November 2006.
Variety, February 17, 1997; September 25, 2006.

Online

"Shooting with Ingmar Bergman," Fathom, http://www.fathom .com/feature/122159/index.html (November 23, 2007).
"Sven Nykvist," *All Movie Guide,* http://www.allmovie.com (November 23, 2007). □

O

Eugene Ormandy

Hungarian-born American conductor Eugene Ormandy (1899-1985) was among the most widely acclaimed symphonic conductors of the twentieth century, molding the Philadelphia Orchestra into a unit that functioned as his personal musical instrument.

Ormandy, as much as any other major conductor, was defined by a relationship with a single institution. As conductor of the Philadelphia Orchestra from the late 1930s until his retirement in 1980 (and for several years after that as a frequent guest), he set a record that still stands for length of tenure with a major orchestra in the United States. "The Philadelphia Orchestra sound—it's me!," he proclaimed confidently, as quoted by Allen Hughes in the *New York Times.* And indeed he could claim credit for the lush string textures that emanated from the orchestra under his baton; a violinist by training, he schooled his players in the techniques that would allow them to produce the sound he wanted.

Entered Prestigious Academy at Age Five

Ormandy was born Jenö Blau on November 18, 1899, in Budapest, Hungary,. His family was Jewish. Ormandy's father, Benjamin Blau, was a dentist but had a passion for music that he passed along to all three of his sons; one of Ormandy's brothers became a New York Philharmonic Orchestra cellist and the other was a fine amateur harpist. Ormandy himself began playing the violin at age three, and he advanced so quickly that he was admitted to Budapest's Royal Academy of Music at the altogether unprecedented

age of five. His teachers at the academy were the best that Hungary had to offer at the time: the Gypsy-influenced virtuoso and composer Jenö Hubay (after whom Ormandy was named) on violin, Zoltán Kodály in composition, and Leo Weiner in theory and music literature.

Ormandy graduated at the age of 14, and after three years of further study he was ready to begin a career as a violinist, joining Germany's Blüthner Orchestra on tour during the last stages of World War I. Back in Budapest at age 20, Ormandy was named head of the violin department at the Royal Academy. He rounded out his education with studies in philosophy at the University of Budapest and then played a series of concerts in Austria and France in 1921. During this tour he began to use the name Jenö B. Ormándy. The source of this name is unclear, and Ormandy mysteriously refused to discuss it. The name Ormándy in Hungarian would mean "person from Ormánd,"; when Ormandy came to the United States he changed his first name, Jenö, to its English form, Eugene.

That move to the United States came about at the end of 1921 as Ormandy, following in the footsteps of many other young European musicians, sought to cash in on an American appetite for Old World classical talent. He was offered $30,000 to play 300 concerts, but when he arrived in New York he found the promoter bankrupt and the tour nonexistent. For two weeks he wandered the streets, looking for work, as his assets dwindled to a single nickel. Finally a fellow Hungarian suggested he audition for the pit orchestra at the Capitol Theatre, a silent movie palace. He was accepted, and the orchestra's conductor, upon discovering his skills, moved him to the position of concertmaster (the lead violinist, who takes short solos and supervises the tuning of the orchestra) within a week. In 1922 Ormandy married his first wife, Stephanie Goldner, a harpist and fellow orchestra

member (and fellow Hungarian). The marriage lasted until 1947, producing two daughters who both died as infants from a blood disease.

The transition from concerts in Europe's musical capitals to the pit orchestra in a movie house might seem to have been a step down for Ormandy, but he later looked back gratefully on this stage of his career. The orchestra had to learn large amounts of new music quickly, and Ormandy developed a prodigious musical memory. In most of his conducting appearances henceforth, he would conduct from memory, without a score. In 1924 he filled in for the orchestra's ailing conductor, and by 1926 he had become its associate director. In the 1920s he recorded several popular and light classical selections with a variety of small orchestral ensembles.

Conducted Outdoor Concerts

Ormandy became a U.S. Citizen in 1927, on his first day of eligibility. That year he met concert manager Arthur Judson after conducting a small orchestra that accompanied a dance recital by the daughter of modern dance pioneer Isadora Duncan. Judson booked Ormandy onto radio programs such as the Dutch Masters Hour and the Jack Frost Melody Moments, and he lined up conducting slots at the popular outdoor summer concert series of the day; Ormandy conducted the New York Philharmonic (then the New York Philharmonic-Symphony) at Lewisohn Stadium in 1929 and the Philadelphia Orchestra in the city's Fairmount Park in 1930 and 1931. In October of 1931, the

legendary Italian conductor Arturo Toscanini was slated to lead the Philadelphia Orchestra as guest conductor but had to cancel due to illness. The orchestra's managers asked Ormandy to take the podium instead.

Judson, as well as Ormandy's friends, pointed out that the position of substitute to the famed Toscanini and the orchestra's flamboyant regular conductor, Leopold Stokowski, was a thankless one. But Ormandy ignored their advice, pointing out that he was already familiar with one of the works slated for the program, Richard Strauss's *Till Eugenspiegel's Merry Pranks,* which he had played while in the Capitol Theatre Orchestra. Ormandy's performance as conductor was hailed as a triumph, and it instantly elevated him in the ranks of rising young conductors. By the time the series of concerts in Philadelphia had ended, Ormandy had already been hired as conductor of the Minneapolis Symphony Orchestra, where he led the orchestra's first recordings for RCA Victor in 1934.

In that year, Stokowski announced that he was cutting his conducting back to a half-time schedule. Ormandy became one of a group of conductors lined up for guest conducting appearances that were really auditions, and in 1936 he was elevated to the position of co-conductor with Stokowski. In 1938 he was elevated to the position of music director, consolidating his position as Stokowski's heir apparent, and in 1941, upon Stokowski's departure, he became the orchestra's principal conductor.

Ormandy's boast that the so-called Philadelphia Sound (otherwise known as the Ormandy Sound) was his own creation was not entirely true. The orchestra's string section was already renowned for its silky tone under Stokowski, who directed the players to use "free bowing" in which each player would draw the bow across the strings independently of the other players. Ormandy inherited a superbly talented string section. But he charted a new course in several key respects, restoring the normal coordinated or "uniform" bowing and favoring a more conservative repertoire than Stokowski had; in place of Stokowski's even balance between new and well-established works, Ormandy instituted a ratio of about 75 percent standards and 25 percent contemporary pieces. And when Ormandy did conduct new music, it was often by a composer such as Dmitri Shostakovich or Samuel Barber, who followed traditional forms, rather than by a radical such as Charles Ives.

Recordings Formed Cornerstones of Catalogue

The Philadelphia Orchestra signed a contract with the Columbia label in 1944, and from then until 1968, when it returned to RCA, Ormandy's recordings formed the backbone of one of the largest catalogues of symphonic music in the world. The classical market began to grow dramatically around 1950, when the new LP medium made recordings of full-length orchestral works much easier to access, and Ormandy's recordings were often the ones the new buyers heard. He specialized in the mainstream repertory of the time—German and Austrian symphonies and concertos from Beethoven up through Brahms, and French impressionist orchestral works. Some of the orchestra's best-selling recordings were made in collaboration with the Mormon Tabernacle Choir.

As a conductor, Ormandy was not an athlete on the podium like Leonard Bernstein and some of his other contemporaries. He marked the beat only lightly, preferring to use his left hand to elicit expressive features. Often the fingers of his left hand would shake lightly, suggesting the vibrato produced by a string player, and Ormandy himself believed that his training as a violinist influenced his conducting. He often pointed out that the Philadelphia Orchestra had its characteristic sound only when he conducted it, creating quite a different impression under guest conductors. Ormandy was not renowned for the originality of his interpretations, but according to Ormandy's obituary in the *New York Times,* written by Allen Hughes, "The more elaborate the orchestral apparatus, the more Ormandy's special gifts became apparent. He was . . . a superb orchestra technician, achieving a finesse and homogeneity of tone matched by few conductors." Beloved by his players, he often lightened the mood with humorous remarks ("I can see none of you are smugglers, that's why it's so loud" appears on one collection of Ormandy quotations maintained by the Arizona State University music department), often unintentional due to his enthusiastic but fractured way of speaking English. In 1950 he married Margaret Hitsch; friends said they hoped she would teach him to have fun, but she reported that he had taught her to work instead.

The Philadelphia Orchestra matched its high level of recording activity with frequent tours, nine of them across the United States, plus trips to Europe, Latin American, and Japan. In 1973 the orchestra went to China, a major political as well as musical event of the period when that country began to open itself culturally to the West after the isolation of the Cultural Revolution. Ormandy participated in a performance in which a local conductor led the Central Philharmonic Orchestra of Beijing in the first movement of Beethoven's Symphony No. 5, and then Ormandy took over for the second movement. "It was a performance very much in the Ormandy manner," according to the *New York Times* obituary, "full, resonant, singing. The Central Philharmonic sounded like a different orchestra, suddenly playing with confidence and rhythmic assurance." Ormandy himself regarded the China tour as one of his greatest accomplishments.

By that time, the advent of jet travel had made Bernstein, Germany's Herbert von Karajan, and other Ormandy contemporaries into international superstars, jumping from orchestra to orchestra and traveling around the world to conduct ensembles on several continents within a single year. Ormandy sometimes took on guest conducting engagements, but it was always clear that Philadelphia was his first priority, and part of his strength was that he maintained the traditional tie between musicians and conductor (although the orchestra experienced episodes of labor strife under his directorship). "This new crop of conductors is marvelously talented, and so eager to make a success in two minutes," Ormandy was quoted as saying by Michael Walsh in *Time.* "There is a very famous one who wants one leg in Berlin, one in London, one hand in Florence, the other in Paris. It can be done, of course, but you must, in the end, belong to one orchestra."

In 1976, as part of the U.S. bicentennial celebrations, Ormandy was knighted by Queen Elizabeth II of England. He retired as the Philadelphia Orchestra's music director at the end of the 1979-80 season, after an unprecedented 42 years at the helm, but remained active as a frequent guest conductor in Philadelphia and elsewhere. At Carnegie Hall in New York on January 10, 1984, he conducted Bartók's lengthy *Concerto for Orchestra,* as usual without a printed score. It was to be his last appearance. Two weeks later he suffered a massive heart attack, and died in Philadelphia on March 12, 1985. Walsh memorialized him with his own words: " "I'm one of the boys, no better than the last second violinist. I'm just the lucky one to be standing in the center, telling them how to play."

Books

Kupferberg, Herbert, *Those Fabulous Philadelphians: The Life and Times of a Great Orchestra,* Scribners, 1969.

The Scribner Encyclopedia of American Lives, Volume 1: 1981-1985, Charles Scribner's Sons, 1998.

Periodicals

New York Times (obituary), March 13, 1985.

Time, March 25, 1985.

Online

"Eugene Ormandy: A Centennial Celebration," Otto E. Albrecht Music Library, University of Pennsylvania, http://www.library .upenn.edu/exhibits/rbm/ormandy/toc.html (December 11, 2007).

"Eugene Ormandy," *All Music Guide,* http://www.allmusic.com (December 11, 2007).

"Eugene Ormandy Quotations," Arizona State University Department of Music, http://www.public.asu.edu/~schuring/ Misc./Ormandy.html (December 11, 2007). □

P

Olof Palme

Swedish political leader Olof Palme (1927-1986), in the words of the *International Herald Tribune*, "is often cited as the greatest Swedish statesman of the 20th century." Over his two stretches as Sweden's prime minister, he was a consistent voice in favor of peace, democracy, and economic equality, and he led Sweden to a place on the world stage that was notable in view of the country's small size.

On the night of February 28, 1986, Palme was gunned down as he walked along a Stockholm street with his wife, Lisbeth. His killing, the first to befall a Swedish leader since King Gustav III was assassinated in 1792, remains one of the greatest unsolved mysteries of the twentieth century; a small-time criminal named Christer Pettersson was convicted of the crime but later released on appeal. Despite, or perhaps because of, his international reputation, Palme was a controversial figure, and over the years since his death Palme's murder has been ascribed, with plausible supporting evidence, to a remarkable variety of international evildoers.

Raised in Comfort

During his time as prime minister, Palme was one of the politicians who led Sweden perhaps closer than any other Western democracy to a socialist political system, financed by a large tax bureaucracy. It was thus sometimes seen as ironic that he personally emerged from the business-oriented class that would later resist his policies. Born on January 30, 1927, in Stockholm, Sweden, he was the son of businessman Gunnar Palme, who died when Olof was seven. Lawyers, bankers, and top government officials were common in his aristocratic family, and his second wife, Lisbeth Beck-Friis, was a baroness. Palme was sent to a top boarding school in Sigtuna, Sweden, where he was groomed as a lawyer and expected to follow one of the family's established patterns. He planned to enroll in law school, but before beginning classes he decided to spend a year in the United States.

It was Palme's experiences in America that put him on the path to political radicalization. He spent the 1947-48 academic year at Kenyon College in Ohio. Perhaps because of the superior education he had received up to that point, he finished all the requirements for a bachelor's degree in just one year of coursework, and was granted that degree in 1948. To celebrate, Palme embarked on a four-month hitchhiking trip around the United States, visiting 34 states and seeing for himself the racial segregation and the vast income disparities that left millions of people mired in poverty in the country that to the rest of the world had seemed a beacon of democracy. Those experiences instilled in Palme the desire to use government as a tool for the elimination of inequality.

Palme returned to Sweden and took personal action in opposition to the Communist Party takeover of the government in what was then Czechoslovakia in 1948: meeting a Czech girl whose position in her homeland was precarious, he married her so that she could join him in Sweden, whereupon the two divorced. Palme returned to Prague, Czechoslovakia, in 1950, for an International Union of Students conference where he, along with other students from Western countries, received a chilly reception. With the world hardening into political spheres of influence dominated by American capitalism and the Communism of the Soviet Union, the ambitious young Swede would come

to imagine a national course unaffiliated with either of those models.

Receiving his law degree from the University of Stockholm in 1951 after joining the government-sponsored Swedish Union of Students, Palme immediately set about climbing the Swedish political ladder. He joined the dominant Social Democratic Party (officially the Social Democratic Labor Party) and landed a job at Sweden's defense ministry, where his talents were spotted by the politician who became his mentor, prime minister Tage Erlander. Erlander, the architect of much of contemporary Sweden's cradle-to-grave system of social services, hired Palme as his speechwriter and private secretary in 1953. Holding that position for nine years, Palme learned the workings of the top levels of Swedish government from the inside. He was elected as a member of Sweden's parliament in 1957. He and his second wife, Lisbeth, had married in 1956, and the couple would raise three sons.

Joined Swedish Cabinet

In 1963 Palme was elevated by Erlander to the rank of cabinet minister without portfolio, and from 1965-67 he served as communications minister. Moving to the position of minister of education, he promoted the inclusion of Marxist thought in school curricula and stirred international controversy for the first time when, in 1968 (a year in which he also appeared in the X-rated Swedish film *I Am Curious (Yellow)*), he marched along with North Vietnam's ambassador to Sweden in a demonstration against U.S. involve-

ment in the Vietnam War. He evolved into an outspoken opponent of U.S. foreign policy, later comparing that country's bombing of Hanoi, Vietnam, to the Nazi German bombing of Guernica, Spain, during the Spanish Civil War. Relations between the United States and Sweden deteriorated as a result, and for a time the two countries came close to a diplomatic rupture as the government of U.S. president Richard Nixon refused to legitimize Sweden's ambassador and recalled its own ambassador to Stockholm.

Yet Palme was hardly a creature of the international left. He criticized the Soviet Union's invasion of Czechoslovakia in 1968 as vociferously as he had opposed American involvement in Vietnam, and to the student protest movement that rolled across Stockholm as well as other Western European cities that year his name was anathema. In 1969 Palme became the leader of the Social Democrats and succeeded the retiring Erlander as prime minister. He was Europe's youngest head of state at the time. Continuing to antagonize the United States, Palme forged an alliance with Cuban leader Fidel Castro. He also emerged as an early leader of the effort to topple South Africa's apartheid regime. He often spoke of the need to find a "third way" between the American and Soviet economic models.

At home, noted Geoffrey Smith of the London *Times,* Palme "was eager for Sweden to move on from a society where there was equality of opportunity to one where there was equality of results as well." His Social Democratic government, undergirded by Swedish prosperity that had resulted in an unemployment rate close to zero, spearheaded an expansion of Sweden's welfare state that included large-scale construction of subsidized housing, social security reform, and generous maternity leave policies, among other benefits. These measures were financed by taxes that were among the world's highest. Sweden's tax bureaucracy became legendary for its heavy-handed ways, and Swedes were troubled when one of their national icons, filmmaker Ingmar Bergman, fled to Germany after complaining of unfair treatment in a tax evasion case.

Combined with a financial crunch in the years following the 1973 Arab oil embargo, that sense of public dissatisfaction was enough to drive Palme from power in 1976; the defeat marked the first time in 44 years that the Social Democrats had been out of power in Sweden. While in opposition, Palme stayed busy as a mediator in both the U.S.-Iran hostage crisis of 1980 and the Iran-Iraq war of the early 1980s. He was returned to power in the Social Democratic victory of 1982, and while his naturally combative personality was undimmed—Palme was described by friends as a man who enjoyed debate for its own sake, regardless of the position or social station of his opponent—he seemed to have mellowed politically. He did stir protests with a controversial plan to turn government-funded investment funds over to the leadership of labor unions.

Gunned Down on Late-Night Walk

On February 28, 1986, Olof and Lisbeth Palme were returning home on foot from an evening at the movies, walking along a well-traveled Stockholm street. As he often did when on a personal outing, he had given his guards the rest of the evening off, considering Stockholm, as most Swedes did, one of the world's safest cities. Just before midnight, someone fired two shots at Palme from behind; one bullet hit him in the back, and a pool of blood, often visited by Swedes over the next days, grew in the snow. He was rushed to Stockholm's Sabbatsberg Hospital but was declared dead shortly after midnight on March 1. No other European head of state had been killed since before World War II.

A taxi driver had immediately called for help after witnessing the shooting, but accusations later flared that police had bungled the initial investigation. According to Michael S. Serrill of *Time,* "Swedish newspapers charged that police were slow in cordoning off the scene of the crime and did not set up roadblocks out of the city until 90 minutes after the murder. Investigators were reportedly so sloppy in examining the scene that the only physical evidence of the shooting, two bullets, was actually found by passersby." Police admitted that they were puzzled by those .357 Magnum cartridges, but observers pointed out that similar ones were being offered for sale at a nearby sporting goods store. As the investigation developed, two cabinet ministers, the chief of Sweden's national police force, and the head of the national police intelligence agency were all forced to resign.

A 43-year-old alcoholic named Christer Pettersson was arrested after witnesses reported seeing him running away from the crime scene, although other witnesses placed him miles away at the time. He was convicted of Palme's murder in 1988, largely on the strength of testimony by Lisbeth Palme, who was herself grazed by a bullet during the shooting. According to the *Economist,* she picked him out of a police lineup, stating, "You can see who's the alcoholic; number 8." The evidence against Pettersson was completely circumstantial, however, with no murder weapon ever recovered and no motive offered, and the conviction was overturned on appeal in 1989. Pettersson, according to the London *Times,* once bragged that "sure as hell it was me who shot him. But they'll never nail me for it. The weapon is gone." During television appearances he made contradictory statements, seeming to admit to the murder but then withdrawing his remarks. Pettersson died in 2004.

By that time, a bewildering variety of theories had been advanced concerning who had actually killed Palme, although his family and top police officials continued to believe that Pettersson was the culprit. The number of conspiracy theories rivaled those attached to the 1963 assassination of U.S. president John F. Kennedy, to which the Palme murder was sometimes compared in terms of its significance for Sweden's national psyche. Candidates for the murder included German left-wing terrorists (who had claimed credit for the shooting shortly after the event), right-wing factions within the ranks of Swedish police, agents of South Africa's apartheid regime, the PKK guerrilla movement associated with the Kurdish ethnic group in Iraq and Turkey, members of the Kurdish Workers' Party in Turkey, and groups in India or Iraq involved in arms dealings with Swedish munitions manufacturer Bofors that Palme had either fostered or tried to stop. Although the twentieth anniversary of Palme's killing in 2006 brought a lower level of public mourning that had been seen ten years earlier, sev-

eral Swedish investigators were still assigned to the case, and the discovery of a gun in a lake in central Sweden at the end of that year brought fresh hopes of new developments. His family established the Olof Palme Memorial Fund for International Understanding and Common Security, which awarded $50,000 annually to a figure active in the pursuit of democracy and human rights. Around the globe, streets and parks had been renamed for Palme.

Books

Bondeson, Jan, *Blood on the Snow: The Killing of Olof Palme,* Cornell University Press, 2005.
Contemporary Newsmakers 1986, Issue Cumulation, Gale Research, 1987.

Periodicals

Daily Mail (London, England), November 22, 2006.
Economist, July 29, 1989.
Europe, November 1996.
Forbes, July 7, 1997.
Houston Chronicle, March 1, 2006.
International Herald Tribune, February 28, 2006.
National Review, March 28, 1986; June 6, 1986.
Nordic Business Report, April 5, 2001; January 21, 2003.
Time, March 10, 1986; March 17, 1986.
Times (London, England), March 3, 1986; October 27, 2004. □

Orhan Pamuk

Turkish novelist Orhan Pamuk (born 1952) was awarded the 2006 Nobel Prize for Literature and became the first writer from his country ever to win the world's most prestigious literary honor. Since the early 1990s Pamuk's books had been garnering critical acclaim on an international level, but in his own country the author is somewhat of a controversial figure for writing about Turkey's checkered history as a democracy. These dualities again greeted the publication of his seventh novel, *Snow,* which appeared in English translation in 2004.

Pamuk was born on June 7, 1952, in Istanbul, the ancient city that straddles the European and Asian continents and for centuries was known as Constantinople, capital of the mighty Byzantine Empire. His mother came from a wealthy textile manufacturing family, while Pamuk's civil engineer father was an executive in his own family's business, which had been founded by Pamuk's grandfather during Turkey's era of rapid modernization in the 1920s and 1930s. Pamuk's father spent time in Paris as a young man, and returned there often when Pamuk was growing up. "My grandfather was a rich person and my father's generation had much money, which they wasted. My childhood was full of my grandmother crying because my father or uncles were selling this or that," he told the London *Guardian*'s Nicholas Wroe.

Dropped Out of Architecture School

Pamuk and his older brother were sent to an American school in Istanbul, where they learned English, and though his family was technically a Muslim one, it was a thoroughly secular household. "In my childhood, religion was something that belonged to the poor and to servants," he recalled in an interview with *Publishers Weekly* writer Judy Stone. "My grandmother—who was educated to be a teacher—used to mock them." Pamuk's grandmother had benefited from sweeping reforms enacted when the man known as the father of modern Turkey, Mustafa Kemal Atatürk (1881-1938), assumed full powers as the president of the newly created Republic of Turkey in 1923. Atatürk banished many long-cherished vestiges of the Ottoman Empire, the powerful Islamic state that had ruled Turkey and much of the Middle East since the early 1300s. Secularism was enforced in all aspects of Turkish life, including equal educational opportunities for women; Atatürk also banned the fez, the brimless hat that was a deeply iconic symbol of male Muslim identity.

Pamuk dreamed of becoming a painter, but studied architecture for a time. In the early 1970s, when he was 22, he abandoned all pretense of college or a career, and instead began an intensive reading course that included the works of Western civilization's most acclaimed modern writers. "People thought, oh, he's a failure," he told Fernanda Eberstadt in an interview that appeared in the *New York Times Magazine* in 1997. "Once every three years my mother opened my bedroom door and said, 'Maybe you should apply to medical school.' "

Pamuk eventually returned to his studies and earned a journalism degree from the University of Istanbul. His first novel, *Cevdet Bey ve ogullari* (Cevdet Bey and His Sons), was published in Turkey in 1982 and became a bestseller. Its title character is a man not unlike Pamuk's own grandfather, whose business empire is mismanaged by sons corrupted by inherited wealth. His next work, *Sessiz ev* (The Silent House), appeared the following year and is set during Turkey's 1980 political crisis, which was yet another of the several military coups in Turkey in the post-Atatürk era.

Heralded as New Voice from East

Pamuk's third novel was the first to appear in English translation. This was *The White Castle,* issued by Carcanet in 1990 five years after its original publication in Turkish. It also reached Western reviewers, and critics on both sides of the Atlantic lavished critical acclaim on Pamuk's riveting tale, set in the 1600s when maritime trade between the Italian city-state of Venice and Constantinople enriched both regions. The story centers on a Venetian scholar who is kidnapped by pirates and sold as a slave in Constantinople; a scientist buys him, and the scholar becomes the scientist's tutor. Over the years, master and slave become more like brothers, and in the end appear to have agreed to switch identities, though this remains unclear in Pamuk's prose. "At a moment when one despairs of there ever being a meeting of minds between the Muslim world and the West," asserted Christopher Lehmann-Haupt in the *New York Times,* Pamuk's novel "comes as a promising antidote."

Writing that review in 1991, Lehmann-Haupt was likely referring to the first Persian Gulf War and the fact that one of the English language's most esteemed writers, Salman Rushdie (born 1947), was forced into hiding after Iran's "Supreme Leader," Ayatollah Ruhollah Khomeini (1902-1989), had issued a *fatwa,* or death sentence, against the British-Indian novelist for passages in his latest novel, *The Satanic Verses,* concerning the founder of Islam, the Prophet Muhammad (c. 570-632). Along with two other Turkish novelists, Pamuk became the first Muslim writer to denounce the Ayatollah's fatwa, and in response the president of Iran issued a formal response hinting that Iran's neighbors—the two countries share a border—"were siding with Rushdie," Pamuk recalled in the interview with Wroe. "I was famous by then, but not that famous. No one knew my address, so I didn't worry too much."

In 1994 Pamuk's fourth novel was published in English translation. *The Black Book,* first published in Turkey as *Kara Kitap* four years earlier, had been written in New York City in the mid-1980s, when Pamuk accompanied his first wife while she studied for a doctoral degree at Columbia University. Its plot follows Galip, a lawyer in Istanbul, whose wife, Ruya, has vanished; her disappearance seems linked to that of her brother, a journalist who wrote articles critical of the military junta-led government. Pamuk's next work appeared in 1997 in English translation as *The New Life.* This story centers around a mysterious new religious cult with an odd religious text as its basis, and the novel "pushes even further the poignant, where-do-we-belong dialectic of isolationism and imitation that has plagued modern Turks," asserted

Eberstadt. "Pamuk feelingly evokes the paranoid weirdness of provincial Turkey—like America, a big, sparsely populated country where housewives, self-made millionaires and retired colonels meet in messianic conspiracies."

Works Explored Deep Conundrums

My Name Is Red was Pamuk's sixth novel, and it set a new sales record in Turkey during its first week in print. Its hero is Enishte Effendi, one of several artists who arrives at the palace of the Ottoman Empire sultan in 1591. The miniaturist painters have been commissioned to illustrate the sultan's biography—though Islamic law expressly forbids all graven images, or representational art—and it seems a murder plot is underfoot within the luxurious but treachery-filled palace walls. Again, the work was hailed as a literary masterpiece in both the English and Turkish languages. Murrough O'Brien, writing in London's *Independent on Sunday,* asserted that "Pamuk depicts the murderee's experience of death so compellingly, and so unbearably, that you have to pinch yourself to remember that he can't have undergone it: the simple shock and annoyance at being struck, the embarrassment in the eyes of the murderer, the body fighting as the soul submits."

Pamuk's next work appeared first in Turkey as *Kar* in 2002 and then in English translation as *Snow* in 2004. Reviewing it for the *New York Times,* Margaret Atwood called the book "not only an engrossing feat of tale-spinning, but essential reading for our times, . . . an in-depth tour of the divided, hopeful, desolate, mystifying Turkish soul." Pamuk uses snow as a metaphor, as Ka, a poet who has returned to Turkey after several years in Europe, is stranded by a major blizzard in a remote village in Anatolia, far from the cosmopolitan cities of Istanbul and Ankara. Ka is puzzled by an unusually high number of suicides of young women in the village, which seems tied to a controversy over the wearing of headscarves in Turkey's public school system. The village itself seems doomed to tragedy, for it was once a distinctly Armenian community. An ethnic group who were among the earliest peoples to officially adopt Christianity, Armenians had a long and troubled history with their neighbors, the Turks. In 1915, in the final days of Ottoman rule, large numbers of Armenians were forcibly removed from such villages by military force; they were deported to Syria on foot, but scores were massacred by Turkish soldiers or died in the desert along the way. An estimated 600,000 Armenians lost their lives between 1915 and 1916, though this number has been disputed for decades, as is the use of the term "genocide" to describe the event.

Prosecuted for Remarks

In February of 2005 Pamuk gave an interview to *Das Magazin,* a Sunday supplement that appears with several Swiss newspapers. In it, he spoke of the aforementioned Armenian catastrophe as well as Turkey's ongoing problems with its Kurdish minority, the world's largest ethnic group without their own homeland. According to Nouritza Matossiann, who discussed the ensuing controversy in the London *Observer,* Pamuk said that "thirty thousand Kurds and a million Armenians were killed in Turkey. Almost no one

dares speak but me, and the [Turkish] nationalists hate me for that." For those two sentences, Pamuk became the target of death threats and was forced to flee his home in Istanbul. He returned to face criminal prosecution under a new law passed in June of 2005.

Article 301 made it a crime for a Turkish person to insult the Republic of Turkey or its legislature; in Pamuk's case, he was charged retroactively, and human rights activists decried both the statute and its retroactive application as a blow to democracy for Turkey. Several prominent Turkish journalists and writers were charged under Article 301, but Pamuk's was the most high-profile case, for he was a writer of international stature whose works had been translated into three dozen languages. There were actually two separate charges, and both were eventually dropped, the second one in January of 2006, just as the justice officials of the European Union (EU) began meetings to review Turkey's judicial system. This is one of several steps necessary for Turkey's acceptance into the 27-member organization of nations, which prides itself on having one of the most impressive human rights charters ever put into force.

Won Nobel Prize

Pamuk was awarded the Nobel Prize for Literature in 2006, which some political analysts viewed as the Nobel Committee's clear rebuke to the rise of Islamic fundamentalism in Turkey and within the growing Muslim immigrant communities in Europe. In his acceptance speech at the awards ceremony, Pamuk spoke at length of his father, who died in 2002 and had once dreamed of being a writer during his sojourns in Paris as a young man. Pamuk also noted that unlike many of his friends, he never feared his father, whom he described as an easygoing, blithe spirit who encouraged his son's literary ambitions and who, upon reading the manuscript of *Cevdet Bey and His Sons,* proclaimed that one day Pamuk would win the Nobel Prize.

But in addressing the question of why his own father never pursued his own dreams of becoming a novelist and poet, Pamuk tried to explain why he—a much more melancholy soul than his father, he also noted—chose it for himself. "When a writer shuts himself up in a room for years on end to hone his craft—to create a world—if he uses his secret wounds as his starting point, he is, whether he knows it or not, putting a great faith in humanity. My confidence comes from the belief that all human beings resemble each other, that others carry wounds like mine—that they will therefore understand. All true literature rises from this childish, hopeful certainty that all people resemble each other."

Periodicals

Guardian (London, England), May 8, 2004.
Independent on Sunday (London, England), August 26, 2001.
New Yorker, November 18, 2002.
New York Times, April 29, 1991; August 15, 2004; October 13, 2006; October 5, 2007.
New York Times Magazine, May 4, 1997.
Observer (London, England), February 27, 2005.
Publishers Weekly, December 19, 1994.

Online

"My Father's Suitcase," Nobelprize.org, http://nobelprize.org/nobel_prizes/literature/laureates/2006/pamuk-lecture_en.html (January 17, 2008). □

Louise Alone Thompson Patterson

American activist Louise Alone Thompson Patterson (1901-1999) participated in the Harlem Renaissance of the 1920s and 1930s, was a close friend of some of its leading literary figures, and spent her life involved in civil rights and other political causes. "She was a leader, an organizer, a humane person who felt deeply about these causes and never wavered in her humane outlook," historian Faith Berry, who knew Patterson, told Elaine Woo of the *Los Angeles Times*.

Proud to be Black

Born Louise Alone Toles in Chicago, Illinois, on September 9, 1901, Patterson was the daughter of bartender William Toles and Lula Brown Toles. After her parents separated, she grew up in the Pacific Northwest with her mother and William Thompson, her stepfather. Patterson adopted her stepfather's last name and was known as Louise Thompson until she married in 1940. She suffered from severe racism while living in towns with no other black children, and channeled her energies into her schoolwork. In 1919 she began studying at the University of California at Berkeley, where she was one of only a few black students.

At Berkeley, Patterson attended a lecture by W.E.B. DuBois, the founder of the National Association for the Advancement of Colored People. DuBois's talk inspired her. "For the first time in my life, I was proud to be black," she said, as quoted by Erik McDuffie in an *American National Biography* entry. After graduating from Berkeley in 1923 with a degree in economics, she briefly returned to Chicago to work as a secretary and pursue graduate studies at the University of Chicago. Soon she began teaching black students, first at a school in Pine Bluff, Arkansas, then at Hampton Institute in Virginia, the alma mater of black activist Booker T. Washington. She lost her job there after supporting a student strike protesting the mostly white administration's policies, which included having the students sing plantation songs to white visitors on Sundays. She also wrote an anonymous letter about the conditions at Hampton to DuBois, who printed it in his publication, *Crisis*.

Joined the Renaissance

Patterson had long aspired to move to New York City, and even before she did so, she began befriending key figures of the Harlem Renaissance, the literary, artistic, and political movement among black intellectuals centered in New York's Harlem neighborhood. In March of 1928, before Patterson left Hampton, Langston Hughes, one of the Harlem Renaissance's most celebrated writers, gave a poetry reading on campus. He and Patterson struck up a friendship there that would last for decades.

In June of 1928, Patterson moved to New York City to study at the New School for Social Research, supported by an Urban League scholarship, and worked for the Urban League in the city as a social worker. Disappointed with what she considered a paternalistic attitude in social work, she eventually left the job. Patterson married the Harlem writer Wallace Thurman in 1928, although they separated after only six months. "I *never* understood Wallace," Patterson later told Arnold Rampersad, as quoted in his biography *The Life of Langston Hughes*. "He took nothing seriously. He laughed about everything. He would often threaten to commit suicide but you knew he would never try it." Most of his friends believed Thurman was gay, but Patterson told Rampersad, "He would never admit that he was a homosexual. *Never, never*, not to me at any rate."

In the fall of 1929, Patterson took a job as secretary to Hughes. She was actually hired by Charlotte Mason, the white patron of Hughes and writer Zora Neale Hurston. Mason later asked Patterson to work as Hurston's secretary as well. Her job soon came to include transcribing a folk comedy Hughes and Hurston were co-writing in 1930, *Mule Bone*. But the two authors had a falling-out, partly over authorship—Hurston attempted to rewrite the play and pass it off as hers alone—and partly over how to pay Patterson for her work. In the process, Hurston became envious of Patterson's closeness to Hughes, even suspecting them of having a romantic relationship, which both strongly denied. The play, never finished, was not performed until 1991.

Meanwhile, in 1930 Mason abruptly terminated her financial relationships with both Hughes and Patterson. She was angry that Hughes had traveled to Washington, D.C., instead of writing, defying Mason's wishes. Patterson, who had liked Mason at first, was shocked and disillusioned. "The way she talked to Langston is the way a woman talks when she's keeping a pimp," she complained, according to Rampersad. " 'I bought you those clothes you are wearing! I took care of you! I gave you this! I gave you that!' " According to Rampersad, the experience led Patterson to "hate the power of money," the thought "that someone because they have money can do to you as they wish and talk to you as they want to. How *dare* they!" The sting of Mason's controlling patronage pushed both Patterson and Hughes toward more radical politics.

Turning Radical

Like many intellectuals in 1930s America, Patterson became sympathetic to socialism and Communism, seeing radical politics as the solution to the Great Depression's poverty, and Communists as rare allies in the fight against American racism. Unlike many of her peers, Thompson remained dedicated to Communist ideas her whole life. She founded the Harlem branch of the Friends of the Soviet Union in the early 1930s and, after the bad experience with Mason, formed an intellectual salon called the Vanguard as an alternative to some Harlem Renaissance figures' dependence on rich patrons. She held Vanguard events in her apartment, including concerts, dances, and Marxist discussions.

In 1932 Patterson organized a trip to the Soviet Union by 22 black American artists and writers, to make a film about racism in the United States, titled *Black and White*. The film was canceled after they arrived, for reasons that remain in dispute: perhaps because the Soviet film company mismanaged the project; or because the Americans rejected the script on the grounds that its Soviet writers did not really understand the United States; or because the Soviet government did not want to hurt its relations with the U.S. government. Despite the project's failure, Patterson remained impressed by Soviet citizens' apparent lack of racism and willingness to demonstrate their respect for black American visitors. "The Russians would push us to the front of the queue line for a bus or ticket, or offer us seats in a crowded streetcar," she later recounted in an essay, quoted by Richard Goldstein of the *New York Times*. "For all of us who experienced discrimination based on color in our own land, it was strange to find our color a badge of honor, our key to the city, so to speak." However, many others on the trip grew distrustful of the Soviets and felt Patterson trusted them too much. They and other critics began calling her "Madame Moscow."

Undaunted, Patterson joined black and Communist efforts to free the Scottsboro boys, nine black teens wrongly convicted of rape in Scottsboro, Alabama, and facing death sentences. In 1933 she organized a march in Washington, D.C., to support the Scottsboro defendants. She officially joined the Communist Party in 1933, studied Marxism at the party's Workers' School, and joined the Communist-affiliated International Workers Order in 1934; she was later named its national secretary. In 1937 she traveled to France for the World Congress Against Racism and Fascism and to Spain as part of a relief delegation supporting the Republican side of the Spanish Civil War. While there, she visited her friend Hughes, who was in Spain to attend the radical International Writers' Congress and write foreign dispatches for black newspapers in the United States.

Once Patterson and Hughes returned from Spain, Hughes felt compelled to blend his love of the theater with radical activism. He turned to Patterson for help, since the powerful IWO, with 145,000 members, was sponsoring many cultural programs. "Langston was at my apartment at 530 Manhattan Avenue one rainy night just after he got back from Spain," Patterson recalled to Rampersad. "'I want a theater, Louise,' Langston told me. 'I'm determined to have one of my own. He was very, very serious, and so I said I would try to help." Patterson and Hughes founded the Harlem Suitcase Theater, a "people's theater" that featured community actors. At Patterson's suggestion, Hughes linked several of his politically minded poems together with blues and spiritual music in a play, *Don't You Want to Be Free?*. The lead role went to Robert Earl Jones, father of the famed actor James Earl Jones. Later, Hughes dedicated *Shakespeare in Harlem*, his 1942 book of poems, to Patterson.

A Lifetime of Activism

In 1940 Patterson married William Patterson, an American Communist Party leader. The couple were longtime friends; they had met at an NAACP meeting in Oakland, California, in 1919. He had helped defend the Scottsboro boys, and in 1946 he founded the Civil Rights Congress, which presented a petition to the United Nations accusing the United States of genocide against blacks.

The Pattersons settled in Chicago, where they had a daughter, Mary Louise Patterson, in 1943. The couple helped found a black cultural center on Chicago's South Side and the Abraham Lincoln Worker's School in Chicago, which operated for three years. During the anti-Communist Red Scare of the early 1950s, U.S. Senator Joseph McCarthy had William Patterson jailed for contempt of Congress when he refused to name the supporters of the Civil Rights Congress.

Patterson was also a friend to the pioneering black singer and actor Paul Robeson, whose leftist political beliefs attracted severe hostility during the anti-Communist McCarthy era of the 1940s and 1950s. In 1949 demonstrators caused a riot at a Robeson concert in Peekskill, New York. To keep such demonstrations from ruining Robeson's career and political efforts, Patterson organized a national tour of black communities for Robeson.

Patterson helped create several activist organizations during her long life. She co-founded the anti-colonial Council of African Affairs with her husband and W.E.B. DuBois in the late 1940s; Sojourners for Truth and Justice, a black women's civil rights group, in 1951; and the American Institute for Marxist Studies, with historian Herbert Aptheker, in the 1960s. In 1970 she headed the New York Committee to Free Angela Davis, the black activist accused of being involved in the murder of a California judge.

Patterson became a key source of information for Langston Hughes's biographers Faith Berry and Arnold Rampersad, and for Zora Neale Hurston biographer Valerie Boyd. She began writing her own memoirs in the late 1980s along with Margaret Wilkerson, but she never completed them, due to failing health in the mid-1990s. The unfinished manuscript is now part of her personal papers at Emory University in Atlanta.

Patterson moved into the Amsterdam Nursing Home in Manhattan in 1997. She died there on August 27, 1999, at age 97. She is survived by her daughter and two granddaughters.

Books

Boyd, Valerie, *Wrapped in Rainbows: The Life of Zora Neale Hurston,* Scribner, 2003.
Rampersad, Arnold, *The Life of Langston Hughes, Volume I: 1902-1941: I, Too, Sing America,* Oxford University Press, 1986.

Periodicals

Black American Literature Forum, Spring 1990.
Los Angeles Times, September 19, 1999.
New York Amsterdam News, September 2, 1999.
New York Times, September 2, 1999.
People's Weekly World, September 7, 1999.

Online

Markowitz, Norman, "Telling it From the Mountaintop," *Political Affairs Magazine (Marxist Thought Online),* http://www.politicalaffairs.net/article/view/105/1/49 (December 16, 2007).

McDuffie, Erik, "Thompson Patterson, Louise," *American National Biography Online,* http://www.anb.org/articles/15/15-01299.html (December 16, 2007). □

Tom Patterson

Canadian journalist Tom Patterson (1920-2005) transformed Stratford, Ontario, from a fading industrial town into a flourishing tourist destination by founding the Stratford Festival in 1953. He is also credited with changing the face of Canadian theater, as his singular vision jump-started the professional theater scene throughout the country. Patterson died on February 23, 2005, in Toronto.

Veteran and Journalist

Patterson was born Harry Thomas ("Tom") Patterson on June 11, 1920, in Stratford, Ontario, Canada. His father was a businessman, but the small industrial town suffered a near mortal blow during the Great Depression (1929-1939). Patterson's recollection of the time was cited by Adam Bernstein of the *Washington Post* as, "Not many people know it, but Stratford had one of the first major strikes of the Depression. The reputation of the town as a home for industry was destroyed. And eventually, the government sent troops in with tanks, and it was like a war." Stratford never really recovered, languishing in obscurity for years until Patterson rejuvenated it at last.

It was to be some time before Stratford's redemption, however. Patterson graduated from his hometown's Collegiate Vocational School before serving as a sergeant in the Canadian Dental Corps from 1939 until 1945. His military service took him abroad and exposed him to culture in Italy and England, a new experience for a young man from a rather grim small town. After World War II ended, he returned to Canada and studied history at the University of Toronto. He received a bachelor's degree in 1948 and went to work as a journalist and associate editor for the Maclean Hunter publishing company on a trade magazine called *Civic Administration.* Before long, though, Patterson began to contemplate an idea that would displace his career in journalism entirely. Indeed, the inkling was to become a veritable mission.

For all Stratford's failings, its founding fathers had possessed adequate foresight when they created and preserved lovely parkland along the banks of its aptly named Avon River. Nor were the current residents insensible to the existence and importance of their famous sister city in England. Still, it was nearly inexplicable that Patterson came to believe that the bucolic riverside would be a likely spot for a Shakespearean theater festival. He did, nonetheless, and he was eventually convinced of the idea's viability. Nicholas Fogg of the London *Guardian* quoted Patterson's recollection of the time from his book *First Stage.* "By 1951, I knew the festival was going to happen. I was going to make it happen." Amazingly, that is precisely what occurred.

Idea Bears Fruit

Patterson's idea was initially buttressed more by way of kismet than perseverance, although that would change. He happened to come across Stratford's then-mayor, David Simpson, at a convention in Winnipeg in 1951. Robert Crew of the *Toronto Star* recounted Patterson's description of that meeting, as given to Crew's fellow reporter Richard Ouzounian: "There was a hell of a lot of liquid being consumed but none of it water," Patterson said. "What do you think about a Shakespearean festival?," [he asked the mayor.] "And [the mayor] said: 'Sounds great to me. That's fine. Go ahead. See what you can do.' " It was, perhaps, not the sort of auspicious wordplay that one would expect to foreshadow the altering of a town's fortunes, but it was more than enough for Patterson.

Buoyed by the vote of confidence, Patterson formed a committee and set about exploring the various possibilities. Armed with relentless enthusiasm, an active imagination, and dogged determination, he was sent by the town of Stratford to New York City to court no less a personage than the famed actor Lawrence Olivier, who was appearing on Broadway at the time. That potential connection was not to be, although he did succeed in getting a somewhat tepid response from the Rockefeller Foundation. Undaunted, Patterson sought out the leading lights of Canadian theater. This approach also proved unsatisfactory until he elicited the advice of theatrical luminary Dora Mavor Moore. Moore had been the first Canadian to graduate from London's Royal Academy of Dramatic Art and had gone on to become a highly acclaimed actor and teacher. She suggested that Patterson contact legendary director Tyrone Guthrie, then working at the venerable Old Vic theater in London. And this time around, Patterson hit pay dirt.

Much to nearly everyone's surprise (except Patterson's, who as a self-described theatrical neophyte, had no real understanding of Guthrie's prominence), Guthrie agreed to come to Canada and evaluate the situation. It was later revealed that the esteemed director had his own agenda, in that he had long wanted to produce Shakespeare on an authentic replica of a stage of the Bard's time, but there is no doubt that Patterson's exuberance swayed him as well. Kenneth Jones of *Playbill* quoted Guthrie's impression of Patterson from the director's book *Renown at Stratford.* "[Patterson] had no great influence to back him, no great reputation, no great fortune. Most of us similarly placed abandon our Great Ideas, write them off as Daydreams, and settle for something less exciting and more practicable. Not so Mr. Patterson. His perseverance was indomitable."

Thus, despite all odds against it, Guthrie signed on as the artistic director of Stratford's first Shakespeare festival. Patterson's strength of purpose and zeal had trumped the naysayers and won the day. And, interestingly, none of his effort was for the love of art or the theater, but rather for the sake of his hometown. As Bernstein quoted him, "The basic interest was in Stratford. It wasn't in Shakespeare or literature." Whatever the motivations had been, however, the play became the thing.

Dream Realized

The Stratford Shakespearean Festival, as it was then called, was slated to open in the summer of 1953. Guthrie's clout in the theater unquestionably lent credibility to the endeavor and helped move matters along. For instance, noted actors Alec Guinness and Irene Worth agreed to star in the inaugural productions of *Richard III* and *All's Well That Ends Well* for expenses only. Prestigious technical experts, such as scenic artist John Collins, designer Tanya Moiseiwitsch, and production manager Cecil Clarke were also imported from England to contribute their assorted talents to the venture. (Moiseiwitsch, it should be noted, designed Guthrie's long-coveted thrust stage from the Shakespearean era for the festival.) Indeed, Patterson's dream began to steam towards reality in fairly short order.

The progress was not without its problems, however. A proposed open-air theater idea had been scrapped early on in favor of a circus tent, and Chicago tent master Skip Manley was brought in to erect the four-ton monstrosity. Guinness, smelling potential disaster far in advance, had insisted on the right to back out if the tent was not in place at least three weeks prior to opening night. Sure enough, the tent was not ready as planned, but crisis was narrowly averted when Guinness was persuaded to rehearse in a nearby barn. Trouble reared its head again upon the tent's completion just one week before opening night, when it was discovered that the concrete floor absorbed all sound. That predicament was solved by a rushed application of matting. Other prospective show-stoppers were both more and less monumental, from financial emergencies to the unexpected need to use Bunsen burners to keep the scenic artist's paint from freezing in the winter, but all contributed to an abiding concern as to whether the festival would ever really open. And perhaps such fears were not truly put to rest until June 13, 1953.

On the evening of June 13, the Stratford Festival presented its first performance, *Richard III*. Noise from a local baseball game did nothing to dim the audience's ardor, and the entire inaugural season played to packed houses that necessitated extending the run from four weeks to six. Patterson's castle in the air had become not only a success but a triumph.

Stratford Festival and Beyond

Within a year of its inception, Patterson's festival repertoire had expanded to include non-Shakespearean plays. Within four years, a permanent theater had been built. And by 1959 it had been graced by a visit from Queen Elizabeth II and Prince Philip of England. Eminent and then-aspiring actors such as James Mason, Christopher Plummer, Hume Cronyn, Peter Ustinov, Julie Harris, Zoe Caldwell, and William Shatner appeared on the festival's stage, and critical acclaim from the Canadian Broadcasting Corporation to Los Angeles to New York helped stoke the fires. A music series was launched, although that was one of the festival's few efforts that did not last long. One of the biggest theatrical undertakings of its time, the Stratford Festival also provided much-needed fuel to the Canadian theater scene and economy. Fine arts schools and new theaters sprouted up across the country, while the coffers of Canada and, most importantly, Stratford, were enhanced. Patterson had, in fact, not merely brought his hometown out of its slump, but had initiated a theatrical renaissance throughout his homeland.

Patterson served as general manager of the Stratford Festival until 1967, but realized after just one season that his strength lay more in ideas than in the day-to-day business of administration. So he turned his remarkable energies elsewhere as well. Among his other pursuits were founding the Canadian Players with actor Douglas Campbell in 1954, becoming founding director of the Canadian Theater Center and a member of the National Theater School's founding committee in 1956, leading a Canadian theater delegation to the Soviet Union in 1956, and serving as general manager of the West Indian Festival of the Arts in 1956. He also founded the Dawson City Gold Rush Festival in 1962 and was general manager of the Ypsilanti Greek Festival in 1966, in addition to serving as associate producer on Guthrie's 1956 film *Oedipus Rex* and as co-producer of the Broadway musical *Foxy* in 1962. Further, he acted as a consultant to various theater companies and festivals all across North America.

Such important contributions to Canadian theater naturally did not go without notice. Patterson's many accolades included the Canadian Drama Award (1954), the President's Award of the Canadian Council of Authors and Artists (1955), the Canadian Centennial Medal (1967), and the Queen Elizabeth II Silver Jubilee Medal (1977). He became a member of the Order of Canada in 1967 and an officer in 1977. In 1978 the city of Stratford dedicated Tom Patterson Island in the Avon River, and in 1991 the Stratford Festival rechristened its Third Stage in his honor. And his was one of the inaugural Bronze Stars placed in front of the festival's Avon Theater in 2002.

By the time the Stratford Festival was celebrating its fiftieth season, Patterson's health was failing. Nonetheless, he was able to make a memorable appearance before the sold-out crowd on the opening night of *Richard III* on July 13, 2002. He rallied in the next couple of years, making his last visit during the 2004 season to see *King Henry VIII (All Is True)*, but his seemingly limitless energy was finally coming to an end. Patterson died on February 23, 2005, in Toronto, at the age of 84. His vision and legacy, however, remained vital and strong, and showed no signs of faltering.

Periodicals

Daily Telegraph (London, England), February 25, 2005.
Guardian (London, England), March 2, 2005.
International Herald Tribune, February 26, 2005.
Plain Dealer (Cleveland, Ohio), February 24, 2005.

Online

Contemporary Authors Online, Gale, 2008. http://galenet.gale group.com/servlet/BioRC (April 14, 2008).

''Moore, Dora Mavor,'' *Canadian Encyclopedia,* http://www.the canadianencyclopedia.com/index.cfm?PgNm = TCE &Params = A1ARTA0005417 (December 15, 2007).

''Patterson, Tom,'' *Canadian Encyclopedia,* http://www.the canadianencyclopedia.com/index.cfm?PgNm = TCE &Params = A1ARTA0009847 (December 2, 2007).

''Stratford Festival Founder Tom Patterson Dies,'' CBC, February 23, 2005, http://www.cbc.ca/story/arts/national/2005/02/23/ Arts/pattersonobit050223.html (December 2, 2007).

''Tom Patterson Dies; Founded Canadian Shakespeare Festival,'' *Washington Post,* February 25, 2005, http://www.washington post.com/wp-dyn/A51928-2005Feb24.html (December 2, 2007).

''Tom Patterson, 84: 'Stage-Struck Boy' Created Festival,'' *Toronto Star,* March 1, 2005, http://www.thestar.com/print Article/108004 (December 2, 2007).

''Tom Patterson, the Father of Canada's Stratford Festival, Dead at 84,'' *Playbill,* February 23, 2005, http://www.playbill.com/ news/print.asp?id = 91362 (December 2, 2007).

''Tom Patterson, Stratford Festival Founder, Dies at 84,'' *New York Times,* February 25, 2005, http://www.nytimes.com/ 2005/02/25/theater/25patter.html?_r = 1&n = Top/Reference/ Times%20Topics/People/S/Shakespeare,%20William&oref = slogin (December 2, 2007). □

Les Paul

American guitarist and inventor Les Paul (born 1915) was responsible for a significant portion of the technical apparatus of contemporary popular music.

H e invented multitrack recording and over-dubbing, using those techniques for the first time in 1947; within a few years they were essential to hundreds of popular record releases, and most popular song recordings are inconceivable without them today. Paul also pioneered other recording sound effects such as reverb, delay, and phase shifting. He was among the first developers of the solid-body electric guitar, which went on to become the defining instrument of rock and roll, and he designed the Gibson Les Paul, one of the two dominant electric guitar makes of the classic rock era. As a recording artist, Paul and his wife, Mary Ford, enjoyed a run of popularity in the late 1940s and early 1950s. In the words of former Led Zeppelin guitarist Jimmy Page, as quoted in a *Melody Maker* interview appearing on the Web site of the Rock and Roll Journal, Paul was ''the man who started everything. He's just a genius.''

Began on Harmonica

Les Paul was born Lester William Polsfuss on June 9, 1915, in Waukesha, Wisconsin. His family shortened their German name, awkward for English speakers, to Polfuss early in his childhood. His parents, George and Evelyn, lived in an apartment next to his father's auto mechanic's shop. When Paul was eight, a local construction worker gave him a har-

monica, which he liked immediately. Soon he was playing in school talent contests. Formal piano lessons went nowhere, but Paul had a knack for entertaining people; he began playing the harmonica on the streets and later added a guitar that he bought for five dollars, earned by picking bugs off potato plants. By the time he was 12, he was taking in $30 in tips every week. He was also an avid electronics experimenter, building a crystal radio when he was nine.

It was hearing guitarists like Eddie Lang on the radio that inspired Paul to take up the instrument, and later he would emulate guitarist Django Reinhardt and other jazz musicians. But his first influences came from country music, in the form of a guitarist named Pie Plant Pete, who performed on the Saturday Night Barn Dance program that was broadcast on Chicago radio station WLS. Pie Plant Pete gave Paul some pointers when he appeared in person in Waukesha, and Paul began to land jobs at service clubs, fraternal organizations, and summer concerts around Waukesha. His high school education was doomed, and he dropped out to pursue music full-time. When he played at Waukesha's Cutler Park, he was frustrated by the limited volume of his acoustic guitar and experimented with using a phonograph needle wedged into the instrument as an electric pickup, attached to a wire plugged into a radio at the other end.

Dubbed ''Rhubarb Red'' for his red hair, Paul began performing in country bands such as Rube Tronson's Cowboys, traveling as far afield as St. Louis. He and local guitarist Sunny Joe Wolverton formed a duet called Sunny Joe and Rhubarb Red. They headed for Chicago to seek out the abundant performing opportunities at the city's Century of Progress Exposition in 1933, and after that world's fair ended, he stayed on in Chicago and snared a pair of radio shows: on station WJJD in the morning he was Rhubarb Red, playing country music, and then he moved over to WIND, playing jazz and using the new name of Les Paul. He also performed around Chicago in a jazz trio that included Jim Atkins, brother of his future collaborator Chet Atkins, and Ernie Newton.

In 1939 this trio took a major step forward when they were signed to perform with Fred Waring and His Pennsylvanians, an orchestra with a show broadcast nationally on NBC radio from New York. Paul played electric guitar in the band. The instrument had appeared in a few jazz and Western swing bands, but in the more conservative Waring group it was unusual enough to stir protests from listeners. Paul flipped a coin to decide whether he should stick to his instincts, and the coin apparently answered in the affirmative. He returned to Chicago to perform with the Ben Bernie big band but continued to spend time in New York as well.

Sought Sustained Guitar Sound

Ever since he had started to play the electric guitar, Paul had dreamed of a different sound than the instrument had produced thus far. Electric guitars of the 1930s tended to produce short blasts of sound, actuated by the player's plucking of the strings and then decaying in much the same way an acoustic guitar chord would. As he played in large dance halls, Paul experimented with ways of creating a more sustained sound. He realized that the sound decayed partly because it was diffused by the soundbox, so he tried filling in the hollow body of the guitar. "I chucked rags in it. I poured it full of plaster of Paris. I tried everything with the guitar to try to get it to not feed back and not sound like an acoustical box," he told Jim O'Donnell of the Rock and Roll Journal. The plaster of Paris idea seemed promising but resulted in an unacceptably heavy guitar. He began working on further refinements during off hours at an Epiphone guitar factory on 14th Street in New York City, while taking time off after an accident in which he received a severe electric shock from a radio transmitter.

Finally, in 1941 Paul constructed a guitar he called the Log, made from a solid four-by-four piece of wood. He noted with satisfaction that he could plug the guitar into an amplifier, pluck a string, go out for a meal, return to his workshop, and hear the note still sounding. Paul is often recognized as the inventor of the solid-body electric guitar. The claim is difficult to evaluate, for guitars were evolving rapidly at the time, and other inventors were pursuing similar paths; the Rickenbacker company had manufactured a solid electric lap steel guitar as early as 1934. But Paul's Log, onto which he soon glued two wings from another Epiphone guitar to make it look more guitar-like, was undoubtedly a major step in the development of the modern electric guitar. Moving to Los Angeles in 1943, Paul quickly attracted the attention of other guitar designers such as Leo Fender.

Paul's Log was so far ahead of its time, in fact, that his first attempts to market the guitar came to nothing. Execu-

tives at Gibson Guitars to whom he showed his project in 1945 or 1946 derided it as a broomstick with a pickup. Paul shelved the guitar temporarily and turned to production work, building a home studio in his garage (using a Cadillac flywheel as a recording lathe) at the urging of singer Bing Crosby, after the two worked together on the recording "It's Been a Long, Long Time." Paul produced songs for other artists who were part of the rapidly growing Los Angeles recording industry, which was oriented toward vocals with instrumental accompaniment rather than the old big bands. He also began to make instrumental electric guitar recordings himself and to experiment with the new technology of tape recordings that had been perfected by the American and German militaries during the war.

In 1947 one of these recordings led to Paul's second breakthrough. Performing an obscure Richard Rodgers-Lorenz Hart composition called "Lover," he recorded eight parts separately (using records in his first attempts, not tape) performing over previously recorded tracks in layers until he had created the finished recording—which required 500 attempts before Paul was satisfied. The new "Les Paul sound" caught on fast, and Paul had hits as a performer on the Capitol label with "Brazil," "Goofus," "Nola," "Little Rock Getaway," and other single releases that marked the first known uses of the overdubbing technique. In 1948 he was injured again in an automobile crash in Oklahoma; for the rest of his life, seven screws held his right arm at an angle that allowed him to play the guitar.

Recorded Duo Hits with Wife

After his recovery, Paul married Colleen Summer, a singer who had worked with the band of Western star Gene Autry. He renamed her Mary Ford for professional purposes, and the two went back into the studio at Capitol. By now Paul had adapted magnetic tape to his multiple-source recording technique, and true multitrack recording was born in such Les Paul and Mary Ford hits as "How High the Moon," which sold a reported 1.5 million copies, and their biggest hit, 1953's "Vaya con Dios," a number one record for nine consecutive weeks. Paul also introduced such now-commonplace effects as reverb and phase shifting in these sessions. Paul and Ford raised an adopted daughter, Colleen, and a biological son, Robert, before their divorce in 1964.

Paul's inventions became standard industry equipment in the 1950s. His solid-body electric guitar became the subject of intense new interest from Gibson after the rival Fender company introduced its Broadcaster model in 1951, and Gibson worked with Paul (the exact nature of his contributions is a matter of debate) to develop a Les Paul model that he played exclusively. The Les Paul and its Fender competitors became fundamental to the sound of rock and roll music as it emerged in the mid-1950s and developed over the rest of the century. Among the Les Paul's famous players were Paul McCartney, Keith Richards, Eric Clapton, and Slash, who conceded that when he acquired his first Les Paul he did not know anything about the man for whom it was named. Ironically, the new music Paul helped make possible put an end to his own career as a hitmaker; the last

Les Paul and Mary Ford recording to reach top chart levels was "Hummingbird," in 1955, although they recorded several LPs for Capitol in the late 1950s and early 1960s.

Health problems, including arthritis, coronary difficulties, and a ruptured eardrum suffered while rough-housing with a friend in 1969 plagued Paul in the 1960s and 1970s, but his creativity was undiminished. In the late 1960s Paul anticipated synthesizer-guitar hybrids by decades with his never-marketed Paulverizer, a guitar that could control prerecorded sounds on tape, and he recorded several solo LPs in the late 1960s. he returned to his country roots in 1976 with the RCA label album *Chester & Lester,* a collaboration with Nashville guitarist Chet Atkins, another star who owed much of the basic vocabulary of his music to Paul's innovations.

In 1984 Paul began appearing weekly at the club Fat Tuesday's in New York's Greenwich Village neighborhood, and he experienced a renewal of attention paid to both his technical and musical contributions. In 1988 the Cinemax cable television network broadcast a Paul tribute concert held at New York's Majestic Theater, featuring guests such as B.B. King, Stanley Jordan, and Eddie Van Halen, and a 1991 four-CD retrospective showcased Paul's skills as a guitarist. A reissued version of "Nola" became a number one hit in China. In 1995 Paul's weekly engagement moved to the Iridium club, and now in his nineties, he has continued to perform regularly in New York. In 2007 he was awarded the U.S. National Medal of Arts by President George W. Bush.

Books

Contemporary Musicians, volume 2, Gale Research, 1989.
Shaughnessy, Mary Alice, *Les Paul: An American Original,* Morrow, 1993.

Periodicals

Entertainment Weekly, November 4, 2005.
Guitar Player, December 2005.
Milwaukee Journal-Sentinel, August 17, 2003.

Online

"Guitarist Les Paul Receives 2007 National Medal of Arts," *Modern Guitars,* http://www.modernguitars.com/archives/004004.html (January 23, 2008).
"Les Paul," *All Music Guide,* http://www.allmusic.com (January 23, 2008).
"Les Paul: Lessons of a Legend," *The Rock and Roll Journal,* http://www.lespaulbiography.com (January 23, 2008). ☐

John Stith Pemberton

American pharmacist John Stith Pemberton (1831-1888) was the inventor of Coca-Cola.

Pemberton was not an amateur tinkerer. He was one of the most successful pharmacists and chemists of his time in Atlanta, Georgia, and he had created several widely distributed products before he began to work on his cola idea. Coca-Cola, moreover, had a famous European predecessor; it did not emerge in a moment of serendipity in Pemberton's laboratory. "He's occasionally portrayed as a wandering medicine man," researcher Monroe Martin King told Jack Hayes of *Nation's Restaurant News.* "But Dr. Pemberton worked in a fully outfitted laboratory and claimed to manufacture every chemical and pharmaceutical preparation used in the arts and sciences." In spite of his other accomplishments, however, Pemberton would probably be forgotten today were it not for his connection with the ubiquitous drink later dubbed the pause that refreshes.

Trained as "Steam Doctor"

John Stith Pemberton was born on January 8, 1831, in the small town of Knoxville, Georgia, near Macon, but he grew up mostly in Rome, in Georgia's Appalachian foothills, and attended schools there. His father, James Clifford Pemberton, was a native of North Carolina. Pemberton returned to Macon to enroll at the Reform Medical College of Georgia there, taking courses in pharmacy and medicine. He was trained as a so-called steam doctor in a system devised by the Massachusetts doctor and herbalist Samuel Thomson—a system that relied on herbal treatments and steam baths that, it was believed, would help patients rid themselves of disease by sweating heavily. Pharmacy and the practice of medicine overlapped considerably in that system and in many of the other novel medical methods of the nineteenth century. He received his degree in Macon at the age of 19.

Later Pemberton acquired a more conventional pharmacy degree, perhaps in Philadelphia. In the early 1850s Pemberton launched a medical-surgical career in Rome. He married Ann Eliza Clifford Lewis, a student at Macon's Wesleyan College, and the pair moved to Columbus, Georgia, in 1853. They had a son, Charles, born the following year. Always on the lookout for financial opportunities bigger than those available to an average small-city pharmacist, he opened a wholesale and retail business selling the raw materials for pharmaceutical remedies sold in apothecary shops and less formal retail environments, such as medicine shows, across the South.

After the outbreak of the Civil War, Pemberton enlisted in the army of the Confederacy in May of 1862 and was made a first lieutenant. He organized the Third Georgia Cavalry Battalion for the defense of Columbus and reached the rank of lieutenant colonel. Pemberton was directly in the line of fire when Union troops under General James Wilson attacked Columbus on Easter Sunday of 1865, and he suffered gunshot and sword wounds in the battle. Pemberton, like many other Civil War veterans, is thought to have become addicted to morphine after using it for pain control as he recovered from these wounds.

After the war's end Pemberton formed a partnership with Columbus physician Austin Walker. He expanded his laboratory with the aim of devising new products and selling medicines and photography supplies. He branched out into cosmetics, finding success with a perfume called

Sweet Southern Bouquet. By 1869 Pemberton was ready to join forces with larger investors in Atlanta, forming the firm of Pemberton, Wilson, Taylor and Company. He moved to Atlanta in 1870 with his family and began to make a name for himself in the growing city's medical establishment, serving as a trustee of Atlanta Medical College (the predecessor to today's Emory University Medical School). Pemberton's labs were state-of-the-art, and they remain in use today as a soil and crop chemical testing facility for the Georgia Department of Agriculture.

Marketed Cocaine-Wine Mixture

Among the successful products Pemberton launched in Atlanta in 1885 was a drink he called Pemberton's French Wine Coca. The product contained coca leaves from South America, which were precursors to cocaine, and Pemberton billed the drink, which was served at pharmacy counters, as a nerve tonic, a mental aid, a headache remedy, and a cure for morphine addiction. Unsurprisingly, it sold well. He admitted to an Atlanta newspaper interviewer that he had based Pemberton's French Wine Coca on an Italian-French product, Vin Mariani, that contained a similar wine-coca mixture and had won the endorsement of no less august a personage than Pope Leo XIII (who had agreed to the use of his image in advertising for the beverage). Pemberton's innovation was to add extracts from other tropical plants: the caffeine-containing kola nut produced by a genus of African trees, and damiana, a Central American shrub leaf reputed to have aphrodisiac properties.

Pemberton's French Wine Coca began to evolve into Coca-Cola when discussion of alcohol prohibition began to circulate within Atlanta's city government in 1886 (it was eventually implemented but lasted only one year). Worried that his newly popular product might soon be outlawed, Pemberton plunged into a fresh round of experimentation at his home on Marietta Street in Atlanta, using a household laboratory where he would work at all hours of the night. He devised an industrial-sized mixing-and-filter apparatus that passed from the house's second story through the floor to the ground level. Samples of his new alcohol-free syrups were sent out to local pharmacies for testing, with Pemberton's nephews assigned to report on customer reactions. One key breakthrough occurred when Pemberton had the idea of adding citric acid to counteract the sweetness of the sugar-based syrup.

By May of 1886 Pemberton was ready with his final formula, which was put on sale in syrup form at Atlanta's Jacob Pharmacy. The idea of bottling it came only in 1894; in the beginning it was a syrup served at the counter, mixed with water to create a beverage with a retail price of five cents. An unsung pharmacy clerk made a brilliant refinement when he found that he had soda water handy and asked a customer whether he could use it in place of plain water. Pemberton formed a new Pemberton Chemical Company to market his new drink, putting his son, Charles (who later died from the ravages of morphine), in charge of production. It was Pemberton's bookkeeper Frank Robinson, who was also one of his partners in the new business, who came up with the name Coca-Cola, referring to the drink's two active ingredients, and devised the antique script logo still in use today.

First-Year Sales of $50

Total Coca-Cola sales for the first year of operations were only $50—a failure in Pemberton's view, for he had spent $70 on supplies. But Robinson believed that exposure was all that was needed and persuaded Pemberton to devote a significant marketing budget to help popularize the new concoction, giving away free drink coupons and advertising Coca-Cola around Atlanta with banners, streetcar placards, and store awnings emblazoned with the message "Drink Coca-Cola." Soon the product was spreading across the city, and Pemberton was convinced it was on its way to national popularity.

Pemberton, however, did not live to reap the profits from his invention. Suffering from stomach cancer, he progressively sold off two-thirds of his interest in the company to other investors, including the transplanted Northern pharmacist Asa G. Candler, as his condition worsened. He retained one-third for his son. In the last months of his life he dragged himself to his laboratory repeatedly in search of further improvements to the Coca-Cola formula, convinced that celery extract was the key to a still more attractive taste. Pemberton died on August 16, 1888, leaving his wife in a difficult financial situation. A struggle for control of Coca-Cola followed his death; the financial machinations that occurred were murky, with rights to both the name Coca-Cola and the formula for the drink under dispute, and it has never been entirely clear how Asa Candler, who was responsible for the growth of Coca-Cola in the 1890s, wrested control of the company from Charles Pemberton and the other investors. By 1905 fresh coca leaves had been removed from Coca-Cola (it still contains spent coca leaves, the part of the plant left over after cocaine is extracted), and by the 1930s the drink was a fixture of American life.

Books

Hays, Constance L., *The Real Thing: Truth and Power at the Coca-Cola Company,* Random House, 2004.

Pendergrast, Mark, *For God, Country, and Coca-Cola: The Definitive History of the Great American Soft Drink and the Company That Makes It,* 2d ed., Basic Books, 2000.

Periodicals

Nation's Restaurant News, February 1996.

Online

"The Chronicle of Coca-Cola," Coca-Cola Company, http://www.thecoca-colacompany.com/heritage/chronicle_birth_refreshing_idea.html (February 11, 2008).

"A History of Coca-Cola," Associated Content, http://www.associatedcontent.com/article/37117/a_history_of_coca cola.html (February 11 2008).

"John Stith Pemberton," article originally published in *Business Heroes Newsletter* (July 1998), http://www.cocaine.org/coca-cola/index.html (February 11, 2008).

"John Stith Pemberton (1831-1888)," New Georgia Encyclopedia, http://www.georgiaencyclopedia.com (February 11, 2008). □

Peyo

Belgian cartoonist Peyo (1928-1992) created a variety of characters over his long career. But only one group became internationally famous: the Smurfs, who were known as the Schtroumpfs in the French-language comics in which they originally appeared.

The Smurfs—contented blue trolls who live inside mushroom-shaped houses in the forest—have had an irresistible appeal to children that transcended cultural boundaries. The printed comics have appeared in 25 languages to date and have served as the basis for a phenomenally popular animated children's television series, television specials, an animated film, and a seemingly omnipresent line of merchandise. Various explanations have been proposed for the Smurfs' success, but one factor certainly worked in Peyo's favor: he maintained control over the Smurfs even after their name became a household word. "I refuse to entrust my business to professionals who would either sell me a bill of goods, or neglect the quality for a larger profit. And on no account will I accept that," he explained in an interview in *Cahiers de la Bande Dessinée* (as quoted in *Contemporary Authors*). "I want to supervise everything so that my little characters stay attractive and the same as they've always been."

Worked in Projection Booth

Peyo's real name was Pierre Culliford. Born in Brussels, Belgium, on June 25, 1928, he was the son of an English stockbroker father and a Belgian mother. He never learned to speak English well, however, and one of his English cousins likewise had trouble with his French nickname Pierrot, pronouncing it Peyo (with the accent on the second syllable). When he began to do small humorous drawings, he took that name as a pseudonym. Peyo quit school at age 16 and got a job as a projectionist's assistant in a movie theater. He attended the Fine Arts Academy in Brussels for a short time as a teen, but otherwise he was completely self-taught.

For several reasons, at the end of World War II Belgium was a hotbed of comic art: the Tintin series of the artist Hergé (Georges Remi) had shown that Belgian artists could gain international popularity, and a vacuum in the production of comics had been created by a ban on American comics during the German occupation of the country. Peyo quickly found employment as an illustrator at a graphic art studio called CBA, and while he was there, he worked on an animated film called *Un cadeau à la fée* and drew some imp-like figures that resembled the future Smurfs. Unfortunately the company went bankrupt, and Peyo was forced to scramble for art-related work amid the shortages and privations of postwar Europe. He painted lampshades for a time and did illustration and design work for advertising agencies, learning the principles of design as he went.

Peyo continued to draw comic strips and graphic stories, and beginning in 1946, he succeeded in getting some of them published in Brussels newspapers. He created a

Native American named Pied-Tendre (Tenderfoot) and his scout Puce (Flea); some of their adventures were published in a supplement to the newspaper called *L'Occident*. Other papers issued adventure strips by Peyo, and one of them, *La Dernière Heure*, published a small Peyo feature about a blond-haired boy in medieval times, a page, named Johan. In 1949 Johan moved to the major *Le Soir* newspaper, to which Peyo also contributed a humorous strip about a kitten named Poussy.

Peyo's aim at the time was to get his foot in the door at the graphic-arts weekly Spirou (then *Le Journal de Spirou*, one of Belgium's most popular youth magazines. He did manage to sell a cover illustration to *Moustique*, another magazine issued by *Spirou*'s publisher Dupuis, but his efforts went nowhere until his friend and fellow cartoonist André Franquin, with whom he had worked at CBA, offered to introduce him to the firm's editors. Peyo diligently reworked some of his Johan comics, changing the page's hair from blond to black, and Johan made his debut in *Spirou* in 1952.

Added Second Character

The feature picked up steam two years later when Peyo added a bumbling but amusing sidekick named Pirlouit, and by the mid-1950s, under the title *Johan et Pirlouit* (Johan and Pirlouit), it was one of the magazine's most popular series. In 1958 (some sources indicate 1957, but the 1958 date comes from an account on the Web site of his publisher, Dupuis), Peyo created a *Johan et Pirlouit* episode called "La Flûte à Six Trous" (The Flute with Six Holes), including a sequence in which Johan and Pirlouit encounter a group of diminutive beings called Schtroumpfs who lived peacefully in the forest. They were only intended to appear in that single episode, but readers reacted favorably enough that Peyo was encouraged to create other Schtroumpfs strips. At first they appeared in small inset panels that suited their small size, but soon they graduated to full-size graphics, and Peyo once again carefully rethought his drawings for the new medium.

The name "Schtroumpf" came about (or at least is anecdotally said to have come about) when Peyo and Franquin were eating dinner in a restaurant, and one (it is unclear which one) said playfully "Passez-moi le schtroumpf" (pass me the smurf) instead of "Passez-mois le sel" (pass me the salt). The exchange gave Peyo the idea not only for the name of his tribe of blue imps, but also for one of the most prominent features of the way they talk: a trademark of Smurf language is that any noun or verb can be replaced with the word "smurf" according to the fancy of the speaker (who might say "let's smurf on over," for example). The idea was guaranteed to catch the attention of youngsters whose vocabularies were growing and who were beginning to experiment with language, and soon it was clear that Peyo was way off the mark with his prediction, issued early in the Smurfs' run in *Spirou* (and quoted in the London *Times*) that "[t]hree years from now, no one will talk about them any more." He had also failed to foresee Pirlouit's success.

The Smurfs were blue simply because Peyo believed children liked that color, and they were based loosely on the trolls who populate Norse folklore. They were, he said (as quoted in the *Times*), supposed to be "three apples high." Peyo's popularity grew to a point where he was able to open a studio of his own, training younger comic artists in his methodical ways. A frequent Peyo collaborator was Yvan Delporte, the editor of *Spirou*. Peyo continued to draw the *Poussy* strips, and in 1960 he introduced a new Dupuis series, *Benoî Brisefer,* about a little boy who has superhuman powers—except when he has a cold. He also created a new strip for *Le Soir* called *Jacky et Célestin.*

Both comics continued to appear through the 1960s and 1970s and spawned their own series of books, but it was the Smurfs that defined Peyo and eventually made him a millionaire. Sometimes he lamented how they had overshadowed his other creations, but he remained involved in producing new Smurf materials until his death. The Schtroumpfs began to appear in the large-format hardback books beloved by European families; two of the initial releases, *Les Schtroumpfs noirs* (The Black Smurfs), and *Histoires Schtroumpfs,* appeared in 1964. They were followed by *Le Schtroumpfissime* (which appeared in English as *The Smurf King*) in 1965 and *La Schtroumpfette* in 1967. That book introduced Smurfette, the only adult female in the Smurf community.

Adapted into Animated Film Versions

An animated French-language Smurf film had a limited release in Belgium in the mid-1960s, and a group of 13-millimeter Smurf short subjects followed. But the real transformation of the Smurfs from graphic art into multimedia

extravaganza began with the 1975 film *La Flûte à Six Schtroumpfs* (The Flute with Six Smurfs), with a score by the dean of French film-music composers, Michel Legrand (who also lent his voice to Smurf characters occasionally). The film was adapted from the *Johan et Pirlouit* episode that had introduced the Smurfs originally. It was released in the United States in 1983 as *The Smurfs and the Magic Flute,* and several Smurf film sequels followed in the wake of its success.

By that time, the Smurfs were a household word in the United States. Stuart R. Ross, who produced *The Smurfs and the Magic Flute,* had secured the U.S. rights to the Smurfs after encountering them on a trip to Belgium, and the Hanna-Barbera animation studio developed a Saturday morning cartoon for the NBC television network after executive Fred Silverman had seen his daughter playing with a Smurf doll (Smurf merchandise was originally imported into the U.S. in advance of the cartoons themselves) and concluded that the Smurfs were a potential hit. The Smurfs made their debut on NBC in 1981 and ran until 1989. They spawned a merchandise line that grew to include clothing, toys, records and compact discs, and various novelty items. A Smurf routine was developed as part of the Ice Capades family skating spectacular. One of the few Smurf-related ventures that failed was a Smurf theme park in Metz, France, that opened in 1981 but was later absorbed by the Six Flags amusement park empire.

The Smurfs were not sharply differentiated from one another, and all of them, with the exception of Smurfette, wore a cone-shaped hat known as a Phrygian cap. They had names like Lazy Smurf that referred to their individual characteristics or sometimes to the kind of work they did, and new Smurfs could be created as needed. Tension in the Smurf universe came from the machinations of Gargamel, a wizard who wants to eat the Smurfs, and his cat Azrael. The vaguely collective nature of Smurf society has occasionally given rise to theories that Peyo intended the series as an allegory with Communist leanings, but evidence for such ideas is slender.

By the early 1990s the Smurfs had appeared in numerous foreign languages other than English, on the way to an eventual total of 25 or more that included Hebrew, Indonesian, and Chinese, in which they were called Ling Shin Ling. The word "smurf," which had been used in Dutch before it was adopted for English-language versions, was retained for many languages in which it sounded euphonious, but the Smurfs became Cumafu in Japanese, Dardassim in Hebrew, and Puffi in Italian. Peyo had help toward the end of his life in managing his worldwide Smurf empire: he and his wife, Nine (whom he married in 1951), raised two children, Thierry and Véronique, and Thierry increasingly took part in managing the family business. Thierry continued to supervise the development of new Smurf enterprises after his father's death in Brussels on December 24, 1992. As of the mid-2000s enthusiasm for the Smurfs showed little sign of abating; a cinematic Smurf trilogy was slated for release in 2008.

Periodicals

New York Times, December 25, 1992.
Times (London, England), January 2, 1993.

Online

''Blue Imps,'' http://www.blueimps.com/peyohistory.html (December 27, 2007).

Contemporary Authors Online, Gale, 2003. http://galenet.gale group.com/servlet/BioRC (December 27, 2007).

''Peyo,'' Dupuis Publishing, http://www.dupuis.com/servlet/jpecat?pgm = VIEW_AUTHOR&lang = UK&AUTEUR_ID = 92 (December 27, 2007).

''Peyo (Pierre Culliford, 1928-1992), Cartoonist,'' Belgium Federal Portal, http://www.belgium.be/eportal/application ?languageParameter = en&pageid = contentPage&docId = 19251 (December 27, 2007).

''Peyo (Pierre Culliford),'' Comiclopedia, http://lambiek.net/artists/p/peyo.htm (December 27, 2007).

''Peyo, the Father of the Smurfs,'' Smurfs official Web site, http://www.smurf.com/peyo-en (December 27, 2007).

''Smurfs at MoCCA,'' http://www.smurfsterocks.com/MoCCA .html (December 27, 2007). □

Manuel Ponce

Mexican composer Manuel Ponce (1882-1948) was and remains one of Mexico's most beloved figures in the world of classical music.

Ponce was the first Mexican composer who consistently introduced elements of the folk and popular music of his country to classical composition. He is also internationally known among guitarists and lovers of guitar music; he was among the first modern composers to write extensively for the guitar, and, through his association with guitarist Andrés Segovia, he played a key role in the revival of the guitar in classical music. Ponce made a variety of contributions to the classical repertory over his long career, never remaining content with a style he had mastered but always forging forward with new musical investigations. In the history of Mexican classical music he is rivaled in importance only by Carlos Chávez.

Manuel María Ponce was born on December 8, 1882, in the small town of Fresnillo, Mexico, in the state of Aguascalientes. He was the twelfth child of his parents, Felipe de Jesus Ponce Leon and María de Jesus Cuellar. Ponce's father had participated in the 1867 revolution that restored Mexico's independence, and when Manuel was born, the family was hiding out in Fresnillo to escape lingering political fallout from that event. They soon moved to the larger town of Aguascalientes, where Ponce spent most of his early life. Ponce's mother loved music and urged her children to study the piano. Ponce's teachers were not musical professionals; he took his first lessons from his older sister Josefina, and he later studied with a local lawyer, Cipriano Avila. Ponce survived both smallpox and measles as a child.

During his teenage years Ponce played the organ at the Church of San Diego in Aguascalientes and wrote several small keyboard pieces. At 18, in search of wider musical experiences, he moved to Mexico City. In 1901 he enrolled at Mexico's National Conservatory of music to study solfèe (sight singing), music theory, analysis, and composition. At this time, musical composition in Mexico was heavily influenced by European models, but from the beginning Ponce showed an interest in writing arrangements of the Mexican folk music he heard around him. Largely self-taught, Ponce already had such a strong grasp of musical fundamentals that he felt the curriculum at the National Conservatory was too easy. After a year he returned to Aguascalientes, took a job teaching at a local music school, and spent time in the city's Jardín de San Marcos park discussing the potential for the creation of Mexican national art forms with a like-minded group of friends.

Determined to challenge himself further, Ponce decided to travel to Europe to study in 1904. He set out for Italy by way of Guadalajara, San Luís Potosí, St. Louis (Missouri) and New York, giving recitals at each stop. He arrived in Bologna, Italy, hoping to study with a local teacher, Enrico Bossi, bringing with him about 40 of his own compositions. In Europe, Ponce encountered a whole new level of musical competition. According to Jorge Barrón Corvera in *Manuel María Ponce: A Bio-Bibliography,* Bossi was unimpressed with Ponce's music, telling the young artist that ''in 1905 one should write music of 1905 . . . or even 1920, but never music of 1830. You have talent, but you lack knowledge of musical technique.'' Nevertheless, Ponce was admitted for some lessons with Bossi and other teachers at Bologna's Liceo Musicale. He had to sell his piano to finance these lessons.

At the end of 1905 Ponce moved on to Germany, studying piano with Edwin Fischer and Franz Liszt's student

Martin Krause. In central Europe, musical nationalism was a hot topic, and Ponce's fellow students in Germany encouraged him to pursue his interest in Mexican music—something that he had the opportunity to do firsthand after he returned to Mexico, broke, in 1906. He had written a body of new music that showed a new level of sophistication reflecting his studies in Europe, and his piano technique was now at concert level.

Criticized for Use of Local Materials

Back in Mexico, Ponce was hired as professor of piano at the National Conservatory, succeeding Mexican composer Ricardo Castro. Mexico was still in the grip of the dictatorship of Porfirio Díz, which emphasized imported products in culture as it did in the realm of technology, and at first Ponce had little success with his nationalist outlook. According to Corvera, Ponce himself later recalled that "the young musician [referring to himself] who in those far gone days initiated the work of preserving and dignifying the little popular tunes, was accused of making music that smelled like *huarache,* or Indian sandals." Among Ponce's students at his private studio during this period was Carlos Chávez. Ponce introduced to his students, and to Mexico in general, the French Impressionist music of Claude Debussy and Maurice Ravel; in 1912 a group of Ponce's students gave an all-Debussy recital at which the 13-year-old Chávez played *Clair de lune.*

The first of Ponce's mature large-scale works date from the period before World War I. Ponce's Piano Concerto had its premiere on June 7, 1912, with the composer at the piano. The work was a traditional Romantic concerto stylistically, but it also contained Mexican folkloric elements. Ponce also composed a variety of small piano pieces, and he continued to arrange Mexican folk music. *Canciones Mexicanas* (Mexican Songs), begun in 1912 and published in 1914, consisted entirely of arrangements for voice and piano of Mexican folk songs—except for "Estrellita" (Little Star), which was an original Ponce composition. That song became an international popular hit, and remains Ponce's single best-known composition. As of 2008 there were at least 180 recordings of it in existence, by performers ranging from the Benny Goodman orchestra to Spanish opera star José Carreras. The idea of copyright, however, was in its infancy at the time, and Ponce never received any royalties for his evergreen song: it quickly became so familiar that publishers and audiences assumed it was a traditional song like the other pieces in Ponce's set.

Ponce began a sustained campaign as a writer and lecturer to promote the use of Mexican materials in classical music, but before he could make much headway, the Mexican Revolution against Díaz's rule broke out, and Ponce decided to escape the disorder by traveling to Havana, Cuba. Ponce lived in Havana from 1915 to 1917, and his stint there produced Cuban-flavored works including a sonata for cello and piano. A 1916 trip to present his music in New York resulted in negative reviews, and Ponce for the rest of his life had a poor relationship with American critics and audiences. His music remains more popular in Latin American than in North America. Ponce married a French

singer, Clema Maurel, on September 3, 1917; the couple had no children. He was active as a music critic and musicologist, writing newspaper and magazine articles in Cuba and founding a new *Revista Musical de México* (Mexican Musical Review) after he returned to Mexico City in 1917. He remained in the Mexican capital until 1925 and was active as a critic there.

The most important musical event in Ponce's life in the early 1920s was his meeting with the Spanish guitarist Segovia in 1923. The meeting came about after Ponce had written a detailed review of one of Segovia's concerts that impressed the guitarist, who had almost single-handedly revived the role of the guitar in classical music. Ponce went on to become a full partner in that revival, soon composing a *Sonata Mexicana* (1925) and a *Thème varié et finale* (Varied Theme and Finale, 1926) for Segovia, and continuing to write for the guitar for the rest of his life.

Took New Lessons in France

In 1925 Ponce decided to challenge himself once again: he traveled to Paris and enrolled in classes with the composer Paul Dukas at the Ecole Normale de Musique; he also took private lessons with Dukas. The move reunited Ponce with Segovia, resulting in a host of new Ponce guitar compositions, and it placed him in the company of progressive European composers. Ponce founded Paris's first Spanish-language music magazine, *La Gaceta Musical,* and emerged with a new backer in Dukas, who said that the top score in his classes at the Ecole Normale was not good enough to express his positive opinion of Ponce. By the end of his stay in Paris in 1933, Ponce, who began as a conservative, Romantic composer, had written works on the leading edge of European composition of the day—the 1929 *Suite bitonal,* for example, demanded that the members of an ensemble play in two different keys at the same time.

Ponce returned to Mexico City in 1933, remaining there for the rest of his life and continuing to compose, teach, and lecture. The following year he became director of the National Conservatory. He brought all of his training and experience together into a mature style heard in several of his most celebrated works: the *Concierto del sur* (Concerto of the South) for guitar and orchestra had its premiere in Montevideo, Uruguay, in 1941, with Segovia on the guitar; it has become a staple of nearly every classical guitarist's repertory, and in general Ponce's music is central to the tradition of classical music for the guitar. Ponce wrote other works for symphony orchestra, including a "divertimento sinfónico" called *Ferial* in 1940 and a concerto for violin and orchestra in 1943. These works, in Corvera's words, "effectively integrate a wide variety of elements from Mexican music: indigenous, mestizo, folk, popular, and even elements from the music of the Spanish motherland. They make use of folkloric material as well as Ponce's own melodies. In addition they convey a 'Mexican sound' through rhythmic, harmonic, and melodic gestures."

Ponce was awarded a number of prizes in his later years, including Mexico's National Prize for Arts and Sciences in 1948, which carried a cash award of 20,000 pesos. In poor health in the late 1940s, he died of uremic poisoning on April 24, 1948. Ponce is remembered as the founder of Mexican musical nationalism, and his music is considered central to the tradition of classical music for the guitar.

Books

Baker's Biographical Dictionary of Music and Musicians, Nicholas Slonimsky, ed. emeritus, Schirmer, 2001.

Corvera, Jorge Barrón, *Manuel María Ponce: A Bio-Bibliography,* Greenwood, 2004.

Online

''Biography,'' International Manuel Ponce Society, http://www .imps.org (February 11, 2008).

''Manuel Ponce,'' *All Music Guide,* http://www.allmusic.com (February 11, 2008).

''Manuel Ponce and the Suite in A minor: Its Historical Significance and an Examination of Existing Editions,'' Doctor of Music thesis, Florida State University (2006), http://etd.lib.fsu .edu/theses/available/etd-12162005-160048/unrestricted/ 02KevinMandervilleTreatise.pdf (February 11, 2008). □

Q

Harriet Quimby

In 1911, less than eight years after the Wright Brothers invented the first successful airplane, Harriet Quimby (1875-1912) became the first U.S. woman to earn her pilot's license. Eight months later, she flew solo across the English Channel, becoming the first woman to accomplish this feat.

Harriet Quimby took to the skies during the early days of flight. Planes of her era were fragile, unreliable machines. Most pilots avoided sustained flights and open water—but not Quimby. Determined to become the first woman to fly across the English Channel, she braved the cold and fog, using nothing but a compass tucked between her knees to guide her way.

Became Journalist

The future aviatress was born May 11, 1875, near Coldwater, Michigan, to farmers Ursula and William Quimby. Around 1884, the family relocated to Arroyo Grande, California, to farm and later opened a general store. In time, they moved to San Francisco, where Quimby, her mother and her sister mixed and packaged herbal remedies, which William Quimby peddled by wagon. The family also earned money sewing sacks for local fruit packers. Ursula Quimby longed for her girls to move beyond their poor beginnings, so as the family became more successful, she made up stories about her daughters' beginnings, telling everyone they came from a wealthy San Francisco farm family and had been schooled abroad.

Initially, Quimby decided to become a journalist, and at the time, women were just breaking into the field. She secured work in San Francisco, first at the *Dramatic Review* and later at the *Call–Bulletin & Chronicle*. Quimby became a celebrity of sorts in San Francisco, drawing admirers through her cunning beauty and ability to turn mundane events into attention–grabbing news stories.

In 1903, Quimby moved to New York City to write for *Leslie's Illustrated Weekly,* a prominent news magazine. She started as a drama critic, writing play reviews, then moved on to features. In 1906, *Leslie's* dispatched Quimby to cover an auto race. While there, Quimby persuaded one of the drivers to give her a ride. Afterward, she learned to drive, which was unusual for women of her day. She gained further notoriety for driving to writing assignments in her yellow "runabout" car.

Took Flight Lessons

In 1910, Quimby was sent to cover an international air competition, which featured aviators racing from New York's Belmont Park to the Statue of Liberty and back. U.S. pilot John Moisant won the race and Quimby left fascinated with the idea of flight. By April 1911, Quimby had enrolled at Moisant's flying school in Long Island. Many schools, including those run by the Wright brothers, would not enroll women. Moisant's sister, Mathilde, began taking lessons about the same time and the two became instant rivals as they competed to become the first U.S.–licensed female pilot.

To avoid the scrutiny and hostility of the male students, Quimby took her lessons in the early–morning hours, disguised as a man. A standard lesson included two to five minutes of air time and cost $2.50 a minute. Despite her best efforts, Quimby could not keep her training secret and soon people showed up at the airfield to catch a glimpse of

the woman who wanted to fly. The *New York Times* dispatched a reporter to cover the story and a feature on Quimby appeared on May 11, 1911. According to the article, when Quimby was asked if she liked flying, she replied, "Well, I'm out here at 4 o'clock every morning. That ought to be answer enough. I took up the sport just because I thought I should enjoy the sensation, and I haven't regretted it. Motoring is all right, and I have done a lot of that, but after seeing monoplanes in the air, I couldn't resist the desire to try the air lanes, where there are neither speed laws nor traffic policemen, and where one needn't go all the way around Central Park to get across Times Square."

On August 1, 1911, after 33 lessons and less than five hours in the air, Quimby won her license, No. 37, from the Aero Club of America. To pass the test, Quimby had to make turns around a pylon, do figure–eights and land the plane within 165 feet of her departure point. Quimby brought her plane to a stop within eight feet of her starting point, setting a new school record for accuracy. Quimby was the second woman in the world to hold a pilot's license. France's Raymonde de Laroche had earned a license earlier in 1910. In an article Quimby wrote for *Leslie's Illustrated Weekly*—and reprinted in *The Pioneers of Flight* by Phil Scott—Quimby described her test–taking experience. "I felt like a bird cleaving the air with my outstretched wings. There was no thought of obstruction or obstacle. There was no fear of falling because the mastery of a well–balanced machine seems complete."

Next, Quimby joined the Moisant Exhibition Team. Attending races and exhibitions was a favorite American pastime during these early days of flight and pilots were paid well. On September 4, 1911, Quimby earned $1,500 for a moonlight flight over Staten Island, New York, which drew 20,000 spectators. Later that month, Quimby beat famed French aviatress Hélène Dutrieu at a meet in New York.

Quimby's exotic flying suit added to her mystique. Female pilots of her time wrestled with clothing because the standard long skirts women wore got whipped around by the wind and tangled in the controls of the open cockpits. Some female pilots wore knickers to solve the problem. Quimby, however, hired a tailor to make her an outfit—a high–collared, purple satin jumpsuit with full bloomers that tucked into the tops of tall lace–up boots. It converted into a traditional skirt after flights and also had a special monk–like hood that shrouded her from the wind. Goggles, gauntlets and a leather jacket completed the outfit.

While outwardly flamboyant, Quimby was a cautious flier. She checked her plane personally before each flight and worked closely with her mechanic. She was also superstitious. She had an antique necklace and bracelet, fashioned from the tusk of a wild boar, which she considered good–luck charms. She also flew with a brass god trinket given to her by a French aviator.

Crossed English Channel

Quimby sailed for London in March 1912, determined to pilot a plane across the English Channel. Once there, she talked the *Daily Mirror* into sponsoring the flight by promising an exclusive story. Quimby decided to fly in a Blériot, a plane named after French pilot Louis Blériot, who completed the first flight over the Channel in 1909. The 50–horsepower Blériot XI was not known for its flying ease. A monoplane, it had one wing that stretched from the fuselage of the plane to each side. These early monoplanes—constructed of wood, canvas and wire—had wings that were prone to twisting in flight, rendering the plane unstable.

By 21st century standards, the Blériot was a bare–bones kind of plane, almost skeletal looking. Only the front half of the fuselage was covered with fabric, while the tail was left exposed. It had a pair of bicycle–like wheels in the front and one controlling lever. The pilot's feet rested on a steering bar, which was connected by wires to the rudder. The pilot sat in a suspended wicker seat with no windshield and was pelted with oil from the revolving engine.

There was no seatbelt, no parachute, no navigation device. Quimby would have to fly with a compass and stay on track because veering more than five miles off course would put her plane over the North Sea. Many pilots had attempted to cross the Channel and died after their planes stalled over the North Sea. Famed English aviator Gustav Hamel caught wind of Quimby's plan and advised against it. He offered to fly for Quimby, to take off from England wearing her trademark suit, then land in an isolated spot in France so they could switch clothes before being discovered. She declined.

Because of high winds, Quimby was unable to test the plane prior to her flight on April 16, 1912. The day dawned cold. Quimby bundled up in layers of silk underwear, a wool flying suit, a raincoat and a sealskin stole. Knowing

Quimby would be at the mercy of the wind and weather 6,000 feet above the earth, Hamel advised her to fly with a hot water bottle in her lap. She took off from Dover, England, around 5 a.m. and quickly hit fog. Quimby guided the plane to different altitudes, searching for a break in the fog. At one point, the plane tilted, causing gas to flood the engine and sputter. As Quimby moved down toward the water planning an emergency landing, however, the gas burned off and the engine returned to normal.

The fog was so thick Quimby could not see the water below, or the coastline. She had to use her watch to gauge how far she had flown. After 22 minutes in the air, she began her descent, hoping to find herself over France. She spied a splotch of white sand and brought the plane to rest near the French town of Hardelot. The people greeted Quimby and carried her on their shoulders into town. That same day, another pilot died trying to cross the Channel. Quimby anticipated instant acclaim for her accomplishment but the next day, the papers were filled with headlines concerning the Titanic, which sank during the night of April 14–15.

Died in Airplane Accident

Quimby returned to the United States and continued flying in exhibitions. On July 1, 1912, she participated in the Harvard–Boston Aviation Meet flying a two–seater 70–horsepower Blériot. Quimby carried a number of passengers around the field, then embarked on a flight with event manager William A.P. Willard on board. As Quimby approached her landing, the plane jolted and she and Willard tumbled out, falling 1,000 feet to their deaths into Dorchester Bay.

The New York Times gave this account of the tragedy the following day: "Five thousand spectators witnessed the accident, which occurred as the machine, a Bleriot monoplane, was volplaning down toward the aviation grounds. Miss Quimby and Willard were thrown from their seats as the machine suddenly turned almost perpendicular in the air, and the two bodies turned over and over as they shot downward. Both victims were found terribly crushed when extricated from the mud of the shallow bay, into which they had sunk deeply."

There were many theories about the accident, from pilot error to machine malfunction. Others thought a gust of wind was to blame. Some thought Willard, sitting directly behind Quimby, shifted his body suddenly, throwing the plane off–balance. The plane had a reputation for instability, particularly when carrying passengers. Ironically, the plane glided to a rest with little damage. Had Quimby and Willard worn seatbelts, they likely would have survived. At the time, however, seatbelts were not a common feature on planes. At the morgue, someone stole Quimby's famous satin costume and her jewelry, which her mother had wanted to donate to the Smithsonian Institution.

After Quimby's death, Mathilde Moisant continued to fly, but noted the risks in an article for the New York Times on August 26, 1928. "Miss Quimby never took chances and frequently chided me for my recklessness. And here I have come out of accident after accident, while Miss Quimby had to lose her life in her very first mishap. It is something like a game of poker, after all, and each one is confident that he will win the next time."

Aviation deaths were common in those days. The deaths of Quimby and Willard marked the 42nd and 43rd aviation fatalities that year. The year before, 73 people died in planes. Had Quimby lived longer, there is no doubting the number of aviation firsts she might have completed. She was already scheduled to fly a bag of mail nonstop from Boston to New York on July 7. One thing Quimby did leave behind, though, was a vision for the future success of commercial aviation. In her writing, she predicted a day when planes would transport people from city to city, though she did not live long enough to see that vision come true.

Books

Kramer, Barbara, Trailblazing American Women: First in their Fields, Enslow Publishers, Inc., 2000.
Langley, Wanda, Women of the Wind: Early Women Aviators, Morgan Reynolds Publishing, 2006.
Scott, Phil, The Pioneers of Flight, Princeton University Press, 1999.

Periodicals

Iris, Fall 2001.
New York Times, May 11, 1911; August 2, 1911; April 17, 1912; July 2, 1912; August 26, 1928.
Smithsonian, January 1984. □

R

Ann Radcliffe

English novelist Ann Radcliffe (1764-1823) wrote a series of Gothic tales in the 1790s just as the literary genre was reaching its peak of popularity among middle- and upper-class women readers in England and America.

Characterized by a suspenseful mixture of romance and horror, the Gothic story unusually centered on an innocent, persecuted heroine threatened by a dark-haired, fierce villain who owns a ghost-haunted or otherwise mystery-steeped castle. The tag "Gothic" came from the fact that these castles or abbeys were usually crumbling piles already several hundred years old by then, built in the late medieval period of the 1300s to the 1500s, when Gothic architecture predominated in England, France, and Italy. "What Radcliffe brought to the Gothic was poetry," noted an essay on her work that appeared in the *St. James Guide to Horror, Ghost & Gothic Writers*. "In all her novels she has lush descriptions of landscape, mostly French and Italian, which seemed more romantic than her native England; and this is not merely background but affects the moods of her characters and comes almost to dominate characters and plot."

Born Ann Ward on July 9, 1764, Radcliffe spent her first eight years in the central London neighborhood of Holborn. Her father, William, was a haberdasher, a term once used for a retailer who sold fabric, buttons, ribbons, and similar items. Both William and his wife, Ann DeWitt Ward, had some prominent figures among members of their extended family: one was William Cheselden (1688–1752), a famous London surgeon who helped elevate the profession in the early eighteenth century and disassociate it from its long-standing alliance with barbers. There was also Thomas Bentley, the business partner to pottery-maker Josiah Wedgewood (1730–1795). Bentley invited Radcliffe's father to take over one of the Wedgwood and Bentley shops in the resort town of Bath, to which they moved in the early 1770s when Radcliffe was eight years old.

Husband Encouraged Her Stories

Few details survive about Radcliffe's formal schooling, though she knew some Latin and appeared to have been quite well-read. In January of 1787, at the age of 22, she married William Radcliffe, a graduate of Oxford University who had abandoned plans for a career in law and switched to journalism. The couple settled in London, where he served as an editor with a newspaper called the *English Chronicle*. They had no children, and it was William Radcliffe who was said to have encouraged his wife's literary ambitions during these first years of their marriage.

Radcliffe made her literary debut with *The Castles of Athlin and Dunbayne: A Highland Story,* which appeared in 1789. The story was set in medieval Scotland, and centered on a young earl named Osbert, who is determined to avenge the untimely death of his father at the hands of a local landowner-rival. With Alleyn, Obsert's mysterious new, apparently common-born friend, he attacks the castle of Baron Malcolm, but then he and Alleyn are taken prisoner within its walls. A pair of romances—one of them involving a young woman who is destined to become the evil baron's bride against her will—rounds out the plot and helps the story conclude on a happy note. The title did not sell well, however, and the handful of critics who reviewed it pointed out several inaccuracies, particularly in her descriptions of the Scottish Highlands.

The Castles of Athlin and Dunbayne had a few elements of the Gothic novel, but Radcliffe would deploy these more fully in her next work, *A Sicilian Romance.* Published in 1790, it features several hallmarks of the genre, including two innocent female protagonists—the sisters Emilia and Julia—who learn that their reprobate father has imprisoned their mother at the family stronghold, the castle of Mazzini in Sicily, while he idles his days away in Naples with his mistress. Again, the work attracted little notice, and later literary scholars have generally dismissed both this and her debut as inferior works of Radcliffe's.

The Romance of the Forest

In 1791, Radcliffe achieved minor celebrity with the publication of *The Romance of the Forest, Interspersed with Some Pieces of Poetry,* the first of her works to enjoy strong sales. Its plot followed the heroine Adeline's quest to unlock the secret of her parentage, and contained several "of what were, even then, Gothic clichés," asserted the *St. James Guide to Horror, Ghost & Gothic Writers* contributor, including "a beautiful young woman being protected, an abbey used by a highwayman as a base, a nightmare featuring a message, a secret chamber, terrible family revelations, injustices and romantic misunderstandings." Critical assessments of the day were mixed, and an essay from Deborah D. Rogers in the *Dictionary of Literary Biography* noted that reviewers "praised Radcliffe's hallmark and pioneering poetical descriptions of landscapes and her creation of suspense but criticized the interspersed verses, anachronisms, improbabilities, excessive descriptions, explained supernatural events, and inadequate characterization."

Despite those shortcomings, *The Romance of the Forest* proved a financial boon to Radcliffe, and her London publisher, Robinson, offered her a 500-pound advance for her next work. This was *The Mysteries of Udolpho: A Romance Interspersed with Some Pieces of Poetry,* which appeared across four volumes in 1794. The story is set in the 1580s as a young, innocent heroine named Emily St. Aubert finds herself locked up in the frightening Castle Udolpho, which appears to be populated by ghosts. Her jailor is an aunt who became Emily's guardian after the death of both parents, along with her aunt's treacherous Italian husband, who schemes to obtain the St. Aubert fortune. The novel figures prominently in the plot of *Northanger Abbey,* English novelist Jane Austen (1775–1817)'s first novel. In Austen's 1818 tale, published posthumously, her heroine Catherine Morland is a devoted reader of Gothic romances, and imagines that the old abbey she is visiting harbors dark secrets along with its owners, the Tilneys, whose son Henry is falling in love with Catherine.

The Mysteries of Udolpho proved a great commercial success for Radcliffe, and like her previous tale, *The Romance of the Forest,* was adapted for the stage. *Fontainville Forest,* a drama by James Boaden, premiered at London's Covent Garden Theater in the summer of 1794, and in January of 1795 *The Mysteries of the Castle* had its debut at the same venue. Despite the popular acclaim, Radcliffe was reportedly sensitive to the harsher words of her literary critics, and strove to improve her prose, characterizations, and plots. She took a break from writing fiction during that same summer of 1794, when she and her husband made an extended trip to visit her mother's relatives in the Netherlands, and continued along Germany's picturesque Rhine River route. Her travel diary was published the following year as *A Journey Made in the Summer of 1794 Through Holland and the Western Frontiers of Germany.*

Abandoned Literary Career

Radcliffe received an 800-pound advance for her next book, *The Italian; or, The Confessional of the Black Penitents,* published by Cadell and Davies over three volumes in 1797. The work owed some creative debt to a popular novel published a year earlier, *The Monk* by Matthew Lewis, a Gothic tale that caused a sensation for its rather daring sexual innuendo, which, in turn, was said to have been inspired in part by Radcliffe's *Udolpho* tale. Unlike her previous works, *The Italian* was set in the relatively recent past, in the 1760s, and did not feature any poetical interludes, which later literary critics found to be the most original element in her writing style. In this plot, the virtuous heroine is named Ellena, and she and the dashing Vincentio di Vivaldi are in love. An Italian monk, Schedoni, conspires to keep them apart, and locks Ellena away in a convent, where the nuns treat her harshly and attempt to force her to take religious vows. Vivaldi comes to rescue her, but their happiness is once more thwarted by Schedoni, who alerts agents of the Holy Inquisition—the Roman Catholic Church's long campaign to ferret out heresy among its believers, sometimes by means of torture—to take the young man into custody. Ellena, meanwhile, is imprisoned in a mansion, and nearly dies at the hands of the mad monk until a revelation that they may be related; he turns out to be her long-lost uncle.

The Italian was the final novel that Radcliffe would publish during her lifetime. Several factors conspired to end her literary career: she had already earned a good sum of money from her work, and in 1797 her husband purchased the *English Chronicle,* which may have placed them on more secure financial footing as well. Her father died in 1798, and her mother died a year later. In between these events, Radcliffe's husband fell ill but recovered, but his nursing care kept her from writing. Furthermore, her inheritances gave her complete financial freedom—although, as an only child she grieved for some time over the deaths of her parents, which also stifled her creative energies. In a journal entry from the year 1800, she wrote: "In this month, on the 24th of July, my dear father died two years since," according to Rogers's *Dictionary of Literary Biography* essay. "On the 14th of last March, my poor mother followed him: I am the last leaf on the tree!"

Radcliffe was a shy writer, uncomfortable with literary acclaim, and had a naturally reclusive personality. These factors combined to make her a somewhat mysterious figure, and there were occasional rumors that she had actually descended into mental illness and was being held somewhere—possibly against her will, like her heroines—out of sight. The gossip was merely imaginative speculation, and Radcliffe was never hidden away; instead she and her husband took extended trips throughout England every summer, and she began to suffer from respiratory ailments, including asthma. She died on February 7, 1823, at the age of 58, from respiratory failure likely caused by pneumonia. She was laid to rest in a chapel in Bayswater, the London neighborhood. One final novel appeared posthumously: *Gaston de Blondeville; and St. Alban's Abbey, with Some Poetical Pieces,* issued by the London house Colburn in 1826. The tale was inspired by her 1802 visit to several historical sites, among them Kenilworth Castle, a ruin dating back to Norman times.

Two volumes of Radcliffe's verse also appeared after her death. Her first biographer was Thomas Noon Talfourd, who wrote a "Memoir of the Life and Writings of Mrs. Radcliffe" for the 1826 publication of *Gaston de Blondeville.* In 1995, another examination of her life and career appeared, bearing the title *Ann Radcliffe: The Great Enchantress.* Its author was Robert Miles. Four years later, Rictor Norton's *Mistress of Udolpho: The Life of Ann Radcliffe* appeared. In the 2007 film *Becoming Jane,* Radcliffe appears as a character, played by Helen McCrory, who meets the young Jane Austen (Ann Hathaway) and encourages her literary ambitions. Such a meeting, however, is not known to have actually occurred.

Books

Rogers, Deborah D., *Dictionary of Literary Biography,* Volume 178: *British Fantasy and Science-Fiction Writers Before World War I,* edited by Darren Harris-Fain, Gale, 1997.
St. James Guide to Horror, Ghost & Gothic Writers, St. James Press, 1998.

Periodicals

Independent on Sunday (London, England), September 21, 2003.
Studies in the Novel, Spring 1997. □

Hal Roach

American filmmaker Hal Roach (1892-1992) was one of the top comedy producers in the early years of Hollywood. Responsible for giving the world such comedic luminaries as Harold Lloyd, Laurel and Hardy, and the *Our Gang* series of short films, his impact was enormous and long-lived. Nor was it limited to movies, as Roach was pioneering in the nascent television industry as well.

Intrepid Youth

Roach was born Harold Eugene Roach on January 14, 1892, in Elmira, New York. His parents were Irish immigrants. His father, Charles H., was an insurance and real estate broker, while his mother, Mabel (Bailey), ran a boardinghouse out of the family home. Young Roach was not particularly cut out for formal schooling, leading to his dismissal from "most every school in Elmira," according to

the Famous People of the Finger Lakes Web site. But he did have a knack for fun, with swimming and playing football among his early passions. He also had the good fortune to witness famed magician Harry Houdini perform at Elmira's Chemung River and, perhaps more notably, cultivate a friendship with eminent author and summer resident Mark Twain. Despite such pleasant distractions, however, the small town charms of his hometown were not sufficient to hold Roach's attention for long.

Roach left school and Elmira while still a teenager. He made his way west, working in a variety of jobs, beginning with selling ice cream. Winding up in Alaska for a time, his resume expanded to include such colorful occupations as gold prospector, mule skinner, trucker, and saloon gambler. Wanderlust eventually propelled him to Seattle, Washington, and finally to Los Angeles, California, in 1912. Roach was just 20 years old then, but he had already experienced adventures of which most people only dream. And he still had 80 productive years ahead of him.

Young, barrel-chested, and possessed of genuine cowboy credentials, which is to say that he could competently ride a horse, Roach soon found work in Hollywood at Universal Pictures as a cowboy extra in silent movies for $25 a week. He struck up a friendship with another extra named Harold Lloyd. The film industry was in its infancy at the time, and the newfound pals were fascinated by the burgeoning new field. Lloyd was content enough as an actor, but Roach aspired to become a producer. Happily,

Roach's coming into a small inheritance put both men on track to realize their goals.

Early Studio Years

Armed with a $3,000 legacy, Roach founded a small production company, which came to be known as the Hal Roach Studios, in 1914. Lloyd came onboard as the company's star comedian for three dollars a day, and Roach began making short films for approximately $350 each. This initial foray into the movie business, however, suffered from a lack of distributors, and Roach took a brief hiatus to work as a director at the Essanay Film Manufacturing Company. A deal with distributor the Pathe Exchange had him back on his own lot by 1916, and history was soon in the making.

Almost from the onset, Roach's studio was known as the "Lot of Fun." Performers, directors, writers, and stage-hands alike were given nearly free rein to do their respective jobs. This management style resulted in a relaxed, congenial atmosphere that employees, naturally, enjoyed immensely. Not incidentally, the studio also started to earn money.

Lloyd was integral to the new studio's increasing success. Mildly popular with his derivative characters of "Willie Work" and "Lonesome Luke," his popularity sky-rocketed with the introduction of his "Glasses Character" in 1917. Lloyd gave the previously untouchable Charlie Chaplin some stiff competition, and Roach's studio was established as a formidable presence in Hollywood.

As his studio prospered, Roach was able to do things he could not do before. Some were personal, such as bringing his parents out to the West Coast and putting his father to work for him. Others were business, such as building up his talent roster to include such stars as Snub Pollard, Will Rogers, and "Sunshine" Sammy Morrison. He scored another coup in 1922 when he released the first of the *Our Gang* series. Comedies based on the trials and triumphs of regular children, the series was hugely successful. It became one of the most enduring of all short subject series (produced by Roach from 1922 to 1938 and MGM from 1938 to 1944), and spawned an equally beloved syndicated television program called *The Little Rascals*. But Roach had even greater contributions to offer.

Laurel and Hardy

Lloyd left the Hal Roach Studios in 1924 to try his hand at setting up his own production firm. While his departure did not bring the studio to a grinding halt, it did leave Roach casting about for a new comedy star. He briefly attempted to make do with animals, but quickly returned to humankind to get audiences chuckling. The *Our Gang* series was still going strong, of course, and writer/director Charley Chase successfully lent his comedic acting skills to the cause, but a more general jumpstart remained just out of reach. Then inspiration struck.

In 1926 Stan Laurel was working as a comedian/director and Oliver Hardy was a supporting actor and vaudeville comedian. Not unlike Roach, Hardy was large and full of life. Laurel, on the other hand, was small and fastidious. Both men, however, were funny, and when Roach hit upon the idea of selling them as a team, he created pure magic.

Part of what set Roach's comedies apart, especially from those of arch rival Mack Sennett, was his attention to story and character in addition to sight gags and slapstick humor. Laurel and Hardy were fine examples of that focus, managing to be distinctly human and indisputably hilarious at the same time. Their inaugural outing together, in Roach's *The Battle of the Century* (1927), set the world's record for custard pie throwing and became one of the most noted comedy short films of all time. Audiences adored the duo, and they were bona fide stars within the year.

The Laurel and Hardy/Roach alliance was to last until 1940, and it survived the perilous transitions from silent films to talkies, and from shorts to feature films. This was particularly significant in that it illustrated Roach's willingness to explore new technologies and keep pace with the changing times, traits not necessarily shared by other independent studio bosses. From shorts such as 1932's *The Music Box,* to features such as 1937's *Way Out West,* to their final effort together in 1940's *Saps at Sea,* Roach and his endearing team created a string of ageless classics still admired and enjoyed in the twenty-first century.

More Changes

Although Laurel and Hardy were the bread and butter of Roach's studio throughout the 1930s, there were other winning performers as well. Chase stayed with Roach until 1936, for instance, starring in his own series of shorts. ZaSu Pitts, Patsy Kelly, Thelma Todd, and Billy Gilbert had their own star turns at the studio, and actors including Jean Harlow, Boris Karloff, Fay Wray, and Janet Gaynor also appeared in Roach vehicles over the years.

Short films became steadily less profitable to produce during the 1930s, as double features began to take center stage. Roach's very last short was 1938's *Hide and Seek,* an *Our Gang* title produced just before he sold the series to MGM. But he had not been ignoring features. He released such popular and disparate movies as 1937's *Topper* (and its sequels), the 1939 drama *Of Mice and Men,* and 1940's *One Million B.C.* But the diminished output necessitated by the time demands of feature films resulted in financial strain on the studio. And World War II left its mark, as Roach received a colonel's commission and made training films for the military in other locales. His studio, dubbed "Fort Roach," was also used for such purposes, employing actors such as Ronald Reagan and Alan Ladd. After the war, though, Roach was once again looking to land on his feet.

Television and Beyond

The aftermath of World War II found Roach scrambling to regain his place in Hollywood. During his absence movie funding had become more difficult to procure, so he set his sights on a new media sensation called television. He was, characteristically, one of the first major film producers to realize the potential of that fledgling industry and, just as true to form, set about to conquer it.

Roach founded the Hal Roach Television Corporation in 1948. Together with his son, Hal Roach Jr., he embarked upon yet another adventure. Father and son produced such programs as *Screen Director's Playhouse, The Stu Irwin*

Show, The Gale Storm Show, and *My Little Margie.* They also rented their facilities for the production of TV series that included *The George Raft Show, Blondie, Amos 'n Andy, The Lone Ranger, Groucho Marx, The Abbott and Costello Show, Racket Squad,* and *The Life of Riley.* For a while, it worked. By 1951 the studio was producing 1,500 hours of television programming, and four years later it had become the biggest producer of filmed television shows. The pioneering and winning streak did not go on forever, however. Roach sold his studio to his son and retired in 1955. It had descended into bankruptcy by the early 1960s, and the entire lot was torn down in 1963.

Although one might reasonably argue that Roach's heyday had passed by the 1950s, his life and times were far from finished. He remained active and productive for decades beyond his official retirement, overseeing distribution of his films, becoming a vital participant on the talk show circuit, and even producing an occasional project. He served, for example, as associate producer of 1966's *One Million Years B.C.,* as well as executive producer of television's *The Little Kidnappers* and *Lantern Hill* (both 1990). Roach was honored with an Academy Award for Lifetime Achievement in 1983, and again by the Academy with a tribute to his work at the 1992 awards ceremony. By that time Roach had reached his one hundredth birthday, an accomplishment for which he was feted from Elmira to Los Angeles to London. Still mentally acute and physically hale as he attained the centenarian rank, his typical irreverence was also intact. Asked about his remarkable longevity by the *Albany Times Union,* Roach said, "I started smoking at the age of 11 and quit two years ago because of a cough. I eat anything I want, whenever I want."

Time finally caught up with Roach on November 2, 1992, when he died in Los Angeles. He was predeceased by his wives, Margaret Nichols (1940) and Lucille Prin (1981), and two of his children, Hal Jr. (1972) and Margaret (1963). What lived on was a legacy of warmth and laughter that would delight many generations to come.

Books

Scribner Encyclopedia of American Lives, Volume 3: 1991-1993, Charles Scribner's Sons, 2001.

Periodicals

Albany Times Union, January 12, 1992.
Times (London, England), January 9, 1992; November 4, 1992.

Online

"Hal Roach," Academy of Motion Picture Arts and Sciences, http://awardsdatabase.oscars.org/ampas_awards/Display Main.jsp?curTime=1197402894498 (December 11, 2007).
"Hal Roach," *All Movie Guide,* http://wm06.allmovie.com/cg/avg.dll?p=avg&sql=2:108408~T1 (December 3, 2007).
"Hal Roach," Film Reference, http://www.filmreference.com/Writers-and-Production-Artists-Po-Ro/Roach-Hal.html (December 3, 2007).
"Hal Roach," Internet Movie Database, http://www.imdb.com/name/nm0730018/ (December 3, 2007).
"Hal Roach," Laurel and Hardy Central, http://laurelandhardy central.com/roach2.htm (December 3, 2007).
"Harold Eugene 'Hal' Roach, Sr. (1892-1992)," Famous People of the Finger Lakes, http://www.ilovethefingerlakes.com/history/famous-people-roach.htm (December 3, 2007). □

Max Roach

Jazz drummer Max Roach (1924-2007) expanded the boundaries of his art. He raised the profile of percussion within American music and served as a pioneer in using his craft as a method for socio-political advocacy for the African-American experience.

Following in the musical footsteps of Big Sid Catlett and Kenny Clarke, Roach—as a member of bands led by such notable talents as Charlie Parker and Dizzy Gillespie—further developed the art of modern jazz drumming. Widely recognized as one of the founders of bebop or modern jazz, Roach refused to recognize such terms in reference to an African-American art form he believed was prejudicially named by those outside the musical community. Described by music writers as a "melodic drummer," Roach retained, within his solo work, logical constructions built creatively around the composition. As a drummer, educator, composer, and political activist, Roach looked to music as a liberating voice. Roach's use of drums and percussion instruments in orchestral ensemble, the integration of non-standard time signatures, and projects involving rap performers, kept him at the forefront of change within jazz and African-American music for more than six decades. His virtuosity as a percussionist set new standards and enriched American music.

Neighborhood Sounds Formed Musical Education Foundation

Maxwell Lemuel Roach was born in Newland, North Carolina, on January 10, 1924. At the age of four, Roach moved with his family to the Bedford-Stuyvesant district of Brooklyn. Roach's mother, a gospel singer, took him to church regularly and it was there that he received his first musical instruction on trumpet and piano. Roach studied keyboard harmony at age eight with his aunt and, within a year, played piano in the summer Bible school of the Concord Baptist Church. Roach's interest in music was heightened by the sounds of his Brooklyn neighborhood. "You could walk down the street; you heard people singing, you heard people playing," he recalled in Ira Gitler's book *Swing to Bop.* "The community was just fraught with music."

Introduced to the drums in high school, Roach joined the school marching band. By listening to radio shows and recordings, he heard the drumming of Jo Jones and swing drummer "Big" Sid Catlett, who recorded with trumpeter Dizzy Gillespie on such influential bebop numbers as "Salt Peanuts." Along with high school friends such as trumpeter Leonard Hawkins and saxophonist Cecil Payne, Roach listened to the latest jazz bands at the Apollo Theatre in Harlem. Playing in Brooklyn rehearsal bands, he read stock arrangements from the band books of Count Basie and

Jimmie Lunceford. On weekends at Coney Island, he performed in the Darktown Follies and accompanied eighteen different acts in one day.

Local jam sessions became the main outlet for the development of Roach's rhythmic ideas. At these fiercely competitive exchanges, Roach's drum technique began to deviate from the standard swing patterns of the period. While still a teenager, Roach often wore a penciled mustache in order to appear old enough to attend after-hours jam sessions at Harlem nightclubs like Monroe's Uptown House on 138th Street and Minton's Playhouse located in the dining room of the Hotel Cecil on 118th Street. At Minton's Roach encountered the house band's innovative drummer, Kenny Clarke, a Brooklyn neighbor who provided him with insight concerning technique and career opportunities. Years later, Clarke recounted in *Klook: The Story of Kenny Clarke*, how he "persuaded," Roach "to study at Julliard so that he could acquire the knowledge to become an all-around musician and do studio work and everything." At this time, Roach also received encouragement from Big Sid Catlett. As Roach told Burt Korall in *Drummin' Men*, "I didn't hear that much of Big Sid, except on records, apart from the little I heard on 52nd Street, but I was influenced by his kindness, his generosity."

Gained Reputation with Finest Bands of the Day

When most of the experienced jazz drummers left New York to serve in the armed forces during World War II,

Roach's musical reputation and his ability to read music allowed him to find employment with some of the finest bands of the day. At age sixteen he played three nights at the Paramount Theatre with Duke Ellington's Orchestra, filling in for the ailing Sonny Greer. In Ira Gitler's *Jazz Masters of the Forties* Roach explained how "I had no rehearsal. The stage came up and I was sitting on Sonny's drums all about me. I followed Duke—his conducting was so hip while he played the piano."

After graduating from Boys High School with full honors in 1942, Roach played regular jobs with white groups, and in the evenings sought out more progressive sounds at Monroe's and Minton's. At these late-night club dates, he established a name for himself as one of the formidable "up-and-coming" modern jazzmen. In 1944, Gillespie and bassist Oscar Pettiford hired Roach for their group based at the Onyx on Fifty-Second Street. From the Onyx, Gillespie booked Roach and several members of a new group across the street at the Down Beat.

In February of 1944 Roach, through the intercession of Dizzy Gillespie, made his recording debut with veteran swing saxophonist Coleman Hawkins on the Keynote label. In the company of Hawkins, Gillespie and other talents such as Budd Johnson and Oscar Pettiford, Roach contributed to the numbers "Disorder at the Border," "Feeling Zero," and "Rainbow Mist." One of the first big-name musicians to hire Roach, Hawkins also nurtured the talents of a number of young modern jazzmen. In the liner notes to *Giants of Jazz: Coleman Hawkins*, Roach considered Hawkins as "the most adventurous of the established musicians of the period." A few months after the session with Hawkins, Roach went on the road with saxophonist Benny Carter's band.

Returning to New York in the spring of 1945, Roach joined the legendary Dizzy Gillespie-Charlie Parker quintet at the Three Deuces on Fifty-Second Street. Although he credited other drummers for his musical development Roach, as he explained in *The Legend of Charlie Parker*, attributed Parker as playing a major role in ". . . the way I play the drums. Bird was really responsible, not just because his style called for a particular kind of drumming, but because he set tempos so fast, it was impossible to play straight." To compensate for the polyrhythmic texture of bebop, Roach abandoned the steady four-four bass pedal and repetitive ride cymbal patterns of earlier jazz drummers. Through the variation of rhythm, he developed what has been called "melodic" drumming—an approach which freed the instrumentalist from his traditional role as strictly a time-keeping accompanist.

With Gillespie's departure from the group, Parker hired 19-year-old trumpeter Miles Davis, who formed a close friendship with Roach. In November of 1945 Roach, along with Gillespie, Davis, and bassist Curly Russell, recorded with Parker on the Savoy label. Released as "Charlie and His Re Boppers," the session yielded the classic numbers "Billie's Bounce," "Now's the Time," and "Thriving on a Riff." The session also included Parker's "Ko Ko"—a landmark bebop number which, as Gary Giddins noted in *Chasin' The Bird*, "braced by the cold winds of Max Roach's drums . . . struck with the violence and calm of a hurricane."

By December of 1945, Parker and Gillespie had replaced Roach in a newly assembled group. Roach then freelanced in Fifty-Second Street clubs with groups led by Coleman Hawkins, Dexter Gordon, and J.J. Johnson. He recorded with Hawkins for the Sonora label, cutting the album *Coppin' the Bop*. His 1947 Dial recordings with Parker included "Scrapple From the Apple," and "Chasin' the Bird." In 1949, Roach attended a session that became part of Miles Davis's ground-breaking *Birth of the Cool* recordings. That same year, he played on pianist Bud Powell's legendary numbers "Tempus Fugit" and the Latin-influenced number "Uno Poco Loco." Around this time Roach also earned a bachelors degree in music theory from the Manhattan School of Music.

Pioneering Efforts Lauded

In his 1952 work, *A History of Jazz in America*, Barry Ulanov lauded Roach as "a rhythmic thinker; his solos are not like swing drummers', not dependent on sheer noise and intensity to make the point." Known for his crisp and precise rhythmic execution and melodic sense, Roach was in demand as both a performer and studio musician. That same year, he joined Charles Mingus and his wife Celia as co-founder of the Debut record label. This short-lived company recorded not only solo projects by Roach and Mingus, but also those of jazzmen such as Miles Davis, Thad Jones, Kenny Dorham, and J.J. Johnson. In May of 1953 Roach and Mingus, along with Gillespie, Parker, and Bud Powell, took part in an all-star concert at Toronto's Massey Hall. The concert, recorded on-stage by Mingus, was later released as the Debut recording *The Quintet: Jazz at Massey Hall*. In *To Be or Not to Bop*, Roach recalled the concert, ". . . everybody was in complete command, everybody had a wonderful time. It was a real happy, happy day."

In 1953, Roach arrived in Hermosa Beach, California to replace drummer Shelly Mann in the Lighthouse All-Stars. During the following year, Roach brought trumpeter Clifford Brown from New York to California and assembled a quintet that included Harold Land, pianist Richie Powell, and bassist George Morrow. In *West Coast Jazz*, Ted Gioia noted that Roach and Brown "were about to become the most prominent members in one of the finest—if not best—jazz combos of the early 1950s." From sessions recorded in Los Angeles during August of 1954, the quintet recorded its first LP *Brown and Roach Incorporated*. This release was followed in 1955 by the album *Clifford Brown and Max Roach*.

These recordings received acclaim from both musicians and music critics. Following the departure of Land from the quintet in 1955, Roach and Brown recruited the talents of saxophonist Theodore Walter "Sonny" Rollins. The horns of Brown and Rollins, along with Roach's inventively propulsive drumming, proved to be a brilliant combination. Rollins' recording debut with the group occurred on the 1956 album, *Clifford Brown and Max Roach at Basin Street*. Like the group's earlier recordings, *At Basin Street* showcased Roach's masterful extended solos. The quintet's success, however, was cut short in June of 1956 when Brown and Powell were killed in an automobile accident. "Max used to tell me all the time how he loved playing with Brownie," related Miles

Davis in his memoir *Miles*. "His death really got to Max and he didn't pull out of it for a long time."

After the deaths of Brown and Powell, Roach performed in a trio with Rollins and bassist George Morrow. In April of 1956, he appeared on saxophonist Johnny Griffin's album, *Introducing Johnny Griffin*. Two months later, he provided accompaniment for Rollins' groundbreaking solo album, *Saxophone Colossus*. A brilliant showcase of material, this album included "St. Thomas," a Caribbean-inspired number in which, as Ira Gitler observed in the album's liner notes, "Max shines in his featured spot, once again demonstrating his musical approach to the drums." Roach's performance on the album *Blue 7* "shows," as Gunther Sculler commented in *Jazz Panorama*, "that exciting drum solos need not be just an un-thinking burst of energy—they can be interesting and meaningful compositions." In December of 1956 Roach, along with bassist Oscar Pettiford, formed the rhythm section for Thelonious Monk's Riverside album *Brilliant Corners*. Roach's contributions to *Brilliant Corners* included playing the tympani on Monk's classic "Bemsha Swing." As Thomas Fetterling remarked in *Thelonious Monk: His Life and Music*, "[Roach] supplanted his kit with tympani, giving the rather simple theme a powerful allure. During [Sonny] Rollins' solo he makes the tympani thunder." In February of 1958, Roach and Pettiford formed a trio with Rollins for the saxophonist's celebrated Riverside album, *Freedom Suite*.

Advocated for Civil Rights

Roach entered the 1960s committed to the struggle against racism. His outspoken views on race were reflected in the 1960 Atlantic album *We Insist! Freedom Now*. In July of the same year, he joined Mingus in a protest against the cancellation of the Newport Jazz Festival by staging a "rebel festival" at the nearby Cliff Walk Manor Hotel. The alternative event attracted such talents as Coleman Hawkins, Jo Jones, Ornette Coleman, and vocalist Anne Marie "Abbey" Lincoln. Soon after the event, in a 1961 issue of *Down Beat*, Roach boldly stated that he would "never again play anything" that did not "have social significance." That same year, Roach infused the voice of racial protest into his recording of *Percussion Bitter, Sweet*. This album showcased a number of original compositions in the company of such musicians as Eric Dolphy, Booker Little, Julian Priester, Clifford Jordan, and Mal Waldron. Vocalist Abbey Lincoln appeared on the tracks, "Garvey's Ghost," which was dedicated to the Jamaican-born black nationalist leader Marcus Garvey, and the ballad "Mendacity," which sardonically mocked American democracy and its promise of racial equality.

Roach married Abbey Lincoln in 1962 and, over the next decade, the two collaborated extensively, even after the marriage eventually ended in divorce. Trained as a rhythm and blues singer, Lincoln expanded her musical horizons by recording with jazz accompanists. In *Down Beat*, Lincoln described the "handsome, sophisticated," Roach as an inspiring companion who "gave me sanctuary." Devoted to expanding the horizons of African-American music, Roach fused jazz with elements of Negro spirituals to create a voice of artistic expression and social protest. As drummer-bandleader, Roach wrote and arranged choral and orchestral works, the first of which appeared on the album *It's Time* in 1962. In September of the same year, Roach and Mingus provided the accompaniment for Duke Ellington's Blue Note recording, *Money Jungle*. The album, which placed Ellington with "two musicians of the next generation, both of whom idolized him, produced some splendidly forthright, if none too well recorded, playing by all three." remarked Brian Priestly in *Mingus.*

In 1971 Roach began teaching at the University of Massachusetts at Amherst, where he became a key figure in establishing a jazz major. That same year, he recorded *Lift Every Voice and Sing*, (dedicated to Paul Robeson) with a twenty-two member gospel choir. In 1972, he founded the M'Boom, a ten-man percussion ensemble featuring over one hundred different Third World instruments, including vibes, steel pans, marimbas and chimes. In 1979 and 1980, he joined pianist Cecil Taylor for a series of concerts and spent the rest of the decade recording with jazzmen such as Abdullah Abrahim, Cecil Bridgewater, and Odoen Pope. Peter Keepnews of the *New York Times*, remembered the Max Roach Double Quartet of the mid-1980s as perhaps Roach's "most ambitious experiment," for in it Roach gave string musicians equal footing with others in the ensemble, allowing them to improvise and swing as never before. In 1987, Roach further pursued his diverse musical vision by contributing to the score of "Swingin' The Dream" an adaptation of William Shakespeare's "Midsummer's Night Dream." During the following year, he appeared with the Japanese drum troupe Kodo, and became the first jazz musician to win a MacArthur Foundation grant for creative genius.

Throughout the 1990s, Roach was involved in numerous collaborations and creative settings. He recorded the two-CD set, *To the Max!*, in 1992 and performed with the Atlanta Symphony Orchestra. Always attentive to new musical ideas, Roach viewed rap as a creative improvisational form and collaborated with MTV's rap-music host Fab Five Freddie in recording the program *From Bebop to Hip-hop*. Roach's sextet performed with the Abyssinian Baptist choir in 1997. In 1998, Roach performed with his So What Brass Quintet, which was comprised of five brass instruments and drums, and with dancers in choreographer Donald Byrd's production "Jazz Train." He performed live until at least 2001, when he appeared with his Quartet at the 2001 JazzFest in New Orleans. Roach's last recording followed in 2002 with trumpeter Clark Terry. Jazz critic Kevin Whitehead found Roach's style on *Friendship* spare when compared with his dynamic recordings from the 1970s, according to his review of the recording for National Public Radio; yet Whitehead concluded that Roach still "phrases with the clarity and grace of a tap dancer."

Roach's musical career offers a timeline of the creative legacy of modern African-American music. His ability to embrace new musical ideas throughout his career exemplified his vast creative vision and boundless desire to interpret the world around him. While alive, Roach took it as his "mission," commented Ben Sidran in *Talking Jazz: An Oral History*, "to keep the long revolution marching forward to a new beat." He died on August 16, 2007, in New York City.

Roach's "superior quality of sound," as Wynton Marsalis observed in a 1988 *New York Times* article about jazz, "is one of the marvels of contemporary music." For his percussive talents, Marsalis described Roach as "a peerless master." For setting standards in American music and for using his music to advocate for his culture, Roach remains a man to be admired.

Books

Bird, The Legend of Charlie Parker, edited by Robert Reisner, Da Capo, 1962.
Davis, Miles, with Quincy Troupe, *Miles: The Autobiography*, Simon & Schuster, 1989.
Fetterling, Thomas, *Thelonious Monk: His Life and Music*, foreword by Steve Lacey, Berkley Hill Books, 1997.
Giddins, Gary, *Chasin' The Bird: The Triumph of Charlie Parker*, Beech Tree, 1987.
Gillespie, Dizzy, *To Be, or Not to Bop*, Doubleday & Company, Inc., 1979.
Gioia, Ted, *West Coast Jazz: Modern Jazz in California 1945-1960*, University of California Press, 1992.
Gitler, Ira, *Jazz Masters of the Forties*, Collier Books, 1966.
———, *The Masters of Bebop*, Da Capo, 2001.
———, *Swing to Bop: An Oral History of the Transition of Jazz in the 1940's*, Oxford University Press, 1985.
Hennesey, Mike, *Klook, The Story of Kenny Clarke*, University of Pittsburgh Press, 1994.
Jazz Panorama: From the Birth of Dixieland, From the Pages of Jazz Review, Collier Books, 1958.
Korall, Burt, *Drummin' Men: The Heartbeat of Jazz, The Swing Years*, Schirmer Books, 1990.
Mathieson, Kenny, *Giant Steps: Bebop and the Creators of Modern Jazz, 1945-65*, Canongate, 1999.
Owens, Thomas, *Bebop: The Music and Its Players*, Oxford University Press, 1995.
Priestly, Brian, *Mingus: A Critical Biography*, Da Capo, 1982.
Sidran, Ben, *Talking Jazz: An Oral History*, Da Capo, expanded edition, 1995.
Taylor, Arthur, *Notes and Tones: Musician-to-Musician Interviews*, Da Capo Press, 1993.
Ulanov, Barry, *A History of Jazz in America*, Viking, 1952.

Periodicals

The Black Perspective in Music, 1990.
Down Beat, March 21, 1968; July 24, 1969; March 16, 1972; September 1989; November 1978; November 1990; February 1992; May 1993; November 1993; November 1998.
Los Angeles Times, August 17, 2007.
Musician, January 1994.
New York Times, July 31, 1988; August 25, 2007.
Philadelphia Tribune, June 12, 1998.
Pulse!, November 1992.
Washington Post, August 17, 2007.

Online

"Marian McPartland's Piano Jazz: Max Roach," *National Public Radio*, www.npr.org/programs/pianojazz/previousguests/summer2007/roach.html (August 27, 2007).
"Max Roach," *DrummerWorld*, www.drummerworld.com/drummers/Max_Roach.html (August 27, 2007).
"Music Review: *Friendship* from Clark Terry and Max Roach," *National Public Radio*, www.npr.org/templates/story/story.php?storyId=1277286 (August 27, 2007).
"Pioneering Jazz Drummer Max Roach Dies at 83," *National Public Radio*, www.npr.org/templates/story/story.php?storyId=12847242 (August 27, 2007).

Other

Liner notes: *Saxophone Colossus,* Prestige, 1956, written by Ira
Gitler; *Giants of Jazz: Coleman Hawkins,* Time Life Records,
1979, written by John McDonough. ☐

Oral Roberts

**American evangelist Oral Roberts (born 1918) was
an early pioneer in televangelism, or using television
to preach the gospel. Roberts, a stutterer-turned-
preacher who survived a bout of deadly tuberculosis
as an adolescent, has been a successful businessman,
author, and educator. "There was no doubting his
charisma—or his results," David van Biema wrote in
Time magazine.**

Early Years

He was born Granville Oral Roberts on January 24,
1918, in Pontotoc County, Oklahoma, near
Bebee. David Edwin Harrell, Jr., in his book *Oral
Roberts: An American Life,* called his birth "the most por-
tentous event in the Roberts family history." He was the
third and last child of Ellis and Claudius Roberts, born on the
farm of his grandfather, Pleasant Roberts. Oral's cousin,
Minnie Lewis, who traditionally named the babies in the
family, called him Oral, adding to the succession of "O"
names in the family. "In later years, reporters were fascinated by the theatrical sound of Oral's name, but cousin
Minnie had no such designs," Harrell wrote. "When asked
in the 1950s if she knew the meaning of Oral's name, she
replied, 'So far as I know, I had never even heard of the word
before.''

Roberts grew up poor, living first on the family farm,
then in Bebee. His family was deeply religious. Poverty
restricted him, and for years he recalled one stinging incident that happened after he was named "king of his class"
in elementary school. When he appeared to escort the
queen, who came from an affluent family, his teacher told
him he still had time to go home and change into his good
clothes. Roberts matter-of-factly said he was wearing his
best clothes. "To his friends Oral appeared unperturbed, but
the incident scarred him," Harrell wrote. "It awakened him
to the debasing stench of poverty."

Roberts emerged from his shyness that was triggered in
no small part by a stuttering problem, and became what
Harrell called "a consummate salesman." He drew on that
survival skill over the years. He was good in sports, and at
times found his parents' emphasis on religious instruction
stifling.

Survived Brush with Death

In February of 1935, Roberts collapsed while competing in a basketball tournament. His coach, Herman Hamil-

ton, drove him to Ada, where the family lived at the time. "A
pall of death settled around the house," Harrell wrote.
Claudius Roberts's father and two older sisters had died of
tuberculosis (TB), a highly contagious bacterium. Roberts
was bedridden, subsisting on raw eggs and milk.

One day his family brought Roberts to a preaching tent
in Ada set up by roving evangelist George W. Moncey. They
encircled Roberts in his rocking chair and told him he
would be saved. Roberts survived his brush with TB.

Roberts, through his father, joined the ministry of the
Pentacostal Holiness Church and wrote for its publication.
He married Evelyn Lutman in 1938; they would have four
children, 13 grandchildren and several great-grandchildren.
She died in 2005. During the 1940s Roberts traveled extensively and published books. He also studied at Oklahoma
Baptist and Phillips Universities. Roberts resigned his pas-
torate in 1947 and purchased his own tent one year later. It
began a career that would eventually include more than
300 crusades on 6 continents.

Television Era Commenced in 1950s

During the 1950s, Roberts turned to a new medium,
television, filming revival crusades under his mobile tent.
Money came in, and Roberts published more books—he
has published about 120 overall. He published his biography, *The Oral Roberts Story,* in 1952. "Oral Roberts insists
that far more than mere mortal ambitions are involved,"
Landrum R. Bolling wrote in the *Saturday Evening Post.*
"These are clear visions to him, unmistakable commands

that God has communicated to him, Anyone who talks in such simple, assured terms in this unbelieving age is bound to be greeted with doubts and derision."

Controversy engulfed Roberts as his ministry flourished. "The very nature of his ministry, its emphasis upon healing by faith, brought countless reports of physical miracles," Bolling wrote. "It also brought charges of deception, fraud, and cruel exploitation of the sick, the crippled, and the dying. The media had a field day with him, as they have had with many others who combine preaching, praying, and healing."

Founded Oral Roberts University

Roberts, who had long harbored the notion of a namesake university, raised $500 million to build it on farmland on the edge of Tulsa, Oklahoma, and an adjoining medical center, City of Faith, which he opened in 1981. The two institutions consumed 500 acres and consisted of "surrealistic buildings dominated by a prayer tower," Muriel Dobbin wrote in *U.S. News & World Report.* Oral Roberts University received its charter in 1963 and accepted students beginning in 1965. The North Central Association of Colleges and Schools granted it full accreditation in 1971.

By 2007 the campus had expanded to 22 major buildings whose value exceeded $250 million. Roberts also founded a retirement complex, University Village. "Roberts's most important credentials are a quick mind, a passion for learning, great curiosity, and great powers of communication—and enormous dedication, faith, and will," wrote Bolling.

Throughout the 1970s, television was still Roberts's primary medium, and it made him a household name in the United States. As the 1970s wound down, Roberts found himself experimenting with various TV formats and discontinuing others. Cable television stations, which focused on narrowcasting, or targeting viewers in smaller, more intense audiences, crowded the landscape.

"The spread of cable systems complicated the religious programming market, as did the proliferation of programs modeled on Robert's innovative techniques," Harrell wrote. Television specials, often on prime time, replaced the healing crusades, which critics called antiquated. "But to Oral they remained honored memories, and in the 1980s crusading reappeared in the ministry, primarily because of the metamorphosis of Richard Roberts [his son] as an evangelist," Harrell wrote.

"God Will Call Me Home"

In 1987 Roberts implored his television audience to send $8 million worth of donations within three months, or God would "call me home," implying that death loomed if his 1.6 million viewers did not respond accordingly. Roberts received more than $9 million, and "God did not call him home," van Biema wrote. Dobbin added: "Also rising is the sound of snickering." Critics pounced on Roberts. "The time has come to laugh," Jenkin Lloyd Jones, the conservative editor of the *Tulsa Tribune,* told Dobbin. His newspaper ran a series of investigative pieces on Roberts, parodied the minister in cartoons and lambasted him in editorials.

The Roberts cash flow prospered. His direct mail mechanism at the time was sending out 27 million letters and magazines annually, urging what he called "faith partners" to buy such trinkets as prayer handkerchiefs, carved angels, and even jigsaw puzzles of Roberts riding his horse, Sonny. The ministry even needed its own ZIP code because it handled so much mail. Roberts stretched his meetings into three-day crusades in the early 1980s, with Richard Roberts often at their center. "Although Richard's crusades by no means attracted the same attention from the press that his father's had three decades earlier, they usually were attended by curious, and often respectful, reporters," Harrell wrote. While the crusades still included their share of conversion and healing testimonials, Richard put his own stamp on them; he was a much better singer than his father, for example. Oral Roberts, meanwhile, wavered between cutting back on his traveling schedule and continuing to do the preaching he loved.

Roberts's organizational structure became more complex after Oral broadened its reach in the mid-1970s. The City of Faith operated under three management boards. Some executives held titles for both the City of Faith and Oral Roberts University. There was also the Oral Roberts Evangelistic Association, which Harrell called "the cockpit of the entire Roberts empire." He added: "The lines of real power within the Oral Roberts organization were not always easy to follow (they were obscured by a maze of titles and powerless sinecures), but there was one ultimate source of all authority—the seventh-floor office of Oral Roberts. . . . All titles aside, power was firmly in Oral's grip, and it trickled down to those in the organization who were closest to him."

Use of Funds Under Glare

The Roberts empire came under scrutiny again in 2007, when the university said it was $52.5 million in debt. Three weeks earlier, three former professors had announced a wrongful termination suit, claiming they were fired after reporting to the school's Board of Regents what they considered to be "moral and ethical lapses" by Richard Roberts, according to van Biema. Richard had inherited the presidency from his father, who had assumed the title of chancellor. The former professors alleged that Richard and his wife, Lindsay, had used university funds to remodel their home 11 times in 14 years and had spent more than $29,000 to send their daughter on a Bahamas vacation. They also alleged that Lindsay Roberts had several times spent the night at a school guest house with an underaged male.

Harry McNevin said he resigned from the Board of Regents over the alleged misuse of funds, according to the Associated Press (AP). "We were dealing in millions," McNevin told Justin Juozapavicius of the AP. McNevin, in the AP interview, said the board virtually "rubber-stamped" the use of millions in endowment money to buy a Beverly Hills, California, mansion and provide Oral Roberts a West Coast office and home.

The investigative groundswell snowballed. Charles Grassley of Iowa, the ranking Republican on the U.S. Senate Finance Committee, announced an investigation into the use of funds by celebrity preachers, which included Oral Roberts University Board of Regents members Creflo Dollar, Kenneth Copeland, and Benny Hinn. Grassley was seeking from ministries such financial records as salaries, spending practices, and perks such as private jets.

Oral Roberts himself, who was semi-retired and living in California, agreed late in 2007 to return and help run the university while Richard took a leave of absence from his annual $228,000 job, pending an investigation. Richard Roberts denied the overspending allegations and said he pays for personal expenses himself. While the university, which charges students $17,580 in annual tuition, is in damage-control mode, the campus is showing its age and construction of a student center, long in the works, is still in question.

Van Biema reported that the school's expensive ventures often bordered on recklessness, citing the buildup of its men's basketball team, which made the National Collegiate Athletic Association (NCAA) tournaments in 2006 and 2007. "But its big-ticket failures in the end have been more telling," van Biema wrote. The school eventually sold its law program to rival preacher Pat Robertson.

Oral Roberts, in an interview with Cable News Network host Larry King on his *Larry King Live* show, said he supported an investigation. "If there is anything out of line, we will bring it into order, like we have always done," Roberts told King, in an article posted on CNN's Web site. Lindsay Roberts, in the same article, called the charges "preposterous." Bishop Carlton Pearson, a Roberts protégé, said Richard Roberts's privileged upbringing may have contributed to the mess. "These kinds of things are common among family-owned and operated businesses and ministries. They don't cross every T and dot every I," Pearson said on CNN.com.

Controversy and Legacy

Oral Roberts University's struggles cast a pall on Roberts as he approached his ninetieth birthday. According to van Biema, *Charisma* magazine editor J. Lee Grady wrote, "I don't know about you, but I'm having flashbacks to 1987." He was referring to scandals that year that were linked to Jimmy Swaggert and Jim Bakker. But John Schmalzbauer of Missouri State University told van Biema that ineffective management may be the issue. "I think the causes must be deeper and more structural," he said.

"The whole affair is a sad denouement for one of the pioneers of televangelism, van Biema wrote. He quoted Randall Palmer, chairman of the religion department at Barnard College in New York, as saying: "I feel badly for him. This must be a blow."

Books

Harrell, David Edwin Jr., *Oral Roberts: An American Life,* Indiana University Press, 1985.

Periodicals

Saturday Evening Post, September 1983.
U.S. News & World Report, March 9, 1987.

Online

"Oral Roberts' Son Accused of Misspending," Associated Press, http://www.wtop.com/index.php?nid=104&sid=1288797 (November 21, 2007).
"Oral Roberts' son denies he misspent school funds," CNN.com, http://www.cnn.com/2007/US/law/10/10/oru.suit/index.html (November 21, 2007).
"Oral Roberts to the Rescue?," *Time,* http://www.time.com/time/nation/article/0,8599,1677098,00.html (November 21, 2007). □

Anita Roddick

British entrepreneur Anita Roddick (1942-2007) was the public face of the Body Shop cosmetics–store chain she founded. Roddick, one of Britain's most successful and visible business executives, was also a strident environmental and animal–rights activist. Roddick "believed that businesses could be run ethically, with what she called 'moral leadership,' and still turn a profit," Sarah Lyall wrote in the *New York Times.* In 2006, one year before she died, Roddick sold the Body Shop and its 2,100 stores to cosmetics giant L'Oréal for €625 million ($1.3 billion).

Early Life

Roddick was born Anita Lucia Perilli on October 23, 1942, in Littlehampton, West Sussex, England. She was the third of four children to Gilda and Donny Perilli, Italian immigrants who made their children work after school and on weekends in the café they owned. They divorced while Roddick was eight—Donny, according to the British *Guardian* newspaper, was alcoholic and prone to violence. Gilda Perilli later married her ex–husband's cousin, Henry—he died of tuberculosis a few years later. When Roddick was 18, her mother admitted that Henry, in fact, was her father, the result of an extramarital affair.

After Roddick attended the Maude Allen Secondary Modern School for Girls, a drama school rejected her application. She took teachers' training at the Newtown Park College of Education in Bath, England, then worked in the morgue at the Paris office of the *International Herald Tribune.* At her next stop, Geneva, Switzerland, she worked briefly in the International Labour Organization's women's rights department.

Roddick spent a year at a kibbutz in Israel before quitting to visit such places as Tahiti, South Africa, and Australia. She applied what she learned during her travels while running the Body Shop. "When you've lived for six months with a group that is rubbing their bodies with cocoa butter, and those bodies are magnificent, or if you wash your hair with mud, and it works, you go on to break all sorts of conventions, from personal ethics to body care," she said, as Lyall quoted her.

Shop Subsidized Husband's Hobby

In 1970, Roddick married Gordon Roddick in Reno, Nevada, when she was pregnant with their second child. They had been together for six years. Early in their marriage, while they were running a bed–and–breakfast lodging and an Italian health–food restaurant, Gordon told Anita he intended to ride horseback from Buenos Aires, Argentina, to New York over 18 months.

Needing to support her children while her husband pursued his hobby, Roddick began to cook moisturizers in her Brighton, England, home in 1975. One year later, she opened her first Body Shop, also in Brighton, based on a similar shop she had seen in Berkeley, California. Her husband helped her negotiate a €4,000 ($8,264) startup loan from a bank. Fifteen skin–care products with far–away names adorned her shelves, in five different bottle sizes to make her product line look more expansive. She originally used dark green paint on the walls, which became the trademark of Body Shops worldwide—to hide patches of mold. Local businessman Ian McGlinn, a former garage owner, provided an additional €4,000 in exchange for a 24 percent stake in the company.

Gordon Roddick, after he returned, provided business and financial savvy to the operation. The passionate Anita, meanwhile, was its face. The Body Shop did not need a marketing department, because she generated enough headlines en route to drawing praise as one of Britain's most successful female business executives. "Loquacious, wacky and opinionated, she was so far outside the normal busi-nesswoman template that it was easy for her to attract free coverage," the *Telegraph* of London wrote.

The Roddicks launched a franchise network and their first store outside the United Kingdom in Brussels, Belgium, in 1978. The company floated on the London Stock Exchange six years later. Its value in 1990 was €800 million ($1.7 billion). The Roddicks had a 30 percent shareholding at the time, making Anita the fourth–richest woman in Britain.

Introduced Activism to Business

Roddick used her business as a pulpit for social causes, including fair treatment of animals, the rain forest, debt relief for poor countries, voting rights, and whales. She believed running a business ethically and profitably were not mutually exclusive. Lyall called her "a woman of fierce passions, boundless energy, unconventional idealism, and sometimes diva–like temperament." In 1985, Roddick pro-moted the save–the–whales campaign by the worldwide organization Greenpeace, prompting Lucy Siegle of the *Guardian* to call it "the first explicit tie–in between products and causes." Roddick linked many of her products to paci-fism, rain–forest preservation, opposition to nuclear power, and, according to Siegle, "sticking two fingers up at corpo-rate greed." Roddick also helped found *Big Issue* magazine in 1990, which homeless people sold and produced.

Her idealism at times collided with the business estab-lishment. In 1999, for example, Roddick was among front–line protesters who were tear–gased outside the World Trade Organization in Seattle, Washington. "Her philippics about the evils of global capitalism, profits and the world trading system sat rather oddly with her status as the leader of a highly profitable multinational corporation with nearly 2,000 outlets in 49 countries," the *Telegraph* wrote. When the Body Shop struggled financially during the 1990s, amid an economic downturn and increasing competition, corporate investors accused the Roddicks of campaigning obsessively for pet causes at the expense of operational efficiency.

Roddick, whom the *Telegraph* described as "highly likeable in many ways, though to some also extremely irritating," was vulnerable to accusations of hypocrisy, par-ticularly from the political left. The company, for example, said none of its products were tested on animals, though other companies had done such testing with ingredients the Body Shop used. In 1989, West Germany's government successfully sued a Body Shop subsidiary for misleading advertising, prompting the company to change its label from "not tested on animals" to "against animal testing." A 1992 documentary by the British television show *Dispatches* also alleged the Body Shop with fraudulent claims, though Roddick sued and won, and in a 1994 article in *Business Ethics*—ironically, a magazine Roddick had endorsed—Jon Entine raised questions about the company's ecological and environmental standards.

She also spoke out against sweatshops, but added, as quoted by Laura Smith-Spark of BBC News, that "only pres-sure from Western consumers can trigger change." She cited garment workers in Bangladesh, denied the three months of maternity leave to which she said they were entitled. "For the women and their infants, this is literally a matter of life and death, since their below–substance wages mean they have no savings in reserve," she said.

Controversial Sale to L'Oréal

Early in the new millennium, rumors persisted that the Body Shop was for sale. Mexican company Grup Omnilife, a seller of direct–to–consumer nutritional supplements, and British cosmetics company Lush were linked with possible takeovers. In 2001 The Body Shop admitted receiving overtures; however, talks with both companies fizzled. Roddick, though, stepped down as company co–chair in 2002.

In March of 2006, an agreement was reached for L'Oréal to take over the Body Shop. The announcement rankled hard–core environmentalists, who said the Paris–based company, whose products include Garnier shampoo and Armani makeup, had a poor record on animal testing. The companies closed on the sale that November. Just before the sale, *Ethical Consumer* magazine had given L'Oréal its lowest possible rating on animal testing. Roddick once said, according to the *Guardian,* "I hate the beauty industry, it is a monster selling unattainable dreams. It lies, it cheats, it exploits women."

Roddick, in an interview with the *Guardian* at her Chichester office in November of 2006, said she still held the same view of the profession. "The beauty industry hasn't changed much. You still have models that look glum—the 'glum cow disease.' You're still thrown on to the trash heap of life if you have wrinkles on her skin or dimples on your bum . . . and models have got[ten] much, much younger, too."

Still, Roddick perceived herself as a "Trojan horse" who hoped to influence policies at L'Oréal. Under the merger agreement, the Body Shop continued to run itself independently, with Roddick serving as an adviser to the French company. "A handful of consumers will never forgive her for L'Oréal, but she seems to be of the opinion that it was worth it," Siegle wrote in the *Guardian.* After Roddick closed on the sale to L'Oréal, she and her husband concentrated their energies on her nonprofit Anita Roddick Foundation. She also published several namesake books through her publishing company. "After 30 years of leading the company I had other avenues to pursue. I wanted to do something with the money I had while I am still able to," she told Claudia Cahalane of the *Guardian.*

Though some analysts argued that L'Oréal overpaid for the Body Shop, the headlines were more positive a year later. An estimate in 2007 by research firm Oddo Securities said sales at the Body Shop will increase at three times the overall L'Oréal pace by 2010 because of rising environmental awareness. Oddo projected Body Shop sales to increase twenty-four percent over three years.

"There is a definite green movement. Consumers' expectations have become much higher in the last couple of years." Tina Gill of Organic Monitor told the *International Herald Tribune.* Organic Monitor compiles marketing data for L'Oréal and U.S. consumer products giant Procter & Gamble, among others. "Mid–to–long term, L'Oréal has really scored a winner," Deutsche Bank analyst Harold Thompson said in the same article. "I think they took all their competitors by surprise."

Contracted Hepatitis While Giving Birth

In February of 2007, Roddick revealed that she had contracted Hepatitis C—which doctors call a "silent killer"—from a blood transfusion in 1971, when she gave birth to her daughter, Samantha. She was diagnosed with the illness in 2004, but went public as her condition worsened. She developed cirrhosis of the liver and needed a transplant. "It's a bit of a bummer, but you groan and move on," she said, as quoted in the *Telepgraph.* Typically, she turned her condition into a crusade. "For starters, she wants to know why the government spends £40 [million] a year promoting the switch from analog to digital television and just £2 [million] on her disease," Siegle wrote.

Amid deteriorating health, Roddick persisted with her causes, and continued to work on her 12–acre home in West Sussex, which she bought in 1999. She cut down on travel, though she shot rapids in Canada's Yukon territory. "Though I've stepped down from the business side of things, the campaigning work is stronger than ever, via the books and my Web site, where I post a new dispatch each week," she said in an interview with Elspeth Thompson of the *Telegraph.* "I'm into more creative solutions now, definitely a lot less confrontational than I was." Still, Thompson wrote, "I did sense, though, that Roddick missed her more public profile."

Mourned as Activist, Business Leader

In early September of 2007, Roddick, whose mother had died recently at age 94, complained of a headache, then collapsed and was taken to St. Richard's Hospital in Chichester, West Sussex. She died after a major brain hemorrhage on September 10. Her husband and daughters Justine and Samantha were with her.

Accolades came in droves for Roddick, who received Order of the British Empire and Dame Commander of the Order of the British Empire awards in 1988 and 2003, respectively. British Prime Minister Gordon Brown called Roddick "one of the country's true pioneers" who inspired businesswomen. "She will be remembered not only as a great campaigner but also as a great entrepreneur," Brown said, as quoted by BBC News. Former co–worker Justin Francis said in the same article, "She had a great passion for life, a great passion for business and for people. She was very warm, very witty, and very clever."

Samantha Roddick, as quoted in the *Telegraph,* called her mother "a hurricane, a tornado—a weather system that reached every horizon and every corner of the world." John Elkington of business consultancy Sustainability, said in the *Guardian,* "Twenty years ago, the business community said to Anita, 'What in god's name are you doing?' Her fair trade ideas were peripheral. But she created the space where it's acceptable to set up an environmental business. Now everyone's doing it. That's a huge achievement."

Online

"And This Time, It's Personal," *Guardian Unlimited,* http://observer.guardian.co.uk/7days/story/0,,2015586,00 .html (November 6, 2007).

"Anita Roddick: A Great Heart in a Tiny Frame," *Telegraph,* http://www.telegraph.co.uk/news/main.jhtml?xml = /news/2007/09/16/nranita116.xml (November 6, 2007).

"Anita Roddick, Body Shop Founder, Dies at 64," *New York Times,* http://www.nytimes.com/2007/09/12/world/europe/12roddick.html?ex = 1347249600&en = 47dcfce375e0811e&ei = 5088&partner = rssnyt&emc = rss   = (November 6, 2007).

"Body Shop in Takeover Talks," BBC News, http://news.bbc.co.uk/2/hi/business/1374801.stm (November 28, 2007).

"Dame Anita Roddick," *Telegraph,* http://www.telegraph.co.uk/news/main.jhtml?xml = /news/2007/09/12/db1201.xml (November 6, 2007).

"Dame Anita Roddick Dies Aged 64," BBC News, http://news.bbc.co.uk/2/hi/uk_news/6988343.stm (November 6, 2007).

"Dame Anita Roddick Dies Aged 64," *Guardian Unlimited,* http://www.guardian.co.uk/uk_news/story/0,,2166382,00.html (November 6, 2007).

" 'I Believe They Are Honourable and the Work They Do is Honourable,' " *Guardian Unlimited,* http://www.guardian.co.uk/business/2006/nov/03/ethicalliving.environment (November 6, 2007).

"L'Oréal's Purchase of Body Shop is Paying Off," *International Herald Tribune,* http://www.iht.com/articles/2007/10/03/bloomberg/bxatm.php (November 28, 2007).

"Roddick Targets 'Sweatshop' Shame," BBC News, http://news.bbc.co.uk/2/hi/uk_news/3624887.stm (November 6, 2007).

☐

Amália Rodrigues

Portuguese vocalist Amália Rodrigues (1920-1999), performing and recording in the Lisbon-based fado style, became a legendary figure in the national musical life of her country and a much-loved ambassador of Portuguese culture abroad.

Rodrigues had an unusually long career, making her debut in 1939 and singing until the last few years of her life. She achieved considerable exposure in the United States in the 1950s but declined opportunities for wider success. Her smoky, passionate singing epitomized fado in its combination of intense emotion, sadness, and nostalgia, merging to create the uniquely Portuguese sentiment known by the untranslatable word *saudade.* When Rodrigues died in 1999 she was mourned as an icon of Portuguese life.

Born During Cherry Blossom Season

Amália da Piedade Rodrigues was born in Lisbon and raised in the industrial Alcântara neighborhood. Her family did not know the exact date of her birth. Rodrigues herself said that she was born on July 1; her birth certificate reads July 23, but a poor family in a still largely underdeveloped Portugal might have taken several weeks to receive that document, and her grandfather's recollection that she was born during cherry blossom season suggests the earlier date. Rodrigues's father was a cobbler and part-time musician who found little success in either field, and Amália was turned over to her grandparents to be raised in Lisbon while most of her family returned to their village of Fundão.

A shy, asthmatic child, Rodrigues liked to stay in her room and sing tangos by Argentine vocalist Carlos Gardel, but her grandfather noticed that people passing on the street would often stop to listen. One of ten children, several of whom did not reach adulthood, Rodrigues grew up in poverty. She enrolled in elementary school at age nine, and once, when she had to buy a second schoolbook for a class, her grandmother asked her why she needed another book, as the first one she had was still in good condition. Leaving school at 12, Rodrigues worked as a seamstress and clothes cleaner to help support her family. When she was 14 her parents and siblings returned to Lisbon, and she went to live with them. She worked in a factory and in her mother's fruit stand. "We never complained about life," she recalled, according to the Portuguese biography site Vidas Lusofonas. "Sure, we knew there were people who were different from us; otherwise there would be no revolutions. But I never heard anybody talk about that."

Rodrigues and her younger sister Celeste occupied what little spare time they had by going to the movies; Rodrigues was fascinated by the 1937 Greta Garbo film *Camille,* and even went so far as to drink vinegar and stand in cold drafts so that she would contract tuberculosis like the Garbo character in the film. As a teenager Rodrigues dreamed of a career as a performer. The reigning style of the day was fado, a gloomy, fatalistic vocal genre that, like Spanish flamenco music, carried influences from Arabic and gypsy music. In 1938 Rodrigues, representing the Alcântara neighborhood, entered and won a "Queen of the Fado" contest. Making inroads into Lisbon's fado scene, she fell in love with guitarist Francisco Cruz and attempted suicide after he at first rejected her. In 1939 she made her debut at a Lisbon fado club, the Retiro da Severa.

That year she married Cruz, but the marriage ended in divorce in the early 1940s. By that time Rodrigues had become a common sight in Lisbon nightspots, singing other popular styles such as tango, Brazilian samba, and waltzes in addition to fado. She was a talented onstage dancer as well. She appeared in a revue called *Ora vai tu,* playing the role of a traditional fado singer who wore a black funeral shawl, and she adopted that clothing as her trademark. Later, when Rodrigues visited America, Hollywood gossip columnist Hedda Hopper suggested that she give up the black shawl for a white dress with plunging neckline and a flower in her hair, but Rodrigues patiently explained the traditional roots of her dark look.

Made Recordings in Brazil

Rodrigues's exposure to international audiences began when she appeared in Madrid, Spain, in 1943. A six-week tour of Brazil in 1944 was extended to three months by popular demand, and the following year she made her first recordings in that country. Recordings from the early part of Rodrigues's career were sparse, however, for her manager, José de Melo, kept her out of the studio in order to boost demand for her live performances. After the end of World War II, Rodrigues's popularity continued to grow both at home and abroad. She appeared in the 1947 film *Capas Negras* (Black Capes), which set box office records in Portugal, and she gave concerts in both London and Paris in 1949. Rodrigues appeared at the Argentina Opera House in Rome, Italy, in 1950, on a bill with musicians who otherwise came exclusively from the operatic field; despite intense stage fright (from which she suffered for her entire career), her appearance was a triumph.

Rodrigues's status as an international star was confirmed when she arrived in New York in 1952 and appeared at the nightclub La Vie en Rose. In 1953 she appeared on the *Eddie Fisher Show,* becoming the first Portuguese singer to perform on American television. She had a major international hit in 1955 with "Colimbra," recorded live at the Olympia Theater in Paris and known in English as "April in Portugal." Rodrigues was offered the chance to record two LPs in the United States, but declined. "If I were to make an album with American songs, I'd have to keep rehearsing and working," she was quoted as saying on the Vidas Lusofonas site. "I like to sing without having to think that I am singing. That's the only way I know how to sing. And if I had to worry about the English lyrics, I'd lose my spontaneity."

Indeed, Rodrigues on stage was a compelling performer, with her head thrown back, seemingly overcome with emotion. Rodrigues broadened the reach of fado, singing songs with texts composed by leading Portuguese poets, but she never lost the despairing essence of fado (which means "fate" in Portuguese). "I have so much sadness in me, I am a pessimist, a nihilist, everything fado demands in a singer, I have in me," she was quoted as saying by Jon Pareles in the *New York Times.* "When I am on my own, alone, tragedy comes, and solitude." Rodrigues married engineer César Seabra in Rio de Janeiro in 1961, and they remained married until Seabra's death in 1997. In 1966 she returned to New York for a concert at Lincoln Center, accompanied by a large orchestra conducted by Andre Kostelanetz.

The sole break in Rodrigues's run of popularity came after the so-called Carnation Revolution of 1974, when Portugal threw off decades of authoritarian rule. For younger Portuguese who helped to bring down the right-wing *Estado Novo* (New State) government, Rodrigues represented the old order in which women were repressed. Rodrigues herself proclaimed that she was apolitical, however, and she had often performed texts by left-wing Portuguese poets and given tacit support to reform forces. By the late 1970s her popularity was as strong as ever.

Later in her life, Rodrigues achieved legendary status. For the first time, she began to write and perform songs of her own. She performed at New York's Carnegie Hall in 1977. In the mid-1980s Rodrigues, a lifelong smoker, was diagnosed with lung cancer; while in New York in 1984 she contemplated suicide, but renounced the idea and continued performing. All of her concerts in her later years were sellouts. Rodrigues appeared in 1990 at the San Carlos Theatre in Lisbon, giving the first fado concert ever held there; her final world tour that year included a stop at Town Hall in New York. Her last vocal performance came in 1994 when the city of Lisbon was designated a capital of culture by the European Union. She released the last of her roughly 170 albums, *For the First Time,* in 1995.

Amália Rodrigues died at her Lisbon home on October 6, 1999. Three days of national mourning followed her death, with large crowds waving white handkerchiefs filling Lisbon's Estrela Square. She was buried at the Prazeres Cemetery in a coffin draped in a Portuguese flag. Rodrigues had lived long enough to see fado decline in popularity and then be revived by younger singers such as Misia, Dulce Pontes, and Madredeus, all of whom acknowledged their debt to Rodrigues. Numerous CD reissues and online downloads of the music of Rodrigues remained available.

Books

Contemporary Musicians, volume 40, Gale, 2003.

Periodicals

Financial Times, November 30, 1999.
New York Times, October 7, 1999; December 3, 2000.
Plain Dealer (Cleveland, OH), July 31, 2001.
Times (London, England), October 7, 1999.

Online

"Amália Rodrigues," Internet Movie Database, http://www.imdb.com/name/nm0735052/bio (April 15, 2008).
"Amália Rodrigues," Vidas Lusofonas, http://www.vidas lusofonas.pt/amalia_rodrigues2.htm (February 5, 2008).
"Portugal mourns the 'voice of its soul,'" BBC News, http://www.news.bbc.co.uk/1/hi/world/europe/469679.stm (February 5, 2008). □

Mikhail Romm

Russian film director and writer Mikhail Romm (1901-1971), like the rest of his generation, was greatly influenced by his country's social upheavals of the early twentieth century. His films, from his treatments of Vladimir Lenin in the 1930s to *9 dney odnogo goda* (Nine Days in One Year) in 1961, aptly reflected the political changes through which he had lived. He was also able to achieve real artistry in a time when propaganda in cinema was the general rule.

Early Life and Influences

Romm was born on January 24, 1901, in Irkutsk, Russia, to Jewish parents who had been exiled to Siberia. His mother was reportedly an avid fan of the theater, and Romm thus came naturally by his love of the arts. He moved to Moscow as a teenager to study sculpture with the famed Anna Golubkina at the Academy of Fine Arts, but military service interrupted his higher education from 1918 until 1921.

It is important to have a basic understanding of the tumultuous times in which Romm came of age, as they necessarily had an impact on his work. In brief, the Social Democratic Labor Party divided into the Bolsheviks (led by Vladimir Lenin and later called the Russian Communist Party) and the Mensheviks (led by Julius Martov) in 1903. In February of 1917, Czar Nicholas II abdicated his throne in response to the protests and demands of the public. This was known as the "February Revolution" and ended the dynasty of the Romanovs. The Russian Parliament, or Duma, which had been established in 1905, quickly installed a prime minister to head a provisional government to replace the czar. The new prime minister did not last long, however, as the Bolsheviks overthrew the government in what became known as the "October Revolution" (still 1917), and Lenin took over the country's leadership. Matters fell into further disarray the following year when a civil war broke out between the Bolsheviks and the Mensheviks. Lenin's Red Army prevailed in 1921, but the hardship and loss of life among the Russian people had been immense (millions died from starvation alone). It was against this dramatic backdrop that Romm had reached adulthood.

Romm served in the Red Army from 1918 until 1921. He began as a soldier and telephone operator before becoming an inspector in the Special Forces for Food Supplies. Happy or unhappy, his military tenure helped provide both rapid maturity and experiences not soon forgotten. After his service, Romm returned to Moscow to complete his studies, graduating from the Academy of Fine Arts in 1925. Throughout the 1920s he pursued a variety of artistic endeavors. Literature was a passion, for example, prompting him to translate the works of such major French authors as Gustave Flaubert and Honore de Balzac into Russian. He also wrote novels and short stories, and worked as a sculptor, interpreter, actor, and journalist. In 1928 he started researching the theory of cinematography, and by the early 1930s, Romm had settled on film as his primary artistic medium.

1932 to 1953

Romm began his movie career in 1932 as the screenwriter and assistant director of an early "talkie" called *Dela i lyudi* (Men and Jobs). His directing debut in 1934 was with the last Russian silent movie produced and the first to be made completely on Russian filmstock. It was an adaptation of a classic by the nineteenth-century French writer Guy de Maupassant, *Boule de Suif* (Pyshka), and was widely seen as one of the finest interpretations of the author's work. (Romm's facility as a translator was of great assistance to him in that effort.) Next up, Romm wrote and directed one of Russia's first "Easterns" (the Soviet answer to the "Western"), *Trinadtsat* (The Thirteen). Released in 1937, its energy and action set a standard for the myriad Russian adventure films that followed it. Not incidentally, the cast included Yelena Kuzmina, who later became Romm's wife.

The year 1937 saw the release of Romm's *Lenin v oktyabre* (Lenin in October). The movie was commissioned by then-Soviet leader Josef Stalin to commemorate the twentieth anniversary of the October Revolution. Although made in just two weeks, the epic saga was well received. It was also an excellent example of the ongoing conflict between art and politics that was indicative of the time. On the one hand, the film's content was actively overseen and guided by Stalin himself, thereby certainly curtailing Romm's artistic autonomy. On the other, Romm was able to inject the project with sufficient artistic credibility that it enhanced his international reputation. A companion piece, *Lenin y 1918* (Lenin in 1918), was released in 1939. It was also successful. Still, it is telling that after Stalin's death in 1953, Romm personally re-edited the Lenin movies, deleting all Stalin references.

Mechta (Dream), starring Faina Ranevskaya, Rostislav Plyatt, Ada Voitsek, and Mikhail Astangov, came out in 1943 and was applauded for its examination of spiritual crises. In 1945 *Chelovek No. 217* (Girl No. 217) was released. It told the story of a Soviet girl captured by fascists. By the late 1940s, however, Romm's reputation began to falter as he bowed to government pressure to produce more propaganda films. Nonetheless, he continued to churn out movies. *Russkiy vopros* (The Russian Question) was based on a play by Konstantin Simonov (1948) and *Sekretnaya missiya* (Secret Mission) was a harrowing tale of a female Soviet spy who comes to a bad end (1950). The release of 1950's *Vladimir Ilich Lenin* (Lenin) was followed up by a historical costume drama about the founding of the Russian Black Sea fleet in 1779 called *Admiral Ushakov,* and by its sequel, *Korabli shturmuyut bastiony* (The Ships from the Bastion), both in 1953. Stalin died in 1953, soon to be succeeded by Nikita Khrushchev. Before long, the Russian cinema and Romm's career would undergo another sea change.

Effect of the Soviet Thaw

In 1956 Romm wore many hats. He wrote the screenplay for *Dolgij put* (A Weary Road), was the creative producer for *Sorok pervyj* (The Forty-First), and directed *Ubiystvo na ulitse Dante* (Murder on Dante Street or The Long Roads). Although the public embraced it, the last effort was a disappointment to Romm, both because his wife was not permitted to appear in it and for artistic reasons. Perhaps partly because of that, he took a job as a film professor at the Russian State Institute of Cinematography (VGIK) in 1957. He still wrote and directed the occasional movie, such as 1957's *Urok istorii* (A Lesson in History) and 1958's *Zhivoj Lenin* (Lenin is Alive), but teaching and writing absorbed most of his time for the next few years. Meanwhile, the Russian motion picture scene had begun its own small revolution.

At a meeting of Communist Party members in 1956, Khrushchev denounced Stalin's crimes and thus ushered in "The Thaw" (a term coined by author and journalist Ilya Ehrenburg). It was a period when the rigid dictates of Stalin regarding Soviet cinema, among other arts, began to relax, or "thaw" out. Film professionals started to breathe more freely and follow their creative instincts in a way not seen in decades. Naturally, as one of the most prominent moviemakers of his generation, Romm could not resist such an exciting prospect. By 1961 he was back in full force and better than ever.

Lasting Influence

Romm's *9 dney odnogo goda* (Nine Days of One Year) came out in 1961 and was an immediate sensation. Mainly filmed on location at a nuclear physics research institute in Siberia, it is the tale of a young physicist who persists in his experiments toward a pioneering discovery to better mankind despite having received potentially lethal doses of radiation. While there was nothing particularly novel in a hero sacrificing himself for the greater good, the movie was groundbreaking in several respects. First, it looked at the ethical pros and cons of nuclear power and radiation. Second, its characters were not drawn as simply good or bad, but embodied a moral ambiguity and self-examination previously unseen in Russian cinema. As David Gurevich of *Images Journal* described them, "The characters derided 'idiots,' both in the USSR and in the West, and wondered whether they themselves were 'positive characters.' They *wondered* about things, period, which constituted a departure from the supremely confident heroes of yore." In short, the movie did not toe the traditional Communist Party line (indeed, the word "Party" was not uttered on screen). And finally, the film's minimalist style was a welcome deviation from the overwrought tendencies of motion pictures of the Stalin Era.

9 dney odnogo goda firmly established Romm at the top of his game, and won a Crystal Globe Award at the Karlovy Vary International Film Festival in 1962. His next project, *Obyknovennyy fashizm* (Ordinary Fascism or A Night of Thoughts), was released in 1965 and was also a major success. It was a documentary about Nazi Germany, narrated by Romm and ostensibly aimed at explaining the advent of fascism in the twentieth century. But it was even more than that, as it unequivocally denounced tyranny and despotism of any kind, in any place. Such a thinly-veiled reference to Stalinism had a difficult enough time with Russian censors in 1965 (they caused nearly half the film's footage to be cut before its release); it surely would have stood no chance at all before the Thaw. *Obyknovennyy fashizm* won the Special Prize of the Jury at the Leipzig DOK Festival in 1965.

Romm continued to teach at VGIK during his resurgence as a filmmaker. There, his influence on the renaissance of his country's cinema was wielded in another, more subtle way, as he cultivated a new crop of disciples to carry on with, and expand, his vision. The last film project Romm embarked upon had a working title of *World Today*, and was, as the name suggests, a further look at the twentieth century. Sadly, he died in Moscow on November 1, 1971, with the film incomplete. Three of his acolytes, Marlen Khutsiyev, Elem Klimov, and German Lavrov, completed the film for their master, however. It was released in 1974 under the title *I vsyo-taki ya veryu* (And Still I Believe). Film critic Neya Zorkaya commented on Romm's vast influence, to Itta Beratova of the *Russian Culture Navigator* in 2001, nearly 100 years after the great filmmaker's birth. "Romm's works continue to impress for their high professionalism, the splendid montage, and the director's insight into human psychology. Many of his pupils became the leading film directors of the next generation: Vasily Shukshin, Andrei Tarkovsky, Grigory Chukhrai, Georgy Danelia, Savva Kulish. Romm was a brilliant storyteller, publicist, and the author of a great number of theoretical works about cinema. He left us an enormous heritage and there is a lot in it that remains to be discovered."

Online

"Film Library by Director," Open Society Archives, http://www .osaarchivum.org/filmlibrary/browse/director?starting = R &val = 29378 (December 2, 2007).

"Mikhail Romm," *All Movie Guide,* http://wc06.allmovie.com/ cg/avg.dll?p = avg&sql = 2:164345~T1 (December 2, 2007).

"Mikhail Romm, Film Director and Teacher," Russia-IC, http://www.russia-ic.com/culture_art/theatre/264/ (December 2, 2007).

"Mikhail Romm," Internet Movie Database, http://www.imdb .com/name/nm0739677/ (December 2, 2007).

"Mikhail Romm," Seagull Films, http://www.seagullfilms.com/ Default.asp?Page = 237 (December 2, 2007).

"Nine Days of One Year," University of Pittsburgh, http://www .rusfilm.pitt.edu/2001/nine.html (December 2, 2007).

"Phenomenon Named Romm," *Russian Culture Navigator,* January 22, 2001, http://www.vor.ru/culture/cultarch153_eng .html (December 2, 2007).

"Russian Film What Was and What Is," *Images Journal,* http://www.imagesjournal.com/issue09/features/russia2/text .htm (December 2, 2007).

"A Time-Line of Russia," Piero Scaruffi, http://www.scaruffi .com/politics/russians.html (December 14, 2007). □

Arthur Rubinstein

Polish-born American pianist Arthur Rubinstein (1887-1982) was one of the foremost pianists of the twentieth century. His remarkable career spanned over 75 years and included more than 6,000 performances and myriad recordings. The work of composer Frederic Chopin was a specialty, but his repertoire was broad and the pianist was among the first to champion the music of Spain. A bon vivant and unrepentant ladies' man, Rubinstein lived his long life to the fullest. And music was his greatest expression of that passion for living.

Piano Prodigy

Rubinstein was born on January 28, 1887, in Lodz, Poland, the youngest of Isaak Rubinstein and Felicia Heyman's seven children. His father owned a small textile factory and the family enjoyed a comfortable lifestyle in the middle of town. Rubinstein did not begin to speak until he was about three years old, but his interest in the piano quickly outweighed any perceived deficits in other areas. He started studying piano around the same time that he learned to talk, and made his performance debut on December 14, 1894, at the age of seven. Three years later,

the young prodigy's mother took him to Berlin to audition for noted violinist Joseph Joachim. Joachim was sufficiently impressed that he agreed to assume responsibility for Rubinstein's musical and general education. Apparently satisfied, Rubinstein's mother returned to Lodz alone, leaving her ten-year-old son in Joachim's hands. The talented little boy never lived with his family again.

Joachim arranged for his charge to study under the demanding eye of Karl Heinrich Barth, who is credited with shaping Rubinstein's singular sound. Rubinstein chafed under Barth's exactitude, but his playing thrived nonetheless. His professional debut took place on December 1, 1900, at Berlin's Beethoven Saal. Only 13 years old at the time, he took the critics by storm with his renditions of such works as Wolfgang Amadeus Mozart's Piano Concerto in A Major and Camille Saint-Saens' Piano Concerto in G Minor (the latter became a signature piece for the pianist). He followed up this initial triumph with other successful concerts, which buoyed his confidence enough that he decided to leave Barth's tutelage and make his own way in 1903.

Rubinstein moved to Paris to continue his studies in 1904. There he met Maurice Ravel and Saint-Saens, as well as the impresario Gabriel Astruc, with whom he signed his first contract. More highly acclaimed European concerts ensued. Then, in 1906, a much-anticipated tour of the United States was booked. Seventy-five concerts were planned, the most important of which was to be performed at Carnegie Hall in New York City. New York, however, did not prove to be as awed by the 19-year-old sensation as Europe had been. The critics found Rubinstein's playing immature and technique lacking. Sorely disappointed and unused to criticism, the young pianist finished the tour and sailed back to Paris, broke and disheartened. It would be four years before Rubinstein gave another public performance.

Uncertain Interlude

Rubinstein's self-imposed professional exile led to financial troubles and depression that culminated in a failed suicide attempt at the age of 21. Happily, that nadir brought about a renewed joy in life that he never relinquished again. The monetary ups and downs continued, but he was famously able to console himself with female companionship and a good party. The latter two were also traits he never outgrew.

In 1910 Rubinstein resumed his career with a well-received concert in Berlin. He toured Europe until the outbreak of World War I in 1914, when he settled in London and was kept occupied at Allied Headquarters as an interpreter (he was fluent in eight languages). His wartime duties did not prevent his continuing to perform, however. In fact, Rubenstein's career was jump-started by a 1914 booking in Spain. Spanish audiences enthusiastically applauded his passionate style, prompting Rubinstein to apply himself immediately to the major composers of that nation. He was soon being saluted as the premier interpreter of such composers as Manuel de Falla and Enrique Granados, and in turn, he became an early ambassador for the merits of Spanish music. His relationship with Spain was cemented by a return tour in 1916 that began as a four-concert booking but was extended to over 100 performances by popular demand. The triumph in Spain was followed by an equally hailed tour of South America, and the two immense successes gave Rubinstein the financial security and peace of mind to enable him to pursue his career with a newfound sense of certainty.

Musical Maturity

Back in Paris in the 1920s, Rubenstein was solidly established as one of the most admired pianists of his time. He began to record, kept an active performance schedule, and resumed his fast-paced lifestyle of wine, women, and song. As he approached 40, however, he began to reevaluate his situation. First, he decided to settle down with a wife and family, so started courting Aniela ("Nela") Mlynarski, the daughter of famed conductor Emil Mlynarski. He married her on July 27, 1932, in London, and the first of their four children was born the following year, when Rubinstein was 46. It was the responsibility of a family that caused the new father to take honest stock of his artistic achievements.

Rubinstein's great gift as a musician also gave rise to his great failing. From childhood, he had possessed an innate ability to absorb scores by simply reading them and to memorize complicated pieces after hearing them just once. This prodigious memory and natural virtuosity gave him a huge advantage over other musicians, both in his ease of learning and in the facility with which he could retain a large repertoire in his head. However, such talents also made him lazy and complacent. He saw no need for practice or proper technique when he could simply coast through a concert, the audience none the wiser about a missed or wrong note, or a muddled phrase. His success in Spain and Latin America, where audiences focused more on temperament and feeling than on technical accuracy, were excellent examples of this phenomenon, but it was by no means limited to those places. Audiences everywhere succumbed to an overall impression of great playing. Rubinstein, however, knew the difference. As did his fellow pianists and, apparently, the critics in New York City. But it was still a few years after he finally conceded his weakness that he at long last began to shore up his technique and become the pianist he was meant to be.

After his marriage, Rubinstein's artistic epiphany gave rise to a new regimen and sense of purpose. He moved his family to a rental property in France and installed a piano in a neighboring stable. There, he spent twelve to sixteen hours a day practicing and honing his technique. Such single-mindedness may have been a bit late, but it was most assuredly not *too* late. Critics and audiences were thrilled with Rubinstein's masterful playing. Even in New York. More than 30 years after his first performance there, the pianist's 1937 Carnegie Hall concert was an unmitigated success.

Extraordinary Career

As World War II loomed, Rubinstein recognized the potential threat of Nazi Germany and moved his family from Paris to the United States in October of 1939. (The entire contents of his house were confiscated by the Nazis, although the pianist's collection of musical manuscripts was returned to his children by the German government in 2006. The children donated the collection to the Juilliard School of Music in October of the following year.) The family first settled in New York City, and then bought a home in Brentwood, California, in 1941. Rubinstein became a U.S. citizen in 1946, although he primarily lived abroad after the war, and continued to record and perform, adding television to his stable of performance venues. He became an avid supporter of the new State of Israel, having lost all his Polish relatives to the Nazis. By the late 1950s, Rubinstein had become an international musical icon.

The tokens and accolades in tribute to Rubenstein were legion. Among many other honors, he was awarded the U.S. Medal of Freedom in 1976 and made a Knight of the Order of the British Empire in 1977. Other honors included citations as a Commander of the Legion of Honor, the Gold Medal of London's Royal Philharmonic Society, and Spain's Cross of Alfonso XII. He also won ten Grammy Awards over the course of his career, in addition to one for Lifetime Achievement in 1994. In 1973 his first autobiography, *My Young Years,* was published. Another, *My Many Years,* appeared in 1980.

Despite a macular disorder that was discovered in 1969, Rubinstein maintained a pace that would give pause to a much younger person. He performed for such pet charities as the National Association for the Advancement of Colored People, the Musicians' Emergency Fund, and the United Jewish Appeal, while continuing to record well into the 1970s. Blindness forced him to retire from performing in 1976. He gave his final Carnegie Hall performance in March and his farewell performance at London's Wigmore Hall that year. Yet he hardly slowed down. Guest appearances, lectures, and world travel remained on his schedule. And, as true to Rubenstein's indomitable spirit as anything else, he left his wife in 1977 for another woman. He was 90 years old at the time.

Rubenstein passed away in his sleep on December 20, 1982, in Geneva, Switzerland, at the age of 95. His extraordinary career encompassed over 75 years, more than 6,000 live performances, and numerous recordings. *Musician Guide*'s Joyce Harrison quoted music critic Harold C. Schonberg's comments from the *New York Times* in 1964: "Vladimir Horowitz may have a more glittering technique, Rudolf Serkin may have a better way with German music, Rosalyn Tureck more of an affinity for Bach, Sviatoslav Richter for Prokofieff and Scriabin, and Claudio Arrau may have a bigger repertory. But no pianist has put everything together the way Rubinstein has. Others may be superior in specific things, but Rubinstein is the complete pianist." Nor can one properly contemplate the illustrious pianist's work without recalling his real passion for music and performing. PBS cited Rubinstein's own words, "On stage, I will take a chance. There has to be an element of daring in great music-making. These younger ones, they are too cautious. They take the music out of their pockets instead of their hearts." Indeed, the manner in which Rubinstein approached music matched the way he lived his life—with no holds barred.

Books

American Decades, Gale Research, 1998.
Contemporary Musicians, Volume 11, Gale Research, 1994.
Scribner Encyclopedia of American Lives, Volume 1: 1981-1985, Charles Scriber's Sons, 1998.

Online

"Arthur Rubinstein," Maurice Abravanel, http://www.maurice-abravanel.com/rubinstein_arthur.html (December 4, 2007).
"Arthur Rubinstein," PBS *American Masters,* http://www.pbs.org/wnet/americanmasters/database/rubinstein_a.html (December 4, 2007).
"Arthur Rubinstein Biography," Musician Guide, http://www.musicianguide.com/biographies/1608000089/Arthur-Rubinstein.html (December 4, 2007).
"Artur Rubinstein (Arthur Rubinstein)," Polish Culture, http://www.culture.pl/en/culture/arykuly/os_rubinstein.artur (December 4, 2007).
"Artur Rubinstein, Piano Virtuoso," Classical Music Lounge, January 30, 2007, http://cmlounge.wordpress.com/2007/01/30/297/ (December 4, 2007).
"Juilliard Acquires Late Pianist Arthur Rubinstein's Papers," *VOA News,* October 19, 2007, http://www.voanews.com/english/archive/2007-10/2007-10-19-voa27.cfm?CFID=166773965&CFTOKEN=19866927 (December 4, 2007).
"School Receives Arthur Rubinstein Collection," *Juilliard Journal,* November 2007, http://www.juilliard.edu/journal/2007-2008/0711/articles/0711_Arthur.html (December 4, 2007).

□

Anna Russell

The British-born Canadian-American comedienne (1911-2006) Anna Russell gained renown among lovers of classical music in the mid-twentieth century by lampooning the object of their affections in her comedic stage routines and recordings.

"The chief danger confronting classical music is the pomposity of its advocates—scholars, performers and critics—and Russell has long been our chief line of defense against this menace," wrote *Washington Post* music critic Joseph McLellan in 1984, as quoted in a 2006 article in the *Post* following the performer's death. Indeed, Russell introduced several generations of listeners to classical music even as she skewered it. The primary focus of her comedy was the grandiose art of opera, most especially the works of its most ambitious practitioner, nineteenth-century German composer Richard Wagner. Russell discovered her comic gift almost by accident, but she expanded on her initial routines consistently over several decades of sellout-level popularity.

Belittled as "Toad"

Given her long association with Canada, Russell's birthplace has sometimes been given, even in obituaries, as London, Ontario, Canada. Citing her birth certificate, however, *The Canadian Encyclopedia* reported that she was born on December 27, 1911, in London, England. Her birth name was Anna (or Ann) Claudia Russell-Brown, and her father, Claud Russell Brown, was a British military engineer and amateur classical pianist. Russell's mother, Beatrice, was Canadian. She bestowed the unflattering nickname of "Toad" on her awkward daughter, and the relationship between the two was never a happy one. Russell was an only child.

Anna got along better with an assortment of older female relatives who encouraged her musical abilities. Her paternal grandmother gave her unintentional comic inspiration with a set of hilarious malapropisms that she produced while attempting to speak French. Anna herself attended a performance of a work called *Facade* by British composer William Walton when she was 12; fascinated by the nonsense texts of the piece, she began to write comic verses herself and set them to music.

Attending St. Felix School in Southwold, England, Russell aspired to a serious career as an opera singer. Her voice was damaged by a field hockey accident that fractured her nose and cheekbone and required reconstructive surgery, but she persisted and entered the Royal College of Music in London in 1934. The school's director, Sir Hugh Allen, greeted one of her vocal recitals with the discouraging suggestion that she consider auditioning at the Palladium, a London vaudeville house. However, the noted British composer Ralph Vaughan Williams was her composition instructor, and she apparently fared better in her courses in musicology and composition than in her voice classes—she graduated in 1939 with a degree in those fields.

Russell nevertheless held onto her operatic dreams. She appeared in small roles with regional British opera companies, and she occasionally gave recitals of folk songs on the British Broadcasting Company (BBC) radio network. Russell was employed full-time by the BBC's education department, but according to Joseph So of the Web site La Scena Musicale, she considered that "a crashing bore." Russell got another unintentional lesson in comedy during a performance of the opera *Cavalleria Rusticana,* in which she was supposed to be thrown to the floor by a male singer during one scene. Instead, she lost her balance and crashed into part of the set, to the accompaniment of gales of laughter from the audience. The effect of this episode on her operatic career remained undetermined, however, as Russell and her mother fled to Canada in 1939 as World War II broke out. They settled in her mother's hometown of Unionville, outside Toronto. In 1943 Russell became a Canadian citizen. She took American citizenship in 1955 but continued to perform in Canada frequently and lived in Unionville for much of her life.

Performed on CBC Radio

Russell's first job in Canada was at a hamburger stand, and she then moved on to the chorus line of a musical. By 1940 she had broken into the live music lineup of the powerful Toronto radio station CFRB, appearing on a program called "Round the Marble Arch" to sing old music hall favorites. Her skills as a comic singer developed in guest slots on the Canadian Broadcasting Corporation program

Jolly Miller Time, and in the early 1940s she cohosted her own variety show, *Syd and Anna,* on station CJBC. She continued to keep one foot in the realm of classical music by working as a rehearsal pianist and understudy with Toronto's Rosselino Opera company, and gradually she began to develop comic routines centered on the classics. Her first appearance as a classical music comedienne came as a last-minute substitute at a music educators' convention.

From there she moved on to solo appearances, one of them sponsored by the Toronto Imperial Order of the Daughters of the Empire. That show caught the attention of Sir Ernest MacMillan, conductor of the Toronto Symphony Orchestra, who invited her to appear as part of an annual Christmas concert of humorous music. Russell's first Toronto Symphony appearance came in 1944, and she was well enough received that the invitation was repeated several times in subsequent years. Russell married a Canadian artist, Charles Goldhamer, but the marriage was short-lived; an earlier marriage in England, to John Denison, had also failed.

Russell's increasing renown in Canada stirred up interest in the United States, and soon she was performing routines like "For Singers with Great Artistry but No Voice" in opera-loving New York City. Mezzo soprano Jennie Tourel was incensed by the routine, thinking that it referred to her personally, and tried unsuccessfully to prevent New York's Carnegie Hall from booking Russell. Tourel's complaint notwithstanding, Russell's 1947 debut at Carnegie Hall marked the beginning of several decades of sustained popularity. Some critics such as the *New York Post*'s Martin Bernheimer championed Russell, although her humor was lost on others. Among her biggest detractors was Claudia Cassidy of the *Chicago Tribune,* on whom Russell took revenge by coining the persistent nickname "Acidy Cassidy," according to Joseph So, writing in *Opera Canada.*

The LP era, which allowed Russell's elaborate comic routines to be captured in recorded form, pushed her career to a new level. Recording for the Columbia label, Russell released the album *Anna Russell Sings?,* which perched atop classical record sales charts for 48 weeks. The album spawned a sequel, *Anna Russell Sings! Again?,* and in 1972 the two earlier albums were re-released as a double LP, *The Anna Russell Album.*

Satirized Wagner Opera Cycle

Russell's comedic targets included the bagpipes ("a very unsanitary instrument," she pointed out) and, in a routine called "How to Write Your Own Gilbert and Sullivan Opera," the stylized plots of light opera's leading Victorian duo. Arranging all her material herself, she peppered her concerts with shorter routines parodying various types of song, including English folksongs (she composed one called "I Wish I Were a Dicky-Bird"), but the centerpiece of her show was a half-hour routine called "The Ring of the Nibelungs (An Analysis)." In that segment, Russell offered a compressed plot summary of composer Richard Wagner's 20-hour operatic Ring Cycle. Russell's version featured a convoluted story with a Norse mythological setting that took on an air of absurdity when stripped down to its essentials and presented in Russell's arch, deadpan Brit-

ish style. "I'm not making this up, you know," Russell would respond, when the audience dissolved in laughter. "Russell always appeared as herself, her comedy rooted in her own slightly starchy upper-middle-class persona," noted Paul Driscoll, writing in *Opera News.*

The line "I'm not making this up, you know," became Russell's trademark and, in 1985, the title of her autobiography. In 1955 she had written another book, *The Power of Being a Positive Stinker,* whose title parodied a popular self-help book of the 1950s called *The Power of Positive Thinking.* Russell never totally renounced her goal of a career in serious opera, and she did take the stage in a few serious roles, including Engelbert Humperdinck's *Hansel and Gretel* in 1953 and Gaetano Donizetti's *The Daughter of the Regiment* in 1977. Russell's routines were also adapted into one-woman Broadway shows (1955's *Anna Russell's Little Show* and 1960's *All by Myself*). Her popularity extended across five continents, as she gave concerts in North America, Britain, South Africa, Malaysia, Hong Kong, Singapore, and Australia; the African trip resulted in an LP, *Anna Russell in Darkest Africa.* Her 1957 concert at London, England's giant Royal Albert Hall was a sellout. Russell recorded three other LPs, *Anna Russell's Guide to Concert Audiences, A Square Talk on Popular Music,* and *A Practical Banana Promotion. The Anna Russell Songbook,* a printed compilation of her material, was published in 1958, and she later headed a company of her own, the B & R Music Publishing Company.

In 1965 Russell retired temporarily but returned to performing in 1973. In 1977 she appeared at Canada's Stratford Festival, and Canadian cities always figured prominently in her itinerary. She embarked on a final world tour in 1983, at the age of 72, and retired for good in 1986. For several years she lived in Unionville, where Anna Russell Way is named after her. Russell's discography began to include the compact disc era when the Sony label issued the album *Encore* in 1998. Some of her 1960s television appearances were released on DVD under the title *Crown Princess of Musical Parody.*

Russell was often assisted in her later years by an Australian woman, Deirdre Prussak, who described their relationship this way in an interview reproduced on the Australian Broadcasting Corporation's Web site: "I knew Anna for 51 years, from when I started being a fan. I then became her secretary years later and then she sort of adopted me . . . so I was upgraded all the way." Russell moved to Bateman's Bay, Australia, in the early 2000s so that she could remain under Prussak's care, and she died there on October 18, 2006, about two months short of her 95th birthday.

Books

Russell, Anna, *I'm Not Making This Up, You Know,* Continuum, 1985.

Periodicals

Daily Telegraph (London, England), October 21, 2006.
Guardian (London, England), October 24, 2006.
Opera Canada, Summer 2000.
Opera News, January 2007.

Times (London, England), October 26, 2006.
Washington Post, October 21, 2006.

Online

"Anna Russell," The Canadian Encyclopedia, http://www.the
canadianencyclopedia.com/index.cfm?PgNm = TCE
&Params = U1ARTU0003065 (January 7, 2008).

"Goodbye Anna Russell," Australian Broadcasting Corporation,
http://www.abc.net.au/southeastnsw/stories/s1768984.htm
(January 7, 2008).
"Remembering Anna Russell (1911-2006)," La Scena Musicale,
http://www.scena.org/columns/reviews/061023-JS-
AnnaRussell.html (January 7, 2008). □

S

Dalip Singh Saund

The Indian American politician Dalip Singh Saund (1899-1973) was the first Asian American elected to the U.S. Congress.

An article on the IMDiversity Web site quoted Don Nakanishi, head of the Asian American Studies Center at the University of California at Los Angeles, as calling Saund "the unsung pioneer of Asian American electoral politics." His life story encompassed financial ups and downs, struggles against discrimination, and an unwavering devotion to the American ideals of freedom and equality that he had read about as a child in India—and to the universal ideals of human dignity that motivated his early activism on behalf of Indian independence and of his fellow Indian Americans. "My guideposts were two of the most beloved men in history, Abraham Lincoln and Mahatma Gandhi," Saund wrote in his autobiography, *Congressman from India.*

Convinced Parents to Start School

Dalip Singh Saund was born on September 20, 1899, in a small village called Chhajalwadi, in northwestern India's Punjab region. He was raised in the Sikh faith and wore a turban, required of some Sikh men, for much of the first part of his life. Saund's family, relatively prosperous, was involved in farming and construction, and one of his brothers went on to become chairman of India's railway board. Saund received the best education India had to offer, attending a boarding school in Baba Bakala, near Amritsar, and Prince of Wales College in Jammu Tawi (now the University of Jammu), and graduating in 1919 with a bachelor's degree in mathematics from Panjab University in Chandigarh.

Although his parents wanted him to enter the service of the British government in India, Saund was determined to go to the United States. He told his parents that he wanted to study food preservation and then return to India to help develop the country's canning industry, and he promised to stay in America for only three years at the most. Saund sailed for the United States in 1920, was processed for admission at Ellis Island in New York, and took a train across the country to San Francisco, eating only milk and bread because he was unfamiliar with the American foods around him.

After a night in a bedbug-ridden hotel room in San Francisco, he settled into a boarding house in Berkeley that had been established by a Sikh temple in Stockton, California. He was almost penniless, but a fellow Indian student told him that since he had an undergraduate degree from India he could enroll at the University of California as a graduate student and pay no tuition charges. Saund studied agriculture for a year but then switched to his earlier passion, mathematics, when he discovered that his previous coursework in India would be accepted by the university. He received his M.A. in 1922 and went on for a Ph.D., mastering the French and German languages as required and receiving his degree in 1924.

Gave Speeches on Gandhi

The beginnings of Saund's career as a public speaker began while he was a student at Berkeley. Mohandas K. Gandhi (later known as Mahatma Gandhi) was gaining international fame for his philosophy of nonviolent resistance to British rule, and Americans were interested to learn more about him from an Indian native. Saund labored over his speeches, turning them into classic pieces of oratory in the Victorian English mold—but he was confounded by the rapid give-and-take necessary to deal with American questioners.

To finance his education, Saund worked over the summer in canning factories in Sunnyvale, Emeryville, and the Sacramento area. A factory superintendent in Emeryville was impressed by Saund and planned to offer him the post of assistant superintendent, but Saund at the time was hoping to gain a position as a mathematics instructor and responded with uncertainty to the manager's questions about his future plans. "It was the first time in my life that I talked myself out of a good job; but certainly not the last," Saund recalled in his autobiography. What he had not reckoned on was a new wave of anti-immigrant sentiment that swept the United States, and California in particular, in the 1920s. Saund and other Indians were barred from citizenship, and after he received his degree he found that jobs, whether in food production or mathematics, were scarce.

Saund sometimes attended Sikh services in Stockton, and there he learned that other Indians had started farms in southern California's newly irrigated Imperial Valley region. With few other prospects, Saund headed south and found a job as a field foreman on a cotton farm owned by some Indian friends. During the day, with the pickers in the field, "I took advantage of the spare time I had on my hands," Saund wrote in his autobiography. "All day, while waiting for the pickers to come in, I read books on literature, poetry, drama, [and] early American history." A friendly librarian in the town of El Centro ordered books for him from the state library in Sacramento, and he began to familiarize himself with the workings of California's government. Saund started a pair of ranches himself, growing lettuce and hay, but he was ruined by the fall in agricultural prices during the Depression. Refusing to declare bankruptcy, he worked long hours at various jobs and paid off all his debts. He still found time to write a book, *My Mother India,* which was a reply to the negative portrayals of his country in Katherine Mayo's popular book *Mother India.*

In 1928 Saund married Marian Kosa, the daughter of a Czech immigrant, who lived with her family in Los Angeles. Under the terms of the Cable Act of 1922, she lost her American citizenship when they married. They moved to Westmorland, California, and raised three children, Dalip Jr., Julie, and Eleanor. The children of the mixed marriage were discriminated against and put in a segregated all-black school, and Marian and the three children eventually returned to Los Angeles in 1942. California writer Tom Patterson, in an article reproduced on the Public Broadcasting System (PBS) Web site, wrote that a relative of his was told by Marian "that she hadn't realized what the prejudice could be and that the children wouldn't be accepted." The family remained close, and Dalip Jr. served as a U.S. military officer during the Korean War.

Joined Toastmasters

Still mostly engaged in farm work, Saund maintained an interest in American political life and, although he was not a citizen and was unable to vote, he joined the Democratic Party after being inspired by the activism of President Franklin Roosevelt on behalf of farmers hard hit by the Depression. With few outlets for his erudition and speaking abilities, he joined a current events club and then a Toastmasters group in the town of Brawley. He won a district contest in San Diego with a speech on Gandhi. In 1946 Saund had the chance to put his skills to work. He formed the Indian Association of America, one of several Indian-American organizations that lobbied for passage of the Luce-Cellar Act, which would open citizenship to Indian immigrants. His efforts were rewarded when President Harry Truman signed the bill into law that year, and Saund promptly applied for citizenship. He became a U.S. citizen in 1949.

By the early 1950s Saund was well known in the Westmorland community as the proprietor of his own company, D.S. Saund Fertilizers, and as a member of organizations such as the March of Dimes. He became chairman of the Imperial County Democratic Central Committee, and in 1952, 1956, and 1960 he served as a delegate to the Democratic National Convention. He seemed to be a logical candidate for higher office, but he had hurdles of discrimination to clear before he achieved that goal. In 1950 he ran for the position of Justice Court Judge in Westmorland and was elected, only to have his election overturned on the technicality that he had not been a citizen long enough before taking office.

Saund ran again in 1952, and his ethnic background was again very much an issue in the campaign. One opponent, as Saund recalled in his autobiography, accosted him in a restaurant and asked, "Doc, tell us, if you're elected, will you furnish the turbans or will we have to buy them ourselves, in order to come into your court?" Saund's mild rejoinder was, "My friend, you know me for a tolerant man. I don't care what a man has on top of his head. All I'm interested in is what he's got inside of it." His remarks were repeated around the community, and helped him win election once again. He took office in January of 1953. Working on several more political campaigns and taking a hard line against Westmorland's reputation as a red light district, Saund accumulated political and community goodwill, and in 1955 he launched his campaign for election to the U.S. House of Representatives from California's 29th District.

That campaign, too, was heated in both the Democratic primary (in which his opponent once again tried to have him disqualified on a citizenship technicality) and in the general election in November of 1956; Saund's Republican opponent, aviator Jacqueline Odlum, ran newspaper advertisements emphasizing his ethnic background, running ads in which the "Dalip Singh" portion of his name was set in large type, while the more ambiguous "Saund" was much smaller. The district had been solidly Republican in previous elections, and Vice President Richard Nixon was one of a host of celebrities who showed up to campaign for Odlum. Nevertheless, with the help of a grassroots effort marked by a massive doorbell-ringing campaign by Saund supporters, he emerged victorious in the November election by a margin of three percentage points. He was reelected convincingly in 1958 and 1960, publishing his book *Congressman from India* during the latter year. Saund was the first Asian American in Congress and the first American of Indian descent elected to any major U.S. political office. He remained the sole U.S. Congressional representative of Indian descent until the election of Bobby Jindal in Louisiana's First District in 2004.

Saund's time in Congress was marked by his support for efforts to improve U.S.-Asian relations, efforts Saund saw as critical to stemming the spread of Communism. He argued for increased development aid as a way to foster citizen support for Asian governments, and in 1958 he made a tour of several Asian countries, including India. Observers in his home region reported that he still spoke the Punjabi language elegantly. Beginning with his first term in 1957, Saund was chosen as a member of the House Foreign Affairs Committee, an unusual honor for a freshman representative.

Saund's political career was cut short by a massive stroke in May of 1962 that left him unable to walk or speak. Although he attempted to keep his name in the running for reelection in 1962, he was unsuccessful. Cared for by his wife at the couple's home in Hollywood, he eventually learned to walk again. Saund died in Hollywood on April 22, 1973.

Books

Notable Asian Americans, Gale, 1995.
Saund, Dalip Singh, *Congressman from India,* Dutton, 1960.
———, *My Mother India,* 1930.

Periodicals

New York Times, April 24, 1973.

Online

"Centennial of Asian American Pioneer Dalip Singh Saund," IMDiversity, http://www.imdiversity.com/villages/asian/history_heritage/archives/nash_dalip_singh_saund.asp (January 9, 2008).
"Dalip S. Saund: The First Asian in U.S. Congress," USAsians, http://us_asians.tripod.com/features-dalip-saund.html (January 9, 2008).
"Dalip Singh Saund: An Asian Indian American Pioneer," Asian American Action Fund, http://www.aaa-fund.org/history/dalip_saund.asp (January 9, 2008).
"Dalip Singh Saund," Dalip Singh Saund Web site, http://www.saund.org/dalipsaund/index.html (January 9, 2008).
"Remembering the US Congressman from India," *The Tribune* (Chandigarh, India), http://www.tribuneindia.com/2002/20020112/windows/main2.htm (January 9, 2008).
"Saund, Dalip Singh," Political Graveyard, http://www.politicalgraveyeard.com (January 9, 2008).
"Triumph and Tragedy of Dalip Saund," Public Broadcasting System (from *California Historian,* June 1992), http://www.pbs.org/rootsinthesand/i_dalip1.html January 9, 2008). □

Vinayak Damodar Savarkar

A freedom fighter, India's Vinayak Damodar Savarkar (1883-1966) began calling for his country's independence from Britain as early as 1900. As a college student, he rallied his peers and became a popular leader of the Hindu Nationalist Movement. Jailed on charges of conspiracy and waging war against the British throne, he spent more than a dozen years in prison and faded into the background of the free India movement. On an international level, Savarkar is not as well-known as other independence leaders like Mahatma Gandhi, but in his homeland, Savarkar remains a household name.

Raised a Hindu

The second of four children, Savarkar was born May 28, 1883, in the western Indian village of Bhagur. At the time of Savarkar's birth, India was a British colony, ruled over by the British Monarchy. Savarkar's father, Damodarpant, was a stern disciplinarian and religious-minded man. His mother, Radhabai, was known as a gentle soul. Most nights before bed, Savarkar's mother insisted the family read from the *Mahabharata* or the *Ramayana.* Both are ancient epic poems that explore the Hindu philosophy and are central teachings of the Hindu faith. They explore the Hindu gods and goddesses and delve into the notion of karma.

At the age of six, Savarkar started attending the village school. He became an insatiable reader, poring over every newspaper or book that came his way. He was particularly interested in history and poetry. When he was 10, Savarkar submitted several of his poems to the newspapers in nearby Pune and they were published by editors who had no idea they came from a child.

Though Savarkar was only a youngster, he was aware of the tensions between the Hindus and Muslims who populated his country. In 1893, the hostility escalated as riots broke out between the two groups in the city of Bombay and also in the Azamgarh district. Many Hindus were killed during the riots and after reading about some of the atrocities committed against his fellow Hindus, Savarkar was determined to seek justice. He flew into a rampage and gathered his friends for a mission. Under Savarkar's direction, they stormed the village mosque and pelted it with stones, breaking the windows and tiles. Around this same time, Savarkar's mother died of cholera and he was grief-stricken.

As a teenager, Savarkar moved to nearby Nasik to attend high school. There, he impressed teachers with his writing and speaking abilities. He wrote ballads for the village chorus and penned an article, "The Glory of Hindustan," which appeared in the local paper. Just as Savarkar was coming into his own, tragedy struck again. His father and uncle died of the plague in 1899 and his brothers were sickened as well, though they recovered. Over the next few years, Savarkar worked to promote the idea of independence for India—and a Hindustan nation in particular. He also married the daughter of Bhaurao Chiplunkar. Savarkar's father-in-law, rich and influential, provided funds for him to continue his education.

Incited India's Independence Movement

In January 1902, Savarkar left Nasik to continue his studies at Fergusson College in nearby Pune. By now, he was more interested in working for India's freedom from British rule than he was in getting an education. In Pune, he promoted the use of Indian–made goods and called for a boycott of all foreign–made products. He despised everything English and told his peers to abstain from purchasing English goods. He gave many speeches at the college aimed at germinating the desire for independence among his peers. A wave of nationalism was sweeping across the country and he wanted his classmates to jump on board.

In his talks, Savarkar discussed some of history's successful revolutions, including those in Italy, the Netherlands, and the United States. He noted the nasty skirmishes associated with quests for independence so his peers would know what the country was in for. Crowds of students gathered to hear him speak. In 1904, he organized an underground revolutionary group called the Abhinava Bharat—or Young India Society. Under Savarkar's direction, the group posted explosive literature critical of the British empire and its treatment of the Indian people.

On October 7, 1905, Savarkar staged his first dissident act when he incited a group of students to burn a pile of foreign clothes. He hoped to launch a boycott of foreign cloth in favor of cloth created on Indian looms. It was the first such bonfire in India. Over the next few decades, as the battle for independence heightened, such bonfires became common and invoked a spirit of nationalism. At the time, though, moderates disapproved of Savarkar's antics. Even Gandhi criticized the bonfire, believing boycott movements had their roots in hatred and violence, which he did not condone. Years later, however, Gandhi endorsed the use of bonfires to destroy imported goods. In general, most of Savarkar's professors admired his intellect but felt uneasy when he touted his revolutionary views. He was fined for his involvement with the bonfire and forbidden to live on campus. Fergusson College was, after all, a state–funded institution with loyalty to the British crown. Savarkar graduated later that year.

Moved to London

In 1906, Savarkar applied for a scholarship to study in London. The scholarship was being offered by Shyamji Krishnavarma, a wealthy Indian who lived in London. According to the autobiography *Veer Savarkar* by Dhananjay Keer, Savarkar wrote this on his application: "Independence and Liberty I look upon as the very pulse and breath of nation. From my boyhood, dear sir, upto this moment of my youth, the loss of Independence of my country and the possibility of regaining it form the only theme of which I dreamt by night and on which I mused by day."

Savarkar's benefactor Krishnavarma himself was interested in the independence movement and readily gave the scholarship to Savarkar. He sailed for London in 1906, intending to study law. While in London, he set about recruiting Indian students who were studying abroad and established the Free India Society to organize students for the revolutionary movement. Back home, the Abhinava Bharat was in contact with revolutionary leaders from Russia, Ireland, Egypt and China. Savarkar envisioned the groups forming a large anti–British front, with each group revolting concurrently against the British empire. Savarkar urged the Abhinava Bharat to prepare for war by arming themselves. They smuggled pistols, hidden in false books, into India. Savarkar even went so far as to send some of his peers to study bomb–making.

Though Savarkar successfully completed his studies and passed England's barrister examination, he had trouble getting his law degree because of his anti–government activities. Administrators told Savarkar he could have his degree on one condition: that he sign a paper saying he would refrain from participating in politics. He, of course, refused.

Jailed for Political Dissidence

By 1909, tensions in India between Savarkar's revolutionaries and the British authorities were mounting. A British magistrate and collector in Nasik, Arthur M.T. Jackson, was assassinated and two bombs were thrown at a British viceroy in a failed assassination attempt. Savarkar's younger brother was arrested in the bomb plot. Authorities in Bombay sent a telegraphic arrest warrant to London and Savarkar was arrested in March 1910. He was placed on a steamship headed for India, where he was to stand trial.

During the voyage, Savarkar slipped through a porthole while the ship was docked in Marseilles, France. He swam for the dock and was chased by British officers. As he ran through the streets, he demanded to be taken to a magistrate because he wanted to seek asylum in France, but it was to no avail. Savarkar was recaptured and turned back over to the authority of the British officers and sent back to Bombay. Savarkar, however, maintained that the French had no right to release him into British custody once he had stepped on French soil and sought refuge as a political prisoner. The matter ended up before the International Hague Tribunal, which ruled the handover had been done in accordance with international law.

Once back in Bombay, Savarkar was put on trial. According to the *New York Times,* he faced charges of "waging war against his Majesty the Emperor of India," "conspiracy to deprive His Majesty of the sovereignty of British India" and procuring and distributing arms. He was sentenced to 50 years and sent to prison in the Andaman Islands, located on the Bay of Bengal. Savarkar's plight made international news and his situation alerted the world to the growing unrest in India.

Life at the prison was grueling. Savarkar spent many days in solitary confinement and had to endure bad food, unsanitary conditions and hard labor. He suffered from dysentery. Many days he picked oakum—a loose hemp or jute fiber that was treated with tar and used to caulk the seams of wooden ships. Other days, he was used like a "workhorse" at the oil mill—forced to walk in circles for hours on end, his physical movements powering the grinding machines.

Later in life, Savarkar wrote a memoir of his prison years titled *My Transportation for Life.* In it, he recounted his first days in jail and the despair that passed over him. "Fifty year of prison–life, alone and in a solitary cell like this! To pass my life, to count the hours of the day as they sounded and rolled on into months and years till they completed the long, inevitable, unredeemed, dark period of fifty years! What a hell on earth? Yet I had to live it.''

Savarkar tried to make the best of his situation. Forbidden to have pencil or paper, he was unable to continue helping the independence movement, though he yearned to write dispatches. He thought of other famous prisoners, including John Bunyan, who wrote *Pilgrim's Progress* from behind bars. Savarkar decided he would use this time to compose an epic poem. As Savarkar composed verses, he scribbled them on the prison walls with thorns and memorized thousands of lines so they could be published later.

Led Hindu Nationalist Movement

In 1921, Savarkar was moved to a jail in Ratnagiri, on India's southwest coast. He was finally released from jail in January 1924 on the condition that he not leave the Ratnagiri district nor have any involvement with politics. After leaving prison, Savarkar wrote plays, poetry, novels and magazine articles. He also urged Indian leaders to abolish the caste system and argued that the ''untouchables''—the people with the lowest social status—should be allowed in the temples because he believed all Hindus were equal. In 1937, the British government eased his restrictions and he became president of the All–India Hindu Mahasabha, a leading force in the Hindu Nationalist Movement.

Savarkar lived to see India become a sovereign nation. In 1947, the British empire granted India its freedom. One of the great leaders of the independence movement, Mahatma Gandhi, was assassinated the following year. The assassin, Nathuram Godse, was a Hindu radical linked to the Hindu Mahasabha, the group Savarkar was heavily involved with. Savarkar was implicated in the murder on charges of conspiracy and stood trial, though he was acquitted. The association damaged Savarkar's reputation and left a stain on his legacy. Decades later, he was still viewed as a hero by some and a radical villain by others, who continued to seek evidence to prove a connection between Savarkar and Godse.

Savarkar died February 26, 1966, in Bombay, India. According to the *New York Times,* upon Savarkar's death, Prime Minister Indira Gandhi, wife of slain leader Mahatma Gandhi, issued a statement saying, ''Mr. Savarkar's name has been a byword for daring and patriotism. He was cast in the mold of a classical revolutionary, and countless people drew inspiration from him. Death removes from our midst a great figure in contemporary India.''

Books

Keer, Dhananjay, *Veer Savarkar,* Popular Prakashan, 1966.
McKean, Lise, *Divine Enterprise: Gurus and the Hindu Nationalist Movement,* University of Chicago Press, 1996.
Savarkar, Veer, *My Transportation For Life,* Prakashan, 1984.

Periodicals

Hindu, December 16, 2003; September 29, 2004.
New York Times, February 15, 1911; February 25, 1911; February 27, 1966.
Statesman (India), June 1, 2003. □

Wolfgang Sawallisch

German orchestral conductor Wolfgang Sawallisch (born 1923) has been one of the best-known and most widely respected figures in the field of classical music, both in his native Germany and in the United States.

Sawallisch's conducting art traced its roots back to the long traditions of German opera. He emerged from a German opera house environment that was directly shaped by the music and personal influence of great composers like Richard Wagner and Richard Strauss. Sawallisch kept to a fairly narrow focus over much of his career; in an age when other conductors such as Leonard Bernstein and Herbert von Karajan became international stars and members of the jet set, he concentrated on the music of a few composers whose music he knew inside and out, and he preferred smaller, high-quality performances to high-profile venues. Yet Sawallisch sought out new challenges in his later years, coming to the United States to assume the leadership of the Philadelphia Orchestra, one of America's most venerated ensembles but one that was troubled when he took the reins.

Career Goals Changed by Performance

Born on August 26, 1923, in Munich, Germany, Wolfgang Sawallisch (suh-VAHL-ish) has lived in that south German city for most of his life. He was given piano lessons from the age of five, quickly showed talent, and at ten announced his goal of becoming a concert pianist. But a visit to the opera in Munich changed his mind. ''At 11 I heard my first opera, coincidentally in the Munich Opera House where I would one day become music director,'' Sawallisch told Mike Bradley of the London *Times.* ''I was so fascinated by the sounds of the orchestra and the singers and the sight of the whole production on the stage that I decided immediately to change my mind and study to be a conductor.''

Munich was one of the centers of German musical life at the time, and Sawallisch soaked up influences from some of the greats of German music. He once saw the aging composer and conductor Richard Strauss conduct a Mozart opera while accompanying it on the harpsichord and inserting little quotations from his own music, to the delight of the audience. Sawallisch's growing mastery of opera was interrupted, however, by the advent of World War II. The teenaged Sawallisch was drafted into the Germany army and sent to the front in Italy, where he was captured and taken prisoner by British forces. He spent three years as a prisoner of war, and was allowed to return home in October of 1945.

By 1947 German musical life had begun to return to normal, and Sawallisch graduated from the Hochschule für Musik (or school of music) in Munich. He landed his first job that year, becoming a repetiteur, or rehearsal conductor, at the Opera Theatre of Augsburg. In 1953, at age 30, he made

mand of Wagner's sprawling, five-hour score won critical admiration, and he remained a regular conductor at Bayreuth until 1962. Eventually, however, he ran afoul of Bayreuth's director, Wieland Wagner, who was Richard Wagner's grandson, and decided to seek out situations where he would have more control.

The younger Wagner was an innovator who wanted to impose his own personality on the staging of Wagner's classics. Sawallisch, by contrast, believed in keeping his own personality in the background. In both opera and symphonic music, his rehearsals were devoted in large measure to drawing out what he saw as the composer's original intention, rather than inserting a specific interpretation on top of what was already there. He studied scores in great detail, paying close attention to the composer's interpretive markings and passing those along to the orchestra members. That placed Sawallisch in contrast to other conductors of the 1950s and 1960s, an era that marked a high point of classical music's popularity in the United States. Other noted conductors of that time, such as the New York Philharmonic's Leonard Bernstein and the Berlin Philharmonic's Herbert von Karajan, often gave performances and made recordings of a given work that differed sharply from those of each other and from other top conductors.

During the 1960s Sawallisch continued to conduct opera and also held orchestral conducting jobs: with the Vienna Symphony Orchestra from 1960 to 1970, and the Hamburg State Philharmonic Orchestra from 1961 to 1973. In the 1970s he achieved world-class posts in both opera and symphony. He became principal conductor of the Orchestre de la Suisse Romande (Orchestra of French-Speaking Switzerland) in Geneva in 1970, remaining there until 1980, and the bulk of his reputation rests on the years he spent with the Bavarian State Opera company in Munich. Beginning as music director in 1971, he became the company's general manager in 1982.

Many of Sawallisch's recordings as a conductor were made in Munich. His recording career began in 1957, and his catalogue grew to include most of the major operas of Wagner and Strauss, as well as Mozart and other German and Austrian composers. Over his career, up to the point when he took over the Philadelphia Orchestra, he conducted Wagner's four-opera, 20-hour *Ring* cycle an astonishing 32 times. Sawallisch rarely took up the baton in Italian opera, preferring to remain with repertory he felt he knew best. He was regarded as one of the top opera conductors in the world, and he regularly received offers of guest conducting engagements from New York's Metropolitan Opera and other top companies, but he restricted his guest conducting engagements mostly to the La Scala opera house in Milan, Italy. As a symphonic conductor he was slightly better-traveled, taking on guest slots with the Israel Philharmonic Orchestra and Tokyo's NHK Symphony, and making a series of acclaimed Beethoven recordings with the Concertgebouw Orchestra of Amsterdam. But for the most part he remained in Central Europe in the orchestral field as well. In personality, unlike many other figures in the world of opera, Sawallisch was described as modest and unassuming.

a splash when he became the youngest person ever to conduct the prestigious Berlin Philharmonic Orchestra, and that year he landed the post of music director—a job that combines conducting duties with choice of repertoire and the larger management of a company's artistic direction—at an opera house in Aachen. He was also the youngest person to hold the post of music director in Germany at the time.

Sawallisch never entirely gave up his ambitions as a pianist, and in 1949 he and violinist Gerhard Seitz took honors as best duo at the Geneva International Competition in Switzerland. He went on to a noteworthy career as an accompanist to classical singers, performing and recording with such stars of German vocal art as Dietrich Fischer-Dieskau and Elisabeth Schwarzkopf; he made his debut in London as an accompanist to Schwarzkopf in 1955. But his career was clearly moving in the direction of conducting. From Aachen he moved to a music directorship at the opera house in Wiesbaden, West Germany, in 1958, and then to the larger Cologne Opera in 1960. There he also became a professor at the Cologne Conservatory.

Clashed with Wagner's Grandson

In 1957 Sawallisch achieved a major breakthrough when he was invited to conduct Wagner's opera *Tristan and Isolde* at the Bayreuth Festival Theater. That opera house, located in Bayreuth in Sawallisch's home region of Bavaria, had been established by Wagner himself and functioned (and continues to function) as a kind of shrine to his music and his vision of a union of all the arts. Sawallisch's com-

Made Philadelphia Debut

For the Philadelphia Orchestra, however, Sawallisch made an exception. He made his first appearance with the orchestra in 1966, at the invitation of its longtime conductor, Hungarian-born Eugene Ormandy, and that first appearance turned into a series of repeat engagements over the years. "I enjoyed that and other contact with the orchestra so much that we began to develop a familiarity," Sawallisch told Bradley. "I was impressed by their discipline, their dedication and their professionalism." When Ormandy's successor, Riccardo Muti, stepped down in the early 1990s, Sawallisch emerged as a top candidate to replace him, and he assumed the position of music director of the Philadelphia Orchestra in 1993, at the age of 70. Echoing President John F. Kennedy's identification of himself as a Berliner 30 years earlier, Sawallisch proclaimed himself a Philadelphian at a splashy outdoor ceremony where he was introduced by Philadelphia mayor Edward Rendell.

The task Sawallisch faced in Philadelphia, at an age when most other conductors had slowed their activities or retired completely, was difficult in several respects. For one thing, he spoke English poorly at the time. For another, the orchestra's overall quality, historically marked by string tone of legendary warmth, was widely thought to have declined under Muti, who showed little interest in the extra-musical socializing usually required of a music director in America, where orchestras sought corporate support. (The level of governmental arts support in Europe was and still remains much higher than in the United States.) But the challenge of working under a system of patronage (contributions from wealthy individuals and organizations) rather than government support appealed to Sawallsich and, he told Bradley, his decision "to forget the past and go forwards was the right decision. It has endowed me with a new youth." The decision was partly motivated by the death of Sawallisch's wife in the years before he came to Philadelphia.

Living and working in America altered Sawallisch's musical perspective. Whereas he had been familiar with the works of only a few American composers while conducting in Europe, the 70-something Sawallisch emerged in Philadelphia as a champion of new American music. He was involved with programming changes that were innovative by any standard: in the year 2000 he devoted the orchestra's entire subscription season to music of the twentieth century, resulting in ticket sales records at a time when other American orchestras were struggling at the box office, and in 1997 he led the orchestra in the first live Internet broadcast mounted by a major symphony orchestra, attracting listeners in more than 40 countries around the world.

Among Sawallisch's most important legacies was his championing of the orchestra's new 2,500-seat Verizon Hall, replacing the durable and physically beautiful but acoustically troublesome Academy of Music. The hall was finished under Sawallisch's tenure and opened to positive reviews, completing a process that Muti, Ormandy, and Leopold Stokowski before him had tried without success to initiate. In 2003, before his retirement as music director, Sawallisch made the first recording undertaken in Verizon Hall, a three-disc set of music by Robert Schumann that was nominated for Grammy Awards in the categories of Best Classical Album and Best Orchestral Performance.

Books

International Dictionary of Opera, 2 vols., St. James, 1993.

Periodicals

Albany Times Union (Albany, NY), September 13, 1990.
Guardian (London, England), July 8, 1994; May 19, 2000.
Financial Times, May 8, 2000.
Seattle Post-Intelligencer, September 28, 2001.
Times (London, England), December 13, 1991; September 16, 1993; May 16, 2000.

Online

"Conductor Laureate," Philadelphia Orchestra, http://www .philorch.org/styles/poa02e/www/conductorlaureate.html (January 16, 2008).
"Wolfgang Sawallisch," *All Music Guide*, http://www.allmusic .com (January 14, 2008).
"Wolfgang Sawallisch—Biography," Wolfgang Sawallisch Foundation, http://www.sawallisch-stiftung.de/index.php ?biography (January 14, 2008).
"Wolfgang Sawallisch (1923)," Remington Studio, http://www .soundfountain.org/rem/remsawal.html (January 14, 2008). □

Adolphe Sax

The Belgian inventor Adolphe Sax (1814-1894) was the originator of the saxophone as well as several other musical instruments.

Sax became something of a footnote in history after his creation was almost forgotten after his death, until it was revived by jazz musicians who barely remembered his name. In his own time, however, Sax made musical headlines. His life story is a rich source of information about music—and musical politics—in the nineteenth century, full of controversy, public scenes, and dramatic reversals of fortune. Sax's life, wrote a contemporary observer quoted on the Web site of the inventor's home city of Dinant, "rises to the heights of a social event."

Developed Interest in Music

Sax was born on November 6, 1814, in Dinant, which was part of France at the time and was then annexed by the Netherlands. The town, known for a particular type of yellow copper, lies in the southern, French-speaking part of what in 1830 became the independent country of Belgium. The oldest of 11 children, he was lucky to survive his childhood, during which he fell from a third-story window (and was given up for dead), swallowed a pin, was burned in a gunpowder accident and burned again by a frying pan, was poisoned three times by varnish fumes, hit on the head with a cobblestone, and nearly drowned in a river. In between these incidents, Sax took naturally to the trade of his father, Charles-Joseph Sax, a cabinetmaker who was

ordered to provide musical instruments for a Dutch army band and turned out to have strong skills in that area.

Sax became his father's apprentice and also pursued the musical side of his education, studying singing and the flute. After the younger Sax's workshop in Paris became successful, their roles were reversed. He hired his father, who had run into financial problems in Belgium, to be his production manager. By the time he was 16, Sax was not only making good examples of existing instruments but also designing new ones. At 20 he exhibited an original 24-key clarinet, and his new bass clarinet won the admiration of François Antoine Habeneck, the conductor of the Paris Opera Orchestra, who was passing through Brussels, Belgium.

Before long, Sax concluded that Belgium was too small for his ambitions. At the Belgian Exhibition (an industrial fair) in 1840 he presented nine inventions, among them an organ, a piano tuning process and a sound-reflecting screen. The judges felt that Sax was too young to receive the gold medal, and instead awarded him the vermeil (gilded silver). Sax was interested in an early version of the saxophone from French opera composer Fromental Halévy, and he made a quick decision to head for Paris, the capital of musical life in the French-speaking world. He had only 30 francs in his pocket.

Lived in Shed

When he arrived in Paris, he was forced to live in a shed and to borrow money in order to get himself established. But his fortunes turned around when Halévy introduced him to Hector Berlioz, who in addition to being France's most con-

troversial composer was also an influential music critic. In 1842 Sax showed Berlioz an early version of the baritone saxophone, an instrument different from any other that had been made up to that time. It had the power of brass instruments, but it was sounded with a reed and had the expressive, voice-like qualities of reed woodwinds. Berlioz sent Sax away with the remark that on the following day Sax would know what he, Berlioz, thought of the instrument. Sax spent a nervous night before picking up the *Journal des Débats,* the most influential arts publication of the day in Paris, where he read Berlioz's words, as quoted in an article contained on the Saxgourmet Web site: "He [Sax] is a calculator, an acoustician, and when required, a smelter, a turner and, if need be, at the same time an embosser. He can think and act. He invents, and he accomplishes."

Berlioz went on to praise the sound of Sax's instrument, which he soon began to produce in seven sizes from sopranino all the way down to double-bass, and it was not long before composers started to write parts for them in the growing opera orchestras of the time. But this was when Sax's troubles began. According to the article on Saxgourmet, he "had exceptional gifts for the gentle art of making enemies." Instrumentalists devoted to rival builders tried to sabotage his innovations, refusing to play Sax's bass clarinets, although Berlioz continued to defend Sax and wrote a piece for the new instrument. And after Sax showed his saxophones at the Paris Industrial Exhibition in 1844, he had to contend with accusations from a German military bandleader named Wieprecht that a pair of German inventors had actually been the first builders to devise both the saxophone and Sax's bass clarinet. German musicians backed up the fraud by ordering Sax's instruments from Paris, buffing out the etching of Sax's name in the brass, and sending the instruments back to France.

Sax defended himself vigorously. The German's accusations were dealt with at a momentous showdown in the German city of Koblenz, attended by such celebrities as the composer Franz Liszt: Wieprecht claimed that he and other German musicians were already familiar with Sax's instruments, but when handed actual examples, he could play the bass clarinet only poorly, and the saxophone not at all. Wieprecht underwent an instant transformation and became one of Sax's new backers, and Sax magnanimously announced that he would wait another year before finalizing his patent application to see if anyone else could produce a genuine saxophone.

Received His Patent

Sax received his patent in 1846 and won his gold medal at the Paris Industrial Exposition in 1849. This did not end his legal problems, however, as lawsuits continued to plague him for years. Sax's workshop sold some 20,000 instruments between 1843 and 1860, but he was not a talented money manager, and sales were not enough to keep him solvent. He filed for bankruptcy three times, in 1852, 1873, and 1877, and he was saved from a fourth debacle only by the intervention of another of his admirers, Emperor Napoleon III. Sax continued to devise improvements to his instruments, and he taught at the Paris Conservatory beginning in 1858.

In 1858 Sax was diagnosed with lip cancer, generally a death sentence at the time, but he was successfully treated by an Afro-French herbalist. He had five children by a Spanish-born mistress, Louise-Adèle Maor, whom he never married, reportedly because he did not want to acknowledge the liaison because he felt her family was too poor. Sax's son Adolphe-Edouard followed him into the business and maintained the Sax workshop into the twentieth century; it was absorbed by the Selmer company, which still exists today, in 1928. Sax wrote a method or learners' manual for the saxophone and continued to promote it vigorously in the field of classical music, but it never caught on strongly in the symphony orchestra.

In 1870 Sax's position at the Paris Conservatory was terminated in the aftermath of the Franco-Prussian War, and he lived his final years in straitened circumstances, kept out of poverty only by a small pension arranged for him by an admirer. By the time of his death on February 7, 1894, at the age of 80, Sax may have feared that his life's work had been compromised; the saxophone was well entrenched in band music but had little presence in the classical sphere. He had no way of knowing that his creation, transplanted to the United States and dispersed around the city of New Orleans by military bandsmen returning from the Spanish-American War around 1900, would evolve into an icon of American music, played enthusiastically by musicians ranging from schoolchildren up to Bill Clinton, the forty-second president of the United States.

Books

Baker's Biographical Dictionary of Musica and Musicians, centennial ed., Nicholas Slonimsky, ed. emeritus, Schirmer, 2001.

Horwood, Wally, *Adolph Sax, 1814-1894: His Life and Legacy,* Bramley, 1980.

Periodicals

Europe, March 1994.
Globe and Mail (Toronto, Canada), July 29, 1994.

Online

"Adolphe Sax," Saxgourmet, http://www.saxgourmet.com/adolph-sax.html (March 18, 2008).

"Adolphe Sax (1814-1894), Inventor of the Saxophone (Historical Excerpts from *Adolphe Sax and His Saxophone,* Saxgourmet, http://www.saxgourmet.com/adolph-sax.html (February 17, 2008).

"Adolphe Sax: Inventor of the Saxophone," City of Dinant Official Web site, http://www.dinant.be/index.htm?lg = 3&m1 = 28&m2 = 88&m3 = 293 (February 17, 2008). □

Irena Sendler

Polish social worker Irena Sendler (1910-2008) saved 2,500 Jewish children from death in the gas chambers of concentration camps run by Nazi Ger-

many during World War II. At the time, Poland was occupied by Nazi troops, and Sendler risked her own life many times over to smuggle young children out of the Warsaw Ghetto, where thousands of the city's Jews were walled in. Honored decades later for her work, Sendler scoffed at the idea that she had behaved heroically as one of the small number of Gentiles who helped rescue Jews from death camps. "The term 'hero' irritates me greatly," a report by Kate Connolly in the London *Guardian* quoted her as saying. "The opposite is true. I continue to have pangs of conscience that I did so little."

Born on February 15, 1910, in Warsaw, Sendler grew up both there and in a small town called Otwock, about 25 miles southeast of the city. During her childhood, Poland belonged to imperial Russia, and her family were practicing Roman Catholics, the predominant religion in the area along with the Jewish faith. Her father was a humanitarian-minded physician who treated Jews in Otwock during typhus outbreaks when other doctors refused to do so. He later died from the disease when Sendler was seven years old. She later recalled that it was a proverb often repeated by her father that served as the inspiration for her own actions: "If you see a person drowning," she told Norman Conard in *NEA Today,* "you must jump into the water to save them, whether you can swim or not."

Joined Resistance Movement

As a young woman, Sendler entered the field of social work, and was 29 years old when World War II broke out in the late summer of 1939. The origin of the conflict was Nazi Germany's occupation of Poland. Horrified by the Nazis' anti-Semitic policies already in place in Germany and now being implemented in Poland under the occupation, Sendler joined the Polish Underground, which aided Polish Jews. By then the Germans were deporting thousands of Jews to large-scale extermination camps on Polish soil, including Auschwitz and Treblinka.

In Warsaw, Sendler had a job with the social welfare department of the municipal government. In 1942, her work in the Polish Underground brought her to the newly formed *Rada Pomocy Zydom,* or Council for Aid to Jews, and known by the codename "Zegota." This was an organization to help Jews, funded in part by the Polish government in exile, and those who belonged to it risked their lives, for in Poland under German rule, if a family was found to be hiding a Jew, all occupants of the house were ordered to be put to death. In December of 1942, Sendler was made head of Zegota's children's division, and given the code name "Jolanta."

Wore Star of David

Earlier, in 1940, Nazi officials in Warsaw had started walling off a section of the city that became known as the Warsaw Ghetto, in order to isolate the city's 400,000 Jews from the rest of the populace. Conditions in the Ghetto were abysmal, with food scarce and poor sanitation leading to outbreaks of deadly diseases. Because Sendler worked for the city government, she received a special permit that allowed her to come and go from the Ghetto. Whenever she passed through its heavily fortified checkpoints, she wore a Star of David on her clothing—as all Jews in lands occupied by Nazi Germany were required to do by law—in order to make her less noticeable to authorities in her secret line of work, and also to show solidarity with the Ghetto's residents.

Sendler also began to carry forged papers that listed her occupation as nurse, which gave her increased access to the Ghetto. This proved especially true when a typhoid fever outbreak occurred and few Germans wished to venture inside to provide aid; instead, they were happy to let Poles do the dangerous work. Sendler's real mission, however, was to search out families with young children in the Ghetto and convince the parents to let her take their children to safety on the outside. There were orphanages as well as families in both the city and countryside who were willing to hide Jewish children, and as word spread that Jews elsewhere were being deported to work camps—which few realized were actually designed to exterminate Europe's Jewish populace via large-scale gas chambers—Poles like Sendler realized that to rescue children from such a fate had now become an urgent humanitarian mission.

Sendler smuggled children out of the Ghetto by various means. Some buildings had secret basements with tunnels that connected to the outside; there was also a municipal court building that had doors on both the Jewish and "Aryan" (non-Jewish) sides, and janitors who often looked the other way when such smuggling operations were being carried out. Often the children were hidden in tool boxes, crates, or other means and loaded onto trucks. Infants had to be quieted with medicine to keep them from crying and thus alerting guards at the checkpoints. There were also dogs who rode along on the truck and were trained to bark in order to cover up any suspicious noises.

Buried Names in a Jar

Once safely outside the Ghetto, the children were taken to host families sympathetic to their plight, or to Roman Catholic orphanages whose nuns were willing to disguise the children as Gentiles. The children received new names, false identity papers, and were given instruction in Catholic rituals and prayers in order to help them blend in. Sendler told her charges, "Do not remember your family, your ways or your one life; you must learn to survive," according to Kirk Shinkle in *Investor's Business Daily.* In order to keep track of the children who left the Ghetto and began living under new identities elsewhere, Sendler wrote down all the relevant information in a special code on used cigarette papers she collected. These lists of names were then put in jars and buried in the yard of a friend's house at 9 Ledarska Street in Warsaw.

On October 20, 1943, the Nazi secret police unit known as the Gestapo raided Sendler's apartment and arrested her. She was taken to Pawiak Prison in Warsaw, a notorious place from which few emerged alive. There she was tortured and her legs and feet broken. She received a death sentence, but on the way to the execution site a Zegota operative managed to bribe a German guard, and she was able to flee. Her name never left the list of those who had been shot that day, however, and after that point she was truly underground. She managed to continue her work, however, and when World War II finally ended in 1945, she hoped to reunite many of the 2,500 children taken out of the Ghetto with their parents. By that point, however, the Ghetto was largely empty, and she was devastated to learn that few of the parents whose names were on her list had survived the Holocaust. Most of the Ghetto families had died at the Treblinka death camp.

Honored by Israel

After the war, Poland became a Soviet ally and fell under one-party Communist rule. Though Sendler was able to reclaim her original identity, she suffered some harassment because she had worked with "Zegota", which had ties to the staunchly anti-Communist Polish government in exile. She married, but because of the campaign against her a son was born prematurely and did not survive. Most of her postwar career was spent helping to found orphanages and nursing homes, and she also worked for the Department of Education for a number of years. The first official recognition of her heroism came in 1965, when she was named one of the "Righteous Among the Nations" by Yad Vashem, the Holocaust Martyrs' and Heroes' Remembrance Authority of Israel. In 2003 she was honored with the Order of the White Eagle, the highest civilian decoration in Poland. Four years later she was nominated for a Nobel Peace Prize.

Sendler's wartime heroism was the inspiration for an educational project in the United States that began in the late 1990s. A high school teacher in Pittsburg, Kansas, named Norm Conard assigned four students to research a brief *U.S. News and World Report* article that mentioned her as one of the war's forgotten names. Conard believed that the magazine had erred in claiming that Sendler had saved some 2,500 Jews, for this number was a good deal higher than the number rescued by Oskar Schindler, a German industrialist named who ran a factory in Krakow and saved 1,200 Jews. Schindler's story was well known, thanks to the 1993 film *Schindler's List* that won an Academy Award for Best Picture. The students affirmed that Sendler had indeed saved that many lives, and their report became the basis for a play they titled *Life in a Jar.* It has been performed in scores of schools in both the United States and Europe. The students were also astounded to learn that Sendler was still alive, though like many senior citizens in the post-Communist world she was living on a very meager income. They began a fundraising effort to send money to her, and a local business leader was so moved by their work that he sponsored their trip to Poland to meet her in person in May of 2001.

Sendler was living in a nursing home in 2006 when a German academic named Joachim Wieler visited her. Wieler told Derren Hayes for the journal *Community Care* that Sendler remained baffled by the attention to her wartime service. "When you know that something is basically at stake, like real life, you do everything to save it. You don't talk about it and discuss it. You do it," she told Wieler. She also noted that there were many others who played a role in saving the children, adding "I did not do it alone."

Sendler died on May 12, 2008, in Warsaw, Poland.

Periodicals

Community Care, May 3, 2007.
Guardian (London, England), March 15, 2007.
Investor's Business Daily, February 4, 2004.
Kansas City Star, May 30, 2002.
NEA Today, September 2002.
Pretoria News (South Africa), May 17, 2007.

Online

"Life in a Jar: The Irena Sendler Project," Irenasendler.org, http://www.irenasendler.org/ (December 15, 2007). □

Francisco Serrão

Portuguese explorer Francisco Serrão (died 1521) achieved minor renown in the annals of his country's navigational history as the first European explorer to sail east past Malacca, the Indonesian state located at the straits of the same name, and into the islands of the Moluccas, located roughly between the Philippines and New Guinea. Serrão was also either a cousin or friend to Ferdinand Magellan (1480–1521), who won financial backing for the first successful circumnavigation of the globe based on reports that Serrão had sent.

V ery little information survives on Serrão prior to his emergence as the captain of one of three ships sent out by the viceroy in India, Afonso de Albuquerque (1453–1515), in 1511. Earlier that year, Albuquerque had set out from the Portuguese enclave of Goa, on India's western coast, with a force of over a thousand men to successfully subdue the state of Malacca. Albuquerque hoped to imprint Portuguese royal authority on the Spice Islands of Banda, too. Known in the modern era as the Malaku Islands, the Bandas were the source of a valuable indigenous tree that produced nutmeg and mace, each of which were prized spices on the European market at the time. The spices were usually sold in Venice by Arab traders who had dominated the Indian Ocean trade for several centuries, and the exorbitant prices charged for both compelled Portugal to seize control of the source for itself.

Commandeered Chinese Junk

Under the command of António de Abreu, three ships left Malacca in November of 1511, heading southeastward into the Java Sea with the help of Malay guides. Serrão served as captain of one of the trio of vessels. They went east through Java and past Bali and other islands known as the Lesser Sundas chain, then north past Amboina to Banda. One report claimed that at the port of Gresik on East Java, Serrão married a Javanese woman who then came along on the remainder of the voyage. After his ship was nearly destroyed, Serrão reached Luco-Pino island (Hitu), where he collected stores of nutmeg, mace, and cloves before acquiring a Chinese junk, or large ship used for trade. The arms his men carried also impressed the local ruler of Hitu, which was engaged in its own battles with Luhu, a nearby island rival.

With his new vessel, Serrão headed on to the Maluku Islands. With him was a crew of 18, comprised of nine Portuguese and nine Indonesians. When their junk was demolished by a reef, they were already warned that the inhabitants of a nearby island were predators known to steal cargo from shipwrecks on that very reef; when the islanders neared the sinking junk in their vessel, Serrão and the Europeans pretended they were merely inept unarmed sailors and not traders. When the scavengers came close enough, Serrão's party turned on them, seized their boat, and forced the local pirates to guide them to Amboina.

Became Advisor to Sultan

Back in Amboina, Serrão received word that the chiefs of two neighboring islands at the north end of the Malukus, Ternate and Tidore, hoped to secure his military expertise. The pair of islands were engaged in a low-level trade war with one another, but because Ternate was the bigger power, Serrão agreed to help and went there with a small band of mercenaries. The Ternate ruler, Sultan Bayan Sirrullah, was so pleased with the success of the mission that he not only paid Serrão the agreed-upon sum, but offered him a permanent salary and lavish living quarters as his personal adviser. Serrão decided not to return to Malacca, but sent a letter to Magellan that the Moluccas were quite far from Malacca, and even so far east that they fell under the Spanish realm as designated by the Treaty of Tordesillas, which divided the unconquered world between the kingdoms of Spain and Portugal. This ignited Magellan's interest in reaching Asia by sailing to the west—across the Atlantic Ocean and around South America—rather than the route the Portuguese had customarily taken to reach India and Indonesia, which followed the shores of the African continent. Magellan showed these letters to Spain's King Charles V (1500–1558), promising him easy access to the Spice Islands for Spain if the crown would agree to finance Magellan's plan for the world's first circumnavigational voyage.

Serrão died in Ternate in 1521, around the same time that Magellan died in the Philippines. Serrão may have been poisoned after falling victim to intrigues at the Sultan's court. His legacy was the trade deal he negotiated on behalf of Portugal for a monopoly on Ternate's cloves and other spices, which endured for another century. He was the first European to reach the northern Moluccas.

Periodicals

Geographical Journal, Including the Proceedings of the Royal Geographical Society, Vol. VII, January-June 1896. ☐

Cecil Sharp

British musicologist Cecil Sharp (1859-1924) made an invaluable contribution to the history of folk music in his travels through Appalachia during World War I. On these expeditions, Sharp extensively documented the folk ballads of the region, which had been brought over as far back as the 1770s from the British Isles by the ancestors of the Appalachian Mountain residents. In their original form, some of these songs dated back to the late medieval period of English, Scottish, and Irish folk music.

Sharp was born in London on November 22, 1859, and grew up in the Denmark Hill area of South London. His father was a slate merchant, and Sharp's love of music was apparently inherited from his mother, Jane Bloyd Sharp. He spent several years at the Uppingham School in Rutland, England, but left at age 15 in order to begin private tutoring in preparation for college. He was a member of the rowing team at Clare College of Cambridge University, where he earned his degree in 1882.

Studied Law in Australia

Later that year Sharp set sail for Australia, where he settled in Adelaide and found work as a clerk with the Commercial Bank of South Australia. He planned to pursue a career in law, and began private study for it—a common practice in the era before law schools came into existence—and served as an associate to Samuel Way, chief justice of the Supreme Court of South Australia. During these years, however, Sharp was also an assistant organist at St. Peter's Cathedral in Adelaide, and the conductor for two choral

societies. He finally abandoned his plans for a law career in 1889 when he became joint director of the Adelaide School of Music. He lectured at the school and also served as conductor of the Adelaide Philharmonic, but a falling-out with I.G. Reimann, the co-director of the Adelaide School, led in part to Sharp's decision to return to England.

Back in England by the end of 1892, Sharp intended to move forward with his career as a composer. In Adelaide he had written the music for two light operas, but few of his works found a publisher or performance venue, and he fared better as a lecturer and instructor. He held positions at a conservatory in the London neighborhood of Hampstead, at Metropolitan College in Holloway, and at Ludgrove, a private school for boys. Periodically felled by asthma and other health issues, he was recuperating from gout over the Christmas holidays in 1899 when he spied a group of Morris dancers from the window. Morris dancers performed in unusually exotic costumes, and their repertoire involved a form of martial dancing whose origins are somewhat mysterious. The term is though to be a derivative of "Moorish" or "Moroccan," and dates back to the 1490s, when dances known as the *moresca* were performed in Spain in celebration of King Ferdinand (1452-1516) and Queen Isabella (1451-1504)'s move to eject the Moors from the Iberian peninsula. In fifteenth-century England, Morris dancers would blacken their faces in what was apparently an imitation of the darker North African Moors, but by Sharp's era they had retained only the bells attached to their boots and their somewhat fanciful North African-inspired garb. By the time that Sharp saw the dancers on the street, the Morris groups were a dying breed, with just a handful of active groups in England left.

Spurred Revival of Morris Dancing

Sharp became fascinated by the Morris dancing phenomenon, and began researching it intensely. The effort led to his 1907 title, *The Morris Book, Part 1: A History of Morris Dancing, With a Description of Eleven Dances as Performed by the Morris-Men of England.* In it, he noted that "the Morris Dance is . . . in spirit, the organized, traditional expression of virility, sound health and animal spirits. It smacks of cudgel-play, of quarter-staff, of wrestling, of honest fisticuffs," he wrote. "It is the dance of folk who are slow to anger, but of great obstinacy—forthright of act and speech: to watch it in its thumping sturdiness is to hold such things as poinards and stilettos, the swordsman with the domino, the man who stabs in the back—as unimaginable things. The Morris dance, in short, is a perfect expression in rhythm and movement of the English character."

Sharp's book helped spur a revival of interest in Morris dancing, and the notations he made to accompany the dances served to instruct a new generation of practitioners. A related work was *The Sword Dances of Northern England,* published in three volumes between 1911 and 1913. This joined Sharp's first published title, *Folk Songs from Somerset,* which had appeared in 1904. With this he began the most significant period of his career as an archivist of folk music of the British Isles. He began traveling through the countryside on his bike during the warmer months to collect these songs, some of which were so old that their actual origins were unknown, and documented the existence of 3,300 such tunes in England alone. Earlier folk music scholars had made similar efforts before him, but Sharp's work was notable in that he made musical notations as well as transcriptions of the lyrics.

Sharp believed that such folk ballads were an important part of the English national heritage, particularly because they served as the artistic expression of simple farmers or tradespeople who were unable to read or write, and had no other formal avenue of artistic expression. The songs told of romantic travails or injustices committed at the hands of aristocratic landowners, and some of them were downright violent or sexually graphic in nature. Sharp began devising a piano accompaniment to some that were more traditionally sung *a cappella* so that they could be taught in schools as part of a new English folk music curriculum.

Made First Foray into Appalachia

In 1911 Sharp founded the English Folk Dance Society, which worked to preserve and promote traditional dances. Just a few months following the onset of World War I, Sharp managed to travel to America to give a lecture tour and contribute to a New York City production of *A Midsummer Night's Dream* by Granville Barker (1877-1946), a well-known actor, director, and expert in Elizabethan-era drama.

Once again waylaid by poor health, Sharp was resting in Lincoln, Massachusetts, from an attack of lumbago when a visitor from North Carolina came calling. Olive Campbell (1882-1954) had been documenting folk songs in the Appalachian Mountain region of the American South, and had heard of Sharp's work in England. She convinced him that the standard scholarly assumption that the English folk songs that came to America in the 1700s with immigrants had not survived was utterly wrong. Campbell asserted that in some of the remoter regions of Appalachia, still untouched by railroads or even formal roads, these songs were still relatively intact in the form in which they migrated across the Atlantic.

Sharp decided to make a journey and investigate for himself. He took with him Maud Karpeles (1885-1976), an English folk-dance aficionado who had been serving as his assistant, and the pair made their first trip into Appalachia over nine weeks in 1916. The trip was conducted by horse-drawn wagon, on horseback, and on foot, into regions of Kentucky, Tennessee, Virginia, and North Carolina that had been largely forgotten by the rest of Americans except for a few missionaries and teachers who occasionally ventured there. Appalachia was both rural and wild, and its people lived in appallingly primitive conditions. "Cut off from all that counted itself as civilization outside their boundaries, these people have grown up in a sort of self-contained isolation, needing little or nothing from the outside, raising on their hillsides most of the food they eat and making the clothes they wear," wrote Richard Aldrich in the *New York Times* in 1924. Noting that the archaic dialects had survived that showed strong links back to speech patterns in parts of England and Scotland, Aldrich noted that the people

"mostly do not read and write. Their songs are traditional, handed down from generation to generation by ear."

When Sharp set out on his first trip, he was advised to take a gun with him, and later admitted, "I have never been so frightened in my life!," according to Tony Scherman in an article that appeared in the *Smithsonian*. Initially the sight of two rather formally attired Britons was alarming to more than a few local residents, who rarely encountered "city folk" who were not there to extract a profit of some sort; there were even rumors that he was there to trick them into signing over their land or water rights. But Sharp's years of experience in coaxing melodies out of equally taciturn English farmers proved to have been excellent practice, and his patience and persistence paid off. On that first trip, he and Karpeles collected some 387 songs.

Returned in 1917

Some of the songs that Sharp found were so old that even English experts like himself were unsure of their dates, placing their origins sometime in the late medieval era. One example is "The Riddle Song," with its opening line, "I gave my love a cherry that had no stone." Another was "The Wife of Usher's Well," which Scherman noted had been documented in the early 1800s, but "was a poor, half-remembered tatter in Scotland. In 1916 in America, mountain singers gave Sharp 18 fine versions of the terrifying ghost ballad in which a woman's three babes haunt her."

As he did in England, Sharp made musical notations of the songs. "To many a mountain singer, most of whom couldn't read music, Sharp's notating was a feat of magic—especially when, sight-reading, he'd actually sing their tunes back to them," wrote Scherman. The *Smithsonian* article also noted that Sharp's initial impressions of the Appalachian "hill people," as they were known in the era, as being transplanted English peasants like those he had encountered—and whose company he much enjoyed—proved to be a false assumption. Instead, he found in the Appalachian residents an absence of "servility which unhappily is one of the characteristics of the English peasant," Scherman quoted him as saying.

Sharp came to love the beauty of the Appalachians as well as the noble character of its people. He returned in the spring of 1917 and spent another 37 weeks with Karpeles collecting songs, fascinated by a culture that seemed to have a limitless supply of leisure time. "Very often, we would call upon some of our friends early in the morning and remain till dusk, sharing the midday meal with the family, and I would go away with the feeling that I had never before been in a more musical atmosphere nor benefited more greatly by the exchange of musical confidences," he wrote in 1917's *English Folk songs of the Southern Appalachians,* as quoted in Aldrich's article.

Left Behind a Trove of Scholarship

Back in England after the end of World War I, Sharp became an inspector of training colleges that taught folk music and dancing, and continued to give well-attended lectures. Long plagued by asthma, he died on June 23, 1924, at the age of 64. Survivors included his wife, Constance Dorothea Birch, whom he had marred in 1893, and their four children. Karpeles did much to ensure that his scholarship survived after his death, readying several more volumes for publication that became standard reference works for those interested in the origins and development of English and American folk music. Morris dancing groups remain active and firmly entrenched in England and Australia, and the English Folk Dance Society he founded back in 1911 merged several years after his death to become the English Folk Dance and Song Society (EFDSS), whose headquarters in London are known as the Cecil Sharp House.

Books

Sharp, Cecil J., with Herbert C. Macilwaine, *The Morris Book, Part 1: A History of Morris Dancing, With a Description of Eleven Dances as Performed by the Morris-Men of England,* Novello and Company, 1907.

Periodicals

New York Times, December 2, 1917; July 20, 1924.
Smithsonian, April 1985. □

Sidney Sheldon

Sidney Sheldon (1917-2007) was the creator of many famous television shows, as well as a prolific writer who penned numerous novels. He was responsible for the creation of television series such as *I Dream of Jeannie,* and for numerous Broadway productions, including *Annie Get Your Gun.* Sheldon then turned his screenwriting talent into a lucrative career penning genre fiction that brought him fame in the world of writing.

Early Life

Sheldon was born in Chicago, Illinois, and grew up in a modest household where his mother and father worked blue collar jobs. Both his parents were school dropouts, and Sheldon himself was not exposed to cultural or intellectual influences until he entered Northwestern University. He studied for a few years, but when the economy took a downturn during the Depression, money problems forced him to give up the college life.

The East and West Coasts

Sheldon moved to New York City to find work. He tried his hand first at composing music, and was able to get some songs down on paper. According to Sheldon's personal Web site, his talent "was first recognized when he worked in the checkroom at the Bismarck Hotel. He gave the orchestra leader, Phil Levant, a song he had written. Levant liked it, created an arrangement out of the piece, and for many nights thereafter, Sheldon would hear his song being played while he checked hats and coats." Sheldon would

return to the world of music much later in his life, but at that time he concentrated on breaking into the realm of writing for the stage.

While living in New York, Sheldon teamed up with a man named Ben Roberts, who later became his screenwriting partner. While waiting for military assignments in the Air Force, Sheldon and Roberts had an opportunity to write for musical theater and for the Broadway stage. The two men had never written anything that had been set to music, but they were willing to give it a try. Their first full production was called *Merry Widow,* and it went on to score 322 performances on Broadway. This made *Merry Widow* the longest running Broadway revival show in history to that time. Sheldon then received his assignment for the Air Force, and went on to serve during World War II. After being discharged early due to health issues, Sheldon moved to Los Angeles, California.

There Sheldon pursued his dream of writing for the movies. He wrote a detailed synopsis of Steinbeck's *Of Mice and Men,* and after submitting it to production houses was accepted for the job of script reader at Metro Goldwyn Mayer (MGM) studios, for $17 dollars a week. While working at MGM, Sheldon created his own scripts in his spare time and collaborated with other employees on story ideas. Sheldon and Roberts worked on various B Movie scripts, eventually getting several produced by small production houses, including a small production studio called Producers Releasing Corporation. The first script that Sheldon and Roberts wrote was called *Dangerous Holiday,* which they sold for a grand total of $500 dollars. This success led to other movies such as *Dangerous Lady* and *Gambling Daughters.*

Sheldon's name eventually got the attention of Dore Schary at MGM. Schary invited Sheldon to work as a screenwriter for the studio, and Sheldon happily accepted. He worked on such titles as *Easter Parade, Annie Get Your Gun,* and *The Bachelor and the Bobby Soxer,* the latter winning Sheldon an Academy Award. Sheldon had originally been concerned that people would not go to see the comedy show because of its strange title. However, his fears were soon put to rest when the movie became a hit.

Sheldon was one of the first people to start writing for television. He left MGM after 12 years of screenwriting to work for the fledgling television industry. ABC Studios hired him to create a show that would star an actress named Patty Duke. Sheldon agreed, and began writing scripts for *The Patty Duke Show.* It was a huge success, and Sheldon ended up writing 78 different scripts for this show. Sheldon was also responsible for the hit show *I Dream of Jeannie.* The show had a unique plot, placing a magical genie in normal everyday situations and playing off the mayhem that results when ordinaryl human beings have their wishes granted. For his work on *I Dream of Jeannie,* Sheldon received an Emmy Award nomination for Outstanding Writing Achievement.

Began Writing Fiction

At age 50, Sheldon's career as a producer and television writer was in full swing. At one point, however, he came up with an idea that was too intricate and detailed to be easily portrayed on the big screen. He felt that the only way to fully realize his vision was to write a book, where he could control all the aspects and details as he saw fit. He wanted to be able to give his characters more depth. As he told the *Seattle Times,* "I got an idea that was so introspective, it entered the character's mind. I didn't know how to do that in a dramatic form. So I gave up. But it was so strong in my mind that I came back to it. That was my first book, *The Naked Face,* about a psychiatrist whom someone was going to murder."

After being turned down by five publishers, Sheldon eventually sold *The Naked Face* to William Morrow Publishers. However, despite winning the Edgar Allen Poe award from the Mystery Writers of America for best first mystery novel, the book did not sell well. Sheldon did not give up, however, and his next book, *The Other Side of Midnight,* sold over three million copies. After this success, Sheldon went on to write many more books, all of them reaching the bestseller lists. Book critics were often not kind to Sheldon's works, calling them "airport reads" and "potboilers," which means books written more for the financial gain of the writer than for any artistic purpose. They were genre books, to be sure, but Sheldon drew on his substantial experience as a television writer and knew how to make his books into page-turners. His fiction continued to sell well, and after a while even the critics warmed up to his stories. He continued to write well into his later years, crafting bestselling stories that captivated the reading public.

The critics acknowledged that Sheldon's fiction, although generally more entertainment than art form, was well crafted, with characters and stories that captured audiences' attention from first page to last. In an interview with *Publishers Weekly,* Sheldon discussed why his characters were so important to him:. "If I wrote a plot that was the most exciting plot in the world and the reader didn't care about the characters, you can forget it. But I could write about someone who needs $20 desperately and make the reader care. It's all in the character." In the interview, Sheldon went on to defend his novels against the accusation that all of his plots seemed similar. "Not one of my books is like another. . . . I'm not a critics' darling and that's fine. I've sold over 300 million books. Forget the critics."

Sheldon had a few common threads that ran throughout his novels. He emphasized female characters, putting them in rags-to-riches situations. His female protagonists usually ended up making something of themselves and re-entering the limelight to exact revenge on the people who had wronged them in the first place. In an article in *The Writer,* Sheldon described his use of up-to-date situations and characters: "My novels and characters remain contemporary because I prefer to write about the most exciting and dynamic period in our history—the present. I also feel that my readers can more easily identify with the characters and their story if it takes place in a contemporary setting."

On his Web site, Sheldon was asked why he turned to writing after all his years in television production. He replied, "I love the freedom that the narrative form provides. When you write a movie, you have a hundred collaborators. But when you write a novel, it's yours. There's this sense of excitement because you invent and control the characters. You decide whether they live or die. I find this type of creative process tremendously stimulating." Indeed, Sheldon's books were so stimulating that they were banned or branded "immoral" by religious figures such as the Rev. Jerry Falwell and the Rev. Tom Williams.

Sheldon Ventured

The only logical next move for an author whose books keep people up at night is to develop comfortable sleepwear. At least, this was Sheldon's thinking in 1995 when he proposed a line of sleepwear for women, called Sidney Sheldon Knightwear. The company that manufactured and marketed this new line was called the Wise Apparel Group. When Sheldon was asked by *WWD* magazine about his inspiration for creating the clothing line, he responded, "I woke up one morning in Bali with the thought of introducing a men's line of robes and sleepwear called Knightwear. My pajamas weren't very comfortable with the humidity—that's what woke me up." Sheldon discussed the plans with his wife, who suggested that he change the idea into a line of sleepwear for women. Sheldon sold the idea, but insisted that he and his wife have sole control over the product. He approved all the designs for the various types of sleepwear.

In 2001 Sheldon went to Nashville, Tennessee, to present a different kind of writing to a much different audience. Sheldon, having mastered the mediums of stage, screen, and page, also hoped to pursue a career in country music. Sheldon brought his own songs with him in the hope that they would be produced. In an article in *Billboard,* Sheldon explained why he was drawn to country music: "Country music is telling a story, and I'm a storyteller. That's why I wanted to get involved in it." Through Sheldon's attorney in Los Angeles he was introduced to Frank Liddell, who worked for Carnival Music, and through Liddell, Sheldon secured appointments with some of Nashville's top song-writers, including Dave Loggins, John Bettis, Mark D. Sanders, Don Cook, and Tia Sillers. With the help of this team of country music writers, Sheldon edited and rewrote many of his songs. Sheldon's first attempt at country song writing left him with more to add to his already formidable repertoire of creations. When asked how writing a song differs from writing a book, he told *Billboard,* "When you write a novel, you take two years to build up a very wide panorama that can go around the world and involve many different people in many different plots. When you write a song, you get to the heart of it and express the sentiment as quickly and as cleverly as you can."

Sheldon died on January 30, 2007, in Rancho Mirage, California, from complications due to pneumonia. He was 89. He had captivated generations of fans with his television shows, Broadway productions and books. His works of fiction have been translated into 51 languages, including Urdu and Swahili.

Books

Authors and Artists for Young Adults. Vol. 65, Thomson Gale, 2005.
Contemporary Popular Writers. St. James Press, 1997.
St. James Encyclopedia of Popular Culture. 5 vols., St. James Press, 2000.

Periodicals

Billboard, March 3, 2001.
Publishers Weekly, August 14, 2000.
Seattle Times, March 5, 2003.
Variety, February 20, 2006.
The Writer, December 1998.
WWD, June 5, 1995.

Online

Contemporary Authors Online. Gale, 2007, http:// galenet.gale group.com/servlet/BioRC (April 15, 2008).
"Sidney Sheldon," Sidney Sheldon Official Web site, http://www .hachettebookgroupusa.com/features/sidneysheldon/index .html (March 11, 2008). □

Simeon, King of Bulgaria

Simeon I the Great (c. 864-927) ruled Bulgaria from 893 to his death in 927, a period that saw a significant enlargement of the kingdom to encompass much of the Balkan peninsula and Bulgaria's corresponding rise to become a cultural center of southeastern Europe. Simeon went to war several times against the mighty Byzantine Empire and closer to home lavished resources on helping the Orthodox Church flourish in his land. His rule ushered in a period of greatness for the Bulgarian Empire over the next two centuries that would never be repeated, and for these achievements he is often called Simeon the Great.

The Bulgars were likely a Turkic people who were originally from Central Asia and came westward on horseback with the Huns, whose hordes swept through Europe in the mid-fifth century under the leadership of Attila (406–453). The Bulgars intermarried with Slavic tribes in the area of southeastern Europe where they eventually settled, and by the start of the eighth century were active traders with the powerful Byzantine Empire to the east. Boris, Simeon's father, was an heir to the Krum dynasty, which ruled Bulgaria after 800, and Boris laid the groundwork for the expansion of the Bulgarian Empire when he ordered his people to abandon their pagan religion and convert to Christianity.

Spent Teen Years in Constantinople

This event of conversion for expansion of the Empire occurred in 865, when Simeon was either an infant or about to be born; the exact date of his birth is unknown. It is known that he was Boris's third son, and his father probably intended for him to enter the priesthood, because he was sent to Constantinople, the Byzantine capital and holy city of the Eastern Orthodox Church, for an education around 878, when he was 13 or 14 years old. While there he became fluent in Greek, the language of religious scholarship in this part of the world at the time, and showed a deep interest in the translation of sacred church texts from Greek into a relatively new written language being used in Bulgaria at the time, known as Old Church Slavonic.

Simeon returned to Bulgaria around 888, and entered a royal monastery in Preslav, a city located in northeastern Bulgaria near the present-day town of Shumen. Preslav was emerging as a great center of learning in southeastern Europe thanks to several new churches built since the Bulgarians' conversion to Christianity, and was home to monasteries where monks copied and translated sacred texts. Simeon joined their ranks, translating works from Greek into Old Church Slavonic, which was the first written language in the Slavic lands, and these were disseminated widely and even reached Russia in the period before Slavs there converted to Christianity. The texts included the gospels as well as the writings of such early church fathers and noted theologians as Athanasius of Alexandria (c. 293–373), who would later become Pope Athanasius I, and John Chrysostom (349–407), the archbishop of Constantinople.

Simeon's brother Vladimir assumed the Bulgarian throne when Boris entered a monastery in 889, but the new king then conspired with nobles in the capital, Pliska, to renounce Christianity and return to paganism. When Boris learned of the scheme, he dethroned his son and installed Simeon instead in 893. The coronation took place in Preslav, which Simeon then decided to make the new capital—a form of rebuke to the treacherous Pliska nobles.

Historians are unsure of why the line of succession skipped Boris's second son, Gavril, in favor of Simeon.

Invaded Neighboring Byzantium

Almost immediately Simeon was faced with a major crisis: the Byzantine Emperor Leo VI (866–912), under pressure from his Greek wife Zoe, rescinded the Bulgarians' trading rights in Constantinople and ordered them to conduct their business in the Greek city of Thessaloniki instead. Bulgarian merchants were outraged, for in Thessaloniki they were forced to pay much higher tariffs, and when an effort to resolve the crisis with Leo through diplomacy failed, Simeon went to war. His troops invaded Byzantium in 894, an act sometimes referred to as Europe's first war over trade.

Byzantium and its capital, Constantinople, were not far from Preslav. Simeon's kingdom sat on the tail end of the European continent, where the Balkan peninsula descended into the kingdom of Thrace, later known as Macedonia, and then farther southward to Greece. Bulgaria possessed valuable access to the Black Sea, and south along that coastline led to the isthmus that connected the European and Asian continents, where Constantinople was located. Simeon's armies initially faced little resistance, because the vast Byzantine Empire was battling back a threat from Arabic invaders on its other side. A third party, the Magyars, then became involved in the conflict. These were a nomadic people who had come from either Central Asia or the Siberian steppes centuries earlier and settled on the steppes of southern Ukraine. The Magyars struck a deal with Byzantium to attack Bulgarian lands while Simeon and his army were away.

War raged for the next two years until Simeon repelled the Magyars at the Battle of Southern Buh in 896. The Bulgarian victory resulted in the forced westward migration of the Magyars, who moved into present-day Hungary and established a kingdom there that also flourished after it converted to Christianity a century later. Simeon then won a victory over the Byzantine army at Battle of Bulgarophygon later in 896, and moved on to lay siege to Constantinople. Finally, Leo agreed to the terms of Simeon's peace treaty, which included the concession of territory between the Black Sea and Strandzha mountain range, return of trading privileges in Constantinople, and an annual tribute, and either a sum of money or goods, payable to Bulgaria from Constantinople.

Conquered Albania and Serbia

Simeon became determined to diminish the power of the Byzantines from the region, and even began to have designs on the throne himself. In 904, he violated the terms of his own peace agreement when a mercenary force he hired captured the Greek city of Thessaloniki. Simeon planned to rid it of its Greek citizens and instead populate the ancient and strategic port with Bulgarians. Leo agreed to further concessions to prevent this from happening, and after this point Simeon's empire expanded to include a large part of Macedonia and the territory of Albania, the latter situated on the coastline of the Adriatic Sea. North of Albania laid the kingdom of Serbia, and here, too, Simeon im-

posed Bulgarian rule. This period witnessed the most significant expansion of the Bulgarian kingdom since its founding by the Krum dynasty.

After the death of Leo in 912, Simeon renewed his efforts to conquer Constantinople when Leo's successor refused to pay the annual tribute. A crisis of succession occurred following the new Byzantine emperor's sudden death in 913, and with the Byzantines under the rule of a council of regents headed by the Nicholas Mystikos, the patriarch of Constantinople—an ecclesiastical office similar to that of archbishop—Simeon's armies attacked Constantinople in the summer of 913. Their success forced the patriarch to grant Simeon formal recognition as "Emperor of the Bulgarians." Included in the new treaty was an arrangement for Simeon's daughter to marry the new Byzantine ruler, Constantine VII, son of Leo. When Zoe—Constantine's mother and Leo's widow—heard of the plot to unite Byzantium with Bulgaria through this match, she returned to Constantinople and in a palace coup ousted her own son.

These events resulted in yet another renewal of hostilities between the Bulgarians and the Byzantine Empire, this time in 917 when the Byzantine army attacked Bulgarian defenses in alliance with both the Magyars and the Serbs, who had chafed under Bulgarian rule. Byzantium possessed one of the most formidable navies in the known world at the time, and deployed it on the Black Sea in August of 917 at the Battle of Anchialos, one of the largest sea battles of the medieval period. Through a combination of strategy and good fortune, Simeon's forces beat back the flotilla from the hills. He then turned to address the treachery of his erstwhile ally, the Serbian prince, Petar Gojniković, sending envoys who tricked Petar into agreeing to meeting, then seized him and took him as a hostage back to Bulgaria, where he died in a dungeon.

Tried to Borrow Arab Navy

Simeon went to war again against Byzantium in 920, this time in a two-year conflict. When tensions flared yet again in 924, he conspired to hire the navy belonging to the Arab Fatimid Empire, based in Cairo, to capture the well-defended Byzantine capital. The founder of the Fatimid caliphate, Ubayd Allah al-Mahdi Billah (birth and death dates unknown), agreed to help, but the envoys sent to arrange the navy were captured in the southern Italian region of Calabria by Byzantine spies, and the plan was foiled. Simeon traveled to Constantinople in the summer of 924 to meet with the new co-emperor, a former admiral named Romanos Lekapenos, and arrange terms of a new peace treaty.

Simeon also began corresponding with Pope John X (died 928) in Rome, who appears to have to seconded Simeon's claim as "Emperor of the Romans," which made him equal in status to the ruler of Byzantium. The Bulgarian Orthodox Church was also elevated to the status of patriarchate, which gave it equal status to the other leading cities of the Orthodox Church—Constantinople, Alexandra, Antioch, and Jerusalem. In the final year of his life Simeon invaded Croatia and made plans to attack Constantinople again, but died of heart failure in his palace in Preslav on May 27, 927. His underage son, Peter I (died 970) succeeded him, with Peter's maternal uncle, George Sursuvul, acting as regent. In a peace treaty concluded in October of 927, Peter was betrothed to Maria, the granddaughter of Romanos, who then took the name Eirene ("peace") after the November wedding.

Simeon left his new capital city, Preslav, an impressive showplace for his empire. More than 20 churches were constructed, with the unique Orthodox-style domes, but none of the towers survived Preslav's decline, which began in the 960s when Kievan Rus invaded, followed by the Byzantines determined to avenge Simeon's years of harassment. The empire was subsumed into the Byzantine Empire completely by 1018.

Books

Crampton, R. J., *A Concise History of Bulgaria,* Cambridge University Press, 2005.
Forbes, Nevill et al., *The Balkans: A History of Bulgaria, Serbia, Greece, Rumania, Turkey,* originally published by Clarendon Press, 1915, Digital Antiquaria, 2004. □

Gobind Singh

The Indian religious leader Guru Gobind Singh (1666-1708) was one of the most important shapers of the Sikh religion.

Gobind was not the founder of Sikhism, a monotheistic faith that arose in India in the fifteenth century. But he is responsible for several of the religion's most visible features and ideals. These include the military ethos of Sikhism, which has included the requirement that some male Sikhs carry a sword at all times. Sikhs view Gobind as the tenth and last human guru of the Sikh faith; he designated a text, the *Guru Granth Sahib,* as the ultimate guru, or teacher, for Sikhs. Gobind's life story played out against a background of military conflict in India, and his ideas transformed Sikhism from the status of a small regional sect to a major world religion that has held significant political power.

Father Executed by Emperor

Gobind Singh was born Gobind Rai Sodhi on December 22, 1666, in Patna in the present-day Indian state of Bihar. His parents were Tegh Bahadur, the ninth Sikh guru, and his wife, Gujari. When he was young the family moved to Anandpur (now Anandpur Sahib, in Punjab state), on the edge of the Himalaya mountains, a city his father had founded. As with many religious leaders, various remarkable stories have been attached to Gobind's childhood. One chronicle, as quoted on the Sikh History Web site, held that Bahadur, dismayed over conflicts between Hindus and Muslims in northern India, said to his son, "Grave are the burdens the earth bears. She will be redeemed only if a truly worthy person comes forward to lay down his head. Distress will then be expunged and happiness ushered in." The child Gobind's reply was that "None could be worthier than yourself to make such a sacrifice." Bahadur turned himself in to the Islamic Mughal emperor, and was executed in 1675 after refusing to renounce his resistance to the empire and convert to Islam.

Before his death, Bahadur named Gobind as his successor, and he was formally proclaimed the Sikh guru on March 29, 1676. At a camp on the shores of the Yamuna River, Gobind was educated in martial arts, hunting, literature, and languages. He learned to write the ancient Indian language of Sanskrit and the Persian of the Mughal court, as well as the Punjabi and the Braj Bhasha variant of Hindi spoken indigenously in northern India. He had a gift for poetry, and in 1684 he composed the epic poem *Var Sri Bhagauti Ji Ki* in the Punjabi language, a tale of a massive conflict between gods and demons rooted in India's ancient literature.

"Poetry as such was, however, not his aim," noted the Sikh History site. "For him it was a means of revealing the divine principle and concretizing a personal vision of the Supreme Being that had been vouchsafed to him." This intense focus on the divine principle was a fundamental tenet of Sikhism, which does not conceptualize the divine in human terms. To this basic orientation, however, Gobind added something new. An expert rider, swimmer, and archer, he grew up in a world of warring states whose conflicts were intensified by religious differences: the Muslim Mughal empire vied for influence in India with local and mostly Hindu leaders of the Rajput order, and adherents of other groups, such as Pathans (today's Pashtuns) of the northwestern subcontinent complicated the situation still more. Singh concluded that it was necessary for the Sikhs to arm themselves and to mold themselves into a fighting force. He ordered that ancient Sanskrit war epics be translated into languages young Sikh men would speak and understand.

Defeated Rajput, Mughal Forces

Gobind benefited from the fact that Rajput clan leaders had their own set of conflicts with the Mughals, some of them centering on taxes and appropriation of resources. Rajput groups in northern India grew worried about Gobind's growing power and raised a unified force to confront him, but his Sikh warriors prevailed in the Battle of Bhangani around 1686. (Dates of many of the major events in Gobind's life are uncertain, and much of what is known about him comes from an autobiographical document called the *Bicitra Natak.*) About a year after that battle, Gobind's army defeated the forces of Alif Kahn, the Mughal governor of the Punjab at Nadaun.

Establishing his compound at Anandpur, Gobind constructed a set of fortresses. He unified the Sikhs under his rule, ordering them to follow his leadership rather than that of local potentates. Married three times, he had four sons, and he consolidated the religious principles that his father and grandfather (who was the sixth Sikh guru) had laid down. As conflict flared in the 1690s between the Mughal emperor Aurangzeb and the Rajput clans, Gobind's power grew. Aurangzeb sent his son, Moazzam, to eliminate the Sikh force, but Moazzam, who promoted a policy of religious tolerance, chose to ignore Gobind and focus his efforts instead on the hill kingdoms.

In 1699 Gobind decided on a dramatic stroke that would permanently sear Sikh values into the minds of his followers. He summoned Sikh males to his headquarters on the Baisakhi harvest festival, which marked the new year for both Hindus and Sikhs. They were instructed not to consult with local religious leaders, and Gobind said that they should arrive with long hair and beards, a practice confined at the time to a few ascetic sects. By the end of March, a large crowd of Sikhs had gathered at Anandpur. Probably on April 13 or 14, 1699 (sources suggest various dates), Gobind engineered, at a single stroke, a new face of Sikhism.

Appeared Before Crowd with Blood-Drenched Sword

Appearing before a large assembly that had just celebrated morning religious services, Gobind brandished his sword and asked (according to the Sikh History site), "Is there present a true Sikh who would offer his head to the Guru as a sacrifice?" The shocked crowd was silent, but finally a man named Daya Ram stepped forward. Gobind led him into a tent and then emerged, alone, with blood dripping from his sword. He repeated his request, and Dharam Das came forward. Again Gobind reappeared with a blood-drenched sword, and he repeated the process three more times. At this point, he revealed to the crowd that he had actually slaughtered five goats. He presented the volunteers, each wearing a turban and carrying a sword, to the crowd and dubbed them *panj piyare,* or the Five Beloved.

Gobind baptized the five men by having them drink a special nectar called *amrit* from a bowl he had sanctified with a double-edged dagger. The men were to be known as *khalsa,* or the pure ones—but other Sikh men could attain the same status by adopting five emblems, each of which began in the Punjabi language with the "k" sound: they should leave their hair and beards uncut (*kais*), carry a comb (*kangha*) in their long hair, wear military knee-length pants (*kachha*), wear a steel bracelet (*kara*) on their right wrists, signifying poverty, and finally, always carry a sword (*kirpan*) to defend the Sikh faith. These emblems collectively were known as *kakkar.* In addition, the members of the *khalsa* community had to take the surname Singh, meaning "lion" (women became Kaur, or princess), to renounce tobacco and alcohol, to agree to eat meat only from an animal killed with a single blow (a sharp contrast to Muslim dietary laws), and to treat women with respect.

It was not required for Sikhs to become *khalsa*; there remained a separate category of Sadjahari Sikhs, or those who needed time to accept the system of conduct. But many did, and they came from the provinces all around Anandpur. Mughal administrators and the Rajput chiefs were alarmed by the emergence of this force of highly motivated warriors, and they resolved that Gobind had to be stopped at all costs. Gobind's hilltop compound at Anandpur resisted a series of attacks between 1700 and 1704, but then came under a deadly blockade by Mughal forces. With his forces decimated in a battle in early December of 1705, Gobind was forced to evacuate Anandpur. His two young sons, Zorawar Singh and Fateh Singh, were captured and executed.

Rather than capitulate, Gobind issued to Aurangzeb a defiant *Zafarnamah* or Epistle of Victory. Reestablishing himself in the Punjabi city of Muktsar, Gobind devoted himself to the preparation of a new version of the *Adi Granth* Sikh scripture that had been compiled by the fifth Sikh guru, Arjun. This became the *Guru Granth Sahib,* which Gobind before his death designated the new guru and final spiritual authority for Sikhs. He also compiled his own writings into a collection called the *Dasam Granth* and wrote his autobiographical *Bicitra Natak.*

Reassembling his forces, Gobind headed for the imperial capital of Delhi, perhaps to protest the killing of his sons. En route he received word that Aurangzeb had died, and that a succession struggle had broken out. Gobind backed the tolerant Moazzam, and Sikh forces backed Moazzam in the decisive battle at Jajau that put him on the Mughal throne. Gobind joined the new emperor on several other military campaigns as he consolidated his rule, following him to the city of Nander in south central India. There, two young Pathan men sent by unknown parties sneaked into Gobind's tent and stabbed him. A British doctor named Cole was brought to try to save his life, but as Gobind tried to swing his sword, his wounds opened anew. He died on October 7, 1708.

Books

Bhattacharya, Sachchidananda, *A Dictionary of Indian History,* George Braziller, 1967.

Encyclopedia of Religion, 2nd ed., edited by Lindsay Jones, Macmillan, 2005.

Kapoor, Sukhbir Singh, *The Ideal Man: The Concept of Guru Gobind Singh,* Khalsa College London Press, 2000.

Periodicals

Coventry Evening Telegraph (Coventry, England), January 6, 2007.

Houston Chronicle, April 17, 1999.

Online

"Nanak X. Guru Gobind Singh ji (1675-1708)," Sikh History, http://www.sikh-history.com/sikhhist/gurus/nanak10.html (February 13, 2008). □

Ellen Johnson Sirleaf

Inaugurated as the president of the African nation of Liberia in January of 2006, Ellen Johnson Sirleaf (born 1938) was the first woman elected as the head of state in any African country.

Sirleaf faced enormous challenges upon taking office. Liberia had been torn by almost two decades of political instability and outright civil war that had killed nearly 10 percent of its citizens. The rest were mired in

poverty, with little access to education, electric power, or basic sanitation. However, she enjoyed grassroots confidence to a degree unusual for a contemporary African leader. Liberians called her "Ma," the "Iron Lady," or simply Ellen. In her first years in office she devoted much of her time to trying to attract international investment and to find ways out of the ruinous levels of foreign debt Liberia had accumulated over its years of trouble.

Of Indigenous Liberian Background

Sirleaf was born Ellen Johnson on October 29, 1938, in the Liberian capital of Monrovia. Her full name has sometimes been given in the hyphenated form of Ellen Johnson-Sirleaf, but her biography on the Web site of the Liberian Embassy in the United States omits the hyphen. Despite her American surname and cosmopolitan image, she was not descended from the African-American slaves who founded the Liberian nation in the nineteenth century and gradually assumed the status of a hereditary elite. Her father was a member of the Gola ethnic group and the son of a village chieftain who had been close to Liberian president Hilary Richard Wright Johnson (1837-1901). As a result of that relationship, Sirleaf's father was brought to the capital of Monrovia, given the name of Johnson, and allowed to obtain an education as a lawyer. He eventually became the first indigenous Liberian (i.e., not one of African-American descent) member of the country's national legislature. Sirleaf's mother was of mixed background; her father was a German trader who had to leave Liberia when the country entered World War I on the American side, and her mother

was a market trader who was adopted by a member of the Liberian elite after her husband fled.

"I am glad that neither my father nor my mother forgot their roots, and so we spent a lot of time with my two illiterate grandmothers, Jenneh and Juah," Sirleaf recalled to members of the All Liberian National Conference in Maryland in 2005, as quoted on the Liberia Past and Present Web site. "We also spent all of [our] vacation time in Julejuah, my father's ancestral village, where I learned most of all that there was to know about village life including the long walks from village to village, swimming and pulling canoe in the Kpo River, fishing with twine made from the palm tree, [and] bird hunting." Sirleaf herself was given the best education her country had available, studying accounting and economics at the College of West Africa in Monrovia.

Marrying James Sirleaf at age 17, she found time to raise four sons in the midst of an impressive educational career; the marriage later ended in divorce. Coming to the United States in the early 1960s, she earned three college degrees. She financed her own education at Madison Business College in Wisconsin, earning an accounting degree there in 1964 after stints as a waitress and drugstore employee in Madison. She earned a second bachelor's degree, in economics, at the University of Colorado in the 1960s, and from 1969 to 1971 she was a student in the graduate program at Harvard University, earning a master's degree in public administration in 1971. She returned home to a post in the Liberian government of President William Tolbert, and she was often sent abroad to cultivate international investment. In 1979 she was elevated to the post of minister of finance, becoming the first woman to hold that office in Liberia.

That began a long period during which Sirleaf attempted to bring professional procedures to Liberia's government against a backdrop of increasing ethnic strife and conflict between the traditional American-descended elites and the country's indigenous patchwork of ethnic groups, which often came into conflict among themselves. She took the side of demonstrators who opposed increases in the government-controlled price of rice, attempted to put in place procedures to curb corruption in government spending, and worked to lessen Liberia's dependence on its long-time but heavily cyclical export staple of iron ore in favor of more reliable foodstuffs such as palm oil and coffee.

Resigned Bank Presidency

Liberia's era of open conflict began with a 1980 military coup that deposed Tolbert (who was executed by firing squad) and installed Liberian army sergeant Samuel K. Doe in power. Doe appointed Sirleaf as director of the Liberian National Bank, but the two soon clashed over the new government's rampant civil rights violations. Sirleaf evaded her mentor's fate by leaving the country and settling in Nairobi, Kenya, where she was hired as the director of the Kenyan division of Citibank. When Doe named himself president in 1984 and putatively allowed the establishment of independent political parties, Sirleaf ran for president in October of 1985 as the candidate of the Liberian Action Party. Doe proclaimed himself the winner of the election, although independent observers proclaimed that Sirleaf would have won had there not been fraudulent practices during the election proceedings.

With that, Sirleaf's existence in her homeland took a sharp turn for the worse. An unsuccessful coup attempt against Doe at the end of 1985 led the dictator to take revenge against his political opponents. Despite her position as an elected Liberian senator, Sirleaf was arrested, jailed, sentenced to ten years in prison, and subjected to psychological torture; soldiers threatened to bury her alive on a beach or to burn off all her hair. After her release in 1986, Sirleaf returned to the United States, and began cultivating support among Liberian exile groups. In the late 1980s she held the post of president at the Equator Bank in Washington, D.C. and at Citibank's African regional office in Nairobi.

When a group of rebel military officers and government officials led by Charles Taylor launched an effort to remove Doe late in 1989, Sirleaf seemed to have a window of opportunity. She supported Taylor, while forces loyal to a third leader, Prince Johnson, captured and executed Doe, and Taylor invited her to join an interim government. The plan soon fell apart, however, as ethnic rivalries flared and Taylor began to wield dictatorial control hardly distinguishable from what the country had experienced under Doe. Sirleaf took a position as assistant administrator at the United Nations Regional Development Program for Africa in 1992, soon becoming the program's director.

Meanwhile, Liberia's situation had devolved into full-scale and ongoing civil war. The real power resided with Taylor, but a group of figurehead leaders was named (none was elected, but one, Ruth Sando Perry, was Africa's first female government leader). When peacekeepers from neighboring countries brought about a pause in ethnic clashes in 1996, free elections were held. Sirleaf quit her UN post and returned to Liberia to run against Taylor. She finished second in a field of 14 candidates, but won only 10 percent of the vote to Taylor's 75 percent.

Criticized U.S. Double Standard

Sirleaf once again faced treason charges in the wake of that election, and again she went into exile. Taylor, however, overplayed his hand by intervening in another civil war in neighboring Sierra Leone in 1999, backing a particularly brutal faction and stirring condemnation both at home and abroad. Sirleaf was a visible face in Washington, criticizing U.S. president Bill Clinton for not committing American forces to end the atrocities in Sierra Leone, even though a European civil war of similar scope in the former Yugoslavia had resulted in American intervention. In 2002 Sirleaf returned to Liberia and was named head of the Unity Party. Taylor responded by banning all political rallies.

In 2003 Liberia's national nightmare ended as Taylor, under UN indictment for war crimes, relinquished power to an interim government led by his subordinate Moses Blah, and went into exile in Nigeria. About 100,000 combatant forces were disarmed, 11 percent of them children who had often been kidnapped and pressed into service by guerrilla forces. The country lost 90 percent of its gross national product and was essentially in ruins, with unemployment running at a staggering 80 percent. Sirleaf was under consideration as interim president, but instead accepted the post of head of the country's Governance Reform Commission. She served in that role from 2003 to 2005 and then announced her candidacy for the presidency in the elections scheduled for 2005, promising to end government corruption. "It would have been much easier for her to quit politics and sit at home like others have done but she has never given up," a Liberian political observer told the BBC News, as noted in a profile on Sirleaf on its Web site.

Sirleaf's chief opponent was George Weah, known as a soccer star and a figure with strong appeal to Liberia's masses of dispossessed young males. Sirleaf, however, appealed to Liberian women and emerged the winner with almost 60 percent of the vote in the head-to-head runoff against Weah on November 8, 2005. According to an article by correspondent Lydia Polgreen in the New York Times, supporters carried signs at her rallies that read "Ellen—she's our man!" Weah alleged that fraud had occurred, but Sirleaf won an across-the-board victory that included support from many male voters, and she was certified the winner by Liberia's national election commission. She was inaugurated as president, and as Africa's first elected female leader, on January 16, 2006. Her security forces destabilized a pair of coup attempts that were hatched after Sirleaf arranged for Taylor's extradition to Sierra Leone to face trial there.

Over her first two years in office, Sirleaf could point to some tangible successes. Foreign debt was forgiven by two of Liberia's biggest creditors, the United States and China, and Indian steelmaker Mittal announced a billion-dollar investment in new mining operations that were set to create 3,500 jobs. Partial water and electric service was restored to Monrovia, and Sirleaf implemented financial controls, in line with the suggestions of international monetary authorities, that increased government revenues. With growth running at 8 percent a year in 2007, Liberia had set out on the long road to recovery. Another significant change, however, was that Liberians now respected their government as a positive force. Samuel Kofi Woods II, the president's minister of labor, told Charlayne Hunter-Gault in an article in Essence magazine that Sirleaf's most important contribution had been the way she had changed the nature of political leadership. "I think now the government has political will," he said, and it was Sirleaf who had brought that will to bear. In 2006 Time magazine named her to its TIME 100 list of important leaders and revolutionaries, which featured an essay by U.S. First Lady Laura Bush stating that Sirleaf's "courage and commitment to her country are an inspiration to me and women around the world."

Books

Newsmakers, Issue 3, Thomson Gale, 2007.

Periodicals

African Business, March 2007.
Economist (US), December 16, 2006.
Essence, October 2006.

New York Times, November 12, 2005.
Time, May 8, 2006.

Online

''Ellen Johnson Sirleaf's tribal roots and Americo Liberian back-ground,'' Liberia Past and Present, http://www.liberiapastand present.org/JohnsonSirleaf/TribalRoots.htm (January 20, 2008).
''President Ellen Johnson-Sirleaf: President of Liberia,'' Join Africa, http://www.joinafrica.com/africa_of_the_week/ellen johnsonliberia.htm (January 20, 2008).
''Profile: Liberia's 'Iron Lady,' '' BBC News, http://news.bbc.co .uk/1/hi/world/africa/4395978.stm] (January 20, 2008).
''Profile of Her Excellency Ellen Johnson Sirleaf,'' Embassy of Liberia, http://www.embassyofliberia.org/biography.htm (January 20, 2008). □

Amalie Skram

Norwegian author Amalie Skram (1846-1905) was one of the key Scandinavian writers in the Naturalist school, which flourished in late nineteenth-century Europe. This literary movement emphasized the mundane ordinariness of everyday life, and was marked by a deeply pessimistic streak that was sometimes infused with passages of a sexually frank nature. Some of Skram's best-known works draw on the time she spent in psychiatric hospitals to cure her of depression.

B orn Berthe Amalie Alver on August 22, 1846, Skram spent her childhood in Bergen, Norway's second largest city. Unlike the capital of Oslo, called Kristiania during Skram's lifetime, Bergen was less centrally located on the Scandinavian peninsula, instead situated on the country's fjord-dotted, mountainous west coast. North Sea fishing was a mainstay of the local economy, but Skram's father, Mons Monsen Alver, together with her mother, Ingeborg Lovise Sivertsen, had a moderately successful farm supply business. She was able to attend a private academy for girls in Bergen, but when she was 17 years old, her parents' business failed. To avoid a stint in a debtors' prison, Mons Alver fled to the United States, leaving his wife to care for Skram and her four brothers.

Pressured into Marriage

The family's financial situation was precarious, and Skram's mother encouraged her to marry an older man, Bernt Ulrik August Mueller, who was a ship's captain. Skram agreed to the match. A 2003 article by Unni Langas in *Scandinavian Studies* quoted Skram's recollections of that time: ''I suffered a misfortune and the misfortune was that I was married before I was properly grown up. Literally. The fault was not only this, that suddenly poverty overtook my home which had previously been such a happy one, but to a greater extent my childish lack of understanding, and my longing to experience something terrible.''

Skram's decision was not an altogether unwise one, for she traveled widely with Mueller because of his line of work. In 1864, about a year after their marriage, they sailed to the West Indies and then on to Mexico, returning the following year. Skram soon became a mother, and by 1869 she and Mueller had two young sons, Jacob and Ludvig August. The couple then embarked on a trip around the world by ship with the boys. Skram's travels afforded her some rich experiences of life outside of Bergen and Scandinavia, which would not have otherwise been available to a woman of her class and era.

Moved to Oslo

Skram's husband was unfaithful, however, and the adjustment of returning to Norway and her role as a homebound wife and mother was also difficult for her. The marriage soured, and she and Mueller separated in 1878; their divorce was finalized two years later. This period of crisis precipitated a nervous breakdown for Skram, and she spent some time in a psychiatric hospital. Afterward, she decided to move to Kristiania with the boys, and became involved in the city's flourishing arts community. She came to know several leading Norwegian writers, among them Arne Garborg (1851-1924) and Bjørnstjerne Bjørnson (1832-1910), and was influenced by the burgeoning Naturalist literary movement that had began to imprint itself on Scandinavian literature. Its leading literary name was France's Émile Zola (1840-1902), and its works were a reaction to the Romantic movement that had dominated the first half of the nineteenth century. Adherents of Naturalism believed that human destiny was shaped by forces already determined by the laws of nature, a bleak view that seemed to resonate with Skram.

Skram's first novel was published in 1882 under the name Amalie Mueller. Little English-language information about this work, called *Høiers Leiefolk,* survives. Two years later, she wed a well-known Danish literary critic, Erik Skram, and in 1885 they moved to Copenhagen, Denmark's capital. A few sources cite Skram's novel that appeared that same year, *Constance Ring,* as her first published work. It incited somewhat of a scandal for Skram back in Norway for its frank depiction of a woman and her sexual liaisons, which were assumed to be autobiographical.

Skram had better success with her four-volume epic novel *Hellemyrsfolket* (People of Hellemyr), published between 1887 and 1898. This saga of a peasant family began with *Sjur Gabriel* (1887), about a fisherman on Norway's rough west coast. Literary critic Laura Marholm Hanson wrote of this first installment in an essay titled ''The Woman Naturalist: Amalie Skram'' that was reprinted in *Twentieth-Century Literary Criticism,* asserting that ''there is not a single false note in the book, and not one awkward description or superfluous word. . . . She describes human beings as they are to be found alone with nature, [and] tells of their never-ending, unfruitful toil, whether field labour or childbearing, the stimulating effect of brandy, the enervating influence of their fear of a harsh God—the God of a severe climate—the shy, unspoken love of the father, and the overworked woman who grows to resemble an animal more and more.''

Depicted Life Aboard Vessel

The next *Hellemyrsfolket* title was *To Venner* (Two Friends), which also appeared in 1887. The story centers on Sjur Gabriel's grandson, who leaves Hellemyr for the open seas as a ship's cabin boy. Hanson gave this novel high praise as well, noting that Skram's portrayal of life aboard a trade vessel that plies the Atlantic Ocean route between Jamaica and Norway was particularly realistic: ''The description of how the entire crew, including the captain, land at Kingston one hot summer night to sacrifice to the Black Venus, and the description of the storm and the shipwreck . . . on the Atlantic Ocean, the gradual destruction of the ship, the state of mind of the crew, and the captain's suddenly awakened piety;—it is all so perfectly life-like, so characteristically true of the sailor class, and so full of local Norwegian colouring, that we ask ourselves how a woman ever came to write it.''

There were two other books in the *Hellemyrsfolket* saga, *S.G. Myre* and *Afkom,* but Skram wrote several other works in the interim. These included *Lucie* in 1888 and *Forrådt* (Betrayal), published in 1891. Among all of Skram's novels, the latter book is the most reflective of the Naturalist literary style. Its protagonist is a young woman named Ory, who marries an older man, a sea captain, and the plot hinges on their disastrous honeymoon. Ory feels repulsion at the idea of her husband touching her, and freezes when others make comments or jokes to her about being a bride on her honeymoon. Criticized as stubborn and immature, she begins to withdraw altogether and seek solace in religion. Writing in the *Times Literary Supplement,* Anna Vaux asserted that ''Ory wields her purity with a biblical wrath which turns her from angel to monster with frightening alacrity.'' A stunning act of violence and madness concludes the story, which Vaux called ''startling and direct in its portrayal of alienation and exclusion.''

Suffered Second Bout of Depression

Another bad marriage was the subject of Skram's next novel, *Fru Inés* (Frau Ines), published in 1891. Similarly, a young woman's financial hardship after a divorce was the theme of Skram's only play, *Agnete.* Her own second marriage had seemed to be a happier match than her first, but she endured another bout of depression after the birth of her daughter Johanne, and in 1894 entered the Copenhagen City Hospital. She was later transferred to a psychiatric hospital near Roskilde, Denmark. The experience became the basis for two novels, both set in a psychiatric hospital and both published in 1895: *Professor Hieronimus* and *På St. Jørgen.* The heroine of both is Else Kant, a painter who is struggling to complete a particularly problematic painting, but the pressures of being a wife and mother prevent her from devoting the necessary time to it. Anxiety breeds insomnia, which triggers depression, and finally she agrees to a ''rest cure'' in a hospital.

At the hospital, Else comes under the care of a well-known psychiatrist, the Professor Hieronimus of the first title, but soon finds herself trapped in a nightmarish cycle—everything she says is perceived as the wrong response, the doctor tells her. According to Langas's article, ''Everything she says and does is interpreted as a sign of her insanity.'' When Else challenges Hieronimus, he deems her irrational, and their exchanges begin to take on the quality of farce, as he seems to deliberately infuriate her. Finally she is transferred to another care facility for the seriously mentally ill.

''Hieronimus Hystericus''

At one point, Else sees the staff handling the body of a woman who spent much of her life in the institution and has recently died. Contemplating her own fate, she returns to her room and begins writing a series of letters to Hieronimus. In the first one, she tells him that she wishes to describe her state of mind without him flying into a rage, and as Langas noted, ''This strategy turns out to be Else's main rhetorical weapon: to adopt the tactics of the enemy as her own. At the same time she writes herself out of the chains of hysteria, she writes him into them. Using this method, the professor is dethroned as a doctor and reinstated as a patient: Hieronimus Hystericus.''

In Else's final letter to the esteemed doctor, she signs herself ''your sincere enemy,'' just as Skram herself had done when she was finally discharged from her Danish psychiatric episode. The real letter had remained on file for a number of years at the hospital, according to Langas, and the episode may have led to the resignation of Dr. Knud Pontoppidan, director of psychiatric care at the Copenhagen Hospital, ostensibly to take a job elsewhere. Pontoppidan was quite well known in his day, but Skram's allegations of mistreatment were not the first to be made against him.

Tale Frightened the Public

Once again, Skram's novels of psychiatric abuse ignited a minor scandal in Norway, and less so in Denmark, which was a more progressive country, but in both places there were calls for legal reform and improved treatment for the mentally ill. *Professor Hieronimus* appeared in English translation in 1899, and a reviewer for *Bookman* called it ''courageous, vital and startlingly vivid.'' The critic noted that while Skram's novel depicts scenes and events that may seem horrific to the average person, ''to read the story is inevitably to feel that such a condition of things does exist somewhere, since it is described with a graphic simplicity that it would be impossible to surpass.''

Skram's second marriage ended in 1899, but she remained in Copenhagen, where she died on March 15, 1905, at the age of 58. Her works were rediscovered by feminists and literary critics only much later in the twentieth century, and a few previously unpublished works appeared in the original Norwegian in the mid-1970s. *Constance Ring* was translated into English in 1988 by Judith Messick and Katherine Hanson, and a second English translation of *Professor Hieronimus* appeared as 1992 with a new title, *Under Observation.*

Books

Twentieth-Century Literary Criticism, edited by Dennis Poupard,
    Volume 25, Gale, 1988.

Periodicals

Bookman, August 1899.
Publishers Weekly, October 12, 1992.
Scandinavian Studies, Spring 2003.
Times Literary Supplement, February 20, 1987. □

Joshua Slocum

**In 1898, Canadian-American mariner Joshua Slocum
(1844-1909) completed a three-year, 46,000-mile
journey around the globe during which time he endured storms, pirates and clashes with some of the
native islanders he encountered along the way. It
was the first recorded, solo circumnavigation of the
earth—an amazing feat at the time, considering
Slocum sailed on a crude, self-built ship with nothing
but a tin clock to track time and a compass, a sextant
and some old charts to guide his way.**

Enchanted by the Sea

The fifth of 11 children, Joshua Slocum was born
February 20, 1844, in Nova Scotia, Canada. His
father, John Slocombe, was a farmer and his mother,
Sarah Slocombe, was a lighthouse keeper's daughter. When
Slocum was eight, the family moved to Westport, Brier
Island, which is located off the tip of Nova Scotia at the
mouth of the Bay of Fundy. There, his father opened a
dockside cobbler's shop, specializing in fisherman's boots.
At 10, Slocum was taken out of school and made to peg
boots for up to 10 hours a day in his father's shop.

During his scarce free moments, Slocum hung out with
local sailors making short trips along the coast. His relationship with his father was stormy and when Slocum was 14,
he tried to escape, finding work as a ship's cook. Fired
almost immediately, Slocum returned home and received a
thrashing. When Slocum was 16, his mother died, and he
left home for good, securing work on the open seas aboard a
ship bound for Dublin, Ireland.

Writing in his memoir, *Sailing Alone Around the
World,* Slocum explained his enchantment with the ocean.
"As for myself, the wonderful sea charmed me from the first.
At the age of eight I had already been afloat along with other
boys on the bay, with chances greatly in favor of being
drowned. When a lad I filled the important post of cook on
a fishing-schooner; but I was not long in the galley, for the
crew mutinied at the appearance of my first duff, and
'chucked me out' before I had a chance to shine as a
culinary artist. The next step . . . found me before the mast in
a full-rigged ship bound on a foreign voyage."

Slocum worked hard and taught himself celestial navigation. He learned to use a sextant—a nautical device that
sailors of his time used to locate a ship's position at sea by
measuring the angles between the stars and the horizon. By
18, Slocum was a second mate and by 1869 he had moved
up the ranks, becoming Captain Slocum. Around this time
he also became a U.S. citizen and changed his name from
Slocombe to Slocum.

Sailed Cargo Around the Globe

In 1870, Slocum delivered a load to Sydney, Australia,
and met Virginia Albertina Walker, a native of New York.
They married on January 31, 1871. As a sea captain's wife,
Virginia Slocum preferred to sail with her husband rather
than stay in port. She learned to use a sextant and could pick
off menacing sharks with a rifle. Their children were born at
sea and Virginia Slocum taught them to read and write as
they voyaged around the world. She made Slocum bolt an
upright piano to the ship's deck so she could teach them
music. It was a rough life, though—three of their seven
infants died at sea, with three boys and one girl surviving.

By the early 1880s, Slocum was skipper—and part
owner—of the 220-foot, tall-masted American windjammer
Northern Light. Used to transport goods during the late 19th
century, a windjammer was the most majestic cargo ship of
its day, with several masts and square sails. While Slocum
was an expert navigator and astute trader, he had a reputation as a brutal leader who pushed his crew mercilessly.
Slocum once gunned down two mutinous seamen. Another

time, he placed an officer in the irons for 53 days. The man pressed charges and a New York court fined Slocum after convicting him on charges of false and cruel imprisonment.

Around 1884, Slocum sold the *Northern Light* and purchased the 138-foot-long *Aquidneck*. On July 25, 1884, while delivering a load of flour to South America, Virginia Slocum died while the *Aquidneck* was moored off the coast of Buenos Aires. She was 34. Slocum rowed her body ashore and buried her in a local cemetery. Slocum's children said he was never the same.

In February 1886, Slocum married a seamstress from Boston named Henrietta Miller Elliot. In December 1887, the *Aquidneck* struck a sandbar off the Brazilian coast. Uninsured, it was a total loss. The family spent the next several months living in a primitive shelter as Slocum and his children built a new vessel so they could sail home. He used native timber and items scrounged from the *Aquidneck*. Slocum fashioned boat clamps from guava trees and melted down the ship's metal to make nails. The 5,500-mile journey home took 55 days, during which they battled storms, sandbars and whales in their primitive craft. They arrived in the United States in October 1888. Slocum returned home nearly broke, having lost his savings with the boat. Over the next few years, he worked odd jobs and unloaded cargo at the waterfront.

Built *The Spray*

In 1892, Slocum ran into an old friend and whaling captain who offered him a ship. When Slocum arrived in Fairhaven, Massachusetts, to pick up the ship—dubbed *The Spray*—he found it sitting in a pasture. The rotting, century-old oyster sloop was in need of a complete overhaul, but it was just the kind of challenge on which Slocum thrived. He built a steam box and pot boiler to steam and bend oak trees from the surrounding woods into a perfectly curved hull. He used yellow pine for planking and rebuilt the ship. Thirteen months later, the 36-foot-long, 14-foot-wide vessel was finished. He used *The Spray* as a charter for small cruises and as a fishing boat, but the vast sea beckoned.

At some point, Slocum resolved to set sail on a grand adventure around the globe. He was happiest at sea and in desperate need of money. Slocum figured he could make money by writing articles about his adventure for newspaper syndication. He stocked his ship's library with Darwin, Mark Twain and Shakespeare and his ship's cupboard with sailor's bread, flour, codfish, potatoes, butter, tea, coffee, pepper, mustard and curry. He also packed a rifle and revolver and was ready to set sail.

Sailed Alone Around the World

Slocum sailed for the open seas on July 2, 1895, setting off from Nova Scotia. In *Sailing Alone Around the World*, Slocum described his first moments at sea: "A thrilling pulse beat high in me. My step was light on deck in the crisp air. I felt that there could be no turning back, and that I was engaging in an adventure the meaning of which I thoroughly understood."

He planned to circle the earth by heading east, passing through the Strait of Gibraltar and into the Mediterranean

Sea. The strait cuts between Spain and Morocco. He arrived in Gibraltar in early August and a British officer warned Slocum that he should change his route to avoid the Mediterranean Sea because it was teeming with pirates. Slocum heeded their advice, reversed course, sailed back across the Atlantic Ocean and toward Cape Horn. He was chased by pirates along the way.

Slocum arrived in Rio de Janeiro, Brazil, on November 5, 1895, and was in Buenos Aires, Argentina, by January 1896. As he neared Cape Horn, the southernmost tip of South America, locals warned Slocum that sailing around the cape would be dangerous because the indigenous Fuegian people who inhabited the area liked to plunder passing ships. On that advice, Slocum decided to avoid the cape and instead pass through the Strait of Magellan, just south of Chile, which would allow passage from the Atlantic to the Pacific. The Strait of Magellan, however, is a difficult 400-mile passage due to erratic currents and williwaws—violent bursts of cold wind that head down from the mountains and are capable of knocking ships over. Slocum made several attempts to sail through the passage and had to do it twice. After his first successful pass, the winds blew him back and he had to start again. It took 62 days.

Slocum encountered the Fuegian people several times but was able to outwit them. Once, several Fuegian canoes came alongside *The Spray*. Slocum hurried into the cabin and came out the other side dressed in different clothes, hoping the Fuegians would think there were several people on board. Ducking inside the cabin, he quickly built a "scarecrow" out of his clothes and attached a line he could tug on to make it move and appear human. As the Fuegians closed in on Slocum, he fired his rifle and, thinking there were at least three armed men on board, the Fuegians fled. Another trick Slocum used was to spread carpet tacks on his deck while he slept at night. At least once, he was awoken by shrieks from a barefooted native who had come aboard. Slocum fired his gun from the cabin and the man jumped overboard.

Slocum arrived at the Juan Fernandez Islands in the South Pacific in April 1896, then headed for Samoa, where he met Fanny Stevenson, widow of famed novelist Robert Louis Stevenson. Stevenson had spent the last several years of his life on the island. Slocum spent several days in Fanny Stevenson's company and when he left, she gave him four volumes of her husband's Mediterranean sailing directories. Slocum enjoyed this leg of the journey, stopping at various islands in the South Pacific. He took part in local celebrations and was often asked to dine with area officials. Next, Slocum went to Australia, where he stayed for 10 months, spending time on the island of Tasmania. Around this time, he began giving lectures about his voyage and charging people to come aboard his boat to earn money to finish the trip.

In December 1897, Slocum rounded the Cape of Good Hope. In May 1898, Slocum crossed the path he had sailed en route to Brazil in October 1895—he had circled the world, but still had a long trek to get back to his starting point. He entered Newport, Rhode Island, on June 27, 1898, dropping anchor at 1 a.m., thus completing his journey.

Disappeared at Sea

The 54-year-old captain, having completed the first solo circumnavigation of the globe, expected a hero's welcome, which he did not receive. Many people doubted his story, believing it impossible to sail around the world alone in such a crude ship. In an article published in the *Smithsonian* on the centennial anniversary of Slocum's voyage, Carlton Pinheiro, a marine museum curator in Rhode Island, said he understood the skeptics.

"Slocum's feat was as remarkable in its time as putting a man on the moon," Pinheiro said. He went on to note that many modern-day sailors will not set out on the open seas without radar, a depth sounder, a GPS and other electronic gear. "It's not surprising that people a hundred years ago were skeptical." After Slocum's logs were examined and he produced papers stamped at 20-some various ports around the globe, people began to believe his story.

For the next few years, Slocum roamed the seaboard giving lectures about the journey and working on his book, *Sailing Alone Around the World,* which was published in 1900. The delicate language and thoughtful passages in this memoir earned him a reputation as a "sea-locked Thoreau."

By 1909, Slocum was itching for another adventure and had a notion to sail the Amazon River. He set sail on November 14, 1909, and was never heard from again. Theories abound as to what became of him. Some believe Slocum had become less attentive to *The Spray* and she was not seaworthy, perhaps busting up in a storm. Others think the vessel, with her faint kerosene running lamp, was plowed down by a steamer in the night. Still others think Slocum headed to some tropical island to live out his days. In 1924, he was declared dead as of the day he set out on his voyage.

Books

Lasky, Kathryn, *Born in the Breezes,* Orchard Books, 2001.

Slocum, Joshua, *Sailing Alone Around the World,* Shambhala Publications, Inc., 1999.

Spencer, Ann, *Alone at Sea: The Adventures of Joshua Slocum,* Firefly Books, 1999.

Teller, Walter, *Joshua Slocum,* Rutgers University Press, 1971.

Periodicals

Cruising World, April 1995.

Maclean's, July 6, 1992.

New York Times, September 22, 1897; July 29, 1956.

Toronto Star, December 13, 1991.

Smithsonian, May 1998. □

Trinh Cong Son

In the words of *Time International* writer Barry Hillenbrand, the Vietnamese singer and songwriter Trinh Cong Son (1939-2001) "provided the audio track" for the Vietnam War.

"Hauntingly sentimental and filled with the sadness of separation and death," Son's songs "always seemed to be drifting from some battered tape player in a cafe or at an army checkpoint on the road to nowhere," wrote Hillenbrand. Son and his music offer an example of the mistrust that may exist between musicians and the governments under which they live and work. He was feared and threatened by both sides during Vietnam's civil war because of his message of peace and reconciliation, and after the war he spent four years as a political prisoner. His music endured, however, and today it remains well known within and even beyond the sphere of speakers of the Vietnamese language.

Parents Were Poets

Trinh Cong Son was born on February 28, 1939, in Dac Lac province, in Vietnam's central highlands, but he grew up in Vietnam's former capital of Hue. He was the oldest of seven children. Both his parents wrote poetry. Son's father made ends meet by working as a bicycle and motorcycle dealer, but he was heavily involved in Vietnamese resistance against French colonial rule and was a member of revolutionary leader Ho Chi Minh's Viet Minh guerrilla army. He was imprisoned for four years during Son's childhood, and after his release the family moved to what was then the city of Saigon.

Son went to school to become a teacher, and he apparently worked in that profession in Hue for several years in the mid-1950s. But he was also driven toward songwriting, and in 1957 he scored his first hit, "Uot Mi" (Wet Eyelashes). After that he gave up teaching to concentrate on songwriting full-time. The song, which told of a young woman mourning the death of her mother, had a melancholy tone that would become characteristic of Son's music in general. Son scored repeated successes in Vietnam over the next several years, with his songs often becoming hits in versions by female vocalist Khanh Ly. "Much of his appeal," wrote his sister Trinh Vinh Trinh in a profile on the Trinh Cong Son Official Web site, "comes from his ability to capture the heartbeat of Vietnam."

With the withdrawal of French colonial forces in 1954, Vietnam had been partitioned into two countries: the Communist Democratic Republic of Vietnam (known as North Vietnam) and the Western-oriented Republic of Vietnam (known as South Vietnam). An insurgency by South Vietnamese guerrillas supporting reunification of the country under Communist rule began in the late 1950s and escalated in the early 1960s, with the United States providing logistical and then on-the-ground support to the South Vietnamese government. Son, who never married or had children, was conscripted into the South Vietnamese army in 1965 but became a draft evader, hiding out in the houses of friends in several cities and on university campuses. Occasionally he came out of hiding for campus performances, eluding arrest with the help of sympathetic students despite constant surveillance and harassment from government secret police.

He continued to write songs, with the sad themes of his lyrics now amplified by the carnage and destruction he witnessed all around him, and his songwriting took on a strong antiwar orientation. Recordings of Son's music were made and smuggled out of his hiding places. His string of hits continued, and his songs also circulated in underground bootleg copies in North Vietnam. One of his biggest hits, a song still known to most Vietnamese, was "Lullaby (Ngu Di Con)," which depicted a mother mourning a son killed in the war. "Rock gently my child, I have done it twice," ran the lyrics, as quoted by Seth Mydans in the *New York Times.* "This body, which used to be so small, that I carried in my womb, that I held in my arms. Why do you rest at the age of 20 years?" A recording of the song notched sales of two million copies in Japan in 1969 and is even said to have earned the fugitive songwriter a gold record award.

Recordings Banned in South Vietnam

The South Vietnamese government banned Son's music, fearing that "Lullaby" and other antiwar pieces would depress support for the war effort. The move did little to dampen Son's popularity, however, as his songs continued to circulate widely in unofficial releases. Khanh Ly continued to record his songs, and copies of her recordings were known in many countries beyond Vietnam. American folk singer Joan Baez even referred to Son as the Bob Dylan of Vietnam, drawing a comparison with the leading U.S. folk singer-songwriter of the time.

After the war ended with South Vietnam's collapse in 1975, Son took an opportunity to perform on Vietnamese radio, singing a song that promoted the idea of reconciliation between North and South. The decision backfired as Son encountered condemnation, both from anti-Communist holdouts who regarded him as a traitor and from the victorious Communist government, which had no interest in promoting reconciliation with its defeated enemy. Many South Vietnamese who had the resources to do so, including Khanh Ly and all of Son's siblings, fled to the United States or Canada, but Son decided to remain in Vietnam. He and his mother were the only members of his family remaining in the country. While on a visit to Hue to see some friends, he was detained and placed under arrest.

Son underwent four years of re-education in the Communist mold. He was sent to work for a peasant family in mountains near Vietnam's border with Laos, dodging unexploded land mines as he tilled rice and cassava fields. After his released in 1979, Son returned to Saigon, which had been renamed Ho Chi Minh City. After this ordeal, he wrote little music in the late 1970s and early 1980s. But he gradually regained his popularity, thanks partly to the popularity of a new female interpreter of his songs, Hong Nhung. Several printed collections of his songs were issued by publishing organs of the Vietnamese government, which would claim after his death, according to a Vietnam News Agency obituary appearing on the Web site of the Danish-Vietnamese Association, that Son "was one of those composers that mingled naturally with the new life in the country after the liberation of southern Viet Nam in 1975." Government surveillance of Son was relaxed, although he told Agence France Presse that "they always seem to know what you are doing."

Took Up Painting

Son resumed his songwriting career in later life, although he told Hillenbrand, "Now that the pain and sadness of war are gone, young people do not really understand me." He composed some 600 songs in all. "I continue to write songs," he was quoted as saying by Mydans, "but they concern love, the human condition, nature. My songs have changed. They are more metaphysical now, because I am not young." Son also began painting in his later years and could often be seen nursing a bottle of scotch in a Ho Chi Minh City cafe. He gave up a five-pack-a-day cigarette habit as his health worsened, but continued to drink whiskey.

Son died in Ho Chi Minh City after a long struggle with diabetes on April 1, 2001. He was buried, not in Ho Chi Minh City's Martyrs' Cemetery, where government-affiliated composers and singers would normally have been interred, but at the rural Go Dura cemetery in Binh Duong province. Government publications initially ignored his death, but it was reported in mass-circulation newspapers, and hundreds of thousands of mourners attended his funeral or followed a procession in which Son's body was carried in a Dodge van left in the country after the departure of U.S. troops. The ceremony was marked by spontaneous outpourings of music and emotion from Vietnamese who were not even born when Son had composed his most famous songs, and his funeral procession is said to have been the second-largest in Vietnamese history, after that of Ho Chi Minh. A memorial to Son was erected in Ho Chi Minh City's Binh Quoi Park, and his songs, especially those written before 1975, remain popular among Vietnamese speakers all over the world. Many have been translated into English, French, German, Japanese, and other languages.

Periodicals

New York Times, April 5, 2001.
Seattle Times, April 3, 2001.
Time International, April 16, 2001.

Online

"About Trinh Cong Son," http://www.myspace.com/trinhcong sonmusic (February 5, 2008).
"Komponisten Trinh Cong Son død," Danish-Vietnamese Association, http://www.davifo.dk/Bio_Trinh_cong_son.htm (February 5, 2008).
"Profile," Trinh Cong Son Official Website, http://www.trinh-cong-son.com/wpma_tcs.html (February 5, 2008).
"Vietnam Mourns Its 'Dylan,' " BBC News, http://news.bbc.co.uk/1/hi/entertainment/music/1260527.stm (February 5, 2008). □

Wladyslaw Starewicz

Russian animator Wladislaw Starewicz (1882-1965) was an early pioneer of stop-motion animation, the technique of using hundreds of individual frames or photographs to create the illusion of movement. His first works used dead insects whose limbs had been

reattached with glue so that they could be manipulated into different poses, but by the 1920s and 1930s Starewicz was creating elaborate animal puppets for his fairy-tale-based fables. "Though often bizarre and not infrequently unsettling, Starewicz's work is exhilarating in its energy, inventiveness, and sardonic humor," noted an *International Dictionary of Films and Filmmakers* essay.

Starewicz was born in Moscow on August 8, 1882, to Polish-Lithuanian parents whose ancestry included Russian and French relatives. Both parents, Aleksander and Antonina Legiecka Starewicz, were from landowning families in what later became Lithuania; at the time, the area was part of imperial Russia. He was raised by his grandmother in the city of Kaunas, and later attended a high school in Tartu, Estonia, where he was allegedly expelled for insubordination.

Made First Film

As a young man, he studied at the Academy of Fine Arts in St. Petersburg, worked as a bookkeeper in the Lithuanian capital of Vilnius, and was a cartoonist for newspapers. He married Anna Zimmerman in 1906, and their daughter Irina was born a year later. In 1913 another daughter arrived, whom they called Jeanne but who was sometimes credited as "Nina Star" in his films. By 1909 he was working at a museum of natural history in Kaunas, and shot his first film, *Nad Nyemen* (Beyond the River Nemunas), that same year. Two more films followed which featured insects taken from exhibitions at the museum: *Zycie Wazek* (The Life of the Dragonfly) and *Walka Zukow* (The Battle of the Stag Beetles).

The Battle of the Stag Beetles was notable for being Starewicz's first foray into stop-action animation. He was fascinated by the fighting that the beetles engaged in, but in order to film them he had to use light, which caused the nocturnal creatures to fall into sleep mode. Finally, he took a pair of dead beetles and sliced off their legs and mandibles, then reattached them using wax so that he could move their limbs freely into various poses. This film became the first animated work in Russian cinema history. Film historians believe he was probably inspired by *Les allumettes animées* (Animated Matches), a 1908 film from French animator Emile Cohl (1857-1938).

Moved to Moscow

Word of Starewicz's talents reached Moscow, and he was offered a job with the film company of Aleksandr Khanzhonkov (1877-1945), the first film studio in Russia. One story holds that the highly regarded Khanzhonkov had contacted Starewicz about a documentary project on Kaunas, but another version noted that Starewicz had won the Christmas masquerade in Vilnius for three years in a row, and word of the eccentric who collected insects and devised outlandish costumes piqued Khanzhonkov's interest enough to offer him a job. Starewicz resettled his family

in Moscow in 1911 and made about two dozen films at the Khanzhonkov studio. These included *The Beautiful Leukanida,* a 1912 beetle fairy tale based on the ancient Greek story of Helen of Troy, and *Mest' kinematografičeskogo operatora,* or "Revenge of the Kinematograph Cameraman," a tale of adultery and betrayal among insects. He also began working with live actors, including his daughter Irina, who starred in 1913's *The Night Before Christmas,* a 41-minute adaptation of the short story by Nikolai Gogol (1809-1852). Another film from that same year, *Terrible Vengeance,* took a gold medal at an international film festival in Milan, Italy, a year later.

During World War I, Starewicz worked for several different film companies as a director of live-action movies, making about 60 in all. With the onset of political turmoil in Russia that began with the October Revolution of 1917, Starewicz and others in the film community who were wary of the revolutionary Bolsheviks decamped from Moscow to Yalta, a Black Sea port in the Crimea. As the Bolshevik-supporting Red Army advanced, Starewicz and his family fled the country permanently. They settled first in Italy, then went on to Paris, where there was a growing community of new Russian émigrés. For a time, Starewicz was a partner in a film company with several other expatriates, but their venture produced just one film, *L'Epouvantail* (The Scarecrow), in 1921.

Frogland

Starewicz eventually moved to a suburb of Paris called Fontenay-sous-Bois, and devoted the remainder of his career to making puppet films. His now-teenaged daughter Irina became his closest collaborator on the two dozen or so films that followed. One of his most visually stunning was *Les Grenouilles qui demandent un roi* (The Frogs That Demand a King, or "Frogland" for its American release), from 1922. It was based on the Aesop fable about a community of frogs who, unable to govern themselves, ask the god Jupiter for a king. Jupiter sends a stork to rule over them, but this places them in danger, because storks eat frogs, and the amphibians must flee underwater. Starewicz probably shot the underwater scenes with the help of an aquarium. Brief clips from it later appeared in the 1996 film *Basquiat,* about New York City artist Jean-Michel Basquiat (1960-1988).

Starewicz's daughter Irina appeared in 1923's *La Voix du rossignol* (The Voice of the Nightingale), a hand-tinted film about a young girl who frees a nightingale. Later in the decade he made his first full-length animated feature, *Le Roman de Renard* (The Tale of the Fox). It was released several years later in Berlin in 1937, then in France in 1941. It was only the third animated feature film made with sound, preceded by *Peludópolis,* a 1931 film from Quirino Cristiani, and *The New Gulliver,* a 1935 Soviet project. Shot in Paris between 1929 and 1931, *The Tale of the Fox* proved an astonishing achievement for other reasons, too. The *International Dictionary of Films and Filmmakers* noted that "one three-minute sequence alone, during the final siege of the Fox's castle of Malpertuis by the forces of King Lion, required 273,000 different movements."

Films Featured Surreal Violence

Another noteworthy work from Starewicz's studio during this era was 1934's *Fétiche Mascotte* (Duffy the Mascot, also known "The Mascot," "Puppet Love," and "The Devil's Ball"). The story centers on a young girl who is ill in bed with scurvy, a vitamin C deficiency. Her grandmother sews a dog puppet, which comes to life because a tear dropped into it, and the dog then travels to the ends of the earth to find the sick little girl an orange. Like many of Starewicz's other works, *The Mascot* is notable for the violence in some scenes, such as the sequence when several "toys struggle to escape from a speeding car," wrote the *International Dictionary of Films and Filmmakers*. "A white-costumed clown jumps clear, only for the wheels of another car to sever his neck. The head rolls into the gutter; the body twitches a couple of times, then lies still."

Starewicz's output slowed down in his later years. A 1947 work titled *Zanzabelle in Paris* won the gold medal for best children's film at the Venice Film Festival. Starewicz died 18 years later on February 26, 1965, leaving his final work unfinished, *Comme chien et chat* (Like Dog and Cat). For decades his name was nearly forgotten in filmmaking annals until some of his works were shown at the 1980 Ottawa Animation Festival. Since then, a few of his older works have been restored, and some have been featured in documentary films on Starewicz. One such retrospective was *The Insect Affair*, which was shown on British television in 1994. Starewicz's "characters," noted David Flusfeder in the *Times* of London, "are not cosy little animals, they're passionate, stupid creatures acting like humans."

Books

International Dictionary of Films and Filmmakers, Volume 4: *Writers and Production Artists,* fourth edition, St. James Press, 2000.

Periodicals

Animation World, May 2000.
Russian Life, November-December 2003.
Times (London, England), December 31, 1994. □

Howard Stringer

In 2005, the Tokyo–based Sony Corporation tapped Welsh–born naturalized American Howard Stringer (born 1942) to lead the company, making him the first foreign chief executive hired to oversee the electronics giant. A native of Wales, Stringer moved to the United States to pursue a career in television, became a citizen and ended up president of the CBS Broadcast Group. After a stint with the Sony Corporation of America—focusing on the company's motion picture and music operations—Stringer was chosen to lead its overseas parent company. Before

Stringer, Sony had a history of hiring only Japanese executives for the top spot.

While the move surprised many corporate analysts, those who were familiar with Stringer believed he would be successful at integrating Asian and Western business models. Former co–workers describe Stringer as a highly gifted executive and praise him as an intelligent, approachable and modest manager who knows how to institute tough, bottom–line decisions while simultaneously listening to employees. "Howard has more charm than a stadium full of people," former CBS colleague and filmmaker Peter Davis told the *New Yorker*'s Mark Singer. "He's clearly very shrewd, but he never seems to be being shrewd."

Emigrated to United States

Stringer was born February 19, 1942, in Cardiff, Wales. His mother, Marjorie Mary (Pook) Stringer, was a teacher and his father, Harry Stringer, served as a squadron leader in Britain's Royal Air Force, seeing active duty during World War II. Because of his father's military career, Stringer moved a lot. The first four years of his life were spent in Wales, but by the time Stringer was 11, he had lived in seven houses in several cities. When he was nine, Stringer attended a small public school in eastern England and earned a reputation as the teacher's pet, irritating his classmates. In turn, they teased the skinny, pre–adolescent

Stringer. Looking for a way to escape, he applied for scholarships to several schools and was accepted by the Oundle School, an independent boarding school north of London.

Writing in the *Oundle Society Newsletter*, Stringer described the transformation that occurred in his life after he earned a scholarship to the elite school. "Oundle, of course, had its ups and downs, but the day I walked into my first dormitory, sat on the bed, munching" a cookie, "knowing that I didn't have to watch my back and that I was going to get the best education possible, was, along with my father's return from the war, the happiest day of my childhood."

After graduating from Oundle, the 6–foot–3–inch Stringer attended Oxford University's Merton College, where he was captain of the rugby team. During his Oxford years, Stringer befriended a number of U.S. students who were studying there as Rhodes Scholars and began fantasizing about life in the United States. Stringer graduated from Oxford in 1964 with a degree in modern history, then set sail for New York City in early 1965 with $200 in his pocket. He eventually landed a job as a log clerk for the popular CBS variety program *The Ed Sullivan Show*. Stringer's duties included gathering the mail and logging caller comments. When viewers phoned in after the Beatles appeared on the show, Stringer put his British accent to work and pretended to be George Harrison as he answered calls.

Fought in Vietnam War

Not long after landing in the United States, Stringer received draft papers. By the mid–1960s, the Vietnam War was in full swing and the United States was ramping up troop support in South Vietnam. At first, Stringer thought there had been a mistake. He told the London *Independent*'s David Usborne that he wrote then–U.S. Attorney General Bobby Kennedy a letter that said, "Look, I've been here for four months and you want me to die for you? Don't you think that's a little premature?" He soon learned that U.S. law permitted resident aliens to be drafted.

Stringer reviewed his options. He considered returning to the United Kingdom but figured he might never be allowed back in the United States if he dodged the draft, so he quit his job and reported for duty. From 1965 to 1967, Stringer served in the U.S. Army, spending just under a year in Vietnam. As Stringer was leaving the war zone, Viet Cong machine gunners hit his transport plane as it sped down the runway. The plane was able to make it to safety and Sgt. Stringer returned home with five medals, including a U.S. Army Commendation Medal for meritorious achievement. Whenever Stringer is asked about his war service, he downplays his awards. "You get some medals for simply showing up," he told the *Guardian*'s Jane Martinson. "And I was actually in charge of medals."

Moved Through Ranks at CBS

After returning from the war, Stringer found his way back to CBS, becoming a news–radio production assistant for WCBS radio in New York. In 1968, Stringer joined the CBS election coverage team as a researcher and swarmed through 26 states in the eight–month run–up to the election. Next, he became a researcher for *CBS Reports*. Launched in 1959, *CBS Reports* was devoted to in–depth documentary reporting on the controversial issues of the day.

By 1976, Stringer had become executive producer of *CBS Reports,* working alongside chief correspondents Dan Rather and Bill Moyers. Stringer wrote, directed and produced a number of highly received investigative reports, including a 1974 feature on the Rockefellers, which won an Emmy Award for Outstanding Documentary Program Achievement. Another segment, titled "The Fire Next Door," provided the impetus for new housing regulations in New York City and captured a 1978 Emmy. In sum, Stringer won nine individual Emmy awards. He was also instrumental in creating several successful news programs, including "48 hours" and "CBS This Morning."

In 1986, Stringer was named president of CBS News and in 1988 became president of the CBS Broadcast Group, which had just experienced its worst prime–time ratings ever and sat behind ABC and NBC in market share. Undaunted, Stringer set about the task of beefing up the network's offerings, courting Hollywood writers and producers for their ideas. In 1993, Stringer snagged David Letterman from NBC, giving CBS a late–night television ratings boost. These, however, were tenuous times at CBS as the network's tight–fisted owner, Laurence Tisch, tightened spending, cutting $30 million from the news budget and touching off a series of layoffs. Despite the cuts, Stringer moved CBS to the front of the network pack.

Stringer quit CBS in 1995 to become chairman and chief executive officer of Tele–TV, a telecommunications start–up that aimed to deliver interactive television and Internet service over the telephone lines. News anchor Dan Rather was quick to mention the void left behind by Stringer's departure from the network after so many years of service. According to the *Washington Post*'s Tom Shales, Rather told colleagues, "We're losing a piece of our heart. Howard Stringer for 30 years has provided an important part of the fiber of CBS and CBS News in particular, as much with his attitude as with his immense creative abilities. Certain organs in an institution's structure can't be removed and randomly replaced. The heart of Howard Stringer is one of them." The job at Tele–TV, however, was short–lived, as the venture folded around 1997.

Joined Sony

In 1998, Stringer became chairman and CEO of the Sony Corporation of America, placing him in charge of Sony's film and music businesses. This arm of the Sony empire was not performing well, having recently written off $3.2 billion to cover losses at Columbia Pictures. In an effort to restore Sony America to profitability, in 2003 Stringer pieced together a 50–50 joint venture with the Bertelsmann Music Group (BMG) to create Sony BMG Music Entertainment, Inc., one of the largest music recording and publishing entities in the world.

He also orchestrated a merger with Metro–Goldwyn–Mayer—MGM. The 2004 deal was a coup for Sony, which outbid other entertainment companies vying to overtake the profitable film studio and gain access to its 4,000–film library that included the well–liked James Bond, Pink Panther and Rocky titles. Besides the business transactions, Stringer laid off 9,000 people. Soon, Sony America was performing well and in 2004, its film studio churned out the No. 2 movie, *Spider–Man II,* which anchored ticket sales and shored up earnings.

On the tails of his success at Sony America, Stringer was hired to become president of the Sony Corporation of Japan. "I thought about taking this job for well over a week because I knew that the reason I got the job was because it was in financial difficulties," Stringer told CBS News in a 2006 interview on "60 Minutes". "And so I knew that I would have to use every personal skill I had to persuade and cajole and convince that for the greater good of the company, we might have to do some tough things."

When Stringer took over Sony in 2005, he was given the gargantuan task of reorganizing and reenergizing the company, which had seen its stock price tumble 75 percent in the preceding five years. While the company's film, music and gaming divisions were performing adequately, its electronics division had lost its dominance in the global market. For a number of years, Sony had been a leader in cutting–edge electronics. In the 1960s, Sony rolled out the must–have Trinitron TV and in the 1970s, the company unveiled the revolutionary Sony Walkman, a pioneer in the portable music player industry. But through the late 1990s and early 2000s, Sony electronics experienced lackluster sales. Sony's PlayStation faced tough competition from Microsoft's Xbox and its televisions struggled to compete with Samsung. In addition, almost every time Sony unveiled a new device, electronics upstarts in South Korea and China rolled out cheap knockoffs.

One of the biggest blows for Sony was the Apple iPod. Sony was slow to launch a competitive digital portable media player because executives worried such devices might cut into profits at Sony BMG Music. The company had plenty of music to market online but worried about piracy. As Sony scrambled to develop a secure download system to prevent piracy, Apple formulated the iPod and online iTunes store, launched the product and scored market dominance.

Faced Challenges at Work, Home

Stringer's first major crisis came at the end of his first year when Sony was forced to recall millions of its laptop batteries, which were prone to overheating and therefore posed a fire risk. The recall was a major setback for Sony's credibility. He also faced challenges from within the company. After a thorough review of assets, in 2006 Stringer announced a restructuring plan to shutter 11 production facilities and eliminate 10,000 jobs—or 7 percent of Sony's global workforce. For Stringer, this was a controversial move and went against the grain of Japan's job–for–life culture. In addition, Stringer faced a language barrier. When he first took the job, he tried to learn Japanese, but realized he would never be fluent enough to communicate effectively. Corporate meetings had to be bilingual, with conversations flowing through multiple translations.

Besides the trials at Sony, Stringer faced challenges in his home life after taking the job. While his family resided in England, he would stop by to visit them as he jet–setted around the globe. During one two–month period in late 2005, Stringer logged 60,000 airline miles flying between Tokyo, England, Boston, Toronto, New York, Beijing, Shanghai, New Delhi, Bombay, Los Angeles and San Jose. Back in England, he remained a virtual unknown, although he received the title of Knight Bachelor from Her Majesty Queen Elizabeth II in 1999. That year, she "knighted" a number of people who had made a significant mark on the 20th century or who were projected to make a mark on the 21st century.

Stringer is one to continually foresee a future where Sony is able to merge content and electronics, creating interactive, on–demand personalized devices. He knows it will be a challenge getting there and knows he will have to tread carefully as he introduces change. But he remains optimistic. As Stringer told CBS News, "This is not a company on its last legs."

Periodicals

Guardian (London), May 5, 2001.
Independent (London), April 28, 1999.
New York Times, March 7, 2005.
Times (London), April 24, 2004; September 24, 2005.
Washington Post, February 24, 1995.

Online

"Senior Management: Sir Howard Stringer," Sony, http://www.sony.com/utilities/printable.php?page=/SCA/bios/stringer.shtml (December 14, 2007).
"Sir Howard Stringer (Ldr 60) Remembers His Arrival at Oundle," *The Oundle Society Summer Newsletter,* http://www.oundlesociety.org/Media/Download/1271/OundleSummer%2005.pdf (December 14, 2007).
"Sir Howard Stringer: Sony's Savior?" CBS News, http://www.cbsnews.com/stories/2006/01/06/60minutes/printable1183023.shtml (December 14, 2007).
"Stringer's Way," *New Yorker,* http://www.newyorker.com/archive/2006/06/05/060605fa_fact1 (December 15, 2007). □

Maria Szymanowska

Polish pianist and composer Maria Szymanowska (1789-1831) was a pioneering figure of significant importance in the history of classical composition and piano performance.

Szymanowska has been called the first musician to take Europe by storm. She toured internationally, meeting and befriending many of the leading intellectual figures of her day, and her piano playing was admired by aristocratic patrons and musical observers alike, including the great German poet Johann Wolfgang von Goethe. Szymanowska may have been the first pianist to play from memory. She wrote more than 100 compositions, and her contributions among a group of early pianist-composers whose music established the piano as an instrument suitable for virtuoso solo displays have been generally underestimated. Both as a pianist and composer, Szymanowska influenced one of the greatest musical figures of the nineteenth century, the Polish-French composer Fryderyk Chopin.

Home Education

Szymanowska was born Maria Agata Wolowska on December 14, 1789, in Warsaw, Poland. She never attended music school; what music schools there were in Warsaw at the time would not have been open to women in any case. Instead she was educated at home by a succession of little-known piano teachers. Her talent was recognized, and she is thought to have been accepted as a student by Jozef Elzner, who was also one of Chopin's early teachers. She gave her first public concert in Warsaw in 1810 at the age of 21, and quickly moved on to give a second concert in Paris, France, one of the music capitals of Europe at the time.

The public concert was not as highly developed as an institution in Szymanowska's time as it would be a few years later. Instead, Szymanowska's parents groomed her as a pianist by inviting well-known guests to their Warsaw home and presenting their daughter as the evening's musical entertainment. These guests included both aristocrats like Prince Antoni Radziwill, and musical guests included Napoleon Bonaparte's kapellmeister (or music director) Ferdinando Paer and violinist Jacques-Pierre-Joseph Rode. All these artists would be of importance in Szymanowska's future career, providing her with a network of contacts she could exploit in her European travels.

In 1810 Szymanowska married Polish aristocrat Jozef Szymanowski, putting her performing career mostly on hold as they raised three children. It is not known what caused the couple's divorce in 1820, something that would have been rare in Catholic Poland, but it is likely that her musical ambitions played a role. She remained close to her children, who stayed in her custody after the divorce, but her surviving correspondence makes no reference to the frequent periods of separation from them that she would have experienced once she resumed her touring life.

Szymanowska used her time off the road profitably: she turned to composition, which could be done at home. Her works were published in Warsaw, Paris, and other European capitals over the next decades. Especially interesting were a set of 20 "Exercises et Préludes" (Exercises and Preludes), published in Leipzig, Germany, by the world-class Breitkopf & Härtel firm in 1819. Like Chopin, Szymanowska wrote pieces that, although designated as exercises, held the attention of pianists and audiences in purely musical terms as well. She wrote some 100 pieces in all, many of them for the piano; others were songs, several of which accompanied the words of Poland's national poet, Adam Mickiewicz.

International Reputation

The influence of Szymanowska on Chopin as a composer is apparent not only in her tendency toward the use of exercise-type forms (known as Etudes in Chopin's case), but also in her attraction to Polish dance forms such as the polonaise and the mazurka. Szymanowska did not invent these forms, which had been used even in the eighteenth century by composers seeking to catch the essence of Polish folk music, but she doubtless provided Chopin with a strong model: the genre distribution of her pieces resembles that of Chopin more closely than that of Irish pianist-composer John Field, the figure generally cited as Chopin's direct predecessor. Szymanowska introduced the nocturne (night piece), which became one of Chopin's favorite genres.

Szymanowska resumed her performing career around 1815 and gradually gained an international reputation. Her public position as a pianist lay somewhere between the world of the aristocratic drawing room of the eighteenth century and the public concert of the nineteenth century exemplified by figures such as Franz Liszt; she might perform for small groups of connoisseurs or for a crowd of perhaps 1,000 people, but rarely to a larger auditorium. Szymanowska began to hit her stride around 1818, when she went to London and began to make the rounds of musical gatherings of the city's top connoisseurs of the arts. She followed up her English tour with appearances in Berlin, Germany, and then, in 1822, she made her first trip to Russia, where she met composers and performers who could easily have been her rivals—Field and Johann Nepomuk Hummel—but who became her friends and backers. Czar Alexander I gave Szymanowska the honorary title of First Pianist of the Royal Princesses Elizabeth and Maria.

In 1823 Szymanowska toured what is now Ukraine, as part of a violin-and-piano duo with Polish violinist Karol Lipinski. She made a three-year tour of Western Europe between 1823 and 1826, reaching the apex of her fame as she performed in Austria, Germany, France, England, Italy, and the Netherlands. She met Goethe at the Austrian resort of Marienbad during this period, and the top composers of the time, including Muzio Clementi, Anton Reicha, Beethoven's student Ferdinand Ries, and the dean of Italian opera composers, Gioacchino Rossini, were unanimous in praising Szymanowska's playing. In the mid-1820s, just before the emergence of Chopin, Liszt, and the other pianists who defined Romantic piano music, she had an unusually high critical reputation and would likely have been well known to these younger figures.

Part of Szymanowska's appeal was that she played from memory. She may have been the first pianist to do this; although that distinction is usually given to Liszt and to Clara Schumann, wife of composer Robert Schumann, Szymanowska is known to have played from memory earlier than either of those performers. At a recital in Poznan, Poland, in 1823, she performed her *Caprice sur la Romance de Joconde* without written-out music, something that was considered unusual enough at the time to attract considerable attention from local newspapers. Szymanowska played with equal facility on the "Walter" model pianos popular in Europe's eastern half and on pianos with the so-called English action that predominated in London and Paris. In the late 1820s she had an English-action piano shipped across Europe to her home in Warsaw.

Headed to Russia

Szymanowska returned home to Warsaw and gave two recitals in January and February of 1827. The young Chopin may have attended these concerts; his career was just gaining momentum in Warsaw, and Szymanowska became one of his biggest backers. When Chopin went to Paris in the late 1820s and was offered instruction of dubious value by the declining virtuoso Kalkbrenner, it was Szymanowska who warned him against Kalkbrenner's attentions. "He [Kalkbrenner] is a scoundrel," Szymanowska said forcefully, according to the Web site of the Chopin Society. "His real aim is to cramp his genius." Scholars believe that Chopin was familiar with Szymanowska's music, and that echoes of her music can be heard in his early works. The ending of Chopin's Etude in A major, Op. 25, No. 1, in particular, appears closely modeled on Szymanowska's Etude No. 18 in E major.

Later in 1827, Szymanowska moved to Russia permanently, settling in Moscow and then in St. Petersburg. She called a halt to her touring career, although she remained active as a performer in her own St. Petersburg apartment. Her home became a center of cultural activity for Poles such as Mickiewicz, who frequented her salons (intellectual and artistic meetings) and later married her daughter Celina. Szymanowska also performed in the homes of Russian aristocrats. A concert program survives from an 1827 musicale at the home of one Countess Dierzhavina, billing "Mrs. Szymanowska" as the featured attraction on a rondo by Hummel and on the grand finale, a potpourri of tunes, perhaps improvised, from the opera *Der Freischütz*.

Publications of Szymanowska's works continued unabated in the late 1820s. But her life was cut short by a cholera epidemic that struck St. Petersburg, and she died there on July 24, 1831. Mickiewicz called her the "Queen of Tones," and the Polish Music Center noted that she was "praised for the brilliance and expressive quality of her tone"; a contemporary observer said that "she made the piano speak and sing." Critical evaluation of Szymanowska's works is still in its infancy. Like the output of Clara Schumann and practically every other female musician with whom she shared the problem of balancing career and family, her music was almost completely neglected for decades after her death. It has only recently begun to be rediscovered.

Books

Baker's Biographical Dictionary of Musicians, centennial ed., Nicolas Slonimsky, ed. emeritus, Schirmer, 2001.

New Grove Dictionary of Music and Musicians, 2nd ed., edited by Sadie Stanley, Macmillan, 2001.

Periodicals

Musical Quarterly, October 1960.

Online

"Biographical Essay About Chopin," Chopin Society, http://www.chopinsociety.org/chopin/biography (February 4, 2008).

"Maria Szymanowska," Polish Music Center, http://www.usc.edu/dept/polish_music/composer/szymanowska.html (February 4, 2008).

"Maria Szymanowska & the Evolution of Professional Pianism," Chopin Foundation of the United States, http://www.chopinfound.brinkster.net/ip.asp?op=MariaSzymanowska (February 4, 2008). □

T

Helen Herron Taft

American First Lady Helen Herron Taft (1861-1943) supported her sometimes reluctant husband, William Howard Taft, from his early judicial posts in Ohio through his presidency and final years as a Supreme Court justice. Ambitious and energetic, Taft had a lifelong interest in politics and was the first presidential spouse to publish her memoirs. Her descendants have remained active in politics and remain one of Ohio's most prominent political families.

Early Life and Career

The fourth of eleven children, Helen Herron Taft was born Helen Herron on June 2, 1861, in Cincinnati, Ohio. Her family was a wealthy and prominent one. Her father, John Herron, was a member of the Ohio senate and a U.S. attorney with connections to two Ohio men who would become U.S. presidents; he had been a college roommate of Benjamin Harrison (twenty-third president, 1889-1893) and a law partner of fellow Cincinnatian Rutherford B. Hayes (nineteenth President, 1877-1881). Her mother, Harriet Collins, was the daughter of a Democratic congressman from New York. Writing in *First Ladies of the United States: A Biographical Dictionary,* Robert P. Watson noted that "Helen grew up accustomed to politics as an intimate part of daily life and developed a strong attraction to political affairs." Legend recounts that when the Herron family was invited to visit the Hayes White House when Taft was a teenager, she was so impressed by her surroundings that she made up her mind to marry a future President.

Taft—called "Nellie" from birth—felt somewhat isolated from her family, being separated from her next surviving older and next surviving younger sister by three years in each direction, and she was often plagued by insecurity and self-criticism during her teen years. Despite this, she excelled as a student, graduating from the Miss Nourse School for Girls in June of 1879 and attending courses at Miami University in Oxford, Ohio. Although few women of the era pursued careers, Taft aspired to have a career, hoping particularly to pursue her love of music. She considered herself unlikely to marry and held high standards for any possible future husband. During the early 1880s Herron made many male acquaintances, including a young court reporter and Yale graduate named William Howard Taft, but none of these acquaintanceships led to serious courtship. Instead, Taft asserted her youthful independence from her parents and society's expectations by smoking cigarettes, drinking beer at Cincinnati's German American beer halls, and in 1882, taking a position as a schoolteacher.

Became a Political Wife

The following year, her friendship with William Taft grew closer; he was, as Carl Sferrazza Anthony observed in *Nellie Taft: The Unconventional First Lady of the Ragtime Era,* "what might be characterized as a 'conservative feminist' . . . that is, one who genuinely believed that women were intellectually equal to men if given full access to education and should be equally salaried and employed, but that most women would probably end up pursuing a traditional role as wife and mother." Taft proposed to Helen and she rejected him at first, but accepted his subsequent

343

she had thrived and fearing that her husband would never regain the attention of major political players. Despite any misgivings, William Taft immensely enjoyed his appointment, and Helen Taft became socially and culturally prominent in Ohio's capital city, Columbus.

Moved to the Philippines

In 1898 the United States assumed control of the Philippine Islands as a result of the Spanish-American War. Two years later President William McKinley appointed William Taft governor of the Philippines, an office which William Taft took with some reservations, but which Helen Taft believed would bring excitement. She studied Filipino culture during her time there and assisted her husband with the challenges presented by his position. She also took advantage of the opportunity to visit Asia. Despite Taft's great success as governor, his growing health problems made it advisable for him to return to the United States. In 1904 the Taft family left Manila for Washington, D.C., when new President Theodore Roosevelt appointed Taft to his cabinet as Secretary of War (now Secretary of State).

Helen Taft found life in Washington difficult. She believed her husband's salary was too low and, as she said in her memoirs, *Recollections of Full Years,* she found "the life of a 'Cabinet lady' newly arrived in the Capital [to be] one of rather monotonous stress." During William Taft's time on Roosevelt's cabinet, his wife acted as his chief adviser and considered ways to raise her husband to higher office, urging Roosevelt to endorse him as a successor. Twice—once during his governorship and once during his years on Roosevelt's Cabinet—William Taft was offered a position on the Supreme Court. Although this job was the one for which he longed above all others, Taft, at the urging of his wife, refused the position both times. Helen Taft continued to press her husband, and in 1908 he became the Republican Party's Presidential nominee.

Became First Lady

Helen Taft was the driving force behind her husband's campaign; Watson wrote that "Taft golfed while Helen organized the campaign." She wrote his speeches and continued to encourage Roosevelt, a popular figure, to show his support for Taft's election. Her efforts on her husband's behalf bore fruit, and he won the 1908 election. Helen Taft rode with her husband on the inaugural parade route, a somewhat scandalous act that set a precedent for future presidential spouses. Unquestionably more enthusiastic about being in the White House than was her husband, Taft continued to serve as his chief adviser, sometimes challenging his decisions and support for certain issues such as prohibition. Her continual drive was temporarily slowed after a stroke partially paralyzed her shortly after Taft took office.

Taft regained her strength and returned to her political role. She supported education measures for women and sat on White House committees. Although previous First Ladies had held influence over their husbands' presidential decisions, none had done so as openly as did Taft; she became the first presidential spouse to give press interviews, speaking about her position as Taft's adviser in national publications.

proposal in 1885. The pair married on June 19, 1886, at the Herron residence in Cincinnati.

In 1887 William Taft was appointed to a vacancy on the Ohio Superior Court, and Helen Taft began teaching kindergarten at her alma mater, the Miss Nourse School for Girls. Two years later the couple's first child, Robert, was born. A daughter, Helen, would follow in 1891 and another son, Charles, in 1897. By 1890 William Taft had been elected to a full five-year term on the Superior Court, and seemed content with his life as judge, husband, and father. However, Helen Taft still held hopes that her husband would be more politically powerful and began encouraging him to move into more prominent national positions. In 1890 she urged him to accept recently elected President Benjamin Harrison's offer of a position as U.S. solicitor general, the federal advocate before the U.S. Supreme Court. That year the Taft family moved to Washington, D.C.

Helen Taft enjoyed life in the nation's capital. She often attended sessions of the House and Senate, observing the proceedings from the visitors' gallery. Politically astute and interested in meeting prominent Washingtonians, she became a frequent guest at social events. When President Harrison nominated William Taft to the federal circuit court in Ohio, Taft—being more interested in the law than in political gain—was pleased; Helen Taft, however, was less enthused. Despite his wife's objections, Taft accepted the position and resigned his Washington post in March of 1892. Helen Taft returned to Ohio with her husband, leaving behind the active political and social circles in which

During her time in the White House, Taft helped modernize the presidency by eliminating horse and buggies in favor of Pierce-Arrow automobiles, and created the annual Washington, D.C., cherry blossom week in the face of opponents who argued that the capital's climate was unsuited for the Japanese trees. She also supported the arts, attending many performances and helping establish a bandstand.

Although Taft relied on his wife's advice, others in Washington used her closeness to the President to attack his abilities. The First Lady could be difficult; she was notoriously hard on the White House staff and sometimes worked to block political appointments of those she did not like. She prevented Nicholas Longworth, a relative of Theodore Roosevelt's, from receiving a diplomatic appointment; this contributed to Roosevelt's decision to withdraw his support from William Taft. This split the loyalties of the Republican Party and led to Roosevelt's subsequent run for president on the Bull Moose ticket in 1912. With Republican support divided between the two candidates, Democratic nominee Woodrow Wilson easily won the electoral vote.

After the debacle of 1912, Taft decided to retire from politics. Helen Taft urged him to run for reelection to the presidency in a future election; however, Taft was appointed as Chancellor Kent Professor of Law and Legal History at Yale University in New Haven, Connecticut. Pleased to be returning to his chosen profession, the law, Taft embraced the position. Helen Taft soon became prominent in New Haven society and was an active supporter of the arts. In 1914 she became the first former First Lady to publish her own memoirs.

Returned to Washington

In 1921 newly inaugurated President Warren G. Harding appointed fellow Ohioan William Taft to the position of chief justice of the Supreme Court. Taft delightedly accepted, finally achieving the position he had always dreamed of attaining. Helen Taft returned to the capital with her husband, although in a somewhat different capacity; Anthony noted that ''she was more removed from [her husband's] work and activities than at any point since his first judicial appointment. . . . Will's new job, in fact, permanently ended the active partnership of the Tafts.'' Uninterested in the field of law, Helen Taft no longer held any sway over her husband's decision-making. However, Taft supported her husband wholeheartedly in his court seat and used her position in Washington to closely follow politics.

Helen Taft also became active in the Colonial Dames, a patriotic society, and was honorary vice president of the Girl Scouts of America. After the death of her husband in 1930, Taft remained resident in Washington, D.C. She died there in 1943 and was buried in Arlington National Cemetery, the first presidential spouse to receive this honor; she was later joined only by Jacqueline Kennedy Onassis.

Throughout her life, Taft worked to support and influence her husband in her political endeavors. Writing in her memoirs, Taft said, ''I confess only to a lively interest in my husband's work which I experienced from the beginning of our association and which nothing in our long life together, neither monotony, nor illness, nor misfortune, has served to lessen.'' She passed this lively interest on to her children; indeed, her most significant legacy may be that of her political family. The eldest Taft child, Robert, served in the U.S. Senate for three terms; his son, Robert Jr., was a Congressman and later senator from Ohio. The third Robert Taft—Helen Taft's great-grandson—served as Ohio's governor from 1999 to 2007. Charles Taft, William and Helen Taft's second son, became mayor of Cincinnati and was the Republican candidate for governor of Ohio in 1952. Helen Taft's place as a strong political figure can still be observed through the importance of the Tafts, and her influence and character have left a mark on history.

Books

American First Ladies, edited by Robert P. Watson, Salem, 2002.
Anthony, Carl Sferrazza, *Nellie Taft: The Unconventional First Lady of the Ragtime Era,* HarperCollins, 2005.
Taft, Helen Herron, *Recollections of Full Years,* Dodd, Mead & Co., 1914.
Watson, Robert P., *First Ladies of the United States: A Biographical Dictionary,* Lynne Rienner Publishers, 2001.

Online

Biography Resource Center Online, http://galenet.galegroup.com/servlet.BioRc (November 26, 2007). □

Marie Taglioni

The Italian-French ballerina Marie Taglioni (1804-1884) revolutionized ballet with her graceful, almost evanescent dancing, introducing the spirituality of Romantic poetry and literature to the world of dance.

Taglioni, under the tutelage and influence of her choreographer father, fundamentally changed the way ballet looked. Dancing en pointe—on the tips of her toes—she created the sensation that she was floating through the air, the perfect incarnation of the sylph or forest spirit she portrayed in her most famous ballet, *La Sylphide.* Her simple white garment, essentially the earliest instance of what became known as the tutu, influenced not only dance but also the world of fashion generally as young women strove to adopt a pale, insubstantial appearance. Taglioni was one of the first true celebrities of 19th-century Europe, inspiring merchandise bearing her image that today would be called product tie-ins. In the words of Carol Lee, writing in *Ballet in Western Culture,* ''Taglioni was one of the very few ballerinas ever to have assisted in creating a new style of dancing,'' and her appearance in *La Sylphide* in 1832 is generally recognized as the beginning of the Romantic era in dance.

Born on April 23, 1804, Marie (also known as Maria) Taglioni was the product of a well-established dance family. Her uncle Salvatore was a dance master in Naples, Italy, and the services of her father, Filippo Taglioni, himself the son of a famous dancer, were in demand all over Europe.

When Marie was born he was living in Stockholm, Sweden, where he had become the head of a ballet company and had married Swedish dancer Sophie Karsten. He later moved on to the Paris Opera, where elaborate dance scenes were interpolated into the sumptuous opera productions of the day. Marie was enrolled in dance lessons but did not seem to be a promising student. She was prim and awkward; her arms were too long; and her classmates and even her teacher called her a hunchback. At the age of six she was dismissed from her class and told to forget about becoming a dancer.

Drilled to Exhaustion

At that point, Filippo Taglioni took over his daughter's education. The 1911 *Encyclopedia Britannica* noted that he was "said to have been pitilessly severe"; Marie's dance practices ran for six hours at a stretch, and she was reportedly so tired at the end of the day that she required help to undress herself before going to bed. The training paid off, however, as Taglioni began to develop unprecedented strength in her leg muscles. Other ballerinas showed strain when dancing en pointe, with the result that choreographers composed only short sequences using the technique. Taglioni, however, could soon dance en pointe almost effortlessly.

At 18, Taglioni made her debut at the Hoftheater in Vienna, Austria, in a production called *La Réception d'une jeune nymphe à la cour de Terpsichore* (The Reception of a Young Nymph at Terpsichore's Court). Like most of the

productions for which Taglioni was famous, it was choreographed by her father. She danced for several years in Vienna before moving west through Munich and Stuttgart, Germany, and in 1827 she made her all-important Paris debut in a dance sequence inserted into the opera *Le Sicilien* (The Sicilian). Before the performance, Taglioni's coach realized that her dancing was so beautiful that the company's regular dancers would probably try to sabotage her performance, so he arranged for her to rehearse with the opera's conductor alone.

Her dancing created the expected sensation; her *New York Times* obituary stated that she achieved a triumph "by her first bound upon the stage." By 1829 she was one of the company's lead ballerinas. As she developed into one of the top dancers in Paris, Taglioni's fame also began to spread across Europe. She danced in Bordeaux, France, in 1828, and in 1830 and 1831 she made several much-heralded appearances in London. Her 1831 starring role in *La Bayadère* placed her in an Indian setting and costume—one of the first manifestations of influence from India in Western dance, although choreographers and audiences of the time knew very little about what Indian dance actually looked like.

Meanwhile, Taglioni was continuing to appear regularly at the Paris Opera. In 1831 Filippo created an interlude called the Ballet of the Nuns to be performed during Meyerbeer's gigantic opera *Robert le Diable;* it had some of the supernatural elements for which Taglioni would become internationally famous. But nothing prepared audiences for *La Sylphide* the following year. That ballet, unconnected with an opera, told the story of a Scottish farmer who falls in love with a sylph, a forest sprite, played by Taglioni. With her father's choreography creating maximum contrast between the rustic movements of the Scottish peasants and her own ethereal grace, Taglioni seemed to float across the stage as she danced en pointe, making an impression that influenced young dancers for several generations to come.

Admired by Victoria

The Scottish setting and the supernatural elements of the ballet were well known to readers of Sir Walter Scott and other Romantic literature, but they were quite new in the visual and kinetic world of ballet. Filippo Taglioni provided his daughter with a steady stream of new ballets that mostly held close to the themes and imagery of *La Sylphide*. One notable Taglioni work of the 1830s was *Brezilia; ou, La Tribu des femmes* (Brazil, or The Tribe of Women), which had its premiere at the Paris Opera in 1835. In 1838's *La gitana,* she portrayed a noblewoman abducted by Gypsies. Taglioni traveled all over Europe with productions of *La Sylphide* itself; among her biggest admirers was London's Princess Alexandrina Victoria, later to become Britain's long-reigning Queen Victoria. In London she commanded the unheard-of sum of 100 pounds per performance

In the midst of these triumphs, Taglioni's personal life was unhappy. She married the Count Gilbert des Voisins— the date is generally given as 1832, but an account of her divorce proceedings written by Edgar Allan Poe places the marriage in 1834. In any event, Taglioni's new husband did not approve of her transcontinental travels and demanded that she give up dancing, which she refused to do. A stormy scene transpired when she returned to Paris from one trip; as she was said to have related in Poe's account (quoted by *Dance Insider*), ''on her return to France she had hoped to find M. des Voisins more disposed to conform to her wishes, but that so far from that being the case he actually shut the door against her; that in this conduct M. des Voisins had offered her a gratuitous injury and insult, which would render it impossible that they could ever live together again as man and wife . . .'' After three years of marriage and two children, she was granted a divorce.

Perhaps the apex of Taglioni's career came during the five seasons she spent performing to capacity crowds at the Imperial Ballet (now the Kirov Ballet) in St. Petersburg, Russia, from 1837 to 1842. Her stay in Russia was interspersed with trips to Vienna, Stockholm, Paris, London, and Milan. Taglioni was beloved by the Russian public, who snapped up caramels and cakes named for her; beauticians also did a brisk business in the Taglioni hairstyle. She nurtured the careers of young Russian ballerinas and contributed to the spectacular development of Russian ballet in the later 19th century. Upon her departure, according to one story, a group of her admirers bid 200 rubles at auction for a pair of her ballet shoes, which they then had cooked, topped with a special sauce, and served. Accounts of Taglioni's career are garnished with a variety of outlandish tales, which, even if unverifiable, attest to the sheer breadth of her popularity.

Retired from Dancing

One of the most famous appearances of the later stages of Taglioni's career came in London in 1845, in a so-called *Pas de quatre*, choreographed by Jules Perrot, that was designed to showcase the talents of Taglioni as well as three of the other great ballerinas of the day: Carlotta Grisi, Fanny Cerrito, and Lucile Grahn. Even in her early 40s, an advanced age for a ballerina, Taglioni was capable of graceful, bounding leaps that transfixed an audience. In 1847 she retired from the stage, moving to a villa on Lake Como in northern Italy. The home became a favored stop on the itineraries of well-heeled tourists.

After a decade, Taglioni felt the pull of the dance world once again and returned to Paris in 1858. She took the post of *inspectrice de la danse* at the Paris Opera, setting up a system of dance exams that was used for decades. But much of her energy was directed toward her student Emma Livry, for whom she created her sole work as choreographer, *Le papillon* (The Butterfly), in 1860. The ballet was a triumph, but Taglioni was shaken by Livry's death in 1863 in a freak accident in which her costume caught fire after brushing a gas lamp being used as a stage light.

Troubles shadowed Taglioni in her old age. She had been financially comfortable when she retired to Italy (the *Times* stated that she had ''a complete museum of jewelry and works of art''), but poor investments begun by her father, further complicated by financial upheavals connected to the Franco-Prussian War of 1870, drained her fortune. Taglioni moved to London, where she took on a few ballet students but mostly instructed young women in the

new social dances, which was more profitable. Among her students was Mary of Teck, later England's queen consort as wife of King George V, and grandmother to Queen Elizabeth II. Mary related proudly in later life that she had been taught to curtsey by Marie Taglioni. Taglioni's name was still widely recognized enough that Vienna's Waltz King, Johann Strauss II, composed a Marie Taglioni Polka incorporating tunes from some of the ballets that had featured her most famous performances.

Marie Taglioni, once the talk of Europe, died destitute in Marseille, France, in 1884. She was buried in Marseille, but her body was later moved to the Père Lachaise Cemetery in Paris (it is marked ''Comptesse des Voisins,'' her title as a married woman). Many of the great dancers of the 1800s are known by little more than their names and a few documentary images—their dances themselves have been lost, for a thorough system of dance notation was not developed until the 20th century. But Taglioni continued to exercise a strong fascination in the minds of young dancers; after an ultimately erroneous report surfaced in 2004 that she was actually buried in Montmartre Cemetery, pointe shoes arrived from all over the world with requests that they be placed on her grave.

Books

Encyclopedia Britannica, 1911 edition.
International Dictionary of Ballet, 2 vols., St. James, 1993.
Lee, Carol, *Ballet in Western Culture: A History of Its Origins and Evolution,* Routledge, 2002.
Migel, Parmenia, *The Ballerinas,* Macmillan, 1972.

Periodicals

New York Times, April 23, 1873.

Online

''Dancer on Wings: Marie Taglioni (1804–1884), Life in Italy, http://www.lifeinitaly.com/heroes-villains/marie-taglioni.asp (December 31, 2007).
''Marie Taglioni,'' Theatre History Online, http://www.peopleplayuk.org.uk/guided_tours/dance_tour/ballet/romantic_taglioni.php (December 31, 2007).
''Marie Taglioni Charms Russia,'' The History of Russian Ballet, http://www.aha.ru/~vladmo/d_txt10.html (December 31, 2007).
''Taglioni's Not in Montmartre,'' *The Dance Insider,* http://www.danceinsider.com/f2004/f1006_1.html (December 31, 2007). □

Thérèse of Lisieux

French saint Thérèse of Lisieux (1873-1897) is revered in the Roman Catholic Church as ''the Little Flower of Jesus'' for the example she set in her short life as a Carmelite nun. At her death at the age of 24, she left behind an autobiography that quickly became a bestseller in France and was translated into dozens of languages. She was elevated to the status

of saint in the Church by Pope Pius XI in one of the fastest canonizations in the history of the Roman Catholicism.

Thérèse was born Marie Françoise Thérèse Martin on January 2, 1873, in Alençon, France. She was the last of nine children born to Louis and Zélie Martin, a watchmaker and lacemaker, respectively, and both extremely devout Catholics. Zélie had a growth in her breast for many years which prevented her from nursing her children, and Thérèse was sent to a wet nurse for the first year of her life. The mother's tumor turned out to be inoperable cancer, and Zélie died when Thérèse was four years old—a grievous blow to the youngster, who was extremely attached to her mother. Afterward, Louis Martin relocated the family to the town of Lisieux in Normandy, where relatives helped care for the children.

Sisters Became Nuns

Thérèse was a serious, clingy child from an early age, unusually fixated on being obedient, and preoccupied with questions about heaven and the afterlife. She was a day student at the Benedictine Abbey school in Lisieux, but her piety was interpreted by others as aloofness and she had few friends. She was primarily raised by her older sisters, and was especially close to Pauline, who was 12 years her senior. When Pauline decided to enter the local order of Carmelite nuns in 1882, Thérèse was inconsolable. "In one

instant, I understood what life was. . . . It appeared to me in all its reality, and I saw it was nothing but a continual suffering and separation," she later wrote, according to Kathryn Harrison's biography *Saint Thérèse of Lisieux.*

Several months later, Thérèse was beset by a three-month-long illness marked by convulsions, nightmares, hallucinations, and occasional comatose states. The family doctor diagnosed it as St. Vitus Dance, more formally known as chorea and characterized by involuntary movements. She was reportedly cured after praying to a statue of the Virgin Mary, whom she believed smiled at her at the instant of the intercession. At this point Thérèse became even more intensely devoted to prayer and penance, later writing, "Suffering became my attraction," she reflected, according to Harrison's book. "It had charms about it which ravished me without my understanding them very well."

In October of 1886 Thérèse's sister Marie also entered the Carmelite convent, and the following Christmas Thérèse claimed to have begun her own process of religious awakening. This was occasioned by a remark her father made after the family returned from midnight Mass services on Christmas Eve, when he grumbled about having to fill the stockings of his youngest child before going to bed. Thérèse overheard the comment, and instead of becoming upset—she was easily wounded by any slight and was prone to histrionics and attention-seeking—she later recalled that by accepting his words without note, she felt transformed into an adult.

Petitioned the Pope

In the spring of 1887, Thérèse decided that she, too, would take religious vows and follow her sisters into the Carmelite order. The local prelate in Lisieux, who had ecclesiastical oversight over the convent, declared that she was far too young at age 14 and needed to wait until she was 21. With her father she secured a meeting with a higher authority, the bishop, in order to plead her case, but it was again rejected. In November of 1887, Thérèse, her father, and sister Céline made a pilgrimage to Rome, where they took part in a general audience before Pope Leo XIII (1810-1903). The custom for pilgrims was to kneel before the pope, kiss his foot and hand, and not address him at all but instead wait for his benediction, but Thérèse asked for his help in joining the Carmelites. Perplexed, Leo turned to the vicar who had accompanied them and the other French pilgrims, and the vicar explained that the teenager's request was being considered by members of the French clergy. At this, Thérèse exclaimed, "Oh Holy Father, if you say yes, everyone will agree!" Leo's reply, according to Harrison's book, was, "Go, go, you will enter if God wills it."

The vicar, likely impressed by Thérèse's otherwise devout conduct on the pilgrimage, agreed to take up her cause, and she became a postulant on April 9, 1888, when she entered the Lisieux Carmelite convent at the age of 15. She was given a long blue dress and black bonnet, and slept in a small and chilly room on a straw mattress. The nuns woke daily at five a.m. for prayer and work, taking their first meal only five hours later. They ate in silence in a dining room that had a human skull affixed to the wall to remind them of the ultimate fate of their physical bodies on earth. The rest of the day was governed by chores and prayer, including two hours of silent contemplation and three and a half hours reciting the Liturgy of the Hours.

Thérèse had been a favorite of the mother superior at Lisieux, Mother Marie de Gonzague, even before she entered the order, and the favoritism shown to her exacerbated bitter divisions already apparent among the nuns, many of whom were much older and resented Thérèse's obvious attempts to demonstrate piety. She became a novice in January of 1889, and made her profession of vows in September of 1890. Three years later she was appointed acting mistress of novices when her sister Pauline succeeded Mother Marie as prioress. Within a year, however, Thérèse's health began to fail, and she was beset by a perpetual sore throat that was eventually diagnosed as tuberculosis. As described in Harrison's book, she wrote to one of her sisters, "Don't worry about me. I am not sick; on the contrary, I have iron health," though she added "God can break iron just like clay."

Prayed to be Consumed by Fire

That sister, Céline, would also enter the Carmelite order, and in June of 1895 Thérèse went with her to ask permission from Pauline, now called Mother Agnes, to make an act of oblation together. This was a solemn offering or presentation to God, and in this case was a request that they be overtaken by Christ entirely and by the process of immolation, or ritual sacrifice, often by burning. Thérèse wrote out the text of the prayer, which read, in part: "I ask you to come and take possession of my soul. . . . I offer myself as a victim of holocaust to your merciful love." A few days later she reported experiencing a burning sensation while saying the Stations of the Cross, and considered this a sign from God that her request had been heard.

Thérèse grew weaker from tuberculosis, and during the Lenten season of 1896 experienced the first hemorrhage of her lung tissue. She was duty-bound to inform Pauline, her superior, of the incident, but asked permission to be allowed to perform her chores and prayers anyway, which Pauline granted. Thérèse's health worsened over the next 18 months, and she was kept awake at night by coughing fits. She submitted to painful applications of mustard plasters, which promoted the formation of blisters and was thought to improve circulation in the ill, only because she believed the pain hastened her path to holiness. By the Lenten season of 1897, she was too weak to stand at times, and became unable to hold down any nourishment due to gangrene in her intestines. As the condition of her lungs worsened, she experienced a feeling of being suffocated, and would repeatedly cry out *Je souffre* (I suffer) and insist that Céline, now her closest caregiver, respond, *Tant mieux,* or "all the better" each time. She died on September 30, 1897, and her last words were accompanied by a glance at the crucifix in her hand, "My God I love you," according to Harrison's book

The Story of a Soul

In the months before Thérèse's death, Pauline had asked her sister to write her memoirs, hoping to record the memories of their happier childhood times before the death

of their mother. Thérèse wrote out three distinct sections: one that chronicled those early years, a second that described her own personal spiritual struggle between 1877 and 1886, and a third section detailing her religious awakening prior to entering the Carmelite convent. Pauline had it printed and sent out as an obituary notice to other Carmelite orders in France, but *Springtime Story of a Little White Flower* was also available to the public and was soon in great demand. A new version was published as *L'histoire d'une âme* (The Story of a Soul), and was widely read by Roman Catholics around the world after its translation into dozens of languages.

In *The Story of a Soul,* Thérèse writes of the difficulties she experienced on her spiritual journey, and the doubts about her faith that befell her at times. "I've got to take myself just as I am, with all my imperfections," she wrote, according to Joel Schorn in *U.S. Catholic,* "but somehow I shall have to find out a little way, all of my own." She also declared that her life's mission was "to scatter flowers—to miss no opportunity of making some small sacrifice . . . always doing the tiniest things right, and doing it for love." This became known as the "Little Way" of St. Thérèse, who is sometimes called "the Little Flower of Jesus." This story of an ordinary teenager from a French middle-class home, who strove to reach spiritual bliss, seemed to resonate among the faithful, and many began to send in letters to the Vatican, the seat of the Church in Rome, claiming that they had prayed to Thérèse to intercede on their behalf and that a miraculous recovery or other extraordinary event had transpired because of it.

The Roman Catholic Church dictates a 50-year waiting period after death before the beatification and canonization process may begin, but in 1910, only 13 years after Thérèse's death, the process was officially opened. Thérèse was beatified in 1923 and canonized on May 17, 1925, by Pope Pius XI (1857-1939), who dubbed her book and the extraordinary response to it a "hurricane of glory." On the centenary of her death, Pope John Paul II (1920-2005) named St. Thérèse of Lisieux a Doctor of the Church, a tremendous honor usually reserved for saints who have been important teachers of the faith. It placed her among ranks that included such theologians as St. Augustine (354-430) and St. Thomas Aquinas (c. 1225-1274), and she was just the third woman in the history of the Church to receive the designation. That same decade, the relics of St. Thérèse made an eight-year-long world tour, and thousands came daily to venerate them in dozens of cities. Her feast day is October 3, and she remains one of the most popular saints of the modern era. Writing in the *New Catholic Encyclopedia,* P. T. Rohrbach attempted to explain her appeal. "In the bull of canonization, Pius XI said that she fulfilled her vocation and achieved sanctity 'without going beyond the common order of things.' This phrase is the key to understanding her message and popularity. Her life was simple, devoid of the drama and major conflict that characterize the lives of so many saints, but in the framework of that simple life she achieved sanctity."

Books

Harrison, Kathryn, *Saint Thérèse of Lisieux,* Lipper/Viking, 2003.

Encyclopedia of Religion, edited by Lindsay Jones, volume 13, second edition, Macmillan Reference USA, 2005.
New Catholic Encyclopedia, volume 13, second edition, Gale, 2003.

Periodicals

Catholic Insight, January-February 1998.
U.S. Catholic, November 2005. □

Danny Thomas

Best remembered as the star of *Make Room for Daddy* during television's first golden age, Danny Thomas (1924-1992) was more than just another nightclub entertainer turned sitcom star. Along with partner Sheldon Leonard, he produced such landmark television series as *The Andy Griffith Show, The Dick Van Dyke Show,* and many others. However, his most enduring contribution was the time and energy he expended while helping establish the St. Jude's Children's Research Hospital.

Started Out in Radio and Nightclubs

According to his 1991 autobiography, *Make Room for Danny,* the man known to millions the world over as Danny Thomas was born Muzyad Yakhoob on January 6, 1914, in Deerfield, Michigan. Baptized at Deerfield's St. Alphonsus Church, his mother had always assumed that her son's name had been changed to Alphonsus, and used it on several legal papers. Finally, the youngster's father decided to legally change the family's last name to Jacobs. Hence the father became Charles Jacobs, the mother Margaret, and young "Muzzy" Yakhoob became Amos Jacobs. That said, even after he adopted his official show business name, longtime friends such as Frank Sinatra simply called him Jake.

The first generation son of Lebanese immigrants, he absorbed much of his family's culture through his close-knit family, and would later use them as the back story for his famed TV sitcom. The elder Jacobs supported his eight sons and one daughter by selling scrap metal and peddling dry goods until he had earned enough to buy a horse farm in Michigan. After losing the farm in a poker game, their father moved to Toledo, Ohio, and spent the rest of his days working in a factory. A natural storyteller, he would fascinate his children with tales of life in Lebanon and his trials and travails as a peddler, which rubbed off on young Thomas.

Living in various ethnic communities, Thomas developed an uncanny ability to mimic accents, including Yiddish, Irish, and Lebanese. Close to his uncle Tony Simon and his Aunt Julia, the boy often lived with them, following them in their various changes of location until he was 15 years old. During the 1920s he sold candy and soda at the

Empire Burlesque Theatre in Toledo. After watching many comedians do their respective acts, he realized that someone could actually make a living being funny. His favorite performer was a dialect comic named Abe Reynolds, who wove Russian and Jewish accents into his monologues in the same fashion that Catskills comedian Myron Cohen did. At the age of 12, Thomas and his brother formed their own short-lived high school act: Ray and Amos Jacobs—Songs, Dances, and Snappy Patter.

After dropping out of high school at age 15, Thomas sold candy at a Burlesque theater in Rochester, New York, before returning to Toledo to work as a punch press operator's assistant at the local Autolite factory. At age 17 he moved in with his uncle David Azar in Detroit, and during the height of the Great Depression made his debut on radio station WMBC's *The Happy Hour Club,* where he met the woman who would eventually become his wife, Rose Marie Mantel. Frequent amateur hour appearances finally led to paying work—$2 a night—at local beer gardens that sold 3.2 and near beer. Telling his ethnic stories and singing songs to ethnic audiences, the youngster was enough of a success to latch onto occasional MC jobs, small dramatic parts on radio, and commercials. However, with a new baby—future *That Girl* star Marlo—and the haphazard nature of show business bookings, the entertainer struggled, and his family was in jeopardy. His wife pleaded for him to quit performing and go into the grocery business.

In later years Thomas claimed that he prayed for guidance to St. Jude Thaddeus, swearing that if he were a show business success, he would build the nearly forgotten apostle a shrine. Certainly Thomas's career began to prosper once he relocated to Chicago in 1940. A master of several different dialects and a fair celebrity impressionist, he began to score work as a character actor on several network radio programs and in commercials, but the employment wasn't steady.

Although he felt it was beneath the dignity of a radio actor to work saloons, Thomas had a family to feed and took a booking at a former Studebaker automobile agency called the 5100 Club. Hoping to avoid the embarrassment of his hometown friends learning about his return to nightclubs, he put two of his brothers' names together and billed himself as Danny Thomas. The name change signaled the beginning of his salad days as a comedian. Constantly refreshing his material ala The Jack Story, Crotchety Calhoun, and Ode to a Wailing Syrian with humorous personal observations, he became an audience favorite and was held over for several months. More important, he attracted a powerful agent, Abe Lastfogel of the William Morris Agency.

Lastfogel asked Thomas to curtail some of the ethnic material in his act, and began booking him for top dollar at nightspots like the Chez Paree in Chicago, La Martinique in New York, the Sands Hotel in Las Vegas, and the Radio City Music Hall. In 1944 the agent landed Thomas the role of Jerry Dingle the postman on Fanny Brice's CBS radio smash The Baby Snooks Show. The canny agent even brokered movie contracts with MGM, Warner Bros., and Columbia pictures for his young variety star. Thomas made five films between 1947 and 1951, most notably the Gus Kahn biopic I'll See You In My Dreams with Doris Day and a schmaltzy remake of Al Jolson's first talkie, The Jazz Singer. Most of Thomas's films were box office successes, but all three studios turned him down as a long-term prospect because the Lebanese-American star refused to get a nose job.

Television's Danny Williams

Still playing nightclubs and theaters, Thomas made his first television appearance as one of the hosts of NBC's Four Star Revue. Mixing fast-paced sketches with jugglers and dance acts worked against the grain of Thomas's comedy. In clubs he could develop a story slowly, then draw the audience in before interjecting a surprising punch-line or, as he called it, "a treacle cutter." After a year, Thomas opted out of the show, which eventually evolved into The Colgate Comedy Hour. After a year back in the clubs, he signed with the upstart ABC network to do a sitcom. The show that writer Mel Shavelson created around him was based on one of Thomas's family stories. While he was on the road, his two young daughters would sleep with their mother. When Thomas came home, the daughters were ushered back to their own room so they could "make room for daddy." A warm-hearted blend of comedy and variety, Make Room for Daddy followed the trials and travails of Danny Williams, a successful entertainer who tried to balance a career and family life. Although ABC initially had far fewer affiliates than the other two major networks, the show was an instant hit and won the Emmy for best new show.

For the first three years, Jean Hagen—who had earned an Oscar nomination for her role in Singing in the Rain—

played his wife Margaret. Sherry Jackson portrayed their daughter, Terry, and Rusty Hamer played son Rusty. By his own admission, Thomas did not get along too well with Hagen, feeling that the former Broadway and Hollywood star looked down on him. Hagen left the show after the 1955/1956 season to take on more serious roles. Rather than replace her with another actress in the same role, the next season's storyline began with reactions to the death of Margaret Williams, making Hagen's the first continuing character role in network television history to be killed off. Although she worked steadily, Hagen's solo career never really regained momentum, and she retired due to ill health in 1964.

Thomas's final season on ABC featured his character as a widower who met a widowed nurse named Kathy O'Hara. Played by red-headed actress Marjorie Lord, the warm yet perky character worked perfectly off of Thomas's slow-burning character. When Thomas moved the show to CBS, she became his character's wife. The show took over the departing I Love Lucy time slot and became a perennial top-ten ratings hit until Thomas voluntarily retired the show in 1964. During its run, the show brought several performers to prominence, including Bill Dana, Hans Conried as Uncle Tonoose, and Angela Cartwright as Kathy's daughter, Linda, who later co-starred on Lost in Space. In one of the minor parts, Sheldon Leonard, a character actor specializing in movie gangster types during the 1930s and 1940s, appeared as Danny Williams's agent and worked behind the scenes as a director. Eventually they became production partners responsible for a slew of hit shows.

Introduced the Andy Griffith and Dick Van Dyke Shows

Lastfogel and the William Morris Agency had the foresight to set Thomas up with his own production company, Danny Thomas Productions. Besides his own show, the comedian's company oversaw the first rural sitcom, The Real McCoys. Starring Walter Brennan and Richard Crenna, the show ran for eight seasons on ABC and CBS. Thomas also introduced popular comedian/actor Andy Griffith as Sheriff Andy Taylor on his own show before spinning it off into the perpetually popular Andy Griffith Show in 1960. Another of television's greatest situation comedies also came from Thomas's company, the Dick Van Dyke Show, which, like his own program, was about working in show business while trying to live a normal family life. One of Thomas's funniest performances came when he portrayed a walnut-eating alien named Kolac in one of Van Dyke's dream sequences. Not all the shows that bore his imprint boasted the same quality, but such programs as The Joey Bishop Show and Gomer Pyle enjoyed solid network runs. In his autobiography, Thomas gave all credit for the success of these shows to his indefatigable partner, Sheldon Leonard. However, even after Leonard departed to form his own company in 1965, Thomas's company produced such hit as The Guns of Will Sonnett and The Mod Squad, the latter co-produced with Aaron Spelling.

Besides making numerous guest appearances on shows hosted by other stars, including his daughter Marlo's series

That Girl, Thomas starred in a series of specials before hosting an hour-long variety and drama series for NBC called *The Danny Thomas Hour* in 1968. Two years later he assembled the cast of his old hit show and retitled it *Make Room for Granddaddy,* which lasted only one season on ABC. Thomas's son, Tony, now a prominent producer in his own right, produced his 1976-77 effort *The Practice,* which featured the comedian in a role he loved, a crusty but caring physician. Less interesting was his role as dentist Ben Douglas in the tepid 1980 Diane Canova vehicle *I'm a Big Girl Now.* Thomas's final television series was the seldom seen 1986 sitcom *One Big Happy Family,* wherein he played an ex-vaudevillian raising his late brother's children. No longer a force on television, Thomas continued playing to capacity crowds at nightclubs and toured with fellow television icons Milton Berle and Sid Caesar in a live show called *The Legends of Comedy.*

A Tireless Philanthropist

Throughout even the busiest times of his career, Thomas always made good on his pledge to build a shrine to St. Jude. The edifice he helped found was the St. Jude's Children's Research Hospital in Memphis, Tennessee, a center where hospital care would be given to all children regardless of their ability to pay. Directed toward the cause by Lastfogel, Thomas began raising money for the project during the early 1950s. After St. Jude's opened in 1962, the comedian publicized the hospital, enlisted all of the biggest names in show business to play the yearly Shower of Stars benefits, and educated the public on the hospital's progress in fighting such diseases as childhood leukemia and Hodgkin's disease. Further, the entertainer donated money from his own pocket. The proceeds from his commercials for Maxwell House coffee and the sale of his share of the Miami Dolphins football team were sent directly to St. Jude's. For his many efforts, Thomas was lauded with numerous awards and honorary doctorates, and was nominated for a Nobel Peace Prize in 1980. The award that meant the most to him was the Congressional Medal of Honor, which was presented to him by his old Hollywood pal President Ronald Reagan on April 16, 1985. Thomas continued working for the cause until his death from a heart attack on February 6, 1991.

Books

Hill, Tom, *TV Land To Go,* Fireside, 2001.

McNeil, Alex, *Total Television,* Penguin Books, 1996, 4th edition.

Thomas, Danny, with Bill Davidson, *Make Room for Danny,* G.P. Putnam's Sons, 1991.

Online

"Danny Thomas," *Internet Movie Database,* http://www.imdb .com/name/nm0858683/bio (April 15, 2008).

"Danny Thomas Story," *St. Jude's Children's Research Hospital,* http://www.stjude.tv/danny_thomas_story.cfm (December 28, 2007).

The Museum of Broadcast Communications, http://www .museum.tv/archives/etv/T/htmlT/thomasdanny/thomas danny.htm (January 1 2008). □

Wallace Henry Thurman

American writer Wallace Henry Thurman (1902-1934) worked as a journalist, editor, novelist and playwright. His most famous novel is "The Blacker the Berry: A Novel of Negro Life," which depicts discrimination among black people based on degrees of skin color. A member of the Harlem Renaissance, Thurman became influential as the editor and publisher of black literary journals, including *Fire!!*

Thurman proved to be a better editor than writer, and his talent and influence helped support New York's young blacks who comprised the artistic movement. For the most part, his plays were not produced while he was alive, and his novels only generated lukewarm enthusiasm. Further, his literary criticism, while perceptive, could often be harsh and even bitter. Later, he would attack the movement he once supported, condemning its members for their standards and pretensions. Today, he is perhaps best known for the innovative, black-oriented literary publications he helped launch. Beset by illness throughout most of his life and troubled with alcohol problems as an adult, he died when he was only 32 years old.

Born in the West

Born in Salt Lake City, Utah, on August 16, 1902, Thurman was the son of Oscar and Beulah Thurman. Wallace Thurman never knew his father, who deserted his family and moved to California. He was raised by his mother and maternal grandmother, Emma Jackson, or "Ma Jack."

While growing up in Salt Lake City, Thurman was a sickly child who spent a great deal of time reading. His remarkably precocious literary tastes included Friedrich Nietzsche, Gustave Flaubert, Charles Baudelaire, Charles Saint-Beuve, Herbert Spencer, Henrik Ibsen, Thomas Hardy, Fyodor Dostoyevsky, Havelock Ellis, and Sigmund Freud. He aspired to be a writer and reportedly penned a novel when he was only ten years old.

Thurman attended public schools in Salt Lake City and graduated from high school in 1919. At the University of Utah, he studied medicine and chemistry. Following his graduation in 1922, he did some post-graduate work at the University of Southern California in Los Angeles, at the time a predominately white academic institution. As a young man, Thurman began formulating personal attitudes that would later inform his writings. Described as a dark-skinned black, he came to resent "Negro society," which at the time tended to favor lighter-skinned members of the race.

Became a Journalist and Publisher

Thurman never completed his graduate work. Instead, he set out to become a journalist, first working as a reporter for the *Los Angeles Sentinel,* an African-American newspaper. He also wrote a column for *Inklings,* another newspaper with a black readership. In 1924 Thurman founded a literary magazine called *Outlet,* which he hoped would help spark the kind of literary movement fostered by the Harlem Renaissance, which was taking place in New York City. However, the magazine only lasted six months.

The following year Thurman moved to New York City, where he became a reporter for *The Looking Glass,* a position he obtained with the help of Theophilus Lewis, a black writer who became his friend and mentor. Thurman also worked as an editor for the publication. The experience led to his becoming the managing editor of the *Messenger* in 1926. Established in 1917 by A. Philip Randolph and Chandler Owen, the periodical focused on political and economic issues that impacted the black community. It was also known as "The World's Greatest Negro Monthly." The co-founders also published short stories and poetry by emerging African-American writers. During his brief tenure as managing editor, Thurman published short works by poet/author Langston Hughes and Zora Neale Hurston, who were leading figures in the Harlem Renaissance. Thurman wrote a short story for the publication, titled "Grist in the Mill," about a racist Southern aristocrat troubled by the fact that he received a life-saving blood transfusion from a black man.

That same year, Thurman left the magazine to take a position as circulation manager for *The World Tomorrow,* a white-owned monthly publication. During this period he also supported himself by writing stories for *True Story,* under the pen names "Ethel Bell Mandrake" and "Patrick Casey."

A Squelched *Fire*

Thurman's second publishing venture (following *Outlet*) would make a more significant impression on the literary world. While living in New York City, Thurman developed a close friendship with Hughes. In the summer of 1926 Hughes asked Thurman to serve as editor of *Fire!!,* a magazine that Hughes was planning with writer Bruce Nugent. As it turned out, Thurman not only edited the publication, he provided much of its funding. Even though it lasted for only one issue, the literary journal is now recognized as the first truly influential African-American magazine of the twentieth century, and it established Thurman's reputation as a daring and unconventional publisher/editor/writer.

The journal's bold name indicated its purpose. In the foreword of the first and only issue (November 1926), Thurman wrote that *Fire!!* would make a vivid impression by "melting steel and iron bars, poking livid tongues between stone apertures and burning wooden opposition with a cackling chuckle of contempt," according to *Notable Black American Men.* This matched the intentions of Hughes, who later revealed that he intended for the publication to "burn up a lot of old, dead conventional Negro-white ideas of the past." Further, he said, it would provide "younger Negro writers and artists" with an "outlet for publication not available."

Appropriately, the avant-garde literary publication's single issue included short stories by Thurman, Hurston, and Gwendolyn Bennett, as well as poetry by Hughes, Countee Cullen, and Arna Bontemps, a play by Hurston, illustrations by Aaron Douglas, and the first part of a novel by Nugent. Despite the bold ambitions of its founders, the journal was quickly scuttled by financial and distribution problems. Moreover, its critical reception was disappoint-

ing: black readers found it too irreverent, old-guard black critics denounced it, and white critics simply ignored it.

Hobnobbed in the Harlem Renaissance

It took Thurman four years to pay for the printing expenses for *Fire!!* During this period of his life, he was often in debt and sometimes unemployed. In addition, his fragile health was worsening. At one point he suffered from a swollen thyroid and other infected glands, and eventually required surgery. Despite his physical condition, he reportedly drank heavily.

Because of his fondness for liquor and parties, Thurman became a popular figure in Harlem social circles, and he mingled with members of the Harlem Renaissance. This vibrant artistic movement included emerging black writers and artists such as Bennett, Bontemps, Cullen, John Davis, Douglas, Jessie Fauset, Rudolph Fisher, Hurston, Nella Larsen, Claude McKay, Nugent, Jean Toomer, and Dorothy West. While Thurman enjoyed the socializing, he did not hold the Renaissance writers in high regard. As far as he could tell, its ranks lacked any important, emerging authors. In turn, Thurman's contemporaries only considered him a marginal literary talent. Still, many of his articles appeared in prestigious publications such as *The New Republic.* This kind of exposure helped establish his reputation as a keen but caustic critic.

Undaunted by the failure of *Fire!!,* Thurman attempted to establish another literary publication that would provide a creative outlet for young black writers. Launched in 1928, the publication, titled *Harlem, A Forum of Negro Life,* folded after only two issues. The first issue included an essay by critic Alain Locke, a book review by Thurman, poetry by Alice Dunbar Nelson and Hughes, fiction by Hughes and George Schuyler, and a theater review by Lewis, who also served as the magazine's editor.

Toward the end of the decade, Thurman worked as an editorial staff member for McFadden Publications and the Macaulay Publishing Company, both located in New York City.

On August 22, 1928, Thurman married Louise Thompson, a teacher and writer, but the union would not last long. Thompson quickly became disenchanted by her husband's heavy drinking, as well as his homosexual tendencies, and she sought a divorce. However, they could not agree upon an alimony settlement. They never divorced, but remained separated.

Wrote Plays

During the late 1920s and early 1930s, Thurman also worked as a playwright, but his efforts met with little success. His first play, *Harlem: A Melodrama of Negro Life in Harlem,* was his most successful, although reviews were mixed. Thurman wrote the play in collaboration with William Jourdan Rapp, a white author and editor who would remain Thurman's lifelong friend. The work premiered on Broadway on February 20, 1929, at the Apollo Theater. It ran for 93 performances in New York and was also staged in Chicago, Los Angeles, and Canada.

Based on a short story Thurman had written and published in *Fire!!,* titled "Cordelia the Crude," the drama focuses on a southern black family that moved to New York City to escape economic hardships, only to have trouble adjusting to the city's urban crime, unemployment, and racial tensions. Black playgoers criticized the work for its focus on the more lurid elements of Harlem life (gambling, drinking, illicit sex). Likewise, critics were put off by its sensationalism. In his review published in *Commonweal,* R. Dana Skinner indicated he was troubled by "the particular way in which this melodrama exploits the worst features of the Negro and depends for its effects solely on the explosions of lust and sensuality." But, at the same time, Skinner found it entertaining and "captured the feel of life."

Thurman again collaborated with Rapp on his second play, *Jeremiah, the Magnificent* (1930), a three-act drama influenced by Marcus Garvey's "back to Africa" movement. For a long time the play remained unpublished, and it was only performed once, after Thurman's death. Thurman wrote two more plays, *Singing the Blues* (1931) and *Savage Rhythm* (1932). Neither were performed or published during Thurman's lifetime.

Published Novels

Along with his publishing and dramatic endeavors, Thurman was a novelist. Today, he his best known for his first novel, *The Blacker the Berry: A Novel of Negro Life.* Published in 1929, the work tackles themes of self-hatred and hypocrisy by targeting a peculiar prejudice existing within black society. The plot relates the story of Emma Lou, a dark-skinned girl denigrated by her more fair-skinned friends and family members. She moves from Los Angeles to Harlem to escape the ostracization engendered by her darker color. When she encounters the same problems in her new environment, she resorts to using skin bleaches and hair straighteners and spurns the advances of darker colored males.

Despite its compelling plot, the book failed to impress critics. It garnered negative reviews in the *New York Times Book Review* and the *New York Herald Tribune,* but Thurman was applauded for his daring in tackling the sensitive subject matter.

Thurman's second novel, *Infants of the Spring* (1932), also set in Harlem, involves a young black writer named Raymond Taylor who lives in a boardinghouse populated by pretentious aspiring writers. Thurman directed satiric barbs at these secondary characters, lambasting their artistic poses and condemning their creativity-stifling decadent lifestyles. Critics suggested that Thurmon based these characters on real-life Harlem Renaissance figures such as Hughes, Hurston, Cullen, Nugent and Douglas. Critics also complained that Thurman tried to tackle too many issues, which ultimately harmed the clarity of the work. At the same time, they complimented Thurman on his candid, realistic depiction of a specific segment of black society.

Thurman wrote only one more novel, *The Interne,* a collaboration with Abraham L. Furman, a white writer whom Thurman met while working at Macaulay Publishing Company. Also published in 1932, the book depicts life at an urban hospital as seen through the eyes of main character Carl Armstrong, an idealistic young white doctor who becomes disillusioned with his profession.

Wrote Screenplays in California

In 1934 Thurman moved to California, where he wrote two screenplays for a film company headed by Bryan Foy, the son of famed vaudevillian Eddie Foy and producer of "B" movies. These screenplays were *Tomorrow's Children* (1934) and *High School Girl* (1935). The latter relates the story of a 17-year-old girl who supports her poor white family. *Tomorrow's Children* was considered a "road show" picture. These kinds of movies were not released through traditional film distribution channels. Because of their sensational subject matter, they were considered special attractions, and they were banned in many cities. *Tomorrow's Children* involved moral and ethical issues related to sterilization, and it featured an on-screen vasectomy. The film was banned in New York City because of its sexually explicit content.

Died in New York City

In California, Thurman continued his unhealthy lifestyle and drank heavily. Eventually he became ill and had to return to New York City in May of 1934, where he was diagnosed with tuberculosis. Despite his poor health, he still drank excessively. In July of that year, he collapsed during his reunion party. He was taken to City Hospital on Welfare Island in New York City. He lingered for six months in a ward for incurable tuberculosis patients. He died on December 21, 1934.

His funeral services were held in New York City on Christmas Eve. In attendance were his estranged wife, Louise Thompson, and members of the Harlem writing community, including Cullen, Douglas and West. He was buried in Silver Mount Cemetery on Staten Island.

Books

Contemporary Black Biography, Volume 16, Gale Research, 1997.
Notable Black American Men, Gale Research, 1998.

Periodicals

Melus, Summer 2003; Fall-Winter 2004.

Online

Contemporary Authors Online, Gale, 2003, http://galenet.gale group.com/servlet/BioRC (October 20, 2007). □

Augustine Tolton

Former slave Augustine Tolton (1854-1897) overcame daunting obstacles to become the second African-American to be ordained a priest in the Roman Catholic Church.

Trained in Rome and ordained in 1886, Tolton served in Quincy, Illinois, and later in Chicago until his premature death in 1897 at the age of 43. He was assigned to small, often desperately poor parishes of black Catholics during an era when this religion was viewed with great prejudice in America as the faith of immigrants. Accounts written by his contemporaries describe him as admirably pious as well as a warm, charismatic leader of his flock.

Tolton was born on the first day of April in 1854, in Ralls County, Missouri. Missouri was a slave state at the time, but its populace—a mix of settlers from both northern and southern states—was bitterly divided over the slavery question. Tolton's mother, Martha Jane Crisley, had come to Missouri with her owners, the Elliotts, a Catholic family from Kentucky. Crisley was a personal maid to Mrs. Elliott and had been baptized in the Roman Catholic Church, as had her husband, Peter Paul Tolton, another Elliott slave. Their two sons—Augustine and his older brother Charley—were baptized in the Church and given religious instruction by Mrs. Elliott, who served as Augustine's godmother.

Entered Parish School

When the U.S. Civil War (1861-1865) broke out in 1861, Tolton was seven years old. His family either escaped in the uproar that ensued in Missouri as various militias from the Union and Confederate sides battled to control the state, or were freed by the Elliotts. In any event, they made their way to a Union Army encampment near Hannibal, where Peter Paul Tolton decided to enlist in the Union Army. His wife, two sons, and a year-old daughter fled across the Mississippi River to Illinois, a free state. Their father died of dysentery later in the war.

Martha Tolton settled in Quincy, the Illinois city located directly across from Hannibal on the banks of the Mississippi. She and her sons worked in a cigar factory which shut down during the winter months, and this hiatus allowed Tolton to begin his first formal schooling. He attended a local public school and then entered the parish school of St. Boniface, one of Quincy's Roman Catholic churches. Some parishioners objected to worshipping alongside the Toltons, however, and to the youngster's presence in the classroom with their children, so Martha switched allegiances to St. Lawrence's, a church run by a sympathetic but strong-willed Irish immigrant priest, Father Peter McGirr, who took sympathy on the family. McGirr installed Tolton in the parish school, ignoring the threats from white parents that they would leave the parish and school, and he became an important mentor to Tolton.

During his teen years, Tolton worked for a local saddle maker, as a custodian at St. Lawrence's (by then renamed St. Peter's), and in a factory. He was drawn to the priesthood but was hampered by his lack of formal schooling. At the time, Roman Catholic religious texts and services were written entirely in Latin, and so McGirr arranged for some local Franciscan priests—who had recently established a Catholic college in Quincy—to begin tutoring him in the classical language. Tolton began his evening classes with the friars around 1873, when he was 19, while McGirr began writing letters to seminaries inquiring if they would accept a black candidate for the priesthood.

Mentors Pulled Strings

No seminary would permit Tolton to enroll, not even one specifically aimed at training missionaries for Africa, and so McGirr and one of the Franciscans, a Father Richard, pleaded with contacts they knew in Rome and the Vatican, the seat of the Roman Catholic Church. They assured their colleagues in the church hierarchy that the 26-year-old Tolton displayed an ardent commitment to his faith, attending Mass sometimes twice daily and often stating his intention to serve as a missionary priest in Africa. Their effort bore fruit, and Tolton was admitted to the College of the Propagation of the Faith, the seminary in Rome that trained missionary priests. Tolton's travel expenses were paid by a fundraising drive spearheaded by McGirr and the other priests in Quincy. The onetime slave arrived in Rome, Christendom's holiest city, in 1880, entered the seminary, and five years later was ordained at St. John Lateran Church in Rome, a structure whose origins as a church dated back to 314 CE.

Tolton's superiors debated over his first assignment as a priest. He hoped to be sent to Africa to work as a missionary, feeling certain that despite his new priest's collar he would still be subject to humiliating racism in the United States, but the decision of church hierarchy was binding, and Tolton complied with it and returned to Illinois. The first Mass he celebrated in the United States was at a church called St. Benedict the Moor in New York City, which served an African-American community of Roman Catholics there. Tolton was feted as a celebrity of sorts, for there was only one other black priest of the faith in the country at the time, Father James Augustine Healy, but he was born to a slave mother and a white father, and was by then serving as Bishop of Portland, Maine.

Back in Quincy, Tolton took over the pastorship of St. Joseph's Catholic Church for Negroes, but the parish struggled financially and had but two dozen members. Still, Tolton emerged as a popular figure in Quincy, and his sermons grew particularly eloquent—enough so that they began attracting more African-American congregants from Protestant churches and even a few whites. His immediate superior in Quincy, however, decreed that integrated church services were forbidden, and some local black ministers reportedly also viewed Tolton as a threat. His fame continued to spread, however, and he was beloved by his parishioners, who called him "Good Father Gus." Contemporary accounts noted that he played the accordion and had an excellent singing voice.

Took Over Chicago Flock

Tolton found it difficult to find potential Roman Catholic converts in Quincy, but his fame had reached other cities, including Chicago. A struggling congregation of black Catholics there petitioned their archbishop to transfer Tolton to their parish, and he moved there in 1889. He took over a small basement church attached to a larger white parish, but church authorities in the city had recently been given a generous donation of $10,000 from a woman named Anna O'Neil to establish a permanent, bricks-and-mortar Roman Catholic church for blacks in the city. Tolton's mother, sister, and several loyal Quincy parishioners eventually followed him to Chicago, and became part of St. Monica's Roman Catholic Church for Negroes, named for the mother of early church theologian St. Augustine, who was African. "These dear people feel proud that they have a priest to look after them," Tolton wrote in one letter to a benefactor, according to *Seattle Times* writer Martha Irvine, and he noted that some blacks of other faiths requested his prayers at their sickbed. "That makes me feel that there is great work for me here."

Tolton also made contact with Mother Katherine Drexel, one of the first American-born Catholics to be canonized a saint after death. Drexel had been born into great wealth but went on to found a religious order and become a generous benefactor to Native American and African-American causes. She provided some additional funds for Tolton's church, then under construction on the corner of 36th Street and Dearborn Avenue. By then Tolton was well-known among Roman Catholics in America and was an active participant in the Congresses of Black Catholics that took place during this era. In the summer of 1892 he spent a month in Boston at a conference of black Catholics, telling his audience at one event, "the Catholic Church considers [ours] a double slavery, that of the mind and that of the body," he said, according to a report that appeared in *Irish World and American Industrial Liberator* newspaper. "She endeavors to free us from both. I was a poor slave boy, but the priests of that Church did not disdain me. . . . It was the priests of the Church who taught me to pray and forgive my persecutors."

St. Monica's, which had some 600 parishioners at its peak, was still under construction when Tolton—already plagued by poor health—traveled to Kankakee, Illinois, in July of 1897, for a religious retreat. On the way home, he was sickened by the heat on a day when the temperature reached 105 degrees. He died on July 9, 1897, at Mercy Hospital in Chicago, at the age of 43. His funeral services took place in Quincy at St. Peter's, the church helmed by Father McGirr, who had died four years earlier. The Tolton grave in Quincy's cemetery became a pilgrimage site for black Catholics.

Tolton's congregation at St. Monica's was later folded into that of St. Elizabeth's, and construction on the church was never completed. The site is near Stateway Park, and across the Dan Ryan Expressway from US Cellular Field, now home of the Chicago White Sox baseball team. Though the number of black Catholics in America grew impressively in the years following his death, few Americans of any color know about Tolton's brief but committed service to the church. One of his contemporary followers is Archbishop Wilton D. Gregory of Atlanta, the first black president of the U.S. Conference of Catholic Bishops. "When he was alive, his life would probably not have been considered that newsworthy," Wilton told Irvine in the *Seattle Times*. "He lived at a time when to be a person of color automatically meant that you were not a person of significance. So the very fact that he was able to accomplish what he accomplished under severe limitations was to his credit."

Periodicals

Atchison Daily Globe (Atchison, KS), December 28, 1893.
Irish World and American Industrial Liberator, (New York, NY), June 11, 1892.
St. Louis Globe-Democrat, February 16, 1887.
St. Louis Post-Dispatch, November 4, 2002.
Seattle Times, January 13, 2007.

Online

Bauer, Roy, "They Called Him Father Gus," http://shamino.quincy.edu/tolton/tolton2.html (May 18, 2007).
"Father Augustine Tolton First Black Priest," *Roots Web*, http://www.rootsweb.com/~momonroe/tolton.htm (July 4, 2007). □

Marie Tussaud

German wax modeler Marie Tussaud (1761-1850) founded the famous London museum that bears her name early in the 1830s, and it remains one of the city's most popular tourist attractions nearly two centuries later.

Tussaud learned the art of creating lifelike figures out of wax during the French Revolution, claiming to have made her first ones directly from the heads of the recently guillotined. "Tussaud experienced sweeping social changes," noted Marianne Brace, a writer for London's *Independent on Sunday*. "She saw the sacramental nature of kingship in the fated Louis XVI give way to the domestic primness of Queen Victoria; the mob transformed into the mass market. Moreover, her blend of entertainment and information was a precursor of a cultural phenomenon existing today," that of the celebrity icon.

The woman known throughout Britain as Madame Tussaud was born Anna Marie Gresholtz (or Grosholtz) on December 7, 1761, in Strasbourg, a city located in the Alsace region between Germany and France. Little is known of her family background, save for information culled from her 1838 volume of memoirs, which later biographers deemed to be riddled with deliberate falsehoods. She claimed, for example, that her father Joseph was a soldier during the Seven Years' War and died in that conflict before she was born; more reliable sources determined that he was descended from a long line of public executioners in the city. Her mother Anne raised her and took her to Bern, Switzerland, when she became housekeeper to a prominent physician in the city, Dr. Philippe Curtius (1741–1794). Sources note that Tussaud was close to Curtius, called him "uncle," and may have actually been his biological daughter.

Moved to Paris

Tussaud became a Swiss citizen, and learned the art of wax sculpting from Curtius, who had become quite skilled in the art from making anatomical models used in medical-

school classes but also had a secret sideline creating erotic tableaux, or staged scenes, for private clients. Wax modeling of human figures dates back to 3000 BC, and became widespread in medieval Europe; wax effigies of kings were used for funeral processions, and those of saints were made for churches when costlier materials were unavailable. Tussaud and her mother apparently followed Curtius to Paris around 1767, where he opened a wax cabinet, or exhibition space, in 1770. His business grew to be quite successful, and over the years divided into two venues: the Palais Royal, which featured tableaux of the French royal family, and the Caverne des Grands Voleurs, or Cavern of the Grand Thieves, which opened on the Boulevard du Temple in 1782. The latter exhibit showcased famous villains throughout history, and was equally as successful as the royal family exhibit.

The first wax figure that Tussaud did on her own was in 1778 to commemorate the passing of the philosopher Jean-Jacques Rousseau (1712–1778). She also completed a likeness of Rousseau's fellow luminary of the age of Enlightenment, the philosopher Voltaire (1697–1778), who also died that year. She claimed to have come to know several prominent figures in pre-Revolutionary France, and asserted she had even given art lessons to the Princess Elizabeth, the sister of Louis XVI, at the Palace of Versailles, but no records survive that support this claim. The French Revolution began in 1789, and at some point Tussaud was apparently targeted as a royalist sympathizer and sentenced to die by guillotine. Before the execution took place, however, it was learned that she was a skilled wax modeler, and she was

spared the blade and instead recruited to make death masks of the most famous guillotine victims, among them the king, Louis XVI (1754–1793) and his wife, Marie Antoinette (1755–1793). This was her version of events; later biographers cast doubt on the story. The "gruesome replicas soon drew appreciative crowds to Curtius's waxworks," asserted *Sunday Times* writer John Carey, "but it seems probable that he and Marie procured the originals by the simple expedient of hiring them from the executioner, rather than via the serial traumas Marie lays claim to."

Left Husband Behind

The turmoil of the Revolution lasted for a decade, and in the meantime Curtius died, leaving all of his property to Tussaud, including the collection of wax figures. A year later, in 1795, she wed François Tussaud, an engineer. Their first child, a daughter, died, but two sons were born, Joseph and François, who would follow their mother into the waxworks business. Tussaud took her collection to England for exhibition in 1802, along with her four-year-old son Joseph, but when the Napoleonic Wars erupted she was prevented from returning to France and forced to remain in London. She negotiated a deal with the operator of a magic lantern show, Philipstal and his Phantasmagoria, to exhibit the wax collection on the lower floor of the Lyceum Theater. "Once in Great Britain, the shrewd businesswoman sniffed which way the wind was blowing," noted Brace in the *Independent on Sunday*. "Curtius's exhibitions may have delighted the *sans culottes* [the working-class radicals of the French Revolution], but Marie set her sights on the burgeoning middle class who wanted respectable family entertainment."

Many of the figures that Tussaud displayed were French luminaries who had died on the guillotine, and this was a subject of intense fascination for the English middle classes. "Exhibitions illustrating the iniquities of the Revolution were popular in Britain," explained Pamela Pilbeam, the author of a Tussaud biography, in an article that appeared in *Business History*. "What made Marie's unique was that she and Curtius had made the figures from the living, or dead, bodies of their subjects. For the first time, English audiences could really see the features of the guillotined king and queen, whose deaths they had mourned." Tussaud's career in England advanced significantly when she won an important commission from the Princess Frederica Charlotte of Prussia (1767–1820), the Duchess of York. This daughter-in-law of England's king asked Tussaud to create a figure of a little boy, a rather heartbreaking request because Frederica's husband had recently left her for his mistress, and the couple was childless.

In the first decade of the nineteenth century, Tussaud traveled extensively with her collection, still using Curtius's name until 1808. She spent time in Edinburgh, Glasgow, and Dublin, and across the English countryside she often staged her exhibits in newly built town exhibition halls, a fashionable civic fad in the era. "Her odyssey was amazing at the time, when almost no married women worked, and when travelling even a short distance was arduous," wrote Pilbeam in *Business History*. "Marie remained on the road for nearly 33 years in total, visiting 75 main towns and some smaller places. The packing and unpacking alone, without the travelling, and model and costume making, would have been herculean tasks for a young person, but Marie set out when she was already middle-aged, with a tiny child, knowing no-one and speaking not a word of English when she began.''

Opened London Wax Museum

In the early 1820s Tussaud was finally reunited with her son François, who joined the business of the traveling exhibit; her husband apparently remained in France permanently after squandering their investments there. In 1835, Tussaud set up her first permanent exhibition space on Baker Street in London, between Dorset and King streets. The museum featured tableaux of famous historical events, such as coronations and peace treaties, and Tussaud staffed the cash table personally until her death. She published an 1838 volume of memoirs that made much of her supposed connections to the French royals and other well-known personas of the era. None other than one of the most famed authors of the era, Charles Dickens (1812–1870), ridiculed ''her cultural pretensions and her flexible approach to the truth in the character of Mrs Jarley in *The Old Curiosity Shop*,'' noted Carey in the *Sunday Times* article.

Tussaud died on April 15, 1850, in London, at the age of 88. Her museum became one of London's most visited tourist attractions, and remained so well into the twenty-first century. Outposts of the original London museum were opened in Las Vegas, New York City, Amsterdam, Hong Kong, and Copenhagen, Denmark. The exhibits at Madame Tussaud's, still located on Baker Street, are regularly updated to reflect current events and entertainers who have attained celebrity status, and members of England's royal family permit museum personnel to take photographs and measurements to update the likenesses that are on permanent display at Tussaud's in London. ''The enduring success of Madame Tussaud's proves what every smart marketing person knows: Ordinary people get a tingle from being in the presence of celebrities, even if the presence is simulated, and even if the celebrities are those of bygone eras,'' noted John Marcom, a writer for *Forbes* magazine. ''Madame Tussaud's is a sort of three-dimensional version of *People Weekly* or *Entertainment Tonight*.''

Periodicals

Business History, January 2003.
Forbes, May 28, 1990.
Independent on Sunday (London, England), August 27, 2006.
Sunday Times (London, England), July 16, 2006. □

V

Rudy Vallee

American vocalist Rudy Vallee (1901-1986) was among the most popular musical performers of the era between World Wars I and II. He is regarded as the first singer to cultivate the amplification-assisted vocal style known as crooning.

Vallee was a pioneer in other respects as well. Quick to realize the potential of radio as it grew explosively in the 1930s, he hosted what may have been the first example of the variety show, featuring appearances by an assortment of well-established and unknown talents. Part of his appeal was visual; Vallee was an idol who commanded near-fanatical devotion from female fans, and whose love life was played out under a media glare. He was a key contributor to the collegiate image that flourished in popular music as late as the 1960s, and he played an important role in fostering the mainstream acceptance of African-American musical performers. Vallee's contributions to the history of American popular song, in short, have arguably been underestimated.

Started Out on Drums

Born Hubert Prior Vallee on July 28, 1901, Rudy Vallee was a native of remote Island Pond, Vermont, near the Canadian border. He was of French-Canadian background and sometimes used the French form of his surname, Vallée. His father, Charles Vallee, was a pharmacist. The family moved to Westbrook, Maine, outside Portland, during Rudy's childhood, and he took immediately to a snare drum his family gave him when he was 11 years old. He was soon teaching himself piano and clarinet in between school,

work at the family pharmacy, and drum duties in his high school band. When he heard the recordings of saxophonist Rudy Wiedoeft, one of the earliest practitioners of the instrument in the popular sphere, Vallee switched from clarinet to saxophone. At first he used an instrument he subleased from an electrician he met through a part-time job at the Strand Theater in Portland.

Wiedoeft was the source of Vallee's show name; reports vary as to whether Vallee himself adopted it as a kind of homage (he learned to play many of Wiedoeft's recordings by ear) or had the name bestowed on him by college friends because of his enthusiasm for the music of the older saxophonist. Vallee had no taste for pharmacy work. At 15 he ran away and joined the U.S. Navy, but was sent home when it became clear that he was under age. Determined to find a way into show business, he won a spot as a wind player in the Strand's live orchestra and began to perform at dances in the area. In 1921 Vallee graduated from high school and enrolled at the University of Maine. The following year he traveled to New York, where he met Wiedoeft, and made a saxophone record called ''Japanese Sunset.''

Transferring to Yale University, Vallee studied philosophy and Spanish (he was later able to sing convincingly in several foreign languages). He largely financed his own education with saxophone gigs inside and outside Yale, and completed his coursework in segments interrupted by money-making performing trips. The 1924-25 academic year was spent in England, where he played in a band at the Savoy Hotel and encountered the British popular song ''My Time Is Your Time,'' the rights of which he purchased. He would later make the song famous. Back in Maine in 1925, Vallee landed a job in the resort town of Old Orchard Beach that involved singing as well as playing saxophone. Frustrated by the problem of being heard in the large dance

opment of the live radio broadcast. Fan mail began to roll in when Vallee and his band were first featured on radio station WABC in February of 1928. Opening the proceedings with a chipper "Heigh ho, everybody," Vallee soon moved to the more powerful station WOR (which was deluged with 50,000 requests after the station offered listeners a copy of Vallee's picture) and then to a network of stations that collectively put him on the air 25 times a week.

Vallee was equally effective in live appearances at such large theaters as the Coliseum and the Palace Theater, performing not only "My Time Is Your Time" but also a song called "The Vagabond Lover" (which he wrote himself) that became the title of his first film, released in 1929. The film was unsuccessful, but the "Vagabond Lover" nickname remained with Vallee for most of the rest of his career.

When he returned to New York after making *The Vagabond Lover* in Hollywood, Vallee premiered a new NBC network radio show that would run for the next ten years; called *The Fleischmann Hour* at first, after its yeast-maker sponsor, it was soon renamed *The Rudy Vallee Show*. Early episodes of the show featured Vallee singing in front of a 16-piece orchestra, but soon the format was broadened to include other artists, some of whom were emerging talents. Famous performers who got early national exposure on Vallee's show included singer Kate Smith, comedians Fred Allen and Jack Benny, and ventriloquist Edgar Bergen. Top stars such as George Gershwin and Eddie Cantor appeared as well, and Vallee got plenty of exposure for his own vocals, singing hits like "Marie," "The Stein Song" (the University of Maine fight song), "Cheerful Little Earful," and, well in advance of the version in the film *Casablanca*, "As Time Goes By." After the run of the program came to an end, Vallee had a starring role in another show, sponsored by the Sealtest dairy; that show, too, was eventually rechristened with his own name.

At a time when the entertainment industry was largely segregated, Vallee took an inclusive stance toward African-American performers. Among those invited to appear on *The Rudy Vallee Show* were dancer Bill "Bojangles" Robinson and jazz singer and pianist Thomas "Fats" Waller. Vallee in turn performed in clubs in the Harlem neighborhood at the invitation of trumpeter and bandleader Louis Armstrong, among others. Throughout the 1930s, Vallee was one of the biggest stars in the United States, and one widely reported rumor held that a woman in the Midwest had shot her husband after he demanded that she tune the radio to a different station during Vallee's Thursday night time slot. It was especially women, from youthful "bobby soxers" to those in middle age, who flocked to Vallee's shows and were attracted to his debonair, Ivy League image. Touring and appearing at his own Villa Vallee theater on 60th Street in Manhattan, Valley earned about $20,000 a week at his peak, often doing three radio broadcasts, an early theatrical show, and club sets at his Villa Vallee.

halls in which he appeared, Vallee unscrewed the bell from his baritone saxophone and used it as a megaphone when he sang.

In the era before electronic amplification, singers (such as the then-dominant Al Jolson) tended to belt out tunes with operatic fervor. Vallee, who had no vocal training at all, produced a very different sound with his megaphone—quiet, conversational, natural, and above all, intimate. The megaphone, which Vallee used well in advance of the microphone-oriented sound of Bing Crosby and other so-called crooners in the 1930s, became his trademark and was adopted by other singers as well. Vallee graduated from Yale in 1927 and headed for New York City with some friends; the group dubbed themselves the Connecticut Yankees, with two violins, two saxophones (including Vallee's) and a piano. In 1928 they auditioned at the Heigh-Ho Club with Vallee on saxophone and another singer on vocals, but the club owner preferred Vallee's simpler style and demanded that he take on the vocal duties. From then on, although he occasionally played saxophone, Vallee was primarily a singer.

Gained Fans Through Live Radio

Although his voice seemed musically undistinguished, Vallee's style was unusual at the time. According to Vallee's obituary in the London *Times*, the term "crooner" was specifically coined to describe Vallee's singing. His success began to grow almost immediately after he was installed at the Heigh-Ho Club, and he was helped along by the devel-

Enlisted in Coast Guard

World War II brought a hiatus in Vallee's career as he enlisted in the military for a second time, this time in the

Coast Guard. He served as conductor of the 11th Naval District Coast Guard Band before returning to radio in 1944. In the late 1930s and early 1940s Vallee also appeared in a series of now mostly forgotten films that included *Sweet Music, Gold Diggers of Paris,* and *The Palm Beach Story.* He also appeared in the stage revues *George White's Scandals of 1931* and *Scandals of 1936.*

Vallee's career as a hit maker was largely over by the end of World War II, but he maintained visibility through a variety of movie roles, including *The Bachelor and the Bobby Soxer* (1947) and *I Remember Mama* (1948). Often he appeared in character roles in comedies, several of them helmed by director Preston Sturges. In 1949 Vallee married Eleanor Kathleen Norris. She was his fourth wife; the Vagabond Lover's three earlier marriages, to Leonie Cauchois, Faye Webb, and Bettyjane Grier, had ended in divorce. Vallee had no children. He felt ill at ease in the new medium of television, but could still command good crowds for live appearances in a one-man show that showcased his talents as a teller of bawdy tales.

Vallee received some of the best reviews of his acting career for the Broadway play *How to Succeed in Business Without Really Trying* (1961), in which he played a bumbling corporate executive with a passion for golf. The show ran for three and a half years and was followed by a film version (1967), in which Vallee appeared with equal success. "I've come a long way from Vermont and Maine on a highway paved, for the most part, with good fortune," he was quoted as saying, according to his obituary in the *New York Times.* Vallee kept performing, often appearing at benefit concerts, until shortly before his death. He died of a stroke following surgery for esophageal cancer, on July 3, 1986, in Hollywood. His body was returned to Westbrook and buried at St. Hyacinth's Cemetery. A collection of his personal materials is housed at the Thousand Oaks Library in Thousand Oaks, California. Three Vallee autobiographies have been published: *Vagabond Dreams Come True* (1929), *My Time Is Your Time* (1962), and *Let the Chips Fall* (1975).

Books

Smith, Bill, *The Vaudevillians,* Macmillan, 1976.
St. James Encyclopedia of Popular Culture, St. James, 2000.
Vallee, Rudy, *Let the Chips Fall,* Stackpole, 1975.

Periodicals

National Review, August 1, 1986.
New York Times, July 4, 1986.
Times (London, England), July 5, 1986.

Online

"Biography," Rudy Vallee Official Web site, http://www.rudy vallee.com (January 7, 2008).
"Rudy Vallee," *All Music Guide,* http://www.allmusic.com (January 7, 2008).
"Rudy Vallee," Solid! The Encyclopedia of Big Band, Lounge, Classic Jazz, and Space-Age Sounds, http://www.parabrisas .com/d_valleer.php (January 7, 2008). □

Loreta Janeta Velasquez

Cuban-American Loreta Janeta Velasquez (1842-1897) gained renown after the publication of her memoirs, *The Woman in Battle*, which recounted her experiences as a spy and solider for the Confederate Army during the American Civil War. Dressed as a man, Velasquez claimed to have been an active participant in the war; although much of her story has been questioned, modern scholars believe her memoirs contain at least some wholly truthful information.

Upbringing in the United States

Born in Havana, Cuba, on June 26, 1842, Loreta Janeta Velasquez was the youngest child of a wealthy family. Her father, a Spaniard, held an official post in Cuba, and her French-American mother was a daughter of a wealthy businessman. When Velasquez was two years old, her father inherited a cattle ranch in San Luis Potosi, Mexico, and the family relocated there. However, the Mexican-American War erupted in 1846, forcing the family to move to St. Lucia in the British West Indies after Velasquez's father joined the Mexican army. The family ranch did not survive the war and the Velasquez family returned to Cuba.

Loreta Velasquez did not remain in Cuba for long. In 1849, she traveled to New Orleans, Louisiana, where she lived with an aunt and attended school. At the age of thirteen, Velasquez married a Texan army officer; although she remained at her aunt's home at first, she soon fled to be with her husband and became estranged from her family. Velasquez had learned to speak English while living in New Orleans and became familiar with military practices due to her husband's army status.

Began Career as a Soldier

Writing in *Cubans in the Confederacy,* Richard Hall observed that Velasquez had "life-long fantasies of being a second Joan of Arc and having adventures in male disguise." Although these dreams had been ignored during Velasquez's early years of marriage, the death of her and her husband's three young children by 1860 changed her focus. Writing in *The Woman in Battle: A Narrative of the Exploits, Adventures, and Travels of Madame Loreta Janeta Velasquez,* Velasquez commented that "my grief at their loss probably had a great influence in reviving my old notions about military glory, and of exciting anew my desires to win fame on the battle-field." Velasquez decided to raise a battalion on her own and then present it to her husband for him to lead. In order to accomplish this, Velasquez perfected walking and speaking as though she were a man and ordered a special article of clothing that made her figure appear manly. After much practice and perfecting of the costume, Velasquez's illusion was complete. Her male disguise, including a false beard and mustache, passed without question.

Acting as "Lieutenant Harry T. Buford," Velasquez was successful in her recruiting mission, returning with a group of new soldiers and fooling even her husband with her disguise. The soldiers Velasquez had recruited would serve in the Civil War in the first half of 1861. However, shortly after Velasquez's return to the training camp at which her husband was stationed in Pensacola, Florida, a personal tragedy struck; her husband died in a training camp accident, leaving Velasquez alone and grief-stricken. In *The Woman in Battle,* Velasquez stated that "I was now alone in the world, and more than ever disposed to take an active part in the war."

Velasquez, accompanied by her African American servant Bob, traveled to Virginia to attempt to receive a commission in the Confederate Army. Although she received no immediate commission, Velasquez was told that an opportunity might arise; indeed, on July 18, 1861, Velasquez and Bob participated in a skirmish at Blackburn's Ford. Velasquez was now eager to show her talents by leading in a larger encounter.

Fought in Battle

The First Battle of Bull Run took place days later, on July 21, 1861, in Manassas, Virginia. This battle marked the first significant confrontation between the Union and Confederate armies. Many if not most of the soldiers on both sides of the battlefield believed that the war would be short and sure to bring victory to their own cause. However, the battle quickly turned difficult, disorderly, and confusing. During the battle, Velasquez fought under the command of General Barnard Bee, near the center of the Confederate line. Velasquez found the battle to be thrilling; in her memoirs, she said of the battlefield that "it was a sight never to be forgotten—one of those magnificent spectacles that cannot be imagined, and that no description, no matter how eloquent, can do justice to." Ultimately, the Confederate army won the day.

Velasquez next participated in combat on October 21, 1861, at Ball's Bluff, Virginia. The carnage of this battle greatly affected Velasquez, and she determined to find other ways to contribute to the Confederate cause. Settling on becoming a spy, Velasquez obtained female clothing and temporarily set aside her guise as "Buford." Traveling to Washington, D.C., Velasquez tried her hand as a spy. Writing in *Patriots in Disguise: Women Warriors of the Civil War,* Richard Hall noted that Velasquez "found it disconcertingly easy to pry information from Union officers and officials, and yearned for an official appointment in the Confederate detective corps to show what she could do." Again taking on male disguise, Velasquez traveled to seek an assignment from General Leonidas Polk.

Acted as Spy

Polk placed Velasquez, in her guise as Buford, into the detective corps; her duties were checking passes and military leave papers. She stayed at the assignment for only a few weeks, however, and in February 1862, Velasquez traveled to Tennessee, where she fought in the battle at Fort

Donelson. When the fort fell to a siege led by Union General Ulysses S. Grant, she tasted military defeat for the first time. The experience disheartened her, although she managed to escape the fort for Nashville, where she recuperated from the battle. She briefly rejoined the detective corps, but left her position following an injury to her foot believing that a surgeon would discover her disguise during treatment.

Returning to New Orleans, Velasquez was in such a poor state that she was arrested twice: first on suspicion of being a spy, and second on suspicion of being a woman. She confessed to the latter charge and was fined and briefly imprisoned. After her release, she sought to leave New Orleans as quickly as possible. In male garb, she enlisted in a company commanded by Captain B. Moses and left with the company for Fort Pillow. Upon her arrival at the fort, Velasquez showed her credentials as an officer to the commander and relinquished her enlisted position. She traveled to meet the Army of East Tennessee. In April 1862, she fought at Shiloh, briefly commanding her original Arkansas company. The Confederate Army experienced another bitter defeat at Shiloh, and Velasquez was wounded while helping to bury the dead. Disillusioned and injured, Velasquez again returned to New Orleans.

In New Orleans, Velasquez resumed female clothing and began working as a spy. For some time, she managed to smuggled needed supplies to Confederate troops, but was eventually arrested. The charges could not be proved, but Velasquez feared for her safety and escaped the city. She reached Richmond, Virginia, only to be arrested on charges of being a woman again. During her imprisonment, she befriended the prison superintendent and with his support became an official part of the secret service. She carried out a few assignments before again being arrested for being a woman in Lynchburg, Virginia.

Returned to Civilian Life

By the summer of 1863 she had traveled to Atlanta. There, she received some letters from her family and learned that an army officer with whom she had had a romantic relationship after the death of her husband, Captain Thomas DeCaulp, was stationed near Spring Hill, Tennessee. Velasquez had seen DeCaulp at Shiloh, but having been in her disguise as Buford, he had been unaware of her identity; other than this, the couple had communicated only by letter for some time, but considered themselves engaged nonetheless. Velasquez began considering marrying DeCaulp and leaving her life as soldier and spy. She soon learned that DeCaulp was in an Atlanta hospital recovering from an illness; she went to him, confessed her secret to him, and soon they were married. The couple took a short honeymoon and DeCaulp died from a relapse of his illness just afterwards.

Unsurprisingly, Velasquez was upset by his death. Not wishing to return to life as a solider, she resumed her career as a spy for the remainder of the war. She appears to have been sanctioned by the Confederate secret service officials at Richmond. Often, Velasquez took on the identity of a "Mrs. Williams" or another widow in order to gain information. For a time, she served as a double agent in Colonel

LaFayette Baker's Federal detective corps. She convinced Baker that she was working to weaken the Confederacy as part of his corps while in fact sabotaging the Union cause and doing all she could to strengthen the Confederate one. Ironically, toward the end of the war Baker assigned Velasquez to track down a particularly elusive and bothersome Confederate spy, not realizing that Velasquez herself was that elusive and bothersome spy. Finally, Velasquez began to fear detection and fled to Europe.

In 1866, Velasquez joined some other Confederates who moved to Venezuela, seeking to form a new Confederate colony there. Shortly before leaving for Venezuela, she married again to a Major Wasson; however, he died soon after their arrival in Venezuela. Velasquez then traveled through Cuba to the United States. She ventured to the American West, marrying her fourth husband in 1868 and having a son by him. The couple seems to have separated, but Velasquez retained custody of her son. By the 1870s, she and her son had settled in Texas, where she wrote her memoirs in order to raise money for their support. Very little is known about Velasquez's life after the period covered by her memoirs, but she seems to have died around 1897.

Velasquez's Reputation

Because practically all of the information regarding Velasquez's life comes from Velasquez herself—and much of that from her somewhat dramatic memoirs—an obvious question arises: how much of Velasquez's story is true? At least some parts of her story appear to be verified by objective evidence. Velasquez's imprisonment in Castle Thunder was reported in the contemporary Richmond *Examiner.* Official military records mentioned a female spy whose assignment in spring 1864 tallied exactly with that discussed by Velasquez in her memoirs. Several contemporary references have record of a woman traveling under the name "Alice Williams" or "Laura Williams" who had served in the Confederate Army under a likely variation of the name Lieutenant Harry T. Buford. An independent study of the Venezuelan Confederate colony appears to confirm Velasquez's account.

Hall noted in *Cubans in the Confederacy,* "exactly how many of the adventures she reports in her memoirs can be accepted as factual is more problematical." Her frequent use of pseudonyms and the misleading information she provided to some contemporary figures serve to muddy the waters regarding her actual movements and activities. In addition, her memoirs were written quickly and presumably from memory over a decade after the events they discuss, certainly leading to at least some factual misrepresentation, if not outright errors. In *Disarming the Nation: Women's Writing and the American Civil War,* Elizabeth Young observed that "Velazquez was censured from the start on . . . textual inauthenticity." Over the years, many have argued that Velasquez's career was simply too sensational to have been true. Only in the past few decades have some scholars begun to reexamine Velasquez's story, declaring it likely that at least parts of it were accurate. Despite the continuing debate over Velasquez's precise contributions to the Confederate cause, it seems unquestionable that her place in history is assured.

Books

Blanton, DeAnne and Lauren M. Cook, *They Fought Like Demons: Women Soldiers in the American Civil War,* Louisiana State University Press, 2002.

Hall, Richard, *Patriots in Disguise: Women Warriors of the Civil War,* Paragon House, 1993.

Leonard, Elizabeth D., *All the Daring of the Soldier: Women of the Civil War Armies,* Norton & Co., 1999.

Tucker, Philip Thomas, ed. *Cubans in the Confederacy,* McFarland & Co., 2002.

Velasquez, Loreta Janeta, *The Woman in Battle: A Narrative of the Exploits, Adventures, and Travels of Madame Loreta Janeta Velasquez,* Dustin, Gilman & Co, 1876.

Young, Elizabeth, *Disarming the Nation: Women's Writing and the American Civil War,* University of Chicago Press, 1999. □

Pauline Viardot

French singer Pauline Viardot (1821-1910) was a star of London and Paris opera houses in the mid-nineteenth century and one of the most acclaimed mezzo-sopranos of her era.

She was a celebrated figure off-stage as well, noted for an intelligent, vivacious personality that bewitched more than one notable literary or musical persona of the era—despite what was often described in the press as Viardot's obvious lack of beauty. Later in this remarkable life, the retired performer devoted herself to teaching, composing her own works, and maintaining a highly regarded Parisian salon. "Her high artistic standards and discreet private life did much to improve the status of singers, particularly in France where, at the beginning of her career, the prejudice against stage people was still deeply entrenched," declared the *International Dictionary of Opera,* of Viardot's legacy.

Born Michele Ferdinande Pauline García, the future star came from a well known family of Spanish opera singers who were living in Paris by the time of her birth on July 18, 1821. Her mother was Joaquina Sitches, a soprano, and her father, Manuel del Popolo Vicente García (1775-1832), was a highly regarded tenor. He originated the role of Count Almaviva in *Il Barbiere di Siviglia* (The Barber of Seville), the famous 1816 opera from composer Gioachino Rossini (1792-1868), who had written the role especially for Viardot's father. During her childhood years, however, it was Viardot's older sister Maria who was the star of the family. Known by her married name as the *La Malibran,* Maria was a soprano who was one of the first genuine divas of opera, known as much for her stunning vocal range and commanding stage presence as for her tempestuous personality. When Viardot was just a toddler, Maria and the García family traveled to New York, where they performed some of the first opera works in the Italian language ever heard in the city.

Succeeded Sister on Stage

Manuel García provided the first music lessons for both of his daughters, as well as for his son, also named Manuel (1807-1906), who would achieve fame as a baritone and teacher later in the century. However, he reportedly used physical abuse as a teaching tool. An apocryphal story often repeated about Viardot and her sister concerns two passers-by who heard blows coming from window of the García apartment, with one remarking to the other, "Don't be afraid. It's García beating his daughter in order to teach her to hit the high notes better," according to an article written for London's *Guardian* newspaper by Erica Jeal. Manuel senior died in 1832, and Viardot's mother took over her musical education at that point. Another unexpected tragedy propelled Viardot to stardom when she was still in her teens: in 1836 her sister Maria fell from a horse during a hunt in England, and spurned medical attention. For a time, she performed on stage with the help of crutches, but the singer who was called the "Enchantress of Nations" died five months later from her injuries.

Hailed as the next star of the family, Viardot made her concert debut in 1837 at the age of 16 in Brussels. In 1839 she debuted in her first opera, Rossini's *Otello*, playing Desdemona, the role her sister had made famous. But Viardot did not possess the same classical loveliness as her sister, and over the course of her career would consistently be described as homely, with hooded eyes, a receding chin, and a figure that remained unvoluptuous. Nevertheless, Viardot did possess the ability to captivate, both on stage and off. After attending one of the *Otello* performances, England's Queen Victoria (1819-

1901) wrote that she was "delighted and astonished at García's Desdemona, it went to one's heart, and those low notes would make one cry," the monarch declared, according to Jamee Ard in an *Opera News* profile of Viardot. Of the evening's star, the Queen noted that Viardot "is an extraordinary creature, but is, oh, so sadly ugly."

Despite such judgments, Viardot was a notorious *femme fatale*. The French poet Alfred de Musset (1810-1857) became the first of many notables to fall under Viardot's spell, which happened when he witnessed one of the 17-year-old's performances. The French feminist and novelist Amantine Aurore Lucile Dupin, who wrote under the pen name George Sand (1804-1876) became a mentor to Viardot, reportedly warning her to avoid de Musset and steering her instead to a more stable match in the form of Louis Viardot, a writer. The two were married in 1840, and by most reports had a happy, prosperous marriage that produced four children. Her husband, who for a number of years served as director of the Théatre Italien in Paris, was also devoted to his wife's career, and served as her manager until she retired. Sand, incidentally, based her 1843 novel *Consuelo* on Viardot, about a Spanish gypsy who becomes one of the opera world's most famous singers. The novel has also been published under the title *The Countess von Rudolstadt*.

Bewitched Turgenev

Soon after her official debut, Viardot was hailed as the next new star of the opera stage. In 1843 she accepted an offer from the St. Petersburg Opera to appear in *Il Barbiere di Siviglia,* and "the Russian critics were dumbfounded" by her talents, noted Jeal. "Then she endeared herself to the audience even further by including a Russian song as Rosina's lesson piece, so beginning an association with Russian music that would eventually see her become one of its most effective conduits to the west."

Viardot continued to appear in St. Petersburg until 1846, but her first season with the house was notable for some off-stage drama. In 1843 the 25-year-old Russian novelist Ivan Turgenev (1818-1883) became enamored of Viardot, and two years later left Russia for good in order to live near—and sometimes with—her and her family. For the next 40 years, Turgenev either kept his own quarters near the Viardot household or lived with them, and became a father figure to the four Viardot children. The actual relationship between Viardot and her well-born Russian admirer remains unclear, but "when Viardot was away on tour, Turgenev threw flowers at her picture at the exact time of her curtain calls onstage," noted Ard. "Echoes of their life together can be seen in Turgenev's works and Pauline can be found in characters such as Irina (*Smoke*) and Natalia (*A Month in the Country*)," Ard asserted.

The latter work cited, *A Month in the Country,* was a play that is believed to have been inspired by Viardot's brief dalliance with another brilliant luminary of the day, the composer Charles Gounod (1818-1893). Turgenev's drama centers around a young man devastated when Natalia, the married woman he adores, spurns him for a younger admirer. Viardot may have also had a relationship—either platonic or otherwise—with the composer Hector Berlioz

(1803-1869). Berlioz wrote one of the lead roles in his opera *Sapho* for her, and the two also collaborated on a new version of the famous opera *Orphée* from Austrian opera pioneer Christoph Willibald Gluck (1714-1787). Their adaptation, which debuted in Paris in 1859, featured a reworking of the title role from tenor to contralto to suit Viardot's voice, was a sensation in Paris and considered the highlight of her career. She played *Orphée* for three years in Paris, and one of her 150 appearances was attended by English novelist Charles Dickens (1812-1870), who deemed it "a most extraordinary performance," according to Ard. Dickens further described it as "pathetic in the highest degree, and full of quite sublime acting."

Composed Dozens of Songs

Viardot had several other notable achievements during her quarter-century on the stage. Berlioz and others wrote some of the opera world's best-known works with her in mind: the French composer wanted her to premier in two roles in his monumental work *Les Troyens*, as both Cassandra and Dido, and a later compatriot, Camille Saint-Saëns (1835-1921) dedicated *Samson et Dalila* to her and once described her voice as "harsh, pungent, like the taste of a bitter orange," according to Ard. Viardot also premiered *Alto Rhapsody* from German composer Johannes Brahms (1833-1897), and originated the roles Fidès in *Le prophète* from Giacomo Meyerbeer (1791-1864) and *Marie-Magdeleine* from Jules Massenet (1842-1912).

Viardot sang in the range from F3 to C6, and though her voice was not as proficient as her late sister's had been, the younger García "appealed to connoisseurs rather than to the wide public—the thinking person's prima donna," noted the *International Dictionary of Opera.* "She was not physically attractive, but she perhaps compensated for this, on and off the stage, by the use of her intelligence and powerful personality. Her voice, too, was not perfect, but she was able to conceal its defects with great skill."

Viardot retired from the stage in 1863 not long after her *Orphée* triumph, but remained active as a private teacher and an instructor on the faculty of the Paris Conservatory. Prior to this the family had lived for a few years in Baden-Baden, Germany, after being forced to leave France because of Louis Viardot's criticism of Emperor Napoleon III (1808-1873). Over the years Viardot composed more than a hundred songs, four operettas, and the opera *Le dernier sorcier.* Her home on the Boulevard Saint-Germain hosted one of the most noteworthy salons in all of Paris during the mid-nineteenth century, attracting gifted artists and writers such as like Eugène Delacroix (1798-1863) and Henry James (1843-1916), along with political figures and other luminaries of the day. It was in her home that the first private performance of Act II of *Tristan und Isolde,* the famed opera by Richard Wagner (1813-1883), was given when the German composer asked Viardot to sight-read the Isolde role with him at one of her salon events in 1860, five years before the opera's premier in Munich.

Viardot also had a home outside Paris in Bougival, which had been given to her by Turgenev in 1874. Their relationship remained a mystery to literary and music schol-ars more than a century later, but the singer once mused, according to Jessica Duchen in London's *Independent,* "Oh, how many bad things I should have done but for that willpower—the almost inseparable sister of my conscience." Both Louis Viardot and Ivan Turgenev died within months of one another in 1883. Reportedly the Russian's final words accompanied a glance at a portrait of Viardot, at which he exclaimed "What marvelous features." Viardot lived for another 27 years in Paris, dying at her home there on May 18, 1910, at age 88. Reportedly her own last words invoked the title of *Norma,* the great opera by Vincenzo Bellini (1801-1835), considered the most difficult of all soprano roles in opera.

The peak years of Viardot's career came long before phonograph recordings of opera stars became commonplace, and no record of her enigmatic voice survives. Her compositions, however, have been rediscovered and used for recitals, such as one given by Frederica von Stade (born 1945), the American mezzo-soprano, at London's Wigmore Hall in 2006. One of the most important legacies left by Viardot, according to music historians, is her early and ardent support of Russian composers like Nicolai Rimsky-Korsakov (1844-1908), Alexander Borodin (1833-1887), and Pyotr Ilyich Tchaikovsky (1840-1893).

Books

International Dictionary of Opera, two volumes, St. James Press, 1993.

Periodicals

Guardian (London, England), February 24, 2006.
Independent (London, England), February 21, 2006.
Opera News, October 2007.
Sunday Times (London, England), February 6, 2005. □

Louis Vuitton

In 1854 a humble Frenchman named Louis Vuitton (1821-1892) founded his own luggage-making company in Paris, specializing in trunks. Due to Vuitton's eye for detail, exquisite craftsmanship and innovative designs, his luggage became a favorite among European aristocrats. More than 150 years later, the company remains a leading producer of luxury leather goods and ready-to-wear fashions and accessories. Louis Vuitton handbags, with the famed beige-on-chestnut LV monogram, remain a staple among the status-conscious crowd the world over.

Start as Luggage Packer

The son of a poor carpenter, Vuitton was born in 1821 in Anchay, France. At the age of 14, Vuitton, unable to find employment in the provinces, left home and walked more than 275 miles to Paris. Along the way, he picked up odd jobs to finance the trip, working as a stable hand and as a kitchen helper. By 1837 Vuitton had settled in Paris, becoming an apprentice to a Parisian trunkmaker named Maréchal.

Besides building trunks, Vuitton worked as a *layetier,* or luggage packer. During this time, when the wealthy traveled on extensive trips, it was common for them to hire an expert to pack their suits and dresses so they would not wrinkle. Vuitton became a well-respected layetier among Paris's upper echelons. By 1853, Vuitton was the personal packer for Empress Eugénie, wife of French Emperor Napoleon III. Besides packing clothes for the empress, Vuitton also created personal luggage for her.

Invented the Modern, Flat-Topped Trunk

Vuitton liked creating custom luggage, and in 1854 he opened his own workshop in downtown Paris. It did not take long for Vuitton to establish himself as an innovative designer of sturdily built luggage. As stagecoach travel gave way to railways and ocean liners, Vuitton modernized the trunk. In the days of stagecoach travel, trunks were toted on top of the coaches and made with domed lids so the water would slide off during rainstorms. To endure the rugged ride and elements, they were made with iron frames and covered with hog skin.

With the advent of railway and ocean liner travel, luggage needs changed and Vuitton was the first to respond. The luggage needed to be durable, yet space-saving, since most travelers would keep it with them. Vuitton hit upon the idea of making flat-topped, stackable trunks, allowing travelers to take more luggage with them. Vuitton built his flat-lidded trunks using a wood frame, which he covered with a canvas he called "Trianon Grey." The trunks were durable, reinforced with strips of wood and brass rivets. They were also waterproof, which impressed clients who were traveling by ocean liner.

An astute businessman, Vuitton coaxed a steamship builder into giving him the designs for the cargo holds. Vuitton then built trunks to fit. He also made sure his trunks would fit under the beds of ocean liner cabins to give travelers more space. For select travelers, he created trunks with interior drawers and hanging space. With an extensive base of clients from his luggage-packing days, Vuitton had a ready market for his new, innovative trunks.

By 1859 sales were steady, and Vuitton decided to move his workshop out of the city and into the countryside north of Paris, near the Seine River. Being close to the river allowed wood for the trunks to be delivered with ease—by water. The Louis Vuitton workshop remains at this site today. In time, Vuitton relocated his family to the area, building an eye-catching mansion with stained-glass windows next to the factory in Asnières-sur-Seine. His family moved into the home in 1878.

Gained Worldwide Fame for Custom Creations

Vuitton first gained international notoriety for his designs in 1869, when the Empress Eugénie took some Vuitton

luggage to Egypt for the inauguration of the Suez Canal, which opened a direct water route between Europe and Asia. The pasha—or leader—of Egypt liked the handcrafted luggage and ordered some for himself.

In time, Vuitton discovered a niche in creating custom-made trunks for specialized purposes. French explorer Pierre Savorgnan de Brazza ordered a specialized "trunkbed" for an 1876 trip to the Congo during which he hoped to discover opportunities for commerce. When the trunk—covered with zinc and lined with lead to make it waterproof—opened, out popped a cot on legs, complete with a horse-hair mattress.

Vuitton's luggage became so popular that other trunkmakers began copying the Vuitton styles and designs. To combat counterfeiting, in 1876 Vuitton replaced the "Trianon Grey" canvas with a more distinguishing beige and brown-striped design. In time, that pattern was copied, too, so in 1888 Vuitton unveiled a new checkerboard canvas with the words "Marque deposée Louis Vuitton" appearing in the material.

As the Louis Vuitton name became more popular, the company extended its reach with more stores. Its first London store opened in 1885. By 1898 the company had opened an outlet inside a John Wanamaker department store, making it one of the first European companies to hit the United States.

Continued Innovative Designs

Vuitton's son, Georges, proved instrumental in helping the company stay ahead of the competition. In 1890 he invented a special lock with five pick-proof tumblers. When Vuitton died in 1892, Georges took over and in 1896 created the now-famous monogram canvas in an effort to combat counterfeiting. Georges Vuitton took his father's initials and incorporated them in a design with abstract geometric flowers to create what remains today one of the most distinctive—and prestigious—luggage patterns ever invented. It is also one of the most copied.

After Vuitton's death, the company continued to prosper by following its founder's vision of offering custom-made, distinct trunks to fit the demands of the day. Vuitton's descendants created another hallmark design in 1926 when they made a special tea trunk for a maharaja of India for use on tiger-hunting expeditions. This moderate-sized leather trunk contained specialized inner compartments to store tea boxes and cakes, a silver tea pot, china tea cups and a silver water jug. A work of art, the case was featured in *Vogue.*

Over the next few decades, Vuitton snapped up a client base that included 1920s American silent movie star Douglas Fairbanks; Japanese Emperor Hirohito, who reigned during World War II; legendary French fashion designer Coco Chanel; and aviator Charles Lindbergh. In the 1960s, the popular English supermodel Twiggy posed with the round-bodied, monogrammed "Papillon" handbag, sending sales surging.

Company Enjoyed Global Success

Although 150 years have passed since Vuitton opened his shop, the company has remained true to its roots. As of

2007, Patrick-Louis Vuitton, a fifth-generation Vuitton, continued to supervise production of special order pieces. Patrick-Louis Vuitton oversees a department of 185 craftsmiths who churn out about 450 unique special order pieces a year. Many things are still done the way Louis Vuitton did them in the 1850s. Specialized pieces are constructed by one crafter from start to finish. The leather handles are stitched by hand and the brass studs are also nailed by hand.

Special requests to meet the demands of twenty-first century travelers keep the workshop busy. One of the company's more recent custom designs was made for a client who wanted a traveling entertainment center—with solar panels—so the client could play DVDs anytime, anywhere. Speaking to *Harper's Bazaar* writer Jamie Huckbody, Jade Hantouche, head of the Louis Vuitton special orders department, described how the designs must adhere to the founder's original vision. "Today, people know exactly what they want and how it should look," Hantouche said. "But at the same time we have to make sure that the piece is Louis Vuitton. Our rule is that if it is not for travelling then it is not a Louis Vuitton product. Another rule is that if two men cannot carry it then it is also not appropriate."

In 1987 Louis Vuitton merged with Moët-Hennessy, a French maker of fine wines, spirits and perfume, to create a new luxury goods conglomerate called LVMH Moët-Hennessy Louis Vuitton. In 2004, as Louis Vuitton celebrated 150 years, it opened its 318th boutique, this one on New York's famed Fifth Avenue, bringing the number of U.S. outlets to 85. From Argentina to China to Japan, Korea, and Vietnam, Louis Vuitton stores dot the globe. In 2007, LVMH reported a net income of $2.9 billion, buoyed by sales of goods bearing the Vuitton label. It all happened because Louis Vuitton decided to build a better trunk.

Books

Byars, Mel, *The Design Encyclopedia,* Laurence King Publishing, 2004.
Contemporary Fashion, edited by Richard Martin, St. James Press, 2002.
Encyclopedia of Clothing and Fashion, edited by Valerie Steele, Charles Scribner's Sons, 2005.

Periodicals

New York Times, December 17, 1989.
Time, February 16, 2004.
Wall Street Journal, June 4, 1987.

Online

"Louis Vuitton, A Hundred and Fifty Years of Passion," French Ministry of Foreign and European Affairs, http://www .diplomatie.gouv.fr/en/article-imprim.php3?id_article =4471 (January 7, 2008).
"100 Years of Louis Vuitton," *Cigar Aficionado,* http://www .cigaraficionado.com/Cigar/CA_Archives/CA_Show_Article/ 0,2322,619,00.html (January 7, 2008).
"Trunk Show," *Harper's Bazaar,* http://www.harpersbazaar.com .au/Fame/2007-11-13_Fame_Interviews_Trunk + show.htm (January 7, 2008).

"The World of Louis Vuitton: Timeline," Louis Vuitton, http://www.louisvuitton.com/web/flash/index.jsp;jsessionid =ZXEYN40K2HYHGCRBXUXFAHYKEG4RAUPU?buy=1 &langue=en_US (January 7, 2008). □

Vladimir Vysotsky

Russian performer Vladimir Vysotsky (1938-1980) was an underground folk hero in the Soviet Union in the 1960s and 1970s, and attained genuine icon status after his untimely death at age 42.

The widely admired poet, singer, and actor is sometimes referred to as the "Bob Dylan" of Soviet Russia for the subversive themes in the lyrics of his songs and in his poetry. In 1981, on the first anniversary of his death, Serge Schmemann wrote in the *New York Times* about the stature accorded Vysotsky both during his lifetime and now, as fans flocked to his gravesite. "Vysotsky's remarkable popularity was, and remains, in the uncanny power of his ballads to reflect the hardships, degradation, hope, humor, profanity, weariness and drunkenness that officially do not exist," Schmemann noted, "but that so many Russians live by."

Origins Obscure

Vysotsky was born on January 25, 1938, in Moscow, during the darkest period of Soviet history, when the country's increasingly authoritarian leader, Josef Stalin (1878–1953) carried out a plan to root out dissent within the party ranks that sent thousands to labor camps for political re-education; countless others were summarily executed. Vysotsky's family was fortunate to escape relatively unscathed, though his father's status as an officer in the Red Army offered little protection in the Stalinist purges. Other sources claim that Vysotsky probably never knew either of his parents. The official story claims that he was half-Jewish, that his bilingual mother worked as a German translator, but his parents divorced when he was still quite young. Another detail notes that he lived in East Germany for a two-year period when his father was stationed at the Soviet military base in Eberswalde, Brandenburg State.

A few sources claim that Vysotsky spent time in a "corrective" colony while still in his teens in the early 1950s, and another asserts that just a few years later he was briefly enrolled at the Moscow Institute of Civil Engineering. His career as a musician seems to have started in Riga, the capital of Latvia—a country that was once part of the Soviet Union—when he began playing the piano in a restaurant, and drew customers with his skillful imitation of American jazz artist Louis Armstrong (1901–1971). After 1959, he began appearing on the stage of the Aleksandr Pushkin Theatre in Moscow, and five years later graduated from the Moscow Art Theatre Drama School.

That same year, Vysotsky joined the company of the newly formed Moscow Theatre of Drama and Comedy on the Taganka, named after the city square it bordered. The

Taganka Theater was founded by director Yuri Lyubimov (born 1917), who became an important friend, mentor, and collaborator to Vysotsky. Lyubimov staged avant-garde productions that borrowed heavily from German playwright Bertolt Brecht (1898–1956)'s idea that theater should spur intellectual debate among the audience. Despite the strong leftist ideals behind Brechtian epic theater, as it was known, Lyubimov and his corps of actors were often the victims of state censorship for being too iconoclastic. "Distinctly dissident in flavor, the theater fought an endless war against Soviet officialdom, which did its best to emasculate the Taganka's productions or ban them altogether," noted Sergie Roy in *Russian Life.* "No wonder people, especially young people, spent endless hours, sometimes whole nights, in lines, waiting for a chance to get a ticket."

Became Popular Film Actor

Two of Vysotsky's best-known roles at the Taganka were as a guitar-playing Hamlet in a 1971 revival of the Shakespeare classic, and in another title role in *Life of Galileo,* a Brecht play that dramatized how the Italian Renaissance-era scientist and thinker was persecuted by church authorities for his theories—an irony not lost on most Soviet citizens. By this point Vysotsky had also established himself as a film actor as well as both an official and an unofficial recording artist: he appeared in wholesome dramas produced by Mosfilm or Lenfim, the largest of the state-run movie studios, and also enjoyed official sanction with the release of "wholesome Soviet tunes about alpinists, friendship, space heroes and the war dead," wrote former *New York Times* bureau chief in Moscow, Hedrick Smith in his 1976 book *The Russians.* Smith named him as one of a trio of subversive singer-songwriters then enjoying tremendous, though unofficial popularity in the Soviet Union at the time, along with Bulat Okudzhava and Aleksandr Galich.

Vysotsky's scores of unofficial tunes, far more biting in their political viewpoints, were originally heard only among the close-knit circle of the Taganka company regulars late at night at alcohol-fueled affairs. He had started to write them back in the early 1960s, and performed them on a slightly out-of-tune acoustic guitar—itself a prized possession in the Soviet world and a symbol of defiance for its connotations to the West and rock 'n' roll. One early example was "The Song of the Criminal Code," in which he sang:

> We don't need novels, stories and inventions. We keep ourselves enlightened all the time. The best of books to me is the collection Of laws that deal with punishment and crime. . . . Just think about these lines, they are quite simple But more expressive than all novels of the world. Behind them there are barracks, wretched people, Cards, fights and scandals, cheating, and harsh word. . . . My heart jumps moaning like a wounded pigeon When I read articles concerning me. Blood hammers in my temples,—I envision: It's cops who hammer at my door, I see.

In discussing these underground songs, the *New York Times*'s Schmemann noted that Vysotsky's "hoarse voice and poorly tuned guitar recalled the tradition of 'Blatnye' songs, the bawdy and profane ballads of inmates and thieves, but his themes were drawn from everyday life: drunks, bad television shows, jealous wives, prison life, trips abroad, pampered intellectuals, war and food lines. The people grumbled and grumbled, the people wanted fair play." Smith, in *The Russians,* wrote that other Vysotsky tunes were especially appealing to intellectuals and artists. "One writer raved to me about a Vysotsky routine aping the clumsy, ungrammatical talk of a factory director," wrote Smith, "an act with calculated appeal for the Moscow intelligentsia who look down their noses at 'our peasant bosses.' "

Married French Actress

Over the years Vysotsky's underground songs were works recorded on reel-to-reel, and then cassette tape recorders, with copies made for trusted friends. This illegal form of distribution was known as *magnetizdat,* and made Vysotsky an underground folk hero throughout the Soviet Union. "The KGB themselves collect his songs," a journalist told Smith. "They know all those camp tunes of his. They like the jargon of thieves that he uses—they are thieves themselves. Vysotsky knows you can criticize different things here and there, but you can't criticize the system, the Party."

Vysotsky seemed to be walking an ideological tightrope in the decade before his death. After marrying Marina Vlady, a French actress, he was allowed to travel back and forth to the West, but occasionally ran afoul of authorities and the privileges he enjoyed would be temporarily revoked. The dual allegiances may have driven him into the singular refuge of the Soviet citizen, vodka, though Vlady later claimed that he became addicted to morphine, too, in his later years.

In early 1979, Vysotsky was allowed to travel to the United States for several concert dates that kicked off with a performance at Brooklyn College and brought him to audiences in Boston and Philadelphia. Eighteen months later, he was dead of heart failure at the age of 42, a premature passing said to have been brought on by substance abuse. He died during the last week of July, just as Moscow was in the full throes of hosting the 1980 Summer Olympic Games. The sole announcement in the state-run news media came in the form of a small notice mourning the loss signed by the Taganka Theater, which his longtime friend Lyubimov had had to battle with authorities to earn permission to have appear in print.

Vysotsky's memorial service at the Taganka Theatre, attended by the leading names in Soviet performing arts, attracted a crowd of 30,000 mourners outside who convened on Taganka Square—a significant event in a society where all public gatherings were tightly controlled. The event took on a subversive air, and the *New York Times*'s Moscow correspondent, Craig R. Whitney, reported that crowds jeered at police, yelling "Shame, shame, shame!" The journalist noted that "the extraordinary scene, with few parallels in modern Soviet history, was a vivid demonstration of the power of the word in this country." It was also believed to be the largest unofficial public demonstration since 1953, when thousands of Soviet citizens genuinely mourned the death of Stalin.

Anniversaries Became Public Spectacles

When Vysotsky was buried at Vagankovskoye Cemetery a few days later, the crowds swelled to an estimated million in number along with those who lined the roads of the procession route. His friend Vadim Tumanov recalled in an interview with the *Russian Life* writer Roy that the vehicle bearing the coffin was swallowed by the crowd. ''Flowers hit against the glass of the hearse like clumps of earth,'' Tumanov said. ''They came flying from every side, thrown by thousands of hands. The car could not start—not only because the whole square was packed with people, but because the driver could not see the road. The flowers covered the whole of the windshield. It became dark inside. Sitting next to Volodya's coffin, I felt as if I was being buried alive together with him.'' Soviet officials reportedly feared that the funeral would become the catalyst for demonstrations against Soviet control, and shifted some troop divisions nearer to Moscow in the event that the crowds of mourners turned into a genuine uprising.

A year after Vysotsky's death, his grave at the Vagankovskoye Cemetery—a burial site dating back to 1771 that is the traditional resting place for Muscovite poets, painters, and singers—was already becoming a shrine and site of pilgrimage. In July of 1981, police barricades were erected to manage the crowds that came, and the crowds grew as the years passed. Vlady had a spectacular statue erected, depicting him as enclosed by angel wings that also seemed to be stifling his spirit. On what would have been his fiftieth birthday, in January of 1988, thousands of Vysotsky's fans turned up, and the occasion seemed to mark a symbolic turning point for the Soviet Union that year: three years into the leadership of Mikhail Gorbachev, the country was becoming more open to new ideas and more honest in discussing its shortcomings. Within a year, private-enterprise initiatives and multiparty elections would hasten the end of the Soviet era. On the January 1988 anniversary, state media outlets featured programming devoted to Vysotsky's life and art. ''On Moscow radio, an announcer said Monday that Mr. Vysotsky had 'offered scathing criticism of the problems we are now living with and fighting against,' '' wrote *New York Times* journalist Felicity Barringer.

Periodicals

Billboard, July 14, 2001.
New York Times, January 22, 1979; July 29, 1980; July 27, 1981; January 27, 1988.
Russian Life, February 1998.
Times (London, England), August 1, 1980; July 24, 1982.

Online

''Vladimir Vysotsky: The Biography,'' http://www.kulichki.com/vv/eng/bio.html (December 1, 2007). □

Bill Walsh

Bill Walsh (1931-2007) was one of pro football's most successful and innovative coaches. Walsh, whose ability to pinpoint and develop talent was uncanny, led the San Francisco 49ers to three Super Bowl championships and created the "West Coast offense," which many teams have adopted. "Walsh's general thinking process was so far outside the box, the box was a $30 cab ride away," Scott Ostler wrote in the *San Francisco Chronicle*.

Early Life

Willliam Ernest Walsh was born on November 30, 1931, in Los Angeles. His father, a laborer, moved the family around California. Walsh was a running back at Hayward High School, near the San Francisco-Oakland area, but had neither the athleticism nor the grades to obtain a college scholarship. He played quarterback for two seasons at the College of San Mateo and wide receiver at San Jose State, though injuries limited his play. He received his bachelor's degree in 1955; that year he married Geri Nardini of Walnut Creek.

After briefly serving in the U.S. Army at Fort Ord near Monterey, California, Walsh returned to San Jose State as a graduate assistant under Bob Bronzan. According to Tom FitzGerald of the *San Francisco Chronicle,* Bronzan was so impressed that when Walsh completed his studies for a master's degree in education in 1959, he wrote in Walsh's placement file, "I predict Bill Walsh will become the outstanding football coach in the United States."

In 1957, Walsh inherited a losing program at Washington Union High School in Fremont and took the school to a 9-1 record and a conference championship. He also drove the team's bus. He spent his next 18 years as an assistant, all the while moving up the ladder. Walsh's first major college job came in 1960 when Marv Levy—who coached the Buffalo Bills to four straight Super Bowl appearances in the 1990s—named him defensive coordinator at the University of California. In 1963 Stanford hired him as an administrative assistant, recruiting coordinator, and defensive backfield coach.

Began as Professional Assistant

In 1966 Walsh took on his first pro football job, as an offensive backfield coach with the Oakland Raiders of the American Football League (AFL). (The upstart AFL merged into the National Football League [NFL] in 1970). He spent two seasons in Oakland, working Super Bowl II as the Raiders lost to the Green Bay Packers. Walsh later credited Raiders' owner Al Davis, a maverick thinker who micromanaged his coaches, as one of his mentors.

Paul Brown, a renowned innovator who had coached the Cleveland Browns to three NFL titles in the 1950s and before that, four in the since-defunct All-American Football Conference, hired Walsh in 1968 as quarterbacks coach and offensive coordinator for the expansion Cincinnati Bengals. Walsh implemented an offense designed to compensate for the Bengals' lack of talent, and essentially planted the seed of the West Coast offense. It consisted primarily of passes so short they were effectively extended handoffs; runners, meanwhile, approached the line in slants rather than straight ahead.

"We couldn't control the football with the run; [opposing] teams were just too strong. So it had to be the

Things fell into place in 1981, after the 49ers lost two of their first three games. They went 15-1 the rest of the way, and reached the Super Bowl with an enthralling 28-27 comeback victory at Candlestick over the Dallas Cowboys. The winning touchdown pass came with 51 seconds remaining, on what San Franciscans called "The Catch," Dwight Clark's gravity-defying snare of Joe Montana's six-yard pass under heavy pressure. In Super Bowl XVI at Pontiac, Michigan, in January of 1982, the 49ers defeated Walsh's former team, Cincinnati, 26-21, largely on a goal line stand in the second half with San Francisco up 19-7. San Francisco would win two more Super Bowls under Walsh—following the 1984 and 1988 seasons—defeating the Miami Dolphins and Cincinnati, respectively.

Professorial, Yet Brutally Competitive

The 49ers, long an afterthought in their own city, became one of the most visible pro franchises under Walsh. "It was the Walsh-Eddie DeBartolo relationship that sealed the deal," Mark Kreidler said on the ESPN.com Web site. "It was that relationship, with the brash young owner hiring the utterly self-confident coach—a hiring settled over a bottle of wine at a landmark San Francisco hotel—that altered the fortunes of a franchise for nearly a quarter century."

Walsh's methods included a professorial exterior that earned him the moniker "The Genius," and differed sharply from those of his peers. The exterior masked his fiercely competitive side, however. "He handled NFL drafts adeptly and polished his management style by studying the leadership of Civil War and World War II generals," FitzGerald wrote. "When it came to cutting veteran players whom [sic] he thought were on the way downhill, he could be ruthless."

He assembled a team that included Montana, a quarterback who had led Notre Dame to a comeback victory in the 1979 Cotton Bowl after the Fighting Irish trailed the University of Houston by 22 points with eight minutes remaining. Montana had 31 fourth-quarter comebacks as a pro, including Super Bowl XXIII, Walsh's last. He led the 49ers to a 92-yard drive in the final 3:20, and fired the winning pass to John Taylor with 34 seconds left in a 20-16 win over the Bengals.

Walsh's short passing game put the ball into the hands of such speedy receivers as Jerry Rice and Freddy Solomon, and opened up the running game for the likes of Roger Craig. The underrated defense featured hard hitters such as linebacker Jack "Hacksaw" Reynolds and defensive back Ronnie Lott. Walsh scripted the game's first 25 plays, freeing players of decision making under extreme game-day stress. "His coaching style called for singular authority," Nancy Gay wrote in the *San Francisco Chronicle*. "The head coach, he believed, was the pre-eminent power broker. And the ultimate fall guy, if things went sour." Walsh's 1984 team lost only once in 19 games, and shredded Miami 38-16 in Super Bowl XIX in Palo Alto, California, on Walsh's old Stanford field.

Fred VonAppe, who coached under Walsh with the 49ers and Stanford, told FitzGerald: "He's a complex man, somewhat of an enigma. I gave up trying to understand him a long time ago. In a way he has the kind of personality that creates a love-hate relationship." Walsh did exhibit a wacky

forward pass, and obviously it had to be a high-percentage, short, controlled passing game," Walsh told FitzGerald. "The old-line NFL people called it a nickel-and-dime offense. They, in a sense, had disregard and contempt for it, but whenever they played with us, they had to deal with it."

Became the Face of 49ers

Walsh left the Bengals when Brown, who gave up coaching to become team president full-time, bypassed him for the head job for another assistant, Bill Johnson. Walsh became a San Diego Chargers assistant in 1976 and returned to college football as head coach at Stanford University in 1977 and 1978. He led the Cardinal to a 17-7 record over those two seasons and victories in the Sun and Bluebonnet bowls.

After the 1978 season, meanwhile, 49ers owner Edward DeBartolo Jr. purged coaching and front-office personnel. San Francisco struggled to a 2-14 record in 1978, its fifth losing season in six years. In came Walsh, and three years later the 49ers won their first Super Bowl. "It was one of the most remarkable turnarounds in recent sports history," FitzGerald wrote. The road there, however, was rocky for Walsh, who almost quit to pursue management, as San Francisco recorded another 2-14 record his first year there. The 49ers, though, improved to 6-10 in 1980, and pulled off the biggest comeback in NFL history, overcoming a 35-7 halftime deficit to defeat the New Orleans Saints at San Francisco's Candlestick Park, 38-35.

side, even in serious moments. He dressed as a bellboy when the team checked into the Pontiac hotel for Super Bowl XVI—one player did not recognize the coach and got into a tug of war over his bags. He also had his assistant coaches dress up as a hooker, pimp, and drug dealer in an effort to steer his players away from narcotics.

Walsh also launched the Minority Coaches Fellowship program designed to open up coaching opportunities for minorities. Art Shell became the first black NFL coach in the modern era, taking over the Raiders in 1989. "Walsh noticed that being colorblind meant being blind to the fact that all the colors were white," Ostler wrote.

Quit after Super Bowl Victory

Disappointment and bitterness intermingled, despite the three championships and a 102-63-1 record at San Francisco. Drug problems beset the 49ers during a strike-truncated 1982 season that followed the first title, and the 49ers missed the playoffs altogether. In 1983 San Francisco rallied from a 21-0 hole in the National Football Conference title game at Washington, only to lose to the Redskins 24-21 on some calls late in the game that Walsh considered questionable. And after the 49ers lost their only playoff game in 1987, at home, despite having sported the league's best record, DeBartolo stripped Walsh of his title as team president.

Tired of DeBartolo's ways, Walsh quit as coach after the 1988 season, breaking into tears in the dressing room after that Super Bowl victory. He gave up his vice presidency in the organization to announce games on the National Broadcasting Corporation (NBC) with Dick Enberg. Walsh, though normally glib, sounded tentative in the booth. Walsh returned to Stanford and coached the Cardinal from 1992 through 1994. In his first year of the comeback, the Cardinal won ten of 13 games, defeating Penn State in the Blockbuster Bowl. It prompted ESPN analyst Beano Cook to say, as quoted by FitzGerald, "If Walsh was a general, he would be able to overrun Europe with the army from Sweden."

In his later years Walsh served as a consultant and was a frequent public speaker. He returned to the 49ers in that capacity in 1996 and then became the team's general manager, but found the organization in shambles amid a revolving-door management and a federal investigation of DeBartolo's application for a riverboat casino license in Louisiana. He surrendered the general manager's title to Terry Donahue in 2001. Tragedy struck Walsh around the turn of the decade; his wife, Geri, was recovering from a massive stroke she suffered in 1998; his mother died in 2002; and his son, Steve, a radio announcer for KGO in the Bay Area, died at age 46 of leukemia.

He returned to Stanford yet again in 2004 to assist athletic director Ted Leland on special projects and fundraising. As interim athletic director, he oversaw the rebuilding of Stanford Stadium, which was completed in 2006. Later that year he resigned as athletic director.

Coaching Tree Extended Far, Wide

Walsh was diagnosed with leukemia in 2004 and died on July 30, 2007. "For me, personally, outside of my dad, he was probably the most influential person in my life. I am

going to miss him," Montana, a Hall of Famer, told the *Los Angeles Times* and McClatchy Newspapers in an article published in the *Seattle Times*.

The "coaching tree," assistants who became successful head coaches on their own, included George Seifert, who succeeded Walsh in San Francisco; Mike Holmgren, who led the Green Bay Packers to a Super Bowl championship; and Dennis Green, who became one the league's few minority coaches when he took over the Minnesota Vikings. In addition, several NFL coaches use Walsh's trademark West Coast offense.

John Madden, a longtime network announcer who coached the Oakland Raiders to the 1977 Super Bowl title, said of Walsh, as quoted in the *Seattle Times*, "Bill's legacy is going to be that he changed offense. What offense is today is what Bill Walsh was. Offense before Bill Walsh was . . . run on first down, run on second down, and if that doesn't work, pass on third down. Bill Walsh passed on first down, passed on second down and used that to set up the run."

Online

"Bill Walsh, 1931-2007: Coach Was Called 'The Genius,' "*Seattle Times*, http://www.seattletimes.nwsource.com/html/seahawks/2003813728_walsh31.html (October 25, 2007).

"Bill Walsh, 1931-2007: Important Dates in the Life and Times of the 49ers Coach," *San Francisco Chronicle*, http://www.seattletimes.nwsource.com/html/seahawks/2003813728_walsh31.html (October 25, 2007).

"Bill Walsh Was More than Just a Coach," *San Francisco Chronicle*, http://www.usatoday.com/sports/football/2007-08-02-4240183605_x.htm (October 25, 2007).

"Former 49er Head Coach Bill Walsh Dies," *San Francisco Chronicle*, http://www.sfgate.com/cgi-bin/article.cgi?f=/c/a/2007/07/30/BAG57LR8OK21.DTL (October 25, 2007).

"Top of the Line: A Legacy Likely to Go Unmatched," *San Francisco Chronicle*, http://www.sfgate.com/cgi-bin/article.cgi?f=/c/a/2007/07/31/SP6TRA0KU2.DTL&hw=Top+of+the+line+Bill+Walsh&sn=010&sc=441 (October 25, 2007).

"Top of the Line: Weird Ways and Times of a Football Icon," *San Francisco Chronicle*, http://www.sfgate.com/cgi-bin/article.cgi?f=/c/a/2007/07/31/SP6TRA0KT3.DTL (October 25, 2007).

"Walsh a Treasure in Bay Area," ESPN.com, http://www.sports.espn.go.com/espn/columns/story?columnist=kreidler_mark&id=2954718 (October 25, 2007). □

Tapio Wirkkala

Finnish artist and designer Tapio Wirkkala (1915-1985) is considered by some to be the "Father of Finnish design." Trained as a sculptor, he is best known for his clean, modern aesthetic, which became the hallmark of Scandinavian-made decorative and everyday objects. He often employed natural shapes, such as in his icy 1970 interpretation of the Finlandia vodka bottle. Today Wirkkala's works are prized by museums and collectors, fetching increasingly high prices.

At the Forefront of a Design Movement

Tapio Wirkkala began designing beautiful, functional objects in the late 1940s and 1950s, when the Scandinavian design movement that defined much of mid-century applied art was in its infancy. Wirkkala's pieces typically echoed organic shapes and utilized natural materials, adding a modern edge; for example, the wood Wirkkala often employed was laminated industrial plywood. Wirkkala spent much of his life in a log cabin in Lapland in the northernmost part of Finland, where the iciness of the landscape inspired many of his best-known pieces.

Tapio Wirkkala was born on June 2, 1915, to Ilmari and Selma Wirkkala, in the small port city of Hanko in the south of Finland. His father designed monuments, and the young Wirkkala was perhaps inspired by this example. In 1933 Wirkkala entered the Central School of Industrial Design in Helsinki, Finland. He studied sculpture at the school, completing the program in 1936. After graduation, Wirkkala began working as a commercial artist for an advertising agency, strengthening his graphic design skills and competing in design competitions outside of his regular job.

In 1939 Wirkkala's professional career was temporarily suspended by the outbreak of war in Europe. During World War II he served in the Finnish military; however, his artistic career continued throughout the war, when he won two design competitions sponsored by the Finnish army. For the first, he successfully designed a knife using boot leather, antlers, and telephone wire. For the other competition, he followed in the steps of his father, designing a monument, titled *Lion,* to honor the capture of the Soviet city Petrozavodsk by Finnish forces in 1941. This latter piece is now on display at the Naval College in Helsinki. Wirkkala's prize for these wins was a lengthy leave from the military. While on this leave of absence, Wirkkala met ceramic artist Rut Bryk at a party, and the two married in 1945. The couple would later have two children: a son, Sami, and a daughter, Maaria. Both of Wirkkala's children are themselves involved with the arts, carrying on the family tradition.

World War II was devastating to Finland, and the country was forced to rebuild its postwar economy. The country turned to design as a basis for new development. Writing in the *Washington Post,* Linda Hales noted that "design—essentially a marriage of art and industry . . . played off a long tradition of art and craft, which Wirkkala was already busy expressing." In 1946 Wirkkala began working for the Iittala glassworks in Helsinki; the company later expanded to include other aspects of design, and Wirkkala designed both art glass and commercial pieces that were produced by the company throughout his career. His first major piece for Iittala was *Kantarelli* (Chanterelle), a glass vase that echoed the shape of the chanterelle mushroom; the piece was exhibited in Milan to much critical praise. Suzanne Slesin commented in the *The New York Times* that these works "first brought [Wirkkala] international acclaim. The organically shaped pieces came to be thought of as the symbols of the best of Finnish design of the 1950's." Iittala produced versions of this design through 1960.

Found International Success

In 1947 Wirkkala drew on his skills as a commercial artist to enter a competition sponsored by the Bank of Finland to design new bank notes for the country. His works won both the first and second prizes, and were later produced as currency. A few years later at the 1951 Milan Triennale, a major international design exhibition, Wirkkala again garnered international recognition, this time for his laminated wood serving pieces, where his work won the Grand Prix at the exhibit. One leaf-shaped plywood serving tray caught the eye of Elizabeth Gordon, an editor at the American magazine *House Beautiful*; the magazine went on to declare the piece "the Most Beautiful Object of 1951." These nature-inspired serving platters channeled the driving theme of the emerging Scandinavian design movement; Wirkkala's biography in *Contemporary Designers* stated that Wirkkala "was a product of an age in Scandinavia when the ideal came to be commonly held that ordinary people had a right to a comfortable home that was both functional and esthetically pleasing."

In 1951 Wirkkala was a co-recipient of the first Frederick Lunning Prize, along with Hans Wegener; the award recognizes outstanding work by Scandinavian designers as selected by their peers. To round out the achievements of this highly successful year for Wirkkala, he was named the artistic director of Helsinki's Central School of Industrial Design; he remained in that position until 1954.

Wirkkala continued to achieve professional and artistic success throughout the ensuing years. On many occasions, Wirkkala or his works served to represent his native land. In addition to the Finnish bank notes of the 1940s, Wirkkala designed four stamps commemorating the 1952 Summer Olympics, which were held in Helsinki. The following year his work appeared in a traveling exhibition put together by the Arts Council of Great Britain. At the Milan Triennale of 1954, Wirkkala not only exhibited but also organized the overall Finnish department of the exhibition, and his work again won a prize. That same year, Wirkkala's work appeared in the United States as part of the traveling "Design in Scandinavia" exhibition. Wirkkala also created the promotional poster and catalogue that supported the exhibition.

In 1955 Wirkkala himself came to the United States to work for a New York City design firm headed by Raymond Loewy. The Smithsonian Institution that year organized a traveling exhibition displaying works by Wirkkala and his wife, a ceramicist. Returning to Europe in 1956, Wirkkala began designing for the respected German design company Rosenthal AG. At about the same time, he established himself as an independent designer. In 1957 he again displayed works at the Milan Triennale, and also won the prestigious Pro Finlandia medal.

Wirkkala helped represent his country on the international stage in 1958, when he organized the Finnish pavilion at Expo 58, popularly known as the World's Fair, in Brussels, Belgium. The artist also exhibited works at this event, winning an award. That same year, some of Wirkkala's works were shown as part of a group exhibition that traveled through parts of South America, including Brazil, Argentina, and Uruguay.

A Decorated Career

In 1960 Wirkkala won the Silver Cutlery Prize given by the New York Museum of Contemporary Crafts; his winning work was shown as part of an accompanying exhibition at the museum. He also took top honors at that year's Milan Triennale. Although best known for his glassware, Wirkkala produced other functional pieces. For example, in 1961 he designed a steel and black nylon reinterpretation of the traditional Finnish puukko knife; this piece, manufactured by the respected knife company Hackman, has remained one of his best known designs.

Wirkkala continued to exhibit throughout the 1960s, with significant shows at Amsterdam, Netherlands; Hamburg, Germany; and Kassel, Germany. He also showed at the Milan Triennale in 1964, winning a silver medal. That same year he was recognized by Great Britain's Royal Society of Arts as an Honorary Royal Designer of Industry. In 1965 he created a sculpture that accompanied a jewelry exhibit at Jablonec, Czechoslovakia. During this time, Wirkkala also won numerous awards for his ceramics pieces.

In 1968 the Finnish Cultural Foundation gave Wirkkala an honorary award; the designer also became chairman of the Finnish Government Industrial Arts Commission, a post he held until 1973. That year was also Wirkkala's last time showing at the Milan Triennale. In about 1972, Wirkkala ceased his work designing exhibitions, although he continued to produce artistic pieces.

Throughout his career, Wirkkala designed pieces that reflected the patterns of nature, particularly the shapes and facets of ice. In 1970 he designed a bottle for the Finnish vodka manufacturer Finlandia. Hales noted that "Wirkkala gave it a surface textured like ice, which conveyed all the romance of the Far North." This piece became perhaps Wirkkala's most recognizable design, and was closely associated with the Finlandia brand for 30 years. In 2000 the company introduced a new design, which some consider to be a lesser artistic work.

Later Years and Legacy

Although Wirkkala became less active during the later 1970s and 1980s, many in the arts communities continued to acknowledge his lifetime of work and furtherance of the Scandinavian design movement. London's Royal College of Art awarded Wirkkala an honorary doctorate in 1971, and the following year he was made an honorary academician in Helsinki. Two Mexican design academies extended honors to Wirkkala in 1982. The Finnish government also made Wirkkala a Knight of the Order of the White Rose, an honorary organization that recognizes meritorious contributions of Finnish nationals.

Wirkkala died on May 19, 1985, at his home in Esbo, Finland, as the result of a heart attack. In 2003 the Tapio Wirkkala-Rut Bryk Foundation was established in Helsinki. According to the Foundation's Web site, "The Foundation seeks to pass on the innovative artistic and intellectual legacy of this designer couple to present-day designers." It holds a large collection of objects and drawings, paintings, and photographs of the works created by Wirkkala and his wife, and boasts many prominent creative and academic individuals on its board of trustees, showing the continued respect and influence of Wirkkala's work more than 20 years after his death. To continue Wirkkala's legacy, the foundation has hosted symposia on topics such as the interconnectivity of design disciplines, the expression of the natural world through art, and the influence of design on culture and society.

Today Wirkkala remains respected as an innovative artist and designer. Many acknowledge his creative influence in the growth and popularity of twentieth-century Scandinavian design; some even call Wirkkala the "Father of Finnish Design." *The Oxford Companion to Twentieth-Century Art* argued that "Wirkkala combined in his a work a feeling for the stark bleakness of the Lapland wilderness with the beauty of the most modern technology." The artistic merit of this combination accounts for the esteem in which collectors and design critics hold Wirkkala's work. The continued popularity of his pieces has led to high auction prices. In the twenty-first century, major exhibitions of Wirkkala's work have been staged at design, architecture, and art museums in his native Finland and around the world. Writing in an exhibition catalog that accompanied one of Wirkkala's shows at the Stedelijik Museum, Wil Bertheux suggested, "Let's . . . be thankful for designers like Wirkkala, who, with love of trade and material, give shape to the everyday things that surround us."

Books

Contemporary Designers, 3rd ed., St. James Press, 1997.
The Oxford Companion to Twentieth-Century Art, edited by Harold Osborne, Oxford University Press, 1981.
The Stedelijk Museum, *Tapio Wirkkala*, 1976.

Periodicals

New York Times, May 23, 1985.
Washington Post, May 4, 2003.

Online

"Finnish Designers: Tapio Wirkkala (1915-1985), " Finnish Design, http://www.finnishdesign.fi/designerbio?id = 899034 (January 10, 2008).
"Tapio Wirkkala," http://www.tapio-wirkkala.de/e/index.shtml (January 10, 2008).
"Tapio Wirkkala," Virtual Finland, http://www.virtual.finland.fi (January 10, 2008).
Tapio Wirkkala Rut Bryk Foundation, http://www.wirkkalabryk.fi (January 9, 2008). □

Witkacy

The Polish artist, playwright, novelist, photographer, and philosopher Stanislaw Ignacy Witkiewicz (1885-1939), who used the single name of Witkacy, produced a richly experimental and often surreal body of work in each of the several forms of expression he took up. Underlying much of his work were the themes of individualism and the power of art as responses to a chaotic and disintegrating universe.

Only moderately well known during his own time and almost completely suppressed during the early decades of Communist rule in Poland, Witkacy posthumously became the subject of a major revival in Poland, and increasingly often abroad, toward the end of the twentieth century. A foe of both Communism and fascism, Witkacy turned into a prophet of hedonism. His writings also refer to illicit drugs and recreational sex, which he saw as hedonistic outlets for people living in fundamentally repressive societies. And, in spite of the madcap, disorganized quality of much of his creative work, Witkacy was an uncannily accurate prophet. In addition to predicting the sensual excesses of the student counterculture, Witkacy foresaw the rise of the modern dictator, the growth in the international power of Chinese Communism, and the attraction of Eastern mysticism for disenchanted youth in the West. His surreal artworks have been shown in several major exhibitions outside Poland, and his sprawling novel *Insatiability* (1930) has been published in English and then issued in a new revised edition in 1996.

Educated at Home

Stanislaw Ignacy Witkiewicz was born in Warsaw, Poland, on February 24, 1885, but grew up in the elegant mountain resort city of Zakopane; some of his first artistic efforts depicted the scenic Tatra Mountains that surrounded the city. His father, also named Stanislaw, was a landscape painter regarded as perhaps Poland's leading artist of the late nineteenth century, and his mother, Maria Pietrzkiewicz, was a pianist and music teacher. The elder Witkiewicz homeschooled his son and made strong attempts to mold him in his own image, but the son took the name Witkacy, derived from his last and middle names, in 1912, after a period of psychoanalysis. Witkacy (vit-KAH-tsuh) was fond of making puns on his new name, sometimes spelling it Vitecasse ("breaks quickly") in the French fashion.

Broadly educated in painting, music, literature, drama, and philosophy, Witkacy wrote his first play, *Cockroaches,* at the age of eight, printing it himself on a toy press. The play depicts an attack by a cloud of airborne roaches that come from America. Among his childhood friends were the pioneering Polish anthropologist Bronislaw Malinowski and the composer Karol Szymanowski. As a teenager Witkacy wrote extensive essays on German philosopher Arthur Schopenhauer and other philosophical subjects, but his first love, and the field in which most of his important ideas first emerged, was art. In the years after 1900 he painted some naturalistic landscapes under his father's influence, but it did not take him long to discover the new currents that were roiling the world of European art.

Travels to Russia and Italy facilitated his explorations, and his paintings took a less representational turn after he saw an exhibition of Paul Gauguin's paintings in Vienna in 1906 and traveled to Paris the following year. He settled in the French region of Brittany for several years and studied with one of Gauguin's Polish students, Wladyslaw Slewinski. Gauguin's flat planes of intense color influenced Witkacy's landscape paintings, but he was also interested in fantastic themes of monsters and horror, and in portraiture that might distort the image of the subject for psychological effect. Portraits would be an especially important segment of his mature output. In 1910 Witkacy wrote a novel, *The 622 Downfalls of Bungo.* By 1913 he had become engaged to Jadwiga Janczewska and had mounted a solo exhibition at the Society of Friends of the Fine Arts in the Polish city of Krakow.

Witkacy's life turned upside down the following year when Janczewska, using Witkacy's gun, committed suicide. He then decided to accompany Malinowski on one of his pioneering research trips to the Trobriand Islands in what is now Papua New Guinea. The relationship of the two men was close but volatile (scholar David A. Goldfarb has suggested that it may have been based on homosexual attraction), and their friendship came to an end after they disagreed violently over the nature of the tribal religious rites they had witnessed. Malinowski saw them as essentially primitive, but Witkacy placed them in the context of his developing ideas about art as a basic human response to the puzzle of existence.

Fought for Russian Army

Returning to Poland, Witkacy agreed to join the Russian military—something he was expected to do, for Russia controlled much of Poland at the time. But his father, who was strongly anti-Russian, was aghast, and died soon afterward. The aristocratic Witkacy was untroubled by life in the army; military conflict supported his philosophical view of the world as violent and chaotic, and he later, according to an article by Adam Shatz in the *Nation,* "claimed to have hit upon his philosophy of art as 'an affirmation of Existence in its metaphysical horror' during an artillery barrage." During this period Witkacy made a photographic self-portrait showing himself, in uniform, reflected in a series of mirrors. He experienced trench warfare during the later stages of World War I and was wounded in Ukraine. Witkacy witnessed the dissolution of the old order, the failure of democratic forces, and the installation of Communism in Russia in 1917.

Soon, however, Witkacy became disillusioned with socialism and returned home to an independent Poland. For much of his life he lived in his hometown of Zakopane, where he was regarded as something of an eccentric intellectual. He had a fondness for odd stunts, such as luring his friends into absurd situations, and, noted Mark Rudnicki on the University of Buffalo's InfoPoland Web site, "He kept a formal list of his friends in order of importance. His best friend would be in the first position and so on. In the event that a 'friend' somehow irritated him or, perhaps, pleased him in some way he would be demoted or promoted on the list as the case may be."

Beginning around 1920, Witkacy entered a period of intense literary productivity. Most of his philosophical treatises date from the early 1920s. In the field of aesthetics, Witkacy outlined what he called the Theory of Pure Form, which argued against realism in art and saw artwork (whether visual or dramatic—he did not count novels, which were necessarily representational, as art, although he wrote several massive novels) as a primal response to the basic conditions of existence. Many of his ideas were summarized in the 1920 book *Introduction to the Theory of Pure Form in the Theatre*. Witkacy also wrote books and essays on social themes. He believed that European society was in decline as the individual artistic spirit was being overwhelmed by the forces of democracy and collectivization, which he saw as closely linked. Witkacy's artistic ideas had parallels with those of early abstract artists such as Russia's Wasily Kandinsky, and his social writings paralleled those of European conservatives such as Oswald Spengler and José Ortega y Gasset. In the breadth of his thinking, however, Witkacy was unique.

Witkacy's career as an adult dramatist began with a play called (in English—Witkacy's punning Polish titles often pose major problems for translators) *Tumor Brainiowicz*, performed in Krakow in 1921. He wrote some 30 plays. Among the most famous are *Gyubal Wahazar* (1921), a play that seemed to anticipate the rise of Adolf Hitler and other leaders who commanded cultlike devotion, and *The Madman and the Nun* (1925), depicting a mental hospital in which it is unclear whether it is the doctors or the patients who are insane. Many of Witkacy's plays went unproduced until after his death; they were rediscovered in the 1950s and 1960s and hailed as precursors of the European theatrical movement known as the Theater of the Absurd.

Established Unorthodox Portrait Studio

Around 1925, with funds running low, Witkacy established the S.I. Witkiewicz Portrait Painting Studio, boasting, according to Shatz, that: "The customer must be satisfied. Misunderstandings are ruled out." Paradoxically, however, Witkacy wrote in a set of studio rules (which he published in 1928, as quoted by Rudnicki) that "Any sort of criticism on the part of the customer is ruled out." Customers could choose from one of five portrait types (with several subtypes) designated by the letters A through E, ranging from the most conventional (type A) to "spontaneous psychological interpretation at the discretion of the firm" (Type E, as translated by Rudnicki). An option was to have Witkacy execute the portrait under the influence of tobacco, alcohol, caffeine, or stronger drugs, singly or in combination, all of which he would list on the painting next to his signature. Originally sold very cheaply, Witkacy's portraits today command prices of more than $5,000 apiece.

Witkacy devoted much of the late 1920s to a pair of novels. *Farewell to Autumn* appeared in 1927, and his most ambitious and controversial work, *Insatiability* (Polish title: *Nienasycenie*), was published in 1930. *Insatiability* was a gigantic satire with elements of science fiction, set in the late twentieth century. It revolves around a brewer's son named Genezip Kapen (the name is a Polish-French pun, for "je ne zipe qu'a peine" meaning "I'm on my last legs" in French) who experiences the last days of European civilization amid a haze of sexual and spiritual adventures: Poland is invaded by a collectivized Chinese army, a "mobile Chinese wall," despite the efforts of Poland's incompetent dictator, Kotzmolochowicz. A Malay mystic purveying a tranquilizing "Murti-Bing pill" appears in the later stages of the novel, anticipating the drugs-as-social-control themes of Aldous Huxley's *Brave New World*.

In the 1930s Witkacy watched uneasily as the rise of Nazism in Germany appeared to confirm his gloomiest prophecies about the brutal conformity toward which modern society was headed. He devoted the bulk of his time to a philosophical treatise, *The Concepts and Principles Implied by the Concept of Existence* (1935), but also found time to write, producing a satirical essay about Poland, *Unwashed Souls*; his last play, *The Shoemaker*; a book on drugs (*Nicotine, Alcohol, Cocaine, Peyote, Morphine, Ether*, 1932); and parts of several new novels. He established the Artistic Theatre in Zakopane (a Witkacy Theatre was founded in Zakopane in 1984 in his honor). In September of 1939, Witkacy and his longtime companion, Czeslawa Korzeniowska, along with many other Poles, fled eastward as Germany invaded Poland from the west. Trapped by the simultaneous advance of Soviet Russian troops from the east, he and Korzeniowska made a suicide pact. He tricked Korzeniowska into avoiding the lethal dose of barbiturates that he himself took on September 18, 1939, in Jeziory, Poland. It was thought that he had been buried in a grave in what is now Ukraine. When the Polish government decided to honor him with a reburial on Polish soil in 1988, his casket was exhumed, but when X-rayed it turned out to contain not Witkacy's remains but those of an unknown Ukrainian woman. His final resting place remains unknown, and it is likely that he played one final prank on an unfriendly world.

Books

The Witkacy Reader, edited by Daniel Gerould, Northwestern University Press, 1992.

Periodicals

Edinburgh Evening News, March 3, 2005.
Nation, May 6, 1996.
New York Times, April 24, 1998.
Science Fiction Studies, November 1979.
Times (London, England), October 25, 1993.
Times Literary Supplement (London, England), July 21, 1978.

Online

"Argonauts of the Western Pacific: S. I. Witkiewicz and Bronislaw Malinowski," Echo: The Virtual Salon of NYC, http://www.echonyc.com/~goldfarb/mal-wtkc.htm (January 8, 2008).
Contemporary Authors Online, Gale, 2008. http://galenet.gale group.com/servlet/BioRC (January 8, 2008).
"Stanislaw Ignacy Witkiewicz," Polish Philosophy Page, http://www.fmag.unict.it/~polphil/PolPhil/Witk/Witk.html (January 8, 2008).
"Stanislaw Ignacy Witkiewicz (Witkacy)," culture.pl, http://www.culture.pl/en/culture/artykuly/os_witkiewicz_stanislaw_ignacy (January 8, 2008).
"Stanislaw Ignacy Witkiewicz; Witkacy (1885–1939)," University of Glasgow Department of Slavonic Studies, http://www.arts.gla.ac.uk/Slavonic/Witkiew.htm (January 8, 2008).
"Witkacy: Stanislaw Ignacy Witkiewicz 1885-1939, Info Poland, http://info-poland.buffalo.edu/classroom/witkacy/witkacy.html (January 8, 2008). □

Wladyslaw II Jagiello, King of Poland

The Lithuanian-Polish monarch Jogaila (c. 1351-1434), known in Polish as Wladyslaw II Jagiello, was a key figure in the history of both Lithuania and Poland during the medieval period.

Geopolitically speaking, the most significant aspect of Jogaila's 57-year reign as Lithuania's monarch was that it inaugurated a union between Lithuania and Poland, known as the Polish-Lithuanian Commonwealth, that would last for centuries, even though the two countries shared little in terms of linguistic or cultural heritage. He brought Christianity to Lithuania, which had been Europe's last pagan state. In Poland he maintained the growth in power and influence that had begun under the Piast dynasty, and, with the assistance of his sainted bride, Jadwiga, reestablished a university that exists today as one of Europe's oldest. In a part of the world long marked by intense national rivalries, perspectives on Jogaila (pronounced "yo-GUY-la") and his legacy have varied according to the locations of those who hold them, but few doubt his overall importance in European history.

Born Into Complex Political Situation

Jogaila's early life has remained elusive to historians. He is generally thought to have been born in the early 1350s in the Lithuanian capital of Vilnius, with Norman Davies, author of *God's Playground: A History of Poland,* suggesting a date of 1351 (some Polish historians have argued in favor of a later date, which would help to explain Jogaila's record of fathering children in late life). His father was Lithuania's grand duke (really a king) named Algirdas, and his mother was a Russian princess. Lithuania in Jogaila's youth was a large kingdom, but one beset by enemies on all sides. These enemies included Russians and Central Asian Tatars to the east, a powerful German religious-military order known as the Teutonic knights to the northwest, and Poland itself, which was growing and unifying.

In 1377 Jogaila ascended to the Lithuanian throne as co-regent with his uncle, Kestutis, but this situation, with agents of the Teutonic Knights doing their best to foment discord, was unstable from the beginning. In 1382 Kestutis was imprisoned on Jogaila's orders, and a few days later he was killed—by whom is not definitively known, but Jogaila himself remains a primary candidate. Kestutis's son Vytautas escaped to German lands and later emerged as Jogaila's rival. External threats, however, kept the lid on Lithuanian internal rivalries.

Jogaila had joined his father in carrying out plundering raids on Polish territory, and he had no particular love for the Polish people, who worshiped what he called the German god and whom he regarded as uncouth (Polish chroniclers would later express surprise that Jogaila bathed and shaved daily). However, the young king realized he was in serious need of allies, and Poland seemed the least expansionist among the possible candidates. Lithuania and Poland had a common enemy in the Teutonic Knights, who occupied prime real estate on the Baltic seacoast and tended when possible to obliterate local governments in the areas they conquered. Although Jogaila's mother was Russian and urged him to make peace with the Russians and marry a Russian princess, his father had been sworn to recover Lithuanian lands lost to the growing Orthodox power to the east.

Another attraction of a Polish alliance from Jogaila's point of view was the availability of the young Polish princess Jadwiga (herself of a varied ethnic background produced by earlier political marriages). For Poland, chartered by the Pope to bring Catholicism to the lands to its east, an alliance also made sense. Negotiations between the two countries began (probably at Poland's initiative), and the Kreva Union Act was signed by Jogaila and a group of Polish barons on August 14, 1385.

Formed Dual State

The agreement (whose text has never surfaced but has been pieced together by historians) made Jogaila King of Poland and specified that Lithuania and Poland would henceforth operate as separate states under a common crown. The Machiavellian instability of political life at the time made both parties feel that the arrangement might well be temporary, as did the lack of cultural continuity between the two countries. The Lithuanian and Polish languages are only slightly related, and Jogaila never learned to speak Polish well (although Latin would have been a language common to some in both courts). Jogaila, now known in Poland as Wladyslaw (or Ladislaus) II Jagiello (pronounced "ya-GYAY-wo," the Polish form of the name Jogaila), would marry Jadwiga, and Christianity would be imposed in Lithuania. Jogaila upheld this part of the deal, translating the Lord's Prayer and the Credo of the Catholic mass into Lithuanian himself. The ancient Lithuanian pagan religion (which, among other beliefs, worshiped pigs as harbingers of the afterlife) went underground and persisted for several centuries.

The effect of these developments on Jadwiga (or Hedwig), who was about 12 years old, can only be guessed. She probably could not even converse with her new husband, with whom she had no language in common, and the marriage remained childless for some years. She threw herself into charitable works, spawning a body of legends that eventually led to her canonization in 1997 by Pope John Paul II. The couple worked to re-establish the University of Krakow, which had fallen into decline after the death of its founder, Poland's King Casimir III. The university flourished after it reopened in 1400, offering courses to both Poles and Lithuanians (in Latin); Jogaila was the first student registered. It is known today as the Jagiellonian University in honor of Jogaila and Jadwiga, who died in 1399 after the birth of a daughter, Elizabeth, who also died.

Especially after Jadwiga's death, Jogaila's status as a foreign king was an ambiguous one. He was naturally treated with suspicion by powerful Poles, who dispatched spies to keep tabs on his activities. Zbigniew Olesnicki, the

Catholic Bishop and later Cardinal of Krakow, emerged as a major antagonist who did what he could to frustrate Jogaila's initiatives, including the recognition of Vytautas, with whom Jogaila had been reconciled, as Lithuania's king. Jogaila's personal life was not particularly happy. He married again at the behest of the Polish nobles, but his second wife, Anna, was unattractive, and Jogaila refused to live with her. She, too, died after bearing a daughter, and Jogaila, to intense local criticism, married a woman named Elizabeth Pilecua whom he chose himself.

In spite of all these factors Jogaila gained a reputation as a linchpin of the Polish state (and when he thought of abdicating and returning to Lithuania, the Poles asked him to stay on). He increased the powers of the Polish nobility. But the most important factor working in his favor was his skill as a diplomat and military leader. Conflicts between the Teutonic Knights and the Slavic peoples intensified in the early 1400s, culminating in 1410 as Jogaila raised a vast army of Polish, Lithuanian, Ukrainian, Tatar, Czech, and Hungarian troops for a surprise invasion of Prussian lands. At the German town of Grünwald, on July 15, 1410, these motley forces faced those of the Germans.

Defeated Teutonic Knights

According to Davies, the Bishop of Pomerania, the Teutonic leader, sent Jogaila a pair of swords with a note stating that it was "for your assistance." Jogaila replied, "We accept the swords you send us, and in the name of Christ, before whom all stiff-necked pride must bow, we do battle." At the battle's end, the technically sophisticated German forces were routed, and the Polish army was credited with technical brilliance, moving men and machinery across the Vistula River on pontoon bridges. Poland obtained rights to free trade along the length of the Vistula, and German national pride received a blow that smarted until the outbreak of World War I more than five centuries later, even though Jogaila was noted as a leader who was merciful to vanquished enemies.

That battle proved to be Jogaila's greatest accomplishment. In later years he tried to undo what he had done and restore Lithuania's full sovereignty, even making common cause with the hated Teutonic Order and other German groups in attempts to install first Vytautas and then his younger brother Svitrigaila on the Lithuanian throne against Polish wishes. In the words of an early historian quoted by Vanda Sruogiene of the *Lithuanian Quarterly Journal of Arts and Sciences,* "old Jogaila was a Lithuanian, and he remained one. Such an action [support of Vytautas], in spite of the consequences, was an idea close to his heart." Ironically, Jogaila is often viewed as a negative figure in Lithuanian historical accounts: he is seen as a leader who helped Poland but set back the cause of Lithuanian identity.

His situation was made more troublesome by the fact that, although he had been married three times and had several children, he had not yet produced a male heir. In 1422, over 70 years old according to most accounts, he married for a fourth time. His new wife was the Lithuanian princess Sofia, known as Sonka, a niece of his second wife. She bore him two sons, although there were rumors that the

children were not Jogaila's own. The sons were too young to take part in the political maneuvering that accompanied the approaching death of the aging Jogaila, however.

The last few years of Jogaila's life were chaotic. Lithuanians who supported the union with Poland managed to deny Svitrigaila the Lithuanian throne and to install one of their own, Zygimantas, as king. Jogaila tried to forestall these developments but no longer had much power. In late May of 1434, Poland suffered through a return of winter weather after spring crops had already begun to sprout. The Polish chronicler Dlugosz, quoted by Sruogiene, told what happened next: "The king, oblivious to the bitter cold, went out into the woods as was his habit, a remnant of his pagan days, to listen to the nightingale and to rejoice in her sweet songs . . . but he caught cold and . . . was taken ill. Finally, fully conscious . . . he fell asleep in the arms of the clergy." He died on June 1, 1434, and was buried in Krakow Cathedral, having fundamentally altered the histories of both the countries he called home.

Books

Biskupski, M.B., *The History of Poland,* Greenwood, 2000.

Davies, Norman, *God's Playground: A History of Poland,* rev. ed., Columbia University Press, 2005.

Lukowski, Jerzy, and Hubert Zawadzki, *A Concise History of Poland,* Cambridge University Press, 2001.

Rowell, S.C., *Lithuania Ascending: A Pagan Empire Within East-Central Europe, 1295-1345,* Cambridge, 1994.

Online

"Jogaila (1350-1434)," *Lithuanian Quarterly Journal of Arts and Sciences* (Winter 1987), http://www.lituanus.org/1987/87_4_04.htm (February 5, 2008). □

Granville T. Woods

Australian-born American inventor Granville T. Woods (1856-1910), dubbed "the black Edison," contributed key inventions to several of the technologies that defined the modern era, including railroad braking, electric railroad systems, and telephony and telegraphy.

During his own life, Woods had to struggle not just for recognition but for financial solvency. He came from modest origins, worked independently, and had no way to market his inventions on his own. For most of his life he had to seek out associates and allies in order to try to realize financial gains from his work. Those allies, well aware of the value of Woods's inventions, used a variety of subterfuges to try to wrest his intellectual property from him, but through a series of lengthy court struggles he resisted their efforts. Woods's story offers many insights into the conditions faced by African-American inventors—and into the roles played by inventors in general during an age when the solo inventor was being supplanted by a different kind of figure, the engineer, employed by a large corporation.

Born in Australia

Many details of Woods's early life have been obscured by contradictory stories told about him, sometimes by Woods himself. His birthplace has often been given as Columbus, Ohio, but his biographer, Rayvon Fouché, relying on census records, Woods's death certificate, and detailed journalistic accounts of Woods's life published in the 1890s, has concluded that he was born in Australia on April 23, 1856. He was of a mixed ethnic background that probably included Australian Aboriginal, Malay, and African elements. As a foreign-born black person, Woods, like other black immigrants, likely found American racial prejudice especially difficult to take. Fouché noted that his "combative spirit, the forthright manner in which he interacted with whites, and his fearless public challenges to white authority—all of which, because of the severe consequences, most African Americans avoided well into the 20th century—indicate that he did not consider himself an American Negro."

It is not known exactly when Woods came to the United States, nor what kind of formal education he received. He apparently spent some time in Columbus. Earlier biographies of Woods have reported that he left school at age ten to learn the trades of machinist and blacksmith, continuing to supplement his education by persuading white friends to check out textbooks from libraries that barred him from entering because of his skin color. In later testimony, however, he said that he began working as a machinist at age 15. He is said to have gone west to work on a railroad, perhaps the Iron Mountain Railroad in Missouri,

to have worked in a mill in Springfield, Illinois, and to have attended an engineering college in the eastern United States. One magazine stated that Woods claimed to be a graduate of the electrical department of Stern's Institute of Technology; another article, quoted by Fouché, stated that "Mr. Woods has a first-class English education, and is an experienced mechanic, having received special training in mechanical engineering." In the year 1878 Woods is variously reported to have served as an engineer on a British ship called the *Ironsides* and to have worked for the Pomeroy Railroad Company in southwestern Ohio.

Reliable records of Woods's activities from the late 1870s onward are available in the form of court testimony he later gave about his creative work as an inventor, largely unearthed by Fouché's research. He apparently moved from the Pomeroy Railroad to the Dayton and Southeastern Railroad around 1879, working there for 13 months and being entrusted with shifting cars in a rail yard in the town of Washington Court House, Ohio, northeast of Cincinnati. He stated that a friendly telegraph operator there instructed him in the scientific fundamentals of telegraphy, but the inventions that he was soon to devise suggested that, however fast he may have been as a learner, he had at some point received more training as an electrical engineer than could be gleaned from a few sessions in a telegraph operator's booth. What seems certain is that Woods obtained a strong working knowledge of the two hottest technologies of the 1880s, railroads and electronic communications. His technical expertise probably explained the relative prestige of the railroad jobs he held as a young man; most African Americans in southern Ohio, a region that reflected the attitudes of points farther south, were relegated to sheer manual labor at the time.

In 1880 Woods experienced the first instance of a problem that would plague him throughout most of his working life: he left the Dayton and Southeastern Railroad after the company failed to pay him the salary he had earned. They issued scrip that local merchants either refused to accept or devalued with huge surcharges. That year, Woods settled in Cincinnati and, possibly working with a brother, Lyates, started a small firm called the Woods Electrical Company. He began to explore the phenomenon of induction, the process of causing an electrical current in a conductor by generating or varying a nearby electromagnetic field. One of his earliest experiments produced an induction-based elevator signaling system, and he began showing drawings of the system to well-heeled Cincinnatians whom he saw as potential investors.

Suffered from Smallpox

Woods's career was soon interrupted, however: in the summer of 1881 he contracted smallpox, which was in its last years as a major threat in the United States. Often fatal, the disease sidelined Woods for most of a year and left him with chronic kidney and liver disease that may have been factors in his early death. Apparently Woods was married at this point; he spoke of having to take extreme measures in order to support his family. Unable to do sustained creative work, he found employers unwilling to hire him in his weakened condition. The only job he could find was at the Queen City Facing Mills, and that company, too, refused to pay him the salary it had agreed on. Woods launched a lengthy court action that recovered only $20 in the end.

By late 1882 and 1883 Woods was once again at work on new inventions. The first patent he received, in 1884, was for an improved type of steam boiler, and he also registered patents on a new telephone signal transmitter and an ingenious process combining features of a telephone and a telegraph machine that he called telegraphony. Rights to that invention were later acquired by Alexander Graham Bell's telephone company. Despite the flow of creative ideas he was experiencing, Woods lacked even the $15 fee necessary to file patents on these inventions. In cases where he did succeed, it was because Cincinnati investors and attorneys, who were becoming aware of his talents and alert to the possibility of a big payoff, fronted him the money.

Woods forged ahead, and by 1885 he had fleshed out his ideas for a true breakthrough invention called the Synchronous Multiplex Railway Telegraph. The system used induction to transmit telegraph messages from moving trains to wires running beside the tracks, thus enabling railroad personnel to monitor the locations of trains in the system—the previous impossibility of which had been the cause of numerous collisions. Woods and another inventor, Lucius J. Phelps, apparently conceived of such a system independently. Woods read of Phelps's work in *Scientific American* magazine and refined his own invention into a system with a wider scope. Using a borrowed battery at the headquarters of the Cincinnati Medicated Mud Bath Company, he constructed a working model, and once again he attracted the attention of well-heeled investors.

The railway telegraph was patented in 1887, but not before Woods had become embroiled in an expensive patent interference proceeding—an attempt by the U.S. Patent Office to determine priority among competing claims—in which Phelps asserted his rights to the invention. The process further sapped Woods's meager financial resources but did bring him a measure of publicity. A *Catholic Tribune* article quoted by Fouché even called him "the greatest inventor in the history of his race, and equal, if not superior to, any inventor in the country." That led two investors, John Gano and Ralph Peters, to back a second Woods Electric Company, this one located across the Ohio River in Kentucky. Meanwhile, Woods had received feelers from the Westinghouse Corporation about a railroad air brake he had developed.

Relationship with Investors Deteriorated

Woods's relationship with Gano and Peters quickly deteriorated, as Woods alleged that they failed to pay him his agreed-upon salary of $50 a month, plus stock options, and did not reimburse him for trips to New York undertaken to promote his inventions. That led to a second set of lawsuits, complicated by the fact that two entities, one in Ohio and one in Kentucky, bore the name Woods Electric Company. By 1890 Woods had managed to sever his ties from Gano and Peters, but he was once again almost penniless.

Woods decided he had to move to New York, the center of American electronics engineering. Over the next ten years, the pattern of his life in Cincinnati repeated itself. Working first as an elevated railway porter for $1.20 a day, and sending most of that money to an ailing sister, Woods shopped his ideas to investors. The key idea Woods worked on in the 1890s was an electric train system. The ancestor of both overhead-powered trams and the "third rail" trains of today, the system Woods had in mind carried enormous potential benefits for investors. Others worked on similar ideas, and Fouché has disputed the often-repeated statement that Woods was the inventor of the third-rail power system. However, with the help of partners in his newly formed American Engineering Company, Woods devised key components of an electric street railway that was built on New York's Coney Island.

Unfortunately, Woods once again found himself in the hands of less-than-honest partners who conspired to cheat him of profits due. His relationship with the American Engineering Company devolved into a violent scene in which Woods confronted company executive James Zerbe over the theft of some of his drawings and ended up in a physical altercation with Zerbe and his son. After a more lengthy court proceeding involving a libel suit filed by Zerbe against Woods—Woods was once again vindicated but drained his savings in defending himself—the partnership was dissolved. The only silver lining was that the court proceedings once again brought Woods a measure of favorable publicity. He succeeded in registering a few more patents, including one in 1900 for a large-scale chicken egg incubator.

The degree to which racism played a part in Woods's troubles remains an open question. Given the fact that the 1890s marked a low point in post–Civil War race relations, he clearly suffered the effects of racial prejudice, and his precarious financial standing resulted from his inability to call upon the sources of capital that would have been available to white inventors. However, the problems Woods faced were shared to some extent by white inventors, including Thomas Edison, and all over the United States and the world freelance inventors like Woods were losing ground to large corporations that had the legal and financial muscle to see the work of engineers through to financial profits.

Woods, in fact, first began to prosper after he worked out a closer arrangement with two of those large corporations, General Electric and Westinghouse, in the last years of his life. Working primarily through an intermediary, H. Ward Leonard, Woods registered 20 patents between 1900 and 1907, most of them for electronic train-control devices. Most of these patents were assigned to General Electric and Westinghouse. Woods was able to purchase a farm in Monsey, New York. He may have married again, with unhappy results. A news account cited by C.R. Gibbs in *Black Inventors: From Africa to America* stated that Woods had filed suit against a Poughkeepsie estate owner, the employer of a maid named Elizabeth who claimed to be married to Woods but said that he had abused her and that she wanted to stay on in her job. Just as Woods began to realize proper remuneration for his life's work, he suffered a stroke on January 28, 1910. He died at Harlem Hospital in New York two days later.

Books

Fouché, Rayvon, *Black Inventors in the Age of Segregation,* Johns Hopkins, 2003.

Gibbs, C.R., *Black Inventors: From Africa to America,* Three Dimensions, 1995.

James, Portia P., *The Real McCoy: African-American Invention and Innovation, 1619-1930,* Smithsonian Institution Press, 1989.

Notable Black American Men, Gale, 1998.

Simmons, William, *Men of Mark: Eminent, Progressive and Rising,* Rewell, 1887.

Periodicals

Jet, June 5, 1995.

Journal of Black Studies, March 1989.

New York Times, December 26, 2004.

Online

"Granville T. Woods: Inventor," The Faces of Science: African Americans in the Sciences, https://webfiles.uci.edu/mc-brown/display/woods.html (December 28, 2007).

"Granville T. Woods: The Multiplex Telegraph," Inventor of the Week, http://web.mit.edu/invent/iow/woods.html (December 28, 2007). ☐

Elizabeth Woodville

English Queen Consort Elizabeth Woodville (c.1437-1492) remains a controversial figure. The wife of King Edward IV, Woodville was cast in a negative light by many both during her time and throughout history. Woodville was mother to many royal children, including the romanticized "Princes in the Tower." Recent scholarship has re-examined her place in history, however, and cast her in a more favorable light.

Daughter of Minor Nobility

The first child of Sir Richard Woodville and Jacquetta of Luxembourg, Elizabeth Woodville was born in about 1437 at Grafton in Northamptonshire, England. Through her mother, she was a descendent of such distinguished luminaries as Charlemagne. Her mother was the widow of John, Duke of Bedford, younger brother of the ruling monarch, Henry V; despite some scandal when the couple married, as Richard Woodville was not of the same level of nobility, the couple enjoyed royal favor. Elizabeth Woodville, along with her younger brothers Anthony and John and younger sister Margaret, spent her earliest years primarily on her family's estate at Grafton. Thomas More claimed that Woodville had served as a maid to Margaret of Anjou, Queen Consort of Henry VI, as a child but some evidence suggests that this is unlikely. More probable is that some time after her seventh birthday, she went to live with another noble family—probably Sir Edward Grey and his

wife Elizabeth—in Leicestershire. At the time, noble parents commonly sent their children to live in other households as a way of developing both personal independence and necessary social or marital contacts. In 1448, Woodville's father became Baron Rivers, a significant elevation in his status.

Some time in the early 1450s, Woodville married Sir John Grey, the son of Sir Edward Grey and his wife. Writing in *Elizabeth Woodville: Mother of the Princes in the Tower,* David Baldwin argued that "it is, perhaps, unlikely that Elizabeth was married at thirteen and a mother at fourteen; but . . . this may be another instance of a family's desire to seal an agreement as quickly as possible taking precedence over the well-being of the bride." Regardless of the exact date of the marriage, it is known that Woodville had two sons by Grey: Thomas, who became the Marquess of Dorset, and Richard. The young family probably lived at one of the Grey family manors in Warwickshire, but very little is known about this time in her history.

Became Queen Consort

Sir John Grey died on behalf of the Lancastrians in the Second Battle of St. Albans during the War of the Roses in 1461. On behalf of the Yorkists, Woodville's mother, Jacquetta of Luxembourg, met with longtime friend Margaret of Anjou, the Queen Consort of deposed ruler Henry VI and head of the Lancastrian armies, to discuss whether the Lancastrian army would move on London. In *Elizabeth Wydeville: The Slandered Queen,* Arlene Okerlund stated:

"As a result of the feminine parley between Margaret and Jacquetta, Margaret limited Lancastrian entry into London to a symbolic force.... That fateful decision destroyed her cause and allowed the troops of Edward, Earl of March to enter the city just days later. Soon, Edward was crowned King Edward IV. The newly-widowed Elizabeth Woodville returned to her family home at Grafton, perhaps then meeting Edward IV for the first time. The new monarch soon pardoned the Woodville family for their participation on the Lancastrian side of the War of the Roses.

In April 1464, Woodville married King Edward IV of England. It remains unclear how the attachment was formed or when the King decided to marry her; a rather colorful legend suggests that Woodville, knowing that Edward IV was hunting in a nearby forest, waited for him with her sons beneath a tree known as the Queen's Oak to ask his assistance with a property agreement she was negotiating. Taken with her beauty and unwillingness to submit to his advances, the King then returned to secretly marry her a few weeks later at her family home in Grafton. Little evidence supports this series of events, but it does seem clear that the engagement and marriage happened quickly and without the knowledge of Edward IV's advisers.

Many in Edward VI's court expected him to form a marriage alliance with a member of an important European ruling family, or at least marry a daughter of a prominent Yorkist family. Baldwin summarized the objections to Woodville by noting that "the new Queen's father was a former Lancastrian who had only been ennobled comparatively recently while she herself was some five years the King's senior, a widow with two young sons." However, Woodville was young, beautiful, and had proven herself capable of bearing healthy sons, an important consideration for a monarch. Her connections to the Lancastrians showed Edward IV was attempting to heal the wounds of the War of the Roses. Any arguments Edward IV's councilors could make were, however, moot as the marriage had already taken place. Elizabeth Woodville was crowned Queen Consort on May 26, 1465.

In early 1466, Woodville gave birth to her first child by Edward IV, Elizabeth. The need for a male heir tinged all royal marriages, but Edward IV remained dedicated to his bride despite the birth of two more royal daughters, Mary in 1467 and Cecily in 1469. (Despite his dedication to his wife, Edward IV often had relationships with other women and sired numerous illegitimate children over the years.) During these early years on the throne, Elizabeth and her Woodville relations developed a negative reputation; many thought that their new influence over Edward IV led to unfairly advantageous marriages and that, generally, the family aimed at building its own power above all other aims. However, Woodville supported Cambridge's Queens' College as well as Eton College, showing that she had at least some domestic aims.

Years of Rebellion

General dissatisfaction with the King grew as well, as some of his subjects believed that little progress had been made since the removal of Henry VI from the throne despite increased taxes. In 1469, the Earl of Warwick, Richard Neville—a relative of Edward IV's who had helped raise him to the monarchy during the War of the Roses—conspired with Edward IV's younger brother George, Duke of Clarence, to undermine Edward IV's power. Edward IV marshaled an army, and Elizabeth Woodville went to Norwich, where she remained for several months. During this time, the conspirators raised an army to battle the King's forces, and successfully captured the King, whom they held captive. Shortly after this coup, Elizabeth Woodville's father and brother were executed; Baldwin argued that "their deaths and the allegations that Jacquetta had used sorcery to make Edward marry her daughter, were really private acts of vengeance designed to remove the barrier which developed between [Warwick] and his royal master." However, Warwick soon discovered that the majority of the nobility were not willing to accept his pretense of ruling the country through Edward IV, and released the King.

Edward IV attempted to reconcile with his rebellious subjects, but the following year they again attempted a coup, this time unsuccessfully. Warwick fled to France, and managed to strike a deal with Margaret d'Anjou. In the summer of 1470, Elizabeth Woodville and her children moved into the Tower of London for protection while Edward IV attempted to raise an army to oust the coming invasion from France. However, the opposition's military advantages forced Edward IV to flee the country. Woodville gathered her family and sought sanctuary at Westminster Abbey. Because the traditions of chivalry usually protected royal women, Okerlund noted that this decision "to join the motley crew in sanctuary at Westminster Abbey indicated not only the extraordinary mayhem in the nation, but her profound distrust of Warwick." There, she gave birth to a son, Edward, on November 2, 1470. She remained in sanctuary until April 1471, when Edward IV returned to London to depose Henry VI from the latter's brief restoration.

Returned to Queenship

Young Edward became Prince of Wales, the official title of the heir to England's throne, in June 1471. Elizabeth Woodville was named the head of the council responsible for the heir's upbringing to the age of 14, and further given the supervisory power over the Prince's daily routine. The following year, Woodville accompanied her son on travels throughout the country. In 1473, Woodville relocated to Ludlow Castle with Prince Edward. There, she gave birth to her second son, Richard, in August 1473. Two years later, the next royal daughter, Anne, was born. Woodville and Edward IV dedicated themselves to arranging suitable matches for their children; Princess Elizabeth, the royal couple's eldest daughter, went on to marry the future Henry VII. Life continued fairly quietly for Woodville for the next several years, excepting two more births: in 1479, she gave birth to Catherine, and the following year to the final royal daughter, Bridget.

In the early 1480s, Edward IV's health began to decline; in April 1483, he died. Edward V soon set out for London from Ludlow Castle. However, supporters of an opposing claimant to the throne, Richard, Duke of Gloucester, took the 12-year-old Edward V into custody en route. Deeming himself the Protector of the young King, Gloucester accompanied the boy to London. There, Gloucester imprisoned both Edward V and his younger brother Richard in the Tower, claiming that Edward IV's marriage to Woodville had been illegitimate and that he, Richard, was thus the true heir to the throne. That July, Gloucester was crowned as King Richard III. The ultimate fate of the "Princes in the Tower" remains unknown to this day, although it seems likely that the boys were executed. Richard III died at the Battle of Bosworth in 1485 and was succeeded by Henry VII.

Death and Legacy

In February 1487, Henry VII forced Woodville to retire to Bermondsey Abbey on arguably spurious charges. She was permitted to have visitors, but little broke the presumably dull routine of her life; the only recorded event during her years at the Abbey was a formal meeting with a group of French ambassadors in November 1489. In the early 1490s, Woodville's health began to decline and she died on June 8, 1492. She was buried quietly in St. George's Chapel alongside her husband; Okerlund commented that "the funeral procession . . . could not have contrasted more starkly with the elaborate processions of her queenly days."

Woodville's greatest legacy was perhaps the great number of her female descendants who became queens. Her daughter married Henry VII and was the mother of not only Henry VIII, but also Margaret, later wife of the King of Scotland, and Mary, later wife of the King of France; Woodville's great-granddaughters included Queen Mary I and the enormously significant Queen Elizabeth I; her great-great-granddaughters included Mary, Queen of Scots and Lady Jane Grey, who ruled England for nine days in July 1553.

While some of her contemporaries respected and even admired Woodville, over the centuries following her death she has generally been regarded distinctly unfavorably. Historians have argued that she connived and intrigued to advance her family's claims to power, and some have made her into an outright villain. Her life and character have been reconsidered by some modern historians and a more favorable picture of her is emerging. Regardless, her contributions to the future of England's history is irrefutable.

Books

Baldwin, David, *Elizabeth Woodville: Mother of the Princes in the Tower,* Sutton, 2002.

Laynesmith, J.L., *The Last Medieval Queens: English Queenship 1445-1503,* Oxford University Press, 2004.

Okerlund, Arlene, *Elizabeth Wydeville: The Slandered Queen* Tempus, 2005.

Smith, George, *The Coronation of Elizabeth Wydeville, Queen Consort of Edward IV, on May 26th, 1465: A Contemporary Account Set Forth from the XV Century Manuscript,* Gloucester Reprints, 1975. □

Jane Cooke Wright

American physician Jane Cooke Wright (born 1919) was a prominent twentieth-century cancer researcher. The daughter of a prominent physician, Jane Cooke Wright followed her father into medicine and eventually became the highest-ranked African-American woman at a major medical institution. Her contributions to the nascent field of chemotherapy have led some to call her "the Mother of Chemotherapy."

Born Into a Medical Family

Born in New York City on November 20, 1919, to Dr. Louis Tompkins Wright and elementary school teacher Corinne Cooke Wright, Jane Cooke Wright came from a long line of pioneers in the field of medicine. Her paternal grandfather, Dr. Ceah Ketcham Wright, was a graduate of the Meharry Medical College in Nashville, Tennessee; after he died, her paternal grandmother married Dr. William Fletcher Penn, the first African-American to graduate from Yale Medical School. This man inspired Wright's father, Louis Tompkins Wright, who attended Harvard Medical School in the face of racial discrimination. Louis Wright later went on to become a successful surgeon and medical researcher and was the first African-American to be a staff physician at a New York City hospital. Writing in *To Fathom More: African American Scientists and Inventors,* Edward Sidney Jenkins commented, "That these men, and the families who supported and encouraged them, could aim so high, even in the shadows of slavery, and achieve such lofty goals, is a striking commentary on their character." Both Jane Cooke Wright and her younger sister, Barbara, followed in the family tradition and became doctors.

Wright was educated in New York City, first at the private Ethical Culture elementary school and later at the Fieldston School, where she particularly enjoyed science and mathematics. She also served as art editor for the yearbook and became captain of the swim team. After graduating from Fieldston in 1938, she attended Smith College in Massachusetts on a scholarship. There, she excelled in her studies and swam on the varsity swim team. She also studied German, living for time in the college's German house. Although she briefly considered pursuing art or physics as a career, Wright settled on medicine. After graduating from Smith in 1942, she enrolled at New York Medical College, again attending on a scholarship due to her academic strength.

Due to World War II, the college required students to complete their studies in only three years, and in 1945 Wright graduated from the college with honors and began an internship at Bellevue Hospital in New York City. She remained at Bellevue for nine months as an assistant in internal medicine. After completing this internship, she continued her training at Harlem Hospital, where she served as a resident in internal medicine in 1947 and 1948. Also in

1947, she married David D. Jones Jr., a graduate of Harvard Law School; the couple would later have two daughters, Jane and Allison. After completing her training, Wright continued to work at Harlem Hospital. In 1949 she took a position as a staff physician with the New York City public school system, and continued to serve as a visiting physician at Harlem Hospital.

Became Cancer Researcher

In 1948 Dr. Louis Tompkins Wright, Jane Cooke Wright's father, had founded the Harlem Hospital Cancer Research Foundation to investigate the possibilities for and effectiveness of chemotherapy drugs in cancer treatment. The following year, Jane Cooke Wright joined the staff of the Harlem Cancer Research Foundation as a clinician; Jenkins noted that "she made the transition from medical practice to medical researcher quickly and smoothly." Much of her work centered on patient trials. Wright studied the reactions of different drugs and chemotherapy techniques on tumors, as well as what her biography in *Notable Scientists: From 1900 to the Present* called "the complex relationships and variations between test animal and patient, tissue sample and patient, and individual patient responses to various chemotherapeutic agents." In 1951 the researchers had some success in using the drug methotrexate to destroy breast cancer cells; up to that time, what little research had been conducted focused on the drug's efficacy with cancers of the lymph nodes or blood, rather than cancerous tumors. With her father, Wright also performed research into the effects of triethylene melamine. When Dr. Louis Tompkins Wright died in 1952, Jane Cooke Wright became the head of the Harlem Cancer Research Foundation.

Other cancer researchers began to acknowledge the importance of the discoveries made by Wright and her team of researchers. During the 1940s and 1950s, chemotherapy was a new, untested cancer treatment that many physicians either disregarded or outright ridiculed for its presumed ineffectiveness in aiding cancer patients. Despite these obstacles, Wright continued to seek out all the information she could find on chemotherapy research and developments, reading widely, attending conferences, and sharing knowledge with other national and international researchers.

Advanced Chemotherapy Treatment

When Wright left the Harlem Cancer Research Foundation in 1955 to take a position at the New York University Bellevue Medical Center, she continued her research. In 1961 she became an adjunct professor of research surgery at the medical center, where she remained until 1967. That year, Wright left to accept a position as associate dean and professor of surgery at New York Medical College; Wright's biography on the National Library of Medicine at the National Institutes of Health Web site noted that "at a time when African American women physicians numbered only a few hundred in the entire United States, Dr. Wright was the highest ranked African American woman at a nationally recognized medical institution." She remained at the college until her retirement, creating a program of study into cancer, heart diseases, and stroke, as well as one to teach

doctors how to use chemotherapy in addition to conducting medical research.

Wright was particularly interested in the effectiveness of a series of chemotherapeutic drugs administered in a specified order, rather than simply as a combination of medicines; her research into this idea was the first of its kind. Wright also began experimenting with different drugs and cancer tissues in order to determine the specific effects of certain drugs and thus increase the effectiveness of chemotherapy treatment for different forms of cancer. Jenkins noted that "this was a significant contribution because then there were few guidelines for any chemotherapy procedures." Wright and her team developed new techniques of administering drugs that ultimately led to an increased reduction of cancer cells via chemotherapy.

In 1960 Wright and her fellow researchers successfully caused a form of skin cancer to regress using chemotherapy. Before this accomplishment, the cancer had been treated with radiation therapy. Wright noticed that by including chemotherapy in early cancer treatments, the lifespan of the treated cancer patients increased by up to ten years.

Because the drugs used in chemotherapy can be harmful to patients, Wright worked to develop treatment guidelines to provide the maximum benefit to patients with a minimum danger of drug intolerance. Wright carefully monitored all chemotherapy patients, lessening or stopping treatment if a person showed signs of damage from the drugs. She also stopped chemotherapy treatment on patients whose tumors disappeared or, in certain circumstances, were greatly reduced in size. Wright had the joy of seeing some of her patients with advanced stages of cancer recover and live for years after chemotherapy treatments.

A Respected Career

Wright's many contributions to the field of chemotherapy included services other than research. In 1957 she traveled to Ghana on a medical mission; four years later she returned to Africa representing the African Research and Medical Foundation. She would later serve as vice-president of that foundation from 1973 to 1984. Wright also led a delegation of medical professionals to China, Eastern Europe, and the Soviet Union as an ambassador of People to People International.

Wright was a member of the highly-respected American Association for Cancer Research, a professional organization dedicated to the study of cancer treatments, and later served on its board of directors. In 1964 she helped found the American Society of Clinical Oncology (cancer medicine); within 15 years, this organization's membership grew from 60 to 8,800. Wright also held membership in the New York City Division of the American Cancer Society, the Medical Advisory Board of the Skin Cancer Foundation, and the New York Cancer Society. In 1971 she became the New York Cancer Society's first female president.

Wright also sat on many government committees. In 1964 President Lyndon B. Johnson invited Wright to serve on the cancer subcommittee of the President's Commission of Heart Disease, Cancer, and Stroke. Her suggestions as part of this commission led to the foundation of regional cancer centers throughout the United States. From 1966 to 1970, Wright served on the National Cancer Advisory Committee, and from 1966 until her retirement she also sat on several committees under the umbrella of the Department of Health and Human Services.

Wright received a number of awards for contributions to cancer research. One of her first came in 1952 from *Mademoiselle* magazine. In 1965 the Albert Einstein College of Medicine awarded Wright its Spirit of Achievement Award; two years later, she was a recipient of the Hadassah Myrtle Wreath award. The following year, Smith College awarded her the Smith Medal. During the 1960s and 1970s Wright was also recognized by the American Association for Cancer Research, the Women's Medical College of Pennsylvania, and Denison University. Later, Wright was featured in a poster series of "Exceptional Black Scientists" released by CIBA-GEIGY and included by the Smithsonian Institution in its traveling exhibit *Black Women: Achievement Against the Odds.*

Retirement Years

Becoming an emeritus professor, Wright retired from the New York Medical College and active cancer research in 1987. In the years since then, she has spent much of her time pursuing her hobbies, which include watercolor painting, reading mystery stories, and sailing. At her Smith College 50-year class reunion in 1992, Wright spoke about the place of cancer during the history of the human race, noting that the increases in life span aided by chemotherapy she had witnessed during her life time "justified her faith in chemotherapy as a major weapon against a tough adversary," according to Jenkins.

In 2006 Wright's personal and professional papers were added to the Sophia Smith collection at the Smith College archives. Also in 2006, the first "Minorities in Can-

cer Research Jane Cooke Wright Lectureship," named in honor of Wright's contributions to the field of cancer research, was awarded by the American Association of Cancer Research to Nigerian scientist and researcher Professor Olufunmilayo Olopade. According to the *Africa News,* "The Lectureship is given to an outstanding scientist who has made meritorious contributions to the field of cancer research and who has, through leadership or by example, furthered the advancement of minority investigators in cancer research." This description encapsulates the legacy of Jane Cooke Wright, whose own contributions to cancer research—including 135 scientific papers and contributions to nine books—have had significant and lasting effects on the field of medicine.

Books

Jenkins, Edward Sidney, *To Fathom More: African American Scientists and Inventors,* University Press of America, 1996.

Notable Black American Women, Book 1, Gale Research, 1992.

Notable Scientists: From 1900 to the Present, Gale Group, 2001.

Sammons, Vivian Ovelton, *Blacks in Science and Medicine,* Hemisphere, 1990.

Periodicals

Africa News, April 18, 2006.

Online

"Changing the Face of Medicine: Dr. Jane Cooke Wright," National Library of Medicine, http://www.nlm.nih.gov/changing thefaceodmedicine/physicians/biography_336.html, (December 30, 2007).

"Jane C. Wright Papers, 1920–2006 Finding Aid," *Sophia Smith Collection, Smith College,* http://asteria.fivecolleges.edu/findaids/sophiasmith/mnsss402.html, (December 30, 2007).

□

Muhammad Yunus

Nobel Prize-winning economist Muhammad Yunus (born 1940) has worked to make microlending and related social business models the norm rather than the exception in developing countries.

Childhood

Muhammad Yunus was born on June 28, 1940, in the Bangladeshi seaport of Chittagong, when the city was still part of India under British rule. His father was Hazi Dula Mia Shoudagar and his mother was Sufia Khatun Yunus. Yunus was the third of 14 children, nine of which survived, and they grew up in the village of Bathua before moving into the city of Chittagong, where their father opened a jewelry shop. Yunus was always active, even in his youth. He participated in the Boy Scouts and even traveled with his troop to Canada in 1955.

Education

Yunus first attended Chittagong Collegiate School, then Chittagong College and eventually Dhaka University. He earned an undergraduate degree in economics at Chittagong College in 1960, and a master's degree from Dhaka University a year later. Yunus then traveled to the United States to attend Vanderbilt University on a Fulbright scholarship, where he married a Russian student named Vera Forostenko. They had a daughter, Monica Yunus, who became an opera soprano. Yunus taught economics classes at Middle Tennessee State University from 1969 until 1972, when the Pakistani civil war ended and Bangladesh was born. He wanted to return to Bangladesh, but his wife chose not to come with their infant daughter. They divorced and Yunus returned, taking a position teaching economics at Chittagong University, where he was invited to head the University's economics department. In 1980 he would marry again, this time to fellow Bangladeshi Afroji Yunus, a physics professor, and they would have a daughter, Dina Yunus.

Bailed Out Bangladesh

Bangladesh is known as one of the poorest places in the world, and has a population close to 120 million people. In 1974 Yunus took his economics class into the local village of Jobra on a field trip, where, according to a now-well-known story, as reported in *Contemporary Heroes and Heroines,* they "met a woman who made bamboo stools, but she earned just two cents for each. She told Yunus and the class that if she could save 20 cents to buy her own supply of bamboo, she would not have to borrow from the dealer who sold it to her; because she owed him money, he was allowed to dictate the price of each stool she sold." Yunus felt that people should be able to sell their wares at a fair price and make enough money to pay their debts, support themselves and and make a little profit. Commercial banks, however, would not issue loans to the poor, because they had no assets, business experience, collateral or often basic literacy skills, a combination that in view of lending institutions, made them the ultimate lending risk.

Yunus saw a great need for a bank that would lend money to the poor, and decided that it could be done at commercial interest rates. He developed an experiment with two other researchers, in which he lent money to a group of borrowers and tracked results. The experiment was successful: the debts to Yunus were repaid in full and on

time. He continued to develop the lending model until he succeeded in founding the Grameen or "Village" Bank in Bangladesh in 1983.

Microlending Began with Grameen Bank

Only the destitute were eligible to borrow from Grameen's community banking system. The system used the pressure of a group of peers to keep borrowers from defaulting. A borrower might get enough to buy a chicken or cow and sell the eggs or milk, while raising and then selling the chicks or calves. The loan amounts were small, but the results turned out to be noteworthy. Yunus quickly learned that men tended to spend loan money on drink, new wives and other personal status items rather than re-investing or saving it, as female borrowers reliably did. As a result, the majority of Grameen borrowers were women, although there have been both religious and social reper-cussions resulting from that practice. Islamic fundamen-talists have attacked Yunus for his efforts to empower women. According to an article in *Fortune* by Sheridan Prasso, "Grameen has provided women the financial means to leave abusive husbands. They own homes in their own names, no longer pay dowries, live longer, have im-proved nutrition and hygiene, and are better able to care for their families. . . . 'I am destroying the culture, yes,' Yunus says, beaming mischievously at the thought. 'Culture is a dynamic thing. If you stay with the same old thing over and over, you don't get anywhere.' "

Reached For the Stars

Yunus has stated on many occasions that his goal is to put poverty in a museum, where it belongs, and he has stated that, with credit as a fundamental human right, peo-ple can rise out of poverty with dignity. A 1986 article in *The Economist* explained the unusual services that Grameen Bank offered: "Borrowers can get cheap seeds, seedlings and ducks, lessons in reading and writing, medi-cal help, and advice on family planning. The bank also dabbles in social engineering: borrowers who accept dowry from their son's bride may have their loan recalled." Ac-cording to a 2007 article in *Social Education,* the Grameen Bank also developed a "social agenda, outlined in four principles: discipline, unity, courage and hard work; and 16 decisions—including the abolition of dowries, attention to environmental causes, and education for all children." A throng of Grameen bank model replicas—often called MFI's or Micro Financing Institutions—have sprung up in other countries and cultures, and Grameen has branched out to include a wealth of telecommunications services and other efforts at economy building.

Congratulation and Criticism

There are many critics, as well as devout enthusiasts, of microlending in general and Yunus in particular, from both the left and right ends of the political spectrum. In a 2007 article in *The American,* writer Tom Bethell was critical of Yunus and the microcredit movement, but granted that Yunus is developing market opportunities in a country that sorely needs them, and added that "he seems to represent an emerging consensus that government-to-government aid enriches only the rulers." Bethell noted that some critics have questioned Grameen's assumption that poor individu-als want to be self-employed instead of earning a paycheck, or that accumulating debt rather than savings will alleviate their poverty.

Social Business

Yunus's current book, *Creating a World Without Pov-erty: How Social Business Can Transform Our Lives* (2007), briefly tells the story of microcredit, then communicates the ways in which the "social" business model can help people while still generating a profit. Many have noted the swiftly growing field of social entrepreneurs and professionals—who espouse more than just the traditional motivation of maximizing profit—who have established a tri-fold bottom line of profit generation, worker welfare and environmental responsibility. More than half the world's population is under 25 years of age, and a great portion of this youth base is openly motivated to seek out a profession that improves life for everyone as well as supporting their own subsistence.

Always one to try and transform theory into reality, Yunus and French food company Danone agreed to partner up and build a yogurt factory in Dhaka, Bangladesh. It opened in November of 2007. Prasso explained the system: "The yogurt . . . would be fortified to curb malnutrition and priced (at 7 cents a cup) to be affordable. Revenue would be reinvested, with Danone only taking out its initial cost of capital. . . . The factory—and ultimately 50 more, if it works—will rely on Grameen microborrowers buying cows to sell it milk on the front end, Grameen microvendors selling the yogurt door to door, and Grameen's 6.6 million members purchasing it for their kids. It will employ 15 to 20 women, and provide income for 1,600 people within a 20-mile radius. Biodegradable cups made from cornstarch, solar panels for electricity, and rainwater collection vats make the enterprise environmentally friendly."

According to Anne W. Howard, writing in the *Chronicle of Philanthropy,* Yunus strongly believes that such social businesses "can solve problems that capitalism, government, and nonprofit groups cannot." She said that Yunus maintained that a social business operates like a "profit maximizing" business . . . by charging for goods and services. "However, its goal is not to return the largest profit to investors but [in Yunus's words] 'to create social benefits for those whose lives it touches.' "

Man and Mission for the Masses

Whether Yunus is described as a "mesmerizing salesman," in Bethell's words, or as "a bona fide visionary," as on the Grameen Web site, the popularity of his personality and professional ideas are not in question. The United Nations declared that 2005 would be known as the Year of Microcredit, and in 2006 Yunus and Grameen Bank were awarded the Nobel Prize for Peace. While it was not the first time the Nobel Committee related peace to the eradication of poverty, they stated that "lasting peace can not be achieved unless large population groups find ways in which to break out of poverty. Microcredit is one such means," as reported on the Infoplease.com Web site. The Committee's choice not only underscored the growing efforts to eradicate poverty, but also opened channels of communication with the Muslim world while highlighting the importance of empowering women.

In 2007 a commemorative postage stamp was issued in Yunus's honor. Celebrities of the music world gathered at a benefit to celebrate the Nobel Laureate with proceeds that went to fight poverty, and early in the year there was media buzz about whether or not Yunus would take his success and popularity into the political arena. Many sources said a party named *Nagarik Shakti* or "Citizen's Power" was being developed by Yunus and his supporters. According to BBC Monitoring South Asia, Yunus sent open letters "to all Bangladeshis urging them to give their opinion on whether he should join politics and launch a party," and "proposed that his party activists would work as 'volunteers' and bear all costs of electing nominees for their constituencies . . . arguing that 'If locals want to see good people elected, they will have to spend their own money.' "

While the political career appears to have been shelved, people from all over the world have continued to shower Yunus with praise. Messages have included thanks to Yunus from many countries, including Kenya, Malaysia, the Peruvian Amazon, New Zealand, Somalia, Italy, and the United States. An article in the *Economist* suggested that "to rid the globe of poverty through credit would require many, many more people with [Yunus's] energy and optimism." A 2006 *PR Newswire* article commented that Yunus "has broken countless rules of banking. . . . He provided loans to the poor, not the rich; to women, not men; in small amounts, not large; and without collateral or excessive paperwork." Despite the inevitable critics, most hope that Yunus will continue breaking the social "rules" that oppress the poor, and that it will inspire others to do the same.

Books

Contemporary Heroes and Heroines: Book III, edited by Terrie M. Rooney, Gale Research, 1998.
The International Authors and Writers Who's Who: 11th Edition, edited by Ernest Kay, Melrose Press Ltd., 1989.
Newsmakers, Thomson Gale, 2007.

Periodicals

The American, May/June 2007.
BBC Monitoring South Asia—Political, February 19, 2007.
Chronicle of Philanthropy, December 13, 2007.
Economist, October 18, 1986; December 12, 1998; November 10, 2007.
Fortune, February 19, 2007.
Hospitals and Health Networks, November 2006.
O, The Oprah Magazine, November 2007.
PR Newswire, December 6, 2006; December 7, 2006; August 21, 2007; October 4, 2007.
Publishers Weekly, November 26, 2007.
Social Education, January-February 2007; April 2007.
St. Petersburg Times (Florida), May 5, 2006.
Texas Monthly, October 2007.
Toronto Sun, November 20, 2006.
UPI News Track, December 10, 2006.
U.S. News and World Report, August 2001.
Western Standard, November 20, 2006.

Online

"About Dr. Yunus," Muhammad Yunus, http://www.muham madyunus.org/ (January 15, 2008).
"Autobiography of Muhammad Yunus," Grameen, http://www .grameen-info.org/book/index.htm (January 15, 2008).
"Muhammad Yunus," Info Please, http://www.infoplease.com/ biography/var/muhammadyunus.html (January 15, 2008).
"Muhammad Yunus: Biography," Book Browse, http://www .bookbrowse.com/biographies/index.cfm?author_number =1380 (January 15, 2008).
"Muhammad Yunus: Biography," Nobel Prize, http://nobelprize .org/nobel_prizes/peace/laureates/2006/ (January 15, 2008).
□

Z

Joe Zawinul

Austrian-born jazz keyboardist Joe Zawinul (1932-2007) helped create the rock-influenced modern jazz style known as fusion, and he is generally credited with introducing the electric piano and the synthesizer to the jazz genre.

The *Daily Telegraph* of London called Zawinul "the most influential European in jazz since Django Reinhardt." Zawinul, like the Belgian guitarist, was descended from Gypsies (and specifically from the Sinti Gypsy subgroup). Zawinul's career encompassed several distinct stages, and he never settled into a fixed style or stopped experimenting. Best known for his years with the pioneering fusion group Weather Report in the 1970s and 1980s, Zawinul was already a veteran of stylistically significant interactions with saxophonist Julian "Cannonball" Adderley and trumpeter Miles Davis when he formed that band, and he went on to contribute to the formation of the world music genre after Weather Report dissolved. In the words of John L. Walters, writing on the Unknown Public Web site, "Many current forms of music, and the myriad sounds, samples and beats that inform them, were influenced or predicted by Zawinul, the grand old man of electronic world jazz fusion."

Started on Accordion

Josef Erich Zawinul was born on July 7, 1932, in Vienna, Austria. Nothing in his background suggested the levels of musical accomplishment to which he would rise, but his mother was an enthusiastic singer and his father, a gas company clerk, sometimes played harmonica.

Zawinul's first instrument was the accordion, on which he entertained his family and for which he retained a lifelong affection. The family had no piano in their small Vienna apartment, but by the time he was six it had become clear that his talents were well beyond the norm, and his family sought out classical piano lessons. The faculty at the Vienna Conservatory were so impressed with the youngster's skills that he was enrolled for free lessons in clarinet, violin, and composition over the next several years. Among his classmates was the experiment-minded classical pianist Friedrich Gilda. Zawinul also formed a dance-music duo with future Austrian president Thomas Lentil.

The key discovery of Zawinul's youth was American jazz, which, having been forbidden during the Nazi era, held a strong fascination for young people in German-speaking regions. Zawinul first heard jazz when he was about 12, and after the end of World War II he heard the playing of jazz pianists Errol Garner and Britain's George Shearing. It did not take him long to settle on a career. "I saw what I wanted to do with my life," he was quoted as saying in the *Daily Telegraph,* "and that was to play with black musicians." By 1952 he was backing Austrian saxophonist Hans Keller and touring Germany and France with a trio of his own. He was obsessed with the idea of coming to the United States. Fellow musicians teased him, at one point arranging a bogus phone summons asking him to join vocalist Ella Fitzgerald on the road; Zawinul, after learning the truth, then ignored a similar but genuine call from trumpeter Clark Terry.

Zawinul finally got his chance when he won a one-semester scholarship to the Berklee College of Music in Boston in 1958, but once he was on American shores he found that he did not need it. Before even finishing his scholarship term, he was snapped up by trumpeter

Maynard Ferguson, in whose band he remained for eight months. Zawinul played keyboards for vocalist Dinah Washington from 1959 to 1961. That year he began a nine-year stint with Adderley, whose music, in contrast to that of radical 1960s players like Ornette Coleman and John Coltrane, retained strong underpinnings of soul music and other popular African-American styles. The saxophonist, spotting how quickly the Austrian pianist had absorbed these idioms, encouraged him to compose, and Zawinul delivered the 1966 hit "Mercy, Mercy, Mercy" as well as several other successful Adderley tunes. Zawinul's solo on "Mercy, Mercy, Mercy" was among the first uses of an electric piano on a jazz recording. Interracial bands were still not common in jazz, and Zawinul sometimes had to crouch on the floor of a car when touring with Adderley's group in the rural South.

Zawinul was a success by any standard, but he was troubled by the idea that he was simply imitating the styles of other musicians, however expertly, rather than functioning as a true jazz creator. Things came to a head when pianist Barry Harris complimented Zawinul on playing that sounded remarkably similar to his own. Zawinul was flattered at first, but after thinking the episode over, decided to pack up his jazz record collection and force himself to strike out in new directions. He enrolled for a new round of classical lessons with pianist Raymond Leventhal in 1966. After seven months of giving lessons, Leventhal stated that he had no more to teach Zawinul, and gave him a silent practice keyboard as a gift.

Turned Down Lucrative Gig

Newly married to his wife Maxine (also recognized as the first African-American *Playboy* bunny), and with a growing family (the couple raised three sons), Zawinul received a tempting offer in the late 1960s: the chance to realize his originally frustrated dream of performing with Ella Fitzgerald. Promoter Norman Granz offered him a salary of $1,400 a week to fill the vacant keyboard spot in Fitzgerald's band, a substantial raise from the $300 a week he was making with Adderley. But Zawinul by that time was closely following Miles Davis's new experiments in fusing rock and jazz, and he felt he had original ideas of his own in that vein. He asked Granz for five minutes to consider the offer and consulted Maxine, who, as Zawinul recalled to Walters, said "No. You do what you have to do. I can make do with $300 and I have time to wait until you have your thing."

An energized Zawinul began to work on a set of new compositions that reflected the emerging fusion trend, and Davis, who had earlier taken notice of Zawinul's "Mercy, Mercy, Mercy" solo and suggested that the keyboardist join his band, paid close attention. Zawinul's "A Silent Way" became the title track for a 1969 Davis LP, and the Zawinul pieces "Pharaoh's Dance" and "Double Image" were prominently featured on Davis's *Bitches Brew* (1970) and *Live–Evil* (1971), both regarded as jazz classics. Zawinul himself appeared on all three albums but never formally joined Davis's band, and when Zawinul released a solo album, simply titled *Zawinul*, in 1970, he refused Davis's suggestion that he appear on the album in turn, telling the trumpeter that his presence would be too powerful. Davis ended up endorsing Zawinul's effort with a set of liner notes.

By that time Zawinul, along with two Davis alumni, saxophonist Wayne Shorter and Czech-born bassist Miroslav Vitous, were on the point of creating a new group of their own. Weather Report came together in November of 1970 and recorded its first eponymously titled debut album in 1971. Signed to the Columbia label, the group was successful from the start with both critics and fans, although the electronic emphasis of the music alienated some jazz traditionalists. Zawinul became increasingly important as a creative force in the group, beginning with the 1973 album *Sweetnighter*, moving from the electric piano to the rapidly developing synthesizer, and finding new potential in an instrument that until then had remained mostly in the pop sphere. Zawinul and Shorter remained the only constants in a revolving cast of group members, and Zawinul found new challenges as talented players such as bassist Jaco Pastorius signed on.

Weather Report's live shows, as captured on the album *8:30* (1979), were unpredictable freeform affairs, and their albums *I Sing the Body Electric* (1971), *Mysterious Traveller* (1974), and *Night Passage* (1980) were fixtures of fast-growing FM radio, popular among jazz, R&B, and pop audiences alike. Most successful of all was *Heavy Weather* (1976), with its Zawinul-composed international hit "Birdland," named in honor of a New York jazz club that was in turn named for bebop saxophone pioneer Charlie Parker, known as "Bird." Zawinul himself opened a Birdland club in his hometown of Vienna.

Released Solo Albums

Weather Report continued to release albums regularly into the mid-1980s, but Zawinul (who was becoming increasingly interested in world music traditions) and Shorter began to evolve in different directions musically, and dissolved Weather Report in 1985. Zawinul released several solo albums, beginning with *Dialects* in 1986, that were virtually one-man shows recorded in his home studio in Pasadena, California. In these recordings, Zawinul gave free rein to his imaginative explorations of the possibilities of the synthesizer. In 1987 Zawinul formed a new group, the Zawinul Syndicate; he would tour with that group, which again included various members over the course of its existence, until the end of his life.

The members of the Zawinul Syndicate increasingly came from non-Western countries, as Zawinul became more and more interested in musical traditions from around the world. The influence went both ways: Zawinul discovered that the Weather Report tune "Black Market" had been used as a theme song on Radio Dakar in the West African nation of Senegal, and in 1991 he produced the *Amen* album of Senegalese star Salif Keita. Subsequently he recruited such musicians as percussionist Arto Tuncboyaciyan, guitarist Amit Chatterjee, and singers Thania Sanchez and Sabine Kabongo. The genre of world music, often featuring local ethnic styles mixed into complex electronic textures, was in its infancy in the early 1990s, and Zawinul was ahead of the curve in experimenting with the cross-cultural mixtures that flowered over the course of the next decade.

Zawinul remained active on a variety of fronts in addition to his work with the Zawinul Syndicate. He performed with his old friend Friedrich Gulda in the late 1980s and early 1990s, and he returned to classical music on a large scale with the symphonic work *Stories of the Danube* in 1993. In 1994 he moved to New York City, and the move enabled him to make faster trips to Europe, where he had maintained musical connections all through his American career. In the early 2000s Zawinul released several new solo albums, *Faces & Places* (2002), *Midnight Jam* (2005), and *Brown Street* (2007).

That year, as the Zawinul Syndicate toured Europe to celebrate its twentieth anniversary, Zawinul was stricken with Merkel cell carcinoma, a rare form of skin cancer. After a month at Wilhelmina Hospital in Vienna, Zawinul died there on September 11, 2007. By that time, fusion jazz had achieved renewed popularity after a period during which it was eclipsed by acoustic styles, and Zawinul increasingly appeared to be one of the true musical prophets of the twentieth century.

Books

Glasser, Brian, *A Silent Way: A Portrait of Joe Zawinul,* Sanctuary, 2001.

Periodicals

Daily Telegraph (London, England), September 12, 2007.
Fort Worth Star-Telegram, September 16, 2007.
Guardian (London, England), September 13, 2007.
New York Times, September 12, 2007.

Star-Ledger (Newark, NJ), September 12, 2007.
Variety, September 17, 2007.

Online

"Joe Zawinul," *All Music Guide,* http://www.allmusic.com (January 1, 2008).
"Joe Zawinul Profile," Unknown Public, http://www.unknownpublic.com/writing/zawinul2.html (January 1, 2008). ☐

Konrad Zuse

Konrad Zuse (1910-1995) is considered by many to be one of the founders of modern computing because of his work on early stage computers and computing languages.

Early Life

Konrad Zuse was born in 1910 in Berlin, Germany. His family moved to East Prussia shortly after he was born, and Zuse spent most of his life there. At a young age, Zuse showed talent in the arts and engineering, and went from making block prints and drawings to building model trains and railroads. As a boy he attended school in the town of Braunsberg, and received an education in the liberal arts. At 17, Zuse's interest in engineering led him to apply to the Berlin Technical School, where he studied the various facets of modern technical engineering. While at school, Zuse built a vending machine that dispensed food and drink, took money, and gave back exact change. However, during his studies Zuse was constantly frustrated at the numerous calculations involved in the processes of engineering. All of these calculations had to be written out and solved by hand.

Inspired to Create a Computing Machine

Zuse soon got a job at the Henschel Aircraft Company as an engineer, supervising the building of aircraft. One of his jobs was to inspect the wings of the plane, and see how much stress could be placed upon them before they would start to break apart. This job required many and diverse calculations that took up a lot of time. It was frustrating work, and Zuse spent many hours with his calculator and a pen. This inspired him to come up with the idea of a machine that would simplify the work involved in calculating advanced mathematics. However, building such a machine would not be simple. Zuse realized that he had to figure out a way for his machine to record and save the various steps involved in doing complex calculations. This required the calculation machine to be able to recognize and store various stages of the mathematical problem.

The Z1 computing machine

Zuse left his job at the aircraft company, and started to work on his invention. Using his parents' living room as a laboratory, he first figured out what his ideal machine would need. He envisioned an input device where he could define

Improvements Made to Computing Machines

Shortly after Zuse completed his first computing machine, one of his friends, Helmut Schreyer, who was also an electric engineer, suggested that Zuse replace the mechanical workings of his computing machine with vacuum tubes and telephone relay switches, to speed up the processing time and increase the efficiency of the machine. Zuse rejected the idea of using vacuum tubes, but he did incorporate the relay switches into his designs.

Zuse created the Z2 computing machine using the relay switches suggested by Schreyer. Built with the telephone relays, it was a bit more unstable than the older mechanical system, because the switches were not always reliable. However, by accommodating these new ideas, Zuse was stepping far ahead of his time, anticipating a future techology.

Zuse's work with these new forms of computation attracted the attention of the German Experimental Aircraft Institute. They had been working unsuccessfully to reduce the number of planes that broke apart during flight because of wear and tear at the wings. The Institute's job was to figure out how to overcome this problem, called fluttering. However, the Institute was not equipped to handle the vast number of calculations required to correct the problem. Zuse was contacted, and a deal was worked out where the Institute would give Zuse funding to build a better computing machine, while at the same time he assisted the Institute in building more wind-resistant planes. Zuse received the grant from the Institute and began working on the Z3, while still using his parents' living room as a base of operations. When it was finished, the Z3 could add, subtract, multiply, divide, and extract a square root. This could be done in a matter of seconds, since the number of relays that Zuse had been able to incorporate was much greater than his previous computing machines.

Innovated

Zuse's computing machines were ahead of their time in both size and portability. Zuse's Z3 took up only a closet's worth of space, and could be moved around at will. Zuse had also invented a push button control panel that allowed the user to input various commands. The device recognized conversion, and could convert decimal numbers into binary numbers and back again at the user's command.

Zuse was also the first person to come up with a programming language for his systems. He incorporated two unique symbols, which are used all the time today in mathematical calculations. They are greater than or equal to ($\geq$) and less than or equal to ($\leq$). Zuse was a technological pioneer even before such terms as hardware or software were commonplace.

World War II

Zuse was recruited by the Third Reich to create computing machines for their forces during World War II. His third computing machine, the Z3, was destroyed when an Allied bomb fell on the house where Zuse and his family

the various parts of the problem, a storage device for saving the various stages of the problem, and an arithmetical module that would work out all the steps of the equation. He would also need some way to link the various parts of the machine together, so they could operate as one. Zuse also planned to add a mechanical keyboard to his device, so he could input the various mathematical problems more efficiently.

With these ideas in mind, Zuse started to work on his project. He was a competent mechanic and draftsman, but his knowledge did not extend into the realm of electrical engineering, a discipline that would have helped him build the machine that he had envisioned. However, this did not dissuade him. Zuse was infinitely more familiar with the two-digit number system of binary arithmetic than he was with the 10-digit number system used by most calculating machines of the time, so Zuse decided that he would program his computing machine to run using binary code. It would be simpler to make a system dependent on only two numbers rather than to keep track of ten. Also, since anything could be expressed through binary code, this would give his machine greater versatility in figuring out complex equations. Zuse's final product consisted of a memory mechanism designed around moving pins in and out of slots, to represent zero or one. Another hidden benefit, Zuse realized, was that because his computing machine was only dealing with two digits, he could keep the space he needed to a minimum, and the resulting machine was very compact. The memory unit that he created took up about a cubic meter of space. Connected to a calculation unit, Zuse's first computing machine, the Z1, was completed around 1938.

lived. Zuse survived, however, and went on to create another computing machine called the S1, similar to the Z3 except that it was not programmable. The S1 computing machines were used to guide unmanned German gliders that carried bombs to targets. These gliders were directed to their targets via remote control, and used the S1 system designed by Zuse to adjust their wings and tail to flying conditions and to the movement of the intended target.

Near the end of the war, Zuse created the Z4, his most advanced system to date. Because his machine was portable, he was able to move it and keep the Allies from discovering and destroying it. He hid the computing machine in a University town by the name of Gottingen, and left it with the Experimental Aircraft Institute, the same institution that he had worked for during the War. His devices were not discovered until much later, when French troops discovered the hidden Z4.

After the French found his machine, word of the new technology spread throughout France and the United States. Members of the scientific community marveled at his computing machine, and they were amazed at how much he had accomplished without any knowledge of similar projects that were being developed at the same time.

Zuse's Later Life

After the war Zuse continued to experiment with computational devices. It took him a long time to release the information about his machines, because even after the war was over he distrusted the Allies and refused to answer their questions about his methods and computing machines.

Zuse soon learned about American scientists that had worked on technological developments during the War. Although the Americans had produced systems that were much larger than Zuse's had been, it was Zuse who brought the science of computing further than anyone had thought possible. He continued designing, and formed his own company, Zuse KG, that continued developing scientific computing systems.

Zuse is still thought to be the true father of modern computing, because of the advanced nature of his inventions.

Books

Computer Sciences, 4 vols., Macmillan Reference USA, 2002.
Notable Scientists: From 1900 to the Present, Gale Group, 2001.

Periodicals

Time, January 3, 1983.

Online

World of Computer Science. Online, Thomson Gale, 2006, Rhttp://galenet.galegroup.com/servlet/BioRC (February 26, 2008).
World of Invention. Online, Thomson Gale, 2006, http://galenet.galegroup.com/servlet/BioRC (February 26, 2008). □

HOW TO USE THE *SUPPLEMENT* INDEX

The *Encyclopedia of World Biography Supplement (EWB)* Index is designed to serve several purposes. First, it is a cumulative listing of biographies included in the entire second edition of *EWB* and its supplements (volumes 1–28). Second, it locates information on specific topics mentioned in volume 28 of the encyclopedia—persons, places, events, organizations, institutions, ideas, titles of works, inventions, as well as artistic schools, styles, and movements. Third, it classifies the subjects of *Supplement* articles according to shared characteristics. Vocational categories are the most numerous—for example, artists, authors, military leaders, philosophers, scientists, statesmen. Other groupings bring together disparate people who share a common characteristic.

The structure of the *Supplement* Index is quite simple. The biographical entries are cumulative and often provide enough information to meet immediate reference needs. Thus, people mentioned in the *Supplement* Index are identified and their life dates, when known, are given. Because this is an index to a *biographical* encyclopedia, every reference includes the *name* of the article to which the reader is directed as well as the volume and page numbers. Below are a few points that will make the *Supplement* Index easy to use.

Typography. All main entries are set in boldface type. Entries that are also the titles of articles in *EWB* are set entirely in capitals; other main entries are set in initial capitals and lowercase letters. Where a main entry is followed by a great many references, these are organized by subentries in alphabetical sequence. In certain cases—for example, the names of countries for which there are many references—a special class of subentries, set in small capitals and preceded by boldface dots, is used to mark significant divisions.

Alphabetization. The Index is alphabetized word by word. For example, all entries beginning with *New* as a separate word *(New Jersey, New York)* come before

Newark. Commas in inverted entries are treated as full stops *(Berlin; Berlin, Congress of; Berlin, University of; Berlin Academy of Sciences)*. Other commas are ignored in filing. When words are identical, persons come first and subsequent entries are alphabetized by their parenthetical qualifiers (such as *book, city, painting*).

Titled persons may be alphabetized by family name or by title. The more familiar form is used—for example, *Disraeli, Benjamin* rather than *Beaconsfield, Earl of.* Cross-references are provided from alternative forms and spellings of names. Identical names of the same nationality are filed chronologically.

Titles of books, plays, poems, paintings, and other works of art beginning with an article are filed on the following word *(Bard, The)*. Titles beginning with a preposition are filed on the preposition *(In Autumn)*. In subentries, however, prepositions are ignored; thus *influenced by* would precede the subentry *in* literature.

Literary characters are filed on the last name. Acronyms, such as UNESCO, are treated as single words. Abbreviations, such as *Mr., Mrs.,* and *St.,* are alphabetized as though they were spelled out.

Occupational categories are alphabetical by national qualifier. Thus, *Authors, Scottish* comes before *Authors, Spanish,* and the reader interested in Spanish poets will find the subentry *poets* under *Authors, Spanish.*

Cross-references. The term *see* is used in references throughout the *Supplement* Index. The *see* references appear both as main entries and as subentries. They most often direct the reader from an alternative name spelling or form to the main entry listing.

This introduction to the *Supplement* Index is necessarily brief. The reader will soon find, however, that the *Supplement* Index provides ready reference to both highly specific subjects and broad areas of information contained in volume 28 and a cumulative listing of those included in the entire set.

INDEX

A

"A"
see Arnold, Matthew

"A.B."
see Pinto, Isaac

AALTO, HUGO ALVAR HENRIK (born 1898), Finnish architect, designer, and town planner **1** 1-2

AARON, HENRY LOUIS (Hank; born 1934), American baseball player **1** 2-3

ABAKANOWICZ, MAGDALENA (Marta Abakanowicz-Kosmowski; born 1930), Polish sculptor **25** 1-3

Abarbanel
see Abravanel

ABBA ARIKA (circa 175-circa 247), Babylonian rabbi **1** 3-4

ABBAS I (1571-1629), Safavid shah of Persia 1588-1629 **1** 4-6

ABBAS, FERHAT (born 1899), Algerian statesman **1** 6-7

ABBAS, MAHMOUD (Abu Masen; born 1935), Palestinian statesman **27** 1-3

Abbas the Great
see Abbas I

Abbé Sieyès
see Sieyès, Comte Emmanuel Joseph

ABBEY, EDWARD (Edward Paul Abbey; 1927-1989), American author and environmental activist **27** 3-5

ABBOTT, BERENICE (1898-1991), American artist and photographer **1** 7-9

ABBOTT, DIANE JULIE (born 1953), British politician and journalist **26** 1-3

ABBOTT, EDITH (1876-1957), American social reformer, educator, and author **26** 3-5

ABBOTT, GRACE (1878-1939), American social worker and agency administrator **1** 9-10

ABBOTT, LYMAN (1835-1922), American Congregationalist clergyman, author, and editor **1** 10-11

ABBOUD, EL FERIK IBRAHIM (1900-1983), Sudanese general, prime minister, 1958-1964 **1** 11-12

ABD AL-MALIK (646-705), Umayyad caliph 685-705 **1** 12-13

ABD AL-MUMIN (circa 1094-1163), Almohad caliph 1133-63 **1** 13

ABD AL-RAHMAN I (731-788), Umayyad emir in Spain 756-88 **1** 13-14

Abd al-Rahman ibn Khaldun
see Ibn Khaldun, Abd al-Rahman ibn Muhammad

ABD AL-RAHMAN III (891-961), Umayyad caliph of Spain **1** 14

ABD AL-WAHHAB, MUHAMMAD IBN (Muhammad Ibn Abd al-Wahab; 1702-1703-1791-1792), Saudi religious leader **27** 5-7

ABD EL-KADIR (1807-1883), Algerian political and religious leader **1** 15

ABD EL-KRIM EL-KHATABI, MOHAMED BEN (circa 1882-1963), Moroccan Berber leader **1** 15-16

Abdallah ben Yassin
see Abdullah ibn Yasin

ABDELLAH, FAYE GLENN (born 1919), American nurse **24** 1-3

ABDUH IBN HASAN KHAYR ALLAH, MUHAMMAD (1849-1905), Egyptian nationalist and theologian **1** 16-17

Abdu-l-Malik
see Abd al-Malik

ABDUL RAHMAN, TUNKU (1903-1990), Former prime minister of Malaysia **18** 340-341

ABDUL-BAHA (Abbas Effendi; 1844-1921), Persian leader of the Baha'i Muslim sect **22** 3-5

ABDUL-HAMID II (1842-1918), Ottoman sultan 1876-1909 **1** 17-18

ABDULLAH II (Abdullah bin al Hussein II; born 1962), king of Jordan **22** 5-7

'ABDULLAH AL-SALIM AL-SABAH, SHAYKH (1895-1965), Amir of Kuwait (1950-1965) **1** 18-19

ABDULLAH IBN HUSEIN (1882-1951), king of Jordan 1949-1951, of Transjordan 1946-49 **1** 19-20

ABDULLAH IBN YASIN (died 1059), North African founder of the Almoravid movement **1** 20

ABDULLAH, MOHAMMAD (Lion of Kashmir; 1905-1982), Indian political leader who worked for an independent Kashmir **22** 7-9

Abdul the Damned
see Abdul-Hamid II

ABE, KOBO (born Kimifusa Abe; also transliterated as Abe Kobo; 1924-1993), Japanese writer, theater director, photographer **1** 20-22

ABE, SHINZO (born 1954), Japanese prime minister **28** 1-3

ABEL, IORWITH WILBER (1908-1987), United States labor organizer **1** 22-23

ABEL, NIELS (1802-1829), Norwegian mathematician **20** 1-2

ABELARD, PETER (1079-1142), French philosopher and theologian **1** 23-25

ABERCROMBY, RALPH (1734-1801), British military leader **20** 2-4

ABERDEEN, 4TH EARL OF (George Hamilton Gordon; 1784-1860), British

397

statesman, prime minister 1852-55 **1** 25-26

ABERHART, WILLIAM (1878-1943), Canadian statesman and educator **1** 26-27

ABERNATHY, RALPH DAVID (born 1926), United States minister and civil rights leader **1** 27-28

ABIOLA, MOSHOOD (1937-1998), Nigerian politician, philanthropist, and businessman **19** 1-3

ABRAHAM (Father Abraham; c. 1996 BCE - c. 1821 BCE), considered the ''father of the world's three largest monotheistic religions **23** 1-3

ABRAHAMS, ISRAEL (1858-1925), British scholar **1** 29

ABRAMOVITZ, MAX (1908-2004), American architect **18** 1-3

ABRAMS, CREIGHTON W. (1914-1974), United States Army commander in World War II and Vietnam **1** 29-31

ABRAVANEL, ISAAC BEN JUDAH (1437-1508), Jewish philosopher and statesman **1** 31

Abreha
  see Ezana

ABU BAKR (circa 573-634), Moslem leader, first caliph of Islam **1** 31-32

ABU MUSA (born Said Musa Maragha circa 1930), a leader of the Palestinian Liberation Organization **1** 32-33

ABU NUWAS (al-Hasan ibn-Hani; circa 756-813), Arab poet **1** 33-34

Abubacer
  see Ibn Tufayl, Abu Bakr Muhammad

ABU-L-ALA AL-MAARRI (973-1058), Arab poet and philosopher **1** 32

ABZUG, BELLA STAVISKY (1920-1998), lawyer, politician, and congresswoman **1** 34-35

ACEVEDO DIAZ, EDUARDO (1851-1924), Uruguayan author and activist **24** 3-4

Achad Haam
  see Ahad Haam

ACHEBE, CHINUA (born 1930), Nigerian novelist **1** 35-37

ACHESON, DEAN GOODERHAM (1893-1971), American statesman **1** 37-38

ACTION, JOHN EMERICH EDWARD DALBERG (1834-1902), English historian and philosopher **1** 38

Activists
  Bangladeshi
    Yunus, Muhammad **28** 386-388

British
  McKellen, Ian Murray **28** 234-237
  Roddick, Anita **28** 298-301
English
  Cunard, Nancy **28** 87-89
French
  Deleuze, Gilles **28** 94-96
Vietnamese
  Son, Trinh Cong **28** 335-336

Activists, American
Asian American issues
  Saund, Dalip Singh **28** 310-312
civil rights
  Patterson, Louise Alone Thompson **28** 272-274
  Roach, Max **28** 292-296
environmental
  Leopold, Aldo **28** 211-213

Actors and entertainers, American
animators
  Hanna and Barbera **28** 156-159
comedians
  Russell, Anna **28** 307-309
  Thomas, Danny **28** 350-352
filmmakers/directors
  Roach, Hal **28** 290-292
film stars
  Lawrence, Florence **28** 209-211
radio
  Vallee, Rudy **28** 359-361
television
  Griffin, Merv **28** 146-149

Actors and entertainers, Canadian
comedians
  Russell, Anna **28** 307-309

Actors and entertainers, European
• GREAT BRITAIN
  comedians
    Hill, Benny **28** 170-172
  filmmakers/directors
    Frears, Stephen Arthur **28** 127-129
  film stars
    McKellen, Ian Murray **28** 234-237
    Mirren, Helen **28** 247-249
  singers
    Haefliger, Ernst **28** 152-154
  stage performers
    McKellen, Ian Murray **28** 234-237
• THE CONTINENT
  animators
    Starewicz, Wladyslaw **28** 336-338
  dancers
    Taglioni, Marie **28** 345-347
  filmmakers/directors
    Chabrol, Claude **28** 67-69
    Romm, Mikhail **28** 303-304
    Starewicz, Wladyslaw **28** 336-338

Actors and entertainers, Japanese
animators
  Miyazaki, Hayao **28** 249-252

ADAM, JAMES (1730-1794), British architect **1** 38-40

ADAM, ROBERT (1728-1792), British architect **1** 38-40

ADAMS, ABIGAIL (Abigail Smith; 1744-1818), American first lady **18** 3-7

ADAMS, ANSEL (1902-1984), landscape photographer and conservationist **1** 40-41

Adams, Brooks
  see Adams, Peter Chardon Brooks

ADAMS, CHARLES FRANCIS (1807-1886), American diplomat and politician **1** 41-42

ADAMS, EDDIE (Edward Thomas Adams; 1933-2004), American photojournalist **25** 3-5

ADAMS, GERALD (born 1948), president of the Sinn Fein Irish political party **1** 42-44

ADAMS, HANK (born 1944), Native American activist **1** 45

ADAMS, HENRY BROOKS (1838-1918), American historian and author **1** 45-47

ADAMS, HERBERT BAXTER (1850-1901), American historian and teacher **1** 47

ADAMS, JAMES LUTHER (1901-1994), American social ethicist, theologian, and defender of religious and political liberalism **1** 47-48

ADAMS, JOHN (1735-1826), American statesman and diplomat, president 1797-1801 **1** 48-51

ADAMS, JOHN COUCH (1819-1892), English mathematical astronomer **1** 51-52

ADAMS, JOHN QUINCY (1767-1848), American statesman and diplomat, president 1825-29 **1** 52-54

ADAMS, PETER CHARDON BROOKS (1848-1927), American historian **1** 54

ADAMS, SAMUEL (1722-1803), American colonial leader and propagandist **1** 55-56

ADAMSON, JOY (Friederike Victoria Gessner; 1910-1980), Austrian naturalist and painter **18** 7-9

ADDAMS, JANE (1860-1935), American social worker, reformer, and pacifist **1** 56-57

Addis Ababa, Duke of
  see Badoglio, Pietro

ADDISON, JOSEPH (1672-1719), English essayist and politician **1** 57-58

ADDISON, THOMAS (1793-1860), English physician **1** 58-59

ADENAUER, KONRAD (1876-1967), German statesman, chancellor of the Federal Republic 1949-63 **1** 59-61

ADLER, ALFRED (1870-1937), Austrian psychiatrist **1** 61-63

ADLER, FELIX (1851-1933), American educator and Ethical Culture leader **1** 63-64

ADLER, LARRY (Lawrence Cecil Adler; 1914-2001), American harmonica player **26** 5-7

ADLER, MORTIMER JEROME (1902-2001), American philosopher and educator **22** 9-11

ADLER, RENATA (born 1938), American author **26** 8-9

Adolphe I
see Thiers, Adolphe

ADONIS ('Ali Ahmad Said; born 1930), Lebanese poet **1** 64-65

ADORNO, THEODOR W. (1903-1969), German philosopher and leader of the Frankfurt School **1** 65-67

ADRIAN, EDGAR DOUGLAS (1st Baron Adrian of Cambridge; 1889-1977), English neurophysiologist **1** 67-69

Adventurers
Slocum, Joshua **28** 333-335

ADZHUBEI, ALEKSEI IVANOVICH (1924-1993), Russian journalist and editor **18** 9-11

AELFRIC (955-circa 1012), Anglo-Saxon monk, scholar, and writer **1** 69-70

AEROSMITH (began 1969), American rock band **24** 4-7

AESCHYLUS (524-456 B.C.), Greek playwright **1** 70-72

AESOP (c. 620 B.C.E.-c. 560 B.C.E.), Greek fabulist **24** 7-8

AFFONSO I (c. 1460-1545), king of Kongo **1** 72

AFINOGENOV, ALEKSANDR NIKOLAEVICH (1904-1941), Russian dramatist **1** 72-73

'AFLAQ, MICHEL (born 1910), Syrian founder and spiritual leader of the Ba'th party **1** 73-74

African American art
see African American history (United States)

African American history (United States)
• SOCIETY and CULTURE
business leaders
Du Sable, Jean Baptiste Pointe **28** 104-106
exploration
Du Sable, Jean Baptiste Pointe **28** 104-106
inventors
Woods, Granville T. **28** 378-381
literature (20th century)
Fisher, Rudolph **28** 121-123
Patterson, Louise Alone Thompson **28** 272-274

Thurman, Wallace Henry **28** 352-354
medicine
Wright, Jane Cooke **28** 383-385
music
Lomax, John Avery **28** 224-225
Roach, Max **28** 292-296
Vallee, Rudy **28** 359-361
religion
Tolton, Augustine **28** 354-356
science
Hall, Lloyd Augustus **28** 154-156
• THROUGH CIVIL WAR
slaves
Keckley, Elizabeth Hobbs **28** 196-199

African Americans
see African American history (United States)

AGA KHAN (title), chief commander of Moslem Nizari Ismailis **1** 74-76

AGAOGLU, ADALET (Adalet Agoglu; born 1929), Turkish playwright, author, and human rights activist **22** 11-13

AGASSIZ, JEAN LOUIS RODOLPHE (1807-1873), Swiss-American naturalist and anatomist **1** 76-78

AGEE, JAMES (1909-1955), American poet, journalist, novelist, and screenwriter **1** 78-79

AGESILAUS II (circa 444-360 B.C.), king of Sparta circa 399-360 B.C. **1** 79-80

AGHA MOHAMMAD KHAN (circa 1742-1797), shah of Persia **1** 80-81

AGIS IV (circa 262-241 B.C.), king of Sparta **1** 81-82

AGNELLI, GIOVANNI (1920-2003), Italian industrialist **1** 82-83

AGNES (c. 292-c. 304), Italian Christian martyr **24** 8-10

AGNESI, MARIA (1718-1799), Italian mathematician, physicist, and philosopher **20** 4-5

AGNEW, DAVID HAYES (1818-1892), American physician **28** 3-5

AGNEW, SPIRO THEODORE (1918-1996), Republican United States vice president under Richard Nixon **1** 83-85

AGNODICE (born ca. 300 BC), Greek physician **20** 5-5

AGNON, SHMUEL YOSEPH (1888-1970), author **1** 85-86

AGOSTINO (1557-1602), Italian painter **1** 86

AGOSTINO DI DUCCIO (1418-1481?), Italian sculptor **1** 86

Agricola
see Crèvecoeur, St. J.

AGRICOLA, GEORGIUS (1494-1555), German mineralogist and writer **1** 86-87

AGRIPPINA THE YOUNGER (Julia Agrippina; 15-59), wife of Claudius I, Emperor of Rome, and mother of Nero **20** 5-8

AGUINALDO, EMILIO (1869-1964), Philippine revolutionary leader **1** 88

Agustin I
see Iturbide, Augustin de

AHAD HAAM (pseudonym of Asher T. Ginsberg, 1856-1927), Russian-born author **1** 88-89

AHERN, BERTIE (Bartholomew Ahern; born 1951), Irish Prime Minister **18** 11-13

AHIDJO, AHMADOU (1924-1989), first president of the Federal Republic of Cameroon **1** 89-90

AHMADINEJAD, MAHMOUD (Mahmoud Ahmadi Nejad; born 1956), Iranian politician **27** 7-10

AIDOO, AMA ATA (Christina Ama Aidoo; born 1942), Ghanaian writer and educator **20** 8-10

AIKEN, CONRAD (1889-1973), American poet, essayist, novelist, and critic **1** 90-91

AIKEN, HOWARD (1900-1973), American physicist, computer scientist, and inventor **20** 10-12

AILEY, ALVIN (1931-1989), African American dancer and choreographer **1** 91-94

AILLY, PIERRE D' (1350-1420), French scholar and cardinal **1** 94

Air pioneers
see Aviators

AITKEN, WILLIAM MAXWELL (Lord Beaverbrook; 1879-1964), Canadian businessman and politician **1** 94-96

AKBAR, JALAL-UD-DIN MOHAMMED (1542-1605), Mogul emperor of India 1556-1605 **1** 96

AKHENATEN (Amenhotep IV; c. 1385-c. 1350 B.C.), Egyptian pharaoh and religious leader **25** 5-7

AKHMATOVA, ANNA (pseudonym of Anna A. Gorenko, 1889-1966), Russian poet **1** 96-97

AKIBA BEN JOSEPH (circa 50-circa 135), Palestinian founder of rabbinic Judaism **1** 97-98

AKIHITO (born 1933), 125th emperor of Japan **1** 98-99

AKIYOSHI, TOSHIKO (born 1929), Japanese musician **24** 10-12

AKUTAGAWA, RYUNOSUKE (Ryunosuke Niihara; 1892-1927), Japanese author **22** 13-14

AL-ABDULLAH, RANIA (Rania al-Yasin; born 1970), Queen Rania of Jordan **25** 8-10

ALAMÁN, LUCAS (1792-1853), Mexican statesman **1** 99-100

Alamein, 1st Viscount Montgomery of
see Montgomery, Bernard Law

ALARCÓN, PEDRO ANTONIO DE (1833-1891), Spanish writer and politician **1** 100-101

ALARCÓN Y MENDOZA, JUAN RUIZ DE (1581?-1639), Spanish playwright **1** 101

ALARIC (circa 370-410), Visigothic leader **1** 101-102

Alau
see Hulagu Khan

ALA-UD-DIN (died 1316), Khalji sultan of Delhi **1** 102-103

ALAUNGPAYA (1715-1760), king of Burma 1752-1760 **1** 103

AL AQQAD, ABBAS MAHMOUD (Abbas Mahmud al Aqqad; 1889-1964), Egyptian author **24** 25-27

ALBA, DUKE OF (Fernando Álvarez de Toledo; 1507-1582), Spanish general and statesman **1** 103-104

Albania (nation, Southeastern Europe)
Simeon, King of Bulgaria **28** 325-327

AL-BANNA, HASSAN (1906-1949), Egyptian religious leader and founder of the Muslim Brotherhood **1** 104-106

Albategnius
see Battani, al-

AL-BATTANI (Abu abdallah Muhammad ibn Jabir ibn Sinan al-Raqqi al Harrani al-Sabi al-Battani; c. 858-929), Arab astronomer and mathematician **25** 10-12

ALBEE, EDWARD FRANKLIN, III (born 1928), American playwright **1** 106-108

Albemarle, Dukes of
see Monck, George

ALBÉNIZ, ISAAC (1860-1909), Spanish composer and pianist **1** 108-109

ALBERDI, JUAN BAUTISTA (1810-1884), Argentine political theorist **1** 109-110

ALBERS, JOSEPH (1888-1976), American artist and art and design teacher **1** 110

ALBERT (1819-1861), Prince Consort of Great Britain **1** 110-112

ALBERT I (1875-1934), king of the Belgians 1909-1934 **1** 112

ALBERT II (born 1934), sixth king of the Belgians **1** 112-113

Albert the Great
see Albertus Magnus, St.

ALBERTI, LEON BATTISTA (1404-1472), Italian writer, humanist, and architect **1** 113-115

ALBERTI, RAFAEL (born 1902), Spanish poet and painter **18** 13-15

ALBERTUS MAGNUS, ST. (circa 1193-1280), German philosopher and theologian **1** 115-116

ALBRIGHT, MADELEINE KORBEL (born 1937), United States secretary of state **1** 116-118

ALBRIGHT, TENLEY EMMA (born 1935), American figure skater **23** 3-6

ALBRIGHT, WILLIAM (1891-1971), American archaeologist **21** 1-3

ALBUQUERQUE, AFONSO DE (circa 1460-1515), Portuguese viceroy to India **1** 118-119

Alcántara, Pedro de
see Pedro II

ALCIBIADES (circa 450-404 B.C.), Athenian general and politician **1** 119-120

ALCORN, JAMES LUSK (1816-1894), American lawyer and politician **1** 120-121

ALCOTT, AMOS BRONSON (1799-1888), American educator **1** 121

ALCOTT, LOUISA MAY (1832-1888), American author and reformer **1** 122

ALCUIN OF YORK (730?-804), English educator, statesman, and liturgist **1** 122-123

ALDRICH, NELSON WILMARTH (1841-1915), American statesman and financier **1** 123-124

Aldrin, Buzz
see Aldrin, Edwin Eugene, Jr.

ALDRIN, EDWIN EUGENE, JR. (Buzz Aldrin; born 1930), American astronaut **18** 15-17

ALDUS MANUTIUS (Teobaldo Manuzio; 1450?-1515), Italian scholar and printer **21** 3-5

ALEICHEM, SHOLOM (Sholom Rabinowitz; 1859-1916), writer of literature relating to Russian Jews **1** 124-125

ALEIJADINHO, O (Antônio Francisco Lisbôa; 1738-1814), Brazilian architect and sculptor **1** 125-126

ALEMÁN, MATEO (1547-after 1615), Spanish novelist **1** 126

ALEMÁN VALDÉS, MIGUEL (1902-1983), Mexican statesman, president 1946-1952 **1** 126-127

ALEMBERT, JEAN LE ROND D' (1717-1783), French mathematician and physicist **1** 127-128

ALESSANDRI PALMA, ARTURO (1868-1950), Chilean statesman, president 1920-1925 and 1932-1938 **1** 128-129

ALESSANDRI RODRIGUEZ, JORGE (born 1896), Chilean statesman, president 1958-1964 **1** 129-130

ALEXANDER I (1777-1825), czar of Russia 1801-1825 **1** 130-132

Alexander I, king of Yugoslavia
see Alexander of Yugoslavia

ALEXANDER II (1818-1881), czar of Russia 1855-1881 **1** 132-133

ALEXANDER III (1845-1894), emperor of Russia 1881-1894 **1** 133-134

ALEXANDER III (Orlando Bandinelli; c. 1100-1181), Italian pope 1159-1181 **24** 12-14

Alexander III, king of Macedon
see Alexander the Great

ALEXANDER VI (Rodrigo Borgia; 1431-1503), pope 1492-1503 **1** 134-135

ALEXANDER VII (Fabio Chigi; 1599-1667), Roman Catholic pope **25** 12-13

ALEXANDER, JANE (nee Jane Quigley; born 1939), American actress **26** 9-12

ALEXANDER, SADIE TANNER MOSSELL (1898-1989), African American lawyer **25** 13-15

ALEXANDER, SAMUEL (1859-1938), British philosopher **1** 141

Alexander Karageorgevich (1888-1934)
see Alexander of Yugoslavia

Alexander Nevsky
see Nevsky, Alexander

ALEXANDER OF TUNIS, 1ST EARL (Harold Rupert Leofric George Alexander; born 1891), British field marshal **1** 135-136

ALEXANDER OF YUGOSLAVIA (1888-1934), king of the Serbs, Croats, and Slovenes 1921-1929 and of Yugoslavia, 1929-1934 **1** 136-137

ALEXANDER THE GREAT (356-323 B.C.), king of Macedon **1** 137-141

Alexeyev, Constantin Sergeyevich
see Stanislavsky, Constantin

ALEXIE, SHERMAN (born 1966), Native American writer, poet, and translator **1** 141-142

ALEXIS MIKHAILOVICH ROMANOV (1629-1676), czar of Russia 1645-1676 **1** 142-143

ALEXIUS I (circa 1048-1118), Byzantine emperor 1081-1118 **1** 143-144

ALFARO, JOSÉ ELOY (1842-1912), Ecuadorian revolutionary, president 1895-1901 and 1906-1911 **1** 144-145

ALFIERI, CONTE VITTORIA (1749-1803), Italian playwright **1** 145-146

ALFONSÍN, RAUL RICARDO (born 1927), politician and president of Argentina (1983-) **1** 146-148

ALFONSO I (Henriques; 1109?-1185), king of Portugal 1139-1185 **1** 148

Alfonso I, king of Castile
see Alfonso VI, king of León

ALFONSO III (1210-1279), king of Portugal 1248-1279 **1** 148-149

ALFONSO VI (1040-1109), king of León, 1065-1109, and of Castile, 1072-1109 **1** 149

ALFONSO X (1221-1284), king of Castile and León 1252-1284 **1** 150-151

ALFONSO XIII (1886-1941), king of Spain 1886-1931 **1** 151

Alfonso the Wise
see Alfonso X, king of Castile and León

ALFRED (849-899), Anglo-Saxon king of Wessex 871-899 **1** 151-153

Alfred the Great
see Alfred, king of Wessex

Algazel
see Ghazali, Abu Hamid Muhammad al-

ALGER, HORATIO (1832-1899), American author **1** 153-154

ALGREN, NELSON (Abraham; 1909-1981), American author **1** 154-155

Alhazen
see Hassan ibn al-Haytham

ALI (circa 600-661), fourth caliph of the Islamic Empire **1** 155-156

ALI, AHMED (1908-1998), Pakistani scholar, poet, author, and diplomat **22** 16-18

Ali, Haidar
see Haidar Ali

ALI, MUHAMMAD (Cassius Clay; born 1942), American boxer **1** 156-158

ALI, SUNNI (died 1492), king of Gao, founder of the Songhay empire **1** 158-159

Ali Ber
see Ali, Sunni

Ali Shah (died 1885)
see Aga Khan II

Ali the Great
see Ali, Sunni

ALIA, RAMIZ (born 1925), president of Albania (1985-) **1** 159

ALINSKY, SAUL DAVID (1909-1972), U.S. organizer of neighborhood citizen reform groups **1** 161-162

AL-KASHI (Ghiyath al-Din Jamshid Mas'ud Al-Kashi; 1380-1429), Iranian mathematician and astronomer **26** 12-13

ALLAL AL-FASSI, MOHAMED (1910-1974), Moroccan nationalist leader **1** 162

ALLAWI, IYAD (born 1945), Iraqi prime minister **25** 15-17

Allegri, Antonio
see Correggio

ALLEN, ELSIE (Elsie Comanche Allen; 1899-1990), Native American weaver and educator **27** 10-11

ALLEN, ETHAN (1738-1789), American Revolutionary War soldier **1** 163-164

ALLEN, FLORENCE ELLINWOOD (1884-1966), American lawyer, judge, and women's rights activist **1** 164-165

ALLEN, GRACIE (1906-1964), American actress and comedian **22** 18-20

ALLEN, PAUL (Paul Gardner Allen; born 1953), American entrepreneur and philanthropist **25** 17-19

ALLEN, PAULA GUNN (born 1939), Native American writer, poet, literary critic; women's rights, environmental, and antiwar activist **1** 165-167

ALLEN, RICHARD (1760-1831), African American bishop **1** 168

ALLEN, SARAH (Sarah Bass Allen; 1764-1849), African American missionary **27** 12-13

ALLEN, STEVE (1921-2000), American comedian, author, and composer **22** 20-22

ALLEN, WOODY (born Allen Stewart Konigsberg; b. 1935), American actor, director, filmmaker, author, comedian **1** 169-171

ALLENBY, EDMUND HENRY HYNMAN (1861-1936), English field marshal **1** 171-172

ALLENDE, ISABEL (born 1942), Chilean novelist, journalist, dramatist **1** 172-174

ALLENDE GOSSENS, SALVADOR (1908-1973), socialist president of Chile (1970-1973) **1** 174-176

Alleyne, Ellen
see Rossetti, Christina Georgina

ALLSTON, WASHINGTON (1779-1843), American painter **1** 176-177

ALMAGRO, DIEGO DE (circa 1474-1538), Spanish conquistador and explorer **1** 177-178

ALMENDROS, NÉSTOR (Nestor Almendrod Cuyas; 1930-1992), Hispanic American cinematographer **27** 13-15

ALMODOVAR, PEDRO (Calmodovar, Caballero, Pedro; born 1949), Spanish film director and screenwriter **23** 6-9

Alompra
see Alaungpaya

Alonso (Araucanian chief)
see Lautaro

ALONSO, ALICIA (Alicia Ernestina de la Caridad dei Cobre Martinez Hoya; born 1921), Cuban ballerina **24** 14-17

ALP ARSLAN (1026/32-1072), Seljuk sultan of Persia and Iraq **1** 178-179

Alpetragius
see Bitruji, Nur al-Din Abu Ishaq al-

Alphonse the Wise
see Alfonso X, king of Castile

AL-SHUKAIRY, AHMAD (1908-1980), Lebanese diplomat and Arab nationalist **25** 20-21

ALTAMIRA Y CREVEA, RAFAEL (1866-1951), Spanish critic, historian, and jurist **1** 179

ALTDORFER, ALBRECHT (circa 1480-1538), German painter, printmaker, and architect **1** 179-180

ALTERMAN, NATAN (1910-1970), Israeli poet and journalist **24** 17-18

ALTGELD, JOHN PETER (1847-1902), American jurist and politician **1** 180-182

ALTHUSSER, LOUIS (1918-1990), French Communist philosopher **1** 182-183

ALTIZER, THOMAS J. J. (born 1927), American theologian **1** 183-184

ALTMAN, ROBERT (1925-2006), American filmmaker **20** 12-14

ALTMAN, SIDNEY (born 1939), Canadian American molecular biologist **23** 9-11

ALUPI, CALIN (Calinic Alupi; 1906-1988), Romanian artist **24** 18-19

Alva, Duke of
see Alba, Duke of

ALVARADO, LINDA (Linda Martinez; born 1951), American businesswoman **25** 21-23

Alvarez, Jorge Guillén y
see Guillén y Alvarez, Jorge

ÁLVAREZ, JUAN (1780-1867), Mexican soldier and statesman, president 1855 **1** 184-185

ALVAREZ, JULIA (born 1950), Hispanic American novelist, poet **1** 185-187

ALVAREZ, LUIS W. (1911-1988), American physicist **1** 187-189

ALVARIÑO, ANGELES (Angeles Alvariño Leira; 1916-2005), Spanish American marine scientist **27** 15-17

AMADO, JORGE (born 1912), Brazilian novelist **1** 189-190

AMBEDKAR, BHIMRAO RAMJI (1891-1956), Indian social reformer and politician **1** 190-191

AMBLER, ERIC (born 1909), English novelist **1** 191-192

Ambrogini, Angelo
see Poliziano, Angelo

AMBROSE, ST. (339-397), Italian bishop **1** 192-193

AMENEMHET I (ruled 1991-1962 B.C.), pharaoh of Egypt **1** 193-194

AMENHOTEP III (ruled 1417-1379 B.C.), pharaoh of Egypt **1** 194-195

Amenhotep IV
see Ikhnaton

Amenophis IV
see Ikhnaton

American art
African American
Lewis, Edmonia **28** 215-217
cartoons
Hanna and Barbera **28** 156-159
Native American
Lewis, Edmonia **28** 215-217
sculpture (19th century)
Lewis, Edmonia **28** 215-217

AMERICAN HORSE (aka Iron Shield; 1840?-1876), Sioux leader **1** 195-198

American literature
African American fiction and drama
Fisher, Rudolph **28** 121-123
autobiography
Keckley, Elizabeth Hobbs **28** 196-199
fantasy
Norton, Andre **28** 257-259

folk themes
Brown, Sterling **28** 51-54
literary criticism
Bloom, Harold **28** 38-40
poetry
Collins, Billy **28** 83-85
science fiction
Dick, Philip K. **28** 96-98
Heinlein, Robert A. **28** 166-168
Herbert, Frank, Jr. **28** 168-170
Norton, Andre **28** 257-259
spiritualist
Castaneda, Carlos **28** 62-64

American Michelangelo
see Rimmer, William

American music
20th century
Appalachian
Sharp, Cecil **28** 321-323
folk and national themes
Lomax, John Avery **28** 224-225
Sharp, Cecil **28** 321-323
jazz
Anderson, Ivie Marie **28** 10-12
orchestral music
Ormandy, Eugene **28** 264-266
popular and show music
Vallee, Rudy **28** 359-361

American Rembrandt
see Johnson, Jonathan Eastman

American Woodsman
see Audubon, John James

AMES, ADELBERT (1835-1933), American politician **1** 198

AMES, FISHER (1758-1808), American statesman **1** 199-200

AMHERST, JEFFERY (1717-1797), English general and statesman **1** 200-201

AMICHAI, YEHUDA (Yehuda Pfeuffer; Yehudah Amichai; 1924-2000), German-Israeli poet **24** 19-21

AMIET, CUNO (1868-1961), Swiss Postimpressionist painter **1** 201-202

AMIN DADA, IDI (born circa 1926), president of Uganda (1971-1979) **1** 202-204

AMINA OF ZARIA (Amina Sarauniya Zazzau; c. 1533-c. 1610), Nigerian monarch and warrior **21** 5-7

AMIS, KINGSLEY (Kingsley William Amis; 1922-1995), English author **28** 5-8

Amitabha Buddha
see Buddha (play)

AMMA (Amritanandamayi, Mata; Ammachi; Sudhamani; born 1953), Indian spiritual leader **28** 8-10

AMORSOLO, FERNANDO (1892-1972), Philippine painter **1** 204

AMORY, CLEVELAND (1917-1998), American author and animal rights activist **26** 14-16

AMOS (flourished 8th century B.C.), Biblical prophet **1** 205

AMPÈRE, ANDRÉ MARIE (1775-1836), French physicist **1** 205-206

AMUNDSEN, ROALD (1872-1928), Norwegian explorer **1** 206-207

AN LU-SHAN (703-757), Chinese rebel leader **1** 239-240

ANAN BEN DAVID (flourished 8th century), Jewish Karaite leader in Babylonia **1** 207-208

Anatomy (science)
pathological
Agnew, David Hayes **28** 3-5

ANAXAGORAS (circa 500-circa 428 B.C.), Greek philosopher **1** 208-209

ANAXIMANDER (circa 610-circa 546 B.C.), Greek philosopher and astronomer **1** 209-210

ANAXIMENES (flourished 546 B.C.), Greek philosopher **1** 210

ANAYA, RUDOLFO ALFONSO (born 1937), Chicano American author **27** 17-19

ANCHIETA, JOSÉ DE (1534-1597), Portuguese Jesuit missionary **1** 210-211

ANDERSEN, DOROTHY (1901-1963), American physician and pathologist **1** 212

ANDERSEN, HANS CHRISTIAN (1805-1875), Danish author **1** 212-214

ANDERSON, CARL DAVID (1905-1991), American physicist **1** 214-215

ANDERSON, IVIE MARIE (Ivy Marie Anderson; 1905-1949), African-American singer **28** 10-12

ANDERSON, JUDITH (1898-1992), American stage and film actress **1** 215-216

ANDERSON, JUNE (born 1953), American opera singer **1** 216-218

ANDERSON, MARIAN (1902-1993), African American singer **1** 218-219

ANDERSON, MAXWELL (1888-1959), American playwright **1** 219-220

ANDERSON, SHERWOOD (1876-1941), American writer **1** 220-221

ANDO, TADAO (born 1941), Japanese architect **18** 17-19

ANDRADA E SILVA, JOSÉ BONIFÁCIO DE (1763-1838), Brazilian-born statesman and scientist **1** 221-222

ANDRÁSSY, COUNT JULIUS (1823-1890), Hungarian statesman, prime minister 1867-1871 **1** 222-223

Andrea da Pontedera
see Andrea Pisano

ANDREA DEL CASTAGNO (1421-1457), Italian painter **1** 223-224

ANDREA DEL SARTO (1486-1530), Italian painter **1** 224-225

ANDREA PISANO (circa 1290/95-1348), Italian sculptor and architect **1** 225-226

ANDREAS-SALOMÉ, LOU (Louise Salomé; 1861-1937), Russian-born German author and feminist **28** 12-14

ANDRÉE, SALOMON AUGUST (1854-1897), Swedish engineer and Arctic balloonist **1** 226

ANDREESSEN, MARC (born 1972), American computer programmer who developed Netscape Navigator **19** 3-5

Andreino
see Andrea del Sarto

ANDREOTTI, GIULIO (born 1919), leader of Italy's Christian Democratic party **1** 226-228

ANDRETTI, MARIO (born 1940), Italian/American race car driver **1** 228-230

ANDREW, JOHN ALBION (1818-1867), American politician **1** 230-231

ANDREWS, BENNY (1930-2006), African American artists **25** 23-25

ANDREWS, CHARLES MCLEAN (1863-1943), American historian **1** 231

ANDREWS, FANNIE FERN PHILLIPS (1867-1950), American educator, reformer, pacifist **1** 231-232

ANDREWS, JULIE (Julie Edwards; born 1935), British singer, actress, and author **25** 25-28

ANDREWS, ROY CHAPMAN (1884-1960), American naturalist and explorer **1** 232-233

ANDRIĆ, IVO (1892-1975), Yugoslav author **24** 21-24

ANDROPOV, IURY VLADIMIROVICH (1914-1984), head of the Soviet secret police and ruler of the Soviet Union (1982-1984) **1** 233-234

ANDROS, SIR EDMUND (1637-1714), English colonial governor in America **1** 234-235

ANDRUS, ETHEL (1884-1976), American educator and founder of the American Association of Retired Persons **19** 5-7

Angel of the Crimea
see Nightingale, Florence

ANGELICO, FRA (circa 1400-1455), Italian painter **1** 235-236

ANGELL, JAMES ROWLAND (1869-1949), psychologist and leader in higher education **1** 236-237

Angelo de Cosimo
see Bronzino

ANGELOU, MAYA (Marguerite Johnson; born 1928), American author, poet, playwright, stage and screen performer, and director **1** 238-239

ANGUISSOLA, SOFONISBA (Sofonisba Anguisciola; c. 1535-1625), Italian artist **22** 22-24

Anna Comnena
see Comnena, Anna

ANNA IVANOVNA (1693-1740), empress of Russia 1730-1740 **1** 240-241

ANNAN, KOFI (born 1938), Ghanaian secretary-general of the United Nations **18** 19-21

ANNE (1665-1714), queen of England 1702-1714 and of Great Britain 1707-1714 **1** 241-242

ANNE OF CLEVES (1515-1557), German princess and fourth wife of Henry VIII **27** 19-21

ANNENBERG, WALTER HUBERT (1908-2002), American publisher and philanthropist **26** 16-18

Annie Get Your Gun (musical)
Sheldon, Sidney **28** 323-325

ANNING, MARY (1799-1847), British fossil collector **20** 14-16

Annunzio, Gabriele d'
see D'Annunzio, Gabriel

ANOKYE, OKOMFO (Kwame Frimpon Anokye; flourished late 17th century), Ashanti priest and statesman **1** 242-243

ANOUILH, JEAN (1910-1987), French playwright **1** 243-244

ANSELM OF CANTERBURY, ST. (1033-1109), Italian archbishop and theologian **1** 244-245

Anson, Charles Edward
see Markham, Edwin

Anthoniszoon, Jeroen
see Bosch, Hieronymus

Anthony, Mark
see Antony, Mark

Anthony, Peter
see Shaffer, Peter Levin

ANTHONY, ST. (circa 250-356), Egyptian hermit and monastic founder **1** 246-248

ANTHONY, SUSAN BROWNELL (1820-1906), American leader of suffrage movement **1** 246-248

Anthony Abbott, St.
see Anthony, St.

Anthony of Egypt, St.
see Anthony, St.

ANTHONY OF PADUA, SAINT (Fernando de Boullion; 1195-1231), Portuguese theologian and priest **21** 7-9

Anthropology (social science)
fossil man
　Dubois, Eugène **28** 106-108
Native Americans
　Castaneda, Carlos **28** 62-64

Anti-Oedipus (book)
Deleuze, Gilles **28** 94-96

ANTIGONUS I (382-301 B.C.), king of Macedon 306-301 B.C. **1** 248-249

ANTIOCHUS III (241-187 B.C.), king of Syria 223-187 B.C. **1** 249-250

ANTIOCHUS IV (circa 215-163 B.C.), king of Syria 175-163 B.C. **1** 250

Antiochus the Great
see Antiochus III

ANTISTHENES (circa 450-360 B.C.), Greek philosopher **1** 250-251

ANTONELLO DA MESSINA (circa 1430-1479), Italian painter **1** 251-252

Antoninus, Marcus Aurelius
see Caracalla

Antonio, Donato di Pascuccio d'
see Bramante, Donato

ANTONIONI, MICHELANGELO (1912-2007), Italian film director **1** 252-253

Antonius, Marcus
see Antony, Mark

ANTONY, MARK (circa 82-30 B.C.), Roman politician and general **1** 253-254

Anushervan the Just
see Khosrow I

Anxiety of Influence, The (book)
Bloom, Harold **28** 38-40

ANZA, JUAN BAUTISTA DE (1735-1788), Spanish explorer **1** 254-255

AOUN, MICHEL (born 1935), Christian Lebanese military leader and prime minister **1** 255-257

Apache Napoleon
see Cochise

APELLES (flourished after 350 B.C.), Greek painter **1** 257

APESS, WILLIAM (1798-1839), Native American religious leader, author, and activist **20** 16-18

APGAR, VIRGINIA (1909-1974), American medical educator, researcher **1** 257-259

APITHY, SOUROU MIGAN (1913-1989), Dahomean political leader **1** 259-260

APOLLINAIRE, GUILLAUME (1880-1918), French lyric poet **1** 260

APOLLODORUS (flourished circa 408 B.C.), Greek painter **1** 261

APOLLONIUS OF PERGA (flourished 210 B.C.), Greek mathematician **1** 261-262

Apostate, the
see Julian

APPELFELD, AHARON (born 1932), Israeli who wrote about anti-Semitism and the Holocaust **1** 262-263

APPERT, NICOLAS (1749-1941), French chef and inventor of canning of foods **20** 18-19

APPIA, ADOLPHE (1862-1928), Swiss stage director **1** 263-264

APPLEBEE, CONSTANCE (1873-1981), American field hockey coach **24** 24-25

APPLEGATE, JESSE (1811-1888), American surveyor, pioneer, and rancher **1** 264-265

APPLETON, SIR EDWARD VICTOR (1892-1965), British pioneer in radio physics **1** 265-266

APPLETON, NATHAN (1779-1861), American merchant and manufacturer **1** 266-267

APULEIUS, LUCIUS (c. 124-170), Roman author, philosopher, and orator **20** 19-21

Apulia, Robert Guiscard, Count and Duke of
see Guiscard, Robert

Aquinas, St. Thomas
see Thomas Aquinas, St.

AQUINO, BENIGNO ("Nino"; 1933-1983), Filipino activist murdered upon his return from exile **1** 267-268

AQUINO, CORAZON COJOANGCO (born 1933), first woman president of the Republic of the Philippines **1** 268-270

Arabic literature
feminist
Mala'ika, Nazik al- **28** 230-232
modern
Mala'ika, Nazik al- **28** 230-232

ARAFAT, YASSER (also spelled Yasir; 1929-2004), chairman of the Palestinian Liberation Organization **1** 270-271

ARAGON, LOUIS (1897-1982), French surrealist author **1** 271-272
Cunard, Nancy **28** 87-89

Arango, Doroteo
see Villa, Pancho

ARANHA, OSVALDO (1894-1960), Brazilian political leader **1** 272-273

ARATUS (271-213 B.C.), Greek statesman and general **1** 273-274

ARBENZ GUZMÁN, JACOBO (1913-1971), president of Guatemala (1951-1954) **1** 274-276

ARBER, AGNES ROBERTSON (nee Agnes Robertson; 1879-1960), English botanist **28** 14-16

Arblay, Madame d'
see Burney, Frances "Fanny"

ARBUS, DIANE NEMEROV (1923-1971), American photographer **1** 276-277

ARCARO, EDDIE (George Edward Arcaro; 1916-1997), American jockey **27** 21-23

Archeologist king
see Ashurbanipal

ARCHIMEDES (circa 287-212 B.C.), Greek mathematician **1** 277-280

ARCHIPENKO, ALEXANDER (1887-1964), Russian-American sculptor and teacher **1** 280-281

ARCINIEGAS, GERMAN (1900-1999), Colombian historian, educator, and journalist **24** 27-29

ARDEN, ELIZABETH (Florence Nightingale Graham; 1878?-1966), American businesswoman **1** 281-282

ARENDT, HANNAH (1906-1975), Jewish philosopher **1** 282-284

ARENS, MOSHE (born 1925), aeronautical engineer who became a leading Israeli statesman **1** 284-285

ARETE OF CYRENE (c. 400 B.C-c. 340 B.C.), Grecian philosopher **26** 18-20

ARÉVALO, JUAN JOSÉ (1904-1951), Guatemalan statesman, president 1944-1951 **1** 285-286

Ari Ha-qodesh
see Luria, Isaac ben Solomon

ARIAS, ARNULFO (1901-1988), thrice elected president of Panama **1** 286-287

ARIAS SANCHEZ, OSCAR (born 1941), Costa Rican politician, social activist,

president, and Nobel Peace Laureate (1987) **1** 287-289

ARINZE, FRANCIS (born 1932), Nigerian Roman Catholic cardinal **26** 20-22

ARIOSTO, LUDOVICO (1474-1533), Italian poet and playwright **1** 289-290

ARISTARCHUS OF SAMOS (circa 310-230 B.C.), Greek astronomer **1** 290-291

ARISTIDE, JEAN-BERTRAND (born 1953), president of Haiti (1990-91 and 1994-95); deposed by a military coup in 1991; restored to power in 1994 **1** 291-293

Aristio
see Unánue, José Hipólito

ARISTOPHANES (450/445-after 385 B.C.), Greek playwright **1** 293-294

ARISTOTLE (384-322 B.C.), Greek philosopher and scientist **1** 295-296

ARIUS (died circa 336), Libyan theologian and heresiarch **1** 297-298

ARKWRIGHT, SIR RICHARD (1732-1792), English inventor and industrialist **1** 298

ARLEN, HAROLD (born Hyman Arluck; 1905-1986), American jazz pianist, composer, and arranger **19** 7-9

ARLT, ROBERTO (Roberto Godofredo Christophersen Arlt; 1900-1942), Argentine author and journalist **23** 11-13

ARMANI, GIORGIO (1935-1997), Italian fashion designer **1** 299-301

ARMINIUS, JACOBUS (1560-1609), Dutch theologian **1** 301-302

ARMOUR, PHILIP DANFORTH (1832-1901), American industrialist **1** 302

ARMSTRONG, EDWIN HOWARD (1890-1954), American electrical engineer and radio inventor **1** 302-303

ARMSTRONG, HENRY (Henry Jackson, Jr.; 1912-1988), American boxer and minister **21** 9-11

ARMSTRONG, LANCE (born 1971), American cyclist **23** 13-15
Merckx, Eddy **28** 241-243

ARMSTRONG, LILLIAN HARDIN (1898-1971), African American musician **23** 15-17

ARMSTRONG, LOUIS DANIEL (1900-1971), African American jazz musician **1** 303-304

ARMSTRONG, NEIL ALDEN (born 1930), American astronaut **1** 304-306

ARMSTRONG, SAMUEL CHAPMAN (1839-1893), American educator **1** 306-307

ARNAZ, DESI (Desiderio Alberto Arnaz y De Acha; 1917-1986), American musician and actor **21** 12-14

ARNE, THOMAS AUGUSTINE (1710-1778), English composer **1** 307-308

ARNIM, ACHIM VON (Ludwig Joachim von Achim; 1781-1831), German writer **1** 308-309

ARNOLD, GEN. BENEDICT (1741-1801), American general and traitor **1** 309-310

Arnold, Franz *see* Lieber, Francis

ARNOLD, HENRY HARLEY (Hap; 1886-1950), American general **1** 310-311

ARNOLD, MATTHEW (1822-1888), English poet and critic **1** 311-313

ARNOLD, THOMAS (1795-1842), English educator **1** 313-314

ARNOLD, THURMAN WESLEY (1891-1969), American statesman **1** 314

ARNOLD OF BRESCIA (circa 1100-1155), Italian religious reformer **1** 314-315

ARNOLFO DI CAMBIO (1245?-1302), Italian sculptor and architect **1** 315-316

ARON, RAYMOND (1905-1983), academic scholar, teacher, and journalist **1** 316-317

Arouet, François Marie *see* Voltaire

ARP, JEAN (Hans Arp; 1887-1966), French sculptor and painter **1** 317-318

ARRAU, CLAUDIO (1903-1991), Chilean American pianist **23** 17-18

ARRHENIUS, SVANTE AUGUST (1859-1927), Swedish chemist and physicist **1** 318-320

ARROYO, MARTINA (born c. 1936), African American opera singer **27** 23-25

Ars, Curé of *see* Vianney, St. Jean Baptiste

ARTAUD, ANTONIN (1896-1948), developed the theory of the Theater of Cruelty **1** 320-321

ARTHUR, CHESTER ALAN (1830-1886), American statesman, president 1881-1885 **1** 321-323

ARTIGAS, JOSÉ GERVASIO (1764-1850), Uruguayan patriot **1** 323

Artists, American
cartoonists
Hanna and Barbera **28** 156-159
photographers
Hine, Lewis Wickes **28** 172-174
sculptors (19th-20th century)
Lewis, Edmonia **28** 215-217

Artists, Belgian
Peyo **28** 280-282

Artists, Bohemian
Hollar, Wenceslaus **28** 180-183

Artists, Czech
Hollar, Wenceslaus **28** 180-183

Artists, English
illustrators
Arber, Agnes Robertson **28** 14-16
painters (20th century)
Lewis, Wyndham **28** 217-219

Artists, Finnish
Wirkkala, Tapio **28** 372-374

Artists, French
cartoonists
Grandville, J.J. **28** 144-146
lithographers
Grandville, J.J. **28** 144-146
sculptors (19th-20th century)
Bartholdi, Frédéric-Auguste **28** 29-31

Artists, German
wax modelers
Tussaud, Marie **28** 356-358

Artists, Japanese
animators
Miyazaki Hayao **28** 249-252

Artists, Polish
Witkacy **28** 374-376

ASAM, COSMAS DAMIAN (1686-1739), German artist **1** 323-324

ASAM, EGID QUIRIN (1692-1750), German artist **1** 323-324

ASBURY, FRANCIS (1745-1816), English-born American Methodist bishop **1** 324-325

ASCH, SHALOM (1880-1957), Polish-born playwright and novelist **1** 325-326

Asclepiades *see* Hippocrates

ASH, MARY KAY WAGNER (born circa 1916), cosmetics tycoon **1** 326-327

ASHARI, ABU AL- HASAN ALI AL- (873/883-935), Moslem theologian **1** 327-328

ASHCROFT, JOHN (born 1942), American statesman and attorney general **23** 18-21

ASHE, ARTHUR ROBERT, JR. (1943-1993), world champion athlete, social activist, teacher, and charity worker **1** 328-330

ASHFORD, EVELYN (born 1957), American athlete **24** 29-32

Ashikaga shogunate *see* Japan—1338-1573

ASHIKAGA TAKAUJI (1305-1358), Japanese shogun **1** 330-332

ASHKENAZY, VLADIMIR (born 1937), Russian musician **22** 24-26

Ashley, 1st Baron *see* Shaftesbury, 1st Earl of

ASHLEY, LAURA (Mountney; 1925-1985), British designer of women's clothes and home furnishings **1** 332-333

Ashley, Lord *see* Shaftesbury, 7th Earl of

ASHLEY, WILLIAM HENRY (circa 1778-1838), American businessman, fur trader, and explorer **1** 333-334

ASHMORE, HARRY SCOTT (1916-1998), American journalist **1** 334-335

ASHMUN, JEHUDI (1794-1828), American governor of Liberia Colony **1** 335-336

ASHRAWI, HANAN MIKHAIL (born 1946), Palestinian spokesperson **1** 336-338

ASHTON, FREDERICK (Frederick William Ashton; 1904-1988), British choreographer **26** 22-24

ASHURBANIPAL (died circa 630 B.C.), Assyrian king 669-ca. 630 **1** 338

ASIMOV, ISAAC (1920-1992), American author **1** 338-341

Askia the Great *see* Muhammad Ture, Askia

ASOKA (ruled circa 273-232 B.C.), Indian emperor of the Maurya dynasty **1** 341-342

ASPASIA (ca. 470-410 BC), Milesian courtesan and rhetorician **22** 26-28

ASPIN, LES (1938-1995), United States congressman and secretary of defense **1** 342-344

Aspirin (drug)
Hoffmann, Felix **28** 179-180

ASPLUND, ERIC GUNNAR (1885-1945), Swedish architect **1** 344

ASQUITH, HERBERT HENRY (1st Earl of Oxford and Asquith; 1852-1928), English statesman, prime minister 1908-1916 **1** 344-346

ASSAD, HAFIZ (born 1930), president of Syria **1** 346-348
Hariri, Rafic **28** 161-163

Assassinations
Lebanon
Gemayel, Bashir **28** 136-138
Hariri, Rafic **28** 161-163
Netherlands
Fortuyn, Pim **28** 125-127
Sweden
Palme, Olof **28** 267-269

ASTAIRE, FRED (Frederick Austerlitz;
1899-1987), dancer and choreographer
1 348-350

ASTELL, MARY (Tom Single, Mr.
Wooton; 1666-1731), English author
24 32-34

ASTON, FRANCIS WILLIAM (1877-
1945), English chemist and physicist **1**
350-351

ASTOR, JOHN JACOB (1763-1848),
American fur trader, merchant, and
capitalist **1** 351-352

ASTOR, NANCY LANGHORNE (1879-
1964), first woman to serve as a
member of the British Parliament
(1919-1945) **1** 352-354

Astrea
see Behn, Aphra

ASTURIAS, MIGUEL ANGEL (born
1899), Guatemalan novelist and poet **1**
354-355

ATAHUALPA (circa 1502-1533), Inca
emperor of Peru 1532-1533 **1** 355-356

ATANASOFF, JOHN (1903-1995),
American physicist **20** 21-22

ATATÜRK, GHAZI MUSTAPHA KEMAL
(1881-1938), Turkish nationalist,
president 1923-1938 **1** 356-357
Nursî, Said **28** 259-261

ATCHISON, DAVID RICE (1807-1886),
American lawyer and politician **1**
357-358

ATHANASIUS, ST. (circa 296-373),
Christian theologian, bishop of
Alexandria **1** 358-359

ATHERTON, GERTRUDE (Gertrude
Franklin Horn Atherton; 1857-1948),
American author **23** 21-23

Athletes
Belgian
Merckx, Eddy **28** 241-243

Athletes, American
football coaches
Walsh, Bill **28** 370-372

ATKINS, CHET (Chester Burton Atkins;
1924-2000), American musician **22**
28-30

ATKINS, VERA (Vera Maria [May]
Rosenberg; 1908-2000), English
intelligence agent **28** 16-18

ATKINSON, LOUISA (Louisa Warning
Atkinson; 1834-1872), Australian
author **22** 30-33

ATLAS, CHARLES (Angelo Siciliano;
1893-1972), American body builder **21**
14-15

Atomic bomb (weapon)
development
Fuchs, Klaus **28** 129-131

ATTAR, FARID ED-DIN (circa 1140-circa
1234), Persian poet **1** 359-360

ATTENBOROUGH, RICHARD SAMUEL
(born 1923), English actor and
filmmaker **18** 21-23

Attic Bee
see Sophocles

ATTILA (died 453), Hun chieftain **1** 360

ATTLEE, CLEMENT RICHARD (1st Earl
Attlee; 1883-1967), English statesman,
prime minister 1945-1951 **1** 361-362

Attorneys general
see statesmen, American

ATWOOD, MARGARET ELEANOR (born
1939), Canadian novelist, poet, critic,
and politically committed cultural
activist **1** 362-364

AUBERT DE GASPÉ, PHILIPPE (1786-
1871), French-Canadian author **1** 364

AUDEN, WYSTAN HUGH (1907-1973),
English-born American poet **1** 364-366

AUDUBON, JOHN JAMES (1785-1851),
American artist and ornithologist **1**
366-367

AUER, LEOPOLD (1845-1930),
Hungarian violinist and conductor **20**
22-24

AUERBACH, RED (Arnold Red Auerbach;
Arnold Jacob Auerbach; 1917-2006),
American Basketball coach **27** 25-28

AUGUSTINE, ST. (354-430), Christian
philosopher and theologian **1** 367-370

AUGUSTINE OF CANTERBURY, ST.
(died circa 606), Roman monk,
archbishop of Canterbury **1** 370-371

Augustine of Hippo
see Augustine, St.

AUGUSTUS (Octavian; 63 B.C.-A.D. 14),
Roman emperor 27 B.C.-A.D. 14 **1**
371-373

AUGUSTUS II (1670-1733), king of
Poland and elector of Saxony **1**
373-374

Augustus the Strong
see Augustus II, (1696-1763)

**AULARD, ALPHONSE FRANÇOIS
VICTOR ALPHONSE** (1849-1928),
French historian **1** 374

Aulnay, Seigneur d'
see Charnisay

AUNG SAN (1915-1947), Burmese
politician **1** 374-375

AUNG SAN SUU KYI (born 1945),
leader of movement toward democracy
in Burma (Myanmar) and Nobel Peace
Prize winner **1** 375-376

Aung Zeya
see Alaungpaya

AURANGZEB (1618-1707), Mogul
emperor of India 1658-1707 **1** 377

AUSTEN, JANE (1775-1817), English
novelist **1** 377-379

AUSTIN, JOHN (1790-1859), English
jurist and author **22** 33-35

AUSTIN, JOHN LANGSHAW (1911-
1960), English philosopher **1** 379-380

AUSTIN, MARY HUNTER (1868-1934),
American author **23** 23-25

AUSTIN, STEPHEN FULLER (1793-1836),
American pioneer **1** 380-381

Austrian music
fusion
Zawinul, Joe **28** 389-391

Authors, American
autobiographies
Keckley, Elizabeth Hobbs **28**
196-199
Velasquez, Loreta Janeta **28** 361-363
critics (20th century)
Bloom, Harold **28** 38-40
essayists (20th century)
Leopold, Aldo **28** 211-213
novelists (20th century)
Dick, Philip K. **28** 96-98
Fisher, Rudolph **28** 121-123
Heinlein, Robert A. **28** 166-168
Herbert, Frank, Jr. **28** 168-170
Norton, Andre **28** 257-259
Sheldon, Sidney **28** 323-325
Thurman, Wallace Henry **28**
352-354
playwrights (20th century)
Sheldon, Sidney **28** 323-325
poets (20th-21st century)
Collins, Billy **28** 83-85
religious writers
Roberts, Oral **28** 296-298
screenwriters
Sheldon, Sidney **28** 323-325
short-story writers (20th century)
Dick, Philip K. **28** 96-98
Fisher, Rudolph **28** 121-123
Heinlein, Robert A. **28** 166-168
Norton, Andre **28** 257-259
spiritualist writers
Castaneda, Carlos **28** 62-64

Authors, Canadian
autobiographers
Slocum, Joshua **28** 333-335

Authors, Chilean
Bolaño, Roberto **28** 42-45

Authors, Dagestani
Gamzatov, Razul **28** 134-136

Authors, English
children's-story writers
Grahame, Kenneth **28** 138-140
critics (18th century)
Chapone, Hester **28** 72-74
critics (20th century)
Amis, Kingsley **28** 5-8
diarists
Fiennes, Celia **28** 118-121
essayists (16th-18th century)
Chapone, Hester **28** 72-74
nonfiction writers
Beeton, Isabella Mary **28** 34-36
Lewis, Wyndham **28** 217-219
novelists (18th century)
Radcliffe, Ann **28** 288-290
novelists (20th century)
Amis, Kingsley **28** 5-8
Baroness Orczy **28** 25-27
Fleming, Ian **28** 123-125
Lewis, Wyndham **28** 217-219
playwrights (17th-18th century)
Centlivre, Susanna **28** 65-67
playwrights (20th century)
Baroness Orczy **28** 25-27
poets (19th century)
Radcliffe, Ann **28** 288-290
poets (20th century)
Cunard, Nancy **28** 87-89
travel writers
Fiennes, Celia **28** 118-121

Authors, Finnish
Canth, Minna **28** 58-60
children's literature
Jansson, Tove Marika **28** 187-189

Authors, French
autobiographers
Thérèse of Lisieux, Saint **28** 347-350
chroniclers
Moitessier, Bernard **28** 252-254
essayists (20th century)
Bazin, André **28** 32-33
Lévy, Bernard-Henri **28** 213-215
essayists (20th-21st century)
Lévy, Bernard-Henri **28** 213-215
film critics
Bazin, André **28** 32-33
nonfiction writers
Deleuze, Gilles **28** 94-96
Moitessier, Bernard **28** 252-254
religious writings
Thérèse of Lisieux, Saint **28** 347-350
travel writers
David-Néel, Alexandra **28** 90-92

Authors, German
essayists
Andreas-Salomé, Lou **28** 12-14
novelists (19th-20th century)
Andreas-Salomé, Lou **28** 12-14

Authors, Hungarian
Baroness Orczy **28** 25-27

Authors, Indian (Asia)
poets
Savarkar, Vinayak Damodar **28** 312-314

religious writers
Krishnamurti, Uppaluri Gopala **28** 201-203

Authors, Iraqi
Mala'ika, Nazik al- **28** 230-232

Authors, Irish
essayists
Moore, Thomas **28** 254-256
poets
Moore, Thomas **28** 254-256

Authors, Norwegian
Skram, Amalie **28** 331-333

Authors, Peruvian
Granda, Chabuca **28** 143-144

Authors, Polish
Witkacy **28** 374-376

Authors, Russian
poets (20th century)
Vysotsky, Vladimir **28** 367-369
screenwriters
Romm, Mikhail **28** 303-304

Authors, Scottish
nonfiction
Cheyne, George **28** 74-76
playwrights
Baillie, Joanna **28** 23-25
poets
Baillie, Joanna **28** 23-25

Authors, Somali
Farah, Nuruddin **28** 114-116

Authors, Swedish
Lindgren, Astrid **28** 219-221

Authors, Turkish
Pamuk, Orhan **28** 269-272

Authors, Vietnamese
Son, Trinh Cong **28** 335-336
Ho, Xuan Huong **28** 174-176

AVEDON, RICHARD (1923-2004), American fashion photographer **1** 381-382

AVERROËS (1126-1198), Spanish-Arabian philosopher **1** 382-383

AVERY, OSWALD THEODORE (1877-1955), Canadian/American biologist and bacteriologist **1** 384-386

Aviators
American
Quimby, Harriet **28** 285-287
French
Blanchard, Jean-Pierre François **28** 36-38

Avicebrón (Avicembril)
see Ibn Gabirol, Solomon ben Judah

AVICENNA (circa 980-1037), Arabian physician and philosopher **1** 386-387

ÁVILA CAMACHO, GEN. MANUEL (1897-1955), Mexican president 1940-1946 **1** 387-388

Ávila, Pedro Arias de
see Pedrarias

AVOGADRO, LORENZO ROMANO AMEDO CARLO (Conte di Quaregna e di Cerreto; 1776-1865), Italian physicist and chemist **1** 388-389

AWOLOWO, CHIEF OBAFEMI (born 1909), Nigerian nationalist and politician **1** 389-390

AX, EMANUEL (born 1949), American pianist **1** 391

AXELROD, JULIUS (1912-2004), American biochemist **28** 18-20

Ayala, Pedro López de
see López de Ayala, Pedro

AYCKBOURN, ALAN (born 1939), British playwright **18** 23-25

AYER, ALFRED JULES (1910-1989), English philosopher **1** 391-393

AYLWIN AZÓCAR, PATRICIO (born 1918), leader of the Chilean Christian Democratic party and president of Chile **1** 393-395

AYUB KHAN, MOHAMMED (1907-1989), Pakistani statesman **1** 395-396

AZAÑA DIAZ, MANUEL (1880-1940), Spanish statesman, president 1936-1939 **1** 396-397

AZARA, FÉLIX DE (1746-1821), Spanish explorer and naturalist **1** 397-398

AZCONA HOYO, JOSÉ (1927-2005), president of Honduras (1986-1990) **1** 398-399

AZHARI, SAYYID ISMAIL AL- (1898-1969), Sudanese president 1965-1968 **1** 399-401

AZIKIWE, NNAMDI (born 1904), Nigerian nationalist, president 1963-1966 **1** 401-402

Azorin
see Ruíz, José Martinez

AZUELA, MARIANO (1873-1952), Mexican novelist **1** 402

B

BÂ, MARIAMA (1929-1981), Senegalese novelist **26** 25-27

BA MAW (1893-1977), Burmese statesman **1** 480-481

BAADER AND MEINHOF (1967-1976), founders of the West German "Red Army Faction" **1** 403-404

BAAL SHEM TOV (circa 1700-circa 1760), founder of modern Hasidism **1** 404-405

BABA, MEHER (Merwan Sheriar Irani; 1894-1969), Indian mystic **24** 35-38

BABAR THE CONQUEROR (aka Zahir-ud-din Muhammad Babur; 1483-1530), Mogul emperor of India 1526-1530 **1** 405-407

BABBAGE, CHARLES (1791-1871), English inventor and mathematician **1** 407-408

BABBITT, BRUCE EDWARD (born 1938), governor of Arizona (1978-1987) and United States secretary of the interior **1** 408-410

BABBITT, IRVING (1865-1933), American critic and educator **22** 36-37

BABBITT, MILTON (born 1916), American composer **1** 410

BABCOCK, STEPHEN MOULTON (1843-1931), American agricultural chemist **1** 410-411

BABEL, ISAAC EMMANUELOVICH (1894-1941), Russian writer **1** 411-412

Baber
see Babar the Conqueror

BABEUF, FRANÇOIS NOEL ("Caius Gracchus"; 1760-1797), French revolutionist and writer **1** 412

Babrak Karmal
see Karmal, Babrak

Babur, Zahir-ud-din Muhammed
see Babar the Conqueror

BACA-BARRAGÁN, POLLY (born 1943), Hispanic American politician **1** 412-414

BACH, CARL PHILIPP EMANUEL (1714-1788), German composer **1** 414-415

BACH, JOHANN CHRISTIAN (1735-1782), German composer **1** 415-416

BACH, JOHANN SEBASTIAN (1685-1750), German composer and organist **1** 416-419

BACHARACH, BURT (born 1928), American composer **22** 38-39

BACHE, ALEXANDER DALLAS (1806-1867), American educator and scientist **1** 420

Baciccio
see Gaulli, Giovanni Battista

BACKUS, ISAAC (1724-1806), American Baptist leader **1** 420-421

BACON, SIR FRANCIS (1561-1626), English philosopher, statesman, and author **1** 422-424

BACON, FRANCIS (1909-1992), English artist **1** 421-422

BACON, NATHANIEL (1647-1676), American colonial leader **1** 424-425

BACON, PEGGY (Margaret Francis Bacon; 1895-1987), American artist and author **25** 29-31

BACON, ROGER (circa 1214-1294), English philosopher **1** 425-427

Bad Hand
see Fitzpatrick, Thomas

BAD HEART BULL, AMOS (1869-1913), Oglala Lakota Sioux tribal historian and artist **1** 427-428

BADEN-POWELL, ROBERT (1857-1941), English military officer and founder of the Boy Scout Association **21** 16-18

BADINGS, HENK (Hendrik Herman Badings; 1907-1987), Dutch composer **23** 26-28

BADOGLIO, PIETRO (1871-1956), Italian general and statesman **1** 428-429

BAECK, LEO (1873-1956), rabbi, teacher, hero of the concentration camps, and Jewish leader **1** 429-430

BAEKELAND, LEO HENDRIK (1863-1944), American chemist **1** 430-431

BAER, GEORGE FREDERICK (1842-1914), American businessman **22** 39-41

BAER, KARL ERNST VON (1792-1876), Estonian anatomist and embryologist **1** 431-432

BAEZ, BUENAVENTURA (1812-1884), Dominican statesman, five time president **1** 432-433

BAEZ, JOAN (born 1941), American folk singer and human rights activist **1** 433-435

BAFFIN, WILLIAM (circa 1584-1622), English navigator and explorer **1** 435-436

BAGEHOT, WALTER (1826-1877), English economist **1** 436-437

BAGLEY, WILLIAM CHANDLER (1874-1946), educator and theorist of educational "essentialism" **1** 437-438

Baha'i (Islamic sect)
Bahá'u'lláh **28** 21-23

BAHÁ'U'LLÁH (Husayn-'Ali', Bahá'u'lláh Mírzá; 1817-1982), Iranian religious leader **28** 21-23

BAHR, EGON (born 1922), West German politician **1** 438-440

BAIKIE, WILLIAM BALFOUR (1825-1864), Scottish explorer and scientist **1** 440

BAILEY, F. LEE (born 1933), American defense attorney and author **1** 441-443

BAILEY, FLORENCE MERRIAM (1863-1948), American ornithologist and author **1** 443-444

BAILEY, GAMALIEL (1807-1859), American editor and politician **1** 444-445

BAILEY, MILDRED (Mildred Rinker, 1907-1951), American jazz singer **23** 28-30

BAILLIE, D(ONALD) M(ACPHERSON) (1887-1954), Scottish theologian **1** 445

BAILLIE, ISOBEL (Isabella Baillie; 1895-1983), British singer **26** 27-29

BAILLIE, JOANNA (1762-1851), Scottish playwright and poet **28** 23-25

BAILLIE, JOHN (1886-1960), Scottish theologian and ecumenical churchman **1** 445-447

BAKER, ELLA JOSEPHINE (1903-1986), African American human and civil rights activist **18** 26-28

BAKER, HOWARD HENRY, JR. (born 1925), U.S. senator and White House chief of staff **18** 28-30

BAKER, JAMES ADDISON III (born 1930), Republican party campaign leader **1** 447-448

BAKER, JOSEPHINE (1906-1975), Parisian dancer and singer from America **1** 448-451

BAKER, NEWTON DIEHL (1871-1937), American statesman **1** 451

BAKER, RAY STANNARD (1870-1946), American author **1** 451-452

BAKER, RUSSELL (born 1925), American writer of personal-political essays **1** 452-454

BAKER, SIR SAMUEL WHITE (1821-1893), English explorer and administrator **1** 454-455

BAKER, SARA JOSEPHINE (1873-1945), American physician **1** 455-456

BAKHTIN, MIKHAIL MIKHAILOVICH (1895-1975), Russian philosopher and literary critic **1** 456-458

Bakufu (shogun military government)
see Japan—1185-1867

BAKUNIN, MIKHAIL ALEKSANDROVICH (1814-1876), Russian anarchist **1** 458-460

BALAGUER Y RICARDO, JOAQUÍN (1907-2002), Dominican statesman **1** 460-461

BALANCHINE, GEORGE (1904-1983), Russian-born American choreographer **1** 461-462

Balanchivadze, Georgi Melitonovitch
see Balanchine, George

BALBOA, VASCO NÚÑEZ DE (circa 1475-1519), Spanish explorer **1** 462-463

BALBULUS, NOTKER (circa 840-912), Swiss poet-musician and monk **11** 434-435

BALCH, EMILY GREENE (1867-1961), American pacifist and social reformer **1** 463-464

BALDWIN I (1058-1118), Norman king of Jerusalem 1100-1118 **1** 464-465

BALDWIN, JAMES ARTHUR (1924-1987), African American author, poet, and dramatist **1** 465-466

BALDWIN, ROBERT (1804-1858), Canadian politician **1** 466-468

BALDWIN, ROGER NASH (1884-1981), American civil libertarian and social worker **25** 31-33

BALDWIN, STANLEY (1st Earl Baldwin of Bewdley; 1867-1947), English statesman, three times prime minister **1** 468-469

Baldwin of Bewdley, 1st Earl
see Baldwin, Stanley

Baldwin of Boulogne
see Baldwin I, king

BALFOUR, ARTHUR JAMES (1st Earl of Balfour; 1848-1930), British statesman and philosopher **1** 469-470

Baline, Israel
see Berlin, Irving

BALL, GEORGE (1909-1994), American politician and supporter of an economically united Europe **1** 470-471

BALL, LUCILLE (Lucille Desiree Hunt; 1911-1989), American comedienne **1** 472-473

BALLA, GIACOMO (1871-1958), Italian painter **1** 473-474

BALLADUR, EDOUARD (born 1929), premier of the French Government **1** 474-475

BALLARD, LOUIS WAYNE (born 1913), Native American musician **26** 29-31

BALLARD, ROBERT (born 1942), American oceanographer **19** 10-12

Ballet (dance)
Taglioni, Marie **28** 345-347

BALLIVIÁN, JOSÉ (1805-1852), Bolivian president 1841-1847 **1** 475

Balloon (aircraft)
hot air
Blanchard, Jean-Pierre François **28** 36-38

BALMACEDA FERNÁNDEZ, JOSÉ MANUEL (1840-1891), Chilean president 1886-1891 **1** 475-476

BALTHUS (Balthasar Klossowski; born 1908), European painter and stage designer **1** 476-477

BALTIMORE, DAVID (born 1938), American virologist **1** 477-478

BALZAC, HONORÉ DE (1799-1850), French novelist **1** 478-480

BAMBA, AMADOU (1850-1927), Senegalese religious leader **1** 481-482

BAMBARA, TONI CADE (1939-1995), African American writer and editor **1** 482-483

BAN KI-MOON (born 1944), South Korean diplomat **27** 29-31

BAN ZHAO (Pan Chao, Ban Hui-ji, Cao Dagu; c. 45-51-c. 114-120), Chinese author and historian **24** 38-40

BANCROFT, ANNE (nee Anna Maria Louisa Italino; 1931-2005), American actress **26** 31-33

BANCROFT, GEORGE (1800-1891), American historian and statesman **1** 483-484

BANCROFT, HUBERT HOWE (1832-1918), American historian **1** 484-485

BANCROFT, MARY (Mary bancroft Badger; 1903-1997), American author and intelligence analyst **27** 31-33

BANDA, HASTINGS KAMUZU (1905-1997), Malawi statesman **1** 485-486

BANDARANAIKE, SIRIMAVO (ALSO SIRIMA) RATWATTE DIAS (born 1916), first woman prime minister in the world as head of the Sri Lankan Freedom party government (1960-1965, 1970-1976) **1** 486-488

Bandinelli, Orlando
see Alexander III, pope

BANERJEE, SURENDRANATH (1848-1925), Indian nationalist **1** 488

Bangladesh (former East Pakistan)
Yunus, Muhammad **28** 386-388

Banking, Bangladeshi
Yunus, Muhammad **28** 386-388

BANKS, DENNIS J. (born 1932), Native American leader, teacher, activist, and author **1** 488-489

BANKS, SIR JOSEPH (1743-1820), English naturalist **1** 489-490

BANNEKER, BENJAMIN (1731-1806), African American mathematician **1** 490-491

BANNISTER, EDWARD MITCHELL (1828-1901), African American landscape painter **1** 491-493

BANNISTER, ROGER (born 1929), English runner **21** 18-20

BANTING, FREDERICK GRANT (1891-1941), Canadian physiologist **1** 493-494

BAÑUELOS, ROMANA ACOSTA (born 1925), Mexican businesswoman and American government official **24** 40-42

BANZER SUÁREZ, HUGO (1926-2002), Bolivian president (1971-1979) **1** 494-496

BAO DAI (born 1913), emperor of Vietnam 1932-1945 and 1949-1955 **1** 496-497

BAR KOCHBA, SIMEON (died 135), Jewish commander of revolt against Romans **2** 5

BARAGA, FREDERIC (Irenej Frederic Baraga; 1797-1868), Austrian missionary and linguist **27** 33-35

BARAK, EHUD (born 1942), Israeli prime minister **1** 497-498

BARAKA, IMAMU AMIRI (Everett LeRoi Jones; born 1934), African American poet and playwright **1** 498-499

BARANOV, ALEKSANDR ANDREIEVICH (1747-1819), Russian explorer **1** 499-500

BARBARA, AGATHA (1923-2002), Maltese politician **27** 36-38

Barbarossa, Frederick
see Frederick I, (1657-1713)

BARBAULD, ANNA (MRS.) (nee Anna Laetitia Aiken; 1743-1825), British author **27** 38-40

BARBEAU, MARIUS (1883-1969), Canadian ethnographer, anthropologist, and author **24** 42-44

BARBER, SAMUEL (1910-1981), American composer **1** 500-501

Barbera, Joseph
see Hanna and Barbera

Barberini, Maffeo
see Urban VIII

BARBIE, KLAUS (Klaus Altmann; 1913-1991), Nazi leader in Vichy France **1** 501-503

Barbieri, Giovanni Francesco
see Guercino

BARBIROLLI, JOHN (Giovanni Battista Barbirolli; 1899-1970), British conductor **24** 44-46

Barbo, Pietro
see Paul II, pope

BARBONCITO (1820-1871), Native American leader of the Navajos **20** 25-27

BARBOSA, RUY (1849-1923), Brazilian journalist and politician **1** 503-504

BARDEEN, JOHN (1908-1991), American Nobel physicist **2** 1-3

Bardi, Donato di Niccolò
see Donatello

BARENBOIM, DANIEL (born 1942), Israeli pianist and conductor **2** 3-4

BARENTS, WILLEM (died 1597), Dutch navigator and explorer **2** 4-5

Baring, Evelyn
see Cromer, 1st Earl of

BARING, FRANCIS (1740-1810), English banker **21** 20-22

BARLACH, ERNST (1870-1938), German sculptor **2** 5-6

BARLOW, JOEL (1754-1812), American poet **2** 6-7

BARNARD, CHRISTIAAN N. (1922-2001), South African heart transplant surgeon **2** 7-8

BARNARD, EDWARD EMERSON (1857-1923), American astronomer **2** 8-9

BARNARD, FREDERICK AUGUSTUS PORTER (1809-1889), American educator and mathematician **2** 9-10

BARNARD, HENRY (1811-1900), American educator **2** 10

BARNES, DJUNA (a.k.a. Lydia Steptoe; 1892-1982), American author **2** 11-13

BARNETT, ETTA MOTEN (1901-2004), African American actress and singer **25** 34-36

BARNETT, MARGUERITE ROSS (1942-1992), American educator **21** 22-24

BARNUM, PHINEAS TAYLOR (1810-1891), American showman **2** 13-15

Barocchio, Giacomo
see Vignola, Giacomo da

BAROJA Y NESSI, PÍO (1872-1956), Spanish novelist **2** 15-16

BARON, SALO WITTMAYER (1895-1989), Austrian-American educator and Jewish historian **2** 16-17

BARONESS ORCZY (Emma Magdalena Rosalia Maria Josefa Orczy; 1865-

1947), Hungarian-British author **28** 25-27

Barozzi, Giacomo
see Vignola, Giacomo da

BARRAGÁN, LUIS (1902-1988), Mexican architect and landscape architect **2** 17-19

BARRAS, VICOMTE DE (Paul François Jean Nicolas; 1755-1829), French statesman and revolutionist **2** 19

BARRE, RAYMOND (1924-1981), prime minister of France (1976-1981) **2** 19-20

BARRÈS, AUGUSTE MAURICE (1862-1923), French writer and politician **2** 20-21

Barrett, Elizabeth
see Browning, Elizabeth Barrett

BARRIE, SIR JAMES MATTHEW (1860-1937), British dramatist and novelist **2** 21-22

BARRIENTOS ORTUÑO, RENÉ (1919-1969), populist Bolivian president (1966-1969) **2** 22-23

BARRIOS, AGUSTIN PÌO (1885-1944), Paraguayan musician and composer **28** 27-29

BARRIOS, JUSTO RUFINO (1835-1885), Guatemalan general, president 1873-1885 **2** 23-24

Barrow, Joe Louis
see Louis, Joe

BARRY, JAMES (Miranda Stuart Barry; 1795-1865), First British female physician **27** 40-41

BARRY, JOHN (1745-1803), American naval officer **2** 24-25

BARRY, MARION SHEPILOV, JR. (born 1936), African American mayor and civil rights activist **2** 25-28

BARRYMORES, American theatrical dynasty **2** 28-30

BARTH, HEINRICH (1821-1865), German explorer **2** 30-31

BARTH, KARL (1886-1968), Swiss Protestant theologian **2** 31-32

BARTHÉ, RICHMOND (1901-1989), African American sculptor **2** 33-34

BARTHOLDI, FRÉDÉRIC-AUGUSTE (1834-1904), French sculptor **28** 29-31

BARTHOLOMAEUS ANGLICUS (Bartholomew the Englishman; Bartholomew de Glanville; flourished 1220-1240), English theologian and encyclopedist **21** 24-25

BARTLETT, SIR FREDERIC CHARLES (1886-1969), British psychologist **2** 34-35

BARTÓK, BÉLA (1881-1945), Hungarian composer and pianist **2** 35-36

BARTON, BRUCE (1886-1967), American advertising business executive and congressman **2** 36-37

BARTON, CLARA (1821-1912), American humanitarian **2** 37-39

BARTON, SIR EDMUND (1849-1920), Australian statesman and jurist **2** 39-40

BARTRAM, JOHN (1699-1777), American botanist **2** 40-41

BARTRAM, WILLIAM (1739-1823), American naturalist **2** 41-42

BARUCH, BERNARD MANNES (1870-1965), American statesman and financier **2** 42-43

BARYSHNIKOV, MIKHAIL (born 1948), ballet dancer **2** 43-44

BASCOM, FLORENCE (1862-1945), American geologist **22** 42-43

Baseball players
see Athletes

BASEDOW, JOHANN BERNHARD (1724-1790), German educator and reformer **2** 44-45

BASHO, MATSUO (1644-1694), Japanese poet **2** 45-48

BASIE, COUNT (William Basie; 1904-1984), pianist and jazz band leader **2** 48-49

BASIL I (circa 812-886), Byzantine emperor 867-886 **2** 49-50

BASIL II (circa 958-1025), Byzantine emperor 963-1025 **2** 50-51

BASIL THE GREAT, ST. (329-379), theologian and bishop of Caesarea **2** 51-52

Basil the Macedonian
see Basil I

Basketball (United States)
see Athletes

BASKIN, LEONARD (1922-2000), American artist and publisher **22** 43-46

BASS, SAUL (1920-1996), American designer of film advertising **21** 25-27

BASSI, LAURA (1711-1778), Italian physicist **20** 27-29

Bassianus
see Caracalla

BATES, DAISY MAE (née O'Dwyer; 1861-1951), Irish-born Australian social worker **2** 52-53

BATES, HENRY WALTER (1825-1892), English explorer and naturalist **2** 53-54

BATES, KATHARINE LEE (1859-1929), American poet and educator **2** 54-55

BATESON, WILLIAM (1861-1926), English biologist concerned with evolution **2** 55-57

BATISTA Y ZALDÍVAR, FULGENCIO (1901-1973), Cuban political and military leader **2** 57-58

BATLLE Y ORDÓÑEZ, JOSÉ (1856-1929), Uruguayan statesman and journalist **2** 58-59

BATTEN, JEAN (1909-1982), New Zealander aviatrix **26** 33-35

BATTLE, KATHLEEN (born 1948), American opera and concert singer **2** 59-60

Battle of the Stag Beetles, The (film) Starewicz, Wladyslaw **28** 336-338

BATU KHAN (died 1255), Mongol leader **2** 60-61

BAUDELAIRE, CHARLES PIERRE (1821-1867), French poet and art critic **2** 61-63

BAUER, EDDIE (1899-1986), American businessman **19** 13-14

Bauer, Georg
see Agricola, Georgius

BAULIEU, ÉTIENNE-ÉMILE (Étienne Blum; born 1926), French physician and biochemist who developed RU 486 **2** 63-66

BAUM, HERBERT (1912-1942), German human/civil rights activist **2** 66-73

BAUM, L. FRANK (1856-1919), author of the Wizard of Oz books **2** 73-74

Baumfree, Isabella
see Truth, Sojourner

BAUR, FERDINAND CHRISTIAN (1792-1860), German theologian **2** 74-75

BAUSCH, PINA (born 1940), a controversial German dancer/choreographer **2** 75-76

BAXTER, RICHARD (1615-1691), English theologian **2** 76-77

BAYLE, PIERRE (1647-1706), French philosopher **2** 77-78

Bayley, Elizabeth
see Seton, Elizabeth Ann Bayley

BAYNTON, BARBARA (1857-1929), Australian author **22** 46-48

BAZIN, ANDRÉ (1918-1958), French film critic **28** 32-33

BBC
see British Broadcasting Corporation

BEA, AUGUSTINUS (1881-1968), German cardinal **2** 79

BEACH, AMY (born Amy Marcy Cheney; 1867-1944), American musician **23** 30-32

BEACH, MOSES YALE (1800-1868), American inventor and newspaperman **2** 79-80

Beaconsfield, Earl of
see Disraeli, Benjamin

BEADLE, GEORGE WELLS (1903-1989), American scientist, educator, and administrator **2** 80-81

BEALE, DOROTHEA (1831-1906), British educator **2** 81-83

BEAN, ALAN (born 1932), American astronaut and artist **22** 48-50

BEAN, LEON LEONWOOD (L.L. Bean; 1872-1967), American businessman **19** 14-16

BEARD, CHARLES AUSTIN (1874-1948), American historian **2** 84

BEARD, MARY RITTER (1876-1958), American author and activist **2** 85-86

BEARDEN, ROMARE HOWARD (1914-1988), African American painter-collagist **2** 86-88

BEARDSLEY, AUBREY VINCENT (1872-1898), English illustrator **2** 88-89

BEATLES, THE (1957-1971), British rock and roll band **2** 89-92

BEATRIX, WILHELMINA VON AMSBERG, QUEEN (born 1938), queen of Netherlands (1980-) **2** 92-93

BEAUCHAMPS, PIERRE (1636-1705), French dancer and choreographer **21** 27-29

BEAUFORT, MARGARET (1443-1509), queen dowager of England **20** 29-31

BEAUJOYEULX, BALTHASAR DE (Balthasar de Beaujoyeux; Baldassare de Belgiojoso; 1535-1587), Italian choreographer and composer **21** 29-30

BEAUMARCHAIS, PIERRE AUGUST CARON DE (1732-1799), French playwright **2** 93-94

BEAUMONT, FRANCIS (1584/1585-1616), English playwright **2** 95

BEAUMONT, WILLIAM (1785-1853), American surgeon **2** 95-96

BEAUREGARD, PIERRE GUSTAVE TOUTANT (1818-1893), Confederate general **2** 96-97

Beaverbrook, Lord
see Aitken, William Maxwell

BECARRIA, MARCHESE DI (1738-1794), Italian jurist and economist **2** 97-98

BECHET, SIDNEY (1897-1959), American jazz musician **22** 50-52

BECHTEL, STEPHEN DAVISON (1900-1989), American construction engineer and business executive **2** 98-99

BECK, LUDWIG AUGUST THEODOR (1880-1944), German general **2** 99-100

BECKER, CARL LOTUS (1873-1945), American historian **2** 100-101

BECKET, ST. THOMAS (1128?-1170), English prelate **2** 101-102

BECKETT, SAMUEL (1906-1989), Irish novelist, playwright, and poet **2** 102-104

BECKHAM, DAVID (David Robert Joseph Beckham; born 1975), British soccer player **26** 36-38

BECKMANN, MAX (1884-1950), German painter **2** 104-105

BECKNELL, WILLIAM (circa 1797-1865), American soldier and politician **2** 105-106

BECKWOURTH, JIM (James P. Beckwourth; c. 1800-1866), African American fur trapper and explorer **2** 106-107

BÉCQUER, GUSTAVO ADOLFO DOMINGUEZ (1836-1870), Spanish lyric poet **2** 107-108

BECQUEREL, ANTOINE HENRI (1852-1908), French physicist **2** 108-109

BEDE, ST. (c. 672-735), English theologian **2** 109-110

BEDELL SMITH, WALTER (1895-1961), U.S. Army general, ambassador, and CIA director **18** 30-33

BEEBE, WILLIAM (1877-1962), American naturalist, oceanographer, and ornithologist **22** 52-54

BEECHAM, THOMAS (1879-1961), English conductor **24** 46-48

BEECHER, CATHARINE (1800-1878), American author and educator **2** 110-112

BEECHER, HENRY WARD (1813-1887), American Congregationalist clergyman **2** 112-113

BEECHER, LYMAN (1775-1863), Presbyterian clergyman **2** 113

Beer, Jakob Liebmann
see Meyerbeer, Giacomo

BEERBOHM, MAX (Henry Maximilian Beerbohm; 1872-1956), English author and critic **19** 16-18

BEETHOVEN, LUDWIG VAN (1770-1827), German composer **2** 114-117

Beethoven of America
see Heinrich, Anthony Philip

BEETON, ISABELLA MARY (Isabella Mary Mayson; Mrs. Beeton; 1836-1865), English author **28** 34-36

BEGAY, HARRISON (born 1917), Native American artist **2** 117-118

BEGIN, MENACHEM (1913-1992), Israel's first non-Socialist prime minister (1977-1983) **2** 118-120

BEHAIM, MARTIN (Martinus de Bohemia; 1459?-1507), German cartographer **21** 30-32

Behmen, Jacob
see Boehme, Jacob

BEHN, APHRA (1640?-1689), British author **18** 33-34

BEHRENS, HILDEGARD (born 1937), German soprano **2** 120-121

BEHRENS, PETER (1868-1940), German architect, painter, and designer **2** 121-122

BEHRING, EMIL ADOLPH VON (1854-1917), German hygienist and physician **2** 122-123

BEHZAD (died circa 1530), Persian painter **2** 123

BEISSEL, JOHANN CONRAD (1690-1768), German-American pietist **2** 123-124

BELAFONTE, HARRY (Harold George Belafonte, Jr.; born 1927), African American singer and actor **20** 31-32

BELASCO, DAVID (1853-1931), American playwright and director-producer **2** 124-125

BELAÚNDE TERRY, FERNANDO (1912-2002), president of Peru (1963-1968, 1980-1985) **2** 125-126

Belgian art
Peyo **28** 280-282

BELGRANO, MANUEL (1770-1820), Argentine general and politician **2** 126-127

BELINSKY, GRIGORIEVICH (1811-1848), Russian literary critic **2** 128

BELISARIUS (circa 506-565), Byzantine general **2** 128-129

BELL, ALEXANDER GRAHAM (1847-1922), Scottish-born American inventor **2** 129-131

BELL, ANDREW (1753-1832), Scottish educator **2** 131-132

Bell, Currer (pseudonym)
see Brontë, Charlotte

BELL, DANIEL (Bolotsky; born 1919), American sociologist **2** 132-133

Bell, Ellis (pseudonym)
see Brontë, Emily

BELL, GERTRUDE (1868-1926), British archaeologist, traveler, and advisor on the Middle East **22** 54-55

BELL BURNELL, SUSAN JOCELYN (born 1943), English radio astronomer **2** 133-134

BELL, VANESSA (Vanessa Stephen; 1879-1961), British painter **25** 36-38

BELLAMY, CAROL (born 1942), American activist and political servant **25** 38-40

BELLAMY, EDWARD (1850-1898), American novelist, propagandist, and reformer **2** 134-135

BELLARMINE, ST. ROBERT (1542-1621), Italian theologian and cardinal **2** 135-136

Bellay, Joachim du
see Du Bellay, Joachim

BELLECOURT, CLYDE (born 1939), Native American activist **2** 136-137

BELLI, GIACONDA (born 1948), Nicaraguan author and activist **24** 48-50

BELLINI, GIOVANNI (circa 1435-1516), Itlaian painter **2** 137-138

BELLINI, VINCENZO (1801-1835), Italian composer **2** 138-139

BELLMAN, CARL MICHAEL (1740-1794), Swedish poet and musician **25** 40-42

BELLO, ALHAJI SIR AHMADU (1909-1966), Nigerian politician **2** 139-140

BELLO Y LÓPEZ, ANDRÉS (1781-1865), Venezuelan humanist **2** 140-141

BELLOC, JOSEPH HILAIRE PIERRE (1870-1953), French-born English author and historian **2** 141

BELLOW, SAUL (1915-2005), American novelist and Nobel Prize winner **2** 141-143

BELLOWS, GEORGE WESLEY (1882-1925), American painter **2** 143

BELLOWS, HENRY WHITNEY (1814-1882), American Unitarian minister **2** 143-144

BELMONT, AUGUST (1816-1890), German-American banker, diplomat, and horse racer **22** 56-57

BELO, CARLOS FELIPE XIMENES (born 1948), East Timorese activist **25** 42-44

Beltov
see Plekhanov, Georgi Valentinovich

BEMBERG, MARIA LUISA (1922-1995), Argentine filmmaker **25** 44-46

BEMBO, PIETRO (1470-1547), Italian humanist, poet, and historian **2** 144-145

BEMIS, POLLY (Lalu Nathoy; 1853-1933), Chinese American pioneer and businesswoman **25** 46-47

BENACERRAF, BARUJ (born 1920), American medical researcher **27** 42-44

BEN AND JERRY, ice cream company founders **18** 35-37

BEN BADIS, ABD AL-HAMID (1889-1940), leader of the Islamic Reform Movement in Algeria between the two world wars **2** 147-148

BEN BELLA, AHMED (born 1918), first president of the Algerian Republic **2** 148-149

BENDIX, VINCENT (1881-1945), American inventor, engineer, and industrialist **19** 18-20

BEN-GURION, DAVID (born 1886), Russian-born Israeli statesman **2** 160-161

BEN-HAIM, PAUL (Frankenburger; 1897-1984), Israeli composer **2** 161-162

BEN YEHUDA, ELIEZER (1858-1922), Hebrew lexicographer and editor **2** 181-182

BENALCÁZAR, SEBASTIÁN DE (died 1551), Spanish conquistador **2** 145-146

BENAVENTE Y MARTINEZ, JACINTO (1866-1954), Spanish dramatist **2** 146-147

BENCHLEY, ROBERT (1889-1945), American humorist **2** 150-151

BENDA, JULIEN (1867-1956), French cultural critic and novelist **2** 151-152

BENEDICT XIV (Prospero Lorenzo Lambertini; 1675-1758), Italian pope **23** 32-35

BENEDICT XV (Giacomo della Chiesa; 1854-1922), pope, 1914-1922 **2** 153-154

BENEDICT XVI (Joseph Alois Ratzinger; born 1927), Roman Catholic pope (2005-) **26** 295-297

BENEDICT, RUTH FULTON (1887-1948), American cultural anthropologist **2** 154-155

BENEDICT, ST. (circa 480-547), Italian founder of the Benedictines **2** 154-155

Benedict of Nursia, St.
see Benedict, St.

BENEŠ, EDWARD (1884-1948), Czechoslovak president 1935-1938 and 1940-1948 **2** 155-157

BENÉT, STEPHEN VINCENT (1898-1943), American poet and novelist **2** 157-158

BENETTON, Italian family (Luciano, Giuliana, Gilberto, Carlo and Mauro) who organized a world-wide chain of colorful knitwear stores **2** 158-159

BENEZET, ANTHONY (1713-1784), American philanthropist and educator **2** 159-160

Bengan Korei
see Muhammad II, Askia

BENJAMIN, ASHER (1773-1845), American architect **2** 162-163

BENJAMIN, JUDAH PHILIP (1811-1884), American statesman **2** 163-164

BENJAMIN, WALTER (1892-1940), German philosopher and literary critic **20** 32-34

BENN, GOTTFRIED (1886-1956), German author **2** 164

BENN, TONY (Anthony Neil Wedgewood Benn; born 1925), British Labour party politician **2** 164-166

BENNETT, ALAN (born 1934), British playwright **2** 166-167

BENNETT, ENOCH ARNOLD (1867-1931), English novelist and dramatist **2** 167-168

BENNETT, JAMES GORDON (1795-1872), Scottish-born American journalist and publisher **2** 168-169

BENNETT, JAMES GORDON, JR. (1841-1918), American newspaper owner and editor **2** 169-170

BENNETT, JOHN COLEMAN (1902-1995), American theologian **2** 170-171

BENNETT, RICHARD BEDFORD (1870-1947), Canadian statesman, prime minister 1930-1935 **2** 171-172

BENNETT, RICHARD RODNEY (born 1936), English composer **2** 172

BENNETT, ROBERT RUSSELL (1894-1981), American arranger, composer, and conductor **21** 32-34

BENNETT, WILLIAM JOHN (born 1943), American teacher and scholar and secretary of the Department of Education (1985-1988) **2** 172-174

Bennett of Mickleham, Calgary, and Hopewell, Viscount
see Bennett, Richard Bedford

BENNY, JACK (Benjamin Kubelsky; 1894-1974), American comedian and a star of radio, television, and stage **2** 174-176

BENTHAM, JEREMY (1748-1832), English philosopher, political theorist, and jurist **2** 176-178

BENTLEY, ARTHUR F. (1870-1957), American philosopher and political scientist **2** 178

BENTON, SEN. THOMAS HART (1782-1858), American statesman **2** 178-179

BENTON, THOMAS HART (1889-1975), American regionalist painter **2** 178-179

BENTSEN, LLOYD MILLARD (1921-2006), senior United States senator from Texas and Democratic vice-presidential candidate in 1988 **2** 180-181

BENZ, CARL (1844-1929), German inventor **2** 182-183

BERCHTOLD, COUNT LEOPOLD VON (1863-1942), Austro-Hungarian statesman **2** 183-184

BERDYAEV, NICHOLAS ALEXANDROVICH (1874-1948), Russian philosopher **2** 184-185

BERELSON, BERNARD (1912-1979), American behavioral scientist **2** 185-186

BERENSON, BERNARD (1865-1959), American art critic and historian **20** 34-35

BERG, ALBAN (1885-1935), Austrian composer **2** 186-187

BERG, PAUL (born 1926), American chemist **2** 187-189

BERGER, VICTOR LOUIS (1860-1929), American politician **2** 189-190

BERGMAN, (ERNST) INGMAR (1918-2007), Swedish film and stage director **2** 190-191
Nykvist, Sven **28** 261-263

BERGMAN, INGRID (1917-1982), Swedish actress **20** 35-37

BERGSON, HENRI (1859-1941), French philosopher **2** 191-192

BERIA, LAVRENTY PAVLOVICH (1899-1953), Soviet secret-police chief and politician **2** 192-193

BERING, VITUS (1681-1741), Danish navigator in Russian employ **2** 193-194

BERIO, LUCIANO (1925-2003), Italian composer **2** 194-195

BERISHA, SALI (born 1944), president of the Republic of Albania (1992-) **2** 195-197

BERKELEY, BUSBY (William Berkeley Enos; 1895-1976), American filmmaker **20** 38-39

BERKELEY, GEORGE (1685-1753), Anglo-Irish philosopher and Anglican bishop **2** 197-198

BERKELEY, SIR WILLIAM (1606-1677), English royal governor of Virginia **2** 198-199

BERLE, ADOLF AUGUSTUS, JR. (1895-1971), American educator **2** 199-200

BERLE, MILTON (1908-2002), American entertainer and actor **18** 37-39

BERLIN, IRVING (1888-1989), American composer **2** 200-201

BERLIN, ISAIAH (1909-1997), British philosopher **2** 201-203

BERLINER, ÉMILE (1851-1929), American inventor **20** 39-41

BERLIOZ, LOUIS HECTOR (1803-1869), French composer, conductor, and critic **2** 203-205
Sax, Adolphe **28** 316-318
Viardot, Pauline **28** 363-365

BERLUSCONI, SILVIO (born 1936), Italian businessman and politician **25** 48-50

BERMEJO, BARTOLOMÉ (Bartolomé de Cárdenas; flourished 1474-1498), Spanish painter **2** 205

BERNADETTE OF LOURDES, SAINT (Marie Bernarde Soubirous; 1844-1879), French nun and Roman Catholic saint **21** 34-36

Bernadotte, Jean Baptiste
see Charles XIV John

BERNANOS, GEORGES (1888-1948), French novelist and essayist **2** 206-207

BERNARD, CLAUDE (1813-1878), French physiologist **2** 208-210

BERNARD OF CLAIRVAUX, ST. (1090-1153), French theologian, Doctor of the Church **2** 207-208

BERNARDIN, CARDINAL JOSEPH (1928-1996), Roman Catholic Cardinal and American activist **2** 210-211

Bernardone, Giovanni di
see Francis of Assisi, St.

BERNAYS, EDWARD L. (1891-1995), American public relations consultant **2** 211-212

BERNBACH, WILLIAM (1911-1982), American advertising executive **19** 20-22

BERNERS-LEE, TIM (born 1955), English computer scientist and creator of the World Wide Web **20** 41-43

BERNHARDT, SARAH (Henriette-Rosine Bernard; 1844-1923), French actress **2** 212-214

BERNIER, JOSEPH E. (Joseph-Elzéan Bernier; 1852-1934), Canadian explorer **23** 35-37

BERNINI, GIAN LORENZO (1598-1680), Italian artist **2** 214-216

BERNOULLI, DANIEL (1700-1782), Swiss mathematician and physicist **2** 216

BERNOULLI, JAKOB (Jacques or James Bernoulli; 1654-1705), Swiss mathematician **23** 37-39

BERNSTEIN, DOROTHY LEWIS (born 1914), American mathematician **2** 217

BERNSTEIN, EDUARD (1850-1932), German socialist **2** 218

BERNSTEIN, ELMER (1922-2004), American composer **27** 44-46

BERNSTEIN, LEONARD (1918-1990), American composer, conductor, and pianist **2** 218-219

Bernstein, Ludvik
see Namier, Sir Lewis Bernstein

Berrettini, Pietro
see Cortona, Pietro da

BERRI, NABIH (born 1939), leader of the Shi'ite Muslims in Lebanon **2** 220-222

BERRIGAN, DANIEL J. (born 1921), activist American Catholic priest **2** 222-223

BERRUGUETE, ALONSO (1486/90-1561), Spanish sculptor **2** 223-224

BERRY, CHUCK (born 1926), African American performer **2** 224-226

BERRY, MARY FRANCES (born 1938), African American human/civil rights activist and official **2** 226-229

BERRYMAN, JOHN (John Allyn Smith, Jr.; 1914-1972), American poet and biographer **19** 22-25

BERTHIER, LOUIS ALEXANDRE (1753-1815), French soldier and cartographer **20** 43-44

BERTHOLLET, CLAUDE LOUIS (1748-1822), French chemist **2** 229-230

BERTILLON, ALPHONSE (1853-1914), French criminologist **2** 230-231

BERTOLUCCI, BERNARDO (born 1940), Italian film director **18** 39-41

BERZELIUS, JÖNS JACOB (1779-1848), Swedish chemist **2** 231-233

BESANT, ANNIE WOOD (1847-1933), British social reformer and theosophist **2** 233-234

Besht
see Baal Shem Tov

BESSEL, FRIEDRICH WILHELM (1784-1846), German astronomer **2** 234-235

BESSEMER, SIR HENRY (1813-1898), English inventor **2** 235-236

BEST, CHARLES HERBERT (1899-1978), Canadian physiologist **2** 236-237

Beta
see Eratosthenes of Cyrene

BETANCOURT, RÓMULO (1908-1990), Venezuelan statesman **2** 237-238

BETHE, HANS ALBRECHT (1906-2005), Alsatian-American physicist **2** 238-239

BETHMANN HOLLWEG, THEOBALD VON (1856-1921), German statesman **2** 239-240

BETHUNE, HENRY NORMAN (1890-1939), Canadian humanitarian physician **2** 240-241

BETHUNE, MARY MCLEOD (1875-1955), African American educator **2** 241-242

BETI, MONGO (Alexandre Biyidi; born 1932), Cameroonian novelist **2** 242-243

BETJEMAN, JOHN (1906-1984), Poet Laureate of Britain 1972-1984 **2** 243-245

Betrayed (Forraadt; book)
Skram, Amalie **28** 331-333

BETTELHEIM, BRUNO (1903-1990), Austrian-born American psychoanalyst and educational psychologist **2** 245-246

BETTI, UGO (1892-1953), Italian playwright **2** 246

BEUYS, JOSEPH (1921-1986), German artist and sculptor **2** 246-248

BEVAN, ANEURIN (1897-1960), Labour minister responsible for the creation of the British National Health Service **2** 248-249

BEVEL, JAMES LUTHER (born 1936), American civil rights activist of the 1960s **2** 250-251

Beverage industry
Pemberton, John Stith **28** 278-279

BEVERIDGE, ALBERT JEREMIAH (1862-1927), American statesman **23** 39-41

BEVERIDGE, WILLIAM HENRY (1st Baron Beveridge of Tuccal; 1879-1963), English economist and social reformer **2** 251-252

BEVERLEY, ROBERT (circa 1673-1722), colonial American historian **2** 252

BEVIN, ERNEST (1881-1951), English trade union leader and politician **2** 252-253

Beyle, Marie Henri
see Stendhal

BHABHA, HOMI JEHANGIR (1909-1966), Indian atomic physicist **2** 253-254

BHAKTIVEDANTA PRABHUPADA (Abhay Charan De; 1896-1977), Hindu religious teacher who founded the International Society for Krishna Consciousness **2** 254-255

BHASHANI, MAULANA ABDUL HAMID KHAN (1880-1976), Muslim leader who promoted nationalism in Assam, Bengal, and Bangladesh **2** 255-257

BHAVE, VINOBA (born 1895), Indian nationalist and social reformer **2** 257-258

BHUMIBOL ADULYADEJ (born 1927), king of Thailand (1946-) representing the Chakri Dynasty **2** 258-259

BHUTTO, BENAZIR (1953-2007), prime minister of Pakistan (1988-1990) **2** 259-261

BHUTTO, ZULFIKAR ALI (1928-1979), Pakistan's president and later prime minister (1971-1979) **2** 261-262

BIALIK, HAYYIM NAHMAN (1873-1934), Russian-born Hebrew poet **2** 262-263

BIBER, HEINRICH VON (Heinrich Ignaz Franz von Biber; 1644-1704), Austrian composer and violinist **26** 38-40

BICHAT, MARIE FRANÇOIS XAVIER (1771-1802), French anatomist, pathologist, and physiologist **2** 263-264

BIDDLE, NICHOLAS (1786-1844), American financier **2** 264-265

BIDWELL, JOHN (1819-1900), American pioneer and agriculturist **2** 265

BIEBER, OWEN (born 1929), American union executive **2** 266-268

BIENVILLE, SIEUR DE (Jean Baptiste Le Moyne; 1680-1768), French colonizer and administrator **2** 268-269

BIERCE, AMBROSE GWINETT (1842-1914?), American journalist and author **2** 269-270

BIERSTADT, ALBERT (1830-1902), American painter **2** 270-271

BIGELOW, JOHN (1817-1911), American journalist, editor, and diplomat **2** 271-272

BIGGE, JOHN THOMAS (1780-1843), English judge and royal commissioner **2** 272

BIGGS, HERMANN MICHAEL (1859-1923), American physician **2** 272-273

Bigordi, Domenico di Tommaso
see Ghirlandaio, Domenico

Bihzad
see Behzad

BIKILA, ABEBE (1932-1973), Ethiopian marathon runner **20** 44-46

BIKO, STEVE (Stephen Bantu Biko; 1946-1977), political activist and writer and father of the Black Consciousness movement in the Union of South Africa **2** 273-274

BILLINGS, JOHN SHAW (1838-1913), American physician and librarian **22** 57-60

BILLINGS, WILLIAM (1746-1800), American composer **2** 274-275

BILLINGTON, JAMES HADLEY (born 1929), American scholar and author **2** 275-276

BILLY THE KID (W.H. Bonney; 1859-1881), American frontiersman and outlaw **2** 277

BIN LADEN, OSAMA (born 1957), Saudi terrorist **22** 60-62

BINET, ALFRED (1857-1911), French psychologist **2** 277-278

BINGHAM, GEORGE CALEB (1811-1879), American painter **2** 278-279

BINGHAM, HIRAM (1875-1956), American explorer **20** 46-48

BINNIG, GERD KARL (born 1947), German physicist **24** 50-52

Biochemistry (science)
neurobiology
Axelrod, Julius **28** 18-20
RNA
Mello, Craig Cameron **28** 238-241

Bird
see Parker, Charles

BIRD, ISABELLA (Isabella Bird Bishop; 1831-1904), English explorer and author **23** 41-42

BIRD, LARRY (born 1956), American basketball player **2** 279-281

BIRD, ROBERT MONTGOMERY (1806-1854), American dramatist and novelist **2** 281-282

BIRDSEYE, CLARENCE (1886-1956), American naturalist, inventor, and businessman **19** 25-27

BIRENDRA (Bir Bikram Shah Dev; 1945-2001), King of Nepal (1972-2001) **2** 282-283

BRIDGET OF SWEDEN (Saint Birgitta of Sweden; Birgitta Birgersdotter; 1303-1373), Swedish Catholic Saint **27** 53-55

BIRINGUCCIO, VANNOCCIO (1480-1539), Italian mining engineer and metallurgist **2** 283

BIRNEY, JAMES GILLESPIE (1792-1857), American lawyer and abolitionist **2** 283-284

BIRUNI, ABU RAYHAN AL- (973-circa 1050), Arabian scientist and historian **2** 284-285

BIRYUKOVA, ALEKSANDRA PAVLOVNA (1929-1990), a secretary of the Central Committee of the Communist party of the Soviet Union and a deputy prime minister (1986-1990) **2** 285-287

BISHARA, ABDULLAH YACCOUB (born 1936), Kuwaiti statesman and first secretary-general of the Gulf Cooperative Council **2** 287-288

BISHOP, BRIDGET (died 1692), Salem, Massachusetts, witch trial defendant **2** 288-290

BISHOP, ELIZABETH (1911-1979), American poet **2** 290-292

BISHOP, ISABEL (1902-1988), American artist **22** 64-67

BISHOP, MAURICE (1944-1983), leader of the New Jewel Movement and prime minister of Grenada (1979-1983) **2** 292-293

Bishop of Broadway
see Belasco, David

BISMARCK, OTTO EDUARD LEOPOLD VON (1815-1898), German statesman **2** 294-296

BITRUJI, NUR AL-DIN ABU ISHAQ AL (circa 1150-1200), Spanish Moslem astronomer **2** 296

BITZER, BILLY (George William Bitzer; 1872-1944), American cinematographer **21** 36-38

BIYA, PAUL (born 1933), president of Cameroon **18** 41-43

Biyidi, Alexandre
see Beti, Mongo

BIZET, GEORGES (1838-1875), French composer **2** 296-297

BJELKE-PETERSEN, JOHANNES ("Joh;" born 1911), Australian politician **2** 297-299

BJERKNES, VILHELM (1862-1951), Norwegian meteorologist **20** 48-50

BJØRNSON, BJØRNSTJERNE (1832-1910), Norwegian author **2** 299-300

BLACK, CONRAD MOFFAT (born 1944), Canadian-born international press baron **2** 300-301

BLACK, HUGO LAFAYETTE (1886-1971), American jurist **2** 301-303

BLACK, JOSEPH (1728-1799), British chemist **2** 303

BLACK, SHIRLEY TEMPLE (born 1928), American actress and public servant **2** 303-305

BLACK ELK, NICHOLAS (1863-1950), Oglala Sioux medicine man **2** 305-306

BLACK HAWK (1767-1838), Native American war chief **2** 308

Black Jack
see Pershing, John Joseph

Black Prince
see Edward the Black Prince

Black Spartacus
see Turner, Nathaniel

Black Spurgeon
see Turner, Henry McNeal

BLACKBEARD (Edward Teach; 1680-1718), English pirate **21** 38-41

BLACKBURN, ELIZABETH HELEN (born 1948), Australian biologist **18** 43-45

Blacker the Berry: A Novel of Negro Life, The (book)
Thurman, Wallace Henry **28** 352-354

BLACKETT, PATRICK M.S. (1897-1974), British physicist **2** 306-307

BLACKMUN, HARRY (1908-1999), United States Supreme Court justice **2** 309-310

"Black-robe Voyageur"
see Lacombe, Albert

Blacks
see African American history (United States); Africa

BLACKSTONE, SIR WILLIAM (1723-1780), English jurist **2** 310-311

BLACKWELL, ANTOINETTE BROWN (1825-1921), American minister and suffragette **21** 41-43

BLACKWELL, ELIZABETH (1821-1910), American physician **2** 311-312

BLACKWELL, EMILY (1826-1910), American physician and educator **19** 27-29

BLAGA, LUCIAN (1895-1961), Romanian poet and philosopher **24** 52-54

BLAINE, JAMES GILLESPIE (1830-1893), American statesman **2** 312-313

BLAIR, BONNIE (born 1964), American athlete **23** 42-44

Blair, Eric Arthur
see Orwell, George

BLAIR, FRANCIS PRESTON (1791-1876), American journalist and politician **2** 313-315

BLAIR, JAMES (1655-1743), British educator and Anglican missionary **2** 315-316

BLAIR, TONY (born 1953), British prime minister **18** 45-47
Brown, Gordon **28** 48-50

BLAKE, EUBIE (James Hubert Blake; 1883-1983), African American composer and pianist **25** 50-53

Blake, Nicholas
see Lewis, Cecil Day

BLAKE, WILLIAM (1757-1827), English poet, engraver, and painter **2** 316-318

BLAKELOCK, RALPH ALBERT (1847-1919), American painter **2** 318

BLAKEY, ART (Arthur Blakey; Abdullah Ibn Buhaina; 1919-1990), African American jazz musician **27** 46-48

BLANC, LOUIS (1811-1882), French journalist, historian, and politician **2** 318-319

BLANC, MEL (1908-1989), American creator of and voice of cartoon characters **2** 319-320

BLANCHARD, FELIX ("Doc" Blanchard; born 1924), American football player and military pilot **21** 43-45

BLANCHARD, JEAN-PIERRE FRANÇOIS (1753-1809), French balloonist **28** 36-38

BLANCHE OF CASTILE (1188-1252), French queen **21** 45-47

BLANCO, ANTONIO GUZMÁN (1829-1899), Venezuelan politician, three-times president **2** 320-321

BLANDIANA, ANA (born Otilia-Valeria Coman, 1942), Romanian poet **2** 321-322

BLANDING, SARAH GIBSON (1898-1985), American educator **2** 322-323

BLANKERS-KOEN, FANNY (Francina Elsja Blankers-Koen; born 1918), Dutch track and field athlete **20** 50-52

BLANQUI, LOUIS AUGUSTE (1805-1881), French revolutionary **2** 323-324

Blashki, Philip
see Evergood, Philip

BLAVATSKY, HELENA PETROVNA (Helena Hahn; 1831-1891), Russian theosophist **22** 67-69

BLEDSOE, ALBERT TAYLOR (1809-1877), American lawyer, educator, and Confederate apologist **2** 324-325

BLEULER, EUGEN (1857-1939), Swiss psychiatrist **2** 325

BLEY, CARLA (nee Carla Borg; born 1938), American composer and pianist **26** 40-42

BLIGH, WILLIAM (1754-1817), English naval officer and colonial governor **2** 325-326

Blixen-Finecke, Baroness
see Dinesen Blixen-Finecke, Karen

BLOCH, ERNEST (1880-1959), Swiss-born American composer and teacher **2** 326-327

BLOCH, ERNST (1885-1977), German humanistic interpreter of Marxist thought **2** 327-328

BLOCH, FELIX (1905-1983), Swiss/American physicist **2** 328-330

BLOCH, KONRAD (born 1912), American biochemist **2** 330-332

BLOCH, MARC (1886-1944), French historian **2** 332-333

BLOCK, HERBERT (Herblock; 1909-2001), American newspaper cartoonist **2** 333-334

BLODGETT, KATHARINE BURR (1898-1979), American physicist **24** 54-56

BLOK, ALEKSANDR ALEKSANDROVICH (1880-1921), Russian poet **2** 335

BLONDIN, JEAN FRANCOIS GRAVELET (Charles Blondin; 1824-1897), French tightrope walker and acrobat **27** 48-50

Bloody Mary
see Mary I

BLOOM, ALLAN DAVID (1930-1992), American political philosopher, professor, and author **2** 335-337

BLOOM, HAROLD (born 1930), American literary critic and educator **28** 38-40

BLOOMBERG, MICHAEL (Michael Rubens Bloomberg; born 1942), American businessman and politician **28** 40-42

BLOOMER, AMELIA JENKS (1818-1894), American reformer and suffrage advocate **2** 337

BLOOMFIELD, LEONARD (1887-1949), American linguist **2** 338

BLOOR, ELLA REEVE ("Mother Bloor"; 1862-1951), American labor organizer and social activist **2** 338-340

BLÜCHER, GEBHARD LEBERECHT VON (Prince of Wahlstatt; 1742-1819), Prussian field marshal **2** 340-341

Bluestocking Circle (women's society, 18th century England)
Chapone, Hester **28** 72-74

BLUFORD, GUION STEWART, JR. (born 1942), African American aerospace engineer, pilot, and astronaut **2** 341-343

BLUM, LÉON (1872-1950), French statesman **2** 343-344

BLUME, JUDY (born Judy Sussman; b. 1938), American fiction author **2** 344-345

BLUMENTHAL, WERNER MICHAEL (born 1926), American businessman and treasury secretary **2** 345-346

BLY, NELLIE (born Elizabeth Cochrane Seaman; 1864-1922), American journalist and reformer **2** 346-348

BLYDEN, EDWARD WILMOT (1832-1912), Liberian statesman **2** 348-349

Blythe, Vernon William
see Castle, I. and V.

Boadicia
see Boudicca

Boanerges
see John, St.

BOAS, FRANZ (1858-1942), German-born American anthropologist **2** 349-351

BOCCACCIO, GIOVANNI (1313-1375), Italian author **2** 351-353

BOCCIONI, UMBERTO (1882-1916), Italian artist **2** 353-354

BÖCKLIN, ARNOLD (1827-1901), Swiss painter **2** 354-355

BODE, BOYD HENRY (1873-1953), American philosopher and educator **2** 355-356

Bodenstein, Andreas
see Karlstadt

Bodhisattva Emperor
see Liang Wu-ti

BODIN, JEAN (1529/30-1596), French political philosopher **2** 356-357

Body Shop (store chain)
Roddick, Anita **28** 298-301

BOEHME, JACOB (1575-1624), German mystic **2** 357

BOEING, WILLIAM EDWARD (1881-1956), American businessman **2** 357-358

BOERHAAVE, HERMANN (1668-1738), Dutch physician and chemist **2** 358-359

BOESAK, ALLAN AUBREY (born 1945), opponent of apartheid in South Africa and founder of the United Democratic Front **2** 359-360

BOETHIUS, ANICIUS MANLIUS SEVERINUS (480?-524/525), Roman logician and theologian **2** 360-361

BOFF, LEONARDO (Leonardo Genezio Darci Boff; born 1938), Brazilian priest **22** 69-71

BOFFRAND, GABRIEL GERMAIN (1667-1754), French architect and decorator **2** 361

BOFILL, RICARDO (born 1939), postmodern Spanish architect **2** 362-363

BOGART, HUMPHREY (1899-1957), American stage and screen actor **2** 363-364

Bohemian art
Hollar, Wenceslaus **28** 180-183

BOHEMUND I (of Tarantò; circa 1055-1111), Norman Crusader **2** 364

BOHLEN, CHARLES (CHIP) EUSTIS (1904-1973), United States ambassador to the Soviet Union, interpreter, and presidential adviser **2** 364-366

BÖHM-BAWERK, EUGEN VON (1851-1914), Austrian economist **2** 366

Böhme, Jakob
see Boehme, Jacob

BOHR, AAGE NIELS (born 1922), Danish physicist **25** 53-55

BOHR, NIELS HENRIK DAVID (1885-1962), Danish physicist **2** 366-368

BOIARDO, MATTEO MARIA (Conte di Scandiano; 1440/41-1494), Italian poet **2** 369

BOILEAU-DESPRÉAUX, NICHOLAS (1636?-1711), French critic and writer **2** 369-371

Boisy, Francis
see Francis of Sales, St.

BOIVIN, MARIE GILLAIN (née Marie Anne Victorine Gillain; 1773-1841), French midwife and author **25** 55-56

BOK, DEREK CURTIS (born 1930), dean of the Harvard Law School and

president of Harvard University **2** 371-372

BOK, EDWARD WILLIAM (1863-1930), American editor and publisher **22** 71-73

BOK, SISSELA ANN (born 1934), American moral philosopher **2** 372-374

BOLAÑO, ROBERTO (1953-2003), Chilean author **28** 42-45

BOLEYN, ANNE (1504?-1536), second wife of Henry VIII **18** 47-49

Bolingbroke, Henry
see Henry IV (king of England)

BOLINGBROKE, VISCOUNT (Henry St. John; 1678-1751), English statesman **2** 374-375

BOLÍVAR, SIMÓN (1783-1830), South American general and statesman **2** 375-377

BOLKIAH, HASSANAL (Muda Hassanal Bolkiah Mu'izzaddin Waddaulah; born 1946), Sultan of Brunei **18** 49-51

BÖLL, HEINRICH (1917-1985), German writer and translator **2** 377-378

BOLTWOOD, BERTRAM BORDEN (1870-1927), American radiochemist **2** 378-379

BOLTZMANN, LUDWIG (1844-1906), Austrian physicist **2** 379-380

BOMBAL, MARÍA LUISA (1910-1980), Chilean novelist and story writer **2** 380-381

Bonaparte, Charles Louis Napoleon
see Napoleon III

BONAPARTE, JOSEPH (1768-1844), French statesman, king of Naples 1806-1808 and of Spain 1808-1813 **2** 381-382

BONAPARTE, LOUIS (1778-1846), French statesman, king of Holland 1806-1810 **2** 382-383

Bonaparte, Napoleon
see Napoleon I

BONAVENTURE, ST. (1217-1274), Italian theologian and philosopher **2** 383-384

Boncompagni, Ugo
see Gregory XIII

BOND, HORACE MANN (1904-1972), African American educator **2** 384-386

Bond, James (character)
Fleming, Ian **28** 123-125

BOND, JULIAN (born 1940), civil rights leader elected to the Georgia House of Representatives **2** 386-387

BONDEVIK, KJELL MAGNE (born 1947), Norwegian politician **27** 51-53

BONDFIELD, MARGARET GRACE (1873-1953), British union official and political leader **2** 388-389

BONDI, HERMANN (1919-2005), English mathematician and cosmologist **18** 51-52

Bonesana, Cesare
see Becarria, Marchese di

BONHAM CARTER, HELEN VIOLET (nee Helen Violet Asquith; 1887-1969), English author and orator **26** 42-44

BONHOEFFER, DIETRICH (1906-1945), German theologian **2** 389-391

BONHEUR, ROSA (Marie Rosalie Bonheur; 1822-1899), French artist **19** 29-31

BONIFACE, ST. (circa 672-754), English monk **2** 391

BONIFACE VIII (Benedetto Caetani; 1235?-1303), pope 1294-1303 **2** 392-393

BONIFACIO, ANDRES (1863-1897), Filipino revolutionary hero **2** 393-394

BONINGTON, RICHARD PARKES (1802-1828), English painter **2** 394-395

BONNARD, PIERRE (1867-1947), French painter **2** 395-396

Bonnie Prince Charlie
see Charles Edward Louis Philip Casimir Stuart

BONNIN, GERTRUDE SIMMONS (Zitkala-Sa; Red Bird; 1876-1938), Native American author and activist **18** 52-54

BONNY, ANNE (Anne Bonn; Anne Burleigh; 1700-1782), Irish American pirate **25** 56-58

BONO (Paul Hewson; born 1960), Irish musician and activist **24** 56-59

BONO, SONNY (Salvatore Bono; 1935-1998), American entertainer and U.S. Congressman **18** 54-56

BONTEMPS, ARNA (Arnaud Wendell Bontempsl 1902-1973), American author and educator **21** 47-50

BONVALOT, PIERRE GABRIEL ÉDOUARD (1853-1933), French explorer and author **2** 396

BOOLE, GEORGE (1815-1864), English mathematician **2** 396-397

BOONE, DANIEL (1734-1820), American frontiersman and explorer **2** 397-398

BOORSTIN, DANIEL J. (born 1914), American historian **2** 398-400

BOOTH, CHARLES (1840-1916), English social scientist **2** 400-401

BOOTH, EDWIN (1833-1893), American actor **2** 401-402

BOOTH, EVANGELINE CORY (1865-1950), British/American humanist **2** 402-403

BOOTH, HUBERT CECIL (1871-1955), English inventor of the vacuum cleaner **21** 50-52

BOOTH, JOHN WILKES (1838-1865), American actor **2** 404

BOOTH, JOSEPH (1851-1932), English missionary in Africa **2** 404-405

BOOTH, WILLIAM (1829-1912), English evangelist, Salvation Army founder **2** 405-406

Boothe, Clare
see Luce, Clare Boothe

BOOTHROYD, BETTY (born 1929), first woman speaker in Great Britain's House of Commons **2** 406-407

BORAH, WILLIAM EDGAR (1865-1940), American statesman **2** 408

BORDEN, GAIL (1801-1874), American pioneer and inventor of food-processing techniques **2** 409

BORDEN, LIZZIE (Lizzie Andrew Borden; 1860-1927), American murderer **28** 45-47

BORDEN, SIR ROBERT LAIRD (1854-1937), Canadian prime minister, 1911-1920 **2** 409-411

BORGES, JORGE LUIS (1899-1986), Argentine author and critic **2** 411-412

Borghese, Camillo
see Paul V, pope

BORGIA, CESARE (1475-1507), Italian cardinal, general, and administrator **2** 412-413

BORGIA, LUCREZIA (1480-1519), Italian duchess of Ferrara **2** 413-416

Borgia, Rodrigo
see Alexander VI, pope

BORGLUM, JOHN GUTZON DE LA MOTHE (1867-1941), American sculptor and engineer **2** 416-417

BORI, LUCREZIA (Lucrezia Gonzá de Riancho; 1887-1960), Spanish American opera singer **23** 44-45

BORJA CEVALLOS, RODRIGO (born 1935), a founder of Ecuador's Democratic Left (Izquierda Democratica) party and president of Ecuador (1988-) **2** 417-418

BORLAUG, NORMAN ERNEST (born 1914), American biochemist who developed high yield cereal grains **2** 418-420

BORN, MAX (1882-1970), German physicist **2** 420-421

BOROCHOV, DOV BER (1881-1917), early Zionist thinker who reconciled Judaism and Marxism **2** 421-422

BORODIN, ALEKSANDR PROFIREVICH (1833-1887), Russian composer **2** 422-423

BORROMEO, ST. CHARLES (1538-1584), Italian cardinal and reformer **2** 423-424

BORROMINI, FRANCESCO (1599-1667), Italian architect **2** 424-425

BOSANQUET, BERNARD (1848-1923), English philosopher **2** 425-426

BOSCH, HIERONYMUS (1453-1516), Netherlandish painter **2** 426-428

BOSCH, JUAN (born 1909), Dominican writer, president, 1963 **2** 428-429

BOSE, SATYENDRANATH (1894-1974), Indian physicist **20** 52-54

BOSE, SIR JAGADIS CHANDRA (1858-1937), Indian physicist and plant physiologist **2** 430-431

BOSE, SUBHAS CHANDRA (1897-1945), Indian nationalist **2** 430-431

BOSOMWORTH, MARY MUSGROVE (Cousaponokeesa;1700-1765), Native American/American interpreter, diplomat, and businessperson **20** 54-56

BOSSUET, JACQUES BÉNIGNE (1627-1704), French bishop and author **2** 431-432

Boston Strong Boy
see Sullivan, John Lawrence

BOSWELL, JAMES (1740-1795), Scottish biographer and diarist **2** 432-434

Botany (science)
plant morphology
Arber, Agnes Robertson **28** 14-16

BOTERO, FERNANDO (born 1932), Colombian artist **24** 59-61

BOTHA, LOUIS (1862-1919), South African soldier and statesman **2** 434-436

BOTHA, PIETER WILLEM (1916-2006), prime minister (1978-1984) and first executive state president of the Republic of South Africa **2** 436-438

BOTHE, WALTHER (1891-1957), German physicist **2** 438-439

Boto, Eza
see Beti, Mongo

BOTTICELLI, SANDRO (1444-1510), Italian painter **2** 439-440

Bou Kharouba, Mohammed Ben Brahim
see Boumediene, Houari

BOUCHER, FRANÇOIS (1703-1770), French painter **2** 440-442

BOUCICAULT, DION (1820-1890), Irish-American playwright and actor **2** 442-443

BOUDICCA (Boadicea; died 61 A.D.), Iceni queen **18** 56-58

BOUDINOT, ELIAS (Buck Watie; Galagina; 1803-1839), Cherokee leader and author **21** 52-54

BOUGAINVILLE, LOUIS ANTOINE DE (1729-1811), French soldier and explorer **2** 443-444

Boulanger, N.A. (pseudonym)
see Holbach, Baron d'

BOULANGER, NADIA (1887-1979), French pianist and music teacher **20** 56-58

BOULEZ, PIERRE (born 1925), French composer, conductor, and teacher **2** 444-445

BOULT, ADRIAN CEDRIC (1889-1983), English conductor **24** 61-64

BOUMEDIENE, HOUARI (born 1932), Algerian revolutionary, military leader, and president **2** 445-446

BOURASSA, JOSEPH-HENRI-NAPOLEON (1868-1952), French-Canadian nationalist and editor **2** 446-447

BOURASSA, ROBERT (born 1933), premier of the province of Quebec (1970-1976 and 1985-) **2** 447-449

Bourcicault, Dion
see Boucicault, Dion

BOURDELLE, EMILE-ANTOINE (1861-1929), French sculptor **2** 449-450

BOURGEOIS, LÉON (1851-1925), French premier 1895-1896 **2** 450-451

BOURGEOIS, LOUISE (born 1911), American sculptor **2** 451-452

BOURGEOIS, LOUYSE (Louise Bourgeois; c. 1563-1636), French midwife **25** 58-60

BOURGEOYS, BLESSED MARGUERITE (1620-1700), French educator and religious founder **2** 452-453

Bourgogne, Jean de
see Mandeville, Sir John

BOURGUIBA, HABIB (1903-2000), Tunisian statesman **2** 453-455

BOURKE-WHITE, MARGARET (1904-1971), American photographer and photojournalist **2** 455-456

BOURNE, RANDOLPH SILLIMAN (1886-1918), American pacifist and cultural critic **2** 456-457

Boursiquot, Dionysius Lardner
see Boucicault, Dion

BOUTROS-GHALI, BOUTROS (born 1922), Egyptian diplomat and sixth secretary-general of the United Nations (1991-) **2** 457-458

BOUTS, DIRK (1415/20-1475), Dutch painter **2** 458-459

Bouvier, Jacqueline Lee
see Kennedy, Jacqueline

BOVERI, THEODOR HEINRICH (1862-1915), German biologist **25** 60-62

BOWDITCH, HENRY INGERSOLL (1808-1892), American physician **2** 459-460

BOWDITCH, NATHANIEL (1773-1838), American navigator and mathematician **2** 460-461

BOWDOIN, JAMES (1726-1790), American merchant and politician **2** 461-462

BOWEN, ELIZABETH (1899-1973), British novelist **2** 462-463

BOWERS, CLAUDE GERNADE (1878-1958), American journalist, historian, and diplomat **2** 463

BOWIE, DAVID (David Robert Jones; born 1947), English singer, songwriter, and actor **18** 58-60

BOWLES, PAUL (1910-1999), American author, musical composer, and translator **19** 31-34

BOWLES, SAMUEL (1826-1878), American newspaper publisher **2** 464

BOWMAN, ISAIAH (1878-1950), American geographer **2** 464-465

BOXER, BARBARA (born 1940), U.S. Senator from California **2** 465-468

Boxers
see Athletes, American—boxers

Boy bachelor
see Wolsey, Thomas

BOYD, LOUISE ARNER (1887-1972), American explorer **22** 73-74

Boyd, Nancy
see Millay, Edna St. Vincent

Boyd Orr, John
see Orr, John Boyd

BOYER, JEAN PIERRE (1776-1850), Haitian president 1818-1845 **2** 468-469

BOYER, PAUL DELOS (born 1918), American biochemist **25** 62-65

BOYLE, ROBERT (1627-1691), British chemist and physicist **2** 469-471

BOYLSTON, ZABDIEL (1679-1766), American physician **2** 471

Boz
see Dickens, Charles

BOZEMAN, JOHN M. (1837-1867), American pioneer **2** 471-472

Bozzie
see Boswell, James

BRACKENRIDGE, HUGH HENRY (1749-1816), American lawyer and writer **2** 472-473

BRACTON, HENRY (Henry of Bratton; c. 1210-1268), English jurist **21** 54-55

BRADBURY, RAY (born 1920), American fantasy and science fiction writer **2** 473-474

Bradby, Lucy Barbara
see Hammond, John and Lucy

BRADDOCK, EDWARD (1695-1755), British commander in North America **2** 474-475

BRADFORD, WILLIAM (1590-1657), leader of Plymouth Colony **2** 475-476

BRADFORD, WILLIAM (1663-1752), American printer **2** 476-477

BRADFORD, WILLIAM (1722-1791), American journalist **2** 477

BRADLAUGH, CHARLES (1833-1891), English freethinker and political agitator **2** 478

BRADLEY, ED (1941-2006), African American broadcast journalist **2** 478-481

BRADLEY, FRANCIS HERBERT (1846-1924), English philosopher **2** 481-482

BRADLEY, JAMES (1693-1762), English astronomer **2** 482-483

BRADLEY, JOSEPH P. (1813-1892), American Supreme Court justice **22** 74-77

BRADLEY, MARION ZIMMER (born 1930), American author **18** 60-62

BRADLEY, OMAR NELSON (1893-1981), American general **2** 483-484

BRADLEY, TOM (1917-1998), first African American mayor of Los Angeles **2** 484-485

BRADMAN, SIR DONALD GEORGE (born 1908), Australian cricketer **2** 485-486

BRADSTREET, ANNE DUDLEY (circa 1612-1672), English-born American poet **2** 486-487

BRADWELL, MYRA (Myra Colby; 1831-1894), American lawyer and publisher **24** 64-66

BRADY, MATHEW B. (circa 1823-1896), American photographer **2** 487-488

BRAGG, SIR WILLIAM HENRY (1862-1942), English physicist **2** 488-489

BRAHE, TYCHO (1546-1601), Danish astronomer **2** 489-490

BRAHMAGUPTA (circa 598-circa 670), Indian mathematician and astronomer **26** 44-46

BRAHMS, JOHANNES (1833-1897), German composer **2** 490-492

BRAILLE, LOUIS (1809-1852), French teacher and creator of braille system **2** 492-493

BRAINARD, BERTHA (Bertha Brainard Peterson; died 1946), American radio executive **28** 47-48

BRAMAH, JOSEPH (Joe Bremmer; 1749-1814), English engineer and inventor **20** 58-59

BRAMANTE, DONATO (1444-1514), Italian architect and painter **2** 493-494

BRANCUSI, CONSTANTIN (1876-1957), Romanian sculptor in France **2** 494-496

BRANDEIS, LOUIS DEMBITZ (1856-1941), American jurist **2** 496-497

BRANDES, GEORG (Georg Morris Cohen Brandes; 1842-1927), Danish literary critic **23** 45-47

BRANDO, MARLON (born 1924), American actor **2** 497-499

BRANDT, WILLY (Herbert Frahm Brandt; 1913-1992), German statesman, chancellor of West Germany **2** 499-500

BRANSON, RICHARD (born 1950), British entrepreneur **19** 34-36

BRANT, JOSEPH (1742-1807), Mohawk Indian chief **2** 500-501

BRANT, MARY (1736-1796), Native American who guided the Iroquois to a British alliance **2** 501-503

BRANT, SEBASTIAN (1457-1521), German author **2** 503-504

BRAQUE, GEORGES (1882-1967), French painter **2** 504-505

Braschi, Gianangelo
see Pius VI

BRATTAIN, WALTER H. (1902-1987), American physicist and co-inventor of the transistor **2** 505-507

Bratton, Henry de
see Bracton, Henry de

BRAUDEL, FERNAND (1902-1985), leading exponent of the *Annales* school of history **2** 507-508

BRAUN, FERDINAND (1850-1918), German recipient of the Nobel Prize in Physics for work on wireless telegraphy **2** 508-509

BRAY, JOHN RANDOLPH (1879-1978), American animator and cartoonist **21** 55-57

BRAZZA, PIERRE PAUL FRANÇOIS CAMILLE SAVORGNAN DE (1852-1905), Italian-born French explorer **2** 509-510

BREASTED, JAMES HENRY (1865-1935), American Egyptologist and archeologist **2** 510-511

BRÉBEUF, JEAN DE (1593-1649), French Jesuit missionary **2** 511-512

BRECHT, BERTOLT (1898-1956), German playwright **2** 512-514

BRECKINRIDGE, JOHN CABELL (1821-1875), American statesman and military leader **22** 77-79

Brède, Baron de la
see Montesquieu, Baron de

BREMER, FREDRIKA (1801-1865), Swedish author **26** 46-48

BRENDAN, SAINT (Brenainn; Brandon; Brendan of Clonfert; c. 486-c. 578), Irish Abbott and explorer **22** 79-80

BRENNAN, WILLIAM J., JR. (born 1906), United States Supreme Court justice **2** 514-515

Brent of Bin Bin
see Franklin, Miles

BRENTANO, CLEMENS (1778-1842), German poet and novelist **2** 515-516

BRENTANO, FRANZ CLEMENS (1838-1917), German philosopher **2** 516-517

BRESHKOVSKY, CATHERINE (1844-1934), Russian revolutionary **2** 517-519

BRESSON, ROBERT (1901-1999), French filmmaker **25** 65-67

BRETON, ANDRÉ (1896-1966), French author **2** 519-520

Bretton, Henry de
see Bracton, Henry de

BREUER, MARCEL (1902-1981), Hungarian-born American architect **2** 520-521

BREUIL, HENRI EDOUARD PROSPER (1877-1961), French archeologist **2** 521-522

BREWSTER, KINGMAN, JR. (1919-1988), president of Yale University (1963-1977) **2** 522-523

BREWSTER, WILLIAM (circa 1566-1644), English-born Pilgrim leader **2** 523-524

BREYER, STEPHEN (born 1938), U.S. Supreme Court justice **2** 524-527

BREYTENBACH, BREYTEN (Jan Blom; born 1939), South African author and activist **24** 66-68

BREZHNEV, LEONID ILICH (1906-1982), general secretary of the Communist party of the Union of Soviet Socialist Republics (1964-1982) and president of the Union of Soviet Socialist Republics (1977-1982) **2** 527-528

BRIAN BORU (940?-1014), Irish king **18** 62-64

BRIAND, ARISTIDE (1862-1932), French statesman **2** 528-529

BRICE, FANNY (1891-1951), vaudeville, Broadway, film, and radio singer and comedienne **3** 1-2

BRIDGER, JAMES (1804-1881), American fur trader and scout **3** 2-3

BRIDGES, HARRY A.R. (1901-1990), radical American labor leader **3** 3-5

BRIDGMAN, PERCY WILLIAMS (1882-1961), American physicist **3** 5-6

BRIGHT, JOHN (1811-1889), English politician **3** 6-7

BRIGHT, RICHARD (1789-1858), English physician **3** 7-8

BRIGHTMAN, EDGAR SHEFFIELD (1884-1953), philosopher of religion and exponent of American Personalism **3** 8-9

BRINK, ANDRE PHILIPPUS (born 1935), South African author **22** 80-83

Brinkley, David
see Huntley and Brinkley

BRISBANE, ALBERT (1809-1890), American social theorist **3** 9

BRISTOW, BENJAMIN HELM (1832-1896), American lawyer and Federal official **3** 9-10

British Broadcasting Corporation
Frears, Stephen Arthur **28** 127-129
Mirren, Helen **28** 247-249

British India
see India (British rule)

BRITTEN, BENJAMIN (1913-1976), English composer **3** 10-11

BROAD, CHARLIE DUNBAR (1887-1971), English philosopher **3** 12

Broadcasting
Brainard, Bertha **28** 47-48

BROCK, SIR ISAAC (1769-1812), British general **3** 12-13

BRODSKY, JOSEPH (Iosif Alexandrovich Brodsky, 1940-1996), Russian-born Nobel Prize winner and fifth United States poet laureate **3** 13-15

Broglie, Louis de
see de Broglie, Louis Victor Pierre Raymond

Brokaw, Clare Boothe
see Luce, Clare Boothe

BROKAW, TOM (Thomas John Brokaw; born 1940), American television journalist and author **25** 67-69

Broken Hand
see Fitzpatrick, Thomas

Bronstein, Lev Davidovich
see Trotsky, Leon

BRONTË, CHARLOTTE (1816-1855), English novelist **3** 17-18

BRONTË, EMILY (1818-1848), English novelist **3** 18-19

Bronte, Duke of
see Nelson, Viscount

BRONZINO (1503-1572), Italian painter **3** 19

BROOK, PETER (born 1925), world-renowned theater director **3** 19-21

BROOKE, ALAN FRANCIS (Viscount Alanbrooke; 1883-1963), Irish military leader **20** 59-61

BROOKE, SIR JAMES (1803-1868), British governor in Borneo **3** 21-22

BROOKE, RUPERT (1887-1915), English poet **3** 22-23

BROOKNER, ANITA (born 1928), British art historian and novelist **3** 23-24

BROOKS, GWENDOLYN (born 1917), first African American author to receive the Pulitzer Prize for Literature **3** 24-26

BROOKS, MEL (Melvin Kaminsky; born 1926), American actor, playwright, and film and theatre producer/director **23** 48-50

BROOKS, PHILLIPS (1835-1893), American Episcopalian bishop **3** 26

BROTHERS, JOYCE (Joyce Diane Bauer; born 1927), American psychologist who pioneered radio phone-in questions for professional psychological advice **3** 26-28

BROUDY, HARRY SAMUEL (born 1905), American philosopher, teacher, and author **3** 28-29

BROUGHAM, HENRY PETER (Baron Brougham and Vaux; 1778-1868), Scottish jurist **22** 83-85

Broun, Heywood, (1888-1939), American journalist Brainard, Bertha **28** 47-48

BROUWER, ADRIAEN (1605/06-1638), Flemish painter **3** 29-30

BROWDER, EARL RUSSELL (1891-1973), American Communist leader **3** 30-31

BROWN, ALEXANDER (1764-1834), American merchant and banker **3** 31-32

BROWN, BENJAMIN GRATZ (1826-1885), American politician **3** 32-33

BROWN, CHARLES BROCKDEN (1771-1810), American novelist **3** 33

BROWN, CHARLOTTE EUGENIA HAWKINS (born Lottie Hawkins; 1882-1961), African American educator and humanitarian **3** 34

BROWN, GEORGE (1818-1880), Canadian politician **3** 35-36

BROWN, GORDON (James Gordon Brown; born 1951), British politician **28** 48-50

BROWN, HELEN GURLEY (born 1922), American author and editor **3** 36-37

BROWN, JAMES (1928-2006), African American singer **3** 37-39

BROWN, JOHN (1800-1859), American abolitionist **3** 39-41

BROWN, JOSEPH EMERSON (1821-1894), American lawyer and politician **3** 41-42

BROWN, LES (Leslie Calvin Brown; born 1945), American motivational speaker, author, and television host **19** 36-39

BROWN, MOSES (1738-1836), American manufacturer and merchant **3** 42-43

BROWN, RACHEL FULLER (1898-1980), American biochemist **3** 43-44

BROWN, ROBERT (1773-1858), Scottish botanist **20** 61-63

BROWN, RONALD H. (1941-1996), African American politician, cabinet official **3** 44-47

BROWN, STERLING (Sterling Allen Brown; 1901-1989), American literary critic **28** 51-54

BROWN, TINA (Christina Hambly Brown; born 1953), British editor who transformed the English magazine *Tatler*, then the United States magazines *Vanity Fair* and the *New Yorker* **3** 47-48

BROWN, TONY (William Anthony Brown; born 1933), African American radio personality **24** 68-70

BROWN, WILLIAM WELLS (1815/16-1884), African American author and abolitionist **3** 48-49

Browne, Charles Farrar *see* Ward, Artemus

BROWNE, SIR THOMAS (1605-1682), English author **3** 49-50

BROWNE, THOMAS ALEXANDER (Rolf Bolderwood; 1826-1915), Australian author **22** 85-87

BROWNER, CAROL M. (born 1955), U.S. Environmental Protection Agency administrator **3** 50-52

BROWNING, ELIZABETH BARRETT (1806-1861), English poet **3** 52-53

BROWNING, ROBERT (1812-1889), English poet **3** 53-55

BROWNLOW, WILLIAM GANNAWAY (1805-1877), American journalist and politician **3** 55-56

BROWNMILLER, SUSAN (born 1935), American activist, journalist, and novelist **3** 56-57

BROWNSON, ORESTES AUGUSTUS (1803-1876), American clergyman and transcendentalist **3** 57-58

Broz, Josip *see* Tito, Marshal

BRUBACHER, JOHN SEILER (1898-1988), American historian and educator **3** 58-59

BRUBECK, DAVE (born 1920), American pianist, composer, and bandleader **3** 59-61

BRUCE, BLANCHE KELSO (1841-1898), African American politician **3** 62-63

BRUCE, DAVID (1855-1931), Australian parasitologist **3** 63

BRUCE, JAMES (1730-1794), Scottish explorer **3** 63-64

Bruce, James (1811-1863) *see* Elgin, 8th Earl of

BRUCE, LENNY (Leonard Alfred Schneider; 1925-1966), American comedian **19** 39-41

Bruce, Robert *see* Robert I (king of Scotland)

BRUCE OF MELBOURNE, 1ST VISCOUNT (Stanley Melbourne Bruce; 1883-1967), Australian statesman **3** 61-62

BRUCKNER, JOSEPH ANTON (1824-1896), Austrian composer **3** 64-65

BRUEGEL, PIETER, THE ELDER (1525/30-1569), Netherlandish painter **3** 65-67

BRÛLÉ, ÉTIENNE (circa 1592-1633), French explorer in North America **3** 67-68

BRUNDTLAND, GRO HARLEM (1939-1989), Norwegian prime minister and chair of the United Nations World Commission for Environment and Development **3** 68-69

Brunei, Sultan of *see* Bolkiah, Hassanal

BRUNEL, ISAMBARD KINGDOM (1806-1859), English civil engineer **3** 69-70

BRUNELLESCHI, FILIPPO (1377-1446), Italian architect and sculptor **3** 70-72

BRUNER, JEROME SEYMOUR (born 1915), American psychologist **3** 72-73

BRUNHOFF, JEAN DE (1899-1937), French author and illustrator **19** 41-42

BRUNNER, ALOIS (born 1912), Nazi German officer who helped engineer the destruction of European Jews **3** 73-74

BRUNNER, EMIL (1889-1966), Swiss Reformed theologian **3** 74-75

BRUNO, GIORDANO (1548-1600), Italian philosopher and poet **3** 75-76

Bruno of Toul (Egisheim) *see* Leo IX, St.

BRUTON, JOHN GERARD (born 1947), prime minister of Ireland **3** 76-77

BRUTUS, DENNIS (born 1924), exiled South African poet and political activist opposed to apartheid **3** 77-78

BRUTUS, MARCUS JUNIUS (circa 85-42 B.C.), Roman statesman **3** 79-80

Brutus, Quintus Caepio *see* Brutus, Marcus Junius

BRYAN, WILLIAM JENNINGS (1860-1925), American lawyer and politician **3** 80-82

BRYANT, PAUL ("Bear;" 1919-1983), American college football coach **3** 82-83

BRYANT, WILLIAM CULLEN (1794-1878), American poet and editor **3** 83-85

BRYCE, JAMES (1838-1922), British historian, jurist, and statesman **3** 85

BRZEZINSKI, ZBIGNIEW (1928-1980), assistant to President Carter for national security affairs (1977-1980) **3** 85-87

BUBER, MARTIN (1878-1965), Austrian-born Jewish theologian and philosopher **3** 87-89

Buccleugh
see Monmouth and Buccleugh Duke of

BUCHALTER, LEPKE (Louis Bachalter; 1897-1944), American gangster **19** 42-44

BUCHANAN, JAMES (1791-1868), American statesman, president 1857-1861 **3** 89-90

BUCHANAN, PATRICK JOSEPH (born 1938), commentator, journalist, and presidential candidate **3** 90-91

BUCHWALD, ART (Arthur Buchwald; 1925-2007), American journalist **27** 55-57

BUCK, JACK (John Francis Buck; 1924-2002), American sportscaster **27** 57-59

BUCK, PEARL SYDENSTRICKER (1892-1973), American novelist **3** 91-93

BUCKINGHAM, 1ST DUKE OF (George Villiers; 1592-1628), English courtier and military leader **3** 93-94

BUCKINGHAM, 2D DUKE OF (George Villiers; 1628-1687), English statesman **3** 94-95

BUCKLE, HENRY THOMAS (1821-1862), English historian **3** 95-96

BUCKLEY, WILLIAM F., JR. (1925-2008), conservative American author, editor, and political activist **3** 96-97

BUDDHA (circa 560-480 B.C.), Indian founder of Buddhism **3** 97-101

BUDDHADĀSA BHIKKHU (Nguam Phanich; born 1906), founder of Wat Suan Mokkhabalārama in southern Thailand and interpreter of Theravāda Buddhism **3** 101-102

Buddhism
scholars of
David-Néel, Alexandra **28** 90-92

Buddhism (Tibet)
David-Néel, Alexandra **28** 90-92

BUDÉ, GUILLAUME (1467-1540), French humanist **3** 102-103

BUDGE, DON (J. Donald Budge; born 1915), American tennis player **21** 57-59

BUECHNER, FREDERICK (born 1926), American novelist and theologian **3** 103-105

BUEL, JESSE (1778-1839), American agriculturalist and journalist **3** 105

Buell, Sarah Josepha
see Hale, Sarah Josepha

BUFFALO BILL (William Frederick Cody; 1846-1917), American scout and publicist **3** 105-106

BUFFETT, WARREN (born 1930), American investment salesman **3** 106-109

BUFFON, COMTE DE (Georges Louis Leclerc; 1707-1788), French naturalist **3** 109-111

BUGEAUD DE LA PICONNERIE, THOMAS ROBERT (1784-1849), Duke of Isly and marshal of France **3** 111

BUICK, DAVID (1854-1929), American inventor and businessman **19** 44-45

BUKHARI, MUHAMMAD IBN ISMAIL AL- (810-870), Arab scholar and Moslem saint **3** 111-112

BUKHARIN, NIKOLAI IVANOVICH (1858-1938), Russian politician **3** 112-113

BUKOWSKI, CHARLES (1920-1994), American writer and poet **3** 113-115

BULATOVIC, MOMIR (born 1956), president of Montenegro (1990-1992) and of the new Federal Republic of Yugoslavia (1992-) **3** 115-116

BULFINCH, CHARLES (1763-1844), American colonial architect **3** 116-117

BULGAKOV, MIKHAIL AFANASIEVICH (1891-1940), Russian novelist and playwright **3** 117

BULGANIN, NIKOLAI (1885-1975), chairman of the Soviet Council of Ministers (1955-1958) **3** 118-119

Bulgaria, People's Republic of (nation, Southeast Europe)
Simeon, King of Bulgaria **28** 325-327

Bulgaroctonus (Bulgar-Slayer)
see Basil II, (1415-1462)

BULL, OLE (Ole Bornemann Bull; 1810-1880), Norwegian violinist and composer **28** 54-56

BULOSAN, CARLOS (1911-1956), American author and poet **21** 59-61

BULTMANN, RUDOLF KARL (1884-1976), German theologian **3** 119-120

BULWER-LYTTON, EDWARD (1st Baron Lytton of Knebworth; 1803-1873), English novelist **22** 87-88

BUNAU-VARILLA, PHILIPPE JEAN (1859-1940), French engineer and soldier **3** 120-121

BUNCHE, RALPH JOHNSON (1904-1971), African American diplomat **3** 121-122

BUNDY, MCGEORGE (born 1919), national security adviser to two presidents **3** 122-124

BUNIN, IVAN ALEKSEEVICH (1870-1953), Russian poet and novelist **3** 124

BUNSEN, ROBERT WILHELM (1811-1899), German chemist and physicist **3** 124-125

BUNSHAFT, GORDON (1909-1990), American architect **3** 125-127

BUNTING-SMITH, MARY INGRAHAM (Polly Bunting; 1910-1998), American educator **27** 59-61

BUÑUEL, LUIS (1900-1983), Spanish film director **3** 127-128

BUNYAN, JOHN (1628-1688), English author and Baptist preacher **3** 128-129

BURBAGE, RICHARD (c. 1567-1619), British actor **24** 70-72

BURBANK, LUTHER (1849-1926), American plant breeder **3** 129-131

BURBIDGE, E. MARGARET (Eleanor Margaret Burbidge; born 1919), British-American astronomer and physicist **26** 48-50

BURCHFIELD, CHARLES (1893-1967), American painter **3** 131-132

BURCKHARDT, JACOB CHRISTOPH (1818-1897), Swiss historian **3** 132-133

BURCKHARDT, JOHANN LUDWIG (1784-1817), Swiss-born explorer **3** 133

BURGER, WARREN E. (1907-1986), Chief Justice of the United States Supreme Court (1969-1986) **3** 133-136

BURGESS, ANTHONY (John Anthony Burgess Wilson; 1917-1993), English author **3** 136-137

BURGOYNE, JOHN (1723-1792), British general and statesman **3** 137-138

BURKE, EDMUND (1729-1797), British statesman, political theorist, and philosopher **3** 138-141

BURKE, KENNETH (born 1897), American literary theorist and critic **3** 141-142

BURKE, ROBERT O'HARA (1820-1861), Irish-born Australian policeman and explorer **3** 142-143

BURKE, SELMA (1900-1995), African American sculptor **3** 143-144

BURLIN, NATALIE CURTIS (Natalie Curtis; 1875-1921), American ethnomusicologist **23** 50-52

BURLINGAME, ANSON (1820-1870), American diplomat **3** 144-145

BURMAN, RAHUL DEV (R. D. Burman; 1939-1994), Indian musician **26** 50-52

BURNE-JONES, SIR EDWARD COLEY (1833-1898), English painter and designer **3** 145-146

BURNET, SIR FRANK MACFARLANE (1899-1985), Australian virologist **3** 146-147

BURNET, GILBERT (1643-1715), British bishop and historian **3** 147

BURNETT, CAROL (born 1933), American television entertainer **23** 52-55

BURNETT, FRANCES HODGSON (Frances Eliza Hodgson Burnett; 1849-1924), English-born American author **18** 64-67

BURNETT, LEO (1891-1971), American advertising executive **19** 45-47

BURNEY, FRANCES "FANNY" (1752-1840), English novelist and diarist **3** 147-148

BURNHAM, DANIEL HUDSON (1846-1912), American architect and city planner **3** 148-149

BURNHAM, FORBES (1923-1985), leader of the independence movement in British Guiana and Guyana's first prime minister **3** 149-151

BURNS, ANTHONY (1834-1862), African American slave **3** 151

BURNS, ARTHUR (1904-1987), American economic statesman **3** 151-153

BURNS, GEORGE (born Nathan Birnbaum; 1896-1996), American comedian and actor **3** 153-155

BURNS, KEN (Kenneth Lauren Burns; born 1953), American documentary filmmaker **20** 63-65

BURNS, ROBERT (1759-1796), Scottish poet **3** 155-156

BURR, AARON (1756-1836), American politician, vice president 1801-1805 **3** 156-159

BURRI, ALBERTO (1915-1995), Italian painter **3** 159-160

BURRITT, ELIHU (1810-1879), American pacifist, author, and linguist **3** 160

BURROUGHS, EDGAR RICE (1875-1950), American author **18** 67-68

BURROUGHS, JOHN (1837-1921), American naturalist and essayist **3** 160-161

BURROUGHS, WILLIAM S. (1914-1997), American writer **3** 162-163

BURROUGHS, WILLIAM S. (William Seward Burroughs; 1855-1898), American inventor **28** 56-57

BURTON, RICHARD (Richard Jenkins; 1925-1984), British actor **3** 163-164

BURTON, SIR RICHARD FRANCIS (1821-1890), English explorer, author, and diplomat **3** 164-166

BURTON, ROBERT (1577-1640), English author and clergyman **3** 166-167

BUSCH, ADOLPHUS (1839-1913), American brewer and businessman **19** 47-49

BUSH, GEORGE (George Herbert Walker Bush; born 1924), United States vice president (1981-1989) and president (1989-1993) **3** 167-169

BUSH, GEORGE WALKER (born 1946), United States president (2001-) **21** 61-64

BUSH, LAURA WELCH (born 1946), American First Lady **25** 69-72

BUSH, VANNEVAR (1890-1974), American scientist and engineer **3** 169-171

BUSH-BANKS, OLIVIA WARD (1869-1944), American author **27** 61-63

BUSHNELL, DAVID (1742-1824), American inventor **21** 64-65

BUSHNELL, HORACE (1802-1876), American Congregational clergyman **3** 171-172

BUSIA, KOFI ABREFA (1914-1978), Ghanaian premier and sociologist **3** 172-173

Business and industrial leaders
Belgian
  Merckx, Eddy **28** 241-243
British
  Roddick, Anita **28** 298-301
Danish
  Christiansen, Ole Kirk **28** 76-78
French
  Vuitton, Louis **28** 365-367
Japanese
  Ibuka, Masaru **28** 184-186
Lebanese
  Hariri, Rafic **28** 161-163
Polish
  Lukasiewicz, Ignacy **28** 225-227

Business and industrial leaders, American
chemical industry
  Dow, Herbert H. **28** 100-102
communications industry
  Brainard, Bertha **28** 47-48
  Cooper, Martin **28** 85-87
  Gross, Al **28** 149-151
  Stringer, Howard **28** 338-340
computer industry
  Burroughs, William S. **28** 56-57
electronics industry
  Stringer, Howard **28** 338-340
entertainment industry
  Griffin, Merv **28** 146-149
financial information industry
  Bloomberg, Michael **28** 40-42
food and beverage industry
  Kellogg, W. K. **28** 199-201
  Marriott, J. Willard **28** 232-234
  Pemberton, John Stith **28** 278-279
hotel industry
  Marriott, J. Willard **28** 232-234
real estate
  Griffin, Merv **28** 146-149
religious enterprises
  Roberts, Oral **28** 296-298

BUSONI, FERRUCCIO BENVENUTO (1866-1924), Italian musician **3** 173-174

BUSSOTTI, SYLVANO (born 1931), Italian composer **3** 174-175

BUSTAMANTE, WILLIAM ALEXANDER (1884-1977), Jamaican labor leader and first prime minister (1962-1967) **3** 175-177

BUTE, 3D EARL OF (John Stuart; 1713-1792), British statesman, prime minister 1762-1763 **3** 177-178

BUTENANDT, ADOLF FRIEDRICH JOHANN (1903-1995), German chemist **25** 72-74

BUTHELEZI, MANGOSUTHU GATSHA (born 1928), chief of the Zulu "homeland" and an important figure in the struggle to end apartheid in South Africa **3** 178-179

BUTLER, BENJAMIN FRANKLIN (1818-1893), American politician and military leader **21** 65-67

BUTLER, JOHN (1728-1796), British Indian agent and Loyalist leader **3** 180

BUTLER, JOSEPH (1692-1752), English philosopher and theologian **3** 180-181

BUTLER, NICHOLAS MURRAY (1862-1947), American educator **3** 181

BUTLER, OCTAVIA E. (1947-2006), African American novelist and essayist **3** 182-183

BUTLER, SAMUEL (1613-1680), English poet **3** 183-184

BUTLER, SAMUEL (1835-1902), English novelist and essayist **3** 183

BUTTERFIELD, JOHN (1801-1869), American financier and politician **3** 184-185

BUTTON, DICK (Richard Totten Button; born 1929), American figure skater and sports commentator **23** 55-57

BUXTEHUDE, DIETRICH (1637-1707), Danish composer and organist **3** 185-186

BYRD, RICHARD EVELYN (1888-1957), American admiral and polar explorer **3** 186-187

BYRD, WILLIAM (1543?-1623), English composer **3** 187-188

BYRD, WILLIAM (1652-1704), English colonial planter and merchant **3** 188-189

BYRD, WILLIAM II (1674-1744), American diarist and government official **3** 189-190

BYRNE, JANE (born 1934), first woman mayor of Chicago **3** 190-191

BYRNES, JAMES FRANCIS (1879-1972), American public official **3** 191-192

BYRON, GEORGE GORDON NOEL (6th Baron Byron; 1788-1824), English poet **3** 193-194

Byzantine Church
see Orthodox Eastern Church

Byzantine Empire (395-1453; Eastern Roman Empire 395-474)
and Bulgaria
Simeon, King of Bulgaria **28** 325-327

Byzantium
see Byzantine Empire (395-1453; Eastern Roman Empire 395-474)

C

CABELL, JAMES BRANCH (1879-1958), American essayist and novelist **3** 195-196

CABET, ÉTIENNE (1788-1856), French political radical **3** 196

CABEZA DE VACA, ÁLVAR NÚÑEZ (circa 1490-circa 1557), Spanish explorer **3** 197

CABEZÓN, ANTONIO (1510-1566), Spanish composer **3** 197-198

CABLE, GEORGE WASHINGTON (1844-1925), American novelist **3** 198-199

CABOT, JOHN (flourished 1471-1498), Italian explorer in English service **3** 199-200

CABOT, RICHARD CLARKE (1868-1939), American physician **3** 200

CABOT, SEBASTIAN (circa 1482-1557), Italian-born explorer for England and Spain **3** 200-201

Caboto, Giovanni
see Cabot, John

CABRAL, AMÍLCAR LOPES (1924-1973), father of modern African nationalism in Guinea-Bissau and the Cape Verde Islands **3** 202-203

CABRAL, PEDRO ÁLVARES (1467/68-1520), Portuguese navigator **3** 203-204

Cabrera, Manuel Estrada
see Estrada Cabrera, Manuel

CABRILLO, JUAN RODRÍGUEZ (died 1543), Portuguese explorer for Spain **3** 204-205

CABRINI, ST. FRANCES XAVIER (1850-1917), Italian-born founder of the Missionary Sisters of the Sacred Heart **3** 205

CACCINI, GIULIO (circa 1545-1618), Italian singer and composer **3** 205-206

CADAMOSTO, ALVISE DA (circa 1428-1483), Italian explorer **3** 206-207

CAEDMON (650-c.680), English Christian poet **20** 66-67

CADILLAC, ANTOINE DE LAMOTHE (1658-1730), French explorer and colonial administrator **18** 69-71

CADMUS, PAUL (1904-1999), American painter **27** 64-66

CAESAR, (GAIUS) JULIUS (100-44 B.C.), Roman general and statesman **3** 207-210

CAESAR, SHIRLEY (born 1938), African American singer **3** 210-211

Caetani, Benedetto
see Boniface VIII

CAGE, JOHN (1912-1992), American composer **3** 211-214

CAGNEY, JAMES (1899-1986), American actor **21** 68-71

CAHAN, ABRAHAM (1860-1951), Lithuanian-American Jewish author **3** 214

Cahiers du cinéma (revolution)
Bazin, André **28** 32-33

CAILLIÉ, AUGUSTE RENÉ (1799-1838), French explorer **3** 214-215

CAIN, JAMES (1892-1977), American journalist and author **19** 50-52

CAJETAN, ST. (1480-1547), Italian reformer; cofounder of the Theatines **3** 215-216

Calabria, Duke of
see Guiscard, Robert

CALAMITY JANE (Martha Jane Cannary; 1852-1903), American frontier woman **3** 216

CALATRAVA, SANTIAGO (born 1951), Spanish/Swiss architect **27** 66-68

Calculating machine (mathematics)
Burroughs, William S. **28** 56-57

CALDECOTT, RANDOLPH (1846-1886), English artist and illustrator **19** 52-55

CALDER, ALEXANDER (1898-1976), American sculptor **3** 216-218

CALDERA RODRÍGUEZ, RAFAEL (born 1916), president of Venezuela (1969-1974) **3** 218-219

CALDERÓN, ALBERTO P. (1920-1998), Hispanic American mathematician **3** 219-220

CALDERÓN, FELIPE (Felipe de Jesús Calderon Hinojosa; born 1962), Mexican politician **27** 68-70

CALDERÓN, PEDRO (1600-1681), Spanish poet and playwright **3** 221-222

CALDERÓN FOURNIER, RAFAEL (born 1949), president of Costa Rica (1990-) **3** 222-223

CALDICOTT, HELEN BROINOWSKI (born 1938), Australian physician and activist **18** 71-73

CALDWELL, ERSKINE (1903-1987), American novelist **3** 223-224

CALDWELL, SARAH (1924-2006), long-time artistic director, conductor, and founder of the Opera Company of Boston **3** 224-226

Calendar (chronology)
Dionysius Exiguus **28** 99-100

Caletti-Bruni, Pietro Francesco
see Cavalli, Pietro Francesco

CALHOUN, JOHN CALDWELL (1782-1850), American statesman **3** 226-228

Caliari, Paolo
see Veronese, Paolo

CALIGULA (12-41), Roman emperor 37-41 **3** 228-229

CALLAGHAN, EDWARD MORLEY (1903-1990), Canadian novelist **3** 229-230

CALLAGHAN, LEONARD JAMES (born 1912), Labor member of the British Parliament and prime minister, 1976-1979 **3** 230-231

CALLAHAN, DANIEL (born 1930), American philosopher who focused on biomedical ethics **3** 231-233

CALLAHAN, HARRY (1912-1999), American photographer **20** 67-69

CALLAS, MARIA (Cecilia Sophia Anna Maria Kalogeropoulos; 1923-1977), American opera soprano **18** 73-75

CALLEJAS ROMERO, RAFAEL LEONARDO (born 1943), president of Honduras (1990-) **3** 233-234

CALLENDER, CLIVE ORVILLE (born 1936), African American surgeon **18** 75-77

CALLES, PLUTARCO ELÍAS (1877-1945), Mexican revolutionary leader **3** 234-235

CALLIMACHUS (circa 310-240 B.C.), Greek poet **3** 235-236

CALLOWAY, CAB (1907-1994), American singer songwriter and bandleader **3** 236-238

CALVERT, CHARLES (3rd Baron Baltimore; 1637-1715), English proprietor of colonial Maryland **3** 238

CALVERT, GEORGE (1st Baron Baltimore; circa 1580-1632), English statesman, founder of Maryland colony **3** 238-239

CALVIN, JOHN (1509-1564), French Protestant reformer **3** 239-242

CALVIN, MELVIN (1911-1986), American chemist **3** 242-243

CALVINO, ITALO (1923-1985), Italian author **3** 243-244

CAMDESSUS, MICHEL (born 1933), French civil servant and managing director of the International Monetary Fund **3** 244-246

Camera
see Photography

Cameron, Elizabeth Bowen
see Bowen, Elizabeth

CAMERON, JULIA MARGARET (1815-1879), British photographer **20** 69-71

CAMERON, SIMON (1799-1889), American politician **3** 246-247

CAMOENS, LUIS VAS DE (Luís de Camoens; Luís Vas de Camões; 1524-1580), Portuguese poet and dramatist **3** 247-249

Camões Luis Vaz de
see Camoëns, Luis Vaz de

CAMPANELLA, ROY (1921-1993), American baseball player **19** 55-57

CAMPANELLA, TOMMASO (Giovanni Domenico Campanella; 1568-1639), Italian philosopher, political theorist, and poet **3** 249

CAMPBELL, ALEXANDER (1788-1866), Irish-born American clergyman **3** 249-250

CAMPBELL, AVRIL PHAEDRA DOUGLAS (KIM) (born 1947), Canada's first woman prime minister **3** 250-252

CAMPBELL, BEBE MOORE (Elizabeth Bebe Moore; 1950-2006), African American author and journalist **27** 71-73

CAMPBELL, BEN NIGHTHORSE (born 1933), Native American United States senator from Colorado **3** 252-253

CAMPBELL, COLIN (Baron Clyde; 1792-1863), English army officer **20** 71-73

CAMPBELL, JOSEPH (1904-1987), American editor and popularizer of comparative mythology **3** 253-255

CAMPIN, ROBERT (circa 1375/80-1444), Flemish painter **3** 255

CAMPION, JANE (born 1954), Australian film director and screenwriter **23** 58-60

CAMPION, THOMAS (Thomas Campian; 1567-1620), English poet and musician **23** 60-62

Campo, Carlos Ibáñez del
see Ibáñez del Campo, Carlos

CAMPOS, ROBERTO OLIVEIRA (1917-2001), Brazilian economist and diplomat **18** 77-79

CAMUS, ALBERT (1913-1960), French novelist, essayist, and playwright **3** 255-257

Canal, Giovanni Antonio
see Canaletto

CANALETTO (1697-1768), Italian painter **3** 257-258

Cancer research
Wright, Jane Cooke **28** 383-385

CANISIUS, ST. PETER (1521-1597), Dutch Jesuit **3** 258

Cannary, Martha Jane
see Calamity Jane

CANNING, GEORGE (1770-1827), English orator and statesman **3** 258-260

CANNON, ANNIE JUMP (1863-1941), American astronomer **3** 260-261

CANNON, JOSEPH GURNEY (1836-1926), American politican **3** 261-262

Canon law (Roman Catholic)
Dionysius Exiguus **28** 99-100

CANOT, THEODORE (1804-1860), French-Italian adventurer and slave trader **3** 262-263

CANOVA, ANTONIO (1757-1822), Italian sculptor **3** 263-264

CANTH, MINNA (Ulrika Vilhelmina Johnson; 1844-1897), Finnish author and feminist **28** 58-60

CANTINFLAS (Mario Moreno Reyes; 1911-1993), Mexican comedian **26** 53-55

CANTOR, EDDIE (Isador Iskowitz; 1892-1964), American singer and comedian **3** 264-265

CANTOR, GEORG FERDINAND LUDWIG PHILIPP (1845-1918), German mathematician **3** 265-266

CANUTE I THE GREAT (c. 995-1035), Viking king of England and Denmark **3** 266-269

CANUTT, YAKIMA (Enos Edward Canutt; 1896-1986), American rodeo performer, actor, stuntman, and film director **21** 71-72

CAO YU (Wan Jibao; Tsao Yu; Xiaoshi; 1910-1996), Chinese playwright **26** 55-57

CAPA, ROBERT (Endre Friedmann; 1913-1954), Hungarian-American war photographer and photojournalist **3** 269-271

Cape Horn: The Logical Route (book)
Moitessier, Bernard **28** 252-254

ČAPEK, KAREL (1890-1938), Czech novelist, playwright, and essayist **3** 271-272

CAPETILLO, LUISA (1879-1922), Puerto Rican labor leader and activist **20** 73-74

Capitol (United States)
see Washington, D.C.—Capitol

CAPONE, AL (Alphonso Caponi, a.k.a. "Scarface;" 1899-1947), American gangster **3** 272-273

CAPOTE, TRUMAN (born Truman Streckfus Persons; 1924-1984), American author **3** 273-275

CAPP, AL (Alfred Gerald Capp; 1909-1979), American cartoonist and satirist **3** 275-276

Cappellari, Bartolommeo Alberto
see Gregory XVI

CAPRA, FRANK (1897-1991), American film director **3** 276-278

CAPRIATI, JENNIFER (born 1976), American tennis player **3** 278-281

CAPTAIN JACK (Kientpoos; circa 1837-1873), American tribal leader **21** 72-74

CARACALLA (188-217), Roman emperor **3** 281-282

Carafa, Giampietro
see Paul IV (pope)

CARAGIALE, ION LUCA (1852-1912), Romanian author **23** 62-64

CARAVAGGIO (1573-1610), Italian painter **3** 282-284

CARAWAY, HATTIE WYATT (1878-1950), first woman elected to the United States Senate in her own right **3** 284-285

CARDANO, GERONIMO (1501-1576), Italian mathematician, astronomer, and physician **3** 285-286

CARDENAL, ERNESTO (born 1925), Nicaraguan priest, poet, and revolutionary **19** 57-59

Cárdenas, Bartolomé de
see Bermejo, Bartolomé

CÁRDENAS, LÁZARO (1895-1970), Mexican revolutionary president 1934-1940 **3** 286-287

CÁRDENAS SOLORZANO, CUAUHTÉMOC (born 1934), Mexican politician **3** 287-288

CARDIN, PIERRE (born 1922), French fashion designer **18** 79-81

CARDOSO, FERNANDO HENRIQUE (born 1931), sociologist and president of Brazil **18** 81-83

CARDOZO, BENJAMIN NATHAN (1870-1938), American jurist and legal philosopher **3** 288-290

CARDUCCI, GIOSUÈ (1835-1907), Italian poet **3** 290-291

CAREW, ROD (born 1945), Panamanian baseball player **3** 291-292

CAREY, GEORGE LEONARD (born 1935), archbishop of Canterbury **3** 293-294

CAREY, HENRY CHARLES (1793-1879), American writer on economics **3** 294-295

CAREY, PETER (born 1943), Australian author **3** 295-297

CAREY, WILLIAM (1761-1834), English Baptist missionary **3** 297

CAREY THOMAS, MARTHA (1857-1935), American educator **3** 297-298

CARÍAS ANDINO, TIBURCIO (1876-1969), Honduran dictator (1932-1949) **3** 298-299

Caricature and Charivari (publication) Grandville, J.J. **28** 144-146

CARISSIMI, GIACOMO (1605-1674), Italian composer **3** 299-300

CARLETON, GUY (1st Baron Dorchester; 1724-1808), British general and statesman **3** 300-301

CARLIN, GEORGE (born 1937), American comedian **3** 301-303

CARLSON, CHESTER F. (1906-1968), American inventor of the process of xerography **3** 303-304

Carlstadt
see Karlstadt

CARLYLE, THOMAS (1795-1881), Scottish essayist and historian **3** 304-305

Carmelites (religious order) Thérèse of Lisieux, Saint **28** 347-350

CARMICHAEL, HOAGY (Hoagland Howard Carmichael; 1899-1981), American songwriter **26** 57-60

CARMICHAEL, STOKELY (1941-1998), African American civil rights activist **3** 305-308

CARNAP, RUDOLF (1891-1970), German-American philosopher **3** 308-309

CARNÉ, MARCEL ALBERT (1909-1996), French film director and screenwriter **26** 60-62

CARNEADES (circa 213-circa 128 B.C.), Greek philosopher **3** 309

CARNEGIE, ANDREW (1835-1919), American industrialist and philanthropist **3** 309-312

CARNEGIE, HATTIE (born Henrietta Kanengeiser; 1889-1956), American fashion designer **3** 313

CARNOT, LAZARE NICOLAS MARGUERITE (1753-1823), French engineer, general, and statesman **3** 313-314

CARNOT, NICHOLAS LÉONARD SADI (1796-1832), French physicist **3** 315

CARO, ANTHONY (born 1924), English sculptor **3** 316

CARO, JOSEPH BEN EPHRAIM (1488-1575), Jewish Talmudic scholar **3** 316-317

Caron, Pierre August
see Beaumarchais, Pierre August Caron de

CAROTHERS, WALLACE HUME (1896-1937), American chemist **3** 317-318

CARPEAUX, JEAN BAPTISTE (1827-1875), French sculptor and painter **3** 318-319

CARR, EMILY (1871-1945), Canadian painter and writer **3** 319

CARR, EMMA PERRY (1880-1972), American chemist and educator **22** 89-91

CARR-SAUNDERS, SIR ALEXANDER MORRIS (1886-1966), English demographer and sociologist **3** 333-334

CARRANZA, VENUSTIANO (1859-1920), Mexican revolutionary, president 1914-1920 **3** 321-322

CARREL, ALEXIS (1873-1944), French-American surgeon **3** 322-323

CARRERA, JOSÉ MIGUEL (1785-1821), Chilean revolutionary **3** 323-324

CARRERA, JOSÉ RAFAEL (1814-1865), Guatemalan statesman, president 1851-1865 **3** 324-325

CARRERAS, JOSE MARIA (born 1946), Spanish opera singer **22** 91-93

Carrick, Earl of
see Robert III

CARRIER, WILLS (1876-1950), American inventer who was the "father of air conditioning" **3** 325-326

CARRINGTON, BARON (born 1919), British politician and secretary-general of the North Atlantic Treaty Organization (1984-1988) **3** 326-327

CARROLL, ANNA ELLA (1815-1893), American political writer and presidential aide **3** 327-331

CARROLL, JOHN (1735-1815), American Catholic bishop **3** 331-332

CARROLL, LEWIS (pseudonym of Charles Lutwidge Dodgson; 1832-1898), English cleric and author **3** 332-333

Carrucci, Jacopo
see Pontormo

CARSON, BEN (born 1951), African American surgeon **18** 83-85

CARSON, CHRISTOPHER "KIT" (1809-1868), American frontiersman **3** 334-335

CARSON, JOHNNY (1925-2005), American television host and comedian **3** 335-337

CARSON, RACHEL LOUISE (1907-1964), American biologist and author **3** 337-338

CARTER, BENNY (Benny Carter, 1907-2003), African American musician **24** 73-75

CARTER, BETTY (Lillie Mae Jones; 1930-1998), American jazz singer **25** 75-77

CARTER, ELLIOTT COOK, JR. (born 1908), American composer **3** 338-339

CARTER, HOWARD (1874-1939), English archaeologist and artist **20** 74-76

CARTER, JAMES EARL ("Jimmy" Carter; born 1924), United States president (1977-1981) **3** 339-342

CARTIER, SIR GEORGE-ÉTIENNE (1814-1873), Canadian statesman **3** 342-343

CARTIER, JACQUES (1491-1557), French explorer and navigator **3** 343-344

CARTIER-BRESSON, HENRI (born 1908), French photographer and painter **19** 59-61

Cartoons
animated
  Hanna and Barbera **28** 156-159
comic strips
  Peyo **28** 280-282

CARTWRIGHT, ALEXANDER (1820-1898), baseball pioneer **21** 74-77

CARTWRIGHT, MARY LUCY (Dame Cartwright; 1900-1998), English mathematician **25** 77-79

CARTWRIGHT, PETER (1785-1872), American Methodist preacher **3** 344-345

CARUSO, ENRICO (1873-1921), Italian operatic tenor **3** 345

Carvalho e Mello, Sebastião José de
see Pombal, Marquês de

CARVER, GEORGE WASHINGTON (1864-1943), African American agricultural chemist **3** 346-347

CARVER, JONATHAN (1710-1780), American explorer and writer **3** 347-348

CASALS, PABLO (born Pau Carlos Salvador Casals y Defill; 1876-1973), Spanish cellist, conductor, and composer **3** 348-350

CASANOVA, GIACOMO JACOPO GIROLAMO, CHEVALIER DE SEINGLAT (1725-1798), Italian adventurer **3** 350-351

CASE, STEVE (born 1958), American businessman **19** 61-64

Casely Hayford, J.E.
see Hayford, J.E. Casely

CASEMENT, ROGER (1864-1916), Irish diplomat and nationalist **20** 76-78

Casey, John
see O'Casey, Sean

CASEY, WILLIAM J. (1913-1987), American director of the Central Intelligence Agency (CIA) **3** 351-353

CASH, JOHNNY (1932-2003), American singer and songwriter **3** 353-355

CASH, JUNE CARTER (Valerie June Carter; 1929-2003), American singer and songwriter **27** 73-75

CASH, W. J. (Joseph Wilbur Cash; 1900-1914), American journalist and author **22** 93-95

CASHIN, BONNIE JEAN (1915-2000), American fashion designer **27** 75-77

CASIMIR III, KING OF POLAND (Kazimierz III; Casimir the Great; 1310-1370), King of Poland (1333-1370) **28** 60-62

CASS, LEWIS (1782-1866), American statesman **3** 355-356

CASSATT, MARY (1845-1926), American painter **3** 356-357

CASSAVETES, JOHN (1929-1989), American filmmaker **22** 96-98

CASSIODORUS, FLAVIUS MAGNUS AURELIUS, SENATOR (circa 480-circa 575), Roman statesman and author **3** 357-358

CASSIRER, ERNST (1874-1945), German philosopher **3** 358-359

Castagno, Andrea del
see Andrea del Castagno

CASTANEDA, CARLOS (Carlos César Salvador Arana Castaneda; Carlos Burungaray; circa 1925-1998), Hispanic American author and anthropologist **28** 62-64

Castel, Charles Irénée
see Saint-Pierre, Abbé de

Castelfranco, Giorgio da
see Giorgione

Castelli, Francesco
see Borromini, Francesco

CASTELO BRANCO, HUMBERTO (1900-1967), Brazilian general, president 1964-1966 **3** 359-360

CASTIGLIONE, BALDASSARE (1478-1529), Italian author and diplomat **3** 360-361

CASTILLA, RAMÓN (1797-1867), Peruvian military leader and president **3** 361

CASTLE, IRENE AND VERNON (1910-1918), ballroom dancers **3** 361-363

CASTLEREAGH, VISCOUNT (Robert Stewart; 1769-1822), British statesman **3** 363-364

CASTRO ALVES, ANTÔNIO DE (1847-1871), Brazilian poet **3** 364-365

CASTRO RUZ, FIDEL (born 1926), Cuban prime minister **3** 365-368

CATHARINE PARR (Katherine Parr; 1512-1548), queen of England and sixth wife of Henry VIII **27** 77-79

CATHER, WILLA SIBERT (1873-1947), American writer **3** 368-369

Catherine II (empress of Russia)
see Catherine the Great (biography)

Catherine de' Médici
see Médici, Catherine de'

CATHERINE OF ARAGON (1485-1536), Spanish princess, first queen consort of Henry VIII of England **18** 85-88

CATHERINE OF SIENA, ST. (1347-1380), Italian mystic **3** 369-370

CATHERINE THE GREAT (1729-1796), Russian empress 1762-1796 **3** 370-372

Catholic Church
see Roman Catholic Church

Catilina, Lucius Sergius
see Catiline (play)

CATILINE (Lucius Sergius Catilina; circa 108-62 B.C.), Roman politician and revolutionary **3** 372-373

CATLIN, GEORGE (1796-1872), American painter **3** 373-374

Cato the Censor
see Cato, Marcus Porcius, the Elder

CATO, MARCUS PORCIUS, THE ELDER (234-149 B.C.), Roman soldier, statesman, and historian **3** 375

CATO THE YOUNGER (Marcus Porcius Cato Uticensis; 95-46 B.C.), Roman politician **3** 374-375

CATS, JACOB (1577-1660), Dutch poet, moralist, and statesman **23** 64-66

CATT, CARRIE CHAPMAN (1859-1947), American reformer **3** 375-376

CATTELL, JAMES MCKEEN (1860-1944), American psychologist and editor **3** 376-377

CATULLUS, GAIUS VALERIUS (circa 84-circa 54 B.C.), Roman poet **3** 377-378

CAUCHY, AUGUSTIN LOUIS (1789-1857), French mathematician **3** 378-380

Cauvin, John
see Calvin, John

CAVAFY, CONSTANTINE P. (Konstantinos P. Kabaphēs; 1863-1933), first modernist Greek poet **3** 381-382

CAVALCANTI, GUIDO (circa 1255-1300), Italian poet **3** 382

CAVALLI, PIETRO FRANCESCO (1602-1676), Italian composer **3** 382-383

CAVAZOS, LAURO FRED (born 1927), American educator and public servant **25** 79-81

Cavelier, René Robert
see La Salle, Sieur de

CAVENDISH, HENRY (1731-1810), English physicist and chemist **3** 383-384

CAVENDISH, MARGARET LUCAS (1623-1673), English natural philosopher **23** 66-67

CAVOUR, CONTE DI (Camillo Benso; 1810-1861), Italian statesman **3** 385-386

CAXIAS, DUQUE DE (Luiz Alves de Lima e Silva; 1803-1880), Brazilian general and statesman **3** 386

CAXTON, WILLIAM (1422-1491), English printer **3** 386-387

CAYTON, SUSIE SUMNER REVELS (1870-1943), African American journalist and newspaper editor **27** 79-81

CBS
see Columbia Broadcasting System (communications)

CEAUSESCU, NICOLAE (1918-1989), Romanian statesman **3** 387-388

CECCHETTI, ENRICO (1850-1928), Italian dancer, choreographer, and teacher **25** 81-83

CECH, THOMAS ROBERT (born 1947), American biochemist **23** 68-70

Cecil, Edward Algernon Robert
see Cecil of Chelwood, Viscount

CECIL OF CHELWOOD, VISCOUNT (Edgar Algernon Robert Cecil; 1864-1958), English statesman **3** 388-389

CELA Y TRULOCK, CAMILO JOSÉ (1916-2002), Spanish author **3** 389-390

CÉLINE, LOUIS FERDINAND (pen name of Ferdinand Destouches; 1894-1961), French novelist **3** 390-391

CELLINI, BENVENUTO (1500-1571), Italian goldsmith and sculptor **3** 391-392

CELSIUS, ANDERS (1701-1744), Swedish astronomer **3** 392

CELSUS, AULUS CORNELIUS (circa 25 B.C.-A.D. 45?), Roman medical author **3** 393

Cenno de' Pepsi
see Cimabue

Censors, Roman
see Statesmen, Roman

CENTLIVRE, SUSANNA (Susanna Carroll; Susanna Rawkins; circa 1666-1723), British author **28** 65-67

Cepeda y Ahumada, Teresa de
see Theresa, St.

Cephas
see Peter, St.

Cerenkov, Pavel
see Cherenkov, Pavel

CERETA, LAURA (Laura Cereta Serina; 1469-1499), Italian author and feminist **24** 75-77

CEREZO AREVALO, MARCO VINICIO (born 1942), president of Guatemala (1986-1991) **3** 393-395

CERF, BENNETT (1898-1971), American editor, publisher, author, and television performer **22** 98-100

CERNAN, GENE (Eugene Andrew Cernan; born 1934), American astronaut **22** 100-102

CERVANTES, MIGUEL DE SAAVEDRA (1547-1616), Spanish novelist **3** 395-398

CÉSPEDES, CARLOS MANUEL DE (1819-1874), Cuban lawyer and revolutionary **3** 398-399

CESTI, PIETRO (Marc'Antonio Cesti; 1623-1669), Italian composer **3** 399-400

CETSHWAYO (Cetewayo; circa 1826-1884), king of Zululand 1873-1879 **3** 400

CÉZANNE, PAUL (1839-1906), French painter **3** 400-402

CHABROL, CLAUDE (born 1930), French filmmaker **28** 67-69

CHADLI BENJEDID (born 1929), president of the Algerian Republic (1979-) **3** 402-404

CHADWICK, FLORENCE (1918-1995), American swimmer **19** 64-66

CHADWICK, SIR EDWIN (1800-1890), English utilitarian reformer **3** 404-405

CHADWICK, SIR JAMES (1891-1974), English physicist **3** 405-406

CHADWICK, LYNN RUSSELL (1914-2003), English sculptor **18** 88-90

CHAGALL, MARC (1887-1985), Russian painter **3** 406-407

CHAHINE, YOUSSEF (born 1926), Egyptian filmmaker **25** 83-86

CHAI LING (born 1966), Chinese student protest leader **19** 67-68

CHAIN, ERNST BORIS (1906-1979), German-born English biochemist **3** 407-408

CHALIAPIN, FEDOR IVANOVICH (1873-1938), Russian musician **24** 77-79

CHALMERS, THOMAS (1780-1847), Scottish reformer and theologian **3** 408-409

CHAMBERLAIN, ARTHUR NEVILLE (1869-1940), English statesman **3** 409-411

CHAMBERLAIN, HOUSTON STEWART (1855-1927), English-born German writer **3** 411

CHAMBERLAIN, JOSEPH (1836-1914), English politician **3** 411-413

CHAMBERLAIN, OWEN (1920-2006), American physicist **25** 86-88

CHAMBERLAIN, WILT (born 1936), American basketball player **3** 413-415

CHAMBERLIN, THOMAS CHROWDER (1843-1928), American geologist **3** 415-416

CHAMBERS, WHITTAKER (Jay Vivian; 1901-1961), magazine editor who helped organize a Communist spy ring in the United States government **3** 416-417

CHAMINADE, CÉCILE LOUISE STÉPHANIE (1857-1944), French composer and pianist **26** 62-64

CHAMORRO, VIOLETA BARRIOS DE (born 1930), newspaper magnate, publicist, and first woman president of Nicaragua (1990) **3** 417-419

CHAMPLAIN, SAMUEL DE (circa 1570-1635), French geographer and explorer **3** 419-421

CHAMPOLLION, JEAN FRANÇOIS (1790-1832), French Egyptologist **3** 421

CHAN, JACKIE (Chan King-Sang; Sing Lung; born 1954), Chinese actor **27** 81-83

Chanakya
see Kautilya

CHANCELLOR, RICHARD (died 1556), English navigator **3** 422

CHANDLER, ALFRED DU PONT, JR. (1918-2007), American historian of American business **3** 422-423

CHANDLER, RAYMOND, JR. (1888-1959), American author of crime fiction **3** 423-425

CHANDLER, ZACHARIAH (1813-1879), American politician **3** 425-426

CHANDRAGUPTA MAURYA (died circa 298 B.C.), emperor of India 322?-298 **3** 426

CHANDRASEKHAR, SUBRAHMANYAN (1910-1995), Indian-born American physicist **3** 426-429

CHANEL, COCO (born Gabrielle Chanel; 1882-1971), French fashion designer **3** 429

CHANEY, LON (Alonzo Chaney; 1883-1930), American actor **19** 68-70

Chang Chiao
see Chang Chüeh

CHANG CHIEN (1853-1926), Chinese industrialist and social reformer **3** 429-430

CHANG CHIH-TUNG (1837-1909), Chinese official and reformer **3** 430-431

CHANG CHÜ-CHENG (1525-1582), Chinese statesman **3** 431-432

CHANG CHÜEH (died 184), Chinese religious and revolutionary leader **3** 432-433

CHANG HSÜEH-CH'ENG (1738-1801), Chinese scholar and historian **3** 433

Ch'ang-k'ang
see Ku K'ai-chih

CHANG PO-GO (died 846), Korean adventurer and merchant prince **3** 433-434

CHANG TSO-LIN (1873-1928), Chinese warlord **3** 434-435

CHANNING, EDWARD (1856-1931), American historian **3** 435

CHANNING, WILLIAM ELLERY (1780-1842), Unitarian minister and theologian **3** 435-436

CHAO, ELAINE (Elaine Lan Chao; born 1953), Asian American government adminstrator **27** 84-86

Chao K'uang-yin
see Zhao Kuang-yin

CHAO MENG-FU (1254-1322), Chinese painter **3** 436-437

CHAPIN, F(RANCIS) STUART (1888-1974), American sociologist **3** 437-438

CHAPLIN, CHARLES SPENCER (1889-1977), American film actor, director, and writer **3** 438-440

CHAPMAN, EDDIE (Arnold Edward Chapman; 1914-1997), British criminal and spy **28** 69-72

CHAPMAN, GEORGE (1559/60-1634), English poet, dramatist, and translator **3** 440-441

CHAPMAN, JOHN (Johnny Appleseed; c. 1775-1847), American horticulturist and missionary **21** 77-78

CHAPMAN, SYDNEY (1888-1970), English geophysicist **3** 441

CHAPONE, HESTER (Hester Mulso; 1727-1801), British author and critic **28** 72-74

CHARCOT, JEAN MARTIN (1825-1893), French psychiatrist **3** 442

CHARDIN, JEAN BAPTISTE SIMÉON (1699-1779), French painter **3** 442-443

CHARGAFF, ERWIN (1905-2002), American biochemist who worked with DNA **3** 444-445

CHARLEMAGNE (742-814), king of the Franks, 768-814, and emperor of the West, 800-814 **3** 445-447

CHARLES (born 1948), Prince of Wales and heir apparent to the British throne **3** 448-450

Charles I (king of Bohemia)
see Charles IV (Holy Roman emperor)

Charles I (king of Spain)
see Charles V (Holy Roman emperor)

CHARLES I (1600-1649), king of England 1625-1649 **3** 450-452

CHARLES II (1630-1685), king of England, Scotland, and Ireland 1660-1685 **3** 452-454

CHARLES II (1661-1700), king of Spain 1665-1700 **3** 454

CHARLES III (1716-1788), king of Spain 1759-1788 **3** 454-455

Charles IV (king of Two Sicilies)
see Charles III (king of Spain)

CHARLES IV (1316-1378), Holy Roman emperor 1346-1378 **3** 455-456

CHARLES IV (1748-1819), king of Spain 1788-1808 **3** 456-457

CHARLES V (1337-1380), king of France 1364-1380 **3** 459-460

CHARLES V (1500-1558), Holy Roman emperor 1519-1556 **3** 457-459

CHARLES VI (1368-1422), king of France 1380-1422 **3** 460-461

CHARLES VII (1403-1461), king of France 1422-1461 **3** 461-462

CHARLES VIII (1470-1498), king of France 1483-1498 **3** 462-463

CHARLES X (1757-1836), king of France 1824-1830 **3** 463-464

CHARLES XII (1682-1718), king of Sweden 1697-1718 **3** 464-466

CHARLES XIV JOHN (1763-1844), king of Sweden 1818-1844 **2** 205-206

CHARLES, RAY (Robinson; born 1932), American jazz musician—singer, pianist, and composer **3** 469-470

CHARLES ALBERT (1798-1849), king of Sardinia 1831-1849 **3** 466

CHARLES EDWARD LOUIS PHILIP CASIMIR STUART (1720-1788), Scottish claimant to English and Scottish thrones **3** 466-467

Charles Louis Napoleon
see Napoleon III

Charles Martel
see Martel, Charles

Charles Philippe (Count of Artois)
see Charles X (king of France)

Charles of Luxemburg
see Charles IV (Holy Roman emperor)

CHARLES THE BOLD (1433-1477), duke of Burgundy 1467-1477 **3** 467-469

Charles the Great
see Charlemagne

Charles the Mad
see Charles VI (king of France)

Charlier, Jean
see Gerson, John

CHARNISAY, CHARLES DE MENOU (Seigneur d'Aulnay; circa 1604-1650), French governor of Acadia **3** 470-471

Charolais, Count of
see Charles the Bold

CHARONTON, ENGUERRAND (circa 1410/15-after 1466), French painter **3** 471

CHARPENTIER, MARC ANTOINE (1634-1704), French composer **3** 471-472

CHARRON, PIERRE (1541-1603), French philosopher and theologian **3** 472

CHASE, MARY AGNES (1869-1963), American botanist **24** 79-81

CHASE, PHILANDER (1775-1852), American Episcopalian bishop and missionary **3** 472-473

CHASE, SALMON PORTLAND (1808-1873), American statesman and jurist **3** 473-475

CHASE, SAMUEL (1741-1811), American politician and jurist **3** 475-476

CHASE, WILLIAM MERRITT (1849-1916), American painter **3** 476-477

CHATEAUBRIAND, VICOMTE DE (1768-1848), French author **3** 477-479

CHATELET, GABRIELLE-EMILIE (1706-1749), French physicist and chemist **22** 102-103

Chatham, 1st Earl of
see Pitt, William, the Elder

CHATICHAI CHOONHAVAN (1922-1998), prime minister of Thailand (1988-1990) 3 479-480

CHATTERJI, BANKIMCHANDRA (1838-1894), Bengali novelist 3 480-481

CHATTERTON, THOMAS (1752-1770), English poet 3 481-482

Chattopadhyay, Sarojini
see Naidu, Sarojini

CHAUCER, GEOFFREY (circa 1345-1400), English poet 3 482-485

CHAUNCY, CHARLES (1705-1787), American Calvinist clergyman and theologian 3 485-486

CHÁVEZ, CARLOS (1899-1978), Mexican conductor and composer 3 486

CHAVEZ, CESAR (1927-1993), American labor leader 3 486-487

CHÁVEZ, DENNIS (1888-1962), Hispanic American politician 3 488-489

CHÁVEZ, HUGO (Hugo Rafael Chávez Frí; born 1954), Venezuelan political and military leader 26 64-66

CHAVEZ, LINDA (born 1947), Hispanic American civil rights activists 3 489-491

CHAVEZ-THOMPSON, LINDA (born 1944), Mexican American businesswoman and labor activist 24 81-83

CHAVIS, BENJAMIN (born 1948), African American religious leader, civil rights activist, labor organizer, and author 3 491-493

CHEEVER, JOHN (1912-1982), American short-story writer 3 493-494

Chekhonte, Antosha (pseudonym)
see Chekhov, Anton Pavlovich

CHEKHOV, ANTON PAVLOVICH (1860-1904), Russian author 3 494-497

CHELMSFORD, 1ST VISCOUNT (Frederic John Napier Thesigner Chelmsford; 1868-1933), English statesman 3 497

Chemistry (science)
and food preservation
Hall, Lloyd Augustus 28 154-156
industrial
Dow, Herbert H. 28 100-102

Chemotherapy (medicine)
Wright, Jane Cooke 28 383-385

CH'EN TU-HSIU (1879-1942), Chinese statesman and editor 3 501-502

Ch'en Wang-tao
see Chih-i

CHENEY, RICHARD B(RUCE) (born 1941), U.S. secretary of defense under George Bush 3 497-499

CHENG HO (1371-circa 1433), Chinese admiral 3 500

CHÉNIER, ANDRÉ MARIE (1762-1794), French poet 3 500-501

Cheops
see Khufu

CHERENKOV, PAVEL ALEKSEEVICH (1904-1990), Russian physicist 3 502-503

CHERNENKO, KONSTANTIN USTINOVICH (1911-1985), the Soviet Union general secretary from February 1984 to March 1985 3 503-504

CHERNYSHEVSKY, NIKOLAI GAVRILOVICH (1828-1889), Russian journalist, critic, and social theorist 3 504-505

CHERUBINI, LUIGI CARLO ZANOBI SALVATORE MARIA (1760-1842), Italian-born French composer 3 505-506

CHESNUT, MARY BOYKIN (1823-1886), Civil War diarist 3 506-508

CHESNUTT, CHARLES WADDELL (1858-1932), African American author and lawyer 20 78-82

Chess (game)
Kasparov, Garry 28 194-196

CHESTERTON, GILBERT KEITH (1874-1936), English author and artist 3 508-509

CHEUNG, KATHERINE (Katherine Sui Fun Cheung; 1904-2003), Chinese American aviator 25 88-90

CHEVALIER, MAURICE (1888-1972), French singer and actor 26 66-68

Chevalier de Saint-Goerge, Joseph Boulogne
see Saint-George, Joseph Boulogne, Chevalier de

CHEVROLET, LOUIS (1878-1941), auto racer and entrepreneur 20 82-84

CHEYNE, GEORGE (1671-1743), Scottish physician and author 28 74-76

Chi Fa
see Wu wang

Ch'i Heng
see Ch'i Pai-shih

CH'I PAI-SHIH (1863-1957), Chinese painter and poet 3 526-527

Chi Tan
see Chou kung

Ch'i Wei-ch'ing
see Ch'i Pai-shih

Chia
see Hui-yüan

CHIA SSU-TAO (1213-1275), Chinese statesman 3 514-515

Chiang Ch'ing
see Jiang Qing

CHIANG CHING-KUO (1910-1988), chairman of the Nationalist party and president of the Republic of China in Taiwan (1978-1988) 3 509-510

CHIANG KAI-SHEK (1887-1975), Chinese nationalist leader and president 3 510-513

Chiaramonti, Luigi Barnabà
see Pius VII

CHIARI, ROBERTO (born 1905), president of Panama (1960-1964) 3 513-514

CHICAGO, JUDY (Judith Cohen; born 1939), American artist and activist 3 515-516

CHICHERIN, GEORGI VASILYEVICH (1872-1936), Russian statesman 3 516-517

CHICHESTER, FRANCIS (1901-1972), British yachter 24 83-85

CHIEN-LUNG (Hung-li; 1711-1799), Chinese emperor (1735-1799) 21 78-79

Ch'ien-lung
see Qianlong

CHIEPE, GAOSITWE KEAGAKWA TIBE (born 1926), intellectual, educator, diplomat, politician, and cabinet minister of external affairs of Botswana 3 517

Chiesa, Giacomo della
see Benedict XV

CHIFLEY, JOSEPH BENEDICT (1885-1951), Australian statesman 3 518

CHIH-I (Chih-k'ai, 538-597), Chinese Buddhist monk 3 518-519

CHIKAMATSU, MONZAEMON (1653-1725), Japanese playwright 23 70-72

CHILD, JULIA MCWILLIAMS (1912-2004), chef, author, and television personality 3 519-520

CHILD, LYDIA MARIA FRANCIS (1802-1880), American author and abolitionist 3 520-521

CHILDE, VERE GORDON (1892-1957), Australian prehistorian and archeologist 3 521-522

Children's literature
see Literature for children

CHILDRESS, ALICE (1920-1994), African American dramatist, author, and poet **3** 522-524

Chilean literature
Bolaño, Roberto **28** 42-45

CH'IN KUEI (1090-1155), Chinese official **3** 524-525

Chingiz-Khan
see Genghis Khan

CHINN, MAY EDWARD (1896-1980), African American physician **3** 525-526

CHINO, WENDELL (1923-1998), Native American tribal leader and activist **27** 86-88

Ch'in-shan
see Yüan, Ma

CHIPPENDALE, THOMAS (1718-1779), English cabinetmaker **4** 1-2

CHIRAC, JACQUES (born 1932), French prime minister **4** 2-3

CHIRICO, GIORGIO DE (1888-1978), Italian painter **4** 4

CHISHOLM, CAROLINE (1808-1877), British author and philanthropist **4** 4-7

CHISHOLM, SHIRLEY ANITA ST. HILL (1924-2005), first African American woman to serve in the United States Congress **4** 7-9

CHISSANO, JOAQUIM ALBERTO (born 1939), a leader of Mozambique's war for independence and later president of Mozambique (1986-) **4** 9-11

CHISUM, JOHN SIMPSON (1824-1884), American rancher **4** 11

CH'I-YING (circa 1786-1858), Chinese statesman and diplomat **4** 12

CHMIELNICKI, BOGDAN (1595-1657), Cossack leader of Ukrainian revolt **4** 12-13

CHOATE, JOSEPH HODGES (1832-1917), American lawyer and diplomat **22** 103-106

CHOATE, RUFUS (1799-1859), American lawyer and statesman **22** 106-107

CH'OE CH'UNG-HON (1149-1219), Korean general **4** 13

Chomedey, Paul de
see Maisoneuve, Sieur de

CHOMSKY, NOAM AVRAM (born 1928), American linguist and philosopher **4** 13-15

CHONG CHUNG-BU (1106-1179), Korean general **4** 15

CHONGJO (1752-1800), king of Korea **4** 15-16

CHOPIN, FRÉDÉRIC FRANÇOIS (1810-1849), Polish-French composer and pianist **4** 16-18
influenced by
Szymanowska, Maria **28** 340-342
performances
Rubinstein, Arthur **28** 305-307

CHOPIN, KATHERINE ("Kate"; born Katherine O'Flaherty; 1851-1904), American writer, poet, and essayist **4** 18-20

Chopinel, Jean
see Jean de Meun

CHOPRA, DEEPAK (born 1946), Indian physician, author, and educator **20** 84-86

Chou, Duke of
see Chou kung

CHOU EN-LAI (1898-1976), Chinese Communist premier **4** 20-22

CHOU KUNG (flourished circa 1116 B.C.), Chinese statesman **4** 22-23

Chou Shu-jen
see Lu Hsün

CHRESTIEN DE TROYES (flourished 12th century), French poet **4** 23-24

CHRÉTIEN, JOSEPH-JACQUES-JEAN "JEAN" (born 1934), French Canadian politician and Canada's 20th prime minister **4** 24-25

Christ, Jesus
see Jesus of Nazareth

CHRISTIAN IV (1577-1648), king of Denmark and Norway 1588-1648 **20** 86-89

Christian Democratic Union (Germany)
Merkel, Angela **28** 243-245

Christianity (religion)
expansion (Bulgarian Empire)
Simeon, King of Bulgaria **28** 325-327
expansion (Lithuania)
Wladyslaw II Jagiello, King of Poland **28** 377-378
oppression
Galerius, Emperor of Rome **28** 132-134

CHRISTIANSEN, OLE KIRK (1891-1958), Danish inventor and entrepreneur **28** 76-78

CHRISTIE, AGATHA (Agatha Mary Clarissa Miller; 1890-1976), best selling mystery author **4** 25-26

CHRISTINA OF SWEDEN (1626-1689), queen of Sweden 1632-1654 **4** 26-29

CHRISTINE DE PISAN (1364/65-circa 1430), French author **4** 29-30

CHRISTO (Christo Vladimiroff Javacheff; born 1935), Bulgarian-born sculptor noted for large-scale environmental artworks **4** 30-31

CHRISTOPHE, HENRI (1767-1820), Haitian patriot and king **4** 32

CHRISTOPHER, WARREN MINOR (born 1925), United States secretary of state **4** 32-33

CHRISTUS, PETRUS (circa 1410-1472/73), Flemish painter **4** 33-34

CHRISTY, EDWIN P. (1815-1862), American minstrel **4** 34-35

CHRYSIPPUS (circa 280-circa 206 B.C.), Greek Stoic philosopher **4** 35-36

CHRYSLER, WALTER PERCY (1875-1940), American manufacturer **4** 36-37

Chrysostom
see John Chrysostom, St.

CHU YUAN-CHANG (Hongwu; T'ai Tsu; Kao-ti; 1328-1398), Chinese emperor (1368-1398) **21** 79-81

CHU, PAUL CHING-WU (born 1941), Chinese-American experimentalist in solid-state physics **4** 37-39

CHU HSI (Chu Fu-tzu; 1130-1200), Chinese scholar and philosopher **4** 40-43

CHU TEH (1886-1976), Chinese Communist military leader **4** 54-55

Chu Ti
see Yung-lo

Chu Yüan-chang
see Hung-wu

Chub
see Ward, Artemus

CHULALONGKORN (Rama V; 1853-1910), king of Thailand 1868-1910 **4** 43-45

CHUN DOO HWAN (born 1931), army general turned politician and president of the Republic of Korea (South Korea); 1981-1988 **4** 45-47

CHUNG, CONNIE (born 1946), American correspondent and resporter **4** 47-48

CHUNG, JU YUNG (1915-2001), Korean businessman **23** 72-74

CHUNG, KYUNG WHA (born 1948), Korean violinist **23** 74-76

Ch'ung Ch'eng
see Shih Ko-fa

Ch'ungnyong, Prince
see Sejong

Chung-shan
see Sun Yat-sen

CHUNG-SHU, TUNG (circa 179-104 B.C.), Chinese man of letters **4** 48-49

CHURCH, FRANK FORRESTER, III (1924-1984), American politician **28** 78-80

CHURCH, FREDERICK EDWIN (1826-1900), American painter **4** 49-50

Church law
see Canon law (Roman Catholic)

Church of Jesus Christ of Latter Day Saints
see Mormons (religious sect)

Church of Rome
see Roman Catholic Church

Churchill, John
see Marlborough, 1st Duke of

CHURCHILL, WINSTON (1871-1947), American novelist **4** 50-51

CHURCHILL, SIR WINSTON LEONARD SPENCER (1874-1965), English statesman **4** 51-53

CHURRIGUERA, JOSÉ BENITO DE (1665-1725), Spanish architect and sculptor **4** 53-54

CHYTILOVÁ, VERA (born 1929), Czech filmmaker **24** 85-87

CICERO, MARCUS TULLIUS (106-43 B.C.), Roman orator and writer **4** 55-58

CID, THE (Cid Campeador; 1043-1099), Spanish medieval warrior **4** 58-59

CILLER, TANSU (born 1946), prime minister of Turkey (1993-) **4** 59-60

CIMABUE (flourished late 13th century), Italian painter **4** 60-61

CIMAROSA, DOMENICO (1749-1801), Italian opera composer **4** 61-62

CINQUE, JOSEPH (circa 1813-circa 1879), West African slave leader **4** 62

Cione, Andrea di
see Orcagna

Cisneros, Francisco Jiménez de
see Jiménez de Cisneros, Francisco

CISNEROS, HENRY G. (born 1947), first Hispanic mayor in Texas **4** 62-64

CISNEROS, SANDRA (born 1954), Hispanic American short story writer and poet **4** 64-65

CISSÉ, SOULEYMANE (born 1940), Malian filmmaker **4** 65-66

CITROËN, ANDRÉ-GUSTAVE (1878-1935), French automobile manufacturer **4** 66-68

Civil rights movement (United States) supporters (white)
Cunard, Nancy **28** 87-89

Civil War, United States (1861-1865)
• ACCOUNTS OF
by historians
Faust, Drew Gilpin **28** 116-118
• CONFEDERACY
spies
Velasquez, Loreta Janeta **28** 361-363
women soldiers
Velasquez, Loreta Janeta **28** 361-363

CLAIBORNE, LIZ (Elizabeth Claiborne Ortenberg; 1929-2007), American businesswoman and clothing designer **4** 68-69

CLAIR, RENÉ (née Ren&eacute Lucien chomette; 1898-1981), French film director and screenwriter **25** 90-93

CLANCY, TOM (born 1947), American author **4** 70-71

CLAPHAM, SIR JOHN HAROLD (1873-1946), English economic historian **4** 71

CLAPP, MARGARET ANTOINETTE (1910-1974), American author, educator, and president of Wellesley College (1949-1966) **4** 71-72

CLAPPERTON, HUGH (1788-1827), Scottish explorer of Africa **4** 72-73

CLAPTON, ERIC (born 1945), English guitarist, singer, and songwriter **18** 90-92

CLARE, JOHN (1793-1864), British Poet **26** 69-71

CLARENDON, 1ST EARL OF (Edward Hyde; 1609-1674), English statesman and historian **4** 73-75

CLARE OF ASSISI, SAINT (Chiara Offreduccio di Favoronne; 1194-1253), Italian relisious leader **23** 76-78

CLARK, GEORGE ROGERS (1752-1818), American Revolutionary War soldier **4** 75-76

CLARK, HELEN ELIZABETH (born 1950), New Zealand prime minister **25** 93-95

CLARK, JOHN BATES (1847-1938), American economist **4** 76-77

CLARK, JOHN MAURICE (1884-1963), American economist **4** 77-78

CLARK, KENNETH B. (born 1914), American social psychologist **4** 78-79

CLARK, KENNETH M. (Lord; 1903-1983), English art historian **4** 79-80

CLARK, MARK WAYNE (1896-1984), American general **4** 80-81

CLARK, TOM CAMPBELL (1899-1977), President Harry S. Truman's attorney general and Supreme Court justice **4** 81-82

CLARK, WILLIAM (1770-1838), American explorer and soldier **4** 82-83

CLARK, WILLIAM ANDREWS (1839-1925), American copper entrepreneur and politician **4** 83-85

CLARKE, ARTHUR CHARLES (1917-2008), English author **18** 92-94

CLARKE, KENNETH HARRY (born 1940), Conservative politician and Great Britain's chancellor of the exchequer (1993-) **4** 85-87

CLARKE, KENNY (Kenneth Spearman Clarke; 1914-1985), African American musician **25** 95-98

CLARKE, MARCUS ANDREW HISLOP (1846-1881), English-born Australian journalist and author **4** 87-88

CLARKE, REBECCA THACHER (1886-1979), English composer and violist **24** 87-89

CLARKE, SAMUEL (1675-1729), English theologian and philosopher **4** 88

Classicism (music)
Ponce, Manuel **28** 282-284

CLAUDE LORRAIN (1600-1682), French painter, draftsman, and etcher **4** 89-90

CLAUDEL, CAMILLE (1864-1943), French sculptor **22** 107-110

CLAUDEL, PAUL LOUIS CHARLES (1868-1955), French author and diplomat **4** 90-91

CLAUDIUS GERMANICUS, TIBERIUS (Claudius I; 10 B.C. -A.D. 54), emperor of Rome 41-54 **4** 91-92

CLAUSEWITZ, KARL VON (Karl Philipp Gottlieb von Clausewitz; 1780-1831), Prussian military strategist **20** 89-91

CLAUSIUS, RUDOLF JULIUS EMANUEL (1822-1888), German physicist **4** 92-94

CLAVER, ST. PETER (1580-1654), Spanish Jesuit missionary **4** 94

CLAY, HENRY (1777-1852), American lawyer and statesman **4** 94-96

CLAYTON, JOHN MIDDLETON (1796-1856), American lawyer and statesman **4** 96-97

CLEARY, BEVERLY (nee Beverly Bunn; born 1916), American author of children's books **22** 110-112

CLEAVER, LEROY ELDRIDGE (1935-1998), American writer and Black Panther leader **4** 97-98

CLEISTHENES (flourished 6th century B.C.), Athenian statesman **4** 98-99

CLEMENCEAU, GEORGES (1841-1929), French statesman **4** 99-101

CLEMENS NON PAPA, JACOBUS (circa 1510-circa 1556), Flemish composer **4** 101

Clemens, Samuel Langhorne
see Twain, Mark

Clemens, Titus Flavius
see Clement of Alexandria

CLEMENT I (died c. 100 A.D.), Bishop of Rome, pope **23** 78-81

CLEMENT V (1264-1314), pope 1304-1314 **4** 101-102

CLEMENT VII (Giulia de Medici; 1478-1534), pope (1523-1534) **21** 81-83

CLEMENT XI (Giovanni Francesco Albani; 1649-1721), Italian pope 1700-1721 **24** 90-92

CLEMENT OF ALEXANDRIA (circa 150-circa 215), Christian theologian **4** 102-103

Clement of Rome, St.
see Clement I, St.

CLEMENTE, ROBERTO (1934-1972), Hispanic American baseball player **19** 70-72

CLEOMENES I (flourished circa 520-490 B.C.), Spartan king **4** 103

CLEOMENES III (circa 260-219 B.C.), king of Sparta 235-219 **4** 103-104

CLEON (circa 475-422 B.C.), Athenian political leader **4** 104-105

CLEOPATRA (69-30 B.C.), queen of Egypt **4** 105-106

Cleophil (pseudonym)
see Congreve, William

CLEVELAND, JAMES (1932-1991), African American singer, songwriter, and pianist **4** 106-108

CLEVELAND, STEPHEN GROVER (1837-1908), American statesman, twice president **4** 108-110

CLIFFORD, ANNE (1590-1676), English author and philanthropist **27** 88-90

CLINE, PATSY (born Virginia Patterson Hensley; 1932-1963), American singer **4** 110-112

CLINTON, DEWITT (1769-1828), American lawyer and statesman **4** 112-113

CLINTON, GEORGE (1739-1812), American patriot and statesman **4** 113-114

CLINTON, SIR HENRY (1738?-1795), British commander in chief during the American Revolution **4** 114-115

CLINTON, HILLARY RODHAM (born 1947), American politician and first lady **4** 115-117

CLINTON, WILLIAM JEFFERSON ("Bill" Clinton; born 1946), 42nd president of the United States **4** 117-119

CLIVE, ROBERT (Baron Clive of Plassey; 1725-1774), English soldier and statesman **4** 119-120

CLODION (1738-1814), French sculptor **4** 121

CLODIUS PULCHER, PUBLIUS (died 52 B.C.), Roman politician **4** 121-122

CLOONEY, ROSEMARY (1928-2002), American singer and actress **27** 90-93

Clopinel, Jean
see Jean de Meun

CLOUET, FRANÇOIS (circa 1516-circa 1572), French portrait painter **4** 122-123

CLOUET, JEAN (circa 1485-circa 1541), French portrait painter **4** 122-123

CLOUGH, ARTHUR HUGH (1819-1861), English poet **4** 123-124

CLOVIS I (465-511), Frankish king **4** 124

Clyens, Mary Elizabeth
see Lease, Mary Elizabeth Clyens

Cnut
see Canute I

COACHMAN, ALICE (Alice Coachman Davis; born 1923), African American athlete **26** 71-73

COBB, JEWEL PLUMMER (born 1924), African American scientist and activist **22** 112-114

COBB, TYRUS RAYMOND (1886-1961), baseball player **4** 124-126

COBBETT, WILLIAM (1763-1835), English journalist and politician **4** 126-127

COBDEN, RICHARD (1804-1865), English politician **4** 127-128

Coca-Cola Company
Pemberton, John Stith **28** 278-279

COCHISE (circa 1825-1874), American Chiricahua Apache Indian chief **4** 128

COCHRAN, JACQUELINE (Jackie Cochran; 1910-1980), American aviator and businesswoman **18** 94-96

COCHRAN, JOHNNIE (1937-2005), African American lawyer **4** 128-131

COCHRANE, THOMAS (Earl of Dundonald; 1775-1860), British naval officer **20** 91-93

COCKCROFT, JOHN DOUGLAS (1897-1967), English physicist **4** 131-132

COCTEAU, JEAN (1889-1963), French writer **4** 132-133

Cody, William Frederick
see Buffalo Bill (poem)

COE, SEBASTIAN (born 1956), English track athlete **20** 93-95

COEN, JAN PIETERSZOON (circa 1586-1629), Dutch governor general of Batavia **4** 133

COETZEE, J(OHN) M. (born 1940), white South African novelist **4** 133-135

COFFIN, LEVI (1789-1877), American antislavery reformer **4** 135

Coffin, Lucretia
see Mott, Lucretia Coffin

COFFIN, WILLIAM SLOANE, JR. (1924-2006), Yale University chaplain who spoke out against the Vietnam War **4** 135-137

COHAN, GEORGE MICHAEL (1878-1942), American actor and playwright **4** 137-138

Cohen, Bennett, (Ben Cohen; born 1951)
see Ben & Jerry

Cohen, George Morris
see Brandes, Georg Morris

COHEN, HERMANN (1842-1918), Jewish-German philosopher **4** 138-139

COHEN, MORRIS RAPHAEL (1880-1947), American philosopher and teacher **4** 139-140

COHEN, WILLIAM S. (born 1940), American secretary of defense **18** 96-98

COHN, FERDINAND (1829-1898), German botanist **20** 95-97

COHN-BENDIT, DANIEL (born 1946), led "new left" student protests in France in 1968 **4** 140-141

COKE, SIR EDWARD (1552-1634), English jurist and parliamentarian **4** 141-142

Colbath, Jeremiah Jones
see Wilson, Henry

COLBERT, JEAN BAPTISTE (1619-1683), French statesman **4** 142-143

COLBY, WILLIAM E. (1920-1996), American director of the Central Intelligence Agency (CIA) **4** 143-145

COLDEN, CADWALLADER (1688-1776), American botanist and politician **4** 145-146

COLE, GEORGE DOUGLAS HOWARD (1889-1959), English historian and economist **4** 146-147

COLE, JOHNNETTA (born 1936), African American scholar and educator **4** 147-149

COLE, NAT (a.k.a. Nat "King" Cole, born Nathaniel Adams Coles; 1919-1965), American jazz musician **4** 149-151

COLE, THOMAS (1801-1848), American painter **4** 151-152

COLEMAN, BESSIE (1892-1926), first African American to earn an international pilot's license **4** 152-154

COLERIDGE, SAMUEL TAYLOR (1772-1834), English poet and critic **4** 154-156

COLERIDGE-TAYLOR, SAMUEL (1875-1912), English composer and conductor **28** 80-83

COLES, ROBERT MARTIN (born 1929), American social psychiatrist, social critic, and humanist **4** 156-157

COLET, JOHN (circa 1446-1519), English theologian **4** 157-158

COLETTE, SIDONIE GABRIELLE (1873-1954), French author **4** 158-159

COLIGNY, GASPARD DE (1519-1572), French admiral and statesman **4** 159-160

COLLETT, CAMILLA (nee Camilla Wergeland; 1813-1895), Norwegian author **26** 73-75

COLLIER, JOHN (1884-1968), American proponent of Native American culture **4** 160-162

COLLINGWOOD, ROBIN GEORGE (1889-1943), English historian and philosopher **4** 162

COLLINS, BILLY (born 1941), American poet **28** 83-85

COLLINS, EDWARD KNIGHT (1802-1878), American businessman and shipowner **4** 162-163

COLLINS, EILEEN (born 1956), American astronaut **4** 163-165

COLLINS, MARVA (born Marva Deloise Nettles; b. 1936), African American educator **4** 165-167

COLLINS, MICHAEL (1890-1922), Irish revolutionary leader and soldier **4** 167-168

COLLINS, WILLIAM (1721-1759), English lyric poet **4** 168-169

COLLINS, WILLIAM WILKIE (1824-1889), English novelist **4** 169-170

COLLOR DE MELLO, FERNANDO (born 1949), businessman who became president of Brazil in 1990 **4** 170-172

Colonna, Oddone
see Martin V

COLT, SAMUEL (1814-1862), American inventor and manufacturer **4** 172-173

COLTRANE, JOHN (1926-1967), African American jazz saxophonist **4** 173-174

COLUM, PADRAIC (1881-1972), Irish-American poet and playwright **4** 174-175

COLUMBA, ST. (circa 521-597), Irish monk and missionary **4** 175-176

COLUMBAN, ST. (circa 543-615), Irish missionary **4** 176

Columbia Broadcasting System (communications)
Stringer, Howard **28** 338-340

COLUMBUS, CHRISTOPHER (1451-1506), Italian navigator, discoverer of America **4** 176-179

COLWELL, RITA R. (born 1934), American marine microbiologist **4** 179-180

COMANECI, NADIA (Nadia Conner; born 1961), Romanian gymnast **18** 98-100

Comedy (performance)
Russell, Anna **28** 307-309

COMENIUS, JOHN AMOS (1592-1670), Moravian theologian and educational reformer **4** 180-181

COMINES, PHILIPPE DE (circa 1445-1511), French chronicler **4** 181

COMMAGER, HENRY STEELE (1902-1998), American historian, textbook author, and editor **4** 181-183

COMMONER, BARRY (born 1917), American biologist and environmental activist **4** 183-185

COMMONS, JOHN ROGERS (1862-1945), American historian **4** 185

Communist party (United States)
members
Patterson, Louise Alone Thompson **28** 272-274

COMNENA, ANNA (1083-1148), Byzantine princess and historian **4** 185-186

COMPTON, ARTHUR HOLLY (1892-1962), American physicist **4** 186-188

Computers and calculating machines
inventors of
Zuse, Konrad **28** 391-393
microprocessors
Hoff, Ted **28** 176-178
programming of
Zuse, Konrad **28** 391-393

COMSTOCK, ANNA BOTSFORD (1854-1930), American artist and natural science educator **20** 97-99

COMSTOCK, ANTHONY (1844-1915), American antivice crusader **4** 188-189

COMSTOCK, HENRY TOMPKINS PAIGE (1820-1870), American gold prospector **4** 189

COMTE, AUGUSTE (1798-1857), French philosopher **4** 189-191

CONABLE, BARBER B., JR. (born 1922), head of the World Bank (1986-1991) **4** 191-192

CONANT, JAMES BRYANT (1893-1978), American chemist and educator **4** 192-193

CONDÉ, PRINCE DE (Louis II de Bourbon 1621-1686), French general **4** 193-194

CONDILLAC, ÉTIENNE BONNOT DE (1715-1780), French philosopher and educator **4** 194-195

CONDORCET, MARQUIS DE (Marie Jean Antoine Nicolas Caritat; 1743-1794), French philosopher and mathematician **4** 195-196

CONE, JAMES HALL (born 1938), American theologian **4** 196-197

CONFUCIUS (551-479 B.C.), Chinese teacher and philosopher **4** 197-200

Congressmen
see Statesmen, American—legislative

CONGREVE, WILLIAM (1670-1729), English dramatist **4** 200-201

CONKLING, ROSCOE (1829-1888), American politician **4** 201-202

CONNALLY, JOHN BOWDEN, JR. (born 1917), Texas governor, political adviser, and confidant to presidents **4** 202-204

CONNERY, SEAN (Thomas Connery; born 1930), Scottish actor **18** 100-102

CONNOLLY, CYRIL (1903-1974), British novelist and literary and social critic **4** 204-205

CONNOLLY, MAUREEN (1934-1969), American tennis player **19** 72-74

CONRAD, JOSEPH (1857-1924), Polish-born English novelist **4** 205-207

CONRAD, PETE (Charles "Pete" Conrad, Jr.; 1930-1999), American astronaut and businessman **22** 114-116

Conservation (United States)
Federal programs
Leopold, Aldo **28** 211-213

CONSTABLE, JOHN (1776-1837), English landscape painter **4** 208-209

CONSTANTINE I (circa 274-337), Roman emperor 306-337 **4** 209-211
rivals
Galerius, Emperor of Rome **28** 132-134

CONSTANTINE XI (Palaeologus; 1405-1453), Byzantine emperor 1448-1453 **4** 211-212

Consulate (France; 1799-1804)
see France—1799-1804

CONTI, NICCOLÒ DE' (circa 1396-1469), Venetian merchant-adventurer **4** 212-213

CONWAY, JILL KATHRYN KER (born 1934), historian interested in the role of women and president of Smith College **4** 213-214

CONYERS, JOHN, JR. (born 1929), African American politician and attorney **26** 75-78

COOGAN, JACKIE (John Leslie Coogan, Jr.; 1914-1984), American actor **21** 83-85

COOK, JAMES (1728-1779), English explorer, navigator, and cartographer **4** 214-215

COOKE, JAY (1821-1905), American merchant banker **4** 215-216

COOLEY, CHARLES HORTON (1864-1929), American social psychologist, sociologist, and educator **4** 216-217

COOLEY, THOMAS MCINTYRE (1824-1898), American jurist and public servant **22** 116-119

COOLIDGE, JOHN CALVIN (1872-1933), president of the United States 1923-1929 **4** 217-219

COOMBS, HERBERT COLE (Nugget; born 1906), Australian economist **4** 219-220

COONEY, JOAN GANZ (born 1929), American television program producer and publicist **19** 74-76

COOPER, ANNIE (Anna Julia Cooper; 1858-1964), African American educator, author, and activist **22** 119-121

Cooper, Anthony Ashley (1621-1683)
see Shaftesbury, 1st Earl of

Cooper, Anthony Ashley (1671-1713)
see Shaftesbury, 3d Earl of

Cooper, Anthony Ashley (1801-1885)
see Shaftesbury, 7th Earl of

COOPER, GARY (Frank James Cooper; 1901-1961), American motion picture actor **21** 85-87

COOPER, JAMES FENIMORE (1789-1851), American novelist and social critic **4** 220-223

COOPER, MARTIN (born 1928), American inventor **28** 85-87

COOPER, PETER (1791-1883), American inventor and manufacturer **4** 223-224

COOPER, THOMAS (1759-1839), English-born American scientist and educator **4** 224

COORS, ADOLPH (Adolph Herrman Kohrs; 1847-1929), American brewer and businessman **19** 76-78

Cooweescoowe
see Ross, John

COPEAU, JACQUES (1879-1949), French dramatic theorist, director, and actor who established the Vieux Colombier **4** 225

COPERNICUS, NICOLAUS (1473-1543), Polish astronomer **4** 226-227

COPLAND, AARON (1900-1990), American composer **4** 227-228

COPLEY, JOHN SINGLETON (1738-1815), American portrait painter **4** 228-230

COPPOLA, FRANCIS FORD (born 1939), American filmmaker and author **18** 102-104

Cordini, Antonio
see Sangallo Family (Antonio the Younger)

CORDOBA, GONZALO FERNANDEZ DE (1453-1515), Spanish military leader **20** 99-100

CORELLI, ARCANGELO (1653-1713), Italian composer and violinist **4** 230-231

CORI, GERTY T. (born Gerty Theresa Radnitz; 1896-1957), American biochemist **4** 231-234

CORINTH, LOVIS (1838-1925), German artist **4** 234

CORMAN, ROGER (born 1926), American film director and producer **21** 87-89

CORNEILLE, PIERRE (1606-1684), French playwright **4** 234-236

CORNELL, EZRA (1807-1874), American financier and philanthropist **4** 236-237

CORNELL, JOSEPH (1903-1972), American artist **4** 237-238

CORNFORTH, JOHN WARCUP (born 1917), Australian chemist **24** 92-94

CORNING, ERASTUS (1794-1872), American merchant and financier **4** 238-239

CORNPLANTER (c. 1732-1836), Seneca village leader **4** 239-241

CORNWALLIS, CHARLES (1st Marquess Cornwallis; 1738-1805), British soldier and statesman **4** 241-243

CORONA, BERT (born 1918), Hispanic American union organizer **4** 243-247

CORONADO, FRANCISCO VÁSQUEZ DE (1510-1554), Spanish explorer and colonial official **4** 247

COROT, JEAN BAPTISTE CAMILLE (1796-1875), French painter **4** 247-249

Corrario, Angelo
see Gregory XII

CORREGGIO (circa 1494-1534), Italian painter **4** 249-251

CORRIGAN, MICHAEL AUGUSTINE (1839-1902), American Catholic archbishop **4** 253

CORRIGAN AND WILLIAMS, founders of the women's peace movement in Northern Ireland **4** 251-253

CORT, HENRY (1740-1800), English ironmaster **4** 254

CORTE REÁL, GASPAR AND MIGUEL, Portuguese explorers **4** 254-255

CORTÉS, HERNÁN (1485?-1547), Spanish conquistador **4** 255-256

Cortines, Adolfo Ruiz
see Ruiz Cortines, Adolfo

CORTONA, PIETRO DA (1596-1669), Italian painter and architect **4** 256

COSBY, WILLIAM HENRY, JR. ("Bill" Cosby; born 1937), American entertainer **4** 257-258

COSELL, HOWARD (Howard William Cohen; 1920-1995), American sportscaster **24** 94-97

COSGRAVE, LIAM (born 1920), Irish foreign minister and prime minister (1973-1977) **4** 258-260

COSIO VILLEGAS, DANIEL (1898-1976), Mexican teacher, civil servant, and author of studies of Mexican history **4** 260-261

Cosmetic industry
Roddick, Anita **28** 298-301

Costilla, Miguel Hidalgo y
see Hidalgo y Costilla, Miguel

COTTEN, ELIZABETH ("Libba"; born Elizabeth Nevills; 1892-1987), African American musician **4** 261-263

COTTON, JOHN (1584-1652), American Congregationalist clergyman **4** 263-265

COUBERTIN, PIERRE DE (Pierre Fredy, Baron de Coubertin; 1863-1937), French organizer of the modern Olympic Games **21** 89-92

COUGHLIN, CHARLES EDWARD (1891-1979), Canadian-American priest and politician **4** 265-266

Coulanges, Numa Denis Fustel de
see Fustel de Coulanges, Numa Denis

COULOMB, CHARLES AUGUSTIN DE (1736-1806), French physicist **4** 266-267

COULTON, GEORGE GORDON (1858-1947), English historian **4** 267

Council of Elders
see French Revolution—Council of Elders

COUNTS, GEORGE S(YLVESTER) (1889-1974), American educator and educational sociologist **4** 267-269

COUPER, ARCHIBALD SCOTT (1831-1892), British chemist **4** 269-270

COUPER, JAMES HAMILTON (1794-1866), American agriculturist **4** 270

COUPERIN, FRANÇOIS (1668-1733), French composer, organist, and harpsichordist **4** 270-271

COURBET, JEAN DESIRÉ GUSTAVE (1819-1877), French painter **4** 271-273

COURLANDER, HAROLD (1908-1996), American folklorist and author **19** 78-80

COURNOT, ANTOINE AUGUSTIN (1801-1877), French mathematician, philosopher, and economist **4** 273

COUSIN, VICTOR (1792-1867), French educator and philosopher **4** 273-274

Cousins, Les (film)
Chabrol, Claude **28** 67-69

COUSINS, NORMAN (1912-1990), editor-in-chief of the Saturday Review and advocate for world peace **4** 274-276

COUSTEAU, JACQUES-YVES (1910-1997), undersea explorer, photographer, inventor, writer, television producer, and filmmaker **4** 276-277
Edgerton, Harold Eugene **28** 109-111

COUSTEAU, JEAN-MICHEL (born 1938), French oceanographer **27** 93-95

COUSY, BOB (Robert Joseph Cousy; born 1928), American basketball player and coach **21** 92-94

COUZENS, JAMES (James Joseph Couzins, Jr.; 1872-1936), American industrialist, politician, and philanthropist **22** 121-125

COVERDALE, MILES (1488-1568), English Puritan **4** 278

COVILHÃO, PEDRO DE (circa 1455-circa 1530), Portuguese explorer and diplomat **4** 278-279

COWARD, NOEL (1899-1973), English playwright, actor, and composer **4** 279-280

COWELL, HENRY DIXON (1897-1965), American composer and pianist **4** 280-281

COWLEY, ABRAHAM (1618-1667), English writer **4** 281-282

COWPER, WILLIAM (1731-1800), English poet **4** 282

COX, ARCHIBALD (born 1912), American lawyer, educator, author, labor arbitrator, and public servant **4** 283-284

COX, HARVEY (born 1929), American theologian and author **4** 284-285

COXE, TENCH (1755-1824), American political economist and businessman **4** 285-286

COXEY, JACOB SECHLER (1854-1951), American reformer and businessman **4** 286-287

COYSEVOX, ANTOINE (1640-1720), French sculptor **4** 287-288

CRABBE, GEORGE (1754-1832), English poet **4** 288

CRAFT, ELLEN (ca. 1826-1897), African American activist **22** 125-127

CRAIG, EDWARD GORDON (1872-1966), European actor, designer, director, and theoretician **4** 288-289

CRANACH, LUCAS, THE ELDER (1472-1553), German painter, engraver, and designer of woodcuts **4** 289-290

CRANDALL, PRUDENCE (1803-1890), American educator **4** 291

CRANE, HART (1899-1932), American poet **4** 291-293

CRANE, STEPHEN (1871-1900), American writer and poet **4** 293-295

Cranes (poem)
Gamzatov, Rasul **28** 134-136

CRANMER, THOMAS (1489-1556), English reformer, archbishop of Canterbury **4** 295-296

CRASHAW, RICHARD (1612/1613-49), English poet **4** 296

CRASSUS DIVES, MARCUS LICINIUS (circa 115-53 B.C.), Roman financier and politician **4** 296-297

CRAVEIRINHA, JOSÉ (born 1922), Mozambican journalist and lyric poet **4** 297-299

CRAWFORD, JOAN (Lucille Fay LeSueur; 1906-1977), American actress **19** 80-82

CRAWFORD, WILLIAM HARRIS (1772-1834), American politician **4** 299-300

CRAXI, BETTINO (1934-2000), statesman and prime minister of the Italian republic (1983-1987) **4** 300-301

CRAY, SEYMOUR (1925-1996), American computer engineer **4** 301-303

CRAZY HORSE (circa 1842-1877), American Indian, Oglala Sioux war chief **4** 303-304

CREEL, GEORGE (1876-1953), American writer and journalist **4** 304-305

CRÉMAZIE, OCTAVE (1827-1879), Canadian poet **4** 305-306

CRERAR, THOMAS ALEXANDER (1876-1975), Canadian political leader **4** 306

CRESSON, EDITH (born 1934), first woman prime minister of France **4** 306-307

CRÈVECOEUR, ST. JOHN DE (1735-1813), French-American farmer and writer **4** 307-308

CRICHTON, (JOHN) MICHAEL (a.k.a. Michael Douglas, Jeffrey Hudson, and John Lange; born 1942), American novelist, screenwriter, and director **4** 308-310

CRICK, FRANCIS HARRY COMPTON (1916-2004), English molecular biologist **4** 310

Crime novel
see Mystery fiction (literary genre)

Criminals, English
Chapman, Eddie **28** 69-72

Crimthann
see Columba, St.

CRISPI, FRANCESCO (1819-1901), Italian statesman **4** 310-311

CRISTIANI, ALFREDO ("Fredy" Cristiani; born 1947), president of El Salvador (1989-) **4** 311-313

CRISTOFORI, BARTOLOMEO (1655-1731), Italian musician and inventor of the piano **21** 94-96

CROCE, BENEDETTO (1866-1952), Italian philosopher, critic and educator **4** 313-314

CROCKETT, DAVID (1786-1836), American frontiersman **4** 314-316

CROGHAN, GEORGE (ca. 1720-1782), American Indian agent and trader **22** 127-129

CROLY, HERBERT DAVID (1869-1930), American editor and author **4** 316-317

CROLY, JANE (Jennie June; 1829-1901), American journalist **21** 96-96

CROMER, 1ST EARL OF (Evelyn Baring; 1841-1907), English statesman **4** 317

CROMWELL, OLIVER (1599-1658), English statesman and general **4** 317-320

CROMWELL, THOMAS (Earl of Essex; circa 1485-1540), English statesman 1532-1540 **4** 320-321

Cromwell of Oakham, Baron
see Cromwell, Thomas

CRONIN, JAMES WATSON (born 1931), American physicist **24** 97-99

CRONKITE, WALTER LELAND, JR. (born 1916), American journalist and radio and television news broadcaster **4** 321-322

CROOK, GEORGE (1828-1890), American general and frontiersman **4** 322-323

CROOKES, SIR WILLIAM (1832-1919), English chemist and physicist **4** 323-324

CROSBY, HARRY LILLIS (Bing; 1903-1977), American singer and radio and television personality **4** 324-326

CROWLEY, ALEISTER (1875-1947), English author and magician **18** 107-109

CROWTHER, SAMUEL ADJAI (circa 1806-1891), Nigerian Anglican bishop **4** 326

CRUMB, GEORGE (born 1929), American composer and teacher **4** 326-328

CRUTZEN, PAUL J. (born 1933), Dutch chemist **27** 95-97

CRUZ, CELIA (1925-2003), Cuban American singer **24** 99-101

CRUZ, OSWALDO GONÇALVES (1872-1917), Brazilian microbiologist and epidemiologist **4** 328-329

CSIKSZENTMIHALYI, MIHALY (born 1934), American psychologist and author **26** 78-80

CUAUHTEMOC (circa 1496-1525), Aztec ruler **4** 329

CUBBERLEY, ELLWOOD PATTERSON (1868-1941), American educator and university dean **4** 329-331

CUDWORTH, RALPH (1617-1688), English philosopher and theologian **4** 331

Cuéllar, Diego Velázquez de
see Velázquez de Cuéllar, Diego

CUFFE, PAUL (1759-1817), African American ship captain and merchant **4** 331-332

CUGAT, XAVIER (1900-1990), Spanish musician **23** 81-82

CUGOANO, OTTOBAH (circa 1757-after 1803), African abolitionist in England **4** 332-333

CUKOR, GEORGE (1899-1983), American film director **19** 82-84

CULLEN, COUNTEE (1903-1946), African American poet **4** 333-334

CULLEN, MAURICE GALBRAITH (1866-1934), Canadian painter **4** 334

CULLEN, PAUL (1803-1879), Irish cardinal **20** 100-103

CUMMINGS, EDWARD ESTLIN (1894-1962), American poet **4** 334-336

CUNARD, NANCY (Nancy Fairbairn; 1896-1965), English poet, publisher, and activist **28** 87-89

CUNHA, EUCLIDES RODRIGUES PIMENTA DA (1866-1909), Brazilian writer **4** 336-337

CUNNINGHAM, GLENN (1909-1988), American track and field athlete **21** 96-99

CUNNINGHAM, IMOGEN (1883-1976), American photographer **19** 84-86

Cunningham, Jane
see Croly, Jane Cunningham

CUNNINGHAM, MERCE (born 1919), American dancer and choreographer **4** 337-338

CUOMO, MARIO MATTHEW (born 1932), Democratic New York state governor **4** 338-339

CURIE, ÈVE (Eve Curie Labouisse; 1904-2007), French musician, author and diplomat **18** 109-111

Curie, Irène
see Joliot-Curie, Irène

CURIE, MARIE SKLODOWSKA (1867-1934), Polish-born French physicist **4** 339-341

CURIE, PIERRE (1859-1906), French physicist **4** 341-344

CURLEY, JAMES MICHAEL (1874-1958), American politician **4** 344-345

CURRIE, SIR ARTHUR WILLIAM (1875-1933), Canadian general **4** 345

CURRIER AND IVES (1857-1907), American lithographic firm **4** 345-346

CURRY, JABEZ LAMAR MONROE (1815-1903), American politician **4** 346-347

CURTIN, ANDREW GREGG (1815-1894), American politician **4** 347-348

CURTIN, JOHN JOSEPH (1885-1945), Australian statesman, prime minister **4** 348-349

CURTIS, BENJAMIN ROBBINS (1809-1874), American jurist, United States Supreme Court justice **4** 349

CURTIS, CHARLES BRENT (1860-1936), American vice president (1929-1932) and legislator **21** 99-100

CURTIS, GEORGE WILLIAM (1824-1892), American writer and reformer **4** 349-350

CURTISS, GLENN HAMMOND (1878-1930), American aviation pioneer **4** 350-351

CURZON, GEORGE NATHANIEL (1st Marquess Curzon of Kedleston; 1859-1925), English statesman **4** 351-352

CUSA, NICHOLAS OF (1401-1464), German prelate and humanist **4** 352-353

CUSHING, HARVEY WILLIAMS (1869-1939), American neurosurgeon **4** 353-354

CUSHMAN, CHARLOTTE (1816-1876), American actress **4** 354-355

CUSTER, GEORGE ARMSTRONG (1839-1876), American general **4** 355-356

CUTLER, MANASSEH (1742-1823), American clergyman, scientist, and politician **4** 356-357

CUVIER, BARON GEORGES LÉOPOLD (1769-1832), French zoologist and biologist **4** 357-359

CUVILLIÉS, FRANÇOIS (1695-1768), Flemish architect and designer **4** 359-360

CUYP, AELBERT (1620-1691), Dutch painter **4** 360-361

Cycling Hall of Fame
Merckx, Eddy **28** 241-243

CYNEWULF (8th or 9th century), Anglo-Saxon poet **20** 103-104

CYPRIANUS, THASCIUS CAECILIANUS (died 258), Roman bishop of Carthage **4** 361-362

CYRIL (OF ALEXANDRIA), ST. (died 444), Egyptian bishop, Doctor of the Church **4** 362

CYRIL, ST. (827-869), Apostle to the Slavs **4** 362

CYRUS THE GREAT (ruled 550-530 B.C.), founder of the Persian Empire **4** 363-364

Czaczkes, Shmuel Yoseph
see Agnon, Shmuel Yoseph

Czech art
Hollar, Wenceslaus **28** 180-183

D

Da Gama, Vasco
see Gama, Vasco da

DA PONTE, LORENZO (Emanuele Conegliano; 1749-1838), Italian librettist and poet **20** 105-106

Dagestani literature and art
Gamzatov, Rasul **28** 134-136

DAGUERRE, LOUIS JACQUES MANDÉ (1787-1851), French painter and stage designer **4** 365-366

DAHL, ROALD (1916-1990), Welsh-born English author **4** 366-367

DAIGO II (1288-1339), Japanese emperor **4** 367-368

DAIMLER, GOTTLIEB (1834-1900), German mechanical engineer **4** 368

DALADIER, ÉDOUARD (1884-1970), French statesman **4** 369

DALAI LAMA (Lhamo Thondup; born 1935), 14th in a line of Buddhist spiritual and temporal leaders of Tibet **4** 369-371

DALE, SIR HENRY HALLETT (1875-1968), English pharmacologist and neurophysiologist **4** 371-373

D'Alembert, Jean
see Alembert, Jean le Rond d'

DALEN, NILS GUSTAF (1869-1937), Swedish engineer and inventor **25** 99-101

DALEY, RICHARD M. (born 1942), mayor of Chicago **24** 102-104

DALEY, RICHARD J. (1902-1976), Democratic mayor of Chicago (1955-1976) **4** 373-375

DALHOUSIE, 1ST MARQUESS OF (James Andrew Broun Ramsay; 1812-1860), British statesman **4** 375-376

DALI, SALVADOR (1904-1989), Spanish painter **4** 376-377

DALLAPICCOLA, LUIGI (1904-1975), Italian composer **4** 377-378

DALTON, JOHN (1766-1844), English chemist **4** 378-379

DALY, MARCUS (1841-1900), American miner and politician **4** 379-380

DALY, MARY (born 1928), American feminist theoretician and philosopher **4** 380-381

DALZEL, ARCHIBALD (or Dalziel; 1740-1811), Scottish slave trader **4** 381-382

DAM, CARL PETER HENRIK (1895-1976), Danish biochemist **4** 382-383

DAMIEN, FATHER (1840-1889), Belgian missionary **4** 383

DAMPIER, WILLIAM (1652-1715), English privateer, author, and explorer **4** 384

DANA, CHARLES ANDERSON (1819-1897), American journalist **4** 384-385

DANA, RICHARD HENRY, JR. (1815-1882), American author and lawyer **4** 385-386

DANDOLO, ENRICO (circa 1107-1205), Venetian doge 1192-1205 **4** 386-387

DANDRIDGE, DOROTHY (1922-1965), African American actress and singer **18** 112-114

Dangerous Liaisons (film)
Frears, Stephen Arthur **28** 127-129

DANIELS, JOSEPHUS (1862-1948), American journalist and statesman **4** 387

Daniels, W. (pseudonym)
see Wallace-Johnson, Isaac

D'ANNUNZIO, GABRIELE (1863-1938), Italian poet and patriot **4** 388

DANQUAH, JOSEPH B. (1895-1965), Ghanaian nationalist and politician **4** 388-389

DANTE ALIGHIERI (1265-1321), Italian poet **4** 389-391

DANTON, GEORGES JACQUES (1759-1794), French revolutionary leader **4** 391-393

DANTZIG, GEORGE BERNARD (1914-2005), American mathematician **26** 81-83

DARBY, ABRAHAM (1677-1717), English iron manufacturer **20** 106-107

DARÍO, RUBÉN (1867-1916), Nicaraguan poet **4** 393-394

DARIUS I (the Great; ruled 522-486 B.C.), king of Persia **4** 394-395

DARROW, CLARENCE SEWARD (1857-1938), American lawyer **4** 396-397

DARWIN, CHARLES ROBERT (1809-1882), English naturalist **4** 397-399

DARWIN, ERASMUS (1731-1802), English physician, author, botanist and inventor **18** 114-116

DARWISH, MAHMUD (born 1942), Palestinian poet **4** 399-401

DAS, CHITTA RANJAN (1870-1925), Indian lawyer, poet, and nationalist **4** 401-402

Dashti
see Jami

DATSOLALEE (Dabuda; Wide Hips; 1835-1925), Native American weaver **22** 130-131

Datta, Narendranath
see Vivekananda

Dau
see Landau, Lev Davidovich

DAUBIGNY, CHARLES FRANÇOIS (1817-1878), French painter and etcher **4** 402

DAUDET, ALPHONSE (1840-1897), French novelist and dramatist **4** 402-403

DAUMIER, HONORÉ VICTORIN (1808-1879), French lithographer, painter, and sculptor **4** 403-405

DAVENPORT, JOHN (1597-1670), English Puritan clergyman **4** 405-406

DAVID (ruled circa 1010-circa 970 B.C.), Israelite king **4** 406-407

DAVID, JACQUES LOUIS (1748-1825), French painter **4** 407-409

DAVID, SAINT (Dewi; 520-601), Welsh monk and evangelist **23** 83-85

DAVID I (1084-1153), king of Scotland **4** 407

DAVID-NÉEL, ALEXANDRA (Eugenénie Alexandrine Marie David; 1868-1969), French explorer and author **28** 90-92

DAVIES, ARTHUR BOWEN (1862-1928), American painter **4** 409-410

DAVIES, RUPERT (1917-1976), British actor **18** 116-117

DAVIES, WILLIAM ROBERTSON (1913-1995), Canadian author **18** 117-119

DAVIGNON, VISCOUNT (ETIENNE) (born 1932), an architect of European integration and unity through the Commission of the European Communities **4** 410-411

DAVIS, ALEXANDER JACKSON (1803-1892), American architect **4** 411

DAVIS, ANGELA (Angela Yvonne Davis; born 1944), African American scholar and activist **4** 412-413

DAVIS, ARTHUR VINING (1867-1962), general manager of the Aluminum Company of America (ALCOA) **4** 413-414

DAVIS, BENJAMIN O., SR. (1877-1970), first African American general in the regular United States Armed Services **4** 414-415

DAVIS, BETTE (1908-1989), American actress **18** 119-121

DAVIS, COLIN REX (born 1927), British conductor **22** 131-133

DAVIS, ELMER HOLMES (1890-1958), American journalist and radio commentator **22** 133-136

DAVIS, GLENN (1925-2005), American football player **21** 101-103

DAVIS, HENRY WINTER (1817-1865), American lawyer and politician **4** 415-416

DAVIS, JEFFERSON (1808-1889), American statesman, president of the Confederacy 1862-1865 **4** 416-418

DAVIS, JOHN (circa 1550-1605), English navigator **4** 419

DAVIS, MILES (1926-1991), jazz trumpeter, composer, and small-band leader **4** 419-421
Zawinul, Joe **28** 389-391

DAVIS, OSSIE (1917-2005), African American playwright, actor, and director **4** 421-422

DAVIS, RICHARD HARDING (1864-1916), American journalist, novelist, and dramatist **4** 422-423

DAVIS, SAMMY, JR. (1925-1990), African American singer, dancer, and actor **4** 423-424

DAVIS, STUART (1894-1964), American cubist painter **4** 424-425

DAVIS, WILLIAM MORRIS (1850-1934), American geographer and geologist **4** 425-426

DAVY, SIR HUMPHRY (1778-1829), English chemist and natural philosopher **4** 426-427

DAWES, HENRY LAURENS (1816-1903), American politician **4** 427

DAWSON, WILLIAM LEVI (1899-1990), African American composer, performer, and music educator **4** 427-428

DAY, DOROTHY (1897-1980), a founder of the Catholic Worker Movement **4** 428-429

DAYAN, MOSHE (1915-1981), Israeli general and statesman **4** 429-431

DAYANANDA SARASWATI (1824-1883), Indian religious leader **4** 431

DE ANDRADE, MARIO (Mario Coelho Pinto Andrade; born 1928), Angolan poet, critic, and political activist **4** 434-435

DE BEAUVOIR, SIMONE (1908-1986), French writer and leader of the modern feminist movement **4** 440-441

DE BOW, JAMES DUNWOODY BROWNSON (1820-1867), American editor and statistician **4** 441-442

DE BROGLIE, LOUIS VICTOR PIERRE RAYMOND (1892-1987), French physicist **4** 442-444

DE FOREST, LEE (1873-1961), American inventor **4** 459-460

DE GASPERI, ALCIDE (1881-1954), Italian statesman, premier 1945-1953 **4** 462-463

DE GAULLE, CHARLES ANDRÉ JOSEPH MARIE (1890-1970), French general, president 1958-1969 **4** 463-465

DE GOUGES, MARIE OLYMPE (born Marie Gouzes; 1748-1793), French author **23** 85-88

DE GOURNAY, MARIE LE JARS (1565-1645), French author **23** 88-90

DE HAVILLAND, SIR GEOFFREY (1882-1965), British aviator and aeronautical engineer **25** 101-103

DE HIRSCH, MAURICE (Baron de Hirsch; 1831-1896), Austro-Hungarian financier and philanthropist **24** 104-106

DE KLERK, FREDRIK WILLEM (born 1936), state president of South Africa (1989-) **4** 466-468

DE KOONING, WILLEM (1904-1997), Dutch-born American painter **4** 468-469

DE LA MADRID HURTADO, MIGUEL (born 1934), president of Mexico (1982-1988) **4** 471-472

DE LA ROCHE, MAZO LOUISE (1879-1961), Canadian author **4** 474-475

DE LEMPICKA, TAMARA (Maria Gorska; Tamara Kuffner; 1898-1980), Polish American artist **24** 106-109

DE LEON, DANIEL (1852-1914), American Socialist theoretician and politician **4** 479-480

DE L'ORME, PHILIBERT (1510-1570), French architect **9** 519

DE MILLE, AGNES (1905-1993), American dancer, choreographer, and author **4** 486-488

DE NIRO, ROBERT (born 1943), American actor and film producer **21** 103-106

DE PISAN, CHRISTINE (1363-1431), French poet and philosopher **24** 109-111

DE QUINCEY, THOMAS (Thomas Quincey; 1785-1859), British author **27** 98-100

De Revoire, Paul
see Revere, Paul

DE SANCTIS, FRANCESCO (1817-1883), Italian critic, educator, and legislator **4** 505

DE SAUSSURE, FERDINAND (1857-1913), Swiss linguist and author **24** 111-113

DE SICA, VITTORIO (1902-1974), Italian filmmaker **21** 106-108

DE SMET, PIERRE JEAN (1801-1873), Belgian Jesuit missionary **4** 509-510

DE SOTO, HERNANDO (1500-1542), Spanish conqueror and explorer **4** 510-511

DE VALERA, EAMON (1882-1975), American-born Irish revolutionary leader and statesman **4** 514-515

DE VALOIS, NINETTE (Edris Stannus; 1898-2001), English choreographer and ballet dancer **25** 103-105

DE VERE, EDWARD (Earl of Oxford; 1550-1604), English author **25** 105-107

DE VRIES, HUGO (1848-1935), Belgian botanist in the fields of heredity and the origin of species **4** 516-518

DE WOLFE, ELSIE (1865-1950), American interior decorator **20** 107-108

Deadwood Dick
see Love, Nat

DEÁK, FRANCIS (1803-1876), Hungarian statesman **4** 431-432

DEAKIN, ALFRED (1856-1919), Australian statesman **4** 432-433

DEAN, JAMES (James Byron Dean; 1931-1955), American actor and cult figure **4** 433-434

DEANE, SILAS (1737-1789), American merchant lawyer and diplomat **4** 435-437

Death of Cleopatra, The (sculpture)
Lewis, Edmonia **28** 215-217

DEB, RADHAKANT (1783-1867), Bengali
reformer and cultural nationalist **4** 437

DEBAKEY, MICHAEL ELLIS (born 1908),
American surgeon **4** 437-438

**DEBARTOLO, EDWARD JOHN, SR.
AND JR.**, real estate developers who
specialized in large regional malls **4**
438-440

DEBS, EUGENE VICTOR (1855-1926),
American union organizer **4** 444-445

DEBUSSY, (ACHILLE) CLAUDE (1862-
1918), French composer **4** 445-447

DEBYE, PETER JOSEPH WILLIAM (1884-
1966), Dutch-born American physical
chemist **4** 447-448

DECATUR, STEPHEN (1779-1820),
American naval officer **4** 448-449

Decimus Junius Juvenalis
see Juvenal

DEE, JOHN (1527-1608), British
mathematician and astronomer **25**
107-110

DEE, RUBY (born Ruby Ann Wallace;
born 1924), African American actor **4**
449-452

DEER, ADA E. (born 1935), Native
American social worker, activist, and
director of Bureau of Indian Affairs **4**
452-454

DEERE, JOHN (1804-1886), American
inventor and manufacturer **4** 455

DEERING, WILLIAM (1826-1913),
American manufacturer **4** 455-456

DEES, MORRIS S., JR. (born 1936),
American civil rights attorney **4**
456-457

DEFOE, DANIEL (1660-1731), English
novelist, journalist, and poet **4**
457-459

DEGANAWIDA (also DeKanahwidah; c.
1550-c. 1600), Native American
prophet, leader, and statesman **4**
460-461

DEGAS, (HILAIRE GERMAIN) EDGAR
(1834-1917), French painter and
sculptor **4** 461-462

DEHLAVI, SHAH WALIULLAH (Qutb-
ud-Din; 1703-1762), Indian religious
leader **28** 92-94

DEISENHOFER, JOHANN (born 1943),
German biochemist and biophysicist
23 90-93

DEKKER, THOMAS (circa 1572-circa
1632), English playwright and
pamphleteer **4** 465-466

**DELACROIX, (FERDINAND VICTOR)
EUGÈNE** (1798-1863), French painter
4 469-471

DELANCEY, STEPHEN (1663-1741),
American merchant and politician **4**
473

DELANY, MARTIN ROBINSON (1812-
1885), African American army officer,
politician, and judge **4** 473-474

Delattre, Roland
see Lassus, Roland de

DELAUNAY, ROBERT (1885-1941),
French abstract painter **4** 475-476

DELBRÜCK, MAX (1906-1981), German-
born American molecular biologist **4**
476-478

DELCASSÉ, THÉOPHILE (1852-1923),
French statesman **4** 478-479

DELEDDA, GRAZIA (Grazia Maria
Cosima Damiana Deledda; 1871-
1936), Italian author **24** 113-115

DELEUZE, GILLES (1925-1995), French
Philosopher **28** 94-96

DELGADO, JOSÉ MATIAS (1768-1832),
Salvadoran political leader **24** 115-117

DELL, MICHAEL SAUL (born 1965),
American businessman **23** 93-95

Della Robbia, Luca
see Robbia, Luca della

DELLINGER, DAVID (born 1915),
American pacifist **4** 480-481

DELORIA, ELLA CLARA (1889-1971),
Native American ethnologist, linguist,
and author **22** 136-138

DELORIA, VINE, JR. (1933-2005), Native
American author, poet, and activist **4**
481-484

DELORS, JACQUES (born 1925), French
president of the European Commission
and chief architect of Western Europe's
drive toward market unity by 1992 **4**
484-486

DEL PILAR, MARCELO H. (1850-1896),
Philippine revolutionary propagandist
and satirist **4** 486

DELAY, TOM (Thomas Dale Delay; born
1947), American politician **26** 83-85

Dementia praecox
see Schizophrenia (medicine)

DEMILLE, CECIL BLOUNT (1881-1959),
American film director and producer **4**
488-490

DEMIREL, SÜLEYMAN (born 1924),
Turkish politician, prime minister, and
leader of the Justice party **4** 490-493

Democratic party (United States)
leaders (California)
Saund, Dalip Singh **28** 310-312
leaders (Idaho)
Church, Frank Forrester, III **28** 78-80

DEMOCRITUS (circa 494-circa 404
B.C.), Greek natural philosopher **4**
493-494

DEMOIVRE, ABRAHAM (1667-1754),
Franco-English mathematician **4**
494-495

DEMOSTHENES (384-322 B.C.), Greek
orator **4** 495-496

DEMPSEY, JACK (William Harrison
Dempsey; 1895-1983), American
boxer **4** 496-497

DEMUTH, CHARLES (1883-1935),
American painter **4** 497-498

DENG XIAOPING (Teng Hsiao-p'ing;
1904-1997), leader in the People's
Republic of China (PRC) in the 1970s
4 498-500

DENIKIN, ANTON (1872-1947), Russian
soldier **20** 108-111

DENKTASH, RAUF (born 1924),
president of the Turkish Republic of
Northern Cyprus (1985-) **4** 500-502

DENNING, ALFRED THOMPSON (Tom
Denning' 1899-1999), British judge
and author **22** 138-140

Dennis, Ruth
see St. Denis, Ruth

DENVER, JOHN (Henry John
Deutschendorf, Jr.; 1943-1997),
American singer and songwriter **27**
100-102

DEODORO DA FONSECA, MANOEL
(1827-1892), Brazilian statesman,
president 1890-1891 **4** 502

DEPARDIEU, GERARD (born 1948),
French actor **27** 102-105

DERAIN, ANDRÉ (1880-1954), French
painter **4** 503

DEREN, MAYA (Eleanora Solomonovna
Derenkovskaya; 1917-1961), Ukrainian
American author and filmaker **23**
95-97

DERRICOTTE, JULIETTE ALINE (1897-
1931), African American educator **22**
140-141

DERRIDA, JACQUES (1930-2004),
French philosopher **4** 503-505

DERSHOWITZ, ALAN MORTON (born
1938), American lawyer **26** 85-87

DESAI, ANITA (née Anita Mazumdar;
born 1937), Indian author **25** 110-113

DESCARTES, RENÉ (1596-1650), French philosopher and mathematician **4** 505-508

Desert Fox
see Rommel, Erwin

Desiderio da Settignano
see Settignano, Desiderio da

Designers
home furnishings
Wirkkala, Tapio **28** 372-374
luggage
Vuitton, Louis **28** 365-367
numismatic
Wirkkala, Tapio **28** 372-374

Despréaux, Nicholas Boileau
see Boileau-Despréaux, Nicholas

DESSALINES, JEAN JACQUES (1758-1806), Haitian nationalist and politician **4** 511-512

Destouches, Louis Ferdinand
see Céline, Louis Ferdinand

Detective stories
see Mystery fiction (literary genre)

DETT, ROBERT NATHANIEL (1882-1943), African American composer, conductor, and music educator **4** 512

Dettonville, Amos
see Pascal, Blaise

DEUTSCH, KARL WOLFGANG (1912-1992), American political scientist **4** 512-514

DEVERS, GAIL (Yolanda Gail Devers; born 1966), American athlete **25** 113-115

DEVLIN, BERNADETTE (McAliskey; born 1947), youngest woman ever elected to the British Parliament **4** 515-516

DEVRIES, WILLIAM CASTLE (born 1943), American heart surgeon **4** 518-519

DEW, THOMAS RODERICK (1802-1846), American political economist **4** 519

DEWEY, GEORGE (1837-1917), American naval officer **4** 520

DEWEY, JOHN (1859-1952), American philosopher and educator **4** 520-523

DEWEY, MELVIL (1851-1931), American librarian and reformer **4** 523-524

DEWEY, THOMAS EDMUND (1902-1971), American lawyer and politician **4** 524

DEWSON, MARY WILLIAMS (Molly; 1874-1962), American reformer, government official, and organizer of women for the Democratic party **4** 525

Dhu'l-Aktaf
see Shahpur II

DIAGHILEV, SERGEI (1872-1929), Russian who inspired artists, musicians, and dancers to take ballet to new heights of public enjoyment **4** 525-527

DIAGNE, BLAISE (1872-1934), Senegalese political leader **4** 527

DIAMOND, DAVID (1915-2005), American composer and teacher **4** 527-529

DIANA, PRINCESS OF WALES (born Diana Frances Spencer; 1961-1997), member of British royal family **4** 529-533

DIAS DE NOVAIS, BARTOLOMEU (died 1500), Portuguese explorer **4** 533-534

DIAZ, ABBY MORTON (nee Abigail Morton; 1821-1904), American author and activist **26** 87-89

Díaz, Manuel Azaña
see Azaña Díaz, Manuel

DÍAZ, PORFIRIO (José de la Cruz Porfirio Díaz; 1830-1915), Mexican general and politician **4** 534-536

Diaz, Rodrigo
see Cid, The

DÍAZ DEL CASTILLO, BERNAL (circa 1496-circa 1584), Spanish soldier and historian **4** 536-537

DÍAZ ORDAZ, GUSTAVO (1911-1979), president of Mexico (1964-1970) **4** 537-538

DICK, PHILIP K. (Philip Kindred Dick; 1928-1982), American science fiction writer **28** 96-98

DICKENS, CHARLES JOHN HUFFAM (1812-1870), English author **4** 538-541

DICKEY, JAMES (1923-1997), American poet **19** 87-89

DICKINSON, EMILY (1830-1886), American poet **4** 541-543

DICKINSON, JOHN (1732-1808), American lawyer, pamphleteer, and politician **4** 543-544

DICKSON, LAURIE (William Kennedy Laurie Dickson; 1860-1935), British inventor and filmmaker **20** 112-113

DIDEROT, DENIS (1713-1784), French philosopher, playwright, and encyclopedist **5** 1-2

DIDION, JOAN (born 1934), American author **20** 113-116

DIEBENKORN, RICHARD (born 1922), American abstract expressionist painter **5** 2-4

DIEFENBAKER, JOHN GEORGE (1895-1979), Canadian statesman **5** 4-5

DIELS, (OTTO PAUL) HERMANN (1876-1954), German organic chemist **5** 5-6

DIEM, NGO DINH (1901-1963), South Vietnamese president 1955-1963 **5** 6-7

DIESEL, RUDOLF (1858-1913), German mechanical engineer **5** 7

DIETRICH, MARLENE (née Marie Magdalene Dietrich; 1901-1992), German actor **25** 115-117

DIKE, KENNETH (Kenneth Onwuka Dike; 1917-1983), African historian who set up the Nigerian National Archives **5** 7-8

DILLINGER, JOHN (1903-1934), American criminal **5** 9

DILTHEY, WILHELM CHRISTIAN LUDWIG (1833-1911), German historian and philosopher **5** 10

DIMAGGIO, JOE (born Giuseppe Paolo DiMaggio, Jr.; 1914-1999), American baseball player **5** 10-11

DIMITROV, GEORGI (1882-1949), head of the Communist International (1935-1943) and prime minister of Bulgaria (1944-1949) **5** 11-13

Din, Muslih-al-
see Sadi

DINESEN BLIXEN-FINECKE, KAREN (a.k.a. Isak Dinesen; 1885-1962), Danish author **5** 13-14

DINGANE (circa 1795-1840), Zulu king **5** 14-15

DINKINS, DAVID (born 1927), African American politician and mayor of New York City **5** 15-18

DINWIDDIE, ROBERT (1693-1770), Scottish merchant and colonial governor **5** 18-19

DIOCLETIAN (Gaius Aurelius Valerius Diocletianus; 245-circa 313), Roman emperor 284-305 **5** 19-20
Galerius, Emperor of Rome **28** 132-134

DIOGENES (circa 400-325 B.C.), Greek philosopher **5** 20-21

DIONYSIUS EXIGUUS (c. 465-c. 530), Roman theologian and mathematician **28** 99-100

DIOP, CHEIKH ANTA (1923-1986), African historian **5** 21-22

DIOP, DAVID MANDESSI (1927-1960), French Guinean poet **24** 117-118

DIOR, CHRISTIAN (1905-1957), French fashion designer **5** 22

DIRAC, PAUL ADRIEN MAURICE (1902-1984), English physicist **5** 23-24

Directory (France; 1795-1799)
see French Revolution-1795-1799 (Directory)

DIRKSEN, EVERETT MCKINLEY (1896-1969), Republican congressman and senator from Illinois **5** 24-26

Discalced Carmelites
see Carmelites (religious order)

DISNEY, WALTER ELIAS (1901-1966), American film maker and entrepreneur **5** 26-27

DISRAELI, BENJAMIN (1st Earl of Beaconsfield; 1804-1881), English statesman, prime minister 1868 and 1874-1880 **5** 27-29

District of Columbia
see Washington, D.C. (federal city)

Dith Pran
see Pran, Dith

DITTERSDORF, KARL DITTERS VON (Karl Ditters; 1739-1799), Austrian musician and composer **25** 117-119

DIVINE, FATHER (born George Baker?; c. 1877-1965), African American religious leader **5** 29-32

DIX, DOROTHEA LYNDE (1802-1887), American reformer **5** 32-33

DIX, OTTO (1891-1969), German painter and graphic artist **5** 33-34

DJILAS, MILOVAN (1911-1995), Yugoslavian writer **5** 34

DO MUOI (born 1917), prime minister of the Socialist Republic of Vietnam (1988-) **5** 53-55

DOBELL, SIR WILLIAM (1899-1970), Australian artist **5** 34-35

DOBZHANSKY, THEODOSIUS (1900-1975), Russian-American biologist who studied natural selection **5** 35-37

DOCTOROW, EDGAR LAURENCE (born 1931), American author **19** 89-91

Documentary photography
Hine, Lewis Wickes **28** 172-174

Dod Grile
see Bierce, Ambrose Gwinett

DODGE, GRACE HOADLEY (1856-1914), American feminist, philanthropist, and social worker **5** 37-38

DODGE, GRENVILLE MELLEN (1831-1916), American army officer and civil engineer **22** 142-145

DODGE, HENRY CHEE (circa 1857-1947), Navajo Tribal leader **26** 89-92

Dodge, Horace Elgin
see Dodge, John Francis and Horace Elgin

DODGE, JOHN FRANCIS (1864-1920) AND HORACE ELGIN (1868-1920), American automobile manufacturers **18** 121-123

Dodgson, Charles Lutwidge
see Carroll, Lewis

DOE, SAMUEL KANYON (1951-1990), Liberian statesman **5** 38-39

DOENITZ, KARL (1891-1980), German naval officer **20** 116-117

DOI TAKAKO (born 1928), chairperson of the Japan Socialist party **5** 39-41

DOLE, ELIZABETH HANFORD (born 1936), American lawyer, politician, and first female United States secretary of transportation **5** 41-43

DOLE, ROBERT J. (born 1923), Republican Senator **5** 43-46

DOLE, SANFORD BALLARD (1844-1926), American statesman **5** 46

DOLLFUSS, ENGELBERT (1892-1934), Austrian statesman **5** 47

DÖLLINGER, JOSEF IGNAZ VON (1799-1890), German historian and theologian **5** 47-48

DOMAGK, GERHARD JOHANNES PAUL (1895-1964), German bacteriologist **5** 48-50

DOMINGO, PLACIDO (born 1941), Spanish-born lyric-dramatic tenor **5** 50-51

DOMINIC, ST. (circa 1170-1221), Spanish Dominican founder **5** 51-52

DOMINO, FATS (Antoine Domino, Jr.; born 1928), African American singer, pianist, and composer **22** 145-147

DOMITIAN (Titus Flavius Domitianus Augustus; 51-96), Roman emperor 81-96 **5** 52-53

Domontovich, Aleksandra M.
see Kollantai, Aleksandra Mikhailovna

DONATELLO (Donato di Niccolò Bardi; 1386-1466), Italian sculptor **5** 55-56

DONATUS (died circa 355), schismatic bishop of Carthage **5** 56-57

DONG, PHAM VAN (born 1906), premier first of the Democratic Republic of Vietnam (DRV) and after 1976 of the Socialist Republic of Vietnam (SRV) **5** 57-59

DONIZETTI, GAETANA (1797-1848), Italian opera composer **5** 59-60

DONLEAVY, JAMES PATRICK (born 1926), Irish author and playwright **19** 91-93

DONNE, JOHN (1572-1631), English metaphysical poet **5** 60-61

DONNELLY, IGNATIUS (1831-1901), American politician and author **5** 62

DONNER, GEORG RAPHAEL (1693-1741), Austrian sculptor **5** 63

DONOSO, JOSÉ (1924-1996), Chilean writer **5** 63-65

DONOVAN, WILLIAM JOSEPH (1883-1959), American lawyer and public servant **22** 147-149

DOOLITTLE, HILDA (1886-1961), American poet and novelist **5** 65-66

DOOLITTLE, JAMES HAROLD (1896-1993), American transcontinental pilot **5** 66-68

Dorchester, 1st Baron
see Carleton, Guy

DORIA, ANDREA (1466-1560), Italian admiral and politician **18** 123-125

DORR, RHETA CHILDE (1868-1948), American journalist **5** 68-69

DORSEY, JIMMY (James Dorsey; 1904-1957), American musician and bandleader **19** 93-95

DORSEY, THOMAS ANDREW (1900-1993), African American gospel singer and composer **22** 149-151

DOS PASSOS, RODERIGO (1896-1970), American novelist **5** 69-71

DOS SANTOS, JOSÉ EDUARDO (born 1942), leader of the Popular Movement for the Liberation of Angola and president of Angola **5** 71-72

DOS SANTOS, MARCELINO (born 1929), Mozambican nationalist insurgent, statesman, and intellectual **5** 72-74

DOSTOEVSKY, FYODOR (1821-1881), Russian novelist **5** 74-77

DOUGLAS, DONALD WILLS (1892-1981), American aeronautical engineer **5** 77

DOUGLAS, GAVIN (circa 1475-1522), Scottish poet, prelate, and courtier **5** 77-78

DOUGLAS, SIR JAMES (1286?-1330), Scottish patriot **5** 80-82

DOUGLAS, MARY TEW (1921-2007), British anthropologist and social thinker **5** 79-80

DOUGLAS, STEPHEN ARNOLD (1813-1861), American politician **5** 80-82

Douglas, Thomas
see Selkirk, 5th Earl of

DOUGLAS, THOMAS CLEMENT (1904-1986), Canadian clergyman and politician, premier of Saskatchewan (1944-1961), and member of Parliament (1962-1979) **5** 82-83

DOUGLAS, WILLIAM ORVILLE (1898-1980), American jurist **5** 83-85

DOUGLAS-HOME, ALEC (Alexander Frederick Home; 1903-1995), Scottish politician **20** 117-119

DOUGLASS, FREDERICK (circa 1817-1895), African American leader and abolitionist **5** 85-86

DOUHET, GIULIO (1869-1930), Italian military leader **22** 151-152

DOVE, ARTHUR GARFIELD (1880-1946), American painter **5** 86-87

DOVE, RITA FRANCES (born 1952), United States poet laureate **5** 87-89

"Doves" (United States politics) see Vietnam war (1956-1976)—opponents (United States)

DOVZHENKO, ALEXANDER (Oleksandr Dovzhenko; 1894-1956), Ukrainian film director and screenwriter **25** 120-122

DOW, CHARLES (1851-1902), American journalist **19** 95-97

DOW, HERBERT H. (Herbert Henry Dow; 1866-1930), American chemist and businessman **28** 100-102

DOW, NEAL (1804-1897), American temperance reformer **5** 89-90

Dow Chemical Co.
Dow, Herbert H. **28** 100-102

DOWLAND, JOHN (1562-1626), British composer and lutenist **5** 90

DOWNING, ANDREW JACKSON (1815-1852), American horticulturist and landscape architect **5** 90-91

DOYLE, SIR ARTHUR CONAN (1859-1930), British author **5** 91-92

DRAGO, LUIS MARÍA (1859-1921), Argentine international jurist and diplomat **5** 92-93

DRAKE, DANIEL (1785-1852), American physician **5** 93-94

DRAKE, EDWIN (1819-1880), American oil well driller and speculator **21** 108-110

DRAKE, SIR FRANCIS (circa 1541-1596), English navigator **5** 94-96

DRAPER, JOHN WILLIAM (1811-1882), Anglo-American scientist and historian **5** 96-97

Drapier, M.B.
see Swift, Jonathan

DRAYTON, MICHAEL (1563-1631), English poet **5** 97-98

DREBBEL, CORNELIUS (Jacobszoon Drebbel; Cornelius Van Drebbel; 1572-1633), Dutch inventor and engineer **28** 102-104

DREISER, (HERMAN) THEODORE (1871-1945), American novelist **5** 98-100

DREW, CHARLES RICHARD (1904-1950), African American surgeon **5** 100-101

DREW, DANIEL (1797-1879), American stock manipulator **5** 101-102

DREXEL, KATHERINE (1858-1955), founded a Catholic order, the Sisters of the Blessed Sacrament **5** 102-103

DREXLER, KIM ERIC (born 1955), American scientist and author **20** 119-121

DREYER, CARL THEODOR (1889-1968), Danish film director **22** 152-155

DREYFUS, ALFRED (1859-1935), French army officer **5** 103-105

DRIESCH, HANS ADOLF EDUARD (1867-1941), German biologist and philosopher **5** 105

DRUCKER, PETER (1909-2005), American author and business consultant **21** 110-112

Drugaya Rossiya (Russian dissident group)
Kasparov, Garry **28** 194-196

Drummond, James Eric
see Perth, 16th Earl of

Drums (musical instrument)
Roach, Max **28** 292-296

DRUSUS, MARCUS LIVIUS (circa 124-91 B.C.), Roman statesman **5** 105-106

DRYDEN, JOHN (1631-1700), English poet, critic, and dramatist **5** 106-107

DRYSDALE, SIR GEORGE RUSSELL (1912-1981), Australian painter **5** 107-109

DU SABLE, JEAN BAPTISTE POINTE (Jean Baptiste Point Desable; c. 1745-1818), African-American explorer and founder of Chicago, IL **28** 104-106

DUANE, WILLIAM (1760-1835), American journalist **5** 109

DUARTE, JOSÉ NAPOLEÓN (1926-1990), civilian reformer elected president of El Salvador in 1984 **5** 109-111

DUBČEK, ALEXANDER (1921-1992), Czechoslovak politician **5** 112-113

DUBE, JOHN LANGALIBALELE (1870-1949), South African writer and Zulu propagandist **5** 113

DU BELLAY, JOACHIM (circa 1522-1560), French poet **5** 113-114

DUBINSKY, DAVID (1892-1982), American trade union official **5** 114-115

DUBNOV, SIMON (1860-1941), Jewish historian, journalist, and political activist **5** 115-116

DUBOIS, EUGÈNE (Marie Eugène Dubois; 1858-1940), Dutch anatomist and paleoanthopologist **28** 106-108

DU BOIS, WILLIAM EDWARD BURGHARDT (1868-1963), African American educator, pan-Africanist, and protest leader **5** 116-118
associates
Patterson, Louise Alone Thompson **28** 272-274

DU BOIS-REYMOND, EMIL (1818-1896), German physiologist **5** 118-119

DUBOS, RENÉ JULES (1901-1982), French-born American microbiologist **5** 119

DUBUFFET, JEAN PHILLIPE ARTHUR (born 1901), French painter **5** 119-120

DUCCIO DI BUONINSEGNA (1255/60-1318/19), Italian painter **5** 121-122

Duce, Il
see Mussolini, Benito

DUCHAMP, MARCEL (1887-1968), French painter **5** 122-123

DUCHAMP-VILLON, RAYMOND (1876-1918), French sculptor **5** 123

Dudevant, Amandine Aurore Lucie Dupin
see Sand, George

Dudley, Anne
see Bradstreet, Anne Dudley

DUDLEY, BARBARA (born 1947), American director of Greenpeace **5** 123-124

Dudley, John
see Northumberland, Duke of

Dudley, Robert
see Leicester, Earl of

DUDLEY, THOMAS (1576-1653), American colonial governor and Puritan leader **5** 124-125

DUFAY, GUILLAUME (circa 1400-1474), Netherlandish composer **5** 125-126

DUFF, ALEXANDER (1806-1878), Scottish Presbyterian missionary **5** 126-127

DUGAN, ALAN (born 1923), American poet **5** 127-128

DUGDALE, RICHARD LOUIS (1841-1883), English-born American sociologist **5** 128-129

DUHEM, PIERRE MAURICE MARIE (1861-1916), French physicist, chemist, and historian of science **5** 129

DUKAKIS, MICHAEL (born 1933), American governor of Massachusetts **5** 130-133

DUKE, DORIS (1912-1993), American philanthropist **24** 118-121

DUKE, JAMES BUCHANAN (1856-1925), American industrialist and philanthropist **5** 133-134

Dukenfield, William Claude
see Fields, W.C.

DULL KNIFE (born Morning Star; c. 1810-1883), Northern Cheyenne tribal leader **5** 135-136

DULLES, JOHN FOSTER (1888-1959), American statesman and diplomat **5** 134-135

DUMAS, ALEXANDRE (1803-1870), French playwright and novelist **5** 136-138

DUMAS, JEAN BAPTISTE ANDRÉ (1800-1884), French Chemist **5** 138-139

DU MAURIER, DAPHNE (Lady Browning; 1907-1989), English author **18** 125-127

DUN, TAN (born 1951), Chinese American musician **24** 121-123

DUNANT, JEAN HENRI (1828-1910), Swiss philanthropist **5** 139-141

DUNBAR, PAUL LAURENCE (1872-1906), African American poet and novelist **5** 141-142

DUNBAR, WILLIAM (circa 1460-circa 1520), Scottish poet and courtier **5** 142-143

DUNBAR, WILLIAM (1749-1810), Scottish-born American scientist and planter **5** 143-144

DUNCAN, ISADORA (1878-1927), American dancer **5** 144-145

DUNHAM, KATHERINE (1910-2006), African American dancer, choreographer, and anthropologist **5** 145-146

DUNMORE, 4TH EARL OF (John Murray; 1732-1809), British colonial governor **5** 147

DUNNE, FINLEY PETER (1867-1936), American journalist **5** 147-148

DUNNIGAN, ALICE ALLISON (1906-1983), African American journalist **25** 122-123

DUNNING, WILLIAM ARCHIBALD (1857-1922), American historian **5** 148-149

DUNS SCOTUS, JOHN (1265/66-1308), Scottish philosopher and theologian **5** 149-150

DUNSTABLE, JOHN (circa 1390-1453), English composer **5** 150-151

DUNSTAN, ST. (circa 909-988), English monk and archbishop **5** 151-152

DUNSTER, HENRY (circa 1609-1659), English-born American clergyman **5** 152-153

DUONG VAN MINH (born 1916), Vietnamese general and politician **18** 285-287

Dupin, Armandine Aurore Lucille
see Sand, George

DUPLEIX, MARQUIS (Joseph François; 1697-1763), French colonial administrator **5** 153

DU PONT, ÉLEUTHÈRE IRÉNÉE (1771-1834), French-born American manufacturer **5** 154

DU PONT, PIERRE SAMUEL (1870-1954), American industrialist **5** 154-155

DU PONT DE NEMOURS, PIERRE SAMUEL (1739-1817), French political economist **5** 155-156

DURAND, ASHER BROWN (1796-1886), American painter and engraver **5** 156-157

DURANT, THOMAS CLARK (1820-1885), American railroad executive **5** 157-158

DURANT, WILLIAM CRAPO (1861-1947), American industrialist **5** 158

DURAS, MARGUERITE (Marguerite Donnadieu; 1914-1996), French author and filmmaker **26** 92-95

DÜRER, ALBRECHT (1471-1528), German painter and graphic artist **5** 159-161

DURHAM, 1ST EARL OF (John George Lambton; 1792-1840), English statesman **5** 161-162

DURKHEIM, ÉMILE (1858-1917), French philosopher and sociologist **5** 162-163

DURRELL, GERALD MALCOLM (1925-1995), British naturalist and conservationist **24** 123-126

DURRELL, LAWRENCE (1912-1990), British author of novels, poetry, plays, short stories, and travel books **5** 163-164

DÜRRENMATT, FRIEDRICH (1921-1990), Swiss playwright **5** 164-165

DUVALIER, FRANÇOIS (Papa Doc; 1907-1971), Haitian president 1957-1971 **5** 165-166

DUVALIER, JEAN CLAUDE (Baby Doc; born 1949), president of Haiti (1971-1986) **5** 166-168

DVOŘÁK, ANTONIN (1841-1904), Czech composer **5** 168-169

DWIGHT, TIMOTHY (1752-1817), American educator and Congregational minister **5** 169

Dyck, Anthony van
see Van Dyck, Anthony

DYLAN, BOB (born Robert Allen Zimmerman; b. 1941), American singer, songwriter, and guitarist **5** 170-171

DYSON, FREEMAN JOHN (born 1923), British-American physicist **5** 171-173

DZERZHINSKY, FELIX EDMUNDOVICH (1877-1926), Soviet politician and revolutionary **5** 173-174

Dzhugashvili, Iosif Vissarionovich
see Stalin, Joseph

E

EADS, JAMES BUCHANAN (1820-1887), American engineer and inventor **5** 175-176

EAKINS, THOMAS (1844-1916), American painter **5** 176-177

EARHART, AMELIA MARY (1897-1937), American aviator **5** 177-179

EARL, RALPH (1751-1801), American painter **5** 179

EARLE, SYLVIA A. (Born Sylvia Alice Reade; born 1935), American marine biologist and oceanographer **5** 180-181

EARNHARDT, DALE (1951-2001), American race car driver **22** 156-158

EARP, WYATT BARRY STEPP (1848-1929), gun-fighting marshal of the American West **5** 181-182

Earthquake (seismology)
Milne, John **28** 245-247

EAST, EDWARD MURRAY (1879-1938), American plant geneticist **5** 182-183

Eastern Catholic Church
see Orthodox Eastern Church

Eastern Orthodox Church
see Orthodox Eastern Church

Eastern Roman Empire
see Byzantine Empire (395-1453;
Eastern Roman Empire 395-474)

EASTMAN, CHARLES A. (1858-1939),
Native American author **5** 183-185

EASTMAN, GEORGE (1854-1932),
American inventor and industrialist **5** 186

EASTMAN, MAX (Max Forrester Eastman;
1883-1969), American poet, radical
editor, translator, and author **5**
187-188

EASTWOOD, ALICE (1859-1953),
American botanist **22** 158-160

EASTWOOD, CLINT (born 1930),
American movie star and director **5**
188-190

EATON, DORMAN BRIDGMAN (1823-
1899), American lawyer and author **5**
190-191

EBADI, SHIRIN (born 1947), Iranian
author and human rights activist **25**
124-126

EBAN, ABBA (Abba Solomon Eban;
1915-2002), Israeli statesman,
diplomat, and scholar **5** 191-192

EBB, FRED (1935-2004), American
lyricist **21** 113-115

EBBERS, BERNIE (born 1941), American
businessman **20** 122-124

EBBINGHAUS, HERMANN (1850-1909),
German psychologist **5** 192-193

EBERT, FRIEDRICH (1871-1925),
German president 1919-1925 **5**
193-194

EBOUÉ, ADOLPHE FELIX SYLVESTRE
(1885-1944), African statesman,
governor of French Equatorial Africa **5**
194

ECCLES, MARRINER STODDARD (1890-
1977), American banker **22** 160-162

ECCLES, SIR JOHN CAREW (1903-1997),
Australian neurophysiologist **5** 195-196

ECEVIT, BÜLENT (1925-2006), Turkish
statesman and prime minister **5**
196-197

Echaurren, Roberto Matta
see Matta Echaurren, Roberto
Sebastian Antonio

ECHEVERRÍA, JOSÉ ESTÉBAN (1805-
1851), Argentine author and political
theorist **5** 197-198

ECHEVERRIA ALVAREZ, LUIS (born
1922), president of Mexico (1970-
1976) **5** 198-200

ECK, JOHANN MAIER VON (1486-
1543), German theologian **5** 200

ECKERT, JOHN PRESPER (1919-1995),
American computer engineer **20**
124-126

ECKHART, (JOHANN) MEISTER (circa
1260-circa 1327), German Dominican
theologian **5** 200-201

ECO, UMBERTO (born 1932), Italian
scholar and novelist **18** 128-130

Empire State Building (New York City)
Hine, Lewis Wickes **28** 172-174

Economics (social science)
microlending
Yunus, Muhammad **28** 386-388

EDDINGTON, SIR ARTHUR STANLEY
(1882-1944), English astronomer **5**
201-202

EDDY, MARY BAKER (1821-1910),
American founder of the Christian
Science Church **5** 202

EDELMAN, GERALD MAURICE (born
1929), American neuroscientist **27**
106-108

EDELMAN, MARIAN WRIGHT (born
1939), lobbyist, lawyer, civil rights
activist, and founder of the Children's
Defense Fund **5** 202-204

EDEN, ANTHONY (1897-1977), English
statesman, prime minister 1955-1957 **5**
204-205

EDERLE, GERTRUDE (born 1906),
American swimmer **19** 98-100

EDGERTON, HAROLD EUGENE (1903-
1990), American inventor **28** 109-111

EDGEWORTH, MARIA (1767-1849),
British author **5** 205-206

EDINGER, TILLY (Johanna Gabriella
Ottelie Edinger; 1897-1967), American
paleontologist **22** 163-164

EDISON, THOMAS ALVA (1847-1931),
American inventor **5** 206-208

EDMISTON, ALTHEA MARIA (Althea
Maria Brown; 1874-1937), African
American missionary **27** 108-111

Education (Europe)
England
Chapone, Hester **28** 72-74

Education (United States)
medical
Agnew, David Hayes **28** 3-5
music
Roach, Max **28** 292-296

EDWARD I (1239-1307), king of England
1272-1307 **5** 208-210

EDWARD II (Edward of Carnarvon;
1284-1327), king of England 1307-27
5 210

EDWARD III (1312-1377), king of
England 1327-77 **5** 211-212

Edward IV (1330-1376)
see Edward the Black Prince

EDWARD IV (1442-1483), king of
England 1461-70 **5** 212-213
relatives
Woodville, Elizabeth **28** 381-383

Edward V, (1471-1483), king of England
1483
Woodville, Elizabeth **28** 381-383

EDWARD VI (1537-1553), king of
England and Ireland 1547-53 **5**
213-214

EDWARD VII (1841-1910), king of Great
Britian and Ireland 1901-10 **5** 214-215

EDWARD VIII (1894-1972), King of
England (1936) and Duke of Windsor
after abdicating his throne **5** 215-217

Edward of Carnarvon
see Edward II

EDWARD THE BLACK PRINCE (1330-
1376), English soldier-statesman **5**
217-218

EDWARD THE CONFESSOR (reigned
1042-1066, died 1066), last king of
the house of Wessex **5** 218-219

EDWARD THE ELDER (died 924), king of
England 899-924 **5** 219-220

Edwards, Eli
see McKay, Claude

EDWARDS, JONATHAN (1703-1758),
American Puritan theologian **5**
220-222

EDWARDS, MELVIN (born 1937),
African-American sculptor **5** 222-223

EDWARDS, SIAN (born 1959), British
conductor **26** 96-98

EGGLESTON, EDWARD (1837-1902),
American Methodist minister and
historian **5** 223-224

EHRENBURG, ILYA GRIGORIEVICH
(1891-1967), Russian author **5**
224-225

EHRLICH, PAUL (1854-1915), German
bacteriologist **5** 225-226

EICHMANN, ADOLF (1906-1962),
German Nazi war criminal **5** 226-227

EIFFEL, ALEXANDRE GUSTAVE (1832-
1923), French engineer **5** 227-228
Bartholdi, Frédéric-Auguste **28** 29-31

EIJKMAN, CHRISTIAN (1858-1930),
Dutch physician and biologist **5** 228

EINHORN, DAVID RUBIN (1809-1879), German theolgian **22** 164-166

EINSTEIN, ALBERT (1879-1955), German-born American physicist **5** 228-231

EISAI (1141-1215), Japanese Buddhist monk **5** 231-232

EISELEY, LOREN COREY (1907-1977), American interpreter of science for the layman **5** 232-233

EISENHOWER, DWIGHT DAVID (1890-1969), American general and statesman, president 1953-61 **5** 233-236

EISENHOWER, MAMIE DOUD (1896-1979), American First Lady **5** 236-237

EISENHOWER, MILTON (Milton Stover Esisenhower; 1899-1985), American adviser to U.S. presidents and college president **5** 237-238

EISENMAN, PETER D. (born 1932), American architect **5** 239-240

EISENSTAEDT, ALFRED (1898-1995), American photographer and photojournalist **19** 100-102

EISENSTEIN, SERGEI MIKHAILOVICH (1898-1948), Russian film director and cinema theoretician **5** 240-242

EISNER, MICHAEL (born 1942), American businessman **19** 102-104

EITOKU, KANO (1543-1590), Japanese painter of the Momoyama period **5** 242

EKWENSI, CYPRIAN (1921-2007), Nigerian writer **5** 242-243

ELBARADEI, MOHAMED (born 1942), Egyptian diplomat **26** 98-100

Elchingen, Duke of
see Ney, Michel

ELDERS, JOYCELYN (born 1933), first African American and second woman U.S. surgeon general **5** 243-246

ELEANOR OF AQUITAINE (circa 1122-1204), queen of France 1137-52, and of England 1154-1204 **5** 246-247

Electronics
Cooper, Martin **28** 85-87

ELGAR, SIR EDWARD (1857-1934), English composer **5** 247-248

ELGIN, 8TH EARL OF (James Bruce; 1811-63), English governor general of Canada **5** 248-249

El-Hajj Malik El-Shabazz
see Malcolm X (film)

Elia
see Lamb, Charles

ELIADE, MIRCEA (1907-1986), Rumanian-born historian of religions and novelist **5** 249-250

ELIAS, TASLIM OLAWALE (1914-1991), Nigerian academic and jurist and president of the International Court of Justice **5** 250-251

Eliezer, Israel ben
see Baal Shem Tov

ELIJAH BEN SOLOMON (1720-1797), Jewish scholar **5** 251-252

ELION, GERTRUDE B. (1918-1999), American biochemist and Nobel Prize winner **5** 252-254

ELIOT, CHARLES WILLIAM (1834-1926), American educator **5** 254

ELIOT, GEORGE (pen name of Mary Ann Evans; 1819-80), English novelist **5** 254-256

ELIOT, JOHN (1604-1690), English-born missionary to the Massachusetts Indians **5** 256-258

ELIOT, THOMAS STEARNS (1888-1965), American-English poet, critic, and playwright **5** 258-261

ELISABETH, EMPRESS OF AUSTRIA (1837-1898), German empress of Austria **28** 111-113

ELIZABETH (Elizabeth Petrovna; 1709-61), empress of Russia 1741-61 **5** 261-263

ELIZABETH I (1533-1603), queen of England and Ireland 1558-1603 **5** 263-266
relatives
Woodville, Elizabeth **28** 381-383

ELIZABETH II (born 1926), queen of Great Britain and Ireland **5** 266-269

ELIZABETH BAGAAYA NYABONGO OF TORO (born 1940), Ugandan ambassador **5** 269-271

ELIZABETH BOWES-LYON (Elizabeth Angela Marguerite Bowes-Lyon; 1900-2002), queen of Great Britain and Ireland (1936-1952) and Queen Mother after 1952 **5** 261-263

ELIZABETH OF HUNGARY (1207-1231), saint and humanitarian **5** 271-272

Elizabethan literature
see English literature—Elizabethan

ELLINGTON, "DUKE" EDWARD KENNEDY (born 1899), American jazz composer **5** 273-274
Anderson, Ivie Marie **28** 10-12

ELLIS, HAVELOCK (Henry Havelock Ellis; 1959-1939), British psychologist and author **20** 126-128

ELLISON, RALPH WALDO (1914-1994), African American author and spokesperson for racial identity **5** 274-275

ELLSBERG, DANIEL (born 1931), U.S. government official and Vietnam peace activist **5** 275-277

ELLSWORTH, LINCOLN (1880-1951), American adventurer and polar explorer **5** 277

ELLSWORTH, OLIVER (1745-1807), American senator and Supreme Court Chief Justice **21** 115-117

ELSASSER, WALTER MAURICE (1904-1991), American physicist **5** 277-278

ELWAY, JOHN (born 1960), American football player **23** 98-100

ELY, RICHARD (1854-1943), American economist and social reformer **21** 117-120

EMERSON, RALPH WALDO (1803-1882), American poet, essayist, and philosopher **5** 278-280

EMINESCU, MIHAIL (1850-1889), Romanian poet **5** 280-281

EMMET, ROBERT (1778-1803), Irish nationalist and revolutionary **5** 281-282

EMPEDOCLES (circa 493-circa 444 B.C.), Greek philosopher, poet, and scientist **5** 282

ENCHI, FUMIKO UEDA (1905-1986), Japanese author **23** 100-102

ENCINA, JUAN DEL (1468-1529?), Spanish author and composer **5** 283

ENDARA, GUILLERMO (born 1936), installed as president of Panama by the U.S. Government in 1989 **5** 283-284

ENDECOTT, JOHN (1588-1655), English colonial governor of Massachusetts **5** 284-285

ENDERS, JOHN FRANKLIN (1897-1985), American virologist **5** 285-286

ENGELS, FRIEDRICH (1820-1895), German revolutionist and social theorist **5** 286-288

Engineering
computer
Hoff, Ted **28** 176-178
electrical
Gross, Al **28** 149-151

ENGLAND, JOHN (1786-1842), Irish Catholic bishop in America **5** 288

English art and architecture
abstract
Lewis, Wyndham **28** 217-219

English literature
children's literature
Grahame, Kenneth **28** 138-140
comedy
Centlivre, Susanna **28** 65-67
diaries and journals
Fiennes, Celia **28** 118-121
gothic
Radcliffe, Ann **28** 288-290
homemaking guides
Beeton, Isabella Mary **28** 34-36
literary criticism
Amis, Kingsley **28** 5-8
modern (novel)
Amis, Kingsley **28** 5-8
Baroness Orczy **28** 25-27
spy novels
Fleming, Ian **28** 123-125
travel
Fiennes, Celia **28** 118-121
Vorticist
Lewis, Wyndham **28** 217-219

English music
classical
Coleridge-Taylor, Samuel **28** 80-83

ENNIN (794-864), Japanese Buddhist
monk **5** 288-289

ENNIUS, QUINTUS (239-169 B.C.),
Roman poet **5** 289

ENRICO, ROGER (born 1944), American
businessman **27** 111-112

ENSOR, JAMES (1860-1949), Belgian
painter and graphic artist **5** 289-290

Environmental activists (European)
Roddick, Anita **28** 298-301

Environmental activists (United States)
Leopold, Aldo **28** 211-213

EPAMINONDAS (c. 425-362 B.C.),
Theban general and statesman **5**
291-292

EPÉE, CHARLES-MICHEL DE L' (1712-
1789), French sign language developer
21 120-122

EPHRON, NORA (born 1941), American
author, screenwriter and film director
18 130-132

EPICTETUS (circa 50-circa 135), Greek
philosopher **5** 292

EPICURUS (circa 342-270 B.C.), Greek
philosopher, founder of Epicureanism
5 292-294

Epimanes
see Antiochus IV (king of Syria)

EPSTEIN, ABRAHAM (1892-1945),
Russian-born American economist **5**
294-295

EPSTEIN, SIR JACOB (1880-1959),
American-born English sculptor **5**
295-296

EQUIANO, OLAUDAH (1745-circa
1801), African author and former slave
5 296-297

ERASISTRATUS (c. 304 B.C.-c. 250 B.C.),
Greek physician and anantomist **5**
297-298

ERASMUS, DESIDERIUS (1466-1536),
Dutch author, scholar, and humanist **5**
298-300

ERASMUS, GEORGES HENRY (born
1948), Canadian Indian leader **5**
300-301

ERATOSTHENES OF CYRENE (circa 284-
circa 205 B.C.), Greek mathematician,
geographer, and astronomer **5** 301-302

ERCILLA Y ZÚÑIGA, ALONSO DE
(1533-1594), Spanish poet, soldier,
and diplomat **5** 302

ERDOS, PAUL (1913-1996), Hungarian
mathematician **22** 166-168

ERDRICH, LOUISE (Karen Louise
Erdrich; born 1954), Native American
author **23** 102-105

ERHARD, LUDWIG (1897-1977),
German statesman, West German
chancellor 1963-66 **5** 302-304

ERIC THE RED (Eric Thorvaldsson;
flourished late 10th century),
Norwegian explorer **5** 304

ERICKSON, ARTHUR CHARLES (born
1924), Canadian architect and
landscape architect **5** 304-306

ERICSON, LEIF (971-circa 1015), Norse
mariner and adventurer **5** 306-307

ERICSSON, JOHN (1803-1889),
Swedish-born American engineer and
inventor **5** 307-308

ERIGENA, JOHN SCOTUS (circa 810-
circa 877), Irish scholastic philosopher
5 308-309

ERIKSON, ERIK HOMBURGER (1902-
1994), German-born American
psychoanalyst and educator **5** 309-310

ERLANGER, JOSEPH (1874-1965),
American physiologist **5** 310-311

ERNST, MAX (born 1891), German
painter **5** 311-312

ERNST, RICHARD (Richard Robert Ernst;
born 1933), Swiss Chemist **27** 112-114

ERSHAD, HUSSAIN MOHAMMAD (born
1930), Bengali military leader and
president of Bangladesh (1982-1990) **5**
312-314

ERSKINE, THOMAS (1750-1823), British
lawyer **22** 168-170

ERTÉ (Romain de Tirtoff; 1892-1990),
Russian fashion illustrator and stage set
designer **5** 314-316

ERVIN, SAM J., JR. (1896-1985), lawyer,
judge, U.S. senator, and chairman of
the Senate Watergate Committee **5**
316-317

ERVING, JULIUS WINFIELD (a.k.a. Dr.
J.; born 1950), African American
basketball player **5** 317-319

ERZBERGER, MATTHIAS (1875-1921),
German statesman **5** 319-320

ESAKI, LEO (Reiona Esaki; born 1925),
Japanese physicist **24** 127-130

ESCALANTE, JAIME (born 1930),
Hispanic American educator **5**
320-321

ESCHER, MAURITS CORNELIS (M.C.
Escher; 1898-1972), Dutch graphic
artist **18** 132-134

ESCOFFIER, AUGUSTE (Georges Auguste
Escoffier; 1846-1935), French chef **21**
122-124

ESENIN, SERGEI ALEKSANDROVICH
(1895-1925), Russian poet **5** 321

Essay on Health and a Long Life, An
(book)
Cheyne, George **28** 74-76

Essex, Earl of (circa 1485-1540)
see Cromwell, Thomas

ESSEX, 2D EARL OF (Robert Devereux;
1567-1601), English courtier **5**
321-322

Estabanico
see Estevan

Estenssoro, Victor Paz
see Paz Estenssoro, Victor

ESTES, RICHARD (born 1932), American
realist painter **5** 322-323

ESTEVAN (a.k.a. Estabanico, Estevanico
the Black; c. 1500-1539), Moroccan
explorer **5** 324-325

ESTHER (Hadasseh; 522-c. 460 B.C.),
queen of Persia **25** 126-128

ESTRADA CABRERA, MANUEL (1857-
1924), Guatemalan president 1898-
1920 **5** 325-326

ESTRADA PALMA, TOMÁS (1835-1908),
Cuban president 1902-1906 **5** 326-327

ETHELRED THE UNREADY (968?-1016),
Anglo-Saxon king of England 978-1016
5 327

EUCKEN, RUDOLF (Rudolf Christof
Eucken; 1846-1926), German
philosopher **25** 128-130

EUCLID (flourished 300 B.C.), Greek
mathematician **5** 327-329

EUDOXUS OF CNIDUS (circa 408-circa 355 B.C.), Greek astronomer, mathematician, and physician **5** 329-330

EUGENE OF SAVOY (1663-1736), French-born Austrian general and diplomat **5** 330-331

EULER, LEONARD (1707-1783), Swiss mathematician **5** 331-332

EURIPIDES (480-406 B.C.), Greek playwright **5** 332-334

EUTROPIUS (fl. 4th century), Roman historian and official **20** 128-130

EUTYCHES (circa 380-455), Byzantine monk **5** 335

Evangelism (religion)
    revivalism
        Roberts, Oral **28** 296-298
    televangelism
        Roberts, Oral **28** 296-298

EVANS, ALICE (1881-1975), American bacteriologist **19** 104-106

EVANS, SIR ARTHUR JOHN (1851-1941), English archeologist **5** 335-336

EVANS, EDITH (1888-1976), English actress who portrayed comic characters **5** 336-337

EVANS, GEORGE HENRY (1805-1856), American labor and agrarian reformer **5** 337-338

Evans, Mary Ann
    see Eliot, George

EVANS, OLIVER (1755-1819), American inventor **5** 338

EVANS, WALKER (1903-1975), American photographer of American life between the world wars **5** 339

EVANS-PRITCHARD, SIR EDWARD EVAN (1902-1973), English social anthropologist **5** 340

EVARTS, WILLIAM MAXWELL (1818-1901), American lawyer and statesman **5** 340-341

EVATT, HERBERT VERE (1894-1965), Australian statesman and jurist **5** 341-343

EVELYN, JOHN (1620-1706), English author **5** 343-344

EVERETT, EDWARD (1794-1865), American statesman and orator **5** 344

EVERGOOD, PHILIP (1901-1973), American painter **5** 345

EVERS, MEDGAR (1925-1963), African American civil rights leader **5** 345-348

EVERS-WILLIAMS, MYRLIE (born Myrlie Louise Beasley; born 1933), civil rights leader, lecturer, and writer **5** 348-350

EWING, WILLIAM MAURICE (1906-1974), American oceanographer **5** 350-351

EWONWU, BENEDICT CHUKA (born 1921), Nigerian sculptor and painter **5** 351-352

Explorers, American
    of American West
        Du Sable, Jean Baptiste Pointe **28** 104-106

Explorers, French
    of Asia
        David-Néel, Alexandra **28** 90-92

Explorers, Portuguese
    of the Far East
        Serrão, Francisco **28** 320-321

EYCK, HUBERT VAN (died 1426), Flemish painter **5** 352-354

EYCK, JAN VAN (circa 1390-1441), Flemish painter **5** 352-354

EYRE, EDWARD JOHN (1815-1901), English explorer of Australia **5** 354

EZANA (flourished 4th century), Ethiopian king **5** 354-355

EZEKIEL (flourished 6th century B.C.), Hebrew priest and prophet **5** 355-356

EZRA (flourished 5th century B.C.), Hebrew priest, scribe, and reformer **5** 356-357

F

FABERGÉ, CARL (Peter Carl Fabergé; Karl Gustavovich Fabergé; 1846-1920), Russian jeweler and goldsmith **21** 125-127

FABIUS, LAURENT (born 1946), prime minister of France in the 1980s **5** 358-359

FACKENHEIM, EMIL LUDWIG (born 1916), liberal post-World War II Jewish theologian **5** 359-361

Facundo, Juan
    see Quiroga, Juan Facundo

Fado (music style; Portugal)
    Rodrigues, Amália **28** 301-302

FADIL AL-JAMALI, MUHAMMAD (born 1903), Iraqi educator, writer, diplomat, and politician **5** 361-362

FADLALLAH, SAYYID MUHAMMAD HUSAYN (born 1935), Shi'i Muslim cleric and Lebanese political leader **5** 362-364

FAHD IBN ABDUL AZIZ AL-SAUD (1920-2005), son of the founder of modern Saudi Arabia and king **5** 364-366

FAHRENHEIT, GABRIEL DANIEL (1686-1736), German physicist **5** 366

FAIDHERBE, LOUIS LÉON CÉSAR (1818-1889), French colonial governor **5** 366-367

Fair, A. A.
    see Gardner, Erle Stanley

FAIR, JAMES RUTHERFORD, JR. (born 1920), American chemical engineer and educator **20** 131-131

FAIRBANKS, DOUGLAS (Douglas Elton Ulman; 1883-1939), American actor and producer **19** 107-108

FAIRCLOUGH, ELLEN LOUKS (1905-2004), Canadian Cabinet minister **5** 367-368

FAIRUZ (née Nuhad Haddad; born 1933), Arabic singer **5** 368-369

FAISAL I (1883-1933), king of Iraq 1921-33 **5** 370-371

FAISAL II (1935-1958), king of Iraq, 1953-1958 **20** 132-132

FAISAL IBN ABD AL AZIZ IBN SAUD (1904-1975), Saudi Arabian king and prominent Arab leader **5** 371-372

FALCONET, ÉTIENNE MAURICE (1716-1791), French sculptor **5** 372

FALLA, MANUEL DE (1876-1946), Spanish composer **5** 372-373

FALLACI, ORIANA (1929-2006), Italian journalist **27** 115-117

FALLETTA, JOANN (born 1954), American conductor **5** 373-375

FALWELL, JERRY (1933-2007), fundamentalist religious leader who also promoted right-wing political causes **5** 375-376

FAN CHUNG-YEN (989-1052), Chinese statesman **5** 376-377

FANEUIL, PETER (1700-1743), American colonial merchant and philanthropist **5** 377

FANFANI, AMINTORE (1908-1999), Italian prime minister **5** 378-379

FANON, FRANTZ (1925-1961), Algerian political theorist and psychiatrist **5** 379-380

Fantasy (literary genre)
    Norton, Andre **28** 257-259

FARABI, AL- (Abou Nasr Mohammed ibn Tarkaw; 870-950), Turkish scholar and philosopher **22** 14-16

FARADAY, MICHAEL (1791-1867), English physicist and chemist **5** 380

FARAH, NURUDDIN (born 1945), Somali author **28** 114-116

FARGO, WILLIAM GEORGE (1818-1881), American businessman **5** 380-381

FARINA, MIMI (Margarita Mimi Baez Farina; 1945-2001), American singer and activist **27** 117-119

FARLEY, JAMES A. (1888-1976), Democratic Party organizer and political strategist **5** 381-383

FARMER, FANNIE MERRITT (1857-1915), American authority on cookery **5** 383

FARMER, JAMES (1920-1999), American civil rights activist who helped organize the 1960s "freedom rides" **5** 383-385

FARMER, MOSES GERRISH (1820-1893), American inventor and manufacturer **5** 385

Farnese, Alessandro (1468-1549)
see Paul III

FARNESE, ALESSANDRO (Duke of Parma; 1545-1592), Italian general and diplomat **20** 132-135

FARNSWORTH, PHILO T. (1906-1971), American inventor of the television **5** 386-387

FAROUK I (1920-1965), king of Egypt 1937-1952 **5** 387-388

FARRAGUT, DAVID GLASGOW (1801-1870), American naval officer **5** 388-389

FARRAKHAN, LOUIS (Louis Eugene Walcott, born 1933), a leader of one branch of the Nation of Islam popularly known as Black Muslims and militant spokesman for Black Nationalism **5** 389-390

FARRAR, GERALDINE (1882-1967), American opera singer **23** 106-108

FARRELL, EILEEN (1920-2002), American singer **27** 119-121

FARRELL, JAMES THOMAS (1904-1979), American novelist and social and literary critic **5** 390-391

FARRELL, SUZANNE (née Roberta Sue Ficker; born 1945), American classical ballerina **5** 391-393

FARRENC, LOUISE (Jeanne Louise Dumont; 1804-1875), French pianist **27** 121-122

FASSBINDER, RAINER WERNER (1946-1982), German filmmaker **26** 101-103

"Father of. . ."
see Nicknames

Fatih
see Mehmed the Conqueror

FAUCHARD, PIERRE (1678-1761), French dentist **26** 103-105

FAULKNER, BRIAN (1921-1977), prime minister of Northern Ireland (1971-1972) **5** 393-395

FAULKNER, WILLIAM (1897-1962), American novelist **5** 395-397

FAURÉ, GABRIEL URBAIN (1845-1924), French composer **5** 397-398

FAUSET, JESSIE REDMON (1882-1961), African American writer and editor **20** 135-138

FAUST, DREW GILPIN (Catherine Drew Gilpin; born 1947), American historian and university president **28** 116-118

FAVALORO, RENE GERONIMO (1923-2000), Argentine physician **24** 131-133

FAWCETT, MILLICENT GARRETT (1847-1929), British feminist **5** 398-400

FAWKES, GUY (Guido Fawkes; 1570-1606), English soldier and conspirator **27** 123-125

FAYE, SAFI (born 1943), Senegalese filmmaker and ethnologist **5** 400-401

FECHNER, GUSTAV THEODOR (1801-1887), German experimental psychologist **5** 401-402

FEE, JOHN GREGG (1816-1901), American abolitionist and clergyman **5** 402-403

FEIFFER, JULES RALPH (born 1929), American satirical cartoonist and playwright and novelist **5** 403-404

FEIGENBAUM, MITCHELL JAY (born 1944), American physicist **5** 404-405

FEIGL, HERBERT (born 1902), American philosopher **18** 135-137

FEIJÓ, DIOGO ANTÔNIO (1784-1843), Brazilian priest and statesman **5** 405-406

FEININGER, LYONEL (1871-1956), American painter **5** 406-407

FEINSTEIN, DIANNE (Goldman; born 1933), politician, public official, and San Francisco's first female mayor **5** 407-408

FELA (Fela Anikulapo Kuti; 1938-1997), Nigerian musician and activist **21** 127-129

FELICIANO, JOSÉ (born 1945), Hispanic American singer and guitarist **19** 109-110

Feliks
see Litvinov, Maxim Maximovich

FELLER, BOB (Robert William Andrew Feller; born 1918), American baseball player **21** 129-131

FELLINI, FEDERICO (1920-1993), Italian film director **5** 408-409

FELTRE, VITTORINO DA (1378-1446), Italian humanist and teacher **5** 409-410

Feminist movement
see Women's rights

Feminists
Finnish
Canth, Minna **28** 58-60
German
Andreas-Salomé, Lou **28** 12-14
Iraqi
Mala'ika, Nazik al- **28** 230-232
Norwegian
Skram, Amalie **28** 331-333
Vietnamese
Ho, Xuan Huong **28** 174-176

FÉNELON, FRANÇOIS DE SALIGNAC DE LA MOTHE (1651-1715), French archbishop and theologian **5** 410-411

FENG KUEI-FEN (1809-1874), Chinese scholar and official **5** 411-412

FENG YÜ-HSIANG (1882-1948), Chinese warlord **5** 412-413

Feodorovich, Pëtr
see Peter III, (Peter Feodorovich; 1728-62)

FERBER, EDNA (1887-1968), American author **5** 413

FERDINAND (1865-1927), king of Romania 1914-1927 **5** 413-414

FERDINAND I (1503-1564), Holy Roman emperor 1555-1564, king of Hungary and Bohemia 1526-64 and of Germany 1531-1564 **5** 414-415

Ferdinand II (king of Aragon)
see Ferdinand V (king of Castile)

FERDINAND II (1578-1637), Holy Roman emperor 1619-1637, king of Bohemia 1617-1637 and of Hungary 1618-1637 **5** 415

FERDINAND II (1810-1859), king of the Two Sicilies 1830-1859 **5** 415-416

Ferdinand III (king of Naples)
see Ferdinand V (king of Castile)

FERDINAND III (1608-1657), Holy Roman emperor 1637-1657, king of Hungary 1626-1657 and of Bohemia 1627-1657 **5** 416-417

Ferdinand V (king of Spain)
see Ferdinand V (king of Castile)

FERDINAND V (1452-1516), king of Castile 1474-1504, of Sicily 1468-1516, and of Aragon 1479-1516 **5** 417-418

FERDINAND VII (1784-1833), king of Spain 1808 and 1814-1833 **5** 418-420

Ferdinand von Hohenzollern-Sigmaringen
see Ferdinand (king of Romania)

FERGUSON, ADAM (1723-1816), Scottish philosopher, moralist, and historian **5** 420-421

FERGUSON, HOWARD (1908-1999), Irish musician and composer **18** 137-138

FERLINGHETTI, LAWRENCE (Lawrence Monsato Ferling; born 1919), American poet, publisher and bookstore owner **27** 125-127

FERMAT, PIERRE DE (1601-1665), French mathematician **5** 421-422

FERMI, ENRICO (1901-1954), Italian-American physicist **5** 422-424

Fermoselle
see Encina, Juan del

FERNÁNDEZ DE LIZARDI, JOSÉ JOAQUIN (1776-1827), Mexican journalist and novelist **5** 424-425

Fernández, José Manuel Balmaceda
see Balmaceda Fernández, José Manuel

Fernando
see Ferdinand

FERNEL, JEAN FRANÇOIS (circa 1497-1558), French physician **5** 425-426

Ferrante
see Ferdinand

FERRARO, GERALDINE (born 1935), first woman candidate for the vice presidency of a major U.S. political party **5** 426-428

FERRER, GABRIEL MIRÓ (1879-1930), Spanish author **5** 428

FERRER, IBRAHIM (1927-2005), Cuban musician **26** 105-107

FERRER, JOSÉ FIGUÉRES (born 1906), Costa Rican politician **5** 428-429

FERRERO, GUGLIELMO (1871-1942), Italian journalist and historian **5** 429-430

FERRY, JULES FRANÇOIS CAMILLE (1832-1893), French statesman **5** 430

FEUCHTWANGER, LION (1884-1958), post-World War I German literary figure **5** 430-432

FEUERBACH, LUDWIG ANDREAS (1804-1872), German philosopher **5** 432

FEYNMAN, RICHARD PHILLIPS (1918-1988), American physicist **5** 432-434

FIBIGER, JOHANNES (Johannes Andreas Grib Fibiger; 1867-1928), Danish bacteriologist and pathologist **21** 131-133

FIBONACCI, LEONARDO (circa 1180-circa 1250), Italian mathematician **5** 434-435

FICHTE, JOHANN GOTTLIEB (1762-1814), German philosopher **5** 435-436

FICINO, MARSILIO (1433-1499), Italian philosopher and humanist **5** 436-437

FIEDLER, ARTHUR (1894-1979), American conductor of the Boston Pops **5** 437-438

FIELD, CYRUS WEST (1819-1892), American merchant **5** 438-439

FIELD, DAVID DUDLEY (1805-1894), American jurist **5** 439-440

FIELD, MARSHALL (1834-1906), American merchant **5** 440-441

FIELD, SALLY (Field, Sally Margaret; born 1946), American actress and director **24** 133-135

FIELD, STEPHEN JOHNSON (1816-1899), American jurist **5** 441-442

FIELDING, HENRY (1707-1754), English novelist **5** 442-444

FIELDS, DOROTHY (1905-1974), American lyricist **26** 107-109

FIELDS, W. C. (stage name of William Claude Dukenfield; 1879-1946), American comedian **5** 444

FIENNES, CELIA (Cecelia Fiennes; 1662-1741), British travel writer and diarist **28** 118-121

Fieschi, Sinibaldo de'
see Innocent IV

FIGUEIREDO, JOÃO BATISTA DE OLIVEIRA (born 1918), Brazilian army general and president (1979-1985) **5** 445-446

Figuéres Ferrer, José
see Ferrer, José Figuéres

FILLMORE, MILLARD (1800-1874), American statesman, president 1850-1853 **5** 447-448

FILMER, SIR ROBERT (died 1653), English political theorist **5** 448

FINCH, ANNE (Anne Kingsmill Finch; 1661-1720), English poet **27** 127-129

FINK, ALBERT (1827-1897), American railroad engineer and economist **21** 133-135

FINKELSTEIN, RABBI LOUIS (born 1895), American scholar and leader of Conservative Judaism **5** 448-450

FINLAY, CARLOS JUAN (1833-1915), Cuban biologist and physician **5** 450

FINNEY, CHARLES GRANDISON (1792-1875), American theologian and educator **5** 450-451

Finnish art
Wirkkala, Tapio **28** 372-374

Finnish literature
Canth, Minna **28** 58-60
Jansson, Tove Marika **28** 187-189

FIORINA, CARLY (Cara Carleton Sneed; born 1954), American businesswoman **25** 131-133

FIRDAUSI (934-1020), Persian poet **5** 451-452

Fire!! (literary journal)
Thurman, Wallace Henry **28** 352-354

FIRESTONE, HARVEY SAMUEL (1868-1938), American industrialist **5** 452-453

FIRESTONE, SHULAMITH (born 1945), Canadian feminist **27** 129-131

FIRST, RUTH (1925-1982), South African socialist, anti-apartheid activist, and scholar **5** 453-454

First Ladies
Harding, Florence Kling **28** 159-161
Hayes, Lucy Webb **28** 163-166
Taft, Helen Herron **28** 343-345

First Triumvirate
see Roman Republic

FISCHER, BOBBY (1943-2008), American chess player **5** 454-456

FISCHER, EMIL (1852-1919), German organic chemist **5** 456-457

FISCHER, HANS (1881-1945), German organic chemist **5** 457-459

FISCHER VON ERLACH, JOHANN BERNHARD (1656-1723), Austrian architect **5** 459-461

FISH, HAMILTON (1808-1893), American statesman **5** 461-462

FISHER, ANDREW (1862-1928), Australian statesman and labor leader **5** 462

FISHER, IRVING (1867-1947), American economist **5** 462-463

FISHER, JOHN ARBUTHNOT (Baron Fisher of Kilverstone; 1841-1920), British admiral **22** 171-173

FISHER, SIR RONALD AYLMER (1890-1962), English statistician **5** 463-464

FISHER, RUDOLPH (Rudolph John Chauncey Fisher; 1897-1934), African American author **28** 121-123

FISK, JAMES (1834-1872), American financial speculator **5** 464-465

Fiske, Helen Marie
see Jackson, Helen Hunt

FISKE, JOHN (1842-1901), American philosopher and historian **5** 465-466

FISKE, MINNIE MADDERN (Mary Augusta Davey; 1865-1932), American "realistic" actress who portrayed Ibsen heroines **5** 466-467

FITCH, JOHN (1743-1798), American mechanic and inventor **5** 467-468

FITCH, VAL LOGSDON (born 1923), American physicist **24** 135-138

Fitz-Boodle, George Savage (pseudonym) *see* Thackeray, William Makepeace

FITZGERALD, ELLA (1918-1996), American jazz singer **5** 468-469

FITZGERALD, FRANCES (born 1940), American author **5** 469-470

FITZGERALD, FRANCIS SCOTT KEY (1896-1940), American author **5** 470-472

FITZGERALD, GARRET (born 1926), Irish prime minister (1981-1987) **5** 472-474

FITZHUGH, GEORGE (1806-1881), American polemicist and sociologist **5** 474

FITZPATRICK, THOMAS (1799-1854), American trapper, guide, and Indian agent **5** 474-475

FIZEAU, HIPPOLYTE ARMAND LOUIS (1819-1896), French physicist **5** 475

FLAGLER, HENRY (1830-1913), American industrialist **21** 135-137

FLAGSTAD, KIRSTEN MALFRID (1895-1962), Norwegian opera singer **25** 133-135

FLAHERTY, ROBERT (1884-1951), American documentary filmmaker **5** 476-477

FLAMININUS, TITUS QUINCTIUS (circa 228-174 B.C.), Roman general and diplomat **5** 477

FLAMSTEED, JOHN (1646-1719), English astronomer **5** 477-478

FLANAGAN, HALLIE (1890-1969), American director, playwright, and educator **5** 478-479

FLANNAGAN, JOHN BERNARD (1895-1942), American sculptor **5** 480

FLAUBERT, GUSTAVE (1821-1880), French novelist **5** 480-482

Flavius Claudius Julianus
see Julian the Apostate

FLEISCHER, MAX (1883-1972), American animator, cartoonist, and inventor **22** 173-175

FLEISCHMANN, GISI (1894-1944), Czechoslovakian leader who rescued many Jews from the Nazi Holocaust **5** 482-483

FLEMING, IAN (Ian Lancaster Fleming; 1908-1964), British author **28** 123-125

FLEMING, PEGGY GALE (born 1948), American figure skater and sportscaster **24** 138-140

FLEMING, SIR ALEXANDER (1881-1955), Scottish bacteriologist **5** 485-486

FLEMING, SIR JOHN AMBROSE (1849-1945), British engineer and scientist **25** 135-138

FLEMING, SIR SANDFORD (1827-1915), Scottish-born Canadian railway engineer **5** 485-486

FLEMING, WILLIAMINA (1857-1911), American astronomer **22** 175-176

FLETCHER, ALICE CUNNINGHAM (1838-1923), American anthropologist **5** 486-487

FLETCHER, JOHN (1579-1625), English playwright **5** 487

FLETCHER, JOSEPH FRANCIS (1905-1991), American philosopher who was the father of modern biomedical ethics **5** 488-489

FLEXNER, ABRAHAM (1866-1959), American educational reformer **5** 489-490

FLINDERS, MATTHEW (1774-1814), English naval captain and hydrographer **5** 490

Flintstones, The (animated television show)
Hanna and Barbera **28** 156-159

Flor de la Canela, La (song)
Granda, Chabuca **28** 143-144

FLOREN, MYRON (Myron Howard Floren; 1919-2005), American musician **27** 131-133

FLORES, CARLOS ROBERTO (Carlos Roberto Flores Facussé;born 1950), Honduran politician **18** 138-140

FLORES, JUAN JOSÉ (1801-1864), South American general, president of Ecuador **5** 491

FLORES, PATRICK FERNANDEZ (born 1929), American archbishop **26** 109-112

FLOREY, HOWARD WALTER (Baron Florey of Adelaide; 1898-1968), Australian pathologist **5** 491-492

FLORY, PAUL (1910-1985), American chemist and educator **5** 492-494

Flow My Tears, The Policeman Said (book)
Dick, Philip K. **28** 96-98

FLOYD, CARLISLE (born 1926), American composer of operas **5** 494-496

FLYNN, ELIZABETH GURLEY (1890-1964), American labor organizer **5** 496-497

FLYNN, JOHN (1880-1951), founder and superintendent of the Australian Inland Mission **5** 497-498

FO, DARIO (born 1926), Italian playwright and actor **18** 140-143

FOCH, FERDINAND (1851-1929), French marshal **5** 498-499

FOKINE, MICHEL (Mikhail Mikhailovitch Fokine; 1880-1942), Russian-American choreographer **26** 112-115

FOLEY, TOM (born 1929), Democratic representative from the state of Washington and Speaker of the U.S. House of Representatives (1989-1995) **5** 499-501

Folk music
England
Sharp, Cecil **28** 321-323
Ireland
Moore, Thomas **28** 254-256
Mexico
Ponce, Manuel **28** 282-284
Portugal
Rodrigues, Amália **28** 301-302
Scotland
Sharp, Cecil **28** 321-323
South American
Barrios, Agustin Pìo **28** 27-29
United States (20th century)
Lomax, John Avery **28** 224-225
Sharp, Cecil **28** 321-323

Folklore (literature)
Brown, Sterling **28** 51-54

FOLKMAN, JUDAH (Moses Judah Folkman; 1933-2008), American physician and medical researcher **22** 176-179

FOLKS, HOMER (1867-1963), American social reformer **21** 137-140

FONDA, HENRY (1905-1982), American actor and producer **20** 138-140

FONDA, JANE (born 1937), actress whose career included films, television, exercise videocassettes, and writing **5** 501-502

FONG, HIRAM LEONG (1907-2004), American politician and businessman **18** 143-144

Fonseca, Manoel Deodoro da
see Deodoro da Fonseca, Manoel

FONSECA, RUBEM (born 1925), Brazilian author **5** 502-504

FONTANA, LAVINIA (1552-1614), Italian artist **22** 179-180

Fontana, Niccolo
see Tartaglia, Niccolo

FONTANE, THEODOR (1819-1898), German author **5** 504

FONTEYN, DAME MARGOT (Margaret "Peggy" Hookham; 1919-1991), classical ballerina who devoted her career to the Royal Ballet in England **5** 504-505

Food industry
Hall, Lloyd Augustus **28** 154-156
Kellogg, W. K. **28** 199-201

FOOT, MICHAEL (born 1913), left-wing journalist and British Labour Party member of Parliament **5** 505-507

Football (sport)
Walsh, Bill **28** 370-372

FOOTE, HENRY STUART (1804-1880), American politician **18** 144-146

Foote, Irene
see Castle, I. and V.

FOOTE, SHELBY (1916-2005), American author **18** 146-148

Forbes, Charles
see Montalembert, Comte de

FORBES, JOHN (1710-1759), British general **5** 507-508

FORBES, MALCOLM (1919-1990), American businessman and publisher **5** 508-509

FORBES, ROBERT BENNET (1804-1889), American merchant and shipowner **5** 509-510

FORD, BETTY (nee Elizabeth Ann Bloomer; born 1921), American first lady **20** 140-142

FORD, BILL (William Clay Ford, Jr.; born 1957), American businessman **19** 110-113

FORD, EDSEL BRYANT (1893-1943), American auto designer and industrialist **18** 148-150

FORD, EILEEN (Eileen Otte; born 1922), American businesswoman and author **19** 113-115

FORD, FORD MADOX (1873-1939), English author and editor **6** 1-2

FORD, GERALD (Leslie Lynch King, Junior; 1913-2006), U.S. Republican vice president (1973) and president (1974-1976) **6** 2-5

FORD, HENRY (1863-1947), American industrialist **6** 5-6

FORD, HENRY, II (born 1917), American industrialist **6** 6-7

FORD, JOHN (1586-1639?), English playwright **6** 7-8

FORD, JOHN SEAN O'FEENEY (circa 1890-1973), American film director **6** 8-9

FORD, PAUL LEICESTER (1865-1902), American bibliographer and novelist **6** 9-10

FORD, TOM (born 1961), American fashion designer and actor **25** 138-140

FORMAN, JAMES (1928-2005), writer, journalist, political philosopher, and leader of the Student Nonviolent Coordinating Committee **6** 10-11

FORMAN, MILOS (Tomas Jan Forman, born 1932), American screenwriter and film director **20** 143-145

FORNÉS, MARÍA IRENE (born 1930), Cuban American playwright and director **24** 140-142

FORREST, EDWIN (1806-1872), American actor **6** 11-12

FORREST, JOHN (1st Baron Forrest of Bunbury; 1847-1918), Australian explorer and politician **6** 12-13

FORREST, NATHAN BEDFORD (1821-1877), American Confederate general **6** 13-14

FORRESTAL, JAMES VINCENT (1892-1949), American statesman **6** 14

FORSSMANN, WERNER (1904-1979), German physician **21** 140-141

FORSTER, EDWARD MORGAN (1879-1970), English novelist and essayist **6** 14-16

FORTAS, ABE (1910-1982), noted civil libertarian who served four years on the Supreme Court (1965-1969) **6** 16-17

FORTEN, JAMES (1766-1842), African American abolitionist and inventor **6** 17-18

FORTH, ELIZABETH DENISON (died 1866), African American landowner and philanthropist **27** 133-135

FORTUNE, DION (Violet Mary Firth; 1890-1946), British author and occultist **22** 180-182

FORTUNE, TIMOTHY THOMAS (1856-1928), African American journalist **6** 18-21

FORTUYN, PIM (Wilhelmus Petrus Simon Foruyn; 1948-2002), Dutch politician **28** 125-127

FOSCOLO, UGO (1778-1827), Italian author, poet, and patriot **6** 21

FOSDICK, HARRY EMERSON (1878-1969), American Presbyterian minister **6** 21-22

FOSSE, BOB (1927-1987), American director, choreographer, and dancer **6** 22-23

FOSSEY, DIAN (1932-1985), world's leading authority on the mountain gorilla **6** 23-24

Fossils
see Paleontology (science)

FOSTER, ABIGAIL KELLEY (1810-1887), American reformer **6** 25

FOSTER, MARIE (1917-2003), African American voting rights activist **25** 140-142

FOSTER, NORMAN (born 1935), British architect **19** 115-117

FOSTER, RUBE (Andrew Foster; 1879-1930), American baseball player and manager **24** 143-145

FOSTER, STEPHEN COLLINS (1826-1864), American composer **6** 25-27

FOSTER, WILLIAM ZEBULON (1881-1961), American Communist party leader **6** 27-28

FOUCAULT, JEAN BERNARD LÉON (1819-1868), French physicist **6** 28-29

FOUCAULT, MICHEL (1926-1984), French philosopher, critic, and historian **6** 29-30

FOUCHÉ, JOSEPH (1759-1820), French statesman **6** 30-31

FOUQUET, JEAN (ca. 1420-ca. 1480), French painter **6** 31

FOURIER, FRANÇOIS CHARLES MARIE (1772-1837), French socialist writer **6** 31-32

FOURIER, BARON JEAN BAPTISTE JOSEPH (1768-1830), French mathematical physicist **6** 32-33

FOWLES, JOHN (1926-2005), English novelist **6** 33-35

FOX, CHARLES JAMES (1749-1806), English parliamentarian **6** 35-37

FOX, GEORGE (1624-1691), English spiritual reformer **6** 37-38

FOX, VICENTE (born 1942), Mexican president **21** 142-143

FOX, WILLIAM (1879-1952), American film producer **21** 143-144

FOYT, A.J. (born 1935), American race care driver **24** 145-147

FRACASTORO, GIROLAMO (Hieronymus Fracastorius; c. 1478-

1553), Italian physician, poet, astronomer, and logician **21** 144-147

FRAENKEL, ABRAHAM ADOLF (Abraham halevi Fraenkel; 1891-1965), Israeli mathematician **23** 109-111

FRAGONARD, JEAN HONORÉ (1732-1806), French painter **6** 38-39

FRANCE, ANATOLE (1844-1924), French novelist **6** 39-40

France (French Republic; nation, Western Europe)
• 1589-1789 (BOURBONS)
  1715-1774 (Louis XV)
    Madame de Pompadour **28** 228-230
• 1940-46 (WORLD WAR II TO 4TH REPUBLIC)
  British operations in
    Atkins, Vera **28** 16-18

Francia
  see France (French Republic; nation, Western Europe)

Francis I (emperor of Austria)
  see Francis II (Holy Roman emperor)

FRANCIS I (1494-1547), king of France 1515-1547 **6** 40-43

FRANCIS II (1768-1835), Holy Roman emperor 1792-1806 and emperor of Austria 1804-1835 **6** 43-44

Francis, Lydia Maria
  see Child, Lydia Maria Francis

FRANCIS FERDINAND (1863-1914), archduke of Austria **6** 44

FRANCIS JOSEPH (1830-1916), emperor of Austria 1868-1916 and king of Hungary 1867-1916 **6** 45-46
  Elisabeth, Empress of Austria **28** 111-113

Francis of Angoulême
  see Francis I (king of France)

FRANCIS OF ASSISI, SAINT (1182-1226), Italian mystic and religious founder **6** 46-47

FRANCIS OF SALES, SAINT (1567-1622), French bishop **6** 47

Francis Stephen of Lorraine, Duke
  see Francis I (Holy Roman emperor)

FRANCIS XAVIER, SAINT (1506-1552), Spanish Jesuit missionary **6** 48

FRANCK, CÉSAR (1822-1890), French composer **6** 48-49

FRANCK, JAMES (1882-1964), German physicist **6** 49-52

FRANCO BAHAMONDE, FRANCISCO (1892-1975), Spanish general and dictator **6** 52-54

FRANCO OF COLOGNE (Franco of Paris; flourished circa 1250-1260), French music theorist **6** 52

FRANK, ANNE (1929-1945), 16-year-old holocaust victim who kept a famous diary **6** 54-56

FRANKENHEIMER, JOHN (1930-2002), American filmmaker **22** 182-185

FRANKENTHALER, HELEN (born 1928), American painter **6** 56-57

FRANKFURTER, FELIX (1882-1965), American jurist **6** 57

FRANKLIN, ARETHA (born 1942), African American singer and songwriter **6** 58-60

FRANKLIN, BENJAMIN (1706-1790), American statesman, diplomat, and inventor **6** 60-64

FRANKLIN, SIR JOHN (1786-1847), English explorer **6** 68-69

FRANKLIN, JOHN HOPE (born 1915), pioneer African American historian **6** 65-67

FRANKLIN, MILES (1879-1954), Australian novelist **6** 68-69

FRANKLIN, ROSALIND ELSIE (1920-1958), British physical chemist and molecular biologist **6** 67-68

FRANKLIN, WILLIAM (circa 1731-1813), American colonial administrator **6** 69-70

FRANKS, TOMMY RAY (born 1945), American military leader **25** 142-144

Franz Josef
  see Francis Joseph

FRASER (PINTER), LADY ANTONIA (born 1932), popular British biographer, historian, and mystery novelist **6** 70-71

FRASER, MALCOLM (born 1930), prime minister of Australia (1975-1983) **6** 71-73

FRASER, PETER (1884-1950), New Zealand prime minister 1940-49 **6** 73-74

FRASER, SIMON (1776-1862), Canadian explorer and fur trader **6** 74-75

FRASER-REID, BERT (born 1934), Jamaican chemist **20** 145-146

FRAUNHOFER, JOSEPH VON (1787-1826), German physicist **6** 75-76

FRAZER, SIR JAMES GEORGE (1854-1941), Scottish classicist and anthropologist **6** 76

FRAZIER, EDWARD FRANKLIN (1894-1962), African American sociologist **6** 77

FREARS, STEPHEN ARTHUR (born 1941), British filmmaker **28** 127-129

FRÉCHETTE, LOUIS-HONORÉ (1839-1908), French-Canadian poet **6** 77-78

FREDEGUND (Fredegunda, Fredegond; c. 550-597), Frankish queen **20** 146-149

FREDERICK I (1123-1190), Holy Roman emperor 1152-1190 **6** 78-79

FREDERICK II (1194-1250), Holy Roman emperor 1215-1250 **6** 79

FREDERICK II (1712-1786), king of Prussia 1740-1786 **6** 81-84

Frederick III (duke of Swabia)
  see Frederick I (Holy Roman emperor)

FREDERICK III (1415-1493), Holy Roman emperor and German king 1440-1493 **6** 84-85

Frederick V (archduke of Austria)
  see Frederick III (Holy Roman emperor)

Frederick Augustus I-II (elector of Saxony)
  see Augustus II-III (king of Poland)

Frederick Barbarossa
  see Frederick I (Holy Roman emperor)

Frederick of Hohenstaufen
  see Frederick II (Holy Roman emperor)

Frederick the Great
  see Frederick II (king of Prussia)

FREDERICK WILLIAM (1620-1688), elector of Brandenburg 1640-1688 **6** 85-86

FREDERICK WILLIAM I (1688-1740), king of Prussia 1713-1740 **6** 86-87

FREDERICK WILLIAM III (1770-1840), king of Prussia 1797-1840 **6** 87

FREDERICK WILLIAM IV (1795-1861), king of Prussia 1840-1861 **6** 87-88

FREDHOLM, ERIK IVAR (1866-1927), Swedish mathematician **24** 147-149

Free French (World War II)
  see France—1940-46

FREED, JAMES INGO (1930-2005), American architect **6** 88-90

FREEH, LOUIS J. (born 1950), director of the Federal Bureau of Investigation (FBI) **6** 90-91

FREEMAN, DOUGLAS SOUTHALL (1886-1953), American journalist **6** 91-92

FREEMAN, ROLAND L. (born 1936), American photographer of rural and urban African Americans **6** 92-93

FREGE, GOTTLOB (1848-1925), German mathematician and philosopher **6** 93-94

FREI MONTALVA, EDUARDO (born 1911), Chilean statesman **6** 94-95

FREIRE, PAULO (born 1921), Brazilian philosopher and educator **6** 95-96

Freire, Rómulo Gallegos
    see Gallegos Freire, Rómulo

FRELINGHUYSEN, THEODORUS JACOBUS (1691-circa 1748), Dutch Reformed clergyman and revivalist **6** 96-97

FRÉMONT, JOHN CHARLES (1813-1890), American explorer and politician **6** 97-98

FRENCH, DANIEL CHESTER (1850-1931), American sculptor **6** 98-99

French art
    cartoons
        Grandville, J.J. **28** 144-146
    monumental sculpture
        Bartholdi, Frédéric-Auguste **28** 29-31

French literature
    essays
        Lévy, Bernard-Henri **28** 213-215
    sea stories
        Moitessier, Bernard **28** 252-254
    travel literature
        David-Néel, Alexandra **28** 90-92

French music
    songs
        Viardot, Pauline **28** 363-365

French Revolution (1789-1799)
    • 1789-1791 (CONSTITUTIONAL MONARCHY)
        terror victims (wax figures of)
            Tussaud, Marie **28** 356-358

FRENEAU, PHILIP MORIN (1752-1832), American poet and journalist **6** 99-100

FRERE, SIR HENRY BARTLE EDWARD (1815-1884), English colonial administrator **6** 100-101

FRESCOBALDI, GIROLAMO (1583-1643), Italian composer and organist **6** 101-102

FRESNEL, AUGUSTIN JEAN (1788-1827), French physicist **6** 102-103

FREUD, ANNA (1895-1982), British psychoanalyst **18** 150-153

FREUD, LUCIAN (born 1922), British painter **20** 149-151

FREUD, SIGMUND (1856-1939), Viennese psychiatrist, founder of psychoanalysis **6** 103-106
    associates
        Andreas-Salomé, Lou **28** 12-14

FREYRE, GILBERTO (1900-1987), Brazilian sociologist and writer **6** 106-107

FREYTAG, GUSTAV (1816-1895), German novelist, dramatist, and critic **6** 107-108

FRICK, HENRY CLAY (1849-1919), American industrialist and financier **6** 108-109

FRIEDAN, BETTY (Betty Naomi Goldstein; 1921-2006), women's rights activist and author **6** 109-111

FRIEDMAN, MILTON (1912-2006), American economist **6** 111-112

FRIEDRICH, CARL JOACHIM (1901-1984), German-born educator who became a leading American political theorist **6** 113-114

FRIEDRICH, CASPAR DAVID (1774-1840), German romantic painter **6** 114-115

FRIEL, BERNARD PATRICK (born 1929), author, teacher, and playwright from Northern Ireland **6** 115-116

FRIEND, CHARLOTTE (1921-1987), American medical researcher **26** 115-117

FRIES, JAKOB FRIEDRICH (1773-1843), German philosopher **6** 116-117

FRINK, ELISABETH (1930-1993), British artist **26** 117-118

FRISCH, KARL VON (1886-1982), Austrian zoologist **6** 117-118

FRISCH, MAX (born 1911), Swiss novelist and dramatist **6** 118-119

FRISCH, OTTO ROBERT (1904-1979), Austrian-British nuclear physicist **6** 119-120

FROBERGER, JOHANN JAKOB (1616-1667), German composer and organist **6** 120-121

FROBISHER, SIR MARTIN (circa 1538-1594), English explorer **6** 121-122

FROEBEL, FRIEDRICH WILHELM AUGUST (1782-1852), German educator and psychologist **6** 122-123

FROHMAN, CHARLES (1860-1915), American theatrical producer **6** 123-124

FROISSART, JEAN (circa 1337-after 1404), French priest, poet, and chronicler **6** 124-125

FROMM, ERICH (1900-1980), German writer in the fields of psychoanalysis, psychology, and social philosophy **6** 125-127

FRONDIZI, ARTURO (1908-1995), leader of the Argentine Radical Party and Argentine president (1958-1962) **6** 127-128

FRONTENAC ET PALLUAU, COMTE DE (Louis de Buade; 1622-1698), French colonial governor **6** 128-130

FRONTINUS, SEXTUS JULIUS (circa 35-circa 104), Roman magistrate, soldier, and writer **6** 130

FROST, ROBERT LEE (1874-1963), American poet **6** 130-133

FROUDE, JAMES ANTHONY (1818-1894), English historian **6** 133-134

FRUNZE, MIKHAIL VASILIEVICH (1885-1925), Soviet military leader **6** 134

FRY, ELIZABETH (1780-1845), British reformer **6** 134-136

FRY, WILLIAM HENRY (1813-1864), American composer **6** 136-137

FRYE, NORTHROP (Herman Northrop Frye; born 1912), Canadian literary scholar **6** 137-139

FUAD I (1868-1936), king of Egypt 1922-1936 **6** 139

FUCHS, KLAUS (Klaus Emil Julius Fuchs; 1911-1988), German-born British physicist and espionage agent **28** 129-131

FUCHS, LEONHARD (1501-1566), German botanist **20** 152-152

FUCHS, SIR VIVIAN (1908-1999), English explorer and geologist **6** 140

FUENTES, CARLOS (born 1928), Mexican author and political activist **6** 141-142

FUERTES, LOUIS AGASSIZ (1874-1927), American naturalist and artist **24** 152-153

FUGARD, ATHOL (born 1932), South African playwright **6** 142-143

FUGGER, JAKOB (Jacob Fugger; 1459-1525), German banker **21** 147-149

Fugitive slaves
    see African American history (United States)

FUJIMORI, ALBERTO KEINYA (born 1938), president of Peru **6** 143-145

FUJITA, TETSUYA (Theodore "Ted" Fujita; 1920-1998), Japanese American meteorologist **27** 135-137

FUJIWARA KAMATARI (614-669), Japanese imperial official **6** 145

FUJIWARA MICHINAGA (966-1027), Japanese statesman **6** 145-146

Fujiwara-no Daijin
see Fujiwara Kamatari

FUKUI, KENICHI (born 1918), Japanese chemist **23** 111-112

FUKUYAMA, FRANCIS (born 1952), American philosopher and foreign policy expert **6** 146-147

FULBRIGHT, JAMES WILLIAM (1905-1995), American statesman **6** 147-149

FULLER, ALFRED (1885-1973), American businessman and inventor **19** 117-118

FULLER, JOHN FREDERICK CHARLES (1878-1966), British soldier and author **22** 185-186

FULLER, META WARRICK (1877-1968), American sculptor **23** 112-114

FULLER, MILLARD (born 1935), American lawyer and social activist **18** 153-155

FULLER, RICHARD BUCKMINISTER (born 1895), American architect and engineer **6** 149-150

FULLER, SARAH MARGARET (1810-1850), American feminist **6** 150-151

FULTON, ROBERT (1765-1815), American inventor, engineer, and artist **6** 151-152

Fulton, Ruth
see Benedict, Ruth Fulton

FU MINGXIA (born 1978), Chinese diver **24** 149-151

FUNK, CASIMIR (1884-1967), Polish-American biochemist **22** 187-189

FURPHY, JOSEPH (1843-1912), Australian novelist **6** 152-153

FÜRÜZAN (Fürüzan Selçuk; born 1935), Turkish author and director **22** 189-190

FUSELI, HENRY (1741-1825), Swiss painter **6** 153-155

FUSTEL DE COULANGES, NUMA DENIS (1830-1889), French historian **6** 155

FUX, JOHANN JOSEPH (1660-1741), Austrian composer, conductor, and theoretician **6** 155-156

G

GABLE, WILLIAM CLARK (1901-1960), American film actor **6** 157-158

GABO, NAUM (1890-1977), Russian sculptor and designer **6** 158-159

GABOR, DENNIS (1900-1979), Hungarian-British physicist who invented holographic photography **6** 159-160

GABRIEL, ANGE JACQUES (1698-1782), French architect **6** 160-161

GABRIELI, GIOVANNI (circa 1557-1612), Italian composer **6** 161-162

Gabrini, Niccola di Lorenzo
see Rienzi, Cola di

GADAMER, HANS-GEORG (1900-2002), German philosopher, classicist, and interpretation theorist **6** 162-163

GADDAFI, MUAMMAR AL- (born 1942), head of the revolution that set up the Libyan Republic in 1969 **6** 163-165

GADSDEN, JAMES (1788-1858), American soldier and diplomat **6** 165-166

GAGARIN, YURI ALEXEIVICH (1934-1968), Russian cosmonaut **6** 166-167

GAGE, MATILDA JOSLYN (1826-1898), American reformer and suffragist **6** 167-169

GAGE, THOMAS (1719/20-1787), English general **6** 169-170

GAGNÉ, ROBERT MILLS (born 1916), American educator **6** 170

GAINSBOROUGH, THOMAS (1727-1788), English painter **6** 170-172

GAINSBOURG, SERGE (Lucien Gainsbourg; 1928-1991), French singer, songwriter and actor **27** 138-141

GAISERIC (died 477), king of the Vandals 428-477 **6** 172

GAITÁN, JORGE ELIÉCER (1898-1948), Colombian politician **6** 172-173

GAITSKELL, HUGH (1906-1963), British chancellor of the exchequer (1950-1951) and leader of the Labour Party (1955-1963) **6** 173-174

Gaius Sallustius Crispus
see Sallust

GALAMB, JOSEPH (Jozsef Galamb; 1881-1955), Hungarian-American engineer **24** 154-155

GALBRAITH, JOHN KENNETH (1908-2006), economist and scholar of the American Institutionalist school **6** 174-177

GALDÓS, BENITO PÉREZ (1843-1920), Spanish novelist and dramatist **6** 177-178

GALEN (130-200), Greek physician **6** 178-180

GALERIUS, EMPEROR OF ROME (Gaius Galerius Valerius Maximianus; circa 250-311), Thracian emperor **28** 132-134

Galilei, Galileo
see Galileo Galilei

GALILEO GALILEI (1564-1642), Italian astronomer and physicist **6** 180-183

GALLATIN, ALBERT (1761-1849), Swiss-born American statesman, banker, and diplomat **6** 183-184

GALLAUDET, THOMAS HOPKINS (1787-1851), American educator **6** 185

GALLEGOS FREIRE, RÓMULO (1884-1969), Venezuelan novelist, president 1948 **6** 185-186

GALLO, ROBERT CHARLES (born 1937), American virologist **22** 191-193

GALLOWAY, JOSEPH (circa 1731-1803), American politician **6** 186-187

GALLUP, GEORGE (1901-1984), pioneer in the field of public opinion polling and a proponent of educational reform **6** 187-189

GALSWORTHY, JOHN (1867-1933), English novelist and playwright **6** 189-190

GALT, SIR ALEXANDER TILLOCH (1817-1893), Canadian politician **6** 190-191

GALT, JOHN (1779-1839), Scottish novelist **18** 156-158

GALTIERI, LEOPOLDO FORTUNATO (1926-2003), president of Argentina (1981-1982) **6** 191-193

GALTON, SIR FRANCIS (1822-1911), English scientist, biometrician, and explorer **6** 193-194

GALVANI, LUIGI (1737-1798), Italian physiologist **6** 194-195

GÁLVEZ, BERNARDO DE (1746-1786), Spanish colonial administrator **6** 195-196

GÁLVEZ, JOSÉ DE (1720-1787), Spanish statesman in Mexico **6** 196

GALWAY, JAMES (born 1939), Irish flutist **18** 158-160

GAMA, VASCO DA (circa 1460-1524), Portuguese navigator **6** 196-198

GAMBARO, GRISELDA (born 1928), Argentine author **23** 115-117

GAMBETTA, LÉON (1838-1882), French premier 1881-1882 **6** 198-199

Gamester, The (play)
Centlivre, Susanna **28** 65-67

GAMOW, GEORGE (1904-1968), Russian-American nuclear physicist, astrophysicist, biologist, and author of books popularizing science **6** 199-200

GAMZATOV, RASUL (Rasul Gamzatovitch Gamzatov; 1923-2003), Dagestani poet **28** 134-136

GANCE, ABEL (1889-1981), French film director **25** 145-147

GANDHI, INDIRA PRIYADARSHINI (1917-1984), Indian political leader **6** 200-201

GANDHI, MOHANDAS KARAMCHAND (1869-1948), Indian political and religious leader **6** 201-204

GANDHI, RAJIV (1944-1991), Indian member of Parliament and prime minister **6** 204-205

GANDHI, SONIA (née Sonia Maino; born 1946), Indian politician **25** 147-149

GAO XINGJIAN (born 1940), French Chinese author **25** 149-151

Gaon, Vilna
see Elijah ben Solomon

GARBO, GRETA (1905-1990), Swedish-born American film star **6** 205-207

GARCIA, CARLOS P. (1896-1971), Philippine statesman, president 1957-61 **6** 207-208

GARCIA, JERRY (Jerome John Garcia; 1942-1995), American musician **21** 150-152

GARCÍA MÁRQUEZ, GABRIEL (born 1928), Colombian author **6** 208-209

GARCÍA MORENO, GABRIEL (1821-1875), Ecuadorian politician, president 1861-1865 and 1869-1875 **6** 209-210

GARCÍA ROBLES, ALFONSO (1911-1991), Mexican diplomat **23** 117-119

Garcia y Sarmientc, Félix Rubén
see Dario, Rubén

GARCILASO DE LA VEGA, INCA (1539-1616), Peruvian chronicler **6** 210-211

GARDINER, SAMUEL RAWSON (1829-1902), English historian **6** 211

GARDNER, AVA (Ava Lavinia Gardner; 1922-1990), American actress **25** 151-154

GARDNER, ERLE STANLEY (1889-1970), American mystery writer **22** 193-195

GARDNER, ISABELLA STEWART (1840-1924), American art patron and socialite **21** 152-155

GARDNER, JOHN W. (1912-2002), American educator, public official, and political reformer **6** 211-213

GARFIELD, JAMES ABRAM (1831-1881), American general, president 1881 **6** 213-214
assassination
Agnew, David Hayes **28** 3-5

GARIBALDI, GIUSEPPE (1807-1882), Italian patriot **6** 215-217

GARLAND, HANNIBAL HAMLIN (1860-1940), American author **6** 217-218

GARLAND, JUDY (1922-1969), super star of films, musicals, and concert stage **6** 218-219

GARNEAU, FRANÇOIS-XAVIER (1809-1866), French-Canadian historian **6** 219-220

GARNER, JOHN NANCE ("Cactus Jack" Garner; 1868-1967), American vice president (1933-1941) **21** 155-157

GARNET, HENRY HIGHLAND (1815-1882), African American clergyman, abolitionist, and diplomat **24** 155-158

GARNIER, FRANCIS (Marie Joseph François Garnier; 1839-1873), French naval officer **6** 220-221

GARNIER, JEAN LOUIS CHARLES (1825-1898), French architect **6** 221-222

GARRETT, JOHN WORK (1820-1884), American railroad magnate **6** 225

GARRETT, THOMAS (1789-1871), American abolitionist **6** 225-226

GARRETT (ANDERSON), ELIZABETH (1836-1917), English physician and women's rights advocate **6** 222-225

GARRISON, WILLIAM LLOYD (1805-1879), American editor and abolitionist **6** 226-228

GARVEY, MARCUS MOSIAH (1887-1940), Jamaican leader and African nationalist **6** 228-229

GARY, ELBERT HENRY (1846-1927), American lawyer and industrialist **6** 229-230

GASCA, PEDRO DE LA (circa 1496-1567), Spanish priest and statesman **6** 230-231

Gascoyne-Cecil, Robert Arthur Talbot
see Salisbury, 3rd Marquess of

GASKELL, ELIZABETH (1810-1865), English novelist **6** 231-232

Gaspé, Philippe Aubert de
see Aubert de Gaspé, Philippe

GATES, WILLIAM HENRY, III ("Bill"; born 1955), computer software company co-founder and executive **6** 232-234

GATLING, RICHARD JORDAN (1818-1903), American inventor of multiple-firing guns **6** 234-235

GAUDÍ I CORNET, ANTONI (1852-1926), Catalan architect and designer **6** 235-236

GAUGUIN, PAUL (1848-1903), French painter and sculptor **6** 236-238

GAULLI, GIOVANNI BATTISTA (1639-1709), Italian painter **6** 238-239

GAULTIER, JEAN PAUL (born 1952), French avant-garde designer **6** 239-240

GAUSS, KARL FRIEDRICH (1777-1855), German mathematician and astronomer **6** 240-242

Gautama, Prince
see Buddha

GAVIRIA TRUJILLO, CESAR AUGUSTO (born 1947), president of Colombia **6** 242-243

GAY, JOHN (1685-1732), English playwright and poet **6** 243-244

GAYE, MARVIN (Marvin Pentz Gay; 1939-1984), American musician **26** 119-123

GAYLE, HELENE DORIS (born 1955), African American epidemiologist and pediatrician **6** 244-245

GAY-LUSSAC, JOSEPH LOUIS (1778-1850), French chemist and physicist **6** 245-246

Geber
see Jabir ibn Hayyan

GEDDES, SIR PATRICK (1854-1932), Scottish sociologist and biologist **6** 246-247

GEERTGEN TOT SINT JANS (Geertgen van Haarlem; circa 1460/65-1490/95), Netherlandish painter **6** 248

GEERTZ, CLIFFORD (1926-2006), American cultural anthropologist **6** 248-249

GEFFEN, DAVID LAWRENCE (born 1943), American record and film producer **23** 119-122

GEHRIG, LOU (Henry Louis Gehrig; 1903-1941), American baseball player **19** 119-121

GEHRY, FRANK O. (née Goldberg; born 1929), American architect **6** 250-251

GEIGER, HANS (born Johannes Wilhelm Geiger; 1882-1945), German physicist **6** 251-253

GEISEL, ERNESTO (1908-1996), Brazilian army general, president of Brazil's national oil company (Petrobras), and

president of the republic (1974-1979)
6 253-255

GEISEL, THEODOR (a.k.a. Dr. Seuss;
1904-1991), American author of
children's books **6** 255-256

Geiseric
see Gaiseric

Gellée, Claude
see Claude Lorrain

GELLER, MARGARET JOAN (born 1947),
American astronomer **6** 256-257

GELLHORN, MARTHA ELLIS (1908-
1998), American journalist and author
27 141-143

GELL-MANN, MURRAY (born 1929),
American physicist **6** 257-258

GEMAYEL, AMIN (born 1942), Lebanese
nationalist and Christian political
leader; president of the Republic of
Lebanon (1982-1988) **6** 258-259
Gemayel, Bashir **28** 136-138

GEMAYEL, BASHIR (1947-1982),
Lebanese political and military leader
28 136-138

GEMAYEL, PIERRE (1905-1984), leader
of the Lebanese Phalangist Party **6**
259-261
Gemayel, Bashir **28** 136-138

GEMINIANI, FRANCESCO SAVERIO
(Francesco Xaviero Geminiani; 1687-
1762), Italian violinist and composer
26 123-125

Gene (biology)
see Genetics (biology)

General Association of German Workers
see Social Democratic party (Germany)

GENET, EDMOND CHARLES (1763-
1834), French diplomat **6** 261-262

GENET, JEAN (1910-1986), French
novelist and playwright **6** 262-263

Genetics (biology)
gene therapy
Mello, Craig Cameron **28** 238-241

Genga, Annibale Francesco della
see Leo XII

GENGHIS KHAN (1167-1227), Mongol
chief, creator of the Mongol empire **6**
263-265

GENSCHER, HANS-DIETRICH (born
1927), leader of West Germany's
liberal party (the FDP) and foreign
minister **6** 265-266

Genseric
see Gaiseric

GENTILE, GIOVANNI (1875-1944),
Italian philosopher and politician **6**
267

GENTILE DA FABRIANO (Gentile di
Niccolò di Giovanni di Massio; circa
1370-1427), Italian painter **6** 266-267

GENTILESCHI, ARTEMISIA (1593-1652),
Italian painter **22** 195-196

GEOFFREY OF MONMOUTH (circa
1100-1155), English pseudohistorian **6**
268

GEORGE I (1660-1727), king of Great
Britain and Ireland 1714-1727 **6**
268-269

GEORGE II (1683-1760), king of Great
Britain and Ireland and elector of
Hanover 1727-1760 **6** 269-270

GEORGE III (1738-1820), king of Great
Britain and Ireland 1760-1820 **6**
270-272

GEORGE IV (1762-1830), king of Great
Britain and Ireland 1820-1830 **6**
272-273

GEORGE V (1865-1936), king of Great
Britain and Northern Ireland and
emperor of India 1910-1936 **6**
273-275

GEORGE VI (1895-1952), king of Great
Britain and Northern Ireland 1936-
1952 **6** 275

GEORGE, DAN (1899-1981), Native
American actor **22** 196-198

George, David Lloyd
see Lloyd George, David

GEORGE, HENRY (1839-1897),
American economist and social
reformer **6** 276

GEORGE, JAMES ZACHARIAH (1826-
1897), American politician and jurist **6**
276-277

GEORGE, STEFAN (1868-1933), German
symbolist poet **6** 277-278

GEPHARDT, RICHARD ANDREW (born
1941), Democratic majority leader in
the House of Representatives **6**
278-280

Gerbert of Aurillac
see Sylvester II

GÉRICAULT, JEAN LOIS ANDRÉ
THÉODORE (1791-1824), French
painter **6** 280-281

GERMAIN, SOPHIE (Marie-Sophie
Germain; 1776-1831), French
mathematician **21** 157-158

German Democratic Republic
see Germany, East (German
Democratic Republic; former nation;
Europe)

German literature
feminist
Andreas-Salomé, Lou **28** 12-14

German music
classical
Sawallisch, Wolfgang **28** 314-316
recordings of
Sawallisch, Wolfgang **28** 314-316

Germanicus, Julius Caesar
see Caligula (play)

Germanicus, Tiberius Claudius
see Claudius Germanicus, T.

Germany, East (German Democratic
Republic; former nation; Europe)
Merkel, Angela **28** 243-245

GERONIMO (1829-1909), American
Apache Indian warrior **6** 281-282

GERRY, ELBRIDGE (1744-1814),
American patriot and statesman **6**
282-283

GERSHOM BEN JUDAH (circa 950-
1028), German rabbi, scholar, and
poet **6** 283-284

Gershon
see Levi ben Gershon

GERSHWIN, GEORGE (1898-1937),
American composer **6** 284-285

GERSHWIN, IRA (Israel Gershvin; 1896-
1983), American lyricist **20** 153-155

GERSON, JOHN (1363-1429), French
theologian **6** 285-286

Gersonides
see Levi ben Gershon

GERSTNER, LOU (Louis Vincent
Gerstner, Jr.; born 1942), American
businessman **19** 121-124

GESELL, ARNOLD LUCIUS (1880-1961),
American psychologist and
pediatrician **6** 286-287

GESNER, KONRAD VON (1516-1565),
Swiss naturalist **6** 287

GESUALDO, DON CARLO (Prince of
Venosa; circa 1560-1613), Italian
composer **6** 287-288

GETTY, JEAN PAUL (1892-1976),
billionaire independent oil producer **6**
288-290

GETZ, STAN (Stanley Getz; 1927-1991),
American saxophonist **27** 143-145

Geyer, Francis
see Harwood, Gwen

GHAZALI, ABU HAMID MUHAMMAD
AL- (1058-1111), Arab philosopher
and Islamic theologian **6** 290-291

GHIBERTI, LORENZO (circa 1381-1455),
Italian sculptor, goldsmith, and painter
6 291-292

GHIRLANDAIO, DOMENICO (1449-
1494), Italian painter **6** 292-293

Ghislieri, Antonio
see Pius V

GHOSE, AUROBINDO (1872-1950), Indian nationalist and philosopher **6** 293-294

GHOSN, CARLOS (born 1954), French business executive **27** 145-147

GIACOMETTI, ALBERTO (1901-1966), Swiss sculptor and painter **6** 294-295

Giambologna
see Giovanni da Bologna

GIANNINI, A. P. (Amadeo Peter; 1870-1949), Italian-American financier and banker **6** 295-297

GIAP, VO NGUYEN (born 1912), Vietnamese Communist general and statesman **6** 297-299

GIBBON, EDWARD (1737-1794), English historian **6** 299-300

GIBBONS, CEDRIC (1893-1960), American film production designer **21** 158-159

GIBBONS, JAMES (1834-1921), American Roman Catholic cardinal **6** 300-301

GIBBS, JAMES (1682-1754), British architect **6** 301-302

GIBBS, JOSIAH WILLARD (1839-1903), American mathematical physicist **6** 302-303

GIBRAN, KAHLIL (1883-1931), Lebanese writer and artist **6** 303-305

GIBSON, ALTHEA (born 1927), African American tennis player **6** 305-306

GIBSON, BOB (Robert Gibson; born 1935), American baseball player **21** 159-162

GIBSON, WILLIAM (born 1914), American author **6** 306-307

GIDDINGS, FRANKLIN HENRY (1855-1931), American sociologist **6** 307-308

GIDE, ANDRÉ (1869-1951), French author **6** 308-309

GIELGUD, JOHN (born 1904), English Shakespearean actor **6** 310-311

GIERKE, OTTO VON (1841-1921), German jurist **6** 311-312

GIGLI, ROMEO (born 1949), Italian designer **6** 312

GILBERT, SIR HUMPHREY (circa 1537-1583), English soldier and colonizer **6** 313

GILBERT, WALTER (born 1932), American molecular biologist **23** 122-124

GILBERT, WILLIAM (1544-1603), English physician and physicist **6** 313-314

GILBERT, SIR WILLIAM SCHWENCK (1836-1911), English playwright and poet **6** 314-315

GILBRETH, FRANK (1868-1924), American engineer and management expert **21** 162-163

GILBRETH, LILLIAN (born Lillian Evelyn Moller; 1878-1972), American psychologist and industrial management consultant **6** 315-317

GILBERTO, JOAO (Joao Gilberto do Prado Pereira de Olivera; born 1931), Brazilian musician **25** 154-156

GILES, ERNEST (1835-1897), Australian explorer **6** 317-318

GILKEY, LANGDON BROWN (1919-2004), American ecumenical Protestant theologian **6** 318-319

GILLARS, MILDRED ELIZABETH (nee Mildred Elizabeth Sisk; 1900-1988), American broadcaster and traitor **26** 125-127

GILLESPIE, DIZZY (born John Birks Gillespie; 1917-1993), African American jazz trumpeter, composer, and band leader **6** 320-322

GILLETTE, KING CAMP (1855-1932), American businessman and inventor **21** 163-166

GILLIAM, SAM (born 1933), American artist **6** 322-323

GILMAN, CHARLOTTE ANNA PERKINS (1860-1935), American writer and lecturer **6** 323-325

GILMAN, DANIEL COIT (1831-1908), educator and pioneer in the American university movement **6** 325-326

GILPIN, LAURA (1891-1979), American photographer **6** 326-327

GILSON, ÉTIENNE HENRY (1884-1978), French Catholic philosopher **6** 327-328

GINASTERA, ALBERTO EVARISTO (1916-1983), Argentine composer **6** 328-329

GINGRICH, NEWT (born 1943), Republican congressman from Georgia **6** 329-332

GINSBERG, ALLEN (1926-1997), American poet **6** 332-333

GINSBURG, RUTH BADER (born 1933), second woman appointed to the United States Supreme Court **6** 333-336

GINZBERG, ASHER (Ahad Ha-Am; means "one of the people;" 1856-

1927), Jewish intellectual leader **6** 336-337

GINZBERG, LOUIS (1873-1953), Lithuanian-American Talmudic scholar **6** 337-338

GINZBURG, NATALIA LEVI (1916-1991), Italian novelist, essayist, playwright, and translator **6** 338-339

GIOLITTI, GIOVANNI (1842-1928), Italian statesman **6** 339-340

GIORGIONE (1477-1510), Italian painter **6** 340-341

GIOTTO (circa 1267-1337), Italian painter, architect, and sculptor **6** 342-345

GIOVANNI, YOLANDE CORNELIA, JR. (born 1943), African American poet **6** 346-347

GIOVANNI DA BOLOGNA (1529-1608), Italian sculptor **6** 345-346

Giovanni da Fiesole, Fra
see Angelica, Fra

Giovanni Pisano
see Pisano, Giovanni

GIPP, GEORGE (1895-1920), American football player **19** 124-126

GIRARD, STEPHEN (1750-1831), American merchant and philanthropist **6** 347-348

GIRARDON, FRANÇOIS (1628-1715), French sculptor **6** 348-349

GIRAUDOUX, JEAN (1882-1944), French novelist, playwright, and diplomat **6** 349-350

GIRTY, SIMON (1741-1818), American frontiersman **6** 350

GISCARD D'ESTAING, VALÉRY (born 1926), third president of the French Fifth Republic **6** 350-352

GISH, LILLIAN (1896-1993), American actress **20** 155-158

GIST, CHRISTOPHER (circa 1706-1759), American frontiersman **6** 352-353

GIULIANI, RUDOLPH WILLIAM (born 1944), mayor of New York City **6** 353-355

GIULIANI, MAURO (Mauro Giuseppe Sergio Pantaleo Giuliani; 1781-1829), Italian guitarist and composer **25** 156-157

GJELLERUP, KARL ADOLPH (1857-1919), Danish author **25** 157-159

GLACKENS, WILLIAM (1870-1938), American painter **6** 355-356

GLADDEN, WASHINGTON (1836-1918), American clergyman **6** 356-357

GLADSTONE, WILLIAM EWART (1809-1898), English statesman **6** 357-360

GLASGOW, ELLEN (1873-1945), American novelist **6** 360-361

GLASHOW, SHELDON LEE (born 1932), American Nobel Prize winner in physics **6** 361-362

GLASS, PHILIP (born 1937), American composer of minimalist music **6** 362-364

GLASSE, HANNAH (Hannah Allgood; 1708-1770), English cookbook author **21** 166-167

GLEDITSCH, ELLEN (1879-1968), Norwegian chemist **23** 124-126

GLENDOWER, OWEN (1359?-1415?), Welsh national leader **6** 364-365

GLENN, JOHN HERSCHEL, JR. (born 1921), military test pilot, astronaut, businessman, and United States senator from Ohio **6** 365-367

GLIDDEN, JOSEPH (1813-1906), American businessman and inventor **21** 167-170

GLIGOROV, KIRO (born 1917), first president of the Republic of Macedonia **6** 367-369

GLINKA, MIKHAIL IVANOVICH (1804-1857), Russian composer **6** 369-370

GLOUCESTER, DUKE OF (1391-1447), English statesman **6** 370-371

Gloucester, Richard, Duke of
see Richard III (play; Shakespeare)

GLUBB, SIR JOHN BAGOT (1897-1986), British commander of the Arab Legion 1939-56 **6** 371-372

GLUCK, CHRISTOPH WILLIBALD (1714-1787), Austrian composer and opera reformer **6** 372-374

GLUCKMAN, MAX (1911-1975), British anthropologist **6** 374-375

GLYN, ELINOR (born Elinor Sutherland; 1864-1943), British author and filmmaker **23** 126-128

Glyndyfrdwy, Lord of Giyndwr and Sycharth
see Glendower, Owen

GOBINEAU, COMTE DE (Joseph Arthur Gobineau; 1816-1882), French diplomat **6** 375-376

GODARD, JEAN-LUC (born 1930), French actor, film director, and screenwriter **19** 126-128

GODDARD, ROBERT HUTCHINGS (1882-1945), American pioneer in rocketry **6** 376-377

GÖDEL, KURT (1906-1978), Austrian-American mathematician **6** 377-379

GODKIN, EDWIN LAWRENCE (1831-1902), British-born American journalist **6** 380

GODOLPHIN, SIDNEY (1st Earl of Godolphin; 1645-1712), English statesman **6** 380-381

GODOY Y ÁLVAREZ DE FARIA, MANUEL DE (1767-1851), Spanish statesman **6** 381-382

GODUNOV, BORIS FEODOROVICH (circa 1551-1605), czar of Russia 1598-1605 **6** 382-383

GODWIN, WILLIAM (1756-1836), English political theorist and writer **6** 383-384

GOEBBELS, JOSEPH PAUL (1897-1945), German politician and Nazi propagandist **6** 384-385

GOEPPERT-MAYER, MARIA (1906-1972), American physicist **6** 385-387

GOETHALS, GEORGE WASHINGTON (1858-1928), American Army officer and engineer **6** 387-388

GOETHE, JOHANN WOLFGANG VON (1749-1832), German poet **6** 388-391

GOGOL, NIKOLAI (1809-1852), Russian author **6** 391-393

GOH CHOK TONG (born 1941), leader of the People's Action Party and Singapore's prime minister **6** 393-395

GOIZUETA, ROBERTO (1931-1997), Cuban American businessman and philanthropist **18** 160-162

GÖKALP, MEHMET ZIYA (1875/76-1924), Turkish publicist and sociologist **6** 395-396

GÖKÇEN, SABIHA (Sabiha Geuckchen; 1913-2001), Turkish aviator **27** 147-149

GOKHALE, GOPAL KRISHNA (1866-1915), Indian nationalist leader **6** 396

GOLD, THOMAS (born 1920), American astronomer and physicist **18** 162-164

GOLDBERG, ARTHUR JOSEPH (1908-1990), U.S. secretary of labor, ambassador to the United Nations, and activist justice of the U.S. Supreme Court **6** 397-398

GOLDBERG, WHOOPI (born Caryn E. Johnson; born 1949), African American actress **6** 398-402

GOLDEN, HARRY (1902-1981), Jewish-American humorist, writer, and publisher **6** 402-403

Goldfish, Samuel
see Goldwyn, Samuel

GOLDIE, SIR GEORGE DASHWOOD TAUBMAN (1846-1925), British trader and empire builder **6** 404

GOLDING, WILLIAM (1911-1993), English novelist and essayist **6** 404-406

GOLDMAN, EMMA (1869-1940), Lithuanian-born American anarchist **6** 406-407

Goldmann, Max
see Reinhardt, Max

GOLDMARK, JOSEPHINE (1877-1950), advocate of government assistance in improving the lot of women and children **6** 407-408

GOLDMARK, PETER CARL (1906-1977), American engineer and inventor **21** 170-172

GOLDONI, CARLO (1707-1793), Italian dramatist, poet, and librettist **6** 408-409

GOLDSMITH, JAMES MICHAEL (1933-1997), British-French industrialist and financier **6** 409-411

GOLDSMITH, OLIVER (1730-1774), British poet, dramatist, and novelist **6** 411-413

GOLDSMITH, OLIVER (1794-1861), Canadian poet **6** 411

GOLDWATER, BARRY (1909-1998), conservative Republican U.S. senator from Arizona (1952-1987) **6** 413-415

GOLDWYN, SAMUEL (1882-1974), Polish-born American film producer **6** 416

GOMBERT, NICOLAS (circa 1500-1556/57), Franco-Flemish composer **6** 416-417

GOMBRICH, ERNST HANS JOSEF (1909-2001), British author and educator **27** 149-151

GÓMEZ, JUAN VICENTE (1857-1935), Venezuelan dictator **6** 417-418

GÓMEZ, MÁXIMO (1836-1905), Dominican-born Cuban general and independence hero **6** 418-419

GÓMEZ CASTRO, LAUREANO ELEUTERIO (1889-1965), Colombian statesman, president **6** 419-420

GOMPERS, SAMUEL (1850-1924), American labor leader **6** 420-422

GOMULKA, WLADISLAW (1905-1982), Polish politician **6** 422-424

GONCHAROV, IVAN ALEKSANDROVICH (1812-1891), Russian novelist **6** 424

GONCHAROVA, NATALIA (1881-1962), Russian painter and theatrical scenery designer **6** 424-426

GONCOURT BROTHERS (19th-century), French writers **6** 426-427

Gondola, Andrea di Pietro dalla
see Palladio, Andrea

Gongon Musa
see Musa Mansa

GÓNGORA Y ARGOTE, LUIS DE (1561-1627), Spanish poet **6** 427-428

GONNE, MAUD (c. 1866-1953), Irish nationalist **20** 158-160

Gonzalez, José Victoriano
see Gris, Juan

GONZÁLEZ, JULIO (1876-1942), Spanish sculptor **6** 428-429

GONZÁLEZ MARQUEZ, FELIPE (born 1942), Socialist leader of Spain **6** 429-431

GONZÁLEZ PRADA, MANUEL (1848-1918), Peruvian essayist and poet **6** 431

GONZALO DE BERCEO (circa 1195-after 1252), Spanish author **6** 431-432

GOOCH, GEORGE PEABODY (1873-1968), British historian and political journalist **6** 432-433

GOODALL, JANE (born 1934), British scientist who studied primates **6** 433-434

GOODE, MAL (Malvin Russell Goode, 1908-1995), African American journalist **27** 151-153

GOODLAD, JOHN INKSTER (born 1917), American education researcher and prophet **6** 434-436

GOODMAN, BENNY (Benjamin David Goodman; 1909-1986), jazz clarinetist and big band leader (1935-1945) **6** 436-438

GOODMAN, ELLEN HOLTZ (born 1941), American journalist **6** 438-439

GOODNIGHT, CHARLES (1836-1926), American cattleman **6** 439

GOODPASTER, ANDREW JACKSON (born 1915), American Army officer active in organizing NATO forces in Europe and adviser to three presidents **6** 439-441

GOODYEAR, CHARLES (1800-1860), American inventor **6** 441

Goon on Earth
see Antiochus IV (king of Syria)

GORBACHEV, MIKHAIL SERGEEVICH (born 1931), former president of the Union of Soviet Socialist Republics. **6** 441-444

GORBACHEV, RAISA MAXIMOVNA (née Titorenko; 1932-1999), first lady of the Soviet Union **6** 444-446

GORDEEVA, EKATERINA (born 1971), Russian ice skater and author **18** 164-166

GORDIMER, NADINE (born 1923), South African author of short stories and novels **6** 446-447

GORDON, AARON DAVID (1856-1922), Russian-born Palestinian Zionist **6** 447-448

GORDON, CHARLES GEORGE (1833-1885), English soldier and adventurer **6** 448-449

Gordon, George Hamilton
see Aberdeen, 4th Earl of

GORDON, JOHN BROWN (1832-1904), American businessman and politician **6** 449-450

GORDON, PAMELA (born 1955), Bermudan politician **18** 166-167

GORDY, BERRY, JR. (born 1929), founder of the Motown Sound **6** 450-451

GORE, ALBERT, JR. (born 1948), Democratic U.S. representative, senator, and 45th vice president of the United States **6** 452-453

Gorenko, Anna Andreyevna
see Akhmatova, Anna

GORGAS, JOSIAH (1818-1883), American soldier and educator **6** 453-454

GORGAS, WILLIAM CRAWFORD (1854-1920), American general and sanitarian **6** 454-455

GORGES, SIR FERDINANDO (1568-1647), English colonizer and soldier **6** 455-456

GORGIAS (circa 480-circa 376 B.C.), Greek sophist philosopher and rhetorician **6** 456

GÖRING, HERMANN WILHELM (1893-1946), German politician and air force commander **6** 457-458

GORKY, ARSHILE (1905-1948), American painter **6** 458

GORKY, MAXIM (1868-1936), Russian author **6** 458-460

GORMAN, R.C. (Rudolph Carl Gorman; 1931-2005), Native American artist **23** 128-130

GORRIE, JOHN (1803-1855), American physician and inventor **21** 172-174

GORTON, SAMUELL (circa 1592-1677), English colonizer **6** 460

GOSHIRAKAWA (1127-1192), Japanese emperor **6** 460-461

GOSHO, HEINOSUKE (1902-1981), Japanese filmmaker **22** 199-200

Gösta
see Gustavus II

Got, Bertrand de
see Clement V

Gothart, Mathis Neithart
see Grünewald, Matthias

Gothic literature
Radcliffe, Ann **28** 288-290

GOTTFRIED VON STRASSBURG (circa 1165-circa 1215), German poet and romancer **6** 461-462

GOTTLIEB, ADOLPH (1903-1974), American Abstract Expressionist painter **6** 462-463

Gottrecht, Friedman
see Beissel, Johann Conrad

GOTTSCHALK, LOUIS MOREAU (1829-1869), American composer **6** 463-464

GOTTWALD, KLEMENT (1896-1953), first Communist president of Czechoslovakia (1948-1953) **6** 464-466

GOUDIMEL, CLAUDE (circa 1514-1572), French composer **6** 466

GOUJON, JEAN (circa 1510-1568), French sculptor **6** 466-467

GOULART, JOÃO (1918-1976), Brazilian statesman **6** 467-469

GOULD, GLENN (1932-1982), Canadian musician **6** 469-470

GOULD, JAY (1836-1892), American financier and railroad builder **6** 470-472

GOULD, STEPHEN JAY (1941-2002), American paleontologist **6** 472-473

Goulden, Emmeline
see Pankhurst, Emmeline

GOUNOD, CHARLES FRANÇOIS (1818-1893), French composer **6** 473-474

GOURLAY, ROBERT (1778-1863), British reformer in Canada **6** 474

GOURMONT, REMY DE (1858-1915), French author, critic, and essayist **6** 475

GOWER, JOHN (circa 1330-1408), English poet **6** 475-476

GOYA Y LUCIENTES, FRANCISCO DE PAULA JOSÉ DE (1746-1828), Spanish painter and printmaker **6** 476-478

Goyakla
see Geronimo

GOYEN, JAN VAN (1596-1656), Dutch painter **6** 478-479

GRACCHUS, GAIUS SEMPRONIUS (ca. 154-121 B.C.), member of a Roman plebeian family referred to as the Gracchi **6** 479-480

GRACCHUS, TIBERIUS SEMPRONIUS (ca. 163-133 B.C.), member of a Roman plebeian family referred to as the Gracchi **6** 479-480

GRACE, WILLIAM RUSSELL (1832-1904), Irish-born American entrepreneur and politician **6** 480-481

GRACIÁN Y MORALES, BALTASAR JERÓNIMO (1601-1658), Spanish writer **6** 481-482

GRADY, HENRY WOODFIN (1850-1889), American editor and orator **6** 482-483

GRAETZ, HEINRICH HIRSCH (1817-1891), German historian and biblical exegete **6** 483

Graham, John
see Phillips, David Graham

GRAHAM, KATHARINE MEYER (1917-2001), publisher who managed *The Washington Post* **6** 483-485

GRAHAM, MARTHA (1894-1991), American dancer and choreographer **6** 485-486

GRAHAM, OTTO (born 1921), American football player and coach **21** 174-176

GRAHAM, SYLVESTER (1794-1851), American reformer and temperance minister **6** 486-487

GRAHAM, WILLIAM FRANKLIN, JR. ("Billy"; born 1918), American evangelist **6** 487-488

GRAHAME, KENNETH (1859-1932), British author **28** 138-140

GRAINGER, PERCY (Percy Aldridge Grainger; George Percy Grainger; 1882-1961), Australian American musician **25** 160-161

Grameen Bank (Bangladesh)
Yunus, Muhammad **28** 386-388

GRAMSCI, ANTONIO (1891-1937), Italian writer and Communist leader **6** 488-489

GRANADOS, ENRIQUE (1867-1916), Spanish composer and pianist **6** 489-490

GRAND DUCHESS OLGA NIKOLAEVNA (Grand Duchess Olga Nikolaevna; 1895-1918), Russian grand duchess **28** 141-143

GRANDA, CHABUCA (Isabel Granda Larco; 1920-1983), Peruvian singer and songwriter **28** 143-144

GRANDVILLE, J.J. (Jean-Ignace-Isidore Gérard; 1803-1847), French artist and cartoonist **28** 144-146

GRANGE, RED (Harold Edward Grange; 1903-1991), American football player **19** 128-130

GRANT, CARY (born Archibald Alexander Leach; 1904-1986), English actor **6** 490-492

GRANT, ULYSSES SIMPSON (1822-1885), American general, president 1869-1877 **6** 492-494

GRANVILLE, CHRISTINE (Krystyna Skarbek; c. 1915-1952), Polish secret agent **27** 153-154

GRANVILLE, EVELYN BOYD (born 1924), African American mathematician **6** 494-496

GRASS, GÜNTER (born 1927), German novelist, playwright, and poet **6** 496-497

GRASSELLI, CAESAR AUGUSTIN (1850-1927), third generation to head the Grasselli Chemical Company **6** 497-498

GRATIAN (died circa 1155), Italian scholar, father of canon law **6** 498-499

GRATTAN, HENRY (1746-1820), Irish statesman and orator **6** 499

GRAU SAN MARTIN, RAMÓN (1887-1969), Cuban statesman and physician **6** 499-500

GRAUNT, JOHN (1620-1674), English merchant and civil servant **21** 176-178

GRAVES, EARL GILBERT, JR. (born 1935), African American publisher **23** 130-132

GRAVES, MICHAEL (born 1934), American Post-Modernist architect **6** 500-502

GRAVES, NANCY STEVENSON (1940-1995), American sculptor **6** 502-504

GRAVES, ROBERT RANKE (1895-1985), English author **6** 504-506

GRAY, ASA (1810-1888), American botanist **6** 506-507

GRAY, HANNAH HOLBORN (born 1930), university administrator **6** 507-508

GRAY, ROBERT (1755-1806), American explorer **6** 508-509

GRAY, THOMAS (1716-1771), English poet **6** 509-510

GRAY, WILLIAM H., III (born 1941), first African American to be elected House Whip for the U.S. House of Representatives **6** 510-511

Grayson, David (pseudonym)
see Baker, Ray Stannard

Greater New York
see New York City (New York State)

GRECO, EL (1541-1614), Greek-born Spanish painter **6** 511-514

GREELEY, ANDREW M. (born 1928), American Catholic priest, sociologist, and author **6** 514-515

GREELEY, HORACE (1811-1872), American editor and reformer **6** 515-517

GREELY, ADOLPHUS WASHINGTON (1844-1935), American soldier, explorer, and writer **6** 517-518

GREEN, CONSTANCE MCLAUGHLIN (1897-1975), American author and historian **6** 518-519

GREEN, EDITH STARRETT (1910-1987), United States congresswoman from Oregon (1954-1974) **6** 519-520

GREEN, THOMAS HILL (1836-1882), British philosopher **6** 520-521

GREEN, WILLIAM R. (1872-1952), American labor union leader **6** 521

GREENAWAY, KATE (Catherine; 1846-1901), English author and illustrator **18** 168-169

GREENBERG, CLEMENT (1909-1994), American art critic **6** 521-523

GREENBERG, HENRY BENJAMIN (Hank; 1911-1986), American baseball player **25** 161-165

GREENBERG, URI ZVI (1898-1981), Israeli author and activist **24** 158-159

GREENE, CATHERINE LITTLEFIELD (1755-1814), American inventor **22** 200-203

GREENE, GRAHAM (born 1904), English novelist and dramatist **6** 523-524

GREENE, GRAHAM (born ca. 1952), Canadian-Native American actor **6** 524-525

GREENE, NATHANAEL (1742-1786), American Revolutionary War general **6** 525-526

Greenfield, Jerry, (born 1951)
see Ben & Jerry

GREENSPAN, ALAN (born 1926), American economist **6** 526-528

GREER, GERMAINE (born 1939), author and authoritative commentator on women's liberation and sexuality **6** 528-530

GREGG, JOHN ROBERT (1867-1948), American inventor of system of shorthand writing **21** 178-180

GREGG, WILLIAM (1800-1867), American manufacturer **6** 530-531

Gregorian calendar
Dionysius Exiguus **28** 99-100

GREGORY I, SAINT (circa 540-604), pope 590-604 **6** 531-532

GREGORY VII (circa 1020-1085), pope 1073-85 **6** 532-534

GREGORY IX (Ugo [Ugolino] di Segni; 1145-1241), Roman Catholic pope (1227-1241) **21** 180-183

GREGORY XII (Angelo Corrario; c. 1327-1417), pope 1406-1415 **18** 169-171

GREGORY XIII (1502-1585), pope 1572-1585 **6** 534

GREGORY XVI (Bartolommeo Alberto Cappellari; Mauro; 1765-1846), Roman Catholic pope 1831-1846 **25** 165-166

GREGORY, LADY AUGUSTA (1852-1932), Irish dramatist **6** 535-536

GREGORY, DICK (Richard Claxton Gregory; born 1932), comedian and civil rights and world peace activist **6** 536-537

GREGORY OF TOURS, SAINT (538-594), Frankish bishop and historian **6** 534-535

Gregory the Great, Saint
see Gregory I, Saint

GRETZKY, WAYNE (born 1961), Canadian hockey star **6** 537-539

GREUZE, JEAN BAPTISTE (1725-1805), French painter **6** 539

GREVER, MARIA (nee Maria de la Portilla; 1894-1951), Mexican musician **24** 159-161

GREY, CHARLES (2nd Earl Grey; 1764-1845), English statesman, prime minister 1830-1834 **6** 539-540

GREY, SIR GEORGE (1812-1898), English explorer and colonial governor **6** 540-541

GREY, ZANE (Pearl Zane Gray; 1872-1939), American author **20** 160-162

GRIBEAUVAL, JEAN BAPTISTE VAQUETTE DE (1715-1789), French army officer **20** 162-163

GRIEG, EDVARD HAGERUP (1843-1907), Norwegian composer **6** 541-542

GRIERSON, JOHN (1898-1972), Canadian and British filmmaker **6** 542-543

GRIFFES, CHARLES TOMLINSON (1884-1920), American composer **6** 543-544

GRIFFITH, DAVID WARK (1875-1948), American film maker **6** 544-545
Lawrence, Florence **28** 209-211

GRIFFIN, MERV (Mervyn Edward Griffin, Jr.; 1925-2007), American television personality and producer **28** 146-149

GRIFFITH, SIR SAMUEL WALKER (1845-1920), Australian statesman and jurist **6** 545-546

GRIFFITH JOYNER, FLORENCE (1959-1998), American athlete **19** 130-133

Grillet, Alain Robbe
see Robbe-Grillet, Alain

GRILLPARZER, FRANZ (1791-1872), Austrian playwright **6** 546-547

Grimaldi, Rainier de
see Rainier III, Prince of Monaco

GRIMKÉ, ANGELINA EMILY (1805-1879) AND SARAH MOORE (1792-1873), American abolitionists and women's rights agitators **7** 1-2

GRIMKÉ, ARCHIBALD HENRY (1849-1930), American editor, author, and diplomat **7** 1-2

GRIMM, JAKOB KARL (1785-1863) AND WILHELM KARL (1786-1859), German scholars, linguists, and authors **7** 3-4

GRIMMELSHAUSEN, HANS JAKOB CHRISTOFFEL VON (1621/22-1676), German author **7** 4-5

GRIS, JUAN (1887-1927), Spanish painter **7** 5-6

GRISHAM, JOHN (born 1955), American author and attorney **7** 6-8

GRISSOM, VIRGIL IVAN (Gus Grissom; 1926-1967), American astronaut **25** 166-168

GROMYKO, ANDREI ANDREEVICH (1909-1988), minister of foreign affairs and president of the Union of Soviet Socialist Republic (1985-1988) **7** 9-11

GROOMS, RED (born 1937), American artist **7** 11-12

Groot, Huig de
see Grotius, Hugo

GROOTE, GERARD (1340-1384), Dutch evangelical preacher **7** 12-13

GROPIUS, WALTER (1883-1969), German-American architect, educator, and designer **7** 13-14

GROS, BARON (Antoine Jean Gros; 1771-1835), French romantic painter **7** 14-15

GROSS, AL (Alfred J. Gross; 1918-2000), Canadian inventor **28** 149-151

GROSS, SAMUEL DAVID (1805-1884), American surgeon, author, and educator **21** 183-185

GROSSETESTE, ROBERT (1175-1253), English bishop and statesman **7** 15

GROSSINGER, JENNIE (1892-1972), American hotel executive and philanthropist **7** 15-17

GROSZ, GEORGE (1893-1959), German-American painter and graphic artist **7** 17-18

GROTIUS, HUGO (1583-1645), Dutch jurist, statesman, and historian **7** 18-19

GROTOWSKI, JERZY (born 1933), founder of the experimental Laboratory Theatre in Wroclaw, Poland **7** 19-20

GROVE, ANDREW (András Gróf; born 1936), American businessman **18** 171-174

GROVE, FREDERICK PHILIP (circa 1871-1948), Canadian novelist and essayist **7** 20-21

GROVES, LESLIE (1896-1970), military director of the Manhattan Project (atom bomb) during World War II **7** 21-22

GRÜNEWALD, MATTHIAS (circa 1475-1528), German painter **7** 23-24

GUARDI, FRANCESCO (1712-1793), Italian painter **7** 24-25

GUARINI, GUARINO (1624-1683), Italian architect, priest, and philosopher **7** 25-26

GUASTAVINO, RAFAEL (Rafael Guastavino Morano; 1842-1908), Spanish-American architect **23** 132-134

GUBAIDULINA, SOFIA (Sofia Asgatovna Gubaydulina; born 1931), Russian composer **26** 127-129

GUCCIONE, BOB, JR. (born ca. 1956), American publisher **7** 26

GUDERIAN, HEINZ (1888-1953), German military leader **20** 163-165

GUDJÓNSSON, HALLDÓR KILJAN (Halldór Laxness; 1902-1998), Icelandic author **25** 169-171

GÜEMES, MARTÍN (1785-1821), Argentine independence fighter **7** 26-27

GUERCINO (Giovanni Francesco Barbieri; 1591-1666), Italian painter **7** 27

GUERICKE, OTTO VON (1602-1686), German physicist **7** 27-28

GUERIN, VERONICA (1959-1996), Irish investigative reporter and journalist **18** 174-176

GUERRERO, LALO (Eduardo Guerrero, Jr.; 1916-2005), Mexican American singer and songwriter **26** 129-131

GUERRERO, VICENTE (1783-1831), Mexican independence fighter, president 1829 **7** 28-30

Guess, George
see Sequoyah

GUEVARA, ERNESTO ("CHE") (1924-1967), Argentine revolutionary and guerrilla theoretician **7** 30-31

GUEYE, LAMINE (1891-1968), Senegalese statesman **7** 31

GUGGENHEIM, DANIEL (1856-1930), American industrialist and philanthropist **21** 185-187

GUGGENHEIM, MEYER (1828-1905), Swiss-born American industrialist **7** 31-32

GUGGENHEIM, PEGGY (nee Marguerite Guggenheim; 1898-1979), American art collector and dealer **26** 131-133

GUICCIARDINI, FRANCESCO (1483-1540), Italian historian and statesman **7** 32-33

GUIDO D'AREZZO (circa 995-circa 1050), Italian music theorist **7** 33

Guido de Cauliaco
see Guy de Chauliac

Guido di Pietro
see Angelico, Fra

GUILLAUME, CHARLES-EDOUARD (1861-1938), Swiss Scientist **25** 171-173

GUILLAUME DE LORRIS (circa 1210-1237), French poet **7** 33-34

GUILLÉN, NICOLÁS (born 1902), Cuban author **7** 34-35

GUILLÉN Y ALVAREZ, JORGE (1893-1984), Spanish poet **7** 35-36

GUINIZZELLI, GUIDO (1230/40-1276), Italian poet **7** 36-37

GUINNESS, ALEC (born 1914), British actor of the stage, films, and television **7** 37-38

GÜIRÁLDEZ, RICARDO (1886-1927), Argentine poet and novelist **7** 38-39

GUISCARD, ROBERT (1016-1085), Norman adventurer **7** 39-40

GUISEWITE, CATHY (born 1950), American cartoonist and author **18** 176-177

Guitar (music)
Barrios, Agustin Pìo **28** 27-29
Ponce, Manuel **28** 282-284

Guitar (musical instrument)
Paul, Les **28** 276-278

GUIZOT, FRANÇOIS PIERRE GUILLAUME (1787-1874), French statesman and historian **7** 40-41

GUMPLOWICZ, LUDWIG (1838-1909), Polish-Austrian sociologist and political theorist **7** 41

GUNN, THOM (born 1929), English poet **18** 177-178

Guns
see Weapons and explosives

GÜNTHER, IGNAZ (1725-1775), German sculptor **7** 41-42

Guru Granth Sahib (Sikh religious text)
Singh, Gobind **28** 327-328

Gustafsson, Greta Lovisa
see Garbo, Greta

GUSTAVUS I (Gustavus Eriksson; 1496-1560), king of Sweden 1523-1560 **7** 42-43

GUSTAVUS II (Gustavus Adolphus; 1594-1632), king of Sweden 1611-1632 **7** 43-45

GUSTAVUS III (1746-1792), king of Sweden 1771-1792 **7** 45-46

GUSTON, PHILIP (1913-1980), American painter and a key member of the New York School **7** 47-48

GUTENBERG, JOHANN (circa 1398-1468), German inventor and printer **7** 48-49

GUTHRIE, EDWIN RAY (1886-1959), American psychologist **7** 49-50

GUTHRIE, TYRONE (1900-1971), English theater director **7** 50-51
Patterson, Tom **28** 274-276

GUTHRIE, WOODROW WILSON ("Woody"; 1912-1967), writer and performer of folk songs **7** 51-52

GUTIÉRRÉZ, GUSTAVO (born 1928), Peruvian who was the father of liberation theology **7** 52-53

GUY-BLACHÉ, ALICE (Alice Blaché; 1873-1968), French filmmaker **26** 133-135

GUY DE CHAULIAC (circa 1295-1368), French surgeon **7** 54

Guzmán Blanco, Antonio
see Blanco, Antonio Guzmán

GUZY, CAROL (Born 1956), American photographer **25** 173-175

Gypsy music
see Folk music—Hungarian

H

H.D.
see Doolittle, Hilda

H.H.
see Jackson, Helen Hunt

HABASH, GEORGE (1926-2008), founder of the Arab Nationalists' Movement (1952) and of the Popular Front for the Liberation of Palestine (PFLP; 1967) **7** 55-56

HABER, FRITZ (1868-1934), German chemist **7** 56-58

HABERMAS, JÜRGEN (born 1929), German philosopher and sociologist **7** 58-60

HABIBIE, BACHARUDDIN JUSUF (born 1936), president of Indonesia **19** 134-136

HADID, ZAHA (Zaha M. Hadid; born 1950), Iraqi-born British architect **27** 155-157

HADRIAN (76-138), Roman emperor 117-138 **7** 60-61

HAECKEL, ERNST HEINRICH PHILIPP AUGUST (1834-1919), German biologist and natural philosopher **7** 61-62

HAEFLIGER, ERNST (Ernst Häflinger; 1919-2007), Swiss singer **28** 152-154

HAFIZ, SHAMS AL-DIN (circa 1320-1390), Persian mystical poet and Koranic exegete **7** 63

HAGEN, UTA THYRA (born 1919), American actress **18** 179-180

HAGEN, WALTER (1892-1969), American golfer **21** 188-190

HAGENS, GUNTHER VON (Guinther Gerhard Liebchen; born 1945), German anatomist **27** 157-159

HAGUE, FRANK (1876-1956), American politician **7** 63-64

HAHN, OTTO (1879-1968), German chemist **7** 64-65

HAHNEMANN, SAMUEL (Christian Friedrich Samuel Hahnemann; 1755-1843), German physician and chemist **21** 190-193

HAIDAR ALI (1721/22-1782), Indian prince, ruler of Mysore 1759-1782 **7** 65-66

HAIG, ALEXANDER M., JR. (born 1924), American military leader, diplomat, secretary of state, and presidential adviser **7** 66-67

HAIG, DOUGLAS (1st Earl Haig; 1861-1928), British field marshal **7** 67-68

HAIGNERE, CLAUDIE ANDRE-DESHAYS (born 1957), French astronaut and government official **25** 176-178

HAILE SELASSIE (1892-1975), emperor of Ethiopia **7** 68-70

HAKLUYT, RICHARD (1552/53-1616), English geographer and author **7** 70

HALBERSTAM, DAVID (1934-2007), American journalist, author and social historian **18** 180-183

HALDANE, JOHN BURDON SANDERSON (1892-1964), English biologist **7** 70-71

HALE, CLARA (nee Clara McBride; 1905-1992), American humanitarian and social reformer **20** 166-168

HALE, EDWARD EVERETT (1822-1909), American Unitarian minister and author **7** 71-72

HALE, GEORGE ELLERY (1868-1938), American astronomer **7** 72-74

HALE, SARAH JOSEPHA (née Buell; 1788-1879), American editor **7** 74-75

HALES, STEPHEN (1677-1761), English scientist and clergyman **7** 75

HALÉVY, ÉLIE (1870-1937), French philosopher and historian **7** 76

HALEY, ALEX (1921-1992), African American journalist and author **7** 76-78

HALEY, MARGARET A. (1861-1939), American educator and labor activist **7** 78-79

HALFFTER, CHRISTÓBAL (born 1930), Spanish composer **7** 79-80

HALIBURTON, THOMAS CHANDLER (1796-1865), Canadian judge and author **7** 80

HALIDE EDIP ADIVAR (1884-1964), Turkish woman writer, scholar, and public figure **7** 80-82

Halifax, 3rd Viscount
see Halifax, 1st Earl of

HALIFAX, 1ST EARL OF (Edward Frederick Lindley Wood; 1881-1959), English statesman **7** 82-83

HALL, ASAPH (1829-1907), American astronomer **7** 83-84

HALL, DONALD (born 1928), New England memoirist, short story writer, essayist, dramatist, critic, and anthologist as well as poet **7** 84-85

HALL, EDWARD MARSHALL (1858-1927), British attorney **22** 204-205

HALL, GRANVILLE STANLEY (1844-1924), American psychologist and educator **7** 85-86

HALL, LLOYD AUGUSTUS (1894-1971), American scientist and inventor **28** 154-156

HALL, PETER REGINALD FREDERICK (born 1930), English theater director **24** 162-165

HALL, PRINCE (circa 1735-1807), African American abolitionist and founder of the first black masonic lodge **26** 136-138

HALL, RADCLYFFE (Marguerite Radclyffe Hall; 1880-1943), British author **20** 168-170

HALLAJ, AL-HUSAYN IBN MANSUR AL (857-922), Persian Moslem mystic and martyr **7** 86-87

HALLAM, LEWIS, SR. AND JR. (Lewis Sr. ca. 1705-1755; Lewis Jr. 1740-1808), American actors and theatrical managers **7** 87

HALLECK, HENRY WAGER (1815-1872), American military strategist **22** 205-207

HALLER, ALBRECHT VON (1708-1777), Swiss physician **7** 87-88

HALLEY, EDMUND (1656-1742), English astronomer **7** 88-89

HALONEN, TARJA KAARINA (born 1943), Finnish president **25** 178-180

HALS, FRANS (1581/85-1666), Dutch painter **7** 89-91

HALSEY, WILLIAM FREDERICK (1882-1959), American admiral **7** 91-92

HALSTED, WILLIAM STEWART (1852-1922), American surgeon **22** 207-209

HAMADA, SHOJI (1894-1978), Japanese potter **26** 138-140

HAMANN, JOHANN GEORG (1730-1788), German philosopher **7** 92

HAMER, FANNIE LOU (born Townsend; 1917-1977), American civil rights activist **7** 93-94

HAMILCAR BARCA (circa 285-229/228 B.C.), Carthaginian general and statesman **7** 94-95

HAMILL, DOROTHY (born 1956), American figure skater **25** 180-183

HAMILTON, ALEXANDER (1755-1804), American statesman **7** 95-98

HAMILTON, ALICE (1869-1970), American physician **7** 98-99

HAMILTON, EDITH (1867-1963), American educator and author **22** 209-211

HAMILTON, SIR WILLIAM ROWAN (1805-1865), Irish mathematical physicist **7** 99-100

HAMMARSKJÖLD, DAG (1905-1961), Swedish diplomat **7** 100-101

HAMM-BRÜCHER, HILDEGARD (born 1921), Free Democratic Party's candidate for the German presidency in 1994 **7** 101-103

HAMMER, ARMAND (1898-1990), American entrepreneur and art collector **7** 103-104

HAMMERSTEIN, OSCAR CLENDENNING II (1895-1960), lyricist and librettist of the American theater **7** 104-106

HAMMETT, (SAMUEL) DASHIELL (1894-1961), American author **7** 106-108

HAMMOND, JAMES HENRY (1807-1864), American statesman **7** 108-109

HAMMOND, JOHN LAWRENCE LE BRETON (1872-1952), English historian **7** 108-109

HAMMOND, LUCY BARBARA (1873-1961), English historian **7** 109

HAMMURABI (1792-1750 B.C.), king of Babylonia **7** 109-110

HAMPDEN, JOHN (1594-1643), English statesman **7** 110-111

HAMPTON, LIONEL (1908-2002), African American jazz musician **22** 211-213

HAMPTON, WADE (circa 1751-1835), American planter **7** 111-112

HAMPTON, WADE III (1818-1902), American statesman and Confederate general **7** 112

HAMSUN, KNUT (1859-1952), Norwegian novelist **7** 113-114

HAN FEI TZU (circa 280-233 B.C.), Chinese statesman and philosopher **7** 124-125

Han Kao-tsu
see Liu Pang

HAN WU-TI (157-87 B.C.), Chinese emperor **7** 136

HAN YÜ (768-824), Chinese author **7** 136-137

HANAFI, HASSAN (born 1935), Egyptian philosopher **7** 114

HANCOCK, JOHN (1737-1793), American statesman **7** 114-116

HAND, BILLINGS LEARNED (1872-1961), American jurist **7** 116

Händel, Georg Friedrich
see Handel, George Frederick

HANDEL, GEORGE FREDERICK (1685-1759), German-born English composer and organist **7** 116-119

HANDKE, PETER (born 1942), Austrian playwright, novelist, screenwriter, essayist, and poet **7** 119-121

HANDLER, RUTH (Ruth Mosko; 1916-2002), American businesswoman **25** 183-185

HANDLIN, OSCAR (born 1915), American historian **7** 121-122

Handschuchsheim, Ritter von
see Meinong, Alexius

HANDSOME LAKE (a.k.a. Hadawa' Ko; ca. 1735-1815), Seneca spiritual leader **7** 122-123

HANDY, WILLIAM CHRISTOPHER (1873-1958), African American songwriter **7** 123-124

HANKS, NANCY (1927-1983), called the ''mother of a million artists'' for her work in building federal financial support for the arts and artists **7** 126-127

HANKS, TOM (Thomas Jeffrey Hanks; born 1956), American actor **23** 135-137

HANNA AND BARBERA (William Hanna, 1910-2001; Joseph Barbera, 1911-2006), American producers and directors of animated cartoons **28** 156-159
Peyo **28** 280-282

HANNA, MARCUS ALONZO (1837-1904), American businessman and politician **7** 127-128

Hanna, William
see Hanna and Barbera

HANNIBAL BARCA (247-183 B.C.), Carthaginian general **7** 128-130

HANSBERRY, LORRAINE VIVIAN (1930-1965), American writer and a major figure on Broadway **7** 130-131

HANSEN, ALVIN (1887-1975), American economist **7** 131-132

Hansen, Emil
see Nolde, Emil

HANSEN, JULIA BUTLER (1907-1988), American politician **7** 132-133

HANSON, DUANE (1925-1990), American super-realist sculptor **7** 133-135

HANSON, HOWARD (1896-1981), American composer and educator **7** 135-136

HAPGOOD, NORMAN (1868-1937), American author and editor **7** 137-138

HARA, KEI (1856-1921), Japanese statesman and prime minister 1918-1921 **7** 138

HARAND, IRENE (born Irene Wedl; 1900-1975), Austrian political and human rights activist **7** 139-145

HARAWI, ILYAS AL- (Elias Harawi; 1930-2006), president of Lebanon **7** 145-146

HARBURG, EDGAR YIPSEL (Irwin Hochberg; E.Y. Harburg; 1896-1981), American lyricist **26** 140-142

Hardenberg, Baron Friedrich Leopold von
see Novalis

HARDENBERG, PRINCE KARL AUGUST VON (1750-1822), Prussian statesman **7** 146-147

HARDIE, JAMES KEIR (1856-1915), Scottish politician **7** 147-148

HARDING, FLORENCE KLING (Florence Kling DeWolfe Harding; 1860-1924), American First Lady **28** 159-161

Harding, Stephen, Saint
see Stephen Harding, Saint

HARDING, WARREN GAMALIEL (1865-1923), American statesman, president 1921-1923 **7** 148-149
wife
    Harding, Florence Kling **28** 159-161

Hardouin, Jules
see Mansart, Jules Hardouin

HARDY, HARRIET (1905-1993), American pathologist **7** 150

HARDY, THOMAS (1840-1928), English novelist, poet, and dramatist **7** 150-152

HARE, ROBERT (1781-1858), American chemist **7** 152-153

HARGRAVES, EDWARD HAMMOND (1816-1891), Australian publicist **7** 153-154

HARGREAVES, ALISON (1962-1995), British mountain climber **26** 142-144

HARING, KEITH (1958-1990), American artist tied to New York graffiti art of the 1980s **7** 154-155

HARINGTON, JOHN (1560-1612), English author and courtier **21** 193-195

HARIRI, RAFIC (1944-2005), politician and businessman **28** 161-163

HARJO, JOY (Born 1951), Native American author, musician, and artist **25** 185-187

HARJO, SUZAN SHOWN (born 1945), Native American activist **18** 183-185

HARKNESS, GEORGIA (1891-1974), American Methodist and ecumenical theologian **7** 155-156

HARLAN, JOHN MARSHALL (1833-1911), American jurist **7** 156-157

HARLAN, JOHN MARSHALL (1899-1971), U.S. Supreme Court justice **7** 157-159

Harlem renaissance (American literature)
Fisher, Rudolph **28** 121-123
Patterson, Louise Alone Thompson **28** 272-274
Thurman, Wallace Henry **28** 352-354

HARLEY, ROBERT (1st Earl of Oxford and Earl Mortimer; 1661-1724), English statesman **7** 159-160

HARNACK, ADOLF VON (1851-1930), German theologian **7** 160

HARNETT, WILLIAM MICHAEL (1848-1892), American painter **7** 160-161

Harold ''Fairhair''
see Harold I

Harold Haardraade
see Harold III

HAROLD I (circa 840-933), king of Norway 860-930 **7** 161-162

HAROLD II (Harold Godwinson; died 1066), Anglo-Saxon king of England of 1066 **7** 162

HAROLD III (1015-1066), king of Norway 1047-1066 **7** 163

Harold the Ruthless
see Harold III

HARPER, FRANCES (Frances Ellen Watkins Harper; 1825-1911), African American author, abolitionist and women's rights activist **18** 185-187

HARPER, JAMES (1795-1869), American publisher **22** 213-216

HARPER, STEPHEN (born 1959), Canadian prime minister **27** 159-161

HARPER, WILLIAM RAINEY (1856-1906), American educator and biblical scholar **7** 163-164

HARPUR, CHARLES (1813-1866), Australian poet and author **22** 216-218

HARRIMAN, EDWARD HENRY (1848-1909), American railroad executive **7** 164-165

HARRIMAN, PAMELA (1920-1997), American ambassador and patrician **18** 187-189

HARRIMAN, W. AVERELL (1891-1986), American industrialist, financier, and diplomat **7** 165-166

HARRINGTON, JAMES (1611-1677), English political theorist **7** 166-167

HARRINGTON, MICHAEL (1928-1989), American political activist and educator **7** 167-169

HARRIOT, THOMAS (1560-1621), English scientist and mathematician **23** 137-139

HARRIS, ABRAM LINCOLN, JR. (1899-1963), African American economist **7** 169-171

HARRIS, BARBARA CLEMENTINE (born 1930), African American activist and Anglican bishop **7** 171-172

HARRIS, FRANK (1856-1931), Irish-American author and editor **7** 172-173

HARRIS, JOEL CHANDLER (1848-1908), American writer **7** 173-174

HARRIS, LADONNA (born 1931), Native American activist **18** 189-191

HARRIS, PATRICIA ROBERTS (1924-1985), first African American woman in the U.S. Cabinet **7** 174-175

HARRIS, ROY (1898-1979), American composer **7** 175-176

HARRIS, TOWNSEND (1804-1878), American merchant and diplomat **7** 176-177

HARRIS, WILLIAM TORREY (1835-1909), American educator and philosopher **7** 177-178

HARRISON, BENJAMIN (1833-1901), American statesman, president 1889-1893 **7** 178-179

HARRISON, GEORGE (1943-2005), English musician **25** 187-191

HARRISON, PETER (1716-1775), American architect and merchant **7** 179-180

HARRISON, WILLIAM HENRY (1773-1841), American statesman, president 1841 **7** 180-181

HARSHA (Harshavardhana; circa 590-647), king of Northern India 606-612 **7** 181-182

Hart, Emma
see Hamilton, Lady; Willard, Emma Hart

HART, GARY W. (born 1936), American political campaign organizer, U.S. senator, and presidential candidate **7** 182-184

HART, HERBERT LIONEL ADOLPHUS (1907-1992), British legal philosopher **22** 218-219

HARTE, FRANCIS BRET (1837-1902), American poet and fiction writer **7** 184-185

HARTLEY, DAVID (1705-1757), British physician and philosopher **7** 185

HARTLEY, MARSDEN (1877-1943), American painter **7** 186

HARTSHORNE, CHARLES (born 1897), American theologian **7** 186-187

HARUN AL-RASHID (766-809), Abbasid caliph of Baghdad 786-809 **7** 188

HARUNOBU, SUZUKI (ca. 1725-1770), Japanese painter and printmaker **7** 188-189

HARVARD, JOHN (1607-1638), English philanthropist **21** 195-197

Harvard College
see Harvard University (Cambridge, Massachusetts)

Harvard University (Cambridge, Massachusetts)
presidents
Faust, Drew Gilpin **28** 116-118

HARVEY, WILLIAM (1578-1657), English physician **7** 189-190

HARWOOD, GWEN (nee Gwendoline Nessie Foster; 1920-1995), Australian poet **26** 144-146

HASAN, IBN AL-HAYTHAM (ca. 966-1039), Arab physicist, astronomer, and mathematician **7** 190-191

Hasan, Mansur ben
see Firdausi

Hasan Ali Shah
see Aga Khan

Hasan ibn-Hani, al-
see Abu Nuwas

HASKINS, CHARLES HOMER (1870-1937), American historian **7** 191-192

Hasong, Prince
see Sonjo

HASSAM, FREDERICK CHILDE (1859-1935), American impressionist painter **7** 192

HASSAN, MOULEY (King Hassan II; 1929-1999), inherited the throne of Morocco in 1961 **7** 194-195

HASSAN, MUHAMMAD ABDILLE (1864-1920), Somali politico-religious leader and poet **7** 194-195

HASTINGS, PATRICK GARDINER (1880-1952), British lawyer and politician **22** 219-221

HASTINGS, WARREN (1732-1818), English statesman **7** 195-196

HATCH, WILLIAM HENRY (1833-1896), American reformer and politician **7** 196

Hathorne, Nathaniel
see Hawthorne, Nathaniel

HATSHEPSUT (ruled 1503-1482 B.C.), Egyptian queen **7** 196-197

HATTA, MOHAMMAD (1902-1980), a leader of the Indonesian nationalist movement (1920s-1945) and a champion of non-alignment and of socialism grounded in Islam **7** 197-199

HAUPTMAN, HERBERT AARON (born 1917), American mathematician **24** 165-167

HAUPTMANN, GERHART JOHANN ROBERT (1862-1946), German dramatist and novelist **7** 199-201

HAUSHOFER, KARL (1869-1946), German general and geopolitician **7** 201

HAUSSMANN, BARON GEORGES EUGÈNE (1809-1891), French prefect of the Seine **7** 201-202

Hauteclocque, Philippe Marie de
see Leclerc, Jacques Philippe

HAVEL, VACLAV (born 1936), playwright and human rights activist who became the president of Czechoslovakia **7** 202-205

HAVEMEYER, HENRY OSBORNE (1847-1907), American businessman **22** 222-224

HAVILAND, LAURA SMITH (1808-1898), American anti-slavery activist **27** 161-163

HAWES, HARRIET ANN BOYD (1871-1945), American archeologist **22** 224-225

HAWKE, ROBERT JAMES LEE (born 1929), Australian Labor prime minister **7** 205-206

Hawkesbury, Baron
see Liverpool, 2nd Earl of

HAWKING, STEPHEN WILLIAM (born 1942), British physicist and mathematician **7** 206-208

HAWKINS, COLEMAN (1904-1969), American jazz musician **7** 208-210

HAWKINS, SIR JOHN (1532-1595), English naval commander **7** 210-211

HAWKS, HOWARD WINCHESTER (1896-1977), American film director **22** 225-226

HAWKSMOOR, NICHOLAS (1661-1736), English architect **7** 211-212

HAWTHORNE, NATHANIEL (1804-1864), American novelist **7** 212-215

HAY, JOHN (1838-1905), American statesman **7** 215-216

HAYA DE LA TORRE, VICTOR RAUL (born 1895), Peruvian political leader and theorist **7** 216-217

HAYDEN, FERDINAND VANDIVEER (1829-1887), American geologist and explorer **22** 227-229

HAYDEN, ROBERT EARL (1913-1980), African American poet **22** 229-231

HAYDEN, THOMAS EMMET (born 1939), American writer and political activist **7** 217-219

HAYDN, FRANZ JOSEPH (1732-1809), Austrian composer **7** 219-221

HAYEK, FRIEDRICH A. VON (1899-1992), Austrian-born British free market economist, social philosopher, and Nobel Laureate **7** 221-223

HAYES, HELEN (1900-1993), American actress **7** 223-224

HAYES, LUCY WEBB (Lucy Ware Webb Hayes; 1831-1889), American Fist Lady **28** 163-166

HAYES, CARDINAL PATRICK JOSEPH (1867-1938), American cardinal **7** 224-225

HAYES, ROLAND (1887-1977), African American classical singer **7** 225-227

HAYES, RUTHERFORD BIRCHARD (1822-1893), American statesman, president 1877-1881 **7** 227-228
wife
    Hayes, Lucy Webb **28** 163-166

HAYFORD, J. E. CASELY (1866-1903), Gold Coast politician, journalist, and educator **7** 228-230

HAYKAL, MUHAMMAD HUSAIN (born 1923), Egyptian journalist and editor of *al-Ahram*(1957-1974) **7** 230-231

HAYNE, ROBERT YOUNG (1791-1839), American politician **7** 231-232

HAYNES, ELWOOD (1857-1925), American inventor and businessman **22** 231-234

HAYS, WILL (William Harrison Hays; 1879-1954), American film censor **21** 197-199

HAYWOOD, ELIZA (Eliza Fowler Haywood; 1693-1756), English author **27** 163-165

HAYWOOD, WILLIAM DUDLEY (1869-1928), American labor leader **7** 232-233

HAYWORTH, RITA (born Margarita Carmen Cansino; 1918-1987), American actress **7** 233-235

HAZA, OFRA (1959-2000), Israeli singer **24** 167-169

Hazaken (Elder)
see Shammai

HAZLITT, WILLIAM (1778-1830), English literary and social critic **7** 235-236

HEAD, EDITH (1898-1981), American costume designer **18** 191-193

HEADE, MARTIN JOHNSON (1819-1904), American painter **7** 236

HEALY, BERNADINE (born 1944), American physician and administrator **7** 237-238

HEANEY, SEAMUS JUSTIN (born 1939), Irish poet, author, and editor **7** 238-240

HEARN, LAFCADIO (1850-1904), European-born American author **7** 240

HEARNE, SAMUEL (1745-1792), English explorer **7** 241-242

HEARST, GEORGE (1820-1891), American publisher and politician **7** 242

HEARST, PATRICIA (born 1954), kidnapped heiress who became a bank robber **7** 242-243

HEARST, PHOEBE APPERSON (1842-1919), American philanthropist **27** 165-167

HEARST, WILLIAM RANDOLPH (1863-1951), American publisher and politician **7** 243-244

HEATH, EDWARD RICHARD GEORGE (1916-2005), prime minister of Great Britain (1970-1974) **7** 244-246

HEAVYSEGE, CHARLES (1816-1876), Canadian poet and dramatist **7** 246

HEBBEL, FRIEDRICH (1813-1863), German poet and playwright **7** 247

HEBERT, JACQUES RENÉ (1757-1794), French journalist and revolutionist **7** 247-248

HECHT, BEN (1894-1964), American journalist, playwright, and Hollywood scriptwriter **7** 248-250

HECKER, ISAAC THOMAS (1819-1888), American Catholic religious founder **7** 250-251

HECKLER, MARGARET MARY O'SHAUGHNESSY (born 1931), American attorney, congressional representative, secretary of health and human services, and ambassador **7** 251-252

HEDIN, SVEN ANDERS (1865-1952), Swedish explorer and geographer **7** 252-253

HEFNER, HUGH (born 1926), founder and publisher of Playboy magazine **7** 253-254

HEGEL, GEORG WILHELM FRIEDRICH (1770-1831), German philosopher and educator **7** 254-256

HEGGESSEY, LORRAINE (born 1956), British television executive **26** 146-148

HEIDEGGER, MARTIN (1889-1976), German philosopher **7** 257-258

HEIDEN, ERIC ARTHUR (born 1958), American skater **24** 169-171

HEIDENSTAM, CARL GUSTAF VERNER VON (1859-1940), Swedish author **7** 258-259

HEIFETZ, JASCHA (1901-1987), American violinist **20** 170-172

HEIGHT, DOROTHY IRENE (born 1912), civil and human rights activist **23** 139-141

HEINE, HEINRICH (1797-1856), German poet and essayist **7** 259-260

HEINLEIN, ROBERT A. (Robert Anson Heinlein; Anson McDonald; 1907-1988), American author **28** 166-168

HEINRICH, ANTHONY PHILIP (1781-1861), American composer **7** 261

HEINZ, HENRY JOHN (H.J. Heinz; 1844-1919), American businessman **19** 136-138

HEISENBERG, WERNER KARL (born 1901), German physicist **7** 261-263

HEISMAN, JOHN WILLIAM (Johann Wilhelm Heisman; 1869-1936), American football coach **24** 171-174

HELLER, JOSEPH (1923-1999), American author **7** 263-265

HELLER, WALTER (1915-1987), chairman of the Council of Economic Advisors (1961-1964) and chief spokesman of the "New Economics" **7** 265-266

HELLMAN, LILLIAN FLORENCE (born 1905), American playwright **7** 267-268

HELMHOLTZ, HERMANN LUDWIG FERDINAND VON (1821-1894), German physicist and physiologist **7** 268-269

HELMONT, JAN BAPTISTA VAN (1579-1644), Flemish chemist and physician **7** 269-271

HELMS, JESSE (born 1921), United States Senator from North Carolina **7** 271-272

HELOISE (c. 1098-c. 1163), French abbess **27** 167-169

HELPER, HINTON ROWAN (1829-1909), American author and railroad promoter **7** 272-273

HELVÉTIUS, CLAUDE ADRIEN (1715-1771), French philosopher **7** 273-274

HEMINGWAY, ERNEST MILLER (1898-1961), American novelist and journalist **7** 274-277

HÉMON, LOUIS (1880-1913), French-Canadian novelist **7** 277

HEMPHILL, JOHN (1803-1862), American jurist and statesman **22** 234-236

HENDERSON, ARTHUR (1863-1935), British statesman **7** 277-278

HENDERSON, DONALD AINSLIE (D.A.; born 1928), American public health official **22** 236-238

HENDERSON, FLETCHER (James Fletcher Henderson; 1897-1952), African American musician **26** 148-150

HENDERSON, RICHARD (1735-1785), American jurist and land speculator **7** 278-279

HENDRIX, JIMI (born Johnny Allen Hendrix; 1942-1970), African American guitarist, singer, and composer **7** 279-283

HENG, CHANG (Zhang Heng; Pingzhi; 78-139), Chinese scientist and author **24** 174-176

HENG SAMRIN (born 1934), Cambodian Communist leader who became president of the People's Republic of Kampuchea (PRK) in 1979 **7** 283-285

HENIE, SONJA (1912-1969), Norwegian figure skater **20** 172-173

Henri I (king of Haiti)
see Christophe, Henri

HENRI, ROBERT (Robert Henry Cozad; 1865-1929), American painter **22** 238-240

Henry (IV, count of Luxemburg)
see Henry VII (Holy Roman emperor)

Henry (prince, Portugal)
see Henry the Navigator

Henry I (Holy Roman emperor)
see Henry I (king of Germany)

HENRY I (876-936), king of Germany 919-936 **7** 285-286

HENRY I (1068-1135), king of England 1100-1135 **7** 286-287

HENRY II (1133-1189), king of England 1154-1189 **7** 287-289

Henry III (king of Navarre)
see Henry IV (king of France)

HENRY III (1017-1056), Holy Roman emperor and king of Germany 1039-1056 **7** 290

HENRY III (1207-1272), king of England 1216-1272 **7** 290-292

HENRY IV (1050-1106), Holy Roman emperor and king of Germany 1056-1106 **7** 292

HENRY IV (1367-1413), king of England 1399-1413 **7** 292-293

HENRY IV (1553-1610), king of France 1589-1610 **7** 293-295

HENRY V (1081-1125), Holy Roman emperor and king of Germany 1106-1125 **7** 295-296

HENRY V (1387-1422), king of England 1413-1422 **7** 296-297

HENRY VI (1421-1471), king of England 1422-61 and 1470-1471 **7** 298-299

HENRY VII (1274-1313), Holy Roman emperor and king of Germany 1308-1313 **7** 299-300

HENRY VII (1457-1509), king of England 1485-1509 **7** 300-302
relatives
Woodville, Elizabeth **28** 381-383

HENRY VIII (1491-1547), king of England 1509-1547 **7** 302-305
relatives
Woodville, Elizabeth **28** 381-383

HENRY, AARON (born 1922), African American civil rights activist **7** 306-307

HENRY, JOSEPH (1797-1878), American physicist and electrical experimenter **7** 307-308

HENRY, MARGUERITE (Margurite Breithaupt; 1902-1997), American author **19** 138-140

HENRY, O. (pseudonym of William Sydney Porter; 1862-1910), American short-story writer **7** 308-309

HENRY, PATRICK (1736-1799), American orator and revolutionary **7** 309-311

Henry of Anjou
see Henry II (king of England)

Henry of Bolingbroke
see Henry IV (king of England)

Henry of Bracton (Bratton)
see Bracton, Henry de

Henry of Derby
see Henry IV (king of England)

Henry of Lancaster
see Henry IV (king of England)

Henry of Navarre
see Henry IV (king of France)

Henry Plantagenet (duke of Normandy)
see Henry II (king of England)

Henry the Fowler
see Henry I (king of Germany)

HENRY THE NAVIGATOR (1394-1460), Portuguese prince **7** 305-306

HENSEL, FANNY MENDELSSOHN (Fanny Cäcilie Mendelssohn-Bartholdy; 1805-1847), German composer and pianist **26** 150-152

HENSON, JIM (James Maury Henson, 1936-1990), American puppeteer, screenwriter, and producer **19** 140-142

HENSON, JOSIAH (1789-1883), African American preacher and former slave **7** 311-312

HENSON, MATTHEW A. (1866-1955), African American Arctic explorer **7** 312-314

HENZE, HANS WERNER (born 1926), German composer **7** 314

HEPBURN, AUDREY (born Edda Van Heemstra Hepburn-Ruston; 1929-1993), Swiss actress and humanitarian **7** 314-316

HEPBURN, KATHARINE (born 1907), American actress on the stage and on the screen **7** 316-317

HEPPLEWHITE, GEORGE (died 1786), English furniture designer **7** 317-318

HEPWORTH, BARBARA (1903-1975), English sculptor **7** 318-319

HERACLIDES OF PONTUS (circa 388-310 B.C.), Greek philosopher **7** 319-320

HERACLITUS (flourished 500 B.C.), Greek philosopher **7** 320

HERACLIUS (circa 575-641), Byzantine emperor 610-641 **7** 320-321

HERBART, JOHANN FRIEDRICH (1776-1841), German philosopher-psychologist and educator **7** 321-322

HERBERG, WILL (1906-1977), Jewish theologian, social thinker, and biblical exegete **7** 322-323

HERBERT, EDWARD (1st Baron Herbert of Cherbury; 1583-1648), English philosopher, poet, diplomat, and historian **7** 324

HERBERT, FRANK, JR. (1920-1986), American author **28** 168-170

HERBERT, GEORGE (1593-1633), English metaphysical poet and Anglican priest **7** 324-326

Herblock
see Block, Herbert

HERDER, JOHANN GOTTFRIED VON (1744-1803), German philosopher, theologian, and critic **7** 327-328

HERGÉ (Georges Remi; 1907-1983), Belgian comics artist **26** 152-154

HERMAN, JERRY (born 1931), American composer and lyricist **20** 173-175

HERNÁNDEZ, JOSÉ (1834-1886), Argentine poet **7** 328-329

HERNÁNDEZ COLÓN, RAFAEL (born 1936), Puerto Rican governor **7** 329-330

HERNDON, ALONZO FRANKLIN (1858-1927), African American businessman **24** 176-178

Hero of Alexandria
see Heron of Alexandria

HEROD THE GREAT (circa 73-4 B.C.), king of Judea **7** 333-334

HERODOTUS (circa 484-circa 425 B.C.), Greek historian **7** 330-333

HERON OF ALEXANDRIA (flourished circa 60), Greek engineer, mathematician, and inventor **7** 334-335

HEROPHILUS (335-280 B.C.), Greek physician and anatomist **25** 191-192

HERRERA, CAROLINA (Maria Carolina Josefina Pacanins y Nino; born 1939), Venezuelan designer **23** 141-143

HERRERA, JUAN DE (circa 1530-1597), Spanish architect **7** 335

HERRERA LANE, FELIPE (1922-1996), Chilean banker and economist **7** 336

HERRICK, ROBERT (1591-1674), English poet and Anglican parson **7** 336-339

HERRIOT, ÉDOUARD (1872-1957), French statesman and author **7** 339-340

HERRMANN, BERNARD (Benny Herrmann; 1911-1975), American composer **21** 199-202

HERSCHEL, CAROLINE (1750-1848), German/English astronomer and mathematician **20** 175-176

HERSCHEL, SIR JOHN FREDERICK WILLIAM (1792-1871), English astronomer **7** 340-341

HERSCHEL, SIR WILLIAM (1738-1822), German-born English astronomer **7** 341-343

HERSHEY, ALFRED DAY (1908-1997), American microbiologist **7** 343-345

HERSHEY, MILTON (1857-1945), American businessman and philanthropist **19** 142-144

HERSKOVITS, MELVILLE JEAN (1895-1963), American anthropologist **7** 345

Hertford, 1st Earl of
see Somerset, Duke of

HERTZ, GUSTAV (1887-1975), German physicist **25** 192-194

HERTZ, HEINRICH RUDOLF (1857-1894), German physicist **7** 346-347

HERTZOG, JAMES BARRY MUNNIK (1866-1942), South African prime minister 1924-39 **7** 347-348

HERUY WÄLDÄ-SELLASÉ (1878-1938), Ethiopian writer and government press director **7** 348-349

HERZBERG, GERHARD (born 1904), German-born Canadian chemist/ physicist **7** 349-350

HERZEN, ALEKSANDR IVANOVICH (1812-1870), Russian author and political agitator **7** 351-352

HERZL, THEODOR (1860-1904), Hungarian-born Austrian Zionist author **7** 352-354

HERZOG, CHAIM (1918-1997), president of the State of Israel **7** 354-355

HERZOG, ROMAN (born 1934), president of the German Federal Constitutional Court (1987-1994) and president of Germany **7** 355-357

HERZOG, WERNER (Werner Stipetic; born 1942), German film director and producer **25** 194-197

HESBURGH, THEODORE MARTIN (born 1917), activist American Catholic priest who was president of Notre Dame (1952-1987) **7** 357-358

HESCHEL, ABRAHAM JOSHUA (1907-1972), Polish-American Jewish theologian **7** 358-359

HESELTINE, MICHAEL (born 1933), British Conservative politician **7** 359-361

HESIOD (flourished circa 700 B.C.), Greek poet **7** 361-362

HESS, MYRA (1890-1965), British pianist **27** 169-171

HESS, VICTOR FRANCIS (1883-1964), Austrian-American physicist **7** 362-363

HESS, WALTER RICHARD RUDOLF (1894-1987), deputy reichsführer for Adolf Hitler (1933-1941) **7** 363-365

HESS, WALTER RUDOLF (1881-1973), Swiss neurophysiologist **7** 365

HESSE, EVA (1936-1970), American sculptor **7** 365-367

HESSE, HERMANN (1877-1962), German novelist **7** 367-369

HESSE, MARY B. (born 1924), British philosopher **7** 369-371

HEVESY, GEORGE CHARLES DE (1885-1966), Hungarian chemist **7** 371

HEWITT, ABRAM STEVENS (1822-1903), American politician and manufacturer **7** 371-372

HEYDRICH, REINHARD (1904-1942), German architect of the Holocaust **20** 176-178

HEYERDAHL, THOR (born 1914), Norwegian explorer, anthropologist and author **18** 194-196

HEYSE, PAUL JOHANN LUDWIG (1830-1914), German author **7** 372-373

HEYWOOD, THOMAS (1573/1574-1641), English playwright **7** 373-374

HIAWATHA (c. 1450), Native American Leader **23** 143-145

Hiawatha's Wedding Feast (choral work) Coleridge-Taylor, Samuel **28** 80-83

HICKOK, JAMES BUTLER ("Wild Bill"; 1837-1876), American gunfighter, scout, and spy **7** 374-375

HICKS, EDWARD (1780-1849), American folk painter **7** 375

HIDALGO Y COSTILLA, MIGUEL (1753-1811), Mexican revolutionary priest **7** 375-377

HIDAYAT, SADIQ (1903-1951), Persian author **7** 377-378

Hideyoshi
see Toyotomi Hideyoshi

Higgins, Margaret
see Sanger, Margaret

HIGGINS, MARGUERITE (1920-1966), American journalist **7** 378-380

HIGGINSON, THOMAS WENTWORTH (1823-1911), American reformer and editor **7** 380

HIGHTOWER, ROSELLA (born 1920), Native American dancer **26** 154-156

Hildebrand
see Gregory VII, Pope

HILDEBRANDT, JOHANN LUCAS VON (1663-1745), Austrian architect **7** 380-381

HILDRETH, RICHARD (1807-1865), American historian and political theorist **7** 382

HILFIGER, TOMMY (born 1952), American fashion designer **19** 144-146

HILL, ANITA (born 1956), African American lawyer and professor **7** 382-385

HILL, ARCHIBALD VIVIAN (1886-1977), English physiologist **7** 385-386

HILL, BENJAMIN HARVEY (1823-1882), American politician **7** 386-387

HILL, HERBERT (1924-2004), American scholar and civil rights activist **7** 387-388

HILL, BENNY (Alfred Hawthorn Hill; 1924-1992), English comedian **28** 170-172

HILL, JAMES JEROME (1838-1916), American railroad builder **7** 388-389

HILL, ROWLAND (1795-1879), British educator, postal reformer, and administrator **21** 202-204

HILLARY, EDMUND (1919-2008), New Zealander explorer and mountaineer **7** 389-390

Hillel Hazaken
see Hillel I

HILLEL I (circa 60 B.C. -circa 10 A.D.), Jewish scholar and teacher **7** 390-391

HILLEMAN, MAURICE RALPH (1919-2005), American microbiologist **26** 156-158

HILLIARD, NICHOLAS (circa 1547-1619), English painter **7** 391-392

HILLMAN, SIDNEY (1887-1946), Lithuanian-born American labor leader **7** 392-393

HILLQUIT, MORRIS (1869-1933), Russian-born American lawyer and author **7** 393-394

HILLS, CARLA ANDERSON (born 1934), Republican who served three presidents as lawyer, cabinet member, and U.S. trade representative **7** 394-396

HILTON, BARRON (William Barron Hilton; born 1927), American businessman **19** 146-148

HILTON, CONRAD (1887-1979), American hotelier **20** 178-180

HIMES, CHESTER BOMAR (1909-1984), American author **22** 242-244

HIMMELFARB, GERTRUDE (born 1922), American professor, writer, and scholar **7** 396-398

HIMMLER, HEINRICH (1900-1945), German Nazi leader **7** 398-399

HINDEMITH, PAUL (1895-1963), German composer **7** 399-400

HINDENBURG, PAUL LUDWIG HANS VON BENECKENDORFF UND VON (1847-1934), German field marshal, president 1925-1934 **7** 400-401

Hindu Nationalist Movement
Savarkar, Vinayak Damodar **28** 312-314

HINE, LEWIS WICKES (1874-1940), American photographer **28** 172-174

Hiner, Cincinnatus
see Miller, Joaquin

HINES, GREGORY OLIVER (born 1946), American dancer and actor **7** 401-403

HINOJOSA, ROLANDO (born 1929), Hispanic-American author **7** 403-405

HINSHELWOOD, SIR CYRIL NORMAN (1897-1967), English chemist **7** 405-406

HINTON, SUSAN ELOISE (born 1950), American novelist and screenwriter **7** 406-407

HIPPARCHUS (flourished 162-126 B.C.), Greek astronomer **7** 407-408

HIPPOCRATES (circa 460-circa 377 B.C.), Greek physician **7** 408-410

HIROHITO (1901-1989), emperor of Japan **7** 410-412

HIROSHIGE, ANDO (1797-1858), Japanese painter and printmaker **7** 412-413

HIRSCHFELD, AL (Albert Hirschfeld; 1903-2003), American caricaturist **25** 197-199

HISS, ALGER (1904-1996), U.S. State Department official convicted of having provided classified documents to an admitted Communist **7** 413-415

HITCHCOCK, ALFRED (1899-1980), English-born film director **7** 415-416

HITCHCOCK, GILBERT MONELL (1859-1934), American publisher and politician **7** 416-417

HITLER, ADOLF (1889-1945), German dictator, chancellor-president 1933-1945 **7** 417-420

HO, DAVID DA-I (born 1952), American AIDS researcher **23** 145-148

HO CHI MINH (1890-1969), Vietnamese revolutionary and statesman **7** 426-428

HO, XUAN HUONG (circa late 18th-circa early 19th century), Vietnamese poet and feminist **28** 174-176

HOBART, JOHN HENRY (1775-1830), American Episcopal bishop **7** 420-421

HOBBES, THOMAS (1588-1679), English philosopher and political theorist **7** 421-423

HOBBY, OVETA CULP (1905-1995), American government official and businesswoman **7** 423-425

HOBHOUSE, LEONARD TRELAWNY (1864-1929), English sociologist and philosopher **7** 425-426

Hobrecht, Jacob
see Obrecht, Jacob

HOBSON, WILLIAM (1793-1842), British naval commander and colonial governor **7** 426

Hobun
see Yamashita, Tomoyuki

HOCKING, WILLIAM ERNEST (1873-1966), American philosopher **7** 428-429

HOCKNEY, DAVID (born 1937), English photographer and artist **7** 429-431

HODGKIN, ALAN LLOYD (born 1914), English physiologist **7** 431-432

HODGKIN, DOROTHY CROWFOOT (1910-1964), English chemist **7** 432-434

HODLER, FERDINAND (1853-1918), Swiss painter **7** 434-435

HOE, RICHARD MARCH (1812-1886), American inventor and manufacturer **7** 435-436

HOFF, TED (Marcian Edward Hoff, Jr.; born 1937), American inventor **28** 176-178

HOFFA, JAMES R. ("JIMMY") (1913-1975), American union leader **7** 436-437

HOFFMAN, ABBIE (1936-1989), American writer, activist, and leader of the Youth International Party **7** 437-439

HOFFMANN, ERNST THEODOR AMADEUS (1776-1822), German author, composer, and artist **7** 439-440

HOFFMANN, FELIX (1868-1946), German chemist and inventor **28** 179-180

HOFFMANN, JOSEF (1870-1956), Austrian architect and decorator **7** 440-441

HOFFMAN, MALVINA CORNELL (1885-1966), American sculptor **23** 148-150

HOFHAIMER, PAUL (1459-1537), Austrian composer, and organist **7** 441

HOFMANN, AUGUST WILHELM VON (1818-1892), German organic chemist **7** 441-442

HOFMANN, HANS (1880-1966), German-American painter **7** 442-443

HOFMANNSTHAL, HUGO VON (1874-1929), Austrian poet and dramatist **7** 443-444

HOFSTADTER, RICHARD (1916-1970), American historian **7** 444-445

HOFSTADTER, ROBERT (1915-1990), American physicist **25** 199-202

HOGAN, BEN (1912-1997), American golfer **19** 148-150

HOGARTH, WILLIAM (1697-1764), English painter and engraver **7** 446-447

HOGG, HELEN BATTLES SAWYER (1905-1993), Canadian astronomer **22** 244-247

Hohenheim, Theophrastus Bombastus von
see Paracelsus, Philippus Aureolus

HOKINSON, HELEN ELNA (1893-1949), American cartoonist **23** 150-152

HOKUSAI, KATSUSHIKA (1760-1849), Japanese painter and printmaker **7** 447-448

HOLBACH, BARON D' (Paul Henri Thiry; 1723-1789), German-born French encyclopedist and philosopher **7** 448-449

HOLBEIN, HANS, THE YOUNGER (1497/98-1543), German painter and graphic artist **7** 449-450

HOLBERG, LUDVIG (Hans Mikkelsen; 1684-1754), Scandinavian author **23** 152-155

HOLBROOK, JOSIAH (1788-1854), American educator **7** 450-451

HÖLDERLIN, JOHANN CHRISTIAN FRIEDRICH (1770-1843), German poet **7** 451-452

HOLIDAY, BILLIE (1915-1959), American jazz vocalist **7** 452-453

Holland
see Netherlands, The

HOLLAND, JOHN PHILIP (1840-1914), Irish-American inventor **7** 453-454

HOLLAR, WENCESLAUS (Wewzel Hollar; Václav Hollar; 1607-1677), Bohemian engraver **28** 180-183

HOLLERITH, HERMAN (1860-1929), American inventor and businessman **19** 151-152

Hollweg, Theobald von Bethmann
see Bethmann Hollweg, Theobald von

HOLLY, BUDDY (Charles Hardin Holley; 1936-1959), American singer, songwriter, and bandleader **22** 247-249

HOLM, HANYA (née Johanna Eckert; born 1893), German-American dancer and teacher **7** 454-455

Holm, Saxe
see Jackson, Helen Hunt

HOLMES, ARTHUR (1890-1965), English geologist and petrologist **7** 455-456

HOLMES, JOHN HAYNES (1879-1964), American Unitarian clergyman **7** 456-457

HOLMES, OLIVER WENDELL (1809-1894), American physician and author **7** 457-458

HOLMES, OLIVER WENDELL, JR. (1841-1935), American jurist **7** 458-459

Holocaust
heroes
Sendler, Irena **28** 318-320
survivors
Karp, Natalia **28** 192-194

HOLST, GUSTAV (1874-1934), English composer **7** 459-460

HOLYOAKE, KEITH JACKA (1904-1983), New Zealand prime minister and leader of the National Party **7** 460-462

HOLZER, JENNY (born 1950), American Neo-Conceptualist artist **7** 462-463

HOMANS, GEORGE CASPAR (1910-1989), American sociologist **7** 463-465

HOMER (ancient), Greek epic poet **7** 468-469

HOMER, WINSLOW (1836-1910), American painter **7** 468-469

Homosexual rights movement
Deleuze, Gilles **28** 94-96
Fortuyn, Pim **28** 125-127
McKellen, Ian Murray **28** 234-237

HONDA, ISHIRO (Inoshiro Honda; 1911-1993), Japanese filmmaker **26** 158-160

HONDA, SOICHIRO (1906-1991), Japanese automaker **7** 469-470

HONECKER, ERICH (1912-1994), German Communist Party leader and head of the German Democratic Republic (1971-80s) **7** 471-472

HONEGGER, ARTHUR (1892-1955), Swiss composer identified with France **7** 472-473

HONEN (1133-1212), Japanese Buddhist monk **7** 473

HOOCH, PIETER DE (1629-after 1684), Dutch artist **7** 473-474

HOOK, SIDNEY (1902-1989), American philosopher and exponent of classical American pragmatism **7** 474-475

HOOKE, ROBERT (1635-1703), English physicist **7** 475

HOOKER, JOHN LEE (1917-2001), African American musician **23** 155-157

HOOKER, RICHARD (1554-1600), English theologian and Church of England clergyman **7** 475-476

HOOKER, THOMAS (1586-1647), English Puritan theologian, founder of Connecticut Colony **7** 476-477

HOOKS, BELL (BORN GLORIA JEAN WATKINS) (born 1952), African American social activist, feminist, and author **7** 477-481

HOOKS, BENJAMIN LAWSON (born 1925), executive director of the NAACP and first African American commissioner of the FCC **7** 481-483

HOOVER, HERBERT CLARK (1874-1964), American statesman, president 1929-1933 **7** 483-485

HOOVER, JOHN EDGAR (1895-1972), American lawyer, criminologist, and FBI director **7** 485-487

HOPE, BOB (born Leslie Townes Hope; born 1903), entertainer in vaudeville, radio, television, and movies **7** 487-489

HOPE, JOHN (1868-1936), African American educator and religious leader **7** 489-490

HOPKINS, ANTHONY (Philip Anthony Hopkins; born 1937), Welsh actor **18** 196-198

HOPKINS, ESEK (1718-1802), American Revolutionary patriot **7** 490-491

HOPKINS, SIR FREDERICK GOWLAND (1861-1947), English biochemist **7** 496

HOPKINS, GERARD MANLEY (1844-1889), English Jesuit poet **7** 492-494

HOPKINS, HARRY LLOYD (1890-1946), American statesman **7** 494-495

HOPKINS, JOHNS (1795-1873), American financier and philanthropist **24** 178-180

HOPKINS, MARK (1802-1887), American educator **7** 495-496

HOPKINS, SAMUEL (1721-1803), American clergyman and theologian **7** 496

HOPKINSON, FRANCIS (1737-1791), American politician, writer, and composer **7** 496-497

HOPPER, EDWARD (1882-1967), American realist painter **7** 497-498

HOPPER, GRACE (born Grace Brewster Murray; 1906-1992), American computer scientist **7** 498-500

HORACE (Quintus Horatius Flaccus; 65-8 B.C.), Roman poet and satirist **7** 500-503

HORNE, HERMAN HARRELL (1874-1946), American philosopher and educator **7** 503-504

HORNE, LENA (born 1917), popular entertainer **7** 504-506

HORNER, MATINA SOURETIS (born 1939), American scholar and administrator **7** 506-508

HORNEY, KAREN DANIELSEN (1885-1952), German-born American psychoanalyst **7** 508-509

HORNSBY, ROGERS (1896-1963), American baseball player and manager **21** 204-206

HOROWITZ, VLADIMIR (1904-1989), American pianist **7** 509-510

HORTHY DE NAGYBÁNYA, NICHOLAS (1868-1957), Hungarian admiral and statesman, regent 1920-1944 **7** 510-512

Horus Neteryerkhet
see Zoser

HORVÁTH, ÖDÖN VON (1901-1938), Hungarian author **26** 160-162

HOSEA (flourished 750-722 B.C.), Hebrew prophet of the kingdom of Israel **7** 512

HO-SHEN (1750-1799), Manchu official in China **7** 512-513

HOSTOS, EUGENIO MARÍA DE (1839-1903), Puerto Rican philosopher, educator, and writer **7** 513-514

Hot Shoppes (restaurant chain)
Marriott, J. Willard **28** 232-234

HOUDINI, HARRY (born Erich Weiss; 1874-1926), American magician and illusionist **7** 514-516

HOUDON, ANTOINE (1741-1828), French sculptor **7** 516-517

HOUNSFIELD, GODFREY (1919-2004), English biomedical engineer **7** 517-519

HOUPHOUËT-BOIGNY, FELIX (1905-1993), Ivorian statesman 1960 **7** 519-520

HOUSE, EDWARD MANDELL (1858-1938), American diplomat **7** 520-521

HOUSMAN, ALFRED EDWARD (1859-1936), English poet **7** 521-522

HOUSSAY, BERNARDO ALBERTO (1887-1971), Argentine physiologist **7** 522-523

HOUSTON, CHARLES HAMILTON (1895-1950), African American lawyer and civil rights leader **7** 523-526

HOUSTON, SAMUEL (1793-1863), American statesman and soldier **7** 526-527

HOUSTON, WHITNEY (born 1963), American singer and actress **19** 152-155

HOVLAND, CARL I. (1912-1961), American psychologist **7** 527-528

HOWARD, JOHN WINSTON (born 1939), Australian prime minister **18** 198-200

HOWARD, OLIVER OTIS (1830-1909), American Union general **7** 528-529

HOWARD, RON (born 1954), American actor, director, and producer **19** 155-158

HOWE, EDGAR WATSON (1853-1937), American author and editor **7** 529

HOWE, ELIAS (1819-1867), American inventor **7** 529-530

HOWE, FLORENCE ROSENFELD (born 1929), feminist American author, publisher, literary scholar, and historian **7** 530-531

HOWE, GEOFFREY (Richard Edward; born 1926), British foreign secretary **7** 531-532

HOWE, GORDIE (born 1928), Canadian hockey player **7** 532-534

HOWE, JOSEPH (1804-1873), Canadian journalist, reformer, and politician **7** 534-535

HOWE, JULIA WARD (1819-1910), American author and reformer **7** 535-536

HOWE, RICHARD (Earl Howe; 1726-1799), English admiral **7** 536-537

HOWE, SAMUEL GRIDLEY (1801-1876), American physician and reformer **7** 537

HOWE, WILLIAM (5th Viscount Howe; 1729-1814), British general **7** 538-539

HOWELLS, WILLIAM DEAN (1837-1920), American writer **7** 539-541

HOWELLS, WILLIAM WHITE (1908-2005), American anthropologist **7** 541-542

Howl's Moving Castle (film)
Miyazaki Hayao **28** 249-252

HOXHA, ENVER (1908-1985), leader of the Communist Party of Albania from its formation in 1941 until his death **8** 1-3

HOYLE, EDMOND (1672-1769), English authority on card games **21** 206-208

HOYLE, FRED (born 1915), English astronomer and author **18** 200-202

HRDLIČKA, ALEŠ (1869-1943), American physical anthropologist **8** 3-4

HROTSVITHA OF GANDERSHEIM (Hrosvit/Roswitha; c. 937-c. 973), German author and nun **25** 202-204

HSIA KUEI (flourished 1190-1225), Chinese painter **8** 4-5

Hsiao Yen
see Liang Wu-ti

HSIEH LING-YÜN (385-433), duke of K'ang-lo, Chinese poet **8** 5-6

Hsien-tze
see Shih Ko-fa

Hsin Shun Wang
see Li Tzu-ch'eng

Hsin-chien, Earl of
see Wang Yang-ming

HSÜAN TSANG (circa 602-664), Chinese Buddhist in India **8** 6-7

HSÜAN-TSUNG, T'ANG (685-762), Chinese emperor **8** 7-8

HSÜN-TZU (Hsün Ch'ing; circa 312-circa 235 B.C.), Chinese philosopher **8** 8

HU SHIH (1891-1962), Chinese philosopher **8** 63-65

HUANG CH'AO (died 884), Chinese rebel leader **8** 8-9

HUANG TSUNG-HSI (1610-1695), Chinese scholar and philosopher **8** 9-10

HUBBARD, L. RON (1911-1986), American author and founder of Scientology **18** 202-204

HUBBLE, EDWIN POWELL (1889-1953), American astronomer **8** 10-11

HUBLEY, JOHN (1914-1977), American animator and filmmaker **21** 208-210

HUCH, RICARDA (1864-1947), German novelist, poet, and historian **8** 11-12

HUDSON, HENRY (flourished 1607-1611), English navigator **8** 12-13

Hueffer, Ford Madox
see Ford, Ford Madox

HUERTA, DOLORES (born 1930), Hispanic American labor activist **18** 204-207

HUERTA, VICTORIANO (1854-1916), Mexican general and politician **8** 13-14

HUGGINS, SIR WILLIAM (1824-1910), English astronomer **8** 14-15

HUGHES, CHARLES EVANS (1862-1948), American jurist and statesman **8** 15-16

HUGHES, HOWARD ROBARD (1905-1976), flamboyant American entrepreneur **8** 16-17

HUGHES, JOHN JOSEPH (1797-1864), Irish-American Catholic archbishop **8** 17-18

HUGHES, LANGSTON (1902-1967), African American author **8** 18-19
Patterson, Louise Alone Thompson **28** 272-274

HUGHES, RICHARD (1900-1976), English author **19** 158-160

HUGHES, TED (1930-1998), English poet laureate **8** 19-21

HUGHES, WILLIAM MORRIS (1864-1952), Australian prime minister 1915-1923 **8** 21-22

HUGO, VICOMTE VICTOR MARIE (1802-1885), French author **8** 22-25

HUI-TSUNG (1082-1135), Chinese emperor and artist **8** 25

HUI-YÜAN (334-416), Chinese Buddhist monk **8** 25-26

HUIZINGA, JOHAN (1872-1945), Dutch historian **8** 26-27

HULAGU KHAN (Hüle'ü; circa 1216-1265), Mongol ruler in Persia **8** 27-28

HULL, BOBBY (Robert Marvin Hull; born 1939), Canadian hockey player **20** 181-183

HULL, CLARK LEONARD (1884-1952), American psychologist **8** 28

HULL, CORDELL (1871-1955), American statesman **8** 28-29

HULL, WILLIAM (1753-1825), American military commander **8** 29-30

Humanitarians
Amma **28** 8-10
Sendler, Irena **28** 318-320
Thomas, Danny **28** 350-352

HUMAYUN (1508-1556), Mogul emperor 1530-1556 **20** 183-185

HUMBOLDT, BARON FRIEDRICH HEINRICH ALEXANDER VON (1769-1859), German naturalist and explorer **8** 30-31

HUMBOLDT, BARON WILHELM VON (1767-1835), German statesman and philologist **8** 31

HUME, BASIL CARDINAL (George Haliburton Hume; 1923-1999), English clergyman and theologian **22** 249-250

HUME, DAVID (1711-1776), Scottish philosopher **8** 31-34

HUMMEL, JOHANN NEPOMUK (1778-1837), Austrian pianist and composer **25** 204-206

HUMPHREY, DORIS (Doris Batcheller Humphrey; 1895-1959), American dancer and choreographer **23** 157-159

HUMPHREY, HUBERT HORATIO, JR. (1911-1978), mayor of Minneapolis, U.S. senator from Minnesota, and vice-president of the U.S. **8** 34-36

HUN SEN (born 1951), Cambodian prime minister **8** 39-42

HUNDERTWASSER, FRIEDENSREICH (Friedrich Stowasser; 1928-2000), Austrian-born visionary painter and spiritualist **8** 36-37

HUNG HSIU-CH'ÜAN (1814-1864), Chinese religious leader, founder of Taiping sect **8** 37-38

Hung-li
see Qianlong

Hungson, Prince
see Taewon'gun, Hungson

HUNG-WU (1328-1398), Chinese Ming emperor 1368-98 **8** 38-39

HUNT, H. L. (1889-1974), American entrepreneur **8** 42-44

HUNT, RICHARD MORRIS (1827-1895), American architect **8** 44

HUNT, WALTER (1796-1859), American inventor **21** 210-212

HUNT, WILLIAM HOLMAN (1827-1910), English painter **8** 44-45

HUNTER, ALBERTA (1895-1984), African American blues singer **23** 160-162

HUNTER, FLOYD (born 1912), American social worker and administrator, community worker, professor, and author **8** 45-46

HUNTER, MADELINE CHEEK (1916-1994), American educator **8** 47-48

HUNTER, WILLIAM (1718-1783), Scottish anatomist **8** 48-49

HUNTINGTON, ANNA HYATT (Anna Vaughn Hyatt; 1876-1973), American sculptor and philanthropist **23** 162-164

HUNTINGTON, COLLIS POTTER (1821-1900), American railroad builder **8** 49

HUNTLEY AND BRINKLEY (1956-1970), American journalists and radio and television news team **8** 49-51

Huntley, Chester Robert, (Chet; 1911-1974)
see Huntley and Brinkley

HUNYADI, JOHN (1385-1456), Hungarian military leader, regent 1446-1452 **8** 51-52

HURD, DOUGLAS (born 1930), English Conservative Party politician and foreign secretary **8** 52-55

HURSTON, ZORA NEALE (1903-1960), African American folklorist and novelist **8** 55-56
Patterson, Louise Alone Thompson **28** 272-274
Thurman, Wallace Henry **28** 352-354

HUS, JAN (a.k.a. John Hus; ca.1369-1415), Bohemian religious reformer **8** 56-59

HUSÁK, GUSTÁV (born 1913), president of the Czechoslovak Socialist Republic (1975-1987) **8** 59-61

HUSAYN, TAHA (1889-1973), Egyptian author, educator, and statesman **8** 61-62

HUSAYNI, AL-HAJJ AMIN AL- (1895-1974), Moslem scholar/leader and mufti of Jerusalem (1922-1948) **8** 62-63

HUSEIN IBN ALI (circa 1854-1931), Arab nationalist, king of Hejaz 1916-1924 **8** 63

Huss, John
see Hus, Jan

HUSSEIN IBN TALAL (1935-1999), king of the Hashemite Kingdom of Jordan (1953-80s) **8** 65-67

HUSSEIN, SADDAM (1937-2006), socialist president of the Iraqi Republic and strongman of the ruling Ba'th regime **13** 415-416

HUSSEINI, FAISAL (1940-2001), Palestinian political leader **19** 160-162

HUSSERL, EDMUND (1859-1938), German philosopher **8** 67-68

HUSTON, JOHN MARCELLUS (1906-1987), American film director, scriptwriter, and actor **22** 250-252

HUTCHINS, ROBERT MAYNARD (1899-1977), American educator **8** 68-69

HUTCHINSON, ANNE MARBURY (1591-1643), English-born American religious leader **8** 69-71

HUTCHINSON, THOMAS (1711-1780), American colonial governor **8** 71-72

Hu-t'ou
see Ku K'ai-chih

HUTT, WILLIAM (William Ian DeWitt Hutt; 1920-2007), Canadian actor and director **27** 171-173

HUTTEN, ULRICH VON (1488-1523), German humanist **8** 72-73

HUTTON, JAMES (1726-1797), Scottish geologist **8** 73-74

HUXLEY, ALDOUS LEONARD (1894-1963), English novelist and essayist **8** 74-75

HUXLEY, JULIAN (1887-1975), English biologist and author **8** 75-77

HUXLEY, THOMAS HENRY (1825-1895), English biologist **8** 77-79

HUXTABLE, ADA LOUISE (nee Ada Louise Landman; born 1921), American journalist **26** 162-165

HUYGENS, CHRISTIAAN (1629-1695), Dutch mathematician, astronomer, and physicist **8** 79-81

Huysmans, Charles Marie Georges
see Huysmans, Joris Karl

HUYSMANS, JORIS KARL (1848-1907), French novelist **8** 81-82

HVIEZDOSLAV (Pavol Országh; Pavol Országh Hviezdoslav; 1848-1921), Slovakian poet **24** 181-182

HYDE, DOUGLAS (1860-1949), Irish author, president 1938-45 **8** 82-83

Hyde, Edward
see Clarendon, 1st Earl of

HYDE, IDA HENRIETTA (1857-1945), American physiologist and educator **22** 252-254

HYMAN, FLO (Flora Jean Hyman; 1954-1986), American volleyball player **26** 165-167

HYMAN, LIBBIE HENRIETTA (1888-1969), American zoologist **8** 83-84

HYPATIA OF ALEXANDRIA (370-415), Greek mathematician and philosopher **8** 85

Hypochondriack
see Boswell, James

I

I Dream of Jeannie (television show)
Sheldon, Sidney **28** 323-325

IACOCCA, LIDO (LEE) ANTHONY (born 1924), American automobile magnate **8** 86-88

IBÁÑEZ DEL CAMPO, CARLOS (1877-1960), Chilean general and president **8** 88

ÍBARRURI GÓMEZ, DOLORES (1895-1989), voice of the Republican cause in the Spanish Civil War **8** 88-90

IBERVILLE, SIEUR D' (Pierre le Moyne; 1661-1706), Canadian soldier, naval captain, and adventurer **8** 90-91

IBN AL-ARABI, MUHYI AL-DIN (1165-1240), Spanish-born Moslem poet, philosopher, and mystic **8** 91

IBN BATTUTA, MUHAMMAD (1304-1368/69), Moslem traveler and author **8** 91-92

IBN GABIROL, SOLOMON BEN JUDAH (circa 1021-circa 1058), Spanish Hebrew poet and philosopher **8** 92

IBN HAZM, ABU MUHAMMAD ALI (994-1064), Spanish-born Arab theologian and jurist **8** 93

IBN KHALDUN, ABD AL-RAHMAN IBN MUHAMMAD (1332-1406), Arab historian, philosopher, and statesman **8** 93-94

Ibn Rushd
see Averroës

IBN SAUD, ABD AL-AZIZ (1880-1953), Arab politician, founder of Saudi Arabia **8** 94-95

Ibn Sina
see Avicenna

IBN TASHUFIN, YUSUF (died 1106), North African Almoravid ruler **8** 95-96

IBN TUFAYL, ABU BAKR MUHAMMAD (circa 1110-1185), Spanish Moslem philosopher and physician **8** 96

IBN TUMART, MUHAMMAD (circa 1080-1130), North African Islamic theologian **8** 96-97

IBRAHIM PASHA (1789-1848), Turkish military and administrative leader **8** 97-98

IBSEN, HENRIK (1828-1906), Norwegian playwright **8** 98-100
associates
Bull, Ole **28** 54-56

IBUKA, MASARU (1908-1997), Japanese inventor and businessman **28** 184-186

ICKES, HAROLD LECLAIRE (1874-1952), American statesman **8** 100-101

ICTINUS (flourished 2nd half of 5th century B.C.), Greek architect **8** 101

IDRIS I (1889-1983), king of Libya 1950-69 **8** 102

IDRISI, MUHAMMAD IBN MUHAMMAD AL- (1100-1165?), Arab geographer **8** 102-103

IGLESIAS, ENRIQUE V. (born 1930), Uruguayan economist, banker, and public official **8** 106-107

IGNATIUS OF ANTIOCH, SAINT (died circa 115), Early Christian bishop and theologian **8** 107-108

IGNATIUS OF LOYOLA, SAINT (1491-1556), Spanish soldier, founder of Jesuits **8** 108-109

IKEDA, DAISAKU (born 1928), Japanese Buddhist writer and religious leader **8** 109-110

IKHNATON (ruled 1379-1362 B.C.), pharaoh of Egypt **8** 110-111

ILIESCU, ION (born 1930), president of Romania (1990-) **8** 111-112

ILITCH, MIKE (born 1929), American businessman **19** 163-165

ILLICH, IVAN (1926-2002), theologian, educator, and social critic **8** 112-114

IMAI, TADASHI (1912-1991), Japanese film director **22** 255-257

IMAM, ALHADJI ABUBAKAR (1911-1981), Nigerian writer and teacher **8** 114-115

IMAMURA, SHOHEI (1926-2006), Japanese film director and producer **25** 207-210

IMAOKA, SHINICHIRO (1881-1988), progressive and liberal religious leader in Japan **8** 115

IMHOTEP (ca. 3000 B.C. - ca. 2950 B.C.), Egyptian vizier, architect, priest, astronomer, and magician-physician **8** 116-117

Imouthes
see Imhotep

INCE, THOMAS (1882-1924), American film producer and director **21** 213-215

INCHBALD, ELIZABETH (Elizabeth Simpson; 1753-1821), British novelist and playwright **27** 174-176

India, Republic of (nation, southern Asia)
• SINCE 1947 (REPUBLIC)
independence
Savarkar, Vinayak Damodar **28** 312-314

Indian literature (Asia)
drama and poetry
Savarkar, Vinayak Damodar **28** 312-314
religious
Krishnamurti, Uppaluri Gopala **28** 201-203

INGE, WILLIAM RALPH (1860-1954), Church of England clergyman, scholar, social critic, and writer **8** 118-119

INGENHOUSZ, JAN (1730-1799), Dutch physician, chemist, and engineer **8** 119-120

INGERSOLL, ROBERT GREEN (1833-1899), American lawyer and lecturer **8** 120-121

INGLIS, ELSIE MAUD (1824-1917), British physician and suffragist **26** 168-170

INGRES, JEAN AUGUSTE DOMINIQUE (1780-1867), French painter **8** 121-123

INNESS, GEORGE (1825-1894), American painter **8** 123-124

INNIS, HAROLD ADAMS (1894-1952), Canadian political economist **8** 124-125

INNOCENT III (Lothar of Segni; 1160/1161-1216), pope 1198-1216 **8** 125-127

INNOCENT IV (Sinibaldo de' Fieschi; died 1254), pope 1243-1254 **23** 165-167

INNOCENT X (Giovanni Battista Pamfili; Giambattista Pamphili; 1574-1655), Italian pope 1644-1655 **24** 183-185

INÖNÜ, ISMET (1884-1973), Turkish military man, statesman, and second president **8** 127-129

Inquisition (Islam Empire)
see Islam—Mihna

Insatiability (book)
Witkacy **28** 374-376

INSULL, SAMUEL (1859-1938), English-born American entrepreneur **8** 130

Integration (racial, United States)
see African American history (United States)

Intel Corporation
Hoff, Ted **28** 176-178

Intelligence Oversight Act of 1980
Church, Frank Forrester, III **28** 78-80

INUKAI, TSUYOSHI (1855-1932), Japanese journalist and statesman **8** 130-131

IONESCO, EUGÈNE (1912-1994), Franco-Romanian author **8** 131-132

IQBAL, MUHAMMAD (c. 1877-1938), Indian Moslem poet and philosopher **8** 132-133

Iraqi literature
Mala'ika, Nazik al- **28** 230-232

IRELAND, JOHN (1838-1918), American Catholic archbishop **8** 133-134

IRELAND, PATRICIA (born 1945), president of the National Organization for Women (NOW) **8** 134-135

IRENE OF ATHENS (ca. 752-803), Byzantine empress 797-802 **8** 135-138

IRIGOYEN, HIPÓLITO (circa 1850-1933), Argentine statesman, twice president **8** 139-140

Irish literature
biographies
Moore, Thomas **28** 254-256
drama and poetry
Moore, Thomas **28** 254-256

Irish music
Moore, Thomas **28** 254-256

Iron Chancellor
see Bismarck, Otto von

Iron Duke
see Alba, Duke of; Wellington, 1st Duke of

Irons, Ralph
see Schreiner, Olive

IRVING, JOHN WINSLOW (John Wallace Blunt Jr.; born 1942), American author **22** 257-259

IRVING, KENNETH COLIN ("K. C."; 1899-1992), Canadian industrialist, the "Paul Bunyan of New Brunswick" **8** 140-141

IRVING, WASHINGTON (1783-1859), American author and journalist **8** 141-143

Irwin, Baron
see Halifax, 1st Earl of

IRWIN, JAMES BENSON (1930-1991), American astronaut **22** 259-261

IRWIN, STEVE (Stephen Robert Irwin; 1962-2006), Australian naturalist and television personality **27** 176-178

ISAAC, HEINRICH (circa 1450-1517), Flemish composer **8** 143-144

ISAACS, JORGE (1837-1895), Colombian novelist **8** 144

Isaacs, Rufus Daniel
see Reading, 1st Marquess of

ISABELLA I (1451-1504), queen of Castile 1474-1504 **8** 144-145

ISABELLA II (1830-1904), queen of Spain 1833-1868 **8** 145-146

ISAIAH (flourished circa 740-701 B.C.), Hebrew prophet **8** 146-147

Isaiah ben Amoz
see Isaiah

ISHERWOOD, CHRISTOPHER (1904-1986), British-born American writer of fiction, drama, film, travel, and autobiography **8** 147-149

ISHI (ca. 1860-1961), Native American aboriginal **22** 261-263

ISIDORE OF SEVILLE, SAINT (560-636), Spanish cleric and encyclopedist **8** 149-150

Islam (religion)
• DOCTRINE
reforms (early)
Dehlavi, Shah Waliullah **28** 92-94
theology and law
Nursî, Said **28** 259-261
• EXPANSION
India and Pakistan
Dehlavi, Shah Waliullah **28** 92-94

Isly, Duke of
see Bugeaud de la Piconnerie, Thomas Robert

ISMAIL PASHA (1830-1895), khedive of Egypt 1863-1879 **8** 150-151

ISOCRATES (436-338 B.C.), Athenian orator **8** 151

ISOZAKI, ARATA (born 1931), Japanese architect **8** 152-153

Israel (ancient king.)
see Jewish history—Biblical Era (Israel)

It Don't Mean a Thing (If It Ain't Got That Swing) (song)
Anderson, Ivie Marie **28** 10-12

Italian, The (book)
Radcliffe, Ann **28** 288-290

ITAMI, JUZO (Ichizo itami; Ichizo Atami; born Ikeuchi Yoshihiro; 1933-1997), Japanese film director, actor and author **22** 263-265

ITO, HIROBUMI (1841-1909), Japanese statesman **8** 153-155

ITURBIDE, AGUSTÍN DE (1783-1824), Mexican military leader **8** 155-156

IVAN III (1440-1505), grand duke of Moscow 1462-1505 **8** 156-157

IVAN IV (1530-1584), grand duke of Moscow, czar of Russia 1547-1584 **8** 157-159

Ivan the Great
see Ivan III

Ivan the Terrible
see Ivan IV

IVANOV, LEV (Lev Ivanovich Ivanov; 1834-1901), Russian dancer and choreographer **24** 185-188

IVES, CHARLES EDWARD (1874-1954), American composer **8** 159-160

Ives, James Merritt, (1824-1895)
see Currier and Ives

IVORY, JAMES (born 1928), American film director and producer **20** 186-188

IWAKURA, TOMOMI (1825-1883), Japanese statesman **8** 160-161

IYENGAR, B.K.S. (Bellur Krishnamachar Sundararaja Iyengar; born 1918), Indian yoga educator and author **27** 178-180

IZETBEGOVIC, ALIJA (born 1926), president of the eight-member presidency of the Republic of Bosnia-Herzegovina **8** 161-163

J

JA JA OF OPOBO (ca. 1820-1891), Nigerian politician **8** 201-204

JABBAR, KAREEM ABDUL (Ferdinand Lewis Alcinor, Junior; born 1947), American basketball player **8** 164-165

JABER AL-SABAH, JABER AL-AHMAD AL- (1926-2006), emir of Kuwait **8** 166-167

JABIR IBN HAYYAN (flourished latter 8th century), Arab scholar and alchemist **8** 167

JABOTINSKY, VLADIMIR EVGENEVICH (1880-1940), Russian Zionist **8** 167-168

JACKSON, ANDREW (1767-1845), American president 1829-1837 **8** 168-172

JACKSON, HELEN HUNT (1830-1885), American novelist **8** 172

JACKSON, HENRY MARTIN (Scoop; 1912-1983), United States senator and proponent of anti-Soviet foreign policy **8** 172-174

JACKSON, JESSE LOUIS (born 1941), U.S. civil rights leader and presidential candidate **8** 174-176

JACKSON, MAHALIA (1911-1972), American singer **19** 166-168

JACKSON, MAYNARD HOLBROOK, JR. (born 1938), first African American mayor of Atlanta, Georgia (1973-81 and 1989-1993) **8** 176-178

JACKSON, MICHAEL JOE (born 1958), one of the most popular singers in history **8** 178-180

JACKSON, PETER (born 1961), New Zealander actor and filmmaker **25** 211-213

JACKSON, REGINALD "REGGIE" MARTINEZ (born 1946), African American baseball player **8** 180-182

JACKSON, ROBERT HOUGHWOUT (1892-1954), American jurist **8** 182-183

JACKSON, SHIRLEY ANN (born 1946), African American physicist **8** 183-184

JACKSON, THOMAS JONATHAN ("Stonewall"; 1824-1863), American Confederate general **8** 184-185

JACOB, JOHN EDWARD (born 1934), African American activist and president of the National Urban League **8** 185-188

JACOBI, ABRAHAM (1830-1919), American physician **8** 188-189

JACOBI, DEREK (born 1938), British actor **19** 168-170

JACOBI, FRIEDRICH HEINRICH (1743-1819), German philosopher **8** 189-190

JACOBI, MARY PUTNAM (1834-1906), American physician **8** 188-189

JACOBS, ALETTA HENRIETTE (1854-1929), Dutch physician and social reformer **26** 171-173

JACOBS, HARRIET A. (1813-1897), runaway slave and abolitionist **8** 190-193

JACOBS, JANE (Jane Butzner; 1916-2006), Canadian author and urban planning activist **27** 181-183

JACOBSEN, JENS PETER (1847-1885), Danish author **8** 193-194

JACOBSON, DAN (born 1929), South African author **22** 266-268

Jacopo, Giovanni Battista di
see Rosso, Il

JACOPONE DA TODI (circa 1236-1306), Italian poet and mystic **8** 194

JACQUARD, JOSEPH MARIE (1752-1834), French inventor **21** 216-218

JAELL, MARIE TRAUTMANN (1846-1925), French pianist and composer **24** 189-191

Jafar, Abu
see Mansur, al-

JAGGER, MICHAEL PHILIP ("Mick"; born 1944), lead singer for the Rolling Stones **8** 194-196

JAHAN, NUR (Mihrunnissa; Nur Mahal; 1577-1646), Indian queen **24** 191-193

JAHANGIR (1569-1627), fourth Mughal emperor of India **8** 196-199

JAHN, HELMUT (born 1940), German-American architect **8** 199-201

Jalal-ed-Din Rumi
see Rumi, Jalal ed-Din

JAMES I (1394-1437), king of Scotland 1406-1437 **8** 206-207

JAMES I (James VI of Scotland; 1566-1625), king of England 1603-1625 **8** 204-206
Drebbel, Cornelius **28** 102-104

JAMES II (1633-1701), king of England, Scotland, and Ireland 1685-1688 **8** 207-208

JAMES III (1451-1488), king of Scotland 1460-1488 **8** 208-209

James VI, king of Scotland
see James I (king of England)

James VII, king of Scotland
see James II (king of England)

JAMES, DANIEL, JR. ("Chappie"; 1920-1978), first African American man in the U.S. to become a four star general **8** 209-211

JAMES, ETTA (Jamesetta Hawkins; born 1938), African American singer **25** 213-215

JAMES, HENRY (1843-1916), American novelist **8** 211-212

JAMES, JESSE WOODSON (1847-1882), American outlaw **8** 212-213

JAMES, P. D. (born 1920), British crime novelist **8** 213-215

JAMES, WILLIAM (1842-1910), American philosopher and psychologist **8** 215-217

JAMESON, SIR LEANDER STARR (1853-1917), British colonial administrator **8** 218

JAMI (Maulana Nur al-Din Abd al-Rahman; 1414-1492), Persian poet **8** 218-219

JAMISON, JUDITH (born 1944), American dancer and choreographer **26** 173-175

JANÁČEK, LEOŠ (1854-1928), Czech composer **8** 219

JANCSO, MIKLOS (born 1921), Hungarian filmmaker **25** 215-217

JANET, PIERRE MARIE FÉLIX (1859-1947), French psychologist **8** 220

JANSEN, CORNELIS (1585-1638), Dutch Roman Catholic theologian **8** 220-221

JANSSON, TOVE MARIKA (Vera Haij; 1914-2001), Finnish author **28** 187-189

Japan (island nation; eastern Asia)
21st century
Abe, Shinzo **28** 1-3

JAQUES-DALCROZE, EMILE (1865-1950), Swiss teacher and composer who developed eurhythmics **8** 221-222

JARA, VICTOR (Victor Lidio Jara Martinez; 1932-1973), Chilean singer and songwriter **27** 183-185

JARREAU, AL (Alwin Lopez Jarreau; born 1940), African American musician **26** 175-177

JARRELL, RANDALL (1914-1965), American poet and critic **8** 222-223

JARUZELSKI, WOJCIECH WITOLD (born 1923), career soldier who became Poland's head of state (1981-1990) **8** 223-225

JARVIK, ROBERT KOFFLER (born 1946), American physician and inventor **25** 217-220

JASPERS, KARL (1883-1969), German philosopher **8** 225-226

JAURÈS, JEAN (1859-1914), French Socialist and politician **8** 226-227

Java man
Dubois, Eugène **28** 106-108

JAWARA, SIR DAUDA KAIRABA (born 1924), Gambian statesman **8** 227-228

JAWLENSKY, ALEXEJ VON (1864-1941), Russian Expressionist painter **8** 228-229

JAWORSKI, LEON (1905-1982), American lawyer and independent prosecutor of Watergate **8** 229-230

JAY, JOHN (1745-1829), American diplomat and jurist **8** 230-232

JAY, WILLIAM (1789-1858), American reformer **8** 232-233

JAYEWARDENE, JUNIUS RICHARD (JR; 1906-1996), leader of the nationalist movement in Ceylon and president of Sri Lanka **8** 233-234

Jazz (music)
Anderson, Ivie Marie **28** 10-12
Roach, Max **28** 292-296
Zawinul, Joe **28** 389-391

Jean de Boulogne
see Giovanni da Bologna

JEAN DE MEUN (circa 1240-1305), French author **8** 234-235

Jean Jacques, Emperor
see Dessalines, Jean Jacques

Jean Paul
see Richter, Johann Paul Friedrich

Jeanne d'Arc
see Joan of Arc

Jeanneret-Gris, Charles Édouard
see Le Corbusier

JEANS, SIR JAMES HOPWOOD (1877-1946), English mathematician, physicist, and astronomer **8** 235-236

JEFFERS, JOHN ROBINSON (1887-1962), American poet **8** 236-237

JEFFERSON, JOSEPH (1829-1905), American actor **8** 237

JEFFERSON, THOMAS (1743-1826), American philosopher and statesman, president 1801-1809 **8** 238-241

JEFFREYS, SIR HAROLD (1891-1989), English mathematician, astronomer, and philosopher **8** 241-242

JELLICOE, JOHN RUSHWORTH (1859-1935), English admiral **8** 242-243

JEMISON, MAE C. (born 1956), African American physician and astronaut **8** 243-244

Jenghiz Khan
see Genghis Khan

JENKINS, ROY HARRIS (born 1920), British Labour politician and author **8** 244-245

Jenkinson, Robert Barks
see Liverpool, 2nd Earl of

JENNER, BRUCE (born 1949), American track and field athlete and motivational speaker **21** 218-221

JENNER, EDWARD (1749-1823), English physician **8** 245-246

JENNEY, WILLIAM LE BARON (1832-1907), American architect and engineer **21** 221-223

JENNINGS, PETER CHARLES (1938-2005), American television journalist **26** 177-179

JENNINGS, ROBERT YEWDALL (1913-2004), British judge who was president of the International Court of Justice **8** 246-247

JENSEN, JOHANNES VILHELM (1873-1950), Danish author **24** 193-196

Jeopardy (television show)
Griffin, Merv **28** 146-149

JEREMIAH (flourished late 7th-early 6th century B.C.), Hebrew priest and prophet **8** 247-248

JEROBOAM I (ruled circa 931-circa 910 B.C.), king of the northern kingdom of Israel **8** 248-249

JEROME, ST. (circa 345-420), Early Christian biblical scholar **8** 249

JESSEL, GEORGE (1898-1981), American screen, stage, radio, and television actor and comedian and film director, composer, and screenwriter **8** 249-251

JESUS BEN SIRA (Sirach; flourished circa 170 B.C.), Jewish sage and author **8** 251

Jesus Christ
see Jesus of Nazareth

JESUS OF NAZARETH (circa 4 B.C. - 29/30 A.D.), founder of the Christian faith **8** 251-255

JEVONS, WILLIAM STANLEY (1835-1882), English economist, logician, and statistician **8** 255-256

JEWETT, SARAH ORNE (1849-1909), American novelist **8** 256

Jewish history
• DISPERSION (EUROPEAN)
in Europe
Casimir III, King of Poland **28** 60-62

JEX-BLAKE, SOPHIA (1840-1912), British physician and women's rights advocate **23** 168-170

JHABVALA, RUTH PRAWER (born 1927), English screenwriter and novelist **18** 208-210

JIANG QING (Madame Mao Zedong; 1914-1991), Chinese revolutionary and leader of the Great Proletarian Cultural Revolution **8** 256-260

JIANG ZEMIN (born 1927), general secretary of the Chinese Communist Party Central Committee **8** 260-261

JIMÉNEZ, JUAN RAMÓN (1881-1958), Spanish symbolist poet **8** 261-262

JIMÉNEZ, LUIS, JR. (Luis Alfonso Jiménez, Jr.; 1940-2006), American artist **27** 185-187

JIMÉNEZ DE CISNEROS, FRANCISCO (1436-1517), Spanish cardinal and statesman **26** 179-181

JIMÉNEZ DE QUESADA, GONZALO (1509-1579), Spanish conquistador **12** 509-510

Jina
see Vardhamana Mahavira

JINNAH, MOHAMMAD ALI (1876-1948), Pakistani governor general 1947-1948 **8** 262-263

JIRASEK, ALOIS (1851-1930), Czech author **25** 220-221

Joachim, Joseph, (1831-1907), German violinist
Rubinstein, Arthur **28** 305-307

Joachim Napoleon (king of Naples)
see Murat, Joachim

JOACHIM OF FIORE (circa 1132-1202), Italian mystic **8** 263-264

JOAN OF ARC (c. 1412-1431), French national heroine **8** 264-265

João (king of Portugal)
see John (king of Portugal)

João I (king of Kongo)
see Nzinga Nkuwu

JOBIM, ANTONIO CARLOS (Tom Jobim; Antonio Carlos Brasileiro de Almeida Jobim; 1927-1994), Brazilian musician **27** 187-189

JOBS, STEVEN (born 1955), American computer designer and co-founder of Apple Computers **8** 265-267

JODL, ALFRED (1892?-1946), German general **18** 210-212

JOFFRE, JOSEPH JACQUES CÉSAIRE (1852-1931), French marshal **8** 267-268

JOFFREY, ROBERT (born Abdullah Jaffa Anver Bey Khan; 1930-1988), American dancer and choreographer **8** 268-270

Jogaila
   see Wladyslaw II Jagiello, King of Poland

Jogu Taishi
   see Shotoku Taishi

JOGUES, ST. ISAAC (1607-1646), French Jesuit missionary and martyr **8** 270-271

JOHANAN BEN ZAKKAI (flourished circa 70 A.D.), Jewish teacher **8** 271-272

JOHANNES IV (1836-1889), Ethiopian emperor 1872-1889 **8** 272-273

JOHN (1167-1216), king of England 1199-1216 **8** 274-275

JOHN II (1319-1364), king of France 1350-1364 **8** 275-276

JOHN II (1455-1495), king of Portugal 1481-1495 **21** 223-225

JOHN III (John Sobieski; 1629-1696), king of Poland **8** 276-277

JOHN XXIII (Angelo Giuseppe Roncalli; 1881-1963), pope 1958-1963 **8** 277-280

JOHN, AUGUSTUS EDWIN (1878-1961), Welsh painter **8** 291

JOHN, ELTON HERCULES (Reginald Kenneth Dwight; born 1947), English singer, songwriter and humanitarian **18** 212-214

JOHN, ST. (flourished 1st century A.D.), Christian Apostle and Evangelist **8** 273-274

JOHN CHRYSOSTOM, ST. (circa 347-407), bishop of Constantinople **8** 280-281

JOHN MAURICE OF NASSAU (1604-1679), Dutch governor general of Netherlands Brazil **8** 281-282

JOHN OF AUSTRIA (1547-1578), Spanish general **20** 189-192

JOHN OF DAMASCUS, ST. (circa 680-750), Syrian theologian **8** 282

John of Fidanza
   see Bonaventure, Saint

JOHN OF GAUNT (5th Duke of Lancaster; 1340-1399), English soldier-statesman **8** 282-283

JOHN OF LEIDEN (1509-1536), Dutch Anabaptist **8** 283

JOHN OF PIANO CARPINI (circa 1180-1252), Italian Franciscan monk **8** 284

JOHN OF SALISBURY (1115/20-1180), English bishop and humanist **8** 284-285

JOHN OF THE CROSS, ST. (1542-1591), Spanish Carmelite mystic **8** 285

JOHN PAUL I (Albino Luciani; 1912-1978), Roman Catholic pope (August 26-September 28, 1978) **8** 286-287

JOHN PAUL II (Karol Wojtyla; 1920-2005), cardinal of Krakow, Poland, and later Roman Catholic pope **8** 287-290

JOHN THE BAPTIST, ST. (flourished circa 29 A.D.), New Testament figure, forerunner of Jesus of Nazareth **8** 290

John the Good
   see John II (king of France)

John the Perfect
   see John II (king of Portugal)

JOHNS, JASPER (born 1930), American painter and sculptor **8** 291-293

JOHNSON, ALVIN SAUNDERS (1874-1971), American economist and editor **8** 293-294

JOHNSON, ANDREW (1808-1875), American statesman, president 1865-1869 **8** 294-295

Johnson, Benjamin F.
   see Riley, James Whitcomb

JOHNSON, BETSEY (born c. 1941), American fashion designer **8** 295-296

Johnson, Charles
   see Brooke, James

JOHNSON, CHARLES SPURGEON (1893-1956), African American educator and sociologist **8** 296-297

JOHNSON, EARVIN, JR. ("Magic"; born 1959), popular African American star of the Los Angeles Lakers basketball team **8** 297-299

JOHNSON, EYVIND (Olof Edvin Verner Johnson; 1900-1976), Swedish author and journalist **25** 221-223

JOHNSON, GUY BENTON (1901-1991), sociologist, social anthropologist, and archaeologist who was a student of African American culture and an advocate of racial equality **8** 299-300

JOHNSON, HIRAM WARREN (1866-1945), American politician **8** 300-301

Johnson, Isaac Wallace
   see Wallace-Johnson, Isaac Theophilus Akunna

JOHNSON, JACK (1878-1946), African American boxer **8** 301-304

JOHNSON, JAMES WELDON (1871-1938), African American author and lawyer **8** 304-305

JOHNSON, SIR JOHN (1742-1830), American loyalist in the American Revolution **8** 305-306

JOHNSON, JOHN HAROLD (1918-2005), American entrepreneur and founder of the Johnson Publishing Company **8** 306-308

JOHNSON, JONATHAN EASTMAN (1824-1906), American painter **8** 308

JOHNSON, LYNDON BAINES (1908-1973), American statesman, president 1963-1969 **8** 308-312

JOHNSON, MARIETTA LOUISE PIERCE (1864-1938), founder and 30-year teacher of an Alabama experimental school **8** 312-313

JOHNSON, MORDECAI WYATT (1890-1976), African American educator and minister **24** 196-198

JOHNSON, PAULINE (Emily Pauline Johnson; Tekahionwake 1861-1913), Canadian poet **23** 170-172

JOHNSON, PHILIP (1906-2005), American architect, critic, and historian **8** 313-314

JOHNSON, RAFER (born 1935), American decathlete and goodwill ambassador **21** 225-227

JOHNSON, ROBERT (1911-1938), African American musician **23** 172-174

JOHNSON, SAMUEL (1696-1772), American clergyman and educator **8** 314-315

JOHNSON, SAMUEL (1709-1784), English author and lexicographer **8** 315-317

JOHNSON, TOM LOFTIN (1854-1911), American entrepreneur and politician **8** 317

JOHNSON, VIRGINIA E. (born 1925), American psychologist and sex therapist **8** 317-319

JOHNSON, WALTER ("Big Train"; 1887-1946), American baseball player and manager **21** 228-230

JOHNSON, SIR WILLIAM (1715-1774), British colonial administrator **8** 319-320

JOHNSON, WILLIAM (1771-1834), American jurist **22** 268-270

JOHNSON, WILLIAM H. (1901-1970), African American painter of the Black experience **8** 320-322

JOHNSTON, FRANCES BENJAMIN (1864-1952), American photographer **23** 174-177

JOHNSTON, HENRY HAMILTON (Sir Harry Johnston; 1858-1927), English administrator, explorer, and author **8** 322-323

JOHNSTON, JOSEPH EGGLESTON (1807-1891), American Confederate general **8** 323

JOHNSTON, JOSHUA (a.k.a. Joshua Johnson; ca. 1765 - ca 1830), African American portrait artist **8** 323-325

JOHNSTON, LYNN (born 1947), Canadian cartoonist and artist **18** 214-216

JOINVILLE, JEAN DE (1224/25-1317), French author **8** 325

Joliot, Jean Frédéric
see Joliot-Curie, Jean Frédéric

JOLIOT-CURIE, IRÈNE (1897-1956), French chemist and physicist **8** 325-327

JOLIOT-CURIE, JEAN FRÉDÉRIC (1900-1958), French physicist **8** 327-328

JOLLIET, LOUIS (1645-1700), French-Canadian explorer, hydrographer, and fur trader **8** 328-329

JOLSON, AL (Asa Yoelson; 1886-1950), American vaudeville, theater, and radio singing performer and film actor **8** 329-330

JOMINI, ANTOINE HENRI (1779-1869), Swiss military strategist **23** 177-179

JONATHAN, CHIEF JOSEPH LEABUA (1914-1987), Lesothoan statesman **8** 330-331

Jones, Edith Newbold
see Wharton, Edith

Jones, Sir Edward Coley Burne
see Burne-Jones, Sir Edward Coley

JONES, ERNEST ALFRED (1879-1958), British psychologist **8** 331-332

JONES, FAY (1921-2004), American architect **8** 332-333

JONES, FREDERICK MCKINLEY (1893?-1961), African American inventor **20** 192-194

Jones, Everett LeRoi
see Baraka, Imamu Amiri

JONES, GEORGEANNA SEEGAR (1912-2005), American physician **26** 181-183

JONES, INIGO (1573-1652), English architect and designer **8** 333-334

JONES, JAMES EARL (born 1931), African American actor **8** 334-337

JONES, JOHN PAUL (1747-1792), American Revolutionary War naval officer **8** 337-338

JONES, LOIS MAILOU (1905-1998), African American artist **20** 194-196

JONES, MARY HARRIS ("Mother"; 1830-1930), Irish immigrant who devoted her life to improving conditions of the working class **8** 338-339

JONES, QUINCY DELIGHT, JR. (born 1933), African American musician-composer-arranger-producer-film and television executive **8** 339-341

JONES, ROBERT EDMOND (1887-1954), American designer of scenes for the theater **8** 341-342

JONES, ROBERT TYRE (Bobby; 1902-1971), American golf great **8** 342

JONES, SAMUEL MILTON (1846-1904), American manufacturer and political reformer **8** 342-343

JONES, WILLIAM (1746-1794), English linguist and judge **27** 189-192

JONG, ERICA (born 1942), American author **18** 216-219

JONSON, BEN (1572-1637), English playwright and poet **8** 343-345

JOPLIN, JANIS (1943-1979), American singer **26** 183-187

JOPLIN, SCOTT (1868-1917), African American composer and instrumental musician **8** 345-347

JORDAENS, JACOB (1593-1678), Flemish painter **8** 347-349

JORDAN, BARBARA CHARLINE (1936-1996), attorney and U.S. congresswoman from Texas **8** 349-350

JORDAN, DAVID STARR (1851-1931), American scientist and educator **8** 350-351

JORDAN, JUNE (1936-2002), Jamaican American poet and activist **8** 351-353

JORDAN, LOUIS (1908-1975), African American bandleader, singer, and instrumentalist **8** 353-355

JORDAN, MICHAEL (born 1963), African American basketball superstar of the Chicago Bulls **8** 355-357

JORDAN, VERNON (born 1935), American civil rights leader **8** 357-358

JOSEPH (circa 1840-1904), American Nez Percé Indian chief **8** 358-359

JOSEPH (dates unknown), biblical figure **25** 223-226

Joseph I (King of Spain)
see Bonaparte, Joseph

JOSEPH II (1741-1790), Holy Roman emperor 1765-1790 **8** 359-360

Joseph ben Mattathias
see Josephus Flavius

JOSEPHUS FLAVIUS (circa 37-100), Jewish historian, diplomat, and military leader **8** 360-361

JOSQUIN DES PREZ (circa 1440-1521), Franco-Flemish composer **8** 361-363

JOULE, JAMES PRESCOTT (1818-1889), English physicist **8** 363-364

Journalists
Finnish
Canth, Minna **28** 58-60

Journalists, American
20th century
Thurman, Wallace Henry **28** 352-354

Journeys of Celia Fiennes, The (book)
Fiennes, Celia **28** 118-121

JOWETT, BENJAMIN (1817-1893), English educator and Greek scholar **8** 364-365

JOYCE, JAMES (1882-1941), Irish author **8** 365-367

JOYNER, MATILDA SISSIERETTA (Sissieretta Jones; 1869-1933), African American singer **23** 179-181

JOYNER-KERSEE, JACKIE (born 1962), American track and field athlete **19** 170-173

JUAN CARLOS I (born 1938), king of Spain **8** 368-369

JUANA INÉS DE LA CRUZ, SISTER (1651-1695), Mexican nun, poet, and savant **8** 367-368

JUÁREZ, BENITO (1806-1872), Mexican statesman, president 1857-1872 **8** 369-372

Judaea (Judea)
see Jewish history—Biblical Era (Judea)

JUDAEUS, PHILO (circa 20 B.C. -circa A.D. 45), Hellenistic Jewish philosopher **12** 282-283

Judah
see Jewish history—Biblical Era (Judah)

JUDAH I (circa 135-circa 220), Jewish scholar **8** 372-373

JUDAH, THEODORE DEHONE (1826-1863), American engineer and railroad promoter **8** 373-374

JUDAH HALEVI (circa 1085-circa 1150), Spanish Hebrew poet **8** 373

Judah Ha-Nasi
see Judah I

JUDAS MACCABEUS (died 160 B.C.), Jewish patriot and revolutionary **8** 374-375

JUDD, CHARLES HUBBARD (1873-1946), psychologist and education reformer **8** 375-376

JUDD, DONALD (1928-1994), American sculptor and art writer **8** 376-377

JUDSON, ADONIRAM (1788-1850), American Baptist missionary in Burma **8** 377-378

JULIA, RAUL (Julia y Arcelay, Raul Rafael Carlos; 1940-1994), American acotr and humanitarian **21** 230-232

JULIAN (The Apostate; Flavius Claudius Julianus; 331-363), Roman emperor 361-363 **8** 378-379

JULIAN, PERCY LAVON (1899-1975), African American chemist and civil rights activist **18** 219-221

JULIAN OF NORWICH (1342-after 1416), English mystic **8** 381

JULIANA (born 1909), queen of the Netherlands (1948-1980) **8** 379-380

JULIAS OF ROME, THE (Julia Domna, ca. 169-ca. 217; Julia Maesa, ca. 164-225; Julia Soamias, died 222; and Julia Mammaea, died 234), empresses of the so-called Severan Dynasty of Rome **8** 381-384

JULIUS II (Giuliano della Rovere; 1443-1513), pope 1503-1513 **8** 384-386

July Monarchy (France)
see France—1830-1848

JUMBLATT, KAMAL (1917-1977), Lebanese ideologue and Druze leader **8** 386-387

JUNAYD, ABU AL-QASIM IBN MUHAMMAD AL (circa 830-910), Islamic mystic **8** 388

June, Jennie
see Croly, Jane Cunningham

JUNG, CARL GUSTAV (1875-1961), Swiss psychologist and psychiatrist **8** 388-389

JUNG, ANDREA (born 1959), American businesswoman **27** 192-194

JUNG, LEO (1892-1987), American Orthodox Jewish Rabbi **8** 390-391

JÜNGER, ERNST (1895-1998), German author **8** 391-392

JUST, ERNEST (1883-1941), American marine biologist **8** 392-393

JUSTIN MARTYR (circa 100-circa 165), Early Christian apologist **8** 395-396

JUSTINIAN I (circa 482-565), Byzantine emperor 527-565 **8** 393-395

JUSTO, AGUSTIN PEDRO (1876-1943), Argentine general, president 1932-1938 **8** 396

JUVARA, FILIPPO (1678-1736), Italian architect and designer **8** 396-397

JUVENAL (Decimus Junius Juvenalis; died after 127), Roman satirist **8** 397-399

Juvenile literature
see Literature for children

K

KABAKOV, ILYA (born 1933), Russian artist **23** 182-184

KABALEVSKY, DMITRI (1904-1987), Soviet composer, pianist, and conductor **8** 400-401

KABILA, JOSEPH (born 1971), president of the Congo **27** 195-197

KABILA, LAURENT (born 1939), Congolese revolutionary and president **18** 222-224

KABIR (circa 1440-circa 1518), Indian religious mystic and poet **26** 188-190

KADALIE, CLEMENTS (circa 1896-1951), South Africa's first Black national trade union leader **8** 401-402

KADÁR, JÁN (1918-1979), Czech filmmaker and screenwriter **25** 227-229

KÁDÁR, JÁNOS (born 1912), Hungarian statesman **8** 402-403

KAFKA, FRANZ (1883-1924), Czech-born German novelist and short-story writer **8** 403-406

KAHANAMOKU, DUKE (1890-1968), Hawaiian swimmer **20** 197-199

KAHLO, FRIDA (1907-1954), Mexican painter **8** 406-407

KAHN, ALBERT (1869-1942), American architect **8** 407-408

KHAN, ALI AKBAR (born 1922), Indian musician **24** 203-206

KHAN, A.Q. (Abdul Quadeer Khan; born 1936), Pakistani metallurgical engineer **27** 205-208

KAHN, LOUIS I. (1901-1974), American architect **8** 408-410

KAIFU TOSHIKI (born 1931), Japanese prime minister (1989-1991) **8** 410-411

KAISER, GEORG (1878-1945), German playwright **8** 411-412

KAISER, HENRY JOHN (1882-1967), American industrialist **8** 412-413

Kakuyu
see Toba Sojo

KALAKAUA, DAVID (1836-1891), king of Hawaiian Islands 1874-1891 **8** 413-414

KALASHNIKOV, MIKHAIL (Mikhail Timofeyevich Kalashnikov; born 1919), Russian inventor **28** 190-192

KALIDASA (flourished 4th-5th century), Indian poet and dramatist **8** 414-415

KALMAN, RUDOLF EMIL (born 1930), Hungarian scientist **24** 199-201

KALMUS, NATALIE (Natalie Mabelle Dunfee; 1883?-1965), American inventor and cinematographer **21** 233-235

Kamako
see Fujiwara Kamatari

Kamakura Period
see Japan—1185-1338

KAMARAJ, KUMARASWAMI (1903-1975), Indian political leader **8** 415

KAMEHAMEHA I (circa 1758-1819), king of the Hawaiian Islands 1795-1819 **8** 416

KAMEHAMEHA III (circa 1814-1854), king of the Hawaiian Islands 1825-1854 **8** 416-417

KAMENEV, LEV BORISOVICH (1883-1936), Russian politician **8** 417-418

KAMERLINGH ONNES, HEIKE (1853-1926), Dutch physicist **8** 418-420

Kamisori
see Tojo, Hideki

Kamitsumiya no Miko
see Shotoku Taishi

KAMMU (737-806), Japanese emperor 781-806 **8** 420

KAMROWSKI, GEROME (1914-2004), American artist **27** 197-199

KANDER, JOHN (born 1927), American composer and lyricist **21** 235-237

KANDINSKY, WASSILY (1866-1944), Russian painter **8** 420-422

KANE, JOHN (1860-1934), Scottish-born American primitive painter **8** 422

KANE, PAUL (1810-1871), Canadian painter and writer **8** 422-423

K'ANG YU-WEI (1858-1927), Chinese scholar and philosopher **8** 426-428

K'ANG-HSI (1654-1722), Chinese emperor 1661-1722 **8** 423-426

Kanis, Saint Peter *see* Peter Canisius, Saint

KANISHKA (ca. 78-ca. 103), Kashan ruler **8** 428-429

Kankan Musa *see* Musa Mansa

KANT, IMMANUEL (1724-1804), German philosopher **8** 430-432

KAO-TSUNG (1107-1187), Chinese emperor **8** 433

KAPITSA, PYOTR LEONIDOVICH (born 1894), Soviet physicist **8** 433-435

KAPLAN, MORDECAI MENAHEM (1881-1983), American Jewish theologian and educator **8** 435-436

KAPP, WOLFGANG (1858-1922), German nationalist politician **8** 436

KAPTEYN, JACOBUS CORNELIS (1851-1922), Dutch astronomer **8** 436-437

KARADZIC, RADOVAN (born 1945), leader of the Serbian Republic **8** 437-440

KARAJAN, HERBERT VON (1908-1989), Austrian conductor **26** 190-192

KARAMANLIS, CONSTANTINE (1907-1998), Greek member of parliament, prime minister (1955-1963; 1974-1980), and president (1980-1985) **8** 440-441

KARAMZIN, NIKOLAI MIKHAILOVICH (1766-1826), Russian historian and author **8** 441-442

KARAN, DONNA (born 1948), American fashion designer and businesswoman **8** 442-444

KARENGA, MAULANA (born Ronald McKinley Everett; born 1941), African American author, educator, and proponent of black culturalism **8** 444-447

Karim, Prince *see* Aga Khan IV

KARIM KHAN ZAND (died 1779), Iranian ruler, founder of Zand dynasty **8** 447

KARLE, ISABELLA (born 1921), American chemist and physicist **8** 447-449

KARLOFF, BORIS (William Henry Pratt; 1887-1969), English actor **26** 192-194

KARLSTADT, ANDREAS BODENHEIM VON (circa 1480-1541), German Protestant reformer **8** 449

KARMAL, BABRAK (born 1929), Afghan Marxist and Soviet puppet ruler of the Democratic Republic of Afghanistan (1979-1986) **8** 449-451

KÁRMÁN, THEODORE VON (1881-1963), Hungarian-born American physicist **8** 451-452

KARP, NATALIA (1911-2007), Jewish Polish pianist **28** 192-194

KARSH, YOUSUF (1908-2002), Canadian photographer **23** 184-187

KARTINI, RADEN AJENG (1879-1904), Indonesian activist **24** 201-203

KARUME, SHEIKH ABEID AMANI (1905-1972), Tanzanian political leader **8** 452-453

KASAVUBU, JOSEPH (circa 1913-1969), Congolese statesman **8** 453-455

Kasimir, Karl Theodore *see* Meyerhold, Vsevolod Emilievich

KASPAROV, GARRY (Garri Kimovich Weinstein; born 1963), Russian chess player and politician **28** 194-196

KASSEBAUM, NANCY (born 1932), Republican senator from Kansas **8** 455-457

KASTRIOTI-SKANDERBEG, GJERGJ (1405-1468), Albanian military leader **23** 187-189

KATAYAMA, SEN (1860-1933), Japanese labor and Socialist leader **8** 457

KAUFFMAN, ANGELICA (Maria Anna Angelica Catherina Kauffman; 1741-1807), Swedish artist **25** 229-231

KAUFMAN, GEORGE S. (1889-1961), American playwright **8** 457-458

KAUFMAN, GERALD BERNARD (born 1930), foreign policy spokesman of the British Labour Party **8** 458-460

KAUFMANN, EZEKIEL (1889-1963), Jewish philosopher and scholar **8** 460

KAUNDA, KENNETH DAVID (born 1924), Zambian statesman **8** 460-461

KAUTILYA (4th century B.C.), Indian statesman and author **8** 462

KAUTSKY, KARL JOHANN (1854-1938), German Austrian Socialist **8** 462-463

KAWABATA, YASUNARI (1899-1972), Japanese novelist **8** 463-464

KAWAWA, RASHIDI MFAUME (born 1929), Tanzanian political leader **8** 464-465

KAYE, DANNY (David Daniel Kaminsky; 1913-1987), American film and stage actor **25** 231-234

KAZAN, ELIA (born 1909), American film and stage director **8** 465-466

KAZANTZAKIS, NIKOS (1883-1957), Greek author, journalist, and statesman **8** 466-468

KEAN, EDMUND (1789-1833), English actor **21** 237-239

KEARNEY, DENIS (1847-1907), Irish-born American labor agitator **8** 468

KEARNY, STEPHEN WATTS (1794-1848), American general **8** 468-469

KEATING, PAUL JOHN (born 1944), federal treasurer of Australia (1983-1991) **8** 469-470

KEATON, BUSTER (Joseph Frank Keaton; 1895-1966), American comedian **20** 199-201

KEATS, JOHN (1795-1821), English poet **8** 470-472

KEFAUVER, CAREY ESTES (1903-1963), U.S. senator and influential Tennessee Democrat **8** 472-474

KEILLOR, GARRISON (Gary Edward Keillor, born 1942), American humorist, radio host, and author **22** 271-273

KEITA, MODIBO (1915-1977), Malian statesman **8** 474-475

KEITEL, WILHELM (1882-1946), German general **18** 224-226

KECKLEY, ELIZABETH HOBBS (Elizabeth Hobbs Keckly; 1818-1907), African American seamstress and author **28** 196-199

KEITH, SIR ARTHUR (1866-1955), British anatomist and physical anthropologist **8** 475-476

KEITH, MINOR COOPER (1848-1929), American entrepreneur **8** 476-477

KEKKONEN, URHO KALEVA (1900-1986), Finnish athlete and politician **23** 189-191

KEKULÉ, FRIEDRICH AUGUST (1829-1896), German chemist **8** 477-478

KELLER, ELIZABETH BEACH (Elizabeth Waterbury Beach; 1918-1997), American biochemist **25** 234-235

KELLER, GOTTFRIED (1819-1890), Swiss short-story writer, novelist, and poet **8** 478-479

KELLER, HELEN ADAMS (1880-1968), American lecturer and author **8** 479-480

KELLEY, FLORENCE (1859-1932), American social worker and reformer **8** 483-484

KELLEY, HALL JACKSON (1790-1874), American promoter **8** 480

KELLEY, OLIVER HUDSON (1826-1913), American agriculturalist **8** 480-481

KELLOGG, FRANK BILLINGS (1856-1937), American statesman **8** 481

KELLOGG, JOHN HARVEY (1852-1943), American health propagandist and cereal manufacturer **21** 239-242
Kellogg, W. K. **28** 199-201

KELLOGG, W. K. (Will Keith Kellogg; 1860-1951), American cereal manufacturer and philanthropist **28** 199-201

KELLOR, FRANCES (1873-1952), American activist and politician **8** 481-482

KELLY, ELLSWORTH (born 1923), American artist **8** 482-483

KELLY, GENE (born Eugene Curran Kelly; 1912-1996), American actor, dancer, and choreographer **8** 484-486

KELLY, GRACE (Grace, Princess; 1929-1982), princess of Monaco **19** 174-176

KELLY, PATRICK (1954-1990), African American fashion designer **22** 273-275

KELLY, PETRA (born 1947), West German pacifist and politician **8** 486-487

KELLY, WALT (Walter Crawford Kelly; 1913-1973), American Cartoonist **22** 275-278

KELLY, WILLIAM (1811-1888), American iron manufacturer **8** 487-488

KELSEY, HENRY (circa 1667-1724), English-born Canadian explorer **8** 488

KELVIN OF LARGS, BARON (William Thomson; 1824-1907), Scottish physicist **8** 488-489

Kemal, Mustapha (Kemal Atatürk)
see Atatürk, Ghazi Mustapha Kemal

KEMAL, YASHAR (born 1922), Turkish novelist **8** 489-491

KEMBLE, FRANCES ANNE (Fanny Kemble; 1809-1893), English actress **8** 491

KEMP, JACK FRENCH, JR. (born 1935), Republican congressman from New York and secretary of housing and urban development **8** 491-493

KEMPIS, THOMAS À (circa 1380-1471), German monk and spiritual writer **8** 493-494

KENDALL, AMOS (1789-1869), American journalist **8** 494

KENDALL, EDWARD CALVIN (1886-1972), American biochemist **8** 495

KENDALL, THOMAS HENRY (Henry Clarence Kendall; 1839-1882), Australian poet **23** 191-194

Kendrake, Carleton
see Gardner, Erle Stanley

KENDREW, JOHN C. (1917-1997), English chemist and Nobel Prize winner **8** 495-496

KENEALLY, THOMAS MICHAEL (born 1935), Australian author **18** 226-228

KENNAN, GEORGE F. (1904-2005), American diplomat, author, and scholar **8** 496-498

Kennedy, Aimee
see McPherson, Aimee Semple

KENNEDY, ANTHONY M. (born 1936), United States Supreme Court justice **8** 498-500

KENNEDY, EDWARD M. (Ted; born 1932), U.S. senator from Massachusetts **8** 500-502

KENNEDY, FLORYNCE RAE (1916-2000), African American activist and lawyer **27** 199-201

Kennedy, Jacqueline Lee Bouvier
see Onassis, Jacqueline Lee Bouvier Kennedy

KENNEDY, JOHN FITZGERALD (1917-1963), American statesman, president 1960-1963 **8** 502-506

KENNEDY, JOHN FITZGERALD, JR. (1960-1999), American icon and publisher **25** 235-238

KENNEDY, JOHN PENDLETON (1795-1870), American author and politician **8** 506-507

KENNEDY, JOHN STEWART (1830-1909), American financier and philanthropist **8** 507-508

KENNEDY, JOSEPH (1888-1969), American financier, ambassador, and movie producer **19** 176-178

KENNEDY, ROBERT FRANCIS (1925-1968), American statesman **8** 508-509

KENNEDY, WILLIAM (born 1928), American author **19** 178-180

Kenny, Charles J.
see Gardner, Erle Stanley

KENNY, ELIZABETH (Sister Kenny; 1886-1952), Australian nursing sister **8** 509-510

KENT, JAMES (1763-1847), American jurist **8** 510-511

KENT, ROCKWELL (1882-1971), American painter and illustrator **8** 511

KENYATTA, JOMO (circa 1890-1978), Kenyan statesman **8** 512-514

KEOHANE, NANNERL OVERHOLSER (born 1940), American feminist activist and university chancellor **18** 229-230

KEPLER, JOHANNES (1571-1630), German astronomer **8** 514-516

KERENSKY, ALEKSANDR FEDOROVICH (1881-1970), Russian revolutionary and politician **8** 516-517

KERKORIAN, KIRK (Kerkor Kerkorian; born 1917), American financier **27** 201-203

KERN, JEROME DAVID (1885-1945), American composer **8** 517-518

Kerosene lamp
Lukasiewicz, Ignacy **28** 225-227

KEROUAC, JEAN-LOUIS LEBRIS DE (Jack; 1922-69), American writer of autobiographical fiction **8** 518-519

KERR, CLARK (born 1911), American economist, labor/management expert, and university president **8** 519-521

KERREY, J. ROBERT (born 1943), Democratic senator from Nebraska and 1992 presidential candidate **8** 521-522

KERRY, JOHN FORBES (born 1943), American political leader **25** 238-240

KESEY, KEN ELTON (1935-2001), American author **27** 203-205

KESSELRING, ALBERT (1885-1960), German field marshal **8** 522-523

KESSLER, DAVID A. (born 1951), commissioner of the Food and Drug Administration **8** 523-524

KETTERING, CHARLES F. (1876-1958), American engineer, industrial pioneer, and apostle of progress **8** 524-525

KEVORKIAN, JACK (born 1928), American pathologist who practiced assisted suicide **19** 180-182

KEY, FRANCIS SCOTT (1779-1843), American poet and attorney **8** 525-527

KEY, VLADIMIR ORLANDO, JR. (1908-1963), American political scientist **8** 527-528

KEYNES, JOHN MAYNARD (1st Baron Keynes of Tilton; 1883-1946), English economist **8** 528-530

KHACHATURIAN, ARAM ILICH (or Khachaturov; 1903-1978), Russian composer **8** 530-531

KHALID BIN ABDUL AZIZ AL-SAUD (1912-1982), Saudi king and prime minister **23** 194-196

KHALIL, SAYYID ABDULLAH (1892-1970), Sudanese general, prime minister 1956-1958 **8** 531-532

KHAMA, SIR SERETSE M. (born 1921), Botswana political leader **8** 532-533

KHAMENEI, AYATOLLAH SAYYID ALI (born 1939), supreme spiritual and political leader of the Islamic Republic of Iran **8** 533-535

Khammurapikh
see Hammurabi

Khmelnitskii, Bogdan
see Chmielnicki, Bogdan

KHOMEINI, AYATOLLAH RUHOLLAH MUSAVI (born 1902), founder and supreme leader of the Islamic Republic of Iran **8** 535-537

KHORANA, HAR GOBIND (born 1922), Indian organic chemist **8** 537-538

KHOSROW I (died 579), Sassanid king of Persia 531-576 **8** 538-539

Khosru
see Khosrow I

KHRUSHCHEV, NIKITA SERGEEVICH (1894-1971), Soviet political leader **8** 539-540

KHUFU (ruled 2590-2568 B.C.), Egyptian king **8** 540-541

Khurram
see Shah Jahan

Khusrau
see Khosrow I

KHWARIZMI, MUHAMMAD IBN MUSA AL- (died circa 850), Arab mathematician, astronomer, and geographer **8** 541

KIBAKI, MWAI (born 1931), Kenyan presidnet **25** 240-242

Kibo-no Mabi
see Makibi, Kibi-no

KIDD, WILLIAM (c. 1645-1701), Scottish pirate **21** 242-244

KIDDER, ALFRED VINCENT (1885-1963), American archeologist **8** 541-542

KIDMAN, SIDNEY (1857-1935), ''The Cattle King'' of Australia **8** 542-544

KIEFER, ANSELM (born 1945), German artist **8** 544-546

KIENHOLZ, EDWARD (born 1927), American Pop artist **8** 546-547

KIERKEGAARD, SØREN AABYE (1813-1855), Danish philosopher **8** 547-549

KIESLOWSKI, KRZYSZTOF (1941-1946), Polish film director **25** 242-244

KILBY, JACK ST. CLAIR (1923-2005), American electrical engineer and inventor **25** 244-246

KILPATRICK, WILLIAM H. (1871-1965), American educator, college president, and philosopher of education **9** 1-3

KIM DAE-JUNG (born 1925), worked for the restoration of democracy and human rights in South Korea after 1971 **9** 3-4

KIM IL-SUNG (born 1912), North Korean political leader **9** 4-6

KIM JONG IL (born 1941), heir-apparent of Kim Il-sung, the founder and leader of the Democratic People's Republic of Korea **9** 6-7

KIM OK-KYUN (1851-1894), Korean politician **9** 7-8

KIM PUSIK (1075-1151), Korean statesman, historian, and general **9** 8-9

Kim Song-ju
see Kim Il-sung

KIM YOUNG SAM (born 1927), South Korean statesman **9** 9-10

KINCAID, JAMAICA (Elaine Potter Richardson; born 1949), African American author **23** 196-199

KINDI, ABU-YUSUF YAQUB IBN-ISHAQ AL- (died 873), Arab philosopher **9** 10-11

KING, B. B. (born Riley B. King; born 1925), African American blues musician, singer, and songwriter **9** 11-14

KING, BILLIE JEAN (born 1943), international tennis star **9** 14-15

KING, CLARENCE (1842-1901), American geologist and mining engineer **9** 15-16

KING, CORETTA SCOTT (1927-2005), American advocate of civil rights, nonviolence, international peace, full employment, and equal rights for women **9** 16-17

KING, ERNEST JOSEPH (1878-1956), American admiral **9** 17-18

KING, FREDERIC TRUBY (1858-1938), New Zealand doctor and founder of the Plunket Society **9** 18-19

KING, MARTIN LUTHER, JR. (1929-1968), African American minister and civil rights leader **9** 20-22

KING, MARY-CLAIRE (born 1946), American geneticist **19** 182-183

KING, RUFUS (1755-1827), American statesman and diplomat **9** 22-23

KING, STEPHEN (a.k.a. Richard Bachman and John Swithen; born 1947), American horror novelist **9** 23-25

KING, WILLIAM LYON MACKENZIE (1874-1950), Canadian statesman **9** 25-26

King of Bourges
see Charles VII (king of France)

KINGMAN, DONG (Dong Moy She Kingman; 1911-2000), Chinese American artist **27** 208-209

KINGSFORD SMITH, SIR CHARLES (''Smithy''; 1897-1935), Australian long-distance aviator **9** 26-28

KINGSLEY, CHARLES (1819-1875), English author and Anglican clergyman **9** 28

KINGSLEY, HENRY (1830-1867), British author **22** 278-280

KINGSLEY, MARY (1862-1900), English explorer and author **20** 201-204

KINGSTON, MAXINE HONG (Maxine Ting Ting Hong; born 1940), Asian-American feminist author **18** 231-232

KINNOCK, NEIL (born 1942), British Labour Party politician **9** 29-30

KINO, EUSEBIO FRANCISCO (1645-1711), Spanish missionary, explorer, and cartographer **9** 30-31

KINOSHITA, KEISUKE (1912-1998), Japanese screenwriter and film director/producer **24** 206-208

KINSEY, ALFRED C. (1894-1956), American zoologist **9** 31-32

KINUGASA, TEINOSUKE (Teinosuke Kogame; 1896-1982), Japanese screenwriter and film director **24** 208-209

KIPLING, JOSEPH RUDYARD (1865-1936), British poet and short-story writer **9** 32-33

KIPNIS, ALEXANDER (1891-1978), Ukrainian American musician **24** 209-211

KIRCH, MARIA WINCKELMANN (1670-1720), German astronomer **20** 204-205

KIRCHER, ATHANASIUS (1601?-1680), German polymath **27** 209-211

KIRCHHOFF, GUSTAV ROBERT (1824-1887), German physicist **9** 33-34

KIRCHNER, ERNST LUDWIG (1880-1938), German expressionist painter **9** 34-35

KIRKLAND, JOSEPH LANE (1922-1999), American labor union movement leader 9 35-37

KIRKLAND, SAMUEL (1741-1808), American Congregationalist missionary 9 37

KIRKPATRICK, JEANE J. (1926-2006), professor and first woman U.S. ambassador to the United Nations 9 37-39

Kirov Ballet Company (GATOB) Taglioni, Marie 28 345-347

KIRSTEIN, LINCOLN (1906-1996), a founder and director of the New York City Ballet 9 39-41

KISHI, NOBUSUKE (1896-1987), Japanese politician 9 41-43

KISSINGER, HENRY ALFRED (born 1923), U.S. secretary of state and co-winner of the Nobel Peace prize 9 43-45

Kitáb-i-Aqdas (book) Bahá'u'lláh 28 21-23

KITCHENER, HORATIO HERBERT (1850-1916), British field marshal and statesman 9 45-46

KITT, EARTHA (nee Eartha Mae Kitt-Fields; born 1927), African American actress and singer 26 194-197

Kiuprili, Ahmed see Köprülü, Ahmed

KIVI, ALEKSIS (Aleksis Stenvall; 1834-1872), Finnish author 25 246-247

KIWANUKA, BENEDICTO KAGIMA MUGUMBA (1922-1972), Ugandan politician 9 46-47

KLEE, PAUL (1879-1940), Swiss painter and graphic artist 9 47-49

KLEIN, A. M. (1909-1972), Canadian journalist, lawyer, novelist, and poet 9 49-50

KLEIN, CALVIN (born 1942), American fashion designer 9 50-52

KLEIN, MELANIE (1882-1960), Austrian psychotherapist 9 52

KLEIST, HEINRICH VON (1777-1811), German author 9 52-53

KLEMPERER, OTTO (1885-1973), German conductor 20 205-207

KLIMA, VIKTOR (born 1947), Austrian chancellor 18 232-234

KLIMT, GUSTAV (1862-1918), controversial Austrian painter 9 53-55

KLINE, FRANZ (1910-1962), American painter 9 55

KLITZING, KLAUS VON (born 1943), German physicist 27 212-214

KLOPSTOCK, FRIEDRICH GOTTLIEB (1724-1803), German poet 9 55-56

KLUCKHOHN, CLYDE (1905-1960), American anthropologist 9 56-57

KLYUCHEVSKY, VASILY OSIPOVICH (1841-1911), Russian historian 9 57-58

KNAPP, SEAMAN ASAHEL (1833-1911), American educator and agricultural pioneer 9 58

Knickerbocker, Diedrich (pseudonym) see Irving, Washington

KNIGHT, FRANK HYNEMAN (1885-1972), American economist 9 58-59

KNIGHT, PHIL (born 1938), American businessman 19 183-186

KNIPLING, EDWARD FRED (1909-2000), American entomologist 9 59-60

KNOPF, ALFRED A. (1892-1984), American publisher 9 60-61

KNOPF, BLANCHE WOLF (1894-1966), American publisher 9 61-62

KNOWLES, MALCOLM SHEPHERD (1913-1997), American adult education theorist and planner 9 62-64

KNOX, HENRY (1750-1806), American Revolutionary War general 9 64

KNOX, JOHN (circa 1505-1572), Scottish religious reformer 9 65-66

KNOX, PHILANDER CHASE (1853-1921), American statesman 9 66-67

KNUDSEN, WILLIAM S. (1879-1948), American auto industry leader 9 67-68

KOBAYASHI, MASAKI (1916-1996), Japanese film director 23 199-201

Kobo Daishi see Kukai

KOCH, EDWARD I. (born 1924), New York City mayor 9 68-69

KOCH, MARITA (Marita Meier-Koch; born 1957), German athlete 26 197-199

KOCH, ROBERT HEINRICH HERMANN (1843-1910), German physician and bacteriologist 9 69-70

KODÁLY, ZOLTÁN (1882-1967), Hungarian composer 9 71

KOESTLER, ARTHUR (1905-1983), author of political novels 9 71-73

KOGAWA, JOY NOZOMI (née Na Kayama; born 1935), Japanese Canadian author and activist 25 247-250

KOHL, HELMUT (born 1930), chancellor of West Germany (1982-1990) and first chancellor of a united Germany since World War II 9 73-74 Merkel, Angela 28 243-245

KOHN, WALTER (born 1923), German-American physicist 27 214-216

KOIZUMI, JUNICHIRO (born 1942), Japanese prime minister 25 250-252

Koizumi, Yakumo see Hearn, Lafcadio

KOJONG (1852-1919), Korean king 9 74-75

KOKOSCHKA, OSKAR (1886-1980), Austrian painter, graphic artist, and author 9 75-76

KOLAKOWSKI, LESZEK (born 1927), philosopher who wrote on broad themes of ethics, metaphysics, and religion 9 76-77

KOLCHAK, ALEKSANDR VASILIEVICH (1873-1920), Russian admiral 9 77-78

KOLLONTAI, ALEKSANDRA MIKHAILOVNA (1872-1952), Soviet diplomat 9 79

KOLLWITZ, KÄTHE (1867-1945), German expressionist graphic artist and sculptor 9 79-81

KONEV, IVAN STEFANOVICH (1897-1973), Soviet marshal 9 81-82

KONOE, PRINCE FUMIMARO (or Konoye; 1891-1945), Japanese premier 1937-1939 and 1940-1941 9 82-83

Kook, Abraham Isaac see Kuk, Abraham Isaac

KOONS, JEFF (born 1955), American artist 9 83-84

KOOP, C. EVERETT (born 1916), American surgeon general 18 235-237

KÖPRÜLÜ, AHMED (Köprülüzade Fazil Ahmed Pasha; 1635-1676), Turkish statesman and general 9 84-85

Koran (Quran; religious book) commentaries on Nursî, Said 28 259-261 translations Dehlavi, Shah Waliullah 28 92-94

KORBUT, OLGA (born 1955), Belarusian gymnast 24 211-213

KORNBERG, ARTHUR (1918-2007), American biochemist 9 85-87

KORNILOV, LAVR GEORGIEVICH (1870-1918), Russian general 9 87-88

Kosan see Yun Sondo

KOSCIUSZKO, TADEUSZ ANDRZEJ BONAWENTURA (1746-1817), Polish

patriot, hero in the American Revolution **9** 88

KOSINSKI, JERZY (Jerzy Nikodem Lewinkopf; 1933-1991), Polish-American author **26** 199-201

KOSSUTH, LOUIS (1802-1894), Hungarian statesman **9** 88-90

Kostrowitsky, Wilhelm Apollinaris de
see Apollinaire, Guillaume

KOSYGIN, ALEKSEI NIKOLAEVICH (1904-1980), chairman of the U.S.S.R. Council of Ministers and head of the Soviet government (1964-1980) **9** 90-91

KOTZEBUE, OTTO VON (1787-1846), Russian explorer **9** 91-92

KOUFAX, SANDY (Sanford Braun; born 1945), American baseball player **20** 208-210

KOUSSEVITZKY, SERGE (Sergey Aleksandrovich Kusevitsky;1874-1951), Russian-born American conductor **24** 213-215

KOVACS, ERNIE (1919-1962), American comedian **19** 186-188

KOVALEVSKY, SOPHIA VASILEVNA (Sonya Kovalevsky; 1850-1891), Russian mathematician **22** 280-282

KOZYREV, ANDREI VLADIMIROVICH (born 1951), Russian minister of foreign affairs and a liberal, pro-Western figure in Boris Yeltsin's cabinet **9** 92-93

KRAMER, LARRY (born 1935), American AIDS activist and author **20** 210-212

KRASNER, LEE (Lenore; 1908-1984), American painter and collage artist **9** 93-94

KRAVCHUK, LEONID MAKAROVYCH (born 1934), president of the Ukraine (1991-1994) **9** 94-95

KREBS, SIR HANS ADOLF (1900-1981), German British biochemist **9** 95-97

KREISKY, BRUNO (1911-1983), chancellor of Austria (1970-1983) **9** 97-98

KREISLER, FRITZ (Friedrich Kreisler; 1875-1962), Austrian violinist **26** 201-203

Kremer, Gerhard
see Mercator, Gerhardus

KRENEK, ERNST (born 1900), Austrian composer **9** 98-99

KREPS, JUANITA MORRIS (born 1921), economist, university professor, United States secretary of commerce (1977-1979), and author **9** 99-101

KRIEGHOFF, CORNELIUS (1815-1872), Dutch-born Canadian painter **9** 101

KRISHNAMURTI, JIDDU (1895-1986), Indian mystic and philosopher **9** 101-103

KRISHNAMURTI, UPPALURI GOPALA (U.G. Krishnamurti; 1918-2007), Indian philosopher and author **28** 201-203

KRLEZA, MIROSLAV (1893-1981), Croatian author and poet **24** 215-217

KROC, RAYMOND ALBERT (1902-1984), creator of the McDonald's chain **9** 103-104

KROCHMAL, NACHMAN KOHEN (1785-1840), Austrian Jewish historian **9** 104-105

KROEBER, ALFRED LOUIS (1876-1960), American anthropologist **9** 105-106

KROGH, SCHACK AUGUST STEENBERG (1874-1949), Danish physiologist **9** 106

KRONE, JULIE (Julieanne Louise Krone; born 1963), American jockey **24** 217-220

KROPOTKIN, PETER ALEKSEEVICH (1842-1921), Russian prince, scientist, and anarchist **9** 107-108

KROTO, HAROLD WALTER (Harold Walter Krotoschiner; born 1939), British Chemist **27** 216-218

KRUGER, STEPHANUS JOHANNES PAULUS ("Paul"; 1825-1904), South African statesman **9** 108-109

KRUPP FAMILY (19th-20th century), German industrialists **9** 109-111

KU CHIEH-KANG (born 1893), Chinese historian **9** 120-121

KUFUOR, JOHN AGYEKUM (born 1938), president of Ghana **27** 218-220

KU K'AI-CHIH (circa 345-circa 406), Chinese painter **9** 125-126

KUANG-HSÜ (1871-1908), emperor of China 1875-1908 **9** 111-112

KUANG-WU-TI (6 B.C. - 57 A.D.), Chinese emperor ca. 25-57 **9** 112-113

KUBITSCHEK DE OLIVEIRA, JUSCELINO (1902-1976), president of Brazil 1956-1961 **9** 113-115

KUBLAI KHAN (1215-1294), Mongol emperor **9** 115-118

KÜBLER-ROSS, ELISABETH (1926-2004), Swiss-born American psychiatrist **9** 118-120

KUBRICK, STANLEY (1928-1999), American filmmaker **18** 237-239

KUCAN, MILAN (born 1941), President of the Republic of Slovenia **18** 239-242

KUHN, MAGGIE (1905-1995), American activist and founder of the Gray Panthers **19** 188-190

KUHN, THOMAS SAMUEL (1922-1996), American historian and philosopher of science **9** 121-123

KUK, ABRAHAM ISAAC (1865-1935), Russian-born Jewish scholar **9** 123-124

KUKAI (774-835), Japanese Buddhist monk **9** 124-125

KUKRIT PRAMOJ, MOMRAJAWONG (M.R.; born 1911), literary figure and prime minister of Thailand (1975-1976) **9** 126-127

KULTHUM, UMM (Ibrahim Umm Kalthum; 1904-1975), Egyptian musician **24** 220-222

Kumara Siladitya
see Harsha

KUMARAJIVA (344/350-409/413), Indian Buddhist monk **9** 127

KUMARATUNGA, CHANDRIKA (Chandrika Bandaranaike; born 1945), Sri Lankan politician **25** 252-254

KUMIN, MAXINE WINOKUR (born 1925), American poet and author **26** 203-206

Kunani
see Suleiman I

KUNDERA, MILAN (born 1929), Czech-born author **9** 128-129

KÜNG, HANS (born 1928), Swiss-born Roman Catholic theologian **9** 129-130

Kung-sun Yang
see Shang Yang

KUNIN, MADELEINE MAY (born 1933), first woman governor of Vermont **9** 130-131

KUNITZ, STANLEY JASSPON (1905-2006), American poet laureate **22** 282-284

KUNSTLER, WILLIAM M. (1919-1995), American civil rights attorney and author **9** 131-133

KUO MO-JO (born 1892), Chinese author **9** 133-134

KUPKA, FRANTISEK (Frank; 1871-1957), Czech painter and illustrator **9** 134-135

Kupper, C.E.M.
see Doesburg, Theo van

Kuprili, Ahmed
see Köprülü, Ahmed

KURON, JACEK (Jacek Jan Kuron; 1934-2004), Polish trade union advisor and politician **28** 203-206

KUROSAWA, AKIRA (1910-1998), Japanese film director **9** 135-137

KUTUZOV, MIKHAIL ILARIONOVICH (1745-1813), Russian field marshal **9** 137-138

KUZNETS, SIMON (1901-1985), American economist, researcher, and author **9** 138-139

Kuznetsov
see Litvinov, Maxim Maximovich

KWANGGAET'O (375-413), Korean statesman, king of Koguryo **9** 139-140

KWANGJONG (925-975), Korean statesman, king of Koryo **9** 140

KWASNIEWSKI, ALEKSANDER (born 1954), Polish politician **27** 220-222

KYD, THOMAS (1558-1594), English dramatist **9** 140-141

KYPRIANOU, SPYROS (born 1932), president of the Republic of Cyprus **9** 141-143

L

LA BRUYÈRE, JEAN DE (1645-1696), French man of letters and moralist **9** 145

LA FARGE, JOHN (1835-1910), American artist and writer **9** 149-150

LA FAYETTE, COMTESSE DE (Marie Madeleine Pioche de la Vergne; 1634-93), French novelist **9** 150-151

LA FLESCHE, FRANCIS (1857-1932), Native American ethnologist **9** 152-154

LA FLESCHE PICOTTE, SUSAN (1865-1915), Native American physician and activist **24** 223-225

LA FLESCHE, SUSETTE (1854-1903), Native American activist and reformer **9** 152-154

LA FOLLETTE, ROBERT MARION (1855-1925), American statesman **9** 155-156

LA FONTAINE, JEAN DE (1621-1695), French poet **9** 156-157

LA GUARDIA, FIORELLO HENRY (1882-1947), American politician, New York City mayor **9** 166-167

LA METTRIE, JULIEN OFFRAY DE (1709-1751), French physician and philosopher **9** 179-180

La Pasionaria
see Ibárruri Gomez, Dolores

LA ROCHEFOUCAULD, FRANÇOIS, DUC DE (1613-1680), French moralist **9** 208-209

LA SALLE, SIEUR DE (René Robert Cavelier; 1643-1687), French explorer and colonizer **9** 210-211

LA TOUR, GEORGE DE (1593-1652), French painter **9** 222

LA VERENDRYE, SIEUR DE (Pierre Gaultier de Varennes; 1685-1749), French-Canadian soldier, explorer, and fur trader **9** 239-240

La Vergne, Marie Madeleine Pioche de
see La Fayette, Comtesse de

Labor leaders
Polish
Kuron, Jacek **28** 203-206

Labour party (England)
Brown, Gordon **28** 48-50

Labriolle
see Velasco Ibarra, José María

LABROUSTE, PIERRE FRANÇOIS HENRI (1801-1875), French architect-engineer **9** 144

Labrunie, Gérard
see Nerval, Gérard de

LACAN, JACQUES (1901-1981), French psychoanalyst **9** 145-147

LACHAISE, GASTON (1882-1935), French-born American sculptor **9** 147

LACHAPELLE, MARIE (1769-1821), French obstetrician and teacher **21** 245-247

Lackland, John
see John (king of England)

LACOMBE, ALBERT (1827-1916), Canadian missionary priest **9** 147-148

LACORDAIRE, JEAN BAPTISTE HENRI (1802-1861), French Dominican preacher **9** 148

LACY, SAM (Samuel Harold Lacy; 1903-2003), African American journalist **26** 207-209

LADD, WILLIAM (1778-1841), American pacifist **9** 149

LADD-FRANKLIN, CHRISTINE (1847-1930), American logician and psychologist **23** 202-204

LAENNEC, RENÉ (René-Théophile-Hyacinthe Laënnec; 1781-1826), French physician and inventor **21** 247-249

LAFAYETTE, MARQUIS DE (Marie Joseph Paul Yves Roch Gilbert du Motier; 1757-1834), French general and statesman **9** 151-152

LAFONTAINE, SIR LOUIS-HIPPOLYTE (1807-1864), Canadian politician **9** 157-158

LAFONTAINE, OSKAR (born 1943), German politician **9** 158-160

LAFORGUE, JULES (1860-1887), French poet **9** 160-161

LAGERFELD, KARL (born 1938), German-French designer of high fashion **9** 161-162

LAGERKVIST, PÄR FABIAN (born 1891), Swedish author **9** 162-163

LAGERLÖF, SELMA OTTILIANA LOVISA (1858-1940), Swedish author **9** 163-164

Lagery, Otto de
see Urban II

LAGOS, RICARDO (born 1938), president of Chile **27** 223-225

LAGRANGE, JOSEPH LOUIS (1736-1813), Italian-born French mathematician **9** 164-166

LAHR, BERT (Irving Lahrheim; 1895-1967), performer and comedian in burlesque, vaudeville, musical comedy, film, and television **9** 167-168

LAING, R. D. (1927-1989), Scottish psychiatrist and author **26** 209-211

LAIRD, MELVIN R. (born 1922), U.S. congressman and secretary of defense **9** 168-170

LAKSHMIBAI (Laksmi Bai; Rani of Jhansi; c.1835-1857), Indian queen and national hero **22** 41-42

LALIBELA (ruled circa 1181-circa 1221), Ethiopian king and saint **9** 170

LALIQUE, RENÉ (1860-1945), French glass and jewelry designer **26** 211-213

LAMAR, LUCIUS QUINTUS CINCINNATUS (1825-1893), American politician and jurist **9** 170-171

LAMARCK, CHEVALIER DE (Jean Baptiste Pierre Antoine de Monet; 1744-1829), French naturalist **9** 171-173

LAMARQUE, LIBERTAD (Libertad Lamarque Bouza; 1908-2000), Argentine entertainer **26** 213-215

LAMARR, HEDY (Hedwig Eva Marie Kiesler; 1913-2000), American actress and inventor **27** 225-227

LAMARTINE, ALPHONSE MARIE LOUIS DE (1790-1869), French poet and diplomat **9** 173-175

LAMAS, CARLOS SAAVEDRA (1878-1959), Argentine scholar, statesman, and diplomat **9** 175-176

LAMB, CHARLES (1775-1834), English author, critic, and minor poet **9** 176-177

Lamb, William
see Melbourne, 2nd Viscount

LAMBSDORFF, OTTO GRAF (born 1926), West German minister of economics **9** 177-179

Lambton, John George
see Durham, 1st Earl of

LAMENNAIS, HUGUES FÉLICITÉ ROBERT DE (1782-1854), French priest and political writer **9** 179

Lamo Dondup
see Dalai Lama

L'AMOUR, LOUIS (Louis Dearborn LaMoore; 1908-1988), American author of westerns **20** 213-215

LAMPMAN, ARCHIBALD (1861-1899), Canadian poet **9** 180-181

LAMPRECHT, KARL (1856-1915), German historian **9** 181

LAMY, JEAN BAPTISTE (1814-1888), French archbishop in the United States **9** 181-182

Lancaster, 5th Duke of
see John of Gaunt

LANCASTER, BURT (Burton Stephen Lancaster; 1913-1994), American actor **20** 215-218

LANCASTER, JOSEPH (1778-1838), English educator **9** 182-183

LAND, EDWIN HERBERT (1909-1991), American physicist, inventor, and manufacturer **9** 183-184

LANDAU, LEV DAVIDOVICH (1908-1968), Soviet theoretical physicist **9** 184-185

Landers, Ann
see Lederer, Esther Pauline

LANDINI, FRANCESCO (circa 1335-1397), Italian composer and poet **9** 185-186

LANDIS, KENESAW MOUNTAIN (1866-1944), American baseball commissioner **22** 285-287

LANDON, ALFRED MOSSMAN (1887-1987), American politician **22** 287-289

LANDOR, WALTER SAVAGE (1775-1864), English poet, essayist and critic **9** 186-187

LANDOWSKA, WANDA (1879-1959), Polish American harpsichordist and pianist **26** 215-218

LANDOWSKI, MARCEL (born 1915), French composer of lyric works **9** 187-188

LANDRY, TOM (Thomas Wade Landry; 1924-2000), American football coach **22** 290-292

LANDSTEINER, KARL (1868-1943), Austrian-born American immunologist **9** 188-189

Lane, Carrie
see Catt, Carrie Chapman

LANE, DICK (Richard Lane; Dick "Night Train" Lane; 1928-2002), American football player **27** 227-229

LANE, FITZ HUGH (1804-1865), American marine painter **9** 189

LANFRANC (circa 1010-1089), Italian theologian, archbishop of Canterbury **9** 189-190

LANG, FRITZ (1890-1976), film director **9** 190-192

LANG, JOHN THOMAS (1876-1975), Australian politician **9** 192-193

LANGDELL, CHRISTOPHER COLUMBUS (1826-1906), American lawyer **23** 204-206

LANGE, DOROTHEA (1895-1965), American photographer **9** 193-194

LANGER, SUSANNE (nee Susanne Katherina Knauth; 1895-1985), American philosopher **26** 218-220

LANGLAND, WILLIAM (circa 1330-1400), English poet **9** 194-195

LANGLEY, SAMUEL PIERPONT (1834-1906), American scientist **9** 195-196

LANGMUIR, IRVING (1881-1957), American chemist **9** 196-197

LANGSTON, JOHN MERCER (1829-1897), American educator and diplomat **9** 197

LANGTON, STEPHEN (c. 1155-1228), English prelate and signer of the Magna Carta **21** 249-251

LANIER, JARON (born ca. 1961), American computer engineer **9** 198-199

LANIER, SIDNEY (1842-1881), American poet, critic, and musician **9** 199-200

LANSING, ROBERT (1864-1928), American lawyer and statesman **9** 200

Lao Lai Tzu
see Lao Tzu

LAO SHÊ (1899-1966), Chinese novelist **9** 200-201

LAO TZU (flourished 6th century B.C.), Chinese philosopher **9** 201-202

LAPLACE, MARQUIS DE (Pierre Simon; 1749-1827), French mathematician **9** 202-204

Larco, Isabel Granda
see Granda, Chabuca

LARDNER, RINGGOLD WILMER (1885-1933), American author **9** 204-205

LAREDO, RUTH (nee Ruth Meckler; 1937-2005), American pianist **26** 220-222

LARIONOV, MIKHAIL (1881-1964), Russian artist **9** 205-206

LARKIN, PHILIP (1922-1986), English poet **9** 206-207

LARKIN, THOMAS OLIVER (1802-1858), American merchant and diplomat **9** 208

LARROCHA, ALICIA DE (Alicia de Larrocha y de la Calle; born 1923), Spanish painist **27** 230-231

LARSEN, NELLA (1893-1963), Harlem Renaissance writer **9** 209-210

LARSON, JONATHAN (1961-1996), American playwright, composer, and lyricist **18** 243-145

LAS CASAS, BARTOLOMÉ DE (1474-1566), Spanish Dominican missionary and historian **9** 211-212

Lasal, Ferdinand
see Lassalle, Ferdinand

LASCH, CHRISTOPHER (1932-1994), American historian and social critic **9** 212-214

LASHLEY, KARL SPENCER (1890-1958), American neuropsychologist **9** 214-215

LASKER, ALBERT (1880-1952), American advertising executive **21** 251-254

LASKER, EMANUEL (1868-1941), German chess grandmaster **20** 218-220

LASKI, HAROLD J. (1893-1950), English political scientist and Labour party leader **9** 215-216

LASKY, JESSE (1880-1958), American film producer **21** 254-256

LASSALLE, FERDINAND (1825-1864), German socialist leader **9** 216

Lasso, Orlando di
see Lassus, Roland de

LASSUS, ROLAND DE (1532-1594), Franco-Flemish composer **9** 216-218

LASSWELL, HAROLD DWIGHT (born 1902), American political scientist **9** 218-219

LÁSZLÓ I, KING OF HUNGARY (ca. 1040-1095), king of Hungary and saint **9** 219-221

LATIMER, HUGH (circa 1492-1555), English Protestant bishop, reformer, and martyr **9** 221

LATIMER, LEWIS (1848-1928), American inventor and electrical engineer **19** 191-193

Latin American literature
fiction
   Bolaño, Roberto **28** 42-45

Latin American music
Paraguay
   Barrios, Agustín Pìo **28** 27-29

LATROBE, BENJAMIN HENRY (1764-1820), English-born American architect **9** 222-224

Latter-Day Saints, Church of the
see Mormons (religious sect)

LATYNINA, LARISA (Larissa Semyonovna Latynina; born 1934), Russian gymnast **26** 222-224

LAUD, WILLIAM (1573-1645), English archbishop of Canterbury **9** 224-225

LAUDER, ESTEE (née Josephine Esthe Menzer, born ca. 1908), founder of an international cosmetics empire **9** 225-226

Laue, Max von
see von Laue, Max

Lauenburg, Duke of
see Bismarck, Otto Edward Leopold von

LAUREL, SALVADOR H. (Doy; born 1928), member of the Philippine Congress and vice-president **9** 226-227

LAUREN, RALPH (Ralph Lipschitz; born 1939), American fashion designer **9** 228-229

LAURENCE, MARGARET (Jean Margaret Wemyss; 1926-1987), Canadian writer **9** 229-230

LAURENS, HENRI (1885-1954), French sculptor **9** 230-231

LAURENS, HENRY (1724-1792), American merchant and Revolutionary statesman **9** 232

LAURIER, SIR WILFRID (1841-1919), Canadian statesman, prime minister 1896-1911 **9** 232-234

LAURO, ACHILLE (1887-1984), Italian business and political leader **9** 234-235

LAUTARO (circa 1535-1557), Araucanian Indian chieftain in Chile **9** 235

LAVAL, FRANCOIS XAVIER DE (1623-1708), French bishop in Canada **9** 235-236

LAVAL, PIERRE (1883-1945), French politician, chief Vichy minister **9** 237-238

LAVALLEJA, JUAN ANTONIO (1778-1853), Uruguayan independence leader **9** 238-239

LAVER, ROD (Rodney George Laver; born 1938), Australian tennis player **25** 257-259

LAVERAN, ALPHONSE (Charles Louis Alphonse Laveran; 1845-1922), French medical researcher **28** 207-209

LAVIGERIE, CHARLES MARTEL ALLEMAND (1825-1892), French cardinal **9** 240

LAVISSE, ERNEST (1842-1922), French historian **9** 241

LAVOISIER, ANTOINE LAURENT (1743-1794), French chemist **9** 241-244

LAVOISIER, MARIE PAULZE (1758-1836), French chemist **22** 292-294

LAW, JOHN (1671-1729), Scottish monetary theorist and banker **9** 244-245

LAW, WILLIAM (1686-1761), English devotional writer **9** 245-246

Lawman
see Layamon

LAWRENCE, ABBOTT (1792-1855), American manufacturer and diplomat **9** 246

LAWRENCE, DAVID HERBERT (1885-1930), English novelist, poet, and essayist **9** 247-248

LAWRENCE, ERNEST ORLANDO (1901-1958), American physicist **9** 248-250

LAWRENCE, FLORENCE (Florence Annie Bridgwood; 1886-1938), Canadian-born American actress **28** 209-211

LAWRENCE, JACOB (born 1917), African American painter **9** 250-251

LAWRENCE, JAMES (1781-1813), American naval officer **9** 251-252

LAWRENCE, SIR THOMAS (1769-1830), English portrait painter **9** 252-253

LAWRENCE, THOMAS EDWARD (1888-1935), British soldier and author **9** 253-254

Lawrence of Arabia
see Lawrence, Thomas Edward

LAWSON, HENRY (1867-1922), Australian poet and short-story writer **9** 254-255

LAWSON, THOMAS WILLIAM (1857-1925), American entrepreneur and reformer **9** 255-256

LAYAMON (flourished circa 1200), English poet **9** 256-257

LAYBOURNE, GERALDINE (born 1947), American businesswoman **26** 224-226

LAYE, CAMARA (1928-1980), Guinean novelist **9** 257-259

LAZARSFELD, PAUL F. (1901-1976), American sociologist **9** 259-260

LAZARUS, EMMA (1849-1887), American poet and playwright **9** 260-261

LAZARUS, SHELLY (Rochelle Braff; born 1947), American businesswoman **27** 231-233

LE BON, GUSTAVE (1841-1931), French social scientist and philosopher **9** 268-269

LE BRUN, CHARLES (1619-1690), French painter, decorator, and draftsman **9** 269-270

LE CARRE, JOHN (born David Cornwell, 1931), British spy novelist **9** 270-271

LECLERCQ, TANAQUIL (Tanny; 1929-2000), French American dancer **27** 234-235

LE CORBUSIER (Charles Édouard eanneret-Gris; 1887-1965), Swiss architect, city planner, and painter **9** 274-275

LE DUAN (1908-1986), North Vietnamese leader and later head of the government of all Vietnam **9** 278-280

LE FANU, JOSEPH SHERIDAN (1814-1873), Irish author **23** 206-208

LE GUIN, URSULA KROEBER (born 1929), American author **18** 249-251

LE JEUNE, CLAUDE (circa 1530-1600), Flemish composer **9** 314-315

Le Moyne, Pierre
see Iberville, Sieur d'

LE NAIN BROTHERS, 17th-century French painters **9** 321-322

LE NÔTRE, ANDRÉ (or Le Nostre; 1613-1700), French landscape architect **9** 328-329

LE PEN, JEAN MARIE (born 1928), French political activist of the radical right **9** 348-350

LE PLAY, GUILLAUME FRÉDÉRIC (1806-1882), French sociologist and economist **9** 350-351

Le Prestre, Sébastien
see Vauban, Marquis de

LE VAU, LOUIS (1612-1670), French architect **9** 360-361

LEA, HENRY CHARLES (1825-1909), American historian **9** 261-262

LEADBELLY (Huddie William Leadbetter; 1885-1949), African American folk singer **23** 208-211
Lomax, John Avery **28** 224-225

LEAKEY, LOUIS SEYMOUR BAZETT (1903-1972), British anthropologist **9** 262

LEAKEY, MARY DOUGLAS (1913-1996), English archaeologist **9** 263-264

LEAKEY, RICHARD ERSKINE FRERE (born 1944), Kenyan researcher in human prehistory and wildlife conservationist **9** 264-265

LEAR, EDWARD (1812-1888), English writer and artist **9** 265-266

LEAR, NORMAN (born 1922), American author and television director and producer **19** 193-195

LEARY, TIMOTHY (1920-1996), American psychologist, author, lecturer, and cult figure **9** 266-267

LEASE, MARY ELIZABETH CLYENS (1853-1933), American writer and politician **9** 268

LEAVITT, HENRIETTA SWAN (1868-1921), American astronomer **23** 211-213

Lebanon, Republic of (nation; southwest Asia)
Gemayel, Bashir **28** 136-138
Hariri, Rafic **28** 161-163

LEBED, ALEXANDER IVANOVICH (1950-2002), Russian general and politician **18** 245-247

LEBLANC, NICOLAS (1742-1806), French industrial chemist **21** 256-258

LECKY, WILLIAM EDWARD HARTPOLE (1838-1903), Anglotrish historian and essayist **9** 271-272

Leclerc, Georges Louis
see Buffon, Comte de

LECLERC, JACQUES PHILIPPE (1902-1947), French general **9** 272-273

LECONTE DE LISLE, CHARLES MARIE RENÉ (1818-1894), French poet **9** 273-274

LECUONA, ERNESTO (Ernesto Sixto de la Asuncion Lecuona y Casado; 1896-1963), Cuban musician **23** 213-216

LED ZEPPELIN (1968-1980), British "Heavy Metal" band **23** 216-218

LEDERBERG, JOSHUA (1925-2008), Nobel Prize winning geneticist **9** 275-277

LEDERER, ESTHER PAULINE (Ann Landers; 1918-2002), American Columnist **25** 255-257

LEDOUX, CLAUDE NICOLAS (1736-1806), French architect **9** 277-278

LEE, MOTHER ANN (1736-1784), religious and social reformer and founder of the Shakers **9** 289-290

LEE, ARTHUR (1740-1792), American statesman and diplomat **9** 288-289

LEE, BRUCE (1940-1973), Asian American actor and martial arts master **18** 247-249

LEE, CHARLES (1731-1782), American general **22** 294-297

LEE, HARPER (Nelle Harper Lee; born 1926), American author **20** 220-222

LEE, MING CHO (born 1930), American scene designer for theater and opera **9** 289-290

LEE, RICHARD HENRY (1732-1794), American patriot and statesman **9** 291-292

LEE, ROBERT EDWARD (1807-1870), American army officer and Confederate general in chief **9** 292-294

LEE, ROSE (Rose Hum; 1904-1964), American sociologist **21** 258-260

LEE, SPIKE (born Sheldon Jackson Lee; born 1957), African American actor, author, and filmmaker **9** 295-299

LEE, TSUNG-DAO (born 1926), Chinese-born American physicist **9** 299-300

LEE, YUAN TSEH (born 1936), Taiwanese American scientist and educator **23** 218-220

LEE HSIEN LOONG (born 1952), Singaporean soldier and deputy prime minister **9** 280-281

LEE KUAN YEW (born 1923), prime minister of Singapore (1959-1988) **9** 281-283

LEE JONG-WOOK (1945-2006), Korean physician and head of the World Health Organization **27** 235-238

LEE TENG-HUI (born 1923), president of the Republic of China (1988-) **9** 283-285

Leefbar Nederland (Livable Netherlands; political party)
Fortuyn, Pim **28** 125-127

LEEKPAI, CHUAN (born 1938), Thai prime minister **24** 225-228

LEEUWENHOEK, ANTON VAN (1632-1723), Dutch naturalist and microscopist **9** 300-301

LEFEBVRE, GEORGES (1874-1959), French historian **9** 301-302

Léger, Alexis Saint-Léger
see Perse, Saint-John

LÉGER, FERNAND (1881-1955), French painter **9** 302-303

LEGHARI, SARDAR FAROOQ AHMED KHAN (born 1940), president of the Islamic Republic of Pakistan **9** 303-305

LEGINSKA, ETHEL (Ethel Liggins; 1886-1970), English American musician **23** 220-222

Legislative Assembly (French Revolution)
see French Revolution—1789-91 (Legislative Assembly), 1792-95 (National Convention)

LEGO Group
Christiansen, Ole Kirk **28** 76-78

LEGUÍA Y SALCEDO, AUGUSTO BERNARDINO (1863-1932), Peruvian president 1908-12 and 1919-30 **9** 305-306

LEHMAN, ERNEST (1915-2005), American screenwriter **26** 226-229

LEHMAN, HERBERT HENRY (1878-1963), American banker and statesman **9** 306-307

Lehmann, Walter
see Harwood, Gwen

LEHMBRUCK, WILHELM (1881-1919), German sculptor **9** 307

LEIBNIZ, GOTTFRIED WILHELM VON (1646-1716), German mathematician and philosopher **9** 307-310

LEIBOVITZ, ANNIE (born 1949), Ameircan photographer **9** 310-312

LEICESTER, EARL OF (Robert Dudley; 1532?-1588), English politician **9** 312-313

Leicester, 6th Earl of
see Montfort, Simon de

LEIGH, MIKE (born 1943), British director and screenwriter **23** 222-225

LEIGH, VIVIEN (Vivian Mary Hartley; 1913-1967), British actress **18** 251-253

LEISLER, JACOB (1640-1691), American colonial leader **9** 313-314

LEITZEL, LILLIAN (born Leopoldina Altitza Pelikan; 1892-1931), German aerialist **23** 225-227

LELY, SIR PETER (1618-1680), German-born painter active in England **9** 315

LEM, STANISLAW (1921-2006), Polish author **27** 238-240

LEMAÎTRE, ABBÈ GEORGES ÉDOUARD (1894-1966), Belgian astronomer **9** 315-316

LEMAY, CURTIS E. (1906-1990), United States combat leader (World War II) and Air Force chief of staff **9** 316-318

LEMBEDE, ANTON (1913-1947), leader of black resistance to white supremacy in South Africa **9** 318-319

LEMIEUX, MARIO (born 1965), Canadian hockey player and team owner **20** 222-224

LEMMON, JACK (John Uhler Lemmon; 1925-2001), American actor **22** 297-299

LEMNITZER, LYMAN LOUIS (Lem; 1899-1988), American soldier-statesman and strategist and NATO architect **9** 319-320

LENARD, PHILIPP (Philipp Eduard Anton von Lenard; 1862-1947), Hungarian-born German physicist **25** 259-261

L'ENFANT, PIERRE CHARLES (1754-1825), French-born American architect **9** 322-323

L'ENGLE, MADELEINE (1918-2007), American author **18** 253-255

LENGLEN, SUZANNE (1899-1938), French tennis player **19** 195-197

LENIN, VLADIMIR ILICH (1870-1924), Russian statesman **9** 323-326
films about
Romm, Mikhail **28** 303-304

LENNON, JOHN (1940-1980), English poet and songwriter **9** 326-328

LEO I (circa 400-461), saint and pope 440-461 **9** 329-330

LEO III (the Isaurian; circa 680-741), Byzantine emperor 717-741 **9** 330-332

Leo VI, (the Wise; 866-912), Byzantine emperor 886-912
Simeon, King of Bulgaria **28** 325-327

LEO IX, SAINT (Bruno of Egisheim; 1002-1054), pope 1049-1054 **9** 332

LEO X (Giovanni de' Medici; 1475-1521), pope 1513-1521 **9** 332-334

LEO XII (Annibale Sermattai della Genga; 1760-1829), Italian Roman Catholic pope (1823-1829) **26** 297-299

LEO XIII (Vincenzo Gioacchino Pecci; 1810-1903), pope 1878-1903 **9** 334-336

Leo Hebraeus
see Levi ben Gershon

LEON, MOSES DE (circa 1250-1305), Jewish mystic **9** 336

LEONARD, DANIEL (1740-1829), American loyalist lawyer and essayist **9** 336-337

LEONARD, SUGAR RAY (Ray Charles Leonard; born 1956), American boxer **24** 228-231

LEONARDO DA VINCI (1452-1519), Italian painter, sculptor, architect, and scientist **9** 337-340

Leonardo of Pisa
see Fibonacci, Leonardo

LEONIDAS I (ca. 530 B.C. - 480 B.C.), Spartan king **9** 340-343

LÉONIN (Leoninus; flourished circa 1165-1185), French composer **9** 343-344

LEOPARDI, CONTE GIACOMO (1798-1837), Italian poet **9** 344-345

LEOPOLD I (1790-1865), king of Belgium 1831-1865 **9** 345-346

Leopold I (Duke of Tuscany)
see Leopold II (Holy Roman emperor)

LEOPOLD II (1747-1792), Holy Roman emperor 1790-1792 **9** 346

LEOPOLD II (1835-1909), king of Belgium 1865-1909 **9** 346-347

LEOPOLD III (1901-1983), king of Belgium 1934-1951 **9** 347-348

LEOPOLD, ALDO (1887-1948), American author and conservationist **28** 211-213

Leopold, Duke of Brabant
see Leopold III (king of Belgium)

Lepoqo
see Moshweshwe

LERDO DE TEJADA, MIGUEL (1812-1861), Mexican liberal politician **9** 351-352

LERMONTOV, MIKHAIL YURIEVICH (1814-1841), Russian poet and prose writer **9** 352-353

LERNER, ALAN JAY (1918-1986), American lyricist and librettist **20** 224-226

LESAGE, ALAIN RENÉ (1668-1747), French novelist and playwright **9** 353-354

LESCOT, PIERRE (1500/1515-1578), French architect **9** 354

LESSEPS, VICOMTE DE (Ferdinand Marie; 1805-1894), French diplomat **9** 354-355

LESSING, DORIS (Doris May Taylor; born 1919), South African expatriate writer **9** 355-357

LESSING, GOTTHOLD EPHRAIM (1729-1781), German philosopher, dramatist, and critic **9** 357-359

LETCHER, JOHN (1813-1884), American politician **9** 359-360

LETTERMAN, DAVID (born 1947), American comedian **26** 229-231

Lettres on the Improvement of the Mind: Addressed to a Young Lady (book)
Chapone, Hester **28** 72-74

LEVANT, OSCAR (1906-1972), American composer and pianist **19** 197-199

LEVERRIER, URBAIN JEAN JOSEPH (1811-1877), French mathematical astronomer **9** 361-362

LÉVESQUE, RENÉ (1922-1987), premier of the province of Quebec, Canada (1976-1985) **9** 362-363

Levi
see Matthew, Saint

LEVI BEN GERSHON (1288-circa 1344), French Jewish scientist, philosopher, and theologian **9** 363-364

LEVI, CARLO (1902-1975), Italian writer and painter **9** 364

LEVI, PRIMO (1919-1987), Italian author and chemist **9** 365-366

LEVI-MONTALCINI, RITA (born 1909), Italian and American biologist who discovered the nerve growth factor **9** 366-368

LÉVI-STRAUSS, CLAUDE GUSTAVE (born 1908), French social anthropologist **9** 371-372

LEVINAS, EMMANUEL (1906-1995), Jewish philosopher **9** 368-369

LEVINE, JAMES (born 1943), American conductor and pianist **9** 369-371

LEVITT, WILLIAM (1907-1994), American real estate developer **19** 199-201

LÉVY, BERNARD-HENRI (BHL; born 1948), French philosopher and author **28** 213-215

LEVY, DAVID (born 1937), Israeli minister of foreign affairs and deputy prime minister **9** 373-374

LÉVY-BRUHL, LUCIEN (1857-1939), French philosopher and anthropologist **9** 374-375

LEWIN, KURT (1890-1947), German-American social psychologist **9** 375-376

LEWIS, ANDREW (circa 1720-1781), American general in the Revolution **9** 376-377

LEWIS, CARL (born Frederick Carlton Lewis; born 1961), African American track and field athlete **9** 377-380

LEWIS, CECIL DAY (1904-1972), British poet and essayist **9** 380

LEWIS, CLARENCE IRVING (1883-1964), American philosopher **9** 381

LEWIS, CLIVE STAPLES (C.S.; 1898-1963), British novelist and essayist **9** 381-382

LEWIS, EDMONIA (Mary Edmomia Lewis; Wildfire; c. 1840-c. 1909), American sculptor **28** 215-217

LEWIS, ESSINGTON (1881-1961), Australian industrial leader **9** 382-384

LEWIS, GILBERT NEWTON (1875-1946), American physical chemist **9** 384-385

LEWIS, HARRY SINCLAIR (1885-1951), American novelist **9** 385-387

LEWIS, JOHN LLEWELLYN (1880-1969), American labor leader **9** 387-388

LEWIS, JOHN ROBERT (born 1940), United States civil rights activist and representative from Georgia **9** 388-390

LEWIS, MATTHEW GREGORY (1775-1818), English novelist and playwright **9** 390-391

LEWIS, MERIWETHER (1774-1809), American explorer and army officer **9** 391-392

LEWIS, OSCAR (1914-1970), American anthropologist **9** 392-393

LEWIS, REGINALD FRANCIS (1942-1993), African American businessman, attorney, and philanthropist **25** 261-263

Lewis, Sinclair
see Lewis, Harry Sinclair

LEWIS, WILLIAM ARTHUR (1915-1991), St. Lucian economist **27** 240-242

LEWIS, WYNDHAM (Percy Wyndham Lewis; 1882-1957), Canadian-born British author and artist **28** 217-219

LEWITT, SOL (1928-2007), American Minimalist and Conceptualist artist **9** 393-395

Li Erh
see Lao Tzu

Li Fei-kan
see Pa Chin

LI HUNG-CHANG (1823-1901), Chinese soldier, statesman, and industrialist **9** 407-409

Li Ma-t'ou
see Ricci, Matteo

LI PENG (born 1928), premier of the People's Republic of China **9** 433-435

LI PO (701-762), Chinese poet **9** 437-439

Li Shih-min
see Tai-tsung, T'ang

LI QINGZHAO (1084-1150), Chinese poet **25** 263-265

LI SSU (c. 280-208 B.C.), Chinese statesman **9** 442-443

LI TA-CHAO (1889-1927), Chinese Communist revolutionist **9** 447

LI TZU-CH'ENG (circa 1606-1645), Chinese bandit and rebel leader **9** 452

LIANG CH'I-CH'AO (1873-1929), Chinese intellectual and political reformer **9** 395-396

LIANG WU-TI (464-549), Chinese emperor of Southern dynasties **9** 396-397

LIAQUAT ALI KHAN (1896-1951), Pakistani statesman **9** 397

LIBBY, LEONA MARSHALL (1919-1986), American nuclear scientist **26** 231-233

LIBBY, WILLARD FRANK (1908-1980), American chemist **9** 397-398

Liberal Democratic party (Japan)
Abe, Shinzo **28** 1-3

Liberia, Republic of (nation; West Africa)
Sirleaf, Ellen Johnson **28** 328-331

Library of Congress (United States)
Archive of American Folk Song
Lomax, John Avery **28** 224-225

LICHTENSTEIN, ROY (1923-1997), American painter, sculptor, and printmaker **9** 398-399

LIE, TRYGVE HALVDAN (1896-1968), Norwegian statesman and UN secretary general **9** 400-401

LIEBER, FRANCIS (circa 1798-1872), German American political scientist **9** 401-402

LIEBERMANN, MAX (1847-1935), German painter **9** 402-403

LIEBIG, BARON JUSTUS VON (1803-1873), German chemist **9** 403-404

LIGACHEV, YEGOR KUZ'MICH (born 1920), member of the Central Committee of the Communist Party of the Soviet Union (1966-1990) **9** 404-406

LIGETI, GYÖRGY (1923-2006), Austrian composer **9** 406-407

LIGHTNER, CANDY (born 1946), American activist and founder of Mothers Against Drunk Driving **19** 201-203

LILBURNE, JOHN (1615-1657), English political activist and pamphleteer **9** 409-410

LILIENTHAL, DAVID ELI (1899-1981), American public administrator **9** 410-411

LILIENTHAL, OTTO (1848-1896), Prussian design engineer **21** 260-262

LILIUOKALANI, LYDIA KAMAKAEHA (1838-1917), queen of the Hawaiian Islands **9** 411-412

LILLY, ELI (1885-1977), American businessman and philanthropist **25** 265-267

Lima e Silva, Luiz Alves de
see Caxias, Duque de

LIMBOURG BROTHERS (flourished circa 1399-1416), Netherlandish illuminators **9** 412-413

LIMÓN, JOSÉ ARCADIA (1908-1972), Mexican American dancer and choreographer **23** 227-229

LIN, MAYA YING (born 1959), American architect **9** 413-415

LIN PIAO (1907-1971), Chinese Communist military and political leader **9** 429-430

LIN TSE-HSÜ (1785-1850), Chinese official **9** 431-432

LIN YUTANG (1895-1976), Chinese author, philosopher, and translator **25** 267-269

LINCOLN, ABRAHAM (1809-1865), American statesman, president 1861-1865 **9** 415-418
in literature and biography
Keckley, Elizabeth Hobbs **28** 196-199

LINCOLN, BENJAMIN (1733-1810), American military officer **9** 418-419

LIND, JAKOV (Heinz "Henry" Landwirth; 1927-2007), Austrian autobiographer, short-story writer, novelist, and playwright **9** 419-420

LIND, JENNY (Johanna Maria Lind; 1820-1887), Swedish coloratura soprano **26** 233-235

LINDBERGH, ANNE MORROW (born 1906), American author and aviator **9** 420-421

LINDBERGH, CHARLES AUGUSTUS (1902-1974), American aviator **9** 421-423

LINDGREN, ASTRID (Astrid Anna Emilia Ericcson; 1907-2002), Swedish author and editor **28** 219-221

LINDSAY, JOHN VLIET (born 1921), U.S. congressman (1959-1965) and mayor of New York (1966-1973) **9** 423-424

LINDSAY, VACHEL (1879-1931), American folk poet **9** 424-425

LINDSEY, BENJAMIN BARR (1869-1943), American jurist and reformer **9** 425-426

LINH, NGUYEN VAN (1915-1998), secretary-general of the Vietnamese Communist Party (1986-1991) **9** 426-427

LINNAEUS, CARL (Carl von Linné; 1707-1778), Swedish naturalist **9** 427-429

LINTON, RALPH (1893-1953), American anthropologist **9** 431

LIPCHITZ, JACQUES (1891-1973), Lithuanian-born American sculptor **9** 432-433

LIPATTI, DINU (Constantin Lipatti; 1917-1950), Romanian musician and composer **28** 222-223

LIPPI, FRA FILIPPO (circa 1406-1469), Italian painter **9** 439

LIPPMANN, GABRIEL (1845-1921), French physicist and inventor **25** 269-271

LIPPMANN, WALTER (1889-1974), American journalist **9** 439-440

LIPPOLD, RICHARD (1915-2002), American Constructivist sculptor **9** 440-442

Lisandrino
see Magnasco, Alessandro

Lisbôa, Antônio Francisco
see Aleijadinho, O

LIST, GEORG FRIEDRICH (1789-1846), German economist **9** 443-444

LISTER, JOSEPH (1st Baron Lister of Lyme Regis; 1827-1912), English surgeon **9** 444-445

LISZT, FRANZ (1811-1886), Hungarian composer **9** 445-447

Literature for children
England
Grahame, Kenneth **28** 138-140
Finland
Jansson, Tove Marika **28** 187-189
Sweden
Lindgren, Astrid **28** 219-221

Lithography (printing process)
Grandville, J.J. **28** 144-146

Lithuania (Lithuanian Soviet Socialist Republic; Europe)
Wladyslaw II Jagiello, King of Poland **28** 377-378

Little, Malcolm
see Malcolm X (film)

LITTLE MILTON (James Milton Campbell; 1934-2005), American blues musician **26** 236-237

LITTLE, ROYAL (born 1896), American textile tycoon **9** 449-451

LITTLE RICHARD (Richard Penniman; born 1932), American rock 'n' roll musician **9** 447-449

Littleton, Mark
see Kennedy, John Pendleton

LITTLE WOLF (1818?-1904), Cheyenne chief **18** 255-257

LITVINOV, MAXIM MAXIMOVICH (1876-1951), Soviet diplomat **9** 451-452

Liu Ch'e
see Han Wu-ti

Liu Chi
see Liu Pang

LIU HSIEH (circa 465-522), Chinese literary critic **9** 452-453

Liu Hsiu
see Kuang-wu-ti

LIU PANG (Han Kao-tsu or Liu Chi; 256 B.C.-195 B.C.), Chinese emperor **9** 453

LIU SHAO-CH'I (born 1900), Chinese Communist party leader **9** 453-455

LIU TSUNG-YÜAN (773-819), Chinese poet and prose writer **9** 455-456

LIUZZO, VIOLA (1925-1965), American civil rights activist **19** 203-205

LIVERIGHT, HORACE B. (1886-1933), American publisher **23** 229-231

LIVERPOOL, 2ND EARL OF (Robert Barks Jenkinson; 1770-1828), English statesman, prime minister 1812-1827 **9** 456-457

LIVIA (ca. 58 B.C. - 29 A.D.), Roman empress, wife of Augustus **9** 457-460

LIVINGSTON, EDWARD (1764-1836), American jurist and statesman **9** 460-461

LIVINGSTON, ROBERT (1654-1728), American colonial politician **9** 461-462

LIVINGSTON, ROBERT R. (1746-1813), American jurist and diplomat **9** 462-463

LIVINGSTONE, DAVID (1813-1873), Scottish missionary and explorer in Africa **9** 463-465

LIVY (Titus Livius; circa 64 B.C.-circa 12 A.D.), Roman historian **9** 465-467

Lizardi, José Joaquín Fernández de
see Fernández de Lizardi, José Joaquín

LLERAS CAMARGO, ALBERTO (1906-1990), Colombian statesman, twice president **9** 467

LLEWELYN AP GRUFFYDD (died 1282), Prince of Wales **9** 468

LLOYD, HENRY DEMAREST (1847-1903), American social reformer **9** 468-469

LLOYD GEORGE, DAVID, (1st Earl of Dwyfor; 1863-1945), English statesman, prime minister 1916-1922 **9** 469-471

LLOYD, HAROLD (1893-1971), American actor **20** 226-229

LLOYD-JONES, ESTHER MCDONALD (born 1901), school personnel specialist who focused on development of the whole person **9** 471-472

LOBACHEVSKII, NIKOLAI IVANOVICH (1792-1856), Russian mathematician **9** 472-474

LOBENGULA (died circa 1894), South African Ndebele king **9** 474-475

LOCHNER, STEPHAN (circa 1410-1451), German painter **9** 475

LOCKE, ALAIN (1886-1954), African American educator, editor, and author **9** 475-478

LOCKE, JOHN (1632-1704), English philosopher and political theorist **9** 478-480

LOCKWOOD, BELVA (1830-1917), American lawyer, suffragist, and reformer **19** 205-207

LODGE, DAVID (born 1935), English novelist **9** 480-482

LODGE, HENRY CABOT (1850-1924), American political leader **9** 482-483

LODGE, HENRY CABOT, JR. (1902-1985), American congressman, senator, ambassador, and presidential adviser **9** 483-485

Lodovico il Moro
see Sforza, Lodovico

LOEB, JACQUES (Isaak Loeb; 1859-1924), German-American biophysiologist **22** 299-301

LOESSER, FRANK (Francis Henry Loesser; 1910-1969), American lyricist **18** 257-259

LOEW, MARCUS (1870-1927), founder of a theater chain and Metro-Goldwyn-Mayer **9** 485-486

LOEWI, OTTO (1873-1961), German-American pharmacologist and physiologist **9** 486-487

LOFTING, HUGH (1886-1947), British author of children's books **19** 207-209

LOGAN, GEORGE (1753-1821), American politician and diplomat **23** 231-234

LOGAN, JAMES (1674-1751), American colonial statesman and jurist **9** 487-488

LOGAN, SIR WILLIAM EDMOND (1798-1875), Canadian geologist **9** 488-489

Loges, François des
see Villon, François

LOISY, ALFRED FIRMIN (1857-1940), French theologian and biblical historian **9** 489-490

LOMAX, ALAN (1915-2002), American folklorist, author and musician **27** 242-244
Lomax, John Avery **28** 224-225

LOMAX, JOHN AVERY (1867-1948), American musicologist **28** 224-225

LOMBARD, PETER (circa 1095-1160), Italian bishop and theologian **9** 490-491

LOMBARDI, VINCE (1913-1970), American football coach **9** 491-492

LOMBARDO, GUY (Gaetano Alberto Lombardo; 1902-1977), Canadian band leader **23** 234-236

LOMBROSO, CESARE (1835-1909), Italian criminologist **9** 493

LOMONOSOV, MIKHAIL VASILEVICH (1711-1765), Russian chemist and physicist **9** 494

London (city; England)
maps of
Hollar, Wenceslaus **28** 180-183

LONDON, JACK (1876-1916), American author **9** 494-495

Londonderry, 2nd Marquess of
see Castlereagh, Viscount

LONG, CRAWFORD WILLIAMSON (1815-1878), American physician **9** 495-496

LONG, HUEY PIERCE (1893-1935), American politician **9** 496-497

LONG, IRENE D. (born 1951), African American aerospace medicine physician **9** 497-498

LONGFELLOW, HENRY WADSWORTH (1807-1882), American poet **9** 499-500

LONGINUS (flourished 1st or 3rd century), Latin author and rhetorician **9** 500-501

LONGSTREET, JAMES (1821-1904), American army officer **22** 301-305

LONGUS (flourished 3rd century), Greek author **20** 229-230

LONNROT, ELIAS (1802-1884), Finnish author and physician **25** 271-273

LONSDALE, KATHLEEN (born Kathleen Yardley; 1903-1971), Irish crystallographer **9** 501-502

LOOS, ADOLF (1870-1933), Viennese architect **9** 502-503

LOOS, ANITA (1893-1981), American actress and writer **21** 262-265

LOPE FÉLIX DE VEGA CARPIO (1562-1635), Spanish dramatist **9** 503-506

LÓPEZ, CARLOS ANTONIO (1792-1862), Paraguayan president-dictator 1844-1862 **9** 506-507

LÓPEZ, FRANCISCO SOLANO (1826-1870), Paraguayan president-dictator **9** 507-508

LÓPEZ, NARCISO (1798-1851), Venezuelan military leader **9** 508

LOPEZ ARELLANO, OSWALDO (born 1921), Honduran military officer and president **20** 230-231

LÓPEZ DE AYALA, PEDRO (1332-1407), Spanish statesman, historian, and poet **9** 508-509

LÓPEZ MATEOS, ADOLFO (1910-1970), president of Mexico (1958-1964) **9** 509-510

LÓPEZ PORTILLO, JOSÉ (born 1920), president of Mexico (1976-1982) **9** 510-511

LORCA, FEDERICO GARCÍA (1898-1936), Spanish poet and playwright **9** 511-513

Lord of the Rings (book; film)
McKellen, Ian Murray **28** 234-237

Lord of the Rings (movie trilogy)
McKellen, Ian Murray **28** 234-237

LORDE, AUDRE (1934-1992), African American poet **9** 513-515

LOREN, SOPHIA (Sofia Villani Scicolene; born 1936), Italian actress and author **18** 259-261

LORENTZ, HENDRIK ANTOON (1853-1928), Dutch physicist **9** 515-516

LORENZ, KONRAD Z. (1903-1989), animal psychologist **9** 516-517

LORENZETTI, PIERRE AND AMBROGIO (flourished 14th century), Italian painters **9** 517-518

Lothar of Segni
see Innocent III

LOTI, PIERRE (1850-1923), French novelist **9** 519-520

LOTT, TRENT (Chester Trent Lott; born 1941), American congressman **18** 262-264

LOTTO, LORENZO (circa 1480-1556), Italian painter **9** 520-521

LOTZE, RUDOLF HERMANN (1817-1881), German idealist philosopher **9** 521-522

LOUIS I (778-840), Holy Roman emperor and king of France and Germany 814-840 **9** 522-523

LOUIS VI (1081-1137), king of France 1108-1137 **9** 523-524

LOUIS VII (circa 1120-1180), king of France 1137-1180 **9** 524-525

LOUIS IX (1214-1270), king of France 1226-1270 **9** 525-526

LOUIS XI (1423-1483), king of France 1461-1483 **9** 526-528

LOUIS XII (1462-1515), king of France 1498-1515 **9** 528-529

LOUIS XIII (1601-1643), king of France 1610-1643 **9** 529-531

LOUIS XIV (1638-1715), king of France 1643-1715 **9** 531-533

LOUIS XV (1710-1774), king of France 1715-1774 **9** 533-534
Madame de Pompadour **28** 228-230

LOUIS XVI (1754-1793), king of France 1774-1792 **9** 534-535

LOUIS XVIII (1755-1824), king of France 1814-1824 **9** 535-536

LOUIS, JOE (Joe Louis Barrow; 1914-1981), American boxer **9** 537-538

LOUIS, MORRIS (Bernstein; 1912-1962), American painter **9** 538-539

LOUIS, PIERRE CHARLES ALEXANDRE (1787-1872), French physician **9** 540

Louis, Saint
see Louis IX (king of France)

Louis d'Orléans
see Louis XII (king of France)

Louis le Dieudonné
see Louis XIV (king of France)

Louis Napoleon
see Napoleon III, Emperor of the French

LOUIS PHILIPPE (1773-1850), king of the French 1830-1848 **9** 536-537

Louis the Great
see Louis XIV (king of France)

Louis the Pious
see Louis I (Holy Roman emperor)

LOVE, NAT (1854-1921), African American champion cowboy **10** 1-2

LOVE, SUSAN M. (born 1948), American surgeon and medical researcher **10** 2-3

LOVECRAFT, H. P. (1890-1937), American author **10** 3-6

LOVEJOY, ARTHUR ONCKEN (1873-1962), American philosopher **10** 6

LOVEJOY, ELIJAH PARISH (1802-1837), American newspaper editor and abolitionist **10** 6-7

LOVELACE, ADA BYRON (Countess of Lovelace, Augusta Ada King Byron; 1815-1852), English mathematician and author **18** 264-266

LOVELACE, RICHARD (circa 1618-circa 1657), English Cavalier poet **10** 7-8

LOVELL, SIR ALFRED CHARLES BERNARD (born 1913), English astronomer **10** 8-9

LOW, JULIETTE GORDON (born Juliette Magill Kinzie Gordon; 1860-1927), American reformer and founder of the Girl Scouts **10** 10-11

LOW, SETH (1850-1916), American politician and college president **10** 11-12

LOWELL, ABBOTT LAWRENCE (1856-1943), American educator and political scientist **10** 12-13

LOWELL, AMY (1874-1925), American poet, critic, and biographer **10** 13

LOWELL, FRANCIS CABOT (1775-1817), American merchant and manufacturer **10** 13-14

LOWELL, JAMES RUSSELL (1819-1891), American poet and diplomat **10** 14-15

LOWELL, JOSEPHINE SHAW (1843-1905), American social reformer and philanthropist **10** 15-16

LOWELL, ROBERT TRAIL SPENCE, JR. (1917-1977), American poet **10** 16-17

LOWIE, ROBERT HARRY (1883-1957), Austrian-born American anthropologist **10** 18

LOWRY, MALCOLM (1909-1957), English author **19** 209-211

LOZIER, CLEMENCE SOPHIA HARNED (1813-1888), American suffragist, reformer, and physician **25** 273-275

LU CHI (261-303), Chinese poet and critic **10** 24

LU CHIU-YUAN (Lu Hsiang-shan; 1139-1193), Chinese philosopher **10** 24-25

LU HSÜN (pen name of Chou Shu-jen; 1881-1936), Chinese author and social critic **10** 35-37

Luang Pradit Manutham
see Pridi Phanomyong

LUBITSCH, ERNST (1892-1947), German-American film director **10** 18-19

LUCARIS, CYRIL (1572-1637), Greek Orthodox patriarch and theologian **10** 20

LUCAS, GEORGE (born 1944), American filmmaker **19** 211-213

LUCAS VAN LEYDEN (1494-1533), Dutch engraver and painter **10** 20-21

LUCE, CLARE BOOTHE (1903-1987), playwright and U.S. congresswoman **10** 21-23

LUCE, HENRY ROBINSON (1898-1967), American magazine editor and publisher **10** 23-24

LUCIAN (circa 120-circa 200), Greek satirist **10** 25-26

LUCIANO, LUCKY (Charles Luciano, Salvatore Lucania; 1897-1962), Italian American mobster **19** 214-215

LUCID, SHANNON (born 1943), American astronaut **19** 215-217

Lucky Jim (book)
Amis, Kingsley **28** 5-8

LUCRETIUS (Titus Lucretius Carus; circa 94-circa 55 B.C.), Latin poet and philosopher **10** 26-27

LUDENDORFF, ERICH FRIEDRICH WILHELM (1865-1937), German general **10** 27-28

LUDLUM, ROBERT (a.k.a. Jonathan Ryder and Michael Shepherd; born 1927), American suspense novelist **10** 28-29

LUDWIG, DANIEL KEITH (1897-1992), American shipping magnate **10** 29-31

LUDWIG, KARL FRIEDRICH WILHELM (1816-1895), German physiologist **10** 31

LUGARD, FREDERICK JOHN DEALTRY (1st Baron Lugard; 1858-1945), British

soldier and colonial administrator in Africa **10** 31-32

Luggage
Vuitton, Louis **28** 365-367

LUHAN, MABEL DODGE (1879-1962), American writer, salon hostess, and patron of artists, writers, and political radicals **10** 32-34

LUHMANN, NIKLAS (born 1927), German sociologist who developed a general sociological systems theory **10** 34-35

LUKÁCS, GYORGY (1885-1971), Hungarian literary critic and philosopher **10** 37-38

Lukar, Cyril
see Lucaris, Cyril

LUKASIEWICZ, IGNACY (1822-1882), Polish pharmacist and inventor of the kerosene lamp **28** 225-227

LUKE, SAINT (flourished A.D. 50), Evangelist and biblical author **10** 38

LUKENS, REBECCA (née Rebecca Webb Pennock; 1794-1854), American industrialist **25** 275-277

LUKS, GEORGE BENJAMIN (1867-1933), American painter **10** 38-39

LULA DA SILVA, LUIZ INÁCIO (Lula; born 1945), president of Brazil **27** 244-247

LULL, RAYMOND (1232/35-1316), Spanish theologian, poet, and missionary **10** 39-40

LULLY, JEAN BAPTISTE (1632-1687), Italian-born French composer **10** 40-41

Lully, Raymond
see Lull, Raymond

LUMET, SIDNEY (born 1924), American filmmaker and television director **22** 305-307

LUMIÈRE BROTHERS (Auguste Marie Louis, 1862-1954, and Louis Jean, 1864-1948), French inventors **10** 41-43

LUMUMBA, PATRICE EMERY (1925-1961), Congolese statesman **10** 43-45

LUNDY, BENJAMIN (1789-1839), American journalist **10** 45-46

LUNS, JOSEPH (1911-2002), West European political leader **10** 46-47

LURIA, ISAAC BEN SOLOMON ASHKENAZI (1534-1572), Jewish mystic **10** 47-48

LUTHER, MARTIN (1483-1546), German religious reformer **10** 48-51

LUTHULI, ALBERT JOHN (1898-1967), South African statesman **10** 51-52

LUTOSLAWSKI, WITOLD (1913-1994), Polish composer **10** 52-53

LUTYENS, EDWIN LANDSEER (1869-1944), English architect **10** 54-55

LUXEMBURG, ROSA (1870-1919), Polish revolutionary **10** 55-56

LUZ, ARTURO ROGERIO (born 1926), Philippine painter and sculptor **10** 56-57

LUZHKOV, YURI MIKHAYLOVICH (born 1936), mayor of Moscow **18** 266-268

LUZZATO, MOSES HAYYIM (1707-1747), Jewish mystic and poet **10** 57-58

LUZZI, MONDINO DE' (circa 1265/70-1326), Italian anatomist **10** 58

LWOFF, ANDRÉ (1902-1994), French microbiologist and geneticist **10** 58-59

LY, ABDOULAYE (born 1919), Senegalese politician and historian **10** 60

LYAUTEY, LOUIS HUBERT GONZALVE (1854-1934), French marshal and colonial administrator **10** 60-61

LYDGATE, JOHN (circa 1370-1449/50), English poet **10** 61-62

LYELL, SIR CHARLES (1797-1875), Scottish geologist **10** 62-63

LYND, HELEN MERRELL (1896-1982), American sociologist and educator **10** 63-64

LYND, ROBERT STAUGHTON (1892-1970), American sociologist **10** 64-65

LYND, STAUGHTON (born 1929), historian and peace militant **10** 65-66

LYNDSAY, SIR DAVID (circa 1485-1555), Scottish poet and courtier **10** 66-67

LYON, MARY (1797-1849), American educator, religious leader, and women's rights advocate **10** 67-69

LYONS, JOSEPH ALOYSIUS (1879-1939), Australian statesman, prime minister 1932-39 **10** 69-70

LYSANDER (died 395 B.C.), Spartan military commander and statesman **10** 70

LYSENKO, TROFIM DENISOVICH (1898-1976), Soviet agronomist and geneticist **10** 71

Lytton of Knebworth, 1st Baron
see Bulwer-Lytton, Edward

M

MA, YO-YO (born 1955), American cellist **20** 232-234

MAAS, PETER (1929-2001), American author **27** 248-251

MAATHAI, WANGARI MUTA (born 1940), Kenyan environmental activist **18** 269-271

MABILLON, JEAN (1632-1707), French monk and historian **10** 72

MABINI, APOLINARIO (1864-1903), Filipino political philosopher **10** 72-73

Mabovitch, Golda
see Meir, Golda

MABUCHI, KAMO (1697-1769), Japanese writer and scholar **10** 73-74

MACAPAGAL, DIOSDADO P. (born 1910), Filipino statesman **10** 74-76

MACAPAGAL-ARROYO, GLORIA (Gloria Arroyo; born 1947), presidnet of the Philippine islands **25** 278-280

MACARTHUR, DOUGLAS (1880-1964), American general **10** 76-78

MACARTHUR, JOHN (circa 1767-1834), Australian merchant, sheep breeder, and politician **10** 78

MACAULAY, CATHARINE (Catherine Sawbridge Macaulay Graham; 1731-1791), British author and feminist **25** 280-282

MACAULAY, HERBERT (1864-1945), Nigerian politician **10** 78-79

MACAULAY, THOMAS BABINGTON (1st Baron Macaulay of Rothley; 1800-1859), English essayist, historian, and politician **10** 79-80

MACBETH (died 1057), king of Scotland 1040-1057 **10** 81

MACBRIDE, SEAN (1904-1988), Irish statesman **19** 218-220

MACCREADY, PAUL (1925-2007), American aeronautical engineer **20** 234-237

MACDONALD, DWIGHT (1906-1982), American editor, journalist, essayist, and critic **10** 81-83

MACDONALD, ELEANOR JOSEPHINE (born 1906), American epidemiologist **10** 83-84

MACDONALD, JAMES RAMSAY (1866-1937), British politician **10** 84-85

MACDONALD, SIR JOHN ALEXANDER (1815-1891), Canadian statesman **10** 85-87

MACDOWELL, EDWARD ALEXANDER (1861-1908), American pianist and composer **10** 87-88

MACEO, ANTONIO (1845-1896), Cuban general and patriot **10** 88-90

MACH, ERNST (1838-1916), Austrian physicist **10** 90-91

MACHADO DE ASSIS, JOAQUIM MARIA (1839-1908), Brazilian novelist **10** 91-92

MACHADO Y MORALES, GERARDO (1871-1939), Cuban general and president **10** 92-93

MACHAUT, GUILLAUME DE (circa 1300-1377), French composer and poet **10** 93-94

MACHEL, SAMORA MOISES (1933-1986), socialist revolutionary and first president of Mozambique **10** 94-96

MACHIAVELLI, NICCOLÒ (1469-1527), Italian author and statesman **10** 97-99

Machine gun
see Weapons and explosives

MACINTYRE, ALASDAIR CHALMERS (born 1929), Scottish-born philosopher and ethicist **10** 99-100

MACIVER, ROBERT MORRISON (1882-1970), Scottish-American sociologist, political philosopher, and educator **10** 100-101

MACK, CONNIE (Cornelius Alexander McGillicuddy; 1862-1956), American baseball player and manager **19** 220-222

MACKAY, JOHN WILLIAM (1831-1902), American miner and business leader **10** 101-102

MACKE, AUGUST (1887-1914), Expressionist painter **10** 102-103

MACKENZIE, ADA (1891-1973), Canadian golfer **24** 232-234

MACKENZIE, SIR ALEXANDER (circa 1764-1820), Scottish explorer, fur trader, and businessman **10** 103-104

MACKENZIE, ALEXANDER (1822-1892), Scottish-born Canadian statesman, prime minister 1873-1878 **10** 104

MACKENZIE, WILLIAM LYON (1795-1861), Scottish-born Canadian journalist, politician, and rebel **10** 104-106

Mackenzie King, William Lyon
see King, William Lyon Mackenzie

MACKERRAS, ALAN CHARLES (Sir Charles Mackerrras; born 1925), Australian conductor **23** 237-239

MACKILLOP, MARY (1842-1909), first Australian candidate for sainthood in the Roman Catholic Church and foundress of the Sisters of Saint Joseph of the Sacred Heart **10** 106-107

MACKINTOSH, CHARLES RENNIE (1868-1928), Scottish artist, architect, and interior/furniture/textile designer **10** 107-108

MACLEAN, GEORGE (1801-1847), Scottish soldier and agent of British expansion **10** 108-109

MACLEISH, ARCHIBALD (born 1892), American poet, playwright, and public official **10** 109-110

MACLENNAN, HUGH (1907-1990), Canadian novelist, essayist, and academic **10** 110-111

MACLEOD, JOHN JAMES RICKARD (1876-1935), Scottish physiologist **24** 234-237

MACMILLAN, DONALD BAXTER (1874-1970), American explorer and scientist **10** 111-112

MACMILLAN, HAROLD (born 1894), British statesman **10** 112-113

MACNEICE, LOUIS (1907-1964), British poet **10** 113-114

MACON, NATHANIEL (1758-1837), American statesman **10** 114-115

MACONCHY, ELIZABETH (Betty Maconchy; 1907-1994), British composer **27** 251-253

MACPHAIL, AGNES CAMPBELL (1890-1954), Canadian activist and politician **24** 237-239

MACQUARIE, LACHLAN (1762-1824), British officer, governor of New South Wales 1810-1822 **10** 115-116

MACQUARRIE, JOHN (1919-2007), Anglican theologian **10** 116-117

MACY, ANNE SULLIVAN (Johanna "Annie" Sullivan; 1866-1936), American teacher **20** 237-239

MADAME DE POMPADOUR (Jeanne-Antoinette Poisson Pompasourr; 1721-1764), French mistress **28** 228-230

Madame Tussaud's Wax Museum Tussaud, Marie **28** 356-358

MADERNO, CARLO (1556-1629), Italian architect **10** 117-118

MADERO, FRANCISCO INDALECIO (1873-1913), Mexican politician, president 1911-13 **10** 118-119

MADHVA (Vasudeva; Madhwa; Anande Tirtha; Purna Prajna; c.1199-c.1276), Indian theologian and philosopher **22** 308-309

MADISON, DOLLY (wife of James Madison, born Dorothea Payne; 1768-1849), American First Lady **10** 119-121

MADISON, JAMES (1751-1836), American statesman, president 1809-1817 **10** 121-123

MADONNA (Madonna Louise Veronica Ciccone, born 1958), American singer and actress **10** 123-125

MAEKAWA, KUNIO (1905-1986), Japanese architect **23** 239-242

Maelwael, Pol, Herman, and Jehanequin see Limbourg Brothers

MAETERLINCK, COUNT MAURICE (1863-1949), Belgian poet, dramatist, and essayist **10** 125-126

MAGELLAN, FERDINAND (1480-1521), Portuguese explorer **10** 126-127 Serrão, Francisco **28** 320-321

MAGENDIE, FRANCOIS (1783-1855), French physiologist **25** 282-285

MAGNANI, ANNA (1908-1973), Italian Actress **26** 238-241

MAGNASCO, ALESSANDRO (1667-1749), Italian painter **10** 127-128

Magnus, Cnaeus Pompeius see Pompey

MAGRITTE, RENÉ (1890-1967), Surrealist painter **10** 128-130

MAGSAYSAY, RAMON (1907-1957), Philippine statesman, president 1953-1957 **10** 130-131

MAHAL, HAZRAT (Iftikarun-nisa; 1820?-1879), Indian revolutionary **18** 271-273

MAHAN, ALFRED THAYER (1840-1914), American naval historian and strategist **10** 131-132

MAHARISHI MAHESH YOGI (1911?-2008), Indian guru and founder of the Transcendental Meditation movement **10** 132-133

MAHATHIR MOHAMAD (born 1925), prime minister of Malaysia **10** 134-135

MAHDI, THE (Mohammed Ahmed; circa 1844-1885), Islamic reformer and Sudanese military leader **10** 137-138

MAHENDRA, KING (Bir Bikram Shah Dev; 1920-1972), ninth Shah dynasty ruler of Nepal (1955-1972) **10** 138-139

MAHERERO, SAMUEL (ca. 1854-1923), Supreme Chief of the Herero naion in southwest Africa **10** 139-142

MAHFUZ, NAJIB (1912-2006), Egyptian novelist **10** 142-144

MAHLER, GUSTAV (1860-1911), Bohemian-born composer and conductor **10** 144-145

MAHMUD II (1785-1839), Ottoman sultan 1808-1839 **10** 145-147

MAHMUD OF GHAZNI (971-1030), Ghaznavid sultan in Afghanistan **10** 147

MAHONE, WILLIAM (1826-1895), American politician and Confederate general **10** 147-148

MAILER, NORMAN KINGSLEY (1923-2007), American author, producer, and director **10** 148-150

MAILLOL, ARISTIDE (1861-1944), French sculptor **10** 150-151

MAIMONIDES (1135-1204), Jewish philosopher **10** 151-152

MAINE, SIR HENRY JAMES SUMNER (1822-1888), English legal historian and historical anthropologist **10** 152

MAISONEUVE, SIEUR DE (Paul de Chomedey; 1612-1676), French explorer and colonizer in Canada **10** 153

MAISTRE, JOSEPH DE (1753-1821), French political philosopher **10** 153-154

MAITLAND, FREDERIC WILLIAM (1850-1906), English historian, lawyer, and legal scholar **10** 154-155

MAJOR, JOHN (born 1943), British prime minister **10** 155-157

MAKARIOS III (Michael Christodoulou Mouskos; 1913-1977), archbishop and ethnarch of the Orthodox Church of Cyprus and first president of the Republic of Cyprus (1959-1977) **10** 157-158

MAKAVEJEV, DUSAN (born 1932), Yugoslav filmmaker **26** 241-243

Make Room for Daddy (television show) Thomas, Danny **28** 350-352

MAKEBA, MIRIAM (Zensi Miriam Makeba; born 1932), South African singer and activist **22** 309-312

MAKEMIE, FRANCIS (1658-1708), Irish-born Presbyterian missionary **10** 158-159

Makhpiyaluta see Red Cloud

MAKI, FUMIHIKO (born 1928), Japanese architect **10** 159-161

MAKIBI, KIBI-NO (693-775), Japanese courtier and statesman **10** 161

MAKO (Makoto Iwamatsu; 1933-2006), Japanese-American actor and director **27** 253-255

MÄKONNEN ENDALKAČÄW (1892-1963), Ethiopian writer and official **10** 161-162

MALA'IKA, NAZIK AL- (Nazek Sadiq al-Malaika; 1923-2007), Iraqi poet, literary critic, and proponent of women's rights **28** 230-232

MALAMUD, BERNARD (1914-1986), American novelist and short-story writer **10** 162-163

MALAN, DANIEL FRANCOIS (1874-1959), South African pastor, journalist, and prime minister 1948-1954 **10** 163-164

Malaria (medicine)
cause of
Laveran, Alphonse **28** 207-209

MALCOLM III (died 1093), king of Scotland 1058-1093 **10** 164-165

MALCOLM X (1925-1965), African American civil rights leader **10** 165-166

MALEBRANCHE, NICOLAS (1638-1715), French philosopher and theologian **10** 166-167

MALENKOV, GEORGY MAKSIMILIANOVICH (1902-1988), head of the Soviet government and leader of its Communist Party (1953) **10** 168

MALEVICH, KASIMIR (1878-1935), Russian painter **10** 168-169

MALHERBE, FRANÇOIS DE (1555-1628), French poet **10** 169-170

MALINOWSKI, KASPAR BRONISLAW (1884-1942), Austrian-born British social anthropologist **10** 170-171

MALIPIERO, GIAN FRANCESCO (1882-1973), Italian composer **10** 171

MALKAM KHAN, MIRZA (1831-1908), Persian diplomat **10** 172

MALLARMÉ, STÉPHANE (1842-1898), French poet **10** 172-173

MALLE, LOUIS (1932-1995), French film director and producer **18** 273-275

MALLON, MARY (Typhoid Mary; 1869-1938), Irish woman who unwittingly infected many with typhoid fever **21** 266-268

MALLORY, GEORGE (1886-1924), English mountain climber **21** 268-271

MALONE, ANNIE TURNBO (Annie Minerva Turnbo Malone; 1869-1957), African American entrepreneur and philanthropist **23** 242-243

MALONE, DUMAS (1892-1986), American historian and editor **10** 174-175

MALORY, SIR THOMAS (flourished 15th century), English author **10** 175-176

MALPIGHI, MARCELLO (1628-1694), Italian anatomist **10** 176-178

MALRAUX, ANDRÉ (1901-1976), French novelist, essayist, and politician **10** 178-180

MALTHUS, THOMAS ROBERT (1766-1834), English economist **10** 180-181

MAMET, DAVID ALAN (born 1947), American author **10** 181-182

MAMUN, ABDALLAH AL- (786-833), Abbasid caliph **10** 183

Man in the High Castle, The (book)
Dick, Philip K. **28** 96-98

Manassa Mauler
see Dempsey, Jack

MANASSEH BEN ISRAEL (1604-1657), Dutch rabbi and theologian **10** 183-184

MANCINI, HENRY (Enrico Mancini; 1924-1994), American composer, pianist, and film music scorer **18** 275-276

MANCO CAPAC (circa 1500-1545), Inca emperor **10** 184-185

MANDELA, NELSON ROLIHLAHLA (born 1918), South African leader **10** 185-186

MANDELA, WINNIE (Nomzamo Winifred Madikizela; born 1936), South African anti-apartheid leader **10** 187-189

MANDELBROT, BENOIT B. (born 1924), Polish-born French-American mathematician who invented fractals **10** 189-191

MANDELSTAM, OSIP EMILYEVICH (1891-1938), Russian poet **10** 191

MANDEVILLE, BERNARD (circa 1670-1733), English satirist and moral philosopher **10** 192

MANDEVILLE, SIR JOHN (flourished 14th century), pen name of English author **10** 192-193

MANET, ÉDOUARD (1832-1883), French painter **10** 193-194

MANGAS COLORADAS (ca. 1790-1863), Apache military leader **10** 194-196

Manhattan Project
see Atomic bomb—development

MANI (216-276/277), Persian prophet **10** 196-197

MANIN, DANIELE (1804-1857), Venetian patriot **10** 197-198

MANKILLER, WILMA (born 1945), Native American activist and Cherokee chief **10** 198-199

MANLEY, MICHAEL NORMAN (1924-1997), Jamaican prime minister (1972-1980) **10** 200-201

MANN, HEINRICH (1871-1950), German novelist, essayist, and social critic **10** 201-202

MANN, HORACE (1796-1859), American educational reformer and humanitarian **10** 202-204

MANN, THOMAS (1875-1955), German novelist and essayist **10** 204-207

MANNERHEIM, BARON CARL GUSTAV EMIL VON (1867-1951), Finnish military leader and statesman, president 1944-46 **10** 207-208

MANNHEIM, KARL (1893-1947), Hungarian-born sociologist and educator **10** 208-209

MANNING, HENRY EDWARD (1808-1892), English cardinal **10** 209-210

MANNIX, DANIEL (1864-1963), Irish-born Australian archbishop **10** 210

Manoel
see Manuel

MANRIQUE, JORGE (1440?-1478), Spanish poet and soldier **10** 210-211

MANSART, FRANÇOIS (1598-1666), French architect **10** 211

MANSART, JULES HARDOUIN (1646-1708), French architect **10** 212

MANSFIELD, KATHERINE (born Kathleen Mansfield Beauchamp; 1888-1923), New Zealander short-story writer and poet **10** 213-214

MANSUR, ABU JAFAR IBN MUHAMMAD AL (712-775), Abbasid caliph **10** 214-215

Mansur, Abu Yusuf Yakub al-
see Yakub Al-Mansur, Abu Yusuf

MANTEGNA, ANDREA (circa 1430-1506), Italian painter and engraver **10** 215-216

MANTLE, MICKEY (1931-1995), American baseball player **10** 216-218

MANUEL I (1469-1521), king of Portugal 1495-1521 **10** 219-220

MANUEL I COMNENUS (circa 1123-1180), Byzantine emperor 1143-1180 **10** 218-219

MANUELITO (1818-1894), Navajo tribal leader **10** 220-222

Manufacturers
see Business and industrial leaders

MANZONI, ALESSANDRO (1785-1873), Italian novelist and playwright **10** 222-224

MANZÙ, GIACOMO (born 1908), Italian sculptor **10** 224-225

MAO ZEDONG (1893-1976), Chinese statesman **10** 225-227

Map (cartography)
Hollar, Wenceslaus **28** 180-183

MAPPLETHORPE, ROBERT (1946-1989), controversial American photographer **10** 227-228

MARADONA, DIEGO (born 1961), Argentine soccer player **20** 239-241

MARAGHI, AL-MUSTAFĀ (1881-1945), Egyptian jurist and educator **10** 228-229

Marah
see Jackson, Helen Hunt

MARAT, JEAN PAUL (1743-1793), French journalist and political leader **10** 230-231

MARBLE, ALICE (1913-1990), American tennis player **21** 271-273

Marbury, Anne
see Hutchinson, Anne Marbury

MARC, FRANZ (1880-1916), German painter **10** 231

MARCEAU, MARCEL (1923-2007), world's greatest practitioner of pantomime **10** 231-233

MARCEL, GABRIEL (1889-1973), French philosopher **10** 233-234

MARCHAND, JEAN-BAPTISTE (1863-1934), French explorer and soldier **10** 234-237

MARCIANO, ROCKY (1923-1969), American boxer **10** 237-238

MARCION (flourished mid-2nd century), Christian theologian **10** 238-239

MARCONI, GUGLIELMO (1874-1937), Italian inventor **10** 239-240

MARCOS, FERDINAND (1917-1989), president of the Republic of the Philippines (1965-1986) **10** 240-242

MARCOS, IMELDA ROMUALDEZ (born 1930), wife of Philippine President Ferdinand Marcos and governor of Metro Manila **10** 242-243

MARCOS DE NIZA, FRIAR (circa 1500-1558), Franciscan missionary in Spanish America **10** 240

Marcus Antonius
see Antony, Mark

MARCUS AURELIUS ANTONINUS (121-180), Roman emperor 161-180 **10** 243-245

MARCUS, STANLEY (1905-2002), American businessman **19** 222-224

Marcus Ulpius Trajanus
see Trajan

MARCUSE, HERBERT (1898-1979), German-American philosopher **10** 245-247

MARCY, WILLIAM LEARNED (1786-1857), American statesman **10** 247-248

MARENZIO, LUCA (1553/54-1599), Italian composer **10** 248

MARGAI, SIR MILTON AUGUSTUS STRIERY (1895-1964), Sierra Leonean physician and statesman **10** 248-249

MARGARET OF ANJOU (1430-1482), queen consort of Henry VI of England **10** 249-250

MARGARET OF DENMARK (born Margaret Valdemarsdottir; 1353-1412), queen of Denmark **10** 250-252

MARGARET OF SCOTLAND, SAINT (1045-1093), wife of Malcolm III of Scotland **10** 252-253

MARGGRAF, ANDREAS (1709-1782), German chemist **21** 273-275

MARGULIS, LYNN (born 1938), American biologist **10** 253-254

Mari Djata
see Sundiata Keita

MARIA THERESA (1717-1780), Holy Roman empress 1740-1780 **10** 256-258

MARIANA, JUAN DE (1536-1624), Spanish Jesuit historian **10** 254-255

MARIÁTEGUI, JOSÉ CARLOS (1895-1930), Peruvian writer **10** 255-256

Maricourt, Pierre de
see Peregrinus, Petrus

MARIE ANTOINETTE (1755-1793), queen of France 1774-1793 **10** 258-259

MARIE DE FRANCE (flourished late 12th century), French poet **10** 259

MARIN, JOHN, III (1870-1953), American painter **10** 259-260

Marin, José Luís Alberto Muñoz
see Muñoz Marín, José Luís

MARINI, MARINO (1901-1980), Italian sculptor **10** 260-262

MARINO, DAN (Daniel Constantine Marino, Jr.; born 1961), American athlete **26** 243-245

MARION, FRANCIS (1732-1795), American Revolutionary War leader **10** 262-263

MARITAIN, JACQUES (1882-1973), French Catholic philosopher **10** 263

MARIUS GAIUS (circa 157-86 B.C.), Roman general and politician **10** 264-265

MARIVAUX, PIERRE CARLET DE CHAMBLAIN DE (1688-1763), French novelist and dramatist **10** 265-266

MARK, SAINT (flourished 1st century), Apostle of Jesus **10** 266-267

MARKHAM, BERYL (1902-1986), British aviator, author, and horse trainer **20** 241-243

MARKHAM, EDWIN (1852-1940), American poet **10** 267

MARKIEVICZ, CONSTANCE (1868-1927), Irish nationalist, labor activist, and feminist **10** 267-271

MARLBOROUGH, 1ST DUKE OF (John Churchill; 1650-1722), English general and statesman **10** 271-272

MARLEY, BOB (Robert Nesta Marley; 1945-1981), Jamaican musician **24** 239-241

MARLOWE, CHRISTOPHER (1564-1593), English dramatist **10** 272-274

MÁRMOL, JOSÉ (1817-1871), Argentine writer and intellectual **10** 274

Maro, Publius Vergilius
see Virgil

MARQUETTE, JACQUES (1637-1675), French Jesuit, missionary and explorer **10** 274-275

Márquez, Gabriel Garcia
see Garcia Márquez, Gabriel

MARRIOTT, ALICE SHEETS (1907-2000), American restaurant and hotel chain executive **27** 255-256
Marriott, J. Willard **28** 232-234

MARRIOTT, J. WILLARD (Bill Marriott; 1900-1985), American hotel and restaurant chain executive **28** 232-234

MARSALIS, WYNTON (born 1961), American trumpeter and bandleader **19** 224-226

MARSH, GEORGE PERKINS (1801-1882), American diplomat, philologist, and conservationist **21** 275-277

MARSH, NGAIO (Edith Ngaio Marsh; 1899-1982), New Zealander author and playwright **19** 226-228

MARSH, OTHNIEL CHARLES (1831-1899), American paleontologist **10** 275-276

MARSH, REGINALD (1898-1954), American painter and printmaker **10** 276-277

MARSHALL, ALFRED (1842-1924), English economist **10** 277-278

MARSHALL, GEORGE CATLETT (1880-1959), American soldier and statesman **10** 278-279

MARSHALL, JOHN (1755-1835), American jurist, chief justice of United States. Supreme Court 1801-1835 **10** 279-281

MARSHALL, PAULE BURKE (born 1929), American author **10** 281-282

MARSHALL, THURGOOD (1908-1993), African American jurist **10** 282-284

MARSILIUS OF PADUA (1275/80-1342), Italian political philosopher **10** 284

MARTEL, CHARLES (circa 690-741), Frankish ruler **10** 285

MARTÍ, JOSÉ (1853-1895), Cuban revolutionary, poet, and journalist **10** 285-286

MARTIAL (Marcus Valerias Martialis; circa 38/41-circa 104), Roman epigrammatist **10** 286-287

MARTIN V (Oddone Colonna; 1368-1431), pope 1417-1431 **10** 287-288

MARTIN, AGNES (1912-2004), American painter **10** 288-289

MARTIN, DEAN (Dino Paul Crocetti; 1917-1995), American entertainer **26** 245-247

MARTIN, GREGORY (circa 1540-1582), British Bible translator and scholar **21** 277-279

MARTIN, LUTHER (1748-1826), American lawyer and Revolutionary patriot **10** 289-290

MARTIN, LYNN MORLEY (born 1939), Republican representative from Illinois and secretary of labor under George Bush **10** 290-292

MARTIN, MARY (1913-1990), popular stage actress, singer, and dancer and a television and film star **10** 292-293

Martin, Violet
see Somerville, E.

MARTIN, WILLIAM MCCHESNEY, JR. (1906-1998), American business executive and federal government official **10** 293-295

MARTIN DU GARD, ROGER (1881-1958), French author **10** 295-296

MARTINEAU, HARRIET (1802-1876), English writer and philosopher **10** 296-297

MARTINEZ, MARIANNE (Marianne von Martinez; Anna Katherina Martinez; 1744-1812), Austrian musician **27** 256-258

MARTINEZ, MARIA MONTOYA (Maria Antonia Montoya; Marie Poveka; Pond Lily; 1881?-1980), Pueblo potter **24** 241-243

MARTÍNEZ, MAXIMILIANO HERNÁNDEZ (1882-1966), president of El Salvador (1931-1944) **10** 297-298

MARTINEZ, VILMA SOCORRO (born 1943), Hispanic American attorney and activist **18** 276-279

Martinez Ruíz, José
see Ruíz, José Martinez

MARTINI, SIMONE (flourished 1315-1344), Italian painter **10** 298-299

MARTINU, BOHUSLAV (1890-1959), Czech composer **10** 299-300

MARTY, MARTIN E. (born 1928), Lutheran pastor, historian of American religion, and commentator **10** 300-301

MARVELL, ANDREW (1621-1678), English poet and politician **10** 301-303

MARX, KARL (1818-1883), German political philosopher **10** 304-308

MARX BROTHERS, 20th-century American stage and film comedians **10** 303-304

MARY, QUEEN OF SCOTS (1542-1587), queen of France and Scotland **10** 308-309

MARY, SAINT (Blessed Virgin Mary; late 1st century B.C.-1st century A.D.), New Testament figure, mother of Jesus **10** 308-309

MARY I (1516-1558), queen of England 1553-1558 **10** 308-309
relatives
    Woodville, Elizabeth **28** 381-383

MARY II (1662-1694), queen of England, Scotland, and Ireland 1689-1694 **10** 309-310

MARY MAGDALENE (Mary of Magdala), Catholic saint and biblical figure **24** 243-246

MASACCIO (1401-1428), Italian painter **10** 312-313

Masafuji
see Mabuchi, Kamo

Masahito
see Goshirakawa

Masanobu
see Mabuchi, Kamo

MASARYK, JAN (1886-1948), Czech foreign minister **20** 243-246

MASARYK, TOMÁŠ GARRIGUE (1850-1937), Czech philosopher and statesman, president 1919-1935 **10** 314-315

MASINISSA, KING OF NUMIDIA (240 B.C. - 148 B.C.), prince of the Massylians who consolidated the Numidian tribes to form a North African kingdom **10** 315-317

MASIRE, QUETT KETUMILE (born 1925), a leader of the fight for independence and president of Botswana **10** 318-319

MASON, BRIDGET (Biddy Mason; 1818-1891), African American nurse, midwife, and entrepreneur **22** 312-314

MASON, GEORGE (1725-1792), American statesman **10** 319-320

MASON, JAMES MURRAY (1796-1871), American politician and Confederate diplomat **10** 320-321

MASON, LOWELL (1792-1872), American composer and music educator **10** 321-322

MASSASOIT (1580-1661), Native American tribal chief **10** 322-324

MASSEY, VINCENT (Charles Vincent Massey, 1887-1967), Canadian governor-general **24** 246-248

MASSEY, WILLIAM FERGUSON (1856-1925), New Zealand prime minister 1912-1925 **10** 324

MASSINGER, PHILIP (1583-1640), English playwright **10** 324-325

MASSYS, QUENTIN (1465/66-1530), Flemish painter **10** 325-326

Mastai-Ferretti, Giovanni Maria
see Pius IX

Master Meng
see Mencius

Master of Flémalle
see Campin, Robert

MASTERS, EDGAR LEE (1869-1950), American author and lawyer **10** 326-327

MASTERS, WILLIAM HOWELL (born 1915), American psychologist and sex therapist **10** 327-328

MASUDI, ALI IBN AL- HUSAYN AL- (died 956), Arab historian **10** 328-329

MASUR, KURT (born 1927), German conductor and humanist **20** 246-248

MATA HARI (Margaretha Geertruida Zelle; 1876-1917), Dutch spy **21** 279-282

MATAMOROS, MARINO (1770-1814), Mexican priest and independence hero **10** 329-330

Mathematics
dating systems
Dionysius Exiguus **28** 99-100
symbols
Zuse, Konrad **28** 391-393

MATHER, COTTON (1663-1728),
American Puritan clergyman and
historian **10** 330-332

MATHER, INCREASE (1639-1723),
American Puritan clergymen, educator,
and author **10** 332-333

MATHEWSON, CHRISTY (Christopher
Mathewson; 1880-1925), American
baseball player **21** 282-284

MATHIAS, BOB (Robert Bruce Mathias;
1930-2006), American track and field
star **21** 284-286

MATHIEZ, ALBERT (1874-1932), French
historian **10** 333-334

MATILDA OF TUSCANY (ca. 1046-
1115), Italian countess **10** 334-336

MATISSE, HENRI (1869-1954), French
painter and sculptor **10** 336-337

MATLIN, MARLEE (born 1965),
American actress **19** 228-230

MATLOVICH, LEONARD (1943-1988),
American gay rights activist **20**
248-250

Matoaka
see Pocahontas (ballet)

MATSUNAGA, SPARK MASAYUKI
(1916-1990), Asian American U.S.
senator **18** 279-281

MATSUSHITA, KONOSUKE (1918-1989),
Japanese inventor and businessman **19**
230-232

Matsys, Quentin
see Massys, Quentin

**MATTA ECHAURREN, ROBERTO
SEBASTIAN ANTONIO** (Matta, 1911-
2002), Chilean artist **24** 248-250

MATTEI, ENRICO (1906-1962), Italian
entrepreneur **10** 337-339

MATTEOTTI, GIACOMO (1885-1924),
Italian political leader **10** 339-340

MATTHAU, WALTER (Walter Matthow;
Walter Matuschanskayasky; 1920-
2000), American Actor **22** 314-316

MATTHEW, SAINT (flourished Ist
century), Apostle and Evangelist **10**
340-341

MATTHEW PARIS (circa 1200-1259),
English Benedictine chronicler **10**
341-342

MATTINGLY, GARRETT (1900-1962),
American historian, professor, and

author of novel-like histories **10**
342-344

MATZELIGER, JAN (1852-1889),
American inventor and shoemaker **19**
232-234

MAUCHLY, JOHN (1907-1980),
American computer entrepreneur **20**
250-252

MAUDSLAY, HENRY (1771-1831),
British engineer and inventor **21**
286-288

MAUGHAM, WILLIAM SOMERSET
(1874-1965), English author **10**
344-345

MAULBERTSCH, FRANZ ANTON (1724-
1796), Austrian painter **10** 345

MAULDIN, BILL (1921-2003), cartoon
biographer of the ordinary GI in World
War II **10** 345-346

**MAUPASSANT, HENRI RENÉ ALBERT
GUY DE** (1850-1893), French author
10 347

MAURIAC, FRANÇOIS (1885-1970),
French author **10** 347-348

MAURICE, JOHN FREDERICK DENISON
(1805-1872), English theologian and
Anglican clergyman **10** 349-350

**MAURICE OF NASSAU, PRINCE OF
ORANGE** (1567-1625), Dutch general
and statesman **10** 348-349

MAURRAS, CHARLES MARIE PHOTIUS
(1868-1952), French political writer
and reactionary **10** 350-351

MAURY, ANTONIA (1866-1952),
American astronomer and
conservationist **20** 252-254

MAURY, MATTHEW FONTAINE (1806-
1873), American naval officer and
oceanographer **10** 351-352

MAUSS, MARCEL (1872-1950), French
sociologist and anthropologist **10**
352-353

MAWDUDI, ABU-I A'LA (1903-1979),
Muslim writer and religious and
political leader in the Indian subcontinent **10** 353-354

MAWSON, SIR DOUGLAS (1882-1958),
Australian scientist and Antarctic
explorer **10** 354-355

MAXIM, SIR HIRAM STEVENS (1840-
1916), American-born British inventor
10 355-356

Maximianus, Gaius Galerius Valerius
see Galerius

Maximilian (emperor of Mexico)
see Maximilian of Hapsburg

MAXIMILIAN I (1459-1519), Holy
Roman emperor 1493-1519 **10**
356-357

MAXIMILIAN II (1527-1576), Holy
Roman emperor 1564-1576 **10**
357-358

MAXIMILIAN OF HAPSBURG (1832-
1867), archduke of Austria and
emperor of Mexico **10** 358-360

MAXWELL, IAN ROBERT (née Ludvik
Hock; 1923-1991), British publishing
magnate **10** 360-361

MAXWELL, JAMES CLERK (1831-1879),
Scottish physicist **10** 361-364

MAY, KARL (1842-1912), German author
26 248-250

**MAYAKOVSKY, VLADIMIR
VLADIMIROVICH** (1893-1930),
Russian poet **10** 364-365

MAYER, JEAN (born 1920), nutritionist,
researcher, consultant to government
and international organizations, and
president of Tufts University **10**
365-366

MAYER, LOUIS BURT (Eliezer Mayer;
1885-1957), American motion picture
producer **19** 234-235

MAYNARD, ROBERT CLYVE (1937-
1993), African American journalist and
publisher **10** 366-367

MAYO, WILLIAM J. AND CHARLES H.
(1861-1939; 1865-1939), American
physicians **10** 367-369

MAYOR ZARAGOSA, FEDERICO (born
1934), Spanish biochemist who was
director-general of UNESCO (United
Nations Educational, Scientific, and
Cultural Organization) **10** 369-371

MAYO-SMITH, RICHMOND (1854-
1901), American statistician and
sociologist **10** 371-372

MAYR, ERNST (1904-2005), American
evolutionary biologist **10** 372-374

MAYS, BENJAMIN E. (1894-1984),
African American educator and civil
rights activist **10** 374-376

MAYS, WILLIE (William Howard Mays,
Jr.; born 1931), African American
baseball player **10** 376-379

Mayson, Isabella Mary
see Beeton, Isabella Mary

MAZARIN, JULES (1602-1661), French
cardinal and statesman **10** 379-380

MAZEPA, IVAN STEPANOVICH (circa
1644-1709), Ukrainian Cossack leader
10 381

Mazzarini, Giulio
see Mazarin, Jules

MAZZINI, GIUSEPPE (1805-1872), Italian patriot **10** 381-383

Mazzola, Francesco
see Parmigianino

M'BOW, AMADOU-MAHTAR (born 1921), director general of UNESCO (United Nations Educational, Scientific, and Cultural Organization) **10** 383-384

MBOYA, THOMAS JOSEPH (1930-1969), Kenyan political leader **10** 384-385

MCADOO, WILLIAM GIBBS (1863-1941), American statesman **10** 385-386

MCAULIFFE, ANTHONY (1898-1975), American army officer **19** 236-239

MCAULIFFE, CHRISTA (nee Sharon Christa Corrigan; 1948-1986), American teacher **20** 254-257

MCCAIN, JOHN SIDNEY, III (born 1936), American politician **25** 285-287

MCCANDLESS, BRUCE (born 1937), American astronaut **23** 243-246

MCCARTHY, EUGENE JOSEPH (1916-2005), American statesman **10** 386-388

MCCARTHY, JOSEPH RAYMOND (1908-1957), American politician **10** 388-389

MCCARTHY, MARY T. (born 1912), American writer **10** 389-391

MCCARTHY, NOBU (nee Nobu Atsumi; 1934-2002), Japanese actress and model **26** 250-252

MCCARTNEY, PAUL (James Paul McCartney; born 1942), British musician **24** 250-253

MCCAY, WINSOR (Zenas Winsor McKay; c. 1871-1934), American cartoonist and animator **21** 288-291

MCCLELLAN, GEORGE BRINTON (1826-1885), American general **10** 391-392

MCCLELLAN, JOHN LITTLE (1896-1977), U.S. senator from Arkansas **10** 392-393

MCCLINTOCK, BARBARA (1902-1992), geneticist and winner of the Nobel Prize in physiology **10** 393-394

MCCLINTOCK, SIR FRANCIS LEOPOLD (1819-1907), British admiral and Arctic explorer **10** 394-395

MCCLOSKEY, JOHN (1810-1885), American cardinal **10** 395

MCCLUNG, NELLIE LETITIA (1873-1951), Canadian suffragist, social

reformer, legislator, and author **10** 396-397

MCCLURE, SIR ROBERT (1807-1873), English explorer and navy officer **10** 398-399

MCCLURE, SAMUEL SIDNEY (1857-1949), American editor and publisher **10** 398-399

MCCORMACK, JOHN WILLIAM (1891-1980), U.S. congressman and Speaker of the House **10** 399-400

MCCORMICK, CYRUS HALL (1809-1884), American inventor, manufacturer, and philanthropist **10** 400-401

MCCORMICK, ROBERT RUTHERFORD (1880-1955), American publisher **10** 401-402

MCCOSH, JAMES (1811-1894), Scottish-American minister, philosopher, and college president **10** 402-403

MCCOY, ELIJAH (1843-1929), American engineer and inventor **19** 239-241

MCCOY, ISAAC (1784-1846), American Indian agent and missionary **10** 403

MCCOY, JOSEPH GEITING (1837-1915), American cattleman **10** 403-404

MCCULLERS, CARSON (Lula Carson Smith; 1917-1967), American novelist and playwright **18** 281-283

MCCULLOCH, HUGH (1808-1895), American banker and lawyer **10** 404-405

MCDANIEL, HATTIE (1898-1952), African American actress **10** 405-408

MCDUFFIE, GEORGE (1790-1851), American statesman **10** 408

MCENROE, JOHN PATRICK, JR. (born 1959), American tennis player **10** 408-411

MCGILL, RALPH EMERSON (1898-1969), American journalist **10** 411-412

MCGILLIVRAY, ALEXANDER (circa 1759-1793), American Creek Indian chief **10** 412

MCGOVERN, GEORGE STANLEY (born 1922), American statesman **10** 412-414

MCGUFFEY, WILLIAM HOLMES (1800-1873), American educator **10** 414-415

MCINTIRE, SAMUEL (1757-1811), American builder and furniture maker **10** 415

MCKAY, CLAUDE (1890-1948), African American poet and novelist **10** 416

MCKAY, DONALD (1810-1880), American ship builder **10** 416-417

MCKELLEN, IAN MURRAY (born 1939), English actor **28** 234-237

MCKIM, CHARLES FOLLEN (1847-1909), American architect **10** 417-418

MCKINLEY, WILLIAM (1843-1901), American statesman, president 1897-1901 **10** 418-420

MCKISSICK, FLOYD B., (1922-1991), African American civil rights leader **10** 420-422

MCLAREN, NORMAN (1914-1987), Canadian filmmaker **25** 287-289

MCLEAN, JOHN (1785-1861), American jurist and politician **10** 422-423

McLeod, Mary
see Bethune, Mary McLeod

MCLOUGHLIN, JOHN (1784-1857), Canadian pioneer and trader **10** 423-424

MCLUHAN, MARSHALL (Herbert Marshall McLuhan; 1911-1980), Canadian professor of literature and culture **10** 424-426

MCMASTER, JOHN BACH (1852-1932), American historian **10** 426-427

MCMILLAN, TERRY (born 1951), African American novelist and short story writer **10** 427-428

MCMURRAY, BETTE CLAIR (1924-1980), American inventor and businesswoman **10** 429

MCNAMARA, ROBERT S. (born 1916), U.S. secretary of defense and president of the World Bank **10** 429-431

MCNAUGHTON, ANDREW (1887-1966), Canadian soldier and diplomat **10** 431-432

MCNEALY, SCOTT (born 1954), American businessman **19** 241-243

MCNICKLE, D'ARCY (born William D'Arcy McNickle; 1904-1977), Native American author, historian, and activist **10** 433

MCPHERSON, AIMEE SEMPLE (1890-1944), American evangelist **10** 434

MCQUEEN, BUTTERFLY (born Thelma McQueen; 1911-1995), African American actress **10** 434-437

MEAD, GEORGE HERBERT (1863-1931), American philosopher and social psychologist **10** 437-438

MEAD, MARGARET (1901-1978), American anthropologist **10** 438-440

MEADE, GEORGE GORDON (1815-1872), American general **10** 440-441

MEANS, RUSSELL (born 1939), Native American activist **10** 441-444

MEANY, GEORGE (1894-1980), American labor leader 10 444

MECIAR, VLADIMIR (born 1942), Slovak prime minister 18 283-285

MEDAWAR, PETER BRIAN (1915-1987), British zoologist 10 444-445

Medical school development (United States)
Agnew, David Hayes 28 3-5

MEDICI, CATHERINE DE' (1519-1589), Italian queen of France 10 445-449

MEDICI, COSIMO DE' (1389-1464), Italian statesman and merchant prince 10 449-450

Medici, Giovanni Angelo de'
see Pius IV

Medici, Giovanni de' (1475-1521)
see Leo X

MEDICI, LORENZO DE' (1449-1492), Italian statesman, ruler of Florence 1469-1492 10 450-451

Medicine
parasitology
Laveran, Alphonse 28 207-209

MEDILL, JOSEPH (1823-1899), American abolitionist editor and publisher 10 451-452

MEDINA, JOSE TORIBIO (1852-1930), Chilean historian and author 24 253-255

MEDUNA, LADISLAS J. (Ladislas Joseph Meduna; 1896-1964), Hungarian neurologist 28 237-238

Meeuwisz, Thonisz
see Van Diemen, Anthony Meuza

MEGAWATI SUKARNOPUTRI (born 1947), Indonesian prime minister 20 257-259

Mehemet Ali
see Mohammed Ali

MEHMED THE CONQUEROR (a.k.a. Mehmed II and Mehmed Celebi; ca. 1432-1481), Turkish sultan 10 452-454

MEHTA, DEEPA (born 1950), Indian-Canadian filmmaker 27 258-261

MEHTA, SIR PHEROZESHAH (1845-1915), Indian statesman 10 455

MEHTA, ZUBIN (born 1936), India born American conductor 10 455-456

MEIER, RICHARD (born 1934), New York architect 10 456-458

MEIGGS, HENRY (1811-1877), American railroad builder 10 458-459

MEIGHEN, ARTHUR (1874-1960), Canadian lawyer, prime minister 1920-21, 1926 10 459-460

Meiji Tenno
see Mutsuhito

MEINECKE, FRIEDRICH (1862-1954), German historian 10 460-461

MEINESZ, FELIX ANDRIES VENING (1887-1966), Dutch geodesist and geophysicist 10 461

MEINONG, ALEXIUS RITTER VON HANDSCHUCHSHEIM (1853-1920), Austrian philosopher 10 461-462

MEIR, GOLDA (1898-1978), Israeli prime minister 10 462-463

MEITNER, LISE (born Elise Meitner; 1878-1968), Austrian-born American nuclear physicist 10 463-466

Melanchthon, Philip
see Melancthon, Philip

MELANCTHON, PHILIP (1497-1560), German theologian and humanist 10 466-467

MELAND, BERNARD EUGENE (born 1899), American historian of liberal theology 10 467-468

MELBA, NELLIE (Helen Porter Mitchell; 1861-1931), Australian opera singer 24 255-257

MELBOURNE, 2ND VISCOUNT (William Lamb; 1779-1848), English statesman, prime minister 1834 and 1835-1841 10 468-469

MÉLIÈS, GEORGES (Marie Goerges Jean Méliès; 1861-1938), French filmmaker and actor 27 261-263

Melikow, Loris
see Hofmannsthal, Hugo von

MELISENDE (1105-1161), French queen 25 289-290

MELLO, CRAIG CAMERON (born 1961), American molecular biologist 28 238-241

MELLON, ANDREW WILLIAM (1855-1937), American businessman 10 469-470

MELLON, RICHARD KING (1899-1970), American business leader and philanthropist 20 259-261

MELNIKOV, KONSTANTIN STEPANOVICH (1890-1974), Russian avant-grant architect 10 470-471

MELVILLE, GEORGE WALLACE (1841-1912), American naval officer and explorer 10 472

MELVILLE, HERMAN (1819-1891), American author 10 472-476

MEMLING, HANS (circa 1440-1494), German-born painter active in Flanders 10 476

MEMMI, ALBERT (born 1920), Tunisian author and sociologist 24 257-259

MEMMINGER, CHRISTOPHER GUSTAVUS (1803-1888), American politician 10 476-477

MENANDER (342-291 B.C.), Athenian comic playwright 10 477-478

MENCHÚ, RIGOBERTA (born 1959), Guatemalan human rights activist who won the Nobel Peace Prize 10 479-480

MENCIUS (circa 371-circa 289 B.C.), Chinese philosopher 10 480-481

MENCKEN, HENRY LOUIS (1880-1956), American journalist, editor, critic, and philologist 10 481-483

MENDAÑA DE NEYRA, ÁLVARO DE (1541-1595), Spanish explorer 10 483

MENDEL, JOHANN GREGOR (1822-1884), Moravian natural scientist and Augustinian abbot 10 483-486

MENDELEEV, DMITRII IVANOVICH (1834-1907), Russian chemist 10 486-488

MENDELSOHN, ERICH (1887-1953), German architect 10 488

MENDELSSOHN, MOSES (1729-1786), German Jewish philosopher 10 488-489

MENDELSSOHN-BARTHOLDY, FELIX JAKOB LUDWIG (1809-1847), German composer 10 489-491

MENDENHALL, DOROTHY REED (1874-1964), American physician 10 491-492

MENDES, CHICO (Francisco Mendes; 1944-1988), Brazilian environmental activist 19 243-245

MENDÈS FRANCE, PIERRE (1907-1982), French prime minister (1954-1955) and politician 10 492-493

MENDES PINTO, FERNAO (1509-1583), Portugese adventurer 10 493-494

MENDOZA, ANTONIO DE (1490-1552), Spanish viceroy in Mexico and Peru 10 494-495

MENDOZA, DANIEL (1764-1836), English boxer 20 261-263

MENELIK II (born Sahle Mariam; 1844-1913), Ethiopian emperor 1889-1913 10 495-497

MENEM, CARLOS SÁUL (born 1930), Peronist president of Argentina 10 497-499

MENÉNDEZ DE AVILÉS, PEDRO (1519-1574), Spanish seaman and colonizer 10 499-500

MENES (King of Egypt; ca. 3420 B.C. - 3345 B.C.), unifier of Egypt **10** 500-502

MENGELE, JOSEF (1911-1979), German physician and war criminal **10** 502-503

MENGISTU HAILE MARIAM (born 1937), head of state of Ethiopia **10** 503-505

MENGS, ANTON RAPHAEL (1728-1779), German painter **10** 505

Meng-tzu
see Mencius

MENKEN, ALAN (born 1949), American composer **20** 263-266

MENNO SIMONS (circa 1496-1561), Dutch reformer **10** 505-506

MENOCAL, MARIO GARCIA (1866-1941), Cuban statesman, president 1913-1921 **10** 506-507

MENON, VENGALIL KRISHNAN KRISHNA (born 1897), Indian statesman **10** 507-509

MENOTTI, GIAN CARLO (1911-2007), Italian-born American composer **10** 509-510

Mental Hospital reform
Scandinavia
Skram, Amalie **28** 331-333

Mental illness
treatments for
Meduna, Ladislas J. **28** 237-238

MENTEN, MAUD L. (1879-1960), Canadian biochemist **24** 259-260

MENUHIN, YEHUDI (1916-1999), American and British violinist and conductor **20** 266-268

MENZIES, SIR ROBERT GORDON (born 1894), Australian statesman **10** 510-511

MENZIES, WILLIAM CAMERON (1896-1957), American film director, producer, and set designer **21** 291-293

Meor Ha-Golah
see Gershom ben Judah

MERCATOR, GERHARDUS (1512-1594), Flemish cartographer **10** 511-512

MERCHANT, ISMAIL (Ismail Noor Mohammed Abdul Rehman; 1936-2005), Indian filmmaker **26** 252-254

MERCKX, EDDY (Edouard Louis Joseph Merckx; born 1945), Belgian cyclist **28** 241-243

MEREDITH, GEORGE (1828-1909), English novelist and poet **10** 512-513

MEREDITH, JAMES H. (born 1933), African American civil rights activist and politician **10** 514-515

MEREZHKOVSKY, DMITRY SERGEYEVICH (1865-1941), Russian writer and literary critic **10** 515-516

MERGENTHALER, OTTMAR (1854-1899), German-American inventor of the Linotype **10** 516-517

MERIAN, MARIA SIBYLLA (1647-1717), German artist and entomologist **20** 268-269

MERICI, ANGELA (St. Angela; 1474-1530), Italian nun and educator **21** 293-295

MÉRIMÉE, PROSPER (1803-1870), French author **10** 517

Merisi, Michelangelo
see Caravaggio

MERKEL, ANGELA (Angela Dorothea Kasner; born 1954), German politician **28** 243-245

MERLEAU-PONTY, MAURICE (1908-1961), French philosopher **10** 518

Merlotti, Claudio
see Merulo, Claudio

MERMAN, ETHEL (Ethel Agnes Zimmermann; 1909-1984), American singer and actress **21** 295-297

Merovingian dynasty
see France—481-751

MERRIAM, CHARLES EDWARD (1874-1953), American political scientist **10** 518-519

MERRILL, CHARLES E. (1885-1956), founder of the world's largest brokerage firm **10** 519-520

MERRILL, JAMES (1926-1995), American novelist, poet, and playwright **10** 521-522

MERTON, ROBERT K. (1910-2003), American sociologist and educator **10** 522-523

MERTON, THOMAS (1915-1968), Roman Catholic writer, social critic, and spiritual guide **10** 523-525

MERULO, CLAUDIO (1533-1604), Italian composer, organist, and teacher **10** 525-526

MESMER, FRANZ ANTON (1734-1815), German physician **10** 526-527

MESSALI HADJ (1898-1974), founder of the Algerian nationalist movement **10** 527-528

MESSERSCHMITT, WILLY (Wilhelm Emil Messerschmitt; 1898-1978), German aircraft designer and manufacturer **25** 291-293

MESSIAEN, OLIVIER (1908-1992), French composer and teacher **10** 528-529

MESSNER, REINHOLD (born 1944), Austrian mountain climber and author **22** 316-318

METACOM (a.k.a. King Philip; 1640-1676), Wampanoag cheiftain **10** 529-531

METCALFE, CHARLES THEOPHILUS (1st Baron Metcalfe; 1785-1846), British colonial administrator **10** 531-532

METCHNIKOFF, ÉLIE (1845-1916), Russian physiologist and bacteriologist **10** 532-533

METHODIUS, SAINT (825-885), Greek missionary and bishop **4** 362-363

Metro-Goldwyn-Mayer (film studio)
Hanna and Barbera **28** 156-159
Sheldon, Sidney **28** 323-325

Metsys, Quentin
see Massys, Quentin

METTERNICH, KLEMENS VON (1773-1859), Austrian politician and diplomat **10** 533-536

Meun, Jean de
see Jean de Meun

Mexican music
Ponce, Manuel **28** 282-284

MEYERBEER, GIACOMO (1791-1864), German composer **10** 536-537

MEYERHOF, OTTO FRITZ (1884-1951), German biochemist **10** 537-539

MEYERHOLD, VSEVOLOD EMILIEVICH (1874-c. 1942), Russian director **10** 539

MFUME, KWEISI (born Frizzell Gray; born 1948), African American civil rights activist and congressman **10** 539-542

MGM
see Metro-Goldwyn-Mayer (film studio)

MI FEI (1051-1107), Chinese painter, calligrapher, and critic **11** 12-13

MICAH (flourished 8th century B.C.), prophet of ancient Israel **10** 542-543

MICHAEL VIII (Palaeologus; 1224/25-1282), Byzantine emperor 1259-1282 **11** 1-2

Michel, Claude
see Clodion

MICHELANGELO BUONARROTI (1475-1564), Italian sculptor, painter, and architect **11** 2-5

MICHELET, JULES (1798-1874), French historian **11** 5-6

MICHELOZZO (circa 1396-1472), Italian architect and sculptor **11** 6-7

MICHELSON, ALBERT ABRAHAM (1852-1931), American physicist **11** 7-8

MICHENER, JAMES (1907-1997), American author **19** 245-247

MICKIEWICZ, ADAM BERNARD (1798-1855), Polish poet **27** 263-265

MIDDLETON, THOMAS (1580-1627), English playwright **11** 8-9

MIDGELY, MARY BURTON (born 1919), British philosopher who focused on the philosophy of human motivation and ethics **11** 9-10

MIES VAN DER ROHE, LUDWIG (1886-1969), German-born American architect **11** 10-12

Mihna
    see Islam—Mihna

MIKAN, GEORGE (1924-2005), American basketball player **21** 297-299

MIKULSKI, BARBARA (born 1936), United States senator from Maryland **11** 13-15

MILÁN, LUIS (circa 1500-after 1561), Spanish composer **11** 15-16

MILES, NELSON APPLETON (1839-1925), American general **11** 16-17

MILHAUD, DARIUS (born 1892), French composer and teacher **11** 17-18

Military leaders, Bulgarian
    Simeon, King of Bulgaria **28** 325-327

Military leaders, Indian (Asian)
    Singh, Gobind **28** 327-328

Military leaders, Lebanese
    Gemayel, Bashir **28** 136-138

Military leaders, Roman
    military emperors
        Galerius, Emperor of Rome **28** 132-134

MILIUKOV, PAVEL NIKOLAYEVICH (1859-1943), Russian historian and statesman **11** 18-19

MILK, HARVEY BERNARD (1930-1978), American politician and gay rights activist **11** 19-21

MILKEN, MICHAEL (born 1946), American businessman **19** 247-249

MILL, JAMES (1773-1836), Scottish philosopher and historian **11** 21

MILL, JOHN STUART (1806-1873), English philosopher and economist **11** 21-23

MILLAIS, SIR JOHN EVERETT (1829-1896), English painter **11** 23-24

MILLAY, EDNA ST. VINCENT (1892-1950), American lyric poet **11** 24-25

MILLER, ARTHUR (1915-2005), American playwright, novelist, and film writer **11** 25-26

MILLER, GLENN (Alton Glenn Miller; 1904-1944), American musician **19** 250-251

MILLER, HENRY (born 1891), American author **11** 26-27

MILLER, JOAQUIN (1837-1913), American writer **11** 27-28

MILLER, PERRY (1905-1963), American historian **11** 28-29

MILLER, SAMUEL FREEMAN (1816-1890), American jurist **11** 29-30

MILLER, WILLIAM (1782-1849), American clergyman **11** 30-31

MILLES, CARL WILHELM EMIL (1875-1955), Swedish sculptor **24** 260-263

MILLET, JEAN FRANÇOIS (1814-1875), French painter **11** 31

MILLET, KATE (born 1934), American feminist author and sculptor **11** 31

MILLIKAN, ROBERT ANDREWS (1868-1953), American physicist **11** 33-35

MILLS, BILLY (Makata Taka Hela; born 1938), Native American runner and businessman **19** 251-253

MILLS, C. WRIGHT (1916-1962), American sociologist and political polemicist **11** 35-36

MILLS, ROBERT (1781-1855), American architect **11** 36-37

MILNE, ALAN ALEXANDER (A.A. Milne; 1882-1956), British author **19** 253-254

MILNE, DAVID BROWN (1882-1953), Canadian painter and etcher **11** 37-38

MILNE, JOHN (1850-1913), English seismologist **28** 245-247

MILNER, ALFRED (1st Viscount Milner; 1854-1925), British statesman **11** 38-39

MILOSEVIC, SLOBODAN (1941-2006), president of Serbia **11** 39-40

MILOSZ, CZESLAW (1911-2004), Nobel Prize winning Polish author and poet **11** 40-42

MILTIADES (circa 549-488 B.C.), Athenian military strategist and statesman **11** 42-43

MILTON, JOHN (1608-1674), English poet and controversialist **11** 43-46

MIN (1851-1895), Korean queen **11** 46-47

MINDON MIN (ruled 1852-1878), Burmese king **11** 47

MINDSZENTY, CARDINAL JÓZSEF (1892-1975), Roman Catholic primate of Hungary **11** 47-49

MINETA, NORMAN YOSHIO (born 1931), Asian American government official **25** 293-295

MINGUS, CHARLES, JR. (1922-1979), African American jazz musician **26** 254-256

Minh, Duong Van
    see Duong Van Minh

MINK, PATSY TAKEMOTO (1927-2003), Asian American congresswoman **18** 287-289

MINNELLI, LIZA (born 1946), American entertainer **26** 256-259

MINTZ, BEATRICE (born 1921), American embryologist **11** 49-50

MINUIT, PETER (1580-1638), Dutch colonizer **11** 50

MIRABAI (Meera Bai; 1498-1547), Indian poet and mystic **24** 263-265

MIRABEAU, COMTE DE (Honoré Gabriel Victor de Riqueti; 1749-1791), French statesman and author **11** 51-52

MIRANDA, CARMEN (Maria do Carmo Miranda da Cunha; 1909-1955), Brazilian singer and actress **26** 259-261

MIRANDA, FRANCISCO DE (1750-1816), Latin American patriot **11** 52-53

Mirandola, Pico della
    see Pico della Mirandola

MIRÓ, JOAN (1893-1983), Spanish painter **11** 53-54

MIRREN, HELEN (Ilyene Lydia Mironoff; born 1945), British actress **28** 247-249

Mirza Malkam Khan
    see Malkam Khan, Mirza

Mises, Dr.
    see Fechner, Gustav Theodor

MISHIMA, YUKIO (1925-1970), Japanese novelist and playwright **11** 54-55

Mrs. Beeton's Book of Household Management
    Beeton, Isabella Mary **28** 34-36

Mr. Tsungli Yaman
see Wen-hsiang

MISTRAL, FREDERIC (1830-1914), French author and philologist **25** 295-297

MISTRAL, GABRIELA (1889-1957), Chilean poet and educator **11** 55-56

MITCHELL, BILLY (1879-1936), American military officer and aviator **20** 269-272

MITCHELL, EDGAR DEAN (born 1930), American astronaut **22** 318-320

MITCHELL, GEORGE JOHN (born 1933), Maine Democrat and majority leader in the United States Senate **11** 56-58

Mitchell, Helen Porter
see Melba, Nellie

MITCHELL, JOHN (1870-1919), American labor leader **11** 58-59

MITCHELL, JONI (Roberta Joan Anderson; born 1943), Canadian American singer **23** 246-248

MITCHELL, MARGARET (Munnerlyn; 1900-1949), American author of Gone With the Wind **11** 59-60

MITCHELL, MARIA (1818-1889), American astronomer and educator **11** 61

MITCHELL, WESLEY CLAIR (1874-1948), American economist **11** 61-62

MITRE, BARTOLOMÉ (1821-1906), Argentine historian and statesman, president 1862-1868 **11** 62-63

MITTERRAND, FRANÇOIS (born 1916), French politician and statesman and president (1981-1990) **11** 63-66

MIYAKE, ISSEY (born 1938), Japanese fashion designer **25** 297-299

MIYAZAKI HAYAO (born 1941), Japanese filmmaker and artist **28** 249-252

MIZOGUCHI, KENJI (1898-1956), Japanese film director **23** 248-250

MIZRAHI, ISAAC (born 1961), American designer **11** 66-67

MLADIC, RATKO (born 1943), Bosnian Serb military leader **11** 68-69

MOBUTU SESE SEKO (Joseph Désiré Mobuto; 1930-1997), Congolese president **11** 69-71

Mo-chieh
see Wang Wei

MODEL, LISETTE (nee Lisette Seyberg; c. 1906-1983), American photographer and educator **19** 254-256

MODERSOHN-BECKER, PAULA (1876-1907), German painter **11** 71-72

MODIGLIANI, AMEDEO (1884-1920), Italian painter and sculptor **11** 72-73

MODIGLIANI, FRANCO (1918-2003), Italian American economist **24** 265-267

MOFFETT, WILLIAM ADGER (1869-1933), American naval officer **21** 299-301

MOFOLO, THOMAS (1876-1948), Lesothoan author **11** 74

MOGILA, PETER (1596/1597-1646), Russian Orthodox churchman and theologian **11** 74-75

Mogul empire
see India—1000-1600

MOHAMMAD REZA SHAH PAHLAVI (1919-1980), king of Iran **11** 75-76

MOHAMMED (circa 570-632), founder of Islam **11** 76-78

Mohammed II (1432-1481)
see Mehmed the Conqueror

MOHAMMED V (Mohammed Ben Youssef; 1911-1961), king of Morocco **11** 79-81

Mohammed Ahmed
see Mahdi, The

MOHAMMED ALI (1769-1849), Ottoman pasha of Egypt 1805-1848 **11** 81-82

Mohammed Ben Youssef
see Mohammed V

MOHOLY-NAGY, LÁSZLÓ (1895-1946), Hungarian painter and designer **11** 82-83

Mohr
see Marx, Karl

MOI, DANIEL ARAP (born Daniel Toroitich arap Moi; born 1924), president of Kenya **11** 83-86

MOITESSIER, BERNARD (1925-1994), French sailor and author **28** 252-254

MOLIÈRE (1622-1673), French dramatist **11** 86-88

Molina, Rafael Leonidas Trujillo
see Trujillo Molina, Rafael Leonidas

MOLINARI, SUSAN K. (born 1958), American newscaster **18** 289-291

MOLINOS, MIGUEL DE (1628-1696), Spanish priest **11** 88-89

MOLOTOV, VYACHESLAV MIKHAILOVICH (1890-1986), Soviet statesman **11** 89-90

MOLTKE, COUNT HELMUTH KARL BERNARD VON (1800-1891), Prussian military leader **11** 90-91

MOLTMANN, JÖURGEN (born 1926), German Protestant theologian **11** 91-92

Molucca Islands
see Spice Islands (Indonesia)

MOMADAY, N. SCOTT (born 1934), Native American author **11** 92-94

MOMMSEN, THEODOR (1817-1903), German historian and philologist **11** 94-95

Momoyama Period
see Japan—1573-1603

MOMPOU, FREDERIC (Federico Mompou i Dencausse; 1893-1987), Spanish composer **26** 261-263

MONAGHAN, TOM (Thomas Stephen Monaghan; born 1937), American businessman and philanthropist **19** 256-258

MONASH, JOHN (1865-1931), Australian soldier, engineer, and administrator **11** 95-96

MONCK, GEORGE (1st Duke of Albemarle; 1608-1670), English general and statesman **11** 96-97

MONDALE, WALTER F. (Fritz; born 1928), United States senator and vice president **11** 97-99

MONDAVI, ROBERT (born 1913), American winemaker **19** 258-260

MONDLANE, EDUARDO CHIVAMBO (1920-1969), Mozambican educator and nationalist **11** 100-101

MONDRIAN, PIET (1872-1944), Dutch painter **11** 101-102

MONET, CLAUDE (1840-1926), French painter **11** 102-104

Monet, Jean Baptiste Pierre Antoine de
see Lamarck, Chevalier de

MONGKUT (Rama IV; 1804-1868), king of Thailand 1851-1868 **11** 104

Monk, George
see Monck, George

MONK, MEREDITH (born 1942), American composer, entertainer, and critic **26** 263-265

MONK, THELONIOUS (1917-1982), African American jazz musician **11** 104-108

MONMOUTH AND BUCCLEUGH, DUKE OF (James Scott; 1649-1685), English claimant to the throne **11** 108-109

MONNET, JEAN (1888-1979), French economist and diplomat **11** 109-110

MONOD, JACQUES (1910-1976), French biologist who discovered messenger RNA **11** 110-111

Monophthalmos
see Antigonus I

MONROE, JAMES (1758-1831), American diplomat and statesman, president 1817-1825 **11** 111-113

MONROE, MARILYN (Norma Jean Baker; 1926-1962), film actress **11** 113-114

MONTAGNIER, LUC (born 1932), French virologist **11** 114-116

MONTAGU, ASHLEY (Israel Ehrenberg; 1905-1999), British-born American anthroplogist and author **22** 320-322

MONTAGU, JOHN, FOURTH EARL OF SANDWICH (1718-1792), English politician and first lord of the admiralty **21** 301-303

MONTAGU, MARY WORTLEY (1689-1762), English poet **18** 291-293

MONTAIGNE, MICHEL EYQUEM DE (1533-1592), French essayist **11** 116-117

MONTALE, EUGENIO (1896-1981), Italian poet and critic **11** 117-118

MONTALEMBERT, COMTE DE (Charles Forbes; 1810-1870), French political writer **11** 118-119

Montalte, Louis de
see Pascal, Blaise

MONTALVO, JUAN MARÍA (1832-1889), Ecuadorian writer **11** 119-120

MONTANA, JOE (born 1956), American football player **11** 120-121

MONTANUS (flourished 2nd century), Early Christian founder of schismatic sect **11** 122

MONTCALM DE SAINT-VÉRAN, MARQUIS DE (1712-1759), French general in Canada **11** 122-123

Montcorbier, François de
see Villon, François

MONTEFIORE, MOSES (1784-1885), English Zionist and philanthropist **20** 272-274

Montenevoso, Principe di
see D'Annunzio, Gabriele

Montereau, Pierre de
see Montreuil, Pierre de

MONTES, ISMAEL (Ismael Montes Gamboa; 1861-1933), president of Bolivia **24** 267-270

MONTESQUIEU, BARON DE (Charles Louis de Secondat; 1689-1755), French man of letters **11** 123-125

MONTESSORI, MARIA (1870-1952), Italian educator and physician **11** 125-126

MONTEVERDI, CLAUDIO GIOVANNI ANTONIO (1567-1643), Italian composer **11** 126-128

MONTEZUMA I (Motecuhzoma I; Moctezuma I; 1397-1469), Aztec ruler **22** 322-324

MONTEZUMA II (c. 1466-1520), Aztec emperor 1502-1520 **11** 128-129

MONTEZUMA, CARLOS (born Wassaja; ca. 1865-1923), Native American physician and political leader **11** 129-132

MONTFORT, SIMON DE (6th Earl of Leicester; 1208-1265), English statesman and soldier **11** 132-133

MONTGOLFIER, JACQUES ÉTIENNE (1745-1799), French inventor and industrialist **11** 133-134

MONTGOLFIER, JOSEPH MICHEL (1740-1810), French inventor and industrialist **11** 133-134

MONTGOMERY, BERNARD LAW (1st Viscount Montgomery of Alamein; born 1887), English field marshal **11** 135-136

MONTGOMERY, LUCY MAUD (1874-1942), Canadian author **11** 136-138

MONTGOMERY, RICHARD (1736-1775), colonial American general **11** 138-139

Montini, Giovanni Battista
see Paul VI

Montreuil, Eudes and Gerbert de
see Montreuil, Pierre de

MONTREUIL, PIERRE DE (flourished circa 1231-1266/67), French architect **11** 139

MONTT TORRES, MANUEL (1809-1880), Chilean statesman, president 1851-1861 **11** 139-140

Monumental sculpture
Bartholdi, Frédéric-Auguste **28** 29-31

MOODIE, SUSANNA (1803-1885), Canadian poet, novelist, and essayist **11** 140-141

MOODY, DWIGHT L. (1837-1899), American evangelist **11** 141-142

MOOG, ROBERT (1934-2005), American inventor **26** 265-267

Moomintrolls (fictional characters)
Jansson, Tove Marika **28** 187-189

MOON, SUN MYUNG (born 1920), founder of the Unification Church **11** 142-143

Moor, the
see Sforza, Ludovico

Moore, Carry Amelia
see Nation, Carry Amelia Moore

MOORE, CHARLES WILLARD (1925-1993), American architect and educator **11** 143-145

MOORE, CHARLOTTE E. (1898-1990), American astrophysicist **11** 145-146

MOORE, GEORGE EDWARD (1873-1958), English philosopher **11** 146

MOORE, HENRY (1898-1986), English sculptor **11** 146-148

MOORE, MARIANNE (1887-1972), American poet and translator **11** 148-149

MOORE, MICHAEL (born 1954), American author and filmmaker **25** 299-302

MOORE, THOMAS (1779-1852), Irish Poet, essayist, and composer **28** 254-256

MORAES, VINICIUS DE (Marcus Vinicius da Cruz de Mello Moraes; 1913-1980), Brazilian songwriter and author **26** 268-269

MORALES, LUIS DE (circa 1519-1586), Spanish painter **11** 150

MORALES-BERMÚDEZ CERRUTI, FRANCISCO (born 1921), president of Peru (1975-1980) **11** 150-151

MORAN, THOMAS (1837-1926), American painter and graphic artist **11** 151-152

MORANDI, GIORGIO (1890-1964), Italian painter of still lifes **11** 152-153

MORAVIA, ALBERTO (1907-1990), Italian author **11** 153-155

MORAZÁN, JOSÉ FRANCISCO (1792-1842), Central American general and statesman **11** 155

MORE, SIR THOMAS (1478-1535), English humanist and statesman **11** 156-157

MOREAU, GUSTAVE (1826-1898), French artist and professor **22** 324-326

MORELOS, JOSÉ MARÍA (1765-1815), Mexican priest and revolutionary leader **11** 157-158

Moreno, Gabriel García
see García Moreno, Gabriel

MORENO, MARIANO (1778-1811), Argentine revolutionary **20** 274-275

MORGAGNI, GIOVANNI BATTISTA (1682-1771), Italian anatomist **11** 158-159

MORGAN, ANN HAVEN (Anna Haven Morgan; 1882-1966), American ecologist and teacher **24** 270-271

MORGAN, CONWAY LLOYD (1852-1936), English psychologist **11** 159-160

MORGAN, DANIEL (circa 1735-1802), American soldier and tactician **11** 160-161

MORGAN, GARRETT A. (1877-1963), African American inventor and publisher **11** 161-162

MORGAN, JOHN (1735-1789), American physician **11** 162-163

MORGAN, JOHN PIERPONT (1837-1913), American banker **11** 163-165

MORGAN, JOHN PIERPONT, II (1867-1943), American banker **11** 165

MORGAN, JULIA (1872-1957), American architect **11** 165-166

MORGAN, JUNIUS SPENCER (1813-1890), American banker **11** 166-167

MORGAN, LEWIS HENRY (1818-1881), American anthropologist **11** 167-168

MORGAN, ROBIN (born 1941), feminist writer, editor, poet, and political activist **11** 168-170

MORGAN, THOMAS HUNT (1866-1945), American zoologist and geneticist **11** 170-171

MORGENTHAU, HANS J. (1904-1979), American political scientist **11** 171-172

MORGENTHAU, HENRY, JR. (1891-1967), American statesman **11** 172-173

MORIN, PAUL (1889-1963), French-Canadian poet **11** 174

MORÍNIGO, HIGINIO (1897-1985), Paraguayan statesman **11** 174-175

MORISON, SAMUEL ELIOT (1887-1976), American historian and biographer **11** 175-176

MORISOT, BERTHE (1841-1895), French painter **21** 303-305

MORITA, AKIO (born 1921), Japanese industrial leader **11** 176-178
Ibuka, Masaru **28** 184-186

MORLEY, JOHN (Viscount Morley of Blackburn; 1838-1923), English statesman and author **11** 178-179

MORLEY, THOMAS (circa 1557-1602/08), English composer and organist **11** 179-180

Mormons (religious sect)
Marriott, J. Willard **28** 232-234

Morning Star (Northern Cheyenne tribal leader)
see Dull Knife

MORO, ALDO (1916-1978), leader of Italy's Christian Democratic Party **11** 180-181

MORRICE, JAMES WILSON (1865-1924), Canadian painter **11** 181-182

MORRILL, JUSTIN SMITH (1810-1898), American legislator **11** 182

MORRIS, GOUVERNEUR (1752-1816), American statesman and diplomat **11** 182-183

MORRIS, LEWIS (1671-1746), American colonial official **11** 183-184

MORRIS, MARK (born 1956), American choreographer **11** 184-185

MORRIS, ROBERT (1734-1806), American financer and statesman **11** 185-187

MORRIS, WILLIAM (1834-1896), English man of letters, artist, and politician **11** 187-188

MORRISON, JIM (James Douglas Morrison; 1943-1971), American singer and songwriter **18** 293-295

MORRISON, TONI (Chloe Anthony Wofford; born 1931), African American novelist **11** 188-190

Morrow, Anne Spencer
see Lindbergh, Anne Morrow

MORROW, DWIGHT WHITNEY (1873-1931), American banker and diplomat **11** 190-191

MORSE, JEDIDIAH (1761-1826), American geographer and clergyman **11** 191-192

MORSE, SAMUEL FINLEY BREESE (1791-1872), American artist and inventor **11** 192-193

MORSE, WAYNE L. (1900-1974), United States senator from Oregon **11** 193-194

Mortimer, Earl
see Harley, Robert

MORTIMER, JOHN CLIFFORD (born 1923), British author of novels, stories, and plays for radio, stage, television, and film **11** 194-195

MORTON, JELLY ROLL (Ferdinand Joseph La Menthe; 1885-1941), African American musician **24** 272-274

MORTON, NELLE KATHERINE (1905-1987), activist for racial justice, teacher of Christian educators, and

proponent of feminist theology **11** 195-197

MORTON, OLIVER HAZARD PERRY THROCK (1823-1877), American politician **11** 197-198

MORTON, WILLIAM THOMAS GREEN (1819-1868), American dentist **11** 198-199

MOSELY-BRAUN, CAROL (born 1947), African American Democratic senator from Illinois **11** 199-200

MOSES (circa 1392-circa 1272 B.C.), Hebrew prophet and lawgiver **11** 200-201

MOSES, EDWIN (born 1955), African American track and field star **20** 275-277

MOSES, GRANDMA (Anna Mary Robertson; 1860-1961), American painter **11** 201-202

MOSES, ROBERT (1888-1981), New York City's builder of public works **11** 202-203

Moses ben Maimon
see Maimonides

Moses ben Nahman
see Nahmanides

MOSHWESHWE (Moshesh; circa 1787-1868), South African king **11** 203-205

Moskowa, Prince of the
see Ney, Michel

MOSQUERA, TOMÁS CIPRIANO DE (1798-1878), Colombian statesman **11** 205-206

MOSSADEGH, MOHAMMAD (Musaddiq; 1882-1967), Iranian nationalist politician and prime minister (1951-1953) **11** 206-207

MÖSSBAUER, RUDOLF (born 1929), German physicist **11** 208-209

Mother Jones
see Jones, Mary Harris

Mother Teresa
see Teresa

Motherwell, Mrs. Robert
see Frankenthaler, Helen

MOTHERWELL, ROBERT (1915-1991), American painter **11** 210-211

Motion pictures (Asia)
Miyazaki Hayao **28** 249-252

Motion pictures (Europe)
Chabrol, Claude **28** 67-69
Frears, Stephen Arthur **28** 127-129
McKellen, Ian Murray **28** 234-237
Mirren, Helen **28** 247-249
Nykvist, Sven **28** 261-263
Romm, Mikhail **28** 303-304

film critics
Bazin, André **28** 32-33

Motion pictures (Russia)
Starewicz, Wladyslaw **28** 336-338

Motion pictures (United States)
cinematographers
Nykvist, Sven **28** 261-263
comedy
Roach, Hal **28** 290-292
film stars
McKellen, Ian Murray **28** 234-237
Mirren, Helen **28** 247-249
filmmakers
Frears, Stephen Arthur **28** 127-129
Roach, Hal **28** 290-292
silents
Lawrence, Florence **28** 209-211

MOTLEY, CONSTANCE BAKER (1921-
2005), African American judge and
attorney **18** 295-297

MOTLEY, JOHN LOTHROP (1814-1877),
American historian and diplomat **11**
211-212

MOTLEY, WILLARD FRANCIS (1909-
1965), African American author **22**
326-328

Motokiyo, Zeami
see Zeami, Kanze

Motorola Company
Cooper, Martin **28** 85-87

MOTT, JOHN R. (1865-1955), American
Protestant leader **11** 212

MOTT, LUCRETIA COFFIN (1793-1880),
American feminist and abolitionist **11**
212-213

MOUNT, WILLIAM SIDNEY (1807-
1868), American painter **11** 213-214

MOUNTAIN WOLF WOMAN
(Kéhachiwinga; Wolf's Mountain
Home Maker; Haksigaxunuminka;
1884-1960), Winnebago
autobiographer **26** 269-272

**MOUNTBATTEN, LOUIS FRANCIS
ALBERT VICTOR NICHOLAS** (1900-
1979), English Navy officer and
viceroy of India **18** 297-299

MOYERS, BILLY DON (''Bill''; born
1934), television journalist, author, and
press secretary to president Lyndon B.
Johnson **11** 214-216

MOYNIHAN, DANIEL PATRICK (''Pat'';
1927-2003), United States senator from
New York **11** 216-218

MOZART, WOLFGANG AMADEUS
(1756-1791), Austrian composer **11**
218-221

Mozee, Phoebe Anne Oakley
see Oakley, Annie

MPHAHLELE, EZEKIEL (a.k.a. Bruno
Eseki; born 1919), South African
author and scholar **11** 221-223

MQHAYI, SAMUEL EDWARD KRUNE
(1875-1945), South African novelist
and poet **11** 223

MUAWIYA IBN ABU SUFYAN (died
680), Umayyad caliph **11** 223-224

MUBARAK, HOSNI (born 1928),
president of Egypt **11** 225-226

MUELLER, OTTO (1874-1930), German
expressionist painter **11** 226-227

Mufti of Jerusalem
see Husagni, Al-Hajj Amin Al-

MUGABE, ROBERT GABRIEL (born
1924), Zimbabwe's first elected black
prime minister **11** 227-229

MUHAMMAD ALI PASHA (Mehmet Ali
Pasha; Muhammad Ali; 1769-1849),
Ottoman Turkish ruler of Egypt **27**
265-267

MUHAMMAD, ELIJAH (Poole; 1897-
1975), leader of the Nation of Islam
(''Black Muslims'') **11** 230-231

MUHAMMAD BIN TUGHLUQ (ruled
1325-1351), Moslem sultan of Delhi
11 229

Muhammad ibn Daud
see Alp Arslan

Muhammad Shah (1877-1957)
see Aga Khan III

MUHAMMAD TURE, ASKIA (circa 1443-
1538), ruler of the West African
Songhay empire **11** 231-232

Muhibbi
see Suleiman I

MÜHLENBERG, HEINRICH MELCHIOR
(1711-1787), German-born American
Lutheran clergyman **11** 232-233

MUHLENBERG, WILLIAM AUGUSTUS
(1796-1877), American Episcopalian
clergyman **11** 233-234

MUIR, JOHN (1838-1914), American
naturalist **11** 234

MUJIBUR RAHMAN, SHEIK (1920-
1975), Bengal leader who helped
found Bangladesh **11** 234-236

MUKERJI, DHAN GOPAL (1890-1936),
Indian author and Hindu priest **22**
328-330

MULDOWNEY, SHIRLEY (born ca.
1940), American race car driver **11**
236-238

MULLER, HERMANN JOSEPH (1890-
1967), American geneticist **11** 238-239

Müller, Johann
see Regiomontanus

MÜLLER, JOHANNES PETER (1801-
1858), German physiologist and
anatomist **11** 239-240

MÜLLER, KARL ALEXANDER (born
1927), Swiss-born solid-state physicist
11 240-241

MÜLLER, PAUL HERMANN (1899-1965),
Swiss chemist **11** 241-242

MULRONEY, MARTIN BRIAN (born
1939), prime minister of Canada **11**
242-246

MUMFORD, LEWIS (1895-1990),
American social philosopher and
architectural critic **11** 246-247

Mun Sun
see Yi Hwang

MUNCH, EDVARD (1863-1944),
Norwegian painter and graphic artist
11 247-248

MUNDELEIN, GEORGE WILLIAM (1872-
1939), American Roman Catholic
cardinal **11** 248-249

Mundinus
see Luzzi, Mondino de'

Munitions
see Weapons and explosives

MUÑOZ MARÍN, JOSÉ LUÍS ALBERTO
(1898-1980), Puerto Rican political
leader **11** 249-250

MUÑOZ RIVERA, LUÍS (1859-1916),
Puerto Rican political leader **11** 250

MUNSEY, FRANK ANDREW (1854-
1925), American publisher **11** 251

MÜNZER, THOMAS (1489?-1525),
German Protestant reformer **11**
251-252

MURASAKI SHIKIBU (circa 976-circa
1031), Japanese writer **11** 252-253

MURAT, JOACHIM (1767-1815), French
marshal, king of Naples 1808-1815 **11**
253-254

MURATORI, LODOVICO ANTONIO
(1672-1750), Italian historian and
antiquary **11** 254-255

MURCHISON, SIR RODERICK IMPEY
(1792-1871), British geologist **11**
255-256

MURDOCH, JEAN IRIS (1919-1999),
British novelist **11** 256-257

MURDOCH, RUPERT (born 1931),
Australian newspaper publisher **11**
257-258

MURILLO, BARTOLOMÉ ESTEBAN
(1617-1682), Spanish painter **11**
258-259

Murjebi, Hamed bin Mohammed el
see Tippu Tip

MURNAU, F.W. (Friedrich Wilhelm Plumpe; 1888-1913), German film director **22** 330-332

Muromachi shogunate
see Japan—1338-1573 (Ashikaga shogunate)

MURPHY, AUDIE (1924-1971), American army officer and actor **18** 299-301

MURPHY, CHARLES FRANCIS (1858-1924), American politician **11** 259-260

MURPHY, FRANK (1890-1949), American jurist and diplomat **11** 260-261

MURRAY, ANNE (Morna Anne Murray; born 1945), Canadian singer **27** 267-269

MURRAY, ARTHUR (Arthur Murray Teichman; 1895-1991), American dance school founder **27** 269-271

MURRAY, GILBERT (George Gilbert Aime Murray; 1886-1957), English scholar **23** 250-253

MURRAY, JAMES (1721-1794), British general **11** 261-262

Murray, John (1732-1809)
see Dunmore, 4th Earl of

MURRAY, JOSEPH (born 1919), American physician **18** 301-303

MURRAY, LESLIE ALLAN (born 1938), Australian poet and literary critic **11** 262-263

MURRAY, PAULI (Anna Pauline Murray; 1910-1985), African American/Native American civil right activist and priest **23** 253-256

MURRAY, PHILIP (1886-1952), American labor leader **11** 264-265

MURRAY, WILLIAM (Lord Mansfield; 1705-1793), English judge **23** 256-258

MURROW, EDWARD ROSCOE (1908-1965), American radio and television news broadcaster **11** 265-266

MUSA MANSA (died 1337), king of the Mali empire in West Africa ca. 1312-1337 **11** 266

MUSGRAVE, THEA (born 1928), Scottish-born composer **11** 266-268

MUSHARRAF, PERVEZ (born 1943), Pakistani head of sate **22** 332-335

MUSIAL, STAN (Stanislaus Musial, Stanley Frank Musial; born 1920), American baseball **19** 260-262

Music
education
Roach, Max **28** 292-296

experimental forms
Zawinul, Joe **28** 389-391
recording of
Haefliger, Ernst **28** 152-154
Lipatti, Dinu **28** 222-223
Ormandy, Eugene **28** 264-266
Paul, Les **28** 276-278

Musicians, American
composers (20th century)
Roach, Max **28** 292-296
conductors
Ormandy, Eugene **28** 264-266
crooners
Vallee, Rudy **28** 359-361
drummers
Roach, Max **28** 292-296
guitarists
Paul, Les **28** 276-278
jazz singers
Anderson, Ivie Marie **28** 10-12
pianists
Rubinstein, Arthur **28** 305-307
preservation of the works of
Lomax, John Avery **28** 224-225
singers
Vallee, Rudy **28** 359-361
songwriters
Paul, Les **28** 276-278

Musicians, Austrian
composers (20th century)
Zawinul, Joe **28** 389-391
keyboardists
Zawinul, Joe **28** 389-391

Musicians, Belgian
Sax, Adolphe **28** 316-318

Musicians, English
composers (19th-20th century)
Coleridge-Taylor, Samuel **28** 80-83
conductors
Coleridge-Taylor, Samuel **28** 80-83
musicologists
Sharp, Cecil **28** 321-323

Musicians, French
composers (19th-20th century)
Viardot, Pauline **28** 363-365
opera singers
Viardot, Pauline **28** 363-365

Musicians, German
conductors
Sawallisch, Wolfgang **28** 314-316
pianists
Sawallisch, Wolfgang **28** 314-316

Musicians, Irish
Moore, Thomas **28** 254-256

Musicians, Jewish
Karp, Natalia **28** 192-194

Musicians, Mexican
Ponce, Manuel **28** 282-284

Musicians, Norwegian
Bull, Ole **28** 54-56

Musicians, Paraguayan
Barrios, Agustin Pio **28** 27-29

Musicians, Peruvian
Granda, Chabuca **28** 143-144

Musicians, Polish
Karp, Natalia **28** 192-194
Rubinstein, Arthur **28** 305-307
Szymanowska, Maria **28** 340-342

Musicians, Portuguese
Rodrigues, Amália **28** 301-302

Musicians, Romanian
Lipatti, Dinu **28** 222-223

Musicians, Russian
singers
Vysotsky, Vladimir **28** 367-369
songwriters
Vysotsky, Vladimir **28** 367-369
support for
Viardot, Pauline **28** 363-365

Musicians, Swiss
Haefliger, Ernst **28** 152-154

Musicians, Vietnamese
Son, Trinh Cong **28** 335-336

MUSIL, ROBERT EDLER VON (1880-1942), Austrian novelist, dramatist, and short story writer **11** 268-269

MUSKIE, EDMUND SIXTUS (1914-1996), United States senator and Democratic vice-presidential nominee **11** 269-271

MUSSET, LOUIS CHARLES ALFRED DE (1810-1857), French poet, dramatist, and fiction writer **11** 271-272

MUSSOLINI, BENITO (1883-1945), Italian Fascist dictator 1922-1943 **11** 272-274

MUSSORGSKY, MODEST PETROVICH (1839-1881), Russian composer **11** 274-276

Mustapha Kemal
see Atatürk, Kemal

MUSTE, ABRAHAM JOHANNES (1885-1967), American pacifist and labor leader **11** 276-277

MUTESA I (circa 1838-1884), African monarch of Buganda **11** 277

MUTESA II (1924-1969), Monarch of Buganda **11** 277-278

MUTIS, JOSÉ CELESTINO (1732-1808), Spanish-Colombian naturalist **11** 278-279

MUTSUHITO (a.k.a. Meiji; 1852-1912), Japanese emperor **11** 279-282

MUYBRIDGE, EADWEARD (1830-1904), English photographer **21** 305-308

MWANGA (circa 1866-1901), Monarch of Buganda **11** 282-283

MYDANS, CARL (1907-2004), American photojournalist **11** 283-284

Myerson, Golda
see Meir, Golda

Myongsong Hwanghu
see Min

MYRDAL, ALVA (1902-1986), Swedish social reformer and diplomat **24** 274-276

MYRDAL, KARL GUNNAR (1898-1987), Swedish economist and sociologist **11** 284

MYRON (flourished circa 470-450 B.C.), Greek sculptor **11** 285

Mysteries of Udolpho, The (book) Radcliffe, Ann **28** 288-290

Mystery fiction (literary genre) Baroness Orczy **28** 25-27 Fisher, Rudolph **28** 121-123

MZILIKAZI (circa 1795-1868), South African warrior leader **11** 285-286

N

NABOKOV, VLADIMIR (1899-1977), Russian-born American writer, critic, and lepidopterist **11** 287-288

NABUCO DE ARAUJO, JOAQUIM AURELIO (1849-1910), Brazilian abolitionist, statesman, and author **11** 288-289

NADELMAN, ELIE (1882-1946), Polish-American sculptor and graphic artist **11** 289-290

NADER, RALPH (born 1934), American lawyer and social crusader **11** 290-291

NADIR SHAH (born Nadir Kouli; 1685-1747), Emperor of Persia **20** 278-281

NAGEL, ERNEST (1901-1985), American philosopher of science **11** 291-292

NAGUMO, CHUICHI (1887-1944), Japanese admiral **19** 263-266

NAGURSKI, BRONKO (Bronislaw Nagurski; 1908-1990), Canadian football player **21** 309-311

NAGY, IMRE (1896-1958), prime minister of Hungary (1953-55, 1956) **11** 292-293

NAHMANIDES (1194-1270), Spanish Talmudist **11** 293-294

NAIDU, SAROJINI (1879-1949), Indian poet and nationalist **11** 294-295

NAIPAUL, V. S. (born 1932), Trinidadian author of English-language prose **11** 295-296

NAISMITH, JAMES (1861-1939), Canadian inventor of basketball **21** 311-313

NAJIBULLAH, MOHAMMAD (born 1947), Soviet-selected ruler of the Republic of Afghanistan **11** 296-298

NAKASONE, YASUHIRO (born 1918), prime minister of Japan (1982-1987) **11** 298-300

Nakayama
see Sun Yat-sen

Naked Needle, A (book) Farah, Nuruddin **28** 114-116

NAMATJIRA, ALBERT (1902-1959), Australian Aboriginal artist **11** 300-301

NAMIER, SIR LEWIS BERNSTEIN (1888-1960), English historian **11** 301-303

NAMPEYO (Numpayu; Tsumana; circa 1859-1942), Hopi-Tewa potter **25** 303-306

NANAK (1469-1538), Indian reformer, founder of Sikhism **11** 303

NANSEN, FRIDTJOF (1861-1930), Norwegian polar explorer, scientist, and statesman **11** 304-305

NAOROJI, DADABHAI (1825-1917), Indian nationalist leader **11** 305

NAPIER, JOHN (1550-1617), Scottish mathematician **11** 306

NAPOLEON I (1769-1821), emperor of the French 1804-1815 **11** 306-310

NAPOLEON III (Louis Napoleon; 1808-1873), emperor of the French 1852-1870 **11** 310-312

Napoleon Bonaparte
see Napoleon I

NARAYAN, JAYAPRAKASH (1902-1979), Indian nationalist and social reformer **11** 312-313

NARAYAN, R. K. (Narayanswami; born 1906), Indian author **11** 313-314

NARIÑO, ANTONIO (1765-1823), Colombian patriot **11** 314-315

NARVÁEZ, PÁNFILO DE (1478?-1528), Spanish soldier and explorer **11** 315

NASH, JOHN (1752-1835), English architect and town planner **11** 316

NASH, JOHN FORBES, JR. (born 1928), American mathematician **22** 336-338

NASH, OGDEN (Frediric Ogden Nash; 1902-1971), American poet **18** 304-306

Nasier, Alcofribas
see Rabelais, François

NASMYTH, JAMES (1808-1890), Scottish engineer and inventor **11** 316-317

Naso, Publius Ovidius
see Ovid

NASSER, GAMAL ABDEL (1918-1970), Egyptian statesman, president 1956-1970 **11** 317-318

NAST, CONDÉ (1873-1942), American publisher **19** 266-268

NAST, THOMAS (1840-1902), American caricaturist and painter **11** 318-319

NATHAN, GEORGE JEAN (1882-1958), American author, editor, and critic **11** 319-321

NATION, CARRY AMELIA MOORE (1846-1911), American temperance reformer **11** 321-322

National Broadcasting Company (NBC) Brainard, Bertha **28** 47-48

National Inventors Hall of Fame Hall, Lloyd Augustus **28** 154-156 Paul, Les **28** 276-278

Nationalism, Asian
India
Savarkar, Vinayak Damodar **28** 312-314

Native Americans (North American) culture
Castaneda, Carlos **28** 62-64

NATIVIDAD, IRENE (born 1948), Asian American activist and women's rights advocate **11** 322-324

NATSUME, SOSEKI (or Kinnosuke; 1867-1916), Japanese novelist and essayist **11** 324-325

Naturalism (literature)
Norway
Skram, Amalie **28** 331-333

NAUMAN, BRUCE (born 1941), American artist **23** 259-261

NAVRATILOVA, MARTINA (born 1956), American tennis player **11** 325-327

NAYLOR, GLORIA (born 1950), African American novelist **11** 328-329

Nazem al-Doleh (al-Molk)
see Malkam Khan, Mirza

NAZZAM, IBRAHIM IBN SAYYAR AL- (died circa 840), Moslem thinker and theologian **11** 329

NBC
see National Broadcasting Co.

N'DOUR, YOUSSOU (born 1959), Senegalese musician **22** 338-340

NE WIN (1911-2002), Burmese political leader **11** 364-365

NEAL, PATRICIA (Patsy Louise Neal; born 1926), American actress **19** 268-270

NEBUCHADNEZZAR (ruled 605-562 B.C.), king of Babylon **11** 330

Necker, Anne Louise Germaine
see Staël, Germaine de

NECKER, JACQUES (1732-1804), French financier and statesman **11** 330-331

NEEL, ALICE (Alice Hartley Neel; 1900-1984), American artist **23** 261-263

NEFERTITI (flourished first half 14th century B.C.), Egyptian queen **11** 331-332

NEGULESCO, JEAN (1900-1993), Romanian film director **24** 277-279

NEHRU, JAWAHARLAL (1889-1964), Indian nationalist, prime minister 1947-1964 **11** 332-334

NEHRU, MOTILAL (1861-1931), Indian lawyer and statesman **11** 334-335

Nehru, Swarup Kumari
see Pandit, Vijaya Lakshmi

NEILL, ALEXANDER SUTHERLAND (1883-1973), Scottish psychologist **11** 335-336

NEILSON, JOHN SHAW (1872-1942), Australian author **22** 340-342

NELSON, HORATIO (Viscount Nelson; 1758-1805), English admiral **11** 336-338

NELSON, RICK (Eric Hillard Nelson; 1940-1985), American musician and actor **21** 314-316

NELSON, WILLIE (Willie Hugh Nelson; born 1933), American singer and songwriter **25** 306-308

NEMCOVA, BOZENA (Barbora Panklova), Czech author **25** 308-310

NEMEROV, HOWARD (1920-1991), American author and third poet laureate of the United States **11** 338-340

NEMIROVICH-DANCHENKO, VLADIMIR IVANOVICH (1858-1943), Russian dramatist **24** 279-281

Neper, John
see Napier, John

NERI, ST. PHILIP (1515-1595), Italian reformer **11** 340

NERNST, WALTHER (born Hermann Walther Nernst; 1864-1941), German chemist and inventor **11** 340-342

NERO CLAUDIUS CAESAR (37-68), Roman emperor 54-68 **11** 342-344

NERUDA, PABLO (Neftalí Ricardo Reyes Basoalto; 1904-73), Chilean poet, Nobel prize winner 1971 **11** 344-345

NERVAL, GÉRARD DE (1808-1855), French poet **11** 345-346

NERVI, PIER LUIGI (1891-1979), Italian architect and engineer **11** 346-348

NESBIT, E(DITH) (Edith Nesbit Bland; Fabian Bland; 1885-1924), English author and activist **23** 263-265

NESSELRODE, COUNT KARL ROBERT (1780-1862), Russian diplomat **11** 348-349

NESTOR, AGNES (1880-1948), American labor leader and lobbyist **26** 273-275

NESTORIUS (died circa 453), Syrian patriarch of Constantinople and heresiarch **11** 349-350

Netaji (führer)
see Bose, Subhas Chandra

NETANYAHU, BINYAMIN (born 1949), Israeli ambassador to the United Nations (1984-1988), head of the Likud Party, and prime minister **11** 350-351

Netherlands, Kingdom of (nation; Europe)
and immigration to
Fortuyn, Pim **28** 125-127
since World War II
Fortuyn, Pim **28** 125-127

NETO, ANTÓNIO AGOSTINHO (1922-1979), Angolan intellectual and nationalist and first president of the People's Republic of Angola **11** 351-352

NEUFELD, ELIZABETH F. (born 1928), American biochemist **11** 352-353

NEUMANN, BALTHASAR (1687-1753), German architect **11** 354-355

Neurobiology
Axelrod, Julius **28** 18-20

Neuropathology (medicine)
Meduna, Ladislas J. **28** 237-238

Neurophysiology (science)
Meduna, Ladislas J. **28** 237-238

Neustadt International Prize for Literature
Farah, Nuruddin **28** 114-116

NEUTRA, RICHARD JOSEPH (1892-1970), Austrian-born American architect **11** 355-356

NEVELSON, LOUISE (1900-1988), American abstract sculptor **11** 356-357

NEVERS, ERNIE (Ernest Alonzo Nevers; 1903-1976), American athlete **20** 281-283

Neville, Richard
see Warwick and Salisbury, Earl of

NEVIN, JOHN WILLIAMSON (1803-1886), American Protestant theologian **11** 357

NEVINS, ALLAN (1890-1971), American historian **11** 357-359

NEVSKY, ALEXANDER (ca. 1220-1262), Russian grand duke and prince **11** 359

New Amsterdam
see New York City (New York State)

New Wave (French filmmaking)
Chabrol, Claude **28** 67-69

New York City (New York State)
• MODERN PERIOD
architecture
Hine, Lewis Wickes **28** 172-174
mayors
Bloomberg, Michael **28** 40-42

NEWBERY, JOHN (1713-1767), English publisher **11** 360-361

NEWCOMB, SIMON (1835-1909), American astronomer **11** 361-362

NEWCOMEN, THOMAS (1663-1729), English inventor and engineer **11** 362

NEWHOUSE, SAMUEL IRVING (1895-1979), American media tycoon **11** 362-364

NEWMAN, BARNETT (1905-1970), American painter **11** 365

NEWMAN, JOHN HENRY (1801-1890), English cardinal and theologian **11** 365-367

NEWMAN, PAUL LEONARD (born 1925), American actor and humanitarian **18** 306-308

NEWTON, HUEY P. (born 1942), co-founder of the Black Panther Party **11** 367-369

NEWTON, SIR ISAAC (1642-1727), English scientist and mathematician **11** 369-372

NEXØ, MARTIN ANDERSON (1869-1954), Danish author **11** 372

NEY, MICHEL (1769-1815), French marshal **11** 372-373

Neyra, Álvaro de Mendaña de
see Mendaña de Neyra, Álvaro de

NEYMAN, JERZY (1894-1981), American statistician **21** 316-318

NGALA, RONALD GIDEON (1923-1972), Kenyan politician **11** 373-374

NGATA, SIR APIRANA TURUPA (1874-1950), Maori leader, politician, and scholar **11** 374-375

Ngengi, Johnstone Kamau
see Kenyatta, Jomo

NGOR, HAING S. (circa 1947-1996), Cambodian American actor and human rights activist **25** 310-312

NGOYI, LILLIAN (1911-1980), South African civil rights activist **20** 283-284

NGUGI WA THIONG'O (James Ngugi; born 1938), Kenyan writer **11** 375-376

Nguyen Ali Quoc (Nguyen That Thanh) see Ho Chi Minh

NI TSAN (1301-1374), Chinese painter **11** 400

Niagara (musical composition) Bull, Ole **28** 54-56

NICHIREN (1222-1282), Japanese Buddhist monk **11** 376-377

NICHOLAS I (1796-1855), czar of Russia 1825-1855 **11** 377-378

NICHOLAS II (1868-1918), czar of Russia 1894-1917 **11** 378-380 Grand Duchess Olga Nikolaevna **28** 141-143

NICHOLAS V (Tommaso Parentucelli; 1397-1455), Italian pope 1447-1455 **26** 299-300

Nicholas of Cusa see Cusa, Nicholas of

NICHOLAS OF ORESME (circa 1320-1382), French bishop, writer and translator **11** 380

NICHOLAS, SAINT (Santa Claus; died 345), Lycian bishop **20** 284-285

NICHOLSON, BEN (1894-1982), English painter **11** 380-381

NICHOLSON, SIR FRANCIS (1655-1728), English colonial governor **11** 381-382

NICKLAUS, JACK (born 1940), American golfer **11** 382-383

Nicknames
Agent Zigzag
Chapman, Eddie **28** 69-72
Biograph girl
Lawrence, Florence **28** 209-211
black Edison
Woods, Granville T. **28** 378-381
earthquake Milne
Milne, John **28** 245-247
father of Prozac Nation
Axelrod, Julius **28** 18-20
father of the mobile phone
Cooper, Martin **28** 85-87
Little Flower of Jesus
Thérèse of Lisieux, Saint **28** 347-350
Mr. Lebanon
Hariri, Rafic **28** 161-163
mother of chemotherapy
Wright, Jane Cooke **28** 383-385
papa flash
Edgerton, Harold Eugene **28** 109-111
Sissi
Elisabeth, Empress of Austria **28** 111-113
the hugging saint
Amma **28** 8-10

Nicola Pisano
see Pisano, Nicola

NICHOLS, MIKE (Michael Igor Peschkowsky; born 1931), American film and theater director and producer **20** 285-288

NICOLSON, HAROLD GEORGE (1886-1968), British diplomat, historian, biographer, critic and journalist, and diarist **11** 383-384

NICOLSON, MARJORIE HOPE (1894-1981), American educator **11** 384-385

NICOMACHUS OF GERASA (circa 60-circa 100), Greek mathematician, philosopher, and musical theorist **25** 312-314

NIDETCH, JEAN (born 1927), founder of Weight Watchers **21** 318-320

NIEBUHR, BARTHOLD GEORG (1776-1831), German historian and statesman **11** 385-386

NIEBUHR, HELMUT RICHARD (1894-1962), American Protestant theologian **11** 386-387

NIEBUHR, REINHOLD (1892-1971), American Protestant theologian **11** 387-388

NIELSEN, CARL AUGUST (1865-1931), Danish composer **11** 388-389

NIEMEYER SOARES FILHO, OSCAR (born 1907), Brazilian architect **11** 389-390

NIETZSCHE, FRIEDRICH (1844-1900), German philosopher and poet **11** 390-392
associates
Andreas-Salomé, Lou **28** 12-14
influence (philosophy)
Deleuze, Gilles **28** 94-96

NIGHTINGALE, FLORENCE (1820-1910), English nurse **11** 392-393

NIJINSKY, VASLAV (1890-1950), Russian ballet dancer **11** 393-395

NIKON, NIKITA MINOV (1605-1681), patriarch of the Russian Orthodox Church 1652-1666 **11** 395

NIMITZ, CHESTER WILLIAM (1885-1966), American admiral **11** 395-396

NIN, ANAIS (1903-1977), American author **11** 397-398

NIN-CULMELL, JOAQUÍN MARÍA (born 1908), American composer, pianist, and conductor **11** 398

Nine Days of One Year (film) Romm, Mikhail **28** 303-304

NIRENBERG, MARSHALL WARREN (born 1927), American biochemist **11** 399-400

Nirvani, Carma
see Kazantzakis, Nikos

NIWANO, NIKKYO (Shikazo Niwano; born 1906), Buddhist Japanese religious leader **11** 400-401

NIXON, RICHARD MILHOUS (1913-1994), president of the United States (1969-1974) **11** 401-404
associates
Marriott, J. Willard **28** 232-234

Niza, Marcos de
see Marcos de Niza, Friar

NIZAMI, KHALIQ AHMAD (born 1925), Indian historian, religious scholar, and diplomat **11** 405

NKOMO, JOSHUA MQABUKO (1917-1999), leading African nationalist in former colony of Rhodesia and president of the Zimbabwe African People's Union **11** 405-407

NKOSI, LEWIS (born 1936), South African author and literary critic **11** 407-408

NKRUMAH, KWAME (Francis Nwa Nkrumah; 1909-1972), Ghanaian statesman, president 1960-1966 **11** 408-410

NOBEL, ALFRED BERNHARD (1833-1896), Swedish chemist **11** 410-411

Nobel Prize winners
literature
Pamuk, Orhan **28** 269-272
peace
Yunus, Muhammad **28** 386-388
physiology and medicine
Axelrod, Julius **28** 18-20
Laveran, Alphonse **28** 207-209
Mello, Craig Cameron **28** 238-241

NOBILE, UMBERTO (1885-1978), Italian explorer and airship designer **11** 411-412

NOBUNAGA, ODA (1534-1582), Japanese general and statesman **11** 413-414

Noech'on
see Kim Pusik

NOETHER, EMMY (born Amalie Emmy Noether; 1882-1935), German American mathematician **11** 414-416

NOGUCHI, ISAMU (1904-1988), American sculptor and designer **11** 416-418

NOLAN, SIDNEY ROBERT (1917-1992), Australian expressionist painter **11** 418

NOLAND, KENNETH (born 1924), American color-field painter **11** 418-419

NOLDE, EMIL (1867-1956), German expressionist painter **11** 419-420

NONO, LUIGI (1924-1990), Italian composer **11** 420-421

NOONUCCAL, OODGEROO (Kath Wlaker; Kathleen Jean Mary Ruska; 1920-1993), Australian Aboriginal poet **27** 272-274

NOOYI, INDRA KRISHNAMURTHY (born 1955), Indian-American business woman **27** 274-276

NORDENSKJÖLD, BARON NILS ADOLF ERIK (1832-1901), Finnish-Swedish polar explorer and mineralogist **11** 421-422

NORDENSKOLD, NILS OTTO GUSTAF (1869-1928), Swedish polar explorer and geologist **11** 422-423

NORDSTROM, JOHN (Johan W. Nordstrom; 1871-1963), American shoe retailer **19** 270-272

NORFOLK, 3D DUKE OF (Thomas Howard; 1473-1554), English soldier and councilor **11** 423

NØRGÅRD, PER (born 1932), Danish composer **23** 265-267

NORIEGA, MANUEL A. (born 1934), strongman of Panama (1980s) forced out in 1989 by the United States **11** 423-425

NORMAN, JESSYE (born 1945), American singer **11** 425-427

Normandy, Duke of
see Charles V(king of France)

NORRIS, BENJAMIN FRANKLIN, JR. (1870-1902), American novelist and critic **11** 427-428

NORRIS, GEORGE WILLIAM (1861-1944), American statesman **11** 428-429

NORTH, FREDERICK (2nd Earl of Guilford; 1732-1792), English statesman **11** 429-430

NORTH, MARIANNE (1830-1890), English naturalist and painter **23** 268-270

NORTHROP, JOHN HOWARD (1891-1987), American biological chemist **11** 430-431

NORTHUMBERLAND, DUKE OF (John Dudley; circa 1502-1553), English soldier and statesman **11** 431-432

NORTON, ANDRE (Alice Mary Norton; 1912-2005), American science fiction and fantasy writer **28** 257-259

Norwegian literature
Skram, Amalie **28** 331-333

Norwegian music
Bull, Ole **28** 54-56

NOSTRADAMUS (born Michel de Notredame; 1503-1566), French physician, astrologist, and author **11** 432-434

Notation (music)
see Music—notation

Notker Balbulus
see Balbulus, Notker

Novak, Joseph
see Kosinsky, Jerzy

NOVALIS (1772-1801), German poet and author **11** 435

Novanglus
see Adams, John

NOVELLO, ANTONIA (Antonia Coello; born 1944), Puerto Rican American pediatrician **18** 308-310

NOYCE, ROBERT (1927-1990), American physicist and inventor **11** 436-437
Hoff, Ted **28** 176-178

NOYES, JOHN HUMPHREY (1811-1886), American founder of the Oneida Community **11** 437-438

NOZICK, ROBERT (1938-2002), American philosopher and polemical advocate of radical libertarianism **11** 438-439

N'si Yisrael
see Bar Kochba, Simeon

NU, U (1907-1995), Burmese statesman **11** 439-441

NUJOMA, SHAFIIHUNA ("Sam"; born 1929), first president of independent Namibia **11** 441-443

Nukada-be, Princess
see Suiko

Núñez de Balboa, Vasco
see Balboa, Vasco Núñez de

NUNN, SAM (born 1938), United States senator from Georgia **11** 443-444

Nur-ad-Din
see Nureddin

Nur al-Din Abd al-Rahman, Maulana
see Jami

NUREDDIN (Malik al-Adil Nur-al-Din Mahmud; 1118-1174), sultan of Syria and Egypt **11** 444-445

NUREYEV, RUDOLPH (born 1938), Russian-born dancer and choreographer **11** 445-446

NURI AL-SA'ID (1888-1958), Iraqi army officer, statesman, and nationalist **11** 446-447

NURMI, PAAVO (1897-1973), Finnish runner **19** 272-274

Nurse, Malcolm Ivan Meredith
see Padmore, George

NURSÎ, SAID (Bediüzzaman Said Nursî; 1876-1960), Turkish theologian **28** 259-261

NUSSLEIN-VOLHARD, CHRISTIANE (born 1942), German biologist **25** 314-316

Nutrition (diet)
Cheyne, George **28** 74-76

Nuvolara, Count of
see Castiglione, Baldassare

NYE, GERALD (1892-1971), American senator **21** 320-323

NYERERE, JULIUS KAMBERAGE (born 1922), Tanzanian statesman **11** 447-449

NYGREN, ANDERS (1890-1978), Lutheran bishop of Lund and representative of the so-called Lundensian school of theology **11** 449-451

NYKVIST, SVEN (Sven Vilhelm Nykvist; 1922-2006), Swedish cinematographer **28** 261-263

NZINGA, ANNA (Pande Dona Ana Souza; 1582-1663), queen of Angola **23** 270-271

Nzinga Mvemba
see Affonso I

NZINGA NKUWU (died 1506), king of Kongo **11** 451-452

O

OAKLEY, ANNIE (1860-1926), American markswoman and Wild West star **11** 453-454

OATES, JOYCE CAROL (born 1938), American author **11** 454-456

OATES, TITUS (1649-1705), English leader of the Popish Plot **11** 456

OBOTE, APOLO MILTON (1925-2005), Ugandan politician **11** 457

OBRADOVIĆ, DOSITEJ (Dimitrije Dositej Obradović 1740?-1811), Serbian author and educator **24** 282-284

OBRECHT, JACOB (1450-1505), Dutch composer **11** 457-458

OBREGÓN, ÀLVARO (1880-1928), Mexican revolutionary general and president **11** 458-459

O'BRIEN, WILLIS (1886-1962), American film special effects pioneer **21** 324-326

Obscure, the
see Heraclitus

O'CASEY, SEAN (1880-1964), Irish dramatist **11** 459-460

Occam, William of
see William of Ockham

OCHOA, ELLEN (born 1958), Hispanic American electrical engineer and astronaut **11** 460-461

OCHOA, SEVERO (1905-1993), Spanish biochemist **11** 461-464

OCHS, ADOLPH SIMON (1858-1935), American publisher and philanthropist **11** 464

OCKEGHEM, JOHANNES (circa 1425-1495), Netherlandish composer **11** 464-465

O'CONNELL, DANIEL (1775-1847), Irish statesman **11** 465-467

O'CONNOR, CARROLL (1924-2001), American actor **22** 343-345

O'CONNOR, JOHN JOSEPH (1920-2000), American Roman Catholic cardinal and archbishop **22** 345-347

O'CONNOR, (MARY) FLANNERY (1925-1964), American author of short stories and novels **11** 467-468

O'CONNOR, SANDRA DAY (born 1930), United States Supreme Court justice **11** 468-470

Octavian (Octavianus, Octavius)
see Augustus

ODETS, CLIFFORD (1906-1963), American playwright and film director **11** 470-471

ODINGA, AJUMA JARAMOGI OGINGA (born 1912), Kenyan politician **11** 471-473

ODOACER (433-493), Germanic chieftain **11** 473

ODRIÁ AMORETTI, MANUEL APOLINARIO (1897-1974), Peruvian army officer, dictator-president, and politician **11** 473-474

ODUM, HOWARD WASHINGTON (1884-1954), American sociologist, educator, and academic administrator **11** 474-476

ODUMEGWU OJUKWU, CHUKWUEMEKA (born 1933), Nigerian army general and rebel **18** 311-313

OE, KENZABURO (born 1935), Japanese author **24** 284-286

OERSTED, HANS CHRISTIAN (1777-1851), Danish physicist **11** 476-478

OERTER, AL (Alfred Adolph Oerter Jr.; 1936-2007), American discus thrower **21** 326-328

OFFENBACH, JACQUES (1819-1880), German-French composer **11** 478-479

OGATA, SADAKO (born 1927), United Nations High Commissioner for Refugees **11** 479-480

OGBURN, WILLIAM FIELDING (1886-1959), American sociologist **11** 480

OGDEN, PETER SKENE (1794-1854), Canadian fur trader and explorer **11** 480-481

OGILVY, DAVID MACKENZIE (1911-1999), British-American advertising executive **11** 481-482

OGLETHORPE, JAMES EDWARD (1696-1785), English general and colonizer **11** 482-483

OGOT, GRACE EMILY AKINYI (born 1930), Kenyan author and politician **11** 483-484

O'HAIR, MADALYN MURRAY (born 1919), American atheist author and radio commentator **11** 484-485

O'HARA, JOHN (1905-1970), American novelist **11** 485

O'HIGGINS, BERNARDO (1778-1842), Chilean soldier and statesman **11** 486

OHM, GEORG SIMON (1789-1854), German physicist **11** 486-487

Oil industry
pipelines and refineries
Lukasiewicz, Ignacy **28** 225-227
Poland
Lukasiewicz, Ignacy **28** 225-227

O'KEEFFE, GEORGIA (1887-1986), American painter **11** 487-489

OKUBO, TOSHIMICHI (1830-1878), Japanese statesman **11** 489-490

OKUMA, SHIGENOBU (1838-1922), Japanese statesman **11** 490

OKYO, MARUYAMA (1733-1795), Japanese artist **23** 272-274

OLAF I TRYGGVASON (968-1000), Viking warrior and king of Norway **11** 490-493

OLAF II (circa 990-1030), king of Norway **11** 493-494

Olaf, St.
see Olaf II

OLATUNJI, MICHAEL BABATUNDE (1927-2003), Nigerian musician and educator **27** 277-279

OLBRICH, JOSEPH MARIA (1867-1908), Austrian Art Nouveau architect and a founder of the Vienna Secession **11** 494-495

Old Arrow-Maker and His Daughter (The Wooing of Hiawatha), The (sculpture)
Lewis, Edmonia **28** 215-217

Old Devils, The (book)
Amis, Kingsley **28** 5-8

OLDENBARNEVELT, JOHAN VAN (1547-1619), Dutch statesman **11** 495-496

OLDENBURG, CLAES (born 1929), American artist **11** 496-498

OLDS, RANSOM ELI (1864-1950), American inventor and automobile manufacturer **18** 313-315

OLIPHANT, MARK (Markus Laurence Elwin Oliphant; 1901-2000), Australian scientist and activist **27** 279-281

OLIPHANT, PATRICK BRUCE (born 1935), American newspaper editorial cartoonist **11** 498-500

OLIVER, JAMES (1823-1908), American inventor and manufacturer **11** 500-501

OLIVETTI, ADRIANO (1901-1960), Italian manufacturer of typewriters, calculators, and computers **11** 501-502

OLIVIER, LAURENCE (1907-1989), English actor and director **11** 502-503

OLLER, FRANCISCO MANUEL (1833-1917), Puerto Rican artist **23** 274-275

OLMSTED, FREDERICK LAW (1822-1903), American landscape architect **11** 503-504

OLNEY, RICHARD (1835-1917), American statesman **11** 504-505

OLSEN, TILLIE (nee Tillie Lerner; 1913-2007), American author **20** 289-291

OLSON, CHARLES (1910-1970), American poet **11** 505-506

OLYMPIO, SYLVANUS E. (1902-1963), first president of the Republic of Togo **11** 506-507

OMAR AL-MUKHTAR (circa 1860-1931), national hero of Libya and member of the Senusy **11** 507-508

OMAR IBN AL-KHATTAB (died 644), second caliph of the Moslems **11** 508-509

OMAR IBN SAID TAL, AL-HAJJ (circa 1797-1864), West African Moslem leader **11** 509-510

OMAR KHAYYAM (1048-circa 1132), Persian astronomer, mathematician, and poet **11** 510-511

ONASSIS, ARISTOTLE (Aristotle Socrates Onassis; 1906-1975), Greek shipping tycoon **24** 286-288

ONASSIS, JACQUELINE LEE BOUVIER KENNEDY (1929-1994), American First Lady **11** 511-513

OÑATE, JUAN DE (circa 1549-circa 1624), Spanish explorer **11** 513-514

ONDAATJE, MICHAEL (Philip Michael Ondaatji; born 1943), Canadian author and poet **18** 315-317

O'NEIL, BUCK (John Jordan "Buck" O'Neil; 1911-2006), African American baseball player **27** 281-283

O'NEILL, EUGENE (1888-1953), American dramatist **11** 514-516

O'NEILL, TERENCE MARNE (1914-1990), Northern Ireland prime minister **11** 516-517

O'NEILL, THOMAS P. ("Tip"; 1912-1994), American politician **11** 517-519

ONG TENG CHEONG (1936-2002), Singapore's fifth president **11** 519-520

ONIZUKA, ELLISON (Ellison Shoji Onizuka; 1946-1986), American Astronaut **25** 317-319

ONSAGER, LARS (1903-1976), American chemist **11** 520-523

OORT, JAN HENDRIK (1900-1992), Dutch astronomer **11** 523-524

Opera (musical form)
    as focus of comedy routines
        Russell, Anna **28** 307-309
    German
        Sawallisch, Wolfgang **28** 314-316

Opera, French
    19th century
        Taglioni, Marie **28** 345-347
        Viardot, Pauline **28** 363-365

OPHÜLS, MAX (Max Oppenheimer; 1902-1957), German film director and screenwriter **23** 275-277

OPPENHEIM, MERET (1913-1985), Swiss Surrealist artist **11** 524-525

OPPENHEIMER, ERNEST (1880-1957), British South African businessman **24** 288-290

OPPENHEIMER, J. ROBERT (1904-1967), American physicist **11** 525-526

Oral Roberts University
    Roberts, Oral **28** 296-298

ORCAGNA (c. 1308-c. 1368), Italian painter, sculptor, and architect **11** 526-527

Ordóñez, José Battle y
    see Batlle y Ordóñez, José

ORELLANA, FRANCISCO DE (circa 1511-1546), Spanish explorer **11** 527-528

ORFF, CARL (1895-1982), German musician **26** 276-278

Orford, 1st Earl of
    see Walpole, Robert

ORIGEN (Origenes Adamantius; circa 185-circa 254), Early Christian theologian **11** 528-529

ORLANDO, VITTORIO EMMANUELE (1860-1952), Italian statesman **11** 529-530

ORLÉANS, CHARLES (1394-1465), French prince and poet **11** 530

ORLÉANS, PHILIPPE II (1674-1723), French statesman, regent 1715-23 **11** 530-531

ORMANDY, EUGENE (Jenö Blau; Jenö B. Ormándy; 1899-1985), American conductor **28** 264-266

OROZCO, JOSÉ CLEMENTE (1883-1949), Mexican painter **12** 1-2

ORR, BOBBY (Robert Gordon Orr; born 1948), Canadian hockey player **12** 2-4

ORR, JOHN BOYD (1st Baron Orr of Brechin; 1880-1971), Scottish nutritionist and UN official **12** 4-5

ORTEGA, DANIEL (born 1945), leader of the Sandinista National Liberation Front and president of Nicaragua **12** 5-7

ORTEGA, KATHERINE DAVALOS (born 1934), Hispanic American government official **25** 319-321

ORTEGA Y GASSET, JOSÉ (1883-1955), Spanish philosopher and essayist **12** 7-8

ORTELIUS, ABRAHAM (Abraham, Ortels; 1527-1598), Flemish cartographer **12** 8-9

Orthodox Eastern Church
    in Bulgaria
        Simeon, King of Bulgaria **28** 325-327

ORTIZ, ALFONSO ALEX (1939-1997), Native American anthropologist and activist **26** 278-280

ORTIZ, SIMON J. (born 1941), Native American author and storyteller **12** 9-12

ORTON, JOHN KINGSLEY ("Joe;" 1933-1967), British playwright **12** 12-14

ORWELL, GEORGE (1903-1950), British novelist and essayist **12** 14-15

Osagyefo
    see Nkrumah, Kwame

OSBORNE, JOHN (1929-1994), English playwright **12** 16-17

OSBORNE, THOMAS MOTT (1859-1926), American reformer **12** 17-18

OSCEOLA (circa 1800-1838), Seminole Indian war chief **12** 18

OSGOOD, HERBERT LEVI (1855-1918), American historian **12** 18-19

OSLER, SIR WILLIAM (1849-1919), Canadian physician **12** 19-20

OSMAN I (Othman; 1259-1326), Turkish warrior-leader who established the Ottoman state as an independent entity **12** 20-22

OSMEÑA, SERGIO (1878-1961), Philippine lawyer and statesman **12** 22-24

OSMOND, DONNY AND MARIE (Donald Clark Osmond; born 1957 and Olive Marie Osmond; born 1959), American singers **27** 283-285

OSTROVSKY, ALEXANDER (Alexander Nikolayevich Ostrocsky; 1823-1886), Russian playwright **26** 280-283

Oswald, F.
    see Engels, F.

OSWALD, LEE HARVEY (1939-1963), presumed assassin of John F. Kennedy **21** 328-330

OTIS, ELISHA GRAVES (1811-1861), American manufacturer and inventor **12** 24

OTIS, HARRISON GRAY (1765-1848), American statesman **12** 25

OTIS, JAMES, JR. (1725-1783), American Revolutionary statesman **12** 25-27

OTTERBEIN, PHILIP WILLIAM (1726-1813), American clergyman **12** 27-28

OTTO I (912-973), Holy Roman emperor 936-973 **12** 28-29

OTTO III (980-1002), Holy Roman emperor 996-1002 and German king 983-1002 **12** 29-30

OTTO, LOUIS KARL RUDOLF (1869-1937), German interpreter of religion **12** 30-32

OTTO, NIKOLAUS AUGUST (1832-1891), German engineer and inventor **21** 331-333

OTTO OF FREISING (circa 1114-1158), German historiographer and philosopher of history **12** 30

Otto the Great
    see Otto I

OUD, JACOBUS JOHANNES PIETER (1890-1963), Dutch architect **12** 32

OUGHTRED, WILLIAM (1574-1660), English mathematician **23** 277-279

OUSMANE, SEMBENE (1923-2007), Senegalese novelist and film maker **12** 32-33

OU-YANG HSIU (1007-1072), Chinese author and statesman **12** 33-34

OVID (Publius Ovidius Naso; 43 B.C. - circa. A.D. 18), Roman elegiac and epic poet **12** 34-36

OVINGTON, MARY WHITE (1865-1951), civil rights reformer and a founder of the National Association for the Advancement of Colored People **12** 36-37

Owain ap Gruffydd
see Glendower, O.

OWEN, DAVID ANTHONY LLEWELLYN (born 1938), English peace envoy in former Yugoslavia for the European Community **12** 37-39

OWEN, SIR RICHARD (1804-1892), English zoologist **12** 39

OWEN, ROBERT (1771-1858), British socialist pioneer **12** 39-40

OWEN, ROBERT DALE (1801-1877), Scottish-born American legislator **12** 40-41

OWEN, RUTH BRYAN (1885-1954), American congresswoman, diplomat, and author **12** 41-43

OWEN, WILFRED (1893-1918), English poet **20** 291-293

Owens, James Cleveland
see Owens, Jesse

OWENS, JESSE (1913-1980), African American track star **12** 43-44

OXENSTIERNA, COUNT AXEL GUSTAFSSON (1583-1654), Swedish statesman **12** 44-45

Oxford, 1st Earl of
see Harley, Robert

Oxford and Asquith, 1st Earl of
see Asquith, Herbert Henry

OYONO, FERDINAND LEOPOLD (born 1929), Cameroonian author and diplomat **24** 290-292

OZ, AMOS (born 1939), Israeli author **12** 45-47

OZAL, TURGUT (born 1927), Turkish prime minister and president **12** 47-49

OZAWA, SEIJI (born 1935), Japanese musician and conductor **12** 49-51

OZU, YASUJIRO (1903-1963), Japanese film director **23** 279-281

P

PA CHIN (pen name of Li Fei-kan; 1904-2005), Chinese novelist **12** 53-54

PAAR, JACK HAROLD (1918-2004), American comedian and radio personality **26** 284-286

PABST, G. W. (Georg Wilhelm Pabst; 1885-1967), Austrian film director **23** 282-284

Pacelli, Eugenio Maria Giuseppe
see Pius XII

Pacheco y Padilla, Juan Vicente Güemes
see Revillagigedo, Conde de

PACHELBEL, JOHANN (1653-1706), German composer and organist **12** 52

PACHER, MICHAEL (circa 1435-98), Austro-German painter and wood carver **12** 53

PACINO, AL (Alfredo James Pacino; born 1940), American actor and film director **23** 284-286

PACKARD, DAVID (1912-1996), cofounder of Hewlett-Packard Company and deputy secretary of defense under President Nixon **12** 54-56

PADEREWSKI, IGNACE JAN (1860-1941), Polish pianist, composer, and statesman **12** 56-57

PADMORE, GEORGE (1902/03-1959), Trinidadian leftist political activist **12** 57-58

PÁEZ, JOSÉ ANTONIO (1790-1873), Venezuelan general and president 1831-46 **12** 58

PAGANINI, NICCOLO (1782-1840), Italian violinist and composer **12** 58-59

PAGE, THOMAS NELSON (1853-1922), American author and diplomat **12** 59-60

PAGE, WALTER HINES (1855-1918), American journalist and diplomat **12** 60-61

PAGELS, ELAINE HIESEY (born 1943), historian of religion **12** 61-62

PAGLIA, CAMILLE (born 1947), American author and social critic **23** 286-288

PAIGE, SATCHEL (Leroy Robert Paige; 1906-1982), African American baseball player **12** 62-65

PAINE, JOHN KNOWLES (1839-1905), American composer **12** 65

PAINE, THOMAS (1737-1809), English-born American journalist and Revolutionary propagandist **12** 66-67

PAISLEY, IAN K. (born 1926), political leader and minister of religion in Northern Ireland **12** 67-69

Pak Chong-hŭi
see Park, Chung Hee

PALACKÝ, FRANTIŠEK (1798-1876), Czech historian and statesman **12** 69-70

PALAMAS, KOSTES (1859-1943), Greek poet **12** 70

Paleontology (science)
prehistoric man
Dubois, Eugène **28** 106-108

PALESTRINA, GIOVANNI PIERLUIGI DA (circa 1525-94), Italian composer **12** 70-72

PALEY, GRACE (1922-2007), American author and activist **22** 348-350

PALEY, WILLIAM (1743-1805), English theologian and moral philosopher **12** 72

PALEY, WILLIAM S. (1901-1990), founder and chairman of the Columbia Broadcasting System **12** 72-75

PALLADIO, ANDREA (1508-1580), Italian architect **12** 75-77

PALMA, RICARDO (1833-1919), Peruvian poet, essayist, and short-story writer **12** 77

PALME, OLOF (Sven Olof Joachim Palme; 1927-1986), Swedish prime minister (1969-1973; 1982-1986) **28** 267-269

PALMER, ALEXANDER MITCHELL (1872-1936), American politician and jurist **12** 77-78

PALMER, ARNOLD DANIEL (born 1929), American golfer **12** 78-80

PALMER, NATHANIEL BROWN (1799-1877), American sea captain **12** 80-81

PALMER, PHOEBE WORRALL (1807-1847), American evangelist **23** 288-290

PALMERSTON, 3D VISCOUNT (Henry John Temple; 1784-1865), English prime minister 1855-65 **12** 81-83

Pamfili, Giovanni Batista
see Innocent X

PAMUK, ORHAN (born 1952), Turkish novelist and Nobel Prize Winner **28** 269-272

PANINI (fl. ca. 5th century BCE), Indian grammarian **24** 293-295

PAN KU (32-92), Chinese historian and man of letters **12** 86-87

PANDIT, VIJAYA LAKSHMI (1900-1990), Indian diplomat and politician **12** 83-84

PANETTA, LEON E. (born 1938), Democratic congressman from California and chief of staff to President Clinton **12** 84-85

PANKHURST, CHRISTABEL HARRIETTE (1880-1948), English reformer and suffragette **22** 350-352

PANKHURST, EMMELINE (1858-1928), English reformer **12** 85-86

PANNENBERG, WOLFHART (born 1928), German Protestant theologian **12** 87-88

PANUFNIK, ANDRZEJ (1914-1991), Polish/British composer and conductor **24** 295-298

PAPANDREOU, ANDREAS (1919-1996), Greek scholar and statesman and prime minister **12** 88-91

PAPINEAU, LOUIS-JOSEPH (1786-1871), French-Canadian radical political leader **12** 91

PARACELSUS, PHILIPPUS AUREOLUS (1493-1541), Swiss physician and alchemist **12** 91-93

Parasitology (science) Laveran, Alphonse **28** 207-209

PARBO, ARVI (born 1926), Australian industrial giant **12** 93-94

PARÉ, AMBROISE (1510-1590), French military surgeon **12** 94-95

PARETO, VILFREDO (1848-1923), Italian sociologist, political theorist, and economist **12** 95-96

PARHAM, CHARLES FOX (1873-1929), American evangelist **23** 291-293

Paris Opera Taglioni, Marie **28** 345-347

Paris, Matthew see Matthew Paris

Paris, School of (art) see French art—School of Paris

PARIZEAU, JACQUES (born 1930), Canadian politician and premier of Quebec **12** 96-99

PARK, CHUNG HEE (1917-1979), Korean soldier and statesman **12** 99-102

PARK, MAUD WOOD (1871-1955), suffragist and first president of the League of Women Voters **12** 102

PARK, ROBERT E. (1864-1944), American sociologist **12** 102-104

PARK, WILLIAM HALLOCK (1863-1939), American physician **12** 104-105

PARKER, ARTHUR CASWELL (1881-1955), Native American anthropologist and museum administrator **26** 286-288

PARKER, CHARLES CHRISTOPHER, JR. (Charlie Parker; 1920-55), American jazz musician **12** 105-106

PARKER, DOROTHY ROTHSCHILD (1893-1967), American writer **12** 106

PARKER, ELY SAMUEL (Ha-sa-no-an-da; 1828-1895), Native American tribal leader **12** 106-108

PARKER, HORATIO WILLIAM (1863-1919), American composer **12** 109

PARKER, QUANAH (c. 1845-1911), Native American religious leader **12** 109-112

PARKER, THEODORE (1810-1860), American Unitarian clergyman **12** 112-113

PARKES, ALEXANDER (1813-1890), British metallurgist and inventor of plastic **21** 334-336

PARKES, SIR HENRY (1815-1896), Australian statesman **12** 113

PARKINSON, C. NORTHCOTE (Cyril Northcote Parkinson; 1909-1993), British historian and humorist **24** 298-300

PARKMAN, FRANCIS (1823-1893), American historian **12** 113-115

PARKS, GORDON (1912-2005), American photographer, composer, and filmmaker **19** 275-277

PARKS, ROSA LEE MCCAULEY (1913-2005), American civil rights leader **12** 115-116

Parma, Duke of see Charles III (king, Spain)

PARMENIDES (flourished 475 B.C.), Greek philosopher **12** 116-117

PARMIGIANINO (1503-1540), Italian painter **12** 117

PARNELL, CHARLES STEWART (1846-1891), Irish nationalist leader **12** 117-119

Parochial schools (United States) see Education (United States)

Parr, Catharine (1802-1899) see Traill, Catharine Parr

PARRINGTON, VERNON LOUIS (1871-1929), American historian **12** 119-120

PARSONS, SIR CHARLES ALGERNON (1854-1931), British engineer **12** 120-121

PARSONS, FRANK (1854-1908), American educator and reformer **12** 121-122

PARSONS, LOUELLA (Louella Oetlinger; 1881-1972), American gossip columnist **21** 336-338

PARSONS, LUCY GONZÁLEZ (1853-1942), Mexican American activist and author **23** 293-295

PARSONS, TALCOTT (1902-1979), American sociologist **12** 122

PÄRT, ARVO (born 1935), Estonian musician **23** 295-297

PARTON, DOLLY (Dolly Rebecca Parton; born 1946), American singer and songwriter **24** 300-302

PARTRIDGE, ERIC (Eric Honeywood Partridge; 1894-1979), New Zealander lexicographer **24** 302-304

PASCAL, BLAISE (1623-1662), French scientist and philosopher **12** 122-124

Pascuccio d'Antonio, Donato di see Bramante, Donato

PASHA, ENVER (1881-1922), Turkish soldier and Young Turk leader **5** 290-291

PASHA, TEWFIK (1852-1892), khedive of Egypt 1879-92 **15** 157-158

Passfield, Baron see Webb, Sidney James

PASTERNAK, BORIS LEONIDOVICH (1890-1960), Russian poet, novelist, and translator **12** 124-125

PASTEUR, LOUIS (1822-1895), French chemist and biologist **12** 125-127

Pasture, Rogelet de le see Weyden, Rogier van der

PATCHEN, KENNETH (1911-1972), American experimental poet and novelist **12** 128-129

PATEL, VALLABHBHAI (1875-1950), Indian political leader **12** 129-130

PATER, WALTER HORATIO (1839-1894), English author **12** 130-131

PATERNO, JOSEPH VINCENT (born 1926), American Football coach **25** 322-324

PATERSON, ANDREW BARTON (1864-1941), Australian folk poet **12** 131-132

PATERSON, WILLIAM (1745-1806), American jurist **12** 132-133

PATIÑO, SIMÓN ITURRI (1862-1947), Bolivian industrialist and entrepreneur **12** 133-134

PATON, ALAN STEWART (1903-1988), South African writer and liberal leader **12** 134-135

PATTERSON, LOUISE ALONE THOMPSON (Louise Alone Toles; Louise Thompson; 1901-1999), African American activist and literary secretary **28** 272-274
Thurman, Wallace Henry **28** 352-354

PATTERSON, TOM (Harry Thomas Patterson; 1920-2005), Canadian theatrical producer **28** 274-276

PATRICK, JENNIE R. (born 1949), African American chemical engineer **12** 136-137

PATRICK, RUTH (born 1907), American limnologist **12** 137-138

PATRICK, SAINT (died circa 460), British missionary bishop to Ireland **12** 135-136

PATTEN, SIMON NELSON (1852-1922), American economist **12** 138-139

PATTERSON, FREDERICK DOUGLAS (1901-1988), African American educator **12** 139-140

PATTON, GEORGE SMITH, JR. (1885-1945), American Army officer **12** 140-141

PAUL I (1754-1801), Russian czar 1796-1801 **12** 143-144

PAUL II (Pietro Barbo; 1417-1471), pope 1464-1471 **25** 324-326

PAUL III (Alessandro Farnese; 1468-1549), pope 1534-49 **12** 144-145

PAUL IV (Giampietro Carafa; 1476-1559), pope 1555-59 **12** 145-146

PAUL V (Camillo Borghese; 1550-1621), Italian pope **23** 297-299

PAUL VI (Giovanni Battista Montini; 1897-1978), pope **12** 146-148

PAUL, ALICE (1885-1977), American feminist and women's rights activist **19** 277-280

Paul, John
see Jones, John Paul, (John Baldwin; born 1946)

PAUL, LES (Lester William Polsfuss (Polfuss); born 1915), American guitarist, inventor, and producer **28** 276-278

PAUL, SAINT (died 66/67), Christian theologian and Apostle **12** 141-143

PAULI, WOLFGANG ERNST (1900-1958), Austrian theoretical physicist **12** 149

Pauline Epistles (New Testament)
see Paul, St.

PAULING, LINUS CARL (born 1901), American chemist **12** 150-152

PAUSANIAS (flourished circa 150), Greek traveler and geographer **25** 326-327

PAVAROTTI, LUCIANO (1935-2007), Italian tenor **12** 152-154

PAVESE, CESARE (1908-1950), Italian novelist, poet, and critic **12** 154-155

PAVLOV, IVAN PETROVICH (1849-1936), Russian physiologist **12** 155-157

PAVLOVA, ANNA (1881-1931), Russian ballet dancer **12** 157-159

Pavón, José Maria Morelos ye
see Morelos, José Maria

PAYNE, JOHN HOWARD (1791-1852), American actor, playwright, and songwriter **12** 159

PAYNE-GAPOSCHKIN, CECILIA (1900-1979), American astronomer **12** 159-161

PAYTON, WALTER (1954-1999), American football player **20** 294-296

PAZ, OCTAVIO (1914-1998), Mexican diplomat, critic, editor, translator, poet, and essayist **12** 161-162

PAZ ESTENSSORO, VICTOR (1907-2001), Bolivian statesman and reformer **12** 163-164

PAZ ZAMORA, JAIME (born 1939), president of Bolivia (1989-) **12** 165-167

PÁZMÁNY, PÉTER (1570-1637), Hungarian archbishop **12** 164-165

PEABODY, ELIZABETH PALMER (1804-1894), American educator and author **12** 167-168

PEABODY, GEORGE (1795-1869), American merchant, financier, and philanthropist **12** 168

PEACOCK, THOMAS LOVE (1785-1866), English novelist and satirist **12** 169

PEALE, CHARLES WILLSON (1741-1827), American painter and scientist **12** 169-171

PEALE, NORMAN VINCENT (1898-1993), American religious leader who blended psychotherapy and religion **12** 171-172

PEALE, REMBRANDT (1778-1860), American painter **12** 172-173

PEARSE, PATRICK HENRY (1879-1916), Irish poet, educator, and revolutionary **12** 173-174

PEARSON, LESTER BOWLES (1897-1972), Canadian statesman and diplomat, prime minister **12** 174-175

PEARY, ROBERT EDWIN (1856-1920), American explorer **12** 175-176

Pecci, Vincenzo Gioacchino
see Leo XIII

PECHSTEIN, HERMANN MAX (1881-1955), German Expressionist painter and graphic artist **12** 176-177

PECK, ANNIE SMITH (1850-1935), American mountain climber **24** 304-306

PECK, MORGAN SCOTT (1936-2005), American author and psychologist **26** 288-291

PECK, ROBERT NEWTON (born 1928), American author of children's literature **12** 177-178

PECKINPAH, SAM (1925-1984), American film director **21** 338-340

PEDRARIAS (Pedro Arias de Ávila; circa 1440-1531), Spanish conqueror and colonial governor **12** 179

PEDRO I (1798-1834), emperor of Brazil and king of Portugal **12** 179-180

PEDRO II (1825-1891), emperor of Brazil 1831-89 **12** 180-181

Pedro III (king, Aragon)
see Peter III, (Peter Feodorovich; 1728-62)

Pedro IV (king, Portugal)
see Pedro I (emperor, Brazil)

PEEL, JOHN (John Robert Parker Ravenscroft; 1939-2004), British disc jockey **27** 286-288

PEEL, SIR ROBERT (1788-1850), English statesman, prime minister 1834-35 and 1841-46 **12** 181-183

Peer Gynt (play; Ibsen)
Bull, Ole **28** 54-56

PÉGUY, CHARLES PIERRE (1873-1914), French poet **12** 183-184

PEI, I. M. (Ieoh Ming Pei; born 1917), Chinese-American architect **12** 184-187

PEIRCE, BENJAMIN (1809-1880), American mathematician **21** 340-342

PEIRCE, CHARLES SANDERS (1839-1914), American scientist and philosopher **12** 187-188

PEIXOTO, FLORIANO (1839-1895), Brazilian marshal, president 1891-94 **12** 188-189

PELAGIUS (died circa 430), British theologian **12** 189-190

PELE (Edson Arantes Do Nascimento Pele; born 1940), Brazilian soccer player **12** 190-191

PELLI, CESAR (born 1926), Hispanic American architect and educator **12** 191-192

PELOSI, NANCY (Nancy D'Alesandro; born 1940), American politician **25** 328-330

PELTIER, LEONARD (born 1944), Native American activist **12** 193-195

PEMBERTON, JOHN STITH (1831-1888), American inventor of Coca-Cola **28** 278-279

PEÑA, PACO (Francisco Peña Pérez; born 1942), Spanish guitarist and composer **23** 299-301

PENDERECKI, KRZYSZTOF (born 1933), Polish composer **12** 195-197

PENDLETON, EDMUND (1721-1803), American political leader **12** 197-198

PENDLETON, GEORGE HUNT (1825-1889), American politician **12** 198

PENFIELD, WILDER GRAVES (1891-1976), Canadian neurosurgeon **12** 198-200

PENN, WILLIAM (1644-1718), English Quaker, founder of Pennsylvania **12** 200-202

PENNEY, J. C. (James Cash Penney; 1875-1971), American chain store executive and philanthropist **12** 202-203

PENNINGTON, MARY ENGLE (1872-1952), American chemist **22** 352-355

PENROSE, BOIES (1860-1921), American senator and political boss **12** 203-204

PENROSE, ROGER (born 1931), British mathematician and physicist **12** 204-205

Pensador Mexicano, El
see Fernández de Lizardi, Josè Joaquin

PENSKE, ROGER (born 1937), American businessman and race car team owner **19** 280-282

PENZIAS, ARNO ALLEN (born 1932), German American physicist **23** 301-304

PEP, WILLIE (William Guiglermo Papaleo; 1922-2006), American boxer **21** 342-344

PEPPER, CLAUDE DENSON (1900-1989), Florida attorney, state representative, U.S. senator, and U.S. representative **12** 205-206

PEPPERELL, SIR WILLIAM (1696-1759), American merchant and soldier **12** 206-207

PEPYS, SAMUEL (1633-1703), English diarist **12** 207-208

PERCY, WALKER (1916-1990), American author **19** 282-284

PEREGRINUS, PETRUS (flourished 1261-69), French scholastic and scientist **12** 208

PEREIRA, ARISTIDES MARIA (born 1923), Cape Verdean president **24** 306-308

PERELMAN, GRIGORY (Grisha Perelman; borm 1966), Russian mathematician **27** 288-290

PERELMAN, S. J. (Sidney Jerome Perelman; 1904-1979), American cartoonist, satirist, and parodist **12** 209-210

PERES, SHIMON (born 1923), head of the Israel Labour Party and Israeli prime minister (1984-1986) **12** 210-211

PERETZ, ISAAC LOEB (1851-1915), Jewish poet, novelist, and playwright **12** 212

PÉREZ, CARLOS ANDRÉS (born 1922), president of Venezuela (1989-1993) **12** 212-214

PÉREZ DE CUELLAR, JAVIER (born 1920), Peruvian foreign service officer and secretary general of the United Nations (1982-) **12** 214-215

PÉREZ ESQUIVEL, ADOLFO (born 1931), Argentine artist and human rights activist **12** 215-217

Pérez Galdós, Benito
see Galdós, Benito Pérez

PÉREZ JIMENEZ, MARCOS (1914-2001), Venezuelan dictator **12** 217-218

PERGOLESI, GIOVANNI BATTISTA (1710-1736), Italian composer **12** 218-219

PERICLES (circa 495-429 B.C.), Athenian statesman **12** 219-221

PERKIN, WILLIAM H. (1838-1907), British chemist **25** 330-332

PERKINS, FRANCES (1882-1965), American statesman and social worker **12** 221-222

PERKINS, GEORGE WALBRIDGE (1862-1920), American businessman and banker **21** 344-347

PERKINS, WILLIAM MAXWELL EVARTS (1884-1947), American editor of fiction who discovered and developed brilliant authors **12** 222-223

PERLASCA, GIORGIO (Jorge Perlas; 1910-1992), Italian activist **25** 332-334

PERLE, GEORGE (born 1915), American musician **12** 223-224

PERLMAN, ITZHAK (born 1945), American musician **18** 318-320

PERÓN, EVA (MARÍA) DUARTE DE (1919-1952), the second wife and political partner of President Juan Perón of Argentina **12** 225-226

PERÓN, ISABEL MARTINEZ DE (born 1931), first woman president of Argentina (1974-1976) **12** 226-228

PERÓN, JUAN DOMINGO (1895-1974), Argentine statesman, president 1946-55 **12** 228-230

PEROT, HENRY ROSS (born 1930), American businessman and activist **12** 230-231

PÉROTIN (Perotinus; flourished circa 1185-1205), French composer and musician **12** 231-232

PERRAULT, CLAUDE (1613-1688), French scientist and architect **12** 232-233

PERRET, AUGUSTE (1874-1954), French architect **12** 233

Perreti, Felice
see Sixtus V

PERRIN, JEAN BAPTISTE (1870-1942), French physicist **12** 233-236

Perry, Edgar A.
see Poe, Edgar Allan

PERRY, HAROLD ROBERT (1916-1991), African American Roman Catholic bishop **12** 236-237

PERRY, MATTHEW CALBRAITH (1794-1858), American naval officer **12** 237-239

PERRY, OLIVER HAZARD (1785-1819), American naval officer **12** 239

PERRY, RALPH BARTON (1876-1957), American philosopher **12** 239-240

PERRY, WILLIAM JAMES (born 1927), President Clinton's secretary of defense (1994-) **12** 240-242

PERSE, SAINT-JOHN (Alexis Saint-Léger Léger; 1887-1975), French poet and diplomat **12** 242-243

PERSHING, JOHN JOSEPH (1860-1948), American general **12** 243-244

Persse, Isabella Augusta
see Gregory, Lady Augusta

PERTH, 16TH EARL OF (James Eric Drummond; 1876-1951), English statesman **12** 244-245

PERUGINO (circa 1450-1523), Italian painter **12** 245-246

PERUTZ, MAX (1914-2002), English crystallographer and biochemist **12** 246-248

Peruvian music
Granda, Chabuca **28** 143-144

Peshkov, Aleksei Maximovich
see Gorky, Maxim

PESOTTA, ROSE (1896-1965), American
union organizer **12** 248-249

PESTALOZZI, JOHANN HEINRICH
(1746-1827), Swiss educator **12**
249-250

PÉTAIN, HENRI PHILIPPE (1856-1951),
French general and statesman **12**
250-252

Peter (emperor, Brazil)
see Pedro

Peter (king, Portugal)
see Pedro

PETER I (Peter the Great; 1672-1725),
czar of Russia 1682-1725 **12** 253-256

PETER I (1844-1921), king of Serbia
1903-18, and of the Serbs, Croats, and
Slovenes 1918-21 **12** 256

PETER III (Pedro; circa 1239-85), king of
Aragon 1276-85 **12** 256-257

PETER, SAINT (died circa 65), apostle
and bishop of Rome **12** 252-253

Peter Canisius, St.
see Canisius, St. Peter

Peter Claver, St.
see Claver, St. Peter

Peter Kanis
see Canisius, St. Peter

Peter Leopold
see Leopold II (emperor)

Peter Lombard
see Lombard, Peter

Peter the Great
see Peter I (czar, Russia)

PETERS, CARL (1856-1918), German
explorer and colonizer **12** 257-258

PETERSON, EDITH R. (born Edith
Elizabeth Runne; 1914-1992),
American medical researcher **12**
258-259

PETERSON, OSCAR (1925-2007),
Canadian pianist **23** 304-306

PETO, JOHN FREDERICK (1854-1907),
American painter **12** 259

PETÖFI, SÁNDOR (1823-1849),
Hungarian poet and revolutionary
leader **23** 306-308

PETRARCH (Francesco Petrarca; 1304-
74), Italian poet **12** 259-261

**PETRIE, SIR WILLIAM MATTHEW
FLINDERS** (1853-1942), English
archeologist **12** 261-262

Petroleum industry
see Oil industry

PETRONIUS ARBITER (died circa 66),
Roman author **12** 262-263

PEVSNER, ANTOINE (1886-1962),
Russian sculptor and painter **12**
263-264

Pevsner, Naum Neemia
see Gabo, Naum

PEYO (Pierre Culliford; 1928-1992),
Belgian cartoonist **28** 280-282
Hanna and Barbera **28** 156-159

PHAEDRUS (c. 15 BC-c. 50), Greek/
Roman fabulists **20** 296-297

Phalangist Party (Lebanon)
Gemayel, Bashir **28** 136-138

Pharmacology (science)
Axelrod, Julius **28** 18-20
Hoffmann, Felix **28** 179-180
Pemberton, John Stith **28** 278-279

PHIBUN SONGKHRAM, LUANG (1897-
1964), Thai statesman, prime minister
1938-44 and 1948-57 **12** 264-265

PHIDIAS (flourished circa 475-425 B.C.),
Greek sculptor **12** 265-267

Philadelphia Orchestra
Ormandy, Eugene **28** 264-266
Sawallisch, Wolfgang **28** 314-316

Philadelphos of Egypt
see Ptolemy II

Philanthropists, American
20th century
Kellogg, W. K. **28** 199-201
Thomas, Danny **28** 350-352

Philanthropists, Lebanese
Hariri, Rafic **28** 161-163

PHILIDOR, FRANÇOIS-ANDRÉ
(François-André Danican-Philidor;
1726-1795), French composer and
chess player **21** 347-349

PHILIP (died 1676), American
Wampanoag Indian chief 1662-76 **12**
267-268

PHILIP (Prince Philip; Philip
Mountbatten; born 1921), Duke of
Edinburgh and husband of Queen
Elizabeth II of the United Kingdom **24**
308-310

Philip I (king of Portugal)
see Philip II (king of Spain)

PHILIP II (382-336 B.C.), king of
Macedon 359-336 **12** 269-271

PHILIP II (Philip Augustus; 1165-1223),
king of France 1180-1223 **12** 268-269

PHILIP II (1527-1598), king of Spain
1556-1598 **12** 271-273

PHILIP III (1578-1621), king of Spain
1598-1621 **12** 273-274

PHILIP IV (the Fair; 1268-1314), king of
France 1285-1314 **12** 274

PHILIP IV (1605-1665), king of Spain
1621-65 **12** 275

PHILIP V (1683-1746), king of Spain
1700-46 **12** 276-277

PHILIP VI (1293-1350), king of France
1328-50 **12** 277-278

Philip Augustus
see Philip II, king of France

Philip of Anjou
see Philip V, king of Spain

Philip the Fair
see Philip IV, king of France

PHILIP THE GOOD (1396-1467), duke
of Burgundy 1419-67 **12** 278-279

Philipon, Charles, (1800-1862), French
journalist
Grandville, J.J. **28** 144-146

PHILLIP, ARTHUR (1738-1814), English
governor of New South Wales **12**
279-280

PHILLIPS, DAVID GRAHAM (1867-
1911), American journalist and
novelist **12** 280-281

PHILLIPS, WENDELL (1811-1884),
American abolitionist and social
reformer **12** 281-282

Philosophers, French
20th century
Deleuze, Gilles **28** 94-96
20th-21st century
Lévy, Bernard-Henri **28** 213-215

Philosophers, Indian (Asia)
Krishnamurti, Uppaluri Gopala **28**
201-203

Philosophers, Polish
Witkacy **28** 374-376

Philosophy
and immanence
Deleuze, Gilles **28** 94-96

PHIPS, SIR WILLIAM (1650/51-95),
American shipbuilder and colonial
governor **12** 283

PHOTIUS (circa 820-891), Byzantine
patriarch **12** 283-284

Photography
as art form
Edgerton, Harold Eugene **28**
109-111
Hine, Lewis Wickes **28** 172-174
film
Nykvist, Sven **28** 261-263
in science
Edgerton, Harold Eugene **28**
109-111

invention and equipment
Edgerton, Harold Eugene **28** 109-111

Phya Kalyan Maitri
see Sayre, Francis

PHYFE, DUNCAN (1768-1854), American cabinetmaker **12** 284-285

PIAF, EDITH (Edith Giovanna Gassion; 1915-63), French music hall/cabaret singer **12** 285-287

PIAGET, JEAN (1896-1980), Swiss psychologist and educator **12** 287-288

PIANKHI (ruled circa 741-circa 712 B.C.), Nubian king **12** 288-289

Piano (musical instrument)
Karp, Natalia **28** 192-194
Lipatti, Dinu **28** 222-223
Rubinstein, Arthur **28** 305-307
Sawallisch, Wolfgang **28** 314-316
Szymanowska, Maria **28** 340-342

PIANO, RENZO (born 1937), Italian architect, lecturer, and designer **12** 289-291

PIAZZOLLA, ASTOR (Astor Pantaleón Piazzolla; 1921-1992), Argentine musician **26** 291-293

Pibul Songgram, Luang
see Songgram, Luang Pibul

PICABIA, FRANCIS (1879-1953), French artist, writer, and bon vivant **12** 291-292

PICASSO, PABLO (1881-1973), Spanish painter, sculptor, and graphic artist **12** 292-295

PICASSO, PALOMA (born 1949), Spanish fashion designer **12** 295-297

PICCARD, AUGUSTE (1884-1962), Swiss scientist **12** 297-298

PICCARD, JACQUES ERNEST JEAN (born 1922), Swiss explorer, scientist, oceanographer, and engineer **18** 320-322

Piccolomini, Aeneas Sylvius de'
see Pius II

PICKENS, THOMAS BOONE JR. (T. Boone Pickens; born 1928), American businessman **19** 284-286

PICKERING, EDWARD CHARLES (1846-1919), American astronomer **12** 298

PICKERING, TIMOTHY (1745-1829), American Revolutionary soldier and statesman **12** 298-299

PICKETT, BILL (1870-1932), American rodeo cowboy **19** 286-288

PICKFORD, MARY (Gladys Louise Smith; 1893-1979), Canadian-American actress, screenwriter, and film producer **19** 288-290

PICO DELLA MIRANDOLA, CONTE GIOVANNI (1463-1494), Italian philosopher and humanist **12** 299-300

PICON, MOLLY (1898-1992), American actress **27** 290-292

PIERCE, FRANKLIN (1804-1869), American statesman, president 1853-57 **12** 300-301

PIERCE, JOHN ROBINSON (born 1910), American electronics engineer and author **21** 349-351

Pierluigi, Giovanni
see Palestrina, Giovanni Pierluigi da

PIERO DELLA FRANCESCA (circa 1415/20-92), Italian painter **12** 301-302

Pierre de Maricourt
see Peregrinus, Petrus

PIGOU, ARTHUR CECIL (1877-1959), English economist **12** 302

PIKE, ZEBULON (1779-1813), American soldier and explorer **12** 302-304

Pilar, Marcelo H. del
see Del Pilar, Marcelo H.

PILLSBURY, CHARLES ALFRED (1842-1899), American businessman **12** 304

PILON, GERMAIN (circa 1535-90), French sculptor **12** 305

PILSUDSKI, JOSEPH (1867-1935), Polish general, president 1918-21 **12** 305-306

PINCHBACK, PINCKNEY BENTON STEWART (1837-1921), African American politician **12** 306-308

Pincherle, Alberto
see Moravia, Alberto

PIN-CHIN CHIANG (Wei-Chih Chiang; Ling Ding; 1904-1986), Chinese author and feminist **24** 310-312

PINCHOT, GIFFORD (1865-1946), American conservationist and public official **12** 308-309

PINCKNEY, CHARLES (1757-1824), American politician and diplomat **12** 309-310

PINCKNEY, CHARLES COTESWORTH (1745-1825), American statesman **12** 310

PINCKNEY, ELIZA (Elizabeth Lucas; 1722-1793), American business woman **25** 334-336

PINCUS, GREGORY GOODWIN (1903-1967), American biologist **12** 310-312

PINDAR (552/518-438 B.C.), Greek lyric poet **12** 312-313

PINEL, PHILIPPE (1745-1826), French physician **12** 313-314

PINERO, ARTHUR WING (1855-1934), English playwright **18** 322-324

Pingwoldang
see Sol Ch'ong

Pinilla, Gustavo Rojas
see Rojas Pinilla, Gustavo

PINKERTON, ALLEN (1819-1884), American detective **12** 314-315

PINKHAM, LYDIA ESTES (1819-1883), American patent medicine manufacturer **21** 351-353

PINKNEY, WILLIAM (1764-1822), American attorney, diplomat, and statesman **22** 355-357

PINOCHET UGARTE, AUGUSTO (1915-2006), Chilean military leader and dictator **12** 315-317

PINTER, HAROLD (born 1930), English playwright **12** 317-318

PINTO, ISAAC (1720-1791), Jewish merchant and scholar **12** 318

PINZÓN, MARTIN ALONSO (1440?-1493), Spanish navigator **22** 358-360

PINZÓN, VICENTE YÁÑEZ (1460?-1524?), Spanish navigator **22** 360-361

PIO, PADRE (Francesco Forgione; 1887-1968), Italian priest **20** 297-299

Pippi Longstocking (fictional character)
Lindgren, Astrid **28** 219-221

PIPPIN, HORACE (1888-1946), African American painter **12** 318-319

PIRANDELLO, LUIGI (1867-1936), Italian playwright novelist, and critic **12** 319-321

PIRANESI, GIOVANNI BATTISTA (1720-1778), Italian engraver and architect **12** 321-322

PIRENNE, JEAN HENRI (Jean Henri Otto Lucien Marie Pirenne; 1862-1935), Belgian historian **12** 322-323

Pisan, Christine de
see Christine de Pisan

PISANELLO (Antonio Pisano; before 1395-1455), Italian painter and medalist **12** 323-324

Pisano
see Pisanello

PISANO, GIOVANNI (circa 1250-1314/17), Italian sculptor **12** 324-325

PISANO, NICOLA (Nicola d'Apulia; circa 1220/25-1278/84), Italian sculptor **12** 325

PISCOPIA, ELENA LUCREZIA CORNARO (1646-1684), Italian philosopher **26** 293-295

PISSARO, CAMILLE (1830-1903), French painter **12** 326-327

PISTON, WALTER (born 1894), American composer **12** 327-328

PITT, WILLIAM, THE ELDER (1708-1778), English statesman **12** 328-329

PITT, WILLIAM, THE YOUNGER (1759-1806), English statesman **12** 329-331

PIUS II (Enea Silvio de'Piccolomini; 1405-64), pope 1458-64 **12** 331

PIUS IV (Giovanni Angelo de' Medici; 1499-1565), pope 1559-65 **12** 332

PIUS V (Antonio Ghislieri; 1504-72), pope 1566-72 **12** 332-333

PIUS VI (Gianangelo Braschi; 1717-99), pope 1775-99 **12** 333-334

PIUS VII (Luigi Barnabà Chiaramonti; 1740-1823), pope 1880-23 **12** 334-335

PIUS IX (Giovanni Maria Mastai-Ferretti; 1792-1878), pope 1846-78 **12** 335-336

PIUS X (Giuseppe Melchiorre Sarto; 1835-1914), pope 1903-14 **12** 336-337

PIUS XI (Ambrogio Damiano Achille Ratti; 1857-1939), pope 1922-39 **12** 337-339
canonizations
Thérèse of Lisieux, Saint **28** 347-350

PIUS XII (Eugenio Maria Giuseppe Pacelli; 1876-1958), pope 1939-58 **12** 339-340

PIZARRO, FRANCISCO (circa 1474-1541), Spanish conquistador in Peru **12** 340-341

PLAATJE, SOLOMON TSHEKISHO (1878-1932), South African writer **12** 341-342

Plaek
see Phibun Songkhram, Luang

PLANCK, MAX KARL ERNST LUDWIG (1858-1947), German physicist **12** 342-344

Plant morphology (botany)
Arber, Agnes Robertson **28** 14-16

PLATH, SYLVIA (1932-1963), American poet and novelist **12** 344-345

PLATO (428-347 B.C.), Greek philosopher **12** 345-347

PLATT, THOMAS COLLIER (1833-1910), American politician **12** 347-348

PLAUTUS (circa 254-circa 184 B.C.), Roman writer **12** 348-350

Plays on the Passions (book)
Baillie, Joanna **28** 23-25

PLAZA LASSO, GALO (1906-1987), Ecuadorian statesman **12** 350-351

PLEKHANOV, GEORGI VALENTINOVICH (1856-1918), Russian revolutionist and social philosopher **12** 351-352

PLENTY COUPS (c. 1848-1932), Native American tribal leader and Crow chief **12** 352-355

Plessis, Armand du
see Richelieu, Armand Jean Du Plessis De

PLINY THE ELDER (23/24-79), Roman encyclopedist **12** 355-356

PLINY THE YOUNGER (circa 61-circa 113), Roman author and administrator **12** 356

PLISETSKAYA, MAYA MIKHAILOVNA (born 1925), Russian ballet dancer **12** 356-358

PLOMER, WILLIAM (William Charles Franklyn Plomer; 1903-1973), South African/British author **24** 312-313

PLOTINUS (205-270), Greek philosopher, founder of Neoplatonism **12** 358-359

PLOTKIN, MARK (born 1955), American ethnobotanist and environmentalist **23** 308-310

PLUTARCH (circa 46-circa 120), Greek biographer **12** 359-360

PO CHÜ-I (772-846), Chinese poet **12** 362-363

POBEDONOSTSEV, KONSTANTIN PETROVICH (1827-1907), Russian statesman and jurist **12** 360-361

POCAHONTAS (circa 1595-1617), American Indian princess **12** 361-362

POE, EDGAR ALLAN (1809-1849), American writer **12** 363-365

Poets Laureate (United States)
Collins, Billy **28** 83-85

POINCARÉ, JULES HENRI (1854-1912), French mathematician **12** 365-366

POINCARÉ, RAYMOND (1860-1934), French statesman **12** 366-368

POIRET, PAUL (1879-1944), French fashion designer **19** 291-293

POITIER, SIDNEY (born 1927), African American actor and director **12** 368-370

POL POT (1928-1998), Cambodian Communist and premier of Democratic Kampuchéa (1976-1979) **12** 382-384

Poland (Polish People's Republic; nation, Eastern Europe)
• EARLY HISTORY
framework of law established
Casimir III, King of Poland **28** 60-62
Jewish immigration
Casimir III, King of Poland **28** 60-62
Polish-Lithuanian Commonwealth
Wladyslaw II Jagiello, King of Poland **28** 377-378

POLANSKI, ROMAN (born 1933), Polish filmmaker and director **23** 310-312

POLANYI, JOHN CHARLES (born 1929), Canadian scientist and Nobel Prize winner **12** 370-372

POLANYI, KARL (1886-1964), Hungarian economic historian **12** 372

POLANYI, MICHAEL (1891-1976), Hungarian medical doctor, physical chemist, social thinker, and philosopher **12** 372-373

Polish literature
Witkacy **28** 374-376

Polish music
Szymanowska, Maria **28** 340-342
Witkacy **28** 374-376

Polish Underground (World War II)
Sendler, Irena **28** 318-320

Politian
see Poliziano, Angelo

POLITKOVSKAYA, ANNA (Anna Stepanova Politkovskaya; 1958-2006), Russian journalist **27** 292-294

POLIZIANO, ANGELO (Politian; 1454-94), Italian poet **12** 373-374

POLK, JAMES KNOX (1795-1849), American statesman, president 1845-49 **12** 374-376

POLK, LEONIDAS LAFAYETTE (1837-1892), American agrarian crusader and editor **12** 376-377

POLKE, SIGMAR (born 1941), German painter **23** 312-315

POLLAIUOLO, ANTONIO (circa 1432-98), Italian painter, sculptor, goldsmith, and engraver **12** 377-378

POLLARD, ALBERT FREDERICK (1869-1948), English historian **12** 378

POLLOCK, JACKSON (1912-1956), American painter **12** 379-380

POLO, MARCO (circa 1254-circa 1324), Venetian traveler and writer **12** 380-382

POLYBIOS (circa 203-120 B.C.), Greek historian **12** 384-385

POLYKLEITOS (flourished circa 450-420 B.C.), Greek sculptor **12** 385-386

POMBAL, MARQUÊS DE (Sebastião José de Carvalho e Mello; 1699-1782), Portuguese statesman **12** 386-387

POMPEY (106-48 B.C.), Roman general and statesman **12** 387-389

POMPIDOU, GEORGES (1911-1974), second president of the French Fifth Republic (1969-1974) **12** 389-390

POMPONAZZI, PIETRO (1462-1525), Italian Aristotelian philosopher **12** 390-391

PONCE, MANUEL (Manuel María Ponce; 1886-1948), Mexican composer and educator **28** 282-284

PONCE DE LEÓN, JUAN (1460?-1521), Spanish conqueror and explorer **12** 391-392

PONIATOWSKA, ELENA (born 1933), Mexican journalist, novelist, essayist, and short-story writer **12** 392-393

Pontedera, Andrea da
see Andrea Pisano

PONTIAC (circa 1720-69), Ottawa Indian chief **12** 393-394

Pontiac's Conspiracy (1763-1766)
Du Sable, Jean Baptiste Pointe **28** 104-106

PONTOPPIDAN, HENRIK (Rusticus; 1857-1943), Danish author **25** 336-338

PONTORMO (1494-1556), Italian painter **12** 394-395

POOL, JUDITH GRAHAM (1919-1975), American physiologist **23** 315-316

POPE, ALEXANDER (1688-1744), English poet and satirist **12** 395-397

POPE, JOHN RUSSELL (1874-1937), American architect in the classical tradition **12** 397-399

POPHAM, WILLIAM JAMES (born 1930), American educator active in educational test development **12** 399-401

POPOVA, LIUBOV SERGEEVNA (1889-1924), Russian and Soviet avant-garde artist **12** 401-402

POPPER, SIR KARL RAIMUND (1902-1994), Austrian philosopher **12** 402

Poquelin, Jean Baptiste
see Molière

PORRES, MARTÍN DE, SAINT (1579-1639), Peruvian patron saint of universal brotherhood **27** 295-297

PORSCHE, FERDINAND SR. (1875-1951), Austrian German automobile designer and engineer **19** 293-295

PORTA, GIACOMO DELLA (circa 1537-1602), Italian architect **12** 402-403

PORTA, GIAMBATTISTA DELLA (1535-1615), Italian scientist and dramatist **12** 403-404

PORTALES PLAZAZUELOS, DIEGO JOSÉ VÍCTOR (1793-1837), Chilean statesman **12** 404

PORTER, COLE ALBERT (1891-1964), American composer **12** 405-406

Porter, Countee Cullen
see Cullen, Countee

PORTER, EDWIN STRATTON (1870-1941), American filmmaker **20** 299-301

PORTER, KATHERINE ANNE (1890-1980), American writer **12** 406-407

Porter, William Sydney
see Henry, O.

PORTINARI, CÂNDIDO (1903-1962), Brazilian painter **12** 407-408

PORTOLÁ, GASPAR DE (circa 1723-1784), Spanish explorer and colonial governor **12** 408

Portuguese music
Rodrigues, Amália **28** 301-302

PORTUONDO, OMARA (born 1930), Cuban singer **26** 302-304

PORTZAMPARC, CHRISTIAN DE (born 1944), French architect **18** 324-326

POSEY, ALEXANDER LAWRENCE (1873-1908), Native American author and politician **26** 304-306

POST, CHARLES WILLIAM (1854-1914), American pioneer in the manufacture and mass-marketing of breakfast cereals **12** 408-409

POST, EMILY PRICE (1873-1960), American authority on etiquette **12** 409-410

Postmasters general
see Statesmen, American

Potawatomi Indians (North America)
Du Sable, Jean Baptiste Pointe **28** 104-106

POTEMKIN, GRIGORI ALEKSANDROVICH (1739-1791), Russian administrator and field marshal **12** 411-412

POTOK, CHAIM (Herman Harold Potok; Chaim Tzvi; 1929-2002), American author **25** 338-341

POTTER, BEATRIX (Helen Beatrix Potter; 1866-1943), English author and illustrator **18** 326-328

POTTER, DAVID M. (1910-1971), American historian **12** 412

POTTER, DENNIS (1935-1994), British essayist, playwright, screenwriter, and novelist **12** 412-414

POULENC, FRANCIS (1899-1963), French composer **12** 414-415

POUND, EZRA LOOMIS (1885-1972), American poet, editor, and critic **12** 415-417
Cunard, Nancy **28** 87-89

POUND, ROSCOE (1870-1964), American jurist and botanist **12** 417-418

POUSSAINT, ALVIN FRANCIS (born 1934), African American psychiatrist **24** 313-316

POUSSIN, NICOLAS (1594-1665), French painter **12** 418-420

POWDERLY, TERENCE VINCENT (1849-1924), American labor leader **12** 420-421

POWELL, ADAM CLAYTON, JR. (1908-1972), African American political leader and Baptist minister **12** 421-422

POWELL, ANTHONY (1905-2000), English novelist **12** 422-423

POWELL, COLIN LUTHER (born 1937), African American chairman of the Joint Chiefs of Staff **12** 424-425

POWELL, JOHN WESLEY (1834-1902), American geologist, anthropologist, and explorer **12** 425-426

POWELL, LEWIS F., JR. (1907-1998), U.S. Supreme Court justice (1972-1987) **12** 426-428

POWERS, HIRAM (1805-1873), American sculptor **12** 428-429

POWHATAN (circa 1550-1618), Native American tribal chief **12** 429-430

POZZO, BROTHER ANDREA, S.J. (1642-1709), Italian artist and architect **25** 341-342

PRADO UGARTECHE, MANUEL (1889-1967), Peruvian statesman **12** 430-431

PRAETORIUS, MICHAEL (circa 1571-1621), German composer and theorist **12** 431-432

PRAN, DITH (born 1942), Cambodian American journalist and activist **18** 328-331

PRANDTAUER, JAKOB (1660-1726), Austrian baroque architect **12** 432

PRASAD, RAJENDRA (1884-1963), Indian nationalist, first president of the Republic **12** 433

PRAXITELES (flourished circa 370-330 B.C.), Greek sculptor **12** 433-434

PREBISCH, RAÚL (1901-1986), Argentine economist active in the United Nations **12** 434-436

PREGL, FRITZ (1869-1930), Austrian physiologist and medical chemist **12** 436-437

PREM TINSULANONDA (born 1920), military leader and prime minister of Thailand (1979-1988) **12** 437

PREMADASA, RANASINGHE (born 1924), president of Sri Lanka (1988-) **12** 437-439

PREMCHAND (1880-1936), Indian novelist and short-story writer **12** 439

PREMINGER, OTTO (1895-1986), Austrian filmmaker and theater producer/director **18** 331-332

PRENDERGAST, MAURICE BRAZIL (1859-1924), American painter **12** 440

PRESCOTT, WILLIAM HICKLING (1796-1859), American historian **12** 440-441

PRESLEY, ELVIS ARON (1935-1977), American singer and actor **12** 441-442

PRESTES, LUIZ CARLOS (1898-1990), Brazilian revolutionary and Communist leader **12** 442-444

PRETORIUS, ANDRIES (1798-1853), South African politician and general **12** 444-445

PRÉVERT, JACQUES (Jacques Henri Marie Prevert; 1900-1977), French poet and filmmaker **27** 297-298

PREVIN, ANDRE (Andreas Ludwig Priwin; born 1929), German American composer and conductor **18** 333-334

PRÉVOST, ABBÉ (1697-1763), French novelist, journalist, and cleric **12** 445-446

Prévost d'Exiles, Antoine François
see Prévost, Abbé

PRICE, FLORENCE BEATRICE (nee Florence Beatrice Smith; 1887-1953), African American composer and music educator **26** 306-308

PRICE, LEONTYNE (Mary Leontyne Price; born 1927), American prima donna soprano **12** 446-447

PRICE, RICHARD (1723-1791), English Nonconformist minister and political philosopher **12** 447-448

PRICHARD, DIANA GARCÍA (born 1949), Hispanic American chemical physicist **12** 448-449

PRIDE, CHARLEY FRANK (born 1938), African American musician **23** 317-319

PRIDI PHANOMYONG (1901-1983), Thai political leader **12** 449

PRIEST, IVY MAUDE BAKER (1905-1975), treasurer of the United States (1953-1960) **12** 450-451

PRIESTLEY, J(OHN) B(OYNTON) (1894-1984), English author of novels, essays, plays, and screenplays **12** 451-452

PRIESTLEY, JOSEPH (1733-1804), English clergyman and chemist **12** 452-453

Prignano, Bartolomeo
see Urban VI

PRIMATICCIO, FRANCESCO (1504-1570), Italian painter, sculptor, and architect **12** 453-454

PRIMO DE RIVERA Y ORBANEJA, MIGUEL (1870-1930), Spanish general, dictator 1923-30 **12** 454-455

PRINCE, HAL (Harold Smith Prince; born 1928), American theatrical producer and director **19** 295-298

PRINCIP, GAVRILO (1894-1918), Serbian nationalist and assassin **21** 353-355

PRINGLE, THOMAS (1789-1834), Scottish author and abolitionist **23** 319-320

PRITCHETT, V(ICTOR) S(AWDON) (born 1900), English short story writer, novelist, literary critic, journalist, travel writer, biographer, and autobiographer **12** 455-457

Prizefighters
see Athletes, American

Pro Football Hall of Fame
Walsh, Bill **28** 370-372

PROCLUS DIADOCHUS (born 410), Byzantine philosopher **12** 457

PROCOPIUS OF CAESAREA (circa 500-circa 565), Byzantine historian **12** 457-458

PROCTER, WILLIAM COOPER (1862-1934), American businessman **19** 298-300

Professor Hieronimus (book)
Skram, Amalie **28** 331-333

PROKOFIEV, SERGEI SERGEEVICH (1891-1953), Russian composer **12** 458-460

PROSSER, GABRIEL (circa 1775-1800), Afro-American slave rebel **12** 460-461

PROTAGORAS (circa 484-circa 414 B.C.), Greek philosopher **12** 461

PROUDHON, PIERRE JOSEPH (1809-1864), French anarchist political philosopher and journalist **12** 461-463

PROULX, E. ANNIE (born 1935), American author **12** 463-465

PROUST, MARCEL (1871-1922), French novelist **12** 465-467

PROXMIRE, WILLIAM (1915-2005), Democratic senator for Wisconsin **12** 467-468

PRUDHOMME, SULLY (Rene Francois Armand Prudhomme; 1839-1907), French author and philosopher **25** 342-344

PRUD'HON, PIERRE PAUL (1758-1823), French painter **12** 469

PRUSINER, STANLEY BEN (born 1942), American biomedical researcher **23** 320-323

PRYOR, RICHARD (1940-2005), American entertainer **19** 300-302

PRZHEVALSKY, NIKOLAI MIKHAILOVICH (1839-1888), Russian general and traveler **12** 469-470

Psychic religion
see Spiritualism (religion)

PTOLEMY I (367/366-283 B.C.), Macedonian general, king of Egypt 323-285 **12** 470-472

PTOLEMY II (308-246 B.C.), king of Egypt 285-246 **12** 472-473

PTOLEMY, CLAUDIUS (circa 100-circa 170), Greek astronomer and geographer **12** 473-474

Public school (United States)
see Education (United States)

Publishers
English
Cunard, Nancy **28** 87-89

Publishers, American
journals
Thurman, Wallace Henry **28** 352-354

Publius Aelius Hadrianus
see Hadrian

PUCCINI, GIACOMO (1858-1924), Italian composer **12** 474-476

PUDOVKIN, V. I. (Vsevolod Illiarionovich Pudovkin; 1893-1953), Russian film director **24** 316-318

PUFENDORF, BARON SAMUEL VON (1632-1694), German jurist and historian **12** 477-478

PUGACHEV, EMELYAN IVANOVICH (1742-1775), Russian Cossack soldier **12** 478-479

PUGIN, AUGUSTUS WELBY NORTHMORE (1812-1852), English architect **12** 479-480

PULASKI, CASIMIR (1747/48-79), Polish patriot **12** 480-481

PULCI, LUIGI (1432-1484), Italian poet **12** 481

PULITZER, JOSEPH (1847-1911), American editor and publisher **12** 481-482

PULLMAN, GEORGE MORTIMER (1831-1897), American industrial innovator **12** 482-483

PUPIN, MICHAEL IDVORSKY (1858-1935), Serbo-American physicist and inventor **12** 483-484

PURCELL, HENRY (1659-1695), English composer and organist **12** 484-485

PURVIS, ROBERT (1810-1898), African American abolitionist **12** 485-486

PURYEAR, MARTIN (born 1941), African American artist **12** 486-487

PUSEY, EDWARD BOUVERIE (1800-1882), English clergyman and scholar **12** 488-489

PUSHKIN, ALEKSANDR SERGEEVICH (1799-1837), Russian poet and prose writer **12** 489-491

PUTIN, VLADIMIR (born 1952), Russian president **21** 355-358
Kasparov, Garry **28** 194-196

PUTNAM, ISRAEL (1718-1790), American Revolutionary War general **12** 491-492

Putnam, Mary Corinna
see Jacobi, Mary Putnam

PUVIS DE CHAVANNES, PIERRE (1824-1898), French painter **12** 492-493

PYLE, ERNIE (Earnest Taylor Pyle; 1900-1945), American war correspondent during World War II **12** 493-494

PYM, FRANCIS (Francis Leslie Pym; 1922-2008), British statesman **12** 494-495

PYM, JOHN (1584-1643), English statesman **12** 495-496

PYNCHON, THOMAS (Thomas Ruggles Pynchon, Jr.; born 1937), American writer **12** 496-498

PYTHAGORAS (circa 575-circa 495 B.C.), Greek philosopher, scientist, and religious teacher **12** 498-499

PYTHEAS (c. 380 B.C.-c. 300 B.C.), Greek explorer **12** 499-500

Q

QABOOS IBN SA'ID (born 1940), ruler of the Sultanate of Oman **12** 501-502

QIANLONG (Ch'ien-lung and Hung-li; 1711-1799), Chinese emperor **12** 502-505

Quaid-i-Azam
see Jinnah, Mohammad Ali

QUANT, MARY (born 1934), British fashion designer and businesswoman **19** 303-305

Quaregna e di Cerreto, Conti di
see Avogadro, Lorenzo Romano Amedeo Carlo

Quarton, Enguerrand
see Charonton, Enguerrand

QUASIMODO, SALVATORE (1901-1968), Italian poet, translator, and critic **12** 506

QUAY, MATTHEW STANLEY (1833-1904), American politician **12** 507

QUAYLE, J(AMES) DANFORTH (born 1947), vice president under George Bush **12** 507-509

Queen, The (film)
Frears, Stephen Arthur **28** 127-129
Mirren, Helen **28** 247-249

QUELER, EVE RABIN (born 1936), American pianist and conductor **26** 309-311

QUERCIA, JACOPO DELLA (1374?-1438), Italian sculptor and architect **12** 509

Quesada, Gonzalo Jiménez de
see Jiménez de Quesada, Gonzalo

QUESTEL, MAE (Maq Kwestel; 1908-1998), American actress and voice-over professional **27** 299-301

Questions About Angels (book)
Collins, Billy **28** 83-85

QUÉTELET, LAMBERT ADOLPHE JACQUES (1796-1874), Belgian statistician and astronomer **12** 510-511

QUEVEDO Y VILLEGAS, FRANCISCO GÓMEZ DE (1580-1645), Spanish poet, satirist, and novelist **12** 511

QUEZON, MANUEL LUIS (1878-1944), Philippine statesman **12** 511-513

QUIMBY, HARRIET (1875-1912), American aviator **28** 285-287

QUINE, WILLARD VAN ORMAN (born 1908), American philosopher **12** 514-515

QUINN, ANTHONY (Antonio Rudolph Oaxaca Quinn; born 1915), Hispanic American actor and artist **20** 302-304

QUINTILIAN (circa 35-circa 99), Roman rhetorician and literary critic **12** 518-519

QUIRINO, ELPIDIO (1890-1956), Philippine statesman **12** 519-520

QUIROGA, HORACIO (1878-1937), Uruguayan writer **12** 520-521

QUIROGA, JUAN FACUNDO (1788/1790-1835), Argentine caudillo **12** 521-522

QUISLING, VIDKIN (1887-1945), Norwegian traitor **20** 304-306

Qur'ān
see Koran (Quran; religious book)

R

Rabbenu Gershom
see Gershom ben Judah

RABEARIVELO, JEAN JOSEPH (1901-1937), Malagasy poet **12** 523-524

RABELAIS, FRANÇOIS (circa 1494-circa 1553), French humanist, doctor, and writer **12** 524-526

RABI, ISIDOR ISAAC (1898-1988), American physicist **12** 526-527

RABIN, YITZCHAK (1922-1995), Israeli statesman **12** 527-529

Rabindranath
see Tagore, Rabindranath

Rabinowitz, Sholem
see Sholem Aleichem

RACHMANINOV, SERGEI VASILIEVICH (1873-1943), Russian composer, pianist, and conductor **12** 531-532

RACINE, JEAN BAPTISTE (1639-1699), French dramatist **12** 532-535

RADCLIFFE, ANN (Ann Ward Radcliffe; 1764-1823), English author and poet **28** 288-290

RADCLIFFE, TED (Theodore Roosevelt Radcliffe; 1902-2005), African American baseball player **26** 312-314

RADCLIFFE-BROWN, A(LFRED) R(EGINALD) (1881-1955), English anthropologist **12** 535-536

RADEK, KARL BERNARDOVICH (1885-1939), Russian Communist leader **12** 536-537

RADHAKRISHNAN, SARVEPALLI (1888-1995), Indian philosopher and statesman **12** 537-538

RADIN, PAUL (1883-1959), American anthropologist and ethnographer **12** 538-539

Radio (communications)
development
Gross, Al **28** 149-151
Ibuka, Masaru **28** 184-186
managers
Brainard, Bertha **28** 47-48
personalities
Vallee, Rudy **28** 359-361

RADISSON, PIERRE-ESPRIT (circa 1636-1710), French explorer **12** 539-540

Radomyslsky, Grigori Evseevich
see Zinoviev, Grigori Evseevich

RAFFLES, SIR THOMAS STAMFORD (1781-1826), English colonial administrator **13** 1-2

RAFINESQUE, CONSTANTINE SAMUEL (1783-1840), French naturalist **21** 359-361

RAFSANJANI, AKBAR HASHEMI (born 1934), president of Iran **13** 3-4

RAHNER, KARL (1904-1984), German Catholic theologian **13** 4-5

RAI, LALA LAJPAT (1865-1928), Indian nationalist leader **13** 5-6

Railroads (United States)
equipment
Woods, Granville T. **28** 378-381

RAIN IN THE FACE (Itonagaju; circa 1835-1905), Native American warrior **26** 314-316

RAINEY, MA (Gertrude Pridgett; 1886-1939), American singer **19** 306-308

RAINIER III, PRINCE OF MONACO (1923-2005), ruler of the principality of Monaco **18** 335-337

RAJAGOPALACHARI, CHAKRAVARTI (1879-1972), Indian nationalist leader **13** 6-7

RAJARAJA I (985-1014), Indian statesman **13** 7

RAJNEESH, BHAGWAN SHREE (Rahneesh Chandra Mohan; 1931-1990), Indian religious leader **13** 7-9

RALEIGH, SIR WALTER (or Ralegh; circa 1552-1618), English statesman, soldier, courtier, explorer, and poet **13** 9-11

Rama IV
see Mongkut

Rama V
see Chulalongkorn

RAMA KHAMHAENG (circa 1239-circa 1299), king of Sukhothai in Thailand **13** 11

RAMAKRISHNA, SRI (1833-1886), Indian mystic, reformer, and saint **13** 11-13

RAMAN, SIR CHANDRASEKHAR VENKATA (1888-1970), Indian physicist **13** 13-14

RAMANUJA (Ramanujacarya; c. 1017-1137), Indian theologian and philosopher **21** 361-362

RAMANUJAN AIYANGAR, SRINIVASA (1887-1920), India mathematician **13** 14-15

RAMAPHOSA, MATEMELA CYRIL (born 1952), general secretary of the National Union of Mineworkers (NUM) in South Africa and secretary general of the African National Congress **13** 15-16

RAMAZZINI, BERNARDINO (1633-1714), Italian physician **21** 362-364

Ramboldini, Vittorino
see Feltre, Vittorino da

RAMEAU, JEAN PHILIPPE (1683-1764), French music theorist and composer **13** 17-18

RAMGOOLAM, SEEWOOSAGUR (1900-1985), president of Mauritius **24** 319-321

RAMON, ILAN (Ilan Wolferman; 1954-2003), Israeli astronaut **25** 345-347

RAMOS, FIDEL VALDEZ (born 1928), president of the Philippines (1992-) **13** 18-19

RAMPAL, JEAN-PIERRE LOUIS (1922-2000), French flutist **22** 362-364

RAMPHAL, SHRIDATH SURENDRANATH (born 1928), Guyanese barrister, politician, and international civil servant **13** 19-20

RAMSAY, DAVID (1749-1815), American historian **13** 21

Ramsay, James Andrew Broun
see Dalhousie, 1st Marquess of

RAMSAY, SIR WILLIAM (1852-1916), British chemist and educator **13** 21-22

RAMSES II (ruled 1304-1237 B.C.), pharaoh of Egypt **13** 22-23

RAMSEY, ARTHUR MICHAEL (1904-1988), archbishop of Canterbury and president of the World Council of Churches **13** 23-25

RAMSEY, FRANK PLUMPTON (1903-1930), English mathematician and philosopher **13** 25

RAMSEY, NORMAN FOSTER, JR. (born 1915), American physicist **13** 25-27

RAMUS, PETRUS (1515-1572), French humanist, logician and mathematician **13** 27-28

RANAVALONA I (c. 1788-1861), Queen of Madagascar **27** 302-304

RAND, AYN (1905-1982), American author and philosoher **20** 307-309

RANDOLPH, A. PHILIP (1889-1979), African American labor and civil rights leader **13** 28-29

RANDOLPH, EDMUND (1753-1813), American statesman **13** 29-30

RANDOLPH, JOHN (1773-1833), American statesman **13** 30

RANDOLPH, PEYTON (1721-1775), American statesman **18** 337-339

RANDS, BERNARD (born 1934), American musician **23** 324-326

RANGEL, CHARLES B. (born 1930), Democratic U.S. representative from New York City **13** 31-32

RANJIT SINGH (1780-1839), ruler of the Punjab **13** 32-33

RANK, OTTO (1884-1939), Austrian psychotherapist **13** 33

RANKE, LEOPOLD VON (1795-1886), German historian **13** 33-35

RANKIN, JEANNETTE PICKERING (1880-1973), first woman elected to the U.S. Congress **13** 35-37

RANNARIDH, PRINCE NORODOM (born 1944), first prime minister of Cambodia **13** 37-39

RANSOM, JOHN CROWE (1888-1974), American poet and critic **13** 39-40

RAPHAEL (1483-1520), Italian painter and architect **13** 40-42

RAPP, GEORGE (1757-1847), German-American religious leader **13** 42-43

RAPPOPORT, SHLOYME ZANUL (S. Ansky; Solomon Ansky), Russian Jewish author and journalist **27** 304-306

Ras Tafari
see Haile Selassie

RASHI (1040-1105), French Jewish scholar and commentator **13** 43

RASMUSSEN, ANDERS FOGH (born 1953), Danish prime minister **27** 306-308

RASMUSSEN, KNUD JOHAN VICTOR (1879-1933), Danish Arctic explorer and ethnologist **13** 44

RASPUTIN, GRIGORI EFIMOVICH (1872-1916), Russian monk **13** 44-45
Grand Duchess Olga Nikolaevna **28** 141-143

RATANA, TAUPOTIKI WIREMU (1870-1939), spiritual and political leader of the New Zealand Maori people **13** 46

RATHBONE, ELEANOR (Eleanor Florence Rathbone; 1872-1946), British politician and social reformer **13** 47-48

RATHENAU, WALTHER (1867-1922), German industrialist and statesman **13** 48-49

RATHER, DAN IRVIN (born 1931), American journalist **24** 321-324

Ratti, Abrogio Damiano Achille
see Pius XI

RATTLE, SIMON DENIS (born 1955), conductor of England's City of Birmingham Symphony Orchestra **13** 49-50

RATZEL, FRIEDRICH (1844-1904), German geographer **13** 50-51

RAU, JOHANNES (1931-2006), German Social Democrat politician **13** 51-52

RAUSCHENBERG, ROBERT (born 1925), American painter and printmaker **13** 52-53

RAUSCHENBUSCH, WALTER (1861-1918), American Baptist clergyman **13** 53-54

Rav
see Abba Arika

RAVEL, MAURICE JOSEPH (1875-1937), French composer **13** 54-55

RAWLS, JOHN (1921-2002), American political philosopher **13** 55-56

RAY, DIXY LEE (1914-1994), marine biologist and governor of Washington **13** 56-57

RAY, JAMES EARL (1928-1998), American assassin **27** 308-310

RAY, JOHN (1627-1705), English naturalist **13** 57-59

RAY, MAN (1890-1976), American painter, photographer, and object maker **13** 59-60

RAY, NICHOLAS (Raymond Nicholas Kienzle; 1911-1978), American film director **22** 364-366

RAY, SATYAJIT (1921-1992), Indian film director **13** 60-61

RAYBURN, SAMUEL TALIAFERRO (1882-1961), American statesman **13** 61-62

RAYLEIGH, 3D BARON (John William Strutt; 1842-1919), English physicist **13** 62

RAZI (Abu Bakr Muhammad ibn Zakariya al-Razi; circa 865-925), Persian physician **13** 63-64

RAZIA (Raziya; c. 1210-1240), sultana of Delhi **23** 326-329

READING, 1ST MARQUESS OF (Rufus Daniel Isaacs; 1860-1935), English lawyer and statesman **13** 64

REAGAN, NANCY DAVIS (Anne Frances Robbins; born 1921), American First Lady and actress **24** 324-327

REAGAN, RONALD W. (1911-2004), governor of California (1967-1975) and U.S. president (1981-1989) **13** 65-68

Realism (literature)
Finnish
Canth, Minna **28** 58-60

Rebecca
see Pocahontas (ballet)

REBER, GROTE (1911-2002), American radio astronomer **21** 364-366

RECORDE, ROBERT (1510-1558), English mathematician **13** 68-69

RECTO, CLARO M. (1890-1960), Philippine nationalist and statesman **13** 69-70

RED CLOUD (1822-1909), American Oglala Sioux Indian chief **13** 70-71

RED JACKET (Sagoyewatha; 1758-1830), Seneca tribal leader **13** 71-73

REDFIELD, ROBERT (1897-1958), American anthropologist **13** 73-74

REDFORD, ROBERT (Charles Robert Redford, Jr.; born 1937), American actor, producer, and director **18** 339-342

REDGRAVE, MICHAEL (1908-1985), English actor **24** 327-329

REDGRAVE, VANESSA (born 1937), British actress and political activist **13** 74-75

REDON, ODILON (1840-1916), French painter and graphic artist **13** 75-76

REDSTONE, SUMNER MURRAY (born 1932), American businessman **23** 329-331

REED, ISHMAEL (Emmett Coleman; born 1938), African American author **23** 331-333

REED, JOHN SILAS (1887-1920), American revolutionist, poet, and journalist **13** 76-77

REED, THOMAS BRACKETT (1839-1902), American statesman and parliamentarian **13** 77

REED, WALTER (1851-1902), American military surgeon **13** 78

REES, LLOYD FREDERIC (1895-1988), Australian artist **13** 78-79

REEVE, CHRISTOPHER (1952-2004), American actor and activist **18** 342-344

REEVE, TAPPING (1744-1823), American jurist **13** 79-80

Reflections on War, Evil, and the End of History (book)
Lévy, Bernard-Henri **28** 213-215

Reform, social
see Social reform

REGAN, DONALD (Donald Thomas Regan; born 1918), American secretary of the treasury and White House chief of staff under Reagan **13** 80-81

REGIOMONTANUS (1436-1476), German astronomer and mathematician **13** 81-82

REHNQUIST, WILLIAM HUBBS (1924-2005), U.S. Supreme Court chief justice **13** 82-84

REICH, STEVE (born 1936), American composer **13** 84-85

REICHSTEIN, TADEUS (1897-1996), Polish-Swiss chemist **13** 85-87

REID, THOMAS (1710-1796), Scottish philosopher, clergyman, and teacher **13** 87-88

REID, WILLIAM RONALD (Bill Reid; 1920-1998), Canadian artist **13** 88-89

Reign of Terror
see French Revolution—1792-95 (Reign of Terror)

REINER, FRITZ (Frederick Martin Reiner; Frigyes Reiner; 1888-1963), Hungarian-American conductor **26** 316-318

REINHARDT, MAX (Max Goldman; 1873-1943), Austrian stage director **13** 89-90

Reizenstein, Elmer
see Rice, Elmer

REJ, MIKOLAJ (Mikolaj Rey; Ambrozy Korczbok Rozek; 1505-1569), Polish writer **26** 318-320

Religious leaders, Baha'I
Bahá'u'lláh **28** 21-23

Religious leaders, Catholic (since 1517)
nuns
Thérèse of Lisieux, Saint **28** 347-350
priests
Tolton, Augustine **28** 354-356

Religious leaders, Evangelical
Roberts, Oral **28** 296-298

Religious leaders, Hindu (India)
Amma **28** 8-10
Krishnamurti, Uppaluri Gopala **28** 201-203

Religious leaders, Islamic
reformers
  Dehlavi, Shah Waliullah **28** 92-94
theologians
  Nursî, Said **28** 259-261

Religious leaders, Sikh (India)
Singh, Gobind **28** 327-328

Reluctant Dragon, The (story)
Grahame, Kenneth **28** 138-140

REMARQUE, ERICH MARIA (Erich Paul
Remark; 1898-1970), German novelist
13 91

REMBRANDT HARMENSZ VAN RIJN
(1606-1669), Dutch painter and etcher
13 91-95

Remi, Geroges
see Hergé

REMINGTON, FREDERIC (1861-1909),
American painter, sculptor, and
illustrator **18** 344-346

REMOND, CHARLES LENNOX (1810-
1873), American black abolitionist **13**
95

RENAN, ERNEST (1823-1892), French
author and philologist **13** 95-96

RENAULT, LOUIS (1877-1944), French
automobile designer and businessman
25 347-349

Rencho
see Nichiren

RENDELL, RUTH (Ruth Grasemann
Rendell; born 1930), English writer of
mysteries and suspense thrillers **13**
96-97

RENI, GUIDO (1575-1642), Italian
painter **13** 97-98

RENNER, KARL (1870-1950), Austrian
statesman, president 1945-50 **13** 98-99

RENO, JANET (born 1938), U.S. attorney
general (1993-2001) **13** 99-101

RENOIR, JEAN (1894-1979), French-
American film director, producer, and
screenwriter **22** 366-369
Bazin, André **28** 32-33

RENOIR, PIERRE AUGUSTE (1841-
1919), French impressionist painter **13**
101-102

RENWICK, JAMES (1818-1895),
American architect **13** 102-103

REPIN, ILYA EFIMOVICH (Il'ia Repin;
1844-1930), Russian artist **24** 330-332

Republic (book; Plato)
see Plato—Republic

RESNAIS, ALAIN (born 1922), French
filmmaker **23** 333-335

RESNIK, JUDITH ARLENE (Judy Resnik;
1949-1986), American astronaut **22**
369-371

RESPIGHI, OTTORINO (1879-1936),
Italian composer **13** 103-104

RESTON, JAMES BARRETT ("Scotty";
born 1909), American journalist and
political commentator **13** 104-105

RETIEF, PIETER (1780-1838), South
African Boer leader **13** 105-106

RETTON, MARY LOU (born 1968),
American gymnast **25** 349-352

REUCHLIN, JOHANN (1455-1522),
German humanist and jurist **13**
106-107

REUTER, PAUL JULIUS VON (Isreal Beer
Josaphat; 1816-1899), French journalist
21 366-367

REUTHER, WALTER PHILIP (1907-1970),
American labor leader **13** 107-108

REVEL, BERNARD (1885-1940),
Talmudic scholar and educator **13**
108-109

REVELS, HIRAM RHOADES (1822-1901),
African American clergyman,
statesman, and educator **13** 109-110

REVERE, PAUL (1735-1818), American
patriot, silversmith, and engraver **13**
110-111

REVILLAGIGEDO, CONDE DE (Juan
Vicente Güemes Pacheco y Padilla;
1740-1799), Spanish colonial
administrator, viceroy of New Spain **13**
111-112

REYES, ALFONSO (1889-1959), Mexican
author and diplomat **13** 112-113

REYES, RAFAEL (1850-1920), Colombian
military leader, president 1904-09 **13**
113

REYMONT, WLADYSLAW STANISLAW
(Wladyslaw Rejment; 1868-1925),
Polish author **25** 352-353

REYNOLDS, ALBERT (born 1932), prime
minister of Ireland **13** 113-115

REYNOLDS, SIR JOSHUA (1723-1792),
English portrait painter **13** 115-116

REYNOLDS, RICHARD JOSHUA JR. (R.J.
Reynolds; 1906-1964), American
businessman and philanthropist **19**
308-310

REZA SHAH PAHLAVI (Reza Khan;
1878-1944), Shah of Iran 1925-41 **13**
116-117

RHEE, SYNGMAN (1875-1965), Korean
independence leader, South Korean
president 1948-60 **13** 117-120

RHETT, ROBERT BARNWELL (1800-
1876), American statesman **13** 120

RHODES, CECIL JOHN (1853-1902),
English imperialist and financier **13**
120-122

RHODES, JAMES FORD (1848-1927),
American historian **13** 122

RHYS, JEAN (Ella Gwendolen Rees
Williams; 1890-1979), English author
19 310-312

RIBERA, JUSEPE DE (1591-1652),
Spanish painter **13** 122-123

Ribonucleic acid (biochemistry)
Mello, Craig Cameron **28** 238-241

RICARDO, DAVID (1772-1823), English
economist **13** 123-124

RICCI, MATTEO (1552-1610), Italian
Jesuit missionary **13** 124-125

RICE, ANNE (born 1941), American
author **13** 125-126

RICE, CONDOLEEZZA (born 1954),
African American national security
advisor **23** 335-338

RICE, ELMER (1892-1967), American
playwright and novelist **13** 126-127

RICE, JOSEPH MAYER (1857-1934),
American education reformer **13**
127-128

RICH, ADRIENNE (born 1929), American
poet **13** 128-130

RICHARD I (1157-1199), king of England
1189-99 **13** 130

RICHARD II (1367-1400), king of
England 1377-99 **13** 130-131

RICHARD III (1452-1485), king of
England 1483-85 **13** 132-133
Woodville, Elizabeth **28** 381-383

Richard, Duke of Gloucester
see Richard III (play; Shakespeare)

Richard the "Lion-Hearted"
see Richard I

RICHARD, MAURICE ("Rocket" Richard;
born 1921), Canadian hockey player
19 312-313

RICHARDS, ANN WILLIS (1933-2006),
Democratic governor of Texas **13**
133-134

RICHARDS, ELLEN H. (born Ellen
Henrietta Swallow; 1842-1911),
American chemist and educator **13**
134-136

RICHARDS, IVOR ARMSTRONG (1893-
1979), English-born American
semanticist and literary critic **13** 137

RICHARDS, THEODORE WILLIAM
(1868-1928), American chemist **13**
137-138

RICHARDSON, HENRY HANDEL (pen
name of Ethel Florence Lindesay
Richardson; 1870-1946), expatriate
Australian novelist **13** 139

RICHARDSON, HENRY HOBSON
(1838-1886), American architect **13**
139-141

RICHARDSON, RALPH DAVID (1902-
1983), British actor **24** 332-334

RICHARDSON, SAMUEL (1689-1761),
English novelist **13** 141-142
Chapone, Hester **28** 72-74

**RICHELIEU, ARMAND JEAN DU
PLESSIS DE** (1585-1642), French
statesman and cardinal **13** 142-144

RICHET, CHARLES ROBERT (1850-
1935), French physiologist **13** 144-145

RICHIER, GERMAINE (1904-1959),
French sculptor **13** 145-146

RICHLER, MORDECAI (1931-2001),
Canadian author **22** 371-373

RICHTER, BURTON (born 1931),
American physicist **25** 354-356

RICHTER, CHARLES F. (1900-1985),
American seismologist **13** 146-148

RICHTER, CONRAD MICHAEL (1890-
1968), American novelist and short-
story writer **13** 148-149

RICHTER, GERHARD (born 1932),
German artist **23** 338-340

RICHTER, HANS (Johann Siegried
Richter; 1888-1976), German-born film
director **13** 149-150

RICHTER, JOHANN PAUL FRIEDRICH
(1763-1825), German humorist and
prose writer **13** 150-151

RICIMER, FLAVIUS (died 472), Germanic
Roman political chief **13** 151-152

RICKENBACKER, EDWARD VERNON
(1890-1973), World War I fighter pilot
and airline president **13** 152-153

RICKEY, WESLEY BRANCH (1881-1965),
innovative baseball executive **13**
153-155

RICKOVER, HYMAN GEORGE (1900-
1986), U.S. Navy officer **13** 155-157

RICOEUR, PAUL (born 1913), French
exponent of hermeneutical philosophy
13 157-158

RIDE, SALLY (born 1951), American
astronaut and physicist **13** 158-160

RIDGE, JOHN ROLLIN (Yellow Bird;
1827-1867), Native American author
22 373-375

RIDGE, THOMAS JOSEPH (born 1946),
American governor of Pennsylvania
and first secretary of the Department of
Homeland Security **24** 334-337

RIDGWAY, MATTHEW BUNKER (1895-
1993), American general **13** 160-161

RIDGWAY, ROZANNE LEJEANNE (born
1935), American diplomat **24** 337-338

RIEFENSTAHL, LENI (born 1902),
German film director **13** 161-163

RIEL, LOUIS (1844-1885), Canadian
rebel **13** 163-164

**RIEMANN, GEORG FRIEDRICH
BERNARD** (1826-1866), German
mathematician **13** 164-165

RIEMENSCHNEIDER, TILMAN (1468-
1531), German sculptor **13** 166

RIENZI, COLA DI (or Rienzo; 1313/14-
1354), Italian patriot, tribune of Rome
13 166-167

RIESMAN, DAVID (1909-2002),
American sociologist, writer, and
social critic **13** 167-168

RIETVELD, GERRIT THOMAS (1888-
1964), Dutch architect and furniture
designer **13** 169

Rigaud, Pierre François de
see Vaudreuil-Cavagnal, Marquis de

RIIS, JACOB AUGUST (1849-1914),
Danish-born American journalist and
reformer **13** 169-170

RILEY, JAMES WHITCOMB (1849-1916),
American poet **13** 170-171

RILKE, RAINER MARIA (1875-1926),
German lyric poet **13** 171-172
Andreas-Salomé, Lou **28** 12-14

RILLIEUX, NORBERT (1806-1894),
American inventor **20** 309-311

RIMBAUD, (JEAN NICOLAS) ARTHUR
(1854-1891), French poet **13** 172-174

RIMMER, WILLIAM (1816-1879),
American sculptor, painter, and
physician **13** 174

**RIMSKY-KORSAKOV, NIKOLAI
ANDREEVICH** (1844-1908), Russian
composer and conductor **13** 174-175

RINGGOLD, FAITH (Faith Jones; born
1930), African American painter,
sculptress, and performer **13** 175-177

RIO BRANCO, BARÃO DO (José Maria
da Silva Paranhos; 1845-1912),
Brazilian political leader **13** 177

RIORDAN, RICHARD JOSEPH (born
1930), American politician; mayor of
Los Angeles **13** 177-179

RIPKEN, CAL, JR. (Calvin Edwin Ripken,
Jr.; born 1960), American baseball
player **18** 346-349

RIPLEY, GEORGE (1802-1880), American
Unitarian minister and journalist **13**
179-180

Riqueti, H. G. V. de
see Mirabeau, Comte de

Risale-i Nur Collection (religious
commentary, Islam)
Nursî, Said **28** 259-261

Rissho Daishi
see Nichiren

RITCHIE, DENNIS MACALISTAIR (born
1941), American computer
programmer **27** 310-311

RITSCHL, ALBRECHT BENJAMIN (1822-
1889), German theologian **13** 180

RITTENHOUSE, DAVID (1732-1796),
American astronomer and instrument
maker **13** 180-181

RITTER, KARL (1779-1859), German
geographer **13** 181-182

Ritter, Mary
see Beard, Mary Ritter

RIVADAVIA, BERNARDINO (1780-
1845), Argentine independence leader,
president 1826-27 **13** 182-183

RIVAS, DUQUE DE (Angel de Saavedra;
1791-1865), Spanish poet, dramatist,
and statesman **13** 398

RIVERA, DIEGO (1886-1957), Mexican
painter **13** 183-184

RIVERA, FRUCTUOSO (circa 1788-
1854), Uruguayan statesman **13**
184-185

RIVERA, JOSÉ EUSTACIO (1888-1928),
Colombian novelist **13** 185-186

Rivera, Luis Muñoz
see Muñoz Rivera, Luís

RIVERS, LARRY (Yitzroch Loiza
Grossberg; 1923-2002), American artist
13 186-187

RIVLIN, ALICE M. (born 1931),
American economist and political
advisor **18** 349-350

RIZAL, JOSÉ (1861-1896), Philippine
national hero **13** 187-189

RNA
see Ribonucleic acid (biochemistry)

ROA BASTOS, AUGUSTO (born 1917),
Paraguayan author **24** 338-341

ROACH, HAL (Harold Eugene Roach;
1892-1992), American filmmaker **28**
290-292

ROACH, MAX (Maxwell Lemuel Roach; 1924-2007), American jazz drummer, composer, and educator **28** 292-296

ROBARDS, JASON (Jason Nelson Robards, JR.; 1922-2000), American Actor **22** 375-378

ROBBE-GRILLET, ALAIN (1922-2008), French novelist **13** 189-190

ROBBIA, LUCA DELLA (1400-1482), Italian sculptor **10** 19-20

ROBBINS, JEROME (Rabinowitz; 1918-1998), American director and choreographer **13** 190-192

ROBERT I (1274-1329), king of Scotland 1306-29 **13** 192-194

ROBERT II (1316-1390), king of Scotland 1371-90 **13** 194

ROBERT III (circa 1337-1406), king of Scotland 1390-1406 **13** 194-195

ROBERT, HENRY MARTYN (1837-1923), American engineer and parliamentarian **21** 367-370

ROBERT, SHAABAN (1909-1962), Tanzanian author who wrote in the Swahili language **14** 128-129

Robert Bruce
see Robert I (king, Scotland)

ROBERTS, FREDERICK SLEIGH (1st Earl Roberts of Kandhar, Pretoria, and Waterford; 1832-1914), British field marshal **13** 195-196

ROBERTS, JOHN GLOVER, JR. (born 1955), American jurist, chief justice of the United States Supreme Court 2005-**26** 320-322

ROBERTS, ORAL (Granville Oral Roberts; born 1918), American evangelist **28** 296-298

Roberts of Kandahar, Pretoria, and Waterford, 1st Earl
see Roberts, Frederick Sleigh

Robertson, Anna Mary
see Moses, Grandma

ROBERTSON, SIR DENNIS HOLME (1890-1963), English economist **13** 196

ROBERTSON, MARION G. (Pat Robertson; born 1930), television evangelist who founded the Christian Broadcasting Network and presidential candidate **13** 196-198

ROBERTSON, OSCAR (born 1938), African American basketball player **20** 311-313

ROBESON, ESLANDA GOODE (born Eslanda Cardozo Goode; 1896-1965), African American cultural anthropologist **23** 340-342

ROBESON, PAUL LEROY (1898-1976), American singer, actor, and political activist **13** 198-199

ROBESPIERRE, MAXIMILIEN FRANÇOIS MARIE ISIDORE DE (1758-1794), French Revolutionary leader **13** 199-201

ROBINSON, EDDIE (1919-2007), African American college football coach **18** 351-352

ROBINSON, EDWIN ARLINGTON (1869-1935), American poet and playwright **13** 201-202

ROBINSON, FRANK, JR. (born 1935), African American baseball player and manager **13** 202-203

ROBINSON, HARRIET HANSON (1825-1911), American author and suffragist **13** 203-207

ROBINSON, JACK ROOSEVELT (Jackie Robinson; 1919-72), African American baseball player; first African American player in the major leagues **13** 207-208

ROBINSON, JAMES HARVEY (1863-1936), American historian **13** 208

ROBINSON, JOAN VIOLET MAURICE (1903-1983), English economist **13** 209-210

ROBINSON, SIR JOHN BEVERLEY (1791-1863), Canadian political leader and jurist **13** 215-217

ROBINSON, JULIA (1919-1985), American mathematician **13** 210-211

ROBINSON, MARY BOURKE (born 1944), first woman president of Ireland **13** 211-213

ROBINSON, MAX (1939-1988), African American television news anchor **13** 213-215

ROBINSON, RANDALL (born 1941), American author and activist **23** 342-345

ROBINSON, SMOKEY (born 1940), African American performer and composer **13** 215-217

ROBINSON, SUGAR RAY (Walker Smith Jr.; 1921-1989), American boxer **19** 313-315

ROBINSON, THEODORE (1852-1896), American painter **13** 217

Robusti, Jacopo
see Tintoretto

ROCA, JULIO ARGENTINO (1843-1914), Argentine general and president **13** 218

ROCARD, MICHEL (born 1930), French left-wing politician **13** 218-220

ROCHAMBEAU, COMTE DE (Jean Baptiste Donatien de Vimeur, 1725-1807), French general **13** 220-221

ROCHBERG, GEORGE (1918-2005), American composer **13** 221-222

ROCHE, KEVIN (born 1922), Irish-American architect **13** 222-224

ROCK, ARTHUR (born 1926), American businessman **19** 316-317

ROCK, JOHN (1825-1866), American physician, lawyer, and abolitionist **21** 370-372

Rock and Roll Hall of Fame
Paul, Les **28** 276-278

ROCKEFELLER, DAVID (born 1915), chairman of the Chase Manhattan Bank **13** 224-225

ROCKEFELLER, JOHN D., JR. (1874-1960), American philanthropist and industrial relations expert **13** 225-226

ROCKEFELLER, JOHN DAVISON (1839-1937), American industrialist and philanthropist **13** 226-228

ROCKEFELLER, NELSON ALDRICH (1908-1979), four-term governor of New York and vice-president of the United States **13** 228-230

ROCKINGHAM, 2D MARQUESS OF (Charles Watson-Wentworth; 1730-82), English statesman **13** 230-231

ROCKNE, KNUTE (1888-1931), American football coach **13** 231

ROCKWELL, NORMAN PERCEVEL (1894-1978), American illustrator **13** 231-233

RODAN, MENDI (Mendi Rosenblum; born 1929), Israeli musician **25** 356-358

RODCHENKO, ALEXANDER MIKHAILOVICH (1891-1956), Russian abstract painter, sculptor, photographer, and industrial designer **13** 233-234

RODDICK, ANITA (Anita Lucia Perilli; Dame Anita Roddick; 1942-2007), British businesswoman and activist **28** 298-301

RODGERS, JIMMIE (James Charles Rodgers; 1897-1933), American musician **19** 317-319

RODGERS, RICHARD CHARLES (1902-1972), American composer **13** 234-236

RODIN, AUGUSTE (1840-1917), French sculptor **13** 236-238

RODINO, PETER WALLACE, JR. (born 1909), Democratic U.S. representative from New Jersey **13** 238-239

RODNEY, GEORGE BRYDGES (1st Baron Rodney; 1718-92), British admiral **13** 239-240

RODÓ, JOSÉ ENRIQUE (1872-1917), Uraguayan essayist and literary critic **13** 240-241

RODRIGUES, AMÁLIA (Amália da Piedade Rodrigues; 1920-1999), Portuguese vocalist **28** 301-302

RODRÍGUEZ DE TÍO, LOLA (1834-1924), Puerto Rican/Cuban poet and nationalist **23** 345-346

ROEBLING, JOHN AUGUSTUS (1806-1869), German-born American engineer **13** 241-242

ROEBLING, WASHINGTON AUGUSTUS (1837-1926), American engineer and manufacturer **13** 243

Roentgen, Wilhelm Conrad
see Röntgen, Wilhelm Conrad

ROETHKE, THEODORE (1908-1963), American poet and teacher **13** 243-244

ROGER II (1095-1154), king of Sicily 1130-54 **13** 244-245

ROGERS, CARL RANSOM (1902-1987), American psychotherapist **13** 245-247

ROGERS, EDITH NOURSE (1881-1960), U.S. congresswoman from Massachusetts **13** 247-248

ROGERS, FRED ("Mr." Rogers; 1928-2003), American television host **18** 352-354

ROGERS, JOHN (1829-1904), American sculptor **13** 248

ROGERS, RICHARD (born 1933), British architect **13** 248-250

ROGERS, ROBERT (1731-1795), American frontiersman and army officer **13** 250-251

ROGERS, WILL (1879-1935), American actor, humorist, journalist, and performer **13** 251-252

ROH TAE WOO (born 1932), president of the Republic of Korea **13** 253-255

Roha (town, Ethiopia)
see Lalibela (town; Ethiopia)

ROHDE, RUTH BRYAN OWEN (1885-1954), U.S. congresswoman **13** 252-253

ROHRER, HEINRICH (Born 1933), Swiss physicist **25** 358-360

ROJAS PINILLA, GUSTAVO (1900-1975), Colombian general and politician **13** 255-256

ROLAND, MADAME (Marie-Jeanne Phlipon; 1754-1793), French author and revolutionary **13** 256-259

ROLDÁN, LUISA IGNACIA (circa 1650-circa 1704), Spanish sculptor **26** 322-324

Rolf
see Rollo

ROLFE, JOHN (1585-1622), English colonist in Virginia **13** 259-260

ROLLAND, ROMAIN (1866-1944), French writer **13** 260

ROLLE OF HAMPOLE, RICHARD (circa 1290-1349), English prose and verse writer **13** 260-261

ROLLING STONES, THE (formed in 1963), rock and roll band **13** 261-264

ROLLINS, CHARLEMAE HILL (1897-1979), African American librarian and author **23** 346-348

ROLLO (Rolf; circa 860-circa 932), Viking adventurer **13** 264-265

RÖLVAAG, OLE EDVART (1876-1931), Norwegian-American writer **13** 265

Roman Catholic Church
Easter
Dionysius Exiguus **28** 99-100

Roman Catholic Church (United States)
19th century
Tolton, Augustine **28** 354-356

Roman Empire
see Rome—217 B.C.-A.D. 476

Roman Republic
see Rome—509-27 B.C.

Romanian music
Lipatti, Dinu **28** 222-223

ROMANOV, ANASTASIA NICHOLAIEVNA (1901-1918), Russian grand duchess **18** 354-357
Grand Duchess Olga Nikolaevna **28** 141-143

Romanticism (dance)
Taglioni, Marie **28** 345-347

ROMBAUER, IRMA VON STARKLOFF (1877-1962), American cookbook author **26** 324-326

Romboutszoon, Theodorik
see Bouts, Dirk

Rome
• 27 B.C.-A.D. 476 (ROMAN EMPIRE) rulers (military despots)
Galerius, Emperor of Rome **28** 132-134

ROMERO, ARCHBISHOP OSCAR (1917-1980), archbishop of San Salvador **13** 265-267

ROMERO BARCELÓ, CARLOS (born 1932), Puerto Rican political leader and governor **13** 267-268

ROMILLY, SAMUEL (1757-1818), English legal reformer **23** 348-351

ROMM, MIKHAIL (Mikhail Ilyich Romm; 1901-1917), Russian filmmaker, artist, and author **28** 303-304

ROMMEL, ERWIN (1891-1944), German field marshal **13** 268-269

ROMNEY, GEORGE (1734-1802), English painter **13** 269-270

ROMNEY, GEORGE (1907-1995), American businessman and politician **20** 313-316

RÓMULO, CARLOS P. (1899-1985), Filipino journalist and diplomat **13** 270-271

RONDON, CANDIDO MARIANO DA SILVA (1865-1958), Brazilian militarist **13** 271

RONSARD, PIERRE DE (1524-1585), French poet **13** 271-273

RÖNTGEN, WILHELM CONRAD (1845-1923), German physicist **13** 273-275

ROOSEVELT, ANNA ELEANOR (1884-1962), American lecturer and author, first lady 1933-45 **13** 275-277

ROOSEVELT, FRANKLIN DELANO (1882-1945), American statesman, president 1933-45 **13** 277-280

ROOSEVELT, THEODORE (1858-1919), American statesman, president 1901-09 **13** 280-283

ROOT, ELIHU (1845-1937), American statesman **13** 283-284

ROOT, JOHN WELLBORN (1850-1891), American architect **21** 372-374

ROREM, NED (born 1923), American composer of art songs **13** 284-286

RORSCHACH, HERMANN (1884-1922), Swiss psychiatrist **13** 286-288

RORTY, RICHARD (1931-2007), American philosopher and man of letters **13** 288-289

ROSA, SALVATOR (1615-1673), Italian painter and poet **13** 289-290

ROSAS, JUAN MANUEL DE (1793-1877), Argentine dictator 1829-52 **13** 290-291

ROSE, PETE (Peter Edward Rose; born 1941), American baseball player **21** 374-376

ROSEBUD YELLOW ROBE (Rosebud yellow Robe-Frantz; 1907-1992), Native American author and educator **26** 390-392

ROSENBERG, JULIUS AND ETHEL (died 1953), Americans executed for atomic espionage **13** 291-293

ROSENWALD, JULIUS (1862-1932), American retailer and philanthropist **13** 293

ROSENZWEIG, FRANZ (1886-1929), Jewish philosopher and writer **13** 294

ROS-LEHTINEN, ILEANA (born 1952), Hispanic American U.S. congresswoman **13** 294-296

ROSMINI-SERBATI, ANTONIO (1797-1855), Italian philosopher and priest **13** 296-297

ROSS, BETSY (Elizabeth Griscom; 1752-1836), American upholsterer who made the first U.S. flag **13** 297-298

ROSS, DIANA (born 1944), African American singer **13** 298-300

ROSS, EDWARD ALSWORTH (1866-1951), American sociologist **13** 300

ROSS, HAROLD (Harold Wallace Ross; 1892-1951), founder and editor of the *New Yorker* magazine **13** 300-302

Ross, Harriet
see Tubman, Harriet Ross

Ross, J. H.
see Lawrence, Thomas Edward

ROSS, SIR JAMES CLARK (1800-1862), English admiral and polar explorer **13** 302-303

ROSS, SIR JOHN (1777-1856), British explorer **22** 378-380

ROSS, JOHN (1790-1866), American Cherokee Indian chief **13** 303-304

ROSS, MARY G. (born 1908), Native American aerospace engineer **13** 304-305

ROSS, NELLIE TAYLOE (1876-1977), American politician **13** 305-306

ROSSELLINI, ROBERTO (1906-1977), Italian film director **20** 316-318

ROSSETTI, CHRISTINA GEORGINA (1830-1894), English poet **13** 307-308

ROSSETTI, DANTE GABRIEL (1828-1882), English painter and poet **13** 308-309

ROSSI, ALDO (born 1931), Italian architect **13** 309-310

ROSSI, LUIGI (circa 1598-1653), Italian composer **13** 310-311

ROSSINI, GIOACCHINO (1792-1868), Italian composer **13** 311-312

ROSSO, IL (Giovanni Battista di Jacopo; 1495-1540), Italian painter **13** 312-313

ROSSO, MEDARDO (1858-1928), Italian sculptor **13** 313-315

ROSTOVTZEFF, MICHAEL IVANOVICH (1870-1952), Russian-born American historian and classical scholar **13** 315

ROSTOW, WALT WHITMAN (1916-2003), American educator, economist, and government official **13** 315-317

ROSTROPOVICH, MSTISLAV LEOPOLDOVICH (Slava Rostropovich; 1927-2007), Russian cellist and conductor **13** 317-318

ROTH, PHILIP (born 1933), American author **13** 318-320

ROTHENBERG, SUSAN (born 1945), American artist **26** 326-328

ROTHKO, MARK (1903-1970), American painter **13** 320-321

ROTHSCHILD, MAYER (1744-1812), German merchant banker **20** 318-320

ROTTMAYR, JOHANN MICHAEL (1654-1730), Austrian painter **13** 321

ROUAULT, GEORGES (1871-1958), French painter and graphic artist **13** 321-322

ROUS, FRANCIS PEYTON (1879-1970), American pathologist and virologist **13** 322-323

ROUSSEAU, HENRI (1844-1910), French painter **13** 323-324

ROUSSEAU, JEAN JACQUES (1712-1778), Swiss-born French philosopher and author **13** 324-328

ROUSSEAU, THÉODORE (1812-1867), French painter and draftsman **13** 328

Rousseau le Douanier
see Rousseau, Henri

ROUSSEL, ALBERT (1869-1937), French composer **13** 328-329

Rouvroy, Claude Henri de
see Saint-Simon, Comte de

Rouvroy, Louis de
see Saint-Simon, Comte de

Rovere, Giuliano della
see Julius II

ROWAN, CARL T. (born 1925), American journalist, author, and ambassador **13** 329-330

ROWLAND, HENRY AUGUSTUS (1848-1901), American physicist **13** 330-331

Rowland, John
see Stanley, Sir Henry Morton

Rowley, Thomas
see Chatterton, Thomas

ROWLING, J.K. (Joanne Rowling; born 1966), British author **25** 360-363

ROXAS, MANUEL (1892-1948), Filipino statesman, president 1946-48 **13** 331-332

ROY, PATRICK (born 1965), Canadian hockey player **23** 351-353

ROY, RAM MOHUN (1772-1833), Bengali social and religious reformer **13** 18

ROYBAL-ALLARD, LUCILLE (born 1941), Hispanic American U.S. congresswoman **13** 332-334

ROYCE, JOSIAH (1855-1916), American philosopher **13** 334-335

ROYDEN, AGNES MAUDE (1876-1956), British preacher, lecturer, and author **13** 335-337

ROYKO, MIKE (1932-1997), American columnist **13** 337-339

ROZELLE, PETE (Alvin Ray Rozelle; 1926-1996), American commissioner of the National Football League (NFL) **19** 319-322

RUBENS, PETER PAUL (1577-1640), Flemish painter and diplomat **13** 339-342

RUBENSTEIN, HELENA (1870-1965), Polish-born beauty expert and businesswoman **13** 342-343

RUBENSTEIN, RICHARD L. (born 1924), American Jewish theologian and writer **13** 343-344

RUBIN, JERRY (1938-1994), activist, writer, lecturer, and businessman **13** 344-346

RUBIN, VERA COOPER (born 1928), American Astronomer **22** 380-382

RUBINSTEIN, ARTHUR (Artur Rubinstein; 1887-1982), Polish American pianist **28** 305-307

RUDKIN, MARGARET FOGARTY (1897-1976), founder and president of Pepperidge Farm Inc. **13** 346-347

RUDOLF I (Rudolf of Hapsburg; circa 1218-91), Holy Roman emperor-elect 1273-91 **13** 347-348

RUDOLPH, PAUL MARVIN (1918-1997), American architect **13** 348-350

RUDOLPH, WILMA (1940-1994), African American track and field athlete and coach **13** 350-352

RUEF, ABRAHAM (1864-1936), American political boss **13** 352-353

RUETHER, ROSEMARY RADFORD (born 1936), American church historian, theologian, writer, and teacher specializing in the area of women and religion **13** 353-354

RUFFIN, EDMUND (1794-1865), American agriculturist **13** 354-355

RUGG, HAROLD (1886-1960), American teacher, historian, and educational theorist **13** 355-357

RUISDAEL, JACOB VAN (1628/29-82), Dutch landscape painter **13** 357-358

RUÍZ, JOSÉ MARTÍNEZ (1873-1967), Spanish writer **13** 358

RUIZ, JUAN (1283?-1350?), Spanish poet **13** 358-359

RUIZ CORTINES, ADOLFO (1890-1973), president of Mexico (1952-1958) **13** 359-360

RUMFORD, COUNT (Benjamin Thompson; 1753-1814), American-born British physicist **13** 360-362

RUMI, JALAI ED-DIN (1207-1273), Persian poet and Sufi mystic **13** 362-363

RUMSFELD, DONALD HAROLD (born 1932), American statesman **23** 353-355

RUNDSTEDT, KARL RUDOLF GERD VON (1875-1953), German field marshal **13** 363-364

RUNEBERG, JOHAN LUDVIG (1804-1877), Finnish poet **25** 363-364

RURIK (died circa 873), Norman warrior **13** 364

RUSH, BENJAMIN (1745-1813), American physician **13** 364-365

RUSH, WILLIAM (1756-1833), American sculptor **13** 365-366

RUSHDIE, AHMED SALMAN (born 1947), Indian/British author **13** 366-368

RUSK, DAVID DEAN (1909-1994), American secretary of state (1961-1969) **13** 368-370

RUSKA, ERNST AUGUST FRIEDRICH (1906-1988), German engineer **13** 370-371

RUSKIN, JOHN (1819-1900), English critic and social theorist **13** 371-372

RUSSELL, ANNA (Anna Claudia Russell-Brown; 1911-2006), British born Canadian-American comedienne **28** 307-309

RUSSELL, BERTRAND ARTHUR WILLIAM (3rd Earl Russell; 1872-1970), British mathematician, philosopher, and social reformer **13** 373-374

RUSSELL, BILL (William Felton Russell; born 1934), African American basketball player and coach **20** 320-322

RUSSELL, CHARLES EDWARD (1860-1941), American journalist and reformer **13** 374-375

RUSSELL, CHARLES MARION (1864-1926), American painter **13** 375-376

RUSSELL, CHARLES TAZE (1852-1916), American religious leader **13** 376-377

RUSSELL, ELIZABETH SHULL (born 1913), American geneticist **13** 377-379

RUSSELL, JAMES EARL (1864-1945), educator and college dean who developed Teachers College **13** 379-380

RUSSELL, JOHN (1792-1878), English statesman, Prime minister 1846-52 **13** 380-381

Russell, 3d Earl
see Russell, Bertrand Arthur William

Russell of Kingston Russell, 1st Earl
see Russell, John

Russian literature
subversive
Vysotsky, Vladimir **28** 367-369

Russian music
ballads
Vysotsky, Vladimir **28** 367-369

RUSSWURM, JOHN BROWN (1799-1851), African American and Liberian journalist, educator, and governor **13** 381-382

RUSTIN, BAYARD (1910-1987), American social activist **13** 382-383

RUTAN, BURT (Elbert L. Rutan; born 1943), American aeronautical engineer **20** 322-325

RUTAN, DICK (Richard Glenn Rutan; born 1938), American aviator **20** 325-326

RUTH, GEORGE HERMAN, JR. (Babe Ruth; 1895-1948), American baseball player **13** 384

Ruth, Dr.
see Westheimer, Ruth Karola

RUTHERFORD, ERNEST (1st Baron Rutherford of Nelson; 1871-1937), British physicist **13** 384-387

RUTLEDGE, JOHN (1739-1800), American jurist and statesman **13** 387-388

RUYSBROECK, JAN VAN (1293-1381), Flemish mystic **13** 388-389

RUYSCH, RACHEL (1664-1750), Dutch artist **24** 341-343

RYAN, LYNN NOLAN (born 1947), American baseball player and author **13** 389-391

RYDER, ALBERT PINKHAM (1847-1917), American painter **13** 391-392

RYERSON, (ADOLPHUS) EGERTON (1803-1882), Canadian Methodist clergyman and educator **13** 392-393

RYLE, GILBERT (1900-1976), English philosopher **13** 393-394

RYLE, MARTIN (1918-1984), British radio astronomer **25** 365-367

S

SÁ, MEM DE (1504-1572), Portuguese jurist and governor general of Brazil **13** 395

Saadi
see Sa'di

SAADIA BEN JOSEPH AL-FAYUMI (882-942), Jewish scholar **13** 396

SAARINEN, EERO (1910-1961), Finnish-American architect and industrial designer **13** 396-398

SAARINEN, ELIEL (1873-1950), Finnish-American architect and industrial designer **13** 396-398

Saavedra, Angel de
see Rivas, Duque de

Saavedra Lamas, Carlos
see Lamas, Carlos Saavedra

SABATIER, PAUL (1854-1941), French chemist **13** 398-399

SÁBATO, ERNESTO (born 1911), Argentine novelist and essayist **13** 399-400

SABBATAI ZEVI (1626-1676), Jewish mystic and pseudo-Messiah **13** 400-401

Sabbatius, Flavius Petrus
see Justinian I

SABIN, ALBERT BRUCE (1906-1993), Polish-American physician and virologist who developed polio vaccine **13** 401-402

SABIN, FLORENCE RENA (1871-1953), American anatomist **13** 402-405

Sabotino, Marchese of
see Badoglio, Pietro

SACAJAWEA (c. 1784-c. 1812), Native American translator/interpreter, and guide **13** 405-408

SACCO, NICOLA (1891-1927) AND VANZETTI, BARTOLOMEO (1887-1927), Italian-born American anarchists **13** 408-410

SACHS, HANS (1494-1576), German poet **13** 410-411

SACHS, NELLY (1891-1970), German-born Jewish poet and playwright **13** 411-412

SACKS, OLIVER WOLF (born 1933), British neurologist **26** 329-331

SADAT, ANWAR (1918-1981), Egyptian president **13** 412-414

SADAT, JIHAN (born 1933), Egyptian women's rights activist **13** 414-415

SADE, COMTE DE (Donatien Alphonse François, Marquis de Sade; 1740-1814), French writer **13** 416-418

SA'DI (circa 1200-1291), Persian poet **13** 418-419

SADI, SHAIKH MUSLIH-AL-DIN
see Sa'di

SADR, MUSA AL- (Imam Musa; 1928-?), Lebanese Shi'ite Moslem religious and political leader **13** 420-422

SAFIRE, WILLIAM (born 1929), American journalist **13** 422-424

SAGAN, CARL E. (born 1934), American astronomer and popularizer of science **13** 424-425

SAGER, RUTH (1918-1997), American biologist and geneticist **13** 425-426

Sagoyewatha
see Red Jacket

SAICHO (767-822), Japanese Buddhist monk **13** 426-428

SAID, EDWARD WADIE (1935-2003), American author and activist **27** 312-314

SAID, SEYYID (1790-1856), Omani sultan **13** 428-429

SAIGO, TAKAMORI (1827-1877), Japanese rebel and statesman **13** 429

Sailing Alone Around the World (book) Slocum, Joshua **28** 333-335

St. Albans, Viscount
see Bacon, Sir Francis

St. Charles Borromeo, Church of
see Karlskirche, The (church, Vienna)

ST. CLAIR, ARTHUR (1736-1818), Scottish-born American soldier and politician **13** 429-430

ST. DENIS, RUTH (1878?-1968), American dancer and choreographer **13** 430-431

SAINT GENEVIEVE (Genovefa; circa 422-512), French religious figure **26** 331-333

St. John, Henry
see Bolingbroke, Viscount

St. Jude's Childrens Research Hospital Thomas, Danny **28** 350-352

ST. LAURENT, LOUIS STEPHEN (born 1882), Canadian statesman **13** 434

SAINTE-BEUVE, CHARLES AUGUSTIN (1804-1869), French literary critic **13** 438

SAINTE-MARIE, BUFFY (Beverly Sainte-Marie; born 1941), Native American singer and songwriter **26** 334-336

SAINT-EXUPÉRY, ANTOINE DE (1900-1944), French novelist, essayist, and pilot **13** 431-432

SAINT-GAUDENS, AUGUSTUS (1848-1907), American sculptor **13** 432

SAINT-JUST, LOUIS ANTOINE LÉON DE (1767-1794), French radical political leader **13** 433

Saint-Léger Léger, Alexis
see Perse, Saint-John

ST. LAURENT, YVES (born 1936), French fashion designer **20** 327-329

SAINT-GEORGE, JOSEPH BOULOGNE, CHEVALIER DE (1745-1799), French musician, athlete and soldier **27** 314-316

SAINT-PIERRE, ABBÉ DE (Charles Irénée Castel; 1658-1743), French political and economic theorist **13** 434-435

SAINT-SAËNS, CHARLES CAMILLE (1835-1921), French composer **13** 435-436

SAINT-SIMON, COMTE DE (Claude Henri de Rouvroy; 1760-1825), French social philosopher and reformer **13** 436-437

SAINT-SIMON, DUC DE (Louis de Rouvroy; 1675-1755), French writer **13** 436

SAIONJI, KIMMOCHI (1849-1940), Japanese elder statesman **13** 438-439

SAKHAROV, ANDREI (1921-1989), Russian theoretical physicist and "father of the Soviet atomic bomb" **13** 439-441

SALADIN (Salah-ad-Din Yusuf ibn Aiyub; 1138-93), Kurdish ruler of Egypt and Syria **13** 441-442

SALAM, ABDUS (1926-1996), Pakistani physicist **24** 344-346

SALAZAR, ANTÓNIO DE OLIVEIRA (1889-1970), Portuguese statesman **13** 442-443

Salcedo, Augusto Bernardino Leguía y
see Leguía y Salcedo, Augusto Bernardino

SALIH, ALI'ABDALLAH (born 1942), president of the Yemeni Arab Republic (North Yemen) and first president of the United Republic of Yemen **13** 443-445

SALINAS DE GORTARI, CARLOS (born 1948), president of Mexico (1988-) **13** 445-447

SALINGER, J. D. (born 1919), American author **13** 447-448

SALISBURY, HARRISON EVANS (born 1908), American journalist **13** 449-451

SALISBURY, 3D MARQUESS OF (Robert Arthur Talbot Gascoyne-Cecil; 1830-1903), English statesman and diplomat **13** 448-449

SALK, JONAS EDWARD (1914-1995), American physician, virologist, and immunologist **13** 451-452

SALLE, DAVID (born 1952), American artist **13** 452-453

SALLINEN, AULIS (born 1935), Finnish composer **25** 368-370

SALLUST (Gaius Sallustius Crispus; 86-circa 35 B.C.), Roman statesman and historian **13** 454

SALOMON, CHARLOTTE (1917-1943), German artist **13** 454-455

SALOMON, HAYM (c. 1740-1785), American financier **20** 329-331

SALVEMINI, GAETANO (1873-1957), Italian historian **13** 455-456

SAMAR, SIMA (born 1957), Afghan physician ans human rights activist **25** 370-372

SAMOSET (1590-1653), Native American chief and interpreter **27** 316-319

SAMPSON, EDITH (nee Edith Spurlock; 1901-1979), African American social worker, judge, and promoter of the United States **23** 356-358

SAMUEL (circa 1056-1004 B.C.), Hebrew prophet, last judge of Israel **13** 457-458

SAMUELSON, PAUL ANTHONY (born 1915), American economist **13** 458-459

San Francisco 49ers (United States football team)
Walsh, Bill **28** 370-372

SAN MARTÍN, JOSÉ DE (1778-1850), Argentine soldier and statesman **13** 468-469

San Martín, Ramón Grau
see Grau San Martín, Ramón

SANA'I, HAKIM (Adam al-Ghaznawi; Abu al-Majd Majdud ibn Adam; c. 1050-c. 1131), Persian mystic poet **24** 346-347

SANAPIA (Mary Poafpybitty; 1895-1979), Comanche medicine woman **23** 358-360

SANCHEZ, SONIA (Wilsonia Benita Driver; born 1934), African American author and educator **24** 347-350

SANCTORIUS (1561-1636), Italian physician and physiologist **13** 459

Sand County Almanac, A (book) Leopold, Aldo **28** 211-213

SAND, GEORGE (1804-1876), French novelist **13** 459-461

SANDAGE, ALLAN REX (born 1926), American astronomer **21** 383-384

SANDBURG, CARL (1878-1967), American poet, anthologist, and biographer **13** 461-462

SANDERS, BARRY (born 1968), African American football player **25** 372-374

SANDERS, COLONEL (Harland David Sanders; 1890-1980), American businessman **19** 323-325

SANDINO, AUGUSTO C. (1894-1934), Nicaraguan guerrilla leader **13** 462-463

Sandracottus
see Chandragupta Maurya

SANDYS, SIR EDWIN (1561-1629), English statesman and colonizer in America **13** 463-464

SANGALLO FAMILY (flourished late 15th-mid-16th century), Italian artists and architects **13** 464-466

SANGER, FREDERICK (born 1918), English biochemist **13** 466-467

SANGER, MARGARET HIGGINS (1884-1966), American leader of birth control movement **13** 467-468

SANMICHELI, MICHELE (circa 1484-1559), Italian architect and military engineer **13** 469-470

SANSOVINO, JACOPO (1486-1570), Italian sculptor and architect **13** 470-471

SANTA ANA, ANTONIO LÓPEZ DE (1794-1876), Mexican general and statesman, six times president **13** 471-472

SANTA CRUZ, ANDRÉS DE (1792-1865), Bolivian general and statesman, president 1829-39 **13** 472-473

SANTAMARIA, BARTHOLOMEW AUGUSTINE (born 1915), Australian Roman Catholic publicist and organizer **13** 473-474

SANTANA, PEDRO (1801-1864), Dominican military leader, three times president **13** 474-475

SANTANDER, FRANCISCO DE PAULA (1792-1840), Colombian general and statesman **13** 475

SANTAYANA, GEORGE (Jorge Agustin de Santayana; 1863-1952), Spanish-American philosopher **13** 475-477

Santorio, Santorio
see Sanctorius

SANTOS-DUMONT, ALBERTO (1873-1932), Brazilian inventor **13** 477-478

Sanzio, Raffaello
see Raphael

SAPIR, EDWARD (1884-1939), American anthropologist **13** 478-479

SAPPHO (circa 625-570 B.C.), Greek lyric poet **13** 479-480

SAPRU, SIR TEJ BAHADUR (1875-1949), Indian lawyer and statesman **13** 480-481

SARAMAGO, JOSE (born 1922), Portuguese author **25** 374-376

SARANDON, SUSAN (Susan Abigail Tomalin; born 1946), American actress and activist **18** 358-360

SARASATE, PABLO DE (Martín Melitón Sarasate y Navascuéz 1844-1908), Spanish violinist and composer **26** 336-338

Saraswati, Swami Dayananda
see Dayananda Saraswati, Swami

SARGENT, JOHN SINGER (1856-1925), American portrait painter **13** 481-482

SARGON II (ruled 722-705 B.C.), king of Assyria **13** 482

SARGON OF AGADE (circa 2340-2284 B.C.), first Semitic king of Mesopotamia **13** 483

SARIT THANARAT (1908-1963), Thai army officer, prime minister 1957-63 **13** 483-484

SARMIENTO, DOMINGO FAUSTINO (1811-1888), Argentine statesman, president 1868-74 **13** 484-485

SARNOFF, DAVID (1891-1971), American television and radio broadcasting executive **13** 485-486
Brainard, Bertha **28** 47-48

SAROYAN, WILLIAM (1908-1981), American short-story writer, dramatist, and novelist **13** 486-487

SARPI, PAOLO (1552-1623), Italian prelate and statesman **13** 487-488

SARRAUTE, NATHALIE TCHERNIAK (1900-1999), French author of novels, essays, and plays **13** 488-490

Sarto, Andrea del
see Andrea del Sarto

Sarto, Giuseppe Melchiorre
see Pius X

SARTON, GEORGE (1884-1956), Belgian-born American historian of science **13** 490-491

SARTRE, JEAN PAUL (1905-1980), French philosopher and author **13** 491-492

SASSETTA (circa 1400-50), Italian painter **13** 492

SASSOON, SIEGFRIED (1886-1967), English poet **13** 492-493

SATANTA (White Bear; 1830-1878), Native American orator and leader of the Kiowa tribe **13** 493-494

SATIE, ERIK (1866-1925), French composer **13** 494-495

SATO, EISAKU (1901-1975), Japanese statesman, prime minister 1964-72 **13** 495-496

Sato, Nobusuke
see Kishi, Nobusuke

SAUER, CARL ORTWIN (1889-1975), American geographer and anthropologist **13** 496-497

SAUGUET, HENRI (born 1901), French composer, writer, and thinker on art and music **13** 497-498

SAUL (circa 1020-1000 B.C.), first King of Israel **13** 498

SAUND, DALIP SINGH (1899-1973), Indian-American U.S. congressman **28** 310-312

Saunders, Sir Alexander Morris Carr
see Carr-Saunders, Sir Alexander Morris

SAUNDERS, SIR CHARLES EDWARD (1867-1937), Canadian cerealist **13** 498-499

SAUNDERS, CICELY (Cicely Mary Strode Saunders; 1918-2005), English doctor and social worker **25** 376-378

SAVAGE, AUGUSTA CHRISTINE (born Augusta Christine Fells; 1892-1962), African American sculptor and teacher **13** 499-501

SAVAGE, MICHAEL JOSEPH (1872-1940), New Zealand labor leader, prime minister 1935-40 **13** 501-502

Savage Detectives, The (book)
Bolaño, Roberto **28** 42-45

SAVARKAR, VINAYAK DAMODAR (Veer Savarkar; 1883-1966), Indian political leader **28** 312-314

SAVIGNY, FRIEDRICH KARL VON (1779-1861), German jurist **13** 502-503

SAVIMBI, JONAS MALHEIROS (1934-2002), founder and leader of UNITA (National Union for the Total Independence of Angola) **13** 503-505

SAVONAROLA, GIROLAMO (1452-1498), Italian religious reformer and dictator of Florence **13** 505-506

SAW MAUNG (born 1928), leader of armed forces that took power in Burma (now Myanmar) in a 1988 military coup **13** 506-507

SAWALLISCH, WOLFGANG (born 1923), German orchestra conductor **28** 314-316

SAX, ADOLPHE (Antoine-Joseph Sax; 1814-1894), Belgian musician and inventor of musical instruments **28** 316-318

Saxophone (musical instrument)
Sax, Adolphe **28** 316-318

SAXE, COMTE DE (1696-1750), marshal of France **13** 507-508

SAY, JEAN BAPTISTE (1767-1832), French economist **13** 508-509

SAYERS, GALE (born 1943), American football player **21** 377-379

SAYRE, FRANCIS BOWES (1885-1972), American lawyer and administrator **13** 509

SAYYID QUTB (1906-1966), Egyptian writer, educator, and religious leader **13** 509-511

SCALFARO, OSCAR LUIGI (born 1918), Christian Democratic leader and president of the Italian Republic **13** 511-512

SCALIA, ANTONIN (born 1936), U.S. Supreme Court justice **13** 513-514

Scandiano, Conte di
see Boiardo, Matteo Maria

SCARGILL, ARTHUR (born 1938), president of the British National Union of Mineworkers **13** 514-515

SCARLATTI, DOMENICO (1685-1757), Italian harpsichordist and composer **13** 515-517

SCARLATTI, PIETRO ALESSANDRO GASPARE (1660-1725), Italian composer **13** 517-518

Scarlet Pimpernel, The (book)
Baroness Orczy **28** 25-27

SCHACHT, HJALMAR HORACE GREELEY (1877-1970), German economist and banker **13** 518-519

SCHAFF, PHILIP (1819-1893), Swiss-born American religious scholar **13** 519-520

SCHAPIRO, MIRIAM (born 1923), Artist **13** 520-521

SCHARNHORST, GERHARD JOHANN DAVID VON (1755-1813), Prussian general **13** 521-522

SCHARPING, RUDOLF (born 1947), minister-president of Rhineland-Palatinate and chairman of the German Social Democratic Party **13** 522-524

SCHECHTER, SOLOMON (1849-1915), Romanian-American Jewish scholar and religious leader **13** 524

SCHEELE, KARL WILHELM (1742-1786), Swedish pharmacist and chemist **13** 525-526

SCHELLING, FRIEDRICH WILHELM JOSEPH VON (1775-1854), German philosopher **13** 526-527

SCHIELE, EGON (1890-1918), Austrian Expressionist painter and draftsman **14** 1-2

SCHIESS, BETTY BONE (born 1923), American Episcopalian priest **18** 360-362

SCHIFF, JACOB HENRY (1847-1920), German-American banker **14** 2-3

SCHILLEBEECKX, EDWARD (born 1914), Belgian Roman Catholic theologian **14** 3-4

SCHILLER, JOHANN CHRISTOPH FRIEDRICH VON (1759-1805), German dramatist, poet, and historian **14** 4-7

SCHINDLER, ALEXANDER MOSHE (1925-2000), American Jewish leader **23** 360-362

SCHINDLER, OSKAR (1908-1974), German businessman and humanitarian **18** 362-365

SCHINDLER, SOLOMON (1842-1915), German-American rabbi and social theorist **14** 7-8

SCHINKEL, KARL FRIEDRICH (1781-1841), German architect, painter and designer **14** 8

Schizophrenia (medicine)
Meduna, Ladislas J. **28** 237-238

SCHLAFLY, PHYLLIS (born 1924), American political activist and author **14** 9-10

SCHLEGEL, FRIEDRICH VON (1772-1829), German critic and author **14** 10-11

SCHLEIERMACHER, FRIEDRICH ERNST DANIEL (1768-1834), German theologian and philosopher **14** 11-12

SCHLEMMER, OSKAR (1888-1943), German painter, sculptor, and stage designer **14** 12-13

SCHLESINGER, ARTHUR MEIER (1888-1965), American historian **14** 13

SCHLESINGER, ARTHUR MEIER, JR. (1917-2007), American historian and Democratic party activist **14** 13-15

SCHLESINGER, JAMES RODNEY (born 1929), American government official **14** 15-16

SCHLICK, FRIEDRICH ALBERT MORITZ (1882-1936), German physicist and philosopher **14** 16-17

SCHLIEMANN, HEINRICH (1822-1890), German merchant and archeologist **14** 17-18

SCHLÜTER, ANDREAS (circa 1660-1714), German sculptor and architect **14** 18-19

SCHMIDT, HELMUT (born 1918), Social Democrat and chancellor of the Federal Republic of Germany (the former West Germany), 1974-82 **14** 19-21

Schmidt, Johann Caspar
see Stirner, Max

SCHMITT, JACK (Harrison Hagan Schmitt; born 1935), American astronaut and geologist **22** 385-386

Schmitz, Ettore
see Svevo, Italo

SCHMOLLER, GUSTAV FRIEDRICH VON (1838-1917), German economist **14** 21

SCHNABEL, ARTUR (1882-1951), Austrian American pianist **27** 319-321

SCHNEERSON, MENACHEM MENDEL (The Rebbe; 1902-1994), Russian-American Hassidic Jewish leader **22** 386-388

SCHNEIDER, ROMY (Rosemarie Magdalena Albach-Retty; 1938-1982), Austrian actress **24** 350-352

SCHNEIDERMAN, ROSE (1882-1972), labor organizer and activist for the improvement of working conditions for women **14** 22-23

SCHNITZLER, ARTHUR (1862-1931), Austrian dramatist and novelist **14** 23-24

SCHOENBERG, ARNOLD (1874-1951), Austrian composer **14** 24-26

SCHOLEM, GERSHOM (1897-1982), Jewish scholar **14** 26

SCHONGAUER, MARTIN (circa 1435-91), German engraver and painter **14** 26-28

SCHÖNHUBER, FRANZ XAVER (1923-2005), German right-wing political leader **14** 28-29

School of Paris (art)
see French art—School of Paris

SCHOOLCRAFT, HENRY ROWE (1793-1864), American explorer and ethnologist **14** 29

SCHOPENHAUER, ARTHUR (1788-1860), German philosopher **14** 29-31

SCHOUTEN, WILLIAM CORNELIUS (circa 1580-1625), Dutch explorer and navigator **14** 31

SCHRAMM, TEXAS ERNEST ("Tex"; 1920-2003), American football team owner **24** 352-355

SCHREINER, OLIVE (Olive Emilie Albertina Schreiner; Ralph Iron; 1855-1920), South African author **23** 362-364

SCHREMPP, JUERGEN (born 1944), German automobile industry executive **20** 331-332

SCHRODER, GERHARD (born 1944), German chancellor **19** 325-327

SCHRÖDINGER, ERWIN (1887-1961), Austrian physicist **14** 31-33

SCHROEDER, PATRICIA SCOTT (born 1940), first U.S. congresswoman from Colorado **14** 33-35

SCHUBERT, FRANZ PETER (1797-1828), Austrian composer **14** 35-37
Haefliger, Ernst **28** 152-154

SCHULLER, GUNTHER (born 1925), American musician **14** 37-38

SCHULZ, CHARLES M. (1922-2000), American cartoonist and creator of "Peanuts" **14** 38-39

SCHUMACHER, KURT (1895-1952), German socialist statesman **14** 40-41

SCHUMAN, ROBERT (1886-1963), French statesman **14** 41

SCHUMAN, WILLIAM HOWARD (1910-1992), American composer and educator **22** 388-391

SCHUMANN, CLARA (Clara Josephine Wieck Schumann; 1819-1896),

German pianist and composer **26** 338-340

SCHUMANN, ROBERT ALEXANDER (1810-1856), German composer and critic **14** 41-43

SCHUMPETER, JOSEPH ALOIS (1883-1950), Austrian economist **14** 43-44

SCHURZ, CARL (1829-1906), American soldier, statesman, and journalist **14** 44-45

SCHUSCHNIGG, KURT VON (1897-1977), Austrian statesman, chancellor of Austria 1934-38 **14** 45-46

SCHÜSSLER FIORENZA, ELIZABETH (born 1938), biblical scholar and theologian **14** 46-48

SCHÜTZ, HEINRICH (1585-1672), German composer **14** 48-49

SCHUYLER, PHILIP JOHN (1733-1804), American Revolutionary War general **14** 49-50

SCHWAB, CHARLES MICHAEL (1862-1939), American industrialist **14** 50-51

SCHWANN, THEODOR (1810-1882), German biologist **14** 51-52

SCHWARTZ, DELMORE (1913-1966), American poet **19** 327-329

Schwartzerd, Philip
see Melancthon, Philip

SCHWARZKOPF, ELISABETH (Dame Olga Maria Elisabeth Friederike Schwarzkopf; 1915-2006), German opera singer **25** 378-380

SCHWARZKOPF, NORMAN (born 1934), American army general **14** 52-54

SCHWEITZER, ALBERT (1875-1965), Alsatian-German philosopher and medical missionary **14** 55-56

SCHWENCKFELD, KASPER VON (1489/90-1561), Silesian nobleman and theologian **14** 56-57

SCHWIMMER, ROSIKA (1877-1948), Hungarian women's rights activist **14** 57-60

SCHWITTERS, KURT (1887-1948), German painter, collagist, typographer, and poet and creator of MERZ-art **14** 60-61

Science fiction (literature)
Dick, Philip K. **28** 96-98
Heinlein, Robert A. **28** 166-168
Herbert, Frank, Jr. **28** 168-170
Norton, Andre **28** 257-259

Scientists, American
biochemists
Axelrod, Julius **28** 18-20

chemists (19th century)
Pemberton, John Stith **28** 278-279
chemists (19th-20th century)
Dow, Herbert H. **28** 100-102
chemists (20th century)
Hall, Lloyd Augustus **28** 154-156
engineers (electrical)
Hoff, Ted **28** 176-178
inventors (19th century)
Burroughs, William S. **28** 56-57
Pemberton, John Stith **28** 278-279
inventors (19th-20th century)
Dow, Herbert H. **28** 100-102
Woods, Granville T. **28** 378-381
inventors (20th century)
Cooper, Martin **28** 85-87
Edgerton, Harold Eugene **28** 109-111
Hall, Lloyd Augustus **28** 154-156
Hoff, Ted **28** 176-178
Paul, Les **28** 276-278
medical researchers
Wright, Jane Cooke **28** 383-385
molecular biologists
Mello, Craig Cameron **28** 238-241
neurophysiologists
Axelrod, Julius **28** 18-20
physicians (19th century)
Agnew, David Hayes **28** 3-5
physicians (20th century)
Wright, Jane Cooke **28** 383-385
surgeons
Agnew, David Hayes **28** 3-5

Scientists, Belgian
inventors
Sax, Adolphe **28** 316-318

Scientists, Canadian
engineers (electrical)
Gross, Al **28** 149-151
inventors
Gross, Al **28** 149-151

Scientists, Dutch
anatomists
Dubois, Eugène **28** 106-108
anthropologists
Dubois, Eugène **28** 106-108
engineers
Drebbel, Cornelius **28** 102-104
inventors
Drebbel, Cornelius **28** 102-104
paleontologists
Dubois, Eugène **28** 106-108

Scientists, English
botanists
Arber, Agnes Robertson **28** 14-16
inventors
Milne, John **28** 245-247
physicists (20th century)
Fuchs, Klaus **28** 129-131
seismologists
Milne, John **28** 245-247

Scientists, French
inventors
Blanchard, Jean-Pierre François **28** 36-38
parasitologists
Laveran, Alphonse **28** 207-209
physicians
Laveran, Alphonse **28** 207-209

Scientists, German
chemists
Hoffmann, Felix **28** 179-180
engineers
Zuse, Konrad **28** 391-393
inventors
Hoffmann, Felix **28** 179-180
Zuse, Konrad **28** 391-393
physicists (20th century)
Fuchs, Klaus **28** 129-131

Scientists, Hungarian
Meduna, Ladislas J. **28** 237-238
neurologists
Meduna, Ladislas J. **28** 237-238

Scientists, Japanese
inventors
Ibuka, Masaru **28** 184-186

Scientists, Polish
inventors
Lukasiewicz, Ignacy **28** 225-227

Scientists, Roman
Dionysius Exiguus **28** 99-100

Scientists, Russian
inventors
Kalashnikov, Mikhail **28** 190-192

Scientists, Scottish
physicians
Cheyne, George **28** 74-76

Scipio Aemilianus
see Scipio Africanus Minor

SCIPIO AFRICANUS MAJOR, PUBLIUS CORNELIUS (236-184/183 B.C.), Roman general **14** 61-62

SCIPIO AFRICANUS MINOR, PUBLIUS CORNELIUS AEMILIANUS (185/184-129 B.C.), Roman general **14** 62-63

Scipio the Elder, Publius Cornelius
see Scipio Africanus Major

SCORSESE, MARTIN (born 1942), American filmmaker and screenwriter **14** 63-65

SCOTT, CHARLOTTE ANGAS (1858-1931), English mathematician **23** 364-367

Scott, Coretta
see King, Coretta Scott

SCOTT, DRED (1795-1858), African American revolutionary **14** 65-66

SCOTT, FRANCIS REGINALD (1899-1985), Canadian poet, political activist, and constitutional theorist **14** 66-67

SCOTT, GEORGE CAMPBELL (1927-1999), American actor and director **22** 391-393

Scott, James
see Monmouth and Buccleugh, Duke of

SCOTT, ROBERT FALCON (1868-1912), English naval officer and polar explorer **14** 67-68

SCOTT, THOMAS ALEXANDER (1823-1881), American railroad builder **21** 393-395

SCOTT, SIR WALTER (1771-1832), Scottish novelist and poet **14** 68-70

SCOTT, WINFIELD (1786-1866), American general **14** 70-71

Scottish literature
Baillie, Joanna **28** 23-25

Scotus
see Duns Scotus, John

SCRIABIN, ALEXANDER NIKOLAYEVICH (1871-1915), Russian composer and pianist **14** 71-72

Scriabin, V. M.
see Molotov, Vyacheslav Mikhailovich

SCRIPPS, EDWARD WYLLIS (1854-1926), American newspaper publisher **14** 72-73

SCULLIN, JAMES HENRY (1876-1953), Australian politician **14** 73

SEABORG, GLENN THEODORE (1912-1999), American chemist and chairman of the Atomic Energy Commission **14** 74-76

SEABURY, SAMUEL (1729-1796), American theologian **14** 76

SEACOLE, MARY (Mary Jane Grant; 1805-1881), African_english nurse and hotelier **27** 321-323

Seafarers
Slocum, Joshua **28** 333-335

SEALE, ROBERT GEORGE (Bobby; born 1936), militant activist and a founder of the Black Panther Party **14** 77-78

SEAMAN, ELIZABETH COCHRANE (1864-1922), American journalist and reformer **14** 78-80

SEARS, RICHARD WARREN (1863-1914), American merchant **24** 355-357

SEATTLE (c. 1788-1866), Native American tribal chief **14** 80-81

Secondat, C.L. de
see Montesquieu, Baron de

Secundus, Gaius Plinius
see Pliny the Elder

Secundus, Gaius Plinius Caecilius
see Pliny the Younger

SEDDON, RICHARD JOHN (1845-1906), New Zealand politician **14** 81-82

Sedges, John (pseudonym)
see Buck, Pearl Sydenstricker

SEDGWICK, ADAM (1785-1873), English geologist **14** 82-83

SEEGER, PETE (born 1919), American folksinger and activist **14** 83-84

SEEGER, RUTH CRAWFORD (Ruth Porter Crawford-Seeger; 1901-1953), American musician **24** 357-359

SEFERIS, GEORGE (Georgios Seferiadis; 1900-71), Greek poet and statesman **14** 84-85

SEGAL, GEORGE (born 1924), American sculptor **14** 85-87

SEGOVIA, ANDRÉS (1893-1987), Spanish guitarist **14** 87-88
Ponce, Manuel **28** 282-284

SEGRÈ, EMILIO (Emilio Gino Segrè; 1905-1989), American Physicist **25** 380-383

Segregation (racial, United States)
see African American history (United States)

SEIBERT, FLORENCE B. (1897-1991), American biochemist **14** 89-90

SEIFERT, JAROSLAV (1901-1986), Czech poet **25** 383-386

Seismology (science)
Milne, John **28** 245-247

SEJO (1417-1468), king of Korea 1453-68 **14** 90-91

SEJONG (1397-1450), king of Korea 1418-50 **14** 91-92

Selassie, Haile
see Haile Selassie

SELENA (Selena Quintanilla-Perez; 1971-1995), Hispanic-American singer **18** 365-367

SELEUCUS I (circa 358-281 B.C.), Macedonian general, king of Babylonia and Syria **14** 92-93

SELIGMAN, EDWIN ROBERT ANDERSON (1861-1939), American economist and editor **14** 93-94

SELIM I (circa 1470-1520), Ottoman sultan 1512-20 **14** 94-95

SELIM III (1761-1808), Ottoman sultan 1789-1807 **14** 95-96

SELKIRK, 5TH EARL OF (Thomas Douglas; 1771-1820), Scottish colonizer in Canada **14** 96

SELLARS, WILFRED (1912-1989), American philosopher **14** 96-98

SELLERS, PETER RICHARD HENRY (1925-1980), British comedy genius of theater, radio, television, and movies **14** 98-99

SELZNICK, DAVID OLIVER (1902-1965), American filmmaker **20** 333-335

SEMENOV, NIKOLAI NIKOLAEVICH (1896-1986), Russian physicist and physical chemist **14** 101

SEMMELWEIS, IGNAZ PHILIPP (1818-1865), Hungarian physician **14** 101-102

SEMMES, RAPHAEL (1809-1877), American Confederate naval officer **14** 102-103

SEN, AMARTYA KUMAR (born 1933), Indian economist **24** 359-361

SEN, RAM CAMUL (1783-1844), Bengali intellectual and entrepreneur **13** 16-17

Senator, Flavius Magnus Aurelius Cassiodorus
see Cassiodorus

SENDAK, MAURICE (born 1928), American author, artist, and illustrator **19** 329-331

SENDER, RAMÓN JOSÉ (1901-1982), Spanish American author **24** 361-363

SENDLER, IRENA (Irena Sendlerowa; born 1910), Polish social worker **28** 318-320

SENECA THE YOUNGER, LUCIUS ANNAEUS (circa 4 B.C.-A.D. 65), Roman philosopher **14** 103-105

SENFL, LUDWIG (circa 1486-circa 1543), Swiss-born German composer **14** 105-106

SENGHOR, LÉOPOLD SÉDAR (born 1906), Senegalese poet, philosopher, and statesman **14** 106-107

SENNACHERIB (ruled 705-681 B.C.), king of Assyria **14** 108

SENNETT, MACK (1884-1960), American film producer and director **14** 108-109

SEQUOYAH (circa 1770-1843), American Cherokee Indian scholar **14** 110-111

Serbian Republic (former kingdom; former republic of Yugoslavia) Simeon, King of Bulgaria **28** 325-327

SERRA, JUNIPERO (Miguel José Serra; 1713-84), Spanish Franciscan missionary, founder of California missions **14** 111-112

SERRANO ELÍAS, JORGE ANTONIO (born 1945), president of Guatemala (1991-1993) **14** 112-113

SERRÃO, FRANCISCO (Francisco Serrano; died 1521), Portuguese explorer **28** 320-321

SERTÜRNER, FRIEDRICH (Friedrich Wilhelm Adam Ferdinand Sertürner; 1783-1841), Prussian pharmacist **21** 379-381

SERVAN-SCHREIBER, JEAN-JACQUES (1924-2006), French journalist and writer on public affairs **14** 113-115

SERVETUS, MICHAEL (circa 1511-53), Spanish religious philosopher **14** 115-116

SESSHU, TOYA (1420-1506), Japanese painter and Zen priest **14** 116-117

SESSIONS, ROGER HUNTINGTON (1896-1985), American composer **14** 117-118

SETON, ELIZABETH ANN BAYLEY (1774-1821), American Catholic leader **14** 118-119

SETON, ERNEST THOMPSON (1860-1946), Canadian author and co-founder of the Boy Scouts of America **14** 119-120

SETTIGNANO, DESIDERIO DA (1428/31-1464), Italian sculptor **4** 509

SEURAT, GEORGES PIERRE (1859-1891), French painter **14** 120-122

Seuss, Dr.
see Geisel, Theodor

SEVAREID, ERIC (Arnold Eric Sevareid 1912-1992), American broadcast journalist and author **22** 395-397

Seven Years War (1756-1763)
French forces
Madame de Pompadour **28** 228-230

SEVERINI, GINO (1883-1966), Italian painter **14** 122

SEVERUS, LUCIUS SEPTIMIUS (146-211), Roman emperor 193-211 **14** 109-110

SEVIER, JOHN (1745-1815), American frontiersman, soldier, and politician **14** 122-123

SEWALL, SAMUEL (1652-1730), American jurist and diarist **14** 123-124

SEWARD, WILLIAM HENRY (1801-1872), American statesman **14** 124-125

SEXTON, ANNE (Anne Gray Harvey; 1928-74), American ''confessional'' poet **14** 125-126

Seymour, Edward
see Somerset, Duke of

SEYMOUR, HORATIO (1810-1886), American politician **14** 126-127

SEYMOUR, JANE (1509-1537), third wife and queen consort of Henry VIII of England **18** 367-368

SEYMOUR, WILLIAM JOSEPH (1870-1922), African American religious leader **27** 323-325

SFORZA, LODOVICO (1452-1508), duke of Milan **14** 127-128

SHAARAWI, HUDA (Nur al-Huda Sultan; 1879-1947), Egyptian women's rights activist **24** 363-365

SHABAKA (ruled circa 712-circa 696 B.C.), Nubian king, pharaoh of Egypt **14** 130

SHABAZZ, BETTY (1936-1997), African American educator, activist, and health administrator **14** 130-132

SHACKLETON, SIR ERNEST HENRY (1874-1922), British explorer **14** 132-133

SHAFFER, PETER LEVIN (born 1926), English/American playwright **14** 133-135

SHAFTESBURY, 1ST EARL OF (Anthony Ashley Cooper; 1621-83), English statesman **14** 135-136

SHAFTESBURY, 3D EARL OF (Anthony Ashley Cooper; 1671-1713), English moral philosopher **14** 136-137

SHAFTESBURY, 7TH EARL OF (Anthony Ashley Cooper; 1801-85), English social reformer **14** 137-138

SHAH JAHAN (1592-1666), Mogul emperor of India 1628-58 **14** 138-139

SHAHN, BEN (1898-1969), American painter, graphic artist, and photographer **14** 139-140

SHAHPUR II (310-379), king of Persia **14** 140-141

SHAKA (circa 1787-1828), African Zulu military monarch **14** 141-142

SHAKESPEARE, WILLIAM (1564-1616), English playwright, poet, and actor **14** 142-145
performances
McKellen, Ian Murray **28** 234-237
Patterson, Tom **28** 274-276

Shakyamuni
see Buddha, the

SHALIKASHVILI, JOHN MALCHASE DAVID (born 1936), chairman of the U.S. Joint Chiefs of Staff **14** 145-147

SHAMIR, YITZCHAK (Yizernitsky; born 1914), Israeli prime minister and leader of the Likud Party **14** 147-149

SHAMMAI (flourished 1st century B.C.), Jewish sage **14** 149

SHANG YANG (circa 390-338 B.C.), Chinese statesman and political philosopher **14** 149-150

SHANGE, NTOZAKE (Paulette Linda Williams; born 1948), African American author **23** 367-369

SHANKARA (Shankaracharya; circa 788-820), Indian philosopher and reformer **14** 150-151

SHANKAR, RAVI (Robindra Shankar; born 1920), Indian musician **22** 397-399

SHANKER, ALBERT (1928-1977), American education leader **14** 151-153

SHANNON, CLAUDE ELWOOD (born 1916), American mathematician **14** 153-154

SHAPEY, RALPH (1921-2002), American composer, conductor, and teacher **14** 154-155

SHAPLEY, HARLOW (1885-1972), American astronomer **14** 155-156

SHARIATI, ALI (1933-1977), "Ideologue of the Iranian Revolution" **14** 156-157

SHARIF, NAWAZ (Niam Nawaz Sharif; born 1949), Pakistani prime minister **19** 331-333

SHARON, ARIEL (Arik; born 1928), Israeli politician and defense minister **14** 157-159

SHARP, CECIL (Cecil James Sharp; 1859-1924), English folklorist and musicologist **28** 321-323

SHARPTON, AL (born 1954), African American civil rights leader and minister **14** 159-162

Sharukin
see Sargon II

SHAW, ANNA HOWARD (1847-1919), American suffragist leader, reformer, and women's rights activist **14** 162-163

SHAW, ARTIE (Arthur Jacob Arshawsky; 1910-2004), American clarinetist and composer **26** 340-342

SHAW, GEORGE BERNARD (1856-1950), British playwright, critic, and pamphleteer **14** 163-164

Shaw, Josephine
see Lowell, Josephine Shaw

SHAW, LEMUEL (1781-1861), American jurist **14** 164-165

SHAW, MARY (born 1943), American computer science professor **14** 165-167

SHAW, RICHARD NORMAN (1831-1912), British architect **14** 167-168

Shaw, T. E.
see Lawrence, Thomas Edward

SHAWN, WILLIAM (1907-1992), American editor **19** 333-335

SHAYS, DANIEL (circa 1747-1825), American Revolutionary War Captain **14** 168

SHCHARANSKY, ANATOLY BORISOVICH (born 1948), prominent figure of the Helsinki Watch Group **14** 168-170

SHEBA (Makeda; Bilqis; c. 1075 BCE-c. 955 BCE), queen of Sheba **24** 365-367

SHEELER, CHARLES (1883-1965), American painter **14** 170-171

SHEEN, FULTON J. (1895-1979), American Roman Catholic bishop and television host **14** 171-172

Shehu
see Uthman don Fodio

Sheikh Ibrahim
see Burkhardt, Johann Ludwig

SHELDON, CHARLES M. (1857-1946), American social reformer who also wrote *In His Steps* **14** 172-174

SHELDON, SIDNEY (1917-2007), American author **28** 323-325

SHELLEY, MARY WOLLSTONECRAFT (1797-1851), English author **14** 174-176

SHELLEY, PERCY BYSSHE (1792-1822), English romantic poet **14** 176-178

Shelomoh Yitzhaki
see Rashi

SHEPARD, ALAN (1923-1998), American astronaut **14** 178-180

SHEPARD, SAM (Samuel Shepard Rogers VII; born 1943), American playwright, rock performer, and film actor **14** 180-181

SHEPPARD, WILLIAM HENRY (1865-1927), African American missionary to Africa **27** 325-327

Spirited Away (film)
Miyazaki Hayao **28** 249-252

SHERATON, THOMAS (1751-1806), English furniture designer **14** 181-182

SHERIDAN, PHILIP HENRY (1831-1888), American general **14** 182-183

SHERIDAN, RICHARD BRINSLEY (1751-1816), British playwright and orator **14** 183-184

SHERMAN, CINDY (Cynthia Morris Sherman; born 1954), American photographer **19** 335-337

SHERMAN, JOHN (1823-1900), American politician **14** 184-185

SHERMAN, ROGER (1721-1793), American patriot **14** 185-186

SHERMAN, WILLIAM TECUMSEH (1820-1891), American general **14** 186-187

SHERRINGTON, SIR CHARLES SCOTT (1857-1952), English physiologist **14** 187-189

SHERWOOD, ROBERT EMMET (1896-1955), American playwright **14** 189-190

SHESTOV, LEV (Lev Isaakovich Schwarzmann; 1866-1938), Russian Jewish thinker and literary critic **14** 190-191

SHEVARDNADZE, EDUARD AMVROSEVICH (born 1928), foreign minister of the U.S.S.R. (1985-1990) **14** 191-193

SHEVCHENKO, TARAS GRIGORYEVICH (1814-1861), Ukrainian poet **24** 367-369

SHIH KO-FA (died 1644), Chinese scholar-soldier **14** 194-195

SHIH LE (274-333), Chinese emperor 330-333 **14** 195

SHIHAB, FU'AD (1903-1973), Father of the Lebanese Army and president of Lebanon (1958-1964) **14** 193-194

Shih-heng
see Lu Chi

SHILS, EDWARD ALBERT (born 1911), American sociologist **14** 195-197

SHINRAN (1173-1262), Japanese Buddhist monk **14** 197

SHIPPEN, EDWARD (1728-1806), American jurist **14** 197-198

SHIRER, WILLIAM L. (born 1904), American journalist and historian who wrote on the history of Nazi Germany **14** 198-199

SHIVAJI
see Śivaji

SHOCKLEY, WILLIAM (1910-1989), American physicist **14** 200-202

SHOEMAKER, GENE (Eugene Merle Shoemaker; 1928-1997), American geologist and planetary scientist **20** 335-338

SHOEMAKER, WILLIE (Billy Lee Shoemaker; born 1931), American jockey and horse trainer **21** 381-383

Shogunate (Japan)
see Japan—1185-1867

SHOLEM ALEICHEM (Sholem Rabinowitz; 1859-1916), Russian-born American author **14** 202-203

SHOLES, CHRISTOPHER LATHAM (1819-1890), American publisher, inventor, and social reformer **21** 383-385

SHOLOKHOV, MIKHAIL ALEKSANDROVICH (1905-1984), Russian novelist **14** 203-204

SHORT, WALTER (1880-1949), American army officer **19** 337-339

SHOSTAKOVICH, DMITRI DMITRIEVICH (1906-1975), Russian composer **14** 204-205

SHOTOKU TAISHI (573-621), Japanese regent, statesman, and scholar **14** 205-207

Showa Tenno
see Hirohito

SHREVE, HENRY MILLER (1785-1851), American steamboat designer and builder **14** 207

SHRIVER, EUNICE KENNEDY (born 1921), American activist **19** 339-341

Shu Ch'ing-ch'un
see Lao Shê

Shu Maung
see Ne Win

SHUB, ESTHER (Esfir Ilyanichna Shub; 1894-1959), Ukrainian filmmaker **24** 369-371

SHUBERT BROTHERS (1883-1963), theatrical managers **14** 207-209

SHULTZ, GEORGE PRATT (born 1920), labor and economics specialist, educator, businessman, and international negotiator **14** 209-211

Shunro
see Hokusai, Katsushika

Shuta
see Liang Wu-ti

SIBELIUS, JEAN JULIUS CHRISTIAN (1865-1957), Finnish composer **14** 211-212

Sicily, Duke of
see Guiscard Robert

SICKERT, WALTER RICHARD (1860-1942), English painter **14** 212-213

SICKLES, DANIEL EDGAR (1819-1914), American politician and diplomat **21** 385-388

SIDGWICK, HENRY (1838-1900), English philosopher and moralist **14** 213

SIDNEY, SIR PHILIP (1554-1586), English poet, courtier, diplomat, and soldier **14** 214-215

SIEBERT, MURIEL (born 1932), American businesswoman **18** 368-370

SIEGEL, BENJAMIN ("Bugsy"; 1906-1947), American gangster **14** 215-216

SIENKIEWICZ, HENRYK (1846-1916), Polish novelist and short-story writer **14** 216-217

SIERRA, JUSTO (1848-1912), Mexican educator, writer, and historian **14** 217

SIEYÈS, COMTE EMMANUEL JOSEPH (1748-1836), French statesman and political writer **14** 217-218

SIFTON, SIR CLIFFORD (1861-1929), politician who helped turn the Canadian West into a premier agricultural area **14** 219-220

SIGISMUND (1368-1437), Holy Roman emperor 1411-37, king of Bohemia 1420-37, and king of Hungary 1385-1437 **14** 220-221

SIGNAC, PAUL (1863-1935), French painter **23** 369-372

SIGNORELLI, LUCA (circa 1445/50-1523), Italian painter **14** 221-222

Sigüenza
see Ferrer, Gabriel Miró

SIHANOUK, PRINCE NORODOM (born 1922), Cambodian nationalist and political leader **14** 222-223

Sikhs (religious sect)
Singh, Gobind **28** 327-328

SIKORSKY, IGOR (1889-1972), Russian-American aeronautical engineer, aircraft manufacturer, and inventor **14** 223-224

SIKORSKI, WLADYSLAW (1881-1943), Polish military leader and prime minister **20** 338-340

SILBER, JOHN (born 1926), American philosopher and educator **14** 224-226

SILES ZUAZO, HERNAN (1914-1996), Bolivian politician **18** 370-373

SILKO, LESLIE (Leslie Marmon Silko; born 1948), Native American author and poet **14** 226-227

SILKWOOD, KAREN (1946-1974), American antinuclear activist **14** 227-229

SILLIMAN, BENJAMIN (1779-1864), American chemist, naturalist, and editor **14** 229-230

SILLS, BEVERLY (Belle Miriam Silverman; 1929-2007), American child performer, coloratura soprano, and operatic superstar **14** 230-231

SILONE, IGNAZIO (1900-1978), Italian novelist and essayist **14** 231-232

Silva, José Bonifácio de Andrada e
see Andrada e Silva, José Bonifácio de

Silva Paranhos, José Maria da
see Rio Branco, Barão do

Silva Xavier, José Joaquim da
see Tiradentes

SILVER, ABBA HILLEL (1893-1963), American rabbi and Zionist leader **14** 232-233

SILVERSTEIN, SHEL (1932-1999), American author and poet **19** 341-343

Sim, Georges
see Simenon, Georges

SIMENON, GEORGES (1903-1989), Belgian novelist **14** 233-234

SIMEON, KING OF BULGARIA (c. 864-927), Emperor of Bulgaria 893-927 **28** 325-327

Simeon ben Jeshua ben Elazar ben Sira
see Jesus ben Sira

SIMMEL, GEORG (1858-1918), German sociologist and philosopher **14** 234-235

SIMMS, WILLIAM GILMORE (1806-1870), American author **14** 235-236

Simon
see Peter, St.

SIMON, CLAUDE (1913-1984), French novelist **25** 386-388

SIMON, CLAUDE HENRI EUGENE (1913-2005), French author **25** 386-388

SIMON, HERBERT ALEXANDER (born 1916), American Nobelist in economics **14** 236-237

SIMON, JULES FRANÇOIS (1814-1896), French philosopher, writer, and statesman **14** 237-238

SIMON, NEIL (Marvin Neil Simon; born 1927), American playwright **18** 373-374

SIMON, PAUL (born 1928), newspaper publisher, Illinois state legislator, lieutenant governor, and U.S. representative and senator **14** 238-239

SIMONE, NINA (Eunice Kathleen Waymon; 1933-2003), African American musician **24** 371-374

SIMONOV, KONSTANTIN MIKHAILOVICH (1915-1979), Soviet poet and novelist **14** 239-240

Simons, Menno
see Menno Simons

SINGH, GOBIND (Gobind Rai Sodhi; 1666-1708), Indian religious leader **28** 327-328

SIMPSON, GEORGE GAYLORD (1902-1984), American paleontologist **14** 240-242

SIMPSON, LOUIS ASTON MARANTZ (born 1923), American poet, critic, and educator **14** 243-244

SIMPSON, WALLIS (Bessie Wallis Warfield Simpson, Duchess of Windsor; 1896-1986), American socialite and wife of Edward VIII, King of England **19** 343-345

SIMS, WILLIAM SOWDEN (1858-1936), American admiral **14** 244

SIN, JAIME L. (1928-2005), Filipino cardinal of the Roman Catholic Church **14** 244-245

SINAN, KODJA MIMAR (1489-1578), Ottoman architect **14** 245-246

SINATRA, FRANCIS ALBERT (Frank Sinatra; 1915-1998), American singer **14** 246-248

SINCLAIR, UPTON BEALE, JR. (1878-1968), American novelist and political writer **14** 248-249

SINGER, ISAAC BASHEVIS (1904-1991), Polish-American author **14** 249-250

SINGER, ISAAC M. (1811-1875), American inventor of the sewing machine **14** 250

SINGER, MAXINE (born Maxine Frank, 1931), American biochemist and geneticist **14** 251-252

SINGER, PETER ALBERT DAVID (born 1946), Australian philosopher and author of Animal Liberation **14** 253-254

SINGH, VISHWANATH PRATAP (born 1931), prime minister of India (1989-1990) **14** 254-256

Singleton, Anne
see Benedict, Ruth Fulton

Sinnott, Michael
see Sennett, Mack

SIQUEIROS, DAVID ALFARO (1896-1974), Mexican mural painter **14** 256

Sirach, Jesus ben
see Jesus ben Sira

SIRANI, ELISABETTA (1638-1665), Italian artist **22** 399-401

SIRICA, JOHN JOSEPH (1904-1992), U.S. district court judge who presided over the Watergate affair **14** 257-258

SIRLEAF, ELLEN JOHNSON (Ellen Johnson-Sirleaf; born 1938), President of Liberia (2006-) **28** 328-331

SISLEY, ALFRED (1839-1899), English-born French artist **26** 342-344

SISMONDI, JEAN CHARLES LÉONARD SIMONDE DE (1773-1842), Swiss-born historian and political economist **14** 258-259

SISULU, NONTSIKELELO ALBERTINA (1918-2003), leader of the anti-apartheid movement in South Africa **14** 259-261

SISULU, WALTER MAX ULYATE (born 1912), leader of the African National Congress (ANC) of South Africa **14** 261-262

SITHOLE, NDABANINGI (born 1920), African nationalist **14** 262-264

SITTING BULL (circa 1834-1890), American Indian leader and medicine man **14** 264-265

SITWELL, DAME EDITH (1887-1964), English poet and critic **14** 265-266

ŚIVAJT (1627-1680), Indian warrior and leader of a Hindu nation **14** 266-267

SIXTUS V (Felice Perreti; 1520-90), pope 1585-90 **14** 267-268

SIZA, ALVARO (Alvaro Joaquim Melo Siza Vieria; born 1933), Portugese architect **18** 375-376

SKELTON, JOHN (circa 1460-1529), English poet and humanist **14** 268-269

Skiagraphos
see Apollodorus

SKINNER, BURRHUS FREDERIC (1904-1990), American experimental psychologist **14** 269-270

SKINNER, CORNELIA OTIS (1901-1979), American actress and author **19** 346-348

Sklodowska, Marie
see Curie, Marie Sklodowska

SKOBLIKOVA, LYDIA PAVLOVNA (born 1939), Russian ice skater **26** 344-346

SKRAM, AMALIE (Berthe Amalie Alver; Amalie Mueller; 1846-1905), Norwegian author **28** 331-333

SLÁNSKÝ, RUDOLF SALZMANN (1901-1952), founding member of the Czechoslovak Communist Party and vice-premier of the former Czechoslovakia **14** 270-271

SLATER, SAMUEL (1768-1835), English-born American manufacturer **14** 272-273

Slee, Margaret
see Sanger, Margaret

SLIDELL, JOHN (1793-1871), American politician **14** 273

SLIM, WILLIAM JOSEPH (a.k.a. Anthony Mills; 1891-1970), English general and governor-general of Australia **18** 377-378

SLOAN, ALFRED PRITCHARD, JR. (1875-1966), American automobile executive **14** 274

SLOAN, JOHN (1871-1951), American painter **14** 274-275

SLOCUM, JOSHUA (Joshua Slocombe; 1844-1909), Canadian mariner, adventurer, and author **28** 333-335

SLUTER, CLAUS (circa 1350-1405/1406), Dutch-Burgundian sculptor **14** 275-276

SLYE, MAUD (1879-1954), American pathologist **14** 276-277

SMALL, ALBION WOODBURY (1854-1926), American sociologist and educator **14** 277

SMALLS, ROBERT (1839-1916), African American statesman **14** 277-278

SMEAL, ELEANOR (Eleanor Marie Cutri Smeal; born 1939), American women's rights activist and president of the National Organization for Women **14** 278-280

SMEATON, JOHN (1724-1792), English civil engineer **14** 280-281

SMETANA, BEDŘICH (1824-1884), Czech composer **14** 281-282

SMIBERT, JOHN (1688-1751), Scottish-born American painter **14** 282

SMITH, ADAM (1723-1790), Scottish economist and moral philosopher **14** 283-284

SMITH, ALFRED EMMANUEL (1873-1944), American politician **14** 284-285

SMITH, BESSIE (1894-1937), African American blues singer **14** 285-287

SMITH, DAVID (1906-1965), American sculptor **14** 287-288

SMITH, DEAN EDWARDS (born 1931), American college basketball coach **18** 378-380

SMITH, DONALD ALEXANDER (1st Baron Strathcona and Mount Royal; 1820-1914), Canadian politician and philanthropist **14** 288-289

SMITH, DORA VALENTINE (1893-1985), American educator **14** 289-290

SMITH, GERRIT (1797-1874), American philanthropist and reformer **14** 290-291

SMITH, IAN DOUGLAS (1919-2007), African prime minister **14** 291-293

SMITH, JAMES MCCUNE (1813-1865), African American physician and author **14** 293-294

SMITH, JEDEDIAH S. (1799-1831), American trapper, fur trader, and explorer **14** 294-295

SMITH, JESSIE CARNEY (Jessie M. Carney; born 1930), African American librarian and educator **24** 374-376

SMITH, JOHN (circa 1580-1631), English colonist in America **14** 295-297

SMITH, JOSEPH (1805-1844), American Mormon leader **14** 297-298

SMITH, LILLIAN EUGENIA (1897-1966), Southern writer and critic of white supremacy and segregation **14** 298-299

SMITH, MARGARET CHASE (1897-1995), first woman elected to both houses of Congress **14** 299-300

SMITH, PAULINE (Pauline Janet Urmson Smith; Janet Tamson; 1882-1959), South African author **23** 372-373

Smith, Robert Barnwell
see Rhett, Robert Barnwell

Smith, Walter Bedell
see Bedell Smith, Walter

SMITH, WILLIAM (1727-1803), American educator and churchman **14** 301

SMITH, WILLIAM EUGENE (1918-1978), American photojournalist **19** 348-350

SMITH COURT, MARGARET JEAN (born 1942), Australian tennis player **24** 376-378

SMITHSON, ROBERT (1938-1973), American sculptor, essayist, and filmmaker **14** 301-303

SMOHALLA (1815-1895), Native American warrior, medicine man, and spiritual leader **14** 303-305

SMOLLETT, TOBIAS GEORGE (1721-1771), English novelist and satirist **14** 305-307

SMUIN, MICHAEL (1938-2007), American dancer-choreographer-director **14** 307-309

Smurfs (cartoon characters)
Peyo **28** 280-282

SMUTS, JAN CHRISTIAN (1870-1950), South African soldier and statesman **14** 309-310

SMYTHSON, ROBERT (1535-1614), English architect **24** 378-381

SNEAD, SAM (Samuel Jackson Snead; 1912-2002), American golfer **21** 388-390

Snow (book)
Pamuk, Orhan **28** 269-272

SNOW, CHARLES PERCY (1905-1972), English novelist and physicist **14** 311-312

SNOW, EDGAR (1905-1972), American journalist and author **14** 312-313

SNOW, JOHN (1813-1858), English physician and epidemiologist **25** 388-390

SNOWE, OLYMPIA (born Olympia Jean Bouchles, 1947), U.S. congresswoman and senator **14** 313-314

SOANE, SIR JOHN (1753-1837), English architect **14** 314-315

SOARES, MÁRIO (Mário Alberto Nobre Lopes Soares; born 1924), first socialist president of Portugal **14** 315-316

SOBCHAK, ANATOLY ALEXANDROVICH (1937-2000), popular democratic leader of Russia elected mayor of St. Petersburg in 1990 **14** 317-318

SOBHUZA II (1899-1982), King of Swaziland **24** 381-383

SOBUKWE, ROBERT MANGALISO (1924-1978), South African politician **14** 318-319

Social Democratic party
Sweden
Palme, Olof **28** 267-269

Social reform
Europe
Canth, Minna **28** 58-60

Social scientists, American
anthropologists (20th century)
Castaneda, Carlos **28** 62-64
educators (20th century)
Bloom, Harold **28** 38-40
historians (20th century)
Faust, Drew Gilpin **28** 116-118

Social scientists, Bangladeshi
Economists
Yunus, Muhammad **28** 386-388

Social scientists, Polish
Sendler, Irena **28** 318-320

SOCRATES (469-399 B.C.), Greek philosopher and logican **14** 320-321

SODDY, FREDERICK (1877-1956), English chemist **14** 321-323

SODERBERGH, STEVEN (born 1963), American film director and screenwriter **25** 390-392

SÖDERBLOM, NATHAN (Lars Jonathan Söderblom; 1866-1931), Swedish Lutheran archbishop **14** 323-324

SOELLE, DOROTHEE (1929-2003), German theologian, political activist, and feminist **14** 324-325

SOL CH'ONG (circa 680-750), Korean Confucian scholar **14** 325-326

Solidarity (independent trade union movement, Poland)
Kuron, Jacek **28** 203-206

SOLÍS, JUAN DÍAZ DE (circa 1470-1516), Spanish explorer **14** 326

SOLOMON (ruled circa 965-circa 925 B.C.), king of the ancient Hebrews **14** 326-327

Solomon bar Isaac
see Rashi

SOLON (active 594 B.C.), Greek statesman and poet **14** 327-328

SOLOVEITCHIK, JOSEPH BAER (1903-1993), Jewish theologian and philosopher **14** 328-329

SOLOVIEV, VLADIMIR SERGEEVICH (1853-1900), Russian philosopher and religious thinker **14** 329-330

SOLZHENITSYN, ALEXANDER ISAYEVICH (born 1918), Soviet novelist **14** 330-332

Somali literature
Farah, Nuruddin **28** 114-116

SOMBART, WERNER (1863-1941), German economic historian **14** 332-333

SOMERSET, DUKE OF (Edward Seymour; 1506-52), English statesman **14** 333-334

SOMERVILLE, EDITH ANNE &Oelig;NONE (1858-1949), Irish author **14** 334-335

SOMERVILLE, MARY (1780-1872), Scottish mathematician, physicist, and geographer **20** 340-342

Somerville and Ross (pseudonym)
see Edith Anna Œnone Somerville

SOMOZA, ANASTASIO (1896-1956), Nicaraguan dictator and military leader **14** 335-336

SOMOZA DEBAYLE, ANASTASIO (1925-1980), president of Nicaragua (1967-1979) **14** 336-337

SON, TRINH CONG (1939-2001), Vietnamese singer and songwriter **28** 335-336

SONDHEIM, STEPHEN (born 1930), American composer and lyricist **14** 337-338

SONDOK (circa 581-647), Korean Queen **25** 392-394

SONG SISTERS (Ailing Song, 1890-1973; Meiling Song, 1898-1919; and Qingling Song, 1890-1981), Chinese political and social activists **14** 338-341

SONGGRAM, LUANG PIBUL (Luang Phibunsongkhram; 1897-1964), Thai prime minister **24** 383-385

Songwriters Hall of Fame
Paul, Les **28** 276-278

SONJO (1552-1608), king of Korea 1567-1608 **14** 341-342

Sonora, Marquess of
see Gálvez, José de

SONTAG, SUSAN (1933-2004), American essayist **14** 342-343

Sony Corporation
Ibuka, Masaru **28** 184-186
Stringer, Howard **28** 338-340

SOPHOCLES (496-406 B.C.), Greek playwright **14** 343-345

SOPWITH, THOMAS OCTAVE MURDOCH (1888-1989), British aviation industrialist and pioneer pilot **14** 345-346

SOR, FERNANDO (Fernando Sors; 1778-1839), Spanish musician **25** 394-396

SORDELLO (ca. 1180-ca. 1269), Italian poet and troubadour **20** 342-343

SOREL, ALBERT (1842-1906), French diplomatic historian **14** 346-347

SOREL, GEORGES (1847-1922), French philosopher **14** 347-348

SORIANO, EDWARD (born 1946), Filipino American military leader **27** 327-329

SOROKIN, PITIRIM A. (1889-1968), Russian-American sociologist **14** 348-349

SOTATSU, TAWARAYA (circa 1570-circa 1643), Japanese painter **14** 349

Soubirous, Bernadette
see Bernadette of Lourdes, St.

SOUFFLOT, JACQUES GERMAIN (1713-1780), French architect **14** 349-350

SOULAGES, PIERRE (born 1919), French painter **14** 350-351

SOULÉ, PIERRE (1801-1870), American politician and diplomat **14** 351-352

SOUSA, HENRIQUE TEIXEIRA DE (born 1919), Cape Verdean novelist **14** 352-353

SOUSA, JOHN PHILIP (1854-1932), American bandmaster and composer **14** 353-354

SOUSA, MARTIM AFONSO DE (circa 1500-64), Portuguese colonizer and statesman **14** 354-355

SOUTER, DAVID H. (born 1939), U.S. Supreme Court justice **14** 355-356

SOUTHEY, ROBERT (1774-1843), English poet and author **18** 381-382

SOUTINE, CHAIM (1894-1943), Russian painter **14** 356-357

SOUVANNA PHOUMA (1901-1984), Laotian prince and premier **14** 357-358

SOWELL, THOMAS (born 1930), American economist and author **19** 350-352

SOYINKA, WOLE (Oluwole Akinwande Soyinka; born 1934), first African to win the Nobel Prize for Literature (1986) **14** 358-359

SPAAK, PAUL HENRI (1899-1972), Belgian statesman and diplomat **14** 359-360

SPAATZ, CARL (1891-1974), American army and air force officer **19** 352-355

Spagnoletto, Lo
see Ribera, Jusepe de

SPALLANZANI, LAZZARO (Abbé Spallanzani; 1729-99), Italian naturalist **14** 360-361

Spanish music
Rubinstein, Arthur **28** 305-307

SPARK, MURIEL SARAH (1918-2006), British author **14** 361-362

SPARKS, JARED (1789-1866), American historian **14** 363

SPARTACUS (died 71 B.C.), Thracian galdiator **14** 363-364

SPAULDING, CHARLES CLINTON (1874-1952), African American business executive **14** 364-365

Speakers of the House
see Statesmen, American

SPEER, ALBERT (1905-1981), German architect and Nazi **19** 355-356

SPEKE, JOHN HANNING (1827-1864), English explorer **14** 366-367

SPELLMAN, CARDINAL FRANCIS JOSEPH (1889-1967), Roman Catholic archbishop **14** 367

SPEMANN, HANS (1869-1941), German experimental embryologist **14** 368-369

SPENCE, CATHERINE HELEN (1825-1910), Australian author and activist **23** 374-375

SPENCER, HERBERT (1820-1903), English philosopher **14** 369-370

SPENCER, SAMUEL (1847-1906), American railroad executive **25** 396-398

SPENDER, STEPHEN HAROLD (born 1909), English poet and critic **14** 370-371

SPENER, PHILIPP JAKOB (1635-1705), German theologian **14** 372

SPENGLER, OSWALD (1880-1936), German philosopher **14** 372-373

SPENSER, EDMUND (circa 1552-99), English poet **14** 373-376

SPERANSKI, COUNT MIKHAIL MIKHAILOVICH (1772-1839), Russian statesman and reformer **14** 376-377

SPERRY, ELMER A. (1860-1930), American inventor **14** 377-379

Spice Islands (Indonesia)
Serrão, Francisco **28** 320-321

SPIEGELMAN, ART (Joe Cutrate; Al Flooglebuckle; Skeeter Grant; born 1948), Swedish American cartoonist **25** 398-400

SPIELBERG, STEVEN (born 1947), American filmmaker **14** 379-381

Spies
for Great Britain
Atkins, Vera **28** 16-18
Chapman, Eddie **28** 69-72
for the Soviet Union
Fuchs, Klaus **28** 129-131
novels about
Fleming, Ian **28** 123-125

SPIES, WALTER (1895-1942), German artist and musician **27** 329-331

SPINOZA, BARUCH (Benedict Spinoza; 1632-77), Dutch philosopher **14** 381-383

Spiritualism (religion)
Krishnamurti, Uppaluri Gopala **28** 201-203

SPITTELER, CARL FRIEDRICH GEORG (Carl Felix Tandem; 1845-1924), Swiss Poet **25** 400-402

SPITZ, MARK (born 1950), American swimmer **23** 376-378

SPOCK, BENJAMIN MCLANE (1903-1998), American pediatrician and political activist and author of *Baby and Child Care* **14** 383-385

Sports
see Athletes, American

SPOTSWOOD, ALEXANDER (1676-1740), British general and colonial governor **14** 385

SPRAGUE, FRANK JULIAN (1857-1934), American electrical engineer and inventor **14** 385-386

SPRINGSTEEN, BRUCE (Bruce Frederick Springsteen; born 1949), American musician **24** 385-388

SPURGEON, CHARLES HADDON (1834-1892), British Christian author and preacher **25** 402-405

SQUIBB, EDWARD ROBINSON (1819-1900), American physician and pharmacist **21** 390-392

Srivastava, Dhanpatrai
see Premchand

SSU-MA CH'IEN (145-circa 90 B.C.), Chinese historian **14** 388-389

SSU-MA HSIANG-JU (circa 179-117 B.C.), Chinese poet **14** 389-390

SSU-MA KUANG (1019-1086), Chinese statesman **14** 390-391

STAËL, GERMAINE DE (1766-1817), French-Swiss novelist and woman of letters **14** 391-392

STAËL, NICOLAS DE (1914-1955), French painter **14** 392

STAHL, GEORG ERNST (1660-1734), German chemist and medical theorist **14** 392-393

STALIN, JOSEPH (1879-1953), Soviet statesman **14** 393-396

STANDING BEAR (1829-1908), Native American tribal leader **24** 388-390

STANDISH, MYLES (circa 1584-1656), English military adviser to the Pilgrims **14** 396-397

STANFORD, LELAND (1824-1893), American railroad builder and politician **14** 397-398

STANISLAVSKY, CONSTANTIN (1863-1938), Russian actor and director **14** 398-399

STANLEY, SIR HENRY MORTON (1841-1904), British explorer and journalist **14** 399-400

STANLEY, WENDELL MEREDITH (1904-1971), American virologist **14** 400-401

STANTON, EDWIN MCMASTERS (1814-1869), American statesman **14** 401-402

STANTON, ELIZABETH CADY (1815-1902), American feminist and reformer **14** 402-403

STAREWICZ, WLADYSLAW (Ladislas Starevich; 1882-1965), Russian animator and filmmaker **28** 336-338

STARHAWK (Miriam Simos; born 1951), theoretician and practitioner of feminist Wicca (witchcraft) in the United States **14** 403-404

STARLEY, JAMES (1831-1881), British inventor and businessman **21** 392-393

STARR, BELLE (Myra Maybelle Shirley; 1848-1889), American outlaw **26** 347-349

Starship Troopers (book)
Heinlein, Robert A. **28** 166-168

STARZL, THOMAS (born 1926), American surgeon **21** 393-395

State, U.S. Secretaries of
see Statesmen, American—Executive (secretaries of state)

Statesmen, American
• LEGISLATIVE
representatives (20th century)
Church, Frank Forrester, III **28** 78-80
Saund, Dalip Singh **28** 310-312
• STATE and LOCAL
mayors (20th century)
Bloomberg, Michael **28** 40-42

Statesmen, Austrian
empresses
Elisabeth, Empress of Austria **28** 111-113

Statesmen, British
prime ministers
Brown, Gordon **28** 48-50

Statesmen, Bulgarian
Simeon, King of Bulgaria **28** 325-327

Statesmen, Dutch
political leaders
Fortuyn, Pim **28** 125-127

Statesmen, English
queen consorts
Woodville, Elizabeth **28** 381-383

Statesmen, German
chancellors (post-1990)
Merkel, Angela **28** 243-245

Statesmen, Hungarian
Elisabeth, Empress of Austria **28** 111-113

Statesmen, Japanese
prime ministers
Abe, Shinzo **28** 1-3

Statesmen, Lebanese
Gemayel, Bashir **28** 136-138
Hariri, Rafic **28** 161-163
presidents
Gemayel, Bashir **28** 136-138

Statesmen, Liberian
Sirleaf, Ellen Johnson **28** 328-331

Statesman, Lithuanian
Wladyslaw II Jagiello, King of Poland **28** 377-378

Statesmen, Polish
Casimir III, King of Poland **28** 60-62
Kuron, Jacek **28** 203-206
Wladyslaw II Jagiello, King of Poland **28** 377-378

Statesmen, Roman
emperors (military)
Galerius, Emperor of Rome **28** 132-134

Statesmen, Swedish
Palme, Olof **28** 267-269

Statue of Liberty (New York City)
Bartholdi, Frédéric-Auguste **28** 29-31

STEAD, CHRISTINA ELLEN (1902-1983), Australian author **23** 378-380

STEEL, DANIELLE (born 1947), American author and poet **14** 404-406

STEEL, DAVID MARTIN SCOTT (born 1938), Scottish member of Parliament and leader of the Liberal Party **14** 406-407

STEEL, DAWN (1946-1997), American movie producer and studio executive **18** 383-384

STEELE, SIR RICHARD (1672-1729), British essayist, dramatist, and politician **14** 407-409

Stefano di Giovanni
see Sassetta

STEFANSSON, VILHJALMUR (1879-1962), Canadian-American Arctic explorer and scientist **14** 409-410

STEFFENS, LINCOLN (1866-1936), American journalist **14** 410-411

STEGNER, WALLACE (1909-1993), American author **19** 356-358

STEICHEN, EDWARD (1879-1973), American photographer, painter, and museum curator **14** 411-412

STEIN, EDITH (1891-1942), German philosopher **14** 412-414

STEIN, GERTRUDE (1874-1946), American writer **14** 414-415

STEIN, BARON HEINRICH FRIEDRICH KARL VOM UND ZUM (1757-1831), Prussian statesman **14** 415-416

STEINBECK, JOHN ERNST (1902-1968), American author **14** 416-417

STEINEM, GLORIA (born 1934), American feminist and journalist **14** 418-419

STEINER, JAKOB (1796-1863), Swiss mathematician **23** 380-382

STEINER, RUDOLF (1861-1925), Austrian philosopher and educator **27** 331-333

STEINITZ, WILHELM (1836-1900), Bohemian American chess player **20** 343-346

STEINMETZ, CHARLES PROTEUS (Karl August Rudolf Steinmetz; 1865-1923),

German-born American mathematician and electrical engineer **14** 419-420

STELLA, FRANK (born 1936), American painter **14** 420-422

STELLA, JOSEPH (1877-1946), Italian-born American painter **14** 422

STENDHAL (Marie Henri Beyle; 1783-1842), French author **14** 422-425

STENGEL, CASEY (Charles Dillon Stengel; 1890-1975), American baseball player and manager **19** 361-363

STENO, NICOLAUS (Niels Stensen; 1638-86), Danish naturalist **14** 425-426

STEPHEN (1096?-1154), king of England 1135-54 **14** 426-427

STEPHEN I (c. 973-1038), king of Hungary **14** 427-428

STEPHEN, SIR LESLIE (1832-1904), English historian **14** 429

STEPHEN HARDING, ST. (died 1134), English abbot and monastic reformer **14** 428-429

STEPHENS, ALEXANDER HAMILTON (1812-1883), American statesman **14** 429-430

STEPHENS, HELEN (1918-1994), American athlete **19** 363-365

STEPHENS, JAMES (1882-1950), Irish novelist and poet **14** 430-431

STEPHENS, URIAH (1821-1882), American labor leader **14** 431-432

STEPHENSON, GEORGE (1781-1848), English railway engineer **14** 432-433

STEPHENSON, ROBERT (1803-1859), English railway engineer **14** 432-433

STEPINAC, ALOJZIJE (1898-1960), Croatian nationalist, Catholic, and anti-Communist **14** 433-435

STEPTOE, PATRICK (1913-1988), British physician **20** 346-348

STERN, ISAAC (born 1920), American violinist **19** 365-367

STERN, OTTO (1888-1969), German-born American physicist **14** 435

STERNE, LAURENCE (1713-1768), British novelist **14** 435-437

STETTINIUS, EDWARD R., JR. (1900-1949), American industrialist and statesman **14** 437-438

STEUBEN, BARON FREDERICK WILLIAM AUGUSTUS VON (1730-1794), German officer in the American Revolution **14** 438-439

STEVENS, GEORGE COOPER (1904-1975), American Film Director and Producer **22** 401-403

STEVENS, JOHN (1749-1838), American engineer and inventor **14** 439-440

STEVENS, JOHN PAUL (born 1920), U.S. Supreme Court justice **14** 440-441

STEVENS, NETTIE MARIA (1861-1912), American biologist and geneticist **14** 441-442

STEVENS, THADDEUS (1792-1868), American politician **14** 442-443

STEVENS, WALLACE (1879-1955), American poet **14** 443-445

STEVENSON, ADLAI EWING (1900-1965), American statesman and diplomat **14** 445-446

Stevenson, Elizabeth Cleghorn
see Gaskell, Elizabeth

STEVENSON, ROBERT LOUIS (1850-1894), Scottish novelist, essayist and poet **14** 446-448

STEVIN, SIMON (Simon Stevinus; 1548-1620), Dutch mathematician **21** 395-398

STEWARD, SUSAN MCKINNEY (nee Susan Marie Smith; 1847-1918), African American physician and activist **24** 390-392

STEWART, ALEXANDER TURNEY (1803-1876), American dry-goods merchant **14** 448-449

STEWART, DUGALD (1753-1828), Scottish philosopher **14** 449

STEWART, ELLEN (born 1920), African-American theater founder and director **20** 348-352

STEWART, JACKIE (John Young Stewart; born 1939), Scottish race car driver **24** 392-395

STEWART, JIMMY (James Maitland Stewart; 1908-1997), American actor **18** 385-386

Stewart, John
see Cugoano, Ottobah

STEWART, MARIA W. MILLER (1803-1879), African American author and activist **24** 395-397

STEWART, MARTHA (nee Martha Kostyra; born 1941), American author, entertainer, and businesswoman **19** 367-369

STEWART, POTTER (1915-1985), liberal U.S. Supreme Court justice **14** 449-451

Stewart, Robert (1769-1822)
see Castlereagh, Viscount

STIEGEL, HENRY WILLIAM (1729-1785), German born American iron founder and glassmaker **14** 451

STIEGLITZ, ALFRED (1864-1946), American photographer, editor, and art gallery director **14** 451-452

STILICHO, FLAVIUS (died 408), Roman general **14** 452-453

STILL, CLYFFORD (1904-1980), American Abstract Expressionist artist **14** 453-454

STILL, WILLIAM (1821-1902), African American abolitionist, philanthropist, and businessman **14** 454-455

STILL, WILLIAM GRANT (born 1895), African American composer **14** 455-456

STILWELL, JOSEPH WARREN (1883-1946), American general **14** 456-457

STIMSON, HENRY LEWIS (1867-1950), American lawyer and statesman **14** 457-458

STIRLING, JAMES (1926-1992), British architect and city planner **14** 458-459

STIRNER, MAX (1806-1856), German philosopher **14** 459-460

STOCKHAUSEN, KARLHEINZ (1928-2007), German composer **14** 460-461

STOCKTON, ROBERT FIELD (1795-1866), American naval officer and politician **14** 461-462

STODDARD, SOLOMON (1643-1728/29), American colonial Congregational clergyman **14** 462-463

STOKER, BRAM (Abraham Stoker; 1847-1912), Irish author **14** 463-464

STOKES, CARL B. (1927-1996), African American politician **14** 464-465

STOLYPIN, PIOTR ARKADEVICH (1862-1911), Russian statesman and reformer **14** 465-466

STONE, EDWARD DURRELL (1902-1978), American architect, educator, and designer **14** 466-468

STONE, HARLAN FISKE (1872-1946), American jurist; chief justice of U.S. Supreme Court 1914-46 **14** 468-470

STONE, I. F. (Isador Feinstein; 1907-1989), American journalist **14** 470-471

STONE, LUCY (1818-1893), American abolitionist and women's suffrage leader **14** 471-472

Stone, Miriam
see Harwood, Gwen

STONE, OLIVER (born 1946), American filmmaker **14** 472-475

STONE, ROBERT ANTHONY (born 1937), American novelist **14** 475-476

STOPES, MARIE (1880-1958), British scientist and birth control advocate **14** 476-478

STOPPARD, THOMAS (Thomas Straussler; born 1937), English playwright **14** 478-479

STORM, THEODOR (1817-1888), German poet and novelist **14** 479-480

STORY, JOSEPH (1779-1845), American jurist and statesman **14** 480-481

Story of Women (film) Chabrol, Claude **28** 67-69

STOSS, VEIT (circa 1445-1533), German sculptor **14** 481-482

STOUFFER, SAMUEL A. (1900-1960), American sociologist and statistician **14** 482-483

STOUT, JUANITA KIDD (1919-1998), African American judge **23** 382-384

STOVALL, LUTHER MCKINLEY (born 1937), American silkscreen artist **14** 483-484

STOWE, HARRIET ELIZABETH BEECHER (1811-1896), American writer **14** 484-485

STRABO (circa 64 B.C.-circa A.D. 23), Greek geographer and historian **14** 485-486

STRACHAN, JOHN (1778-1867), Canadian Anglican bishop **14** 486-487

STRACHEY, GILES LYTTON (1880-1932), English biographer and critic known for his satire of the Victorian era **14** 487-488

STRACHEY, JOHN (Evelyn John St. Loe Strachey; 1901-1963), British author and politician **20** 352-354

STRADIVARI, ANTONIO (circa 1644-1737), Italian violin maker **14** 488-490

STRAFFORD, 1ST EARL OF (Thomas Wentworth; 1593-1641), English statesman **14** 490-491

STRAND, MARK (born 1934), fourth Poet Laureate of the United States **14** 491-493

STRAND, PAUL (1890-1976), American photographer **19** 369-371

STRANG, RUTH MAY (1895-1971), American educator **14** 493-494

Stranger in a Strange Land (book) Heinlein, Robert A. **28** 166-168

STRASBERG, LEE (Israel Strasberg; 1901-82), American acting instructor, director, and founding member of the Group Theatre **14** 494-495

Stratford Festival (Canadian live theater festival) Patterson, Tom **28** 274-276

Strathcona and Mount Royal, 1st Baron see Smith, Donald Alexander

STRAUS, ISIDOR (1845-1912), American merchant **14** 496

STRAUSS, DAVID FRIEDRICH (1808-1874), German historian and Protestant theologian **14** 496-497

STRAUSS, FRANZ JOSEF (1915-1988), West German politician **14** 497-498

STRAUSS, JOHANN, JR. (1825-1899), Austrian composer **14** 498-499

STRAUSS, LEO (1899-1973), German Jewish Socratic political philosopher **14** 499-500

STRAUSS, LEVI (Loeb Strauss; 1829-1902), American businessman **20** 354-356

STRAUSS, RICHARD (1864-1949), German composer and conductor **14** 500-501

STRAUSS, ROBERT SCHWARZ (born 1918), Democratic fundraiser and strategist **14** 501-502

STRAVINSKY, IGOR FEDOROVICH (1882-1971), Russian-born composer **14** 502-506

STRAWSON, SIR PETER FREDRICK (1919-2006), English philosopher **14** 506-507

STREEP, MERYL LOUISE (born 1949), American actress **23** 384-387

STREETON, SIR ARTHUR ERNEST (1867-1943), Australian landscape painter **14** 507-508

STREISAND, BARBRA (Barbara Joan Streisand; born 1942), American entertainer **18** 386-388

STRESEMANN, GUSTAV (1878-1929), German statesman and diplomat **14** 508-509

Strickland, Susanna see Moodie, Susanna

STRINDBERG, AUGUST (1849-1912), Swedish author **14** 509-511

STRINGER, HOWARD (born 1942), Welsh-American businessman **28** 338-340

STROESSNER, ALFREDO (1912-2006), Paraguayan statesman **14** 511-512

STRONG, JOSIAH (1847-1916), American clergyman and social activist **14** 512-513

STROZZI, BARBARA (Barbara Valle; 1619-1677), Italian composer and singer **26** 350-351

STRUSS, KARL (1886-1981), American photographer and cinematographer **21** 398-399

Strutt, John William see Rayleigh, 3d Baron

STRUVE, FRIEDRICH GEORG WILHELM VON (1793-1864), German-born Russian astronomer and geodesist **14** 513

Stuart, Charles see Charles I and II (king of England)

Stuart, Charles Edward Louis Philip Casimir see Charles Edward Louis Philip Casimir Stuart

STUART, GILBERT (1755-1828), American painter **14** 513-515

STUART, JAMES EWELL BROWN (Jeb; 1833-64), Confederate cavalry officer **14** 515-516

Stuart, John see Bute, 3d Earl of; Cugoano, Ottobah

STUDENT, KURT (1890-1978), German general **20** 356-358

STUDI, WES (born Wesley Studie; born circa 1944), Native American actor **15** 1-2

STURGES, PRESTON (Edmund Preston Biden; 1898-1959), American playwright, screenwriter, director, and businessman **19** 371-374

STURLUSON, SNORRI (1179-1241), Icelandic statesman and historian **14** 310-311

STURT, CHARLES (1795-1869), British officer, explorer, and colonial administrator **15** 2-3

STURTEVANT, A. H. (Alfred Henry Sturtevant; 1891-1970), American geneticist **15** 3-5

STUYVESANT, PETER (circa 1610-72), Dutch colonial administrator **15** 5-6

STYRON, WILLIAM (1925-2006), American southern writer of novels and articles **15** 6-8

SUÁREZ, FRANCISCO (1548-1617), Spanish philosopher and theologian **15** 8

Suárez de Figueroa, Gòmez see Garcilaso de la Vega, Inca

SUAZO CÓRDOVA, ROBERTO (born 1927), physician and president of Honduras (1982-1986) **15** 8-10

Submarines
development
Drebbel, Cornelius **28** 102-104

SUCKLING, SIR JOHN (1609-1642),
English poet and playwright **15** 10-11

SUCRE, ANTONIO JOSÉ DE (1795-
1830), Venezuelan general, Bolivian
president 1826-28 **15** 11-12

SUDERMANN, HERMANN (1857-1928),
German dramatist and novelist **15**
12-13

SUETONIUS TRANQUILLUS, GAIUS
(circa 70-circa 135), Roman
administrator and writer **15** 13

SUHARTO (1921-2008), second
president after Indonesia's
independence **15** 14-15

SUI WEN-TI (541-604), Chinese emperor
15 16-18

SUIKO (554-628), empress of Japan 593-
628 **15** 15-16

SUKARNO (1901-1970), Indonesian
statesman, president 1945-66 **15** 18-20

SULEIMAN I (the Magnificent; 1494-
1566), Ottoman sultan 1520-66 **15**
20-21

SULLA, LUCIUS CORNELIUS I (138-78
B.C.), Roman general, dictator 82-79
B.C. **15** 21-22

SULLIVAN, SIR ARTHUR SEYMOUR
(1842-1900), English composer **15** 23

SULLIVAN, ED (Edward Vincent Sullivan;
1902-1974), American television
emcee, screenwriter, and author **19**
374-376

SULLIVAN, HARRY STACK (1892-1949),
American psychiatrist **15** 23-24

SULLIVAN, JOHN LAWRENCE (1858-
1918), American boxer **15** 24-25

SULLIVAN, LEON HOWARD (1922-
2001), African American civil rights
leader and minister **15** 25-27

SULLIVAN, LOUIS HENRI (1856-1924),
American architect **15** 27-28

SULLY, THOMAS (1783-1872), English-
born American painter **22** 403-404

Sultan of Brunei
see Bolkiah, Hassanal

SULZBERGER, ARTHUR OCHS (born
1926), publisher of the *New York
Times* **15** 28-30

SULZBERGER, ARTHUR OCHS JR. (born
1951), American newspaper publisher
19 376-378

SUMMERSON, JOHN (John Newenham
Summerson; 1904-1992), English
architectural historian **27** 333-335

SUMNER, CHARLES (1811-1874),
American statesman **15** 30-31

SUMNER, WILLIAM GRAHAM (1840-
1910), American sociologist and
educator **15** 32

Sun Djata
see Sundiata Keita

SUN YAT-SEN (1866-1925), Chinese
statesman, leader of republican
revolution **15** 35-39

SUNDAY, WILLIAM ASHLEY ("Billy";
1862-1935), American evangelist **15**
32-33

SUNDIATA KEITA (circa 1210-circa
1260), founder of Mali empire in West
Africa **15** 33-34

Sung T'ai-tsu
see Zhao Kuang-yin

Surgery (medical)
Agnew, David Hayes **28** 3-5

Surrealism (art)
Europe
Witkacy **28** 374-376
precursors
Grandville, J.J. **28** 144-146

Surrealism (literature)
influence of
Witkacy **28** 374-376

SU-SHIH (Su Tung-p'o; 1037-1101),
Chinese author and artist **15** 39-40

Suspense story
see Mystery fiction (literary genre)

SUTHERLAND, GRAHAM (1903-1980),
English painter **15** 40-41

SUTHERLAND, JOAN (born 1926),
Australian opera singer **22** 404-407

SUTTER, JOHN AUGUSTUS (1803-
1880), German-born American
adventurer and colonizer **15** 41-42

SUTTNER, BERTHA VON (born Countess
Bertha Kinsky; 1843-1914), Austrian
author and activist **15** 42-44

SUVOROV, ALEKSANDR VASILIEVICH
(1730-1800), Russian general **15** 44-45

Suyang, Prince
see Sejo

SUZMAN, HELEN (born 1917), member
of the South African House of
Assembly for the Progressive Party **15**
45-46

SUZUKI, DAISETZ TEITARO (1870-
1966), Japanese translator, teacher,
and interpreter of Zen Buddhist
thought **15** 46-47

SVEVO, ITALO (pseudonym of Ettore
Schmitz; 1861-1928), Italian novelist
15 47-48

SWAMINATHAN, M.S. (Monkombu
Sambasivan Swaminathan; born 1925),
Indian agricultural geneticist **25**
405-407

SWAMMERDAM, JAN (1637-1680),
Dutch naturalist **15** 48-49

Swedberg, Emanuel
see Swedenborg, Emanuel

Sweden, Kingdom of (nation, Northern
Europe)
neutralist policies
Palme, Olof **28** 267-269

SWEDENBORG, EMANUEL (1688-1772),
Swedish scientist, theologian, and
mystic **15** 49-50

Swedish art and literature
Lindgren, Astrid **28** 219-221

SWEELINCK, JAN PIETERSZOON (1562-
1621), Dutch composer, organist, and
teacher **15** 50-51

SWIFT, GUSTAVUS FRANKLIN (1839-
1903), American businessman **22**
407-409

SWIFT, JONATHAN (1667-1745),
English-Irish poet, political writer, and
clergyman **15** 51-54

SWINBURNE, ALGERNON CHARLES
(1837-1909), English poet, dramatist,
and critic **15** 54-55

SWITZER, MARY E. (1900-1971),
American champion of rehabilitation
15 55-56

SWOPE, GERARD (1872-1957), president
of General Electric **15** 56-58

Sword of Gideon
see Münzer, Thomas

SYDENHAM, BARON (Charles Edward
Poulett Thomson; 1799-1841), English
merchant and politician **15** 59-60

SYDENHAM, THOMAS (1624-1689),
English physician **15** 59-60

Sydenstricker, Pearl
see Buck, Pearl Sydenstricker

SYED AHMED KHAN (1817-1898),
Moslem religious leader,
educationalist, and politician **15** 60

Sylphide, La (ballet)
Taglioni, Marie **28** 345-347

SYLVESTER I (died 335), pope (314-335)
24 397-399

SYLVESTER II (Gerbert of Aurillac c.
940-1003), French pope 998-1003 **25**
407-408

SYLVIS, WILLIAM (1828-1869),
American labor leader **15** 60-61

SYNGE, EDMUND JOHN MILLINGTON
(1871-1909), Irish dramatist **15** 61-62

Synthesizer (music)
Zawinul, Joe **28** 389-391

SZELL, GEORGE (György Szell; 1897-1970), Hungarian-American conductor **26** 351-354

SZENT-GYÖRGYI, ALBERT VON (1893-1986), Hungarian-American biochemist **15** 62-64

SZILARD, LEO (1898-1964), Hungarian-born nuclear physicist **15** 64-66

SZOLD, HENRIETTA (1860-1945), American Jewish leader **15** 66-67

SZYMANOWSKA, MARIA (Maria Agata Wolowska; 1789-1831), Polish pianist and composer **28** 340-342

SZYMANOWSKI, KAROL (1882-1937), Polish composer **15** 67-68

SZYMBORSKA, WISLAWA (born 1923), Polish author **25** 408-410

T

TABARI, MUHAMMAD IBN JARIR AL- (839-923), Moslem historian and religious scholar **15** 69-70

TABOR, HORACE AUSTIN WARNER (1830-1899), American mining magnate and politician **15** 70

TACITUS (56/57-circa 125), Roman orator and historian **15** 70-72

TAEUBER-ARP, SOPHIE (1889-1943), Swiss-born painter, designer, and dancer **15** 73-74

TAEWON'GUN, HŬNGSON (1820-1898), Korean imperial regent **15** 74-75

Tafari, Lij (or Ras)
see Haile Selassie

TAFAWA BALEWA, SIR ABUBAKAR (1912-1966), Nigerian statesman, prime minister 1957-1966 **15** 75

TAFT, HELEN HERRON (Nellie Taft; 1861-1943), American First Lady **28** 343-345

TAFT, LORADO (1860-1936), American sculptor **15** 75-76

TAFT, ROBERT ALPHONSO (1889-1953), American senator **15** 76-78

TAFT, WILLIAM HOWARD (1857-1930), American statesman, president 1909-1913 **15** 78-81
family
Taft, Helen Herron **28** 343-345

TAGLIONI, MARIE (Maria Taglioni; 1804-1884), French ballet dancer **28** 345-347

TAGORE, RABINDRANATH (1861-1941), Bengali poet, philosopher, social reformer, and dramatist **12** 529-531

TAHARQA (reigned circa 688-circa 663 B.C.), Nubian pharaoh of Egypt **15** 81-82

TAINE, HIPPOLYTE ADOLPHE (1828-1893), French critic and historian **15** 82-83

T'ai Tsung
see T'ai-tsung, T'ang

T'AI-TSUNG, T'ANG (600-649), Chinese emperor **15** 83-84

T'ai-tzu
see Hung-wu

Taizong
see T'ai-tsung, T'ang

TAKAHASHI, KOREKIYO (1854-1936), Japanese statesman **15** 84-85

Takauji, Ashikaga
see Ashikaga Takauji

TAKEMITSU, TORU (1930-1996), Japanese composer **26** 355-357

TAL, JOSEF (Josef Gruenthal; born 1910), Israeli composer, pianist, and professor of music **15** 85-86

TALBERT, MARY MORRIS BURNETT (1866-1923), American educator, feminist, civil rights activist, and lecturer **15** 86-88

Tale of the Fox, The (film)
Starewicz, Wladyslaw **28** 336-338

Taliaferro, Booker
see Washington, Booker Taliaferro

TALLCHIEF, MARIA (born 1925), Native American prima ballerina **15** 88-89

TALLEYRAND, CHARLES MAURICE DE (Duc de Tallyrand-Périgord; 1754-1838), French statesman **15** 89-90

TALLIS, THOMAS (circa 1505-85), English composer and organist **15** 91

TALMA, LOUISE JULIETTE (1906-1996), American composer and educator **27** 336-338

TALON, JEAN (1626-1694), French intendant of New France **15** 91-92

TAM, VIVIENNE (Yin Yok Tam; born 1957), Chinese American designer **24** 400-402

TAMARA (Tamar; 1159-1212), Queen of Georgia (1184-1212) **23** 388-390

TAMBO, OLIVER REGINALD (1917-1993), serves as acting president of the African National Congress **15** 92-94

TAMERLANE (1336-1405), Turko-Mongol conqueror **15** 94-95

TAMIRIS, HELEN (Helen Becker; 1905-1966), American dancer and choreographer **23** 390-392

Tan (historian)
see Lao Tzu

TAN, AMY (born 1952), American author **15** 95-96

TANAKA, KAKUEI (1918-1993), prime minister of Japan (1972-1974) **15** 96-98

TANEY, ROGER BROOKE (1777-1864), American political leader, chief justice of U.S. Supreme Court **15** 98-99

TANGE, KENZO (1913-2005), Japanese architect and city planner **15** 99-101

TANGUY, YVES (1900-1955), French painter **15** 101

TANIZAKI, JUNICHIRO (1886-1965), Japanese novelist, essayist, and playwright **15** 101-102

TANNER, HENRY OSSAWA (1859-1937), African American painter **15** 102-103

T'AO CH'IEN (365-427), Chinese poet **15** 104-105

T'ao Yüan-ming
see T'ao Ch'ien

TAO-AN (312-385), Chinese Buddhist monk **15** 103-104

TAO-HSÜAN (596-667), Chinese Buddhist monk **15** 105

Tao-lin
see Shih Ko-fa

TAPPAN BROTHERS (19th century), American merchants and reformers **15** 105-106

TAQI KHAN AMIR-E KABIR, MIRZA (circa 1806-52), Iranian statesman **15** 106-107

TARBELL, IDA MINERVA (1857-1944), American journalist **15** 107-108

TARDE, JEAN GABRIEL (1843-1904), French philosopher and sociologist **15** 108-109

TARKINGTON, NEWTON BOOTH (1869-1946), American author **15** 109

TARKOVSKY, ANDREI ARSENYEVICH (1932-1986), Russian film director **23** 392-395

TARLETON, SIR BANASTRE (1754-1833), English soldier; fought in American Revolution **15** 110

TARSKI, ALFRED (1902-1983), Polish-American mathematician and logician **15** 110-111

TARTAGLIA, NICCOLO (1500-1557), Italian mathematician **15** 111-112

TARTINI, GIUSEPPE (1692-1770), Italian violinist, composer, and theorist **15** 112-113

Tashufin, Yusuf ibn
see Ibn Tashufin, Yusuf

TASMAN, ABEL JANSZOON (circa 1603-59), Dutch navigator **15** 113-114

TASSO, TORQUATO (1544-1595), Italian poet **15** 114-116

TATA, JAMSETJI NUSSERWANJI (Jamshedji Nasarwanji Tata; 1839-1904), Indian businessman **24** 402-404

TATE, ALLEN (1899-1979), American poet, critic and editor **15** 116

TATLIN, VLADIMIR EVGRAFOVICH (1885-1953), Russian avant garde artist **15** 117-118

TATI, JACQUES (Jacques Tatischeff; 1908-1982), French actor and director **22** 410-412

Tatti, Jacopo
see Sansovino, Jacopo

Taubman, George Dashwood
see Goldie, Sir George Dashwood Taubman

TAUSSIG, HELEN BROOKE (1898-1986), American physician **15** 118-120

TAWNEY, RICHARD HENRY (1880-1962), British economic historian and social philosopher **15** 120-121

TAYLOR, BROOK (1685-1731), English mathematician **15** 121-122

TAYLOR, EDWARD (circa 1642-1729), American Puritan poet and minister **15** 122-123

TAYLOR, EDWARD PLUNKET (1901-1989), Canadian-born financier and thoroughbred horse breeder **15** 123-124

TAYLOR, ELIZABETH ROSEMUND (born 1932), American film actress **15** 124-125

TAYLOR, FREDERICK WINSLOW (1856-1915), American industrial manager and production engineer **21** 400-402

TAYLOR, JOHN (1753-1824), American politician and political theorist **15** 126

TAYLOR, MAXWELL (1901-1987), American soldier-statesman-scholar **15** 126-127

TAYLOR, MILDRED D. (Mildred Delois Taylor; born 1943), African American author **24** 404-407

TAYLOR, SUSIE KING (1848-1912), African American nurse **15** 127-128

TAYLOR, ZACHARY (1784-1850), American statesman; president 1849-1850 **15** 128-130

TCHAIKOVSKY, PETER ILYICH (1840-1893), Russian composer **15** 130-132

TCHEREPNIN, ALEXANDER (Nikolayevich; 1899-1977), Russian-French and later American composer **15** 132-133

Tchernikowsky, Saul
see Tschernichowsky, Saul

TE KANAWA, KIRI (born 1944), lyric soprano from New Zealand **15** 136-137

Téllez, Gabriel
see Tirso de Molina

TEBALDI, RENATA (Renata Ersila Clotilde Tebaldi; 1922-2004), Italian opera singer **26** 357-359

TECUMSEH (circa 1768-1813), American Shawnee Indian tribal chief **15** 133

TEDDER, ARTHUR (1890-1967), British military leader **19** 379-381

TEGGART, FREDERICK J. (1870-1946), comparative historian, librarian, sociologist, and educator who initiated sociology at the University of California **15** 133-134

TEILHARD DE CHARDIN, MARIE JOSEPH PIERRE (1881-1955), French theologian and paleontologist **15** 134-136

TEKAKWITHA, KATERI (Catherine Tegakovita; 1656-1680), Native American nun **23** 395-397

Telegraph (communications)
development
Woods, Granville T. **28** 378-381

TELEMANN, GEORG PHILIPP (1681-1767), German composer **15** 137-138

Telemanque
see Vesey, Denmark

Telephone (communications)
Gross, Al **28** 149-151

TELESIO, BERNARDINO (1509-1588), Italian philosopher of nature **15** 138-139

Television (Asia)
Miyazaki Hayao **28** 249-252

Television (Great Britain)
personalities
Hill, Benny **28** 170-172

Mirren, Helen **28** 247-249
producers
Frears, Stephen Arthur **28** 127-129

Television (United States)
animated cartoons
Hanna and Barbera **28** 156-159
evangelists
Roberts, Oral **28** 296-298
executives
Stringer, Howard **28** 338-340
personalities
Griffin, Merv **28** 146-149
Thomas, Danny **28** 350-352
producers
Griffin, Merv **28** 146-149
Hanna and Barbera **28** 156-159
Roach, Hal **28** 290-292
Stringer, Howard **28** 338-340
Thomas, Danny **28** 350-352
scriptwriters for
Sheldon, Sidney **28** 323-325

TELKES, MARIA (Maria DeTelkes; 1900-1995), Hungarian American scientist **24** 407-409

TELLER, EDWARD (born 1908), Hungarian-American physicist **15** 139-141

Temperance movement (United States)
supporters
Hayes, Lucy Webb **28** 163-166

Temple, Henry John
see Palmerston, 3d Viscount

TEMPLE, WILLIAM (1881-1944), ecumenicist and archbishop of Canterbury **15** 141-143

Temüjin
see Genghis Khan

TEN BOOM, CORRIE (Cornelia Ten Boom; 1892-1983), Dutch author **25** 411-413

Tendzin Gyatso
see Dalai Lama

TENGKU, ABDUL RAHMAN ("the Tengku"; born 1903), first prime minister of the Federation of Malaya and later of Malaysia **15** 340-341

TENNENT, GILBERT (1703-1764), American Presbyterian clergyman and evangelist **15** 143-144

TENNYSON, ALFRED (1st Baron Tennyson; 1809-92), English poet **15** 144-146

TENSKWATAWA (Lalewithaka; 1775-1836), Shawnee religious leader **20** 359-362

TENZING NORGAY (born 1914), Nepalese mountain climber **20** 362-364

TER BORCH, GERARD (1617-1681), Dutch painter **15** 146

TERENCE (Publius Terentius After; 195-159 B.C.), Roman comic playwright **15** 146-148

TERESA (Mother Teresa; Agnes Gonxha Bojaxhiu; 1910-1997), Catholic nun and missionary; Nobel Prize for Peace recipient **15** 148-151

TERESA OF AVILA (Teresa Sanchez de Cepeda y Ahumada; 1515-1582), Spanish nun **20** 364-366

TERESHKOVA, VALENTINA (born 1937), Russian cosmonaut **15** 151-152

TERKEL, LOUIS ("Studs"; born 1912), American radio personality and author **15** 152-153

TERMAN, LEWIS MADISON (1877-1956), American psychologist **15** 153-154

TERRA, GABRIEL (1873-1942), Uruguayan politician, president 1933-38 **15** 154-155

TERRELL, MARY CHURCH (Mary Eliza Church Terrell; 1863-1954), African American activist and feminist **23** 397-399

Terror, Reign of
see French Revolution—1792-95 (Reign of Terror)

TERRY, ELLEN (Dame Ellen Alice [or Alicia] Terry; 1847-1928), English actress **24** 409-411

TERTULLIAN (Quintus Septimius Florens Tertullianus; circa 160-circa 220), North African theologian and apologist **15** 155-156

TESLA, NIKOLA (1856-1943), Croatian-American inventor and electrical engineer **15** 156-157

Teutonic Knights (military order)
Wladyslaw II Jagiello, King of Poland **28** 377-378

TEWODROS II (1820-1868), emperor of Ethiopia **15** 158-159

THACKERAY, WILLIAM MAKEPEACE (1811-1863), British novelist **15** 159-161

THALBERG, IRVING (1899-1936), American filmmaker **20** 366-368

THALES (circa 624-circa 545 B.C.), Greek natural philosopher **15** 161

THANT, U (1909-1974), Burmese statesman and UN secretary general **15** 161-162

THARP, MARIE (1920-2006), American geologist and oceanographic cartologist **15** 162-164

THARP, TWYLA (born 1941), American dancer and choreographer **15** 164-165

THARPE, ROSETTA NUBIN (1915-1973), African American musician **24** 411-413

THATCHER, MARGARET HILDA (born 1925), prime minister of Great Britain (1979-1990) **15** 165-168

Thayendanegea
see Brant, Joseph

THAYER, ELI (1819-1899), American reformer, agitator, and promoter **15** 168

THAYER, SYLVANUS (1785-1872), American educator and engineer **15** 168-169

THEANO (born c. 546 BC), Greek mathematician and physician **23** 399-401

Theater
Canadian
Patterson, Tom **28** 274-276
festivals
Patterson, Tom **28** 274-276

THEILER, MAX (1899-1972), American epidemiologist and microbiologist **15** 169-170

THEMISTOCLES (circa 528-462 B.C.), Athenian politician **15** 170-171

Themistogenes of Syracuse
see Xenophon

THEOCRITUS (circa 310-circa 245 B.C.), Greek poet **15** 171-172

Theodore II (emperor of Ethiopia)
see Tewodros II

THEODORIC THE GREAT (453/454-526), king of the Ostrogoths **15** 175-176

THEODOSIUS (circa 346-395), Roman emperor 379-395 **15** 176

THEORELL, AXEL HUGO THEODOR (born 1903), Swedish biochemist **15** 176-177

Theos Soter
see Ptolemy I

Theosophy (philosophy)
Krishnamurti, Uppaluri Gopala **28** 201-203

Theotokopoulos, Domenikos
see Greco, El

THEREMIN, LEON (Lev Sergeivitch Termen; 1896-1993), Russian inventor **24** 413-415

THERESA, SAINT (Theresa of Ávila; 1515-82), Spanish nun **15** 178-179

THÉRÈSE OF LISIEUX, SAINT (Marie Françoise Thérèse Martin; 1873-1897), French nun and Roman Catholic saint **28** 347-350

THEROUX, PAUL (born 1941), expatriate American writer of fiction and of chronicles of train travels **15** 179-180

Thibault, Jacques Anatole François
see France, Anatole

THIBAUT IV (Thibaut I of Navarre; 1201-53), Count of Champagne and Brie **15** 180-181

Thiene, Gaetano da
see Cajetan, St.

THIERS, LOUIS ADOLPHE (1797-1877), French journalist, historian, and statesman **15** 181-182

THIEU, NGUYEN VAN (1923-2001), South Vietnamese president **15** 182-183

Thiry, Paul Henri
see Holbach, Baron D'

THOMAS, ALMA WOODSEY (1891-1978), African American artist **23** 401-403

THOMAS, CLARENCE (born 1948), U.S. Supreme Court justice **15** 186-188

THOMAS, DANNY (Muzyad Yakhoob; 1924-1992), Lebanese-American comedian and humanitarian **28** 350-352

THOMAS, DAVE (R. David Thomas; 1932-2002), American businessman **18** 389-397

THOMAS, DYLAN MARLAIS (1914-1953), British poet **15** 188-190

THOMAS, GEORGE HENRY (1816-1870), American general **15** 190-191

THOMAS, HELEN (born 1920), American journalist **19** 381-384

THOMAS, NORMAN MATTOON (1884-1968), American Socialist politician, author, and lecturer **15** 191-192

Thomas, Paul
see Mann, Thomas

THOMAS, THEODORE (1835-1905), American orchestral conductor **15** 192-193

THOMAS, WILLIAM ISAAC (1863-1947), American sociologist and educator **15** 193

Thomas à Becket
see Becket, St. Thomas

Thomas à Kempis
see Kempis, Thomas à

THOMAS AQUINAS, SAINT (circa 1224-74), Italian philosopher and theologian **15** 183-186

Thomas of Kempen
see Thomas à Kempis

Thomas of London
see Becket, St. Thomas

THOMASIUS (1655-1728), German philosopher and jurist **15** 193-194

Thompson, Benjamin
see Rumford, Count

THOMPSON, DALEY (Francis Ayodele Thompson; born 1958), English track and field athlete **20** 368-370

THOMPSON, DAVID (1770-1857), Canadian explorer, cartographer, and surveyor **15** 194-195

THOMPSON, DOROTHY (1894-1961), conservative American journalist **15** 195-196

THOMPSON, EMMA (born 1959), British author and actress **27** 338-340

THOMPSON, HUNTER STOCKTON (born 1939), American journalist **15** 196-198

THOMPSON, TOMMY (born 1941), American politician **25** 413-415

Thomson, Charles Edward Poulett
see Sydenham, Baron

THOMSON, SIR GEORGE PAGET (1892-1975), English atomic physicist **15** 198-199

THOMSON, JAMES (1700-1748), British poet **15** 199-200

THOMSON, SIR JOSEPH JOHN (1856-1940), English physicist **15** 200-201

THOMSON, KENNETH (1923-2006), Canadian print and broadcast journalism magnate **15** 201-202

THOMSON, TOM (1877-1917), Canadian painter **15** 202

THOMSON, VIRGIL (1896-1989), American composer, critic, and conductor **15** 202-203

Thomson, William
see kelvin of Largs, Baron

THOREAU, HENRY DAVID (1817-1862), American writer and transcendentalist **15** 203-205

THOREZ, MAURICE (1900-1964), headed the French Communist Party from 1930 to 1964 **15** 206-207

THORN, GASTON (born 1928), prime minister of Luxembourg **15** 207-208

THORNDIKE, EDWARD LEE (1874-1949), American psychologist and educator **15** 208-209

THORNDIKE, SYBIL (Dame Agnes Sybil Thorndike; 1882-1976), English actress and manager **24** 415-417

THORPE, JIM (James Francis Thorpe; 1888-1953), American track star and professional football and baseball player **15** 209-211

THORVALDSEN, BERTEL (Albert Bertel Thorvaldsen; 1770-1848), Danish sculptor **23** 403-406

Thorvaldsson, Eric
see Eric the Red

Thrillers (films)
Chabrol, Claude **28** 67-69

THUCYDIDES (circa 460-circa 401 B.C.), Greek historian **15** 211-212

THUKU, HARRY (1895-1970), Kenyan politician **15** 212-213

Thünström, Louis Leon
see Thurstone, Louis Leon

THURBER, JAMES GROVE (1894-1961), American writer and artist **15** 213-214

THURMAN, WALLACE HENRY (Patrick Casey; Ethel Belle Mandrake; 1902-1934), African American author and journalist **28** 352-354
Patterson, Louise Alone Thompson **28** 272-274

THURMOND, JAMES STROM (born 1902), American lawyer and statesman **15** 214-215

Thurstein, Domine de
see Zinzendorf, Count Nikolaus Ludwig von

THURSTONE, LOUIS LEON (1887-1955), American psychologist **15** 215-216

THUTMOSE III (1504-1450 B.C.), Egyptian king **15** 216-217

TIBERIUS JULIUS CAESAR AUGUSTUS (42 B.C. -A.D. 37), emperor of Rome 14-37 **15** 217-218

Tibet (Chinese autonomous region)
exploration
David-Néel, Alexandra **28** 90-92

TIECK, LUDWIG (1773-1853), German author **15** 218-219

T'ien-wang
see Hung Hsiu-ch'üan

TIEPOLO, GIOVANNI BATTISTA (1696-1770), Italian painter **15** 219-220

TIFFANY, LOUIS COMFORT (1848-1933), American painter and designer **15** 220-221

TIGLATH-PILESER III (ruled 745-727 B.C.), king of Assyria **15** 221-222

TILBERIS, ELIZABETH (Elizabeth Jane Kelly; Liz Tilberis; 1947-1999), British journalist **27** 340-342

TILDEN, BILL (William Tatem Tilden II; 1893-1953), American tennis player **20** 370-372

TILDEN, SAMUEL JONES (1814-1886), American politician **15** 222-223

TILLEY, SIR SAMUEL LEONARD (1818-1896), Canadian statesman **15** 223-224

TILLEY, VESTA (Matilda Alice Victoria Powles; 1864-1852), British entertainer **26** 359-361

TILLICH, PAUL JOHANNES (1886-1965), German-American Protestant theologian and philosopher **15** 224-225

TILLMAN, BENJAMIN RYAN (1847-1918), American statesman and demagogue **15** 225-226

TILLY, GRAF VON (Johann Tserclaes; 1559-1632), Flemish general **20** 372-374

TIMERMAN, JACOBO (1923-1999), Argentine journalist and human rights advocate **15** 226-228

Timur
see Tamerlane

TINBERGEN, JAN (1903-1994), Dutch economist **15** 228-229

TINBERGEN, NIKOLAAS (1907-1988), English ethologist and zoologist **15** 229-230

TING, SAMUEL CHAO CHUNG (born 1936), American nuclear physicist **23** 406-408

TINGUELY, JEAN (1925-1991), Swiss sculptor **15** 230-232

TINTORETTO (1518-1594), Italian painter **15** 232-234

TIPPETT, MICHAEL KEMP, SIR (1905-1998), English composer and conductor **15** 234-235

TIPPU TIP (Hamed bin Mohammed bin Juma bin Rajab el Murjebi; circa 1840-1905), Zanzibari trader **15** 235-236

TIPU SULTAN (1750-1799), Moslem ruler of Mysore **15** 236

TIRADENTES (José Joaquim da Silva Xavier; 1748-92), Brazilian national hero **15** 237

TIRPITZ, ALFRED VON (1849-1930), German admiral and politician **20** 374-376

TIRSO DE MOLINA (1584-1648), Spanish dramatist **15** 237-238

TISCH BROTHERS (1923-), real estate developers **15** 238-240

TISELIUS, ARNE WILHELM KAURIN (1902-1971), Swedish biochemist **15** 240-241

TITCHENER, EDWARD BRADFORD (1867-1927), English-American psychologist **15** 241-242

TITIAN (1488/90-1576), Italian painter **15** 242-244

TITO, MARSHAL (1892-1980), Yugoslav president **15** 244-246

TITULESCU, NICOLAE (1882-1941), Romanian statesman **15** 246-247

Titus Flavius Domitianus Augustus see Domitian

TITUS FLAVIUS VESPASIANUS (39-81), Roman general, emperor 79-81 **15** 247-248

Titus Petronius Niger see Petronius Arbiter

TOBA SOJO (1053-1140), Japanese painter-priest **15** 248-249

TOBEY, MARK (1890-1976), American painter **15** 249-250

TOCQUEVILLE, ALEXIS CHARLES HENRI MAURICE CLÉREL DE (1805-1859), French statesman and historian **15** 250-251

TODD, ALEXANDER (1907-1997), English chemist **15** 251-253

TODD, MIKE (Avron Hirsch Goldenbogen; 1907-1958), American theater and film producer **21** 402-404

TODD, REGINALD STEPHEN GARFIELD (1908-2002), prime minister of Southern Rhodesia and supporter of Zimbabwean independence **18** 391-393

TOER, PRAMOEDYA ANANTA (1925-2006), Indonesian author **27** 342-345

TOGLIATTI, PALMIRO (1893-1964), Italian statesman and a founder of the Italian Communist Party **15** 253-254

TOGO, HEIHACHIRO (1847-1934), Japanese admiral **20** 376-379

Togu Gakushi see Makibi, Kibi-Ho

TOJO, HIDEKI (1884-1948), Japanese general, premier 1941-44 **15** 254-256

TOKUGAWA IEYASU (1542-1616), founder of Tokugawa shogunate **8** 103-106

Tokugawa shogunate see Japan—1603-1867

TOKYO ROSE (Ikuko Toguri; Iva Toguri d' Aquino; Iva Toguri; 1916-2006), Japanese American broadcaster and businesswoman **27** 345-348

TOLAND, GREGG (1904-1948), American cinematographer **21** 405-407

TOLAND, JOHN (1670-1722), British scholar **15** 256

TOLEDANO, VICENTE LOMBARDO (1894-1968), Mexican intellectual and politician **15** 256-257

TOLEDO, FRANCISCO DE (1515-1584), Spanish viceroy of Peru **15** 257-259

TOLKIEN, J. R. R. (1892-1973), English author **15** 259-261

TOLLER, ERNST (1893-1939), German playwright **15** 261

TOLMAN, EDWARD CHACE (1886-1959), American psychologist **15** 261-262

TOLSTOY, LEO (1828-1910), Russian novelist and moral philosopher **15** 262-265

TOLTON, AUGUSTINE (1854-1897), African-American Roman Catholic priest **28** 354-356

Tom and Jerry (cartoon) Hanna and Barbera **28** 156-159

TOMONAGA, SIN-ITIRO (1906-1979), Japanese physicist **15** 265-266

TONEGAWA, SUSUMU (born 1939), Japanese biologist **24** 417-420

TÖNNIES, FERDINAND (1855-1936), German sociologist **15** 266-267

TOOMBS, ROBERT AUGUSTUS (1810-1885), American statesman **15** 267-268

TOOMER, JEAN (Nathan Eugene Pinchback Toomer; 1894-1967), American author **23** 408-410

T'o-pa Hung see Wei Hsiao-wen-ti

TORQUEMADA, TOMAS DE (1420-1498), leader of the Spanish Inquisition **21** 407-409

Torre, V. R. Haya de la see Haya de la Torre, Victor Raúl

TORRENCE, JACKIE (1944-2004), American storyteller **19** 384-386

Torres, Manuel Montt see Montt Torres, Manuel

TORRICELLI, EVANGELISTA (1608-1647), Italian mathematician and physicist **15** 268-269

TORRIJOS, OMAR (1929-1981), Panamanian strongman **15** 269-270

TORSTENSSON, LENNART (1603-1651), Swedish military leader **20** 379-381

TOSCANINI, ARTURO (1867-1957), Italian conductor **15** 270-271

Tosei see Basho, Matsuo

TOSOVSKY, JOSEF (born 1950), banker and prime minister of the Czech Republic **18** 393-395

TOULMIN, STEPHEN EDELSTON (born 1922), British-American ethical philosopher **15** 271-273

TOULOUSE-LAUTREC, HENRI DE (1864-1901), French painter **15** 273-274

TOURAINE, ALAIN (born 1925), French sociologist **15** 274-275

TOURÉ, SAMORY (1830-1900), Sudanese ruler and state builder **15** 275-277

TOURÉ, SÉKOU (1922-1984), African statesman, president of Guinea **15** 275-277

TOURGÉE, ALBION WINEGAR (1838-1905), American jurist and writer **15** 277-278

TOUSSAINT L'OUVERTURE, FRANÇOIS DOMINIQUE (1743-1803), Haitian military leader **15** 278-279

TOWER, JOAN (born 1938), American composer **15** 279-281

TOWNES, CHARLES HARD (born 1915), American physicist **15** 281-282

TOWNSEND, FRANCIS EVERITT (1867-1960), American physician **15** 282-283

Toymakers Christiansen, Ole Kirk **28** 76-78

TOYNBEE, ARNOLD JOSEPH (1889-1975), English historian and philosopher of history **15** 283-284

TOYODA, EIJI (born 1913), Japanese automobile manufacturing executive **15** 284-286

Toyo-mike Kashiki-ya-hime see Suiko

TOYOTOMI HIDEYOSHI (1536-1598), Japanese warrior commander **15** 286-289

TRACY, SPENCER BONAVENTURE (1900-1967), American film actor **15** 289-290

TRAILL, CATHARINE PARR (1802-1899), Canadian naturalist and author **15** 291

TRAJAN (Marcus Ulpius Trajanus; circa 53-117), Roman emperor 98-117 **15** 291-292

Tranquilli, Secondino see Silone, Ignazio

Transistors (electrical)
Ibuka, Masaru **28** 184-186

TRAVERS, P.L. (Pamela Lyndon Travers; Helen Lyndon Geoff; 1988-1996), British author **27** 348-350

TRAVIS, WILLIAM BARRET (1809-1836), American cavalry commander **15** 292-293

TREITSCHKE, HEINRICH VON (1834-1896), German historian and publicist **15** 293-294

TREMBLAY, MICHEL (born 1942), Canadian author **27** 350-352

TREVELYAN, GEORGE MACAULAY (1876-1962), English historian **15** 294-295

TREVINO, LEE (born 1939), American golfer **24** 420-422

TREVOR, WILLIAM (born 1928), British novelist, television dramatist, playwright, and short-story writer **15** 295-297

TRIMBLE, DAVID (William David Trimble; born 1944), Irish political leaders **19** 386-388

TRIMMER, SARAH (Sarah Kirby; 1741-1810), English author and educator **27** 352-353

TRIPPE, JUAN TERRY (1899-1981), American overseas aviation industry pioneer **15** 297-298

TRIST, NICHOLAS PHILIP (1800-1874), American lawyer and diplomat **15** 298-299

Triumvirates (Rome)
see Rome—Roman Republic

TROELTSCH, ERNST (1865-1923), German theologian, historian, and sociologist **15** 299-300

TROGER, PAUL (1698-1762), Austrian painter **15** 300

TROLLOPE, ANTHONY (1815-1882), English novelist **15** 300-302

TROTA OF SALERNO (Trotula of Salerno; c. 11th century), physician **24** 423-424

TROTSKY, LEON (1879-1940), Russian revolutionist **15** 302-305

TROTTER, MILDRED (1899-1991), American anatomist **15** 305-306

TROTTER, WILLIAM MONROE (1872-1934), African American newspaper editor and protest leader **15** 306-307

TRUDEAU, GARRETSON BEEKMAN ("Garry"; born 1948), comic-strip artist, playwright, and animator **15** 308-309

TRUDEAU, PIERRE ELLIOTT (born 1919), leader of the Liberal Party and Canada's prime minister (1968-1984) **15** 309-311

TRUFFAUT, FRANÇOIS (1932-1984), French film director and critic **15** 311-313
Bazin, André **28** 32-33

TRUJILLO MOLINA, RAFAEL LEONIDAS (1891-1961), dictator of the Dominican Republic **15** 313-314

TRUMAN, HARRY S. (1884-1972), American statesman, president 1945-53 **15** 314-316

TRUMBO, DALTON (James Dalton Trumbo; 1905-1976), American screenwriter **21** 409-411

TRUMBULL, JOHN (1756-1843), American painter **15** 316-317

TRUMBULL, LYMAN (1813-1896), American statesman **15** 317-318

TRUMP, DONALD JOHN (born 1946), American real estate developer **15** 318-319

TRUONG CHINH (1909-1988), Vietnamese Communist leader **15** 319-320

TRUTH, SOJOURNER (circa 1797-1883), African American freedom fighter and orator **15** 320-321

TRYON, WILLIAM (1729-1788), English colonial governor in America **15** 321

Tsai-t'ien
see Kuang-hsü

TS'AI YÜAN-P'EI (1867-1940), Chinese educator **15** 322

TS'AO TS'AO (155-220), Chinese general, statesman, and folk hero **15** 322-323

TSCHERNICHOWSKY, SAUL (1875-1943), Hebrew poet, translator, and physician **15** 323

TSENG KUO-FAN (1811-1872), Chinese statesman, general and scholar **15** 324-325

TSHOMBE, MOÏSE KAPENDA (1919-1969), Congolese political leader **15** 325-326

TSIOLKOVSKY, KONSTANTIN EDUARDOVICH (1857-1935), Russian scientist **15** 326-328

TSO TSUNG-T'ANG (1812-1885), Chinese general and statesman **15** 328-329

TSOU YEN (flourished late 4th century B.C.), Chinese philosopher **15** 329-330

Tsui-weng
see Ou-yang Hsiu

TU FU (712-770), Chinese poet **15** 335-336

TUBMAN, HARRIET ROSS (circa 1820-1913), African American Underground Railroad agent **15** 330-331

TUBMAN, WILLIAM VACANARAT SHADRACH (1895-1971), Liberian statesman, president 1943-71 **15** 331

TUCHMAN, BARBARA (born 1912), American Pulitzer Prize-winning historian and journalist **15** 331-332

TUCKER, C. DELORES (Cynthia DeLores Nottage; 1927-2005), African American civil rights activist **18** 395-397

TUCKER, GEORGE (1775-1861), American historian **15** 332-333

TUCKER, PRESTON (1903-1956), American businessman and automobile designer **18** 397-399

TUDJMAN, FRANJO (1922-1999), Croatian president **15** 333-335

Tughlak, Mohamed
see Muhammad bin Tughluq

TUGWELL, REXFORD GUY (1891-1979), American politician, educator, and public servant **15** 336-339

Tukulti-apal-Eshara
see Tiglath-pileser III

TULL, JETHRO (1674-1741), English agriculturist and inventor **21** 411-413

TUNG CH'I-CH'ANG (1555-1636), Chinese calligrapher, painter, and historian **15** 339-340

TÚPAC AMARU, JOSÉ GABRIEL (1742-1781), Peruvian revolutionist, last of the Incas **15** 341

TUPOLEV, ANDREI NIKOLAEVICH (1888-1972), Soviet aeronautical engineer and army officer **15** 341-342

TUPPER, SIR CHARLES (1821-1915), Canadian statesman, prime minister 1896 **15** 342-343

TURA, COSIMO (1430-1495), Italian painter **15** 343-344

TURABI, HASSAN ABDULLAH AL- (born 1932), major leader of the Sudan's Islamic fundamentalist movement **15** 344-345

TURENNE, VICOMTE DE (Henri de la Tour d'Auvergne; 1611-1675), French military commander **20** 381-383

TURGENEV, IVAN SERGEYEVICH (1818-1883), Russian novelist, dramatist, and short-story writer **15** 345-348
Viardot, Pauline **28** 363-365

TURGOT, ANNE ROBERT JACQUES (Baron de l'Aulne; 1721-81), French economist **15** 348-349

TURING, ALAN MATHISON (1912-1954), British mathematician **15** 349-350

Turkey, Republic of (nation, Asia Minor & South East Europe) and Islam
Nursî, Said **28** 259-261

Turkish literature
Pamuk, Orhan **28** 269-272

TURNER, FREDERICK JACKSON (1861-1932), American historian **15** 350-351

TURNER, HENRY MCNEAL (1834-1915), African American racial leader **15** 351-352

TURNER, JOSEPH MALLORD WILLIAM (1775-1851), English painter **15** 352-354

TURNER, LANA (Julia Jean Mildred Frances Turner; 1920-1995), American actress **19** 388-390

TURNER, NATHANIEL (1800-1831), African American slave leader **15** 354

TURNER, TED (Robert Edward Turner; born 1938), American television entrepreneur **15** 355-357

TURNER, TINA (Anna Mae Bullock; born 1939), African American singer, dancer, and actress **15** 357-359

TUSSAUD, MARIE (Madame Tussaud; Anna Marie Gresholtz Tussaud; Anna Mari Grosholtz; 1761-1850), German wax modeler and museum founder **28** 356-358

TUTANKHAMEN (reigned 1361-1352 B.C.), twelfth king of the Eighteenth Egyptian Dynasty **15** 359-360

TUTU, ARCHBISHOP DESMOND (born 1931), South African Anglican archbishop and opponent of apartheid **15** 360-361

TUTUOLA, AMOS (born 1920), Nigerian writer **15** 361-362

TWACHTMAN, JOHN HENRY (1853-1902), American painter **15** 362-363

TWAIN, MARK (Samuel Langhorne Clemens; 1835-1910), American humorist and novelist **15** 363-366

TWAIN, SHANIA (Eileen Regina Edwards; born 1965), Canadian singer-songwriter **26** 361-363

TWEED, WILLIAM MARCY (1823-1878), American politician and leader of Tammany Hall **15** 366-367

TYLER, ANNE (born 1941), American author **15** 367-368

TYLER, JOHN (1790-1862), American statesman, president 1841-45 **15** 368-369

TYLER, MOSES COIT (1835-1900), American historian **15** 369-370

TYLER, RALPH W. (born 1902), American educator/scholar **15** 370-371

TYLER, ROYALL (1757-1826), American playwright, novelist, and jurist **15** 371-372

TYLOR, SIR EDWARD BURNETT (1832-1917), English anthropologist **15** 372-373

TYNDALE, WILLIAM (circa 1495-1536), English biblical scholar **15** 373-374

TYNDALL, JOHN (1820-1893), Irish physicist **15** 374

Typhoid Mary
see Mallon, Mary

TYRRELL, GEORGE (1861-1909), Irish-English Jesuit priest and theologian **15** 374-375

TYRRELL, JOSEPH BURR (J.B. Tyrrell; 1858-1957), Canadian geologist and explorer **23** 410-412

TZ'U-HSI (1835-1908), empress dowager of China 1860-1908 **15** 375-376

U

UBICO Y CASTAÑEDA, GENERAL JORGE (1878-1946), president of Guatemala (1931-1944) **15** 377-378

UCCELLO, PAOLO (1397-1475), Italian painter **15** 378-379

UCHIDA, MITSUKO (born 1948), Japanese pianist **23** 413-415

UEBERROTH, PETER VICTOR (born 1937), Former baseball commissioner **15** 379-381

UELSMANN, JERRY (born 1934), American photographer **20** 384-385

UHLENBECK, KAREN (born 1942), American mathematician **15** 381-382

ULANOVA, GALINA (1910-1998), Russian ballerina **15** 382-383

ULBRICHT, WALTER (1893-1973), East German political leader **15** 383-384

ULFILAS (circa 311-circa 382), Arian bishop of the Visigoths **15** 384

ULPIAN, DOMITIUS (died 228), Roman jurist **15** 385-386

Umayado no Miko
see Shotoku Taishi

Umdabuli we Sizwe
see Mzilikazi

UNAMUNO Y JUGO, MIGUEL DE (1864-1936), Spanish philosopher and writer **15** 386-387

UNÁNUE, JOSÉ HIPÓLITO (1755-1833), Peruvian intellectual, educator, and scientist **15** 387-388

Underground Railroad
see African American history—Slavery and abolition (Underground Railroad)

UNDERHILL, JOHN (circa 1597-1672), American military leader and magistrate **15** 388

Underwater exploration
Edgerton, Harold Eugene **28** 109-111

UNDSET, SIGRID (1882-1949), Norwegian novelist **15** 388-389

Unfaithful Woman, The (film)
Chabrol, Claude **28** 67-69

UNGARETTI, GIUSEPPE (1888-1970), Italian poet **15** 389-390

UNITAS, JOHNNY (John Constantine Unitas; 1933-2002), American football player **20** 385-387

United Provinces
see Netherlands, The

UNSER, AL, SR. (born 1939), American race car driver **23** 415-417

UPDIKE, JOHN (born 1932), American author of poems, short stories, essays, and novels **15** 390-392

UPJOHN, RICHARD (1802-1878), English-born American architect **15** 392

URBAN II (Otto de Lagery; 1042-99), pope 1088-99 **15** 393

URBAN VI (Bartolomeo Prignano; 1318-89), pope 1378-89 **15** 394

URBAN VIII (Maffeo Barberini; 1568-1644), Italian Roman Catholic pope (1623-1644) **26** 301-302

URBAN, MATT (1919-1995), American solider **19** 391-392

UREY, HAROLD CLAYTON (1893-1981), American chemical physicist and geochemist **15** 394-396

URQUIZA, JUSTO JOSÉ (1801-1870), Argentine dictator, general, and statesman **15** 396-397

URRACA (c. 1078-1126), Queen of Leon-Castilla) **23** 417-418

UTAMARO, KITAGAWA (1753-1806), Japanese printmaker **15** 397

UTHMAN DON FODIO (1755-1816), Moslem teacher and theologian **15** 397-398

Uticensus, Marcus Porcius Cato
see Cato the Younger

V

Vaca, Álvar Núñez Cabeza de
see Cabeza de Vaca, Álvar Núñez

VADIM, ROGER (Roger Vadim Plemiannikov; 1928-2000), Russian/ French filmaker and author **22** 413-415

VAGANOVA, AGRIPPINA YAKOVLEVNA (1879-1951), Russian ballet dancer and teacher **24** 425-427

VAIL, THEODORE NEWTON (1845-1920), American businessman **23** 419-421

VAJPAYEE, ATAL BEHARI (born 1926), prime minister of India **19** 393-395

VALADON, SUZANNE (Marie Clémentine Valadon; 1865-1935), French artist and model **27** 354-356

VALDEZ, LUIS (born 1940), Hispanic American playwright and filmmaker **15** 399-400

VALDIVIA, PEDRO DE (circa 1502-53), Spanish conquistador and professional soldier **15** 400-401

VALENS, RITCHIE (Richard Steven Valenzuela; 1941-1959), Hispanic American musician **22** 415-417

VALENTI, JACK JOSEPH (1921-2007), presidential adviser and czar of the American film industry **15** 401-403

VALENTINO, RUDOLPH (Rodolfo Alfonso Raffaelo Pierre Filibert de Valentina d'Antonguolla Guglielmi; 1895-1926), Italian/American actor **20** 388-390

VALENZUELA, LUISA (born 1938), Argentine author **23** 421-423

VALERA Y ALCALÁ GALIANO, JUAN (1824-1905), Spanish novelist and diplomat **15** 403

VALERIAN (Publius Licinius Valerianus; circa 200-circa 260), Roman emperor 253-260 **15** 404-405

VALÉRY, PAUL AMBROISE (1871-1945), French poet, philosopher, and critic **15** 405-406

VALLA, LORENZO (circa 1407-57), Italian humanist **15** 406

VALLANDIGHAM, CLEMENT LAIRD (1820-1871), American politician **15** 406-407

VALLE INCLÁN, RAMÓN MARIA DEL (circa 1866-1936), Spanish novelist, playwright, and poet **15** 407-408

VALLEE, RUDY (Hubert Prior Vallee; 1901-1986), American vocalist **28** 359-361

VALLEJO, CÉSAR ABRAHAM (1892-1938), Peruvian poet **15** 408-409

VAN BUREN, MARTIN (1782-1862), American statesman, president 1837-41 **15** 410-411

VAN DER GOES, HUGO (flourished 1467-82), Flemish painter **15** 416-417

VAN DIEMEN, ANTHONY MEUZA (1593-1645), Dutch colonial official and merchant **15** 420

VAN DOESBURG, THEO (1883-1931), Dutch painter **15** 421

VAN DONGEN, KEES (Cornelis Theodorus Marie Van Dongen; 1877-1968), Fauvist painter, portraitist, and socialite **15** 421-422

VAN DUYN, MONA (1921-2004), first woman to be appointed poet laureate of the United States **15** 422-423

VAN DYCK, ANTHONY (1599-1641), Flemish painter **15** 423-425

VAN DYKE, DICK (Richard Wayne Van Dyke; born 1925), American actor, author, and producer **25** 416-418

VAN EEKELEN, WILLEM FREDERIK (born 1931), Dutch secretary-general of the Western European Union **15** 426-427

VAN GOGH, VINCENT (1853-1890), Dutch painter **15** 427-429

VAN HORNE, SIR WILLIAM CORNELIUS (1843-1915), American-born Canadian railroad entrepreneur **15** 429-430

VAN PEEBLES, MELVIN (Melvin Peebles; born 1932), American film director and producer, actor, author, and musician **21** 414-416

VAN RENSSELAER, KILIAEN (circa 1580-1643), Dutch merchant and colonial official in America **15** 430-431

VAN VECHTEN, CARL (1880-1964), American writer and photographer **18** 400-402

VAN VLECK, JOHN HASBROUCK (1899-1980), American physicist **25** 418-420

VANBRUGH, SIR JOHN (1664-1726), English architect and dramatist **15** 409-410

VANCE, CYRUS R. (1917-2002), American secretary of the army and secretary of state **15** 411-413

VANCE, ZEBULON BAIRD (1830-1894), American politician **15** 413-414

VANCOUVER, GEORGE (1758-1798), English explorer and navigator **15** 414-415

VANDER ZEE, JAMES (1886-1983), photographer of the people of Harlem **15** 418-419

VANDERBILT, CORNELIUS (1794-1877), American financier, steamship and railroad builder **15** 415-416

VANDERBILT, GLORIA (born 1924), American designer, artist, and author **19** 395-397

VANDERLYN, JOHN (1775-1852), American painter **15** 417

VANDROSS, LUTHER (1951-2005), American singer **26** 364-366

VANE, SIR HENRY (1613-1662), English statesman **15** 425-426

Vannucci, Pietro
see Perugino

VAN'T HOFF, JACOBUS HENDRICUS (1852-1911), Dutch physical chemist **15** 431-432

Vanzetti, Bartolomeo
see Sacco, Nicola and Vanzetti, Bartolomeo

VARDHAMANA MAHAVIRA (circa 540-470 B.C.), Indian ascetic philosopher **10** 135-137

Varennes, Pierre Gaultier de
see La Verendrye, Sieur de

VARÈSE, EDGARD (1883-1965), French-American composer **15** 432-433

VARGAS, GETULIO DORNELLES (1883-1954), Brazilian political leader **15** 433-434

VARGAS LLOSA, MARIO (born 1936), Peruvian novelist, critic, journalist, screenwriter, and essayist **15** 434-436

VARMUS, HAROLD ELIOT (born 1939), medical research expert and director of the National Institutes of Health (1993-1999) **15** 436-437

VARNHAGEN, FRANCISCO ADOLFO DE (1816-1878), Brazilian historian **15** 437-438

VARRO, MARCUS TERENTIUS (116-27 B.C.), Roman scholar and writer **15** 438-439

VARTHEMA, LUDOVICO DI (circa 1470-circa 1517), Italian traveler and adventurer **15** 439-440

Vasa, Gustavus
see Gustavus I

VASARELY, VICTOR (1908-1997), Hungarian-French artist **15** 440-442

VASARI, GIORGIO (1511-1570), Italian painter, architect, and author **15** 442-443

VASCONCELOS, JOSÉ (1882-1959), Mexican educator and author **15** 443-444

Vassa, Gustavus
see Equiano, Olaudah

VAUBAN, SEBASTIEN LE PRESTRE DE (1633-1707), French military engineer **18** 402-404

VAUDREUIL-CAVAGNAL, MARQUIS DE (Pierre Fransçois de Regaud; 1698-1778), Canadian-born governor of New France **15** 444

VAUGHAN, HENRY (1621/22-95), British poet **15** 444-445

VAUGHAN, SARAH LOIS (1924-1990), jazz singer **15** 445-446

VAUGHAN WILLIAMS, RALPH (1872-1958), English composer **15** 446-447

VAUGHT, WILMA L. (born 1930), U.S. Air Force officer **24** 427-429

VAVILOV, NIKOLAI IVANOVICH (1887-1943), Russian botanist and geneticist **15** 447-448

VÁZQUEZ, HORACIO (1860-1936), president of the Dominican Republic 1903-04 and 1924-30 **15** 448-449

VÁZQUEZ ARCE Y CEBALLOS, GREGORIO (1638-1711), Colombian artist **23** 423-425

VEBLEN, THORSTEIN BUNDE (1857-1929), American political economist and sociologist **15** 449-450

Vecellio, Tiziano
see Titian

Vega Carpio, Lope Félix
see Lope de Vega

Vega, Inca Garcilaso de la
see Garcilaso de la Vega, Inca

Vegetarianism (diet)
Cheyne, George **28** 74-76

VELASCO, JOSÉ MARÍA (1840-1912), Mexican painter **15** 450-451

VELASCO, LUIS DE (1511-1564), Spanish colonial administrator **15** 450-451

VELASCO ALVARADO, JUAN (1910-1977), Peruvian army officer who seized power in 1968 **15** 451-452

VELASCO IBARRA, JOSÉ MARÍA (1893-1979), Ecuadorian statesman, five time president **15** 452-454

VELASQUEZ, LORETA JANETA (1842-1897), Cuban American soldier and spy **28** 361-363

VELÁZQUEZ, DIEGO RODRÍGUEZ DE SILVA Y (1599-1660), Spanish painter **15** 454-456

VELÁZQUEZ, NYDIA MARGARITA (born 1953), Hispanic American politician **15** 456-459

VELÁZQUEZ DE CUÉLLAR, DIEGO (circa 1465-1523), Spanish conqueror, founder of Cuba **15** 459

VELDE, HENRY VAN DE (1863-1957), Belgian painter, designer, and architect **15** 419-420

Venerable Bede
see Bede, St.

Venezia, Domenico di Bartolomeo da
see Veneziano, Domenico

VENEZIANO, DOMENICO (Domenico di Bartolomeo da Venezia; 1410?-1461), Italian painter **15** 459-460

VENIZELOS, ELEUTHERIOS (1864-1936), Greek statesman **15** 460-461

VENTURI, ROBERT (born 1925), American architect **15** 461-463

VERA, YVONNE (1964-2005), Zimbabwean author **23** 425-427

VERCINGETORIX (circa 75-circa 46 B.C.), Celtic chieftain and military leader **19** 397-399

VERDI, GIUSEPPE FORTUNINO FRANCESCO (1813-1901), Italian opera composer **15** 463-465

VERLAINE, PAUL MARIE (1844-1896), French poet **15** 465-466

VERMEER, JAN (1632-1675), Dutch painter **15** 466-467

VERNE, JULES (1828-1905), French novelist **15** 467-469

VERONESE, PAOLO (1528-1588), Italian painter **15** 469-470

VERRAZANO, GIOVANNI DA (circa 1485-circa 1528), Italian navigator and explorer **15** 470-471

VERROCCHIO, ANDREA DEL (1435-1488), Italian sculptor and painter **15** 471-472

VERSACE, GIANNI (1946-1997), Italian fashion designer **19** 399-401

VERTOV, DZIGA (Denis Abramovich Kaufman; 1896-1954), Russian film director **26** 366-368

Verulam, 1st Baron
see Bacon, Sir Francis

VERWOERD, HENDRIK FRENSCH (1901-1966), South African statesman, prime minister 1958-66 **15** 472-473

VESALIUS, ANDREAS (1514-1564), Belgian anatomist **15** 473-475

VESEY, DENMARK (1767-1822), American slave leader **15** 475

VESPASIAN (9-79), Roman emperor 69-79 **15** 475-476

Vespasianus, Titus Flavius
see Titus Flavius Vespasianus

VESPUCCI, AMERIGO (1454-1512), Italian navigator **15** 476-478

Veuster, Joseph de
see Damien, Father

VIANNEY, ST. JEAN BAPTISTE (1786-1859), French priest **15** 478-479

VIARDOT, PAULINE (Michele Ferdinande Pauline García; 1821-1910), French singer and composer **28** 363-365

Viaud, Julien
see Loti, Pierre

VICENTE, GIL (circa 1465-circa 1536), Portuguese dramatist and poet **15** 479-480

Vichy France
see France—1940-46

VICO, GIAMBATTISTA (1668-1744), Italian philosopher and jurist **15** 480-481

Victor, Alfred
see Vigny, Comte de

VICTOR AMADEUS II (1666-1732), Duke of Savoy, king of Sicily, and king of Sardinia **15** 482-483

VICTOR EMMANUEL II (1820-1878), king of Sardinia 1849-61 and of Italy 1861-78 **15** 483-484

VICTOR EMMANUEL III (1869-1947), king of Italy 1900-46 **15** 484-485

VICTORIA (1819-1901), queen of Great Britain and Ireland 1837-1901 and empress of India 1876-1901 **15** 485-487

VICTORIA, TOMÁS LUIS DE (circa 1548-1611), Spanish composer **15** 487-488

Victorian literature
see English literature—Victorian

VICTORIO (circa 1820-1880), Apache warrior **26** 368-370

VIDAL, EUGENE LUTHER GORE (born 1925), American author of novels, essays, plays, and short stories **15** 488-490

VIDAL DE LA BLACHE, PAUL (1845-1918), French geographer **15** 490

VIDELA, JORGE RAFAÉL (born 1925), military president of Argentina (1976-1981) who violated human rights **15** 490-492

Vidiguerira, Count of
see Gama, Vasco da

VIEIRA, ANTÔNIO (1608-1697), Portuguese orator and Jesuit missionary **15** 492

Vietnam War (1956-1976)
opponents of
Son, Trinh Cong **28** 335-336
opponents of (United States)
Church, Frank Forrester, III **28** 78-80

Vietnamese literature
Ho, Xuan Huong **28** 174-176

Vietnamese music
Son, Trinh Cong **28** 335-336

VIGEE LEBRUN, ELISABETH (1755-1842), French painter **19** 402-403

VIGELAND, GUSTAV (1869-1943), Norwegian sculptor **25** 420-422

VIGILIUS (died 555), pope (537-555) **23** 427-429

VIGNOLA, GIACOMO DA (1507-1573), Italian architect **15** 493-494

VIGNY, COMTE DE (Alfred Victor Vigny; 1797-1863), French poet **15** 494-495

VIGO, JEAN (Jean Bonaventure de Vigo; 1905-1934), French filmmaker **23** 429-431

VIKE-FREIBERGA, VAIRA (born 1937), Latvian president **25** 422-424

VILLA, JOSE GARCIA (1914-1997), Filipino poet **24** 429-431

VILLA, PANCHO (Francisco Villa; 1878-1923), Mexican revolutionary **15** 495-496

VILLA-LOBOS, HEITOR (1887-1959), Brazilian composer **15** 496-497

VILLANI, GIOVANNI (circa 1270-1348), Italian chronicler **15** 497-498

VILLANUEVA, CARLOS RAÚL (1900-1975), Venezuelan architect **24** 431-432

VILLARD, OSWALD GARRISON (1872-1949), American journalist **15** 498-499

Villegas, Francisco Gómez de Quevedo y
see Quevedo y Villegas, Francisco Gómez de

VILLEHARDOUIN, GEFFROI DE (circa 1150-1213), French historian and soldier **15** 499

VILLEDA MORALES, RAMON (1909-1971), Honduran president, 1957-1963 **20** 390-392

VILLEPIN, DOMINIQUE DE (Dominique Marie François René Galouzeau de Villepin; born 1953), French prime minister and poet **26** 370-372

Villiers, George
see Buckingham, 1st Duke of; Buckingham, 2d Duke of

VILLON, FRANÇOIS (1431-after 1463), French poet **15** 499-501

Vimeur, Jean Baptiste Donatien de
see Rochambeau, Comte de

VINCENT, JOHN HEYL (1832-1920), American educator and religious leader **15** 502-503

VINCENT DE PAUL, ST. (1581-1660), French priest **15** 501-502

VINCENT OF BEAUVAIS (circa 1190-1264), French writer and theologian **21** 416-418

Vine, Barbara
see Rendell, Ruth

VINOGRADOFF, SIR PAUL GAVRILOVITCH (1854-1925), Russian educator and historian **15** 503

VINSON, FRED (Frederic Moore Vinson; 1890-1953), chief justice of the U.S. Supreme Court **15** 503-505

Violin (musical instrument)
Bull, Ole **28** 54-56

VIOLLET-LE-DUC, EUGÈNE EMMANUEL (1814-1879), French architect and theorist **15** 505-506

VIRCHOW, RUDOLF LUDWIG CARL (1821-1902), German medical scientist, anthropologist, and politician **15** 506-507

VIRGIL (Publius Vergilius Maro; 70-19 B.C.), Roman poet **15** 507-510

VISCONTI, GIAN GALEAZZO (Duke of Milan; 1351-1402), Italian despot **15** 510-511

VISCONTI, LUCHINO (Don Luchino Visconti DiModrone; 1906-1976), Italian film and stage director **25** 424-427

Viseu, Duke of
see Henry the Navigator

Vishinsky, Andrei
see Vyshinsky, Andrei

Vishnugupta
see Kautilya

VISSER 'T HOOFT, WILLEM ADOLF (1900-1985), Reformed churchman and ecumenist who was the first general secretary of the World Council of Churches **15** 511-512

VITORIA, FRANCISCO DE (circa 1483-1546), Spanish theologian and political theorist **16** 1-2

VITRY, PHILIPPE DE (1291-1360), French poet, composer, and churchman-statesman **16** 2

VITTORINI, ELIO (1908-1966), Italian novelist, editor, and journalist **16** 2-3

Vittorino da Feltre
see Feltre, Vittorino da

VIVALDI, ANTONIO (1678-1741), Italian violinist and composer **16** 3-4

VIVEKANANDA (1863-1902), Indian reformer, missionary, and spiritual leader **16** 4-5

VLADIMIR I (died 1015), grand prince of Kievan Russia 980-1015 **16** 5-6

Vladimir, St.
see Vladimir I

VLAMINCK, MAURICE (1876-1958), French painter **16** 6

VOEGELIN, ERIC (1901-1985), German-Austrian political theorist **16** 6-8

VOGEL, HANS-JOCHEN (born 1926), West German political leader **16** 8-9

VOGEL, SIR JULIUS (1835-1899), New Zealand statesman, twice prime minister **16** 9-10

VOGELWEIDE, WALTHER VON DER (circa 1170-1229), German poet, composer, and singer **16** 10-11

VOLCKER, PAUL (born 1927), chairman of the U.S. Federal Reserve Board (1979-1987) **16** 11-12

VOLTA, ALESSANDRO (1745-1827), Italian physicist **16** 12-14

VOLTAIRE (1694-1778), French poet, dramatist, historian, and philosopher **16** 14-16
associates
Madame de Pompadour **28** 228-230

VON AUE, HARTMANN (Aue von Hartman; c.1160 - c.1250), German poet and troubadour **22** 417-419

VON BINGEN, HILDEGARD (Hildegard of Bingen; 1098-1179), German composer, scientist, and theologian **22** 240-242

VON BRAUN, WERNHER (1912-1977), German-born American space scientist **16** 17-18

VON FURSTENBERG, DIANE (Diane Simone Michelle Halfin; born 1946), American fashion designer and businesswoman **16** 20-21

VON HÜGEL, BARON FRIEDRICH (1852-1925), philosopher of Christianity **16** 21-22

VON LAUE, MAX (1879-1960), German physicist **16** 23-24

VON MEHREN, ROBERT BRANDT (born 1922), American lawyer who helped create the International Atomic Energy Agency **16** 24-25

VON MISES, LUDWIG (born 1881), Austrian economist and social philosopher **16** 25

VON NEUMANN, JOHN (1903-1957), Hungarian-born American mathematician **16** 27-28

VON PAPEN, FRANZ (1879-1969), conservative German politician who helped prepare the way for the Third Reich **16** 28-29

VON RAD, GERHARD (1901-1971), German theologian **16** 29-30

VON STROHEIM, ERICH (Erich Oswald Stroheim; 1885-1957), Austrian actor and director **21** 418-420

VON TROTTA, MARGARETHE (born 1942), German filmmaker and actor **25** 427-429

VONDEL, JOOST VAN DEN (1587-1679), Dutch poet and dramatist **16** 19-20

VONNEGUT, KURT, JR. (1922-2007), American author **16** 25-27

VORSTER, BALTHAZAR JOHANNES (1915-1983), South African political leader **16** 30-32

Vorticism
Lewis, Wyndham **28** 217-219

VOS SAVANT, MARILYN (born 1946), American columnist and consultant **16** 32-33

VUILLARD, JEAN ÉDOUARD (1868-1940), French painter **16** 36

VUITTON, LOUIS (1821-1892), French luggage maker and businessman **28** 365-367

VYSHINSKY, ANDREI (1883-1954), state prosecutor in Stalin's purge trials and head of the U.S.S.R.'s foreign ministry (1949-1953) **16** 36-37

VYSOTSKY, VLADIMIR (Vladimir Semyonovich Vysotsky; 1938-1980), Russian singer and poet **28** 367-369

W

WAALS, JOHANNES DIDERIK VAN DER (1837-1923), Dutch physicist **15** 417-418

WADE, BENJAMIN FRANKLIN (1800-1878), American lawyer and politician **16** 38-39

WAGNER, HONUS (Johannes Peter Wagner; 1874-1955), American baseball player **20** 393-395

WAGNER, OTTO (1841-1918), Austrian architect and teacher **16** 39-40

WAGNER, RICHARD (1813-1883), German operatic composer **16** 40-43

WAGNER, ROBERT F. (1910-1991), New York City Tammany Hall mayor (1954-1965) **16** 44-45

WAGNER, ROBERT FERDINAND (1877-1953), American lawyer and legislator **16** 43

WAGONER, G. RICHARD (Richard Wagoner, Jr.; born 1953), American businessman **25** 430-432

Wahlstatt, Prince of
see Blücher, G. L. von

WAINWRIGHT, JONATHAN MAYHEW (1883-1953), American general **16** 45-46

WAITE, MORRISON REMICK (1816-1888), American jurist, chief justice of U.S. Supreme Court 1874-88 **16** 46

WAITE, TERRY (born 1939), official of the Church of England and hostage in Lebanon **16** 47-48

WAITZ, GRETE (nee Grete Andersen; born 1953), Norwegian runner **24** 433-436

WAJDA, ANDRZEJ (Andrzei Wajda; born 1926), Polish film director and screenwriter **25** 432-434

WAKEFIELD, EDWARD GIBBON (1796-1862), British colonial reformer and promoter **16** 48-49

WAKSMAN, SELMAN ABRAHAM (1888-1973), American microbiologist **16** 49-50

WALCOTT, DEREK ALTON (born 1930), West Indian poet and dramatist **16** 50-51

WALCOTT, MARY VAUX (Mary Morris Vaux; 1860-1940), American artist and naturalist **25** 434-437

WALD, FLORENCE S. (Florence Sophie Schorske; born 1917), American founder of the hospice movement **24** 436-437

WALD, GEORGE (born 1906), American biochemist interested in vision **16** 51-53

WALD, LILLIAN (1867-1940), American social worker and reformer **16** 53-54

WALDEMAR IV (Wlademar Atterdag; 1320-1375), King of Denmark, 1340-1375 **20** 395-397

WALDHEIM, KURT (1918-2007), Austrian statesman and president **16** 54-55

WALDO, PETER (flourished 1170-84), French religious leader **16** 55-56

WALDSEEMÜLLER, MARTIN (circa 1470-circa 1518), German geographer and cartographer **16** 56

WALESA, LECH (born 1943), Polish Solidarity leader and former president **16** 57-59
Kuron, Jacek **28** 203-206

WALKER, ALICE MALSENIOR (born 1944), African American novelist, poet, and short story writer **16** 59-61

WALKER, MADAME C. J. (Sarah Breedlove; 1867-1919), African American entrepreneur **16** 61-62

WALKER, DAVID (1785-1830), African American pamphleteer and activist **16** 62-63

WALKER, JOSEPH REDDEFORD (1798-1876), American fur trader **16** 63-64

WALKER, LEROY TASHREAU (born 1918), U.S. sports official, university chancellor, educator, and track coach **16** 64-65

WALKER, MAGGIE LENA (1867-1934), American entrepreneur and civic leader **16** 65-66

WALKER, MARGARET (born 1915), American novelist, poet, scholar, and teacher **16** 67

WALKER, MARY EDWARDS (1832-1919), American physician and feminist **23** 432-434

WALKER, ROBERT JOHN (1801-1869), American politician **16** 67-68

WALKER, WILLIAM (1824-1860), American adventurer and filibuster **16** 68-69

WALL, JEFF (born 1946), Canadian photographer and artist **23** 434-436

WALLACE, ALFRED RUSSEL (1823-1913), English naturalist and traveler **16** 69-70

WALLACE, DEWITT (1889-1981), American publisher and founder of *Reader's Digest* **16** 70-71

WALLACE, GEORGE CORLEY (1919-1998), American political leader **16** 71-72

WALLACE, HENRY (1836-1916), American agricultural publicist and editor **16** 73

WALLACE, HENRY AGARD (1888-1965), American statesman, vice-president 1940-44 **16** 73-74

WALLACE, LEWIS (1827-1905), American general and author **16** 74-75

WALLACE, SIPPIE (Beulah Belle Thomas; 1898-1986), African American singer **24** 437-440

WALLACE, SIR WILLIAM (circa 1270-1305), Scottish soldier **16** 75-76

WALLACE-JOHNSON, ISAAC THEOPHILUS AKUNNA (1895-1965), West African political leader and pan-Africanist **16** 76-77

Wallach, Meyer
see Litvinov, Maxim Maximovich

WALLAS, GRAHAM (1858-1932), English sociologist and political scientist **16** 77-78

WALLENBERG, RAOUL (1912-?), Swedish diplomat **16** 78-80

WALLENSTEIN, ALBRECHT WENZEL EUSEBIUS VON (1583-1634), Bohemian soldier of fortune **16** 80-81

WALLER, THOMAS WRIGHT (Fats; 1904-43), American jazz singer, pianist, organist, bandleader, and composer **16** 81-82

Walls of Jericho, The (book)
Fisher, Rudolph **28** 121-123

WALPOLE, ROBERT (1st Earl of Oxford; 1676-1745), English statesman **16** 82-84

WALRAS, MARIE ESPRIT LÉON (1834-1910), French economist **16** 84-85

WALSH, BILL (William Ernest Walsh; American football coach), 1931-2007 **28** 370-372

WALSH, STELLA (Stanislawa Walasiewiczowna; 1911-1980), Polish American athlete **19** 404-406

WALSH, THOMAS JAMES (1859-1933), American statesman **16** 85-86

WALTER, JOHANN (1496-1570), German composer **16** 86

WALTERS, BARBARA (born 1931), American network newscast anchor **16** 86-88

WALTON, ERNEST (1903-1995), Irish physicist **16** 88-90

WALTON, IZAAK (1593-1683), English writer and biographer **16** 90-91

WALTON, SAM MOORE (1918-1992), American businessman who co-founded Wal-Mart **16** 91-92

WALTON, SIR WILLIAM TURNER (1902-1983), English composer **16** 91-92

WANG, AN (1920-1990), Chinese-American inventor, electronics expert, and businessman **16** 93-95

WANG AN-SHIH (1021-1086), Chinese reformer, poet, and scholar **16** 95-97

WANG CHING-WEI (1883-1944), Chinese revolutionary leader **16** 98

WANG CH'UNG (27-circa 100), Chinese philosopher **16** 98-99

WANG FU-CHIH (1619-1692), Chinese philosopher **16** 99-101

WANG GUANGMEI (1921-2006), Chinese first lady **27** 357-358

WANG KON (877-943), Korean king **16** 101

WANG MANG (45 B.C. -A.D. 23), Chinese statesman, emperor 9-23 **16** 101-103

WANG MING (Chen Shaoyu; 1904-74), leader of the "Internationalist" group within the Chinese Communist Party **16** 103-104

WANG PI (226-249), Chinese philosopher **16** 104-105

WANG T'AO (1828-1897), Chinese reformer and scholar **16** 105-106

WANG, VERA ELLEN (born 1949), Asian American fashion designer **24** 440-442

WANG WEI (699-759), Chinese poet and painter **16** 106-108

WANG YANG-MING (1472-1529), Chinese philosopher and government official **16** 108-109

WARBURG, OTTO (1883-1970), German biochemist **16** 109-111

WARBURG, PAUL MORITZ (1868-1932), German-American banker **16** 111-112

WARD, AARON MONTGOMERY (1843-1913), American merchant **16** 112

WARD, ARTEMUS (1834-1867), American journalist and humorist **16** 112-113

WARD, JAY (J Troplong Ward; 1920-1989), American television producer **21** 421-423

Ward, Julia
see Howe, Julia Ward

WARD, LESTER FRANK (1841-1913), American paleobotanist and sociologist **16** 113-114

WARD, NANCY (Tsituna-Gus-Ke; Nanye'hi; Ghihau; 1738-1822), Cherokee tribal leader **23** 436-438

WARHOL, ANDY (Andrew Warhola; ca. 1927-1987), American pop artist and film maker **16** 114-115

WARMERDAM, DUTCH (Cornelius Warmerdam; 1915-2001), American pole vaulter **21** 423-425

WARNER, JACK (Jacob Eichelbaum; 1892-1978), American film producer and studio executive **19** 406-408

WARNOCK, HELEN MARY WILSON (born 1924), British philosopher **16** 115-117

WARREN, EARL (1891-1974), American jurist, chief justice of U.S. Supreme Court 1953-69 **16** 117-120

WARREN, MERCY OTIS (1728-1814), American writer **16** 120-121

WARREN, ROBERT PENN (1905-1989), American man of letters **16** 121-122

Warsaw (city, Poland)
Sendler, Irena **28** 318-320

Warwick, John Dudley, Earl of
see Northumberland, Duke of

WARWICK AND SALISBURY, EARL OF (Richard Neville; 1428-71), English military and political leader **16** 122-123
Woodville, Elizabeth **28** 381-383

WASHAKIE (circa 1804-1900), Native American Shoshoni tribal leader **16** 123-125

WASHINGTON, BOOKER TALIAFERRO (1856-1915), African American educator and racial leader **16** 125-126

Washington, D.C. (federal city)
cherry blossom festival
Taft, Helen Herron **28** 343-345

WASHINGTON, GEORGE (1732-1799), American Revolutionary commander in chief, president 1789-97 **16** 126-129

WASMOSY, JUAN CARLOS (born 1939), president of Paraguay (1993-) **16** 129-130

WASSERMANN, JAKOB (1873-1934), German author **16** 130-131

WATERHOUSE, BENJAMIN (1754-1846), American physician **16** 131-132

WATERS, ETHEL (1896-1977), African American singer and actress **25** 437-439

WATERS, MAXINE (born 1938), African American congresswoman **16** 132-134

WATERS, MUDDY (born McKinley Morganfield; 1915-1983), African American blues musician **16** 134-136

WATSON, ELKANAH (1758-1842), American merchant and banker **16** 136

WATSON, JAMES DEWEY (born 1928), American biologist **16** 137-138

WATSON, JOHN BROADUS (1878-1958), American psychologist **16** 138-139

WATSON, THOMAS EDWARD (1856-1922), American lawyer and politician **16** 139

WATSON, THOMAS J. (1874-1956), American business executive **16** 140

WATSON, THOMAS J. JR. (1914-1993), American businessman **19** 408-410

WATSON-WATT, SIR ROBERT ALEXANDER (1892-1973), British scientific civil servant **16** 140-141

Watson-Wentworth, Charles
see Rockingham, 2d Marquess of

WATT, JAMES (1736-1819), British instrument maker and engineer **16** 141-143

WATTEAU, ANTOINE (1684-1721), French painter **16** 143-144

WATTLETON, FAYE (Alyce Faye Wattleton, born 1943), African American women's rights activist **18** 405-407

WATTS, ALAN WILSON (1915-1973), naturalized American author and lecturer **16** 144-145

WATTS, ISAAC (1674-1748), English hymnist and theologian **26** 373-375

WATTS, J.C. (Julius Caesar Watts, Jr.; born 1957), African American politician **18** 407-409

WAUGH, EVELYN ARTHUR ST. JOHN (1903-1966), English author **16** 145-147

WAUNEKA, ANNIE DODGE (1910-1997), Navajo nation leader and Native American activist **18** 409-410

WAVELL, ARCHIBALD PERCIVAL (1st Earl Wavell; 1883-1950), English general, statesman, and writer **16** 147-148

wax modeling (art)
Tussaud, Marie **28** 356-358

WAYLAND, FRANCIS (1796-1865), American educator and clergyman **16** 148-149

WAYNE, ANTHONY (1745-1796), American soldier **16** 149-150

WAYNE, JOHN (Marion Mitchell Morrison; 1907-79), American actor **16** 150-151

Weapons and explosives
Kalashnikov, Mikhail **28** 190-192

WEAVER, JAMES BAIRD (1833-1912), American political leader **16** 151-152

WEAVER, PAT (Sylvester Laflin Weaver, Jr.; 1908-2002), American television executive **19** 410-413

WEAVER, ROBERT C. (1907-1997), first African American U.S. cabinet officer **16** 152-153

WEBB, BEATRICE POTTER (1858-1943), English social reformer **16** 153-154

WEBB, SIDNEY JAMES (Baron Passfield; 1859-1947), English social reformer, historian, and statesman **16** 154-155

WEBBER, ANDREW LLOYD (born 1948), British composer **16** 155-156

WEBER, CARL MARIA FRIEDRICH ERNST VON (1786-1826), German composer and conductor **16** 156-157

WEBER, LOIS (1881-1939), American film director **26** 375-378

WEBER, MAX (1864-1920), German social scientist **16** 157-160

WEBER, MAX (1881-1961), American painter **16** 160

WEBERN, ANTON (1883-1945), Austrian composer **16** 160-162

WEBSTER, DANIEL (1782-1852), American lawyer, orator, and statesman **16** 162-164

WEBSTER, JOHN (circa 1580-circa 1634), English dramatist **16** 164

WEBSTER, NOAH (1758-1843), American lexicographer **16** 164-166

WEDEKIND, FRANK (Benjamin Franklin Wedekind; 1864-1918), German dramatist, cosmopolite, and libertarian **16** 166-167

WEDGWOOD, CICELY VERONICA (1910-1997), British writer and historian **16** 167-168

WEDGWOOD, JOSIAH (1730-1795), English potter **16** 168-169

WEED, THURLOW (1797-1882), American politician **16** 169-170

WEEMS, MASON LOCKE (1759-1825), American Episcopal minister and popular writer **16** 170

WEGENER, ALFRED LOTHAR (1880-1930), German meteorologist, Arctic explorer, and geophysicist **16** 170-171

WEI HSIAO-WEN-TI (467-499), Chinese emperor **8** 5

WEI JINGSHENG (born 1950), Chinese human rights activist **18** 410-412

Wei, Prince of
see Ts'ao Ts'ao

Wei Yang
see Shang Yang

WEI YÜAN (1794-1856), Chinese historian and geographer **16** 180-181

WEIDENREICH, FRANZ (1873-1948), German anatomist and physical anthropologist **16** 171-172

WEIL, SIMONE (1909-1943), French thinker, political activist, and religious mystic **16** 172-174

WEILL, KURT (1900-1950), German-American composer **16** 174-175

Wei-mo-ch'i
see Wang Wei

WEINBERG, STEVEN (born 1933), Nobel Prize-winning physicist **16** 175-177

WEINBERGER, CASPER WILLARD (born 1917), U.S. public official under three presidents **16** 177-178

Weinstein, Nathan
see West, Nathanael

WEISMANN, AUGUST FREIDRICH LEOPOLD (1834-1914), German biologist **16** 178-180

WEISSMULLER, JOHNNY (Peter John Weissmuller; 1904-1984), American swimmer and actor **21** 425-427

WEIZMAN, EZER (1924-2005), Israeli air force commander and president of Israel (1993-) **16** 181-182

WEIZMANN, CHAIM (1874-1952), Israeli statesman, president 1949-52 **16** 183-184

WELCH, JACK (John Francis Welch, Jr.; born 1935), American businessman **19** 413-415

WELCH, ROBERT (1899-1985), founder of the John Birch Society **16** 184-185

WELCH, WILLIAM HENRY (1850-1934), American pathologist, bacteriologist, and medical educator **16** 185-186

Weld, Mrs. Theodore
see Grimké, Angelina Emily

WELD, THEODORE DWIGHT (1803-1895), American reformer, preacher, and editor **16** 186

WELDON, FAY BIRKINSHAW (born 1931 or 1933), British novelist, dramatist, essayist, and feminist **16** 186-188

WELENSKY, SIR ROY (1907-1991), Rhodesian statesman **16** 188

WELK, LAWRENCE (1903-1992), American bandleader and television host **22** 420-422

WELLES, GIDEON (1802-1878), American statesman **16** 188-190

WELLES, ORSON (1915-1985), Broadway and Hollywood actor, radio actor, and film director **16** 190-191

WELLES, SUMNER (1892-1961), American diplomat **16** 191-192

Wellesley, Arthur
see Wellington, 1st Duke of

WELLESLEY, RICHARD COLLEY (1st Marquess Wellesley; 1760-1842), British colonial administrator **16** 192-193

WELLHAUSEN, JULIUS (1844-1918), German historian **20** 397-400

WELLINGTON, 1ST DUKE OF (Arthur Wellesley; 1769-1852), British soldier and statesman **16** 193-195

WELLS, HERBERT GEORGE (1866-1946), English author **16** 195-196

WELLS, HORACE (1815-1848), American dentist **16** 196

WELLS, MARY GEORGENE BERG (born 1928), American businesswoman **16** 197-198

WELLS-BARNETT, IDA B. (1862-1931), American journalist and activist **16** 198-199

WELTY, EUDORA (born 1909), American author and essayist **16** 199-201

WENDERS, WIM (Ernst Wilhelm Wenders; born 1945), German filmmaker **26** 378-380

WEN T'IEN-HSIANG (1236-1283), Chinese statesman **16** 203

WENCESLAS (Vaclav; c. 903-c. 935), Czech feudal lord **20** 400-402

WENCESLAUS (Wenceslaus IV of Bohemia; 1361-1419), Holy Roman emperor 1376-1400, and king of Bohemia 1378-1419 **16** 201-202

Wen-chen
see Yen Li-pen

Wen-ch'eng
see Wang Yang-ming

Wen-ho
see Liu Hsieh

WEN-HSIANG (1818-1876), Manchu official and statesman **16** 202-203

Wentworth, Thomas
see Strafford, 1st Earl of

WENTWORTH, WILLIAM CHARLES (1790-1872), Australian statesman, writer, and explorer **16** 203-204

WERFEL, FRANZ (1890-1945), Austrian poet, novelist, and playwright **16** 204-205

WERNER, ABRAHAM GOTTLOB (1749-1817), German naturalist **16** 205-207

WERNER, HELMUT (born 1936), German business executive **19** 415-417

WERTHEIMER, MAX (1880-1943), German psychologist **16** 207-208

Wesel de Bruxella, Andras ven
see Vesalius, Andreas

WESLEY, CHARLES (1707-1788), English hymn writer and preacher **16** 208-209

WESLEY, JOHN (1703-1791), English evangelical clergyman, preacher, and writer **16** 209-210

WEST, BENJAMIN (1738-1820), English American painter **16** 210-212

WEST, CORNEL (born 1953), American philosopher **16** 212-213

WEST, DOROTHY (1907-1998), African American author **27** 359-361

WEST, JERRY (born 1938), American basketball player and coach **21** 428-430

WEST, MAE (Mary Jane West; 1893-1980), American actress **19** 417-419

WEST, NATHANAEL (1903-1940), American novelist **16** 213-214

WESTHEIMER, RUTH KAROLA (a.k.a. "Dr. Ruth;" born 1928), German American psychologist, author, and media personality **16** 214-215

WESTINGHOUSE, GEORGE (1846-1914), American inventor and manufacturer **16** 215

Westmacott, Mary
see Christie, Agatha

WESTMORELAND, WILLIAM CHILDS (1914-2005), commander of all American forces in the Vietnam War (1964-1968) and chief of staff of the U.S. Army **16** 216-217

WESTON, EDWARD (1886-1958), American photographer **19** 419-421

WESTWOOD, VIVIENNE (born 1941), British designer **16** 217-218

WEXLER, NANCY (born 1945), American psychologist **16** 218-219

WEYDEN, ROGIER VAN DER (1399-1464), Flemish painter **16** 219-221

WHARTON, EDITH (1861-1937), American author **16** 221

What Is Cinema? (book)
Bazin, André **28** 32-33

WHEATLEY, PHILLIS (circa 1753-84), African American poet **16** 221-222

Wheel of Fortune (television show)
Griffin, Merv **28** 146-149

WHEELOCK, ELEAZAR (1711-1779), American clergyman and educator **16** 222-223

WHEELOCK, LUCY (1857-1946), American educator **26** 380-382

WHEELWRIGHT, WILLIAM (1798-1873), American entrepreneur **16** 223-224

WHIPPLE, FRED LAWRENCE (1906-2004), American astronaut and astrophysicist **25** 439-441

WHIPPLE, GEORGE HOYT (1878-1976), American pathologist **16** 224-225

WHISTLER, JAMES ABBOTT MCNEILL (1834-1903), American painter, etcher, and lithographer **16** 225-226

WHITE, ANDREW DICKSON (1832-1918), American educator and diplomat **16** 226-227

WHITE, BYRON R. (1917-2002), deputy U.S. attorney general and associate justice of the U.S. Supreme Court **16** 227-228

WHITE, E. B. (Elwyn Brooks White; 1899-1985), American essayist and author of children's books **16** 228-230

WHITE, EDWARD DOUGLASS (1845-1921), American jurist, chief justice of U.S Supreme Court **16** 230-231

WHITE, ELLEN GOULD (Ellen Gould Harmon White; 1827-1915), American religious leader and reformer **23** 438-440

WHITE, KEVIN H. (born 1929), mayor of Boston (1967-1983) **16** 231-232

WHITE, LESLIE A. (1900-1975), American anthropologist **16** 232-233

WHITE, PATRICK VICTOR MARTINDALE (1912-1990), Australian novelist and playwright **16** 233-235

WHITE, REGGIE (Reginald Howard White; 1961-2004), African American football player and minister **26** 382-385

WHITE, RYAN (1971-1990), American AIDS activist **19** 421-423

WHITE, STANFORD (1853-1906), American architect **16** 235-236

WHITE, T. H. (1915-1986), American journalist **16** 236-237

WHITE, WALTER FRANCIS (1893-1955), general secretary of the National Association for the Advancement of Colored People **16** 238-239

WHITE, WILLIAM ALANSON (1870-1937), American psychiatrist **16** 239-240

WHITE, WILLIAM ALLEN (1868-1944), American journalist **16** 240-241

WHITEFIELD, GEORGE (1714-1770), English evangelist **16** 241-242

WHITEHEAD, ALFRED NORTH (1861-1947), English-American mathematician and philosopher **16** 242-244

WHITELEY, OPAL IRENE (Françoise d'Orléans; 1897-1992), American author **27** 361-363

WHITING, SARAH FRANCES (1847-1927), American astronomer and educator **24** 442-444

WHITLAM, EDWARD GOUGH (Gof; born 1916), prime minister of Australia (1972-1975) **16** 244-245

WHITMAN, CHRISTINE TODD (born c. 1947), American politician **16** 245-248

WHITMAN, MARCUS (1802-1847), American physician, missionary, and pioneer **16** 248-249

WHITMAN, NARCISSA (Narcissa Prentiss Whitman; 1808-1847), American missionary **27** 363-366

WHITMAN, WALT (1819-1892), American poet **16** 249-251

WHITMIRE, KATHRYN JEAN NIEDERHOFER (born 1946), first female mayor of Houston, Texas (1982-1992) **16** 252-253

WHITNEY, ELI (1765-1825), American inventor and manufacturer **16** 253-254

WHITNEY, JOSIAH DWIGHT (1819-1896), American chemist and geologist **16** 254-255

WHITNEY, MARY WATSON (1847-1921), American astronomer **23** 440-442

WHITTAKER, CHARLES EVANS (1901-1973), U.S. Supreme Court justice **16** 255-256

WHITTIER, JOHN GREENLEAF (1807-1892), American poet **16** 256-257

WHITTLE, SIR FRANK (1907-1996), English Air Force officer and engineer **16** 257-258

WHORF, BENJAMIN LEE (1897-1941), American linguist **27** 366-368

WIDNALL, SHEILA E. (born 1938), American aeronautical engineer **16** 258-259

WIELAND, CHRISTOPH MARTIN (1733-1813), German poet and author **16** 260-261

WIEMAN, HENRY NELSON (1884-1975), American philosopher and theologian **16** 261-262

WIENER, NORBERT (1894-1964), American mathematician **16** 262-263

WIESEL, ELIE (born 1928), writer, orator, teacher, and chairman of the United States Holocaust Memorial Council **16** 263-264

WIESENTHAL, SIMON (1908-2005), Ukrainian Jew who tracked down Nazi war criminals **16** 264-266

WIGGLESWORTH, MICHAEL (1631-1705), American Puritan poet and minister **16** 266-267

WIGMAN, MARY (Marie Wiegmann; 1886-1973), German dancer, choreographer, and teacher **16** 267-268

WIGNER, EUGENE PAUL (1902-1995), Hungarian-born American physicist **16** 268-269

WILBERFORCE, WILLIAM (1759-1833), English statesman and humanitarian **16** 269-270

WILBUR, RICHARD PURDY (born 1921), translator and poet laureate of the United States (1987-1988) **16** 271-272

WILDE, OSCAR FINGALL O'FLAHERTIE WILLS (1854-1900), British author **16** 272-273

WILDER, AMOS NIVEN (1895-1993), American New Testament scholar, poet, minister, and literary critic **16** 273-274

WILDER, BILLY (Samuel Wilder; 1906-2002), American film director, screenwriter, and producer **21** 430-432

WILDER, LAURA INGALLS (1867-1957), American author and pioneer **18** 413-414

WILDER, LAWRENCE DOUGLAS (born 1931), first African American elected governor in the United States **16** 274-276

WILDER, THORNTON NIVEN (1897-1975), American novelist and playwright **16** 276-277

Wildlife conservation
Leopold, Aldo **28** 211-213

WILES, ANDREW J. (born 1953), English mathematician **23** 442-444

WILEY, HARVEY WASHINGTON (1844-1930), American chemist **16** 277-278

Wilhelm II
see William II (emperor of Germany)

WILHELMINA (1880-1962), queen of the Netherlands 1890-1948 **16** 278-279

WILKES, CHARLES (1798-1877), American naval officer **16** 279-280

WILKES, JOHN (1727-1797), English politician **16** 280-281

WILKINS, SIR GEORGE HUBERT (1888-1958), Australian explorer, scientist, and adventurer **16** 281-282

WILKINS, MAURICE HUGH FREDERICK (1916-2005), English biophysicist **18** 415-416

WILKINS, ROY (1901-1981), African American civil rights leader **16** 282-283

WILKINSON, ELLEN (1891-1947), British Labour politician and crusader for the unemployed **16** 283-284

WILKINSON, JAMES (1757-1825), American army general and frontier adventurer **16** 284-286

WILL, GEORGE FREDERICK (born 1941), syndicated columnist and television commentator **16** 286-287

WILLAERT, ADRIAN (circa 1480-1562), Franco-Flemish composer active in Italy **16** 287-288

WILLARD, EMMA HART (1787-1870), American educator and author **16** 288-289

WILLARD, FRANCES ELIZABETH CAROLINE (1839-1898), American temperance and women's suffrage leader **16** 289-290

William (duke of Normandy)
see William I (king of England)

William I (prince of Orange)
see William the Silent

WILLIAM I (the Conqueror; 1027/28-1087), king of England 1066-1087 **16** 290-291

WILLIAM I (1772-1843), king of the Netherlands 1815-40 **16** 291-292

WILLIAM I (1797-1888), emperor of Germany 1871-88 and king of Prussia 1861-88 **16** 292-293

WILLIAM II (William Rufus; circa 1058-1100), king of England 1087-1100 **16** 293-294

WILLIAM II (1859-1941), emperor of Germany and king of Prussia 1888-1918 **16** 294-295

William III (prince of Orange) see William III (king of England)

WILLIAM III (1650-1702), king of England, Scotland, and Ireland 1689-1702 **16** 295-296

WILLIAM IV (1765-1837), king of Great Britain and Ireland 1830-37 **16** 296-297

WILLIAM OF MALMESBURY (circa 1090-circa 1142), English historian **16** 297-298

WILLIAM OF OCKHAM (circa 1284-1347), English philosopher and theologian **16** 298-299

WILLIAM OF SENS (Guillaume de Sens; died 1180), French architect **21** 432-434

WILLIAM OF TYRE (circa 1130-84/85), French archbishop, chancellor of the Latin Kingdom of Jerusalem **16** 299-300

William the Conqueror see William I (king of England)

WILLIAM THE SILENT (1533-1584), prince of Orange and stadholder of the Netherlands **16** 300-302

WILLIAMS, BERT (Egbert Austin Williams; 1874-1922), African American comedian and songwriter **27** 368-370

Williams, Betty see CORRIGAN and WILLIAMS

WILLIAMS, DANIEL HALE (1856-1931), African American surgical pioneer **16** 302-303

WILLIAMS, EDWARD BENNETT (1920-1988), American lawyer and sports club owner **22** 422-424

WILLIAMS, HANK (Hiram King Williams; 1923-1953), American singer and songwriter **20** 402-404

WILLIAMS, HENRY SYLVESTER (1869-1911), Trinidadian lawyer and pan-African leader **16** 303-304

WILLIAMS, JODY (born 1950), American political activist **25** 441-443

WILLIAMS, JOE (Joseph Goreed; 1918-1999), American singer **20** 404-407

WILLIAMS, MARY LOU (Mary Lou Burley; Mary Elfrieda Scruggs; Mary Elfreda Winn; 1910-1981), African American musician **23** 444-446

Williams, Ralph Vaughan see Vaughan Williams, Ralph

WILLIAMS, ROGER (circa 1603-83), Puritan clergyman in colonial America **16** 304-305

WILLIAMS, SHIRLEY VIVIEN TERESA BRITTAIN (born 1930), British politician **16** 305-306

WILLIAMS, TED (Theodore Samuel Williams; 1918-2002), American baseball player **19** 423-426

WILLIAMS, TENNESSEE (Thomas Lanier Williams; born 1914), American dramatist and fiction writer **16** 306-308

WILLIAMS, WILLIAM CARLOS (1883-1963), American poet and pediatrician **16** 308-309

WILLS, HELEN (1905-1998), American tennis player **19** 426-428

Willy, Colette see Colette, Sidonie Gabrielle

WILLYS, JOHN (1873-1935), American businessman **20** 407-409

WILMOT, DAVID (1814-1868), American politician **16** 312-313

WILMUT, IAN (born 1944), British embryologist **20** 409-411

WILSON, ALEXANDER (1766-1813), Scottish-American ornithologist and poet **16** 313-314

WILSON, AUGUST (Frederick August Kittell; 1945-2005), African American playwright **16** 314-316

WILSON, CHARLES ERWIN (1890-1961), engineer, businessman, and secretary of defense **16** 316-317

WILSON, CHARLES THOMSON REES (1869-1959), Scottish physicist **16** 317-318

WILSON, EDMUND (1895-1972), American critic **16** 318-319

WILSON, EDWARD OSBORNE (born 1929), American biologist **16** 319-320

Wilson, Harold see Wilson, James Harold

WILSON, HARRIET E. (circa 1827-circa 1863), African American author **16** 320-322

WILSON, HENRY (1812-1875), American politician **16** 322-323

WILSON, JAMES (1742-1798), American statesman **16** 323-324

WILSON, JAMES HAROLD (born 1916), English statesman, prime minister 1964-70 **16** 324-325

WILSON, JOSEPH CHAMBERLAIN (1909-1971), American businessman **16** 325-326

WILSON, KENNETH GEDDES (born 1936), American scientist **23** 446-448

WILSON, PETE (born 1933), American politician **16** 326-329

WILSON, RICHARD (1713/14-82), British painter **16** 329-330

WILSON, THOMAS WOODROW (1856-1924), American statesman, president 1913-21 **16** 330-332

WINCKELMANN, JOHANN JOACHIM (1717-1768), German archeologist **16** 332-333

Wind in the Willows, The (book) Grahame, Kenneth **28** 138-140

Windsor, Duchess of see Simpson, Wallis

Windsor, Duke of see Edward VIII

WINFREY, OPRAH GAIL (born 1954), America's first lady of talk shows **16** 333-336

Winfrith see Boniface, St.

WINNEMUCCA, SARAH (a.k.a. Thocmetony; circa 1844-1891), Native American rights activist **16** 336-338

WINSLOW, EDWARD (1595-1655), Pilgrim leader in colonial America **16** 338-339

WINTHROP, JOHN (1588-1649), American colonial politician and historian **16** 339-341

WINTHROP, JOHN (1606-1676), American colonial statesman and scientist **16** 341

WINTHROP, JOHN (1714-1779), American educator and scientist **16** 341-342

WIRKKALA, TAPIO (1915-1985), Finnish designer and sculptor **28** 372-374

WIRTH, LOUIS (1897-1952), American sociologist and activist **21** 434-436

WISE, ISAAC MAYER (1819-1900), American Jewish religious leader **16** 342-343

WISE, JOHN (1652-1725), American Congregational minister **16** 343-344

WISE, ROBERT (Robert Earl Wise, Jr.; 1914-2005), American filmmaker **26** 385-387

WISE, STEPHEN SAMUEL (1874-1949), American Jewish religious leader **16** 344-345

WISEMAN, FREDERICK (born 1930), American documentary filmmaker **16** 345-346

WITHERSPOON, JOHN (1723-1794), Scottish-born American Presbyterian divine and educator **16** 346-348

WITKACY (Stanislw Ignacy Witkiewicz; 1885-1939), Polish artist, playwright, novelist, and philosopher **28** 374-376

WITT, JOHAN DE (1625-1672), Dutch statesman **16** 348-349

WITTE, COUNT SERGEI YULYEVICH (1849-1915), Russian statesman **16** 349-350

WITTGENSTEIN, LUDWIG (1889-1951), Austrian philosopher **16** 350-351

WITZ, KONRAD (circa 1410-46), German painter **16** 351-352

WLADYSLAW II JAGIELLO, KING OF POLAND (Jagiello; c. 1351-1434), Lithuanian-Polish monarch, 1377-1434 **28** 377-378

WO-JEN (1804-1871), Chinese official **16** 352

WOLF, FRIEDRICH AUGUST (1759-1824), German classical scholar and philologist **16** 352-353

WOLFE, JAMES (1727-1759), English general **16** 354-355

WOLFE, THOMAS CLAYTON (1900-1938), American novelist **16** 355-356

WOLFE, THOMAS KENNERLY, JR. ("Tom"; born 1931), American journalist and novelist **16** 356-357

WOLFF, BARON CHRISTIAN VON (1679-1754), German philosopher **16** 358

WOLFF, HUGH (born 1953), American conductor **16** 358-360

WOLFRAM VON ESCHENBACH (circa 1170-circa 1230), German writer **16** 360-361

WOLFSON, HARRY AUSTRYN (1887-1974), American scholar and educator **16** 361-362

WOLLSTONECRAFT, MARY (Mary Wollstonecraft Godwin; 1759-1797), English writer **26** 387-389

Wollstonecraft, Mary
see Shelley, Mary Wollstonecraft

WOLPE, STEFAN (1902-1972), German-born composer **16** 362-364

WOLSELEY, GARNET (1833-1913), Irish army officer **20** 411-413

WOLSEY, THOMAS (circa 1475-1530), English statesman and cardinal **16** 364-366

Women aviators
Quimby, Harriet **28** 285-287

Women military personnel
Velasquez, Loreta Janeta **28** 361-363

Women politicians
Liberian
Sirleaf, Ellen Johnson **28** 328-331

Women religious leaders
Amma **28** 8-10

Women scholars
Faust, Drew Gilpin **28** 116-118

Women's history
Faust, Drew Gilpin **28** 116-118

Women's rights
Arabic
Mala'ika, Nazik al- **28** 230-232
Asian
Ho, Xuan Huong **28** 174-176
equal education opportunity
Chapone, Hester **28** 72-74
social reformers
Ho, Xuan Huong **28** 174-176
Mala'ika, Nazik al- **28** 230-232

WONDER, STEVIE (Stevland Judkins Morris; born 1950), American singer, songwriter, and musician **19** 428-430

WONG, ANNA MAY (born Wong Liu Tsong; 1905-1961), Asian American actress **16** 366-367

Wood, Annie
see Besant, Annie Wood

Wood, Edward Frederick Lindley
see Halifax, 1st Earl of

WOOD, FERNANDO (1812-1881), American politician **16** 367-368

WOOD, GRANT (1891-1942), American painter **16** 368-369

WOOD, LEONARD (1860-1927), American Army officer and colonial administrator **16** 369-370

WOOD, ROBERT ELKINGTON (1879-1969), American Army officer and business executive **16** 370-371

WOODHULL, VICTORIA C. (1838-1927), American women's rights activist **16** 371-372

WOODRUFF, ROBERT W. (1889-1985), American businessman and philanthropist **16** 372-374

WOODS, GRANVILLE T. (1856-1910), African American inventor **28** 378-381

WOODS, ROBERT ARCHEY (1865-1925), American social worker **16** 374

WOODS, TIGER (born 1975), African American/Asian American golfer **18** 416-418

WOODSON, CARTER GODWIN (1875-1950), African American historian **16** 374-376

WOODSWORTH, JAMES SHAVER (1874-1942), Canadian humanitarian, reformer, and political leader **16** 376

WOODVILLE, ELIZABETH (Elizabeth Wydeville; c. 1437-1492), English queen consort **28** 381-383

WOODWARD, COMER VANN (born 1908), American historian **16** 378-379

WOODWARD, ELLEN S. (1887-1971), director of work relief programs for women during the New Deal **16** 379-381

WOODWARD AND BERNSTEIN, investigative reporting team of Woodward, Robert Upshur (born 1943), and Bernstein, Carl (born 1944) **16** 376-378

WOOLF, VIRGINIA STEPHEN (1882-1941), English novelist, critic, and essayist **16** 381-382
Cunard, Nancy **28** 87-89

WOOLMAN, JOHN (1720-1772), American Quaker merchant and minister **16** 382-383

WOOLWORTH, FRANK WINFIELD (1852-1919), American merchant **16** 383-384

WOOTTON, BARBARA ADAM (1897-1988), British social scientist and member of Parliament **16** 384-385

WORDSWORTH, WILLIAM (1770-1850), English poet **16** 385-388

WORK, HENRY CLAY (1832-1884), American songwriter **27** 370-372

WORK, MONROE (1866-1945), American sociologist and publisher **16** 388-389

Work Projects Administration
see Works Progress Administration (WPA)

Works Progress Administration (WPA)
see also Federal Arts Project

World War II (1939-1945)
• ALLIES
Great Britain (intelligence operations)
Atkins, Vera **28** 16-18
Great Britain (secret agents)
Chapman, Eddie **28** 69-72
Poland
Sendler, Irena **28** 318-320
secret agents
Chapman, Eddie **28** 69-72
United States (industry)
Gross, Al **28** 149-151

WORNER, MANFRED (born 1934), West German statesman **16** 389-390

WORTH, CHARLES FREDERICK (1825-1895), English-born French fashion designer **21** 436-438

WOVOKA (a.k.a Jack Wilson; circa 1856-1932), Native American religious leader and mystic **16** 390-393

WOZNIAK, STEVE (Stephen Gary Wozniak; born 1950), American inventor and computer designer **19** 430-432

WPA
see Works Progress Administration (WPA)

WREN, SIR CHRISTOPHER (1632-1723), English architect **16** 393-394

WRIGHT, CARROLL DAVIDSON (1840-1909), American statistician and social economist **16** 396

WRIGHT, ELIZUR (1804-1885), American reformer **16** 396-397

WRIGHT, FRANCES (1795-1852), Scottish-American socialist, feminist, and reformer **16** 397-398

WRIGHT, FRANK LLOYD (1869-1959), American architect **16** 398-401

WRIGHT, JANE COOKE (born 1919), African American cancer researcher **28** 383-385

Wright, Orville
see Wright, Wilbur, and Orville

WRIGHT, RICHARD (1908-1960), African American author **16** 401-402

WRIGHT, WILBUR (1867-1919) AND ORVILLE (1871-1948), American aviation pioneers **16** 394-396

WRIGLEY, WILLIAM, JR. (1861-1932), American businessman and baseball team owner **20** 413-415

WRINCH, DOROTHY MAUD (1894-1976), British mathematician, biochemist and educator **24** 444-446

WU CHAO (Wu Hou/Wu Tse T'ien; 625-705), Empress of China, 690-705 **20** 415-417

Wu Chao
see Wu Tse-t'ien

WU CHIEN-SHIUNG (1912-1997), American physicist **19** 432-434

Wu, Emperor
see Liang Wu-ti

WU P'EI-FU (1874-1939), Chinese warlord **16** 404-405

WU TAO-TZU (circa 689-after 758), Chinese painter **16** 405-406

WU TSE-T'IEN (623-705), empress of China **16** 408

WU WANG (died circa 1116 B.C.), first ruler of the Chou dynasty of China 1122-1116 B.C. **16** 408-409

WU YI (born 1938), Chinese government trade negotiator **25** 443-445

WUNDT, WILHELM MAX (1832-1920), German psychologist and philosopher **16** 402-403

WUORINEN, CHARLES (born 1938), American composer, conductor, and pianist **16** 404

WU-TI (a.k.a. Han Wuti; 156 B.C.-circa 87 B.C.), Chinese emperor **16** 406-408

WYANT, ALEXANDER HELWIG (1836-1892), American painter **16** 409-410

WYATT, SIR THOMAS (1503-1542), English poet and diplomat **16** 410-411

WYCHERLEY, WILLIAM (circa 1640-1716), English dramatist **16** 411-412

WYCLIF, JOHN (1330/32-84), English theologian and reformer **16** 412-413

WYETH, ANDREW NEWELL (born 1917), American painter **16** 413-415

WYLER, WILLIAM (1902-1981), American film director **22** 424-426

WYNETTE, TAMMY (Virginia Wynette Pugh; 1942-1998), American musician **27** 372-374

WYNN, EARLY (Gus Wynn; 1920-1999), American baseball player **20** 417-419

WYTHE, GEORGE (1726-1806), American jurist **16** 415

X

Xavier, St. Francis
see Francis Xavier, St.

XENAKIS, IANNIS (born 1922), Greek-French composer and architect **16** 416-418

XENOPHON (circa 430-circa 355 B.C.), Greek historian, essayist, and military expert **16** 418-420

XERXES (ruled 486-465 B.C.), king of Persia **16** 420

XIANG JINGYU (born Xiang Qunxian; 1895-1928), Chinese feminist **16** 421-422

XU GUANGQI (a.k.a. Kuang-ch'i Hsü; 1562-1633), Chinese politician **16** 422-425

Y

Yabuki, Sugataro
see Katayama, Sen

Yakolev, Aleksandr
see Herzen, Aleksandr Ivanovich

YAKUB AL-MANSUR, ABU YUSUF (reigned 1184-99), Almohad caliph in Spain **16** 426

Yale University (New Haven, Connecticut)
literature
Bloom, Harold **28** 38-40

YALOW, ROSALYN S. (Sussman; born 1921), American physicist who developed radioimmunoassay **16** 427-428

Yamabe
see Kammu

YAMAGATA, ARITOMO (1838-1922), Japanese general **16** 428-429

YAMAMOTO, HISAYE (born 1921), Japanese American author **25** 446-448

YAMAMOTO, ISOROKU (born Takano Isoroku; 1884-1943), Japanese admiral **16** 429-433

YAMANI, AHMED ZAKI (born 1930), Saudi Arabian lawyer and minister of petroleum and mineral resources (1962-1986) **16** 433-435

YAMASHITA, TOMOYUKI (1885-1946), Japanese general **16** 435-436

YANCEY, WILLIAM LOWNDES (1814-1863), American politician **16** 436-437

YANG, CHEN NING (born 1922), Chinese-born American physicist **16** 437-438

Yang Chien
see Sui Wen-ti

Yaqui Indians (North America)
Castaneda, Carlos **28** 62-64

YARD, MARY ALEXANDER ("Molly"; 1912-2005), American feminist, political organizer, and social activist **16** 438-439

YASUI, MINORU (1917-1987), Asian American attorney **16** 440-444

Yatsumimi no Miko
see Shotoku Taishi

YEAGER, CHUCK (born 1923), American pilot **16** 444-445

YEAGER, JEANA (born 1952), American pilot **23** 449-451

YEATS, WILLIAM BUTLER (1865-1939), Irish poet and dramatist **16** 445-447

YEH-LÜ CH'U-TS'AI (1189-1243), Mongol administrator **16** 447-449

YEKUNO AMLAK (ruled circa 1268-1283), Ethiopian king **16** 449

YELTSIN, BORIS NIKOLAEVICH (1931-2007), president of the Russian Republic (1990-) **16** 449-452

YEN FU (1853-1921), Chinese translator and scholar **16** 452

YEN HSI-SHAN (1883-1960), Chinese warlord **16** 452-453

YEN LI-PEN (died 673), Chinese painter **16** 453-454

YERBY, FRANK (Frank Garvin Yerby; 1916-1991), American Author **25** 448-450

YERKES, ROBERT MEARNS (1876-1956), American psychologist **16** 454-455

Yeshayhu
see Isaiah

YEVTUSHENKO, YEVGENY ALEXANDROVICH (born 1933), Soviet poet **16** 455-456

Yi Ha-ŭng
see Taewon'gun, Hŭngson

YI HWANG (1501-1570), Korean philosopher, poet, scholar, and educator **16** 457

Yi Kong
see Sonjo

Yi Kŭm
see Yongjo

YI SNG-GYE (1335-1408), Korean military leader, founder of the Yi dynasty **16** 458-459

Yi Song
see Chongjo

Yi Song-gye
see Yi Sng-gye

Yi Sung-man
see Rhee, Syngman

YI SUNSIN (1545-1598), Korean military strategist and naval hero **16** 459-461

Yi T'aewang
see Kojong

Yi To
see Sejong

Yi Yu
see Sejo

YO FEI (Yo P'eng-chü; 1103-41), Chinese general **16** 462

YOGANANDA (Mukunda Lal Ghose; 1893-1952), Indian yogi **16** 462-463

YÔNGJO (1694-1776), king of Korea 1724-76 **16** 461-462

YORITOMO, MINAMOTO (1147-1199), Japanese warrior chieftain **16** 463-464

York, Edward, Duke of
see Edward IV

YOSHIDA, SHIGERU (1878-1967), Japanese diplomat and prime minister **16** 464-465

Yoshimichi Mao
see Kukai

YOSHIMUNE, TOKUGAWA (1684-1751), Japanese shogun **16** 465-466

YOULOU, FULBERT (1917-1972), Congolese president **16** 466-467

YOUNG, ANDREW JACKSON JR. (born 1932), African American preacher, civil rights activist, and politician **16** 467-469

YOUNG, BRIGHAM (1801-1877), American Mormon leader and colonizer **16** 469-470

YOUNG, COLEMAN ALEXANDER (1918-1997), first African American mayor of Detroit **16** 470-471

YOUNG, CY (Denton True Young; 1867-1955), American baseball player **24** 447-449

YOUNG, LESTER WILLIS ("Prez";1909-59), American jazz musician **16** 471-473

YOUNG, LORETTA (Gretchen Michaela Young; 1913-2000), American Actress **22** 427-430

YOUNG, OWEN D. (1874-1962), American industrialist and monetary authority **16** 473-474

YOUNG, STARK (1881-1963), drama critic, editor, translator, painter, playwright, and novelist **16** 474-475

YOUNG, THOMAS (1773-1829), English physicist **16** 475-476

YOUNG, WHITNEY MOORE, JR. (1921-1971), African American civil rights leader and social work administrator **16** 476-477

Young Pretender
see Charles Edward Louis Philip Casimir Stuart

YOUNGER, MAUD (1870-1936), American suffragist and trade unionist **26** 392-395

YOUNGHUSBAND, SIR FRANCIS EDWARD (1863-1942), English soldier and explorer **16** 477

YOURCENAR, MARGUERITE (Marguerite Antoinette Ghislaine; 1903-87), French novelist, poet, essayist, dramatist, world traveller, and translator **16** 477-479

YÜAN, MA (flourished circa 1190-circa 1229), Chinese painter **10** 379

YÜAN MEI (1716-1798), Chinese author **16** 479-480

YÜAN SHIH-K'AI (1859-1916), Chinese military leader **16** 480-481

YUDHOYONO, SUSILO BAMBANG (born 1949), president of Indonesia **27** 375-377

YUKAWA, HIDEKI (1907-1981), Japanese physicist **16** 481-482

YUN SONDO (1587-1671), Korean sijo poet **16** 483

YUNG-LO (1360-1424), Chinese emperor **16** 482-483

YUNUS, MUHAMMAD (Mohammad Yunus; born 1940), Bangladeshi economist and developer of microlending **28** 386-388

Yü-yü
see Hsia Kuei

YZAGUIRRE, RAUL (Raul Humberto Yzaguirre; born 1939), Hispanic American civil rights leader **24** 449-452

YZERMAN, STEVE (born 1965), Canadian hockey player **23** 451-453

Z

ZACH, NATHAN (Natan Sach; born 1930), Israeli poet **24** 453-455

ZADKINE, OSSIP JOSELYN (1890-1967), Russian sculptor **16** 484

ZAGHLUL PASHA, SAAD (1859-1927), Egyptian political leader **16** 485-486

ZAH, PETERSON (born 1937), Native American leader and activist **16** 486-487

ZAHARIAS, MILDRED DIDRIKSON ("Babe"; 1913-56), Olympic athlete and golfer **16** 487-488

ZAHIR SHAH, MUHAMMAD (1914-2007), Afghani King **22** 431-433

ZAKHAROV, ROSTISLAV VLADIMIROVICH (1907-1975), Russian choreographer **26** 396-398

Zaldívar, Fulgencio Batista Y
see Batista y Zaldívar, Fulgencio

ZAMYATIN, EVGENY IVANOVICH (Yevgeny Zamyatin; 1884-1937), Russian author **26** 398-400

ZANGWILL, ISRAEL (1864-1926), Jewish author and philosopher **16** 488-489

ZANUCK, DARRYL F. (1902-1979), American film producer and executive **19** 435-437

ZAPATA, EMILIANO (circa 1879-1919), Mexican agrarian leader and guerrilla fighter **16** 489-490

Zarathustra (prophet)
see Zoroaster

ZARLINO, GIOSEFFO (1517-1590), Italian music theorist and composer **16** 490-491

ZARQAWI, ABU MUSSAB AL- (Ahmed Fadeel al-Khalayleh; 1966-2006), Jordanian terrorist **27** 378-380

ZATOPEK, EMIL (born 1922), Czechoslovakian runner **20** 420-422

ZAWINUL, JOE (Josef Erich Zawinul; 1932-2007), Austrian keyboardist and composer **28** 389-391

ZAYID BIN SULTAN AL-NAHYAN (born 1923), president of the United Arab Emirates (1971-) **16** 491-492

ZEAMI, KANZE (1364-1444), Japanese actor, playwright, and critic **16** 492-493

ZEDILLO PONCE DE LEON, ERNESTO (born 1951), president of Mexico **16** 493-495

ZEFFIRELLI, FRANCO (born 1923), Italian stage, opera, and film director, set designer, and politician **18** 419-421

ZELAYA, JOSÉ SANTOS (1853-1919), Nicaraguan statesman, three-time president **16** 495-496

ZEMURRAY, SAMUEL (1877-1961), Russian-born U.S. fruit importer **16** 496-497

ZENGER, JOHN PETER (1697-1746), American printer **16** 497-498

Zenko kokushi
see Eisai

Zennichimaru
see Nichiren

ZENO OF CITIUM (335-263 B.C.), Greek philosopher **16** 499-500

ZENO OF ELEA (born circa 490 B.C.), Greek philosopher and logician **16** 500

ZENOBIA (died 273), queen of Palmyra **16** 500-503

ZETKIN, CLARA (1857-1933), German political activist **16** 504-505

ZETSCHE, DIETER (born 1953), German businessman **27** 380-382

ZHANG YIMOU (born 1950), Chinese filmmaker **27** 382-384

ZHAO KUANG-YIN (a.k.a. Song Tai Zu or Sung T'ai Tsu; 927-976), Chinese emperor **16** 505-508

ZHAO ZIYANG (Zhao Xiusheng; 1919-2005), Chinese statesman **16** 508-509

ZHIRINOVSKY, VLADIMIR VOLFOVICH (born 1946), Russian politician **16** 509-510

ZHIVKOV, TODOR (1911-1998), leader of the Bulgarian Communist Party and head of the Bulgarian government (1962-) **16** 510-512

ZHUKOV, GEORGI KONSTANTINOVICH (1896-1974), Russian general **16** 512-513

ZIA, HELEN (born 1952), Asian American activist and journalist **18** 421-423

ZIA UL-HAQ, MOHAMMAD (1924-1988), president of Pakistan (1978-1988) **16** 513-515

ZIAUR RAHMAN (1936-1981), Bangladesh president (1975-1981) **16** 515-516

ZIDANE, ZINÉDINE (Zizou; Yazid Zidane; born 1972), French soccer player **27** 384-387

ZIEGFELD, FLORENZ (1869-1932), American musical producer **16** 516-517

Zik
see Azikiwe, Nnamdi

ZIMMERMANN, BERND ALOIS (1918-1970), German composer **16** 517-518

ZIMMERMANN BROTHERS, German artists **16** 518

ZINDEL, PAUL (1936-2003), American children's author and playwright **18** 423-425

ZINE EL ABIDINE BEN ALI (born 1936), president of Tunisia **16** 518-520

ZINN, HOWARD (born 1922), American political scientist and historian **16** 520-521

ZINNEMANN, FRED (Alfred Zinnemann; 1907-1997), Austrian-American filmmaker **26** 400-402

ZINOVIEV, GRIGORI EVSEEVICH (1883-1936), Soviet politician **16** 521-522

ZINZENDORF, COUNT NIKOLAUS LUDWIG VON (1700-1760), German-born Moravian clergyman **16** 522-523

ZIZEK, SLAVOJ (born 1949), Slovenian philospher **27** 387-389

ZNANIECKI, FLORIAN (1882-1958), Polish-American sociologist and educator **16** 523-524

ZOË (circa 978-1050), Byzantine empress 1028-34 **16** 524-525

ZOG I (Ahmed Bey Zog; 1895—1961), Albanian king **16** 525-526

ZOLA, ÉMILE (1840-1902), French novelist **16** 526-528

ZORACH, WILLIAM (1887-1966), American sculptor and painter **16** 528

ZOROASTER (flourished 1st millennium B.C.), prophet and founder of Iranian national religion **16** 528-530

ZORRILLA DE SAN MARTIN, JUAN (1855-1931), Uruguayan poet and newspaperman **16** 530-531

ZOSER (flourished circa 2686 B.C.), Egyptian king **16** 531

ZUKERMAN, PINCHAS (born 1948), Israeli musician **22** 433-435

ZUKOR, ADOLPH (1873-1976), American film producer and executive **19** 437-439

ZUMÁRRAGA, JUAN DE (circa 1468-1548), Spanish churchman, first archbishop of Mexico **16** 531-532

ZUMWALT, ELMO RUSSELL, JR. ("Bud"; 1920-2000), commander of U.S. naval forces in Vietnam **16** 532-534

ZUNZ, LEOPOLD (1794-1886), German-born Jewish scholar **16** 534

ZURBARÁN, FRANCISCO DE (1598-1644), Spanish painter **16** 534-535

ZUSE, KONRAD (1910-1995), German engineer and inventor **28** 391-393

ZWILICH, ELLEN TAAFFE (born 1939), American composer **16** 536-537

ZWINGLI, HULDREICH (1484-1531), Swiss Protestant reformer **16** 537-538

ZWORYKIN, VLADIMIR KOSMA (1889-1982), Russian-American physicist and radio engineer **16** 539-540